SOUTH AFRICA YEARBOOK 2003/04

Foreword

In this 10th anniversary year since we achieved democracy, we can, as South Africans, take pride in the progress that freedom has brought. We can be confident of our ability as a nation, working together, to meet the enormous challenges of fully achieving our goal of a better life for all.

The pages of this *South Africa Yearbook* attest to the progress and the challenges, the difficulties and opportunities.

It has been the historic mission of this generation of South Africans to confront and overcome apartheid's pervasive legacy. The transformation of our society, and the reconstruction and development of our country have been and remain our strategic goals. Central to the realisation of these goals is the restoration of the dignity of all South Africans and the eradication of poverty.

As we approach the end of the First Decade of Freedom, we can assert with confidence that social, political and economic stability prevails in our country, previously divided and torn by conflict; that many millions have gained access to basic services and benefits once denied them; and that the culture of human rights and democracy has taken root. South Africa, once isolated from the international community by the inhumanity of apartheid, now plays its part in Africa and the world, contributing to the collective effort to promote peace, development and human rights. The tide has turned.

Government's partnership with the people of South Africa, in a national effort to build a better life for all, has been critical to the progress made. The people's contract for a better tomorrow is taking shape.

While we take pride in the progress that has been made, we are acutely aware of the massive challenges that remain before the accumulated legacy of poverty and underdevelopment can be eradicated. We are learning the lessons of our experience and resolve to build on what has been achieved.

The *South Africa Yearbook 2003/04* reflects that experience and that determination. As we celebrate 10 years of freedom in South Africa, we do so as a people united for a better South Africa and a better world.

President Thabo Mbeki
November 2003

South Africa Yearbook 2003/04
Tenth edition
Originally published as *South Africa Official Yearbook*
ISSN 0302-0681

Editor Delien Burger

Assistant editors Anri Cronjé and Elias Tibane

Photographs supplied by the GCIS, unless otherwise specified.

Proofreader Kathleen Bartels for Wordsmiths

Design and layout Thabo Matlejoane of STE Publishers

Indexer Mirié van Rooyen

Suggested reading lists Prof Reuben Musiker

Compiled, edited and published by Government Communications (GCIS),
Private Bag X745, Pretoria, 0001
Telephone: (012) 314 2911, Fax: (012) 323 3831
Website: *www.gcis.gov.za*

Co-published by STE Publishers, PO Box 93446, Yeoville 2143 Tel: +27 11 484 7824

Trade distributor: Pan Macmillan S.A. Tel: +27 11 325-5220

Publishing consultant: Zann Hoad – Sharp Sharp Media +27 11 442-8707

Printed and bound in the Republic of South Africa by Formeset Printers

ISBN 1-919855-18-1
ISSN 1022-9515
Library of Congress Catalogue Card Number: 57-40609

The *South Africa Yearbook* is compiled and edited by the GCIS. The editorial staff has taken all reasonable care to ensure correctness of facts and statistics. However, any person requiring formal confirmation of any data in the *Yearbook*, or more detailed specific information, should consult the contributors. The information is also available on *Government Online* [*ww.gov.za*].
Unless otherwise specified, the information contained in this book was the latest available in October 2003.

Contents

Chapter 1
The land and its people   1-29

The people   1
  Languages   1
Bill on the Commission for the Promotion and Protection of Cultural, Religious and Linguistic Communities   5
Religion   5
  Religious groups in South Africa   5
  Christian churches   5
  African Independent Churches (AICs)   6
  Afrikaans churches   6
  The Roman Catholic Church   6
  Other Christian churches   7
  African traditionalists   7
  Other religions   7
The land   8
  The oceans   8
  The coasts   8
  Relief features   8
  Climatic features   9
  Rainfall   9
  Temperatures   9
  Frost, humidity and fog   9
  Sunshine   9
The provinces   10
  Western Cape   10
  Eastern Cape   12
  KwaZulu-Natal   14
  Northern Cape   16
  Free State   18
  North West   20
  Gauteng   21
  Mpumalanga   24
  Limpopo   25

Chapter 2
History   31-49

The early inhabitants   31
The early colonial period   32
The British colonial era   33
The mineral revolution   35
The Anglo-Boer/South African War (October 1899 – May 1902) and its aftermath   37
Segregation   38
Apartheid   40
The end of apartheid   42
The first decade of freedom   44

Chapter 3
Overview: 10 years of freedom   51-63

Progress in the first decade   51
  Reconstruction and development   51
  What the democratic State inherited   51
  Ten-year review   51
  Measuring change   52
Governance Cluster   52
  The State has become a people-centred State   52
Social Cluster   53
  Boosting the income of the poor   53
  Broadening access to social services   53
  Boosting ownership of assets and access to opportunities   58
Economy Cluster   58
  Performance of the economy   58
  State-enterprise restructuring   59
  Expanding economic opportunities   59
Justice, crime prevention and security   59
  National Crime Prevention Strategy (NCPS)   59
  High-priority crimes   60
International relations   60
  Diplomatic normalisation   60
  Marketing and branding South Africa   60
  International relations for growth and development   61
  Promoting human rights, peace, security and stability   61
  Strengthening multilateralism and co-operation   61
Challenges of the next decade   61
  Influence of the State   61
  The social transition   62
  The global setting   63
  Challenges and opportunities   63

Chapter 4
Agriculture   65-103

Strategic plan for South African Agriculture   65
Agriculture economy   67

Sustainable resource-use and management	68
Production	71
Field crops and horticulture	71
Livestock	75
Game-farming, aquaculture and bee-keeping	76
Production input	77
Veterinary services	77
Pest control	78
Migratory pest control	79
Marketing	80
Land administration	81
Food security	81
National Food Pricing Monitoring Committee (FPMC)	82
Regional issues	82
International issues	83
Risk management	83
Drought management	83
Agricultural risk insurance	83
Credit and assistance	83
Agribusiness Promotion and Industry Relations (APIR)	83
National LandCare Programme	84
Land and Agricultural Development Bank of South Africa (Land Bank)	86
AgriSA	87
Agricultural Business Chamber (ABC)	87
National African Farmers' Union	88
Economic empowerment	88
Institutional capacity-building	89
Training and research	89
Trade relations	90
Import and export control	92

Land Affairs	**93-103**
Deeds registration	93
Cadastral surveys	94
Surveys and mapping	95
Surveys	96
Spatial planning and information	97
Land-reform implementation, management and co-ordination	99
Land-reform systems and support services	100
Commission on the Restitution of Land Rights	101

Chapter 5
Arts and culture	**105-127**
Policy and legislation	105
Funding	105
National symbols	105
National anthem	105
National flag	106
National coat of arms	106

National orders	106
National symbols	108
Arts and culture organisations	108
National Heritage Council	108
South African Heritage Resources Agency (SAHRA)	108
South African Geographical Names Council (SAGNC)	108
National Arts Council (NAC)	110
Performing Arts Companies	110
Business Arts South Africa	111
Arts and Culture Trust	111
Other cultural organisations	111
Arts and culture initiatives	112
Education and training in arts and culture	112
Cultural tourism	113
Cultural villages	114
The Cultural Industries Growth Strategy	114
Arts festivals	115
Theatre	116
Music	116
Orchestras	117
Dance	117
Visual arts	118
Photography	118
Architecture	118
Rock art	118
Crafts	119
Design	119
Literature	120
Film	120
The Film and Publication Board	121
Museums	121
Archives and heraldry	125

Chapter 6
Communications	**129-159**
Policy	130
Telecommunications	131
Regulators and licensing	131
Information technology	132
Internet	133
Public Internet Terminals (PITs), Multi-purpose Community Centres (MPCCs) and Citizen Post Offices (CPOs)	134
International co-operation	134
Telkom	135
Mobile communications	137
The postal sector	138
Policy and legislation	138
Postal services regulatory framework	139
South African Post Office	139
International and regional co-operation	142
The media	142
Media freedom	142
Broadcasting	142
Cross-media control and local content	143

Independent Communications Authority of South Africa	144
Broadcasting role-players	144
Print	147
Media organisations and role-players	152
News Agencies	153
Training centres	153
Journalism awards	154
Media diversity	155
Advertising	156

Chapter 7
Economy   161-207

Domestic output	162
Domestic expenditure	163
Price inflation	164
Exchange rates	165
Foreign trade and payments	166
Department Trade and Industry	168
International trade and economic development	169
Trade relations	169
Africa	169
Trade with Europe	171
The Americas	172
Asia	174
Multilateral economic relations	175
Export and investment promotion	176
Enterprise and industry development	178
The Enterprise Organisation	180
Innovation and technology	180
Skills research	181
Workplace Challenge Programme	181
National Industrial Participation Programme (NIPP)	181
Manufacturing	182
Competition policy	182
Small, medium and micro enterprises	183
Institutional support framework	184
Restructuring of State assets	187
Progress of restructuring process	187
Consumer and corporate regulation	192
Community-Based Public Works Programme	192
Expanded Public Works Programme (EPWP)	193
Construction industry	194
Strategic asset management	195
Black Economic Empowerment	196
Broad-Based Black Economic Strategy	196
Black Business Supplier Programme (BBSP)	197
Employment and Skills development	197
National Skills Authority (NSA)	199
National Skills Fund	199
Unemployment Insurance Fund (UIF)	200
Occupational health and safety (OHS)	200

Labour relations	201
Legislation	201
Code of Good Practice	201
Directorate: Collective Bargaining	201
Commission for Conciliation, Mediation and Arbitration (CCMA)	202
Directorate: Employment Equity	202
International co-operation	203
Directorate: Employment Standards	203

Chapter 8
Education   209-231

Education structures	209
Ministry of Education	209
National and provincial Department of Education	210
Statutory bodies	210
Council of Education Ministers	210
Heads of Education Departments Committee	210
Council for Quality Assurance in General and Further Education and Training (Umalusi)	211
South African Qualifications Authority	211
Council for Higher Education	211
South African Council for Educators (SACE)	212
National Board for Further Education and Training (NBFET)	212
Education Labour Relations Council	212
National Student Financial Aid Scheme	212
Financing education	213
Conditional grants to provinces	213
Equity in education expenditure	213
Education policy	214
Legislative framework	214
Tirisano	215
New policy developments	216
General education and training	218
Further education and training	219
Higher education	220
Adult Basic Education and Training	222
Education of learners with special education needs	222
Early Childhood Development	223
The School Register of Needs	224
Human Resource Development Strategy	224
HIV/AIDS	225
Partnerships, international relations and funding	225
Teacher unions	225
Non-governmental organisations (NGOs)	225
Public-private partnerships	226
The international community	226
Highlights in Education since 1994	227
Library and information services sector	228

Chapter 9
Environmental management   233-265

Environmental Impact Assessments (EIAs)	234
State of the environment	234
World Summit of Sustainable Development (WSSD)	235
Biological diversity	235
Savanna Biome	237
Nama-Karoo biome	237
Grassland biome	237
Succulent Karoo biome	238
Fynbos biome	238
Forest biome	238
Thicket biome	239
Desert biome	239
Preserving genetic diversity	239
Conservation areas	240
Botanical gardens	244
Zoological gardens	245
Breeding centres	246
Aquaria	247
Snake parks	247
Marine resources	247
State of marine resources	248
Legislation	251
Transformation	251
Harbours	251
International relations	252
4x4s	252
Conservation challenges	252
Climatic and atmospheric change	252
Erosion and desertification	253
Waste management	254
Water-quality management	256
Air pollution	257
Marine pollution	257
Coastal management	258
Chemicals	259
Recycling	260
Urban conservation	260
Environmental injustices	260
International co-operation	261
United Nations Framework Convention on Climate Change (UNFCCC)	261
Convention on International Trade in Endangered Species	262
Montreal Protocol	262
Private-sector involvement	263

Chapter 10
Finance   267-303

Fiscal policy framework	267
Debt management	269
Legislation	270
The Public Finance Management Act	271
State expenditure	273
National Treasury	273
South Africa's anti money-laundering system	274
Financial and Fiscal Commission	275
Budget Council	275
Macro-economic strategy	276
South African Revenue Service	277
Tax system	277
International tax agreements for the avoidance of double taxation	278
Agreements for mutual administrative assistance between customs administrations	278
Sources of revenue	278
Organisational performance	282
Budget estimates and revenue outcome	282
2003 tax proposals	283
Gambling and lotteries	283
Auditor-General	284
Financial sector	285
South African Reserve Bank	285
Monetary policy	286
Financial Services Board	289
The banking industry	290
The microlending industry	291
Insurance companies	292
Other financial institutions	292
Development Bank of Southern Africa (DBSA)	292
Land and Agricultural Development Bank	293
Participation mortgage-bond schemes	293
Stokvels	293
Unit trusts	293
Financial intermediaries and advisors	294
Retirement funds and friendly societies	294
Financial markets	295
Primary capital-market activity	295
Secondary capital-market activity	295
Money markets	296
Exchange controls	299
Institutional investors	299
South African corporates	299
Emigrants' funds	300
JSE Securities Exchange	300
Bond Exchange of South Africa	301
Primary debt markets	301
Market performance	302
Main indices	302
Regulation	302
Guarantee Fund	302

Chapter 11
Foreign relations   305-339

South Africa and Africa	305
Organisation of African Unity (OAU)/ African Economic Community (AEC)/ African Union (AU)	305

New Partnership for Africa's Development (NEPAD)	309
Conference on Security, Stability, Development and Co-operation in Africa (CSSDCA)	311
Southern Africa	311
Development co-operation	315
South Africa and the Southern African Development Community	315
Relations with central Africa	318
Relations with North and West Africa and the Horn of Africa	319
Relations with Asia and the Middle East	323
Asia	323
The Middle East	327
Relations with the Americas	329
United States of America	329
Canada	329
The Caribbean	330
Latin America	330
Relations with Europe	331
Multilateral diplomacy	333
International organizations	334

Chapter 12
Government system 341-371

The Constitution	341
The Preamble	341
Fundamental rights	341
Government	341
Parliament	341
National Assembly	342
National Council of Provinces	342
Law-making	343
The President	343
The Deputy President	343
Cabinet	343
Deputy Ministers	344
Traditional leadership	344
Houses of Traditional Leaders	345
Provincial government	345
Local government	348
South African Local Government Association (SALGA)	348
Municipalities	349
Legislation	350
Programmes	350
Government and communication	353
International Marketing Council (IMC)	353
Co-operative governance	354
Elections	354
Disaster management	355
The Public Service	355
Size of the Public Service	355
Restructuring of the Public Service	356
Macro-organisational issues	356
Community Development Workers (CDWs)	356
Strengthening institutional performance	357
Service-delivery improvement	357
Labour relations and conditions of service	358
Fighting corruption	359
Senior Management Service	359
Human resource management	359
Human resource development	360
HIV/AIDS	360
Public-service information	360
Government Information Technology Officers' (GITO) Council	361
State Information Technology Agency (SITA)	361
International and African Affairs	362
Governance and Administration Cluster	362
Public Service Commission (PSG)	363
Affirmative action	365
Training	365
Home Affairs	366
Civic services	366
Citizenship matters	366
Migration	367
Visas	367
Control of travellers	368
Control of sojourn	368
Permanent residence	368
Temporary residence	368
Removal of undesirable persons	369

Chapter 13
Health 373-397

Statutory bodies	373
Health authorities	373
National	373
Provincial	373
Primary healthcare	374
Health policy	374
Telemedicine	375
Legislation	375
National School Health Policy	375
Medicines administration	376
Health team	376
Physicians	376
Oral health professionals	377
Pharmacists	377
Nurses	377
Supplementary health services	378
Allied health professions	378
Provincial Health Departments	378
National Health Laboratory Service	79
South African Vaccine Producers and State Vaccine Institute	379
The role of local government	379
Non-profit health sector	380
Costs and medical schemes	381
Community health	382

Polio and measles	382
Integrated management of Childhood Illness	382
Malaria	383
Tuberculosis	384
HIV/AIDS	385
Reproductive health	387
Traditional medicine	389
Tobacco control	389
Alcohol and substance abuse	390
Violence against women	391
Violence prevention	391
Birth defects	391
Chronic diseases, disabilities and geriatrics	392
Occupational health	393
Mental health	393
Quarantinable diseases	394
Consumer goods	394
Nutrition	394

Chapter 14
Housing 399-415

Legislation and policy	401
Rental Housing Act, 1999 (Act 50 of 1999)	401
Home Loan and Mortgage Disclosure Act, 2000 (Act 63 of 2000)	401
Housing Consumer Protection Measures Act, 1998 (Act 95 of 1998)	401
Housing Amendment Act, 2001 (Act 4 of 2001)	402
Draft Social Housing Bill	402
Community Reinvestment (Housing) Bill	402
Public-Sector Hostel Redevelopment Programme	402
Funding	403
Capacity-building	403
National Housing Capacity-Building and Training Programme	403
Housing subsidies	404
Housing institutions	407
National Home-Builders Registration Council	407
National Housing Finance Corporation (NHFC)	408
National Urban Reconstruction and Housing Agency (NURCHA)	409
Servcon Housing Solutions	410
Thubelisha Homes	411
Social Housing Foundation (SHF)	411
South African Housing Fund	412
People's Housing Process	413
Rural Housing Loan Fund (RHLF)	413
Urban renewal	414
Urban Upgrading and Development Programme (UUDP)	414
Settlement policy and urban development	414

Chapter 15
Justice and correctional services 417-453

Administration of justice	417
Transformation of the justice system	417
National Prosecuting Authority of South Africa (NPA)	418
State Legal Services	422
Human rights	423
Crime prevention	423
Integrated Justice System	423
e-Justice	424
Legislation	425
Compulsory HIV-Testing of Alleged Sexual Offenders Bill, 2003	427
Court and other legal structures	428
Constitutional Court	428
Supreme Court of Appeal	429
High Courts	429
Circuit local divisions	430
Regional Courts	430
Magistrate's Courts	430
Civil jurisdiction	430
Small Claims Court	431
Other civil courts	431
Criminal jurisdiction	431
Other criminal courts	432
Legal practitioners	432
Masters of the High Court	433
Rules Board for Courts of Law	433
Justice College	433
Office of the Family Advocate	433
Legal Aid	434
Office of the Public Protector	435
Magistrate's Commission	435
South African Law Reform Commission	435
Judicial Service Commission	436
South African Human Rights Commission (SAHRC)	436
Commission on Gender Equality (CGE)	437
Truth and Reconciliation Commission (TRC)	438
International Affairs	438
Human-rights issues	439
Correctional services	441
Safe custody of prisoners	441
Incarceration	441
Safety and security	442
Classification	443
Categories	443
The privilege system	444
Physical care and hygiene	444
Provision of rehabilitation services	445
Community corrections	448
Facility management and capital works	450
Administration	450
Human resources	451
Community involvement	451
Anti-corruption	451

Chapter 16
Minerals and energy 455-483

Policy	455
Mine environmental management	457
Excellence in Mining Environmental Management (EMEM) Award System	458
Mining industry	458
Mineworkers	459
Mine health and safety	459
Human resource development	460
Chamber of Mines	461
Junior and small-scale mining	461
Mineral wealth	462
Gold	464
Coal	464
Platinum-group metals	464
Base minerals	465
Ferrous minerals	465
Industrial minerals	465
Processed minerals	465
Other minerals	465
Energy	466
Energy in the economy	466
Energy efficiency	466
Energy demand by the economic subsector	467
Coal	467
Nuclear power	468
Liquid fuels	471
Gas	473
Infrastructure	473
Electricity	475
Restructuring of the electricity supply industry (ESI)	475
Restructuring of the electricity distribution industry (EDI)	476
National Electricity Regulator	476
Integrated National Electrification Programme	477
Mini-grid hybrid systems	478
Southern African Power Pool	478
Biomass	479
Renewables	479
Solar	480
Wind	481
Hydro	481
Energy and the environment	482

Chapter 17
Safety, security and defence 485-515

Safety and security	485
Secretariat for Safety and Security	486
Independent Complaints Directorate	486
South African Police Service	487
Strategic overview and key objects	487
Divisions	488
Police projects	491
International obligations and involvement in Africa	495
Defence	496
Defence Secretariat	497
Legislation	497
Functions of the South African National Defence Force	498
Tasks of the South African National Defence Force	498
Corporate strategy	499
Organisational structure	500
Operations	502
Management of transformation	503
Force employment	503
Important developments	505
Requirement of main equipment	508
Facilities, land and environment	509
Armaments	509
Armaments Corporation of South Africa	509
Denel Group of South Africa	510
National Conventional Arms Control Committee	512
Intelligence services	512

Chapter 18
Science and technology 517-547

Policy	517
National Research and Development (R&D) Strategy	517
National Advisory Council on Innovation (NACI)	517
Public understanding of science, engineering and technology (Puset)	518
Technology diffusion and transfer	519
National Biotechnology Strategy (NBS)	520
Godisa Programme	521
Poverty-Reduction Programme	521
Science Councils	522
National Research Foundation	522
Agricultural Research Council	527
Council for Scientific and Industrial Research (CSIR)	530
Mintek	532
Human Sciences Research Council (HSRC)	534
Medical Research Council (MRC)	536
Council of Geoscience (CGS)	538
South African Bureau of Standards (SABS)	539
Other scientific and research organisations and structures	540
Biotechnology Partnership for Africa's Development (Biopad)	540
Sasol	541
Iscor	541
Eskom	541
National Health Laboratory Service (NHLS)	541

Bureau for Economic Research	541
National Institute for Tropical Diseases	542
General research areas	542
Antarctic research	542
Mine-safety research	543
Energy research	543
Agriculture research	543
Water research	543
Environmental research	544
Fisheries research	545
Coastal and marine research	545
Private-sector involvement	546

Chapter 19
Social development 549-563

Legislation	550
Older Persons Bill	550
New child-care legislation	550
Social Assistance Bill	551
Social Assistance	551
Payment of social grants	552
Improving the existing system of social assistance	553
Poverty-Relief Programme	553
Food security	554
Responding to the impact of HIV/AIDS	555
Home-based/community-based care	555
Services for children infected or affected by HIV/AIDS	556
Developing capacity	557
Research	557
Partnerships	557
Promoting and protecting rights of vulnerable groups	558
Children and youths	558
Women	558
People with disabilities	559
Victim-Empowerment Programme (VEP)	559
One-stop centres for abused women and children	560
Anti-rape strategy	560
Non-profit organisations (NPOs)	560
Statutory bodies	561
National Development Agency (NDA)	561
Relief Boards	561
Central Drug Authority (CDA)	561

Chapter 20
Sport and recreation 565-579

Sports Tourism Project	567
Young Champions Project	568
South African Sports Commission	568
Recognition of sport and recreational bodies	568
Hosting of and bidding for major international sports events	569
National colours	569
Sports Information and Science Agency (SISA)	569
Dispute-Resolution Centre	570
Projects	570
Transformation in sport	571
Sports Transformation Charter	571
Ministerial Task Team into High-Performance Sport	571
Presidential Sports Awards	572
Sports Organisations	572
National Olympic Committee of South Africa (NOCSA)	572
Disability Sport South Africa (DISSA)	572
Boxing South Africa	573
South African Institute for Drug-Free Sport (SAIDS)	573
Recreation	574
2003 sports highlights	575
Cricket	575
Tennis	575
Golf	575
Motorsport	576
Boxing	576
Hockey	576
Surfing	576
Swimming	576
Special Olympics	577
Athletics	577
Equestrian	577
Soccer	577
Squash	578
Cycling	578
All Africa Games	578
Rugby	578
2004 sports events	578

Chapter 21
Tourism 581-617

Tourism policy	582
Poverty-relief funding	583
Marketing	584
Human resource development	586
Hints for the tourist	587
Accommodation	588
Tourist safety	589
Tourism in the provinces	589
Western Cape	598
Northern Cape	600
Free State	602
Eastern Cape	604
Limpopo	605
North West	606
Mpumalanga	607
Gauteng	609
KwaZulu-Natal	612

Chapter 22
Transport — 619-649

Policy — 619
  Public-transport subsidies — 619
  Black Economic Empowerment (BEE) — 620
  Non-motorised transport — 621
  Transport safety — 621
  New Partnership for Africa's Development (NEPAD) — 621
Agencies — 622
  South African National Roads Agency Ltd — 622
  South African Maritime Safety Authority — 622
  Cross-Border Road Transport Agency — 623
  Civil Aviation Authority — 623
Transnet Limited — 623
Road transport — 624
  National roads — 624
  Provincial roads — 625
  Spatial Development Initiatives (SDIs) — 625
  Municipal roads — 625
  Toll roads — 625
  Road-traffic signs — 626
  Credit-card format (CCF) licences — 627
Public transport — 627
  National transport Register — 627
  Urban transport — 628
  Cross-border transport — 630
  Goods transport — 631
  Road-traffic safety — 631
  Road-traffic control — 634
  Road Accident Fund (FAF) — 634
Rail transport — 635
  Spoornet — 636
  Social-investment activities — 638
  Metrorail — 638
  South African Rail Commuter Corporation — 639
Civil aviation — 640
  Airports — 640
  Scheduled airlines — 642
  Aviation safety and security — 642
Ports — 643
Pipelines — 645
Maritime affairs — 645
  Maritime administration, legislation and shipping — 645
  Training — 646
  Search-and-rescue services — 646
  Maritime safety — 648

Chapter 23
Water Affairs and Forestry — 651-671

Water for all — 653
  Community Water Supply and Sanitation (CWSS) Programme — 653
  Municipal Infrastructure Grant (MIG) — 654
  Free Basic Water — 654
Water policy — 654
  Water Services Act, 1997 (Act 108 of 1997) — 655
  National Water Act, 1998 — 656
  Draft Water Services White Paper — 656
Water resource management — 657
  Water management institutions — 658
  Working for Water Programme — 659
  Flood and drought management — 660
  Dams and water schemes — 660
  Drainage and hydrology — 661
  Lakes and pans — 662
  Groundwater resources — 662
Forestry — 662
  Managing the forests — 663
  Indigenous high-canopy forest — 668
  Scrub forest and woodlands — 668
  Planted forests — 668
  Plantation yields — 669
  Primary wood-processing — 669
  Research and training — 669
  Community forestry — 670

Addendum — 672-693

Index — 694-736

Shaun Harris/PictureNET

chapter 1
The land and its people

South Africa is a country where various cultures merge to form a unique nation, proud of its heritage.

The country boasts some of the world's most breathtaking scenery and features an amazing display of bird and wildlife species, which include the well-known Big Five (lion, leopard, elephant, buffalo and rhino).

South Africa's biggest asset is its people; a rainbow nation with rich and diverse cultures. South Africa is often called the cradle of humankind, for this is where archaeologists discovered 2,5-million-year-old fossils of our earliest ancestors, as well as 100 000-year-old remains of modern man.

The people

The results of the second democratic Census (Census 2001) were released in July 2003.

On the night of 10 October 2001, there were 44 819 778 people in South Africa. Of these, 79% classified themselves as African; 9,6% as white; 8,9% as coloured; and 2,5% as Indian/Asian.

A total of 21 685 415 people in South Africa are male, and 23 662 839 female.

The South African population consists of the following groups: the Nguni people (consisting of the Zulu, Xhosa, Ndebele and Swazi); the Sotho-Tswana people, who include the Southern, Northern and Western Sotho (Tswana); the Tsonga; the Venda; Afrikaners; the English; coloureds; Indians, and those who have immigrated to South Africa from the rest of Africa, Europe and Asia and maintain a strong cultural identity. A few members of the Khoi and the San also live in South Africa.

Languages

The South African Constitution, 1996 (Act 108 of 1996), states that everyone has the right to use the language and to participate in the cultural life of his or her choice, but no one may do so in a manner inconsistent with any provision of the Bill of Rights. Each person also has the right to instruction in the language of his or her choice where this is reasonably practicable.

Official languages

To cater for South Africa's diverse peoples, the Constitution provides for 11 official languages, namely Afrikaans, English, isiNdebele, isiXhosa, isiZulu, Sepedi, Sesotho, Setswana, siSwati, Tshivenda and Xitsonga.

Recognising the historically diminished use and status of the indigenous languages, the Constitution expects government to implement positive measures to elevate the status and advance the use of these languages.

According to Census 2001, isiZulu is the mother tongue of 23,8% of the population, followed by isiXhosa (17,6%), Afrikaans

◀ Although South Africans come from many cultural traditions, they belong to one nation, a dynamic blend of age-old customs and modern ways, building a South African society to create a better life for all.

(13,3%), Sepedi (9,4%), and English and Setswana (8,2% each).

The least spoken indigenous language in South Africa is isiNdebele, which is spoken by 1,6% of the population.

Language policy

The National Language Policy Framework (NLPF) was launched in 2003 and is guided by the following principles:
- promoting and protecting linguistic and cultural diversity
- supporting democracy through entrenchment of language equity and language rights
- asserting the view that multilingualism is a resource
- encouraging the learning of other South African languages.

The National Language Service (NLS) will lay the basis for the South African Languages Bill. Despite the fact that some groundwork has already been done by the NLS relating to the language provisions set out in the Constitution, the NLPF calls for more radical implementation strategies.

The NLPF is a national framework which will have to be implemented by provincial and local governments. It is critical that these levels of governance align their language policies with the NLPF. They will also have to take into account regional circumstances and the needs and preferences of local communities.

Considering the nature and the history of the previously marginalised languages, more effort will have to be put into the development of these languages.

There is a need to identify priority areas with a view of supporting existing structures for the development of these languages. It is important to note that the implementation of the NLPF will increase the demand for translation and editing work and interpreting services, especially in the African languages.

The growing need for the services of professional language practitioners will create a demand for further training and educational resources. This will result in job opportunities for people who are linguistically skilled and will contribute to poverty alleviation in South Africa.

The Department of Arts and Culture has taken steps to promote the indigenous languages of South Africa.

One of the projects viewed critically by the Department in terms of bringing services to the people, is the Telephone Interpreting Service of South Africa (TISSA).

The NLS has also produced a multilingual *AIDS Manual* containing substantial terminology that should help to bridge the gap between different language communities and the primary healthcare providers who serve them.

The NLS has also focused on education-terminology projects, particularly for the natural sciences and technology, the economic and management sciences, and the human and social sciences.

The NLS is committed to preventing the country's languages, specifically the African languages, from losing their functionality and becoming redundant. The NLS regards the development of human language technologies as imperative if online dictionaries, terminology lists and other products are to be provided in all 11 official languages of South Africa, including spellcheckers for the 10 indigenous languages.

South Africa has 12 public holidays:
New Year's Day – 1 January
Human Rights Day – 21 March
Good Friday – Friday before Easter Sunday
Family Day – Monday after Easter Sunday
Freedom Day – 27 April
Workers' Day – 1 May
Youth Day – 16 June
National Women's Day – 9 August
Heritage Day – 24 September
Day of Reconciliation – 16 December
Christmas Day – 25 December
Day of Goodwill – 26 December
If any of these days falls on a Sunday, the following Monday becomes a public holiday.

The land and its people

Telephone Interpreting Service of South Africa

The TISSA was launched in March 2002. This is a ground-breaking project to facilitate access to public services in South Africans' languages of choice.

In this project, interpreters bridge language barriers via telephone. It is the first project of its kind in South Africa.

The TISSA is a project of the Department of Arts and Culture and is jointly funded by the Pan South African Language Board (PaNSALB).

With TISSA, the Department is on par with international standards of well-known telephone interpreting services in other multilingual countries such as Australia, the United States of America and many European countries. TISSA caters for the needs of the speakers of the 11 official languages of South Africa, thus promoting the use of indigenous languages. By April 2003, TISSA was operational in about 40 police stations countrywide.

A videophone facility for sign-language interpreting was launched in August 2002.

Language usage in government

National and provincial governments may use any two or more official languages for the purposes of government, taking into account usage, practicality, expense, regional circumstances and the needs and preferences of the population. The Constitution states that all official languages should enjoy parity of esteem and be treated equitably.

National departments tend to produce multilingual documents for communication with the public (information brochures, annual reports, letters, and to a lesser extent, government notices and bills). For internal communication purposes, documents are mainly created in English. Internal newsletters are often produced in more than one language.

Hansard, a verbatim record of the Parliamentary debate, contains all speeches in the language(s) in which they were delivered, followed by an English translation where necessary.

The NLPF provides for multilingual *Hansard* publications which, in the case of provincial legislatures, will use languages as determined by regional circumstances.

Pan South African Language Board

The purpose of the Board is to promote multilingualism in South Africa by:
- creating conditions for the development and equal use of all official languages
- fostering respect for and encouraging the use of other languages in the country
- encouraging the best use of the country's linguistic resources to enable South Africans to free themselves from all forms of linguistic discrimination, domination and division.

The functions of PaNSALB are to:
- initiate research to promote the development of
  - all official languages
  - the Khoi and San languages
  - South African Sign Language
- initiate research aimed at
  - developing previously marginalised languages in South Africa
  - strengthening rights relating to language and the status of languages (as at 27 April 1994)
  - promoting multilingualism
  - utilising South Africa's language resources and preventing exploitation, domination and division by any language
  - making recommendations on language legislation, practice and policy

---

A national Multilingualism Consultative Conference, entitled *The Future of Multilingualism in South Africa: From Policy to Practice*, was held in Johannesburg in June 2003.

The aim of the Conference was to discuss and consult stakeholders on whether the South African Languages Bill captures the spirit of the Constitution's provisions on language, and whether it appropriately reflects the content of the National Language Policy Framework.

- advising on the co-ordination of language planning in South Africa.

PaNSALB may on its own initiative, or upon receipt of a written complaint, investigate the alleged violation of any language right, policy or practice. It may also summon any person, body or state organ to give evidence.

Pan South African Language Board Amendment Act, 1999

The PaNSALB Amendment Act, 1999 (Act 10 of 1999), provided the Board with a progressive shift from being a watchdog State organ to addressing the language-development needs of South Africans.

PaNSALB's explicit role is to create conditions for the development and equal use of all official languages. It must initiate, facilitate and empower agencies within both State structures and civil society to contribute towards the development of all official languages.

The Amendment Act provides for the establishment of National Lexicography Units (NLUs) for all official languages. The purpose of these Units is to compile monolingual explanatory, and other, dictionaries to satisfy the needs of the different linguistic communities.

National Lexicography Units

Eleven NLUs have been established and registered as Section 21 companies since 2000, namely:
- Afrikaans: *Buro van die Woordeboek van die Afrikaanse Taal* (WAT)
- English: Dictionary Unit for South African English (DSAE)
- isiNdebele: *IsiHlathululi-Mezwi SesiNdebele*
- isiXhosa: isiXhosa NLU
- isiZulu: *Isikhungo Sesichazamazwi SesiZulu*
- siSwati: *Silulu SesiSwati* NLU
- Setswana: Setswana NLU
- Sesotho: *Sesiu sa Sesotho* NLU
- Sesotho sa Lebowa: Sesotho sa Lebowa Dictionary Unit
- Tshivenda: Tshivenda NLU
- Xitsonga: Xitsonga NLU.

The Government supports the development and preservation of languages within a bilingual or multilingual policy. In the past, the country had a bilingual policy and the Government supported two dictionary offices, namely WAT in Stellenbosch, Western Cape and DSAE in Grahamstown, Eastern Cape. With 11 official languages, 11 national dictionary offices need government support.

The NLUs are financed on a monthly basis by PaNSALB.

PaNSALB established the 11 official NLUs at tertiary institutions within the boundaries of the geolinguistic area where most of the language users of the particular language are situated. The existing official dictionary offices (WAT and DSAE) remained where they were.

National language bodies

National language bodies have been established for all 11 official languages.

The Khoi and San national language bodies were officially launched in October 1999 in Upington, Northern Cape, to promote and develop the Khoi and San languages. In addition, they assist PaNSALB in its endeavours to promote multilingualism as a national resource. They conduct surveys in communities where the Khoi and San languages are spoken, to record and standardise new terminology and words. They also liaise closely with other professional bodies that can help to enrich and expand the Khoi and San languages.

These advisory bodies assist PaNSALB to take meaningful decisions regarding the standardisation, orthography, terminology and literature issues of each language.

Protection of language rights

Section 11 of the PaNSALB Act, 1995 (Act 59 of 1995), requires the Board to investigate any alleged violation of any language right, policy or practice. It is imperative to conduct such an investigation in order to determine whether there is any substance to the complaint lodged. Should it be found that the complaint is valid, the next process would be mediation, conciliation or negotiation. In the event of these failing, a hearing would follow.

The Section does not require a formal investigation procedure. The initial stages of the investigation procedure are informal. PaNSALB is furthermore empowered by Section 11(5) to negotiate or mediate in language conflict and attempt conciliation. Mediation, consultation and conciliation form part of the 'jurisdictional requirements' of the Act. Section 12(2) obliges PaNSALB to report and alert Parliament to problems.

From its inception to the end of March 2003, 317 written complaints had been lodged with PaNSALB.

During the 2002/03 financial year, 83 complaints were lodged compared with 67 complaints in the previous year. Some 55,4% of complaints lodged during 2002/03 targeted government departments, particularly the Department of Labour's Compensation Commissioner. This is significantly higher than the 28% recorded during 2001/02. Some 10,8% of complaints targeted local authorities compared with 16% of complaints recorded during 2001/02.

Bill on the Commission for the Promotion and Protection of Cultural, Religious and Linguistic Communities

This Bill was published to give effect to Section 185 of the Constitution and was approved by Cabinet in 2001. The Commission's main purpose will be to promote respect for the rights and interests of the various cultural, religious and linguistic communities in South Africa. In addition, the Bill delegates the Commission to:
- promote and develop peace, friendship, humanity, tolerance and national unity among cultural, religious and linguistic communities on the basis of equality, non-discrimination and free association
- recommend the establishment or recognition of other councils for a community or communities in South Africa.

To achieve its goals, the Commission will have the power to:
- monitor, investigate, research, educate, lobby, advise and report on any issue concerning the rights of cultural, religious and linguistic communities
- facilitate the resolution of conflict or friction between any such community and an organ of State
- receive and deal with complaints and requests by cultural, religious or linguistic communities
- convene an annual national conference of delegates from various cultural, religious and linguistic communities in South Africa and governmental and non-governmental role-players.

The names of 53 short-listed candidates for the Commission were released on 31 July 2003. The candidates were interviewed in August and September 2003 with a view to selecting the final 26 names which will be submitted to the President.

Religion

Religious groups in South Africa

Almost 80% of South Africa's population follows the Christian faith. Other major religious groups are the Hindus, Muslims and Jews. A minority of South Africa's population do not belong to any of the major religions, but regard themselves as traditionalists or of no specific religious affiliation.

Freedom of worship is guaranteed by the Constitution, and the official policy is one of non-interference in religious practices.

Christian churches

There are many official and unofficial ecumenical relations between the various churches.

The most important of these is perhaps the South African Council of Churches (SACC), even though it is not representative of the full spectrum of churches.

The major African indigenous churches, most of the Afrikaans churches, and the Pentecostal and charismatic churches are, as a rule, not members of the SACC, and usually have their own co-ordinating liaison bodies.

Church attendance in South Africa is favourable in both rural and urban areas, and the churches are well served by a large number of clerics and officials.

On the whole, training for the ministry is thorough and intensive, and based on a variety of models. Patterns of ministry vary greatly.

Apart from the work of the churches, a number of Christian organisations operate in South Africa, doing missionary work, giving aid and providing training. (A comprehensive register appears in the *South African Christian Handbook 2003/04*.)

The broadcasting of religious radio and television programmes underlines the importance of religion in South Africa. Many newspapers carry a daily scriptural message, and various religious magazines and newspapers are produced.

African Independent Churches (AICs)

The largest grouping of Christian churches is the AICs, and one of the most dramatic aspects of religious affiliation has been the rise of this movement.

Although these churches originally resulted from a number of breakaways from various mission churches (the so-called 'Ethiopian' churches), the AICs have developed their own dynamics and momentum and continue to flourish. The majority are no longer regarded as Ethiopian churches, but rather Zionist or Apostolic churches. The Pentecostal movement also has its independent offshoots in this group.

The Zion Christian Church is the largest of these churches in South Africa and the largest church overall. More than a million members gather twice a year at Zion City, Moria, near Polokwane in Limpopo, at Easter and for the September festival. Traditionally, Easter is the religious highlight of the year. Church members, estimated to number four million, are not obliged to make the pilgrimage, but have loyally observed the tradition for more than 80 years.

The 4 000 or more independent churches have a membership of more than 10 million, making this movement the single most important religious group in South Africa.

The independent churches attract people from rural and urban areas. There are, for example, hundreds of separate churches in rural KwaZulu-Natal and at least 900 from all ethnic groups in the urban complex of Soweto alone. In the northern KwaZulu-Natal and Mpumalanga areas, these churches serve more than half the population.

Afrikaans churches

The *Nederduitsch Gereformeerde* (NG) family of churches in South Africa – the Dutch Reformed churches – represents some 3,5 million people. The *NG Kerk* is the largest of the three churches with a total of about 1 200 congregations countrywide. The other churches are the United Reformed Church of South Africa and the smaller Reformed Church in Africa, with predominantly Indian members. The *Nederduitsch Hervormde Kerk* and the *Gereformeerde Kerk* are regarded as sister churches. There are several other churches with Afrikaans-speaking adherents, some with very large memberships. The *NG Kerk* also has six fully fledged English-language congregations, one congregation for Dutch-speaking people and four for Portuguese-speaking people. In total, there are about 2 000 members in each of these congregations.

The Roman Catholic Church

In recent years, the Roman Catholic Church

The land and its people

has grown strongly in number and influence, even though South Africa is predominantly Protestant. It works closely with other churches on the socio-political front.

Other Christian churches

Other established churches in South Africa include the Methodist Church, the Church of the Province of Southern Africa (Anglican Church), various Lutheran and Presbyterian churches and the Congregational Church.

Although the different Baptist groups are not large, they represent a strong church tradition. Together these churches form the nucleus of the SACC.

The largest traditional Pentecostal churches are the Apostolic Faith Mission, the Assemblies of God and the Full Gospel Church, but there are numerous others. Many of them enjoy fellowship in groups such as the Church Alliance of South Africa, and operate in all communities.

A number of charismatic churches have been established in recent years, such as His People Christian Church. The sister churches of the charismatic churches, together with those of the Hatfield Christian Church in Pretoria, are grouped under the International Fellowship of Christian Churches.

Also active in South Africa, among the smaller groups, are the Greek Orthodox and Seventh Day Adventist churches.

Number of individuals by religion, based on Census 2001

Religion	Members	%
Christian	35 750 636	79,8%
African traditional	125 903	0,3%
Judaism	75 555	0,2%
Hinduism	551 669	1,2%
Islam	654 064	1,5%
Other	283 814	0,6%
No religion	6 767 165	15,1%
Undetermined	610 971	1,4%
Total	44 819 778	–

African traditionalists

Because the traditional religion of the African people has a strong cultural base, the various groups have different rituals, but there are certain common features.

A Supreme Being is generally recognised, but ancestors are of far greater importance, being the deceased elders of the group. They are regarded as part of the community, indispensable links with the spirit world and the powers that control everyday affairs. These ancestors are not gods, but because they play a key part in bringing about either good or ill fortune, maintaining good relations with them is vital and they have to be appeased regularly by a variety of ritual offerings.

While an intimate knowledge of herbs and other therapeutic techniques, as well as the use of supernatural powers, can be applied to the benefit of the individual and the community, some practitioners are masters of black magic, creating fear among people. As a result of close contact with Christianity, many people find themselves in a transitional phase somewhere between traditional African religion and Christianity.

Other religions

Most Indians retained their Hindu religion when they originally came to South Africa. Today, some two-thirds of South Africa's Indians are Hindus.

The Muslim community in South Africa is small, but growing strongly. The major components of this community are the Cape Malays, who are mainly descendants of Indonesian slaves, as well as 20% of people of Indian descent.

The Jewish population is less than 100 000. Of these, the majority are Orthodox Jews.

Buddhism is barely organised in South Africa. The number of Parsees has decreased, while there is a small group of Jains in Durban. The Baha'i faith is establishing groups and temples in various parts of the country.

The land

The Republic of South Africa occupies the southernmost part of the African continent, stretching latitudinally from 22° to 35° S and longitudinally from 17° to 33° E.

Its surface area is 1 219 090 km^2. It has common boundaries with the republics of Namibia, Botswana and Zimbabwe, while the Republic of Mozambique and the Kingdom of Swaziland lie to the north-east. Completely enclosed by South African territory in the south-east is the mountain Kingdom of Lesotho.

To the west, south and east, South Africa borders on the Atlantic and Indian oceans. Isolated, 1 920 km south-east of Cape Town in the Atlantic, lie Prince Edward and Marion islands, annexed by South Africa in 1947.

The oceans

South Africa is surrounded by the ocean on three sides – to the west, south and east – and has a long coastline of about 3 000 km. This coastline is swept by two major ocean currents – the warm south-flowing Mozambique-Agulhas Current and the cold Benguela. The former skirts the east and south coasts as far as Cape Agulhas, while the Benguela Current flows northwards along the west coast as far as southern Angola.

The contrast in temperature between these two currents partly accounts for important differences in climate and vegetation between the east and west coasts of South Africa. It also accounts for the differences in marine life. The cold waters of the west coast are much richer in oxygen, nitrates, phosphates and plankton than those of the east coast. Consequently, the South African fishing industry is centred on the west coast.

The coasts

The coastline itself is an even, closed one with few bays or indentations naturally suitable for harbours. The only ideal natural harbour along the coastline is Saldanha Bay on the west coast. However, the area lacks fresh water and offers no natural lines of penetration to the interior.

Most river-mouths are unsuitable as harbours because large sandbars block entry for most of the year. These bars are formed by the action of waves and currents, and by the intermittent flow, heavy sediment load and steep gradients of most South African rivers. Only the largest rivers, such as the Orange and Limpopo, maintain narrow permanent channels through the bars. For these reasons, the country has no navigable rivers.

Relief features

The surface area of South Africa falls into two major physiographic categories: the interior plateau, and the land between the plateau and the coast. Forming the boundary between these two areas is the Great Escarpment, the most prominent and continuous relief feature of the country. Its height above sea level varies from approximately 1 500 m in the dolerite-capped Roggeveld scarp in the south-west, to a height of 3 482 m in the KwaZulu-Natal Drakensberg.

Inland from the Escarpment lies the interior plateau, which is the southern continuation of the great African plateau stretching north to the Sahara Desert.

The plateau itself is characterised by wide plains with an average height of 1 200 m above sea level.

Surmounting the plateau in places are a number of well-defined upland blocks. The dissected Lesotho plateau, which is more than 3 000 m above sea level, is the most prominent. In general, the Escarpment forms the highest parts of the plateau.

Between the Great Escarpment and the coast lies an area which varies in width from 80 to 240 km in the east and south, to a mere 60 to 80 km in the west. At least three major subdivisions can be recognised: the eastern plateau slopes, the Cape folded belt and adjacent regions, and the western plateau slopes.

The land and its people

Climatic features

The subtropical location, on either side of 30°S, accounts for the warm temperate conditions so typical of South Africa, making it a popular destination for foreign tourists.

The country also falls squarely within the subtropical belt of high pressure, making it dry, with an abundance of sunshine.

The wide expanses of ocean on three sides of South Africa have a moderating influence on its climate. More apparent, however, are the effects of the warm Agulhas and the cold Benguela Currents along the east and west coasts respectively. While Durban (east coast) and Port Nolloth (west coast) lie more or less on the same latitude, there is a difference of at least 6°C in their mean annual temperatures.

Gale-force winds are frequent on the coasts, especially in the south-western and southern coastal areas.

Rainfall

South Africa has an average annual rainfall of 464 mm, compared with a world average of 860 mm. About 20% of the country has a total annual rainfall of less than 200 mm, 48% between 200 and 600 mm, while only about 30% records more than 600 mm. In total, 65% of the country has an annual rainfall of less than 500 mm – usually regarded as the absolute minimum for successful dry-land farming.

In Cape Town, the capital city of the Western Cape, the average rainfall is highest in the winter months, while in the capital cities of the other eight provinces, the average rainfall is highest during summer.

South Africa's rainfall is unreliable and unpredictable. Large fluctuations in the average annual rainfall are the rule rather than the exception in most areas of the country. Below-average annual rainfall is more commonly recorded than above-average total annual rainfall. South Africa is periodically afflicted by drastic and prolonged droughts, which often end in severe floods.

Temperatures

Temperature conditions in South Africa are characterised by three main features. Firstly, temperatures tend to be lower than in other regions at similar latitudes, for example, Australia. This is due primarily to the greater elevation of the subcontinent above sea level.

Secondly, despite a latitudinal span of 13 degrees, average annual temperatures are remarkably uniform throughout the country. Owing to the increase in the height of the plateau towards the north-east, there is hardly any increase in temperature from south to north as might be expected.

The third feature is the striking contrast between temperatures on the east and west coasts.

Temperatures above 32°C are fairly common in summer, and frequently exceed 38°C in the lower Orange River valley and the Mpumalanga Lowveld.

Frost, humidity and fog

Frost often occurs on the interior plateau during cold, clear winter nights, with ice forming on still pools and in water pipes. The frost season is longest (from April to October) over the eastern and southern plateau areas bordering on the Escarpment. Frost decreases to the north, while the coast is virtually frost-free. Average annual relative humidity readings show that, in general, the air is driest over the western interior and the plateau. Along the coast, the humidity is much higher and at times may rise to 85%. Low stratus clouds and fog frequently occur over the cool west coast, particularly during summer. The only other area that commonly experiences fog is the 'mist belt' along the eastern foothills of the Escarpment.

Sunshine

South Africa is famous for its sunshine. Generally speaking, April and May are the most pleasant months when the rainy season over the summer-rainfall region has ended, and before the rainy season in the winter-rainfall area has begun. At this time of year, the hot summer weather has abated and the winds are lighter than during the rest of the year.

In certain areas, however, notably the hot, humid KwaZulu-Natal coast, Mpumalanga and Limpopo, June and July are the ideal holiday months.

The provinces

In terms of the Constitution of South Africa, the country is divided into nine provinces, each with its own Legislature, Premier and executive councils. The provinces with their own distinctive landscapes, vegetation and climate, are the Western Cape, the Eastern Cape, KwaZulu-Natal, the Northern Cape, Free State, North West, Gauteng, Mpumalanga and Limpopo. (See Chapter 21: *Tourism*.)

Western Cape

The Western Cape is situated on the south-western tip of the African continent. It is a region of majestic mountains, well-watered valleys, wide, sandy beaches and breathtaking scenery.

The cold Atlantic Ocean along the west coast is a rich fishing area, while the warmer Indian Ocean skirts the province's southern beaches.

Visitors to the Western Cape can disembark at Cape Town International Airport or at the Port of Cape Town in the shadow of Table Mountain. A network of roads also leads to Cape Town, the capital, also known as the Mother City.

Other important towns in the province include Vredenburg-Saldanha, an important harbour for iron exports and the fishing industry; Worcester and Stellenbosch in the heart of the winelands; George, renowned for indigenous timber and vegetable produce; Oudtshoorn, known for its ostrich products and the world-famous Cango Caves, and Beaufort West on the dry, sheep-farming plains of the Great Karoo.

The Western Cape boasts one of the six accepted floral kingdoms of the world. Although the smallest of them all, the Western Cape floral kingdom, locally called *fynbos*, contains more plant species than the whole of Europe. These include the famous proteas and heathers.

The Knysna-Tsitsikamma region has the country's biggest indigenous forests. This is a fairyland of ancient forest giants, ferns and colourful birdlife. Products of the forests include sought-after furniture made from the indigenous yellowwood, stinkwood and white pear.

The tourism sector is perceived as the most important growth force in the Western Cape.

The people

More than 4,5 million people live in the Western Cape on 129 370 km^2 of land. The majority of them are Afrikaans-speaking, while the other main languages are isiXhosa and English. The Western Cape has the highest adult-education level in the country, with only 5,7% of people aged 20 years or older having undergone no schooling (Census 2001). The province has a strong network of higher-education institutions.

The official unemployment figure for the province, 12,1%, is the lowest in the country according to the Labour Force Survey 2001.

Agriculture and marine fishery

The Western Cape is rich in agriculture and fisheries.

Primary industries, i.e. agriculture, forestry and fishing, and mining and quarrying contributed 5,4% to the Gross Domestic Product (GDP) of the province in 2001, which translates to R7 287 million (Census 2001).

The agricultural sector plays a key role as an agent of growth, accounting for more than 9% of provincial employment, more than 55% of all South African agricultural exports, and 23% of the national agricultural contribution to GDP.

The sheltered valleys between the mountains provide ideal conditions for the cultiva-

The land and its people

tion of top-grade fruits, such as apples, table grapes, olives, peaches and oranges. In the eastern part of the Western Cape region, a great variety of vegetables is cultivated.

The province can be divided into three climatic regions. The area around the Cape Peninsula and the Boland, further inland, is a winter-rainfall region with sunny, dry summers.

Towards George, along the south coast, the climate gradually changes to year-round rainfall, while inland, towards the more arid Great Karoo, the climate changes to summer rainfall.

The Western Cape is known as one of the world's finest grape-growing regions. Many of its wines have received the highest accolades at international shows.

The Klein Karoo region around Oudtshoorn, besides being famous for its Cango Caves, is the centre of the ostrich-farming industry in South Africa. Fine leatherware, ostrich feathers and meat are exported to destinations all over the world. The Swartland district around Malmesbury and the Overberg around Caledon form the bread basket of the country.

The inland Karoo region around Beaufort West, and the Bredasdorp district produce wool and mutton, as well as pedigree merino breeding stock.

Western Cape

Capital: Cape Town
Principal languages: Afrikaans 55,3%
isiXhosa 23,7%
English 19,3%
Population: 4 524 335
Area (km²): 129 370
% of total area: 10,6%
GGP* at current prices (2001): R136 062 million
% of total GDP:** 13,8%

* GGP (Gross Geographical Product) = GDP of a region
** GDP (Gross Domestic Product)

Other animal products include broiler chickens, eggs, dairy products, beef and pork. Racehorse-breeding is another important industry.

The west coast of the province is washed by the cold Benguela Current. The plankton-rich Current is considered to be one of the world's richest fishing grounds. This resource is protected against overfishing by foreign vessels, by means of a 200 km commercial-fishing zone and a strict quota system.

The province is well-known for the wide variety of seafood offered at restaurants along the scenic coastline. Snoek, Cape lobster, abalone, calamari, octopus, oysters and mussels are among the most sought-after piscatorial delights.

The Western Cape is the only province with the status of being free of African horse-sickness. This means that the province is the only offset point for the export of horses, which brought the country millions of Rands in foreign revenue.

The province has also established itself as the leading facilitator in the export of ostrich meat to Europe, and boasts the most export abattoirs in the country from which products to the value of about R1 billion are exported.

The provincial Department of Agriculture's ostrich-breeding herd at Oudtshoorn is the only one in the world for which production data for several generations of ostriches can be connected to their pedigrees.

Industry

The *White Paper on Preparing the Western Cape for the Knowledge Economy of the 21st Century* was accepted by Parliament in 2001.

The province maintains economic growth rates slightly higher than national averages, resulting in its share of the national economy growing to about 14%. At the same time, unemployment rates have been significantly below the national average, despite significant immigration.

The finance, real estate and business services are the biggest money-makers for the province, contributing some 26,6% to the province's GDP (Census 2001). During 2001, this translated to R36 211 million.

An exciting development for the province and South Africa is the emergence of the first information communications technology cluster.

The head offices of all but one of South Africa's petroleum companies are located in Cape Town.

The city also houses the head offices of many of South Africa's insurance giants and national retail chains. With over 170 000 people employed in the clothing and textile industry, it is the single most significant industrial source of employment in the Western Cape.

The biggest segment of South Africa's printing and publishing industry is also situated in Cape Town.

While Epping, Parow, Retreat and Montagu Gardens have been the core industrial areas in the past, new developments are arising in the Saldanha-Vredenburg area as a spin-off from the vast Saldanha Steel project.

The West Coast Investment Initiative, which forms part of the Government's Spatial Development Initiative (SDI) programme, was launched on 25 February 1998.

Tourism

The Western Cape's natural beauty, complemented by a history of hospitality, excellent wine and colourful cuisine, truly makes the province one of the world's greatest tourist attractions.

The tourism industry in the Western Cape contributes 13,0% to the total GDP of the province (Census 2001).

The tourism successes of Cape Town and the Western Cape over the last 10 years have been highlighted by the following:
- Besides the upgrading of traditional sites like Cape Point and the National Botanical Gardens at Kirstenbosch, there have been a number of other significant improvements.
- Robben Island is successfully run as a museum and heritage site, with ferry boats taking visitors to and from the Nelson Mandela Gateway at the Victoria and Alfred Waterfront.
- Table Mountain's cableway has been revamped. The carts now revolve while travelling up and down the Mountain, providing visitors with 360 degrees of breathtaking views.
- The District Six and Bo-Kaap Museums continue to host new and exciting material on these two historical residential areas.
- The Cape Town International Convention Centre was opened by President Thabo Mbeki on 28 June 2003. This world-class facility boasts 10 000 m^2 of exhibition- and trade-show space and two auditoriums with seating for 1 500 and 620 people respectively, as well as spacious and deluxe banqueting and function rooms of varying sizes, including a magnificent 2 000 m^2 ballroom with majestic views.

A study conducted by the University of Cape Town's Graduate School of Business, projects that the Convention Centre will create about 47 000 new jobs and bring in about R25 billion to the province over a period of 10 years.

Eastern Cape

The Eastern Cape, a land of undulating hills, endless, sweeping sandy beaches, majestic mountain ranges and emerald green forests, is in surface area the second largest of the nine provinces.

The region boasts a remarkable natural diversity, ranging from the dry, desolate Great Karoo to the lush forests of the Wild Coast and the Keiskamma Valley, the fertile Langkloof, renowned for its rich apple harvests, and the mountainous southern Drakensberg region at Elliot.

The main feature of the Eastern Cape is its astonishing coastline lapped by the Indian

The land and its people

Ocean. With its long stretches of undisturbed sandy beaches, rocky coves, secluded lagoons and towering cliffs, the coastline provides the province with a rich natural tourist attraction.

The graceful curve of Algoa Bay provides an ideal setting for the Port of Port Elizabeth while there are also good harbour facilities at East London. The province is serviced by three airports situated in Port Elizabeth, East London and Umtata.

The architecture of many of the cities and towns reflects the rich heritage of the people. The capital is Bisho. Other important towns in the province include Uitenhage, which has important motor vehicle-manufacturing and related industries; King William's Town, rich in early settler and military history; Grahamstown, also known as the City of Saints because of its more than 40 churches; Graaff-Reinet, with its interesting collection of historic buildings; Cradock, the hub of the Central Karoo; Stutterheim, the forestry centre of the province; Aliwal North, famous for its hot sulphur springs; and Port St Johns, the largest town on the Wild Coast.

In the Eastern Cape, various floral habitats meet. Along the coast, the northern tropical forests intermingle with the more temperate woods of the south. This makes for an interesting forest habitat of various species endemic to this region.

Age-old forests occur at Keiskammahoek, Dwesa, Port St Johns and Bathurst; dune forests are found at Alexandria; and mangroves along the Wild Coast.

Rolling grasslands dominate the eastern interior of the province, while the western central plateau is savanna bushveld. The northern inland is home to the aromatic, succulent Karoo.

The people

The Eastern Cape has 6 436 763 people living on about 169 600 km^2 of land.

The language most spoken is isiXhosa, followed by Afrikaans and English.

The province has a number of tertiary institutions. Despite the high quality of education facilities, 22,8% of the population aged 20 years or older have never received any schooling, and 6,3% have completed some form of higher education (Census 2001).

In 2001, the unemployment rate of the province stood at 14,8% (Labour Force Survey 2001).

Agriculture, fishing and forestry

The Eastern Cape has excellent agricultural and forestry potential. The fertile Langkloof Valley in the south-west has enormous deciduous fruit orchards, while the Karoo interior is an important sheep-farming area. Angora wool is also produced here.

The Alexandria-Grahamstown area produces pineapples, chicory and dairy products, while coffee and tea are cultivated at Magwa. People in the former Transkei region are dependent on cattle, maize and sorghum-farming. An olive nursery has been developed in conjunction with the University of Fort Hare to form a nucleus of olive production in the Eastern Cape.

Extensive exotic forestry plantations in the high rainfall areas of Keiskammahoek provide employment for large numbers of the population. The province is a summer-rainfall region with high rainfall along the coast, becoming gradually drier behind the mountain ranges into the Great Karoo.

Eastern Cape

Capital: Bisho
Principal languages: isiXhosa 83,4%
Afrikaans 9,3%
English 3,6%
Population: 6 436 763
Area (km^2): 169 580
% of total area: 13,9%
GGP at current prices (2001): R81 027 million
% of total GDP: 8,2%

The basis of the province's fishing industry is squid, some recreational and commercial fishing for line fish, some collection of marine resources, and access to line-catches of hake.

Ostrich exports are doing very well. The provincial Department of Africulture has been hailed for the support it is giving this industry. Each ostrich-export establishment has a resident official veterinarian, which is a requirement for exporting ostrich products to the European Union. This industry earns the province some R94,4 million per year in foreign revenues.

The game industry is enjoying unprecedented demand in the international market. The health-conscious consumer is increasingly demanding lean organic game meat. The gross foreign earnings from this industry amount to R23,5 million.

Industry

The metropolitan economies of Port Elizabeth and East London are based primarily on manufacturing, the most important being motor manufacturing. The province is the hub of South Africa's automotive industry.

With two harbours and three airports offering direct flights to the main centres, and an excellent road and rail infrastructure, the province has been earmarked as a key area for growth and economic development.

To facilitate integrated planning, sensitive to the environment, the province is implementing a consultative process involving community participation. It includes the Fish River SDI, the Wild Coast SDI and two Industrial Development Zones (IDZs), namely the West Bank (East London) and the Coega IDZs. The latter, 20 km east of the Port Elizabeth-Uitenhage metropoles, was the first IDZ to be earmarked and is one of the biggest initiatives ever undertaken in South Africa. Plans for the development of the area as an export-orientated zone include the building of a deepwater port.

The IDZs at Coega (Ngqura) and East London, and the West Coast SDI, continue to be the province's economic flagships.

The final commitment by the French investment and industrial company Pechiney was to invest R18,6 billion in an aluminium smelter at Coega. The R40-million contract for building the IDZ village was awarded largely to emerging small, medium and micro enterprises, and includes female contractors.

The East London IDZ has been awarded an operator's licence.

The forestry developments and the construction of the N1 toll road as part of the Wild Coast SDI is expected to create more than 20 000 jobs. An additional 5 000 jobs are expected to be created in the mining sector through upstream and downstream investment.

KwaZulu-Natal

Aptly called South Africa's garden province, this verdant region forms the east coast of South Africa, stretching from Port Edward in the south, northwards to the Mozambique boundary. It is a province with a subtropical coastline, sweeping savanna in the east, and the magnificent Drakensberg mountain range in the west. The warm Indian Ocean washing its beaches makes it one of the country's most popular holiday destinations.

Visitors to KwaZulu-Natal can either disembark at Durban International Airport or the Durban Harbour, or make use of the extensive national road network.

Durban is one of the fastest-growing urban areas in the world. Its port is the busiest in South Africa and is one of the 10 largest in the world.

KwaZulu-Natal is the only province with a monarchy specifically provided for in its Constitution.

Pietermaritzburg and Ulundi are joint capitals of the province.

Other important towns include Richards Bay, an important coal-export harbour, and

The land and its people

many coastal holiday resorts, such as Port Shepstone, Umhlanga Rocks and Margate. In the interior, Newcastle is well-known for steel production and coal-mining, Estcourt for meat processing, and Ladysmith and Richmond for mixed agriculture. The KwaZulu-Natal coastal belt yields sugar cane, wood, oranges, bananas, mangoes and other tropical fruit.

Some of South Africa's best-protected indigenous coastal forests are found along the subtropical coastline of KwaZulu-Natal, for example, at Dukuduku and Kosi Bay. It is also along this coast that the magnificent St Lucia Estuary and Kosi Bay lakes are located. In 1999, the Greater St Lucia Wetlands Park was declared a World Heritage Site.

Separating KwaZulu-Natal from the mountain Kingdom of Lesotho, the Drakensberg runs 200 km along the western boundary of the province.

The northern part of the province, south of the Swaziland border, is typical African savanna, providing a natural backdrop for its rich wildlife, protected in several game parks.

The people

KwaZulu-Natal has 9 426 017 people living on 92 100 km^2 of land. The principal language spoken is isiZulu, followed by English and Afrikaans. Remnants of British colonialism, together with Zulu, Indian and Afrikaans traditions make for an interesting cultural mix in the province.

The province counts several universities, technikons and various other educational institutions among its assets.

A total of 21,9% of the population of the province aged 20 and above have received no form of education (Census 2001).

KwaZulu-Natal has a relatively poorly skilled labour force. The economy therefore experiences a shortage of skilled human resources.

Agriculture and industry

KwaZulu-Natal was the second highest contributor to the South African economy during 2001, at 15,5% (Census 2001) of GDP.

However, the province recorded the second highest unemployment rate in the country at 17,7%. (Labour Force Survey 2001).

The Port of Durban handles the greatest volume of sea-going traffic in southern Africa.

As this Port plays such a crucial role in the South African economy, it will be the first concession for a container terminal in the country.

Heavy minerals are mined at Richards Bay. In recent times, the province has undergone rapid industrialisation owing to its abundant water supply and labour resources. Industries are found at Newcastle, Ladysmith, Dundee, Richards Bay, Durban, Hammarsdale, Richmond, Pietermaritzburg and Mandeni.

The sugar-cane plantations along the Indian Ocean coastal belt form the mainstay of the economy and agriculture of the region. The coastal belt is also a large producer of subtropical fruit, while the farmers in the hinterland concentrate on vegetable, dairy and stock-farming. Another major source of income is forestry, in the areas around Vryheid, Eshowe, Richmond, Harding and Ngome. Ngome also has tea plantations.

The summer-rainfall coastal regions of this province are hot and humid with a sub-

---

KwaZulu-Natal

Capital: (Joint capitals) Pietermaritzburg and Ulundi
Principal languages: isiZulu 80,9%
English 13,6%
Afrikaans 1,5%
Population: 9 426 017
Area (km^2): 92 100
% of total area: 7,6%
GGP at current prices (2001): R152 703 million
% of total GDP: 15,5%

tropical climate. The KwaZulu-Natal Midlands between the coastal strip and the southern Drakensberg Escarpment are drier, with extremely cold conditions in winter and snow on the high-lying ground. In the north, the subtropical strip extends further around the Kingdom of Swaziland, to the edge of the Escarpment.

For the past three years, the provincial Department of Agriculture and Environmental Affairs has been gearing itself to launch a programme of Unlocking Agricultural Potential, often termed the Green Revolution, which aims at virtually quadrupling the overall provincial agricultural production over the next 20 years. The Green Revolution has three main elements. The first is the intensification of agricultural production. To this end, the Department has made a start with a R10-million Mechanisation Programme, which will for the first time put tractors and modern farm machinery within reach of previously disadvantaged farmers. The second is land reform, where the Department has already settled new farmers on 30 000 hectares (ha) of former State land. The last is the *Xoshindlala* (chase away hunger) Programme, a food-security programme that has more than a 1 000 small food-production projects running in various parts in the province.

The Department has managed to win the full support of national government for the early relocation of the Durban International Airport to La Mercy. The Department has further strengthened the Dube Trade Port project, incorporating the King Shaka International Airport, thus making it an economic and logistics hub that will be the first of its kind in Africa. The province has committed R50 million per annum over five years to this project.

Since 2001, local business has invested over R15 billion in new investment in the province. Exports are on the increase in key economic sectors with good prospects for even greater achievements through the Toyota expansion and growth in aluminium production and the textile sector.

Northern Cape

The Northern Cape lies to the south of its most important asset, the mighty Orange River, which provides the basis for a healthy agricultural industry. The landscape is characterised by vast arid plains with outcroppings of haphazard rock piles. The cold Atlantic Ocean forms the western boundary.

This region covers the largest area of all the provinces and has the smallest population. Its major airports are situated at Kimberley, the capital, and Upington. The Northern Cape is serviced by an excellent road network, which makes its interior easily accessible from South Africa's major cities, harbours and airports.

Important towns are Upington, centre of the karakul sheep and dried-fruit industries, and the most northerly wine-making region of South Africa; Springbok, in the heart of the Namaqualand spring-flower country; Kuruman, founded by the missionary Moffat; De Aar, hub of the South African railway network; Sutherland, the coldest town in the country; and the sheep-farming towns of Carnarvon, Colesberg, Kenhardt and Prieska.

Apart from a narrow strip of winter-rainfall area along the coast, the Northern Cape is a semi-arid region with little rainfall in summer. The weather conditions are extreme – cold and frosty in winter, with extremely high temperatures in summer.

The largest part of the province falls within the Nama-Karoo biome, with a vegetation of low shrubland and grass, and trees limited to water courses. The area is known worldwide for its spectacular display of spring flowers which, for a short period every year, attracts thousands of tourists.

This biome is home to many wonderful plant species, such as the elephant's trunk (*halfmens*), tree aloe (*kokerboom*) and a variety of succulents.

The province has several national parks and conservation areas. The Kalahari Gemsbok National Park, together with the Gemsbok National Park in Botswana, is Africa's first

The land and its people

transfrontier game park, known as the Kgalagadi Transfrontier Park. It is one of the largest nature-conservation areas in southern Africa and one of the largest remaining protected natural ecosystems in the world. The Park provides unfenced access to a variety of game between South Africa and Botswana and has a surface area of more than two million ha.

The Ai-Ais-Richtersveld Transfrontier Conservation Park spans some of the most spectacular scenery of the arid and desert environments in southern Africa. Bisected by the Orange River, which forms the border between South Africa and Namibia, it comprises the Ai-Ais Hot Springs Game Park in Namibia and the Richtersveld National Park in South Africa. Some of the distinctive features in the area include the Fish River Canyon (often likened to the Grand Canyon in the United States of America) and the Ai-Ais Hot springs. This arid zone is further characterised by a unique and impressive variety of succulent plant species.

Nowhere is the Orange River more impressive than at the Augrabies Falls, which ranks among the world's greatest cataracts on a major river. The Augrabies Falls National Park was established to preserve this natural wonder.

Northern Cape

Capital: Kimberley
Principal languages: Afrikaans 68,0%
Setswana 20,8%
isiXhosa 6,2%
Population: 822 727
Area (km²): 361 830
% of total area: 29,7%
GGP at current prices (2001): R19 585 million
% of total GDP: 2,0%

The people

The Northern Cape is sparsely populated and houses some 822 727 people on 361 830 km² of land. About 68% of the people speak Afrikaans. Other languages spoken are Setswana, isiXhosa and English.

The official unemployment rate of the Northern Cape is 14,4% (Labour Force Survey).

The last remaining true San (Bushman) people live in the Kalahari area of the Northern Cape. The whole area, especially along the Orange and Vaal Rivers, is rich in San rock engravings. A good collection can be seen at the McGregor Museum in Kimberley. The province is also rich in fossils.

Agriculture and industry

The Northern Cape is an important contributor to South Africa's primary production and has considerable potential for the beneficiation of these primary commodities.

However, the province only contributed 2,0% to the economy of South Africa in 2001, making it the smallest contributor among all the nine provinces (Census 2001).

The province is displaying a tremendous growth in value-added activities, including game farming.

Food production and processing for the local and export market is growing significantly.

Underpinning the growth and development plan of the province are the investment projects that link up with the existing plans of the Namaqua Development Corridor. The focus is on the beneficiation and export of sea products.

The economy of a large part of the Northern Cape, the interior Karoo, depends on sheep-farming, while the karakul-pelt industry is one of the most important in the Gordonia district of Upington.

The province has fertile agricultural land. In the Orange River Valley, especially at Upington, Kakamas and Keimoes, grapes and fruit are intensively cultivated.

Some 14 million crates of table grapes were produced in 2001/02, mainly for the export market. In line with grape production being higher than expected, raisins also showed a significant increase with the South African Dried Fruit Co-op paying out more than R200 million to some 200 producers.

Wheat, fruit, peanuts, maize and cotton are produced at the Vaalharts Irrigation Scheme near Warrenton.

Mining

The Northern Cape is rich in minerals. The country's chief diamond pipes are found in the Kimberley district. In 1888, the diamond industry was formally established with the creation of De Beers Consolidated Mines. Alluvial diamonds are also extracted from the beaches and sea between Alexander Bay and Port Nolloth.

The Sishen Mine near Kathu is the biggest source of iron ore in South Africa, and the copper mine at Okiep is one of the oldest mines in the country. Copper is also mined at Springbok and Aggenys. The province is also rich in asbestos, manganese, fluorspar, semi-precious stones and marble.

Until recently, the majority of small- to medium-scale alluvial operations were concentrated along or near the current Vaal River system. With the rapidly depleting deposits available for mining, there has been a gradual shift towards the Orange River system, with Trans-Hex holding 50% of concessions issued along the Orange River. Two recent larger scale investments also show continued prospects in this sector.

Free State

The Free State lies in the heart of South Africa, with the Kingdom of Lesotho nestling in the hollow of its bean-like shape. Between the Vaal River in the north and the Orange River in the south, this immense rolling prairie stretches as far as the eye can see.

The capital, Bloemfontein, has a well-established institutional, educational and administrative infrastructure and houses the Supreme Court of Appeal. The province has a well-known university and many other training institutions.

Important towns include Welkom, the heart of the goldfields and one of the few completely pre-planned cities in the world; Odendaalsrus, another gold-mining town; Sasolburg, which owes its existence to the petrol-from-coal installation established there; Kroonstad, an important agricultural, administrative and educational centre; Parys, on the banks of the Vaal River; Phuthaditjhaba, well-known for the beautiful handcrafted items produced by the local people, and Bethlehem, gateway to the Eastern Highlands of the Free State.

The national road, which is the artery between Gauteng and the Western and Eastern Cape, passes through the middle of the Free State.

The people

The Free State is the third-largest province in South Africa.

It houses some 2 766 775 people on about 129 480 km^2 of land. The main languages spoken are Sesotho and Afrikaans. Some 16% of people aged 20 years or older have received no schooling (Census 2001). The official unemployment rate according to the Labour Force Survey of September 2001 is 17,6%.

Many of the towns display a cultural mix clearly evident in street names, public buildings, monuments and museums. Dressed-sandstone buildings abound on the Eastern Highlands, while beautifully decorated Sotho houses dot the grasslands. Some of South Africa's most valued San rock art is found in the Free State. The districts of Bethlehem, Ficksburg, Ladybrand and Wepener have remarkable collections of this art form.

Agriculture

This summer-rainfall region can be extremely cold during the winter months, especially towards the eastern mountainous regions where temperatures can drop as low as 9,5 °C.

The land and its people

The western and southern areas are semi-desert.

Known as the 'granary of the country', the Free State has cultivated land covering 3,2 million ha, while natural veld and grazing cover 8,7 million ha.

Field crops yield almost two-thirds of the gross agricultural income of the province. Animal products contribute a further 30%, with the balance coming from horticulture.

Ninety per cent of the country's cherry crop is produced in the Ficksburg district, while the two largest asparagus canning factories are also situated in this district. Soya, sorghum, sunflowers and wheat are cultivated, especially in the eastern Free State, where farmers specialise in seed production. About 40% of the country's potato yield comes from the high-lying areas of the Free State.

Mining

The mining industry is the biggest employer in the Free State. Investment opportunities are substantial in productivity-improvement areas for mining and related products and services.

South Africa is the world's largest producer of gold. A gold reef of over 400 km long, known as the Goldfields, stretches across Gauteng and the Free State, the largest gold-mining complex being Free State Consolidated Goldfields with a mining area of 32 918 ha.

Some 82% of the region's mineral production value is derived from this activity, primarily in the Goldfields region, which comprises the districts of Odendaalsrus, Virginia and Welkom. Roughly 30% of South Africa's gold is obtained from this region, and the province qualifies for fifth position as a global producer.

The Harmony Gold Refinery, situated in Virginia, is allowed to sell one-third of its total annual gold production to jewellery manufacturers, and has the facilities to ensure that the correct quality is maintained at all times. Harmony Gold Refinery and Rand Refinery are the only two gold refineries in South Africa.

Gold mines in the Free State also supply a substantial portion of the total silver produced in the country, while considerable concentrations of uranium occurring in the gold-bearing conglomerates of the goldfields are extracted as a by-product.

Bituminous coal is mined in the province and converted to petrochemicals at Sasolburg.

Diamonds from this region, extracted from kimberlite pipes and fissures, are of a high quality.

The largest deposit of bentonite in the country occurs in the Koppies district.

Manufacturing

The Free State, best known for its maize production has, in the last decade, reduced its dependency on the primary sector and become a manufacturing economy.

In 2001, the manufacturing industry contributed 13,2% to the total value added at basic prices.

Some 14% of the province's manufacturing is classified as being in high-technology industries, which is the highest percentage of all the provincial economies.

This growth in high-tech industries is significant in the context of the changing contribution of the gold-mining industry to Gross Geographic Product (GGP).

Free State
Capital: Bloemfontein
Principal languages: Sesotho 64,4%
Afrikaans 11,9%
isiXhosa 9,1%
Population: 2 766 775
Area (km²): 129 480
% of total area: 10,6%
GGP at current prices (2001): R53 900 million
% of total GDP: 5,5%

The province's three-tier development strategy centres on competitiveness, empowerment, capacity-building and beneficiation.

Manufacturing is the second-largest sector in the regional economy. Among the most important activities are the chemical products manufactured by Sasol and the further beneficiation of agricultural products. A wide variety of industries have developed around the production of basic chemicals from coal.

North West

North West is centrally located in the subcontinent with direct road and rail links to all of the southern African countries, and its own airport. The province borders on Botswana and is fringed by the Kalahari desert in the west and the Witwatersrand area in the east.

The province is divided into five regions, namely the Central, Bophirima (towards the west), Southern, Rustenburg and Eastern Regions.

Most economic activity is concentrated in the Southern Region (between Potchefstroom and Klerksdorp), Rustenburg, and the Eastern Region, where more than 83,3% of GGP of the province is produced.

The Klerksdorp and Rustenburg Regions together produce about 67% of the province's GGP while covering 33% of the surface area. Forty-eight per cent of the province's population reside here.

The people

Of the 3 669 349 people in the North West, 65% live in the rural areas. In spite of its small population, it is estimated that 9% of all the poor people in the country live in the North West. The poverty rate is estimated at 57%. As far as educational attainment and skills availability are concerned, the North West lags behind the South African average.

The province has the lowest number of people aged 20 years and older (5,9%) who have received higher education. The literacy rate is in the region of 57%. As part of the Department of Education's proposed plans for higher education, the existing four higher learning institutions will be merged to form two.

During 2003, as part of the Year of Further Education and Training project, three mega institutions, Taletso, ORBIT and Vuselela, were established to provide technical and vocational training to the youth. These institutions have been incorporated into many of the former education and technical colleges and manpower centres.

Mining

Although the 'platinum province' is the third-slowest contributor to South Africa's GDP, it is the dominant province in mineral sales.

Mining contributes 33,2% to the economy and 17,8% of total employment in the North West. Diamonds are mined at Lichtenburg, Koster, Christiana and Bloemhof, while Orkney and Klerksdorp have gold mines.

Between February 2002 and February 2003, additional investments in the mining industry created more than 3 000 jobs, at an investment value of more than R4 billion.

The area surrounding Rustenburg and Brits boasts the largest single platinum-production area in the world. Marble is also mined here. Fluorspar is exploited at Zeerust.

Manufacturing

Manufacturing is almost exclusively dependent on the performance of a few sectors in which the province enjoys a competitive advantage. These are fabricated metals, food, and non-metallic metals.

According to figures from Statistics South Africa and Global Insight, it is estimated that North West's manufacturing sector grew by 1,7% in 2002.

Much of this growth was driven by the manufacturing sector's links with agriculture and mining.

Industrial activity is centred around the

The land and its people

towns of Brits, Klerksdorp, Vryburg and Rustenburg.

The Brits industries concentrate mostly on manufacturing and construction, while those at Klerksdorp are geared towards the mining industry, and those at Vryburg and Rustenburg towards agriculture.

The Platinum SDI can unlock further development. It is situated on the Coast-to-Coast highway that links the Port of Maputo in Mozambique to Walvis Bay in Namibia.

Approximately 200 potential project opportunities in tourism, manufacturing, agriculture and mining have been identified.

As a result of the Platinum SDI, more than R3 billion was injected into the South African economy. During its construction phase, the project created some 3 000 direct and 12 000 indirect and induced jobs.

By 2003, progress had been made regarding the Mafikeng IDZ around the Mafikeng Airport. The aim of the IDZ is to create jobs and enhance the economic potential of the Central Region, the entire North West and the Southern African Development Community Region.

Efforts are under way to secure international status for the Mafikeng Airport.

By February 2003, the province had completed a holistic North West Economic Development and Industrial Strategy which forms part of the wider North West 2012 Development Plan.

North West

Capital: Mafikeng
Principal languages: Setswana 65,4%
Afrikaans 7,5%
isiXhosa 5,8%
Population: 3 669 349
Area (km^2): 116 320
% of total area: 9,5%
GGP at current prices (2001): R72 230 million
% of total GDP: 7,3%

Agriculture

Agriculture is of extreme importance to the North West. It contributes about 13% of the total GGP and 19% to formal employment.

The province is an important food basket in South Africa. Maize and sunflowers are the most important crops; the North West is the biggest producer of white maize in the country.

Some of the largest cattle herds in the world are found at Stellaland near Vryburg, which explains why this area is often referred to as the 'Texas of South Africa'. Marico is also cattle-country. The areas around Rustenburg and Brits are fertile, mixed-crop farming land.

Twenty-eight different types of projects of new household food-security projects were implemented throughout the North West during 2002. Participants in these projects included 1 500 women and 700 youths.

The provincial Department of Agriculture has also developed a comprehensive veterinary programme for evaluating and improving dairy facilities for export purposes.

Gauteng

Although the smallest of the nine provinces, Gauteng (Sotho word for the place of gold) is the powerhouse of South Africa and the heart of its commercial business and industrial sectors.

In 2001, the largest contribution to South Africa's economy was made by Gauteng, at 33,9% (Census 2001).

Gauteng was also recorded as having the highest unemployment rate (19,9%).

The three most important sectors contributing to GGP are financial and business services, logistics and communications, and mining.

The growth and development plans for the province are underpinned by the Blue IQ projects.

These consist of 11 different mega projects in economic infrastructure development, in the areas of technology, tourism, transport and high-value-added manufacturing.

The aim is to attract some R100 billion in direct investment over the next 10 years. In excess of R2 billion has already been allocated by the Gauteng Provincial Government to facilitate these investment projects.

Gauteng's main cities are Johannesburg, the largest city in southern Africa, and Pretoria, the administrative capital of the country.

The province blends cultures and colours and first- and third-world traditions into a spirited mix that is flavoured by many foreign influences.

Gauteng's primary attraction is business opportunity, but there is more to this province. There is a wealth of culture to be found in the museums, galleries, art routes and historical battlefields.

Most overseas visitors enter South Africa via Johannesburg International Airport.

Johannesburg, nicknamed Egoli (place of gold), is the capital of the province and is a city of contrasts. Mine-dumps and headgear stand proud as symbols of its rich past, while modern architecture rubs shoulders with examples of 19th-century engineering prowess. Gleaming skyscrapers contrast with Indian bazaars and African *muti* (medicine) shops, where traditional healers dispense advice and traditional medicine.

The busy streets ring out with the calls of fruit-sellers and street vendors. An exciting blend of ethnic and western art and cultural activities is reflected in theatres and open-air arenas throughout the city.

South of Johannesburg is Soweto, a city developed as a township for black people under the apartheid system. Most of the struggle against apartheid was fought in and from Soweto. Soweto is estimated to be inhabited by over two million people, their homes ranging from extravagant mansions to make-shift shacks. Soweto is a city of enterprise and cultural interaction. It is a popular tourist destination with sites such as Kliptown, where the Freedom Charter was drawn up, the home of former President Nelson Mandela, the Hector Petersen Memorial site, restaurants and shopping malls. It boasts one of the largest hospitals on the continent, the Chris Hani-Baragwanath Hospital.

Some 50 km north of Johannesburg lies Pretoria.

As administrative capital of South Africa, the city is dominated by government services and the diplomatic corps of foreign representatives in South Africa.

Pretoria is renowned for its colourful gardens, shrubs and trees, particularly beautiful in spring when some 50 000 jacarandas envelop the avenues in mauve. The city developed at a more sedate pace than Johannesburg, and town planners had the foresight to include an abundance of open spaces. Pretoria has more than 100 parks, including bird sanctuaries and nature reserves.

An air of history pervades much of central Pretoria, especially Church Square, around which the city has grown. Many buildings of historical and architectural importance have been retained or restored to their former splendour.

North of Pretoria is the industrial area of Rosslyn and the township of Soshanguve. To the east is Cullinan, known for its diamonds.

Other important Gauteng towns include Krugersdorp and Roodepoort on the West Rand, and Germiston, Springs, Boksburg, Benoni, Brakpan and Kempton Park on the East Rand. The hominid sites at Swartkrans, Sterkfontein and Kromdraai (also known as the Cradle of Humankind) are a World Heritage Site.

Vanderbijlpark and Vereeniging in the south of the province are major industrial centres,

---

The 284 m-long Nelson Mandela Bridge, built in honour of the former President, was officially opened in July 2003.

The Bridge, which cost the Gauteng Government R85 million, forms part of the R300 million Blue IQ inner-city renewal project driven by the Provincial Government and the City of Johannesburg.

while Heidelberg, Nigel and Bronkhorstspruit to the east are important agricultural areas.

Although the province is highly urbanised and industrialised, it contains wetlands of international importance, such as Blesbokspruit near Springs.

The people

Gauteng is the most densely populated province in South Africa. It houses almost nine million of the country's people. The level of urbanisation is 97%.

Gauteng has the most important educational and health centres in the country. Pretoria boasts the largest residential university in South Africa, the University of Pretoria, and what is believed to be the largest correspondence university in the world, the University of South Africa (UNISA).

Another attribute of Pretoria is the number of scientific institutes in and around the city, for example the Council for Scientific and Industrial Research, Onderstepoort Veterinary Institute and the South African Bureau of Standards.

According to the 2001 Census findings, only 8,4% of adults in the province have received no schooling.

Johannesburg has two residential universities. There are several teacher-training colleges, technical colleges and technikons in the province. Many of the existing technikons, satellite university campuses and universities will merge, as part of the Department of Education's plan for higher education.

More than 60% of South Africa's research and development takes place in Gauteng.

Manufacturing

The manufacturing sector in Gauteng has over 9 300 firms, employing more than 600 000 people. Industries that have contributed significantly to this output are basic iron and steel; fabricated and metal products; food; machinery, electrical machinery, appliances and electrical supplies; vehicle parts and accessories; and chemical products.

Technology

The economy of the province is being re-aligned to move away from traditional heavy industry markets and low value-added production towards sophisticated high value-added production, particularly in information technology, telecommunications and other high-tech industries. The burgeoning 'high-tech' corridor in Midrand (halfway between Pretoria and Johannesburg) is the most rapidly developing area in the country.

Agriculture and industry

Gauteng's agricultural sector is geared to provide the cities and towns of the province with daily fresh produce, including dairy products, vegetables, fruit, meat, eggs and flowers.

A large area of the province falls within the so-called maize triangle. The districts of Bronkhorstspruit, Cullinan and Heidelberg hold important agricultural land, where ground-nuts, sunflowers, cotton and sorghum are produced.

This summer-rainfall area has hot summers and cold winters with frost. Hail is common during the summer thunderstorms.

Gauteng is an integrated industrial complex with major areas of economic activity in five subregional areas, namely the Vaal Triangle;

Gauteng

Capital: Johannesburg
Principal languages: isiZulu 21,5%
Afrikaans 14,4%
SeSotho 13,1%
English 12,5%
Population: 8 837 178
Area (km^2): 17 010
% of total area: 1,4%
GGP at current prices (2001): R333 171 million
% of total GDP: 33,9%

the East, West and Central Rand; and Pretoria. The Vaal Triangle has a strong manufacturing sector; the West Rand concentrates on primary mining; and the Central Witwatersrand is dominated by the manufacturing and finance sectors, with mining-capital playing a major role. All sectors rely heavily on the Vaal Dam (on the Vaal River), from where water is piped across the province.

Gauteng has a greater proportion of its labour force in professional, technical, managerial and executive positions than any other province.

Johannesburg houses the JSE Securities Exchange, the largest in Africa.

The province's economic magnetism draws a large inflow of migrant labour from poorer regions in the country. It is the province with the highest per-capita income.

Mpumalanga

Mpumalanga means 'place where the sun rises'. It is bordered by Mozambique and Swaziland in the east, and Gauteng in the west. It is situated mainly on the high plateau grasslands of the Middleveld, which roll eastwards for hundreds of kilometres. In the northeast, it rises towards mountain peaks and then terminates in an immense escarpment. In some places, this escarpment plunges hundreds of metres down to the low-lying area known as the Lowveld.

The area has a network of excellent roads and railway connections, making it highly accessible. Because of its popularity as a tourist destination, Mpumalanga is also served by a number of small airports.

The Cabinet approved the designation of Kruger Mpumalanga Airport as an international airport in April 2003. This entailed the transfer of the status of Nelspruit International Airport to the Kruger Mpumalanga Airport, with the former downgraded to 'national airport' status.

Nelspruit is the capital of the province and the administrative and business centre of the Lowveld. Witbank is the centre of the local coal-mining industry; Standerton, in the south, is renowned for its large dairy industry; Piet Retief in the south-east is a production area for tropical fruit and sugar, while a large sugar industry is also found at Malelane in the east; Ermelo is the district in South Africa that produces the most wool; Barberton is one of the oldest gold-mining towns in South Africa; and Sabie is situated in the forestry heartland of the country.

The Maputo Corridor, which links the province with Gauteng and Maputo in Mozambique, heralds a new era in terms of economic development and growth for the region.

As the first international toll road in Africa, the Corridor aims to attract investment, unlock local economic potential of the landlocked parts of the country and thus generate sustainable economic growth that will lead to sustainable high-quality jobs.

The best-performing sectors in the province include mining, manufacturing and services. Tourism and agroprocessing are potential growth sectors in this province.

The province falls mainly within the grassland biome. The Escarpment and the Lowveld form a transitional zone between this grassland area and the savanna biome. Long sweeps of undulating grasslands abruptly change to the thickly forested ravines and thundering waterfalls of the Escarpment, only to change again to present the subtropical wildlife splendour of the Lowveld.

Sabie and Graskop provide a large part of the country's total requirement for forestry products. These forestry plantations are an ideal backdrop for ecotourism opportunities, with a variety of popular hiking trails, a myriad waterfalls, patches of indigenous forest, and a variety of nature reserves.

Lake Chrissie is the largest natural freshwater lake in South Africa, and is famous for its variety of aquatic birds, especially flamingos.

The people

Even though it is one of the smaller provinces

The land and its people

(some 79 490 km² in surface area), Mpumalanga has a population of more than three million people.

According to the 2001 Census results, some 27,5% of those aged 20 years or older have not undergone any schooling, while the population growth rate is higher than the national average. The main languages spoken are siSwati, isiZulu and isiNdebele.

Mpumalanga's unemployment rate stood at 16,5% in September 2001 (Labour Force Survey 2001).

Agriculture and forestry

This is a summer-rainfall area divided by the Escarpment into the Highveld region with cold frosty winters and the Lowveld region with mild winters and a subtropical climate.

The Escarpment area sometimes experiences snow on high ground. Thick mist is common during the hot humid summers.

An abundance of citrus fruit and many other subtropical fruits – mangoes, avocados, litchis, bananas, pawpaws, granadillas, guavas – as well as nuts and a variety of vegetables are produced here.

Nelspruit is the second-largest citrus-producing area in South Africa. It is responsible for one-third of the country's export in oranges. The Institute for Tropical and Subtropical Crops is situated here.

The natural forests of the area could not supply enough timber for the burgeoning mining industry in the early days of gold-mining. Plantations of exotic trees, mainly pine, gum and Australian wattles, were established to supply wood for the mine props. These trees grew so well that the Sabie area became the biggest single region of forestry plantations in South Africa.

Groblersdal is an important irrigation area which yields a wide variety of products such as citrus fruit, cotton, tobacco, wheat and vegetables.

Carolina-Bethal-Ermelo is sheep area. Potatoes, sunflower seeds, maize and peanuts are also produced in this region.

Industry

Mpumalanga is very rich in coal reserves. The country's biggest power stations, three of which are the biggest in the southern hemisphere, are situated here. Unfortunately, these cause the highest levels of air pollution in the country. Secunda, where the country's second petroleum-from-coal installation is situated, is also located in this province.

One of the country's largest paper mills is situated at Ngodwana, close to its timber source. Middelburg produces steel and vanadium, while Witbank is the biggest coal producer in Africa.

Mpumalanga

Capital: Nelspruit
Principal languages: siSwati 30,8%
isiZulu 26,4%
isiNdebele 12,1%
Population: 3 122 990 million
Area (km²): 79 490
% of total area: 6,5%
GGP at current prices (2001): R70 621 million
% of total GDP: 7,2%

Limpopo

Limpopo lies within the great elbow of the Limpopo River and is a province of dramatic contrasts – from true Bushveld country to majestic mountains, primeval indigenous forests, latter-day plantations, unspoilt wilderness areas and a patchwork of farming land.

Limpopo has a strong rural basis. Its growth strategy centres on addressing infrastructure backlogs, the alleviation of poverty and social development.

Underpinning the growth and development strategies in the province are the Phalaborwa SDI and the N1 Corridor, which encompasses

South Africa Yearbook 2003/04

agroprocessing and mining-beneficiation activities.

Regional economic integration takes the form of the 'Golden Horse Shoe', which aims to create a single reserve that will arch from the Kruger National Park in the east to Botswana in the west. The culturally and historically significant Mapungubwe site will be included in this development initiative.

Limpopo is the gateway to the rest of Africa. It is favourably situated for economic co-operation with other parts of southern Africa as it shares borders with Botswana, Zimbabwe and Mozambique.

The highest average real-economic-growth rate recorded in South Africa between 1995 and 2001 was that of Limpopo, with an average growth rate of 3,8% (Census 2001).

Polokwane is the capital city and lies strategically in the centre of the province.

The Great North Road through the centre of the province strings together a series of interesting towns. Bela-Bela, with its popular mineral spa, is near the southern border of the province.

Further north lies Modimolle with its table-grape industry and beautiful Waterberg range; Mokopane; Polokwane; Makhado (until recently known as Louis Trichardt) at the foot of the Soutpansberg mountain range; and Musina, with its thick-set baobab trees.

The crossing into Zimbabwe is at Beit Bridge, where the South African section of this important route north into Africa ends.

Other important Limpopo towns include the major mining centres of Phalaborwa and Thabazimbi, and Tzaneen, producer of tea, forestry products and tropical fruits.

The Maputo Corridor will link the province directly with Maputo Port, creating development and trade opportunities, particularly in the south-eastern part of the province.

This province is in the savanna biome, an area of mixed grassland and trees, which is generally known as Bushveld. A trip through this summer-rainfall area soon convinces one that this is tree country.

The biggest section of the Kruger National Park is situated along the eastern boundary of Limpopo with Mozambique.

The people

In Limpopo, 5 273 642 million people live on about 123 910 km^2 of land. The main languages spoken are Sepedi, Xitsonga and, Tshivenda.

According to the Census 2001 results, more than a third of those in Limpopo aged 20 years and above have not received any form of eduation or schooling.

The official unemployment rate for Limpopo stood at 15,5% in September 2001 (Labour Force Survey 2001).

Several museums and national monuments bear testimony to ancient peoples and fearless pioneers who braved the unknown in days of yore. Living museums include the Bakone Malapa Museum near Polokwane, where Bapedi tribesmen practise age-old skills for the benefit of visitors, and the Tsonga Open-Air Museum near Tzaneen. Mapungubwe (place of the jackal) Hill, some 75 km from Musina, used to be a natural fortress for its inhabitants from about AD 950 to 1200.

Valuable archaeological discoveries, including many golden artefacts, have been made in this area, as well as in the northern part of the Kruger National Park.

Limpopo

Capital: Polokwane
Principal languages: Sepedi 52,1%
Xitsonga 22,4%
Tshivenda 15,9%
Population: 5 273 642
Area (km^2): 123 910
% of total area: 10,2%
GGP at current prices (2001): R63 646 million
% of total GDP: 6,5%

Agriculture

The Bushveld is cattle country. Controlled hunting is often combined with ranching.

Sunflowers, cotton, maize and peanuts are cultivated in the Bela-Bela-Modimolle area. Modimolle is also known for its table-grape crops.

Tropical fruit, such as bananas, litchis, pineapples, mangoes and pawpaws, as well as a variety of nuts, are grown in the Tzaneen and Makhado areas. Extensive tea and coffee plantations create many employment opportunities in the Tzaneen area.

Zebediela, one of the largest citrus estates in the country, is situated south of Polokwane.

The largest tomato farm in South Africa lies between Tzaneen and Makhado.

Extensive forestry plantations are found in the Makhado and Tzaneen districts. Plantations of hard woods for furniture manufacturing have also been established.

Many of the rural people practise subsistence farming.

The northern and eastern parts of this summer-rainfall region are subtropical with hot, humid summers and mist in the mountainous parts. Winter throughout the province is mild and mostly frost-free.

Industry

Limpopo is rich in minerals, including copper, asbestos, coal, iron ore, platinum, chrome, diamonds, phosphates and gold.

The province is a typical developing area, exporting primary products and importing manufactured goods and services. It has a high potential and capacity with the right kind of economic development, and is an attractive location for investors. Resources such as tourism, rain-fed agriculture, minerals and an abundant labour force available in the province offer excellent investment opportunities.

South Africa Yearbook 2003/04

Acknowledgements

Original text by Theuns and Heila van Rensburg
Eastern Cape Provincial Government
Free State Provincial Government
Gauteng Provincial Government
KwaZulu-Natal Provincial Government
Limpopo Provincial Government
Mpumalanga Provincial Government
Northern Cape Provincial Government
North West Provincial Government
Pan South African Language Board
Statistics South Africa
Western Cape Provincial Government
www.gov.za

Suggested reading

Absalom, E. *'Previously called' Coloured People – Past and Present: 350 years.* Rehoboth (Namibia): CBH Publishers, 2001.
Atlas of Southern Africa and the World. Halfway House: Southern Book Publishing, 1992.
Beall, J., Crankshaw, O. and Parnell, S. *Uniting a Divided City: Governance and Social Exclusion in Johannesburg.* London: Earthscan Publications, 2002.
Bekker, S. and others. *Shifting African Identities.* Pretoria: Human Sciences Research Council, 2001.
Bowes, B. and Pennington, S., eds. *South Africa: The Good News.* Johannesburg: Good News, 2002. Includes authors such as Kader Asmal, Cheryl Carolus, Tom Lodge, Trevor Manuel, Cyril Ramaphosa and Frederick van Zyl Slabbert.
Deacon, H.H. and Deacon, J. *Human Beginnings in South Africa. Uncovering the Secrets of the Stone Age.* Cape Town: David Philip, 1999.
De Gruchy, J.W. *Christianity and Democracy.* Cape Town: David Philip, 1995.
De Gruchy, J.W. *The Church Struggle in South Africa.* Cape Town: David Philip, 1992.
De Klerk, W. *Afrikaners, Kroes, Kras, Kordaat.* Cape Town: Human and Rousseau, 1999.
Du Toit, Z.B. *Die Nuwe Toekoms: 'n Perspektief op die Afrikaner by die Eeuwisseling.* Pretoria: JP van der Walt, 1999.
Elphick, R. and Davenport R., eds. *Christianity in South Africa: A Political, Social and Cultural History.* Cape Town: David Philip, 1997.
Erasmus, Z. *Coloured by History, Shaped by Place: New Perspectives on Coloured Identity in Cape Town.* Cape Town: Kwela Books, 2001.
Fodor's South Africa: The Complete Guide to the Cities, Winelands and Game Parks, with Zimbabwe and Botswana. 2nd new edition. Compiler: A. Barbour. New York: Fodor's Travel Publications, 1998.
Fox, R. and Rowntree K., eds. *The Geography of South Africa in a Changing World.* Cape Town: Oxford University Press Southern Africa, 2000.
Free State, The Winning Province. Johannesburg: Chris van Rensburg Publications, 1997.
Freund, B. and Padayachee, V. *Durban Vortex: South African City in Transition.* Pietermaritzburg: University of Natal Press, 2002.
Gall, S. *The Bushmen of Southern Africa: Slaughter of the Innocence.* London: Chatto & Windus, 2001.
Germond, P. and de Gruchy, S. *Homosexuality and Christian Faith in South Africa.* Cape Town: David Philip, 1997.
Giliomee, H. *The Afrikaners: Biography of a People.* Cape Town: Tafelberg, 2003.
Haldenwang, B.B. *A Socio-demographic Profile of the Southern African Development Community Region.* Stellenbosch: Institute for Futures Research, University of Stellenbosch, 1997.
Illustrated Guide to the Game Parks and Nature Reserves of Southern Africa. 3rd ed. Cape Town: Reader's Digest Association, 1997.
James, W., Caliquire D. and Cullinan., K., eds. *Now That We Are Free: Coloured Communities in Democratic South Africa.* Cape Town: Institute for Democracy in South Africa, 1996.
Jenkins, E.R., Raper, P.E. and Moller, L.A. *Changing Place Names.* Durban: Indicator Press, 1996.

The land and its people

Johannesburg: Africa's World City. Johannesburg: Centre for Development and Enterprise, 2002.
Katz, R. and others. *Healing Makes Our Hearts Happy: Spirituality and Cultural Transformation Among the Kalahari Jul'hoansi.* Rochester, Vermont: Inner Traditions International, 1997.
Knobel, J. *The Magnificent Natural Heritage of South Africa.* Llandudno, South Africa: Sunbird Publishing, 1999.
Kollenberg, A. et al., eds. *Jewish Life in the South African Communities. Vol 1. The Northern Great Escarpment, The Lowveld, The Northern Highveld, The Bushveld.* Johannesburg: South African Friends of Beth Hatefutsoth, 2002.
Lively, A. *Masks: Bleakness, Race and the Imagination.* Oxford: Oxford University Press, 2000.
Magubane, P. *Vanishing Cultures of South Africa: Changing Customs in a Changing World.* Cape Town: Struik, 1998.
Majodina, Z., ed. *The Challenge of Forced Migration in Southern Africa.* Pretoria: Africa Institute of South Africa, 2001.
Moon, B.P. and Dardis, C.F. *Geomorphology of Southern Africa.* Halfway House: Southern Book Publishers, 1992.
Morrell, R. ed. *Changing Man in Southern Africa.* Pietermaritzburg: University of Natal Press, 2001.
Preston-Whyte, R.A. and Tyson, P.D. *Atmosphere and Weather of Southern Africa.* Cape Town: Oxford University Press, 1989.
Rogerson, C. and McCarthy, J., eds. *Geography in a Changing South Africa: Progress and Prospects.* Cape Town: Oxford University Press, 1992.
Schadeberg, J. *Soweto Today.* Pretoria: Protea Book House, 2002.
Schadeberg, J. *The San of the Kalahari.* Pretoria: Protea Book House, 2002
Shain, M. and Mendelsohn, R., eds. *Memories, Dreams and Realities: Aspects of the South African Jewish Experience.* Johannesburg: Jonathan Ball, 2002.
Shimoni, G. *Community and Conscience: The Jews in Apartheid South Africa.* Johannesburg: David Philip, 2003.
Simon, D., ed. *South Africa in Southern Africa: Reconfiguring the Region.* Oxford: James Currey; Cape Town: David Philip, 1998.
Smith, A. and others. *The Bushmen of Southern Africa: A Foraging Society in Transition.* Cape Town: David Philip, 2000.
Smith, A. and others. *The Cape Herders: A History of the Khoikhoi of Southern Africa.* Cape Town: David Philip, 2000.
Tyson, P. D. *Climatic Change and Variability in Southern Africa.* Cape Town: Oxford University Press, 1986.
Van Rooyen, J. *The New Great Trek: The Story of South Africa's White Exodus.* Pretoria: University of South Africa, 2000.
Van Zyl Slabbert, F. *Afrikaner, Afrikaans.* Cape Town: Tafelberg, 1999.
Venter, L. *In the Shadow of the Rainbow.* Sandton: Heineman, 2001.
Villa-Vicencio, C. *Civil Disobedience and Beyond: Law, Resistance and Religion in South Africa.* Cape Town: David Philip, 1990.

Truth and Reconciliatio...

chapter 2
History

The early inhabitants

There seems to be general agreement among scholars that humankind had its earliest origins in Africa. South Africa is rich in fossil evidence of the evolutionary history of the human family, going back several million years. The discovery of the skull of a Taung child in 1924; the latest discoveries of hominid fossils at Sterkfontein caves, recently declared a World Heritage Site; and the ground-breaking work done at Blombos Cave in the Southern Cape, have all put South Africa at the forefront of palaeontological research into the origins of humanity. Modern humans have lived in the region for over 100 000 years.

The small, mobile bands of Stone Age hunter-gatherers, who created a wealth of rock art, were the ancestors of the Khoekhoe and San of historical times. The Khoekhoen and San (the 'Hottentots' and 'Bushmen' of early European terminology), although collectively known as the Khoisan, are often thought of as distinct peoples.

The former were those who, some 2 000 years ago, adopted a pastoralist lifestyle herding sheep and, later, cattle. Whereas the hunter-gatherers adapted to local environments and were scattered across the subcontinent, the herders sought out the pasturelands between modern-day Namibia and the Eastern Cape, which, generally, are near the coast.

At around the same time, Bantu-speaking agropastoralists began arriving in southern Africa, bringing with them an Iron Age culture and domesticated crops. After establishing themselves in the well-watered eastern coastal region of Southern Africa, these farmers spread out across the interior plateau, or 'highveld', where they adopted a more extensive cattle-farming culture. Chiefdoms arose, based on control over cattle, which gave rise to systems of patronage and hence hierarchies of authority within communities. Cattle exchanges formed the basis of polygamous marriage arrangements, facilitating the accumulation of social power through control over the labour of kin groups and dependants.

Metallurgical skills, developed in the mining and processing of iron, copper, tin and gold, promoted regional trade and craft specialisation. At several archaeological sites, such as Mapungubwe and Thulamela in the Limpopo Valley, there is evidence of sophisticated political and material cultures, based in part on contact with the East African trading economy. These cultures, which were part of a broader African civilisation, predate European encroachment by several centuries. Settlement patterns varied from

◀ The Truth and Reconciliation Commission helped inculcate a commitment to accountability and transparency in South Africa's public life, at the same time helping to heal the wounds inflicted by the inhumanities of the apartheid era.

31

the dispersed homesteads of the fertile coastal regions in the east, to the concentrated towns of the desert fringes in the west.

The farmers did not, however, extend their settlement into the western desert or the winter-rainfall region in the south-west. These regions remained the preserve of the Khoisan until Europeans put down roots at the Cape of Good Hope. This meant that the farmers were little affected by the white presence for the first century during which European settlement expanded from the Western Cape.

Currently, aided by modern science in uncovering the continent's past, which forms part of the African Renaissance, South Africa is gaining a greater understanding of its rich pre-colonial past and African achievements that were to be disrupted and all but hidden from sight in the period that followed.

The early colonial period

Portuguese seafarers, who pioneered the sea route to India in the late 15th century, were regular visitors to the South African coast during the early 1500s. Other Europeans followed from the late 16th century.

In 1652, the Dutch East India Company (VOC) set up a station in Table Bay (Cape Town) to provision passing ships. Trade with the Khoekhoe(n) for slaughter stock soon degenerated into raiding and warfare. Beginning in 1657, European settlers were allotted farms by the colonial authorities in the arable regions around Cape Town, where wine and wheat became the major products. In response to the colonists' demand for labour, the VOC imported slaves from East Africa, Madagascar, and its possessions from the East Indies.

By the early 1700s, the colonists had begun to spread into the hinterland beyond the nearest mountain ranges. These relatively independent and mobile farmers (*trekboers*), who lived as pastoralists and hunters, were largely free from supervision by the Dutch authorities.

As they intruded further upon the land and water sources, and stepped up their demands for livestock and labour, more and more of the indigenous inhabitants were dispossessed and incorporated into the colonial economy as servants. Diseases such as smallpox, which was introduced by the Europeans in 1713, decimated the Khoisan, contributing to the decline of their cultures. Unions across the colour line took place and a new multiracial social order evolved, based on the supremacy of European colonists. The slave population steadily increased since more labour was needed.

By the mid-1700s there were more slaves in the Cape than there were 'free burghers' (European colonists). The Asian slaves were concentrated in the towns, where they formed an artisan class. They brought with them the Islam religion, which gained adherents and significantly shaped the working-class culture of the Western Cape. Slaves of African descent were found more often on the farms of outlying districts.

In the late 1700s, Khoisan bands offered far more determined resistance to colonial encroachment across the length of the colonial frontier. From the 1770s, colonists also came into contact and conflict with Bantu-speaking chiefdoms some 700 km east of Cape Town. A century of intermittent warfare ensued during which the colonists gained ascendancy first over the Khoisan and then over the Xhosa-speaking chiefdoms to the east. It was only in the late 1800s that the subjugation of these settled African societies became feasible. For some time their relatively sophisticated social structure and economic systems fended off decisive disruption by incoming colonists, who lacked the necessary military superiority.

At the same time, a process of cultural change was set in motion, not least by commercial and missionary activity. In contrast to the Khoisan, the black farmers were by and large immune to European diseases. For this and other reasons they were to greatly outnumber the whites in the population of white-ruled South Africa, and were able to preserve important features of their culture. A spate of State-building was launched beyond the frontiers of European settlement. Perhaps because of population pressures, combined with the actions of slave traders in Portuguese territory on the east coast, the old order was upset and the Zulu kingdom emerged as a highly centralised State. In the 1820s, the innovative leader Shaka established sway over a considerable area of south-east Africa and brought many chiefdoms under his dominion.

As splinter groups conquered and absorbed communities in their path, the disruption was felt as far north as central Africa. Substantial states, such as Moshoeshoe's Lesotho and other Sotho-Tswana chiefdoms, were established, partly for reasons of defence. The *mfecane* or *difaqane*, as this period of disruption and State formation became known, remains the subject of much speculative debate.

But the temporary disruption of life on the Highveld served to facilitate Boer expansion northwards from the 1830s, and provided a myth of the 'empty land' which whites employed to justify their domination over the subcontinent in the 20th century.

The British colonial era

In 1795, the British occupied the Cape as a strategic base against the French, controlling the sea route to the East.

After a brief reversion to the Dutch in the course of the Napoleonic wars, it was retaken in 1806 and kept by Britain in the post-war settlement of territorial claims. The closed and regulated economic system of the Dutch period was swept away as the Cape Colony was integrated into the dynamic international trading empire of industrialising Britain.

A crucial new element was evangelicalism, brought to the Cape by Protestant missionaries. The evangelicals believed in the liberating effect of 'free' labour and in the 'civilising mission' of British imperialism. They were convinced that indigenous peoples could be fully assimilated into European Christian culture once the shackles of oppression had been removed.

The most important representative of the mission movement in South Africa was Dr John Philip, who arrived as superintendent of the London Missionary Society in 1819. His campaign on behalf of the oppressed Khoisan coincided with a high point in official sympathy for philanthropic concerns.

One result was Ordinance 50 of 1828, which guaranteed equal civil rights for 'people of colour' within the colony and freed them from legal discrimination. At the same time, a powerful anti-slavery movement in Britain promoted a series of ameliorative measures, imposed on the colonies in the 1820s, and the proclamation of emancipation, which came into force in 1834. The slaves were subject to a four-year period of 'apprenticeship' with their former owners on the grounds that they must be prepared for freedom, which came on 1 December 1838.

Although slavery had become less profitable because of a depression in the wine industry, Cape slave-owners rallied to oppose emancipation. The compensation money, which the British treasury paid out to sweeten the pill, injected unprecedented liquidity into the stagnant local economy. This brought a spurt of company formation, such as banks and insurance companies, as well as a surge of investment in land and wool sheep in the drier regions of the colony, in the late 1830s. Wool became a staple export on which the Cape economy depended for its further development in the middle decades of the century.

For the ex-slaves, as for the Khoisan servants, the reality of freedom was very different from the promise. As a wage-based economy developed, they remained a dispossessed and exploited element in the population, with little opportunity to escape their servile lot.

Increasingly, they were lumped together as the 'coloured' people, a group which included the descendants of unions between indigenous and European peoples and a substantial Muslim minority who became known as the 'Cape Malays' (misleadingly, as they mostly came from the Indonesian archipelago). The coloured people were discriminated against on account of their working-class status as well as their racial identity. Among the poor, especially in and around Cape Town, there continued to be a great deal of racial mixing and intermarriage throughout the 1800s.

In 1820, several thousand British settlers, who were swept up by a scheme to relieve Britain of its unemployed, were placed in the eastern Cape frontier zone as a buffer against the Xhosa chiefdoms.

The vision of a dense settlement of small farmers was, however, ill-conceived and many of the settlers became artisans and traders. The more-successful became an entrepreneurial class of merchants, large-scale sheep farmers and speculators with an insatiable demand for land.

Some became fierce warmongers who pressed for the military dispossession of the chiefdoms. They coveted Xhosa land and welcomed the prospect of war involving large-scale military expenditure by the imperial authorities. The Xhosa engaged in raiding as a means of asserting their prior claims to the land. Racial paranoia became integral to white frontier politics. The result was that frontier warfare became endemic through much of the 19th century, during which Xhosa war leaders such as Chief Maqoma became heroic figures to their people.

By the mid-1800s, British settlers of similar persuasion were to be found in Natal. They too called for imperial expansion in support of their land claims and trading enterprises.

Meanwhile, large numbers of the original colonists, the Boers, were greatly extending white settlement beyond the Cape's borders to the north, in the movement that became known as the Great Trek, in the mid-1830s. Alienated by British liberalism, and with their economic enterprise usurped by British settlers, several thousand Boers from the interior districts, accompanied by a number of Khoisan servants, began a series of migrations northwards. They moved to the Highveld and Natal, skirting the great concentrations of black farmers on the way by taking advantage of the areas disrupted during the *mfecane*.

When the British, who were concerned about controlling the traffic through Port Natal (Durban), annexed the territory of Natal in 1843, those emigrant Boers who had hoped to settle there returned inland. The *Voortrekkers* (as they were later called) coalesced in two land-locked Republics, the South African Republic (Transvaal) and the Orange Free State. There, the principles of racially exclusive citizenship were absolute, despite the trekkers' reliance on black labour. With limited coercive power, the Boer communities had to establish relations and develop alliances with some black chiefdoms, neutralising those who obstructed their intrusion or who posed a threat to their security.

Only after the mineral discoveries of the late 1800s did the balance of power swing decisively towards the colonists. The Boer Republics then took on the trappings of real statehood and imposed their authority within the territorial borders that they had notionally claimed for themselves.

The Colony of Natal, situated to the south of the mighty Zulu State, developed along very different lines from the original colony of settlement, the Cape. The size of the black population left no room for the assimilationist vision of race domination embraced in the Cape. Chiefdoms consisting mainly of refugee groups in the aftermath of the *mfecane* were persuaded to accept colonial protection in return for reserved land and the freedom to govern themselves in accordance with their own customs. These chiefdoms were established in the heart of an expanding colonial territory.

Natal developed a system of political and legal dualism, whereby chiefly rule was entrenched and customary law was codified. Although exemptions from customary law could be granted to the educated products of the missions, in practice they were rare. Urban residence was strictly controlled and political rights outside the reserves were effectively limited to whites. Natal's system is widely regarded as having provided a model for the segregationism of the 20th century.

Natal's economy was boosted by the development of sugar plantations in the sub-tropical coastal lowlands. Indian-indentured labourers were imported from 1860 to work the plantations, and many Indian traders and market gardeners followed.

These Indians, who were segregated and discriminated against from the start, became a further important element in South Africa's population. It was in South Africa that Mohandas Gandhi refined from the mid-1890s the techniques of passive resistance, which he later effectively practised in India. Although Indians gradually moved into the Transvaal and elsewhere, they remain concentrated mainly in Natal.

In 1853, the Cape Colony was granted a representative legislature in keeping with British policy, followed in 1872 by self-government. The franchise was formally non-racial but also based on income and property qualifications. The result was that Africans and 'coloured' people formed a minority – although in certain places a substantial one – of voters.

What became known as the 'liberal tradition' in the Cape depended on the fact that the great mass of Bantu-speaking farmers remained outside its colonial borders until late in the 19th century. Non-racialism could thus be embraced without posing a threat to white supremacy.

Numbers of Africans within the Cape colony had had sufficient formal education or owned enough property to qualify for the franchise. Political alliances across racial lines were common in the eastern Cape constituencies. It is therefore not surprising that the eastern Cape became a seedbed of African nationalism, once the ideal and promise of inclusion in the common society had been so starkly violated by later racial policies.

The mineral revolution

By the late 19th century, the limitations of the Cape's liberal tradition were becoming apparent. The hardening of racial attitudes that accompanied the rise of a more militant imperialist spirit coincided locally with the watershed discovery of mineral riches in the interior of southern Africa. In a developing economy, cheap labour was at a premium, and the claims of educated Africans for equality met with increasingly fierce resistance.

At the same time, the large numbers of Africans in the chiefdoms beyond the Kei River and north of the Gariep (Orange River), then being incorporated into the Cape Colony, posed new threats to racial supremacy and white security, increasing segregationist pressures.

Alluvial diamonds were discovered on the Vaal River in the late 1860s. The subsequent discovery of dry deposits at what became the city of Kimberley drew tens of thousands of people, black and white, to the first great industrial hub in Africa, and the largest diamond deposit in the world. In 1871, the British, who ousted several rival claimants, annexed the diamond fields, which fell in sparsely populated territory to the west of the main corridors of northward migration. The Colony of Griqualand West thus created was incorporated into the Cape Colony in 1880. By 1888, the consolidation of diamond claims had led to the creation of the huge De Beers monopoly under the control of Cecil Rhodes. He used his power and wealth to become Prime Minister of the Cape Colony (1890 – 1896) and, through his chartered British South Africa Company, conqueror and ruler of modern-day Zambia and Zimbabwe.

The mineral discoveries had a major impact on the subcontinent as a whole. A railway network linking the interior to the coastal ports revolutionised transportation and energised agriculture. Coastal cities such as Cape Town, Port Elizabeth, East London and Durban experienced an economic boom as port facilities were upgraded.

The fact that the mineral discoveries coincided with a new era of imperialism and the scramble for Africa, brought imperial power and influence to bear in southern Africa as never before.

Independent African chiefdoms were systematically subjugated and incorporated by their white-ruled neighbours. The most dramatic example was the Zulu War of 1879, which saw the Zulu State brought under imperial control, during which King Cetshwayo's impis inflicted a celebrated defeat on British forces at Isandlwana. In 1897, Zululand was incorporated into Natal. The South African Republic (Transvaal) was annexed by Britain in 1877. Boer resistance led to British withdrawal in 1881, but not before the Pedi (northern Sotho) State, which fell within the Republic's borders, had been subjugated. The indications were that, having once been asserted, British hegemony was likely to be reasserted. The southern Sotho and Swazi territories were also brought under British rule but maintained their status as imperial dependencies, so that both the current Lesotho and Swaziland escaped the rule of local white regimes.

The discovery of the Witwatersrand goldfields in 1886 was a turning point in the history of South Africa. It presaged the emergence of the modern South African industrial State.

Once the extent of the reefs had been established, and deep-level mining had proved to be a viable investment, it was only a matter of time before Britain and its local representatives again found a pretext for war against the Boer Republics of Transvaal and the Orange Free State.

The demand for franchise rights for English-speaking immigrants on the goldfields (*Uitlanders*) provided a lever for applying pressure on the Government of President Paul Kruger.

Egged on by the deep-level mining magnates, to whom the Boer Government seemed obstructive and inefficient, and by the expectation of an *Uitlander* uprising, Rhodes launched a raid into the Transvaal in late December 1895. The raid's failure saw the end of Rhodes' political career, but Sir Alfred Milner, British High Commissioner in South Africa from 1897, was determined to overthrow Kruger's Government and establish British rule throughout the subcontinent. The Boer Government was eventually forced into a declaration of war in October 1899.

The mineral discoveries had a radical impact on every sphere of society. Labour was required on a massive scale and could only be provided by Africans, who had to be drawn away from the land.

Many Africans did respond with alacrity to the opportunities presented by wage labour, travelling long distances to earn money to supplement rural enterprise in the homestead economy.

In response to the expansion of internal markets, Africans exploited their farming skills and family labour to good effect to increase production for sale. A substantial black peasantry arose, often by means of share-cropping or labour tenantry on white-owned farms.

For the white authorities, however, the chief consideration was ensuring a labour supply and undermining black competition on the land. Conquest, land dispossession, taxation and pass laws were designed to force black men off the land and channel them into labour markets, especially to meet the needs of the mines.

Gradually, the alternatives available to them were closed, and the decline of the homestead economy made wage labour increasingly essential for survival. The integration of Africans into the emerging urban and industrial society of South Africa should have followed these developments, but short-term, recurrent labour migrancy suited employers and the authorities, which sought to entrench the system.

The closed compounds pioneered on the diamond fields, as a means of migrant labour control, were replicated at the gold mines. The preservation of communal areas from which migrants could be drawn had the effect of lowering wages, by denying Africans rights within the urban areas and keeping their families and dependants on subsistence plots in the reserves.

Africans could be denied basic rights if the fiction could be maintained that they did not belong in 'white South Africa' but to 'tribal societies' from which they came to service the 'white man's needs'. Where black families secured a toehold in the urban areas, local authorities confined them to segregated 'locations'. This set of assumptions and policies informed the development of segregationist ideology and, later (from 1948), apartheid.

The Anglo-Boer/South African War (October 1899 – May 1902) and its aftermath

The War that followed the mineral revolution was mainly a white man's war. In its first phase, the Boer forces took the initiative, besieging the frontier towns of Mafeking (Mafikeng) and Kimberley in the northern Cape, and Ladysmith in northern Natal. Some colonial Boers rebelled, however, in sympathy with the Republics. But after a large expeditionary force under Lords Roberts and Kitchener arrived, the British advance was rapid. Kruger fled the Transvaal shortly before Pretoria fell in June 1900.

The formal conquest of the two Boer Republics was followed by a prolonged guerrilla campaign. Small, mobile groups of Boers denied the imperial forces their victory, by disrupting rail links and supply lines.

Commandos swept deep into colonial territory, rousing rebellion wherever they went. The British were at a disadvantage owing to their lack of familiarity with the terrain and the Boers' superior skills as horsemen and sharpshooters. The British responded with a scorched-earth policy. This included farm burnings, looting and the setting-up of concentration camps for non-combatants, in which some 26 000 Boer women and children died from disease. The incarceration of black (including coloured) people in the path of the War in racially segregated camps has been absent in conventional accounts of the War and has only recently been acknowledged.

They too suffered appalling conditions and some 14 000 (perhaps many more) are estimated to have died.

At the same time, many black farmers were in a position to meet the demand for produce created by the military, or avail themselves of employment opportunities at good wages. Some 10 000 black servants accompanied the Boer commandos, and the British used Africans as labourers, scouts, dispatch riders, drivers and guards.

The War also taught many Africans that the forces of dispossession could be rolled back if the circumstances were right. It gave black communities the opportunity to recolonise land lost in conquest, which enabled them to withhold their labour after the War. Most supported the British in the belief that Britain was committed to extending civil and political rights to black people.

In this they were to be disappointed, as in the Treaty of Vereeniging that ended the War the British agreed to leave the issue of rights for Africans to be decided by a future self-governing (white) authority. All in all, the Anglo-Boer/South African War was a radicalising experience for Africans.

Britain's reconstruction regime set about creating a white-ruled dominion by uniting the former Boer Republics (both by then British colonies) with Natal and the Cape.

The most important priority was to re-establish white control over the land and force the Africans back to wage labour. The labour-recruiting system was improved, both internally and externally. Recruiting agreements were reached with the Portuguese authorities in Mozambique, from where much mine labour came.

When, by 1904, African sources still proved inadequate to get the mines working at pre-War levels, over 60 000 indentured Chinese were brought in. This precipitated a vociferous outcry from proponents of white supremacy in South Africa and liberals in Britain.

By 1910, all had been repatriated, a step made easier when a surge of Africans came forward from areas such as the Transkeian territories and the northern Transvaal, which had not previously been large-scale suppliers of migrants. This was the heyday of the private recruiters, who exploited families' indebtedness to procure young men to labour in the mines. The Africans' post-War ability to withhold their labour had been undercut by government action, abetted by drought and stock disease.

The impact of the Anglo-Boer/South African War as a seminal influence in the development of Afrikaner nationalist politics became apparent in subsequent years.

The Boer leaders – most notably Louis Botha, Jan Smuts and J.B.M. Hertzog – played a dominant role in the country's politics for the next half century. After initial plans for anglicisation of the defeated Afrikaners through the education system and numerical swamping through British immigration were abandoned as impractical, the British looked to the Afrikaners as collaborators in securing imperial political and economic interests.

During 1907 and 1908, the two former Boer Republics were granted self-government but, crucially, with a whites-only franchise. Despite promises to the contrary, black interests were sacrificed in the interest of white nation-building across the white language divide. The National Convention drew up a constitution and the four colonies became an independent dominion called the Union of South Africa on 31 May 1910.

The 19th-century formally non-racial franchise was retained in the Cape but was not extended elsewhere, where rights of citizenship were confined to whites alone.

It was clear from the start that segregation was the conventional wisdom of the new rulers. Black people were defined as outsiders, without rights or claims on the common society that their labour had helped to create.

Segregation

Government policy in the Union of South Africa did not develop in isolation, but against the backdrop of black political initiatives. Segregation and apartheid assumed their shape, in part, as a white response to Africans' increasing participation in the country's economic life and their assertion of political rights. Despite the Government's efforts to shore up traditionalism and retribalise them, black people became more fully integrated into the urban and industrial society of 20th-century South Africa than happened elsewhere on the continent. An educated élite of clerics, teachers, business people, journalists and professionals grew to be a major force in black politics.

Mission Christianity and its associated educational institutions exerted a profound influence on African political life, and separatist churches were early vehicles for African political assertion. The experiences of studying abroad, and in particular, interaction with black people struggling for their rights elsewhere in Africa, the United States of America and the Caribbean, played an important part. A vigorous black press, associated in its early years with such pioneer editors as J.T. Jabavu, Pixley Seme, Dr Abdullah Abdurahman, Sol Plaatje and John Dube, served the black reading public.

At the same time, African communal struggles to maintain access to the land in rural areas posed a powerful challenge to the white State.

Traditional authorities often led popular struggles against intrusive and manipulative policies. Government attempts to control and co-opt the chiefs often failed.

Steps towards the formation of a national political organisation of coloureds began around the turn of the century, with the formation of the African Political Organisation in 1902 by Dr Abdurahman mainly in the Cape Province. The African National Congress (ANC), founded in 1912, became, however, the most important black organisation drawing together traditional authorities and the educated African élite in common causes.

In its early years, the ANC was concerned mainly with constitutional protest. Worker militancy emerged in the wake of the First World War, and continued through the 1920s.

It included strikes and an anti-pass campaign given impetus by women, particularly in the Free State, resisting extension of the pass laws to them. The Industrial and Commercial Workers' Union, under the leadership of Clements Kadalie, was (despite its name) the first populist, nationwide organisation representing blacks in rural as well as urban areas. But it was short-lived. The Communist Party, formed in 1921 and since then a force for both non-racialism and worker organisation, was to prove far longer-lasting. In other sections of the black population too, the turn of the century saw organised opposition emerging. Gandhi's leadership of protest against discriminatory laws gave impetus to the formation of provincial Indian congresses, including the Natal Indian Congress formed by Ghandi in 1894.

The principles of segregationist thinking were laid down in a 1905 report by the South African Native Affairs Commission and continued to evolve in response to these economic, social and political pressures. In keeping with its recommendations, the first Union government enacted the seminal Natives Land Act in 1913.

This defined the remnants of their ancestral lands after conquest for African occupation, and declared illegal all land purchases or rent tenancy outside these reserves.

The reserves ('homelands' as they were subsequently called) eventually comprised about 13% of South Africa's land surface. Administrative and legal dualism reinforced the division between white citizen and black non-citizen, a dispensation personified by the Governor-General who, as 'Supreme Chief' over the country's African majority, was empowered to rule them by administrative fiat and decree.

The Government also regularised the job colour bar, reserving skilled work for whites and denying African workers the right to organise.

Legislation, which was consolidated in the Natives (Urban Areas) Act, 1923, entrenched urban segregation and controlled African mobility by means of pass laws. The pass laws were intended to enmesh Africans in a web of coercion designed to force them into labour and keep them there under conditions and at wage levels that suited white employers, and to deny them any bargaining power.

In these and other ways, the foundations of apartheid were laid by successive governments representing the compromises hammered out by the National Convention of 1908 to 1909 to effect the union of English- and Afrikaans-speaking whites.

Divisions within the white community remained significant, however. Afrikaner nationalism grew as a factor in the years after union.

It was given impetus in 1914, both by the formation of the National Party (NP), in a breakaway from the ruling South African Party, and by a rebellion of Afrikaners who could not reconcile themselves with the decision to join the First World War against Germany. In part, the NP spoke for Afrikaners impoverished by the Anglo-Boer/South African War and dislodged from the land by the development of capitalist farming.

An Afrikaner underclass was emerging in the towns, which found itself uncompetitive in the labour market, as white workers demanded higher wages than those paid to blacks.

Soon, labour issues came to the fore. In 1920, some 71 000 black mineworkers went on strike in protest against the spiralling cost of living, but the strike was quickly put down by isolating the compounds where the migrant workers were housed.

Another threat to government came from white workers. Immigrant white workers with mining experience abroad performed much of the skilled and semi-skilled work on the mines. As mine-owners tried to cut costs by using lower-wage black labour in semi-skilled jobs, white labour became increasingly militant. These tensions culminated in a bloody and dramatic rebellion on the goldfields in 1922, which the Smuts Government put down with military force. In 1924, a Pact government under Hertzog, comprising Afrikaner nationalists and representatives of immigrant labour, ousted the Smuts regime.

The Pact was based on a common suspicion of the dominance of mining capital, and a determination to protect the interests of white labour by intensifying discrimination against blacks. The commitment to white labour policies in government employment such as the railways and postal service was intensified, and the job colour bar was reinforced, with one of its main objectives to address what was known as a 'poor-white problem'.

In 1934, the main white parties fused to combat the local effects of a worldwide depression. This was followed by a new Afrikaner nationalist breakaway under Dr D.F. Malan.

In 1936, white supremacy was further entrenched by the United Party with the removal of the Africans of the Cape Province who qualified from the common voters' roll. Meanwhile Malan's breakaway NP was greatly augmented by an Afrikaner cultural revival spearheaded by the secret white male Afrikaner *Broederbond* and other cultural organisations during the year of the *Voortrekker* Centenary Celebrations (1938), as well as anti-war sentiment from 1939.

Apartheid

After the Second World War, in 1948, the NP, with its ideology of apartheid that brought an even more rigorous and authoritarian approach than the segregationist policies of previous governments, won the general election. It did so against the background of a revival of mass militancy during the 1940s, after a period of relative quiescence in the 1930s when black groups attempted to foster unity among themselves.

The change was marked by the formation of the ANC Youth League in 1943, fostering the leadership of figures such as Nelson Mandela, Oliver Tambo and Walter Sisulu (who passed away in May 2003), who were to inspire the struggle for decades to come.

In the 1940s, squatter movements in peri-urban areas brought mass politics back to the urban centres.

The 1946 mineworkers' strike was a turning point in the emergence of a politics of mass mobilisation.

As was the case with the First World War, the experience of the Second World War and post-War economic difficulties enhanced discontent. For those who supported the NP, its primary appeal lay in its determination to maintain white domination in the face of rising mass resistance; uplift poor Afrikaners; challenge the pre-eminence of English-speaking whites in public life, the professions and business; and abolish the remaining

History

imperial ties. The State became an engine of patronage for Afrikaner employment. The Afrikaner *Broederbond* co-ordinated the Party's programme, ensuring that Afrikaner nationalist interests and policies attained ascendancy throughout civil society.

In 1961, the NP Government under Prime Minister H.F. Verwoerd declared South Africa a Republic, after winning a whites-only referendum on the issue. A new currency, the Rand, new flag, anthem and coat of arms were formally introduced. South Africa, having become a Republic, had to apply for continued membership of the Commonwealth – in the face of demands for an end to apartheid, South Africa withdrew its application and a figurehead president replaced the Queen (represented locally by the Governor-General) as Head of State.

In most respects, apartheid was a continuation, in more systematic and brutal form, of the segregationist policies of previous governments.

A new concern with racial purity was apparent in laws prohibiting interracial sex and provisions for population registration requiring that every South African be assigned to one discrete racial category or another.

For the first time, the coloured people, who had always been subjected to informal discrimination, were brought within the ambit of discriminatory laws. In the mid-1950s, government took the drastic step of overriding an entrenched clause in the 1910 Constitution of the Union so as to be able to remove coloured voters from the common voters' roll. It also enforced residential segregation, expropriating homes where necessary and policing massive forced removals into coloured 'group areas'.

Until the 1940s, South Africa's racial policies had not been entirely out of step with those to be found in the colonial world. But by the 1950s, which saw decolonisation and a global backlash against racism gather pace, the country was dramatically opposed to world opinion on questions of human rights. The architects of apartheid, among whom Dr Verwoerd was pre-eminent, responded by elaborating a theory of multinationalism. Their policy, which they termed 'separate development', divided the African population into artificial ethnic 'nations', each with its own 'homeland' and the prospect of 'independence', supposedly in keeping with trends elsewhere on the continent. This divide-and-rule strategy was designed to disguise the racial basis of official policy-making by the substitution of the language of ethnicity. This was accompanied by much ethnographic engineering as efforts were made to resurrect tribal structures. In the process, the Government sought to create a significant collaborating class.

The truth was that the rural reserves were by this time thoroughly degraded by overpopulation and soil erosion. This did not prevent four of the 'homeland' structures (Transkei, Bophuthatswana, Venda and Ciskei) being declared 'independent', a status which the vast majority of South Africans, and therefore also the international community, declined to recognise. In each case, the process involved the repression of opposition and the use by the Government of the power to nominate and thereby pad elected assemblies with a quota of compliant figures.

Forced removals from 'white' areas affected some 3,5 million people and vast rural slums were created in the homelands, which were used as dumping grounds. The pass laws and influx control were extended and harshly enforced, and labour bureaux were set up to channel labour to where it was needed. Hundreds of thousands of people were arrested or prosecuted under the pass laws each year, reaching over half a million a year from the mid-1960s to the mid-1970s. Industrial decentralisation to growth points on the borders of (but not inside) the homelands was promoted as a means of keeping blacks out of 'white' South Africa.

In virtually every sphere, from housing to education to healthcare, central government took control over black people's lives with a view to reinforcing their allotted role as 'temporary sojourners', welcome in 'white' South Africa solely to serve the needs of the employers of labour. But these same programmes of control became the focus of resistance. In particular, the campaign against the pass laws formed a cornerstone of the struggle.

The end of apartheid

The introduction of apartheid policies coincided with the adoption by the ANC in 1949 of its Programme of Action, expressing the renewed militancy of the 1940s. The Programme embodied the rejection of white domination and a call for action in the form of protests, strikes and demonstrations. There followed a decade of turbulent mass action in resistance to the imposition of still harsher forms of segregation and oppression.

The Defiance Campaign of 1952 carried mass mobilisation to new heights under the banner of non-violent resistance to the pass laws. These actions were influenced in part by the philosophy of Mohandas Ghandi.

A critical step in the emergence of non-racialism was the formation of the Congress Alliance, including the ANC, South African Indian Congress, the Coloured People's Congress, a small white congress organisation (the Congress of Democrats), and the South African Congress of Trade Unions.

The Alliance gave formal expression to an emerging unity across racial and class lines that was manifested in the Defiance Campaign and other mass protests of this period, which also saw women's resistance take a more organised character with the formation of the Federation of South African Women.

In 1955, a Freedom Charter was drawn up at the Congress of the People in Soweto. The Charter enunciated the principles of the struggle, binding the movement to a culture of human rights and non-racialism. Over the next few decades, the Freedom Charter was elevated to an important symbol of the freedom struggle.

The Pan-Africanist Congress (PAC), founded by Robert Sobukwe and based on the philosophies of 'Africanism' and anti-communism, broke away from the Congress Alliance in 1959.

The State's initial response, harsh as it was, was not yet as draconian as it was to become. Its attempt to prosecute more than 150 anti-apartheid leaders for treason, in a trial that began in 1956, ended in acquittals in 1961. But by that time, mass organised opposition had been banned.

Matters came to a head at Sharpeville in March 1960, when 69 anti-pass demonstrators were killed when police fired on a demonstration called by the PAC. A state of emergency was imposed and detention without trial was introduced.

The black political organisations were banned and their leaders went into exile or were arrested. In this climate, the ANC and PAC abandoned their long-standing commitment to non-violent resistance and turned to armed struggle, combined with underground organisation and mobilisation as well as mobilisation of international solidarity.

Top leaders, including members of the newly formed military wing *Umkhonto we Sizwe* (Spear of the Nation), were arrested in 1963. In the 'Rivonia trial', eight ANC leaders, including Nelson Mandela, were convicted of sabotage (instead of treason, the original charge) and sentenced to life imprisonment.

The 1960s was a decade of overwhelming repression and relative political disarray among blacks in the country. Armed action was contained by the State.

The resurgence of resistance politics from the early 1970s was dramatic. The Black Consciousness Movement, led by Steve Biko (who was killed in detention in 1977), re-awakened a sense of pride and self-esteem

History

in black people. News of the brutal death of Biko reverberated around the globe and led to unprecedented outrage.

As capitalist economies sputtered with the oil crisis of 1973, black trade unions revived. A wave of strikes reflected a new militancy that involved better organisation and was drawing new sectors, in particular intellectuals and the student movement, into mass struggle and debate over the principles informing it.

The year 1976 marked the beginning of a sustained anti-apartheid revolt. In June, school pupils of Soweto rose up against apartheid education, followed by youth uprisings all around the country.

By the 1980s, the different forms of struggle – armed struggle, mass mobilisation and international solidarity – were beginning to integrate and coalesce.

The United Democratic Front and the informal umbrella, the Mass Democratic Movement, emerged as legal vehicles of democratic forces struggling for liberation. Clerics played a prominent public role in these movements. The involvement of workers in resistance took on a new dimension with the formation of the Congress of South African Trade Unions and the National Council of Trade Unions.

Popular anger was directed against all those who were deemed to be collaborating with the Government in the pursuit of its objectives, and the black townships became virtually ungovernable. From the mid-1980s, regional and national states of emergency were enforced.

Developments in neighbouring states, where mass resistance to white-minority and colonial rule led to Portuguese decolonisation in the mid-1970s and the abdication of Zimbabwe's minority regime in 1980, left South Africa exposed as the last bastion of white supremacy

Under growing pressure and increasingly isolated internationally, the Government embarked on a dual strategy, introducing limited reform coupled with intensifying repression and militarisation of society, with the objective of containing the pressures and increasing its support base while crushing organised resistance.

An early example of reform was the recognition of black trade unions to try to stabilise labour relations. In 1983, the Constitution was reformed to allow the coloured and Indian minorities limited participation in separate and subordinate Houses of Parliament. The vast majority of these groups demonstrated their rejection of the tricameral dispensation through massive boycotts of elections, but it was kept in place by the apartheid regime despite its visible lack of legitimacy. Attempts to legitimise Community Councils as a vehicle for participation of Africans outside the Bantustans in local government met a similar fate.

Militarisation included the ascendancy of the State Security Council, which usurped the role of the executive in crucial respects, and a succession of states of emergency as part of the implementation of a comprehensive counter-insurgency strategy to combat what, by the mid-1980s, was an endemic insurrectionary spirit in the land.

However, by the late 1980s, popular resistance was taking the form of mass defiance campaigns, while struggles over more localised issues saw broad sections of communities mobilised in united action. Popular support for released political prisoners and for the armed struggle was being openly expressed.

In response to the rising tide of resistance, the international community strengthened its support for the anti-apartheid cause. A range of sanctions and boycotts was instituted, both unilaterally by countries across the world and through the United Nations (UN). These sanctions were called for in a co-ordinated strategy by the internal and external anti-apartheid movement in South Africa

F.W. de Klerk, who had replaced P.W. Botha as State President in 1989, announced at the opening of Parliament in February 1990 the unbanning of the liberation movements and release of political prisoners, notably Nelson Mandela. A number of factors led to this step. International financial, trade, sport and cultural sanctions were clearly biting. Above all, even if South Africa was nowhere near collapse, either militarily or economically, several years of emergency rule and ruthless repression had clearly neither destroyed the structures of organised resistance, nor helped establish legitimacy for the apartheid regime or its collaborators. Instead, popular resistance, including mass and armed action, was intensifying.

The ANC, enjoying popular recognition and legitimacy as the foremost liberation organisation, was increasingly regarded as a government-in-waiting. International support for the liberation movement came from various countries around the globe, particularly from former socialist countries and Nordic countries as well as the Non-Aligned Movement (NAM). The other liberation organisations increasingly experienced various internal and external pressures and did not enjoy much popular support.

It was obvious that Botha's strategy of reform initiatives combined with repression had failed to stabilise the internal situation.

To outside observers, and also in the eyes of growing numbers of white South Africans, apartheid stood exposed as morally bankrupt, indefensible and impervious to reforms. The collapse of global communism, the negotiated withdrawal of Cuban forces from Angola, and the culmination of the South-West African People's Organisation's liberation struggle in the negotiated independence of Namibia – formerly South-West Africa, administered by South Africa as a League of Nations mandate since 1919 – did much to change the mindset of whites. No longer could whites demonise the ANC and PAC as fronts for international communism.

White South Africa had also changed in deeper ways. Afrikaner nationalism had lost much of its *raison d'être*. Many Afrikaners had become urban, middle class and relatively prosperous. Their ethnic grievances and attachment to ethnic causes and symbols had diminished.

A large part of the NP's core constituency was ready to explore larger national identities, even across racial divides, and yearned for international respectability. Apartheid increasingly seemed more like a straitjacket than a safeguard. In 1982, disenchanted hardliners had split from the NP to form the Conservative Party, leaving the NP open to more flexible and modernising influences. After this split, factions within the Afrikaner élite openly started to pronounce in favour of a more inclusive society, causing more friction with the NP Government, which increasingly became militaristic and authoritarian.

A number of business, student and academic Afrikaners held meetings publicly and privately with the ANC in exile. Secret talks were held between the imprisoned Nelson Mandela and government Ministers about a new dispensation for South Africa with blacks forming a major part of it.

Inside the country, mass action became the order of the day. Petty apartheid laws and symbols were openly challenged and removed. Together with a sliding economy and increasing international pressure, these developments made historic changes inevitable.

The first decade of freedom

After a long negotiation process, sustained despite much opportunistic violence from the right wing and its surrogates, and in some instances sanctioned by elements of the State, South Africa's first democratic election was held in April 1994 under an interim Constitution.

History

The interim Constitution divided South Africa into nine new provinces in place of the previous four provinces and 10 'homelands', and provided for a Government of National Unity to be constituted by all parties with at least 20 seats in the National Assembly.

The ANC emerged from the election with a 62% majority. The main opposition came from the NP, which gained 20% of the vote nationally, and a majority in the Western Cape. The Inkatha Freedom Party (IFP) received 10% of the vote, mainly in its KwaZulu-Natal base. The NP and the IFP formed part of the Government of National Unity until 1996, when the NP withdrew.

The ANC-led Government embarked on a programme to promote the reconstruction and development of the country and its institutions. This called for the simultaneous pursuit of democratisation and socio-economic change, as well as reconciliation and the building of consensus founded on the commitment to improve the lives of all South Africans, in particular the poor. It required the integration of South Africa into a rapidly changing global environment.

Pursuit of these objectives has been a consistent focus of government during the first decade of freedom, seeking the unity of a previously divided society in working together to overcome the legacy of a history of division, exclusion and neglect.

Converting democratic ideals into practice required, among others, initiating a radical overhaul of the machinery of government at every level, towards service delivery, openness and a culture of human rights. It has required a more integrated approach to planning and implementation to ensure that the many different aspects of transformation and socio-economic upliftment cohere with maximum impact.

A significant milestone in the democratisation of South Africa was the exemplary Constitution-making process, which in 1996 delivered a document that has evoked world-wide admiration.

So too have been the elections subsequent to 1994 – all conducted peacefully, with high levels of participation compared to the norm in most democracies, and accepted by all as free and fair in their conduct and results.

Local government elections during 1995 and 1996, and then again in 2000 after the transformation of the municipal system, gave the country its first democratically elected non-racial municipal authorities.

Since 2001, participatory democracy and interactive governance have been strengthened through the practice of *Imbizo*, in which members of the executive, in all three spheres of government, including The Presidency, regularly engage directly with the public around implementation of programmes of reconstruction and development.

The second democratic national election in 1999 saw the ANC majority increase to just short of two-thirds and the election of Mr Thabo Mbeki as President in succession to Mr Nelson Mandela. It saw a sharp decline of the NP (now the New National Party [NNP]) and its replacement by the Democratic Party, led by Mr Tony Leon, as the official opposition in Parliament. These two parties formed the Democratic Alliance, which the NNP left in 2001.

Although the new Constitution does not provide for a Government of National Unity, the Government continued to include representatives of opposition parties, namely the IFP, later the Azanian People's Organisation, and the NNP.

The Truth and Reconciliation Commission (TRC), under the leadership of Archbishop Desmond Tutu, helped inculcate a commitment to accountability and transparency in South Africa's public life, at the same time helping to heal wounds inflicted by the inhumanities of the apartheid era.

During 2003, Parliament accepted the Government's response to the final report of the TRC. Out of 22 000 individuals or surviving families appearing before the Commission, 19 000 were identified as needing urgent reparation assistance – virtually all, where the necessary information was available, received interim reparations. As final reparations, government is providing a once-off grant of R30 000 to individuals or survivors who appeared before, and were designated by, the TRC, over and above the programmes for material assistance. There will also be systematic programmes to project the symbolism of the struggle and the ideal of freedom. These include the Freedom Park Monument and other symbols and monuments, and such matters as records of history, remaking of cultural and art forms, and geographical and place names.

The ethos of partnership informed the establishment of the National Economic Development and Labour Council. It brings together government, business, organised labour and development organisations to confront the challenges of growth and development for South Africa in a turbulent and globalising international economy.

The Presidential Jobs Summit in 1998 and the Growth and Development Summit (GDS) in June 2003 brought these sectors together to collectively take advantage of the conditions in South Africa for faster growth and development. At the GDS, a comprehensive set of agreements were concluded to address urgent challenges in a practical way and speed up job-creating growth and development.

Partnership between government and civil society has been further strengthened by the creation of a number of working groups through which sectors of society – business, organised labour, higher education, religious leaders, higher education, youth and women – engage regularly with the President.

From the start, government placed emphasis on meeting basic needs through programmes for socio-economic development such as the provision of housing, piped water, electricity, education and healthcare, as well as social grants for those in need.

The impact of these programmes is seen in the increased proportion of South Africans who now have access to these basic services. This has been achieved despite a social revolution reflected in smaller household sizes (with the number of households growing almost three times faster than the population) and therefore many more households needing basic services.

Another priority has been the safety and security of citizens, requiring both transforming the police into a service working with the community, and overcoming grave problems of criminality and a culture of violence posed by the social dislocations inherited from the past.

On the economic front, the key objectives have been job creation, poverty eradication, reduction of inequality and overall growth. There has been progress in rebuilding the economy, in particular with the achievement of macro-economic stability and the initiation of programmes of micro-economic reform. But unemployment remains a major challenge – the number of jobs created has not been enough, as the economically active population has grown faster, and the economy needs more skilled workers.

The integration of South Africa into the global political, economic and social system has been a priority for democratic South Africa. As a country isolated during the apartheid period; an African country; a developing country; and a country whose liberation was achieved with the support of the international community, it has been of critical importance to build political and economic links with the countries and regions of the world, and to work with others for an international environment more favourable to development across the world, and in Africa and South Africa in particular.

The South African Government is committed to the African Renaissance, which is based on consolidation of democracy, economic development and a co-operative approach to resolving the challenges the continent faces.

South Africa hosted the launch of the African Union (AU), a step towards further unification of Africa in pursuit of socio-economic development, the Organisation of African Unity (OAU) having fulfilled its mandate to liberate Africa. President Mbeki chaired the AU for its founding year, handing over the chair to President Joaquim Chissano of Mozambique in July 2003. Through the New Partnership for Africa's Development (NEPAD), the development programme of the AU, South Africa works with the rest of the continent and its partners in the industrialised world for the development and regeneration of the African continent.

Democratic South Africa has sought to play an active role in international and multilateral organisations. During the first decade of its freedom, it acted at various times as chair of the Southern African Development Community, NAM, AU and the Commonwealth Heads of Government meeting. It has played host to several international conferences, including the United Nations Conference on Trade and Development in 1996, 2000 World AIDS Congress, World Conference Against Racism in 2001, World Summit on Sustainable Development in 2002, and the World Parks Congress in 2003.

In 2004, South Africa will celebrate 10 years of freedom. South Africans have made much progress in pursuit of their goals. Many challenges face the nation as it enters the second decade of its freedom, at the beginning of the 21st century.

During 2003, government initiated a 10-Year Review to reflect on its performance in achieving its mandate and assess the challenges of the coming period.

Some of these challenges are shared with the rest of the world, especially developing countries. Globalisation, the digital divide, poverty, HIV and AIDS, and creating conditions conducive to sustainable development are some of the critical issues for which the nation is seeking solutions in partnership with others.

Other challenges are specific to South Africa. Prominent among those identified are: the further strengthening of social partnerships for the development of South African society, and the eradication of poverty, improving the performance of the State, addressing the consequences of the social transition that has followed the end of apartheid, and improving the regional environment and implementing NEPAD.

The fabric of South African society is continually changing, creating not only new challenges but also greater stability and peace, and laying the foundation for a society in which the individual and collective human potential of the nation can come to full fruition.

Acknowledgement

This history chapter has evolved year by year, based on initial text from the Institute for Historical Research, University of the Western Cape.

Suggested reading

Alexander, P. *Workers, War and the Origins of Apartheid: Labour and Politics in South Africa, 1939 – 1948*. Cape Town: David Philip, 2001.
An extraordinary 20th century. Johannesburg: Star Independent Newspapers, 1999.
Beinart, W. *Twentieth Century South Africa*. 2nd ed. Cape Town: Oxford University Press, 2001.
Berger, L.R. *In the Footsteps of Eve: The Mystery of Human Origins*. Washington: National Geographic Society, 2000.
Bond, P. *Elite Transition: From Apartheid to Neoliberalism in South Africa*. Pietermaritzburg: University of Natal Press, 2000.
Bonner, P. and Segal, L. *Soweto: A History*. Cape Town: Maskew Miller Longman, 1998.

Brink, E. and others. *Soweto: 16 June 1976.* Cape Town: Kwela Books, 2001.
Bulbulia, F. and Isiakpere, F. eds. *Council of the Elders: A Tribute to the Veterans of the South African Liberation Struggle.* Lagos: Minaj Publishers, 1997.
Callinicos, L. *People's History of South Africa.* Johannesburg: Ravan Press, 1981 – 1993. 3 vols.
Coleman, M. ed. *A Crime Against Humanity: Analysing the Repression of the Apartheid State.* Bellville: Mayibuye Books, University of the Western Cape, 1998.
Davenport, T.R.H. *The Transfer of Power in South Africa.* Cape Town: David Philip, 1998.
Davenport, T.R.H. and Saunders, C. *South Africa: A Modern History.* 5th ed. London: Macmillan, 2000.
De Gruchy, J. ed. *The London Missionary Society in Southern Africa: Historical Essays.* Cape Town: David Philip, 1999.
Drew, A. *Discordant Comrades: Identities and Loyalties of the South African Left.* Pretoria: University of South Africa, 2002.
Driver, C.J. *Patrick Duncan: South African and Pan-African.* Cape Town: David Philip, 2000.
Dubow, S. *The African National Congress.* Johannesburg: Jonathan Ball, 2000.
Du Pre, R.H. *Separate But Unequal: The Coloured People of South Africa: A Political History.* Johannesburg: Jonathan Ball, 1994.
Ebrahim H. *The Soul of a Nation: Constitution-Making in South Africa.* Cape Town: Oxford University Press, 1998.
Evans, M.M. *Encyclopedia of the Boer War.* Oxford: ABC – Clio, 2000.
Field, S. ed. *Lost Communities, Living Memories.* Cape Town: David Philip, 2001.
Frankel, G. *Rivonia's Children: Three Families and the Price of Freedom in South Africa.* Johannesburg: Jonathan Ball, 1999.
Frankel, P. *An Ordinary Atrocity: Sharpeville and its Massacre.* Johannesburg: Witwatersrand University Press, 2001.
Freund, B. *The Making of Contemporary Africa: The Development of African Society Since 1800.* 2nd ed. London: Macmillan, 1998.
Hadland, A. and Rantao, J. *Life and Times of Thabo Mbeki.* Rivonia, Johannesburg: Zebra Press, 1997.
Hamilton, C. *Terrific Majesty: The Powers of Shaka Zulu and the Limits of Historical Intervention.* Cape Town: David Philip, 1998.
Hammond-Tooke, D. *The Roots of Black South Africa: An Introduction to the Traditional Culture of the Black People of South Africa.* Johannesburg: Jonathan Ball, 1993.
Harris, J.E. *Africans and their History.* 2nd ed. New York: Meridian, 1998.
Honikman, A. *In the Shadow of Apartheid.* Johannesburg: Quartz Press, 1998.
Hopkins, P. and Grange, H. *The Rocky Rioter Teargas Show: The Inside Story of the 1976 Soweto Uprising.* Cape Town: Zebra, 2001.
Isichei, E. *A. History of African Societies to 1870.* Cambridge: University Press, 1997. Southern Africa discussed in Chapter 22, pp. 409 – 430.
Johnson, R.W. and Schlemmer L. *Launching Democracy in South Africa. The First Open Election, 1994 – 1996.* New Haven: Yale University Press, 1996.
Johnson, R.W. and Welsh, D. *Ironic History: Liberalism in Post-liberation South Africa.* Cape Town: Oxford University Press, 1998.
Joyce, P. *Concise Dictionary of South African Biography.* Cape Town: Francolin, 1999.
Kathrada, A. *Letters from Robben Island: A Selection of Ahmed Kathrada's Prison Correspondence.* 2nd ed. Zebra Press, 2000.
Keegan, T. *Colonial South Africa and the Origins of the Racial Order.* Cape Town: David Philip, 1996.
Laband, J.P.C. *Rope of Sand: The Rise and Fall of the Zulu Kingdom in the Nineteenth Century.* Johannesburg: Jonathan Ball, 1995.
Le May, G.H.L. *The Afrikaners: A Historical Interpretation.* Oxford: Blackwell Publishers, 1995.
Lodge, T. *Bus Stop for Everyone.* Cape Town: David Philip, 2002. 2nd ed.
Marks, S.C. *Conflict Resolution during South Africa's Transition to Democracy.* Washington: United States Institute of Peace Press, 2000.
Mathebula, M. *800 Years of Tsonga History.* Polokwane: Sharp-Shoot Publishing, 2002.
Matshikiza, T. and Matshikiza, J. *With the Lid Off: South African Insights from Home and Abroad, 1959 – 2000.* Johannesburg: M & G Books, 2000.
Maylam, P. *A History of the African People of South Africa: From the Early Iron Age to the 1970s.* Cape Town: David Philips, 1995.
Mbeki, G. *The Struggle for Liberation in South Africa: A Short History.* Cape Town: David Philip, 1997.
McKinley, D.T. *The ANC and the Liberation Struggle: A Critical Political Biography.* London: Pluto Press, 1997.

History

Meiring, P. *Chronicle of the Truth Commission: A Journey through the Past and Present into the Future of South Africa.* Vanderbijlpark: Carpe Diem Books, 1999.
Mitchell, P. *The Archaeology of Southern Africa.* Cape Town: Cambridge University Press, 2002.
Mostert, N. *Frontiers: The Epic of South Africa's Creation and the Tragedy of the Xhosa People.* London: Jonathan Cape, 1992.
Musiker, N. and Musiker, R. *A Concise Historical Dictionary of Greater Johannesburg.* Cape Town: Francolin, 2000.
Naidoo, I. *Island in Chains: Ten Years on Robben Island.* London: Penguin, 2000.
Ndlovu, S.M. *The Soweto Uprisings: Counter-Memories of June 1976.* Randburg: Ravan Press, 1998.
New Dictionary of South African Biography: Volume 2. Editor: N.E. Sonderling. Pretoria: Human Sciences Research Council, 1999.
Nuttall, S. and Coetzee, C. eds. *Negotiating the Past: The Making of Memory in South Africa.* Cape Town: Oxford University Press, 1998.
O'Meara, D. *Forty Lost Years: The Apartheid State and the Politics of the National Party.* Johannesburg: Ravan Press, 1996.
Omer-Cooper, J.D. *History of Southern Africa.* 2nd ed. Cape Town: David Philip, 1994.
Pakenham, T. *The Scramble for Africa 1876 – 1912.* Johannesburg: Jonathan Ball, 1991.
Penn, N. *Rogues, Rebels and Runaways: Eighteenth Century Cape Characters.* Cape Town: David Philip, 2000.
Prah, K.K. *Beyond the Colour Line: Pan-Africanist Disputations.* Florida: Vivlia, 1997.
Rantete, J.M. *The African National Congress and the Negotiated Settlement in South Africa.* Pretoria: Van Schaik, 1998.
Reader's Digest Illustrated History of South Africa. 3rd ed. Cape Town: Reader's Digest, 1994.
Reynolds, A. ed. *Election '99: South Africa from Mandela to Mbeki.* Cape Town: David Philip, 1999.
Ross, R. *Concise Cambridge History of South Africa.* Cambridge: 1999.
Sachs, A. *The Soft Vengeance of a Freedom Fighter.* 2nd ed. Cape Town: David Philip, 2000.
Sampson, A. *Mandela: The Authorised Biography.* Johannesburg: Jonathan Ball, 1999.
Saunders, C. and Southey, N. *A Dictionary of South African History.* 2nd ed. Cape Town: David Philip, 2001.
Schoeman, K. *The Griqua Captaincy of Philippolis, 1826 – 1861.* Pretoria: Protea Book House, 2002.
Seekings, J. *The UDF: A History of the United Democratic Front in South Africa, 1983 – 1991.* Cape Town: David Philip, 2000.
Smith, C. *Mandela.* Cape Town: Struik, 1999.
Spies, S. B. *Methods of Barbarism: Roberts, Kitchener and the Civilians of the Boer Republics: January 1900 – May 1902.* Johannesburg: Jonathan Ball, 2001.
Suttner, R. *Inside Apartheid's Prison: Notes and Letters of Struggle.* Pietermaritzburg: University of Natal Press, 2001.
Terreblanche, S. *A History of Inequality in South Africa, 1652 – 2002.* Pietermaritzburg: University of Natal Press, 2002.
Thompson, D. and Watson, B. *They are Africans Who Worked Toward the Liberation, Unity and Solidarity of Africa and African People Throughout the World.* Cape Town: Kwela Books, 2000.
Truth and Reconciliation Commission. Final Report. 5 vols. Distributors: Cape Town: Juta, 1998.
Van der Merwe, H.W. *Peacemaking in South Africa: A Life in Conflict Resolution.* Cape Town: Tafelberg, 2000.
Wadley, L. ed. *Our Gendered Past: Archaeological Studies of Gender in Southern Africa.* Johannesburg: Witwatersrand University Press, 1997.
Waldmeir, P. *Anatomy of a Miracle: The End of Apartheid and the Birth of the New South Africa.* London: Penguin Books, 1998.
Webster, R. *At the Fireside: True South African Stories.* Cape Town: Spearhead, 2002.
Welsh, F. *History of South Africa.* London: Harper Collins, 1998.
Wilson, M. and Thompson L.M. eds. *Oxford History of South Africa.* Oxford: Clarendon Press, 1969 – 1971. 2 vols.
Worden, N. *Concise Dictionary of South African History.* Cape Town: Francolin, 1998.
Worden, N. *The Making of Modern South Africa: Conquest, Segregation and Apartheid.* Blackwell, Oxford 1994.

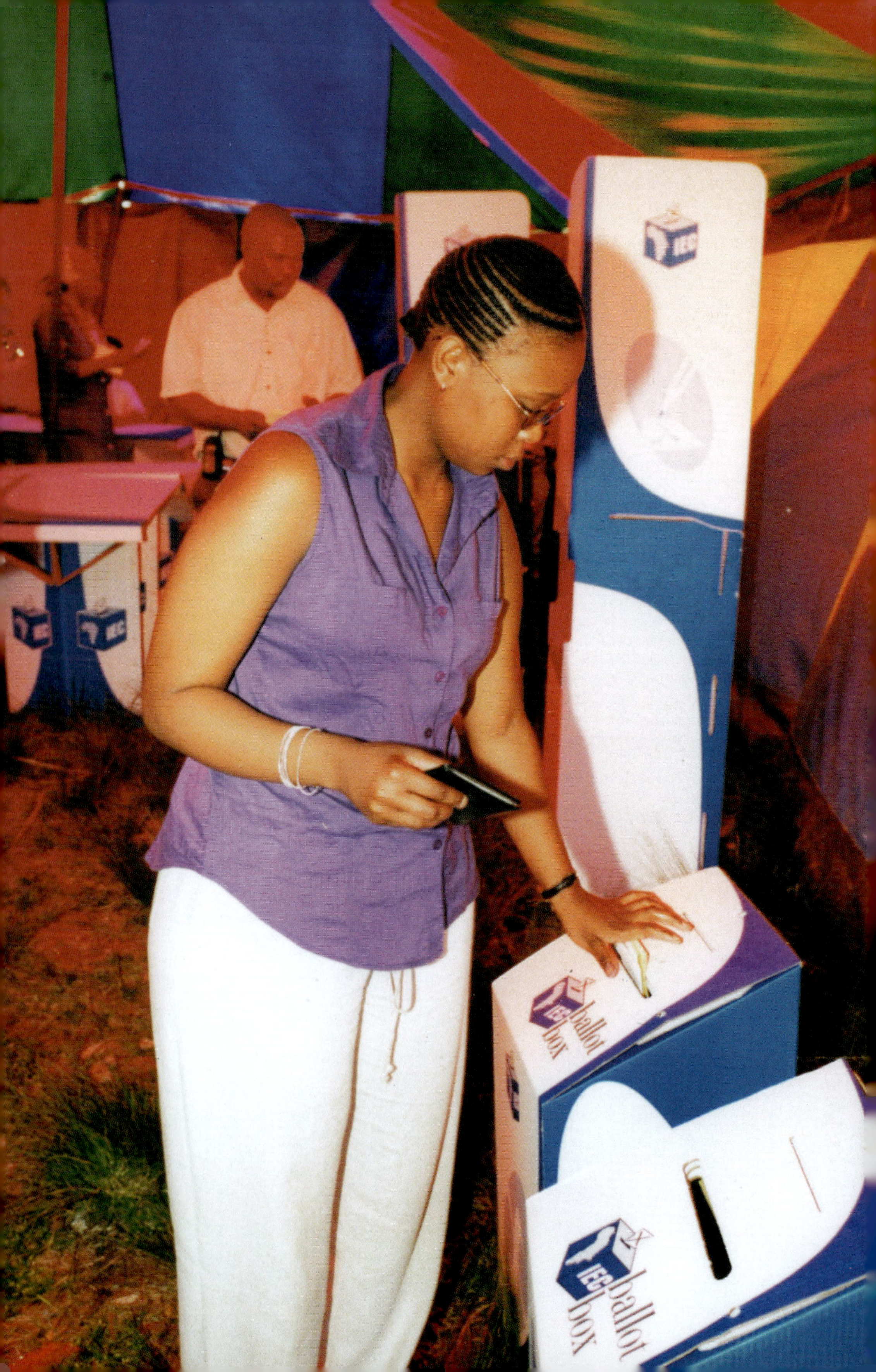
IEC
IEC ballot box
IEC ballot box

chapter 3

Overview – 10 years of freedom

Progress in the first decade

Reconstruction and development

Since 1994, in line with the Reconstruction and Development Programme (RDP), government has set out to dismantle apartheid social relations and create a democratic society based on equity, non-racialism and non-sexism. New policies and programmes have been put in place to dramatically improve the quality of life of all South Africans.

The RDP, the core of all post-1994 policies, has as its objectives:
- meeting basic needs
- building the economy
- democratising the State and society
- developing human resources and nation-building.

What the democratic State inherited

Black people were denied the franchise, society was divided along racial lines, and the social exclusion and neglect of the majority was a matter of State policy.

◀ South Africa's first democratic election on 27 April 1994 was a historic culmination of a peaceful transition from the oppressive apartheid regime to a democratic government founded on the fundamental principles of freedom, equality and justice for all, among others.

Economically, the country was isolated and the economy was in crisis. Growth declined to below 1% per annum in the decade before 1994, and by the early 1990s had come to a standstill.

Public-sector debt was ballooning out of control.

The police and justice system violated most human and civil rights and was mainly used to defend apartheid. The South African Defence Force was fighting a low-intensity war against the liberation movement. Until after the 1994 election, parts of the country lived under a state of war, and assassinations and bombings of political opponents were rife.

Governance was largely defined by a national-security doctrine with little respect for the rule of law. The State became more isolated, more corrupt and more dependent on extra-judicial measures to sustain itself. By the late 1980s, the country had become ungovernable, the social fabric torn apart by apartheid and social conflict.

Ten-year review

Government has been assessing how far it has achieved its objectives in the past decade. It has also begun to assess the challenges of the next decade. This review is focused on government's performance. It is expected that organisations in sport, arts

South Africa Yearbook 2003/04

Broadening access to social services

From the Census 2001	1996	2001
Households with access to clean water	80,0%	85,0%
Households using electricity for lighting	57,6%	69,7%
People who have completed Grade 12 schooling	16,3%	20,4%
Households in formal housing	57,5%	63,8%
Households with chemical or flush toilets	50,5%	51,9%

Output of government's social programmes

From department reports		1994 – 1998	1999 – 2002	Since 1994
Water	People gaining access via community programmes	3,0 million	5,4 million	8,4 million
Electricity	Grid connections	2,3 million	1,5 million	3,8 million
Housing	Subsidised houses built or under construction	0,74 million	0,72 million	1,46 million
Land redistribution	Hectares distributed	0,44 million	1,36 million	1,8 million
	Households in transfers	30 061	107 417	137 478
Land restitution	Claims lodged	68 878		68 878
	Claims settled	3 964	32 525	36 489
	Hectares restored	0,23 million	0,27 million	0,57 million

and culture; universities; professionals and the intelligentsia; trade unions; and the private sector will make their own assessments. These, together with government's review will help the nation evaluate itself in the first decade of freedom.

The review is based on research by people inside and outside government. Departments were also asked to assess their own performance. A detailed report is available at *South Africa Government Online* (www.gov.za).

Measuring change

In assessing the change, the review uses the best statistics available. But so great are the differences between the apartheid State and the democratic State that direct comparisons are often impossible. The official statistics of the past also underestimated the impact of apartheid on the majority of South Africans by excluding the so-called 'independent' *Bantustans*.

Governance Cluster

The State has become a people-centred State

New Constitution and laws

The Constitution of the Republic of South Africa, 1996 (Act 108 of 1996), and over 780 pieces of legislation have created a framework for reshaping South Africa.

Transforming the Public Service

Bantustan and central government civil services have been integrated into a single public service. Representivity targets have almost been met – Africans make up 72% of the Public Service but there should be more women in senior positions and people with disabilities.

The Public Finance Management Act, 1999 (Act 1 of 1999), and a medium-term budget cycle have improved accountability, budgeting and financial management.

Access to services is being improved by Multi-Purpose Community Centres (one per district by the end of 2004 and expanding to each municipality in the next decade), the introduction of Community Development Workers and the e-Government *batho pele* (people first) Gateway.

Better service delivery
Policy and implementation are more integrated thanks to government's Cluster approach, provincial co-ordination, Integrated Development Plans in local government and the recently introduced National Planning Framework. There are still serious capacity problems affecting especially provincial and local service delivery and in central government middle management.

Fighting corruption
A Code of Conduct for the Public Service is now part of the regulations for every public servant. The 1999 National Anti-Corruption Summit created a powerful platform for the National Campaign Against Corruption and helped establish whistle-blowing mechanisms, special corruption courts and the National Anti-Corruption Forum. New laws to fight corruption include the Promotion of Access to Information Act, 2000 (Act 2 of 2000), and the recent Prevention of Corruption Bill.

The National Directorate of Public Prosecutions and South African Police Service (SAPS) have acted against corrupt officials and white-collar crime. About 80% of corruption cases in government reported in the media are discovered by government.

Social Cluster

Programmes to alleviate poverty have improved the lives of millions.

Boosting the income of the poor
Social grants, formerly allocated on a racial basis, have been equalised and extended to all who are in need and eligible. Beneficiaries have increased from 2,6 million in 1994 to 5,1 million in 2003. The poorest 20% of households receive the largest amount from grants. However, the full impact will only be realised when all those who are eligible are registered.

Broadening access to social services
Programmes to broaden access to services have improved the lives of millions of South Africans:
- Electricity, water and sanitation – As the table on page 52 shows, many more people have access to these basic services.
- Education – Adult literacy is up from 83% in 1996 to 89% in 2001, and for 15- to 24-year-olds from 83% to 96%. The matric pass rate rose from 54% in 1996 to 69% in 2002.
- Health
  - Primary healthcare has expanded, with free healthcare for women and children under six. Upgrading and building new clinics have resulted in 701 additional clinics.
  - The integrated nutrition programme, which reached 89% of the targeted learners in 1994, now reaches 94% or 4,58 million children.
  - Government's comprehensive response to HIV and AIDS has expanded rapidly. Expenditure increased tenfold from R30 million in 1994 to R342 million in 2001/02, and is set to increase tenfold again to R3,6 billion in 2005/06. HIV infection, after rapidly increasing in the 1990s, stabilised after 1999 – 22,4% in 1999, 24,5% in 2000, 24,8% in 2001 and 26,5 in 2002. For pregnant women under 20 years, the infection rate has decreased consistently for the last few years.
  - The tuberculosis-control programme increased treatment rates from 60%

10 YEARS OF FREEDOM
south africa 1994 - 2004

'Never, never and never again shall it be that this beautiful land will again experience the oppression of one by another and suffer the indignity of being the skunk of the world.'

President Nelson Mandela, 10 May 1994, Inauguration address

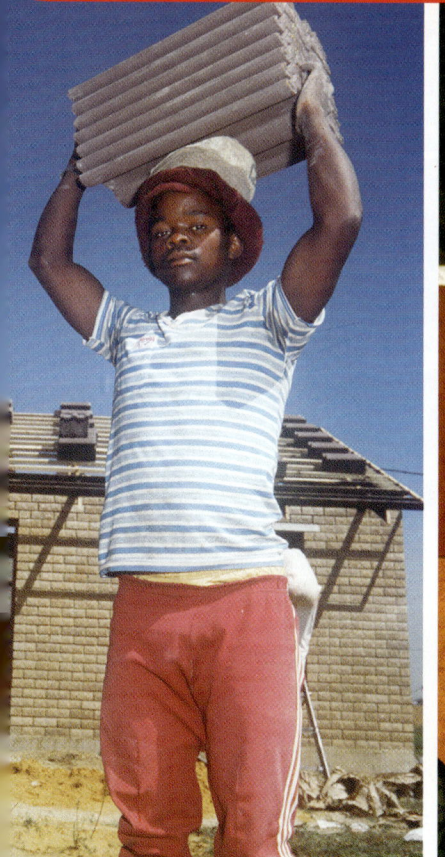

THE ROAD TO RECONCILIATION.

'We have no doubt that our policies have been and are a correct response to the practical reality we inherited. The changes taking place in our country attest to this. The lives of our people are changing for the better.'

President Thabo Mbeki, 14 February 2003 State of the Nation Address

10 YEARS OF FREEDOM
south africa 1994 - 2004

to 65% between 1996 and 1999, but treatment interruptions and transfers have kept cure rates below the targeted 85%.

Boosting ownership of assets and access to opportunities

Housing
Over 1,9 million subsidies have been approved for new houses, and 480 000 houses built in the apartheid era have been transferred to occupants under the discount benefit scheme.

Land reform
Between 1994 and 2002, some 0,5 million hectares (ha) were restored through land restitution while 1,8 million ha were distributed.

Communications and culture
Access to means of communication has grown rapidly – by 2001, 32% of households had cellphones, 42% access to land lines, 73% had radios in the home, and 54% television sets. Plans are under way to fully implement the constitutional recognition of all 11 languages of South Africa as official languages.

Addressing social exclusion
Discriminatory laws have been repealed. New measures to prevent social exclusion include tenure and land reform; steps towards gender equality, including recognition of customary marriages; employment equity; maternity benefits; recognition of surnames; attending to sexual harassment; and affirmative action. Specially targeted programmes protect the elderly, people with disabilities and children, as well as vulnerable workers such as domestic and farm workers.

Preserving the environment
Government has focused on fairer distribution of rights of access to natural resources and benefits of conservation areas.

Economy Cluster

Government's economic policies have turned around an economy that was in crisis. Almost continuous growth since 1994 has created jobs, but not enough to keep up with the increasing number of people looking for employment.

Performance of the economy
- Stability – Government's policies have freed resources for social expenditure by reducing the interest it has to pay on debt. The Budget deficit fell from 9,5% in 1993 to 1% in 2002/03, and public-sector debt fell from 60% to 50%.
- Investment – Investment has been low (16 – 17% of Gross Domestic Product) compared with successful developing countries, but has begun to improve in the last three years.
- Growth – Negative per-capita growth in the decade before 1994 has changed to average growth of 2,8% a year since then. Real growth per person in South Africa has increased just over 1% per year since 1994.
- Employment – Between 1995 and 2002, the number of people employed grew by 1,6 million from 9,6 million to 11,2 million. However, the number of people unemployed also grew by 2,4 million because many more people were seeking work. While many unskilled workers are unemployed, there are also shortages of skilled workers in many sectors.
- Trade reform and industrial restructuring – Government's industrial policy and efforts to promote an international trade environment that favours development have improved the balance of trade and brought a shift to higher valued-added exports.
- Labour legislation – Great progress in labour relations laws has given employers and employees more certainty and security in their relationship. This is reflected in the huge fall in person-strike-days per year.

State-enterprise restructuring

Restructuring has focused mainly on telecommunications, energy, defence and transport. The aim has been to broaden access to services; reduce costs and raise revenue to reduce public debt, at the same time minimising the impact on employment; and promote Black Economic Empowerment. In the process, R24 billion has been raised to reduce public debt, and share-ownership has been widened. Lowering costs and improving service quality will require further improvement in the regulatory environment.

Expanding economic opportunities

Small-business development
Initiatives such as the Small Business Council, Khula Enterprise Finance Corporation and Ntsika Enterprise Promotion Agency have made some impact, but not enough.

Skills development
Government has directed resources towards education and skills training and set up Sector Education and Training Authorities (SETAs) for each sector of the economy, financed by a skills levy on the pay roll. Although the SETAs have been slow in meeting their objectives and employers slow to take advantage of them, performance is improving.

Empowerment
Empowerment in the workplace is continuing, albeit slowly. Black people in top management grew from 12% to 13% between 2000 and 2001; and in senior management, from 15% to 16%. Black ownership of public companies was 9,4% in 2002 compared with 3,9% in 1997 (and was virtually non-existent before 1994). The figures for women in the workplace are not much different.

Justice, crime prevention and security

Transformation and integration of a crime prevention system that once focused on shoring up apartheid has helped to all but end political violence, deal with terrorism and stabilise crime. But better service delivery needs more capacity-building, citizen involvement and eradication of corruption. Moral regeneration and nation-building are also essential for effective crime prevention.

National Crime Prevention Strategy (NCPS)
The NCPS has several elements:
- The National Crime Combating Strategy ('Operation Crackdown') is beginning to make an impact. Serious crime levels in South Africa are continuing to come down or stabilise.
- Except for robbery and malicious damage to property, most of the 20 categories of serious crime have either stabilised or decreased since 1994.
- Since 1994, murder has decreased by 30,7%.
- Though the trend of robberies has continued to increase, almost 50% of robberies now relate to cellphone theft or misplacement, with high reporting rates for insurance purposes.
- High-profile robberies (vehicle hijacking, hijacking of trucks, cash-in-transit robbery and bank robbery) have come down significantly since they were first recorded in 1996.
- The Integrated Justice System has brought about shorter cases, better-quality dockets and higher conviction rates (up from 78% in 1999 to 81% in 2002). The introduction of Saturday and additional courts has helped.
- Attacking the causes of crime is part of the national strategy requiring further implementation, including the social crime-prevention initiatives that are part of Integrated Rural Development, Urban Renewal and Moral Regeneration.

- Community policing has made policing more effective. Community Police Forums and the partnership with Business Against Crime have reduced street crime by 80% in targeted city centres.
- Prison overcrowding is being relieved by opening new prisons, alternative sentencing, correctional supervision, an awaiting-trial prisoner project, parole, and an improved rehabilitation programme. Escapes were reduced from 1 244 in 1996 to 325 in 2002.

High-priority crimes

Sexual-assault crimes
The incidence of rape increased by 10% after 1994, then stabilised for some years and in 1999 began to decline once more to 1994 levels.

Organised crime and corruption
Action against criminal syndicates helped to bring down vehicle hijacking by 33,7% and bank-related crimes by 52,2% since 1996 – and white-collar crime by 24% since 1994. Over 200 syndicates were neutralised out of the 300 that were identified and investigated.

Border control
The South African National Defence Force has assisted the SAPS in controlling borders, resulting in the deportation of thousands of illegal immigrants and the confiscation of stolen vehicles and illegal firearms. New controls and upgrading of infrastructure at ports of entry will combat cross-border crime and other threats to national security.

Taxi violence
Violence in the taxi industry has been curbed by more effective regulation and prosecution of perpetrators, though sporadic attacks and extortion of funds from members of taxi associations continue.

Illegal firearms
Over 80 000 illegal firearms have been destroyed. New measures include regulating ownership of legal firearms and reducing the number of illegal firearms.

Terrorism
Urban terrorism in the Western Cape was ended by co-ordinated operations and the conviction of perpetrators, but socio-economic factors that sustain gangsterism and violence still need attention. Right-wing terrorist plans were uncovered in 2002, leading to the confiscation of weapons, prevention of assassination plans, and more than 20 prosecutions. The Government is implementing United Nations (UN) resolutions relating to international terrorism.

International relations

South Africa's post-1994 success in defining its place in the world is remarkable given its size. This required thoroughly revising the mission of national security and the principles underpinning the country's international relations, as well as transforming South Africa's institutions to align them with the new democracy.

Diplomatic normalisation
South Africa has normalised its relations with the world and is actively promoting its own interests and those of the South in all significant regional, continental and multilateral institutions.

The country has hosted many international conferences and events since 1994. These include the Non-Aligned Movement (NAM) Summit (1998), Commonwealth Heads of Government Meeting (1999), UN AIDS Conference (2000), UN World Conference Against Racism (2001), World Summit on Sustainable Development (2002), and the African Union (AU) Summit (2002).

Marketing and branding South Africa
The Government has, since the late 1990s,

Overview

been actively imaging, branding and marketing South Africa, both directly and by supporting initiatives like Proudly South African, hosting hallmark events, and creating the International Investment Council, Inter-national Marketing Council and International Task Force on Information Society and Development.

Tourism has surged – from 5,7 million international tourist arrivals in South Africa in 1998 to 6,4 million in 2002.

International relations for growth and development

Trade
Trading networks and markets have been expanded and diversified through, among others, bilateral and multilateral negotiations and expanding relations with South America, Asia and Africa.

Regional integration in southern Africa
A democratic South Africa has promoted regional integration in the context of the Southern African Development Community (SADC) and the New Partnership for Africa's Development (NEPAD). The restructuring of SADC will provide member states with a comprehensive development agenda.

Continental affairs
South Africa played an active role in reconstituting the Organisation of African Unity (OAU) into the AU as a more effective continental body, and developing NEPAD as the AU's socio-economic programme. The African Peer Review Mechanism has been established as a voluntary mechanism to ensure that policies and practices of participating states conform to the Declaration on Democracy, Political, Economic and Corporate Governance.

Global affairs
Since 2001, South Africa has worked to keep Africa and the South on the G8 agenda, and engaged with international financial institutions to promote a global financial system more favourable to developing countries.

Science and technology (S&T)
Some 30 bilateral agreements have been signed for S&T in the past nine years. There are several major S&T initiatives in South Africa with strong international participation, including the HIV/AIDS Vaccine Initiative.

Promoting human rights, peace, security and stability
South Africa works with other African states and multilateral organisations like the UN, OAU/AU and SADC to promote international respect for human rights, democracy and good governance. South Africa has been part of regional and continental initiatives to assist the Zimbabwean people to resolve their problems, and has assisted with peace-keeping in Ethiopia/Eritrea, the Democratic Republic of the Congo and Burundi.

Strengthening multilateralism and co-operation
In order to advance the interests of developing countries, South Africa has worked to promote a rules-bound international political and economic order; and to transform North-South relations through dialogue while consolidating South-South collaboration by participation in groupings like the NAM, United Nations Conference on Trade and Development, SADC and the AU.

Challenges of the next decade

The next decade's challenges arise from lessons learnt in the first decade of freedom and new challenges created by the first stage of transformation.

Influence of the State
The record of implementation shows that government's successes have often, though

not always, been in areas in which it has had significant control and less so where its influence has been indirect:
- There has been considerable progress in building a new constitutional order, three spheres of government and more integrated administration – but many areas of service delivery require much improved performance by the Public Service.
- There has been great extension and deracialisation of social services, with striking impact on women's rights. However, many people entitled to grants are still unregistered or poorly serviced.
- Good progress in economic areas under government control (fiscal and monetary policy, and trade and industrial policy) has not been matched where new agencies or partnerships are involved – small business, human resource development, restructuring of State-owned enterprises, equity and empowerment. Government has had even less success in areas depending significantly on private-sector and civil-society investment and employment creation.
- National security has been enhanced, the rule of law established, and institutions transformed. However, due to aspects of the social transition, insufficient civil-society involvement, and new forms of organised crime, the gains in crime prevention could have been better.
- Internationally, government has made progress beyond its limited resources as the country has reintegrated in the international arena.

The social transition

Four social trends in the first decade of freedom shape the challenges ahead.
- Households – From 1996 to 2001, the South African population grew 11% from 40,4 million to 44,8 million. The number of households grew by 30% from 9,7 million to 11,8 million, as households became smaller. 'Unbundling' of households, together with freedom and improvement in the quality of life, are resulting in fewer extended families.
- Economically active population – The population grew by about 2% a year from 1995 to 2002 but the economically active population grew by about 4% a year – from 11,5 million to 15,4 million. The number of jobs grew by 12% (after accounting for jobs lost) but the economically active population grew by 35%. New job seekers are not only young adults but also older people who in the old order did not consider themselves part of the labour market, many of them African women from rural areas.
- Economy – While all the main sectors grew between 1995 and 2002, there was a shift from public services, construction and mining to financial and business-service sectors (where employment doubled). This is

---

Pushing back the frontiers of poverty

What difference are government interventions making in the lives of the poor?

People's means of living depend on income from wages and other economic activity together with the 'social wage' (the impact of social spending including social grants and access to social services – education, healthcare, water, sanitation, electricity, etc.).

Since 1993, government's social spending has shifted to the poor. Between 1993 and 1997, social spending increased for the poorest 60% of households – especially the poorest 20% – and decreased for the 40% who are better off. It increased for Africans and decreased for others. It increased three times more in rural areas than metropolitan areas, and doubled in other urban areas.

To see the impact of social spending, look first at distribution of income alone and then add the value of benefits from social spending.

The Gini coefficient measures income inequal-ity – 1,0 for extreme inequality and 0,0 for complete equality. In 1993, social spending made almost no difference to the Gini coefficient (it was 0,68). In 2000, it was 0,57 for income alone, but became 0,35 when social spending was included.

Social services are improving the quality of life of the poor and reducing inequality.

consolidating 'two economies' in one country. One is advanced and skilled, becoming more globally competitive. The second is mainly informal, marginalised and unskilled. Despite impressive gains in the first economy, the benefits have yet to reach the second economy, which could fall even further behind without decisive government intervention.
- Migration – There has been a shift from rural to big urban areas. Twenty per cent of people in the main urban areas are new migrants. This adds pressure on urban service delivery and economic opportunities, and causes loss of people and opportunities in rural areas. It affects social relations and links to authority structures, reducing the potential for people to interact on a collective basis.

The impact of these trends is likely to be compounded depending on what happens with HIV/AIDS and other demographic factors.

These social trends, added to the apartheid backlog, help to explain the scale of the past decade's challenges and some of the limitations in progress, for example in unemployment, poverty alleviation and combating crime. Nevertheless, there has been significant progress in dealing with these problems.

The global setting

As South Africans enter the second decade of freedom, the global environment is uncertain, with increasing tension, unilateralism and unresolved international trade issues. But despite this, there are also new opportunities for developing countries to assert their interests.

While many current developments contain seeds for Africa's marginalisation, there are opportunities for the continent to mobilise support for its plight and that of the other poor regions. Among governments and citizens of developed countries there is potential to focus attention on the common objectives of humanity contained in the UN Millennium Declaration. South Africa's history, its location, the size of its economy in the continent, and its current endeavours and outlook equip it to play a critical role in this regard.

Challenges and opportunities

The experience of a decade of reconstruction and development, social trends and the global context point to some major challenges as the country enters the second decade of freedom.

If South Africans are to make continued progress towards the fundamental objective of a united, non-racial, non-sexist and democratic society – then they need a major intervention to reinforce the consolidation of democracy with measures aimed at integrating society into a growing economy from which they can benefit. This requires:
- a framework defining a shared destiny, as a basis for social partnership
- better performance by the State
- addressing consequences of the social transition
- improving the southern African environment and implementing NEPAD.

Guy Stubbs/Touchline Images

chapter 4
Agriculture

The aim of the Department of Agriculture is to lead and support agriculture and promote rural development through:
- access to sufficient, safe and nutritious food
- eliminating skewed participation and inequity in the sector
- maximising growth, employment and income in agriculture
- enhancing the sustainable management of natural agricultural resources and ecological systems
- ensuring effective and efficient governance
- ensuring knowledge and information management.

The agricultural sector operates in an ever-changing environment marked by, among others, the impact of climatic conditions on seasonal output, the rise in food prices and the continued decline in employment in the sector. The Department is therefore faced with the challenge to respond quickly and appropriately to these changing conditions, without sacrificing its long-term goals of transforming the sector.

In 1994, the Department inherited an agricultural sector that was not inclusive and did not reflect the demography of the South African society. It was also highly regulated with subsidies and financial concessions available to commercial farmers, often at a high cost to government.

The Department was faced with the enormous challenge of addressing poverty, landlessness and a general skewed participation of black people, youth and women in the sector.

Government's response has been to ensure that the right of access to sufficient food and water, healthcare and social security is fundamental in the programmes implemented in the new democracy.

Within the context of implementation it is clear that government's role in terms of, policy-making and appropriate allocation of resources, needs to be complemented by the beneficiaries of government policy to partnerships which can result in innovation and the creation of jobs and income-generating opportunities.

Strategic Plan for South African Agriculture

The vision for the agricultural sector implies sustained profitable participation in the South African agricultural economy by all stakeholders. It recognises the need to maintain and increase commercial production, to build international competitiveness and to address the historical legacies that resulted in skewed access and representation.

The Strategic Plan consists of three core strategies:

◀ Land redistribution is a major policy instrument used for alleviation of asset poverty. Since 1994, 1,8 million hectares (ha) have been transferred to about 137 478 households.

South Africa Yearbook 2003/04

Exports						
	1998	1999	2000	2001	2002	Average: five years
Total South African products ('000 000)	147 547	165 143	210 022	245 448	308 054	215 243
Total agricultural products ('000 000)	13 699	14 774	15 820	20 075	25 460	17 966
Agriculture as % of total exports	9,3	8,9	7,5	8,2	8,3	8,3

Source: Directorate: Agricultural Statistics, Department of Agriculture

- equitable access and participation: the objectives of this strategy are to ensure equitable access to and participation in agricultural opportunities, to deracialise land and enterprise ownership and to unlock the full entrepreneurial potential in the sector
- global competitiveness and profitability: the aim of this strategy is to enhance profitability through sustained global competitiveness in the agricultural sector's input supply, primary production, agriprocessing and agritourism industries
- sustainable resource management: this strategy aims to enhance farmers' capacity to use resources in a sustainable manner and to ensure the wise use and management of natural resources.

Role-players identified the following priority programmes and actions:

- implementing a broad-based safety and security strategy for good working and social stability, trust and confidence
- fostering a shared vision for agriculture, good governance and social partnerships
- fast-tracking a programme of land redistribution for agricultural development and processes of empowerment for targeted groups
- transforming agricultural research and transferring technology and education to be more responsive to markets
- redefining the mandate of agricultural marketing and international trade in the post-control board era against great global competition and demands for market access, infrastructure and information
- building credible agricultural, statistical, and economic analysis systems that will be accessible to all farmers and enterprises
- building an agricultural risk-management system to ensure that agricultural enterprises will recover, grow and develop after natural disasters
- developing an effective integrated risk-management system for plant and animal-health systems, price and income systems and natural disasters
- establishing the integrated rural financial-services systems
- targeting investments in rural-development nodes to provide livelihoods, infrastructure, irrigation, electricity, telecommunications, transportation, training and skills development
- establishing an agricultural co-operation programme for Africa to spearhead the role of agriculture in the New Partnership for Africa's Development (NEPAD)
- lowering the overall cost of production.

The following outcomes are expected from the successful pursuit of these strategic objectives:

- increased wealth creation in agriculture and rural areas
- increased sustainable employment in agriculture
- increased income and foreign exchange earnings
- reduced poverty and inequalities in land and enterprise ownership
- improved farming efficiency
- improved national and household food security

- stable and safe rural communities, reduced levels of crime and violence, and sustained rural development
- improved investor confidence and greater domestic and foreign investment in agricultural activities and rural areas
- pride and dignity in agriculture as an occupation and sector.

The national Department of Agriculture, the National African Farmers' Union (NAFU) and AgriSA have established an institutional framework to oversee the process of implementing the Strategic Plan. Through this mechanism, they have been able to stimulate the emergence of mentorships intended to ensure that the beneficiaries of land reform and agricultural development make good use of their land.

A sum of R3,7 million was transferred to the provinces in 2002 as a training component of the comprehensive farmer-support package. In the 2003/04 financial year, the Department allocated R10 million for this purpose.

The Plan challenges the partners to work for public-private partnerships in the area of research and development.

The National Agricultural Research Forum, a consultative forum where government, public entities, and educational institutions, are involved in agricultural research and technology development and transfer, in collaboration with the private sector, was launched in May 2002.

The Forum enables the partners to share best practice and work for synergy in the optimisation of existing capacity. Prior to 1994, statistics on agriculture focused on the white commercial sector and were not reliable regarding the former homeland areas and black participation.

By April 2003, the Department was working with Statistics South Africa to conduct an agricultural census as a source of more reliable information on the sector.

Preliminary results were expected to be released by December 2003. The census, funded by the Department to the tune of R17 million, will be updated every five years.

A survey on rural households, targeting five communal areas was completed in 2003. The data, which for the first time provides some useful information on communal rural agriculture, will improve the quality of planning and effectiveness of government interventions.

Agricultural economy

South Africa has a dual agricultural economy, comprising a well-developed commercial sector and a predominantly subsistence-orientated sector in the rural areas. About 13% of South Africa's surface area can be used for crop production. High-potential arable land comprises only 22% of the total arable land. Some 1,3 million hectares (ha) are under irrigation.

The most important factor limiting agricultural production is the availability of water. Rainfall is distributed unevenly across the country. Almost 50% of South Africa's water is used for agricultural purposes. The country can be subdivided into a number of farming regions according to climate, natural vegetation, types of soil and the type of farming practised. Agricultural activities in these regions range from intensive crop production and mixed farming in winter-rainfall and high summer-rainfall areas, to cattle-ranching in the bushveld and sheep-farming in the more arid regions.

Primary agriculture contributes about 3% to Gross Domestic Product (GDP) of South Africa and less than 9% of formal employment. However, there are strong backward and forward linkages into the economy, so that the agro-industrial sector is estimated to comprise 15% of GDP.

Today, South Africa is not only self-sufficient in virtually all major agricultural products, but in a normal year it is also a net food exporter. However, with very low average rainfall and high variability within and between seasons, agriculture is vulnerable to the effects of drought. When there is a major drought, strong downward pressure is placed on GDP. In good years, however, the contribution of agriculture can be vital to lifting the economy.

> South Africa doesn't have ideal conditions for crop production. Less than 12% of its land is arable, and serious climatic constraints, such as periodic droughts, hinder agricultural production. Despite these circumstances, productivity must increase to meet the food needs of the growing population. Recent developments in biotechnology have brought hope in tackling the challenges of increasing food production. Genetic modification provides a way of meeting the growing demand for food without placing even greater pressure on scarce resources.
>
> The Genetically Modified Organisms (GMO) Act, 1997 (Act 15 of 1997), was implemented on 1 December 1999, making provision for the regulation of GMOs in South Africa, particularly new biosafety assessments. In terms of the Act, permits are issued for trials and the commercial release of any GMO crops in the country, to ensure contained cultivation and reduced environmental impact. The objectives of the Act are to increase crop yield while protecting biodiversity. By mid-2001, the Department of Agriculture had approved the planting of three commercial Genetically Modified (GM) crops, i.e. insect-resistant cotton, herbicide-resistant cotton and insect-resistant maize.
>
> There are no GM crops planted for human consumption in South Africa. There are no fresh GM fruit and vegetables on sale in the country. Imported engineered soya is used in processed meat and other locally produced food.
>
> In terms of the GMO Act, 1997, the Advisory Committee, comprising scientific experts, conducts risk assessments to determine if a particular GMO is safe for humans, animals and the environment. The Foodstuffs, Cosmetics and Disinfectants Act, 1972 (Act 54 of 1972), oversees the safety of food in South Africa.
>
> During a meeting between the Minister of Environmental Affairs and Tourism, Mr Mohammed Valli Moosa, and his provincial counterparts, in June 2003, it was decided that there was a need to strengthen regulations governing GMOs.
>
> The revision must ensure that the public is enabled to make better-informed decisions when purchasing goods made from GM products.
>
> It was also resolved that serious consideration was needed around the labelling of GM products.

During 2002, the seasonally adjusted real value added by the agriculture, forestry and fishing industry increased by 3,9% compared with 2001. This was ascribed mainly to an increase in the production of maize and other field crops.

Despite the farming industry's declining share of GDP, it remains vitally important to the economy, and the development and stability of the southern African region.

For the past five years, agricultural exports have contributed on average approximately 8% (9% in 2002) of total South African exports.

Normally, South Africa is a net exporter of agricultural products in Rand value. The largest export groups are wine, citrus, sugar, grapes, maize, fruit juice, wool, and deciduous fruit such as apples, pears, peaches and apricots. Other important export products are non-alcoholic beverages, cigars and cigarettes, food preparations, meat, avocados, pineapples, peanuts, preserved fruit and nuts, hides and skins, and dairy products.

Sustainable resource-use and management

South Africa, at most times, is able to meet its own food requirements with considerable food exportation. However, the inherent limitations of the natural resource base and variable climate require land users to be very circumspect in how they use and manage these resources, so as to retain their productive capacity. Improved information about the potential and limitations of the natural resource base is essential for good management decisions. An inventory of soils, terrain forms and climate (land types) was undertaken by the Agricultural Research Council's (ARC) Institute for Soil, Climate and Water.

The Land Type (soil, climate and terrain) Survey for the whole of South Africa will assist land-use planning and management decision-making. Data from this and other more detailed soil and climate surveys are integrated into a comprehensive Geographic Information

System (GIS), which allows for assessment of agricultural potential and land suitability.

Although it is generally recognised that soil degradation is a problem, there has been little reliable data systematically collected over time. Soil degradation is largely related to the decline in soil organic matter. Monoculture cereal production, intensive tillage, short-to-no fallow, and limited crop rotation have contributed to this in the commercial sector. Excessive fuelwood collection, inappropriate land-use, population density and overgrazing are the main causes of soil degradation in the communal areas. In addition, it is estimated that about 60% of the cropland area is moderately to severely acid, and probably at least 15% is affected by subsoil acidity.

Physical degradation of South Africa's agricultural land results in soil erosion by both water and wind. It has been estimated that water erosion affects about 6,1 million ha of cultivated soil in South Africa, and wind erosion about 10,9 million ha. Another degradation problem is compaction within the soil profile, especially on fine sandy soils where, for example, maize yields can be adversely affected by some 30% to 40%.

Urban spread, industrialisation and mining also impact on the sustainable use of agricultural land. Opencast coal-mining in Mpumalanga is an example of this pressure.

The Conservation of Agricultural Resources Act, 1983 (Act 43 of 1983), allows the national Department of Agriculture to exercise control over the utilisation of South Africa's natural agricultural resources. The Act provides for the conservation of these resources by maintaining the land's production potential, combatting and preventing erosion, protecting vegetation and combatting weeds and invader plants. The Act generally applies to all agricultural land in South Africa, except for the sections dealing with weeds and invader plants, which also apply to urban areas.

Specific requirements and prohibitions applicable to land users are detailed in control measures, published as regulations of the Conservation of Agricultural Resources Act, 1983. Certain activities, such as the cultivation of virgin land and burning of veld, are subject to prior approval, while others are prescribed as 'best practice' in the interest of sustainable land-use. The Act further provides for the implementation of schemes, of which two are still functioning. These are the Weed Control Scheme that is administered nationally and the Soil Conservation Scheme that is administered by the provinces.

In order to promote natural agricultural resource conservation, policies, norms, standards and guidelines have been developed, as has a national agricultural resource audit division and a conservation GIS. At farmer level, conservation committees can be appointed to promote the conservation of the natural agricultural resources in the area concerned, in order to achieve the objectives of the Act. The national Department of Agriculture's Inspection Service does compliance-monitoring at farm level in all provinces.

South Africa is a signatory to a number of international agreements and conventions that require the matter of sustainable resource-use and management to be addressed in a responsible way. Agenda 21 is an action plan and blueprint for sustainable development, and was one of five documents adopted by more than 178 governments at the United Nations (UN) Conference on Environment and Development (UNCED) in Rio de Janeiro in 1992. Specific to sustainable resource-use is Chapter 14 on promoting sustainable agriculture and rural development.

International conventions that apply to aspects of sustainable resource-use are the Convention on Biological Diversity, the UN Framework Convention on Climate Change, and the Convention to Combat Desertification (CCD). The CCD requires South Africa to draw up a National Action Programme, which will be integrated into a regional programme for the Southern African Development Community

(SADC) region. All these activities are receiving attention under the leadership of the Department of Environmental Affairs and Tourism, involving all stakeholders, including the national Department of Agriculture and the provinces.

One of the key programmes of the national Department of Agriculture that addresses sustainable use and management of natural resources is the National LandCare Programme (NLP). (See page 84.)

Gross value of agricultural production, 2002 ('000 t)	
Field crops	
Maize	13 906
Wheat	4 213
Hay	1 778
Grain sorghum	382
Sugar cane	3 284
Ground-nuts	322
Tobacco	529
Sunflower seed	2 160
Cotton	155
Other	1237
Total	**27 966**
Horticulture	
Viticulture	2 088
Citrus	2 915
Subtropical fruit	941
Deciduous and other fruit	4 396
Vegetables	3 522
Potatoes	2 438
Other	1 124
Total	**17 424**
Animal products	
Wool	1 269
Poultry and poultry products	10 767
Cattle and cattle slaughtered	5 289
Sheep and goats slaughtered	1 413
Pigs slaughtered	1 090
Fresh milk	2 794
Milk for dairy products	1 391
Other	1 558
Total	**25 571**
Grand total	**70 961**

Preliminary Source: Agricultural Statistics: Department of Agriculture

Research institutes of the ARC and some universities have been contracted to undertake various research projects on matters relating to the sustainable use of agricultural resources. The practices of minimum tillage and no-till crop-production are again being actively promoted in KwaZulu-Natal and Mpumalanga, aimed not only at commercial farmers, but also at smaller and subsistence farmers.

An agreement has been signed with the Food and Agriculture Organisation (FAO) of the UN for a project on conservation agriculture.

In terms of the projects, which is financed by the Technical Co-operation Programme, a survey of the conservation agriculture practices in South Africa will be done, workshops conducted, and visits to other African and South American countries organised.

The aim of the project is to formulate a strategy for implementing conservation agriculture in South Africa.

The National Water Act, 1998 (Act 36 of 1998), places strong emphasis on equity in access to water, including water for agriculture. A feature of the development of water sources for agriculture has been the lack of co-ordination of initiatives and support interventions.

A proposal for the integrated management of water use in agriculture has been drafted.

The national Department undertook two projects to improve stockwater provision to small-scale farmers. In terms of the projects, existing boreholes are rehabilitated, pumps repaired, and new boreholes provided where water audits indicate that additional supplies are needed. Operations commenced in the Sekhukhune cross-border and Chris Hani districts, and were later expanded to QwaQwa and Kalahari-Kgalagadi districts. Eventually all the priority nodes will be included.

The Farmers' Charter, a commitment by farmers, government and other stakeholders for the sustainable use of natural resources, was launched in 2002 during the World Summit on Sustainable Development.

Agriculture

Production

In general, the prices of agricultural products increased by 26% from 2001 to 2002. Prices of field crops increased by 35%, horticultural products by 23%, and livestock products also by 23%. The net income of the farming sector increased from R10 591 million in 2001 to R20 277 million in 2002. The country is self-sufficient where primary foods are concerned, with the exception of wheat, oil-seeds, rice, tea and coffee.

Field crops and horticulture

The largest area of farmland is planted with maize, followed by wheat and, to an extent, sugar cane and sunflowers.

The maize industry plays a very important role in the economy. Maize is the largest locally produced field crop, and the most important source of carbohydrates in the SADC for animal and human consumption. South Africa is the main maize producer in the SADC with an average production of approximately 9,1 metric tons (mt) per annum over the past 10 years.

It is estimated that more than 9 000 commercial producers of maize are responsible for the major part of the South African crop, while the rest is produced by many thousands of small-scale producers.

Production of important field crops and horticultural products, 2002 ('000 t)	
Maize	10 073
Wheat	2 331
Sugar cane	23 013
Grain sorghum	255
Ground-nuts	133
Sunflower seed	965
Deciduous and other soft fruit	1 602
Citrus fruit	1 896
Subtropical fruit	616
Vegetables	2 050
Potatoes	1 540

Preliminary Source: Agricultural Statistics, Department of Agriculture

Maize is produced mainly in the North West, the north-western, northern and eastern Free State, the Mpumalanga Highveld, and the KwaZulu-Natal Midlands. Local commercial consumption of maize amounts to approximately 7,5 mt and surplus maize is usually exported.

Wheat is produced in the winter-rainfall areas of the Western Cape and the eastern parts of the Free State. Production in the Western Cape is the highest, but there are considerable annual fluctuations.

Barley is produced mainly on the southern coastal plains of the Western Cape. The area where barley is planted was estimated at 72 400 ha for the 2002/03 production season, and production was estimated at 183 260 t.

Ground-nuts are grown mainly in the Free State, North West and Northern Cape. Groundnut plantings decreased by 47%, from 94 160 ha in 2001/02 to 50 300 ha in 2002/03.

The ARC developed a sampling technique for estimating grain-crop areas, yield and production. It is the first time that a GIS, Global Positioning System, Remote Sensing Imagery and Internet-based data have been integrated into a system to provide information to the National Crop Estimation Committee. The Committee can now make a more reliable estimate of grain-crop production for South Africa, which has a major impact on markets, pricing and futures trading.

South Africa is the world's 11th-largest producer of sunflower seed. Sunflower seed is produced in the Free State, North West and on the Mpumalanga Highveld, as well as in Limpopo.

For many years, Oudtshoorn, De Rust and Douglas were the only areas in South Africa in which lucerne seed was produced in reasonable quantity. Today, the Oudtshoorn district is responsible for about 90% of the lucerne seed produced in South Africa. A lucerne plant can produce 100 to 120 lucerne bales per hectare every three weeks, provided enough water is available.

Sorghum is cultivated mostly in the drier parts of the summer-rainfall areas such as Mpumalanga, Free State, Limpopo and North West.

South Africa is ranked as the world's 12th-largest sugar producer. Sugar cane is grown in 15 cane-producing areas extending from northern Pondoland in the Eastern Cape, through the coastal belt and Midlands of KwaZulu-Natal, to the Mpumalanga Lowveld. An estimated 2,5 mt of sugar is produced per season. About 50% of this is marketed in southern Africa. The remainder is exported to numerous markets in Africa, the Middle East, North America and Asia. Based on actual sales and selling prices in 2002/03, it is estimated that the South African sugar industry contributed R2,0 billion to South Africa's foreign exchange earnings.

Deciduous fruit is grown mainly in the Western Cape and in the Langkloof Valley in the Eastern Cape. Smaller production areas are found along the Orange River and in the Free State, Mpumalanga and Gauteng. This industry's export-earnings represent 11% of the country's total earnings from agricultural exports. In 2002, apples made up the largest percentage of the crop (38%), while pears totalled 21% and grapes 19%. Approximately 76% of the total crop was produced in the Western Cape, 11% in the Northern Cape, and 13% in the Eastern Cape.

The wine and spirits industry in South Africa is a very important part of the agricultural sector. South Africa is ranked as the eighth-largest wine producer in the world. It is also pioneering an integrated production system, including an environmentally friendly approach to wine-making. Preliminary guidelines, to proactively address the environmental impact of winery and distillery-effluent water were proposed for implementation by the wine industry at an international workshop. The workshop, organised for the first time in South Africa, also led to the identification of research gaps.

In 2002, South African wine-growers produced a grape harvest of 8,3 hectolitres, of which 66% was used in wine-making. About 106 330 ha of land are under cultivation with about 317 million vines. About 84% of wines are still produced by co-operatives. Some 4 390 primary wine producers employ about 67 000 people. According to the South African Wine and Spirits Export Association, the export of white wine increased from 20 million litres (ML) in 1992 to 218 ML in 2002.

The long-awaited Wine and Spirits Agreement between South Africa and the European Union (EU) was signed on 28 January 2002.

It is anticipated that the Agreement will improve access into the large European market for South African wine and spirits. Applying an annual duty-free tariff quota of 42 ML will ensure better access for South African wines. In addition, the EU will make available an amount of 15 million Euro for restructuring the South African wine and spirits industry. The signing of these agreements is an essential step in formalising South Africa's co-operation with the EU in the wine and spirits trade.

Since 1 January 2000, the Directorate: Marketing of the Department of Agriculture has issued export permits for sparkling wines in terms of the Trade, Development and Co-operation Agreement (TDCA) between South Africa and the EU for 472 500 litres to be exported at reduced levels of duty to the European community.

Export permits for 42,02 ML white and red wine have been issued since March 2002, when the Wine and Spirits Agreement came into effect.

Part of the Agreement involves phasing out names traditionally used in South Africa for specific types of wines. The names 'port' and 'sherry' will be phased out over five years for exports to non-SADC markets, starting from 1 January 2000. They must be phased out of all markets after 12 years. South Africa will also phase out the names *grappa*, ouzo, *korn/kornbrand*, *jägertee* and *pacharan* within five years of signing the agreement.

Agriculture

The EU is the largest destination for South African wines, accounting for 75% of total exports in this sector in 2002. At the same time, it is the largest supplier of imported wine and spirits to the South African market.

Citrus production is largely limited to the irrigation areas of Limpopo, Mpumalanga, the Eastern and Western Cape, and KwaZulu-Natal.

Pineapples are grown in the Eastern Cape and northern KwaZulu-Natal. Other subtropical crops such as avocados, mangoes, bananas, litchis, guavas, pawpaws, granadillas, and macadamia and pecan nuts are produced mainly in Mpumalanga and Limpopo at Levubu and Letaba, and in the subtropical coastal areas of KwaZulu-Natal and the Eastern Cape.

About 40% of the country's potato crop is grown in the high-lying areas of the Free State and Mpumalanga. Limpopo, the Eastern, Western and Northern Cape, and the high-lying areas of KwaZulu-Natal are also important production areas. About two-thirds of the country's total potato crop is produced under irrigation.

Of the total crop, 50% is delivered to fresh-produce markets and a further 16% is processed. The South African potato-processing industry grew by more than 100% over the past five years. This growth took place primarily in the three main disciplines of the processing industry, namely crisps, chips and French fries. Production of frozen French fries (41% of the total processed potato products in South Africa) has increased over the last couple of years.

In terms of gross income to the grower (apart from potatoes, which contribute 40%), tomatoes, onions, green mealies and sweetcorn are probably the most important vegetable crops.

These crops contribute 37% to the income derived from vegetables. Tomatoes are produced countrywide, but mainly in Limpopo, the Mpumalanga Lowveld and Middleveld, the Pongola area of KwaZulu-Natal, the southern parts of the Eastern Cape, and the Western Cape.

Onions are grown in Mpumalanga; in the districts of Caledon, Ceres and Worcester in the Western Cape; and at Venterstad and the adjoining areas in the southern Free State.

Cabbages are also grown countrywide, but are more concentrated in Mpumalanga and the Camperdown and Greytown districts of KwaZulu-Natal.

Cotton is cultivated in Mpumalanga, Limpopo, Northern Cape, KwaZulu-Natal and North West. It constitutes 74% of natural fibre and 42% of all fibre processed in South Africa. Cotton is grown under irrigation as well as in dry-land conditions. Cotton under irrigation usually contributes almost as much to the national crop as that grown in dry-land conditions, although the number of hectares under dry-land conditions are much more than those under irrigation. Seventy-five per cent of local production is harvested by hand.

Virginia tobacco is produced mainly in Mpumalanga and Limpopo, with smaller quantities of Oriental tobacco being produced in the Western and Eastern Cape. There are more than 1 000 growers in the country, who produce an annual average of 34 million kilograms on about 24 000 ha of land. The crop represents 173 different grades of Virginia, and five different grades of Oriental, tobacco.

Honeybush tea grows mainly in the coastal and mountainous areas of the Western Cape

---

The South African Government announced in January 2003 that it would be donating R170 million towards food aid in southern Africa.

South Africa's donation to the World Food Programme (WFP) is expected to finance 100 000 tons of mealies, which will be distributed to the famine-stricken areas of Zimbabwe, Malawi, Zambia, Lesotho, Mozambique and Swaziland.

It forms part of government's plan to spend R400 million per year for the next three years to fight famine in southern Africa.

The country's donation to the WFP was the biggest ever made by an African country.

but also in certain areas of the Eastern Cape. From a small beginning in 1993, the honeybush has grown to a commercial crop, with a production of more than 100 t of processed tea per annum. In the last eight years, the industry has seen an improvement in the quality of tea and the establishment of export standards, the construction of a large processing and packaging facility in Mossel Bay, increased consumer awareness, appearance of several brand names on supermarket shelves, and a growing overseas market.

The South African Honeybush Tea Association was established in 1999 to enable producers of this beverage to formalise their industry in response to the growing demand for their product.

The ARC is developing a method to create interspecies crosses between different honeybush tea species.

Rooibos tea is an indigenous herb produced mainly in the Cedarberg area of the Western Cape. In 2002, the demand for *rooibos* was estimated to be 3 500 t compared with 3 200 t exported in 2000. The active producers of *rooibos* tea are estimated at 320, ranging from small to large farming enterprises.

Ornamental plants are produced throughout the country, but production aimed particularly at the export market is concentrated in the central parts of Limpopo, Mpumalanga and Gauteng. Ornamental-plant production includes nursery plants, cut flowers and pot plants. The country's most important plant export products are gladioli, proteas, bulbs, chrysanthemum cuttings and roses.

Amaryllis bulbs are a lucrative export product to the United States of America (USA). In support of the protea and *fynbos* industry, the ARC is involved in several ongoing research activities. During 2002/03, about 1 613 accessions of the indigenous *fynbos* were maintained by the ARC at Elsenburg and 3 000 seedlings from 110 candidate cultivars of *fynbos* were produced. The ARC completed a project on p*roteaceae* breeding and production, which was funded by the 5th Framework Programme of the EU.

The *fynbos* Industry is being transformed from 'wild harvesting' to 'cultivation', with an array of cultivars planted. Further *fynbos* species have potential for development as crops, provided the necessary research funding can be secured. Dried flowers form an important component of the *fynbos* industry. A large variety of proteas, conebushes and other products are well-established in the marketplace.

Ornamental plants are produced throughout the country, with greenhouse and open-field production concentrated mainly in Limpopo, Mpumalanga and Gauteng. The protea industry is mainly concentrated in the Western Cape.

South Africa's indigenous flowers, such as, gladioli, nerine, freesia and gerbera, have undergone many years of extensive research in Europe and have become major crops throughout the world.

On 6 June 2003, the Deputy Minister of Trade and Industry, Ms Lindiwe Hendricks, opened a R7-million pineapple-processing plant in East London, Eastern Cape.

Collondale Cannery is one of only two pineapple-processing factories in South Africa. The company has installed a plant with a new evaporator specifically imported for processing pineapple-juice concentrate.

South Africa accounts for 6% of the world's pineapple production. The world market is dominated by Thailand, Indonesia, the Phillipines and Kenya. South African pineapples are traditionally less sweet and more acidic than those of its competitors. A blend between South African pineapple concentrate and that of its competitors results in a sweeter product, but with the distinctive pineapple taste that is unique to the South African product.

The new plant illustrates the value of investment in production-capacity for export sales and job creation. The new Collondale plant incorporates the latest technology that will enable the company to increase its production of pineapple-juice concentrate by 50%. All of this will be exported, generating sales of R7 million per year.

Agriculture

Livestock numbers, 2001 – 2002 (million)		
	2001	2002
Cattle	13,5	13,6
Sheep	28,8	29,0
Pigs	1,6	1,6
Goats	6,8	6,7

Source: Agricultural Statistics, Department of Agriculture

South Africa is the leading exporter of protea cut flowers, accounting for more than half of proteas sold on the world market. South African proteas and so-called Cape greens (*fynbos*) are mainly marketed in Europe.

Livestock

Livestock is farmed in most parts of South Africa. Numbers vary according to climatic conditions. Stock-breeders concentrate mainly on the development of breeds that are well-adapted to diverse climatic and environmental conditions. The latest estimates for cattle and sheep are 13,6 million and 29,0 million, respectively. South Africa normally produces 85% of its meat requirements, while 15% is imported from Namibia, Botswana, Swaziland, Australia, New Zealand and European countries.

The livestock industry is currently the largest national agricultural sector. The local demand for products, which generally outstrips production, creates a dependence on imports, even though there are untapped production reserves within communal farming.

In June 2003, three men from southern Africa won the World Shearing Championships held in Scotland in the United Kingdom.

Eliot Ntsombo of Lesotho was crowned world champion for the eighth time, with Zwelile Hans of South Africa in second place. Hans has been champion for the past two years.

Samuel Nkomoyi, also of South Africa, took third position.

The best sheep-shearers from all over the world competed for the coveted title.

South Africa has been a member of the Golden Shears organisation, which organises the tournaments, since 1998.

The ARC aims to broaden access to this market opportunity, increase efficiency of the livestock-production chain, and improve product quality and safety through research and development support. This will be achieved through focused attention on animal nutrition and environment; breeding genetics and reproduction physiology; health products; food security and safety; and marketing and economics across the different animal species.

Dairy-farming is practised throughout South Africa, with the highest concentration of dairy farms in the eastern and northern Free State, North West, the KwaZulu-Natal Midlands, the Eastern and Western Cape, the Gauteng metropolitan area, and the southern parts of Mpumalanga.

The ARC fully participates in the Multiple Across-Country Evaluation for all four major dairy breeds in South Africa, namely Holstein, Jersey, Guernsey and Ayrshire. A new rye grass cultivar bred by the ARC improves the milk production of a Jersey herd by 0,9 litres per cow per day, and the production of a Holstein herd by 1,5 litres per cow per day.

The South African Milk Federation co-ordinates industry matters, including the information and research functions financed by means of voluntary levies. Market forces determine prices. The dairy industry is an important employer as some 4 300 milk producers employ about 60 000 farm workers and indirectly provide jobs to some 40 000 people. Milk production for 2002/03 was estimated at 1,94 ML.

Cattle ranches are found mainly in the Eastern Cape, parts of the Free State and Kwa-Zulu-Natal, Limpopo and the Northern Cape. The indigenous Afrikaner and Nguni, and the locally developed Bonsmara and Drakensberger, are popular beef breeds, but British, European and American breeds, such as Brahman, Charolais, Hereford, Angus, Santa Gertrudis, Simmentaler and Sussex are maintained as pure breeds and used in cross-breeding.

The Taurus Livestock Improvement Co-operative (in Irene, Gauteng) is one of the companies providing the country's beef farmers with an annual average of some 110 000 units of semen, and the dairy industry with 580 000 units of semen, for use in artificial insemination.

Sheep-farming is concentrated mainly in the Northern and Eastern Cape, Western Cape, Free State, and Mpumalanga, with Ermelo in Mpumalanga being one of the largest wool-producing districts. Most sheep are fine-woolled Merinos (50%). Other breeds include the locally developed Afrino (a woolled mutton breed adapted to arid conditions), the South African Mutton Merino, the Dohne and the Merino Land Sheep. Non-wool breeds such as the Dorper, a highly productive, locally developed mutton breed for arid regions, and the woolled Merino account for most of South Africa's mutton production.

The indigenous meat-producing Boer goat accounts for about 30% of all commercial goats. The Angora goat is used for mohair production. South Africa has about 3 500 Angora farmers.

Compared with the mainly extensive cattle and sheep industries, the poultry and pig industries are more intensive and are located on farms near metropolitan areas such as Gauteng, Durban, Pietermaritzburg, Cape Town and Port Elizabeth. The predominant pig breeds are the South African Landrace and the Large White.

The Agricultural Research Council (ARC) has established a BioStore database of biological material and DNA for game and indigenous farm animals. This facilitates the identification of animals at species and subspecies level. Biological samples are processed and stored in vials in individually marked boxes at -40° C. By June 2003, the BioStore contained 7 425 biological samples from 53 different species, representing blood, hide, hair, organs, meat and gut.

The Species Identification Service mainly utilises biological samples from the BioStore as control samples to be included for forensic analyses and the identification of meat and meat products.

South Africa's annual poultry meat production is estimated at 950 000 t. Broiler production contributes about 82% to total poultry-meat production, with the rest made up of mature chicken slaughter (culls), small-scale and backyard poultry production, ducks, geese, turkeys and other specialised white-meat products.

Commercial producers slaughtered an estimated 541 million broilers during 2002. The gross value of broilers and other fowls slaughtered during this period is estimated at R8 252 million, which makes it the most important contributor to the value of agricultural production in South Africa.

South Africa accounts for 72% of world sales of ostrich products, namely leather, meat and feathers. The Klein Karoo Co-operative is one of the world's largest producers and exporters of ostrich products. According to the Co-operative, there is a big increase in the demand for ostrich meat abroad.

Game-farming, aquaculture and bee-keeping

South Africa has more game and a wider variety of game species than most countries. Game-farming has grown over the years, and today it is a viable industry with great economic potential. The main game areas are in Limpopo, North West, Mpumalanga, Free State, Eastern Cape, the Karoo, the Kalahari in the Northern Cape, and the thorn scrub of KwaZulu-Natal.

Despite periodic droughts in the past, game numbers have consistently increased. The South African Game Ranchers' Organisation, as well as local organisations in each province, service the industry.

A descriptive game-production model has been developed for optimising intensive animal production on game farms. The model has the potential to increase the global produce of the game industry by between 8% and 15%.

The aquaculture industry in South Africa continues to make meaningful progress in cultivation technology, marketing strategy, marketing practice and scientific innovation. Mussels, trout, tilapia, ratfish, oysters and *waterblommetjies* (Cape pondweed) are the major aquaculture species. Mussel-farming occurs mainly at Saldanha Bay. The Abalone Farmers' Association of South Africa has been instrumental in formulating product standards.

The South African honey industry is still small, worth some R27 million annually. The ARC presents bee-keeping courses and provides on-farm support for between 12 and 18 months.

Production input

Fertilisers, farm feeds and agricultural and stock remedies are known as agricultural production input. A Draft Bill makes provision for the registration of products such as animal feed, fertilisers and pesticides to enhance agricultural production, and the registration of persons involved with the application of such products. The Draft Bill will repeal the Fertilisers, Farm Feeds, Agricultural Remedies and Stock Remedies Act, 1947 (Act 36 of 1947), and was expected to be published for comment in 2003.

The internationally proposed classification and labelling systems have been accepted for agricultural and stock remedies. These systems, locally referred to as the RSA Classification and Labelling System, have been in use since 1993. The System also makes provision for the use of CropLife International's pictograms on product labels.

Complaints about a specific agricultural production resource are investigated immediately, and administrative or legal action is taken against offenders when necessary.

Samples of all raw material and animal feed are taken regularly and tested for pathogenic contamination. This action, and the steps that follow when contamination is detected, assures the public of food safety.

Veterinary services

State Veterinary Services constantly guard against the introduction of animal diseases from outside South Africa, and existing animal diseases, which may be detrimental to the economy of South Africa and to human and animal health, are controlled and combated. Stock in the high-risk areas is inspected at short intervals.

The Directorate: Animal Health of the national Department of Agriculture sets norms and standards for the delivery of veterinary services in South Africa.

The Animal Diseases Act, 1984 (Act 35 of 1984), soon to be replaced by the Animal Health Act, 2002 (Act 7 of 2002), provides the necessary powers to control diseases such as foot-and-mouth disease (FMD), swine fever, rabies and anthrax. In May 2002, after three small oubreaks of FMD in 2000/01, South Africa, excluding the Kruger National Park and surrounding game reserves, gained recognition as an FMD-free zone.

Trade with various countries in animals and animal products has resumed.

The ARC has been contracted by government to provide an FMD vaccine for Zimbabwe. The vaccine will be delivered over a two-year period at a cost of R12 million. FMD has become a regional problem, with outbreaks in Botswana, Mozambique, Malawi and Zimbabwe.

Surveillance systems are in place to ensure that all agricultural products entering and leaving the country are free of disease and thus safe for human consumption. All ports are thoroughly monitored, making sure that imported and exported goods are disease-free.

Particular emphasis is placed on the control of borders to neighbouring countries to prevent the introduction of FMD.

Although national livestock-disease schemes have reduced the incidence of both tuberculosis and brucellosis since the 1960s and early 1970s, these diseases remain a concern.

Comprehensive attempts are made to control the increasing incidence of rabies throughout South Africa, especially in KwaZulu-Natal. To further strengthen South Africa's internal measures to combat animal diseases, the Department of Agriculture allocated R5 million for the development and rehabilitation of dipping infrastructure, which will ensure that there is adequate surveillance for tick-borne diseases, especially in the communal areas.

Highlights in the last decade include the introduction of the electronic Animal Disease Information System for South Africa and a laboratory management system, as well as the implementation of quality-control systems in official veterinary laboratories.

The increased co-operation with other African countries, especially within the SADC region, provides a considerable boost to animal-disease control as a result of the adoption of regional strategies for transboundary diseases. This approach will also prove valuable in the light of animal-disease challenges that may emerge due to transfrontier wildlife-conservation areas.

Another significant development is the export of horses with an estimated value in excess of R200 million in 2002.

The Meat Safety Act, 2000 (Act 40 of 2000), stipulates that meat inspections and hygiene control must be carried out by qualified meat-inspection personnel at abattoirs to prevent the transmission of diseases through meat to humans and animals.

The Directorate: Food Safety and Quality Assurance prescribes and audits essential standards implemented at provincial level. Imported and exported meat is monitored, and a national residue-monitoring programme has been implemented.

The former Directorate: Onderstepoort Biological Products (OBP) is a State-owned public company. It has the capacity and the technology to produce veterinary vaccines for the whole of Africa. The OBP is the sole or main producer of at least 15 vaccines for African animal diseases, and eight vaccines in the world for tropical diseases.

The institution is now positioned to produce even more vaccines for diseases relevant to the African continent. A vaccine bank is also being established to assist in the rapid response to disease outbreaks in the country and region. The facility will be upgraded at a cost of R37 million during the 2004/05 financial year. About R27 million has been generated internally for this purpose.

The OBP provides vaccines to fight major outbreaks of diseases such as CBPP (lung-sickness in cattle), lumpy-skin disease, Rift Valley fever, horse sickness and anthrax. The OBP has also joined the Pan African Vaccine Network to supply rinderpest and lung-sickness vaccines for Africa, and is involved in projects of the *Office International des Epizooties* (OIE), the World Health Organisation and the EU to supply vaccines to African countries.

OBP sales have increased in the last three years from 8% to around 37%.

The ARC is involved in the development of a new-generation vaccine against Newcastle disease, while major progress has been made towards a recombinant vaccine against heart-water. Heart-water is the most predominant tick-borne disease in the country affecting livestock.

South Africa's first veterinary recombinant subunit vaccine is in sight. The ARC has formulated a prototype African horse-sickness (AHS) virus vaccine. Technology has also been established to serotype any AHS virus within only two days, as opposed to current serological techniques which deliver results of AHS diagnosis after 14 days or longer.

The ARC is also involved in the development of an ethnoveterinary database.

Pest control

The Department of Agriculture is involved in the chemical and biological control of invader

Agriculture

plants. In total, an infestation of 48 000 ha of queen of the night has been controlled, partly in co-operation with the Working for Water Programme of the Department of Water Affairs and Forestry.

The Department is active in another campaign to control the weed *Cereus jamacaru*, which has invaded an area of approximately 255 000 ha. It spans four provinces, stretching from Loskop Dam in the east to Zeerust in the west, and from Modimolle in the north to Hartbeespoort Dam in the south. The cactus seriously reduces groundwater supply and the agricultural potential of the land. In some parts, the weed is also being controlled in collaboration with the Working for Water Programme. (See Chapter 23: *Water Affairs and Forestry*).

The Department is actively spreading biological control agents on other weed species such as *Harissia martinii, Sesbania punicea* and some aggressive *Opuntia spp.*

The ARC is involved in:
- the successful biocontrol of red water fern and *Acaciapycnantha*
- producing a new field guide for alien plant invaders
- the registration of Garlon 4 to control *Prosopis spp.* and *Ulex europaeus.*

Host-specificity testing was completed for the leaf-mining fly *Calycomyza eupatorivora*, for the biological control of chromolaena in South Africa, and permission was obtained to release five new species of biological control agents against their target weeds. The Plant Pathogenic and Plant Protecting Bacterial Culture has been registered with the World Federation of Culture Collections.

During 2002, the ARC released the first guide to the identification of potentially dangerous invasive aquatic plants in South Africa. The book, entitled *Invasive Aquatic Plants,* can also be used in other SADC countries.

The ARC publication, *Alien Weeds and Invasive Plants,* describes 234 species of alien weeds and invasive plants in South Africa. Comprehensive information is provided about all declared weeds and invaders, and the regulations concerning their control.

Most countries have established Maximum Residue Limits (MRLs) for pesticides used in the control of pests and diseases, not only to safeguard consumer health, but also to minimise the presence of these residues in the environment.

As a condition of market access, products exported must comply with these residue standards. To ensure compliance with legislation, monitoring samples are drawn for analysis during quality inspections.

Exporters and producers are obliged to:
- comply with the requirements of the correct, approved use and application of pesticide remedies
- keep records of the chemical remedies used in spray programmes and as a post-harvest treatment, and provide this information on request to the responsible authorities
- verify the MRLs with their importer or agent in the relevant country
- keep up with the registration and re-registration processes of pesticides within South Africa as well as in importing countries
- inform the Directorate: Plant Health and Quality of any rejections by importing country authorities due to residues.

In June 2003, the Directorate was in the process of establishing a database for regulatory purposes, based on South African registered pesticides and the MRLs per crop, established by the country's major export trading partners.

Migratory pest control

In terms of the Agricultural Pests Act, 1983 (Act 36 of 1983), the Department is continuously involved in the control of migratory pests such as the quelea, locust and blackfly.

Scientists of the ARC discovered a relationship between locust outbreaks, the Normalised Difference Vegetation Index, and rainfall, which will be used to forecast interseasonal locust outbreaks. The brown-locust-forecasting model will directly enhance the operational efficiency of the Brown Locust Early Warning System which is currently under development to support the country's Disaster Management Programme.

This research contributes towards maximising South Africa's ability to provide timely and reliable forecasts of brown-locust outbreaks, both for its own food-security needs and those of neighbouring countries in the brown-locust invasion area.

The Information Core for Southern African Migrant Pests (ICOSAMP) network, which is managed by the ARC, has attained international recognition through the incorporation of its monthly bulletin (*ICOSAMP News*) into two global networks, *IPMnet News* and *Monthly Situation Reports of the Africa Emergency Locust and Grasshopper Assistance project*.

The South African Pest Control Association (SAPCA) is the official representative of the pest-, termite- and woodborer-control industries. All SAPCA-qualified inspectors have to apply for registration with the Department of Agriculture.

South Africa liaises with other countries and international organisations to ensure technology transfer on the control of pests.

Marketing

In order to achieve the Government's aim with regard to the upliftment of small, medium and micro enterprises and the commercialisation of the emerging farming sector, the Directorate: Domestic Marketing was created under the Department of Agriculture. One of the first tasks of this Directorate was to plan and organise a marketing course for extension officers. This was done in close collaboration with the FAO. The Directorate developed a training manual on the basics of agricultural marketing. The manual is in pictorial form specially designed for emerging farmers. In July 2003, the first series was ready for printing and distribution.

The Directorate is also involved in the administration and issuing of negotiated market-access import and export permits for a range of agricultural products. It has amended the permits-allocation policy to make provision for increased allocations to new importers and small and medium enterprises.

In terms of the Marketing of Agricultural Products Act, 1996 (Act 47 of 1996), which replaced the 1968 Marketing Act, all of the old control boards (schemes) in terms of the 1968 Act had to be abolished by 5 January 1998.

Once these control boards had been disbanded, structures were put in place to serve the agricultural industry.

Commodities that were regulated by the time the Marketing of Agriculture Products Act, 1996 came into operation were canned and deciduous fruit, citrus, cotton, dairy, sorghum, lucerne seed, maize, meat, mohair, oilseeds, winter cereals, and wool.

The National Agricultural Marketing Council (NAMC) is a statutory body which primarily provides advice to the Minister of Agriculture and Land Affairs. One of the tasks of the NAMC is to provide the Minister with a report on the current status of a specific industry and make recommendations on how to enhance the viability of the relevant industry. The NAMC also proposes measures to increase the participation of previously disadvantaged individuals in all facets of the agricultural sector.

The NAMC continues to do important work in monitoring the agricultural marketing environment in order to promote the existence of a more diverse and competitive sector. The Outreach Programme – which empowers emerging farmers with information – had reached 1 400 such farmers by June 2003.

Attendance at agricultural shows, farmers' days, conferences and workshops offers the NAMC the opportunity to disseminate information to farmers.

Agriculture

The Directorate: Plant Health and Quality of the Department of Agriculture is responsible for setting the standards for certain agricultural and related products. This includes aspects such as composition, quality, packaging, marking and labelling, as well as physical, physiological, chemical and microbiological analyses.

These standards are published in terms of the Agricultural Product Standards Act, 1990 (Act 119 of 1990), and the Liquor Products Act, 1989 (Act 60 of 1989), in the form of regulations for products sold on local markets, and as standards and requirements for products that are intended for export.

The Directorate developed the Production Unit Code Registration for deciduous as well as subtropical fruits. This is aimed at ensuring the traceability of the origin of the products.

Another international development to ensure safe food of good quality through good agricultural and manufacturing practices is the control of management systems. These ensure a more structured approach to the control of identified hazards than what can be achieved through traditional inspection and quality procedures.

Land administration

The Department of Agriculture, through the Directorate: Farmer Settlement and Development, controls and administers 673 253 ha of State agricultural land.

State agricultural land is divided as follows:
- some 581 864 ha of land expropriated by the South African Development Trust
- some 91 388 ha of commercial land purchased from insolvent estates and properties transferred by the Department of Public Works in terms of Section 7 of the Disposal Act, 1961 (Act 48 of 1961).

The primary goal of the Directorate is the internal administration of State agricultural land with the aim of farmer settlement and ownership reform.

Food security

A decision was taken at the Cabinet *lekgotla* of 2000 to design an integrated food-security strategy that would streamline, harmonise and integrate actions/programmes that address food security in the country. The Integrated Food Security Strategy was adopted at MinMec (forum of national and provincial Ministers), resulting in consultative workshops at national and provincial level.

A joint plan-of-action was agreed on with provincial Departments of Agriculture.

National departments provided a list of their existing food-security programmes and committees that could be linked to the Food Security Strategy.

The Cabinet approved the Integrated Food Security and Nutrition Programme in July 2002 as one of the key programmes of the Social Cluster. The vision of the Programme is to ensure the universal physical, social and economic access to sufficient, safe and nutritious food by all South Africans, at all times, to meet their dietary and food preferences for an active and healthy life. Its goal is to eradicate hunger, malnutrition and food insecurity by 2015.

In March 2003, the Minister of Social Development, Dr Zola Skweyiya; the Minister of Health, Dr Manto Tshabalala-Msimang; and the Minister of Agriculture and Land Affairs, Ms Thoko Didiza, met with their provincial counterparts to further strengthen government's Integrated Food Security and Nutrition Programme and accelerate its delivery to the poorest of the poor.

In July 2003, the Cabinet noted the progress being made in implementing the Integrated Food Security and Nutrition Programme, and the challenges of linking the beneficiaries to the formal social safety net, including the provision of agricultural starter packs.

To ensure that beneficiary households do not relapse into vulnerability, Cabinet decided to extend the food parcel to the original Band

A beneficiaries covered during the 2002/03 allocation (244 000 households) for another three months, to provide for reasonable time frames in implementing the model. Band A households spend less than R200 per month on food.

The Directorate: Plant Health and Quality drafted the Draft Food Security Bill to ensure not only food safety, but also the quality of agricultural products, including fresh fruit and vegetables, exported within the current control system. By implementing the prevention-is-better-than-cure rule, control is transferred from end-product testing to the design and manufacture of such products.

In any international exchange of plants and plant products, there is a risk that pests and diseases might be introduced into the territory of the importing country. In view of this, the South African Government is a signatory member of various multinational agreements. The most important, in terms of safeguarding the country's agricultural resources and natural environment, are the International Plant Protection Convention (IPPC) and the World Trade Organisation Agreement on the Application of Sanitary and Phytosanitary Measures (WTO-SPS).

During working-committee discussions with officials from the Human Rights Commission and the UN Council for Human Rights, the Draft Bill was hailed as the first of its kind to comprehensively address all pertinent food-related issues. The document will be used as a basis for discussions in Africa and the UN. Normal procedures on new legislation and policy guidelines will follow when discussions are finalised.

During April 2003, the Minister of Agriculture and Land Affairs announced that the Department was investigating the feasibility of longer-term food security measures.

These include a comprehensive regional food-security strategy, strategic grain reserves and food stamps, and improved information management.

National Food Pricing Monitoring Committee (FPMC)

The FPMC was established in January 2003 in terms of Section 7 of the Marketing of Agricultural Products Act, 1996. The Committee is tasked with monitoring the prices of food, particularly basic foodstuffs, and investigating any sharp or unjustified food-price increases.

The Committee engages with industry and regulators like the Competition Commission in conducting its investigations. The first task of the FPMC was to investigate the competitiveness of production operations and price-formation mechanisms within the value chains of basic foodstuffs.

The investigation will provide recommendations on required productivity improvements in areas of market inefficiencies and distortions, incidents of predatory pricing and monopolistic tendencies, as well as collusive and discriminatory practices.

The Directorate also facilitated the implementation of the *Yiyo Lena* public-private partnership through which the Minister of Agriculture and Land Affairs invited the business community to voluntarily contribute towards alleviating the impact of high food prices experienced since the beginning of 2001.

As a short-term measure, Premier Foods, Metcash South Africa and Afgri volunteered to introduce a *Yiyo Lena* 12,5-kg maize meal brand at the subsidised price of R25,99 to households in identified national poverty hot spots.

Distribution of the subsidised maize meal commenced on 31 October 2002 and continued until January 2003. In the initial allocation of the monthly quota of about 80 000 bags, priority was given to those stores located in the poverty-stricken areas of the Eastern Cape, KwaZulu-Natal and parts of Limpopo.

Regional issues

South Africa participated in various training programmes of the SADC Food Security Training Programme. The country also parti-

Agriculture

cipates in the Regional Advisory Committee (RAC) of the Programme.

A Regional Food Security Training Programme (RFSTP) has been developed over a five-year period as endorsed by the RAC. From January 2000, the activities of the RFSTP focus on three main areas: strengthening the supply of food-security training services; strengthening the effective demand for training; and developing and sustaining regional markets for food-security-related training services.

The SADC has instituted the Subcommittee for Plant Protection, tasked with harmonising phytosanitary requirements in southern Africa. South Africa is also one of some 52 members of the Inter-African Phytosanitary Council, which was established in 1954. Regional plant protection organisations such as these are able to provide valuable co-ordination for the activities and objectives of the IPPC at local level.

International issues

As a signatory to the Rome Declaration, South Africa has committed itself to the implementation of the World Food Summit Plan of Action. For this purpose, South Africa reports annually to the World Committee for Food Security. South Africa is also collaborating with the FAO on the implementation of the Special Programme for Food Security within the context of the Integrated Sustainable Rural Development Programme.

South Africa is an active participant in other international standard-setting bodies vital to its global market share, such as the IPPC and Codex Alimentarius.

Risk management

The Government is moving forward with the development of an agricultural risk-management programme that includes agricultural risk insurance as one of the major tools in managing agricultural production risk.

A working group to devise agricultural disaster-management plans has been established. These plans cover awareness, avoidance, mitigation and transfer of risk.

Drought management

The Draft Drought Management Strategy will be discussed with all stakeholders, such as provinces and municipalities. The Strategy will place the responsibility of coping with drought back on the normal production system. This will cause farmers to exercise greater prudence and make themselves less vulnerable to the effects of drought.

Agricultural risks insurance

The Department of Agriculture has drafted an Agricultural Risks Insurance Bill, a risk transfer which will assist farmers in managing production risk. This tool will assist farmers to recover from natural disasters. The insurance-based risk management programme allows the farmer, government and the private sector to share the risk involved in agricultural production.

Credit and assistance

The agricultural sector has, to date, been a net borrower, in that it borrows more than it saves. In fact, the total debt of South African farmers has grown by about 10% a year since 1995 – reaching R28 220 million by the end of 2002, compared with R9 495 million at the end of 1984.

The six major sources of credit for farmers are: banks (39%), agricultural co-operatives and agribusinesses (14%), the Land Bank (28%), private creditors (9%), other creditors and financial institutions (8%), and the State (2%).

Agribusiness Promotion and Industry Relations (APIR)

The Directorate: APIR is a newly established unit in the Department of Agriculture, charged with promoting participation and equity sharing towards an inclusive, equitable and prosperous agricultural sector.

The ultimate aims are:
- unlocking the economic potential of idle to underutilised resources of emergent groups by
  - instilling self-confidence and self-esteem through organisational skills, basic business management principles and technical skills
  - encouraging and supporting them to take charge of their lives by facilitating the opening of opportunities/markets and accessing productive resources
  - allowing/affording them the opportunity to contribute to the growth and wealth of their economy.
- facilitating restructuring and expansion of existing agribusinesses to enhance their competitiveness and contribution to the sector as well as the economy as a whole.

National LandCare Programme

The vision of the NLP is for communities and individuals to adopt an ecologically sustainable approach to the management of South Africa's environment and natural resources, while improving their quality of life. This means that people must use the soil, water and vegetation resources in a responsible manner to ensure that future generations will also be able to use them to their benefit. It also implies that cultivation, livestock grazing and harvesting of natural resources should be managed in such a manner that no further degradation (such as soil erosion, nutrient loss, loss of components of the vegetation, and increased run-off of water) occurs.

The NLP's objectives are to:
- promote partnerships between communities, the private sector, and government in the management of natural resources
- establish institutional arrangements to develop and implement policies, programmes and practices that will encourage the sustainable use of natural resources
- encourage opportunities for the development of business enterprises that focus on sustainable resource management
- enhance the long-term productivity of natural resources.

LandCare themes are grouped into two areas, namely focused investment (Watercare, Veldcare, Soilcare and Juniorcare) and small community grants.

LandCare is developing and implementing integrated approaches to natural resource management in the country, which are efficient, sustainable, equitable and consistent with the principles of ecologically sustainable development. LandCare partners have consequently designed key strategies for sustainable natural-resource management.

Serious concerns about land and water degradation, which impacts on sustainable resource use, are identified in each province, and specific projects address these issues.

In cases of serious catchment-wide degradation and erosion, the root causes are investigated. In some cases, physical control structures are needed to ensure that water run-off control takes place. The Department of Agriculture's Subdirectorate: Key Soil Conservation Works designs and constructs such structures in terms of the Conservation of Agricultural Resources Act, 1983.

Projects are under way in Limpopo, Mpumalanga, North West, KwaZulu-Natal and the Eastern Cape.

The purpose of this strategy is to empower resource-poor communities to develop LandCare groups and activities through awareness, training and education. This includes communication strategies directed towards rural community groups and young people. The strategy formulates policy and legislation to develop incentives for natural-resource management.

The aim is to establish and implement a monitoring system to evaluate progress, assess contemporary issues and provide a basis for planning and research.

The Department also aims to promote its National Policy on Agricultural Land and

Agriculture

Resource Management in all spheres of government and other stakeholders.

There are 346 LandCare projects throughout the country, funded to an amount of R240 million.

The Australian Government, through the Australian Agency for International Development, funded a R15-million capacity-building programme for LandCare over a period of three years, from April 2001 to April 2004. An additional R6 million was added to the programme in 2002 during the World Summit on Sustainable Development.

Focused investment

The Watercare theme targets Limpopo in particular, because of water shortages and the importance of water for irrigation in the province. This theme establishes a framework for managing land and preventing the silt-up of dams for irrigation. Watercare works in partnership with the community to develop action plans for managing and restoring irrigation schemes. The rehabilitation of irrigation schemes increases water supply and household food security. Furthermore, Watercare promotes the development of techniques for water-resource management and encourages opportunities for training in this field.

Under the Watercare project, 28 schemes have been revitalised. There are 138 small-holder schemes in Limpopo. A business plan for the revitalisation of small-holder irrigation schemes has been developed. It aims at revitalising the remaining 105 schemes in Limpopo over a six-year period from 2003 to 2009. The Limpopo Government has committed R252 million to this plan.

Veldcare promotes best grazing-systems and erosion-prevention practices to improve production. It develops and maintains agricultural activities in accordance with the principles of ecologically sustainable development within North West. Economic and social development opportunities are realised by improving grazing areas and maintaining viable grazing areas throughout rural communities.

Soilcare encourages rural farmers in KwaZulu-Natal, the Eastern Cape and Mpumalanga to build innovative structures to combat soil erosion. This includes reducing the depletion of soil fertility and acidity. Through Soilcare, sustainable agricultural production systems are introduced, such as diversification, management of input and conservation tillage.

The objectives of Juniorcare are to empower previously disadvantaged youth through training in facilitation and leadership skills.

This includes the promotion of food security at home and at schools, awareness of sustainable agriculture, and stimulating the formation of youth clubs and projects that aim to promote other components of LandCare. Juniorcare addresses the needs of young

---

The Northern Cape Government, in partnership with Haymake Investments and Gili Greenworld, launched a paprika factory in Springbok, Northern Cape, in March 2003.

The factory, worth R55 million, is one of South Africa's supreme irrigational emerging farmer empowerment projects, called the Goodhouse Paprika Project.

The factory's core business is the production of paprika spice and paprika oleo-resin (concentrated) to be exported to Europe, the United States of America, Mexico, the Far East and the Middle East.

It has created 78 permanent jobs and projected sales for the first six years are estimated at R276 million.

The raw material for the factory is supplied by the emerging Goodhouse Agricultural Corporation, comprising 55 small-scale black farmers who acquired Land Redistribution Agricultural Development Grants from the Department of Land Affairs and loans from the Land Bank.

Each beneficiary has been allocated 10 hectare (ha) for the cultivation of paprika. A total of 550 ha of irrigational land will be developed along the Orange River.

The Northern Cape Government has invested R17 million (25% shareholding) in the factory, on behalf of the emerging farmers of Goodhouse.

people in an integrated way and involves interdisciplinary approaches.

Land and Agricultural Development Bank of South Africa (Land Bank)

The Land Bank operates as a development finance institution within the agricultural and agribusiness sectors regulated by the Land and Agricultural Development Bank Act, 2002 (Act 15 of 2002), that repealed the Land Bank Act, 1944 (Act 13 of 1944), on 10 June 2002.

The Bank has a mandate from government to support the development of the agricultural sector as a whole. The Bank's key strategic intent is to achieve financial sustainability focusing on social and development impact. Meeting client needs with cost-effective and competitive products and services; building an efficient, representative and committed workforce; and promoting good relations with stakeholders are critical elements of this strategy. The Bank provides a comprehensive range of retail and wholesale financial products and services designed to meet the needs of commercial and developing farmers and agriculture-related businesses.

The Bank offers loan products to the agricultural industry for the financing of fixed property, equipment, livestock, standing crops and orchards, and farming input costs. The needs of individual farmers are catered for through loan products distributed via the Bank's network of 27 retail branches situated in agricultural centres throughout South Africa, as well as 45 satellite branches. The financing needs of agricultural co-operatives and agribusiness are met through loan products distributed by the Bank's specialist Corporate Finance Units, situated in Pretoria and Cape Town.

The Bank extends loans to agribusiness and makes equity investments, opening the way to diversify and grow the portfolio. Diversification is important for long-term financial sustainability. The Bank receives no ongoing grants or subsidies from government. It raises its funds on local and international money markets. The Bank's conservative financial approach and good results are reflected in a premium risk rating, enabling it to access funds at favourable rates.

Products and services

The Land Bank empowers various farming communities, especially the poorest of the poor. Through the Bank's creative funding programmes and initiatives, women in rural areas have been able to empower themselves and take charge of their lives.

By April 2003, the Bank had assisted a total of 14 000 black clients who are not beneficiaries of government-supported Land Redistribution for Agricultural Development (LRAD).

The Bank is increasingly reaching out to a client base that was traditionally not served by the country's financial institutions. A total of 7 900 LRAD beneficiaries have also received financial assistance through the Bank.

Corporate and development finance

The number of loans advanced to development clients increased by 35% from 66 846 in 2000 to 90 155 in 2001. During this period, some 4 116 loan applications amounting to R192 million for the Silver and Bronze products, and 28 loans amounting to R328 million in respect of development products were approved. The total value of loans extended to development clients, compared with the previous year, increased by 8% from R413 million in 2000 to R446 million in 2001.

In 2001, government introduced a grant for LRAD, which has provided an opportunity for future financing of land-acquisition by historically disadvantaged persons. The Land Bank has been appointed by the Department of Agriculture to administer this grant and will provide additional loans for land-acquisition and input-costs to qualifying beneficiaries.

Black Economic Empowerment (BEE)

In agriculture, BEE is seen as the driving force

Agriculture

towards stimulating growth and wealth. The sector has proactively tried to address BEE issues in its joint strategic plan.

The main challenge facing the sector is to harmonise its strategic plan with the Government's BEE strategy, codes and norms. An initial brainstorming workshop was held with key stakeholders on 28 August 2002, to recommend a policy framework that can be used as a platform for policy debates, consultations and ultimate guidelines in agriculture.

The Department's top management has, in principle, approved the recommendations. A refined document has been submitted to the Minister for clearance before the Department embarks on targeted external consultations with industries and other departments.

Microfinance

To address the widespread need for microfinance in rural areas, the Land Bank introduced the Step Up scheme in April 1998. This enables people with no security to borrow an initial amount of R250. If clients repay the loan on time they can 'step up' to a R500 loan, continuing to a maximum loan of R18 000.

At this stage, many Step Up clients have a track record that qualifies them for the Land Bank's high- to medium-risk categories.

Agri SA

Agri SA is an independent producer organisation consisting of provincial agricultural unions, commodity organisations and co-operatives and agricultural businesses owned by farmers. The main objective of Agri SA is to negotiate the best possible economic and social conditions for agricultural producers in South Africa. To attain this objective, it strives to organise the farming population and agricultural business into a united front.

The highest authority within the structure of the organisation lies with the Agri SA Annual Congress, where all three legs of organised agriculture are represented.

The General Council of Agri SA, which consists of representatives from the Provincial Chamber, Commodity Chamber and Agribusiness Chamber, gives continuous attention to matters of general interest concerning the farming community. An executive committee, consisting of Agri SA's president, deputy president and the chairpersons of the three Chambers, makes the day-to-day decisions within the accepted policy of the organisation.

Agri SA also has a number of functional committees specialising in matters which are relevant to the farming community, such as economic issues, safety, labour, land affairs, etc. In addition, they are major employers, developers and sources of added-value.

Agricultural Business Chamber (ABC)

The ABC is a sectoral body representing an important component of South Africa's business sector. The ABC's members represent total assets of almost R30 billion and an annual agricultural business turnover of approximately R50 billion.

Together, ABC members operate more than 2 000 service centres countrywide and have a total employee-complement of more than 100 000. In many rural areas, members of the ABC are the business hub of the community and make a key contribution to maintaining the rural infrastructure.

The ABC is an integral part of the Agri SA Group, and associates with Business South Africa and international bodies such as the International Federation of Agricultural Producers, the International Chamber of Commerce and the International Agribusiness Management Association.

The ABC strives to support its member organisations by creating an environment within which they are able to operate as competitive and innovative business enterprises.

The Chamber represents agricultural companies, agricultural co-operatives, agricultural co-operatives in the developing agricultural sector, companies which arose out of the conversion of agricultural co-operatives, and other agricultural business enterprises and organisations.

Agricultural businesses play a significant role in the economy of South Africa as handlers, processors and marketers of agricultural products, and as suppliers of production input and services.

Agribusiness as an economic sector

Agribusiness can be divided into two categories: non-co-operative business ventures and co-operatives or transformed co-operatives.

Non-co-operative business ventures, also known as profit companies, are involved in the production and distribution of agricultural equipment and production requisites, and the marketing of agricultural products.

Co-operatives dominate the distribution of intermediate requisites and the handling, processing and marketing of agricultural products.

Agricultural co-operatives or agribusinesses are regarded as the farmers' own independent business organisations. There are close to 1 000 primary agricultural co-operatives and agribusinesses throughout the country. They supply their members with production input such as seed, fertiliser, fuel and repair services. They also provide credit and extension services, and handle a large percentage of their members' produce.

There are more than 15 central co-operatives in the country, which aim to supply the primary co-operatives with specific services, such as processing and marketing of agricultural products, insurance services for crops, short-term cover, and farming requisites. The structure of agribusiness has changed substantially since the deregulation of the agricultural sector into a free-market economy in 1994. Many co-operatives transformed into private companies, consolidations and mergers occurred, international groups entered South Africa, and agribusinesses listed on the Johannesburg Securities Exchange (JSE).

Agribusinesses are involved in the production and distribution of agricultural equipment and production requisites, and in the marketing and processing of agricultural products.

South African agribusiness is increasingly challenged to perform competitively and the ABC's Competitive Index indicates an upward trend, especially since 1998. This implies that value-adding processes in South African agriculture are becoming more competitive. The input sectors also indicate a positive trend in competitiveness. These positive trends are supported by growing agricultural exports and sustained increases in the Agribusiness Confidence Index.

The co-operative movement in South African agriculture is expected to grow. A new Co-operative Bill is under consideration and it is envisaged that this enabling legislation will make co-operatives accessible to all communities through outgrower projects, contracting, and share equity schemes.

The Co-operative Development Initiative is one of many efforts to facilitate such linkages and support a 'growth-with-equity' development path for South African agriculture.

National African Farmers' Union

NAFU strives to promote the interests of the disadvantaged farming sector by lobbying for access to support services and empowering its members through effective communication and capacity-building programmes.

Economic empowerment

The Department of Agriculture funds NAFU's capacity-building programme. Further funding is provided by the US Department of Agriculture.

Bergville Maize Milling Co-operative was also co-ordinated and funded by the national Department of Agriculture.

The Zijamele Farmers Co-operative training programme was co-ordinated by the Department and rendered by Africare as an implementing agent.

The Department also co-ordinates the Presidential Mechanisation Lead Projects.

Institutional capacity-building

The Department of Agriculture has developed a databank for agricultural human resource capacity for South Africa.

In collaboration with the Economic Development Institute of the World Bank, the Department has designed and developed training courses for rural restructuring and development. The Youth Entrepreneurship Programme was launched in 1999.

The Department co-ordinated and funded the development of the National Emerging Red Meat Producers' Organisation. This includes the formation of provincial structures and the provision of organisational leadership training.

Training and research

South African agriculture has a strong research component. Many of the people involved are world leaders in their respective fields. The ARC, an autonomous statutory body set up in terms of the Agricultural Research Act, 1990 (Act 86 of 1990), is the largest agricultural research organisation in Africa.

The ARC provides research support to the Department of Agriculture and the nine provincial departments of agriculture. ARC scientific expertise supports most of the Department of Agriculture's regulatory directorates such as the Directorate: Public Veterinary Health, the Directorate: Animal Health, the Directorate: Plant Health and Quality, the Directorate: Agricultural Resource Conservation, and the Directorate: Agricultural Production Input. The ARC also supports other agricultural institutions such as the Registrar of Livestock Improvement and Identification, the Registrar of Brands, the South African Veterinary Council, and the Perishable Products Export Control Board.

The ARC serves the whole continuum of farmers, from the small-scale subsistence sector, through the emergent commercial sector, to fully fledged commercial farmers. Research can be scale-neutral or directed to the specific needs of small-scale or commercial farmers.

The ARC publishes various reports, field guides and other multimedia information products directed at all levels of agriculture in South Africa and the rest of Africa. Various specialised training courses and information days are presented and attended by farmers and delegates from South Africa and neighbouring countries. Participatory research, specialised exhibitions, training courses and open days (with practical demonstrations) are used to reach the small-scale farmer.

South Africa has a number of specialised agricultural high schools and regular schools offering a comprehensive range of agricultural subjects. Prospective farmers are trained at 11 agricultural colleges: Elsenburg (Western Cape), Cedara and Owen Sitole (KwaZulu-Natal), Grootfontein Agricultural College at the Grootfontein Agricultural Development Institute (run by the Department of Agriculture), Glen (Free State), Potchefstroom (North West), Lowveld (Mpumalanga), Fort Cox and Tsolo (Eastern Cape), and Tompi Seleka and Madzivhandila (Limpopo). Diploma courses are also offered at various technikons. Degree courses are offered at the faculties of agriculture of various universities.

Veterinary surgeons are trained at the University of Pretoria's Faculty of Veterinary Sciences at Onderstepoort. The former Faculty of Veterinary Sciences at the Medical University of South Africa has amalgamated with the University of Pretoria. State veterinarians are assisted countrywide by animal health technicians who have a National Diploma in Animal Health. A National Diploma in Veterinary Technology is offered by Technikon Pretoria (soon to become Tshwane University of Technology) to enable student veterinary laboratory technicians of the Department of Agriculture and the private sector to become fully qualified.

Meat inspectors in the provincial Directorate: Veterinary Services assist State veterinarians with meat inspections at abattoirs in South Africa. They complete a three-year diploma course to become environmental health officers and are designated by the Directorate to become meat inspectors. Meat examiners must complete a National Certificate in meat-examining for red meat or poultry. A similar course is being developed for the ostrich industry.

The marked lack of interest in agricultural engineering as a career choice has been widely debated. Food processing, packaging, storage and transport, computers, and sales and service opportunities are all off-farm activities that fall within the ambit of the agricultural engineer. The Universities of Technology (technikons) at Pretoria, Bloemfontein and Cape Town offer civil engineering with agricultural courses. The Universities of Pretoria and Natal offer degree courses in agricultural engineering.

Trade relations

The Department of Agriculture has reviewed its foreign representation and all previous foreign representatives of the Department and the ARC have been recalled. Foreign offices have been reopened in Washington DC (USA), Beijing, (People's Republic of China), Brussels (Belgium) and Rome (Italy). The main functions of these foreign representatives are to provide South Africa with information on agricultural developments, particularly issues that impact on policy; and to liaise with all agricultural organisations in host and neighbouring countries on matters of mutual interest.

Liaison with foreign missions is promoted by arranging agricultural tours and briefing sessions for the diplomatic corps.

The Directorate: International Relations facilitates and co-ordinates international activities on both multilateral and bilateral bases.

The Directorate: International Trade analyses international trade and marketing policies and advises on multilateral and bilateral agricultural trade policy. The Department is responsible for dealing with matters concerning agricultural relations with other countries and organisations, such as the Southern African Customs Union (SACU), the trade and industry sectors of the SADC, the World Trade Organisation (WTO) and the International Grains Convention.

The Department maintains bilateral trade agreements with countries in Africa, including Lesotho, Malawi, Swaziland and Zimbabwe. The Department is also involved in negotiations with the USA, Southern Common Market (Mercosur), and the European Free Trade Association, as well as within the WTO individually, and as a member of the Cairns group.

Work relating to agricultural relations in the field of trade is done in co-operation with the Departments of Trade and Industry and of Foreign Affairs. The Department of Agriculture is a member of the FAO; the Consultative Group on International Agricultural Research; the Food, Agriculture and Natural Resources Sector of the SADC; the International Seed-Testing Association; the Organisation for Economic Co-operation and Development's Seed Schemes; the Union for the Protection of New Varieties of Plants; and the Cairns Group.

The Directorate: International Trade is responsible for the implementation of South Africa's commitments in terms of the WTO Marrakech Agreement. These commitments include the reduction of tariffs, export subsidies and domestic support given to agriculture. Almost all of these commitments were met by the conversion of quantitative import restriction to tariffs, as well as the deregulation of the agricultural marketing system. In addition, the Department is creating market access opportunities by implementing the minimum market-access commitments contained in the agreement.

WTO agricultural negotiations entered their third phase in March 2002. This phase was scheduled to be completed by 31 March 2003, with the completion of modalities (quantifiable reduction of commitments) and rule-related elements for further reform. This deadline could not be met due to many differences being negotiated.

In June 2003, the negotiations were continuing.

The Directorate: Marketing issues import permits for various agricultural products at reduced levels of duty.

South Africa's objectives in the agricultural negotiations arena are to achieve a substantial reduction in domestic support and export subsidies, mainly from developed countries. Other objectives are to achieve a substantial improvement of market access for South African agricultural exports; and to ensure that South Africa's commitment, in terms of domestic support, fully covers the development needs of the country.

The Department is developing trade relations with other countries. This includes the implementation of the agricultural aspects of the SACU Agreement, the SADC Protocol on Trade, and the SA-EU TDCA.

A substantive restructuring is aimed at graduating the SADC into a regional trading bloc. Key features of this restructuring include the grouping of the 21 sectors into clusters under four directorates at the SADC Secretariat, and the establishment of SADC national committees to co-ordinate their respective individual member-state interests relating to the SADC.

By July 2003, the organisation was also finalising the Regional Indicative Strategic Development Programme in order to provide a clear direction in line with SADC policies and programmes over the long term.

The SA-EU TDCA was implemented on 1 January 2000. The Department has introduced a system whereby market opportunities under the Agreement can be fully utilised. This includes providing information to potential exporters, as well as the administration of export quotas granted to South Africa under the Agreement. Since 1 January 2000, the Department has issued export permits for various products such as wine, canned fruit, fruit juice, cut flowers, proteas, cheese, and frozen strawberries to be exported to the EU at reduced levels of duty.

The South African Government has signed a framework agreement with Mercosur (a treaty establishing a common market between Argentina, Brazil, Paraguay and Uruguay). This agreement lays down the framework for negotiations of a free trade agreement (FTA). The third round of negotiations took place in Pretoria in December 2002. The Department is part of the Government's negotiating team representing agricultural interests. The Department is also preparing its position regarding possible FTAs with China, India, Nigeria and Kenya.

In addition to these agreements, the Department represents the Government at the International Grains Convention. It is responsible for implementing and administering the agricultural components of the bilateral agreements with Zimbabwe, Malawi and Mozambique. Import permits for agricultural products are issued in terms of the trade agreements with Zimbabwe and Malawi.

The Department is investigating and evaluating export opportunities for agricultural products on world markets. A subdirectorate was formed to deal specifically with issues related to the strategic repositioning of the agricultural export sector. Strategic market research and formulating new industry strategies for exports are priorities. Export-led development projects are also being considered as a means to alleviate poverty.

The ARC participates in various co-operative research agreements, international organisations and networks. These include the Special Programme for African Agricultural Research and FAO. South Africa is a partner in research projects that are funded by the EU under its 4th Framework Programme. The Biotechnology Action Committee of the UN's Educational, Scientific and Cultural Organisation established its Biotechnology Education and Training Centre for Africa at the

ARC-Roodeplaat Vegetable and Ornamental Plant Institute. The ARC-Onderstepoort Veterinary Institute is the OIE Regional Collaborating Centre and the Reference Centre for FMD.

At national level, the ARC supports various government departments in deliberations regarding international agreements and disputes, for example the Convention on Biodiversity, the Kyoto Protocol on Global Change, the Montreal Protocol, Genetically Modified Organisms and Indigenous Knowledge Systems.

Import and export control

The aim of the Import Export Policy Unit of the Directorate: Animal Health is to formulate and support policies to reduce sanitary (health) risks in the import and export of animals and animal products.

Applications to import animals and animal products are evaluated in accordance with the Animal Diseases Act, 1984, the Meat Safety Act, 2000 and international standards (e.g. the OIE Code and Codex Standards). Import requirements vary according to the product and the animal-health situation in individual countries.

South Africa is an active member of the OIE. Disease reports are received from the OIE and by direct contact with the veterinary administration in the exporting countries.

Trade in animal and animal products is based on a series of requirements considered appropriate by the importing country to prevent the entry of diseases.

South Africa is a signatory member of the WTO-SPS. As a signatory member of the IPPC, South Africa subscribes to the principles of equal market access and international co-operation in protecting human, animal and plant health. The WTO-SPS acknowledges the IPPC as the relevant organisation to draft and adopt standards for phytosanitary measures.

These international organisations promote free trade in plants and plant products, and at the same time acknowledge the rights of member countries to protect plant health.

The Directorate: Plant Health and Quality, of the Department of Agriculture, is the designated National Plant Protection Organisation of South Africa and has an obligation to fulfil the requirements of the WTO-SPS and the IPPC.

The Department is one of the key regulatory State departments with the authority to enforce laws enacted by Parliament to protect the South African consumer, the environment and other national interests. The Department's regulatory activities with regard to plants and plant products are primarily enforced by the Directorate: Plant Health and Quality and the Directorate: Genetic Resources. In addition, South Africa's Customs Service participates in this effort by detaining imported goods when requirements have not been met.

The Directorate: Plant Health and Quality promotes and regulates the availability of healthy and productive plant material and the quality of agricultural products in South Africa. It administers the Agricultural Pests Act, 1983, the Liquor Products Act, 1989 and the Agricultural Product Standards Act, 1990. Import control is vital to prevent the introduction of potentially harmful foreign pests. Prospective importers of plants and plant products have to apply for an import permit for those controlled goods not published in *Government Gazette R1013* of 1989. A pest-risk analysis, based on scientific data, is conducted, and specific phytosanitary requirements are set out according to the phytosanitary risk(s) involved. These conditions are then stipulated in the permit issued to the importer. Importers are obliged to present the material to the Executive Officer of the Act or the official representative for inspection. Should the imported material comply with all conditions, permission will be granted for release to the importer. In cases of non-compliance, the risks will be evaluated and managed by a decision on mitigation, destruction or return to the country of origin.

Should any potentially harmful pest be introduced into and become established in South Africa, the Directorate: Plant Health and Quality will conduct a survey to determine the distribution of the organism, draft an eradication programme, liaising with other relevant parties, and possibly co-ordinate and participate in the eradication programme.

Despite strict precautions in the past, several harmful alien organisms have become established in specific production areas in South Africa, causing substantial losses to agriculture. Control measures are published to prevent or combat the spread of these organisms to other areas in the country. Quarantine services ensure imported plant material and biological control agents are appropriately handled to guarantee that harmful alien organisms do not enter and become established in the country.

In export control, South Africa has to comply with the import conditions of the specific country or group of countries it is exporting to, by issuing phytosanitary certificates. The Directorate furthermore maintains a database on the import conditions and procedures of various countries and the occurrence of harmful organisms within South Africa. It renders advisory and identification services, carries out field inspections and conducts laboratory tests as requested by the importing country.

All consignments of plants and plant products intended for export are inspected, evaluated and certified by the Directorate.

This ensures a high standard of phytosanitary control, which contributes to international credibility and phytosanitary accountability, and promotes international trade in agricultural products. Close international liaison with regard to export programmes and their execution is very important to establish and maintain world markets for South African produce. Export control is further supported by the analysis of fresh produce for chemical residues, to ensure it complies with international standards and norms and enhances international trade. These procedures include sampling commodities presented for export, and using highly specialised and sophisticated methods to determine the status of the products. These analytical results are used as input when deciding whether to release products for export.

Land Affairs

The Department of Land Affairs is responsible for the following functions:
- financial management
- corporate services
- deeds registration
- cadastral surveys
- surveys and mapping
- spatial planning and information
- land reform, implementation management and co-ordination
- land reform systems and support services.

Deeds registration

The registration of deeds is a national competency. The aim of the Deeds Registry is to maintain a public register of land as well as an efficient system of registration aimed at affording security of title to land and rights to land.

There are nine Deeds Offices in South Africa, situated in Pretoria, Cape Town, Johannesburg, Pietermaritzburg, Bloemfontein, Kimberley, King William's Town, Vryburg and Umtata.

To comply with Section 9 of the Constitution, 1996 (Act 106 of 1996), the Department plans for the establishment of a Deeds Registry in all nine provinces. The first of the new Deeds Registries will be established in Nelspruit, Mpumalanga. The State Information Technology Agency has been requested to put forward proposals for the establishment of a digital archive in Nelspruit. It is anticipated that the establishment of the office will be completed by the second quarter of 2004.

Deeds Offices are responsible for the:
- registration of real rights to land
- maintenance of land registers
- provision of land-registration information
- preservation of registration records for archival purposes.

Deeds and documents lodged with the Deeds Registries are examined by deeds controllers for accuracy regarding the content, as well as for compliance with common, case and statutory law and attachments against the property.

Holders of a title deed registered in the Deeds Office are therefore assured of the security of their title to the property. The average turnaround time from lodgement to registration is 10 working days.

The Chief Directorate: Deeds Registration has developed a bar-code-based document-tracking system (DOTS) for implementation in Deeds Registries. DOTS was born out of the need to eliminate the disappearance of deeds and documents during the registration process. DOTS' ability to track deeds and documents through the various processes within the Deeds Registry has repeatedly proved its worth. In addition, the system provides Deeds Registries with valuable statistical information which is being used for managerial purposes.

Deeds Offices supply registration information in support of all units in the Department conducting research for land-reform purposes.

The Document Copy System is a service supplied by the Chief Directorate: Deeds Registration whereby users can request that a copy of a deed or document (which is stored on microfilm) be transmitted to them by fax.

Cadastral surveys

The Chief Directorate: Cadastral Surveys' project for the upgrading of townships surveyed under the former Department of Development Aid has made it possible for thousands of people to register their properties as freehold where previously they had only held lesser land rights. The upgrading process has been completed in the Western and Eastern Cape as well as in KwaZulu-Natal. Progress in the remaining provinces has been steady and the entire process was expected to be completed in 2003.

The process of development of the Cadastral Information System (CIS) continued in 2002/03. Major developments were carried out on key components of the System. Many modules have moved from a full maintenance to maintenance-free or periodical maintenance status.

Service delivery has improved and good turnaround times have been maintained in the four Offices of the Surveyor-General.

Processing periods of less than 15 working days in the examination of cadastral documentation are being maintained.

The turnaround times were made possible by the continued improvement of procedures, the restructuring of offices, and the enhanced CIS, which is operational in the Office of the Surveyor-General. Ease of access to accurate spatial data has been provided through the enhanced usability and continual updating of the spatial database. Clients have ready access to such data, both in electronic and hard-copy format.

A decision to supply government, provincial and local authorities with free digital data (diagram and general plan images) has been accepted with great enthusiasm.

The website of the Chief Surveyor-General contains information and links to a number of other related sites. Information can be downloaded from the site and spatial data contained within the offices of the Surveyor-General can be viewed.

Two Client Service Centres have been designed and established at the Pretoria and Cape Town Surveyor-General Offices.

The highly technical, user-friendly Centres serve approximately 100 to 150 clients a day. They are also able to supply a legal registration

Agriculture

help-desk function to attorneys, land surveyors and other professionals in the property industry.

Services provided to other government departments include the preparation of documentation relating to awarding tenders to private land-survey firms for the survey of State land. Assistance is given to the Land and Tenure Reform Branch and Land Claims Commissions (regional and provincial) in the form of surveys; the provision of cadastral information; the undertaking of field inspections; the undertaking of investigations to determine magisterial boundaries; and the upgrading of data on the former Transkei, Bophuthatswana, Venda and Ciskei states. A tendering process is administered by the Surveyor-General Offices for the appointment of land surveyors on request from either unit.

The use of cadastral spatial data is increasing continuously and is also being applied as overlays in aerial photography.

The formal and informal cadastral spatial data have proved invaluable in providing assistance to components dealing with land reform and restitution. Enhancements to the spatial data will continue to be made with a view to providing services in support of land reform and orderly development.

Surveys and mapping

The aim of the Chief Directorate: Surveys and Mapping is to maintain an integrated national control survey system, a national mapping programme, a national aerial-photography programme, and associated geospatial products. The Chief Directorate's spatial data are a valuable resource, essential for orderly and sustainable development.

The Chief Directorate contributed to the process of spatial development and, in particular, to the land-reform programme by supplying accurate and up-to-date spatial data. To increase sustainable land-use, the Chief Directorate renders support in the form of assistance with land restitution/reform research.

It also provides spatial information to other departments and parastatal organisations that require spatial data for their own development programmes. The Chief Directorate provides assistance for land-reform projects by supplying maps, aerial photography and other essential geospatial information. Direct assistance is also provided for restitution research and land-reform projects.

The Chief Directorate aligns its aerial photography and map-production programmes to the requirements of local, provincial and national government departments through the National Advisory Survey Committee. The change to digital map-production methods continues. Almost all data-capturing and cartographic processes are now digital. The integrated national control survey system consists of a countrywide network of control points with accurately determined positions and/or heights. This network provides the spatial reference framework for the country.

The Chief Directorate is in the process of installing a network of 38 active GPS (global positioning system) base stations, known as TrigNet. By March 2003, 32 base stations had been established and operationalised. It is expected that the remaining stations will be established by 2004.

The data generated by the network provide users with the means to achieve high position-accuracy using stand-alone GPS receivers.

Capacity-building is given high priority by the Chief Directorate. The project strives to develop and enhance the map-skills of people using spatial information in the workplace and schools.

Between April 2002 and March 2003, the Chief Directorate had eight students on the in-house pupil-survey-officer programme, and 25 students received high-quality experiential training. Of these 25 students, 17 from the Special Bursary Scheme were accommodated in the 2003 academic year.

The Special Bursary Scheme was extended by almost 47% compared with the previous year. An increase from 38 students in 2002 to 56 students in the 2003 academic year was achieved.

Mapping is a crucial resource for decision-making and development – and is one of the most important deliverables of the Chief Directorate to support orderly spatial planning and sustainable land-use. Of the national mapping-series, the 1:50 000 topographical map series is the largest-scale map-series providing full coverage of South Africa. Small-scale maps (1:250 000 and 1:500 000) are produced from the 1:50 000 map series.

The popular large-scale 1:10 000 orthophoto map-series provides coverage of predominantly built-up areas, areas of economic importance, and areas experiencing rapid development. This series currently covers approximately 25% of the country. Aeronautical charts and other wall maps are also produced. These maps must be continuously revised to reflect the change in landscape and other geospatial features.

The Chief Directorate maintains a topographical information system that contains the major features (roads, railways, built-up areas, contours and rivers) of the entire 1:50 000 national map-series in digital format.

A digital elevation model is available in horizontal intervals of 400 m, 200 m in mountainous areas and 50 m for the major metropolitan and development areas. These valuable national assets are continually improved upon and maintained, to satisfy the nation's need for digital spatial information.

Individuals and organisations, both public and private, utilise these data sets for planning, engineering, and social and scientific purposes. The database serves as a fundamental data set for the country and is utilised by, among others, Statistics South Africa for census planning and the Independent Electoral Commission for the delineation of voting areas.

The Chief Directorate is a full member of the National Airspace Committee and produces aeronautical charts for the southern African region that are vital to the interests of air safety. The Chief Directorate provides up-to-date charts that reflect changes to airspace with respect to the Future Airspace Management Efficiency Programme.

The Chief Directorate enhanced effective government empowerment by building capacity through active assistance to other national departments. The Department of Environmental Affairs and Tourism was assisted with the mapping of Antarctica and Marion Island, and the Wetlands GIS project.

The Chief Directorate is a key stakeholder of, and co-funded, the National Land Cover 2000 Project.

This project is of great importance to sustainable development, utilising highly advanced satellite imagery which enables the classification of land cover to the detail of 1 ha. Detailed information can be analysed and classified to display a specific cultivation and provide users of spatial information with much-improved and more realistic information. The areas covered by the first phase of the project are KwaZulu-Natal, Mpumalanga, Limpopo, Gauteng, Swaziland and Lesotho.

The Chief Directorate plays a leading role in the African Reference Framework Project, which aims at harmonising and linking spatial reference systems across Africa and which will connect Africa to the rest of the world. This will support access to regional spatial information in support of various development projects.

Surveys

The aim is to undertake field surveys in order to acquire control survey, mapping and specialised survey data, aerial photography and ancillary data; to process the survey and mapping data collected through the processing of network adjustments, aerial triangulation, photogrammetric compilation and map data processing; to maintain national control survey network monuments, and to collect and provide permanent GPS base-station network data.

Agriculture

The integrated national control survey system is the backbone of the survey and geospatial industry. The system consists of a network of approximately 62 000 control points distributed throughout the country. The network is made up of about 28 000 trigonometric beacons, 24 000 town-survey marks and 10 000 elevation benchmarks. The co-ordinates of these marks are referenced to the Hartebeesthoek 94 datum, which, in turn, is referenced to the International Terrestrial Reference Frame. Cadastral, engineering and mapping surveys are referenced to this datum, which facilitates the exchange of data, uniform standards of accuracy and reduced costs of survey and spatial data to the public.

The Chief Directorate's archive of aerial photography, dating back to 1934, is expanded annually with the acquisition of new photography covering approximately 20% of the country. Aerial-photography programmes and priorities are determined in co-operation with local, provincial and national government departments. The archive is used for mapping, land-resource planning, infrastructure development and legal and land restitution matters.

The Chief Directorate is a permanent member of the South African Geographic Names Council (SAGNC). New names collected during field work for mapping are submitted to the SAGNC for consideration. The Chief Directorate also completed a digital database of geographic names and prepared draft digital gazetteers of each province. Some 57 000 previously acquired geographical names were also submitted for approval.

Spatial planning and information

Part of the transformation of South Africa as a country and as a society requires the fundamental restructuring of settlement patterns to ensure greater equity and efficiency. It is common knowledge that the effluences of colonialism, apartheid and the modernist society have adversely affected settlement patterns. Among the manifestations of this challenge are:
- racially segregated settlements
- urban sprawl
- disintegrated land-use patterns
- unsustainable service costs (transport subsidies alone account for R2 billion annually).

In addressing these challenges, the Department is focusing specifically on aspects within its statutory mandate, i.e. spatial planning, land-use management and spatial information. The *White Paper on Spatial Planning and Land-Use Management* was completed and approved by Cabinet on 27 June 2001. The White Paper is built on the concept of Integrated Development Plans. As a spin-off from this, the Land-Use Management Bill was drafted and consultation with relevant stakeholders has taken place.

The *White Paper on Spatial Planning and Land-Use Management* sets out the policy directives that will guide the legislation necessary to regulate spatial planning and land-use management. The core tenets of the White Paper and the Bill are that:
- Development plans from all spheres of government must be reflected in a spatial development framework. This will enhance interpretation, implementation and monitoring.
- Development plans must include an analysis of strategically located land and a recommendation of how best such land should be utilised, in an attempt to make settlement patterns more equitable and efficient.
- The principles of equity, efficiency, integration, environmental sustainability and good and fair governance should guide all development planning decisions.

During 2002, extensive consultation and bilateral discussions with interested parties were undertaken. These include the South African Council for Town and Regional Planners, the

South African Property Owners' Association, the South African Local Government Association, and Western Cape and Gauteng Provincial Administrations' representatives.

The Planning Professions Act, 2002 (Act 36 of 2002), repealed the Town and Regional Planner's Act of 1984. By March 2003, mechanisms to implement the Act were in an advanced stage.

With regard to capacity-building, support was given to the Mpumalanga Development Tribunal, established in terms of the Development Facilitation Act, 1995 (Act 67 of 1995), to consider and decide on land-development applications. Training on the integration of land-reform projects, in particular restitution projects, into the integrated development-planning process at municipal level, was conducted for the Free State Land Reform Provincial Office as well as the Free State and Northern Cape Regional Land Claims Commissions.

The implementation of the Policy and Guidelines for the Integration of Environmental Planning into Land Reform has been significantly delayed as a result of funding problems experienced after the withdrawal of the Danish Government. The implementation of the Guidelines will ensure greater sustainability of projects resulting from the land reform and land restitution programme. It was anticipated that implementation of the Guidelines would begin during 2003.

South Africa hosted the 21st International Cartographic Conference and 12th General Assembly of the International Cartographic Association in Durban in August 2003.

Various issues were discussed under the theme *Cartographic Renaissance*. These included:
- challenges and solutions of geographical data-capturing for developing countries
- spatial data-sharing for a developing world
- organisational and policy issues for sustainable development
- applied cartography and the Geographic Information System in development programmes and projects, showing development spatially.

The process of monitoring and evaluating Spatial Development Frameworks (SDFs) developed at municipal level in terms of the relevant legislation, will gain speed with the promulgation of the Land-Use Management Bill. During 2002, an investigation into capacity and information gaps at both provincial and local government level was conducted. Investigations into the status quo of the SDFs were also undertaken. The results of these investigations were expected in 2003.

The Land-Use Management Bill proposes a set of directive principles to guide land-use management practices in the country. It aims to establish standards and tools for effective decision-making in land development processes.

The Spatial Information Bill provides for greater access to spatial information, standards to enhance interoperability, and the institutional framework to govern and regulate the sector.

During 2002, additional consultative workshops were held. The Chief Directorate undertook a study to determine whether provincial and local government departments have adequate access to spatial information as well as the capacity to compile SDFs as required by the Land-Use Management Bill. The results of the study will enable the Chief Directorate to determine how best to assist provincial and local government departments to compile SDFs.

To improve and facilitate access to spatial information, the Spatial Data Discovery Facility (SDDF) has been maintained and expanded to link 22 nodes. It also contains information concerning approximately 3 259 spatial data sets, an increase of 1 980 records, through the web. The Council for Scientific and Industrial Research Environmentek and the Demarcation Board are in the process of creating nodes and will populate them with more records. The Spatial Information Bill, when enacted, will encourage more data custodians to capture metadata, thus creating the critical mass neccessary for the SDDF to become the one-stop portal for geospatial metadata.

Agriculture

The National Spatial Information Framework, in conjunction with the South African Bureau of Standards (SABS), is developing four standards. These include the Minimum Data Content of the Framework Data and the Unique Feature Identification Standard. A test bed will be developed to establish guidelines for the implementation of the Unique Feature Identification Standard. The Land Cover Classification Standard has been completed and submitted to the SABS for comment.

The Deeds Registry of the Department of Land Affairs has a proud record that goes back to the preservation of land records on paper since 1666. With the rapid increase in the popularity of the Internet as a global information tool, the Deeds Office recognised an opportunity to expand its clients to include the Internet browser. The Chief Registrar of Deeds developed a less-expensive method of giving the public access to deeds registration information called *DeedsWeb*.

With *DeedsWeb*, any person with the necessary web-browser software can access the Deeds Office database and obtain up-to-date registration information upon payment of the prescribed fee. DeedsWeb has many advantages for service delivery and has the potential for generating additional revenue for the Deeds Registration Trading Account.

A characteristic of DeedsWeb is that it paved the way for an electronic network that will ultimately also be used by the Department's proposed electronic Deeds Registration System (e-DRS). The e-DRS will provide a revolutionary method for electronically lodging, processing and registering statutory land rights as well as full ownership of land (freehold).

This System will primarily benefit previously disadvantaged sectors of the community living in rural areas, informal settlements or low-cost housing schemes. Deeds Offices have maintained their service delivery record by keeping the turnaround time for deeds from lodgement to registration at an average of 10 days in spite of the annual increase in lodge-ments.

Since the launch of *DeedsWeb* in December 2001, some 14 227 requests were lodged through the service during March 2003 alone.

The functionalities on DeedsWeb have been expanded to include requests for transfers, bulk searches and billing information.

To prevent fraudulent subsidy claims being submitted by persons claiming to be first home-owners, the Department of Housing supplied this Chief Directorate with 2 182 454 names for verification against 6 153 222 registered properties on *DeedsWeb*.

Land-reform implementation, management and co-ordination

The Chief Directorate: Land Reform Implementation Management and Co-ordination is located in the Branch: Land and Tenure Reform.

The Chief Directorate's aim is the actual delivery of land and tenure reform. This is primarily done through nine provincial Land Reform Offices and 36 operational regions (district and/or satellite Land Reform Offices).

Important policy and systems developments that have enhanced delivery and will further broaden its scope are the following:

- The approval of version seven of the Grants and Services Document that regulates the use of grants. This version enables spending against LRAD structures.
- Financial and responsibility management delegations in terms of the Provision of Land and Assistance Act, 1993 (Act 126 of 1993), as well as the related structures for project assessment and approval at district and provincial level, which were finalised in 2001.
- The LRAD planning agreement with the Land Bank in August 2001.

In August 2001, the Department entered into an agency agreement with the Land Bank for the implementation of the LRAD, particularly for projects with a loan component.

The LRAD Programme was officially launched by the Minister of Agriculture and Land Affairs at Nkomazi in Mpumalanga in August 2001 and paved the way for implementation in other provinces.

The Nkomazi Project involved 241 LRAD grant beneficiaries. A sugar-cane-growing project at Nkomazi, where the participants had harvested their crop of sugar cane after a year of production, made gross earnings of about R100 000, far more than the R65 000 they had planned to earn. The main objective of the LRAD, in line with the Department's mission to

South Africa Yearbook 2003/04

provide access to land and to extend land rights to the previously disadvantaged communities, is to redistribute white-owned agricultural land to black people.

By March 2003, progress was being made in resolving cases in KwaZulu-Natal and Mpumalanga, where the majority of labour tenants are found. This is not only being achieved in terms of provision of land, but also by ensuring that the land is used productively to improve the quality of life of the labour tenants.

The Glenbella Project in Estcourt, KwaZulu-Natal, benefits 59 households who have received 800 ha of land. This land is being utilised for small-scale farming and ecotourism, with the assistance of the farm-owner who serves as a mentor for the emerging farmers.

In Mpumalanga, a number of labour tenants are involved in serious agricultural production. The Inkululeko project in Langverwacht, Wakkerstroom, owned by four families who were previously labour tenants, involves intensive maize production and livestock farming. They are not only producing for subsistence purposes but have also been able to produce a surplus which they are selling to a number of secure markets.

In the Piet Retief area, also in Mpumalanga, another labour-tenant project called Khubedu boasts about 58 families who are also producing a surplus of maize and beans.

From August 2001 until December 2002, the Department transferred a total of 295 024 ha to 140 227 beneficiaries.

During the first quarter of 2002/03, the Department transferred 214 farms through the LRAD programme, yielding 185 609 ha to 6 769 beneficiaries. In total, 8 139 ha were transferred to previously disadvantaged beneficiaries, including labour tenants.

Land-reform systems and support services

The objectives of the Land and Tenure Reform Programme are:
- increased sustainable land-use
- better access to land-administration services
- reaching land-redistribution targets
- decrease in State-owned land
- increased State-land vesting
- increased security of land tenure.

The Communal Land Rights Bill was expected to be finalised by the end of 2003. The Bill aims not only to ensure ownership of assets by families in rural areas, but also to encourage small-scale and co-operative agricultural production, thereby improving food security.

Total number of properties on the Deeds Registration System Database

Deeds Office	Township erven	Scheme units	Agricultural holdings	Portions of farms	Total
Pretoria	1 787 556	172 272	47 486	200 418	2 207 732
Cape Town	1 576 029	143 405	Nil	136 202	1 855 636
Johannesburg	906 318	104 449	Nil	Nil	1 010 767
Pietermaritzburg	814 433	123 640	Nil	92 268	1 030 241
Bloemfontein	450 302	19 848	6 992	59 661	536 803
Kimberley	84 868	651	866	4 782	91 167
King William's Town	154 732	5 769	Nil	11 541	172 042
Vryburg	71 712	181	4 005	11 373	87 271
Umtata*	61 235	18	Nil	115	61 368
Total 2002/03	5 907 185	570 133	59 346	516 360	7 053 027
Total 2001/02	5 707 437	550 404	59 080	514 837	6 831 758

* Database not complete

Source: Department of Land Affairs website

Commission on the Restitution of Land Rights

In 1995, the Commission on the Restitution of Land Rights was established in terms of the Restitution Act, 1994 (Act 22 of 1994), which aims to:
- provide equitable redress and restoration to victims of dispossessions, particularly the landless and the poor
- contribute towards the equitable redistribution of land in South Africa
- promote reconciliation through the restitution process
- facilitate development initiatives by bringing together all relevant stakeholders, especially provincial governments and municipalities.

Initially, the Commission adopted a judicial approach to the processing of more than 68 000 claims, which meant that all claims would be referred to the specialised Land Claims Court for adjudication. It soon became clear that the court-driven process was antagonistic and painstakingly slow.

Amendments made to the Act in 1999 gave powers to the Minister of Agriculture and Land Affairs to make awards based on negotiated settlement agreements. This administrative approach has resulted in a phenomenal and exponential increase in the number of claims settled to date.

By 2002, approximately 68 000 claims had been lodged, of which 72% were urban and 28% rural. A total of 36 489 claims had been settled, involving about 85 000 households. Urban claims mostly involved financial compensation for victims of forced removals; the total compensation made by December 2002 was R1,2 billion. For rural claimants, the restitution mainly takes the form of restoration of land, and by December 2002, approximately 571 232 ha had been restored at a cost of approximately R442 million.

The protracted and contentious claim of Mangethe in KwaZulu-Natal, involving 199 households, was settled out of court.

The Khumalo land-claim in KwaZulu-Natal saw more than 7 292 ha restored to 250 households, who will use the land for producing their own food, grazing and housing. About 500 ha of this land will be used for game-farming where the claimants are key stakeholders.

In Gauteng and the North West, rural claims that have been settled include Koppieskraal, Byl, Concordia, Holgat, Khaukwe, Walmansdal, Mooiland, Zamenskomst, Kleinwain and Rama.

In the Eastern Cape, nine rural claims in Keiskammahoek, as well as Luswazi and Mankaku near Kokstad have been settled. The claimants decided to put the restitution award towards development projects, including agriculture, forestry, infrastructure and rural livelihood projects. The municipalities of Amatole and Amahlati are playing a central role in the implementation of these projects.

In the Northern Cape and Free State, the rural claims settled include Komani San, Palmietfontein, Herschel, Andriesfontein and Dakpoort. The settlement of the Komani San community land-claim was a highlight and breakthrough in 2003, after protracted negotiations between South African National Parks (SANParks), the San community and other State departments.

Some 30 000 ha of the Kalahari National Park was transferred to the community. SANParks has embraced the principle of the involvement of the new land-owners in the sustainable management of the Park.

In Mpumalanga, land-claims settled included Bakoni baPetla and Botshabelo, while in Limpopo it was Dzwerani in Giyani.

Some of the challenges faced in processing the rural claims included difficulty in obtaining relevant documentation and information; unresolved disputes; unregistered and unsurveyed land rights; and poor infrastructure, which often hampered accessibility.

The Commission is intent on meeting the President's directive that all claims should be resolved by 2005.

South Africa Yearbook 2003/04

Acknowledgements

Agricultural Research Council
Department of Agriculture
Department of Land Affairs
Land Bank
National Agricultural Marketing Council
www.gov.za

Suggested reading

African Farm Management Conference (1998: Stellenbosch, South Africa) *Farm and Farmer Organisation for Sustainable Agriculture in Africa*, 26 – 30 January 1998, Stellenbosch, South Africa.
Agriculture in South Africa. 5th ed. Johannesburg: Chris van Rensburg, 1994.
Agricultural Land Reform in South Africa: Policies, Markets and Mechanisms. Cape Town: Oxford University Press,1996.
Auerbach, R.M.B. *Design for Participation in Ecologically Sound Management of South Africa's Mlazi River Catchment*. Wageningen: Landbouwuniversiteit, 1999.
Bundy, C. *Rise and Fall of the South African Peasantry*. 2nd ed. Cape Town: David Philip, 1988.
Compiled by Ntsekhe, W.P. and Farrell, J. *The Conservation Ideal: The Fourth Decade: Being the SARCCUS Record for the Period 1981 to 1990*. Pretoria: SARCCUS, 1998.
Cross, C.R. and Haines, R.J. eds. *Towards Freehold: Options for Land Development in South Africa's Black Rural Areas*. Cape Town: Juta, 1988.
De Klerk, M. ed. *Harvest of Discontent: The Land Question in South Africa*. Cape Town: Institute for a Democratic South Africa, 1991.
Devereux, S. and Maxwell, S. eds. *Food Security in Sub-Saharan Africa*. Pietermaritzburg: University of Natal Press, 2003.
De Villiers, B. ed. *Land Claims and National Parks*. Pretoria: HSRC, 1999.
Environmental Development Agency. *People's Farming Workbook*. 3rd revised ed. Cape Town: David Philip, 1999.
Employment Trends in Agriculture in South Africa/Statistics South Africa and National Department of Agriculture. Pretoria: Stats SA, 2000.
Jeeves, A.H. and Crush, J. eds. *White Farms, Black Labour: The State and Agrarian Change in Southern Africa, 1910 – 1950*. Pietermaritzburg: University of Natal Press, 1997.
Jiggins, J. *Breaking New Ground: Options for Agricultural Extension and Development in South Africa*/Janice Jiggins. Johannesburg, South Africa: Land and Agriculture Policy Centre, 1997.
Johnson, R.W. *Farmers and Farm Workers in KwaZulu-Natal: Employment Conditions, Labour Tenancy, Land Reform, Attitudes and Relationships*. R.W. Johnson and L. Schlemmer. Johannesburg: Helen Suzman Foundation, 1998.
Johnson, R.W. and Schlemmer, L. *Attitudes and Relationships*. Johannesburg: Helen Suzman Foundation, 1998.
Keegan, T.J. *Facing the Storm: Portraits of Black Lives in Rural South Africa*. Cape Town: David Philip, 1988.
Kirsten, J., van Zyl, J. and Vink, N. *The Agricultural Democratisation of South Africa*. Project co-ordinators: Cape Town: Published for Africa Institute for Policy Analysis and Economic Integration by Francolin Publishers., 1998.
Kok, P. and Pietersen, J. *Agriculture and Agroprocessing*. Pretoria: Human Sciences Research Council (HSRC), 2000.
Kruger E. *Farmer to Farmer: A Story of Innovation and Solidarity*. Scottsville: Farmer Support Group, University of Natal, 1998.
Land Reform and Agrarian Change in Southern Africa: An occasional paper series. Bellville, RSA: University of the Western Cape. No. 10, 12(1999).
Letsoabo, E.M. *Land Reform in South Africa: A Black Perspective*. Johannesburg: Skotaville, 1987.
Levin R. and Weiner, D. eds. *Community Perspectives on Land and Agrarian Reform in South Africa*. Chicago: MacArthur Foundation, 1994.
Marcus, T. *Commercial Agriculture in South Africa: Modernising Super Exploitation*. London: Zed Books, 1989.
Marcus, T., Eales, K. and Wildschut, A. *Land Demand in the New South Africa*. University of Natal: Indicator Press, 1996.

Agriculture

Meer, S. ed. *Women, Land and Authority: Perspectives from South Africa.* Cape Town: David Philip in association with the National Land Committee, 1997.

Nieuwoudt, L. and Groenewald J., eds. *The Challenge of Change: Agriculture, Land and the South African Economy.* Pietermaritzburg: University of Natal Press, 2003.

Nemutanzhela, T. *Ploughing Amongst the Stones: The Story of 'Betterment' in the Zoutpansberg 1939 – 1944.* Johannesburg: Ravan Press, 1999.

Palmer, R. *Contested Land in Southern and Eastern Africa: A Literature Survey.* London: Oxfam, 1997.

People's Farming Workbook. 2nd ed. Cape Town: Environmental and Development Agency Trust, 1998.

People's Farming Workbook. Cape Town: David Philip, 1995.

People's Farming Workbook. 2nd ed. Cape Town: David Philip for Environmental Development Agency Trust, 1998.

Southey, J. *Footprints in the Karoo: A Story of Farming Life.* Johannesburg: Jonathan Ball, 1990.

Tainton, N, ed. *Pasture Management in South Africa.* Pietermaritzburg: University of Natal Press, 2000.

The Dynamics of the South African Export Basket. Compiled by the Department of Economic Research and Development, Industrial Development Corporation of South Africa (IDC), Ltd. Sandton, RSA, 1996.

The Nutritional Content of South African Beef. Compiled by H.C. Schönfeldt et al. – Pretoria: South African Meat Board, 1996.

Thomson, J. *Genes for Africa.* Cape Town: UCT Press, 2002.

Van der Walt, A.J. *Land Reform and the Future of Land Ownership in South Africa.* Cape Town: Juta, 1991.

Van Onselen, C. *The Seed is Mine: The Life of Kas Maine: A South African Sharecropper, 1894 – 1985.* Cape Town: David Philip, 1996.

Van Rooyen, J., Groenewald J. and Kirsten, J eds. *Agricultural Policy Reform in South Africa.* Pretoria: University of Pretoria, 1998.

Wethli, E. *The South African Chicken Book: How to Start a Small Business Keeping Chickens.* Berold, R. ed; illustrator: Gilbert, L. Kenwyn, RSA: Juta, 1999.

Winburg, M. *Back to the Land.* Johannesburg: Porcupine Press, 1996.

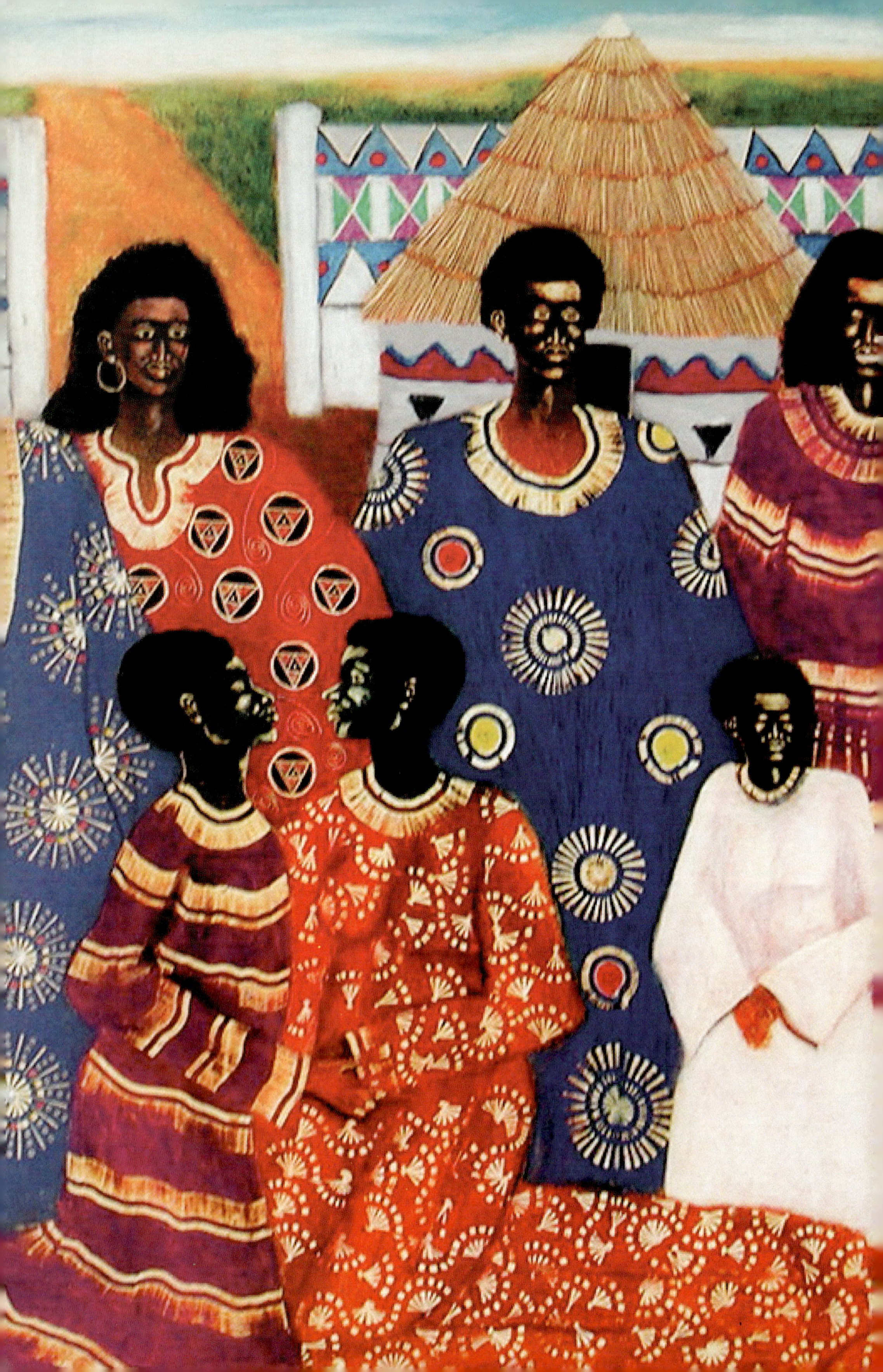

chapter 5

Arts and culture

The Department of Arts and Culture deals with matters pertaining to arts and culture, develops the economic potential in cultural industries, alleviates poverty through job creation, takes part in the strategy to brand South Africa as a sought-after tourism destination, and renders State archive and heraldic services at national level.

Policy and legislation

The Council of Culture Ministers makes important decisions on policy matters of national impact, and consists of the Minister and Deputy Minister of Arts, Culture, Science and Technology and those members of provincial executive councils responsible for arts and culture.

Funding

Since the turn of the century, the budget for the Department of Arts and Culture has seen an annual growth rate of 18,3%. Institutions are seen as key partners in unlocking creativity and implementing arts policy.

For the next three-year financial cycle, the Department is dedicating considerable resources to this sector. The allocation for the 2003/04 financial year was R30 million,

◀ *The Sad Farewell* by KwaZulu-Natal artist, S'fiso ka Mkame. The Department of Arts and Culture supports a number of projects to promote the visual arts.

the allocation for the 2004/05 financial year is R45 million, and in the 2005/06 financial year, the budget is expected to be R60 million.

The Department is responsible for 27 public entities including museums, art galleries, the National Zoological Gardens, the National Archives and the six playhouses.

The Department's capital-works budget has grown by more than 100%, from R81,5 million in 2002/03 to R168,05 million in 2003/04. Examples of how this money is spent and the investments made in the Department's institutions included R7,8 million for the Qunu component of the Nelson Mandela Museum; R6,3 million to the Voortrekker Museum; R5,5 million to the Northern Flagship Institution; R3,1 million to the National Museum; and R17 million to the Robben Island Museum, R4,5 million of which was allocated to the long-term project of repairing the breakwater wall on the Island.

National symbols

National anthem

The national anthem of South Africa is a combined version of *Nkosi Sikelel' iAfrika* and *The Call of South Africa* (*Die Stem van Suid-Afrika*) and is played at all State occasions. *The Call of South Africa* was written by C.J. Langenhoven in May 1918. The music was composed by the Rev. M.L. de Villiers in 1921. *Nkosi Sikelel' iAfrika* was composed in 1897 by Enoch Sontonga, a Methodist mission school teacher.

The words of the first stanza were originally written in isiXhosa as a hymn.

Seven additional stanzas in isiXhosa were later added by the poet Samuel Mqhayi. It became a popular church hymn that was later adopted as an anthem at political meetings. It has been translated into most of South Africa's official languages.

National flag

The national flag of the Republic of South Africa was brought into use on Freedom Day, 27 April 1994. The design and colours are a synopsis of the principal elements of the country's flag history.

The central design of the flag, beginning at the flag-pole in a 'V' form and flowing into a single horizontal band to the outer edge of the fly, can be interpreted as the convergence of diverse elements within South African society, taking the road ahead in unity. The flag was designed by the State Herald.

When the flag is displayed vertically against a wall, the red band should be to the left of the viewer with the hoist or the cord seam at the top. When it is displayed horizontally, the hoist should be to the left of the viewer and the red band at the top. When the flag is displayed next to or behind the speaker at a meeting, it must be placed to the speaker's right. When it is placed elsewhere in the meeting place, it should be to the right of the audience.

National coat of arms

South Africa's coat of arms was launched on Freedom Day, 27 April 2000.

A central image of the coat of arms is the well-known secretary bird with its uplifted wings. Above the bird is the rising sun, a force that gives life while representing the flight of darkness and the triumph of discovery, knowledge and understanding of things that have been hidden, and illuminating the new life that is coming into being. Below the bird is the protea, an indigenous flower of South Africa, which represents beauty, the aesthetic harmony of all its cultures, and South Africa flowering as a nation. The ears of wheat are emblems of the fertility of the land, while the tusks of the African elephant, reproduced in pairs to represent men and women, symbolise wisdom, steadfastness and strength.

At the centre stands a shield, which signifies the protection of South Africans from one generation to the next. Above it, repose a spear and a *knobkierie*. Together, they assert the defence of peace rather than a posture of war. This shield of peace, which also suggests an African drum, conveys the message of a people imbued with a love of culture. Its upper part is a shield being imaginatively represented by the protea.

Contained within the shield are some of the earliest representations of humanity in the world. Those depicted were the very first inhabitants of the land, namely the Khoisan people. These figures are derived from images on the Linton Stone, a world-famous example of South African rock art. The motto of the coat of arms, !Ke e:/xarra//ke, written in the Khoisan language of the /Xam people, means 'diverse people unite' or 'people who are different joining together'.

National orders

The new national orders were unveiled by President Thabo Mbeki on 27 April 2002, at the Freedom Day celebrations in Bloemfontein, Free State. These national orders are the highest awards that the country can bestow on individual South Africans and eminent foreign leaders and personalities.

The Order of Mapungubwe is awarded to South African citizens for excellence and exceptional achievement. It reflects the ancient Kingdom of Mapungubwe, which existed in the northern corner of South Africa a millennium ago.

The Order of the Baobab is awarded to South African citizens for distinguished service of above and beyond the ordinary call of duty. It is awarded for exceptional contribu-

The national anthem

Nkosi sikelel' iAfrika
Maluphakanyisw' uphondo lwayo,
Yizwa imithandazo yethu,
Nkosi sikelela, thina lusapho lwayo.

Morena boloka setjhaba sa heso,
O fedise dintwa le matshwenyeho,
O se boloke, O se boloke setjhaba
sa heso,
Setjhaba sa South Afrika –
South Afrika.

Uit die blou van onse hemel,
Uit die diepte van ons see,
Oor ons ewige gebergtes,
Waar die kranse antwoord gee,

Sounds the call to come together,
And united we shall stand,
Let us live and strive for freedom,
In South Africa our land.

tions towards building democracy and human rights, nation-building and community service, and peace and security.

The Baobab tree is known throughout Africa, and its many legends and mysteries represent the spirituality of the South African nation. It is an essential meeting place for communities and plays an important role in the health of the people because of its medicinal properties.

The Order of the Companions of O.R. Tambo is awarded to Heads of State and other personalities for promoting peace, co-operation and friendship towards South Africa.

O.R. Tambo was a great humanitarian, a selfless internationalist and a committed African, who, among others, developed a movement of solidarity against racism and apartheid throughout the world.

In September 2003, the Cabinet approved a set of additional national orders. The new orders will honour individuals who have rendered distinguished service for democracy and human rights (Order of Luthuli); those who have shown outstanding bravery in the face of great danger (Mendi Decoration for Bravery); and for excellence in the fields of arts, culture, literature, music, journalism and/or sport (Order of Ikhamanga).

National symbols
South Africa's national symbols are:
- National animal: springbuck
- National bird: blue crane
- National fish: galjoen
- National flower: king protea
- National tree: real yellowwood.

Arts and culture organisations

National Heritage Council
The National Heritage Council Act, 1999 (Act 11 of 1999), established a framework and institution that co-ordinate the heritage sector, including archives, museums, heritage resources, geographical names and libraries.

In addition to funding projects in these areas, the Council will serve as a policy advisory body to the Minister, lobby for and raise additional funding, determine strategy and promote international liaison.

The Council was expected to be established during the 2003/04 financial year.

South African Heritage Resources Agency (SAHRA)
The National Heritage Resources Act, 1999 (Act 25 of 1999), established SAHRA, which replaced the National Monuments Council. This body manages the heritage resources of the country in co-operation with similar new provincial agencies, by implementing legislation in line with international trends in the heritage resources field.

South African Geographical Names Council (SAGNC)
The SAGNC is an advisory body appointed by the Minister of Arts, Culture, Science and Technology in terms of the South African Geographical Names Council Act, 1998 (Act 118 of 1998). The Council advises the Minister on the transformation and standardisation of official geographical names in South Africa.

The objectives of the SAGNC are to:
- facilitate the establishment of provincial geographical names committees
- ensure the standardisation, transformation and implementation of geographical names
- promote the use of standardised South African geographical names at international level
- promote awareness of the economic and social benefits of the standardisation of geographical names.

The Council has jurisdiction over all names of geographical features and entities falling within the territories over which the South African Government has sovereignty or jurisdiction acquired by treaty.

The following principles are adhered to:

National symbols and orders

National bird: blue crane

National fish: galjoen

National animal: springbuck

National tree: real yellowwood

National flower: king protea

The Order of the Baobab

The Order of Mapungubwe

The Order of the Companions of O.R. Tambo

The Order of Luthuli

The Mendi Decoration for Bravery

The Order of Ikhamanga

- each individual feature entity should have only one official name
- the following types of geographical names should generally be avoided:
  - approved names of places elsewhere in South Africa
  - names of places in other countries, and names of countries
  - names that are blasphemous, indecent, offensive, vulgar, unaesthetic or embarrassing
  - names that are discriminatory or derogatory with regard to race, colour, creed, gender, political affiliation or other social factors
  - names consisting of personal names without a generic element
  - names that may be regarded as an advertisement for a particular product, service or firm
  - names of living persons.

The Council is reviewing names that have not previously been submitted for approval. Names that appear to have racist connotations have been referred to relevant authorities and communities for comment and suggested substitutes.

As the national body, the SAGNC has been assigned, among its duties, to facilitate the establishment of Provincial Geographical Names Committees (PGNCs). According to the Act, the Council must set guidelines for the operation of PGNCs and municipalities in their respective areas of jurisdiction.

Publications of the Council are available on the departmental website under Heritage Chief Directorate. Applications for approval of a changed or new name can also be processed online by visiting *www.dac.gov.za*.

National Arts Council (NAC)

The responsibilities of the NAC of South Africa are to develop, promote and support the arts.

Before 2002, the NAC operated mainly as a funding organisation. At the beginning of 2003, a section dealing specifically with policy and strategy was established. The NAC is now responsible for policy research and advice to the Minister on arts policy matters.

During 2003, government increased its grant to the NAC to enable the organisation to award sustained grants to the Performing Arts Companies (PACs) and institutions. Major companies were awarded grants over a period of three years. This enabled the NAC to make more funds available for regular project funding.

The budget of the NAC has increased to R42 million over the past two years.

Strategic projects and initiatives were also identified. These include projects in crafts, literature, theatre and dance.

In addition, the NAC has formed strategic partnerships with provincial and local authorities involved in arts and culture and organisations such as Create SA, the South African Broadcasting Corporation (SABC), Business Arts South Africa (BASA), the National Film and Video Foundation (NFVF), the Arts and Culture Trust (ACT) and government departments with similar interests and priorities.

In the international sphere, the NAC runs the South African-Norwegian Education and Music Education Programme which is jointly financed by the Norwegian and the South African Governments. There are now possibilities for other international jointly funded projects. Networking also takes place through the International Federation of Arts Councils and Culture Agencies.

The NAC has moved away from being an arts bank to a truly supportive, developmental and policy-making body engaged in arts debates and dialogue. In the coming years, the NAC will strengthen this role while striving at the same time to promote excellence and creativity.

Performing Arts Companies

The PACs, currently established in terms of Section 21 of the Companies Act, 1973 (Act 61 of 1973), assist in creating a sustainable

performing arts industry based on access, excellence, diversity and redress. They encourage the development of the full range of performing arts. The PACs include the:
- State Theatre (Pretoria)
- Playhouse Company (Durban)
- ArtsCape (Cape Town)
- Market Theatre (Johannesburg)
- Windybrow Theatre (Johannesburg)
- Performing Arts Council of the Free State (Bloemfontein).

The total budget for PACs is approximately R80 million per annum.

The Department has earmarked R14 million to playhouses for capital works in 2003/04.

Business Arts South Africa

BASA was launched in 1997 as a joint initiative between the Government, through the Department of Arts and Culture, and the business sector, to assist in securing the future of the arts industry. BASA's aim is to promote and encourage sustainable partnerships between the business and the arts sectors to their mutual benefit and that of the community at large. With funding from the Government, BASA has introduced what was initially called a 'matching grant scheme', now known as the 'supporting grant scheme', whereby additional funds are made available to support the sponsorships of arts organisations or events.

This creates an incentive for business to sponsor the arts, on the basis of identifying strategic marketing or promotional opportunities through such sponsorship. It also provides the arts sector with an opportunity to approach sponsors on the basis of potential benefits to their business. In addition, BASA is actively seeking to lift the profile of the arts in South Africa, and to develop business skills within the arts community to demonstrate the real value for the sponsor and to encourage business to retain its involvement.

BASA is a member of the International Network of Business Arts Associations, linking with similar organisations internationally.

Business Day continues to partner BASA in its annual awards which acknowledge the importance of private sponsorships in the development of the arts.

Arts and Culture Trust

ACT was launched in October 1994 to finance, and manage funding for, the arts in South Africa. The Trust, with former President Nelson Mandela as its chief patron, has Nedbank, Sun International, the Ministry of Arts, Culture, Science and Technology, Vodacom, and the Dutch Government as its major funders. The Trust also seeks to build a better arts and culture dispensation through proactive initiatives such as:
- forums, conferences and campaigns around strategic issues, such as support for the arts through the National Lottery
- the annual ACT Awards, which recognise the important contributions of role-players such as administrators, journalists and educators
- establishing mutually beneficial relationships between itself and the arts and culture community as part of its *Culture-Helping-Culture* Campaign.

Other cultural organisations

There have always been a number of non-governmental organisations (NGOs) and community-based cultural organisations operating in South Africa. The majority of these organisations have never received State support. Since March 1996, however, the emphasis in funding has shifted to assisting organisations, communities and projects which were previously not considered for funding.

Freedom Day on 27 April 2004 will be a special occasion as it will mark 10 years of democracy in South Africa. In planning for this national celebration, the Department of Arts and Culture has been allocated an amount of R80 million, spread over two financial years.

Arts and culture initiatives

The Legacy Project

Monuments, museums, plaques, outdoor art, heritage trails and other symbolic representations create visible reminders of, and commemorate, the many aspects of South Africa's past.

The Legacy Project was approved by the Cabinet as a mechanism to establish commemorative structures, that will be based on a coherent set of principles and criteria. The Legacy Project principles were developed taking into consideration the need for redress, consultation with affected parties, environmental sensitivity and linking heritage with economic development. In essence, the Legacy Project seeks to maintain coherence in aligning the resources and expertise of Government to establish a system to acknowledge and honour a largely neglected part of South Africa's heritage. At the same time, it seeks to change the nature of commemoration by creating spaces that are people-friendly and accessible. The Legacy Project includes the:

- Women's Monument: A monument to commemorate the contribution of the women of South Africa to the struggle for freedom was unveiled by President Thabo Mbeki on 9 August 2000 at the Union Buildings in Pretoria. The ceremony marked the day, in 1956, when 20 000 women marched to the Union Buildings to protest against the Government's pass laws.
- Chief Albert Luthuli Legacy Project: The Department is restoring the home of Chief Albert Luthuli in Stanger, KwaZulu-Natal, to pay homage to South Africa's first Nobel Peace Prize winner. The house will become a declared cultural institution.
- Battle of Blood River/Ncome Project: Following the unveiling of the Ncome Monument on 16 December 1998, the Ncome Museum was opened on 26 November 1999.
- Samora Machel Project: The Samora Machel Monument in Mbuzini, Mpumalanga was unveiled on 19 January 1999.
- Nelson Mandela Museum: The Museum was opened on 11 February 2000. It is being developed as a single component comprising three elements, namely a museum in Umtata, a youth centre at Qunu and a visitors' centre in Mvezo, where the former President was born. Thanks to donations, the scheme has mushroomed into a series of halls, shops and gardens.
- Constitution Hill Project: The Old Fort Prison in Hillbrow, Johannesburg, is being developed into a multidimensional and multi-purpose precinct that will house the Constitutional Court and accommodate various constitutional commissions. The project was expected to be completed in 2003.
- Khoisan Project: Consultation with relevant role-players at national, provincial and local level has been initiated to promote and protect the Khoisan heritage.
- Freedom Park Project: Construction of the Freedom Park Project, a memorial to the anti-apartheid struggle to be built on Salvokop in Pretoria, began in 2002, and is scheduled for completion in time for the 10th anniversary of the first democratic election on 27 April 2004. The following physical elements are proposed: a garden of remembrance, memorial, museum and a number of commercial facilities. Some R50 million was allocated to the Freedom Park Project in 2002/03. The Project was launched by President Mbeki on 16 June 2002.

Education and training in arts and culture

Training is critical for the development of arts and culture, to achieve both the developmental and economic potential of the sector. The sector needs to absorb the new policy environment set out in the South African

Qualifications Authority Act, 1995 (Act 58 of 1995), and the Skills Development Act, 1998 (Act 97 of 1998), which fall within the ambit of the National Qualifications Framework (NQF). Training also needs to be market-driven and in line with current thinking on human resource development.

Strategic objectives include:
- ensuring the continued provision of quality, accredited arts education and training by the non-formal sector and community arts centres
- developing the capacity of people with disabilities to participate more effectively in the arts
- developing a range of sector-specific programmes and curricula in arts, culture and heritage management accredited under the NQF, and a range of new cultural management skills directly relevant to the challenges facing the sector
- bringing together people committed to effective teacher-training in the arts and to develop a sectoral plan of action to address challenges, career paths and employment opportunities
- curriculum development and accreditation.

The Department of Arts and Culture, in partnership with the Department of Labour and the Media, Advertising, Publishing, Printing, Packaging Sector Education Training Authority, (MAPPPSETA), will embark on a R117-million skills-training programme for the creative industries, including crafts, film, music and live events, over the next three years.

Those eligible for the Create SA Project include freelance or self-employed workers in the creative industries, as well as new entrants into the labour market, from school-leavers to the unemployed. By 2005, it is expected that 6 000 people from around the country would have benefited from learnerships and skills programmes as part of Create SA.

The Create SA Project has registered 14 learnerships and 12 skills programmes. Some of the work-based and work-relevant national qualifications being developed, registered and implemented by Create SA include national certificates in craft production, craft micro-enterprise, film and video production and music technology.

More information is available at *www.createsa.org.za*.

The new education policy reflects a clear commitment to introduce effective and transformed education in arts and culture, to learners in the formal and non-formal sectors, as a fundamental part of lifelong learning. The *White Paper on Arts, Culture and Heritage* commits the Department to play a significant facilitative role in arts and culture education and training. A subdirectorate has been established to manage this process.

Cultural tourism

Cultural tourism is one of the most rapidly growing sectors of the multibillion-Rand international tourism industry, and is an area in which South Africa is well-placed to compete. Professional and innovative museums, galleries and theatres are key attractions for cultural tourists. Based on the success of crafts and cultural projects, the Department will spend R95 million of poverty-alleviation funding towards this end over the next few years.

A 1997 survey into cultural-tourism activities in three Spatial Development Initiatives (SDIs) yielded a wealth of information. The survey identified areas in which government intervention could help cultural workers to benefit from such tourism.

The research suggested the Lubombo, Wild Coast and Maputo Corridor SDIs as focus areas.

Cultural festivals, African-cuisine projects, cultural villages, heritage routes and storytelling were highlighted as activities that could attract revenue to these areas. Working closely with resorts, national parks and other tourist destinations and attractions, cultural producers, consumers and tourists can be joined together in an economic network.

Cultural villages

Most tourists visiting South Africa are eager to explore the country's cultural diversity. At the same time, an increasing number of local tourists want to learn more about the people they were separated from under apartheid. (See Chapter 21: *Tourism*.)

Various projects around the country offer insight into South Africa's cultural wealth, ranging from traditional dances and rituals in rural areas, to excursions into the urban and township milieux that give South Africa its defining features. These include Khaya Lendaba near Port Elizabeth; the Basotho Cultural Village situated in the QwaQwa Nature Reserve near Harrismith, Free State; the Makhosini Cultural Village and Tourism Initiative in the Valley of Kings at Umgungundlovu in KwaZulu-Natal; Lesedi Cultural Village near Johannesburg; Tlholego in Magaliesburg; the KoMjekejeke Cultural Village north of Pretoria; the Mapoch Ndebele Village in Winterveld, north-west of Pretoria; the Gaabo Motho Cultural Village in Mabopane; the Rainbow Cultural Village west of the Hartbeespoort Dam, North West; Botshabelo in Middelburg, Mpumalanga; and Shangana in Hazyview, Mpumalanga.

The Cultural Industries Growth Strategy

For a number of years, the Department of Arts and Culture has been working with partners such as the Department of Trade and Industry to develop and implement the Cultural Industries Growth Strategy. This Strategy has made meaningful contributions to the lives of thousands of people, while contributing to the growth of the tourism and marketing sectors and enriching South Africa's identity at a local and international level.

The Cabinet has identified cultural industries as economic key growth areas. An amount of R20 million was allocated to cultural industries in 2002/03.

The aim of the Cultural Industries Growth Strategy is to enhance the potential of South African cultural industries to contribute to job and wealth creation. The project began with a research and strategy-development phase, which resulted in detailed analyses of the craft, film and television, music and publishing industries.

The key recommendations were:
- developing education and training opportunities
- increasing local and international demand for cultural products
- encouraging the industries to work together
- generating information
- continuing to raise the profile of the cultural industries in the media and in government departments.

Projects under way include:
- Crafts: By February 2003, the Department of Arts and Culture had, through the Council of Scientific and Industrial Research's (CSIR) craft-development projects and, as part of a macro poverty-alleviation project initiated by the Department, paid out R1 million each to two projects in some of the poorest parts of the Eastern Cape and Free State. A total of R2 million has been invested in the Sekhukune project in the Northern Cape and over R4,5 million has been endowed as part of the Urban Renewal Neighbourhood Branding Project in Gauteng. In addition, the Department supported a R2,3-million craft and cultural-development project in the St Lucia Wetlands, and funded numerous other craft and culture-development projects with spin-off benefits for the community, such as wealth creation and employment opportunities. The CSIR's craft project in the Eastern Cape created some 275 jobs.

Dynamic strategies are being used, and where jobs are not created directly, training is given in such a way that self-employment opportunities are opened up, swelling the capacity of small,

Arts and culture

medium and micro enterprises. By February 2003, the St Lucia project had enabled the training of 692 people.
- Film and television: The film industry has taken the initiative to establish a cluster to collaborate on projects to develop the industry.
- Music: After an investigation by the Music Industry Task Team, the Department identified key priority areas. They are:
  - Developing and/or implementing an effective and enabling legislative framework.
  - Education and training in the music industry. The Department of Arts and Culture is working with the Department of Labour to address this.
  - Investigating the livelihood of the music industry.
  - Promoting and resourcing the music industry.
  - Facilitating the establishment of an export council for the music industry. The project is facilitated by the Music Industry Development Initiative (MIDI) Trust (comprising MIDI, major record companies, independent labels and other stakeholders).
  - Liaising with the Department of Home Affairs to establish a new accreditation system to monitor the activities of foreign artists in the country.

As part of the 40th anniversary of the Organisation of African Unity/Africa Day celebrations, the Department of Arts and Culture hosted the Southern African Development Community (SADC) Multidisciplinary Festival in Pretoria from 18 to 25 May 2003.

The Festival focused on skills development that catered for music, dance, theatre, story-telling, a crafts fair and a creative arts and heritage exhibition. Representatives from SADC countries participated in the Festival.

Performances took place at Church Square and the State Theatre, as well as at shopping malls in Mamelodi and Atteridgeville.

- Ensuring that the needs of the arts sector are incorporated in SETA structures.
- Publishing: The Print Industries Cluster is continuing its strategic work to develop the sector.
- Urban renewal: The Department has designed pilot projects in urban renewal areas such as Alexandra, Cape Town, Port Elizabeth, Pretoria and Durban amounting to R10 million. These projects will promote the economic empowerment of South African artists, sculptors, painters and crafters.
- SETAs: The Department has been integrally involved in mobilising the arts and culture sector to form SETAs according to the Skills Development Act, 1998. This has led to the Department commissioning a sector-skills strategy, and arts and culture being located in the MAPPPSETA.

Arts festivals

The National Arts Festival, held annually in July in Grahamstown, Eastern Cape, is one of the largest and most diverse arts gatherings of its kind staged in Africa, rating favourably with similar international festivals. It showcases southern African talent in all arts disciplines.

There is also growing interest and participation from artists in other African countries and from the rest of the world.

The *Klein Karoo Nasionale Kunstefees* is a vibrant festival for the performing arts, presented mainly, but not exclusively, in Afrikaans. It is held annually in Oudtshoorn, Western Cape, at the end of March. Disciplines include drama, cabaret, and contemporary and classical music.

The Arts Alive International Festival, Johannesburg's annual festival of music, dance, theatre and performance-poetry, was hosted by the city for the 12th time in September 2003.

Heritage reclamation festivals are also emerging at local level in communities destroyed by apartheid such as Sophiatown and Vrededorp (Fietas) in Johannesburg.

Other festivals that attract visitors at both national and international level are Oppikoppi, Calabash, *Aardklop*, The One City Festival, the Awesome Africa Music Festival in Durban, and *Macufe* in Bloemfontein.

The Department of Arts and Culture and the NAC support numerous festivals throughout South Africa, including the North Sea Jazz Festival, Port St Johns Festival, Morgan's Bay Festival and the Grahamstown National Arts Festival.

The Department of Arts and Culture and the Department of Environmental Affairs and Tourism have established a forum of festival directors to maximise tourism opportunities.

Theatre

The performing arts marketed South Africa to overseas audiences most effectively during the 1980s, specifically through theatre and musical productions. As a result, South African theatre is internationally acclaimed as unique and of top-class standard.

The well-known Market Theatre in Johannesburg kept South African theatre alive through the apartheid years. The Market Theatre's reputation is based on its local content productions. A growing number of directors are doing original South African works. A new trend is the establishment of smaller theatres which is making this artform more accessible to South Africans from all walks of life.

Early in 2003, two South Africans, dance choreographer Robyn Orlin and actor Craig Urbani, were nominated for the highly prestigious Laurence Olivier Awards.

Orlin was nominated in the category Outstanding Achievement in Dance and Urbani was nominated in the category Best Performance in a Supporting Role in a Musical or Entertainment.

Music

South African music is characterised by its fusion of diverse musical forms.

South Africa has nurtured the development of an array of distinctive styles of music and it has contributed to music heard on the continent throughout the ages.

These styles range from South African jazz, which describes a range of music from early *marabi*-inspired sounds in the late-1930s and 1940s by bands like the Marry Blackbirds Orchestra, to current performers such as trumpeter Hugh Masekela.

Kwaito music is very popular. It combines elements of rap, reggae, hip-hop and other musical styles into a distinctly South African style. Popular *kwaito* musicians include Arthur Mafokate, Bongo Muffin, TKZee, Mandoza and Mdu.

Music is one of the key cultural industries covered by the Cultural Industrial Growth Strategy report and Government has committed itself to harnessing its potential. In addition to its cultural value, music plays an important economic role in the country, generating significant copyright revenue. Music sales in 2000 had a total retail value of just over R1 billion and provided employment for more than 20 000 people. This figure does not include the number of jobs created through live events.

The Department of Arts and Culture secured funds from the Poverty-Alleviation Fund for Job Creation in the Arts and Culture Industry. *Music in Public Places* is one of the strategies for young artists' development and the promotion of South African music.

The project focuses on live performances and selling South African music in public places such as airports and stations. The project targets emerging artists, who are given the opportunity to perform and sell their

---

In March 2003, the celebrated South African novelist Andre P. Brink won the Commonwealth Writers Prize for Africa for the novel, *The Other Side of Silence*. Previous South African winners include Zakes Mda, Sello Duiker, Nadine Gordimer and J.M. Coetzee.

Arts and culture

products. The Department has also funded the *South African Music Directory*.

The North Sea Jazz Festival secured South Africa's position on the international jazz circuit when it took place for the first time on African soil in March 2001. The North Sea Jazz Festival – Cape Town has a unique programming formulary. With a 50/50 talent split between Africa and the rest of the world, the South African Festival allows for local musicians to take their rightful place alongside international artists.

The ninth South African Music Awards were presented on 5 April 2003 at Sun City in the North West. Mzekezeke won awards for Artist of the Year and Song of the Year. Other winners included:

- Best Selling Release: Revolution
- Best Female Artist: Sibongile Khumalo
- Best Male Artist: Hugh Masekela
- Best Jazz Vocal Album: Linda Kekana
- Best African Pop Album: Mafikizolo.

South African Music Week was introduced to schools across the country for the first time during 2003, as part of government's awareness campaign to promote South Africa's culture and heritage. The Minister of Education, Prof. Kader Asmal, announced at the launch of the 2003 South African Music Week that the Department of Education was considering ways of establishing and funding schools specialising in music and performing arts.

Orchestras

As a means to meet the needs of a rapidly changing funding environment, the Department developed a policy requiring partnerships between local, provincial and national government to support these entities.

In 2002, the first agreement was reached in KwaZulu-Natal, with the orchestra in that province receiving R3 million from the Department of Arts and Culture. In 2003, this partnership was extended to the Western Cape and Gauteng, with agreements to ensure that a total of R9 million was allocated by the Department. Orchestras will be developing training programmes to ensure greater representation and participation by young black South Africans.

Dance

South African dance is unique in its vitality, energy. More and more South African dance companies and individual dancers and choreographers are being invited to perform at festivals throughout Europe, Australia and the United States of America (USA).

Contemporary work ranges from normal preconceptions of movement and performance art or performance theatre to the completely unconventional.

Added to this is the African experience, which includes traditional dance inspired by wedding ceremonies, battles, rituals and the trifles of everyday life.

An informal but highly versatile performance venue in Johannesburg, The Dance Factory, provides a permanent platform for all kinds of dance and movement groups.

The Wits Theatre (attached to the University of the Witwatersrand) is also a popular dance venue. It is home to the annual First National Bank Dance Umbrella, which usually takes place over three weeks from the end of February. It is complemented by workshops and performances by visiting international groups. The festival provides a platform for the full spectrum of southern African contemporary dance.

Only new and indigenous choreography is accepted in the Dance Umbrella and no previous experience is required. The concept has also been launched in Cape Town, Bloemfontein, Durban and Grahamstown.

Started in 1934 as the University of Cape Town Ballet Company, the Cape Town City Ballet is the oldest ballet company in the country. Ninety-nine per cent of the dancers employed by the company are local artists.

South Africa Yearbook 2003/04

Visual arts

The Department of Arts and Culture supports a number of projects that promote the visual arts.

These range from arts publications and women-empowerment programmes to national and international exhibitions and infrastructure funding.

The Department considers the visual arts, crafts and design as integral to arts and culture. In its development of the arts, it is particularly interested in the application of interdisciplinary technology to art.

The Department is currently investigating the establishment of an arts bank. This lending library will loan artwork to government departments and the private sector.

Photography

Various South African photographers have been acclaimed for their art and documentary work. A growing number of South African photographers are producing documentaries, coffee-table books and other material.

National and international photographic salons are held in South Africa annually, and various national awards are bestowed on outstanding local photographers.

Architecture

South Africa has a rich architectural heritage, to which all the cultural groups in the country have contributed. The statutory organisation SAHRA conserves buildings of historical or architectural value. To date, more than 4 000 buildings, sites and other objects (including trees) have been declared national monuments.

Heritage SA is the most important non-profit private organisation that conserves and restores buildings of historical and architectural importance.

An interdepartmental committee has been established in conjunction with the Department of Housing to investigate the role of arts, culture and heritage in the design and delivery of housing.

Rock art

There are many traces of ancient cultures who roamed the country in the distant past. The San people left a priceless and unique collection of Stone Age paintings and engravings in South Africa, the largest in the world. The mountains, especially the Drakensberg range and the Cape mountains, are home to fascinating rock art panels.

Rock engravings are scattered throughout the interior on flat rock surfaces and boulders. The artworks mainly depict hunter-gatherers and their relationship with the animal world, historical events, and interaction with and observation of newcomers encroaching upon their living space. Indigenous people with spears and Nguni cattle; Khoi-Khoin fat-tailed sheep; European settlers on horseback with rifles and wagons; ships; and soldiers in uniform were captured in surprising detail.

On the sandstone canvases are immortalised visions of the artists' spiritual world, depicting complex symbols and metaphors to illustrate the supernatural powers and potency they received from nature.

The oldest dated rock art in South Africa, an engraved stone, was discovered in a living floor some 10 200 years old at the Wonderwerk Cave near Kuruman in the Northern Cape.

The oldest painted stones (6 400 years) were recovered at Boomplaas Cave in the Cango Valley near Oudtshoorn.

Early in 2003, filming of Antjie Krog's book *Country of My Skull* started in Cape Town. The film stars Juliette Binoche and Samuel L. Jackson and is directed by John Boorman.

The book, which features Krog's experiences as a journalist reporting on the Truth and Reconciliation Commission, sold more than 14 000 copies in 10 months.

The screenplay was written by the South African-born writer Ann Peacock.

Arts and culture

Three painted stones were also found at the Klasies River Caves, which yielded the second-oldest stone, dating back 3 900 years.

The Department of Arts and Culture is supporting a number of related projects, including a rock heritage project in Clanwilliam in the Western Cape.

Crafts

The crafts industry in South Africa employs about one million people. The crafts they produce are exported all over the world.

The development of South Africa's crafts industry is an ongoing priority for government through the Department of Arts and Culture. There are numerous role-players involved in various initiatives to develop this sector.

The National Crafts Development Initiative, spearheaded by the NAC and supported by several national bodies, is one such example, providing a platform for growing the local market by staging craft fairs at various levels.

The work of various bodies and institutions can be categorised into areas such as training, marketing, information provision, supply of raw material, co-ordination, and funding or financing.

The Department, in partnership with other government departments and role-players, aims to address the co-ordination of the sector, develop a national strategy for craft financing, marketing and development, and find a suitable vehicle to develop and grow exports of South African craft products.

The biggest intervention from government and other craft development agencies is with regard to training. It covers areas such as product development, product design and diversification, sustainable use of raw material, craft techniques and skills, costing and pricing, marketing and selling, how to rub a crafts business, and financial management and business administration.

Examples include the rural development projects in Limpopo, where the CSIR linked with various rural craft projects to develop new products. In Thohoyandou, the Ifa textile project is producing fashionable handbags in traditional Venda design, while the crafters of the Lubombo SDI in northern KwaZulu-Natal have incorporated minimal interventions in their designs to produce butter dishes, thus creating new marketing opportunities.

The Department has 115 craft projects in all nine provinces. The products of these and other projects can be viewed in a number of places, including two State-assisted outlets at the Bus Factory in Newtown, Johannesburg, and the Boardwalk in Port Elizabeth.

Design

After examining the status of the design industry in South Africa, the Department of Arts and Culture launched a number of initiatives aimed at creating centres of expertise. These have promoted collaborative ventures between the private and public sectors, in areas of product design, and the use of computer-aided design engineering. The initiatives involve the following:
- The launch of the National Product Development Centre at the CSIR. This initiative operates within a national framework, optimising the contributions of service-providers throughout the country in the area of design technology.
- The successful launch and promotion of the computer-aided design initiative at the CSIR, which is linked to the technology station at the Free State University of Technology (Technikon) as well as similar institutions in KwaZulu-Natal and the Eastern Cape.

Early in October 2003, South African novelist J.M. Coetzee won the 2003 Nobel Prize for Literature. Coetzee was born in Cape Town in 1940. His novels, which include *Disgrace*, *Waiting for the Barbarians* and *In the Heart of the Country*, are 'characterised by well-crafted composition, pregnant dialogue and analytical brilliance', the Swedish Academy said in its citation.

- The establishment of the Cape Craft and Design Institute.
- Awarding two learnerships in design with the Create SA Project to help emerging designers.
- The sixth International Design Indaba, held in Cape Town in February 2003.

Literature

South Africa has a vibrant and rich oral tradition. This form of expression goes back many centuries and has been passed down from generation to generation as an important way of sharing advice, remembering history, telling stories, and reflecting on contemporary society.

At the end of September 2000, the African Languages Literary Museum was opened at the University of South Africa (UNISA), Pretoria.

All indigenous languages are catered for, and authors featured include Prof. Maja Serudu, E.M. Ramaila, O.K. Matsepe and Semakaleng Monyaise. The Museum also features books, manuscripts, old typewriters used by some African writers, antiques, and authors' portraits.

There is an English literary museum in Grahamstown and an Afrikaans museum in Bloemfontein.

The Department of Arts and Culture has assisted the Print Industries Cluster Council to establish a writers' network.

Film

During 2002/03, the Cultural Industries Growth Strategy programme evaluated the film and video sector, which is an important job-creator and income generator. A report suggested that the industry generated up to R4 billion in 2001 in Cape Town alone. In partnership with the NFVF, the Department of Arts and Culture is proactively working with provincial governments in further developing their film industries. In addition, the African Film and Broadcast Conference was held at Sithengi, in Cape Town (funded by the Department of Arts and Culture to the tune of R350 000), in November 2002.

Sithengi is South Africa's annual film and television market with extensive African and international appeal.

The NFVF, which was formed with the promulgation of the NFVF Act, 1997 (Act 73 of 1997), is the key co-ordinator and promoter of this industry.

The Department of Arts and Culture has allocated R35 million over the next few years for the establishment of a film fund for the NFVF. The fund is expected to attract international investment.

Through established industry players, South Africa offers film facilitation, logistics and administration-management services which ensure the successful production of films in South Africa. This is achieved through world-class facilities and professional film facilitators.

The establishment of film offices in the provinces is meant to support the above-mentioned services.

South Africa is at the cutting-edge in film, in terms of imagination, technology and product quality, with a wealth of experienced, talented and skilled people, both at management and operational level. Combined with the advanced technology employed across the industry, this talent provides foreign investors and producers with an excellent support infrastructure.

A number of large South African media companies have acquired production companies to increase their capabilities in the media and entertainment sector. The revenue generated from television production constitutes approximately 36% of the total annual film/television revenue.

The increase in the number of television channels available to South African viewers has resulted in an increased demand for local programming due to local-content quotas. In South Africa, locally produced television productions are extremely popular with viewers.

South African broadcasters are exploring opportunities to distribute local productions

Arts and culture

into the rest of Africa through direct sales and a form of bartering, where content is exchanged for advertising airtime. This is expected to increase the demand for locally produced television content.

The three largest film distributors in South Africa are Ster-Kinekor, UIP and Nu-Metro. Ster-Kinekor has a specialised art circuit called Cinema Nouveau with theatres in Johannesburg, Cape Town, Durban and Pretoria.

The Film and Publication Board

The Films and Publications Amendment Act, 1999 (Act 34 of 1999), provides for the regulation of films and publications intended for distribution and/or exhibition in South Africa.

The Act recognises the right of all South Africans to freely choose what they wish to see or read. It encroaches on constitutional rights and freedoms only where there is a risk of harm. The Act provides for an invasion of privacy only where child pornography is concerned. The implementation of the Act has been entrusted to the Film and Publication Board, which consists of members appointed through a process of public nominations, and is broadly representative of the South African population in terms of ethnicity, gender, religion and experience.

The Film and Publication Board no longer censors, but instead classifies movies for age appropriateness. Its main focus is to protect children against harmful and disturbing material, while allowing adults to make informed decisions about what they want and do not want to see, or allow their children to see or not to see. There is no pre-classification of magazines. Publications are classified only when a valid complaint about a certain publication is lodged with the Board.

In terms of the legislation, the Board may ban the distribution of visual material containing:
- sexual acts involving persons under the age of 18 years or who appear to be under the age of 18 years
- bestiality
- explicit violent acts that promote violence
- material that promotes religious hatred
- explicit violent acts coupled with sexual conduct.

Although such material, classified as XX, is only banned from distribution, the possession of child pornography is a criminal offence. People found guilty of possessing child pornography face up to five years in prison for each item found. The Act has been amended to include the regulation and control of child pornography on the Internet and a more precise definition of what constitutes child pornography. The Act also provides for the regulation of trade in previously banned, sexually explicit material. Adult shops that do not comply with the requirements of the Act could be closed by the Board for up to a year.

The Film and Publication Board is funded by an annual grant of approximately R4 million. A total of 60% of the budget is spent on the remuneration of film examiners.

Museums

Museums are the windows to the natural and cultural heritage of a country. South Africa can justifiably be called the museum country of Africa, with the earliest of its museums dating back to the first half of the 19th century. Today, more than 300 of the approximately 1 000 museums in Africa are situated in South Africa. They range from museums of geology, history, the biological sciences and

---

According to attendance figures issued by CineMARK in July 2003, cinema attendance increased by 3,4% over the 12-month period from July 2002 to June 2003 against the same period in the previous year. The six-month average of January to June 2003, compared with the same period in 2002, indicated a 6,6% overall increase. When comparing the month of June with the same period in the prior year, results show attendances peaking at 2 002 166 in 2003 against the figure of 1 614 444 in June 2002, resulting in a phenomenal 24% increase.

the arts, to mining, agriculture, forestry and many other disciplines. Most of the country's national museums are declared cultural institutions (national museums that have framework autonomy and are managed by their own councils) and fall under the overall jurisdic-tion of the Department of Arts and Culture. They receive an annual subsidy from the Department, but are otherwise autonomous.

According to the Cultural Institutions Act, 1998 (Act 119 of 1998), a new streamlined system under which the declared institutions operate was established on 1 April 1999. In terms of this Act, the declared museum institutions in Gauteng and Cape Town are grouped together into two new organisations, known as Flagship Institutions. While the components of these two museum flagships (the museums from which they have been constituted) continue to operate as semi-independent museums with regard to their core functions (collecting, preservation, research and education), other functions, particularly administration, financing and human resource management, have been centralised.

The following museums currently report to the Minister of Arts and Culture in terms of the Cultural Institutions Act, 1998:
- Northern Flagship Institution, Pretoria
- Iziko Museums, Cape Town
- Natal Museum, Pietermaritzburg
- National Museum, Bloemfontein
- Afrikaanse Taalmuseum, Paarl
- National English Literary Museum, Grahamstown
- Voortrekker Museum, Pietermaritzburg
- War Museum of the Boer Republics, Bloemfontein
- Robben Island Museum, Cape Town
- William Humphreys Art Gallery, Kimberley
- Engelenburg House Art Collection, Pretoria
- Nelson Mandela Museum, Umtata.

The Northern Flagship consists of the National Cultural History Museum (NCHM) and its former satellite museums (Kruger House, Tswaing Crater Museum, Willem Prinsloo Agricultural Museum, Pioneer Museum, Sammy Marks Museum and the Coert Steynberg Museum), the Transvaal Museum of Natural History in Pretoria, and the South African National Museum of Military History in Johannesburg.

The Southern Flagship (renamed Iziko Museums of Cape Town) consists of the South African Museum, South African Cultural History Museum and its satellite museums, the South African National Gallery, the William Fehr Collection, and the Michaelis Collection.

In terms of the Cultural Institutions Act, 1998, the declared museums in other provinces continue to operate as before. These include the National Museum and the Anglo-Boer War Museum (Bloemfontein), the William Humphreys Art Gallery (Kimberley), the Natal Museum and the Voortrekker Museum (Pietermaritzburg), the South African Institute for Aquatic Biodiversity in Grahamstown, and the Foundation for Education, Science and Technology in Pretoria, which manages a science and technology museum. The aforementioned two museums fall under the Department of Science and Technology.

The Act also provides for a National Museums Division, comprising the Flagship museums and other declared museums.

The Robben Island Museum is very popular. It was established as a national monument and museum, and declared as South Africa's first World Heritage Site in 1999.

Guided tours are offered to historical sites on the Island, including the cell in which former President Nelson Mandela was imprisoned. The Robben Island Museum has its own council and is a separate declared institution, independent of Iziko.

The breakwater wall at the Robben Island Museum is to be repaired at a cost of R21 million, while R11 million will be spent on jetties at the West Quay of the Waterfront, and R10 million on the Museum's general maintenance and upgrading.

Arts and culture

For the 2003/04 financial year, a total of R13,5 million has been allocated from a project totalling R25 million to establish the Qunu component of the Nelson Mandela Museum and R7,6 million has been allocated for the upgrading of the Bhunga building.

A further R9 million will be spent on installing air-conditioning and additional storage facilities at the Iziko Museums, and R5,5 million for installing air-conditioning in the public gallery at the Natal Museum.

The Tswaing Crater Museum will receive R4 million for development, and R1,6 million will go towards the upgrading of the Kruger House Museum.

Apart from the declared museums that fall under the Department, there are also a number of other national museums, which are administered by central government departments or research councils. Notable examples are the Museum of the Council for Geoscience (Pretoria); the Theiler Veterinary Science Museum at Onderstepoort (Pretoria); the South African Air Force Museum at Air Force Base Zwartkop (Pretoria) with its satellites in Cape Town, Port Elizabeth and Durban; the museum of the Department of Correctional Services (Pretoria); and the Porcinarium (the world's first pig museum) outside Pretoria on the Irene campus of the Agricultural Research Council.

A number of museums fall directly or indirectly under the provincial government departments responsible for Arts and Culture. In some provinces, these museums render museum support services at provincial level, while other provinces, notably Gauteng, KwaZulu-Natal, Western Cape and the Free State, have separate museum-service organisations.

However, many museum and heritage services are also rendered by the declared national museums on a consultancy basis. Many municipalities also manage museums. Other museums fall under universities and university departments or are owned and managed by private-sector companies, NGOs and individuals.

The largest museums are situated in Johannesburg, Pretoria, Cape Town, Durban, Pietermaritzburg and Bloemfontein. The best-known natural history collections in South Africa are housed in the Iziko Museums and the Northern Flagship Institution, as well as in the following:
- Natal Museum, Pietermaritzburg
- National Museum, Bloemfontein (fossils)
- McGregor Museum, Kimberley
- East London Museum (coelacanth)
- South African Institute for Aquatic Biodiversity, Grahamstown (fish)
- Port Elizabeth Museum
- Durban Museum of Natural History.

The best-known cultural-history collections are housed in the Iziko Museums and the Northern Flagship Institution, as well as in the following:
- National Museum, Bloemfontein
- Natal Museum, Pietermaritzburg
- Durban Local History Museum
- Museum Africa, Johannesburg.

Among the art museums are the following:
- The South African National Gallery, Cape Town
- Johannesburg Art Gallery
- Pretoria Art Museum
- William Humphreys Art Gallery, Kimberley.

The South African Cultural History Museum in Cape Town houses the oldest cultural history collection in the country – in a magnificent old building to which modern facilities have been added.

The South African Museum (Cape Town) showcases the natural history of South Africa, as well as relics of the early human inhabitants of the subcontinent. The huge Whale Hall houses possibly the most impressive of all its exhibitions. This is also the only collection in South Africa with a planetarium attached to it.

The Transvaal Museum in Pretoria houses the skull of Mr Ples (until recently known as Mrs Ples), a 2,5-million-year-old hominid fossil, and depicts the origin and development of life in South Africa, from the most primitive unicellular form of life to the emergence of mammals and the first human beings. It has a collection of early human fossils.

The Tswaing Meteorite Crater is situated to the north-west of Pretoria. It supports the Presidential Imperatives by combining a museum with a cultural-development initiative.

The NCHM (former African Window) in Pretoria is a centre for the preservation and communication of the culture and heritage of all South Africans. It explores cultural diversity and commonalities, links the present and the past to offer a better understanding of both, and nurtures the living culture of all South Africans. In addition, the Museum works with institutions and community-based organisations to host film festivals, arts and crafts exhibitions, seminars, conferences, festivals and other cultural events.

Mining is best represented by the De Beers Museum at the Big Hole in Kimberley, where visitors can view the biggest hole ever made by man with pick and shovel. It includes an open-air museum, which houses many buildings dating back to the era of the diamond diggings.

Another important mining museum is at Pilgrim's Rest, Mpumalanga, where the first economically viable goldfield was discovered. The entire village has been conserved and restored. It boasts beautiful examples of houses from the period of the gold rush, as well as an early mining camp and a complete reduction works.

Agriculture in South Africa is depicted mainly at two museums. These are Kleinplasie in Worcester, Western Cape, which showcases the wine culture and the characteristic architecture of the winelands, and the Willem Prinsloo Agricultural Museum between Pretoria and Bronkhorstspruit in Gauteng. The latter houses two 'house' museums, and runs educational programmes based on their extensive collection of early farming implements, vehicles of yesteryear, and indigenous farm animals. Both museums are famous for their *mampoer* and *witblits* – liquor distilled from fruit and grapes.

The Absa Museum and Archives in Johannesburg, which belongs to Amalgamated Banks of South Africa (Absa), aims to preserve the banking group's more than 110 years of history. It also houses a unique and very valuable coin and banknote collection.

The Apartheid Museum in Johannesburg offers a realistic portrayal of the political situation in the townships of South Africa during the 1970s and 1980s. Exhibitions in the Museum feature, among other things, audio-visual footage recorded during the apartheid era.

One of the most common types of museum in South Africa is the 'house' museum. Examples include an entire village nucleus in Stellenbosch; Groot Constantia in the Western Cape, which is an example of the lifestyle of the wealthy wine farmer; the mansion of the millionaire industrialist Sammy Marks, outside Pretoria; the Victorian affluence mirrored in Melrose House, Pretoria; and the Kruger House Museum in Pretoria, former residence of President Paul Kruger. Simpler architectural variations have not been neglected, for instance the pioneer dwelling in Silverton, Pretoria, and the humble farmhouse at Suikerbosrand near Heidelberg in Gauteng. There are several open-air museums which showcase the black cultures of the country, for example Tsongakraal near Letsitele, Limpopo; the Ndebele Museum at Middelburg, Mpumalanga; the Bakone Malapa (Northern Sotho) Museum at Polokwane, Limpopo; and the South Sotho Museum at Witsieshoek, Free State.

South Africa has two national military history museums. The South African Museum for Military History in Johannesburg reflects the military history of the country, while the War Museum in Bloemfontein depicts the Anglo-Boer/South African War in particular. The famous battlefields of KwaZulu-Natal, Northern Cape and North West are also worth a visit.

Also on the cards for 2003/04 was a major upgrading of the South African Military History

Museum at a cost of R13 million.

The work of the War-graves division of the SAHRA includes the upkeep of the graves of victims of the struggle for the liberation of South Africa.

Archives and heraldry

Archives of governmental bodies are transferred to archive repositories after a period of 20 years, and are accessible to the public and the office of origin. National Archives functions in terms of the National Archives of South Africa Act, 1996 (Act 43 of 1996).

The archives of central government are preserved in the National Archives Repository in Pretoria; and provincial archives repositories in Pretoria, Cape Town, Pietermaritzburg, Durban, Ulundi, Port Elizabeth and Bloemfontein house archives dating from before 1910 as well as the relevant provincial archives. Records centres for archives younger than 20 years exist in Pretoria, Bloemfontein and Cape Town.

The retrieval of information from archives is facilitated by the national automated archival information system (*www.national.archives.gov.za*), which includes national registers of manuscripts, photographs and audio-visual material. National Archives also renders a comprehensive record-management service for current records, aimed at promoting efficient administration.

An important aspect of the Act is its mandate to National Archives to collect non-public records with enduring value of national significance. In so doing, National Archives is obliged to pay special attention to aspects of the nation's experience neglected by archives of the past. A key project in this regard is the Oral History Project, which seeks to build the National Archives' capacity to document the spoken word and to develop a national oral history programme. The automated National Register of Oral Sources is an important element of the project. The Act also provides government with a measure of control over private collections. Archives are taken to the people through co-ordinated national and provincial archive services. At the same time, National Archives is responsible for trying to ensure effective, transparent and accountable management of all public records.

The National Archives in Pretoria include the National Film, Video and Sound Archives. Its primary functions are to obtain and preserve films, videotapes and sound recordings of archival value, and to make these available for research and reference purposes.

The Bureau of Heraldry is responsible for the registration of coats of arms; badges and other emblems such as flags, seals, medals and insignia of rank and offices of order; as well as the registration of names and uniforms (colours) of associations and organisations, such as universities.

The Timbuktu Manuscripts Project was officially launched by President Mbeki and President Amadou Toumani Toure of Mali as Africa's very first New Partnership for Africa's Development cultural project on Africa Day, 25 May 2003.

The preservation of the Timbuktu Manuscripts is a Presidential Project co-ordinated by The Presidency and the Department of Arts and Culture through the National Archives.

President Mbeki first noted the existence of these manuscripts, which are believed to be more than 800 years old, during a visit to the *Institut Des Hautes et de la Recherche Islamique* (IHERI-AB) as part of his State visit to Mali in 2001.

He subsequently undertook that South Africa would assist with the preservation of the Manuscripts through exchange training and infrastructure-development programmes.

The National Archives of South Africa will lead the programme to build the infrastructure and develop skills in conservation and preservation management for the staff at IHERI-AB. A Trust Fund for the preservation of the Manuscripts was launched on 29 May 2003.

South Africa Yearbook 2003/04

Acknowledgements

Department of Arts and Culture
Department of Home Affairs
Film and Publication Board
National Arts Council
National Cultural History Museum
www.gov.za

Suggested reading

Arnold, M. *Women and Art in South Africa*. Cape Town: David Philip, 1996.
Agordoh, A.A. *Studies in African Music*. Ghana: New Age Publications, 1994.
Bassett, S.T. *Rock Paintings of South Africa*. Cape Town: David Philip, 2001.
Becker, R. and Keene, R. *Art Routes: A Guide to South African Art Collections*. Johannesburg: Witwatersrand University Press, 2000.
Berman, E. *Art and Artists of South Africa*. 3rd ed. Halfway House: Southern Book Publishers, 1992.
Berman, E. *Painting in South Africa*. Halfway House: Southern Book Publishers, 1993.
Blignaut, J. and Botha, M. *Movies, Moguls and Mavericks: South African Cinema, 1979 – 1991*. Cape Town: Vlaeberg, 1992.
Botha, M. and Van Aswegen, A.H. *Images of South Africa: The Rise of the Alternative Film*. Pretoria: Human Sciences Research Council, 1992.
Breakey, B. and Gordon, S. *Beyond the Blues: Township Jazz in the '60s and '70s*. Cape Town: David Philip, 1997.
Brink, A. *Reinventing a Continent: Writing and Politics in South Africa, 1982 – 1995*. London: Secker and Warburg, 1996.
Campbell, J. ed. *Directory of South African Contemporary Art Practices*. Cape Town: Contemporary Art Publishers, 1999.
Caplan, D. *In Township Tonight: South Africa's Black City Music and Theatre in South Africa*. Johannesburg: Ravan, 1985.
Chapman, M. *Southern African Literatures*. Pietermaritzburg: University of Natal Press, 2003.
Cole, M. *Collectables*. Johannesburg: South African Antique Dealers Association and BDFM Publishers, 2003.
Contemporary South African Art: The Gencor Collection. Johannesburg: Jonathan Ball, 1997.
Crwys-Williams, J. *Penguin Dictionary of South African Quotations*. 2nd ed. Sandton: Penguin Books, 1999.
De Gruchy, J. ed. *London Missionary Society in Southern Africa: Historical Essays in Celebration of the Bicentenary of the LMS in Southern Africa, 1799 – 1999*. Cape Town: David Philip, 1999.
Diawara, M. *African Cinema: Politics and Culture*. Johannesburg: Witwatersrand University Press, 1992.
Dikeni, S. *Soul Fire: Writing the Transition*. Pietermaritzburg: University of Natal Press, 2002.
Directory of South African Contemporary Art. Vol. 1. (Painting, 1997/98). Stanford, Western Cape: Contemporary Arts Publishers, 1997.
Fletcher, J. *Story of Theatre in South Africa: A Guide to its History from 1780 – 1930*. Cape Town: Vlaeberg, 1994.
Fisher, R.C., le Roux, S. and Marè, E. eds. *Architecture of the Transvaal*. Pretoria: University of South Africa, 1998.
Germond, P. and de Gruchy, S. eds. *Aliens in the Household of God: Homosexuality and Christian Faith in South Africa*. Cape Town: David Philip, 1997.
Goldblatt, D. *South Africa: The Structure of Things Then*. Cape Town: Oxford University Press, 1998.
Grundlingh, K. ed. *Line of Sight*. Cape Town: South African National Gallery, 2001.
Gray, S. ed. *Modern South African Stories: Revised Selection*. Johannesburg: Jonathan Ball, 2002.
Gunner, L. ed. *Politics and Performance: Theatre, Poetry and Song in Southern Africa*. Johannesburg: Witwatersrand University Press, 1993.
Harris, V. *Exploring Archives: An Introduction to Archival Ideas and Practice in South Africa*. National Archives of South Africa, Pretoria, 2000.
Hauptfleisch, T. *Theatre and Society in South Africa: Some Reflections in a Fractured Mirror*. Pretoria: Van Schaik, 1997.
Herreman, F. ed. *Liberated Voices: Contemporary Art from South Africa*. New York: Museum for African Art, 1999.
Jackson, G.S. *Outside Insights: Quotations for Contemporary South Africa*. Cape Town: Human and Rousseau, 1997.
Kalu, A.C. *Women, Literature and Development in Africa*. Trenton, New Jersey, Africa World Press, 2001.
Kaschula, R.H. ed. *African Oral Literature: Functions in Contemporary Contexts*. Claremont: New Africa Books, 2001.

Arts and culture

Kaschula, R. *The Bones of the Ancestors are Shaking.* Cape Town: Juta, 2002.
Kavanagh, R.M. *Theatre and Cultural Struggle in South Africa.* London: ZED Books, 1985.
Kavanagh, R.M. *Making People's Theatre.* Johannesburg: Witwatersrand University Press, 1997.
Kivnick, H.Q. *Where is the Way: Song and Struggle in South Africa.* New York: Viking Penguin, 1990.
Krige, R. and Zegeye, A. eds. *Culture in the New South Africa after Apartheid.* Cape Town: Kwela Books, 2001.
Kourie, C. and Kretzschmar L. eds. *Christian Spirituality in South Africa.* Pietermaritzburg: Cluster Publications, 2000.
Larlham, P. *Black Theatre, Dance and Ritual in South Africa.* Ann Arbor, Michigan (US): UMI Research Press, 1985.
Layiwold, D. ed. *Rethinking African Arts and Culture.* Cape Town: CASAS, 2000.
Levinsohn, R.R. *Art and Craft of Southern Africa.* Johannesburg: Delta Books, 1984.
Lewis-Williams, D. ed. *Stories that Float from Afar: Ancestral Folklore of the San of the Southern Africa.* Cape Town: David Philip, 2000.
Lewis-Williams, D. and Blunt, G. *Fragile Heritage: A Rock Art Fieldguide.* Johannesburg: Witwatersrand University Press, 1998.
Lewis-Williams, D. and Dowson, T. *Discovering Southern African Rock Art.* Cape Town: David Philip, 2000.
Lewis-Williams, D. *Images of Mystery: Rock Art of the Drakensberg.* Cape Town: Double Storey Books, 2003.
Losambe, L. and Sarinjeive, D. eds. *Pre-Colonial and Post-Colonial Drama and Theatre in Africa.* Cape Town: New Africa Books, 2001.
Magubane, P. and Klopper, S. *African Heritage: Arts and Crafts; African Heritage: Ceremonies; African Heritage: Dress and Adornment.* Cape Town: Struik, 2002.
Marschall, S. *Community Mural Art in South Africa.* Pretoria: University of South Africa, 2002.
Moffett, H. and Mphahlele, E. eds. *Seasons Come to Pass.* Cape Town: Oxford University Press, 2002.
Miles, E. *Land and Lives: A Story of Early Black Artists.* Cape Town: Human and Rousseau, 1997.
Molefe, Z.B. and Mzileni, M. *A Common Hunger to Sing: A Tribute to South Africa's Black Women of Song, 1950 to 1990.* Text by Z.B. Molefe; photographs by M. Mzileni. Cape Town: Kwela Books, 1997.
Morris, J. *Speaking with Beads: Zulu Beads from Southern Africa.* Text by E. Preston Whyte. London: Thames and Hudson, 1994.
Muwanga, C. *South Africa: A Guide to Recent Architecture.* London: Ellipsis, 1998.
Music Africa Directory, 1997. Sandton: Sun Circle, 1997 – Annual.
Nettleton, A. and Hammond-Tooke, W.D. *African Art in South Africa: From Tradition to Township.* Johannesburg: Donker, 1989.
Nuttall, S. and Michael, C. eds. *Senses of Culture: South African Culture Studies.* Cape Town: Oxford University Press, 2001.
Okurè, T. ed. *To Cast Fire Upon the Earth: Bible and Mission Collaborating in Today's Multicultural Global Context.* Pietermaritzburg: Cluster Publications, 2000.
Orkin, M. *Drama and the South African State.* Johannesburg: Witwatersrand University Press, 1991.
Over the Rainbow: An Anthology of African Verse. Scottburgh: Poetry Institute of Africa, 1997.
Picton-Seymour, D. *Victorian Buildings in South Africa.* Cape Town: Balkema, 1977.
Petersen, B. *Monarchs, Missionaries and African Intellectuals: African Theatre and the Unmasking of Colonial Marginality.* Johannesburg: Witwatersrand University Press, 2000.
Plastow, J. ed. *African Theatre: Women.* Johannesburg: Witwatersrand University Press, 2002.
Radford, D. *A Guide to the Architecture of Durban and Pietermaritzburg.* Cape Town: David Philip, 2002.
Saron, G. *The Jews of South Africa: An Illustrated History to 1953,* edited by N. Musiker. Johannesburg: South African Jewish Board of Deputies, 2001.
Schadeberg, J. *The Black and White Fifties: Jurgen Schadeberg's South Africa.* Pretoria: Protea Book House, 2001.
Strauss, P. *Africa Style in South Africa.* Johannesburg: Jonathan Ball, 1994.
Tomaselli, K. ed. *Cinema of Apartheid: Race and Class in South African Film.* Bergvlei: Random Century, 1989.
Van Graan, M. and Ballantyne, T. *The South African Handbook on Arts and Culture, 2002 – 2003.* Cape Town: David Philip, 2002.
Van Rensburg, J.J. *The Paradigm Shift: An Introduction to Postmodern Thought and its Implications for Theology.* Pretoria: Van Schaik, 2000.
Williamson, S. and Jamal, A. *Art in South Africa: The Future Present.* Cape Town: David Philip, 1996.
Winburg, M. *My Eland Heart. The Art of the !Xu and Khwe.* Cape Town: David Philip, 2001.
Woodhouse, H C. *Bushman Art of Southern Africa.* Durban: Art Publishers, 2003.
Zebra Register of South African Artists and Galleries. Vol. 3. Bethal, Clarence (OFS): DM & R Marketing, 2003

16 JUNE
LOST THEIR LIVES BECAUSE OF BANTU
EDUCATION,
ALTHOUGH YOU HAVE PASSED
ON I WOULD
LIKE TO THANK
YOU FOR THE FREEDOM WE NOW HAVE!
Oppression
Inequality
WE ARE CELEBRATING

chapter 6

Communications

The Department of Communications is the centre of policy-making and policy review for the postal, telecommunications and broadcasting sectors in the country. This includes policy-making that affects State-owned enterprises (SOEs) such as Telkom SA Ltd, the South African Post Office (SAPO) (Pty) Ltd, Sentech, the South African Broadcasting Corporation (SABC), National Electronic Media Institute of South Africa (NEMISA), as well as the regulators – the Independent Communications Authority of South Africa (ICASA) and the Universal Services Agency (USA). All these, including the Department, fall under the Cabinet portfolio of the Ministry of Communications.

The Department aims to enable ordinary people to have access to information and communication technologies (ICTs). This includes the following services:
- telemedicine – enabling rural clinics to get diagnoses from specialists at urban medical centres
- tele-education – enabling the country to reverse the illiteracy rate through distance education
- convenience measures such as teleshopping and telebanking.

The development of policies includes the following domains:
- Assessment of technological changes and trends, and their business- and public-impact.
- Research, development and dissemination of specific policies, including the extension of services.
- Research and development of telecommunications, postal and broadcasting legislation required by the Ministry, regulatory authorities and SOEs.
- High-level skills development through the Institute for Satellite and Software Applications (ISSA), situated in Grabouw in the Western Cape. It is a partnership programme on virtual-reality research with Miralab at the University of Geneva. The research focuses on the development of different scientific tools for diagnostic and educational purposes.
- Analysis and development of competition policies and encouragement of business development.
- Analysis of tariffs, licence fees and other sources of funding.
- Encouragement of local content and the local manufacturing industry.

Other role-players in these fields include Government Communications (GCIS) and the Department of Science and Technology.

◀ The Department of Communications is developing strategies to improve the services delivered by community telecentres and e-schools cyber labs to insure the delivery of multimedia services such as e-education, e-health, e-business development of small, medium and macro enterprises, as well as co-operatives, e-government services and other socio-economic development programmes.

Policy

The Department's policy-making objectives ensure that the development of the information and communication sectors is well-regulated, and that the services provided are accessible to all. In addition, policy development since 1998/99 has sought to restructure SOEs, introduce competition, accelerate the penetration of services into underserviced communities, and streamline the regulatory framework.

Developing a stable and predictable regulatory regime on e-commerce is central to the Department's vision of moving South Africa into the knowledge economy.

The Electronic Communications and Transactions Act, 2002 (Act 25 of 2002), will pave the way for a secure environment for e-commerce transactions. It provides for the:
- facilitation and regulation of electronic communications and transactions
- development of a national e-strategy
- promotion of universal access to electronic commerce, and the use of e-commerce by small, medium and micro enterprises (SMMEs)
- human resource development in electronic transactions
- prevention of the abuse of information systems, and encourages the use of e-government services.

The legislation also provides for the appointment of a panel to facilitate the establishment of the board of the Section 21 Domain Name Authority, cyber-inspectors. In July 2003, the Minister of Communications, Dr Ivy Matsepe-Casaburri, announced the names of the nine-member board of the .za Domain Name Authority.

The Telecommunications Amendment Act, 2001 (Act 64 of 2001), was passed in November 2001 to give effect to the policy of managed liberalisation of the South African telecommunications market.

The amendments also paved the way for the awarding of an international and multimedia licence to Sentech, the largest signal distributor for broadcasting in Africa.

It also provides for the licensing of operators in underserviced areas with a teledensity of less than 5%. The majority of these are in the Integrated Sustainable Rural Development Programme (ISRDP) nodal points. The Department held provincial workshops on opportunities for telecommunications licences in these areas to raise awareness among the relevant communities. This process will bring about the most significant ownership and involvement in the communications sector by black people and women in South Africa. The amendments provide for a new public emergency telephone service and an emergency number, 112. A pilot project has been established in Klerksdorp, North West.

In May 2002, the Minister of Communications issued an invitation to apply for a 51% stake in the Second National Operator (SNO). Applications were received from two consortiums, but ICASA recommended that neither of the applicants was in a position to take up the 51% equity stake. The Minister concurred with the recommendation and set about preparing an alternative process that would facilitate the way forward. The Minister subsequently applied Section 35(A) of the Telecommunications Act of 1996, (Act 103 of 1996), as amended, which provides for the Minister, in specific instances, to determine the manner in which applications may be made, and the licensing process and conditions that will apply.

The Department of Communications has embarked on a process to develop a policy framework to facilitate the convergence of technologies in the information and communication technologies environment.

A feasibility study has been conducted in this regard and a national Colloquium was convened in July 2003 with stakeholders and interest groups to share ideas and experiences that will inform policy options.

On 31 March 2003, the Minister issued an invitation to express interest to apply for a 51%-stake. Two submissions were received by ICASA.

In August 2003, ICASA announced that, notwithstanding the applicants' individual strengths with regard to the evaluation criteria, they still fell short of the envisaged rival to Telkom owning a 25-year licence and controlling a 51% equity stake.

THe process to appoint a SNO continues.

Telecommunications

Telecommunications is the fastest-growing industry in South Africa. Government recognises the centrality of the telecommunications and information technology (IT) sectors in economic development and its telecommunications policy has played a cardinal role in revolutionising the industry.

South Africa ranks 23rd in telecommunications development and 17th in Internet-use in the world.

Regulators and licensing

Independent Communications Authority of South Africa

The proclamation of the ICASA Act, 2000 (Act 13 of 2000), in May 2000 paved the way for the merger of the South African Telecommunications Regulatory Authority (SATRA) and the Independent Broadcasting Authority (IBA) into ICASA.

The core responsibilities of ICASA include the regulation of South Africa's communications industry as stipulated in the telecommunications and broadcasting laws. ICASA's main goal is to create regulatory certainty in an environment where technological developments are growing at a rapid pace. ICASA promotes:

- growth in telecommunications and broadcasting
- economic growth and development of society
- national and international investment
- universal service and access
- participation of previously disadvantaged groups
- levelling the playing-fields by ensuring fair competition
- protecting public interest and consumer rights.

Radio and television broadcasters, as well as all telecommunications service-providers, are licensed by ICASA. In addition, ICASA plans frequency spectrum and type, and approves telecommunications equipment.

Policies and regulations are developed for interconnection, licence fees and tariffs. Monitoring is an integral part of the Authority's regulatory function. ICASA monitors the use of numbering, frequency spectrum, use of equipment, consumer monitoring, and broadcasters' compliance with their licence conditions.

Universal Service Agency

The USA was launched in May 1997. It is a statutory body created in terms of the Telecommunications Act, 1996, and its objectives include advising the Minister on ways to bring about universal access and service, and co-ordinating initiatives by service providers such as Telkom, Vodacom, Mobile Telephone Network (MTN) and Cell C. It extends access to telecommunications by working

---

With the financial aid of the Prince of Wales' International Business Leaders Forum, the New Digital Partnership for South Africa was launched in 2003.

The Partnership acquires used computers from multinational organisations, refurbishes them, and deploys them in schools across the country. In the course of 2003, the Partnership was expected to receive 67 000 computers. A roll-out plan was finalised in conjunction with the Department of Education.

The factory for the refurbishment of the computers is located at the Institute for Satellite and Software Applications.

with community-based organisations (CBOs), non-governmental organisations (NGOs), donor organisations and businesses.

The Telecommunications Amendment Act, 2001 also provides for increasing the mandate of the USA through its management of the Universal Service Fund. The Fund is used to reinforce the development of infrastructure in underserviced communities. In addition, support is given to schools procuring IT equipment to access the Internet.

Information technology

Knowledge Management Unit

The Knowledge Management Unit of the Department of Communications promotes awareness of knowledge management among stakeholders, particularly within government, focusing on local government.

The Unit aims to:
- take advantage of the convergence of communication technologies in the areas of telecommunications, broadcasting, IT and multimedia
- increase the human resource capability of the communications sector
- make South Africa globally competitive by becoming a hub of multimedia development, particularly through the opening up of opportunities for historically disadvantaged communities
- contribute towards an African communication strategy that will help build an information backbone to ensure the success of Africa's renewal.

By July 2003, the Knowledge Management Unit had:
- chaired the Executive Committee of the Knowledge Management Society of southern Africa
- chaired the inaugural meeting of the South African Bureau of Standards (SABS) Technical Committee on Knowledge Management Standards, which was held in March 2003
- overseen the completion of the analysis for a User Requirement Service for the implementation of knowledge management, done at ISSA.

State Information Technology Agency (SITA)

On 29 January 1999, SITA was incorporated as a private company, with the State as sole shareholder, to provide IT-related services exclusively for the Public Service. It officially opened its doors on 1 April 1999. (See Chapter 12: *Government system*.)

arivia.kom

The State-owned IT company, arivia.kom, which became fully operational on 8 January 2001, is the product of a merger between ITS (the IT division of Eskom), Datavia (the IT division of Transnet) and Ariel Technologies (the IT division of Denel). The combined value of the three entities is estimated at R644 million, whereas the value of the merged model for the three entities is about R846 million, with Eskom, Transnet and Denel as direct shareholders.

Its key focus is to deliver IT infrastructure solutions and focused business solutions, and to engage further in e-ventures to exploit opportunities in e-commerce.

Presidential International Advisory Council on Information Society and Development

The aim of the Presidential International Advisory Council on Information Society and Development is to assist government in narrowing the digital divide between South Africa and the rest of the world. The Council consists of Chief Executive Officers (CEOs) from major international ICT corporations, and industry experts. The Council meets once a year to exchange ideas.

Presidential National Commission on Information Society and Development

President Thabo Mbeki also established

Communications

the Presidential National Commission on Information Society and Development to mobilise national knowledge and build common approaches. This body recommends strategies to bridge the digital divide and helping to develop an ICT policy framework.

Institute for Satellite and Software Applications

ISSA continues its work in satellite development and remote sensing, telecommunications, and software and network engineering. The Institute has changed from a primary academic training institute to become a product developer. Some of the projects developed by the Institute include a satellite development group that is building a micro-satellite able to scan water- and electricity-meter readings from above – saving municipalities millions of Rands and providing ratepayers with more reliable accounts; a computer-virus monitoring centre; and an electronic testing facility that enables the industry to test products locally instead of in foreign laboratories.

ISSA's collaboration with the Carnegie Mellon University (CMU) in the United States of America (USA) in 2002 saw nine females complete their studies for a master's Degree in IT (software engineering). Some of the graduates of the programme have returned to establish the Software Evaluation Centre (SEC), which was chartered to stop the acquisition of inferior software that does not meet the requirements specified; provide support for software evaluation; and provide recommendations for the acquisition of software. In 2003, the SEC worked on software standards and the validation and evaluation of software for the Department, SAPO and other parastatals. Meanwhile, 11 others have commenced their training in the same course.

ISSA has successfully facilitated the conclusion of an agreement between the University of Stellenbosch and CMU for the introduction of an honours Degree in software engineering during the 2003 academic year, presented jointly by the computer science faculties of the University of Stellenbosch and CMU. Fourteen students were selected by ISSA to commence their studies during the 2003 academic year.

Through collaboration between the Department of Communications, Microsoft and Netscope training-solutions providers, 2002 saw the commencement of a Microsoft Certified Solutions Developer training programme at ISSA. Sixteen science graduates registered for this course in 2002.

ISSA also presents training towards specialised high-level qualifications in Cisco, Microsoft, Oracle and Unix Networking. In 2002, 50 students were registered for these courses. These formed the core of the personnel constituting the backbone infrastructure for authentication in the electronic communications and transactions regime. These students were instrumental in maintaining ISSA's website and Intranet, as well as in developing websites of their own.

ISSA graduates are assisted in forming their own IT networks and software-engineering companies.

Internet

According to a study by World Wide Worx,

In March 2003, the Minister of Trade and Industry, Mr Alec Erwin, officially launched the country's first information communications technology (ICT) and electronics marketing and promotion campaign at a cost of R1,8 million.

Savant is a public-private partnership between the Government and industry, designed to be the vanguard of the South African ICT and electronics sector.

The campaign will focus on promoting areas in which South Africa holds a competitive advantage – IT training and certification, call centres, wireless development, niche software and infrastructure development.

Savant will make use of extensive promotional material, advertisements and marketing exercises, both locally and abroad.

some 2,89 million South Africans (one out of every 15) had access to the Internet by the end of 2001. The number was expected to grow to around 3,1 million by the end of 2002. This makes South Africa the largest Internet consumer in Africa.

The primary role of the Directorate: Internet, established by the Department of Communications, is to increase access and use of the Internet by all South Africans. Specific focus is given to historically disadvantaged communities and the youth.

The Directorate aims to realise the social and economic benefits of the Internet by expanding participation and facilitating access.

Public Internet Terminals (PITs), Multi-Purpose Community Centres (MPCCs) and Citizen Post Offices (CPOs)

To roll out and implement the sustainable plan of communications infrastructure and related services to rural communities and those from historically disadvantaged areas, the Department of Communications is collaborating with GCIS to establish MPCCs. This is in line with the objectives of the ISRDP/Urban Rural Strategy initiatives. By November 2003, 48 MPCCs had been launched. The Department's role in this strategic project is to provide communications infrastructure in the form of computer terminals connected to the Internet, telephony as well as PITs.

CPOs provide a dedicated, specially designed space inside existing post offices, especially in the rural areas, where communities have access to both traditional communications services, and new and emerging electronic communications services.

A phased approach has been adopted in the roll-out of the CPOs. Seven pilot sites were earmarked for roll-out before the end of the 2003/04 financial year. The roll-out of the remaining 11 sites will take place in 2004/05.

Another joint venture between the Department of Communications and SAPO is the establishment of PITs. These are located in post offices and other access sites around the country, and are intended to bring electronic communications services and Internet facilities to the public. Through PITs, the public has access to government forms and information, e-mail facilities, the Internet and education services.

In the 2001/02 financial year, 100 PITs were established countrywide.

International co-operation

South Africa is a member of the Council of the International Telecommunications Union, an arm of the United Nations (UN). Several governments, international organisations and donor agencies have pledged financial and technical support to help strengthen the South African IT industry.

The money will be used to fund research projects to identify sustainable ways of enlarging the industry. This could include seed capital to fund research or manufacturing projects, assessing how rural hospitals could benefit from telemedicine, or how effective computer-based education is in schools.

The African Telecommunications Union (ATU), which succeeded the Pan-African Telecommunications Union (PATU) in December 1999, has launched the African Connection Project. The Project provides for sector restructuring through new policy and regulatory frameworks that will facilitate much-needed investment.

The ATU provides a forum for African governments, as well as public, private and social-sector organisations involved in ICT, to formulate policies and strategies aimed at improving access to information infrastructure, and promoting its use as a tool for stimulating economic development and enhancing poverty reduction.

Six key African telecommunications projects have been prioritised: telemedicine, telehealth, tele-education, tele-agriculture, infrastructure development, telecentre/Internet access, and centres of excellence. South Africa chairs the Ministerial Oversight Committee (MOC).

The MOC was established by the then PATU at its Sixth Ordinary Session Conference of Plenipotentiaries in 1998.

The Minister of Communications, in her capacity as the chairperson of the MOC, hosted the MOC meeting in Magaliesburg, in May 2003. The meeting, which was attended by Africa's Ministers of ICT, deliberated on key issues on the continent affecting the sector.

The Ministry remains dedicated to the advancement of telecommunications in Africa. The majority of the continent's 53 Communications Ministers have committed themselves to this goal.

The Minister attended the 29th Session of the Board of the Regional Commonwealth in the Field of Communications (RCC) from 29 to 30 June 2003 in St Petersburg, Russia. Over the next few years, modern policy and legislative frameworks will have to be considered by the participating governments, regulatory systems established, and a pool of African expertise harnessed for co-ordinated spectrum management and frequency planning.

The Minister stressed the importance of the World Summit on the Information Society (WSIS). The WSIS will be held in two phases. The first phase of the WSIS took place in Geneva, Switzerland, from 10 to 12 December 2003. The second phase will take place in Tunis, Tunisia, from 16 to 18 November 2005.

The Summit will bring together Heads of State, Executive Heads of UN agencies, industry leaders, NGOs, media representatives and civil society. The roles of the various partners in ensuring smooth co-ordination of the practical establishment of the information society around the globe will also be discussed.

Telkom

The social and political transformation in South Africa in 1994, not only marked the beginning of a new economy, but also set the platform for an era of telecommunications transformation.

On 7 May 2002, the South African telecommunications landscape faced one of its most important transformations – the end of Telkom's period of exclusivity, which opened the door to competition. During this time, Telkom transformed itself into a competitive player, providing total communications solutions in the ICT sector.

During its five-year period of exclusivity, the company was required to comply with a number of conditions and obligations relating to milestone targets, as set out in its licence.

The Public Switched Telecommunications Services licence included service and fixed-line roll-out targets. Telkom substantially met all of these targets with the exception of the residential fault-rate target, targets relating to service provision in underserviced villages, and the replacement of analogue lines with digital lines. The company narrowly missed the aggregate fixed-line roll-out target as it decided to refrain from rolling out lines in areas that were not economically viable.

In 1997, Telkom embarked on an extensive five-year capital-investment programme in the fixed-line business. The fixed-line capital investment for the five years ended 31 March 2002 was R41,7 billion, of which R27,9 billion was to be used for network modernisation and line roll-out in order to comply with licence obligations and prepare for competition.

The state-of-the-art National Network Operations Centre enables Telkom to be more proactive in anticipating, localising and isolating problems like congestion and cable breaks so that they can be corrected promptly. During 2002, further developments were made to the fixed and mobile networks, and operational systems, which further enhanced Telkom's network capability.

Telkom invested in the SAT-3/WASC/SAFE submarine cable system, which provides increased fibre-optics-transmission capability between South Africa and international destinations.

On 5 March 2003, Telkom successfully listed on the JSE Securities Exchange (JSE) and the New York Stock Exchange.

After the Initial Public Offering (IPO), the South African Government owns 39,3% of Telkom's issued share-capital, Thintana Communications LLC – a beneficiary owned by SBC Communications and Telekom Malaysia – owns 30%, Ucingo Investments owns 3%, and the public owns 27,7%.

Telkom maintained market leadership in the mobile sector through its 50% ownership of the Vodacom Group. Group revenue grew 10% during 2002/03, reaching R37,6 billion. The 10% growth was primarily due to a fixed-line tariff increase, the growth in fixed-line data services, and Vodacom's growth in mobile customers.

Other highlights included:
- consumer packages being introduced, such as the discounted package on pre-selected numbers, a free basic voice-mail service, and value-added services from the TalkPlus range
- strong growth (15,4%) in prepaid lines and supporting products
- a huge increase in network usage as a result of 101% growth in Internet users
- the introduction of Assymetric Digital Subscriber Lines which helped data-revenue grow by 15,2%
- the introduction of CyberTrade Xchange, an e-commerce B2B platform
- the launch of a range of information-security products
- voice-over Internet Protocol developments

The initial public offering (IPO) of Telkom on the JSE Securities Exchange and the New York Stock Exchange on 5 March 2003 was positively received. Some R3,9 billion was realised on the first day of the IPO, making it the biggest initiative so far in government's programme to restructure State-owned enterprises and the second-largest global IPO in 2003.

connecting international carriers in Europe, the USA and Africa
- corporate voice service installation improving by 87% to 0,4 days
- business voice service installation improving by 60% to two days
- ISDN service installation improving by 52% to 15 days
- faults per 1 000 business lines improving from 265 to 242.

During 2002/03, Telkom took some major steps to manage the impact of reducing staff numbers. Alternative strategies to avoid job losses were introduced, including establishing Telkom's Agency for Career Opportunities.

The Agency creates new opportunities for its employees whose jobs may have been affected by the changing nature of the communications industry.

Sixty-two per cent of the 37 employees at management level who entered the Agency in November 2002 have been appointed internally.

Telkom Foundation

The Telkom Foundation enables Telkom to play an active role in South Africa's socio-economic development.

Telkom founded the Foundation in 1998. With a budget of R100 million over a period of five years, its principal objective was to contribute to the transformation of disadvantaged communities through sustainable development programmes.

On 1 April 2002, the Foundation was established as an autonomous legal entity of Telkom SA Limited and a non-profit organisation. It is now registered as a trust, with a board of trustees and its own CEO. Despite its autonomy, the Foundation remains Telkom's sole corporate social-investment arm tasked with co-ordinating the company's social-investment activities.

The Foundation continues to pursue a philosophy of empowerment and sustainable development through its focus on:

Communications

- mathematics, science and technology
- the empowerment of women, children and people with disabilities
- education and training.

During 2002/03, the Foundation's expenditure amounted to R39 million. Some 42% was allocated to mathematics, science and technology, 32% to empowerment projects, and 11% to education and training. A further 15% was spent on general projects.

Establishing partnerships with national and provincial role-players in government and NGOs, ensuring full community involvement, and building relationships with stakeholders and structures in previously disadvantaged communities, lie at the core of its philosophy.

Economic empowerment

Empowerment spending

Since 1997, Telkom has spent close to R14 billion to meet its empowerment objectives, constantly refining its focus to meet the changing needs of the empowerment process.

Centres of Excellence (CoEs)

This is a collaborative programme between Telkom, the telecommunications industry and government to promote postgraduate research in communications technology and allied social sciences, and to provide facilities that encourage young scientists and engineers to pursue their interests in South Africa.

Launched in 1997, the programme has already improved local telecommunications and IT skills, yielding substantial benefits for the academic institutions involved. It has helped Telkom and its local technology partners to solve technical problems and cut costs. Telkom's corporate partners are also reaping rewards as the work undertaken at the CoEs is relevant to their areas of business.

Since the inception of the postgraduate research programme, approximately R150 million has been realised for telecommunications research in South Africa.

There are currently 14 Centres located at tertiary institutions around the country. Approximately 350 students conduct post graduate telecommunications research through the CoE programme. Seventy of these receive support from Telkom to conduct full-time research.

In addition to developing skills in science, engineering and technology, the Centres aim at creating partnerships between historically disadvantaged and advantaged institutions, to jointly focus on a specific aspect of telecommunications research. This approach provides for the transfer of skills to, and the upliftment of, previously disadvantaged institutions.

Sponsorships

Telkom has a clear sponsorship strategy, centred on a programme of national events designed to enable, encourage and support talented South Africans, while positively promoting the Telkom brand. Telkom has committed R8,25 million over three years to Proudly South African, an organisation established to create jobs, increase demand for South African products and services, and encourage companies to improve their quality and competitiveness.

Proudly South African's membership criteria are based on the principles of sound environmental policies, fair labour practice and unwavering commitment to quality and meaningful local production value.

Mobile communications

South Africa, with the operators Vodacom, MTN and Cell C, is the fourth-fastest growing mobile-communications market in the world. By October 2003, there were 15 million cellular users in the country and the figure is expected to grow to 21 million by 2006.

The country's third cellular licence was granted to Cell C in June 2001. It started operating on 17 November 2001. Cell C (Pty) Ltd is wholly owned by 3C Telecommunications (Pty) Ltd, which in turn is 60% owned by Oger Telecom South Africa, a division of Saudi Oger, and 40% by Cell SAF. It also brought in Verizon Communications, the biggest cellular operator in the USA, as its operating partner. Cell C started operating on an 084 prefix number range. Three service-providers, namely Cell C, Nashua Mobile and Autopage Cellular, have been working together to connect South Africans to the 084 network. Cell C signed a 15-year roaming agreement with Vodacom in July 2001.

By August 2003, Cell C had more than 1,5 million subscribers. Cell C's business plan envisages creating 2 500 direct and 15 000 indirect jobs within four to five years, encompassing individuals from all previously disadvantaged sectors. Women account for more than 40% of the total staff complement, which by August 2003 was over 1 200.

The company is making extensive use of local organisations and contractors to ensure that funds are injected into the South African economy. It has invested more than R2,5 billion in goods and services since its launch, with more than R990 million of this benefiting historically disadvantaged individuals.

Cell C aims to achieve 20% of the market-share by 2007.

Cell C has six active-roaming agreements in Namibia, Mozambique, Spain, the Ivory Coast, Mauritius and Swaziland, and has entered into roaming agreements with an additional 49 international operators.

Vodacom is South Africa's leading cellular network with a 61% share of the market. More than 95% of all new connections are prepaid customers. Telkom is the majority shareholder of Vodacom, with a 50% interest. Other stakeholders are Vodafone (31,5%), Rembrandt Group Ltd (13,5%), and Hosken's Consolidated Investments (5%).

By July 2003, Vodacom was providing a service to almost seven million customers in South Africa, Tanzania, Lesotho and the Democratic Republic of the Congo.

More than 5 000 Vodacom base stations provide coverage to 93% of the South African population.

MTN was the first cellular provider in the world to have mobile coverage of 60 000 km^2, obtain a cellular licence in Africa, and launch prepaid cellular packages in South Africa, as well as a special package for the deaf community.

MTN's network coverage in South Africa embraces almost 900 000 km^2 (including sea) and provides telecommunications access to 94,5% of the population. MTN's other African operations include Uganda, Swaziland, Rwanda, Cameroon and Nigeria. MTN has close to five million subscribers.

MTN was the first African network to be awarded the international quality certifications ISO 9001 for its Network and IT divisions, ISO 9002 for its Customer Services Department, and ISO 14001 for its Environmental Management System.

The Telecommunications Act, 1996 provides for 1 800 MHz spectrum (as well as 2,4 GHz – 3G spectrum), to be issued to existing operators, the SNO and underserviced area operators. A key element in this process is the determination of access fees and universal service obligations (USOs) for the allocation of the frequency spectrum.

The Department of Communications negotiated these issues, including new service fees and additional USOs, with the industry. The proposed obligations will include:
- the supply of 250 000 free phones and numbers to public emergency services over a period of five years
- the provision of Internet and phone links, including computers in schools
- public pay phones in accessible places in rural areas and MPCCs
- the issuing of some four million free SIM cards over a period of five years.

The postal sector

Policy and legislation

The cornerstone of national policy for the postal sector is the provision of a universal service at an affordable price and acceptable standard of service for all citizens. In order to ensure this, a USO is placed on the SAPO. In order to offset the cost of providing a basic service in low-density, rural or uneconomical areas, it has also been common practice to confer exclusive rights and privileges, i.e. a monopoly on the provision of the basic letter service.

A USO is an obligation to provide specified services to the whole community, even though these services may not be commercially viable in their own right. The universal postal service implies that all citizens will have equal access to a basic letter service:
- that is reasonably accessible to all people
- at a single uniform rate of postage
- at the lowest price consistent with meeting all its obligations, financial and otherwise
- to places outside the country
- at a standard of performance which reasonably meets the needs of the population.

The adoption of the *White Paper on Postal Policy* in May 1998 paved the way for legislative reform, which resulted in the Postal Services Act, 1998 (Act 124 of 1998), which repealed certain sections of the Post Office Act, 1958 (Act 44 of 1958). The Postal Services Act, 1998 came into operation in January 1999.

In terms of the Post Office Act, 1958, SAPO enjoyed exclusive rights and privileges, including a monopoly on letter mail up to 2 kg.

The South African Post Office (SAPO) has developed an educational tool in collaboration with READ Educational Trust. The project focuses on:
- establishing links between SAPO and communities
- increasing awareness, knowledge and community perception of SAPO
- positioning the company positively in the communities it serves
- promoting the use of SAPO's products and services
- building the image of SAPO.

By February 2003, 900 schools had been visited and 4 000 books distributed.

According to the Postal Services Act, 1998, SAPO continues to enjoy certain exclusive rights and privileges. The monopoly is now on letter mail up to 1 kg.

In addition, SAPO is obliged to operate under a 25-year licence with explicit universal service targets and other terms and conditions. The monopoly and compliance with the terms and conditions of the licence will be reviewed and monitored by the regulator.

New projects of the postal policy section include the establishment of a Postal Training Institute for the postal industry, and postal security improvements, both local and regional.

Postal services regulatory framework

The Postal Regulator, established in terms of the Postal Services Act, 1998, is responsible for exercising regulatory functions in relation to the reserved and unreserved postal services. The Regulator encourages the expansion of postal services and promotes the interests of postal-service users in terms of the cost of reserved services. The Regulator is also responsible for issuing postal licences and monitoring compliance with licence conditions by the operators.

South African Post Office

SAPO Ltd was established in terms of Section 3 of the Post Office Act, 1958 as a government business enterprise to provide postal and rela-ted services to the South African public. SAPO reports to the Minister of Communications. The Government subsidy to SAPO was terminated on 31 March 2000. This was in anticipation of SAPO becoming a viable profit-making business. However, the turnaround strategy did not succeed and the organisation sustained further losses in 2000/01 and 2001/02. To help improve the finances of SAPO, to enable it to continue rolling out postal infrastructure, the subsidy was re-introduced in 2001/02 with an initial allocation of R600 million. A further R300 million a year has also been allocated for the medium term.

The principal function of SAPO is to supply postal services within and outside of South Africa. SAPO may also conduct subsidiary and incidental businesses and activities relating to postal services.

Principal activities

SAPO is expected to break even at the end of the 2003/04 financial year, for the first time in the many years of its existence.

The improved state of affairs is partly due to the following undertakings and achievements:
- in the financial year ending March 2003, SAPO managed to cut down its operating losses to R154 million, down 50% from a R351 million-loss in 2001/02 and a R580 million-loss in 2000/01
- in line with SAPO's commitment to social and economic transformation, in the last three years, its Black Economic Empowerment spend increased from 6% to 35,4%, representing R321 million being spent on previously disadvantaged companies.

Business re-engineering

In the ensuing years, SAPO will concentrate on financial services (15% at present) and courier business (18% at present), and develop expertise in these areas. SAPO intends to grow its financial services and courier business to 20% each. The decline in mail volumes and the emergence of ICTs, which have brought about new realities, have necessitated this business re-engineering process.

This transformation has put SAPO among the top 15 post offices in the world that have transformed their revenue streams.

The main areas of business are the delivery of domestic and international letters, and courier and parcel services.

Products and services

SAPO handles an average of six million letters a day, 70% of which are prepaid mass-mailed letters sent by companies using franking machines. All franking machine systems in operation in South Africa operate on remote meter-settings. The system enables the user to frank, date and seal an article, print a return address and count the items in the same time as it takes to have a stamp affixed, thus saving time and money. The exact postage due can be franked onto an envelope or label, as opposed to affixing a number of postage stamps to make up the postage due. Machine inspections are done on the clients' premises.

Counter service

In addition to letter mail and parcel services, SAPO offers a range of other mail services, including courier services; agency services such as pension payments; and the collection of third-party payments on behalf of organisations such as Telkom, the SABC and local government. It also offers savings and money-transfer services through the Postbank.

Securemail

Securemail is a business unit aimed at handling security-sensitive items such as credit cards. It handles more than 2,5 million credit cards a year.

It was established with the full co-operation of major financial institutions to minimise postal theft and fraud. Since its inception,

---

The South African Post Office (SAPO) has adopted an attitude of zero tolerance towards crime. Corrupt employees are dealt with severely, irrespective of their position in the company. From April 2002 to December 2002, 277 employees were dismissed for postal crimes, 13 of whom were in management positions. Since April 2002, 59 persons (including members of the public) were arrested for postal crime.

In May 2003, SAPO was nominated into the Top Five post offices in the world for the most secure mail services, during the International Mail Awards held in Rome, Italy.

Communications

there has been a significant decrease in credit card theft. Over 99% of cards handled are now successfully delivered.

Freight and courier services
The Courier and Freight Group (Pty) Ltd of SAPO became the biggest distribution company in southern Africa when it took over the customer base of Fast Forward. Services available are:
- parcel distribution, express and courier services
- mini-container services
- parcel and mini-container services to neighbouring countries
- document exchange
- Speed Services Couriers.

Philatelic services
The sale of postage stamps is traditionally associated with SAPO. Annually, SAPO prints more than 384 million of these tiny works of art. Stamps not only play an important role in the daily postal delivery system, but also serve the interests of a great many stamp collectors and philatelists by keeping pace with historic events and parading the country's rich culture and diverse artistic splendour. SAPO's Philatelic Division serves stamp collectors and dealers throughout the world. Apart from counter sales and mail orders, the Division operates a deposit account system whereby new issues are automatically mailed to stamp collectors all over the world.

Stamps for 2003 included issues to celebrate the Cricket World Cup, the 175th Anniversary of King Shaka's assassination, 100 years of flight (aviation), Africa Day and a collection on life in informal settlements.

Mail volumes
SAPO services over 40 million South Africans and numerous public and private institutions. It delivers mail items to over 7,5 million delivery points.

Postal network
SAPO has some 2 760 postal outlets countrywide and 30 mail processing centres. The management of the post offices, agencies, local hubs and delivery depots in the provinces is done through postal regions. The network is being rebalanced for access and more equitable services, especially in historically disadvantaged areas. South Africa has a network of postal routes across which mail is conveyed to and from cities, towns, villages and hamlets.

SAPO uses road transport on most of the major routes in the country for the dispatch of domestic surface mail. Sea mail is carried to all parts of the world as and when ships are available. Closed surface-mail dispatches are forwarded to more than 90 countries and received from more than 75, while closed airmail dispatches are forwarded to more than 65 and received from more than 100 countries. Some 45 airlines transport mail to South Africa and about 33 airlines transport mail from the country. The international air and surface parcel service of SAPO is available to some 220 countries.

Delivery standards and service performance
SAPO uses various systems to measure service performance. Each of the systems is in operation nationally and provides operational and management information which is monitored weekly at a video conference at the National Control Centre.

To ensure quick and accurate mail delivery, the use of correct postal codes is essential. Postal codes may be obtained from the Internet at *www.sapo.co.za* or through the PostCoder software package (toll-free number 0800 110 980).

Address provision
The provision of addresses to previously underserviced areas continues. This project aims to ensure that every citizen of South Africa, irrespective of location in the country or

economic status, has an address. SAPO delivers mail to 6,5 million addresses. Of these, 3,4 million are street addresses and three million are post boxes. The aim is to install five million additional address boxes within the next few years.

Postbank
Postbank is aiming at remaining a profitable entity within SAPO's infrastructure. It services its target market through a carefully defined and expanded mix of innovative and traditional products, using cost-effective distribution channels, including SAPO's network.

Postbank is in the process of refining and expanding its product range to cater for the needs of the 'unbanked' part of the South African population. This will include providing loan facilities and other basic banking products.

As part of the restructuring process, Postbank is being corporatised to ensure that it plays a greater role in development activities. These include addressing the financial-service needs of low-income communities and improving access to credit for small businesses. The Department is currently investigating an appropriate governance and regulatory framework for Postbank. Its aim is to ensure adequate protection of public deposits and the associated contingent liability to government, while also ensuring the bank's ability to meet its mandate.

International and regional co-operation
South Africa is a member of the Universal Postal Union (UPU). The country participates in technical assistance programmes within the UPU, and uses its international accounting facility. It also participates in other international bodies such as the Pan African Postal Union, Council of Commonwealth Postal Administrations and the Southern African Transport and Communications Commission.

South Africa, through the Department of Communications, is a signatory to international treaties, conventions and agreements. It co-operates and works in partnership with other postal administrations through either bilateral or multilateral agreements relating to letters, parcels and postal financial services.

The media

Media freedom
According to the Bill of Rights, as contained in South Africa's Constitution, 1996 (Act 108 of 1996), everyone has the right to freedom of expression, which includes:
- freedom of the press and other media
- freedom to receive or impart information or ideas
- freedom of artistic creativity
- academic freedom and freedom of scientific research.

Several laws, policies and organisations act to protect and promote press freedom in South Africa.

The first Press Freedom Index by Reporters Without Barriers, released late in 2002, ranked press freedom in South Africa as 26th in the world.

Finland, Iceland, Norway and the Netherlands share first place on the Index. South Africa shares its place with Austria and Japan.

Broadcasting

Policy and legislation
The Broadcasting Act, 1999 (Act 4 of 1999), and the IBA Act, 1993 (Act 153 of 1993), are aimed at establishing and developing a broadcasting policy to regulate and control all broadcasting to:
- contribute to democracy, nation-building, the provision of education, and strengthening the moral fibre of society
- encourage ownership and control of broadcasting services by people from historically disadvantaged communities

Communications

- ensure fair competition in the sector
- provide for a three-tier system of public, commercial and community broadcasting services
- establish a strong and committed public broadcaster to service the needs of all South Africans.

The Act defines the objectives of the South African broadcasting system, the structure of the SABC, and the roles of the various sectors in meeting these objectives. It also guarantees the independence of the SABC as public broadcaster. Section 8 of the Broadcasting Act, 1999 sets out the objectives of the SABC.

The SABC is being corporatised and restructured in order to better fulfil its mandate of meeting the needs of its audiences. These include accurate and credible news and current affairs programmes; local content programming in languages reflecting the country's cultural diversity; educational programming to advance lifelong learning; and programming targeted at children, women and people with disabilities.

The Act deals with the restructuring of the SABC to fit into the changing broadcasting environment. The Act requires that the SABC board establishes two management boards to focus on the public and commercial services. Under the new dispensation, the public broadcasting wing will execute and meet its public-service mandate free from commercial interests. The commercial wing will be allowed to generate profit to be self-sustainable.

The Broadcasting Amendment Act, 2002 (Act 64 of 2002), was proclaimed on 7 March 2003. It brings into effect, among others, the new Code of Conduct for Broadcasters.

Implementation of the Act will result in a better definition of public and commercial broadcasting services.

The SABC has developed, for the first time, editorial policies for news and other programming that covers issues including content accuracy and impartiality. The policies are open to public comment.

The Broadcasting Amendment Act, 2002 provides for the establishment of two regional television licences: the first for the northern region, to cater for the Sesotho, Xitsonga, Tshivenda and Sepedi languages; and the second for the southern region, to cater for the Nguni languages.

The *White Paper on Broadcasting* provided for the establishment of the Digital Broadcasting Advisory Body. Early in 2001, the Minister jointly launched the Digital Advisory Body and the Broadcast Production Advisory Body, consisting of representatives from all broadcasting stakeholders, to promote the production of local content, the production of material that will meet the needs of the community sector, and the foreign sale of local products. The Digital Broadcast Advisory Body works very closely with the Department of Communications. The Body advises the Minister on technology issues, with particular reference to digital broadcasting and the economic and other implications of converting from analogue to digital transmission techniques.

Cross-media control and local content

The schedule to the Broadcasting Act, 1999 provides for certain amendments to Section 50 of the IBA Act, 1993. It states the specific parameters for cross-media ownership, pending the investigation called for in the White Paper to review the limitations on cross-media control.

ICASA also has to investigate the level of foreign ownership. Early in 2003, the level of ownership of private radio and television stations permitted for a foreigner was 20%.

The Government believed that this should be raised to increase investment.

ICASA released a position paper requiring local radio and television stations to increase their quotas of locally produced content as of August 2003. New quotas for public and community radio stations were doubled to 40%, while qoutas for private and public commercial stations were raised to 25%. New quotas for television were increased to 55% for public broadcasters, 30% for commercial private and public free-to-air stations, and 8% for pay stations.

Independent Communications Authority of South Africa

In May 2000, the ICASA Act, 2000 was proclaimed, paving the way for the merger of SATRA and the IBA and the establishment of ICASA.

Broadcasting role-players

Radio

The first radio broadcasts in South Africa took place under the auspices of a broadcasting committee of the South African Railways. The first experimental broadcast was undertaken in Johannesburg on 18 December 1923 by the Western Electric Company.

During 1924, the Associated Scientific and Technical Association of South Africa began regular broadcasts in Johannesburg. The Cape Peninsula Publicity Broadcasting Association began a similar service, and the Durban Municipality followed suit with its own regular broadcasts.

The first radio station, JB Calling, went on air in July 1924.

By 1926, legislation had become necessary. Under the Radio Act, 1926 (Act 20 of 1926), all radio transmission and reception was placed under the control of the Postmaster-General.

Following the contribution made by Sir John Reith, the then Director-General of the British Broadcasting Corporation (BBC), the SABC was established on 1 August 1936.

The SABC is the country's public broadcaster. It introduced its own national news service on 17 July 1950, with daily news bulletins on the English service, the Afrikaans service, and Springbok Radio.

Radio Zulu, Radio Xhosa and Radio Sesotho were established on 1 June 1960.

The SABC's national radio network comprises 20 stations which, combined, reach an average daily adult audience of 20 million.

For its internal coverage, Radio News uses about 13 editorial offices, a countrywide network of about 1 300 correspondents, and more than 2 000 news contacts.

World news is provided by international news agencies and strategically situated foreign correspondents.

Copy supplied to Radio News from various sources amounts to almost a million words a day, and is compiled round the clock into 300 news bulletins and 22 current affairs programmes broadcast daily on the SABC's radio services. There is a public broadcasting service radio station for each language group.

The SABC also started an external service along the lines of the BBC World Service and the Voice of America in 1966. Called Radio South Africa, the channel was funded by the Department of Foreign Affairs.

In the early 1990s, the channel's name was changed to Channel Africa as part of the transformation of the image and the role of the public broadcaster. It is targeted at audiences in Africa and the Indian Ocean islands, and offers an all-African radio service. As a broadcaster from Africa to Africa, it concentrates on providing programmes with a specific African content.

Channel Africa is part of the State-owned portfolio which is being administered by the SABC on behalf of government.

Channel Africa comprises four language services, reaching millions of listeners throughout Africa. Broadcasts are in English, French, Kiswahili and Portuguese.

Private radio stations

The following private radio stations have been granted licences by ICASA: Classic FM in Gauteng; Cape Talk MW in the Western Cape; P4, a jazz station in Cape Town with a sister station in Durban; Kaya FM, a multilingual youth radio station in Gauteng; Y-FM, broadcasting in Johannesburg in isiZulu, Sesotho and English; Radio KFM; Radio Algoa; Radio Oranje; Highveld Stereo; Radio 702 in Gauteng; East Coast Radio; and Radio Jacaranda. Stations such as Radio Jacaranda, Highveld Stereo, Radio Oranje, Radio Algoa and East Coast Radio were initially SABC stations, but were sold to private owners to diversify radio ownership in South Africa as part of the transformation of the public broadcaster.

In August 2002, ICASA revoked the licences of Punt Geselsradio in Johannesburg and Cape Town, after having considered and applied a recommendation by the Broadcasting Monitoring Complaints Committee (BMCC).

Community radio stations

Over the past 10 years, 94 community radio broadcasting and 10 commercial licences were awarded. The Multimedia Unit of the Department of Communications instituted both infrastructure, and support and programme-production support, through the provision of 42 community radio station licences to communities, and 50 000 minutes of programming produced to cover disability, children, women, HIV/AIDS, and crime. NEMISA, established in 1998, was set up to offer all-round, integrated training in broadcasting and multimedia transformational needs.

It is estimated that 88% of the rural population listens to the radio in a seven-day period, compared to 79% in 1994.

Television

SABC

A one-channel television service was introduced on 5 January 1976.

Today, the SABC's national television network comprises four full-spectrum free-to-air channels, two satellite pay-TV channels aimed at audiences in Africa, and Bop-TV, which the SABC runs on behalf of the State. Combined, the free-to-air channels broadcast in 11 languages and reach a daily adult audience of almost 17 million people via the terrestrial signal distribution network and a satellite signal.

There are more than four million licensed television households in South Africa. South Africa is the country with by far the largest television audience in Africa.

About 50% of all programmes transmitted are produced in South Africa. Locally produced television programmes are augmented by programmes purchased abroad, and by co-productions undertaken with other television programming organisations. Television news is fed by SABC news teams reporting from all parts of the country, using modern portable electronic cameras and line-feed equipment via more than 220 television transmitters. *Ad hoc* satellite feeds are arranged from wherever news events occur.

News bulletins are broadcast in all 11 official languages.

M-Net

M-Net, South Africa's first private subscription television service, was launched in 1986. Today, it has over 1,23 million subscribers in 49 countries across the African continent.

M-Net, which is listed on the JSE, features broad-ranging programme scheduling on its two terrestrial channels in South Africa.

In November 1999, it also made its debut on the Nigerian Stock Exchange, making it the first South African company to list in Nigeria.

The main M-Net channel focuses on movies and sport, but also offers a general entertainment line-up of children's programmes, series, and magazine programmes.

It has a daily two-hour 'open window' when unencoded programmes (available to viewers without decoders), including the country's longest-running local soap opera, *Egoli – Place of Gold*, are screened.

The second channel, Community Services Network, offers niche sports programming and specialised community channels for the local Indian, Portuguese, Italian, Jewish, and Christian communities.

Development of the local film and television industries is a priority, and is supported by the New Directions project, which identifies and mentors emerging film-makers; and the M-Net All Africa Awards, which recognise excellence in films made across the African continent. These projects, which play a dynamic role in nurturing and investing in the film and television industry, are among a number of initiatives and co-productions funded by M-Net's commissioning and productions department, MagicWorks.

M-Net's licence has been renewed until 2010.

Satellite broadcasting

MultiChoice Africa (MCA), was formed in 1995 to manage the subscriber services of its sister company, M-Net. It became the first African company on the continent to offer digital satellite broadcasting

This innovation has been the hallmark of MCA, culminating in its presence in over 50 countries throughout Africa. MCA provides television entertainment through its DStv, Indian, Portuguese and Arabic bouquets, to 638 000 subscribers in South Africa and a total of 860 000 subscribers across 50 countries on the African continent and adjacent Indian Ocean islands. This is done through franchises and joint ventures. Operations include subscriber-management services and digital satellite television platforms broadcasting 55 video and 48 audio channels 24 hours a day. Included are six data channels which were the first interactive television offerings on the continent. In addition, interactive services like TV-Mail and TV-Shopping are also available in South Africa.

MCA's technological roll-out has included the launch of data channels and W4 satellite over west Africa, which has made digital satellite television acquisition cheaper. An added benefit has been the Africanisation of channels where local stations and languages are accommodated in the countries where MCA is broadcasting.

MCA is 100% owned by the MIH Group, which is listed on the JSE, NASDAQ in New York, and AEX in Amsterdam.

Free-to-air television

The *White Paper on Broadcasting Policy*, released in June 1998, provided for the extension of free-to-air, pay and regional television services. On 30 March 1998, the consortium Midi Television was awarded the first privately owned free-to-air television licence.

The station they operate, e.tv, is a commercial service dependent on advertising. It does not charge subscription fees. The e.tv channel started broadcasting on 1 October 1998. News broadcasts and a 24-hour service were introduced early in 1999.

Signal distribution

The signal distributor Sentech will be developed into a multimedia company, which will provide infrastructure for digital broadcasting in South Africa as well as international gateway telecommunications.

Sentech, the official signal carrier of the SABC, launched its new business initiatives in June 2002. Until then, Sentech's mandate entailed the provision of its network for use by other operators, and the provision of telecommunications services direct to customers or end-users.

In July 2003, the Independent Communications Authority of South Africa (ICASA) released a *Position Paper and Regulations on Sports Broadcasting*, that allows the majority of South Africans to enjoy their favourite sport of rugby, cricket, soccer and the Olympic Games on free-to-air TV channels.

ICASA listed the Summer Olympic Games, All Africa Games, FIFA Soccer World Cup, the Rugby Super 12 (only if a South African team is competing) and the Confederation of African Football's Champions League as events of national interest.

Communications

As part of its new business initiatives, Sentech will add to the launch of the submarine cable, which links Africa with Europe and the Far East, by entering the international telecommunications market and providing the necessary infrastructure for African inter-connectivity.

Sentech has started the phased roll-out of its Multimedia Network. The Multimedia Business was expected to be launched before the end of 2003. Sentech's International Gateway is operational and the company has signed its first customer, namely one of the South African mobile operators. Commercial agreements with other operators are to be concluded in due course. The international gateway infrastructure is being expanded in anticipation of increased voice traffic.

Sentech is also a co-sponsor of the Information Systems Electronics and Telecommunications Technologies Sector Education and Training Authority (SETA), with the expressed aim of introducing technology to people in the rural areas around the country.

Print

Technical handling of the print media in South Africa rates among the best in the world. On the editorial side, concerns have been raised about the general quality of content from a journalistic point of view. Research has shown that journalists lack certain basic skills and the juniorisation of newsrooms has impacted negatively on most of the major publications.

The roots of the print media in South Africa can be traced back to the 19th century, when the first issue of a government newspaper, the *Cape Town Gazette and African Advertiser/Kaapsche Stads Courant and Afrikaansche Berigter*, was published in 1800.

The first independent publication, *The South African Commercial Advertiser*, was published in 1824 by Thomas Pringle and John Fairbairn. Eighteen issues later it was banned, and reappeared only after various representations had been made to the authorities in London.

South African newspapers and magazines are mainly organised into press groups, which have burgeoned over the years as a result of take-overs.

The major press groups are Independent Newspapers (Pty) Ltd, Media24 Ltd, CTP/Caxton Publishers and Printers Ltd, and Johnnic Publishing Ltd.

Other important media players include Primedia, Nail (New Africa Investments Limited) and Kagiso Media. Nail has unbundled into a commercial company (New Africa Capital) and a media company (New Africa Media).

Since 1994, the major press groups have embarked on programmes to boost black empowerment in media ownerships.

Newspapers

Most South African newspapers are based on the British model. Management and editorial departments are controlled separately.

The size of the country – 1 500 km separating the main centres of Cape Town and Johannesburg – still precludes national dailies in the true sense of the word. Some of the bigger titles and specialist newspapers like *Business Day* are distributed in metropolitan areas. The only truly national newspapers are the four Sunday newspapers, *Sunday Times*, *Rapport*, *Sunday Independent* and *Sunday Sun*, and the weekly newspaper *City Press*. All are published simultaneously in various cities, using the printing facilities of related dailies. A number of newspapers have introduced separate weekend editions of their daily newspapers, e.g. *Saturday Star*, *Saturday Dispatch* and *Post Weekend*.

The *Sunday World*, launched in March 1999, soon lost its initial popularity. It was relaunched in 2000 as the *Sowetan Sunday World* and almost doubled its circulation. But the biggest success story of 2002 belongs to the *Daily Sun*. This Gauteng newspaper launched by Media24 in July 2002, has become the biggest daily in South Africa. Imitating the tabloid format and the controversial content line that appears in its British namesake, *The Sun,* it took the South African daily market by storm. An Afrikaans version, *Son,* has been launched in the Western Cape and Gauteng and all indications are that it will be successful.

There are 17 dailies, seven Sunday papers and 24 weeklies in South Africa. Almost 161 Community Press Association or country newspapers, most of which are weekly tabloids, serve particular towns or districts in the country, by covering local affairs and carrying local advertising. Most are published in English and Afrikaans. The most popular publication day is Friday.

Newspapers appearing only in certain neighbourhoods are also part of this section. They are known as 'knock-and-drops' or 'freebies' as they are distributed free of charge. They have a guaranteed readership with advertising being their only source of income. More than 3,5 million newspapers in this sector are distributed weekly.

In 2002, the Audit Bureau of Circulation (ABC) listed more than 90 such papers. They are distributed mainly in urban areas and number in the hundreds when unlisted ones are considered. Press groups such as Media24 and CTP/Caxton are major players in this field.

Since 1996, local newspapers, freebies and corporate newspapers have ventured into reporting in indigenous languages as well. With 11 official languages, it can be expected that more home-language publications will emerge. Separate newspapers for different cultural groups are still preferred, with English as the popular language of choice.

Circulation

Newspapers

Most of the dailies showed a slight decrease in circulation during the period July to December 2002, owing to the decline in sales during the festive season. Weekly newspapers saw more impressive growth of 8,2% for 2002, compared with 2001 figures. This growth is attributed to increased black readership of English newspapers.

According to the All Media Products Survey (AMPS) 2002B readership survey compiled by the South African Advertising Research Foundation (SAARF):

- The total newspaper readership increased slightly to 45% or 13,324 million readers.
- Daily readership also increased significantly to 17,1% or 5,045 million as opposed to 16% in the past. A significant increase in readers between the ages of 16 and 24 was also noted. The average number of papers per reader also showed an average increase at 1,27 papers per reader, which was up from 1,25 in AMPS 2002A.
- Daily newspapers showed remarkable stability on a paper-by-paper basis, supporting the theory that the introduction of the newspapers *Daily Sun* and *Isolezwe* (Independent Newspapers' isiZulu newspaper in KwaZulu-Natal) brought real growth to the sector, attracting new readers to the mix.
- Weekly papers had a 39,6% or 11,72 million readership.
- Weekly newspapers maintained their previous levels with market penetration at 30,8%. The average number of weekly newspapers per reader was 1,89 as opposed to 1,91 in the AMPS 2002A survey.
- Readership of community papers remained stable, with total penetration at 21,9%. The only province to register a readership change was the Northern Cape, which saw its readership falling from 29,8% to 20%.

The growth in the Sunday market is an indication that black readership is picking up. These papers showed healthy figures while dailies traditionally read by black people, namely the *Sowetan, Star* and *Citizen,* did not show any increase in circulation. The *Sowetan* saw a disappointing drop from more than 200 000 readers in 2001 to less than 160 000 in 2002.

Although the literacy of the South African population increased by more than 20% from 1991 to 1995, this has not been reflected in the circulation figures of traditional English newspapers. This is attributed to aliteracy among South Africans (aliteracy refers to people who can read, but choose not to).

The battle for the top position in the Sunday market continued throughout 2002. *Sunday Times* did not experience a decrease in circulation, but *City Press* and the *Sowetan Sunday World* received stiff competition from the *Sunday Sun*.

The soccer newspaper, *Laduma*, steadily drew more and more readers during 2002 and its circulation topped 200 000.

The Cape Town newspapers did especially well with their weekend editions. *Die Burger* and especially the *Weekend Argus* outsold their daily editions.

Magazines

The ABC figures for the period July to December 2002 indicated a relatively static overall magazine market with circulation down an overall 2% in comparison with the ABC figures for the same period in 2001, which is echoed by the AMPS figures. Considering the explosion of titles in the market over the last few years, magazine sales have remained constant and the focus for publishers remains on retail sales.

The business-to-business magazine market was larger than the consumer market, but only by a small margin. Most titles were highly niched with small circulations.

In terms of magazine sectors, the men's magazine sector showed an increase in circulation across all three titles and the women's magazine market remained highly competitive. The year 2003 saw the launch of two more titles into these specific markets – *Razor* for men and *Glamour* for women.

The major publishers in the magazine industry are Media24, Caxton, Johnnic, Associated Magazines and Ramsay Son & Parker.

Distribution

In cities, newspapers rely heavily on street sales and door-to-door delivery. Cafés and general stores provide additional selling points. In rural areas, newspapers are distributed mainly by special truck deliveries, often covering hundreds of kilometres in a single run. The cost of bulk transport by air is very high.

Sold magazines with the largest circulation, July – December 2002

Name	Frequency	Language	Audited circulation
Huisgenoot	W	A	347 519
You	W	E	231 648
Sarie	M	A	162 642
Rooi Rose	M	A	141 155
True Love	M	E	134 098
Reader's Digest	M	E	119 373
TV Plus	M	B	118 015
People	F	E	113 285
The Motorist	Q	B	110 348
Cosmopolitan	M	E	102 984

The abbreviations used are the following: W (weekly), F (fortnightly), E (English), M (monthly), Q (quarterly), A (Afrikaans), B (bilingual)

Source: Audit Bureau of Circulation

South Africa Yearbook 2003/04

Daily and weekly papers

Name	Publisher	Contact information	Frequency	Language	Audited circulation Jul – Dec 2002
Beeld (Daily)	Media 24	PO Box 333, Auckland Park, 2006 T. 011 713-9000 / F. 011 713-9956 E-mail: beeld@beeld.com	MD, M-F	A	101 212
Beeld (Saturday)	Media 24	PO Box 333, Auckland Park, 2006	W, Sat	A	85 039
Burger, Die (Daily)	Media 24	PO Box 692, Cape Town, 8000	MD, M-F	A	106 499
Burger, Die (Saturday)	Media 24	PO Box 692, Cape Town, 8000 T. 021 406-2121 / F. 021 406-2911	W, Sat	A	116 370
Business Day	BDFM Publishers (Pty) Ltd	PO Box 1742, Saxonwold, 2132 T. 011 280-3000 / F. 011 280-5600 E-mail: bday@tml.co.za	MD, M-F	E	41 653
Cape Argus, The	Independent Newspapers Cape Ltd	PO Box 56, Cape Town, 8000 T. 021 488-4911 / F. 021 488-4075 E-mail: josepha@ctn.independent.co.za	AD, M-F	E	78 423
Cape Times (Daily)	Independent Newspapers Cape Ltd	PO Box 56, Cape Town, 8000 T. 021 488-4911 / F. 021 488-4762 E-mail: chriswh@independent.co.za	MD, M-F	E	48 774
Citizen, The (Daily)	Caxton Publishers & Printers Ltd	PO Box 7712, Johannesburg, 2000 T. 011 713-2901 / F. 011 713-9985 E-mail: news@citizen.co.za	MD, M-F	E	80 886
Citizen, The (Saturday)	Caxton Publishers & Printers Ltd	PO Box 7712, Johannesburg, 2000	W, Sat	E	
City Press	RCP Media Bpk	PO Box 3413, Johannesburg, 2000 T. 011 713-9001 / F. 011 713-9985 E-mail: news@citypress.co.za	W, Sun	E	188 546
Daily Dispatch	Dispatch Media (Pty) Ltd	PO Box 131, East London, 5200 T. 031 308-2381 / F. 011 308-2111	AD, M-F	E	32 806
Daily News	Independent Newspapers KZN	PO Box 47549, Greyville, 4023 T. 031 308-2911 / F. 013 308-2111 E-mail: tbruce@nn.independent.co.za	AD, M-F	E	51 091
Daily Sun	Media 24	PO Box 333, Auckland Park, 2006 T. 011 877 6000	MD, M-F	E	71 742
Diamond Fields Advertiser	Independent Newspapers Gauteng Ltd	PO Box 610, Kimberley, 8300 T. 053 832-6261 / F. 053 832-1141 E-mail: pbe@independent.co.za	MD, M-F	E	8 432
East Cape Weekend	Times Media Eastern Cape	PO Box 1121, Port Elizabeth, 6000 T. 041 504 7911	W, Sat	E	32 399
Herald (Daily)	Times Media Eastern Cape	PO Box 1117, Port Elizabeth, 6000 T. 041 504-7911 / F. 041 554-966 E-mail: epherald@tmecl.co.za	MD, M-F	E	31 689
Herald (Saturday)	Times Media	PO Box 1117, Port Elizabeth, 6000 T. 041 504-7911 / F. 041 554-966 E-mail: epherald@tmecl.co.za	W, Sat	E	23 775
Ilanga	Mandla Matla Publishing Co (Pty) Ltd	PO Box 2159, Durban, 4000 T. 031 309-4350 / F. 031 309-3489	BW, Th Mo	Z	92 143
Isolezwe	Independent Newspapers KZN	PO Box 47549, Greyville, 4023	MD, M-F	Z	34 057
Independent on Saturday, The	Independent Newspapers KZN	PO Box 47549, Greyville, 4023 T. 031 308-2500 / F. 013 308-2111	W, Sat	E	61 331
Mail and Guardian	M&G Media (Pty) Ltd	PO Box 32362, Braamfontein, 2017 T. 011 727-7000 / F. 011 727-7111 E-mail: newsroom@mg.co.za	W, Fr	E	37 057
Mercury, The	Independent Newspapers KZN	PO Box 47549, Greyville, 4023	MD, M-F	E	39 053

Communications

Name	Publisher	Contact information	Frequency	Language	Audited circulation Jul – Dec 2002
Natal Witness	Natal Witness Pr & Pub Co (Pty) Ltd	PO Box 362, Pietermaritzburg, 3200 T. 033 355-2127 / F. 033 355-1122 E-mail:news@witness.co.za	MD, M-S	E	23 477
Post	Independent Newspapers KZN	PO Box 47549, Greyville, 4023 T. 031 308-2424 / F. 031 308-2427 E-mail: khalil@independent.co.za	W, Wed	E	37 592
Pretoria News (Daily)	Independent Newspapers Gauteng Ltd	PO Box 439, Pretoria, 0001 T. 012 300-200 E-mail: tle@pretorianews.co.za	AD, M-F	E	28 038
Pretoria News (Saturday)	Independent Newspapers Gauteng Ltd	PO Box 439, Pretoria, 0001 T. 012 300-200	W, Sat	E	15 904
Rapport	RCP Media	PO Box 333, Auckland Park, 2006 T. 011 713-9002 E-mail:aleroux@rapport.co.za	W, Sun	A	338 702
Saturday Dispatch	Dispatch Media (Pty) Ltd	PO Box 131, East London, 5200 T. 031 308-2381 / F. 011 308-2111	W, Sat	E	28 278
Saturday Star, The	Independent Newspapers Gauteng Ltd	PO Box 1014, Johannesburg, 2000 T. 011 633-9111 / F. 011 834-7520 E-mail: starnews@star.co.za	W, Sat	E	136 191
Soccer-Laduma	CT Media (Proprietor)	PO Box 787, Sea Point, 8060 T. 021 685-3838 / F. 021 685-3852	W, Thu	E	200 645
Southern Cross, The	Catholic Newspapers & Pub Co Ltd	PO Box 2372, Cape Town, 8000 T. 021 465 5007	W, Sun	E	10 186
Sowetan	New Africa Publications (NAP) Ltd	PO Box 6663, Johannesburg, 2000 T. 011 471-4000 / F. 011 474-8834 E-mail: editor@sowetan.co.za	MD, M-F	E	154 747
Sowetan Sunday World	Times Media Ltd & NAP	PO Box 6663, Johannesburg, 2000 T. 011 471-4200 / F. 011 471-4164 E-mail:newsed@sundayworld.co.za	W, Sun	E	130 603
Star, The	Independent Newspapers Gauteng Ltd	PO Box 1014, Johannesburg, 2000 T. 011 633-9111 / F. 011 836-6186 E-mail:starnews@star.co.za	MD, M-F	E	164 364
Sunday Independent, The	Independent Newspapers Gauteng, Ltd	PO Box 1014, Johannesburg, 2000 T. 011 633-9111 / F. 011 834-7520 E-mail:newstips@independent.co.za	W, Sun	E	40 151
Sunday Sun	RCP Media Ltd	PO Box 8422, Johannesburg, 2000 T. 011 713-9001 / F. 011 713-9956	W, Sun	E	137 544
Sunday Times	Times Media Ltd	PO Box 1742, Saxonwold, 2132 T. 011 280-3000 / F. 011 280-5150 E-mail: suntimes@tml.co.za	W, Sun	E	504 295
Sunday Tribune	Independent Newspapers KZN	PO Box 47549, Greyville, 4023 T. 031 308-2911 / F. 011 308-2715 E-mail: clarke@independent.co.za	W, Sun	E	109 500
Volksblad, Die (Daily)	Media24	PO Box 267, Bloemfontein, 9300 T. 051 404-7600 / F. 051 430-6949 E-mail: mvanrooyen@volksblad.com	MD, M-F	A	28 207
Volksblad, Die (Saturday)	Media24	PO Box 267, Bloemfontein, 9300 T. 051 404-7600 / F. 051 430-6949	W, Sat	A	24 464
Weekend Argus	Independent Newspapers Cape Ltd	PO Box 56, Cape Town, 8000 T. 021 488-4528	W, Sat & Sun	E	103 901

The abbreviations used are the following: MD (morning daily), AD (afternoon daily), BW (bi-weekly), Mo-Fr (Monday to Friday), Mo (Monday), Tu (Tuesday), W (Wednesday), Th (Thursday), Fri (Friday), Sat (Saturday), Sun (Sunday), A (Afrikaans), E (English), Z (Zulu), n/a (not available)

Source: Audit Bureau of Circulation

Newspaper Circulation Services and Magazine Circulation Services handle all Johnnic Publishing's circulation. The Afrikaans press group, Media24 (*Nasionale Nuusdistribueerders*), handles most of its distribution itself.

Online media
Most of the bigger publications have websites on the Internet. There are more than 600 'netzines' listed as online publications in South Africa, with at least 16 of them specialising in daily news. The *Mail and Guardian* has received worldwide acclaim as the best online publication in Africa.

Media organisations and role-players
Several organisations and associations play an important role in the media field.

Print Media South Africa (PMSA), formed in 1996, is an umbrella organisation administering individual bodies, namely the Newspaper Association of Southern Africa (the oldest communication organisation, established in 1882), Magazine Publishers Association SA, and the Community Press Association of Southern Africa. Allied to PMSA, but not a constituent member, is the ABC, responsible for auditing and verifying print-media circulation figures.

The South African National Editors' Forum (SANEF) was conceived at a meeting of the Black Editors' Forum, the Conference of Editors, and senior journalism educators and trainers, in October 1996.

SANEF's membership includes editors and senior journalists from the print, broadcast and online/Internet media, as well as journalism educators from all the major training institutions in South Africa.

SANEF has facilitated the mobilisation of the media in the *Partnership Against AIDS* Campaign and in campaigns to end violence against women and children.

Various seminars and debates have been held on media freedom and transformation, especially in relation to gender and technology. SANEF is involved in training initiatives and in setting practical standards in journalism education.

In January 1997, the Forum of Black Journalists, consisting only of black journalists, was launched to tackle issues which directly affect black journalists.

On 1 July 1997, the office of the independent Press Ombudsman was opened in Johannesburg. Members of the public who have complaints or concerns about reports in newspapers and magazines can submit their grievances to the Ombudsman.

Should they not be satisfied with the resultant ruling, they can lodge an appeal with an independent appeal panel. The office of the Press Ombudsman was set up by the PMSA, SANEF, the Media Workers' Association of South Africa, and the South African Union of Journalists (SAUJ).

As self-regulating mechanisms of the media industry, the Press Ombudsman and the appeal panel act in accordance with the Constitution, 1996, and embrace the spirit of transformation in South Africa.

The Freedom of Expression Institute (FXI) was formed in January 1994 following the merger of two organisations involved in campaigning for freedom of expression during the apartheid years, namely the Campaign for Open Media and the Anti-Censorship Action Group.

The FXI also established the Media Defence Fund to sponsor freedom-of-expression court

---

In April 2003, the Presidential Press Corps was launched by President Thabo Mbeki and the South African National Editors' Forum (SANEF).

The move followed the Sun City talks, in 2001, between government and SANEF, where SANEF undertook to bring together a team of journalists in a bid to improve information-sharing between journalists and The Presidency.

President Mbeki said the move would pave the way for a better understanding between journalists and government.

Communications

cases on behalf of media representatives who are not able to afford the legal costs.

Another body that protects freedom of speech is the Freedom of Commercial Speech Trust, which was instituted in 1997. Backed by the marketing communication industry and supported by organised business and consumer organisations, the Trust focuses on transparent negotiation with legislators.

The SAUJ has fought consistently and primarily for a free and independent media, and acceptable working conditions for its members. To this end, the SAUJ has signed formal agreements with most employer groupings, and participates in structures aimed at fostering and enhancing media freedom.

The Broadcasting Complaints Commission of South Africa is an independent self-regulatory body which serves as a voluntary watchdog to adjudicate complaints from the public about programmes flighted by members subscribing to its code of conduct. It is empowered by its members, which include the SABC, M-Net, Radio 702 and Trinity Broadcasting Network. However, the Commission does not deal with X-rated material which, under criminal law, is prohibited.

The BMCC was established under Sections 21 and 22 of the IBA Act, 1993.

It monitors broadcasting licensees for their compliance with, or adherence to, the terms, conditions and obligations of:
- their broadcasting licences
- the Code of Conduct for Broadcasting Services
- the Code of Advertising Practice.

The BMCC receives and adjudicates complaints from the public with regard to licence conditions, and is also entitled to initiate its own investigations into suspected non-compliance by a broadcaster.

If a member of the public is concerned that a broadcaster is not observing its licence conditions, that person may lodge a complaint with ICASA. If a broadcaster is found to be guilty of contravening its licence conditions, the BMCC makes recommendations to ICASA about action that should be taken.

Material that could be considered X-rated must be submitted to the Film and Publication Board prior to being shown. (See Chapter 5: *Arts and culture*.)

The mission of the National Association of Broadcasters is to protect the interests of broadcasting as a whole, at the same time interfacing with ICASA on matters such as freedom of speech.

Other press organisations operating in the country are the Foreign Correspondents' Association of South Africa, the Printing Industries Federation of South Africa, the South African Typographical Union, the Specialist Press Association, the South African Guild of Motoring Journalists, Professional Photographers of South Africa, the Media Institute of Southern Africa, and press clubs in major centres.

News agencies

The South African Press Association (SAPA), which is a national news agency, is a co-operative, non-profit news-gathering and distribution organisation operating in the interests of its members and the public. SAPA's foreign news is received from Associated Press (AP) and its representatives in London.

The main foreign news agencies operating in South Africa are AFP, AP, *Deutsche Presse Agentur*, Reuters and United Press International.

Other agencies are the Eastern Cape News Agency, African Eye News Service in Mpumalanga, and Network Radio News.

Training centres

Over 40 institutions offer media training in South Africa.

Tertiary institutions include various universities of technology (technikons) and universities such as Pretoria Technikon, Rhodes, Potchefstroom, Stellenbosch and Witwatersrand Universities; and organisations such as the

Cape Town Film and Television School; the SABC's Television Training Centre; the Radio Freedom Institute; the Institute for the Advancement of Journalism; and NEMISA, a government-funded training institute specialising in broadcasting, news media and multimedia skills.

During 2002/03, about 45 producers from more than 30 community radio stations were trained in production skills by NEMISA. Onsite training was conducted in five provinces and producers were trained in the art of making programmes relating to women, children, HIV/AIDS, and the disabled.

NEMISA also conducted targeted training programmes in the form of two-week long courses for the community radio sector. Some 35 radio stations benefited from this intervention.

Towards the latter part of 2002, NEMISA conducted a three-month intensive course for a group of 26 Nigerian radio and television broadcasters. The course was the first of its kind delivered by a South African institution to a delegation of experienced broadcasters on the African continent. In 2003/04, the Institute aims to increase products and services on offer to broadcasters across the continent.

By February 2003, there were 50 learners studying towards this qualification at the Institute. Thirty learners were expected to complete this programme in May 2003. The electives on this course, leading to specialisation, were in the areas of animation, information design, and advertising. The qualification enjoys joint-accreditation status by both the South African Council on Higher Education and the Malaysia Multimedia University.

During 2002/03, the language portals project was undertaken by NEMISA, with 26 individuals from across South Africa assigned the task of producing content in indigenous languages. This was the first project of its nature in South Africa. It will have a fundamental effect on the manner in which media is consumed in the country.

The second graduation ceremony for the Institute was held on 4 July 2003. During 2003, NEMISA administered the Khuluma Radio Project, a three-year skills-development programme for community media.

The Media, Advertising, Publishing, Printing, and Packaging (MAPPP) SETA was gazetted on 15 March 2000.

It has six advisory committees, with representatives from labour, business and government, which advise on:
- print media
- advertising
- publishing
- printing
- packaging
- film and electronic media.

The MAPPP SETA is responsible for co-ordinating a sector training plan across the media industry, and assesses the quality of training courses that are run by the industry.

Parallel to this, the South African Qualifications Authority (SAQA) has approved the establishment of several standards-generating bodies for the media industry.

Similar bodies were implemented for journalism training and communication studies. These bodies are substructures of the National Standards Body 04 (language and communication), which co-ordinates standard-setting in the communication and language sectors.

Journalism awards

The most important awards include the:
- Mondi Paper Magazine and Newspaper Awards
- Nat Nakasa Award for Courageous Journalism
- SAPPI Magazine Publishers Association of South Africa PICA Awards
- Sanlam Community Press Awards
- Vodacom awards for journalism across all mediums
- South African Breweries (SAB) Journalism Awards.

Communications

Winners of major annual press trophies

	Frewin*	McCall**	Cronwright***	Hultzer****	Joel Mervis*****
1999	Beeld	The Mercury	Western Transvaal Record	Vaal Weekly	Naweek-Beeld
2000	Beeld	Business Day	Record District Mail	Vaal Weekly	Naweek-Beeld
2001	The Star	The Mercury	Sandton Chronicle	Potchefstroom Herald	Rapport
2002	Beeld	Natal Witness	Paarl Post	Potchefstroom Herald	Rapport

* Best urban daily newspaper with a circulation exceeding 50 000
** Best daily with a circulation under 50 000
*** Best community newspaper with a circulation exceeding 8 000
**** Best community newspaper with a circulation below 8 000
***** Best urban weekly

Source: PMSA

The Nat Nakasa Award for Courageous Journalism was won by chief photographer of the *Star*, Debbie Yazbek, in 2003. Yazbek made history by being the first photographer to walk away with this prestigious Award, which recognises integrity, fearlessness, courage and determination in journalism.

Anne-Marie Lombard and Alpheus Sibane of the TV programme *Special Assignment* walked away with the Vodacom Journalist of the Year Award for 2003.

Kim Cloete, also from the SABC, won a Cable News Network Award for Best Report on an ongoing issue.

The Fuji Photographer of the Year was Halden Krog of *Beeld*.

Robyn Chalmers from *Business Day* was the Sanlam Financial Journalist of the Year.

The Sanlam Community Press Journalist of the Year was Samantha Wade of the *Newcastle Advertiser*.

Johan Esterhuizen of *Rapport* was the SAB Sports Writer of the Year.

Media diversity

Media diversity in any country is regarded as a sign of the status of its democracy. South Africa is on its way to achieving as much diversity as possible.

Media Development and Diversity Agency (MDDA)

The MDDA Act, 2002 (Act 14 of 2002), provides for the establishment of an independent, statutory body, which is to be jointly funded by government, the media industry and other donors, and which must act in terms of the Public Finance Management Act, 1999 (Act 1 of 1999).

President Mbeki has appointed a nine-member board which will govern the MDDA, ushering in a new dawn for media development and diversity initiatives in South Africa, especially for the community and small commercial-media sector.

In terms of the financing of the MDDA, the Act provides for the Agency to be an independent and statutory body, jointly funded by government and the media industry. The Agency is also enabled by the Act to approach donor organisations to mobilise further funding. Although jointly funded, the MDDA will function independently and at arm's length from all funding sectors.

This arrangement represents the building of an unprecedented partnership that will enable government, the media industry and donors to work together towards addressing the legacy of imbalances in access to the media.

The MDDA published draft regulations outlining its plans for supporting community and small media in July 2003.

The draft regulations set out which media organisations qualify for financial assistance, what kind of assistance these media organisations can expect from the MDDA, and how to apply.

The public had until 1 September 2003 to comment on the draft regulations. According to the regulations, about 60% of grant money available would go towards community media projects, 25% to small commercial-media and 5% to research projects.

GCIS committed R3 million to the MDDA for 2002/03 and an additional R7 million for 2003/04.

Advertising

The top advertising agencies in 2003, as recognised in the *AdFocus* supplement in *Financial Mail* were kulula.com for Advertiser of the Year, Net#work BBDO (Agency of the Year), morrisjones&co (Small Agency of the Year) and CIA Nota Bene (Media Agency of the Year). Colin Ramparsadh and Grant Willemse of Saatchi and Saatchi South Africa won the Roger Garlick Youth Award for innovative media strategies, for their Osram Light Bulbs *Studio Lights* campaign.

South African agencies are also active in Africa. The top three are: McCann-Erickson Africa, Ogilvy Africa and FCB Africa.

Advertising awards

The Loerie Awards are the best-known South African awards that recognise excellence in advertising. These Awards, established by the Association of Marketers in 1978, cover 16 mutually exclusive media categories: television, international television, cinema, radio, newspaper, magazine, international print and poster, outdoor advertising (above-the-line) and design (below-the-line) campaigns, graphic design, promotional marketing, audiovisual, corporate events, digital interactive, and student.

Excess monies are ploughed directly back into the industry, in the form of bursaries for underprivileged advertising and marketing students via the Loerie Education Trust Fund and as a donation to the Advertising Benevolent Fund.

The 2003 Loerie winners included TBWA Hunt Lascaris, which won six awards in the television category, one in the cinema category and five awards in the radio category.

Other winners included Net#work BBDO, HarrisonHuman Bates, Ogilvy & Mather RS-TM and the Association of Advertising Agencies.

The MultiChoice VUKA! Awards encourage the making of Public Service Announcements (PSAs) in southern Africa, and are open to both newcomer and professional film-makers. A PSA is a commercial produced for a registered charity, NGO or a worthy cause. These worthy causes need media exposure in order to generate awareness and raise funds for social, economic or environmental issues.

The Consumer Magazine Awards were divided into 13 categories. The overall winner was *Y - Yired*, which also won the Youth Category.

Other winners in the respective categories included:
- *Shape*, published by Touchline Media, under both the Women's Magazines and Health and Spirituality categories.
- *House and Leisure*, (Associated Magazines), under Home and Garden.
- *Visi*, (New Media Publishing), under Design and Decor. It also won the Award for Excellence in Magazine Design.
- *Men's Health* (Touchline Media), under Men's Health.
- *You* and *Huisgenoot* (Media 24) were joint winners under Family Magazines.
- *Golf Digest* (Touchline Media), under Sport.
- *Getaway* (Ramsay, Son and Parker), under Travel, Wildlife and Conservation.
- *Baby and Me* (Associated Magazines), under Parenting.
- *Landbouweekblad* (Media 24), under Business.
- *Car* (Ramsay, Son and Parker), under Motoring.
- *Insig* (New Media Publishing), under Entertainment and Leisure.

Communications

The annual Pendoring Awards reward excellence in Afrikaans advertising and have developed into an awareness-builder of the importance of advertising in Afrikaans. Above-the-line categories consist of radio, television, cinema, magazines, newspapers, outdoor advertising and campaigns. Other categories are below-the-line, new media and student.

Pendoring received a total of 303 entries in 2003 from 50 advertising agencies, internal marketing departments and training institutions. FCB Cape Town collected the biggest bundle of Pendoring Awards in 2003. They won five categories while the company's Johannesburg branch scooped winner status in three categories.

Deon Wiggett of TBWA/Gavin Reddy walked away with the sought-after Prestige Prize.

A number of agencies were awarded golden trophies for the first time since the inception of the Pendorings, namely BesterBurke, HarrisonHumanBates, KingJames, TBWA/Gavin Reddy and Grey Worldwide.

Net#work BBDO received three Pendorings (two silver and one gold).

Other marketing communication awards

Two of the fastest growing areas in marketing communication are direct marketing and sponsorship.

The Assegai Awards were established in 1998 to honour excellence in direct marketing strategic-prowess and innovation, with an emphasis on results. The Association of Marketers established the Raptor Awards in 1999. These Awards recognise excellence in different South African sponsorship categories, namely sport, arts, environment and broadcast. In sponsorship campaigns, various advertising and promotional activities are integrated to leverage the overall effectiveness of the campaign.

During 2002, more than R1,4 billion and R1,2 billion was spent on sport sponsorships and the leveraging of sport sponsorships, respectively.

International exposure

South African agencies are very visible at international events such as the Cannes International Advertising Festival. This Festival is widely accepted as the leading global advertising event. Thousands of delegates, representing the global advertising fraternity, spend many days and nights viewing and screening more than 10 000 entries.

Lowe Bull from Gauteng won two Golden Lions at Cannes in 2003, while TBWA Hunt Lascaris (Gauteng, Durban and Cape Town), won two bronze awards.

At global advertising events certified by the CDF, TBWA Hunt Lascaris (Gauteng) broke away from the rest of the field and achieved 12 710 points through their performance in the Loerie, Cannes, Clios, The One Show and Eagles events.

Online and offline advertising

The collapse of the dot-com world in 2000 led to a substantial slump in online advertising.

The Internet is still used as an entertainment medium and information source, but the biggest growth in Internet usage seems to be in business-to-business communication.

According to AMPS figures, adspend on the Internet between December 2001 and November 2002 was R45,5 million. This amounted to a mere 0,4% of total adspend.

Search-engine marketing is one of the fastest-growing types of online advertising in South Africa.

In South Africa, Internet usage remained stable at 4,6% of the population in 2002 compared with 2001, according to the SAARF.

Advertising ethics and the Advertising Standards Authority (ASA)

The ASA is an independent body set up and paid for by the marketing communication industry to regulate advertising in the public interest through a system of self-regulation. The ASA works closely with government, statutory bodies, consumer organisations and the industry to ensure that the content of advertising meets the requirements of the Code of Advertising Practice, the guiding document of the ASA. The Code is based on the International Code of Advertising Practice, prepared by the International Chamber of Commerce. This is internationally accepted as the basis for domestic systems of self-regulation. The Code is drawn up by the ASA in collaboration with representatives of the marketing communication industry, and is amended from time to time to meet the changing needs of both the industry and society.

This Code is supplemented by individual codes, which are determined by the various member organisations or negotiated with government institutions.

The ASA is the protector of the ethical standards of advertising in South Africa, and protects consumers against manipulative advertising and unfair claims.

Acknowledgements

Audit Bureau of Circulations
biz–community.com
Department of Communications
Dr Neels van Heerden, University of Pretoria
Government Communications
Mr P Diederichs, Department of Journalism, Pretoria Technikon
Print Media SA
South African Broadcasting Corporation
South African Post Office
South African National Editors' Forum
Telkom Ltd
www.gov.za

Suggested reading

A Post Office for the People. Mellville: Chris van Rensburg, 1997.
Chapman, M. ed. *The Drum Decade*. Pietermaritzburg: University of Natal Press, 2001.
Chapman, M. ed. *The Drum Decade: Stories from the 1950s*. Pietermaritzburg: University of Natal Press, 2001.
Prof. de Beer, A. S. ed. *Mass Media towards the Millennium: The South African Handbook of Mass Communication*. 2nd ed. Pretoria: Van Schaik, 1998.
Duncan, J. *Broadcasting and the National Question*. Johannesburg: Freedom of Expression Institute (FXI), 2002.
Duncan, J. and Seleoane, M. eds. *Media and Democracy in South Africa*. Pretoria: Human Sciences Research Council (HSRC) and FXI, 1998.
Fardon, R. and Furness, G. eds. *African Broadcast Cultures: Radio in Transition*. Editors: Cape Town: David Philip, 2000.
Gerber, R. and Braun, R. *New Connections: Telecommunications in a Changing South Africa*. Rondebosch: University of Cape Town Press, 1998.
Goldstuck, A. *Hitchhiker's Guide to the Internet: A South African Handbook*. Wynberg, Sandton: Zebra Books, Struik Publications, 1995.
Jacobs, S. and others. *Real Politics: The Wicked Issues*. Cape Town: Institute for a Democratic South Africa, 2001.
Jackson, G. S. *Breaking Story: The South African Press*. Boulder: Westview Press, 1993.
Johnson, S. *Strange Days Indeed*. London: Bantam, 1993.
Kaplan, D. *The Crossed Line: The South African Communications Industry in Transition*. Johannesburg: University of the Witwatersrand Press, 1990.

Kok, P. and Pietersen, J. *Information and Communication Technologies*. Pretoria: HSRC, 2000 (National Research and Technology Project).
Louw, E. *South African Media Policy: Debates of the 1990s*. Durban: Centre for Cultural and Media Studies, University of Natal, 1993.
Manoim, I. *You Have Been Warned: The First Ten Years of the Mail and Guardian*. London: Viking, 1996.
Merrett, C. *A Culture of Censorship: Secrecy and Intellectual Repression in South Africa*. Cape Town: David Philip and University of Natal Press, 1994.
Oosthuizen, L. *Media Ethics in the South African Context*. Cape Town: Juta, 2002.
Owen, K. *These Times: A Decade of South African Politics*. Johannesburg: Jonathan Ball, 1992.
Retief, J. *Media Ethics: An Introduction to Responsible Journalism*. Cape Town: Oxford University Press South Africa, 2002.
Reynolds, H. and Richard, N. *Women Today: A Celebration: Fifty Years of South African Women*. Cape Town: Kwela Books, 2003.
Ronning, H. and Kasoma, F.P. *Media Ethics*. Cape Town: Juta, 2002
Shaw, G. *The Cape Times: An Informal History*. Cape Town: David Philip, 1999.
Stein, S. *Who Killed Mr Drum?* Cape Town: Mayibuye Books, 1999.
Switzer, L. and Adhikari, M. eds. *South Africa's Resistance Press: Alternative Voices in the Last Generation Under Apartheid*. Ohio: Ohio University Centre for International Studies, 2000.
Tyson, H. *Editors Under Fire*. Sandton: Random House, 1993.
Verwoerd, W. and Mabizela, M. *Chief Truths Drawn in Jest: Commentary on the TRC through Cartoons*. Cape Town: David Philip, 2000.
Wilhelm, P. *The State We're in*. Randburg: Ravan, 1999.
Young, L. *The All Africa Internet Guide*. Johannesburg: M&G Books, 2002.

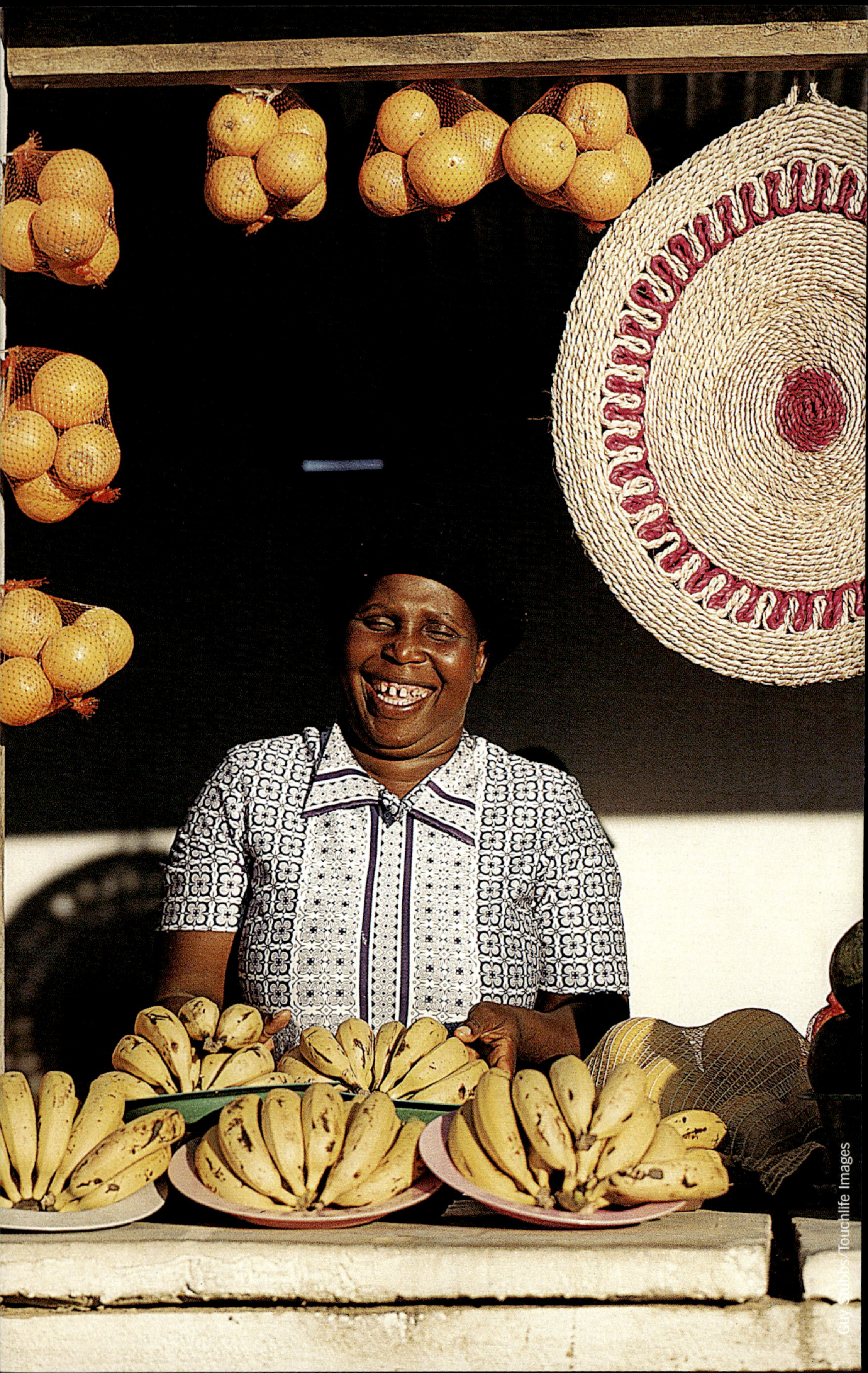

Guy Stubbs/Touchlife Images

chapter 7
Economy

After the steady decline in annual Gross Domestic Product (GDP) growth during the apartheid years, the country has begun to experience economic growth since 1994.

Significant economic achievements have been recorded since 1994, including macro-economic stabilisation, a profound restructuring of the real economy, and substantial export success.

The critical challenge of strengthening the link between economic growth and export success with employment creation, poverty alleviation, and a marked reduction in inequalities, remains.

South Africa will have growth rates rising to a projected 4% by 2005, with Consumer Price Inflation excluding mortgage rates (CPIX) falling to around 5% per annum by 2005.

Furthermore, for the first time in more than a decade, GDP is benefiting from positive input from all components – gross fixed investment, household consumption expenditure and government expenditure.

The easing of Balance of Payments constraints, supported by a strong trade balance and a positive domestic economic outlook, helps the latter. Among emerging markets, South Africa increasingly stands out as a success story.

Supporting this is one of the lesser-known achievements of the South African economy – a dramatic rise in productivity levels since 1994, after two decades of stagnant or declining productivity preceding the first democratic election. This extends to fixed-capital productivity, while labour productivity and unit labour costs are converging. This is further reinforced by the almost complete disappearance of illegal strikes and plant stoppages.

In 2002, manufacturing grew by 5,4%, which was the fastest growth rate since 1995. The decline in employment in manufacturing has eased and there are encouraging signs of possible employment growth in this sector. Although the weak global conditions, compounded by the crisis in the Middle East, were expected to lead to softer conditions in manufacturing in 2003, this should be viewed against the impressive growth rate in 2002. A lowering inflation rate, cuts in interest rates, and reductions in personal income tax, will support significant increases in domestic consumer expenditure, thus increasing domestic demand.

Forecasts by the Bureau for Economic Research, based on surveys of manufacturing enterprises, predict continued strong growth in manufacturing output over the next four years. In terms of manufacturing

◀ The South African Women Entrepreneurs Network was established to assist aspiring and existing women entrepreneurs in the small business sector to find solutions to the wide range of gender-related obstacles that have an adverse impact on their businesses. The Network addresses these constraints by advocating appropriate policy changes, building capacity and facilitating the access of women to business resources and information.

Real Gross Domestic Product

Percentage change at seasonally adjusted and annualised rates

Sector	2001					2002				
	1st qr	2nd qr	3rd qr	4th qr	Year	1st qr	2nd qr	3rd qr	4th qr	Year
Primary sectors	-3,8	-0,8	-2,0	-2,2	-1,6	3,6	4,7	2,7	0,1	1,4
Agriculture	-6,8	-2,2	-0,8	0,5	-1,7	7,6	8,8	4,9	0,3	4,0
Mining	-1,4	0,2	-2,9	-4,3	-1,5	0,6	1,6	1,1	-0,1	-0,6
Secondary sectors	2,1	2,2	0,1	5,4	3,5	3,3	5,0	3,0	2,2	3,4
Manufacturing	1,7	1,9	-0,1	6,9	3,6	3,8	5,8	3,6	1,6	4,0
Tertiary sectors	3,8	3,4	3,3	3,3	3,4	2,7	3,4	2,9	2,8	3,1
Non-agricultural sectors	3,0	2,9	2,1	3,4	3,1	2,7	3,7	2,8	2,5	3,0
Total	2,3	2,6	1,8	3,2	2,8	3,0	3,8	2,9	2,4	3,0

Source: South African Reserve Bank *Quarterly Bulletin*, March 2003

output, the sector is expected to be 40% bigger in 2007 than it was in 1995.

Ranked against other economies, South Africa's global competitiveness has consistently improved over the last few years, whether measured in terms of business efficiency, government efficiency, infrastructure or economic performance. Mirroring this is a steady rise in manufacturing production, while the quality of that production, measured in terms of defects per unit, is steadily rising.

Manufacturing for export has replaced commodities as the centrepiece of the South African economy, far exceeding mining in importance. A prime example of this is the automotive industry which, since 1996, has taken off to remarkable heights, growing tenfold by 2002, in terms of vehicles and components. At the end of August 2002, annual growth in manufacturing exports was 8,7%, according to the Bureau for Economic Research.

Investment grew by 6,3% and is expected to continue to grow around 6% a year from 2003 to 2006. According to the Bureau for Economic Research, the net majority of firms reported an increase in total fixed investment, from 11% to 29%. These investment plans will drive the growth in manufacturing output over the next four years. The primary sector expanded by 3,7%, driven by solid growth in the platinum-group metal and agricultural sectors. Buoyed by investment in the manufacturing sector, and the strong growth in construction spending, the secondary sector expanded steadily in the first three quarters of 2002, helping to create new employment opportunities.

Domestic output

The South African economy grew by 3% in 2002 as a whole, a growth rate that was marginally higher than the 2,8% attained in 2001. Even though the economy lost some growth momentum in the second half of 2002, economic growth still outpaced the rate of expansion in many parts of the world.

After South Africa's real GDP increased at quarter-to-quarter seasonally adjusted and annualised growth rates of 3,0%, 3,8% and 2,9% in the first three quarters of 2002, the economy grew at a rate of 2,4% in the last quarter of 2002. This slowdown in growth can be attributed mainly to slower growth in the real value added by the secondary sectors of the economy.

Growth in real value added by the primary sectors improved from a decline of 1,6% in 2001 to 1,4% in 2002. This was due to the

Real gross domestic expenditure

Percentage change at seasonally adjusted and annualised rates

Components	2001					2002				
	1st qr	2nd qr	3rd qr	4th qr	Year	1st qr	2nd qr	3rd qr	4th qr	Year
Final consumption expenditure by households	3,3	2,5	2,8	3,5	3,1	3,4	3,5	2,9	2,3	3,1
Final consumption expenditure by general government	3,5	3,6	3,7	3,8	3,3	3,5	3,5	3,7	4,2	3,7
Gross fixed capital formation	3,9	3,1	2,2	5,5	3,2	6,9	7,8	8,7	11,5	6,5
Domestic final demand	3,5	2,8	2,8	3,9	3,2	4,0	4,2	4,0	4,2	3,8
Change in inventories (R billion)	0,4	-2,3	4,0	4,7	1,7	6,4	0,4	4,5	6,2	4,4
Gross domestic expenditure	3,1	1,7	5,9	4,9	2,3	5,4	-0,6	7,4	5,0	4,2

Source: South African Reserve Bank *Quarterly Bulletin*, March 2003

agricultural sector improving from a decline of 1,7% in 2001 to 4% in 2002. Increased field-crop production contributed generously to this performance. The mining sector declined by 0,6%. Subdued global demand for metals and minerals and the dampening effect of the stronger Rand on export earnings towards the last part of 2002 might also have constrained mining production somewhat.

Despite the slowdown in manufacturing output in the second half of 2002, this sector was the major contributor to growth in the secondary sectors in 2001 and 2002. Quarter-to-quarter growth rates ranging between 1,6% and 5,8% lifted the growth in real manufacturing value added, for 2002 as a whole, to 4%, a slight acceleration from the 3,6% growth in 2001. This was due to the improved price competitiveness which South African producers enjoyed in export markets, as a result of the lower exchange value of the Rand for the greater part of 2002.

The year-on-year growth in the real value added by the tertiary sectors slowed down slightly from 3,4% in 2001 to 3,1% in 2002. Sturdy quarter-to-quarter growth rates ranging between 2,7% and 3,4% were recorded during 2002.

Domestic expenditure

Growth in real expenditure for 2002 as a whole amounted to 4,2%, compared with growth of 2,3% in 2001. Heightened investment activity contributed substantially to the acceleration of expenditure growth in 2002. In contrast with GDP, the growth in gross domestic expenditure was stronger during the second half of 2002.

Final domestic demand also accelerated growth in 2002, from 3,2% in 2001 to 3,8% in 2002.

The growth in real final consumption expenditure by households remained at 3,1% for both 2001 and 2002.

Similarly, the quarter-to-quarter growth recorded in this aggregate during 2002 resembled that of 2001. The quarterly growth rates in real final consumption expenditure by households slowed down somewhat during the second half of 2002.

Despite this development, final consumption expenditure by households as a ratio to gross domestic expenditure increased marginally from 64,2% in 2001 to 64,3% in 2002. Expenditure on non-durable goods weakened noticeably towards the second part of 2002. This could be attributed to a

Financial account of the balance of payments (R million), 1996 – 2002

	1996	1997	1998	1999	2000	2001	2002
Financial account							
Direct investment							
Liabilities	3 515	17 587	3 104	9 184	6 158	58 404	7 929
Assets	-4 485	-10 831	-9 841	-9 659	-1 878	27 357	4 216
Net direct investment	-970	6 756	-6 737	-475	4 280	85 763	12 145
Portfolio investment							
Liabilities	17 983	51 563	50 452	83 883	11 793	-24 000	5 348
Assets	-8 407	-20 983	-30 077	-31 537	-25 628	-43 626	-9 619
Net portfolio investment	9 576	30 580	20 375	52 346	-13 835	-67 626	-4 271
Other investment							
Liabilities	7 492	-1 330	6 534	-9 322	10 828	-10 226	-1 162
Assets	-2 704	-8 957	-2 872	-10 034	947	-12 324	12 016
Net other investment	4 788	-10 287	3 662	-19 356	11 775	-22 550	10 854
Balance on financial account	13 394	27 049	17 300	32 513	2 220	-4 413	18 728

Source: South African Reserve Bank

slowdown in the growth of real outlays on food and beverages, and a decline in real outlays on petroleum products. Households economised on their petrol consumption as a result of several price increases during the year.

The high food price increases in 2002 also affected the demand for these products.

Real final consumption expenditure by general government accelerated slightly from 3,3% in 2001 to 3,7% in 2002. This was the net result of a marked increase in expenditure on goods and services other than labour services.

Final consumption expenditure by general government to GDP effectively maintained the level of about 19% for both 2001 and 2002.

The third component of real final domestic demand, i.e. fixed capital formation, accelerated from 3,2% in 2001 to 6,5% in 2002.

Stronger growth rates were registered towards the end of 2002.

Public corporations in particular fuelled these growth rates. The ongoing expansion of the Coega Harbour Project in the Eastern Cape contributed amply to real capital outlays. General government as well as private business enterprises also accelerated their outlays on capital expenditure for 2002 as a whole.

The upward momentum in real gross fixed capital formation since the fourth quarter of 1999 accelerated during 2002, thereby propelling gross domestic expenditure.

Quarterly growth rates of capital expenditure during 2002 accelerated from 6,9% in the first quarter to 11,5% in the fourth quarter – sharing the highest quarterly growth rate since the second quarter of 1996.

Real inventory investment occurred at a faster rate during 2002 than in 2001. This took place against the background of strong domestic demand. The ratio of industrial and commercial inventories to GDP outside of agriculture increased accordingly from 15% in 2001 to 15,7% in 2002.

Price inflation

Consumer Price Inflation (CPI) fell from 15,3% in 1991 to 5,4% in 2000, rising to 5,7% in 2001 and 10,1% in 2002. The steady decline of CPI during the 1990s was the result of sound monetary and fiscal policies and the opening of the economy to international trade and capital flows. In more recent years, movements in the CPI have been determined mainly by

Economy

Production and consumer price indices, 1995 – 2001

Period	Production prices of goods for domestic use (Production prices 2000 = 100)			Consumer prices (2000 = 100)			
	Goods produced in South Africa	Imported goods	All goods	Food (Goods)	All goods (Goods)	Services	All items
1996	79,4	75,0	78,1	76,1	76,2	79,6	77,7
1997	85,5	78,7	83,6	83,3	82,4	86,9	84,4
1998	88,6	81,1	86,6	88,4	87,3	93,8	90,2
1999	93,2	87,4	91,6	92,7	97,7	94,9	94,9
2000	100,0	100,0	100,0	100,0	100,0	100,0	100,0
2001	107,8	110,0	108,4	105,4	105,6	105,6	105,7
2002	122,4	127,1	123,8	122,0	116,4	113,9	115,4

Source: South African Reserve Bank

changes in mortgage interest costs, petrol and food prices, and import and export parity pricing, which generally lift price inflation.

CPIX accelerated from 6,6% in 2001 to 10,0% in 2002, reaching 11,2% in March 2003. According to Reserve Bank models, there was a 60% chance that CPIX would fall below 6% in the final quarter of 2003 and remain at this level in 2004.

Independent surveys and the yield differential between conventional 10-year government bonds and inflation-linked debt show that inflation expectations are falling. Lower oil and food prices and a slowdown in the United States (US) economy, coupled with a marked appreciation in the exchange rate of the Rand, are helping to reduce external pressure on domestic inflation.

Production price inflation has risen sharply in recent years. The annual increase in the all-goods production price index accelerated from 3,5% in 1998 to 5,8% in 1999, 9,2% in 2000, 8,4% in 2001, and 14,2% in 2002.

Factors underlying the acceleration during 2002 included the rise in the prices of energy and food, the depreciation of the Rand against a basket of currencies in the closing months of 2001, and the somewhat faster increases than before in the production prices of South Africa's major trading partners.

Changes in production prices have fallen considerably from a year-on-year inflation rate of 15,4% in September 2002 to 5,1% in March 2003. Lower rates of increase in the prices of imported and domestically produced goods assisted the slowdown in production price inflation in the opening months of 2003. The two main drivers slowing production price inflation were the substantial appreciation in the exchange rate of the Rand, and moderating food price inflation at both the agricultural and manufacturing level. The easing in food price inflation resulted from good crops and the strengthening of the Rand, which has a direct influence on the determination of domestic food prices. Slowing domestically produced goods inflation in mid-2003 was not only reliant on lower food prices, but extended to lower prices for all goods except transport equipment, metal products, petroleum products, coal, rubber and plastics.

Exchange rates

The weighted exchange rate of the Rand, which declined by 34,4% between the end of December 2000 and the end of December 2001, bounced back by 26% between the end of December 2001 and the end of December 2002. The strengthening of the external value of the Rand coincided with surpluses on the current account and financial accounts of the Balance of Payments of the country.

The improvement of the external value of the Rand occurred mainly in the fourth quarter of 2002 when, on balance, the nominal effective exchange rate of the Rand strengthened by 17,8% – the largest movement in any single quarter since the first quarter of 1986. Factors that probably supported the improvement in the country's international reserves and the strengthening of the external value of the Rand during 2002 and early 2003 were:
- the sound macro-economic policies of the South African monetary and fiscal authorities
- positive statements about South Africa's credit outlook by international credit-rating agencies and the International Monetary Fund (IMF)
- the interest rate differential between South Africa and other economies, which widened significantly during 2002 and invited capital flows into South Africa
- a general reduction in risk aversion towards emerging-market asset classes
- uncertainty about the health of the US economy and the associated weaker trend in the value of the US Dollar
- an improvement in South Africa's terms of trade
- speculation against currency risk, which probably aided the strength of the Rand (e.g. importers might have been induced not to cover forward their expected foreign exchange purchases and/or to sell back existing forward cover)
- perceptions regarding South Africa's status as a safe haven improved during 2002 following increased geopolitical tensions.

The external value of the Rand weakened somewhat on a trade-weighted basis during January 2003, despite the announcement of the date for the privatisation of the State-owned telecommunications company Telkom.

Heightened risk aversion among international investors in anticipation of a war in Iraq, and a widespread decline in the value of financial asset prices, caused non-resident investors to reduce their holdings of domestic fixed-interest and equity securities during January 2003.

The weighted exchange rate of the Rand declined by 1,0% from the end of December 2002 to the end of January 2003. However, in February 2003 the Rand strengthened again, taking the overall increase of its nominal effective value to 7,1% from the end of December 2002 to the end of February 2003.

The net average daily turnover in the domestic market for foreign exchange, which had declined to US$7,3 billion in the third quarter of 2002, rose to US$8,2 billion in the fourth quarter of 2002 – its highest level since the fourth quarter of 2001. The value of transactions involving non-residents increased from US$4,4 billion per day to US$5,0 billion per day during the same period. Participation by resident parties increased from US$2,9 billion per day in the third quarter of 2002 to US$3,3 billion per day in the fourth quarter.

Foreign trade and payments

The South African economy weathered the turbulent global economic conditions well in 2002/03. This was evident from the improvement in the Balance of Payments on current account, which reverted from a deficit of R2,9 billion in 2001 to a surplus of R3,3 billion in 2002. This was the first time since 1994 that a surplus was recorded for a full calendar year. The improvement mainly occurred as a result of an increase in total export earnings, which was only partly offset by the higher value of merchandise imports.

Consequently, the trade balance recorded a surplus of R46,2 billion for 2002 compared with a surplus of R41,0 billion in 2001. Expressed as a ratio to GDP, the current account balance amounted to a surplus of 0,3% in 2002 from a deficit of 0,3% in 2001.

In the first half of 2002 the value of merchandise exports rose sharply, but levelled off in the second half. For the 2002 calendar year as a whole, the nominal value of merchandise exports rose by 21,0% to R283,0 billion, from R233,2 billion in 2001.

An analysis of changes in the value of exports by product category indicates that sizeable increases were registered across all the major categories, especially manufactured goods. The Rand prices of exported goods increased on average by 26,2% in 2002, mainly due to a decline in the weighted exchange rate of the Rand.

The strengthening of commodity prices over the same period further supported this increase.

Weaker global economic conditions dampened the demand for locally produced goods, causing the physical quantity of exports to fall by 4,0%. However, this decline was fully offset by the increase in the domestic unit price of exported goods.

The reversal of the current account deficit in 2002 was also brought about by the increase, of 44,7%, in the value of net gold exports from R29,2 billion in 2001 to R42,6 billion in 2002.

This resulted from an increase in the average realised price of gold, which rose by 38,7% from R2 338 per fine ounce to R3 242 per fine ounce over this period. Despite the uncertainties in global financial markets and concerns about the possibility of a war against Iraq, the average fixing price on the London market rose from US$271 per fine ounce in 2001 to US$310 per fine ounce in 2002.

The seasonally adjusted and annualised value of merchandise imports remained fairly stable during the first three quarters of 2002. In the last quarter of 2002, the nominal value of merchandise imports advanced due to domestic demand. For the whole of 2002, the value of merchandise imports increased by 26,3% compared with an increase of 16,55% in 2001.

The physical quantity of goods from abroad remained muted in the first three quarters of 2002 and accounted on average for about 18,8% of gross domestic expenditure. In the fourth quarter of 2002, foreign suppliers satisfied about 20% of aggregate domestic demand. In 2002, the volume of imported goods increased by only 3,6%, whereas the Rand price rose by 21,9%, owing mainly to the weakening of the external value of the Rand.

Net service, income and transfer payments, which declined from R51,93 billion in the second quarter of 2002 to R44,5 billion in the third quarter, receded further to R38,7 billion in the fourth quarter. The improvement services in the balance on the account resulted from a sharp decline in dividends declared on foreign direct investment (FDI) in the economy, which caused a contraction in the net investment-income payments to non-residents.

Investors dividend paid on foreign portfolio investment also declined in 2002, following non-residents' disinvestment from shares listed on the JSE Securities Exchange (JSE). For 2002 as a whole, the shortfall on the services and income account amounted to R42,9 billion compared with a deficit of R43,9 billion in 2001.

Strong capital inflows into the economy during the first half of 2002 were curtailed in the second half of the year owing to negative investor sentiment.

Net financial inflows to the value of R33,1 billion were recorded in the first half of 2002. These flows, however, almost completely fell away in the second half of the year.

A deficit of R0,2 billion and a small surplus of R0,6 billion in the third and fourth quarters of 2002 respectively, were recorded on the financial account of the Balance of Payments.

For 2002 as a whole, the financial account registered a surplus of R33,5 billion, compared with a surplus of R10,3 billion in 2001.

FDI flows into South Africa, which were positive in the first three quarters of 2002, turned negative to the value of R0,7 billion in the fourth quarter. Direct outward investment recorded an inflow (i.e. a reduction in foreign investment assets) of R4,2 billion in 2002, compared with an inflow of R27,4 billion in 2001. For 2002 as a whole, a net inflow of direct investment capital to the value of R12,1 billion was requested.

The net outward movement of portfolio capital declined from R67,1 billion in 2001 to R4,3 billion in 2002. The substantial net outflows in 2001 were related mainly to the restructuring of Anglo-American/De Beers.

Other foreign investment in South Africa, consisting mainly of loans, trade finance and bank deposits, declined from an outflow of R10,2 billion in 2001 to an outflow of R1,2 billion in 2002. Over the same period, South African entities reduced their other foreign investment assets by R12,0 billion.

The country's net international reserves increased by R36,6 billion during 2002, due mainly to a healthy surplus on the financial account during the first half of 2002, and to a lesser extent, the improvement on the current account of the Balance of Payments. Total gross gold and foreign exchange reserves decreased from R152,8 billion at the end of December 2001 to R132,6 billion at the end of December 2002.

In US dollar terms, South Africa's total gross international reserves rose from US$12,6 billion to US$15,4 billion over the same period.

Import cover, i.e. the value of gross international reserves expressed as a ratio of the value of imports of goods and services, declined from 23,5 weeks at the end of 2001 to 17,5 weeks at the end of 2002.

The nominal effective exchange rate of the Rand appreciated by 26,0% from the end of 2001 to the end of 2002. This strengthening in the external value of the Rand coincided with surpluses on the current and financial accounts of the Balance of Payments.

Department of Trade and Industry

The key objectives of the Department of Trade and Industry are to:
- grow investments and exports
- grow markets for South African products abroad
- grow small, micro and medium enterprises (SMMEs)
- grow women-owned enterprises
- redress inequities in the economy by bringing the previously disadvantaged into the mainstream
- grow the Southern African Development Community (SADC) region and assist with the New Partnership for Africa's Development (NEPAD)
- reduce geographic/spatial development inequalities by spreading investment over the provinces
- create a fair and efficient marketplace for business and consumers alike.

Two critical policy developments occurred in 2002/03. In April 2002, the Department released the Integrated Manufacturing Strategy (IMS) for discussion, and a new Marketing Division for the Department was introduced.

The IMS provides a platform for the Department's programmes and projects as contained in the Medium Term Strategy Framework. Institutional arrangements have been introduced to promote the strategic and operational alignment of the various divisions of the Department, and the public entities comprising the Department of Trade and Industry, with the objectives of the IMS. Version 2 of the IMS is under way.

The Marketing Division was introduced to develop and implement a marketing strategy that gives effect to the Department's commit-

---

The Department of Trade and Industry's train, the Business Express, travels to small towns and villages throughout South Africa as part of the Department's awareness drive to reach small and medium enterprises in all corners of the country.

The function of the Business Express is to explain what government is doing to support small businesses.

Economy

ment to becoming a customer-orientated and responsive organisation.

International trade and economic development

The International Trade and Economic Development (ITED) Division of the Department has as its central brief increasing South Africa's access to markets worldwide by negotiating international trade agreements, where possible on preferential terms. The ITED also seeks to ensure that the country's commitments are honoured in the multilateral, rules-based trading system underpinned by the World Trade Organisation (WTO).

The ITED's global economic strategy considers sustainable growth as its departure point. It is not developed in isolation, but is part of South Africa's broad industrial strategy. It was formulated in light of the country's relations with the SADC, the rest of Africa, NEPAD, and economic relations with developed and developing trading partners in the North and the South.

Since 1994, the Rand value of both South Africa's exports and imports in manufactured goods has grown steadily. South Africa's export base is diversifying rapidly with success having been achieved most notably in processed agricultural goods, automobiles, and a number of categories of industrial machinery.

As with all other economies, South Africa's success is intimately tied to that of the region and the continent of which it is part. ITED is committed to the pursuit of market access for South Africa, more effective efforts at sub-regional and continental integration, and the strategic and positive engagement of the region and the continent in the WTO.

Policy and programme developments in international trade development include:
- Continuing negotiations with India, Brazil and Nigeria. A 25% rise in South African exports to India has already been achieved.
- Continuing negotiations with Mercosur, a trading bloc of six Latin American countries, namely Argentina, Bolivia, Brazil, Chile, Paraguay and Uruguay.
- The administration of various binational commissions (BNCs) with other governments.
- The implementation of the new Southern African Customs Union (SACU) agreement concluded in September 2001, in which ITED played a pivotal role.
- Strengthening the trade capacity of the SADC.
- Preparing for and participating in a new trade-round under the auspices of the WTO.
- Ongoing analysis of trade threats and opportunities.
- Replacing the Board of Tariffs and Trade (BTT) with the new Commission for International Trade Administration (CITA), an independent regulatory agency. CITA will take over BTT's function of administering the tariff regime and is set to play a central role within SACU on tariff and related issues.

Trade relations

Africa

Africa forms the focus of South Africa's global economic strategy. Partnerships with countries on the continent are therefore considered vital and strategic.

South Africa's economy is inextricably linked to that of the southern African region and its own success is linked to the economic recovery of the continent through NEPAD. The developmental challenges must be viewed in light of the mutually beneficial economic and developmental impact on South Africa and Africa's self-enforcing and economic existence.

Africa is an important market for South African exports. In 2002, approximately 16% of South Africa's exports were destined for the continent. Unfortunately, this was not mirrored by imports from the continent, which accounted for only 4% of South Africa's total imports.

This trade imbalance has largely been offset by South Africa's investment on the continent,

aimed at infrastructural projects designed to enhance the productive capacities of African economies. In addition to bilateral trade relations and the normal aspects involved in forging economic relationships, the Department of Trade and Industry is committed to increasing South Africa's involvement in large capital projects on the continent. The following areas have been prioritised:
- infrastructure and logistics (roads, ports, etc.)
- energy and information communications technology (ICT)
- water and waste management
- transport
- construction
- oil and gas infrastructure
- agribusiness
- mining
- human resource development.

The Department, through Trade and Investment South Africa (TISA), has established trade and investment promotion offices on the continent for the purpose of facilitating trade and investment flows.

The Department is providing supportive services to NEPAD, which is playing a critical role in catalysing trade and economic development on the continent. In southern Africa, South Africa seeks to restructure regional arrangements promoting industrialisation. The Department supports a process whereby integrated manufacturing platforms form the basis for an integrated regional industrial strategy. This entails using southern Africa as an integral part of supply chains for globally competitive manufacturing processes.

Through a combination of sectoral co-operation, policy co-ordination and trade integration, South Africa's regional policy aims to achieve a dynamic regional economy capable of competing effectively in the global economy.

For instance, South Africa works closely with its neighbours in engaging effectively with multilateral international institutions and agreements, from the WTO to the African-Caribbean-Pacific (ACP) Declaration.

Southern African Development Community

The centrepiece of South Africa's foreign economic policy is the SADC, constituted by Angola, Botswana, the Democratic Republic of the Congo (DRC), Lesotho, Malawi, Mauritius, Mozambique, Namibia, the Seychelles, South Africa, Swaziland, Tanzania, Zambia and Zimbabwe.

Two-way trade between South Africa and the SADC member states is characterised by the prevailing trade imbalance in terms of exports *vis-a-vis* imports from the region. Within the SADC, a smaller group of countries, South Africa, Botswana, Lesotho, Namibia and Swaziland (BLNS countries), have organised themselves into SACU.

The SACU shares a common tariff regime without any internal barriers. Customs revenues are shared according to an agreed formula.

A sizeable share of South Africa's exports (currently estimated at over R15 billion) are destined for SACU and other SADC countries. Trade with SADC countries has increased significantly, from R16 billion to approximately R32 billion during the period 1998 to 2002. However, in 2002, there was a significant increase in the amount of imports from the region, to approximately R4,2 billion. This gives an overall export: import ratio of 8:1. There is a definite need to reverse this trend and close the trade imbalance between South Africa and its SADC partners.

The Department of Trade and Industry (dti), through its Consumer and Corporate Regulation Division, hosts the Annual dti Awards for Consumer Champions. The Awards recognise the contribution of individuals and organisations in protecting consumer rights and ensuring that quality goods are provided, and that high standards of service are established and maintained.

Individual consumer advocates, journalists, non-governmental and community-based organisations as well as industry associations are eligible for the Awards.

Mozambique has become the main destination for South Africa's exports into Africa, absorbing well over R6 billion of South Africa's exports. Mozambique now accounts for 18% of South African exports into Africa, in comparison with Zimbabwe at 16%.

South Africa's imports from the region are focused on a few countries, with the top 10 countries accounting for between 80% and 90% of total imports from Africa. Zimbabwe is South Africa's top supplier in Africa, followed by Mozambique, Malawi, Zambia and Angola.

Strong links guide South Africa's interests and objectives in the southern African region between the domestic and regional economy. As the market for a large proportion of South Africa's high value-added exports, the growth of these domestic industries is inextricably linked to the growth of the region's economies. Growth in South African manufactured exports to SADC countries in 2001/02 grew by 13,9%, despite regional setbacks.

SADC Free Trade Agreement

Tremendous progress has been achieved in negotiations, including the implementation phase of the SADC Protocol on Trade on 1 September 2000 which encompasses the establishment of a SADC Free Trade Area (FTA) by 2008.

A Trade Implementation Unit was set up at the SADC Secretariat to co-ordinate the day-to-day implementation of the Protocol. Furthermore, the Cut, Make and Trim Unit (relating to agreements in clothing and textiles) reiterated its decision to eliminate core non-tariff barriers that have led to cumbersome procedures, and that have, in turn, tended to impede intra-SADC trade. These developments are expected to enhance the SADC's capacity to participate in regional and international trade.

South African Customs Union

The new SACU agreement is in place and further opens the door to a SACU FTA. New institutional features include the Council of Ministers, responsible for taking decisions on all matters pertaining to the SACU agreement; a SACU tariff body, responsible for making recommendations on tariff and trade remedies to the Council; a small SACU Secretariat, responsible for rendering administrative and support services to SACU structures; and a dispute settlement mechanism similar to the one in place in the SADC.

SACU members agreed on the establishment of national bodies responsible for receiving tariff applications from each member state. Consensus was also reached on a new revenue-sharing formula.

Trade with Europe

Europe is the largest source of investment for South Africa and accounts for almost half of South Africa's total foreign trade. Seven of South Africa's top 10 trading partners are European countries. In 2001/02, South African manufactured exports to Europe grew by 19,8%.

Both bilateral development co-operation and multilateral development programmes through the European Union (EU) form a substantial element of South Africa's reconstruction and development. Relations with Europe, with the EU as the pivot, are crucial economically.

The United Kingdom (UK), with its historic links with South Africa, is South Africa's third-largest trading partner and the largest foreign investor in South Africa. Germany is South Africa's second-largest trading partner and an influential member of the EU. The Germany-South Africa BNC intends expanding the strong commercial links that already exist between the two countries.

South Africa is the Netherlands' main trading partner in Africa, with exports totalling R740 million in 2002. Likewise, the Netherlands is one of South Africa's top 10 trading partners and offers prospects of increased involvement in the EU, especially in light of the Trade, Development and Co-operation Agreement (TDCA) signed with the EU.

Between 1999 and 2002, Spain invested R2,02 billion in South Africa, making it the fourth-largest new investor in South Africa in 2002.

The Netherlands is the fifth-largest destination for South African exports (R12,6 billion in 2002) and the fifth-largest investor in South Africa (R17,4 billion in 2000).

European Union

The historic TDCA, which was provisionally implemented on 1 January 2000, established an FTA between South Africa and the EU. South Africa will grant duty-free access to 86% of EU imports over a period of 12 years, while the EU will liberalise 95% of South Africa's imports over a 10-year period.

The Agreement is a key component of South Africa's trade policy since the EU is the country's largest trade and investment partner, accounting for about 40% of South Africa's total world trade. The expected impact on trade and investment flows between South Africa and the 15 EU member states will contribute towards the restructuring of the South African economy and its long-term economic growth potential.

The Agreement covers trade and related issues, and co-operation in the economic, social and political fields. It also provides a legal framework for ongoing EU financial assistance in grants and loans for development co-operation, which amounts to some R900 million per annum.

Statistics compiled by the South African Revenue Service show that increasing use is being made of the tariff preferences in the Agreement and more so on the export side. South African exports under the FTA exceed imports from the EU.

The wine and spirits agreements between South Africa and the European Community were signed in February 2002, concluding the TDCA and firmly establishing South African wines and spirits exports in its major market.

At the same time, the negotiators achieved precedent-setting agreements on extremely contested areas relating to geographical indicators, intellectual property and trademark protection.

Cotonou Agreement

South Africa is a member state of the ACP Group, but a qualified member of the Cotonou Agreement (signed on 23 June 2000 in Cotonou, Benin), in the sense that, in the case of trade and development co-operation, the TDCA takes precedence over the Cotonou Agreement. The Cotonou Agreement is a trade and aid framework between the EU and 77 members of the ACP countries. Its main aim is to reverse the economic and technological marginalisation of ACP countries in the global trade and investment arena.

The Agreement states that future EU-ACP relations will be characterised by the following:
- a stronger political partnership between the EU and the ACP
- decentralised co-operation, which involves the active participation of civil society and the private sector in the planning of national development strategies
- reformed financial co-operation programmes of the European Development Fund's financial resources amounting to 24 billion Euro
- WTO-compatible Regional Economic Partnership Agreements, essentially covering all trade, and implemented over 10 to 12 years as of 1 January 2008.

The Americas

North America

The USA is South Africa's number one trading partner in terms of total trade (the sum of exports and imports) recorded in 2002 and the first six months of 2003. Exports to the USA rose in nominal terms from R30 billion in 2001 to R35 billion in 2002. Imports from the USA increased in nominal terms from R25 billion to R31 billion from 2001 to 2002.

Economy

Since 2000, trade has been in South Africa's favour with trade surplus increasing in nominal terms from R3,4 billion to R7,6 billion between 2000 and 2002.

The USA tends to export higher value-added products to South Africa while South African exports to the USA consist largely of unprocessed and semi-processed material.

South Africa is a beneficiary of the USA's Generalised System of Preferences (GSP), which grants duty-free treatment for more than 4 650 products.

South Africa is also a beneficiary of the Africa Growth and Opportunity Act (AGOA), which was promulgated in October 2000. In terms of AGOA, an additional 1 783 products were added to the existing GSP products, but only until September 2008. AGOA also allows duty-free entry of clothing and selected textiles into the USA subject to certain criteria and policy reforms. By 2003, about 38 countries had qualified under AGOA, including Swaziland, Ivory Coast, the DRC and Gambia.

South Africa signed the Trade and Investment Framework Arrangement (TIFA) with the USA in 1999. The TIFA Council took over the role of the Trade and Investment Committee, which was to address private-sector concerns requiring government intervention.

The South African-USA Bilateral Co-operation Forum replaced the BNC between the two countries. A sign of the healthy relationship between South Africa and the USA was South Africa's exemption from new US steel tariffs imposed in 2002.

Canada is South Africa's second-largest trading partner in North America. Since the lifting of sanctions in 1994, bilateral trade between the two countries has been on the increase, from R903 million in 1993 to R4,2 billion in 2002.

Canada extended a quota on clothing and textile products from South Africa to enter its market at a better than 'Most Favoured Nation' tariff rates. The Trade and and Investment Co-operation Arrangement, signed in 1998, sought to enhance bilateral trade and investment.

South Africa is a beneficiary of Canada's General Preferential Tariff (GPT). GPT rates range from duty-free to reductions in the 'Most Favoured Nation' rates. South Africa has a Memorandum of Understanding (MoU) with Canada relating to the export of clothing and textile products to that country.

Latin America

South Africa's major trading partners in Latin America are Brazil, Argentina, Chile, Mexico and Peru. South Africa and Mercusor signed a Framework Agreement in December 2000 in Brazil. It commits both parties to negotiate and conclude an FTA. However, as the first step towards achieving this goal, the parties agreed to exchange preferences in certain sectors in the early stages of the negotiation process.

Trade between South Africa and Mercusor grew substantially from R2,7 billion in 1994 to R6 billion in 2000. Both South Africa and Brazil regard each other as strategic partners with co-operation taking place in multilateral forums such as the WTO. Notwithstanding South Africa's strong ties with Mercusor, Chile is becoming an increasingly important partner for South Africa. South African mining companies are heavily involved in mining activities in Chile.

Trade between South Africa and Mexico grew from R922 million in 1999 to R1,4 billion in 2000. The balance of trade has been in South Africa's favour for a number of years.

Bilateral trade between South Africa and the Andean Community (Peru, Ecuador, Bolivia, Colombia and Venezuela) has been growing at a relatively slow pace since 1994. The Andean Community, more specifically Colombia and Peru, offers great potential for South African companies participating in the mining industry.

Asia

South and south-east Asia and Australasia

South Africa is a member of the Indian Ocean Rim Association for Regional Co-operation (IOR-ARC), a project-based regional economic grouping of 19 countries washed by the Indian Ocean.

This group covers the eastern coastline of Africa, the Arabian peninsula, southern Asia and Singapore, Indonesia and Australia.

South Africa's participation in the IOR-ARC is guided by the framework of its global economic strategy, which envisages the strengthening of strategic partnerships and economic ties between developing and less-developed countries. The ultimate objective is to advance the economic interests of the South in a global economic system characterised by increasing marginalisation of the poor and advancement in the developed North.

Between 1995 and 2002, the IOR-ARC accounted for a small, but significant, average of a 14% share of South Africa's global trade.

Total trade with India has been increasing rapidly since 1994. According to the latest figures, total two-way trade between the two countries stands at over US$2 billion, with the trade balance in South Africa's favour.

South Africa's objective is to strengthen and deepen economic links through strong business and governmental co-operation between the two countries. The Joint Ministerial Commission (JMC) provides an institutional mechanism for Ministerial consultations on political and economic matters, and has facilitated several initiatives including a trade agreement, co-operation on defence issues, science and technology co-operation programmes, capacity-building through the India Technical Co-operation Programme, MoUs on Telecommunications, co-operation on small and medium enterprise (SME) development, and sector co-operation through the India-South Africa Commercial Alliance.

The bilateral relationship between South Africa and India has led to negotiations for an FTA between India and SACU.

Relations with Australia have also been cemented via the JMC. Total trade with Australia amounted to R12,8 billion in 2002. South African manufactured exports to Australia grew by 17,3% in 2001/02.

Bilateral trade with south-east Asia increased rapidly off a low base from 1990. This trade is more or less evenly spread between Singapore, Malaysia, Indonesia and Thailand. The percentage of total south-east Asian trade of any single country ranges between 19% and 28%.

South Africa has built its strongest ties in south-east Asia with Malaysia, which is the second-largest investor in South Africa since 1994. Malaysian investments, on a cumulative basis, total approximately R6,67 billion and are concentrated in telecommunications, energy and oil, and property. Thailand is increasingly coming into focus as a key partner for South Africa.

North-east Asia

Japan is South Africa's largest trading partner in Asia and its fourth-largest overall trading partner. It also became South Africa's third-largest export destination during 2002. At the end of 2002, total trade between the two countries stood at R43,9 billion. The Partnership Forum, designed to strengthen bilateral ties between Japan and South Africa, meets regularly.

South Korea is a large trading partner for South Africa in Asia. Total bilateral trade in 2002 amounted to R10,04 billion.

By September 2003, investment from South Korea totalled around US$55 million.

Economic and trade relations between South Africa and the People's Republic of China have grown rapidly since the formal establishment of diplomatic relations. The two countries engage regularly on economic issues through the JMC, and relations are at the point where an FTA is being explored. Total trade with China amounted to R19,08 billion in 2002. This represented an increase of over 40% in the Rand value of trade in 2001. South African exports to Taiwan amounted to R5,12 billion in 2000, while imports amounted to R5,42 billion in the same period.

Multilateral economic relations

The WTO, in partnership with the Bretton Woods Institutions, the World Bank and the IMF, has been setting the parameters for and directing the economic policies of governments around the world.

This has had serious implications for the content, evolution and trajectory of economic development strategies being pursued by developing countries, including South Africa. As the process of globalisation is being questioned, it is imperative for South Africa to influence and shape the configurations of the emerging system of global governance. This is best done by participating actively and effectively in all multilateral forums, to ensure that its particular economic interests and developmental objectives, as well as those of the African continent, are taken into account.

United Nations Conference on Trade and Development (UNCTAD)

UNCTAD is an important resource organisation for South Africa and the continent. The main goals of the organisation are to:
- maximise the trade, investment and development opportunities of developing countries
- help developing countries face challenges arising from globalisation and integration into the world economy on an equitable basis.

This is pursued through research and policy analysis, intergovernmental deliberations, technical co-operation, and interaction with civil society and the business sector. UNCTAD is focusing much of its energy on assisting developing countries to prepare for mandated and possible future negotiations in the WTO.

World Trade Organisation

South Africa regards its membership of the WTO as very important because of the enhanced security and certainty in the multilateral trading system provided by WTO rules.

The country is an active participant and contributor towards a strengthened multilateral trading system whose benefits are equitably distributed across the world community. South Africa wants to participate in the shaping of global governance to ensure beneficial and full integration of its economy into the global trading system.

South Africa's efforts to build an alliance of developing countries within the WTO, based on a common approach and consensus on key issues, bore fruit in late 2001, when an agreement was reached to launch a new round of trade negotiations, this time with a developmental agenda.

Following the collapse of negotiations at the fifth Ministerial Conference of the WTO in Cancun, Mexico, in September 2003, South Africa's Minister of Trade and Industry, Mr Alec Erwin, said that the Group of 20+, which includes Brazil, Argentina, South Africa, India, China and Nigeria, were able to present a balanced proposal on the way forward. The Group indicated in these negotiations that there was a possibility of achieving meaningful outcomes for developing countries in the areas of market access, domestic support and export competition in agriculture, while understanding the concerns of food security and rural development, and those of least-developed countries.

Regarding the critical and complex issues of agriculture, some important advances have been made in the areas of domestic support, market access and export subsidies.

Cairns Group

The Cairns Group is an association of countries exporting agricultural products with the objective of free and fair trade in the global agricultural market. It participates as a group in WTO agricultural negotiations. The Group consists of Argentina, Australia, Bolivia, Brazil, Canada, Chile, Colombia, Costa Rica, Fiji, Guatemala, Indonesia, Malaysia, New Zealand, Paraguay, Philippines, South Africa, Thailand and Uruguay.

In June 2003, the South African Government hosted the Growth and Development Summit, aimed at bringing together government and its social partners to take advantage of the conditions for faster growth and development that exist in South Africa.
The major commitments and agreements reached included the following:
- All social partners made commitments to work towards creating more and better jobs and decent work for all, through public-investment initiatives in partnership with the private sector.
- Business committed to investing R145 billion over the next five years in the automotive, chemical, mining and oil sectors.
- All social partners committed to addressing the investment challenge through encouraging investors to invest 5% of their investible income in appropriate financial instruments that are to be developed. They agreed that the share of low-income housing financed by private-sector bonds should increase.
- All social partners committed to advancing equity, developing skills, creating opportunities for all and extending services through government's Broad-Based Black Economic Empowerment initiative with a R10-billion pledge by government over the next five years. Business also undertook to contribute resources to the joint Employment Equity Campaign. A commitment was also made with business and the Public Service to register at least 72 000 unemployed learners for learnerships by May 2004.
- All social partners made commitments to engage in local action and implementation for development – government undertook to expand the number of Multi-Purpose Community Centres from 37 to 60 over the next 18 months and intensify the *Imbizo* and *Letsema* Campaigns while strengthening local government structures and Integrated Development Plans. Labour, through the Job Creation Trust, will support small-scale projects that contribute to employment and skills development. Business entities at local level will work with the Department of Trade and Industry to provide services to emerging businesses.

World Economic Forum (WEF)

The WEF, an annual meeting of world economic leaders, held in Davos, Switzerland, has become the world's global business summit. South Africa is well-represented at the Forum.

Export and investment promotion

A central task of the Department of Trade and Industry is to promote value-added exports and to attract investment. The vision is one of a restructured and adaptive South African economy, characterised by growth, employment and equity (regional, spatial, gender and racial).

The Department is continuing to shift its focus from demand-driven to supply-side driven measures, and to increase its focus on SMME development. The emphasis is also on customer-defined assistance. The new suite of incentives also relies on private-sector interventions, and affects a wider range of sectors such as tourism, agribusiness, biotechnology, cultural industries, and other priorities identified by government.

Old manufacturing support schemes, such as the Tax Holiday Scheme, the Small Medium Manufacturing Development Programme, the Regional Industrial Development Programme and the Simplified Regional Industrial Development Programme, are being replaced with a suite of six incentives, some of which are still being finalised. The components of the suite are:
- Small Medium Manufacturing Enterprise Development Programme
- Skills Support Programme
- Critical Infrastructure Facility
- Industrial Development Zones (IDZs)
- Foreign Investment Grant
- Strategic Investment Programme.

More attention will be paid to the neglected and hard to reach, but numerically significant, micro-enterprise sector. A Micro Investor Programme is under way, as well as the South African Women Entrepreneurs' Network, (SAWEN) which caters more broadly for women

Economy

in business in all sectors, alongside the Technology for Women in Business (TWIB) Programme.

The Competitiveness Fund allocates 48% of its spending to SMME projects, while the revised Export Marketing and Investment Assistance (EMIA) Programme also focuses on SMMEs, with 68% of its funds going to this sector.

Trade and Investment South Africa

The core business of TISA, a division of the Department of Trade and Industry, is developing South Africa's industries. In 2002, a decision was taken to change TISA's status as a Section 21 company to a fully fledged division of the Department.

This change in status supported a department-wide restructuring and integration process for maximum efficiency and an unswerving customer focus. After going through a significant transformation process, including the development of a new mission and organisational structure, TISA is now ready to deliver on the demands of sector development. The latter is geared towards promoting growth, employment and equity, and TISA's core functions include co-ordination, developing and promoting exports and investment, and creating and changing policy.

TISA houses all the sector business units, sector support services, Export Marketing and Investment Assistance (EMIA), foreign operations and foreign service management.

In May 2002, the Cabinet approved the Micro-Economic Reform Strategy (MRS), which proposes micro-economic improvement in priority sectors in the South African economy. The Department's contribution to the MRS, the IMS, gives priority to the develoment of these sectors. As such, TISA's mandate has been broadened from investment and export promotion to an all-encompassing agenda of sector development. These priority sectors have been selected on the basis of their potential to contribute to economic growth, employment and equity. They also cover a wide spectrum of the economy, ranging from agroprocessing to ICTs.

TISA is also aggressively targeting new high-growth, knowledge-intensive sectors, while refining its existing target markets, sector strategies and internal performance measurements. At the same time, TISA will restructure its overseas representation, prioritising these on the basis of opportunity and demand. Another priority will be the broadening of the involvement of emerging entrepreneurs in international trading and investment activities, particularly those from historically disadvantaged communities.

From March 2003, TISA was responsible for developing the following set of priority sectors:
- agroprocessing
- chemical and allied industries
- clothing, textiles, leather and footwear
- cultural industries
- exportable services (business process outsourcing)
- ICTs and electronics
- metals and mineral-based industries
- tourism
- transport industries (automotive, aerospace, marine and rail).

The Export Credit Finance Guarantee Scheme for SMEs has been introduced. The Scheme facilitates finance for SMEs that lack working capital to procure material and services for the execution of an export order, and/or financing export trade debtors for a period of up to 180 days. Pre- and post-shipment finance can be obtained for export orders. Finance is provided by banks and can constitute up to 90% of export orders.

Guarantees are issued by the Credit Guarantee Insurance Corporation (CGIC) and are reinsured by the Department. The exporter has to be an independently owned business whose total assets do not exceed R5 million, or whose labour force does not exceed 200 employees. The loan application should not exceed R1 million and not be less than R50 000.

The Export Finance Scheme for Capital Projects is becoming more popular among financial institutions and contractors. Through this Scheme, exporters of capital projects are able to compete internationally by offering prospective overseas buyers competitive repayment rates denominated in US Dollars. Such credit facilities are available over a maximum repayment period of 10 years.

Africa, and southern Africa in particular, has proved to be a popular market for South African exporters of capital projects. There has also been an increase in insurance cover extended to South African short-term exports.

Export credit insurance provides an exporter with insurance protection against financial loss owing to non-receipt of payment of a legally enforceable debt, due and payable by a non-South African importer to the exporter for goods and services delivered. Insurance is available through the CGIC with reinsurance provided by the Department.

Businesses wishing to import or export goods that are subject to control may obtain permits from the Director of Imports and Exports, Private Bag X192, Pretoria, 0001, or phone 0861 843 384. Permits must be renewed annually. Registration with the local Controller of Customs and Excise is required of all factories subject to excise duties, as well as all enterprises that import on a regular basis.

Information regarding specifications for existing or new products, and guidance on quality control, is available from the South African Bureau of Standards (SABS). Excise duty is levied on certain locally produced goods, of which potable spirits, beer, cigarettes, tobacco, motor vehicles and certain petroleum products yield the highest revenue.

International Investment Council

The Council meets twice a year to advise President Thabo Mbeki on investment promotion and other economic issues.

The focus of discussions at a meeting near Kleinmond in the Western Cape in March 2003 was on how South Africa could further increase the rate of economic growth and employment creation.

The Council provided advice on how the new Black Economic Empowerment (BEE) Policy announcements could be communicated effectively to the international community.

It met again in September 2003 in Port Elizabeth, in the Eastern Cape.

Enterprise and industry development

Enterprise development remains an important area of co-operation across all three spheres of government. In order for South Africa's economy to grow in a manner that will create decent work for entrants into the labour market, it is necessary that new enterprises be created and that existing enterprises become more competitive.

The Department's Enterprise and Industry Development Division (EIDD) has, as its particular concern, moving trade and industrial policy in South Africa towards an internationally competitive status, capitalising on the country's competitive and comparative advantages. The emphasis is also on the worldwide trend towards knowledge-intensive economies, and on creating an environment for vigorous enterprise development through the development of suitable policies and strategies. Special attention is also given, as in the case of exports and investment, to BEE and regional growth within the SADC.

Considerable policy and advocacy work has been done by the EIDD, specifically in the areas of logistics and infrastructure, human resource development, technical infrastructure and technology and innovation.

Government's industrial policy strives to achieve a balance between greater openness, and improvement in local competitiveness. South Africa has made great strides in

Economy

opening the domestic economy to international competition, which include:
- a market-related and competitive exchange rate
- no restrictions on the type or extent of foreign investments
- strengthening the competition policy
- abolishing exchange control for non-residents and substantial reduction in that applicable to residents
- a significant reduction in tariff barriers, ahead of the WTO timetable, resulting in the lowest (trade-weighted) average rate of protection in the SADC region
- a proactive strategy to attract foreign strategic equity partners into the process of restructuring State assets
- the availability of attractive investment incentives to enhance international competitiveness and technology transfer with the means to facilitate FDI.

One of South Africa's key industrial policies remains its commitment to fostering sustainable industrial development in areas where poverty and unemployment are at their highest. This objective is implemented through the Spatial Development Initiatives (SDIs), which focus high-level support on areas where socio-economic conditions require concentrated government assistance, and where inherent economic potential exists. The SDI programmes focus government attention on the various national, provincial and local government spheres, with the goal of fast-tracking investments and maximising synergies between various types of investments.

The SDI programme consists of 11 local SDIs and four IDZs at varying stages of delivery. They are the following:
- SDIs: Maputo Development Corridor; Lubombo SDI; Richards Bay SDI, including the Durban and Pietermaritzburg nodes; Wild Coast SDI; Fish River SDI; West Coast Investment Initiative; Platinum SDI; Phalaborwa SDI; and Coast-2-Coast Corridor.
- IDZs: Gauteng, Coega, East London, Saldanha and Richards Bay.

The SDI concept may have a variety of focuses, such as:
- Industrial – KwaZulu-Natal and Fish River SDIs
- Agrotourism – Lubombo and Wild Coast SDIs
- Sectoral mix – Maputo Development Corridor
- IDZs – Coega, Saldanha and East London.

IDZs are located near major transport nodes such as ports or airports. The benefits of IDZs are: support to investing companies, especially for greenfield's development projects; access to transport for exporting purposes; waiver of import duties for products that are produced for export; and subsidies in the provision of skills training for employees.

In 2001, work started on the Coega Deep Water Harbour and industrial development near Port Elizabeth. It is expected that 10 000 jobs will be created during the construction phase of the Harbour and industrial zone. In January 2002, the Minister of Trade and Industry awarded a provisional operator's licence to the Coega Development Corporation (CDC), enabling it to operate the Coega IDZ.

The South African Government, in collaboration with the Commonwealth Business Council (CBC) and the New Partnership for Africa's Development Secretariat, hosted the Africa Investment Forum in Johannesburg in April 2003.

The Forum built on the success of the Commonwealth-Africa Investment Forum held in Abuja, Nigeria in April 2002.

The sessions focused on key investment issues such as infrastructure development and finance, expanding regional markets, information and communications technology, and agriculture.

It also focused on developing the CBC's pioneering work on the themes of corporate governance and accounting standards, as well as confronted the issue of how business tackles HIV, AIDS, malaria and tuberculosis. Sector coverage included power, transport, water and sanitation, telecommunications, and oil and gas.

The Forum is designed to create opportunities for partnerships between the public and private sectors.

By the end of March 2003, the CDC had awarded contracts worth more than R500 million for various projects at the IDZ.

Investments committed for the Coega Project – both the IDZ and the deep water port of Ngqura – amount to R800 million for infrastructure developed by the IDZ, R2,4 million for the port, and R1,8 billion for the upgrading of electrical lines to the Nelson Mandela Metro by power utility Eskom.

The French aluminium group Pechiney selected Coega over other sites in Canada and Australia for the first of a new generation of smelters.

The US$600-million contract to build and manage the smelter has been awarded to the South African project facilitation group, Bateman, and French oilfield services and construction group, Technip-Coflexip, in a 50-50 partnership.

By mid-2003, the Coega Village, a R40-million construction village to house Coega workers, was being built. The 520-unit village will accommodate the skilled core staff of construction companies from outside the Nelson Mandela Metro.

A R7,6-million business centre is also being built in the Village. Work began in November 2002 and is expected to be completed by May 2004.

The Enterprise Organisation

The Enterprise Organisation of the Department of Trade and Industry provides incentives to stimulate or catalyse investment in infrastructure, human resource development, integrated manufacturing and related activities, small business development, specific regions, and technology and innovation.

The programme has four subprogrammes, namely:
- Investment incentives that promote higher rates of domestic and FDI in targeted sectors of the economy, through tax incentives and cash grants for investment.
- Infrastructure investment incentives that promote investment in critical economic infrastructure by leveraging private-sector investment through public-private partnerships to provide world-class infrastructure.
- IMS support measures that promote the competitiveness of enterprises by supporting the diffusion of world-class management practices and technology; beneficiation and value-added regional production; equity and economic participation; knowledge intensity and services integration; and the support of integrated value matrices.
- Empowerment support measures that promote the growth of enterprises owned and managed by women and black people. During 2002, eight strategic investment projects were approved. The total expected investment value is R2,4 billion. The projects were awarded a tax allowance of R1,7 billion. They are expected to create 1 458 direct and some 8 085 indirect jobs.

Innovation and technology

Venture capital

The Venture Capital Fund is a joint initiative between the Department of Trade and Industry and the Council for Scientific and Industrial Research (CSIR) with the aim of providing early-stage capital, and to a lesser extent, expansion capital, for technology-based SMMEs, and management support for investee companies.

Technology Transfer Centre (TTC)

The TTC is to be established by the CSIR as an agent to provide the following services to industry in South Africa:
- negotiating and drafting assistance agreements related to technology transfers
- technology-transfer training
- technology evaluation, assessment and selection services related to technology transfer
- technology advisory services
- match-making between technology sellers

and buyers and appropriate financial institutions
- if required, direct and/or indirect financial assistance for technology-transfer activities.

Incubators

A Technology Business Incubator is a facility that provides a variety of services under controlled conditions to create an environment favourable for developing, nurturing and accelerating growth of new, technology-based companies. The support services provided include physical space, business development and technical services.

The Department directly funds four incubators, namely the Furniture Technology Centre (Furntech) in George, Western Cape, specialising in training, demonstration and incubation in furniture technologies; the National Fibre Centre in Port Elizabeth, specialising in research and development and incubation in natural fibres; the Downstream Aluminium Centre for Technology in Richards Bay, KwaZulu-Natal, specialising in training and incubation in the beneficiation of aluminium; and the Mpumalanga Stainless Steel Initiative in Middelburg, Mpumalanga, specialising in incubation in the beneficiation of stainless steel.

Godisa is an initiative of the Department of Trade and Industry, the Department of Science and Technology and the EU to fund and support incubators. The EU supports three pilot projects, namely the Innovation Support Centre situated in Cato Manor, Durban, KwaZulu-Natal, which commercialises embedded technologies; the Demonstration Centre situated at Mintek in Randburg, Gauteng, which demonstrates equipment to small-scale miners all over South Africa; and the Technology Incubator, situated at the CSIR in Pretoria, specialising in incubating software for wireless technologies. Five other incubators have been established, namely the:
- Acorn Incubator at the University of Cape Town, specialising in medical-device technologies
- EgoliBio in Modderfontein, Gauteng, focusing on biotechnologies
- Timbali Incubator in Nelspruit, Mpumalanga, focusing on floriculture technologies
- Chemin Incubator at the Port Elizabeth University of Technology, focusing on fine chemicals technologies
- Brainworks Incubator in Sunninghill, Johannesburg, focusing on information, communications and electronic technologies. (See Chapter 18: *Science and technology.*)

Skills research

A project to identify skills needs in all the priority sectors is currently under way in partnership with respective Sector Education and Training Authorities (SETAs). The aim is to guide human-capital investment decisions made by enterprises, individuals and communities.

Workplace Challenge Programme

This supply-side Programme of the Department (administered by the National Productivity Institute), assists enterprises and industries to improve their productivity and competitiveness. The Programme focuses on improving workplace collaboration, adopting world-class manufacturing and workplace practices, and disseminating best practices.

The focus of the Programme has been on the manufacturing and processing sectors.

National Industrial Participation Programme (NIPP)

A number of large government contracts may be awarded to foreign suppliers on the basis of competitiveness and appropriate technology, which could act as a drain on foreign reserves, with a reduction in local industrial and commercial activities. The NIPP of the Department is designed to address these issues. In terms of the Industrial Participation (IP) Policy and Guidelines, all State and parastatal purchase and lease contracts (goods and services) signed after 1997, and exceeding a certain level of imported content, are subject to an IP obligation. No contract can be awarded to a tenderer if the latter has not satisfied the IP requirements.

The IP obligation is benchmarked on the imported content of the contract. Any contract with an imported content equal to or exceeding US$10 million has an IP obligation. The obligation amounts to 30% of the imported content. IP arrangements to satisfy the obligation include investments, subcontracting, export promotion, licensor production, supply arrangements, and research and development collaboration. These economic activities have to be generated in seven years.

The NIPP has been very successful in boosting direct investment in South Africa's economy. By April 2003, approximately R2 billion worth of investment had created new jobs and generated R7 billion in exports and domestic sales. Some 155 projects had been financed through the NIPP.

Manufacturing

South Africa's manufacturing sector growth has averaged 4% per annum every year since 1994 in terms of production volumes. By late 2001, it was growing at over 5%.

Key functions of the Department include:
- supporting increased investment in the manufacturing sector
- enhancing the establishment of new manufacturing entities
- supporting new sustainable and profitable manufacturing entities.

In order to provide direction to the economy and to provide the Council of Trade and Industry Institutions with a framework in which to operate, the Department released its IMS in 2002.

Some of the key aspects of the IMS involves the following:
- improving market access for South African products in key markets
- promoting beneficiation and value addition so that value is added to the many natural resources already present in the country
- finding ways to harness the skills and expertise in South Africa so that they can be sold to other countries.

The IMS also identifies the need to capture local knowledge. It encourages big corporations and large companies to make greater use of small businesses, as well as promoting greater integration between the different sectors of the economy so that they add value to each other.

BEE, small business development, increased use of ICT, job creation, and a more equitable geographic spread of investment and economic activities, will be addressed in the implementation of the IMS.

By March 2003, the Motor Industry Development Plan (MIDP) had transformed South Africa's motor industry into a dynamic export business.

From 11 500 vehicles worth R750 million in 1996, the MIDP resulted in 130 000 cars worth R15 billion being exported in 2002. The number of exported cars is expected to reach 200 000 per annum.

Competition policy

The Competition Act, 1998 (Act 89 of 1998), which came into effect on 1 September 1999, is aimed at anti-competition practices, elimi-

---

The Strategic Investment Programme (SIP) of the Department of Trade and Industry is a significant incentive for investments.

The SIP aims to increase private-sector investment in innovative, profitable and wealth-creating business enterprises in South Africa, while simultaneously creating job opportunities within the industrial sector. Some 10 projects have been approved, attracting about R2,97 billion in investments. The provinces with SIP projects include Gauteng, KwaZulu-Natal, Mpumalanga, Western Cape and Eastern Cape.

The Programme is working towards developing and growing priority sectors in the provinces, which include agroprocessing in Mpumalanga and Limpopo, clothing and textiles in KwaZulu-Natal, and call centres in Gauteng.

Economy

nating abuse of dominant positions and the strengthening of merger control. The Act provides for the establishment of a Competition Commission, Competition Tribunal and Competition Appeal Court to replace the former Competition Board. The Act aims to outlaw the following main areas of business practice:
- Restrictive practices between businesses, or between businesses, their supplier(s) and customers, which hinder competition. These include price-fixing, collusive tendering, and restricting output, investment and market sharing.
- The abuse of a dominant position which, according to the Act, is defined as a market share of 35% or more.

The Competition Second Amendment Act, 2000 (Act 39 of 2000), included an amendment to provisions which allowed the Minister to change the thresholds in relation to merger control and abuse of dominance only every five years. Section 3(1)(d) was amended to cater for concurrent jurisdiction over competition matters between competition authorities and sector regulators. Furthermore, the Minister can now change the thresholds for merger controls and abuse of dominance whenever the need arises.

In addition to the Act, new rules for proceedings in the Competition Commission and the Competition Tribunal, new thresholds for the notification of mergers and acquisitions, as well as new forms, became effective. In terms of the new regulations, the lower threshold for mergers has been raised from R50 million for combined annual turnover/asset value to R200 million, while the value of the primary target firm/asset value has been raised from R5 million to R30 million. Furthermore, the fees for merger notification have been significantly reduced and simplified. A single fee for intermediate mergers of R75 000 has been introduced. Prior to the amendments, fees for intermediate mergers ranged from R5 000 to R250 000. The fee for large mergers has been halved from R500 000 to R250 000.

The Competition Commission also has an obligation to evaluate the impact of mergers and acquisition activity on employment.

Small, medium and micro enterprises

The Enterprise, Commerce and Industry Development Division of the Department of Trade and Industry is responsible for policy and strategy development; programme development, monitoring and evaluation; consultation; and relationship-building in the areas of BEE and enterprise development, SMMEs, co-operatives, business regulation, consumer protection and sector development. The central focus is on the Department's approach to the issues of BEE, gender equity (women-owned enterprises), and an emerging focus on co-operatives as an alternative mechanism for addressing the need for emerging entrepreneurs to pool resources to compete effectively. The Department has new ventures in each of these areas, including TWIB, attention to legislative and regulatory reform, and a new BEE strategy cross-cutting all the Department's programmes.

Small business development is critical to the development of South Africa's economy, the levels of equity and as a mechanism for the creation of jobs in the country.

The key objectives of government's National Strategy for Small Business are to:
- create an enabling environment for small enterprise
- level the playing fields between big and small businesses, as well as between rural and urban businesses
- facilitate greater equalisation of income, wealth and earning opportunities, and address the legacy of apartheid-based disempowerment of black business
- support the advancement of women in all business sectors
- create long-term jobs

- stimulate sector-focused economic growth
- strengthen cohesion between small enterprises
- prepare small business to meet the challenges of an internationally competitive economy.

The National Small Business Amendment Bill, which is to amend the National Small Business Act, 1996 (Act 102 of 1996), provides for the following:

- Creating a voice for small business: Due to the closure and liquidation of the National Small Business Council, it is necessary that the Council be removed from the legislation.
- Ensuring that the mandate of the Ntsika Enterprise Promotion Agency is more focused and that some of the functions provided by the institution, which overlap with the functions of others, be removed. Ntsika has already embarked on a process to rectify the situation.
- Extending the due date for the tabling of the Annual Small Business Review in Parliament, streamlining the process of appointing directors for Ntsika, and enhancing information on the schedule of the Act with regard to the definition of small business.

These changes are necessary to ensure that a legitimate voice is created to articulate the needs of SMMEs. The purpose of this body would be to advise government on critical issues such as:

- the impact of current and new legislation on small business
- the identification of areas of market failure for small businesses so that appropriate support and intervention can be provided
- the constraints, needs and communication mechanisms to interface with small businesses
- formulating methods to monitor support services to the small business sector.

Other initiatives to support small business include the consolidation of existing successful programmes such as Ntsika's Mentorship Programme, assistance with entering export markets and the expansion of local infrastructure, and support for the provision of business development services.

Institutional support framework

Ntsika Enterprise Promotion Agency

Ntsika's mission is to render non-financial support services to the SMME sector through a broad range of intermediaries. This is achieved through initiatives in the areas of management and entrepreneurship development, marketing and business linkages, research and business development services, and targeted assistance. The achievements of Ntsika can be categorised into capacity-building of the retail distribution network and direct services to SMMEs through these retailers.

Ntsika has established a network of 170 Local Business Service Centres across the country, which offer business counselling, advice, training and information to SMMEs. Ntsika also offers a Tender Advice Centre Programme that has helped various SMMEs win tenders to the value of R87 million.

The Trade and Investment Development Programme is a three-track programme that assists potential exporters to become competitive and fully fledged exporters. Ntsika also has an active Small Exporter Development Programme in place.

Transfers to Ntsika will increase from R40 million in 2002/03 to R42,4 million in 2005/06.

Khula Enterprise Finance

Khula is a wholesale agency which provides financial support for small businesses through intermediaries. Its financial products include loans, a national credit-guarantee scheme, grants, institutional capacity-building, equity funds and mentorship schemes. The achievements of Khula can be categorised into support to financial intermediaries as retail distribution networks, and direct services to SMMEs.

The Thuso Mentorship Network provides entrepreneurs with pre-loan business plans and post-loan support in the form of technical expertise management.

Khula is expanding the Network to enhance access to business advice and mentoring. Eight offices have been opened since the Network started operating in 2001, with two more to open in Kimberley and Polokwane.

By March 2003, Khula had assisted approximately 190 000 South Africans through its network of retail finance intermediaries and micro-credit outlets, 72% of whom were women.

From April to December 2002, Khula facilitated the creation of some 126 764 jobs.

During 2002, Khula provided 800 enterprises with R145 million worth of credit guarantees on their loans. It also provided wholesale loan finance to the value of R77 million to SMME lending agencies. Khula also implemented a rural micro enterprise lending programme which assisted more than 26 000 micro enterprises.

National Co-ordinating Office of the Manufacturing Advisory Office (NAMAC)

The NAMAC's role is to supply high-quality advisory and information services to new and existing SMMEs to ensure improvement in their quality, competitiveness and productivity.

The Department of Trade and Industry proposed during its 2003/04 budget vote that NAMAC's allocation be increased from R45 million to R80 million for the 2003/04 financial year.

The additional funding saw the expansion of NAMAC offices to all provinces in South Africa, the extension of its Business Referral and Information Network to 415 locations, increased support in the provision of franchise information and the establishment of one-stop shops for business support services. Some of NAMAC's achievements include providing support to 1 400 enterprises, the creation of 1 800 new jobs in those enterprises, and ensuring that more than 15 000 jobs were sustained through the interventions of the Manufacturing Advisory Centres.

Technology for Women in Business

The TWIB aims to enhance the use of technology by women in business, promote innovation among women, and encourage young girls and women to choose careers in science and technology.

The Department hosted a TWIB conference with the theme *Technology Access – Linkages and Opportunities* in Nelspruit in August 2003. More than 600 female entrepreneurs from across the country attended.

One of the key issues discussed during the conference was how female entrepreneurs can access the products and services offered by the Department.

An entrepreneur from KwaZulu-Natal, Tholakele Hadebe, won the 2003 TWIB Award, which is awarded annually to honour women who have successfully exploited technology to grow their business or enterprise.

Hadebe is the owner of Tholubonge Pottery, which manufactures dinner sets and coffee mugs for the local and overseas markets.

South African Women Entrepreneurs Network

The SAWEN was established to assist aspiring and existing women in business. The Network advocates policy changes, builds capacity, and facilitates the access of women to business resources and information.

SAWEN signed a MoU with the JSE in May 2003. In accordance with the MoU, the JSE will train these women entrepreneurs in the workings of stock, commodity and bond markets, the operations of the JSE, and how to engage with these markets and institutions.

National Empowerment Fund (NEF) Trust

The NEF Trust was established to facilitate the redressing of economic inequality from past unfair discrimination against historically disadvantaged individuals (HDIs). The NEF Trust is primarily capitalised through receiving shares of State-owned enterprises (SOEs) undergoing restructuring. It is envisaged that the Trust will promote BEE through the following: an investment trust that will market investment units to HDIs; a portfolio trust that will warehouse the shares of SOEs, which will thereafter be sold to HDIs; and an equity management fund to provide venture capital among HDIs. The Fund buys shares in privatisation utilities from government, at a discount of up to 20%, to resell to previously disadvantaged people.

One of the NEF's functions is investor education to ensure awareness of the economic environment and basic economic literacy. The Fund operates at three levels, initially targeting low-income individual earners, and progressing towards savings clubs and equity finance agreements for SMMEs.

Industrial Development Corporation (IDC)

The IDC plays an increasingly important role in both supporting and assisting with venture capital in the formation of new SMEs. Tourism is just one of the latest sectors targeted.

Over the last five years, the IDC has facilitated the creation of 70 000 jobs and approved projects responsible for generating more than R20 billion per annum in export earnings.

The IDC also facilitated investments of more than R21 billion into South Africa, and made significant progress in the support of BEE through providing loan finance to the value of R1,4 billion to historically disadvantaged businesses. Almost 60% of the IDC projects were in rural and peri-urban areas and 1 200 SMEs received loan finance.

Business Partners Ltd

Business Partners Ltd is a specialist investment group, providing customised and integrated investment, mentorship, and property management services for SMEs in South Africa.

The group has been investing in entrepreneurs for over 20 years, providing private equity of up to R15 million for viable start-ups, expansions, outright purchases, management buy-outs and buy-ins, franchises, tenders and contracts. It also provides a range of value-added services including property broking, property management, consulting and mentorship.

Business Partners announced a R500-million investment budget for 2003/04. R200 million of the total was allocated to entrepreneurs from previously disadvantaged communities, and R162,5 million was allocated for investment in businesses owned and run by women.

Manufacturing remains the country's single largest economic sector. This is reflected in the fact that R104 million has been earmarked for investment in this sector.

Another industry sector that is showing important growth is the business and personal-services sector, which is reflected in the new budget with a R91-million allocation. Entrepreneurs in this sector include health professionals in private practice and companies offering various other business and professional services, including legal services.

Business Partners' property portfolio, which provides for the premises needs of entrepreneurs, consists of 320 properties across South Africa.

These premises are occupied by 3 600 tenants employing a staff complement of 27 000 people. The group's dedicated mentorship division also provides value-added services, including counselling, specialist management consulting, and turnaround and sectoral assistance.

Business Partners is an unlisted public company whose major shareholders include the Department of Trade and Industry (through Khula Enterprise Finance), Remgro, the Business Partners Employee Share Trust,

Economy

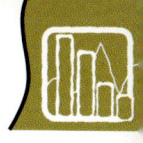

Sanlam, BHP Billiton SA, Amalgamated Banks of South Africa, Nedcor, FirstRand, Old Mutual Nominees, Standard Bank Investment Corporation of South Africa, Anglo American Corporation of South Africa, De Beers Holdings and Standard Bank Nominees.

A new Franchise Fund was launched in conjunction with the Umsobomvu Youth Fund. This Fund will extend the group's capacity to facilitate new job creation for HDIs.

The group is easily accessible, operating through 22 offices nationwide. It offers free initial consultations to existing or potential entrepreneurs with a viable business plan. It also offers a user-friendly business planning model on its website at *www.businesspartners.co.za*.

Restructuring of State assets

The Department of Public Enterprises has been tasked with redressing the imbalances created by apartheid, through the accelerated restructuring of SOEs in an integrated and coherent manner to promote economic growth and socio-economic development. The Department manages and directs the restructuring of SOEs in such a way that they:
- perform optimally in a globally competitive market
- maximise the distribution of wealth across South Africa
- facilitate investment in underdeveloped areas

The Department of Trade and Industry's Competitiveness Fund was launched in Durban, KwaZulu-Natal in September 2003.

The Fund is a cost-sharing grant that provides financial support to entrepreneurs for up to 50% of their eligible costs.

All registered South African private-sector companies qualify for assistance. However, companies must have a clearly stated objective to support competitiveness.

The Fund committed more than R200 million to more than 1 300 companies during its first phase of operation.

- promote equity for black people in skills, assets and income.

The Department's Restructuring Programme has been designed around a multiple array of strategies or mixes of options, to foster the maximisation of shareholder interest, defined in multidimensional terms. Restructuring therefore refers to the matrix of options that includes:
- redesign of business management principles within enterprises
- attraction of strategic equity partners or concessionaires
- the divestment of equity in whole or in part, as appropriate
- employment of various turnaround strategies.

At the enterprise and sector level, restructuring involves:
- improving the efficiency and effectiveness of the entity
- accessing globally competitive technologies
- mobilising private-sector capital and expertise
- creating effective market structures in sectors.

At the macro-economic level, restructuring aims to:
- attract foreign investment
- reduce public borrowing requirements
- assist in the development of an economic context that promotes industrial competitiveness and fuels economic growth.

Progress of restructuring process

During 2002, government carried out 11 transactions, bringing the number of transactions concluded since 1997 to 27.

These included outright disposals, equity sales, participation of BEE groups, dividend payments, proceeds from the rationalisation of interests across SOEs, and the Telkom Initial Public Offering (IPO). By mid-2003, total proceeds amounted to R35,5 million, with the National Revenue Fund absorbing just under R22,5 billion. Income for 2002 was R8,126 billion.

The 2002/03 financial year yielded R7,4 billion in proceeds. The bulk of this amount was made up of R4,1 billion from Telkom's IPO and R1,1 billion from the MTN management buy-out.

In addition, the disposal of 51% of Apron Services yielded R117 million, and the Turbomeca/Denel Aerospace joint venture resulted in R50 million accruing to the fiscus.

Eskom declared a dividend of R549 million and PetroSA (formerly the Central Energy Fund), a dividend of R1,5 billion.

Telkom listing

Amidst turbulent equity markets, the South African Government finalised the listing of the country's dominant telecommunications company, Telkom. Primary listing on the JSE occurred on 4 March 2003 and was followed by a secondary listing on the New York Stock Exchange.

A total of 154 199 467 ordinary shares were offered to the public at a listing price of R28 per share. A total of R4,3 billion was raised through the offering. To date, this was the largest global IPO and the largest telecommunications IPO in Europe, the Middle East and Africa since the listing of Burberry in July 2002.

Government believes that the Telkom IPO is the flagship of BEE. During mid-2003, the share price on the JSE was R31,11, representing a 39% rise in value since listing. Telkom's ordinary shares have outperformed both the FTSE/JSE Top 40 and the European Benchmark Index.

Accessing more than 125 000 individuals was a significant achievement in developing a new equity-investment culture in South Africa. More than R720 million of demand was generated from retail investors in South Africa and the USA.

The South African retail offer represented 12 012 992 shares or 8% of the IPO, which was at the top end of the initially anticipated 5% to 10% range. More than 100 000 applications were new participants in the equity market.

More than 80 000 applications were received under the Khulisa offer, including *stokvels* that received full allocations. Approximately 56% of Khulisa applications were from HDIs.

A total of 168 institutional investors from South Africa, the USA and Europe participated in the offering.

Forestry

Progress in restructuring the commercial forestry assets of the State in 2002/03 centered around three significant forestry assets, namely Komatiland Forests (Pty) Ltd, Mountain to Oceans (MTO) (Pty) Ltd and Amatola Forestry (Pty) Ltd. It was anticipated that in 2003/04 all three forestry assets would be completed and the assets transferred to the successful bidders.

During 2002/03, two forestry packages were sold to successful bidders, namely Singisi Forests (Eastern Cape) and SiyaQhubeka (KwaZulu-Natal).

The second phase of the restructuring of Komatiland Forests was started in February 2003. More than 30 companies expressed interest in the package. The Bid Evaluation Committee recommended six bidders for short-listing. The Cabinet approved these bidders in March 2003.

The Cabinet was expected to announce the preferred bidder by the end of 2003, with negotiations completed before 31 March 2004.

After the implementation of this transaction, 75% of the equity in Komatiland will be disposed of. Employees will hold 9%, a community trust will hold 10%, and government will hold a residual 6%.

By September 2003, negotiations with CTR, the preferred bidder of the MTO package in the Western Cape, were at a final stage. Negotiations were also at a final stage with Rance, the preferred bidder for the Amatola package in the Eastern Cape.

The South African Forestry Company Limited (Safcol)-Cape conversion is a long-

Economy

term process that will achieve government's aim of making significant land available to previously disadvantaged individuals and communities in both the western and southern Cape. Areas have been identified and the following land-uses proposed: conservation, agriculture, housing and forestry.

The Singisi consortium (Safcol-Singisi), which purchased the Singisi assets, included 168 communities surrounding the forest areas. This process directly influenced the lives of 11 600 people and increased the employment in the Company to 2 300 people.

SiyaQhubeka Forests (SQF) recorded its intention, subject to prevailing market conditions, to sell into the local market and limit the export of unbeneficiated products.

SQF undertook to ensure that within five years of the effective date, at least 50% of the management would be from historically disadvantaged groups.

SQF further undertook to provide appropriate assistance and support to facilitate the growth and development of SMMEs, and to afford employees first option to take up contracts.

Hospitality industry

At the beginning of 2002/03, 12 of the original 15 Aventura resorts remained State assets.

Bloemfontein, Aldam and Christiana were sold for R23 million in 2001. The sale proceeds were used to reduce the company's overdraft. The proceeds from the sale in 2002 of the next four resorts, namely Eiland, Heidelbergkloof, Kareekloof and Roodeplaat, which were sold individually for a sum of R32 million, were also used to settle the overdraft.

The packaged sale of the last eight resorts, namely Loskopdam, Blydepoort, Tshipise, Gariep, Plettenberg, Warmbaths, Badplaas and Swadini, followed a public process which attracted more than 30 proposals that were narrowed down to two short-listed candidates.

The Cabinet approved the choice of the Forever Siyonwaba Consortium as the preferred bidder in May 2003.

In accordance with comprehensive negotiations, the Consortium will retain all employees for a minimum period of three years, and pay a gross purchase price of R200 million. Government has allowed the deduction of R58 million to cover Club Privé debenture liabilities, the price for future holiday accommodation for Club Privé members until 2010, and certain other liabilities. Government will receive a net amount of R101 million.

Government Printing Works (GPW)

During 2002/03, government decided to incorporate GPW as a fully fledged public enterprise. To this end, processes were commenced to establish the necessary legal framework. Work has commenced on developing a business plan for the entity. This was expected to be finalised in 2003/04.

Denel

It was announced in April 2003 that government had decided to terminate discussions with British Aerospace (BAE) Systems surrounding a 30% disposal of Denel, the State-owned high-technology engineering and defence industrial undertaking.

BAE Systems had been selected as the preferred bidder for Denel in 2000. A thorough and complex series of negotiations ensued. Despite recording significant progress, agreement could not be reached on a number of commercial and contractual arrangements to the satisfaction of government.

Since 2000, government has successfully concluded the formation of Turbomeca Africa, a new aerospace engine and maintenance facility, comprising 51% of Turbomeca, France and 49% of Denel Airmotive. Denel itself also shed some of its loss-making, non-core entities during this period.

Denel improved its order book from less than R1 billion in 1998 to more than R10 billion in 2003. Denel continues to generate technology transfers into the company, through its participation in the Strategic

Defence Package acquisition by the South African National Defence Force.

Denel and BAE Systems will continue to participate in joint production ventures and programmes where possible, and the relationship between the two companies remains amicable and healthy, particularly in relation to the offset packages of the Hawk and Gripen programmes.

Government will continue to seek international partners for Denel as the company continues to grow and develop its product and technology ranges. (See Chapter 17: *Safety, security and defence.*)

Energy sector

Based on the *White Paper on Energy Policy 1998*, the Cabinet approved proposals for electricity generation and transmission sector reforms in April 2001. The managed liberalisation approach outlined by the Cabinet has driven restructuring in this sector. Cabinet policy on energy sector restructuring outlined the following objectives, namely to:
- introduce competition into generation
- divest 30% of generation capacity, with a minimum of 10% to BEE groups
- establish a multimarket model for wholesale electricity trading
- create a separate national transmission company.

As a result, two separate restructuring processes were established, namely the electricity distribution industry (EDI) restructuring project under the leadership of the Department of Minerals and Energy, and the Electricity Supply Industry (ESI) restructuring project under the leadership of the Department of Public Enterprises.

In terms of the Eskom Conversion Act, 2001 (Act 13 of 2001), Eskom was incorporated as a company with effect from 1 July 2002. A Board of Directors has been appointed for Eskom Holdings Limited.

The EDI restructuring process gained momentum during 2002 after the approval of the EDI Blueprint by government in September 2001. The Blueprint outlines the process whereby the electricity distribution function of Eskom will become separate from Eskom and merge with municipal electricity undertakings to form six Regional Electricity Distributors.

Government has also indicated its intention to restructure the generation and transmission sectors of the ESI in order to introduce competition into the generation sector, to facilitate BEE and to encourage private-sector participation.

In the medium term, government will establish a separate State-owned transmission company that will be independent of the generation and retail business, with ring-fenced transmission system operation and market operation functions. Initially, this transmission company will be a subsidiary of Eskom, and will eventually be established as a separate State-owned transmission company before any investments are made in current or new generation capacity. (See chapter 16: *Minerals and energy*)

Spoornet

Spoornet, the largest division of Transnet, is responsible for the entire State rail freight transport and long-distance passenger services. It also operates the Blue Train, a luxury train service that is in the process of being concessioned to a hospitality sector operator.

Spoornet's major challenge for 2002/03 was its recapitalisation needs and resulting capacity problems. In this period, some critical upgrades and refurbishment were completed to maintain current capacity levels, with expansion in certain areas critical to the economy and clients. However, the bulk of the recapitalisation programme was expected to commence in the 2003/04 financial year.

The deteriorating position of light and low-density lines are in the process of being addressed by an agreement between national and provincial government, Spoornet management and organised labour.

Economy

The proposal to establish a separate division that will concentrate on these lines was expected to be completed in 2003/04. This intervention will focus on management, capital expenditure and operations on aligning rail operations with the development strategies and initiatives of provincial government. This will increase traffic on these lines, reduce the degradation of provincial secondary roads and act as a stimulus and support to local and regional economic development. (See Chapter 22: *Transport*.)

Ports restructuring

The *White Paper on National Commercial Ports Policy, 2001* seeks to ensure that there is an affordable, internationally competitive, efficient and safe port service for national and inter-national shippers and receivers. Guided by the policy objective to improve the competitiveness of commercial ports, the Department focuses on preparing for the transfer of port operations to private-sector operators via leases or concessions.

Central to the new Ports Policy is the establishment of a National Ports Authority to perform a landlord role responsible for infrastructure provision and management of the publicly owned port estate. The new entity was launched at the end of August 2003.

Severe congestion problems experienced with container handling in the port of Durban in the latter part of 2002 drew attention to the damaging implications of bottlenecks in the transport system for the economy and job creation.

The Cabinet announced at the end of July 2003 that the transaction for the Durban Container Terminal would be expedited, additional resources would be mobilised to ease congestion at the Durban, Cape Town and Port Elizabeth terminals and special measures would be put in place to improve efficiency. (See Chapter 22: *Transport*.)

South African Airways (SAA)

During 2002/03, the SAA Restructuring Task Team concentrated its efforts on the structural alignment of SAA operations with government's objectives for SOEs. It was expected that the final SAA restructuring model would be completed in 2003/04 and would have to take into account the weakness in global aviation and volatility that had impacted negatively on SAA's revenues, as well as the requirements of the Fleet Upgrade Programme. It will also support the focus on developing air services in Africa to lend support for NEPAD.

The developmental role of State-owned enterprises

SOEs are critically important to the economy of South Africa, as the restructuring of these enterprises has released financial resources to be utilised for socio-economic programmes throughout the country.

Government considers the strategic employment of SOE procurement budgets as instruments of BEE that complement ongoing transformation. During 2002, Eskom, Transnet and Denel had a combined discretionary procurement budget of just under R34 billion, of which just more than R9 billion was BEE-centred. Transnet committed 54,6% of its procurement-spend to BEE, followed by Eskom with 21,2% and Denel with 15%.

Eskom and Transnet spread their BEE procurement across manufacturing, production, resource and professional services. Eskom's BEE-spend also included a significant 33,7% of coal purchases. Denel plans to increase the supply of local-content products and services from black suppliers to 40% of manufacturing, including marine freight services, engineering services, electrical components and raw material.

Progress continues with employment equity and SOEs' contribution towards education, training and skills development aimed at scholars and students. Safcol, Eskom, Transnet and Denel are very active in this area.

Consumer and corporate regulation

The Consumer and Corporate Regulation Division within the Department of Trade and Industry is responsible for administering the regulation of the liquor, gambling and lottery industries, as well as commercial, competition and consumer-protection policies.

The South African Company Registration Office and the South African Patents and Trademarks Office, funded from this programme, have been merged into the Companies and Intellectual Property Registration Office (CIPRO). The overall objective is to ensure that the market is fair, efficient and transparent.

Corporate and consumer regulation has become a creative endeavour that seeks to serve the interests of both business and consumers, and to create a modern and globally competitive national economy. A corporate law-reform project and making amendments to the intellectual property rights regime are ongoing activities.

The CIPRO was established as a trading entity in 2002 and is expected to become self-sustainable by July 2004.

The CIPRO improved the registration of enterprises by facilitating more than 100 000 close corporations in 2002/03. It also improved the availability of registration forms, simplified the procedures, and improved the use of technology in the tracking and management of documents.

The Department is engaged in corporate law-reform processes that are likely to result in new functions for CIPRO.

Public works programmes

The National Public Works Programme (NPWP) is a framework through which public works programmes can be aligned with the social and economic development of the country, including rural poverty-alleviation and transformation of the construction industry.

The Community-Based Public Works Programme (CBPWP) and the Construction Industry Development Programme constitute the NPWP.

Community-Based Public Works Programme

The CBPWP is an essential component of the Government's Integrated Sustainable Rural Development Programme (ISRDP). The Programme is geared to achieve poverty relief and infrastructure investment by:
- targeting identified poverty pockets in rural areas
- capacity-building within local communities and local governments
- maximising job creation
- targeting rural women, in particular female-headed households with dependants
- incorporating operation and maintenance to ensure sustainability of assets
- constructing useful infrastructure to improve access to trade opportunities
- skills training appropriate to project requirements.

A total of 560 CBPWP projects were implemented in the 2002/03 financial year, employing some 13 982 workers.

In 2001/02, the Department of Public Works allocated R10 million for the establishment of Multi-Purpose Community Centres (MPCCs) as part of government's roll-out strategy to build at least one MPCC in each of the country's 61 district councils by the end of 2003/04.

By June 2003, the Department had assisted with the establishment of 14 MPCCs.

When it comes to social-cohesion-related projects, MPCCs play a crucial role in addressing the needs of the people, together with Community Production Centres (CPCs), which are established with the Department of Agriculture to promote sustainable, commercially driven and market-orientated communal agricultural ventures.

About 15 Centres have been established in most of the nine provinces.

The very first CPC, the Lambasi CPC in the Eastern Cape, produces an average of 2 500 tons (t) of maize every year on approximately 500 hectares (ha). Sales of mealies (1 300 t) have on average realised R2,6 million per annum, while the 80 000 chickens sold during the 2002/03 financial year netted R1,3 million.

At the Ncora CPC in the Eastern Cape, cabbage sales from 10 ha over a month totalled R40 000.

At the Umzimkhulu Highlands CPC in the Eastern Cape, some 100 ha of the total 640 ha has been planted with maize.

Partnerships with the Department of Agriculture's Mass Food Production Programme will extend benefits to about 400 households.

The Keiskammahoek CPC in the Eastern Cape entered into a community private partnership between smallholding farmers and dairy producer, Clover.

At the Elandskraal CPC in Limpopo, the community is benefitting from the rehabilitation of irrigation infrastructure, while approximately 290 small farmers are engaged in reaping the winter wheat crop.

The Upper Arabie CPC in Limpopo covers approximately 540 ha and is supported by some 400 small-scale farmers. The community will benefit from the rehabilitation of irrigation infrastructure.

The Cairn Lemon CPC in Mpumalanga has a management partnership agreement with a commercial farmer. The community is benefitting from the rehabilitation of bulk water supply, the development of a lemon orchard, and the rehabilitation of irrigation infrastructure. The CPC has secured a market with Coca-Cola.

In KwaZulu-Natal, the Ndaya CPC comprises approximately 18 ha and is managed by a group of 18 local women and five men. The CPC produces a variety of crops. Profits are shared between members, and dividends are based on the members' contribution to the crop production. The CPC has a nursery that provides the seedlings for cropping.

At the Makhathini Flats CPC in KwaZulu-Natal, the Department of Public Works has completed the infrastructure provision. The provincial Department of Agriculture is busy with production and development.

The Schmidtsdrift CPC in the Northern Cape serves 770 households who farm with goats and sheep. The provisioning of fencing and the rehabilitation of the water supply will enable them to graduate from subsistence to commercial farming.

Between 1999 and 2003, the CBPWP and other construction initiatives of the Department of Public Works had:
- created a total of 106 000 temporary jobs
- employed a total of 39 125 women
- employed 41 323 youths
- employed 2 249 people with disabilities.

Expanded Public Works Programme (EPWP)

Following the announcement of the establishment of the EPWP in February 2003, the Department of Public Works has been taking concrete steps to ensure that the concept of an EPWP is fully understood and supported within and outside government.

The proposed EPWP is a key intervention by government based on the recognition that infrastructure development is one of the primary drivers of growth, employment and development.

The aim of the EPWP will be to facilitate and create employment opportunities for the poor and vulnerable, through integrated and co-ordinated labour-intensive approaches to government infrastructure delivery and service provision.

The objectives of the EPWP are:
- job creation
- poverty alleviation
- investment in social and economic infrastructure
- human resource development through the training of participants.

The key focus areas in which the Department

of Public Works is in a position to optimise contributions include:
- labour-based methods: optimal use of labour while ensuring cost-effectiveness and safeguarding quality, primarily within the construction industry
- emerging contractor support programme: SMME development and support to have resources circulate within communities and create capacity for maintenance
- procurement policy: ensures policy responsiveness, uniformity and adjustment in all spheres of government
- monitoring and evaluation: ensure mechanisms to track development and focus on objectives and targets.

The Programme will realign current governmental infrastructure and maintenance investments, targeting initiatives such as:
- national, provincial and local government infrastructure investment and service delivery
- SOE infrastructure, and community and poverty-alleviation programmes.

All public-sector departments and SOEs will be expected to formally respond to the EPWP, indicating which of the overall targets they will contribute to.

The alignment and co-ordination of programmes within the ISRDP and the Urban Renewal Strategy have been identified as of upmost importance.

Construction industry

To promote the construction industry as an asset to the country and attract young students to the industry, the Department of Public Works will be driving a campaign to establish a Construction Industry Development Week.

Another initiative will be the Incubator Programme which aims to provide sustainable work opportunities, training and access to finance for black construction enterprises of significant size, and to develop them to achieve the status of established construction enterprises.

Projects between R2 million and R25 million will be identified exclusively for these enterprises over a period of time.

Construction Industry Development Board (CIDB)

The Board's mandate is to:
- drive an integrated industrial development strategy
- provide strategic leadership to construction industry stakeholders to stimulate growth, reform and improvement of the construction sector for effective delivery and the industry's enhanced role in the country's economy.

Projects that are being prioritised and developed include:
- Roll-out of procurement and public-sector delivery best practice to address improved spending of the infrastructure budget.
- The *Know Your Rights and Responsibilities* Campaign.
- The Register of Projects and Register of Contractors are being developed to promote improved demand- and supply-side performance. The Construction Registration Service constitutes a licensing vehicle to drive the principal objectives of industry development – improved performance, delivery, sustainable growth and transformation. It is expected that this service will be ready for roll-out by April 2004.
- Establishing a body of knowledge and a website as a resource to the industry.
- Developing CIDB governance procedures.
- Taking forward important work flowing from the Department's commissioned reports on the *Status Quo of the Industry, Investment Review* and *Construction Industry Indicators*..

According to the Construction Industry Development Board Act, 2000 (Act 38 of 2000), the CIDB must constitute a construction industry stakeholder forum. The forum's main objective is to inform the CIDB on matters that affect the development of the industry.

Council for the Built Environment (CBE)

The CBE was launched in April 2002. It ensures proper co-ordination between government and the built environment professions, and proper application of policies by the respective councils. The CBE also promotes a range of new priorities and acts as an appeal body for affected professionals and members of the public.

Built environment professions

The decline in the quantity and quality of built environment professionals is of serious concern. The average age of built environment professionals is 50 and is increasing annually. In order to address this, the Department of Public Works is engaging with the public and and private sectors to develop a strategy and implementation plan to deal with this issue, as it is critical to the development of the industry.

Emerging Contractor Development Programme (ECDP)

In 2001/02, the number of contractors registering on the ECDP database continued to rise. The number increased to over 3 257 compared to 2 153 in the previous year. As these are emerging contractors, it is a challenge to access them, validate their credentials and manage their development and growth. The ECDP is exploring a practical development strategy to incubate targeted emerging contractors for a set period, which will ensure a sustainable award of contracts and provision of capacity-building interventions.

Access to finance

Access to finance remains the single major problem facing black contractors, but efforts to promote access to finance are beginning to show positive results. Within the Strategic Empowerment Programme, the Department of Public Works has succeeded in mobilising the support of Standard Bank, Khula and the IDC to provide access to bridging finance for working capital, and performance guarantees to all qualifying contractors awarded contracts within the Strategic Projects Initiative Programme. Contractors requiring financing of R1 million and less are referred to Standard Bank and Khula, while those requiring more than R1 million are catered for by the IDC.

The Department is still exploring mechanisms to broaden this finance facility. Further relief to emerging contractors has been brought about by the waiver of guarantees for projects up to R2 million, and by the intensified campaign to shorten payment cycles.

Women in construction

Since the launch of the Strategic Empowerment Programme for Women in Construction in August 2001, some R188 million worth of construction-related work involving more than 79 projects have been awarded to women-owned enterprises.

Projects in 2003 included work by 400 workers on the R19-million Repair and Maintenance Project at the Leeuwkop Prison, north of Johannesburg. The R16-million repair phase was completed in March 2003.

Strategic asset management

The Department of Public Works is faced with the challenge of managing government's property portfolio in order to maximise returns and reduce costs. The Department employed a Strategic Asset Management Partner, made up of a consortium of six local and international companies, to fulfil the Asset Management function. The Strategic Asset Management Framework will guide the whole of government on the management of State properties.

The Strategic Asset Management Partner is busy with a detailed analysis of the portfolios of the various government departments.

During 2002/03, the Department disposed of 835 properties totalling 63 544 ha, with an estimated market value of R55,2 million.

Of these:
- 803 properties (63 140 ha) were for land-reform purposes

- 19 properties (359 ha) were for low-cost housing and related infrastructure
- 13 properties (45 ha) with a market value of R24,7 million were for commercial purposes.

In addition, two properties valued at R983 000 were acquired in exchange for State land.

The Department's maintenance budget of R557 million was fully utilised.

Since its implementation, the Repair and Maintenance Programme has grown to 654 contracts to the value of R2,8 billion.

Black Economic Empowerment

The Department of Trade and Industry, in partnership with several non-profit industry organisations, namely the Black Information Technology (IT) Forum, the Electronic Industries Federation, the Insurance Institute of South Africa, the IT Association, and the South African Electrotechnical Export Council, has developed a database of BEE companies in the IT, telecommunications and electronics sectors.

Phase 1 of the project was funded by the Department, the South African Electrotechnical Export Council and the Electronics Industry Federation.

The BEE company database is available on the Department's website, *www.thedti.gov.za*, and lists more than 250 small, medium and large BEE companies.

Broad-Based Black Economic Empowerment Strategy

Government launched its Broad-Based BEE Strategy on 24 March 2003.

The BEE Strategy aims to address human resource development, employment equity, enterprise development, preferential procurement and investment, ownership and control of enterprises, and economic assets. The Strategy is the result of an extensive consultation process by government and private-sector role-players which included the BEE Commission, the Department of Trade and Industry, the National Economic Development and Labour Council (NEDLAC) and the President's Black Business and Big Business Working Groups.

The successful implementation of the BEE Strategy will be evaluated against the following policy objectives:
- a substantial increase in the number of black people who have ownership and control of existing and new enterprises
- a significant increase in the number of black-empowered and black-engendered enterprises
- a significant increase in the number of black people in executive and senior management positions of enterprises.

The Minister of Trade and Industry appointed the BEE Task Team in April 2003 to finalise legislation and devise the guidelines outlined in the Broad-Based BEE Strategy. The Task Team will serve until the Advisory Council on BEE is appointed.

Government introduced a Broad-Based BEE Bill in Parliament in August 2003 to establish an enabling framework for the promotion of BEE in South Africa.

In particular, the legislation will allow the Minister to issue guidelines and codes of good practice on BEE, as well as establish a BEE Advisory Council to advise the President on the implementation of BEE and related matters.

Government will utilise various regulatory means to achieve its BEE objectives, including using a balance scorecard to measure progress made in achieving BEE by enterprises and sectors. The use of a common scorecard by different stakeholders provides a basic framework against which to benchmark the BEE process.

The scorecard will measure three core elements of BEE, namely:
- direct empowerment through ownership and control of enterprises and assets
- human resource development and employment equity
- indirect empowerment through preferential procurement and enterprise development.

The scorecard will be issued as a Code of Good Practice. The Code will allow for a measure of flexibility so that it can be adapted to the particular circumstances of specific sectors or enterprises, while at the same time bringing a measure of standardisation to the definition and measurement of BEE.

In particular, government will apply BEE criteria, as set out in the scorecard, whenever it:
- grants a licence to engage in a specific regulated economic activity, e.g. gambling or mining
- grants a concession to a private enterprise to operate an asset or enterprise on behalf of the State
- sells an asset or an SOE
- enters into a public-private partnership
- engages in any economic activity.

A total of R2,2 billion was allocated to fund BEE initiatives in the 2002/03 financial year.

The Isibaya Fund contributed an amount of R321 million and the Umsobomvu Fund, R461 million.

Over the past five years, to December 2002, there was an increase of 39% in empowerment funding from 14% of the total number in 1998 (R56,4 milion). This figure increased to R1,2 billion in the first six months of 2002/03.

Black Business Supplier Programme (BBSP)

The Department of Trade and Industry launched the BBSP in April 2003.

The BBSP is a 20:80 cost-sharing cash grant incentive scheme, which offers support to black-owned enterprises in South Africa. The scheme provides such firms with access to business development services that assist them to improve their core competencies, upgrade managerial capabilities, and restructure to become more competitive.

It is aimed at growing black-owned enterprises by fostering links between black SMMEs and corporate and public-sector enterprises.

Any enterprise that is majority black-owned (50 plus one share), has a significant number of black managers, and has a minimum trading history of one year, qualifies for the Programme.

Enterprises with a maximum annual turnover of R12 million also qualify.

The maximum grant that a single enterprise can qualify for is limited to R100 000.

Employment and skills development

Employment and skills development continue to be high on the Government's agenda.

In June 2003, at the Growth and Development Summit (GDS), government, business, trade unions and community leaders agreed on a range of programmes and initiatives designated to create jobs, reduce unemployment and further boost skills development. It was agreed to promote and expand the leadership programme, an innovative approach to training that combines practical and theoretical learning, and which, together with more traditional apprenticeships, should provide substantial new training opportunities, particularly for young, unemployed people. The GDS also saw a renewed commitment by employers and trade unions to strengthen the 25 Sector Education and Training Authorities (SETAs). These tripartite organisations were established in March 2000 to identify and meet skills needs in each sector of the economy.

The Department of Labour is reviewing the Skills Development Act, 1998 (Act 97 of 1998).

The proposed changes will strengthen the Minister of Labour's powers to regulate and monitor the work of the SETAs and align their reporting with the Public Finance Management Act (PFMA), 1999 (Act 1 of 1999).

The new measures will include the following:
- it will be mandatory for SETAs to enter into an annual service level agreement with the Department of Labour
- regulation of SETA administration: the Minister's current discretionary powers to set the limit on the funds SETAs can utilise for

administrative purposes will be extended to include determining staff salaries and allowances paid to Board members
- equity considerations: it will be obligatory for each SETA to address the question of equity for its governing body and staff composition
- employment and skills development agencies: small firms and non-governmental organisations will be able to take on the administrative functions associated with learnerships
- private employment agencies: the changes will give the Department the power to deregister unscrupulous private employment agencies and compel them to close down.

Other changes include empowering the Minister to effect changes to the scope of a SETA's coverage or the merger of SETAs. The Bill also clarifies the Minister's position regarding the takeover of the administration of a SETA.

The number of registered learnership programmes had more than doubled between 2001/02 and 2002/03 to 478.

This was in line with the targets set in the National Skills Development Strategy (NSDS). The number of learners enrolled for learnerships was almost seven times greater in March 2003 compared with the same period in 2002.

The National Skills Fund (NSF) funded 577 scholarships and about 2 700 undergraduate bursaries in areas of scarce skills.

The implementation of the NSDS, with regular assessments of progress in meeting its objectives and targets, continues.

During 2002, the Department of Labour allocated R1,3 billion for SETAs, to be used over three years for strategic skills-development projects.

According to the Department of Labour, the involvement of small enterprises in learnership programmes remained low. To address this, the Department announced changes in the skills-grants regulations, designed to reduce the demands on smaller companies.

The Department has also embarked on a *Learnership* Campaign.

Workshops have been conducted with stakeholders to develop strategic plans around learnership implementation, funding, marketing and communication, group training for SMMEs, and employment-service functions such as recruitment and the placement of learners.

The Campaign has three phases. Phase one is expected to be completed in March 2004, phase two will be rolled out from 2005 to 2009 and phase three, from 2010 to 2014.

The Department has appointed various task teams to develop plans with regard to:
- an outline of learnership implementation education and training provision and related matters that require urgent attention, obstacles and proposed solutions, etc.
- the marketing and communication of the Campaign
- the funding that will be necessary to sustain the Campaign and the effective utilisation of current resources available to SETAs.

The 25 SETAs are responsible for about R2,5 billion each year collected through the skills-levy system. The SETAs make grants available, principally to employers, who provide skills plans and report on their implementation.

The SETAs are also responsible for the learnership programme and the implementation of strategic sector-skills plans. The SETAs have discretionary funds, drawn from their levy income, that can be used for projects designed to assist in the achievement of sector priorities, including the design and implementation of learnerships.

The Department signs an annual MoU with each SETA.

This MoU sets out commitments to contributing to the achievement of the National Skills Development Strategy targets and reporting requirements. Twenty-four SETAs concluded an MoU with the Department of Labour for the 2002/03 financial year.

There are still issues to be resolved to ensure the accurate and timely reporting of the work of SETAs and the appropriate analysis of this data.

The Department and the SETAs are committed to transparency and full accountability to the various stakeholder groups the NSDS seeks to serve.

National Skills Authority (NSA)

The NSA, made up of employer, worker, community, government, and education- and training-provider representatives, was established in 1999 to advise the Minister of Labour on all aspects of skills development. The Authority completed its first three-year period of office and was reconstituted during 2002.

The NSA has set itself key priorities and an action plan. It has advised the Minister on amendments to legislation and on policy issues concerning the NSF. The NSA routinely monitors the implementation of the NSDS and its members are involved in the planning of the annual National Skills Conference. During 2003, the NSA started consultations on the NSDS, which will be reviewed and launched in its revised form at the National Skills Conference towards the end of 2004.

National Skills Fund

The NSF is administered by the Department of Labour. It is made up of 20% of the total skills levy paid by employers and is used to address significant national skills priorities.

Funds are allocated through a range of funding windows. The NSA provides advice on each window and the criteria to be used to determine the allocation of funds.

The principal funding windows deal with strategic projects, social development initiatives, innovation and research, and a bursary programme to support students to study in areas of scarce skills.

Nineteen strategic projects to the value of R1,3 billion have been approved over a three-and-a-half-year period. In May 2002, the Minister of Labour, Mr Membathisi Mdladlana, launched the strategic projects.

The strategic grants have been made to SETAs to meet specific sector priorities, including the design and development of learnerships, small business development, the promotion of strategic occupations, Adult Basic Education and Training (ABET), and dealing with the labour market effects of HIV and AIDS.

Some 14 innovation and research projects were approved, most of which are concerned with research methodologies in relation to skills development. During 2002, some 577 postgraduate bursaries were awarded and 2 688 undergraduates received financial support from the NSF.

In addition to this, the NSF supports the Department of Trade and Industry's SME Development Programme and Strategic Industrial Programme through the provision of funds to support training.

Key highlights of the strategic projects during 2002 included:
- a total of 1 069 shop stewards received training on HIV/AIDS
- a total of 810 mathematics and accounting teachers benefitted from street finance projects
- some 3 200 and 2 900 learners respectively completed ABET programmes and SMME support training and bridging courses as part of the Learnerships and Skills Programme
- some 219 bursaries were awarded to learners
- 320 assessors completed training.

The Social Development Funding Window (SDFW) of the NSF was used to train unemployed people to become self-employed, employers or employees.

In 2002, a total of R152 million was spent on training 37 491 unemployed people. More than 26 300 of them were placed in income-generating opportunities, representing a 70% placement rate compared with 36% in 2001.

The SDFW allocated R77 million to poverty-alleviation projects which benefitted about 23 670 people, mainly rural women and youth.

An example of these partnerships is the Working for Water project, where the Department handles the skills development aspect. Another example at local level is the partnership with the O.R. Tambo District Municipality in the Eastern Cape, where R8 million was allocated for skills development.

Unemployment Insurance Fund (UIF)

The Unemployment Insurance Amendment Bill was tabled in the National Assembly on 17 September 2003. The proposed amendments are part of the successful turnaround strategy being implemented by the UIF, based on four main pillars. These are legislative reform, IT, human resources and institutional restructuring.

The successful and ongoing implementation of this strategy has already resulted in an increase in the UIF's income from R2,1 billion in 2001 to R3,8 billion in 2002/03.

The Fund also continued to provide benefits to unemployed workers. Despite the fact that 2002/03 saw a decline in unemployment and illness benefits, the UIF experienced an increase in benefits paid to workers on maternity leave and dependants of deceased contributors. By February 2003, the UIF had received more than 608 000 claims and made 470 000 payments with a total benefit value of R2,2 billion.

The Fund has a surplus of R1,4 billion from a previous string of deficits. As part of the turnaround strategy, expenditure was contained in an attempt to return to financial health and create the financial strength needed to bring about lasting change.

Part of the new policy framework is an annual actuarial evaluation. In the 2002/03 evaluation, the actuary concluded that the Fund was in a sound financial state on a cashflow basis. In line with sound financial practice, the Fund implemented a reserve policy in the 2002/03 financial year.

From 2003, employers who employ domestic workers (including gardeners), must register with the UIF if the employee works for more than 24 hours a month.

The first payments to the UIF had to be made by 7 May 2003. Failure to pay by the seventh day of every month can result in an employer having to pay interest on the outstanding amount. A penalty of 10% will also be incurred.

By June 2003, more than 530 000 employers had registered their employees with the UIF, while the number of employer declarations stood at 413 111, with a total of R8,2 million received in contributions. This translates to more than 67% of employers having registered.

By September 2003, more than 560 000 domestic workers were registered.

The Unemployment Insurance Amendment Bill also regularises the status of domestic, seasonal and other workers.

One of the proposed amendments to be made to the Unemployment Insurance Act, 2001 (Act 63 of 2001), includes an amendment to Section 63 that workers with more than one employer will be entitled to unemployment benefits should they lose their jobs.

Occupational health and safety (OHS)

The OHS legislative framework consists of the OHS Act, 1993 (Act 85 of 1993), and its regulations.

Ensuring compliance with legislation is the responsibility of the Department's Inspection and Enforcement Service Business Units. This is accomplished by conducting inspections and investigations and providing information, advice and statutory services.

The Department of Labour embarked on a vigorous OHS campaign, focusing on OHS awareness, capacity-building for inspectors and backlog reduction.

Proactive, reactive and blitz inspections were conducted, with an emphasis on education and law enforcement.

Economy

The number of inspections increased from 51 751 to 87 815 in the 2002/03 financial year.

To contain the problem of the OHS backlog, which had accumulated over many years, the Department developed a backlog reduction strategy, which reduced the backlog at an average of 21% per month. It was expected that the outstanding OHS backlog would be completed before March 2004.

Training
During 2002/03, the Department of Labour developed and implemented a major OHS training initiative for labour inspectors. The training was aimed at enhancing inspectors' knowledge and enforcement of the OHS Act, 1993 and its regulations and general health and safety foundations. During 2002, some 284 inspectors received safety training.

Labour relations

Two main areas of focus in 2002/03 were the amendments to the Labour Relations Act, 1995 (Act 66 of 1995), and the Basic Conditions of Employment Act, 1997 (Act 75 of 1997), as well as the historical introduction of minimum wages and setting of working conditions for domestic and agricultural workers.

The labour-law amendments that were promulgated during 2002 sought to enable the Registrar of Labour Relations to act against bogus unions and employer organisations.

On 28 January 2003, the Minister of Labour announced steps to be taken by the Department of Labour to identify and weed out trade unions and employer organisations that are not genuine. Some 18 trade unions and 11 employer organisations were named.

The names of 158 trade unions and 41 employers' organisations who had failed to meet the requirement of the Labour Relations Act, 1995 to annually submit audited financial statements, were also made public. Legal notices to this effect were published in the *Government Gazette* on 30 January 2003.

This gave an opportunity for interested parties to make representations on possible cancellations.

By mid-2003, there were 362 trade unions and 240 registered employer organisations operating in South Africa. This compared well with the 282 trade unions and 192 employers' organisations that were registered on 11 November 1996 when the Labour Relations Act, 1995 came into effect.

Legislation
The amendments to the Labour Relations Act, 1995 and the Basic Conditions of Employment Act, 1997 came into effect on 1 August 2002. The objective of these amendments is to address policy imperatives of government to create jobs, promote and develop small business, improve the protection of vulnerable workers, and stimulate investment.

Code of Good Practice
The Code of Good Practice on Key Aspects of Disability was finalised and published on 19 August 2002. The Code guides employers on how to treat people with disabilities in the workplace. The Technical Assistance Guidelines of the Code on managing HIV/AIDS in the workplace have also been finalised.

Directorate: Collective Bargaining
The Directorate's role is to:
- administer the Labour Relations Act, 1995
- register trade unions, employer organisations, and bargaining and statutory councils
- publish bargaining council agreements and the extension of agreements to non-parties

---

The Department of Labour has launched an education campaign called *Sizakala* (get help), which is aimed at informing workers on the procedures they need to follow when claiming from the Compensation Fund in the event of getting injured at work.

The campaign also informs workers about occupational health and safety issues in the workplace.

- promote and monitor collective bargaining
- achieve appropriate balance between security and flexibility.

Commission for Conciliation, Mediation and Arbitration (CCMA)

During 2002, the governing body of the CCMA approved amendments to fee tariffs and new rules for the conduct of proceedings before the CCMA, which were published as part of the Labour Relations Act, 1995.

Since the implementation of the amendments in August 2002, the following cases have been recorded:
- five pre-dismissal arbitrations in terms of Section 188A
- 10 applications for facilitation by the CCMA in large-scale retrenchments in terms of Section 189A
- referrals where the provisions of Section 191 were utilised.

Some 605 applications were also made to certify enforcement of awards as an order of the Labour Court in accordance with Section 143.

Conflict was reduced through attempting to resolve protest actions referred to NEDLAC in terms of Section 77 of the Act.

Directorate: Employment Equity

The Directorate monitors enforcement and provides support and advice on the implementation and enforcement of the Employment Equity Act, 1998 (Act 55 of 1998).

According to a survey conducted by the Department of Labour from 2001 to 2002, the number of industrial actions (strikes) in South Africa had declined by 43%.

The number of workdays lost through strikes decreased from 953 610 in 2001 to 615 723 in 2002.

Other findings of the survey included a decline in the number of workers taking part in industrial actions between 2001 (90 392) and 2002 (66 250), and that 68,1% of the reported industrial actions were resolved through negotiations between employers and employees.

The Directorate's staff, partnered with labour inspectors in the provincial offices of the Department, conduct workplace inspections on employment equity. Private-sector employers as well as organs of State throughout the country were targeted for inspection.

This exercise enabled inspectors to focus on employment-equity inspections, and the Directorate to assess the training and skills needs of inspectors.

The Directorate facilitated employment-equity enforcement training for 355 labour inspectors and trainers in all provincial offices.

Government's priority is to promote diversity in the workplace to ensure that the workforce of business, Government and non-governmental organisations (NGOs) is representative of the broader demographics of society. This is being achieved through the implementation of the Employment Equity Act, 1998.

A key aspect of this legislation is the collection of data on progress being made by designated employers. The deadline for the submission of employment-equity reports by employers who employ more than 150 workers was 1 October 2003.

Figures produced by the Commission of Employment Equity earlier in 2003 reflected progress of 1% in relation to new black entrants into top management positions.

Employment Conditions Commission (ECC)

The ECC meets monthly to discuss matters relating to employment conditions.

Challenges for 2003/04 included:
- Implementing sectoral determinations for workers in the minibus taxi, welfare and hospitality sectors.
- Completing and implementing the National Programme of Action on the Eradication of Child Labour in South Africa.
- Continuing to work with the Child Labour Intersectoral Group, which is made up of other government departments, trade

Economy

unions, NGOs and employer representatives. This includes raising awareness, monitoring and enforcing child labour cases.
- Raising awareness on the promulgation of new sectoral determinations through launches and other campaigns, and maintaining visibility in the domestic worker and agricultural sectors.
- Ensuring the effective implementation of a permit system for children working in the performing arts.

Employment Equity Registry

The Directorate: Employment Equity captures and maintains employment equity reports submitted by designated employers. This makes it possible to measure the extent of employment equity in the workplace. This includes designated employers with 50 or more workers.

A Public Register is maintained in terms of Section 41 of the Employment Equity Act, 1998.

The list is regularly updated and periodically published in the *Government Gazette*.

International co-operation

During 2002, the US Agency for International Development provided donor funding for work on the following projects:

A Labour Force Survey released by Statistics South Africa in March 2003 revealed that in September 2002, there were an estimated 28,0 million people aged between 15 and 65 years in the country.

The official unemployment rate at the time was estimated to be 30,5%.

Among these people some 15,9 million were economically active, 11,0 million of whom were employed, and 4,8 million unemployed. In addition, 12,1 million were not economically active, of whom:
- 4,9 million were full-time scholars
- 1,1 million were full-time homemakers
- 1,2 million were disabled or chronically ill, hence unable to work
- 0,9 million were either too young or too old to work
- 0,2 million were retired.

- research to determine employment equity best practices
- development of a Code of Good Practice on the Employment of People with Disabilities
- development of technical assistance guidelines for the Code of Good Practice on the Employment of People with Disabilities.

Donor funding from the International Labour Organisation (ILO) was used to prepare technical assistance guidelines for the Code of Good Practice Key Aspects of HIV/AIDS and Employ-ment. The US Department of Labour made funding available for research to determine the extent of compliance with the Employment Equity Act, 1998 in the private sector.

Directorate: Employment Standards

The Directorate's role is to implement the Basic Conditions of Employment Act, 1997. It also assists the ECC with fulfilling its statutory functions. This includes conducting investigations into working conditions and advising the Minister on the establishment of sectoral determinations.

Sectoral determinations

The most important sectoral determinations recently established include the following:
- **Agricultural sector**

  The sectoral determination for the agricultural sector was published on 2 December 2002, setting minimum wages and conditions of employment for the sector.

  Since 1 March 2003, every farmer in South Africa is legally obliged to pay a minimum wage to their employees.
- **Domestic workers**

  The sectoral determination for the domestic worker sector was published on 15 August 2002, setting mimimum wages and conditions of employment.

  The Minister of Labour announced in August 2003 that the minimum wage for domestic workers would increase by at least

8% on 1 November 2003, pending the year-on-year Consumer Price Inflation (CPI) rate.

In predominantly urban areas, the wage was initially set at R4,51 per hour for domestic workers working an ordinary 27 hours or less per week – from November 2003 it will be at least R4,87 per hour – and a minimum of R4,10 for those working more than 27 hours will be adjusted to at least R4,42. In the rural areas, workers working 27 hours or less per week will receive an increase to a minimum salary of R3,95 per hour, while the remainder will increase to R3,59.

Domestic and farm workers have been included in the Unemployment Insurance Contributions Act, 2002 (Act 4 of 2002), which came into effect on 1 April 2002.

- **Wholesale and retail sector**

Minimum wages and basic employment conditions were determined for workers in the wholesale and retail sector in December 2002.

The determinations, which came into effect on 1 February 2003, replaced the old wage determination for the commercial distributive trade in certain areas. It furthermore incorporates, for the first time, workers from the former homelands of South Africa.

In the former Transkei, Bophuthatswana, Venda and Ciskei, concessions have been made to allow for the phasing in of the minimum wage. Initially, employers in these regions will pay 30% less than other areas, with annualised increases aimed at reaching the same levels as the wages for other areas by 1 February 2005.

The wage levels are set at hourly, weekly or monthly levels. Wages are set for a three-year period, with a 8,8% increase per annum in the second and third years.

The determinations allow for commission-based payment of salespersons and allow employees a 40-hour week, on condition that they work at least three Sundays a month, taking other days of the week off to rest.

- **Private security sector**

The Sectoral Determination for the private security sector, which sets out basic employment standards and minimum wages for security guards, was published in the *Government Gazette* on 13 July 2003.

The sectoral agreement, which came into effect on 16 June 2003 and is in line with international best practice, is set for a period of three years.

The determination sets minimum wages at levels ranging from R911 in rural areas to R2 533 in urban areas. The wages represent an overall increase for entry levels in excess of 7% every year for three years.

In a shift from earlier security wage determinations, wages are no longer set on an hourly basis, but on a monthly basis. This not only fixes the wages of security officers, but can also be regarded as an upgrading of the profession.

Other conditions of employment include the stipulation of night shift allowances and improvements to maternity benefits over the next three years.

Eradication of child labour

During 2002, the Department of Labour:
- developed training material on child labour and conducted training sessions in all the provinces
- made a presentation on child labour to the Parliamentary Portfolio Committee
- received the MoU on the ILO's International Programme on the Elimination of Child Labour and forwarded it to the ILO for scrutiny and approval
- published reports on the Survey of Activities of Young People
- implemented an enforcement policy for child labour contraventions arising out of the results of the survey and which is in line with the Basic Conditions of Employment Act, 1997
- commenced provincial and sectoral workshops on the development of a National

Programme of Action to eradicate child labour.

The Basic Conditions of Employment Act, 1997 prohibits the employment of children under 15 years or those who are minimum school-leaving age. The Act protects children between 15 and 18, establishing whether the employment is appropriate for the age of the child; whether the workplace risks the child's well-being, education, physical or mental health; or spiritual, moral or social development; and whether it has been prohibited through regulations.

However, special provision can be made to accommodate the employment of children in the performance of advertising, sport, artistic or cultural activities.

Acknowledgements

Business Partners Ltd
Department of Labour
Department of Public Works
Department of Trade and Industry
Estimates of National Expenditure 2003, published by the National Treasury
Office for Public Enterprises
South African Reserve Bank
SouthAfrica.info
www.gov.za

Suggested reading

Abedian, I. and Standish, B. eds. *Economic Growth in South Africa: Selected Policy Issues.* Cape Town: Oxford University Press, 1992.
Abratt, R. *Contemporary Cases in South African Marketing.* Cape Town: New Africa Books, 2002.
Ackerman, R. *Hearing Grasshoppers Jump: The Story of Raymond Ackerman as told to Denise Pritchard.* Cape Town: David Philip, 2001.
Adam, H., Van Zyl Slabbert, F. and Moodley, K. *Comrades in Business: Post-Liberation Politics in South Africa.* Cape Town: Tafelberg, 1997.
African National Congress. *The Reconstruction and Development Programme.* Johannesburg: Umanyano Publications, 1994.
Alemayehu, M. *Industrialising Africa: Development Options and Challenges for the 21st Century.* Trenton, N.J.: Africa World Press, 2000.
Barker, F. *South African Labour Market.* Pretoria: Van Schaik, 2003.
Barnard, N. and Du Toit, J. *Understanding the South African Macro-Economy.* Pretoria: Van Schaik, 1992.
Baskin, J. ed. *Against the Current: Labour and Economic Policy in South Africa.* Johannesburg: Ravan Press, 1996.
Bendix, S. *Industrial Relations in South Africa.* 3rd edition. Cape Town: Juta, 1996.
Bendix, S. *Basics of Labour Relations.* Cape Town: Juta, 2000.
Best Companies to Work for in South Africa. Cape Town: Zebra Press, 2000.
Bhorat, H, et al. *Fighting Poverty: Labour Markets and Inequality in South Africa.* Lansdowne: University of Cape Town Press, 2001.
Black, Calitz, Steenkamp and Associates. *Public Economics for South African Students.* Cape Town: Oxford University Press South Africa, 2003.
Bond, P. *Commanding Heights and Community Control: New Economics for a New South Africa.* Johannesburg: Ravan Press, 1991.
Bond, P. *South Africa Meets the World Bank, International Monetary Fund and International Finance.* Cape Town: University of Cape Town Press, 2001.
Botha, H. and Botha, J. *Guide to The New Basic Conditions of Employment Act.* Lynnwood Ridge: Practition IR Publication, 1998.
Bothma, C. H. *E-Commerce for South African Managers.* Cape Town: New Africa Books, 2001.
Cameron, B. *Financial Freedom for Women.* Cape Town: Zebra Books, 2002.
Cheadle, H. and others. *Current Labour Law 1998: An Annual Review of Key Areas of Labour Law.* Cape Town: Juta, 1998.

Clark, I. and others. *More Small Business Opportunities in South Africa.* 2nd ed. Cape Town: Zebra, 1996.
Consultative Business Movement. *Building a Winning Nation: Companies and the Reconstruction and Development Programme.* Randburg: Ravan Press, 1994.
Coetzee J. K. and others, eds. *Development: Theory, Policy and Practice.* Cape Town: Oxford University Press, Southern Africa, 2001.
Compiler: Erasmus, J. *Coping Structures of the Unemployed.* Pretoria: Human Sciences Research Council (HSRC), 1999.
Corporate Social Investment and Development Handbook. Rivonia: BML, 1998. Annual.
Creating Action Space: The Challenge of Poverty and Democracy in South Africa. Cape Town: Institute for Democratic South Africa (IDASA) and David Philip, 1998.
Doing Business in South Africa. 5th ed. Editor: J. Reuvid. London: Kegan Paul, 2001.
Du Toit, J. and Falkema, H.B. *The Structure of the South African Economy.* Johannesburg: Southern Book Publishers for ABSA Bank, 1994.
Employee Participation and Workplace Forums. Editor: M. Anstey. Kenwyn: Juta, 1997.
Fine, B. and Rustomjee, Z. *The Political Economy of South Africa: From Minerals-Energy Complex to Industrialisation.* Johannesburg: Witwatersrand University Press, 1996.
Ginsberg, A. *South Africa's Future: From Crises to Prosperity.* Basingstoke, Hampshire: Macmillan, 1998.
Grossett, M. and Venter, R. *Labour Relations in South Africa: A Comprehensive Guide for Managers and Practitioners.* Johannesburg: International Thomson Publications, 1998.
Hetherington, I. *Heroes of the Struggle.* Kempton Park: National Industrial Chamber, 1998.
Hickey, A. and van Zyl, A. *2002 South African Budget Guide and Dictionary.* Cape Town: IDASA, 2002.
Howe, G. and Le Roux, P. eds. *Transforming the Economy: Policy Options for South Africa.* Pietermaritzburg: University of Natal Indicator Project South Africa, 1992.
Huber, M. and Sack, P. *Employing a Domestic Worker.* Welgemoed (Cape): Metz Press, 1997.
Hugo, P. ed. *Redistribution and Affirmative Action: Working on the South African Political Economy.* Halfway House: Southern Book Publishers, 1992.
Huysamen, D. *Rehumanised Productivity Improvement.* Randburg: Knowledge Resources, 1999.
IBC's Guide to Doing Business in South Africa, 1997. Highlands North, Johannesburg: International Business Centres, 1997. Annual.
Investment in South Africa. Johannesburg: KPMG, 1997.
Isaacs, S. *South Africa in the Global Economy: Understanding the Challenges: Working Towards Alternatives.* Durban: University of Durban, Trade Union Research Project, 1997.
Jeffrey, A. *Business and Affirmative Action.* Johannesburg: South African Institute of Race Relations, 1996.
Khosa, M. ed. *Empowerment through Economic Transaction.* Pretoria: HSRC, 2001.
Kiloh, M. and Sibeko, A. *A Fighting Union: An Oral History of the SA Railway and Harbour Workers' Union 1936–1998.* Johannesburg: Ravan Press, 2000.
Kok, P. and Pietersen, J. *Manufacturing and Materials.* Pretoria: HSRC, 2000.
Kuzwayo, M. *Marketing through Mud and Dust.* Cape Town: David Philip, 2000.
Lighthelm, A. A. *The Southern African Development Community (SADC): A Socio-Economic Profile.* Pretoria: Bureau of Market Research, University of South Africa, 1997. (Research report no 4)
Lipton, M. *Capitalism and Apartheid: South Africa, 1910 – 1986.* Cape Town: David Philip, 1986.
Lowry, D. *Twenty Years in the Labour Movement: The Urban Training Project and Change in South Africa, 1971 – 1991.* Johannesburg: Wadmore, 1999.
Macleod, G. *Cultural Considerations: A Guide to Understanding Culture, Courtesy and Etiquette in South African Business.* Cape Town: Spearhead, 2002.
Maganya, E. and Houghton, R. eds. *Transformation in South Africa? Policy Debates in the 1990s.* Braamfontein, Johannesburg: Institute for African Alternatives, 1996.
Mahdi, P. M. *Black Economic Empowerment in the New South Africa. The Rights and the Wrongs.* Randburg: Knowledge Resources, 1997.
Making Affirmative Action Work: A South African Guide. Rondebosch: IDASA, 1995.
Marais, H. *South Africa's Limits to Change: The Political Economy of Transformation.* 2nd reprint. Rondebosch: University of Cape Town Press, 1999.
Marais, H. *South Africa: Limits to Change: The Political Economy of Transition.* 2nd ed. Cape Town: University of Cape Town, 2001.
May, J. ed. *Poverty and Inequality in South Africa: Meeting the Challenge.* Cape Town: David Philip, 2000.

Economy

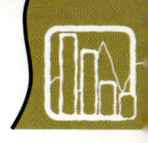

Mbigi, L. *In Search of the African Business Renaissance: An African Cultural Perspective.* Randburg: Knowledge Resources, 2000.
McGregor's Who Owns Whom in South Africa: Millennium Edition. Grant Park, Johannesburg: Purdey Publishing, 1999.
Mengisteab, K. and Logan, I. eds. *Beyond Economic Liberalisation in Africa: Structural Adjustment and The Alternatives.* London: Zed Books, 1995.
Micro-Finance in Rural Communities in Southern Africa. Pretoria: HSRC, 2002.
Mills, G. *Poverty to Prosperity: Globalisation, Good Government and African Recovery.* Johannesburg: South African Institute of International Affairs and Cape Town: Tafelberg, 2002.
Mostert, J W et al. *Micro-Economics.* Cape Town: Juta, 2002.
Naidoo, R. *Corporate Governance: Essential Guide for SA Companies.* Cape Town: Double Storey, 2003.
Nattrass, N. *Profits and Wages: The South African Economic Challenge.* Johannesburg: Penguin, 1992.
Nattrass, N. and Ardington, E. eds. *Political Economy of South Africa.* Cape Town: Oxford University Press, 1990.
Nattrass, N, Wakeford, J. and Muradzikwa, S. *Macro-Economics: Theory and Policy in South Africa.* Cape Town: David Phillip, 2000.
Nel, P. S. and others. *Successful Labour Relations: Guidelines for Practice.* Pretoria: Van Schaik, 1998.
Nicholson, J. *Measuring Change: South Africa's Economy since 1994.* Durban: Trade Union Research Project, University of Natal, 2001.
Nicholson, J. and others, eds. *User's Guide to the South African Economy.* Durban: Y Press, 1994.
Parsons, R. *The Mbeki Inheritance: South Africa's Economy, 1990 – 2004.* Randburg: Ravan Press, 1999.
Preston-Whyte, E. and Rogerson, C. eds. *South Africa's Informal Economy.* Cape Town: Oxford University Press, 1994.
Qunta, C. *Who's Afraid of Affirmative Action: A Survival Guide for Black Professionals.* Cape Town: Kwela Books, 1995.
Ramphele, M. *The Affirmative Action Book: Towards an Equity Environment.* Rondebosch: IDASA, 1995.
Roussouw, D. *Business Ethics in Africa.* Cape Town: Oxford University Press, 2002.
Roux, A. *Everyone's Guide to the South African Economy.* 4th ed. Wynberg, Sandton: Zebra Books, 1996.
Rumney, R. and Wilhelm, J. eds. *Movers and Shakers: An A – Z of South African Business People.* Sandton: Penguin Books, 1999.
Schlemmer, L. and Levitz, C. *Unemployment in South Africa: The Facts, The Prospects and an Exploration of Solutions.* Johannesburg: South African Institute of Race Relations, 1998.
Schutz, H, ed. *Organisational Behaviour – A Contemporary South African Perspective.* Pretoria: Van Schaik, 2003.
Schrire, R. ed. *Wealth or Poverty: Critical Choices for South Africa.* Cape Town: Oxford University Press, 1992.
Sen, A. *Development as Freedom.* Oxford: University Press, 1999.
Simpson, J. and Dore, B. *Marketing in South Africa.* Pretoria: Van Schaik, 2002.
Shaw, M. *Finding the Rainbow: Organisational Culture: The Key to Corporate Performance.* Johannesburg: Ravan Press, 1997.
Smollan, R. *Black Advancement in the South African Economy.* Johannesburg: Macmillan Boleswa, 1993.
Sono, T. *From Poverty to Poverty. Themba Sono's Five Steps to Real Transformation.* Sandton: FMF Books, 1999.
South African Industrial Relations: Theory and Practice. Editor: P.S. Nel. 3rd ed. Pretoria: Van Schaik, 1997.
South Africa's Most Promising Companies. Cape Town: Zebra Press, 2000.
Tustin, C. and Geldenhuys, D. *Labour Relations: the Psychology of Conflict and Negotiation.* 2nd ed. Cape Town: Oxford University Press Southern Africa, 2000.
Van Zyl, C. et al. *Understanding South African Financial Markets.* Pretoria: Van Schaik, 2003.
Von Holdt, K. *Transition from Below: Forging Trade Union and Workplace Change in South Africa.* Pietermaritzburg: University of Natal Press, 2003.
Vosloo, W. B. ed. *Entrepreneurship and Economic Growth.* Pretoria: HSRC, 1994.

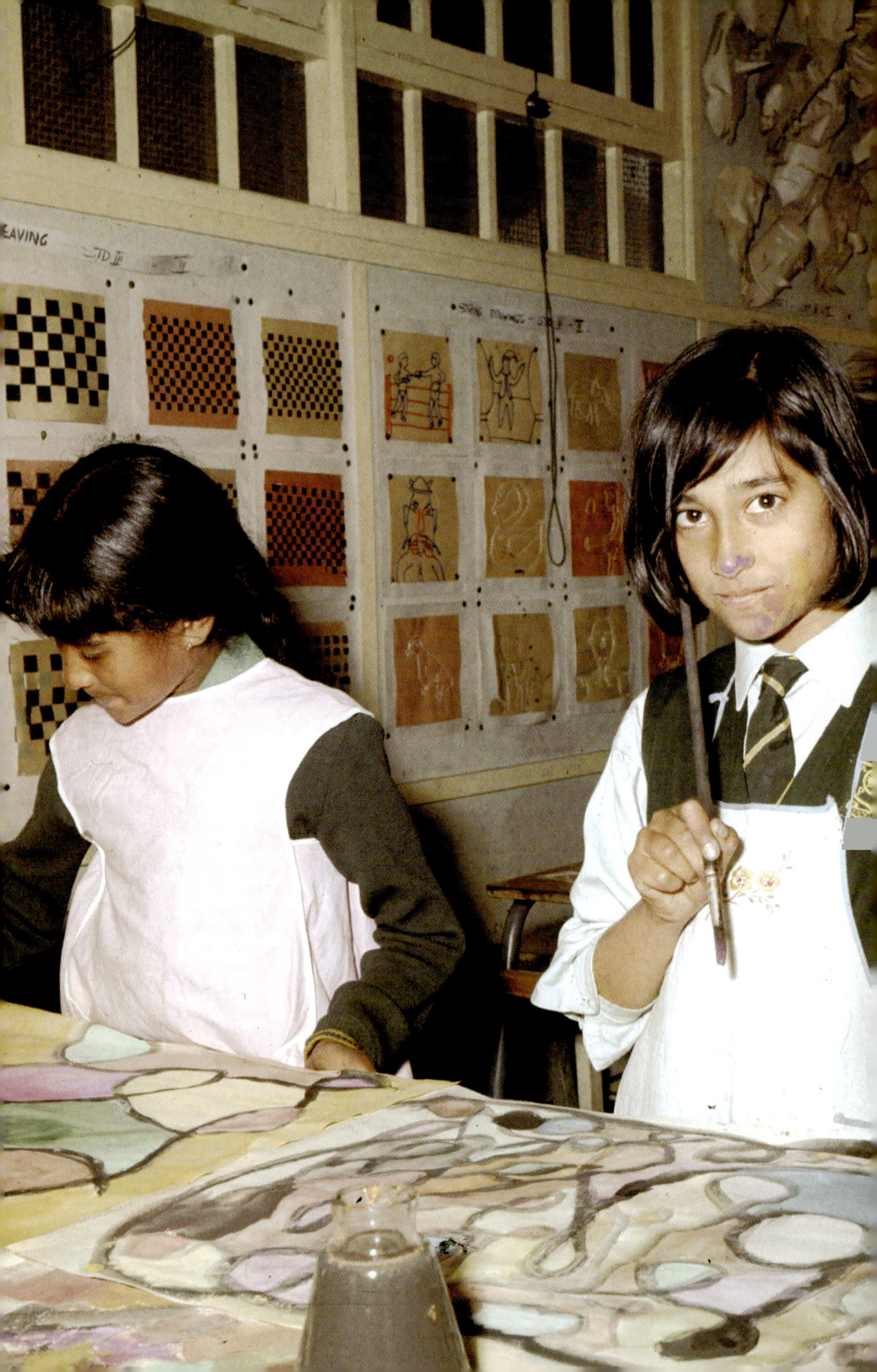

chapter 8
Education

Education is not only pivotal to economic prosperity, but also plays a crucial role in enabling South Africans to improve the quality of their lives and contribute to a peaceful, productive and democratic nation.

According to the Bill of Rights contained in the Constitution of the Republic of South Africa, 1996 (Act 108 of 1996), everyone has the right to a basic education, including adult basic education and further education, which the State, through reasonable measures, must make progressively available and accessible.

Education is one of the most important long-term investments a country can make. There has been a significant increase in the education budget-allocation under the post-apartheid democratic Government, from R31,8 billion in 1994 to R69 063 billion in 2003. At almost 6% of Gross Domestic Product, South Africa has one of the highest rates of government investment in education in the world.

Formal education in South Africa is categorised according to three levels. The General Education and Training (GET) band consists of the Reception Year (Grade R) and learners up to Grade 9, as well as an equivalent Adult Basic Education and Training (ABET) qualification. The Further Education and Training (FET) band consists of all education and training from the National Qualifications Framework (NQF) Levels 2 to 4 (equivalent to Grades 10 – 12 in schools) and the National Technical Certificate 1 to 3 in FET colleges. The Higher Education (HE) band consists of a range of degrees, diplomas and certificates up to and including postdoctoral degrees. These levels are integrated within the NQF provided by the South African Qualifications Authority (SAQA) Act, 1995 (Act 58 of 1995).

By mid-2003, the South African public education system accommodated more than 11,7 million school learners, 448 868 university students, 216 499 technikon students, and over 356 000 FET college students. There were 27 458 primary, secondary, combined and intermediate schools with 354 201 educators.

Universities, technikons and technical colleges are undergoing rationalisation, which will reduce the overall number of institutions through mergers.

Education structures

South Africa has a single national education system, which is organised and managed by the national Department of Education and the nine provincial Departments.

Ministry of Education
The National Education Policy Act, 1996 (Act 27 of 1996), gives the Minister of Education the power to determine national norms and

◀ By mid-2003, the South African public education system accommodated more than 11,7 million school learners.

standards for education-planning, provision, governance, monitoring and evaluation. The principle of democratic decision-making must be exercised within the context of overall policy goals. In determining policy, the Minister must take into account the competence of provincial legislatures and the relevant provisions of any provincial law relating to education.

National and provincial Departments of Education

The Constitution has vested substantial power in the provincial legislatures and governments to run educational affairs (other than universities and universities of technology – until recently, technikons), subject to a national policy framework. The national Department of Education is responsible for formulating policy, setting norms and standards, and monitoring and evaluating all levels of education. It also funds HE institutions through subsidies and by providing financial support to students through the National Student Financial Aid Scheme (NSFAS).

Provincial Departments of Education are responsible for all aspects of school education, as well as ABET, Early Childhood Development (ECD) and FET at colleges. The South African Schools Act, 1996 (Act 84 of 1996), further devolves responsibility to school level by delegating the governance of public schools to democratically elected school governing bodies consisting of parents, educators, non-educator staff, and (in secondary schools) learners.

Relations with provincial Departments of Education are guided by national policy, within which the provincial Departments have to set their own priorities and implementation programmes. The National Education Policy Act, 1996 formalised relations between national and provincial authorities, and established the Council of Education Ministers (CEM) and the Heads of Education Departments Committee (HEDCOM) as intergovernmental forums to collaborate in developing the education system.

The role of the national Department is to translate the education and training policies of government and the provisions of the Constitution into a national education policy and legislative framework.

It is the responsibility of the Department to ensure that:
- all levels of the system adhere to these policies and laws
- mechanisms are in place to monitor and enhance quality in the system
- the system is on par with international developments.

The core activities of the Department are to:
- provide research and policy review
- provide planning and policy development
- provide support to the provinces and HE institutions in their implementation of national policy, norms and standards
- monitor the implementation of policy, norms and standards to assess their impact on the quality of the educational process, and identify policy gaps.

Statutory bodies

Council of Education Ministers

The CEM, consisting of the Minister of Education, the Deputy Minister of Education, and the nine provincial executive council members (MECs) for Education, meets regularly to discuss the promotion of national education policy, share information and views on all aspects of education in South Africa, and co-ordinate action on matters of mutual interest.

Heads of Education Departments Committee

The HEDCOM consists of the Director-General of the Department of Education, the Deputy Directors-General of the Department, and the heads of provincial Education Departments. The functions of the Committee include facilitating the development of a national education system, sharing information and views on national education, co-ordinating administrative action on matters of mutual interest, and advising the Department on a range of specified matters related to the proper functioning of the national education system.

Council for Quality Assurance in General and Further Education and Training (Umalusi)

On 11 April 2003, the Minister of Education, Prof. Kader Asmal, officially launched Umalusi, a statutory council that reports to the Ministry of Education. It replaced the South African Certification Council in June 2002.

The Council ensures that education- and training-providers have the capacity to deliver and also assesses qualifications and learning programmes to ensure that they conform to set standards.

The Council has a five-point programme:
- quality assurance of providers
- quality assurance of qualifications and learning programmes
- quality assurance of assessments
- issuing of certificates
- monitoring and reporting on quality in education and training.

South African Qualifications Authority

The SAQA, which is a statutory body established in 1995, is answerable to the Ministers of Labour and of Education.

The SAQA, via the NQF, ensures that South African qualifications are of the highest quality, and internationally comparable. The functions of the Authority are to oversee the:
- development of the NQF by formulating and publishing policies and criteria for the registration of bodies responsible for establishing education and training standards or qualifications, and for the accreditation of bodies responsible for monitoring and auditing achievements in terms of such standards and qualifications
- implementation of the NQF by ensuring the registration, accreditation and assignment of functions to the referred bodies, as well as the registration of national standards and qualifications on the NQF.

The NQF is a set of principles and guidelines in which records of learner achievement are registered, to enable national recognition of acquired skills and knowledge, thereby ensuring an integrated system that encourages lifelong learning. The NQF also attempts to move the measurement of achievement in education and training away from input towards outcomes.

The SAQA's Centre for the Evaluation of Educational Qualifications determines the equivalence between foreign and South African qualifications in the South African context.

The integration of a seamless system, encompassing ECD, GET, ABET, FET and HE is achieved through the development of the NQF.

Thirty-one Education and Training Quality Assurance Bodies have been accredited, including the Council on Higher Education (CHE) and 25 Sector Education and Training Authorities (SETAs). There are 6 945 qualifications registered with the NQF.

Council on Higher Education

The CHE was established by the Higher Education (HE) Act, 1997 (Act 101 of 1997), and is responsible for advising the Minister on all aspects of HE, in particular funding arrangements, language policy, and the appropriate shape and size of the system.

It is also responsible for designing and implementing a system for quality assurance in HE. It promotes student access to HE, publishes an annual report on the state thereof, and convenes an annual summit for stakeholders. The Council also holds executive responsibility for quality assurance through its permanent subcommittee, the Higher Education Quality Committee (HEQC).

The HEQC was awarded Education and Training Quality Assurer status by SAQA in 2001.

South African Council for Educators (SACE)

The SACE functions under the auspices of the SACE Act, 2000 (Act 31 of 2000), and is responsible for the registration, promotion and professional development of educators, and setting, maintaining and protecting their ethical and professional standards. It aims to enhance the status of the teaching profession. Almost 30 000 educators registered with the SACE in 2002, bringing the total number of registered educators to 430 000. The Council relies on initial registration fees and monthly levies from educators as its main source of revenue.

The Ministry of Education, together with the SACE and the Education Labour Relations Council (ELRC) embarked on the *Proud to be a Teacher* Campaign during 2003. The Campaign is aimed at uplifting the status of teachers and mobilising young South Africans to join the teaching profession.

The Code of Conduct of the SACE took effect on 1 January 2000. The Code determines the ethical rules of the profession which educators must adhere to.

The SACE is dedicated to ensuring adherence to the Code, which includes dealing with complaints. Serious offenders can lose the right to teach.

The Ethics Division of the SACE received 241 complaints during 2002. Some 36 investigations and 30 hearings were held, resulting in 16 educators being struck off the roll.

In May 2003, South Africa's home-grown television programme, *Takalani Sesame Street*, won the International Grand Prix Award for Best Children's Programme, at the World Media Festival in Hamburg, Germany. The programme, designed to help children prepare for school, is a joint project of the Department of Education and SABC Education.

The SACE partners the Department of Education and the ELRC in facilitating the upgrading of teacher qualifications. By mid-2003, approximately 10 000 educators benefited from programmes leading up to the National Professional Diploma in Education.

National Board for Further Education and Training (NBFET)

The NBFET was launched in June 1999 in terms of the National Education Policy Act, 1996. It provides the Minister with independent and strategic advice on matters relating to the transformation of FET. The Board may, on its own initiative, advise the Minister on any aspect of FET as well as:
- national FET policy, goals and priorities
- norms and standards, including funding
- norms and the terms, purposes and conditions of earmarked grants
- reports on FET from provincial advisory bodies.

Education Labour Relations Council

The ELRC is a bargaining council for the education sector. The Council consists of equal representation of the employer (the national and provincial Departments of Education) and the employees (trade unions representing educators and other employees in the sector). The ELRC aims to create effective and constructive labour relations in the education sector, and to ensure the promotion and transformation of education at all levels within society.

National Student Financial Aid Scheme

The NSFAS is responsible for:
- allocating loans and bursaries to eligible students in public HE
- developing criteria and conditions for the granting of loans and bursaries to eligible students in consultation with the Minister
- raising funds, recovering loans, maintaining

and analysing a database, and undertaking research for the better utilisation of financial resources
- advising the Minister on related matters.

In 2003/04, the Department utilised R850 million in loans and bursaries to support students from the poorest communities in receiving tertiary education. Of the R850 million, R210 million came from repaid loans, an amount which is expected to grow annually.

Financing education

In the 2003/04 financial year, R69 063 billion was allocated to education. This amount included R8 380 billion for universities and technikons, and R53 102 billion for college and school education.

Financial planning in the Department occurs within the Government's Medium Term Expenditure Framework, which, through its three-year budgeting horizon, facilitates sustainable and properly planned financing. An average amount of R243 million has been allocated per year over the medium term (2002/03 – 2005/06) for financial management and quality enhancement in school education.

Conditional grants to provinces

A Conditional Grant for improved financial management and education quality in provincial education systems was established in 1999.

Provincial Education Departments formulated projects to be funded through this Conditional Grant, based on the framework of priorities established by the Minister of Education after consultation with provincial MECs. The priority areas for this Grant include:
- whole-school evaluation, school record-keeping, quarterly reports on school attendance and school supervision
- regular assessment of learner performance
- school safety
- improvement in the quality of Senior Certificate Examinations
- professional development of principals, with an emphasis on the induction of new appointees
- developing functional and effective school-governing bodies
- orientation and ongoing professional development of educators for Curriculum 2005
- provincial strategic planning and the availability of credible and reliable data for planning and budgeting
- working systems and processes, including financial systems, procurement procedures and personnel practices.

Equity in education expenditure

Equity between and within provinces is achieved through three mechanisms, namely the equitable division of national revenue between provinces, making use of the Equitable Shares Formula (ESF), the National Norms and Standards for School Funding, and the National Post Provisioning Norms.

The Government's ESF promotes financial equity between provinces, through the distribution of national revenue to provinces on the basis of relative need and backlogs. In the area of education, the size of the school-age population and the number of learners enrolled in public ordinary schools are taken into account, as well as capital-investment needs.

In March 2003, the South African National Defence Force donated part of its Klippan Military Base, outside Mafikeng in North West, to the provincial Department of Education.

The R30-million facility, excluding the radar section of the Base, is to be transformed into an educational facility for pupils from farm schools.

It will be used to integrate 25 farm schools around Mafikeng, Zeerust and parts of Lichtenburg, and will house 600 lodgers and 230 day pupils, aged between seven and 15 years (Grades 1 to 9).

The province has some 390 farm schools in total.

The North West Education Department has budgeted R9,7 million over the next three years to renovate and upgrade facilities at the Base.

The National Norms and Standards for School Funding, which became national policy in 1999, are aimed at achieving equality and poverty redress at schools in terms of non-personnel expenditure within a province. The Norms are clearly progressive, with 60% of a province's non-personnel expenditure going to the poorest 40% of learners in public schools. The poorest 20% of learners receive 35% of non-personnel resources, while the richest 20% receive 5%.

Considering that about 90% of provincial education expenditure goes towards personnel costs, the distribution of personnel, in particular educators, is a key driver of equity within provinces. Equity in this regard is promoted by the National Post Provisioning Norms. These Norms have contributed to the narrowing of inequalities with regard to educator:learner ratios and the availability of more educator posts in historically disadvantaged areas.

Education policy

Legislative framework
Education policy is informed by the following legislation:
- The National Education Policy Act, 1996 is designed to identify the policy, legislative and monitoring responsibilities of the Minister of Education, and to formalise relations between national and provincial authorities. It established CEM and HEDCOM as intergovernmental forums to collaborate in developing the education system, and provides for the determination of national policies in general and further education and training, including curriculum assessment, language policy and quality assurance. The Act embodies the principle of co-operative governance.
- The South African Schools Act, 1996 promotes access, quality and democratic governance in the schooling system. It ensures that all learners have access to quality education without discrimination, and makes schooling compulsory for children aged seven to 15, or learners reaching the ninth grade, whichever occurs first. It also provides for two types of schools – independent schools and public schools. The Act's provision for democratic school governance through school-governing bodies is in place in public schools countrywide. The school-funding norms outlined in the Act prioritise redress and target poverty in funding allocations to the public schooling system.
- The FET Act, 1998 and the *Education White Paper 4 on FET (1998)* provide the basis for developing a nationally co-ordinated system, comprising the senior-secondary component of schooling and technical colleges. It requires that FET institutions, created in terms of the new legislation, develop institutional plans, and provides for programme-based funding and a national curriculum for learning and teaching.
- The HE Act, 1997 makes provision for a unified and nationally planned system of HE, and creates the statutory CHE which advises the Minister and is responsible for quality assurance and promotion. The HE Act, 1997, *Education White Paper 3 on HE (1997)*, and the National Plan for HE form the basis for the transformation of the HE sector.
- The Employment of Educators Act, 1998 (Act 76 of 1998), regulates the professional, moral and ethical responsibilities and competencies of educators.
- ABET Act, 2000 (Act 52 of 2000), provides for the establishment of public and private adult-learning centres, funding for ABET provisioning, the governance of public centres, and quality-assurance mechanisms for the sector.
- The SAQA Act, 1995 provides for the creation of the NQF, which establishes the framework for a national learning system that integrates education and training at all levels.

- The SACE Act, 2000 provides for the establishment of a Council to undertake the registration of educators; promote the professional development of educators; and set, maintain and protect ethical and professional standards for educators.

The Education Laws Amendment Act, 2002 (Act 50 of 2002), and the HE Amendment Act, 2002 (Act 63 of 2002), came into effect during 2002.

The Education Laws Amendment Act, 2002 makes provision for amending the South African Schools Act, 1996, to give clarity and certainty regarding the admission age to Grades R and 1 at public and independent schools. As a result of the amendment, the minimum age of admission has been lowered by six months. The compulsory school-going age remains seven to 15 years, or completion of Grade 9. A new section was also inserted to prohibit initiation practices at schools.

The HE Amendment Act, 2002 clarifies and brings legal certainty to labour and student matters regarding the mergers of public HE institutions, and provides clarity on the authority to take the decision to merge and to give a name and physical location to a new institution.

The HE Amendment Bill, 2003 provides for the establishment of National Institutes for HE in Mpumalanga and Northern Cape. The Institutes will serve as the administrative and governance hubs for the provision of HE in response to regional needs. The Institutes are not intended to offer their own academic programmes, but will co-ordinate HE in these provinces, including the sharing of infrastructure and resources.

A new section was inserted into the Employment of Educators Act, 1998 to enable a provincial Department to appoint new recruits or applicants after a break in service, without requiring a recommendation from a governing body. It also enables the fair distribution of qualified educators by allowing provinces to distribute such educators, especially to schools in rural areas.

A new section was inserted into both the FET Act, 1998 and the ABET Act, 2000, prohibiting corporal punishment in educational institutions and centres.

Tirisano

In January 2000, the *Tirisano* (meaning working together) plan was operationalised. Through it, the Department has achieved greater stability in the system, enhanced basic school functionality, improved the ability of provincial education systems to manage human and financial resources, and ensured a clear focus on delivery.

Since 2001, the Department has been able to shift its focus from creating an integrated education framework and providing basic systemic functionality, to institutional renewal and enhanced effectiveness, focusing on teaching; learning; curriculum and whole-school development; learner performance; increased participation in further and HE; mathematics, science and technology; building good citizenship through the promotion of values, and targeting those communities that are part of government-wide programmes for rural and urban development.

The nine priorities of *Tirisano* are to:
- deal urgently and purposefully with HIV/AIDS by utilising the education and training system
- ensure the successful running of provincial systems through successful co-operative governance
- reduce illiteracy among adults and youths over the next five years
- develop schools as centres of community life
- end conditions of physical degradation in South African schools
- develop the professional abilities of the teaching force
- ensure the success of active learning through outcomes-based education (OBE)
- create a vibrant FET system, which will equip youths and adults to achieve social goals

- build a rational and seamless HE system that will embrace the intellectual and professional challenges facing South Africans in the 21st century.

These priorities have been organised into the following six core programme areas that will guide the activities of the Department over the next five years:
- HIV/AIDS
- school effectiveness and teacher professionalism
- literacy
- FET and HE
- organisational effectiveness of the national and provincial Departments of Education
- values in education.

New salary and post structure

In March 2003, the Minister of Education unveiled a new pay and post structure for teachers. The new salary system comprises 16 notches.

Two key features of the new post and pay structure are:
- the creation of a senior teacher category in schools, which allows teachers to remain in the classroom without sacrificing career opportunities
- different career paths for teachers, which will allow them to choose between a teaching, learning or management option.

The Policy on Drug Abuse in Schools was gazetted in 2002. The policy makes a very clear statement about the unacceptability of drugs and other illegal substances in schools, and proposes firm action, including suspension and expulsion, where necessary.

The policy also recognises that substance abuse is a complex problem and that interventions must be relevant to the particular context. In all cases, a supportive response, aimed at correcting the problem, is encouraged. Random drug testing and searches are prohibited, and should only be conducted where reasonable suspicion exists. In all cases, parents must be involved as soon as possible.

Nicotine use by pupils, teachers and visitors is prohibited.

New policy developments

Improving access to free and quality basic education

School fees are charged for children to attend school. The amount is set at an annual public meeting of the school governing body where parents vote on the amount to be paid. Parents who cannot afford to pay, or who can only afford a lesser amount, are granted an exemption or reduction in the amount they must pay.

In response to government's concern about the relatively high costs of school education, the Department of Education undertook a Review of the Financing, Resourcing and Costs of Education in Public Schools.

The Review, which was released for public comment in March 2003, highlighted practices within the system and in society that drive increases in the cost of education, and gave recommendations on how to curtail practices that lead to the marginalisation of learners, especially those from poor families.

A Plan of Action to improve access to free and quality education for all was subsequently developed and approved by the Cabinet. The Plan was made public on 17 June 2003.

The Plan includes mechanisms to ensure:
- Greater interprovincial equity so that learners with similar levels of poverty receive the same minimum level of school funding.
- The abolition of compulsory school fees, where adequate levels of resourcing are reached, for 40% of learners in the poorest schools.
- A national norm based on a minimum basic package of R450 per school term in 2003, which will be allocated per learner for non-personnel recurrent items, starting with the poorest 20% of learners. Adequate-per-learner funding for the poorest 60% of learners in the poorest schools will be phased in over three years.
- The granting of automatic fee exemptions to learners who qualify for certain social service grants and payments.

Religion in education

After extensive public consultation, the National Policy on Religion and Education was launched on 9 September 2003. The Policy aims to strengthen the role and place of religion in schools, which is an important aspect of the campaign for moral regeneration.

In line with the principle of equal recognition of all religions, enshrined in the Constitution, the non-prescriptive Policy emphasises the prohibition of practices which are discriminatory and which lead to a loss of respect, or undermine the dignity of a person.

In terms of the Policy, a public school must cater in an equitable fashion for all religions, in order to bring about mutual respect and appreciation for the diverse cultures and religions of the country. The Policy restates the need for children to be educated about religion, in an impartial and fair way, so that they can be better informed. The Department of Education has developed age-appropriate outcomes for each of the Grades, which will form part of the compulsory and examinable Life Orientation Programme.

Religious groupings were invited to assist in the development of suitable teaching material and in the training of educators, to ensure support for the Programme.

As a core element of the National Curriculum Statement, no pupil may be exempt from this Programme and no educator may refuse to teach it.

Agreement on target shooting in schools

In April 2003, the CEM gave their support for the use of airguns instead of .22 rifles in the sport of target shooting at schools. This is in line with the view of the Ministers of Safety and Security and of Education that schools should be declared gun-free zones.

The South African National Defence Force (SANDF) loaned guns which are currently in the possession of schools, and the CEM gave their support for the collection of all existing .22 rifles in schools by the SANDF.

A national task team, comprising the Directors-General of the Department of Education and of Sport and Recreation South Africa, as well as the Commissioner of the South African Police Service, will liaise with the relevant sporting federations to discuss the possible development and promotion of target shooting as a sport in schools in an equitable and safe manner.

e-Education

On 27 August 2003, the Cabinet approved the *Draft White Paper on e-Education*. It sets out government's response to a new information and communications technology (ICT) environment in education. Government wants to ensure that every school has access to a wide choice of diverse and high-quality communications services.

The goal is to ensure that every learner is ICT-capable by 2010, and that all schools are connected to the Internet by that time. The need for teacher-training and ICT equipment was recognised, which would require additional resources from provincial budgets and other innovative sources.

By September 2003, agreements had been signed between the Department of Education and the private sector, including Microsoft,

---

The Department of Education launched the Girls' Education Movement (GEM) in Parliament in March 2003. As part of its objectives, GEM hopes to:
- provide opportunities for girls to develop and exercise their leadership and technical skills
- tap the potential of boys, women and men to work in partnership with girls to promote girls' education in Africa; and through education, create more equitable and just African societies.

GEM is an organisation representing children in Africa which was initiated in Kampala, Uganda in 2001.

It comprises children in schools and communities throughout Africa, who work in different ways to improve the lives of African girls.

It also aims to ensure that girls receive an adequate education, especially in science and technology.

Sentech, the Telkom Foundation, and the Digital Partnership Programme.

The services offered by the initiative will enhance lifelong learning and provide unlimited opportunities for personal growth and development. This includes the ICT development of teachers and managers, and the availability of high-quality content resources.

General Education and Training

General school education is structured according to three phases, namely the Foundation Phase, Intermediate Phase and Senior Phase, and constitutes the compulsory component of the education system. The progressive provision of a Grade R prior to Grade One started in 2002.

Currently, the Foundation Phase lasts three years. Basic learning activities during this Phase centre around three learning programmes, namely literacy, numeracy and life skills. One additional language is introduced in Grade 3.

During the three-year Intermediate Phase, learning activities centre on five learning programmes, namely language literacy and communication; mathematical literacy, mathematics and mathematical sciences; arts and culture; life orientation, human, social, environmental and management sciences; and natural sciences and technology.

The Senior Phase accounts for Grades 7 to 9. During these years, learners have to master the following learning programmes: language literacy and communication; mathematical literacy, mathematics and mathematical sciences; arts and culture; life orientation; human and social sciences; economic management sciences; natural sciences; and technology. Grade 9 signals the end of compulsory schooling and ends with a GET certificate, which is Level 1 on the NQF.

Curriculum 2005

Curriculum 2005 is the brand name of the National Curriculum Framework introduced into schools in 1998 and based on the concept of OBE.

OBE regards learning as an interactive process between and among educators and learners. The focus is on what learners should know and be able to do (knowledge, skills, attitudes and values). It places strong emphasis on co-operative learning, especially group work involving common tasks. The goal is to produce active and lifelong learners with a thirst for knowledge and a love of learning.

The revised Curriculum will be phased in, starting with Grades R to 3 in 2004.

The revised Curriculum Statement is available in all 11 official languages as well as in Braille. This Statement is much simpler to work with and provides much more guidance to teachers about expectations and standards. In addition, a teacher's guide has been prepared, which assists the educator in developing appropriate learning programmes to achieve the specified outcomes.

A national core team provided training to officials from every province, including curriculum specialists, subject advisors and other key staff. They, in turn, have been training school principals, who are expected to provide instructional leadership in their schools and to educators.

The National Curriculum Statement, Grades 10 – 12, was approved by the CEM and by the Cabinet. It will be accompanied by a new Further Education and Training Certificate (FETC), which will replace the current Senior Certificate. While the new Curriculum will be introduced in Grade 10 in 2006, the new Certificate will be introduced in Grade 12 in 2008.

The FETC, which will require higher levels of performance in each subject, will greatly enhance the Department's ability to predict learners' future performances, by explicitly stating levels of learner performance. The FETC will not prejudge learners' potential by differentiating them into Higher and Standard Grades.

School admission policy

Pupils normally enrol for Grade 1 education at the beginning of the year in which they turn seven years of age, although earlier entry at the age of six is allowed if the child meets specified criteria indicating that he/she has reached a stage of school readiness.

When applying for admission, parents must present the school with an official birth certificate and proof that the child has been immunised against communicable diseases.

For non-South African citizens, a study permit, temporary or permanent residence permit, or evidence of application for permission to stay in South Africa, is also required.

Further Education and Training

FET consists of all learning and training from NQF Levels 2 to 4, or the equivalent of Grades 10 to 12 in the school system and National Technical Certificate 1 to 3 in FET colleges. Learners enter FET after the completion of the compulsory phase of education in Grade 9 or via the ABET route. The long-term vision of this sector includes the development of a co-ordinated FET system, providing high-quality, flexible and responsive programmes and opportunities for a learning society. The short-to-medium-term focus is on addressing the weaknesses and deficiencies of the current system, while simultaneously laying the foundations for the system to be built over the next 20 years.

Government declared 2003 the Year of FET, in recognition of the vital role FET plays in the development of the country's human resources.

Curriculum development in Further Education and Training

The FET Curriculum is shifting away from the traditional divides between academic and applied learning, theory and practice, and knowledge and skills. The new Curriculum moves towards a balanced learning experience that provides flexible access to lifelong learning, higher education and training, and productive employment in a range of occupational contexts.

FET comprises three different pathways, namely academic, vocationally orientated and occupation-specific. The Curriculum consists of three components of learning: fundamental, core and elective. Curriculum development in FET regards the 12 learning fields of the NQF as its point of departure.

By May 2003, a Draft National Curriculum Framework, setting the parameters for the development of responsive programmes was in place.

Further Education and Training colleges

South African learners need a range of skills and knowledge to keep up with modern technology. Remote rural areas need to be reached, and adult learners need the opportunity to retrain for a second or third career. small-business entrepreneurs also need courses catering for their needs, and industry and the community need to be provided with productive people who see learning as a lifelong occupation, within an economy that is being restructured to meet the demands of globalisation.

In this context, the creation of a dynamic, responsive and high-quality FET system to promote wider access and social inclusion, encourage lifelong learning, meet the human resource development needs of the country, contribute towards urban renewal and rural development, and develop an entirely new citizenry in the country, became imperative.

As a result, a major transformation of the FET sector took place during 2002, in which the existing 152 technical colleges were merged to form 50 multicampus FET colleges.

The colleges provide:
- high-level skills training
- a balanced training programme, emphasising both theoretical and practical skills linked to specific industry requirements
- vocational training, which continually exposes students to the demands of the work environment.

The new system operates under a single governing council appointed to oversee effective and accountable management across and within the various FET college campuses and sites.

The recorded increase in student intake, the development of new programmes and increased participation in learnerships bear testimony to the potential for growth in this sector.

Higher education

The role of HE in the South African education system is threefold:
- Human resource development: the mobilisation of human talent and potential through lifelong learning, to contribute to the social, economic, cultural and intellectual life of a rapidly changing society.
- High-level skills training: the training and provision of person power to strengthen the country's enterprises, services and infrastructure. This requires the development of professionals with globally equivalent skills, but who are socially responsible and conscious of their role in contributing to the national development effort and social transformation.
- Production, acquisition and application of new knowledge: national growth and competitiveness are dependent on continuous technological improvement and innovation, driven by a well-organised and vibrant research and development system which integrates the research and training capacity of HE with the needs of industry and of social reconstruction.

Transformation and reconstruction of the Higher Education system

The *Education White Paper 3: A Programme for the Transformation of HE* and the HE Act, 1997 provide the policy and legislative framework for the transformation of the HE system.

National Plan for Higher Education

The National Plan for HE was released in March 2001. The Plan establishes indicative targets for the size and shape of the HE system, including overall growth and participation rates, institutional and programme mixes, and equity and efficiency goals.

It provides a framework and outlines the process for the restructuring of the system. It also provides signposts for the development of institutional plans.

The key proposals of the Plan are that:
- the participation rate in HE will be increased from 15% to 20% in the long term, i.e. 10 to 15 years
- there will be a shift in the balance of enrolments over the next five to 10 years between the humanities; business and commerce; and science, engineering and technology from the current ratio of 49:26:25 to 40:30:30 respectively
- institutions will establish student-equity targets with the emphasis on programmes in which black and female students are underrepresented, and develop strategies to ensure equity of outcomes
- institutions will develop employment-equity plans with clear targets for rectifying race and gender inequities
- institutional diversity will be achieved through the approval of a distinct mission and academic-programme profile for each institution
- the academic programme mix at each institution will be determined on the basis of

---

In February 2003, the Minister of Education, Prof. Kader Asmal, announced the completion of the building of classrooms and schools in KwaZulu-Natal and the Eastern Cape, two of the four provinces earmarked for infrastructure development in the country.

Together with Limpopo and Mpumalanga, the provinces are part of a comprehensive programme of assistance to South Africa by the Japanese Government. The assistance includes a school-building programme to the value of about R200 million.

The four provinces account for the largest portion of school-infrastructure backlogs in the country.

its current programme profile, as well as its demonstrated capacity to add new programmes
- redress for historically black institutions will be linked to agreed missions and programme profiles, including developmental strategies to build capacity
- a single dedicated distance-education institution will be established through the merger of the University of South Africa (UNISA) and Technikon South Africa, and the incorporation of the distance education campus of Vista University into the merged institution
- research will be funded through a separate formula based on research output, including, at a minimum, master's and doctoral graduates and research publications
- earmarked funds will be allocated to build research capacity, including scholarships to promote postgraduate enrolments
- the institutional landscape will be restructured through collaboration at the regional level in programme development, and delivery and rationalisation, particularly of small and costly programmes.

As part of the process of implementing the National Plan, the Minister of Education appointed a National Working Group to advise him on the restructuring of the institutional landscape of the HE system. The Working Group investigated the feasibility of consolidating HE provision by reducing the number of institutions, but not the number of regional delivery sites.

In May 2002, the Cabinet approved the ground-breaking proposals for the transformation and reconstruction of HE.

As part of the transformation process, a National HE Information and Applications Service was established in 2003 to provide Grade 12 learners with easily accessible information on study opportunities in HE.

Institutional restructuring

The proposed institutional landscape establishes a new institutional and organisational form, namely comprehensive institutions formed by merging universities and technikons. This will strengthen the provision of technikon programmes by ensuring that they are available throughout the country, particularly in rural areas which are currently inadequately serviced in terms of technikon provision.

In October 2003, the Minister of Education announced the new names of the merged institutions of higher learning.
- The merged Universities of Potchefstroom, North West and Vista (Sebokeng campus) will be called the North West University.
- The University of Pretoria will retain its name after incorporating the Mamelodi Campus of Vista University.
- UNISA will retain its name after merging with the Vista University Distance Education Campus.
- Technikons Pretoria, North West and Northern Gauteng will be called the Tshwane University of Technology.
- Technikon Witwatersrand and the Soweto and East Rand Campuses of Vista University will merge with the Rand Afrikaans University in 2005 and be called the University of Johannesburg.
- The Medical University of South Africa (Medunsa) and the University of the North will merge to become the University of Limpopo.
- The University of Port Elizabeth, Port Elizabeth Technikon and Port Elizabeth Campus of Vista will be called the Nelson Mandela Metropolitan University from 2005.
- The University of Transkei, Border Technikon and the Eastern Cape Technikon will be called the Eastern Cape University of Technology.
- The East London Campus of Rhodes University will be incorporated into the University of Fort Hare.
- The Universities of Cape Town and the Witwatersrand will remain unchanged.
- Cape Technikon and Peninsula Technikon will be called the Cape Peninsula University of Technology.

Adult Basic Education and Training

The ABET Act, 2000 and the regulations for a National ABET Board provide a legislative framework for the establishment, governance and funding of ABET centres. Through the Adult Education and Training Multi-Year Implementation Plan (MYIP), the quality of ABET provisioning and delivery is improving.

The National ABET Board, an advisory body to the Minister which receives reports from all sectors on the progress of the MYIP, replaced the interim ABET advisory body in 2002.

The most recent Household Survey placed illiteracy at a level of 93% – up from 86% in 1994. Between 1999 and 2002, over one million learners attended and successfully completed literacy and ABET programmes.

The South African National Literacy Initiative (SANLI) was established in 2000 with the purpose of engaging with all organisations involved in the development and delivery of literacy, to mobilise resources for these organisations, and to improve and assure the quality of their programmes. SANLI pledged to ensure that one million of the estimated 3,3 million illiterate people in South Africa can read and write by 2004. It noted that this could only be achieved through extensive partnerships.

The Department established the South African Literacy Agency to significantly reduce adult illiteracy through:
- mobilising voluntary services in support of a nationwide literacy initiative
- developing training programmes for volunteer educators
- designing, developing and procuring reading and resource material
- setting up local literacy units
- establishing and maintaining a database of learners and providers
- servicing the needs of learners and educators.

As part of the Literacy Strategy, the Department is also ensuring the development of frameworks for the provision of ABET in line with the NQF.

As part of the advocacy campaign to mobilise learners, National Adult Learners' Week was launched as an annual event on 1 September 2000, and award ceremonies are held on International Literacy Day (8 September) to honour and applaud the courage and achievements of adult learners and their educators.

SANLI managed to mobilise sufficient resources, largely from the United Kingdom's (UK) Department for International Development (DFID) and the European Union (EU), to enable it to present literacy classes to more than 200 000 newly enrolled adult learners in 2003. The majority of these learners were from the Eastern Cape and Limpopo, where the effects of illiteracy compound the difficulties experienced by the rural poor.

Masifunde Sonke is another project set up by the Ministry of Education to address the challenges of illiteracy, and to promote a love of reading. The project is tasked to profile reading, and to encourage stakeholders to promote reading. The project is being used to 'spread the word', and numerous reading promotion messages are seen on television channels and heard on radio, owing to the strong working relationship with the SABC.

The Democracy in the Classroom Project was launched in August 2003. It is the result of a partnership between the DFID, the Independent Electoral Commission of South Africa, and the ABET Institute of UNISA, in collaboration with SANLI.

Education of learners with special education needs

The Ministry appointed the National Commission on Special Needs in Education and Training (NCSNET) and the National Committee on Education Support Services (NCESS) in October 1996, to investigate and make recommendations on all aspects of special needs and support services in education and training in South Africa. A joint report of the findings of these two bodies was presented to the

Minister in November 1997, and the final report was published in February 1998.

The NCSNET and NCESS recommended that the education and training system develop inclusive and supportive centres of learning that would enable all learners to participate actively in the education process. They could then develop and extend their potential and participate as equal members of society.

The report suggested that the key strategies required to achieve this, included:
- Transforming all aspects of the education system.
- Developing an integrated system of education.
- Infusing special needs and support services throughout the system.
- Pursuing the holistic development centres of learning to ensure a barrier-free physical environment and a supportive and inclusive psychosocial learning environment, and developing a flexible curriculum, which can be accessed by all learners.
- Promoting the rights and responsibilities of parents, teachers and learners.
- Providing effective development programmes for educators, support personnel and other relevant human resources.
- Fostering holistic and integrated support (intersectoral collaboration) by developing a community-based support system. This includes a preventative and developmental approach to support.
- Developing funding strategies that will ensure redress, sustainability and, ultimately, access to education for all learners.

The Ministry released a Consultative Paper based on these recommendations in 1999. The submissions and feedback of social partners, role-players and the wider public were collated, and informed the writing of the *Education White Paper 6 on Special Needs Education: Building an Inclusive Education and Training System*, released in July 2001. The White Paper outlines a 20-year plan for an inclusive education and training system across all bands of education.

The Directorate: Inclusive Education implements inclusive education in classrooms and education institutions across the country. Their main tasks include removing barriers to learning experienced by learners with disabilities, and integrating learners with special needs into mainstream schools.

Early Childhood Development

In July 2000, the final report on the National ECD Pilot Project was released. The Project tested the interim ECD policy, particularly as it was related to Grade R. The report presented some evidence that the existing norms and standards were appropriate for the practitioners, but recommended that they be refined to eliminate vagueness.

An audit of over 23 000 ECD sites was conducted in 2001, which revealed that the ECD field is dominated by the non-governmental sector. Where departmental provision exists, it usually caters for children from the age of three years to school-going age. It is estimated that about 90% of children under the age of nine in South Africa do not have access to ECD prior to attending school.

ECD centres must be registered with municipalities and their activities are controlled by the provincial Education Departments. These regulations are applicable to public as well as private pre-primary schools.

The SACE Act, 2000 provides for the registration of ECD practitioners. In terms of the Act, all educators must be registered before they can be responsible for the care and education of children. When ECD practitioners are registered, they undergo professional development sponsored by the Council and are subject to the Code of Ethics.

The *White Paper 5 on ECD*, which establishes a national system of provision of Grade R for children aged five, was launched in May 2001. The medium-term goal is for all children entering Grade 1 to have participated in an accredited Grade R programme by 2010.

The White Paper also focuses on expanding ECD provision, correcting imbalances, ensuring equitable access and improving the quality and delivery of ECD programmes. These interventions aim to break the cycle of poverty by increasing access to ECD programmes, particularly of poor children.

The ECD policy focuses on the phasing-in of a nationally accredited Grade R Programme for five-year-olds, collaboration with other government departments in making provision for children from birth to five years old, as well as special programmes for five-year-olds.

The School Register of Needs

The School Register of Needs provides an important benchmark for addressing historical inequities.

Considerable progress has been made since 1994 in correcting these inequities. The School Register of Needs 2000 Survey recorded significant improvements in school infrastructure and access to basic services countrywide.

The Register reported less overcrowding in institutions overall, with a decline in the average number of learners in a classroom from 43 (in 1996) to 35 (in 2000). Except in Mpumalanga, learner:classroom ratios also decreased. Classroom shortages decreased from 49% (1996) to 40% (2000). In 1996, 40% of all schools nationwide had no access to water. By 2000, this was reduced to 34%. There was a 68% improvement in the provision of sanitation, although 16,6% of learners remained without toilet facilities. Fifty-nine per cent of schools had no telephones in 1996. This percentage was reduced to 34% in 2000.

On the other hand, the biggest decline was in the number of schools in excellent and good condition, indicating that investment in infrastructure had not been adequately maintained. The number of buildings in good condition declined from 9 000 to 4 000, with at least 12 000 school buildings in need of repair.

Recent years have seen an improvement in infrastructure spending, especially on school education. The provincial education capital budget, which was R2,01 billion in the 2002/03 financial year, increased to R2,5 billion in 2003/04, with a projected increase to R3,02 billion in 2004/05. In particular, emphasis on classroom provision has reduced classroom backlogs drastically. Some 3 750 classrooms were built in 2002/03, while 4 330 were expected to be built by the end of the 2003/04 financial year.

Human Resource Development Strategy

In April 2001, the Ministries of Education and of Labour jointly launched the Human Resource Development Strategy for South Africa, entitled *A Nation at Work for a Better Life for All*. The Strategy is underpinned by a set of institutional arrangements, including SETAs, and the general reshaping of further and higher education to meet the human resource development needs of the country.

The Strategy will ensure integrated human resource development planning and implementation, monitored on a national, regional and sectoral level. Progress will be measured against approved indicators.

The key mission of the Strategy is to maximise the potential of people in South Africa, through the acquisition of knowledge and skills, to set in place an operational plan and the necessary arrangements to ensure that everyone achieves productivity and works competitively to improve the quality of life.

The goals of the Strategy include improving the social infrastructure of the country, reducing disparities in wealth and poverty, developing a more inclusive society, and improving South Africa's position on the International Competitiveness Table.

The benefits to the country of the successful implementation of this Strategy over the

Education

next five to 10 years will be significant. Primarily, the integration of different government policies will help to increase economic growth and employment, improve the standard of living for all, broaden participation in the labour market, and produce a more educated and trained citizenry.

HIV/AIDS

The Ministry of Education works alongside the Ministry of Health to ensure that the national education system plays its part in stemming HIV/AIDS, and ensuring that the rights of all those infected with the disease are fully protected.

This priority has been operationalised into three objectives of the *Tirisano* implementation plan. Each is linked to anticipated outcomes and performance indicators. The three programmes are:
- awareness, information and advocacy
- HIV/AIDS within the curriculum
- planning for HIV/AIDS and the education system.

The Ministry's policy on HIV/AIDS for learners and educators has been converted into an accessible booklet aimed at educators, school-governing bodies and district officials. One million copies were distributed nationwide, coinciding with a media communication campaign.

On 9 June 2003, the CEM announced a three-year strategic plan, which is consistent with the national five-year plan. The new plan focuses on:
- limiting the spread of HIV and AIDS through life-skills education – a component which had been exceptionally effective by mid-2003, with the training of 130 000 educators, and over 60% of schools offering the programme
- providing social support to educators and learners who are affected
- managing the impact of HIV and AIDS on the education system.

Partnerships, international relations and funding

Central to the education policy framework is the contention that a high-quality education sector cannot be built by government alone. It depends on creative and dynamic partnerships between the public sector, civil society and international partners. Several working partnerships have been, and are being, consolidated as the capacities of various sectors to contribute to educational development are better understood.

The Department of Education, the three teacher unions, the SACE, the ELRC and the Education, Training and Development Practices SETA signed a historic declaration at the National Education Convention in November 2002, in which they committed themselves to work together to achieve education transformation goals.

Teacher unions

The majority of educators are organised into three teacher unions, namely the National Professional Teachers' Organisation of South Africa, the South African Teachers' Union and the South African Democratic Teachers' Union. A labour-relations framework has been jointly agreed to by the Ministry of Education and the unions. This encompasses both traditional areas of negotiation and issues of professional concern, including pedagogy and quality-improvement strategies.

Non-governmental organisations (NGOs)

NGOs are emerging as important partners in educational transformation and are often a source of creativity and innovation. The Department of Education is working with NGOs and the private sector to expand relationships, particularly in the areas of educator training, school improvement, ABET, ECD and FET, as well as evaluation, research and monitoring. The private sector in particular is increasingly engaging in the provision of basic education by funding FET initiatives, building schools in needy communities, and supporting the provision of teaching and learning equipment.

Public-private partnerships

The success of key national initiatives (including SANLI) relies largely on partnerships with the private and NGO sectors.

Several partnerships have been consolidated, providing working models of educational transformation through public-private partnerships. The Business Trust, a partnership between business and government, works in education through three NGOs, namely the READ Educational Trust, Joint Education Trust, and the National Business Initiative Colleges Collaboration.

The international community

The international community's contribution to education transformation is important. The Department co-operates with United Nations (UN) agencies and with numerous donors to improve access to basic, further and higher education. Development co-operation partners such as the Australian Agency for International Development, Flanders, France, Germany, Italy, Japan International Co-operation Agency, the Swiss Agency for Development and Co-operation, the Danish Agency for Development Assistance, the United States Agency for International Development, the Swedish International Development Agency, the Canadian International Development Agency, DFID (UK), the Netherlands, the Irish Agency for International Development, the Finnish Government and the EU have been instrumental in the provision of technical and financial assistance to the national and provincial Departments of Education.

In February 2003, South Africa and France signed a R6,6-million agreement for the improvement of education in Gauteng.

Two groups of 14 learners received training by attending two month-long internships in France on a 'train-the-trainer' basis. The project, expected to be expanded to Limpopo, KwaZulu-Natal and the Eastern Cape, aims at setting up nine Education Action Zones in the province, and will also build capacity in the areas of administration and management, especially for school principals.

The Governments of the UK and Northern Ireland are making available R226 million to the Limpopo Department of Education. The assistance, which will be spread over six years (2003 – 2009), is known as the *Khanyisa* Education Support Programme.

The Programme aims to improve learning achievement, support, and service delivery across the whole education system.

The Ministry has also played a leading role in the development of the Southern African Development Community Protocol on Education and Training, which aims to achieve equivalence, harmonisation and standardisation of education in the region.

International partnerships and South-South exchanges are fostered particularly within the African continent.

The Department has a strong collaborative relationship with the UN Educational, Scientific and Cultural Organisation. A key initiative of the collaboration is the development of national Education For All (EFA) action plans. As part of regional consultations on the implementation, the Department participates in assessing progress in the elaboration of the EFA plans of countries in sub-Saharan Africa, and exchanges information and best practice on the development of these plans. South Africa has reaffirmed its commitment to the Ministers of Education of African member states to make the experience, expertise and existing infrastructure of South African HE available to the rest of Africa.

Highlights in education since 1994

The first years of democratic government witnessed significant reform in education, which included dismantling apartheid structures to create a unified education system consisting of one national and nine provincial Departments of Education. Thus, a more equitable system of financing education, and a policy framework to reflect the values and mandate of the new Government were created, putting in place democratic governance structures and democratising relations within the education system. A basis for lifelong learning, and transforming learning at school level by offering a new learner-centred, outcomes-based school curriculum to reflect the values and ethos of a new democratic order, were established.

The African Institute for Mathematical Sciences (AIMS), a new state-of-the-art educational centre, was formally launched on 18 September 2003 in Muizenberg, Cape Town.

The Department of Science and Technology has spent over R1 million on the AIMS programme which linked to centres and networks of excellence in science and technology. The centres and networks of excellence focus strongly on human resource development and are aimed at popularising science in South Africa and across the African continent.

AIMS is an international initiative combining the three universities in the Western Cape, Cambridge and Oxford in the United Kingdom, and the University of Paris-Sud in France. Its goal is to strengthen scientific and technological capacity across the African continent. Initially, it will focus on a unique residential nine-month postgraduate course, developing strong foundations in mathematical research skills as well as providing an overview of many of the most exciting cutting-edge fields in science.

Through advertising on the web, AIMS has recruited 30 of Africa's top graduate students, from Algeria to Zimbabwe, who on completion, will boost the African networks of excellence. In time, the student body will grow to 60. Students and lecturers are accommodated at the AIMS educational centre, allowing for maximal interaction. The centre has outstanding computer, library and lecture-hall facilities.

Major achievements in education over the past decade have included:
- Improving access to primary and secondary schooling, with near universal enrolment in primary schooling and 86% enrolment in secondary schooling achieved by 1998. The participation rate among girls is also among the highest in the world.
- Access to school education was further improved by exempting poor learners from paying school fees, and outlawing discrimination against, and exclusion of, learners who cannot afford school fees. A plan of action to progressively increase access to free education for all was made public in June 2003.
- Enhancing access to HE institutions through the establishment of the NSFAS in 1996. The Scheme disbursed over R2,6 billion to almost half a million students in HE institutions between 1996 and 2001.
- Improving the performance of learners throughout the schooling system and especially in the Grade 12 Senior Certificate examination, where the pass rate has improved from 53% in 1999 to 68% in 2002. The examinations were also subjected to a quality assurance exercise by the Scottish Qualifications Authority, which certified the examinations as being of a high standard. The National Systemic Evaluation System has also been established to monitor and evaluate the performance of learners and for quality assurance.
- Improving the qualifications of educators, with the proportion of underqualified educators being reduced from 36% in 1994 to 26% in 1998.
- Establishing more equitable learner:educator ratios, from an average of 43:1 in 1996 to 35:1 in 2000, through redeployment and post-provisioning strategies in favour of areas of greatest need.
- Increasing per-capita expenditure on learners, from R2 222 in 1994 to R3 253 in 2000, and achieving interprovincial equity.

- Restructuring the FET and HE systems to make their programmes more relevant to the needs of students and the economy, and to reconfigure their institutional landscapes from an apartheid structure to a rationalised one that eliminates unnecessary duplication and promotes growth, rejuvenation and co-operation.
- Nurturing the growth of democracy, and the promotion of values and moral regeneration through the establishment of the South African History Project and the Values in Education Initiative. The Manifesto on Values, Education and Democracy, produced in 2001, laid the basis for a comprehensive and ongoing advocacy campaign, and provided a practical framework for instilling and reinforcing the values of the new South Africa in learners and promoting the concepts of democracy, national pride and identity in the classroom.
- Establishing a National Strategy for Mathematics, Science and Technology Education in 2001. The Strategy identifies 102 schools with a specific mandate to promote, especially among girls, study in these fields.
- Reducing illiteracy and aliteracy among the population through the establishment of SANLI, the reading advocacy project *Masifunde Sonke*, and ABET programmes.

Library and information services sector

South African libraries have developed over a period of more than 150 years. The world's first free public library service was established by Lord Charles Somerset in 1820, by levying a tax on the sale of wine. When he returned to England, tax reforms by the new governor spelt the end of the free library; but it formed the basis of what is today the National Library of South Africa in Cape Town.

By 1900, subscription libraries were operating in most towns and cities, financed by annual membership fees and, in most cases, grants from local authorities. An investigation in the 1930s by the Carnegie Corporation of New York found most of these libraries inadequate and poorly funded. The necessity for government support to ensure free public libraries was recognised.

By the 1950s, all four provinces of the Union of South Africa had ordinances that set out the functions of local and provincial government, and public library development gathered momentum.

In 1985, librarians commissioned UNISA to investigate the role that libraries can and should play in developing South Africa. The result was that greater emphasis was placed on providing material that would support formal and informal education. Outreach programmes to schools and pre-schools received priority. Many libraries started presenting literacy classes for adults.

South Africa's growing library and information services (LIS) sector includes a national library, public/community libraries, special libraries, government libraries and HE libraries. By mid-2003, South Africa had more than 11 373 libraries, with 77 HE libraries, 9 416 school libraries, 79 government departmental libraries, one national library with two branches and 1 800 public libraries provided by provincial and local government (library services and metro libraries). Less than 10% of secondary schools have school libraries.

The nine provincial library authorities provide, in partnership with local government, extensive public library services. Public libraries, among other services, increasingly render community and general information services, and provide study material and facilities for school and tertiary students.

The approximately 1 800 public libraries in the country have to provide services to a total population of about 44,8 million. According to Census 2001 figures, this translates to one library service point for every 25 000 people.

The HE libraries hold the bulk of South Africa's scientific and scholarly information resources and fulfil more than half of all the interlibrary loan requests. Pressures on HE libraries include redistribution of educational resources, rising prices and declining student numbers. These libraries have responded by forming consortia, looking at access, and exploring digital resources.

Special libraries refer to libraries which consist of subject-specialised collections, including private organisations' libraries and government departmental libraries.

Policy Framework for School Libraries

The Department of Education is working on the Policy Framework for School Libraries. This draft document locates itself within the context of socio-political and educational transformation that is driven by the new legislative framework and the educational paradigm shift to OBE.

The draft policy argues that teachers and learners will only be able to access an OBE curriculum if they have access to learning resources. This has implications for the way school libraries conceptualise, manage and provide resources. The draft policy recommends different models of school libraries to provide access to resources for learners, and draws attention to the relationship between the school library, the curriculum and learning resources. It also supports the view that the school library is a facility ideally suited to providing learners with a wide range of curriculum-orientated resources in diverse media forms, as required by an OBE system.

Library Association of South Africa (LIASA)

Librarians recognise the value that association membership and participation offers them. The LIS sector professionals have established the LIASA to unite all the institutions and persons engaged in the LIS sector in South Africa. LIASA's mission advocates and supports the provision of an efficient, user-orientated and excellent LIS that aspires to enhance equitable access to information for all communities in South Africa. However, unlike lawyers, doctors and dentists who may be required to be members of a legally constituted association in order to practise, librarians are under no legal obligation to belong to State, national or professional groups. LIASA's role in the profession is therefore to:

- provide a direct channel of communication between every member and the Association through a number of publications, in print and electronic format
- provide opportunities for continuous training and development
- provide access to professional expertise
- act as a powerful advocate for the LIS sector
- provide authoritative policy advice to government and other agencies
- provide an active and consultative process of governance in which the membership is encouraged to be involved
- facilitate development and networking of members through the structures of the organisation in branches, interest groups, etc.
- organise and support international and regional events such as the Standing Conference of Eastern, Central and Southern African Library and Information Associations, and International Federation of Library Associations and Institutions.

South Africa Yearbook 2003/04

Education

Acknowledgements

BuaNews
Department of Arts and Culture
Department of Education
National Library of South Africa
South African Qualifications Authority
www.gov.za

Suggested reading

Badat, S. *Black Student Politics, Higher Education and Apartheid: From SASO to SANSCO. 1968 – 1990*. Pretoria: Human Sciences Research Council (HSRC), 1999.
Bot, M. and Pienaar, L. *TUATA: Transvaal United African Teachers' Association*. Pretoria: HSRC, 1999.
Burger, J.F. and Vermaak, A. *Directory of HSRC-rated Courses Offered in the Private Education and Training Sector*. Pretoria: HSRC, 1999.
Bursary Register for the 1998 Academic Year. Johannesburg: Motivational Guides on Education, Training and Career Orientation, 1998.
Chinapah, V. *With Africa for Africa: Towards Quality Education for All*. Pretoria: HSRC, 2000.
Christie, P. *Right to Learn: The Struggle for Education in South Africa*. 2nd ed. Randburg: Ravan Press, 1991.
Cross, M. *Resistance and Transformation: Education, Culture and Reconstruction in South Africa*. Johannesburg: Skotaville, 1992.
Cross, M. and other eds. *Dealing with Diversity in South African Education: A Debate on the Politics of a National Curriculum*. Kenwyn: Juta, 1998.
Du Toit, C.W. and Kruger, J.S. eds. *Multireligious Education in South Africa*. Pretoria: 1998.
Fleisch, B.D. *Managing Educational Change: the State and School Reform in South Africa*. Sandton: Heinemann, 2002.
Graaf, J. and others. *Teaching in the Gap: Implementing Education Policy in South Africa in the Nineties*. Hatfield: Via Afrika, n.d.
Harber, C. *State of Transition*. Oxford: Symposium Books, 2001.
Harley, A. and others. *A Survey of Adult Basic Education in South Africa in the 90s: Commissioned by the Joint Education Trust (JET)*. Johannesburg: Sached, 1996.
Hartshorne, K. *Crisis and Challenge: Black Education, 1910 – 1990*. Cape Town: Oxford University Press, 1992.
Kallaway, P. ed. *The History of Education under Apartheid 1948 – 1994*. Cape Town: Pearson Education, 2002.
Kallaway, P. *Apartheid and Education: The Education of Black South Africans*. Johannesburg: Ravan Press, 1990.
Kraak, A. ed. *Changing Modes: New Knowledge Production and Its Implications for Higher Education in South Africa*. Pretoria: HSRC, 2000.
Kraak, A. and Young, M. eds. *Education in Retrospect*. Pretoria: HSRC and Institute of Education, 2001.
Mboya, M.M. *Beyond Apartheid: The Question of Education for Liberation*. Cape Town: Esquire Press, 1993.
Mncwabe, M.P. *Post-Apartheid Education*. Lanham, Maryland (US): University Press of America, 1993.
Mokadi, A. *A Portrait of Governance in Higher Education: Taking a Stand for Education*. Johannesburg: Sedibeng Publishing House, 2002.
Morrow, W. and King, K. eds. *Vision and Reality: Changing Education and Training in South Africa*. Cape Town: University of Cape Town, 1998.
Nicolaou, G. and Nicolaou, E. *The School Guide Book*. Johannesburg: G.E.N. Publishing, 1998.
Pretorius, F. ed. *Outcomes-Based Education in South Africa*. Randburg: Hodder and Stoughton, 1999.
Saunders, S. *Vice-Chancellor on a Tightrope: A Personal Account of Climactic Years in South Africa*. Cape Town: David Philip, 2000.
Sekete, P. and others. *Deracialisation and Migration of Learners in South African Schools*. Pretoria: HSRC, 2001.
Steyn, J.C. *Education for Democracy*. Durbanville: Wachwa Publishers, 1997.
Walters, S. ed. *Globalisation, Adult Education and Training: Impact and Issues*. London: Zed Books; Cape Town: CACE Publications, 1997.

Guy Stubbs/Touchlife Images

chapter 9
Environmental management

Environmental management in South Africa is the responsibility of various government institutions. At central government level, the Department of Environmental Affairs and Tourism is the central policy-formulating and co-ordinating body.

The vision of the Department is to lead environmental management and tourism in the interest of sustainable development and to contribute to the improvement of the quality of life of all South Africans by:
- promoting the sustainable development, utilisation and protection of the country's natural and cultural resources
- establishing responsible tourism that ensures environmental sustainability and contributes to job creation and a better quality of life for all
- harnessing the skills, experience and knowledge of the environment of all South Africans
- fostering equitable access to the benefits derived from the country's natural and cultural resources

◀ The ground hornbill is an endangered species. As the largest co-operative breeding birds in the world they are of great interest to scientists. The current status of the ground hornbill has been judged by the WorldWide Fund (WWF) and South African Green Trust as justifying a conservation, research and introduction project.

- empowering the South African public, communities and organisations through participation, environmental education, capacity-building, research and information services
- working with all relevant stakeholders and spheres of government in the spirit of good governance
- ensuring that all international participation and obligations are undertaken in accordance with South Africa's environmental policies and principles.

Other Departments involved include Agriculture, Water Affairs and Forestry, Minerals and Energy, and Health.

At regional level, the provincial conservation agencies are major role-players, and independent statutory organisations such as the South African National Parks (SANParks) and National Botanical Institute (NBI) are valuable partners in the country's total conservation effort.

In accordance with the National Environment Management Act, 1998 (Act 107 of 1998), the Committee for Environmental Co-ordination was established to harmonise the work of government departments on environmental issues, and to co-ordinate environmental implementation and national management plans at provincial level. The Act sets principles for effective management of the environment, which all organs of the

State have to comply with in their decision-making. The Act also makes provision for the National Environmental Advisory Forum, where stakeholders and experts advise the Minister of Environmental Affairs and Tourism on environmental-management issues.

The National Environmental Management Act, 1998 requires government and provincial departments to compile Environmental Implementation Plans (EIPs) and Environmental Management Plans, providing a legal framework for environmental development.

By June 2003, the national and provincial Departments of Environmental Affairs had put in place a comprehensive set of EIPs. The national Department has approached the Office of the Auditor-General for assistance in developing a mechanism to monitor compliance with the EIPs.

Reports providing the status of these EIPs can be viewed on the Department's website at www.environment.gov.za.

Each province may promulgate its own ordinances dealing with hunting, fishing and the protection of fauna and flora.

Environmental Impact Assessments (EIAs)

One of the most far-reaching interventions around co-operative governance in the last decade has been the introduction of EIAs. Some EIAs are considered at national level, but the vast majority of development applications are processed by provinces.

In 2002, the Department processed 88 EIAs, which comprised projects estimated at a value of R43 billion. These included:
- the N4 platinum toll highway which is to form part of the main link between the West Coast and East Coast
- Coega industrial development and Coega Harbour
- the construction of an underground natural gas pipeline from Mozambique's Temane and Pande gas fields to Secunda in Mpumalanga
- the development of support infrastructure within the Great Limpopo Transfrontier Park (GLTP)
- twenty-nine applications related to government's Poverty-Relief Programme.

State of the environment

The greatest challenge for South Africa and the rest of the world is to improve the quality of human life for both present and future generations, without depleting its natural resources. This can only be achieved through a healthy natural environment which supplies raw material; absorbs and treats waste products; and maintains water, soil and air quality.

Food security, water provision and climatic stability depend on having properly functioning ecosystems, stable levels of biodiversity, sustainable rates of resource extraction, and a minimal production of waste and pollution.

To this end, the United Nations (UN) General Assembly Conference on Environment and Development developed and adopted Agenda 21 in 1992 as the global strategy for sustainable development.

South Africa has taken several steps to implement Agenda 21 at national and local level, including reforming environmental policies, ratifying international agreements and participating in many global and regional sustainable-development initiatives.

World Wetlands Day: 2 February
National Water Week: 19 March to 25 March
Earth Day: 20 March
World Water Day: 22 March
World Meteorological Day: 23 March
World Environment Day: 5 June
World Desertification Day: 17 June
National Arbor Week: 1 to 7 September
International Day for the Protection of the Ozone Layer: 16 September
World Tourism Day: 27 September
World Habitat Day: 4 October
National Marine Day: 20 October

Environmental management

World Summit on Sustainable Development (WSSD)

Johannesburg hosted the WSSD, which took place from 26 August to 4 September, 2002.

Representatives of nearly 200 countries with widely divergent positions attended. The agreements reached in Johannesburg are a guide to action that will take forward the UN Millennium Summit Declaration's goal of halving world poverty by 2015, as well as decisions taken by world bodies since the Rio Earth Summit in 1992.

Among the victories of the Summit was the launch of over 300 partnerships, including 32 energy initiatives, 21 water programmes and 32 programmes for biodiversity and ecosystem management.

The biggest success was getting the world to turn the UN Millennium Declaration into a concrete set of programmes and mobilise funds for these programmes. The WSSD focused on the most marginalised sectors of society, including women, youth, indigenous people and people with disabilities.

The Implementation Plan includes programmes to deliver water, energy, healthcare, agricultural development, a better environment for the world's poor, and targets for the reduction of poverty and protection of the environment.

New targets set at the Summit will have enormous impact:
- The number of people without basic sanitation will be halved by 2015. In 2001, the world's leaders agreed to halve the number of people without access to safe drinking water by 2015.
- Biodiversity loss is to be reversed by 2010, and collapsed fish stocks restored by 2015.
- Chemicals with a detrimental health impact will be phased out by 2020.
- Energy services will be extended to 35% of African households over the next 10 years.

The Minister of Environmental Affairs and Tourism, Mr Mohammed Valli Moosa, chaired the 11th Session of the UN Commission on Sustainable Development in New York in April 2003.

Ministerial input at the meeting, a follow-up to the WSSD, included aspects such as ways in which the sectors involved in the WSSD should address the issues raised.

A Multi-Year Programme of Work was drawn up according to different thematic clusters for the work which is to be done by 2016/17. The main themes identified are as follows:
- 2004/05: Water, Sanitation and Human Settlements
- 2006/07: Energy for Sustainable and Industrial Development, Air Pollution/Atmosphere Climate Change
- 2008/09: Agriculture, Rural Development, Land, Drought, Desertification, Africa
- 2010/11: Transport, Chemicals, Waste Management, Mining and a 10-Year framework of programmes on Sustainable Consumption and Production Patterns
- 2012/13: Forests, Biodiversity, Biotechnology, Tourism, Mountains
- 2014/15: Oceans and Seas, Marine Resources, Small Island Developing States, Disaster Management and Vulnerability
- 2016/17: Overall Appraisal of Implementation of Agenda 21, the Programme for the Further Implementation of Agenda 21, and the Johannesburg Plan of Implementation.

Biological diversity

South Africa enjoys the third-highest level of biodiversity in the world. The country's rich natural heritage is vast and staggering in its proportions. For example, over 3 700 marine species occur in South African waters and nowhere else in the world. The remarkable richness of South Africa's biodiversity is largely the result of the mix of tropical Mediterranean and temperate climates and habitats occurring in the country. Some 18 000 vascular plant species occur within South Africa's boundaries, of which 80% occur nowhere else. More plant species occur within 22 000 hectares (ha) of the

Biodiversity values in South Africa

	Biome	Veld type	Number of species				
			Plant	Mammal	Bird	Amphibian	Reptile
Eastern Cape	6	29	6 383	156	384	51	57
Free State	3	19	3 001	93	334	29	47
Gauteng	2	9	2 826	125	326	25	53
KwaZulu-Natal	3	19	5 515	177	462	68	86
Limpopo	2	14	4 239	239	479	44	89
Mpumalanga	2	20	4 593	160	464	48	82
Northern Cape	4	20	4 916	139	302	29	53
North West	2	10	2 483	138	384	27	59
Western Cape	6	19	9 489	153	305	39	52

Source: Department of Environmental Affairs and Tourism. Plant defined as angiosperm and gymnosperm. Data taken from the National Herbarium Pretoria Computerised Information System database, May 2003.
Biome counts taken from Rutherford (1997) with thicket from Low & Rebelo (1998)
Veld types taken from Acocks (1988)

Cape Peninsula National Park than the whole of the British Isles or the whole of New Zealand.

In addition to South Africa's extraordinarily varied plant life, a wealth of animal life exists in the region. The country hosts an estimated 5,8% of the world's total mammal species, 8% of bird species, 4,6% of the global diversity of reptile species, 16% of the total number of marine fish species, and 5,5% of the world's classified insect species. In terms of the number of mammal, bird, reptile and amphibian species which occur in this country only, South Africa is the 24th-richest country in the world and the fifth-richest in Africa.

The National Environmental Management: Biodiversity Bill was approved by the Cabinet for submission to Parliament in April 2003.
The Bill aims to ensure the management and conservation of the biological diversity of South Africa, the sustainable use of biological resources, and the fair and equitable sharing of benefits arising from the use and application of genetic resources and material.
The Bill also provides for the establishment of the National Biodiversity Institute, replacing the National Botanical Institute. The Biodiversity Institute will regulate and manage botanical gardens, and act as an advisory and consultative body to State organs and biodiversity stakeholders on matters relating to biodiversity.
The National Council of Provinces approved the Bill in August 2003.

South Africa is home to a diversity of spiders – 66 families comprising more than 6 000 species. The country also boasts 175 species of scorpion.

South Africa's marine life is similarly diverse, partly as a result of the extreme contrast between the water masses on the east and west coasts. Three water masses – the cold Benguela Current, the warm Agulhas Current and oceanic water – make the region one of the most oceanographically heterogeneous in the world. According to the *White Paper on the Conservation and Sustainable Use of South Africa's Biological Diversity*, over 10 000 plant and animal species – almost 15% of the coastal species known worldwide – are found in South African waters, with about 12% of these occurring nowhere else.

The easiest way to describe the country's natural heritage is on the basis of a systematic classification of regions, or biomes. A biome can be defined as a broad ecological unit representing a major life zone, which extends over a large area, and contains relatively uniform plant and animal life closely connected with environmental conditions, especially climate.

The White Paper states that South Africa is one of six countries in the world with an entire plant kingdom within its national confines. Known as the Cape Floral Kingdom, this area

Environmental management

has the highest recorded species diversity for any similar-sized temperate or tropical region in the world.

Other biomes in the country are also of global conservation significance; for example, one-third of the world's succulent plant species is found in South Africa.

There are eight major terrestrial biomes, or habitat types, in South Africa. These biomes can, in turn, be divided into 70 veld types.

The degree to which each of these biomes is threatened varies, depending on the fertility of the soil, the economic value derived from use of the area, human population pressures, and the extent to which the biome is conserved in protected areas.

Savanna biome

This biome is an area of mixed grassland and trees, and is generally known as bushveld.

In the Northern Cape and Kalahari sections of this biome, the most distinctive trees are the camel thorn (*Acacia erioloba*) and the camphor bush (*Tarchonanthus camphoratus*). In Limpopo, the portly baobab (*Adansonia digitata*) and the candelabra tree (*Euphorbia ingens*) dominate. The central bushveld is home to species such as the knob thorn (*Acacia nigrescens*), bushwillow (*Combretum spp.*), monkey thorn (*Acacia galpinii*), mopani (*Colophospermum mopane*) and wild fig (*Ficus spp.*) In the valley bushveld of the south, euphorbias and spekboom trees (*Portulacaria afra*) predominate.

An abundance of wild fruit trees provide food for many birds and animals in the savanna biome.

Grey louries, hornbills, shrikes, flycatchers and rollers are birds typical of the northern regions. The subtropical and coastal areas are home to Knysna louries, purple-crested louries and green pigeons. Raptors occur throughout the biome.

The larger mammals include lion, leopard, cheetah, elephant, buffalo, zebra, rhinoceros, giraffe, kudu, oryx, waterbuck, hippopotamus and many others.

Approximately 8,5% of the biome is protected. The Kruger National Park, Kgalagadi Transfrontier Park, Hluhluwe-Umfolozi Park, Greater St Lucia Wetlands Park (GSWLP), and other reserves are located in the savanna biome.

Nama-Karoo biome

This biome includes the Namaland area of Namibia and the Karoo area of South Africa.

Because of low rainfall, rivers are nonperennial. Cold and frost in winter and high temperatures in summer demand special adaptations from plants. The vegetation of this biome is mainly low shrubland and grass, with trees limited to water courses. The bat-eared fox, black-backed jackal, ostrich, suricate and ground squirrel are typical of the area.

Only 1% of the Nama-Karoo biome falls within officially protected areas, of which the Karoo and Augrabies National Parks are the largest.

Overgrazing and easily eroded soil surfaces are causing this semi-desert to creep slowly in on the neighbouring savanna and grassland biomes.

Grassland biome

This biome is a summer-rainfall area with heavy thunderstorms and hail, and frost in winter. A number of perennial rivers such as the Orange, Vaal, Pongola, Kei and Umzimvubu originate in, and flow through, the area. Trees

---

From 8 to 17 September 2003, South Africa, under the leadership of South African National Parks, hosted the Fifth World Parks Congress in Durban, KwaZulu-Natal – the single most important event of its kind for dealing with issues of conservation and environmental protection. South Africa was requested to host the event in recognition of the country's successful park management system and transfrontier parks initiatives.

The theme of the Congress was *Benefits Beyond Boundaries*.

Some 2 300 participants, including experts in the field of protected area management from across the world, attended.

are scarce and are found mainly on hills and along river beds. Karee (*Rhus lancea*), wild currant (*Rhus pyroides*), white stinkwood (*Celtis africana*) and several acacia species are the most common.

The grassland biome has the third-largest number of indigenous plant species in the country.

Eight mammal species endemic to South Africa occur in a wild state in this biome. Three of these, namely the black wildebeest, blesbok and eland, do not occur outside the grassland biome.

The area is internationally recognised as an area of high species endemicity insofar as birds are concerned. Birds commonly found in the area include the black korhaan, blue crane, guinea-fowl and other grassland birds.

Only 1,1% of the grassland biome is officially protected. The wilderness areas of the KwaZulu-Natal Drakensberg are the most significant.

Succulent Karoo biome

One of the natural wonders of South Africa is the annual blossoming of the Namaqualand wild flowers (mainly of the family *Asteraceae*), which transforms the semi-desert of the Northern Cape into a fairyland. After rain, the drab landscape is suddenly covered from horizon to horizon with a multicoloured carpet (from August to October, depending on the rainfall).

This is a winter-rainfall area with extremely dry and hot summers. Succulents with thick, fleshy leaves are plentiful. Most trees have white trunks to reflect the heat.

The quiver tree (*Aloe dichotoma*) and the human-like elephant's trunk (*Pachypodium namaquanum*) are prominent in the Richtersveld. Grass is scarce.

The animal life is similar to that of neighbouring biomes (*fynbos* and Nama-Karoo).

The Richtersveld, Tankwa-Karoo and Namaqua National Parks have improved the conservation status of this biome considerably.

Fynbos biome

The *fynbos* biome is one of the six accepted floral kingdoms of the world. This region covers only 0,04% of the land surface of the globe.

Fynbos is found mainly in the Western Cape. It is a winter-rainfall area, and the *fynbos* vegetation is similar to that of mediterranean regions.

Fynbos is the name given to a group of evergreen plants with small, hard leaves (such as those in the Erica family). It is made up mainly of three groups of plants, namely the proteas, the heathers and the restios, and incorporates a diversity of plant species (more than 8 500 kinds, over 6 000 of which are endemic).

The *fynbos* biome is home to the protea, for which South Africa is renowned. The biome also contains flowering plants, now regarded as garden plants, such as freesia, tritonia, sparaxis and many others.

Protected areas cover 13,6% of the *fynbos* biome and include the Cape Peninsula and Agulhas National Parks.

The biome is not very rich in bird and mammal life, but does include the grysbok, the geometric tortoise, the Cape sugar-bird and the protea seed-eater, which are endemic to the area. The mountains are the habitat of the leopard, baboon, several types of eagle, honey-badger, caracal and rhebuck.

Forest biome

South Africa has few forests. The only forests of significance are the Knysna and Tsitsikamma forests in the Western and Eastern Cape, repectively.

Other reasonably large forest patches that are officially protected are in the high-rainfall areas of the eastern escarpment, and on the eastern seaboard. Forest giants such as yellowwood (*Podocarpus spp.*), ironwood (*Olea capensis*) and lemonwood (*Xymalos monospora*) dominate.

The indigenous forests are a magical world of ferns, lichens, and colourful forest birds such as the Knysna lourie, the endangered

Cape parrot and the rameron pigeon. Animals include the endangered samango monkey, the bushpig, the bushbuck and the delicate blue duiker.

Thicket biome

Subtropical thicket ranges from closed shrubland to low forest, dominated by evergreen succulent trees, shrubs and vines.

It is often impenetrable and has little herbaceous cover. Roughly 20% of the species in the thicket biome are endemic to the biome.

Desert biome

True desert is found under very harsh environmental conditions which are even more extreme than those found in the succulent Karoo and the Nama-Karoo biomes. The climate is characterised by summer rainfall, but also high levels of summer aridity. Rainfall is highly variable from year to year. Desert is found mostly in Namibia, although it does occur in South Africa in the lower Orange River valley.

The vegetation of the desert biome is characterised by the dominance of annual plants (often annual grasses). This means that after a rare season of abundant rain, the desert plains can be covered with a sea of short annual grass, whereas in drier years, the plains appear bare with the annual plants persisting in the form of seeds.

Perennial plants are usually encountered in specialised habitats associated with local concentrations of water. Common examples of such habitats are broad drainage lines or washes. Nearer to the coast, the role of coastal fog also governs the distribution of certain species commonly associated with the desert.

The desert biome includes an abundant insect fauna which includes many tenebrionid beetles, some of which can utilise fog water. There are also various vertebrates including reptiles, springbuck, ostrich, gemsbuck, snakes and geckos.

Some areas in the desert biome are formally protected in the Richtersveld National Park.

Preserving genetic diversity

South Africa, with its wide range of natural resources, is an ideal proponent to apply the principle of sustainable use of these resources. There is a wide range of benefits derived from the conservation of biodiversity. A large portion of the South African population is directly dependent on biological resources for subsistence purposes, including the gathering, harvesting or hunting of plants and animals as a source of food, medicine, shelter and trade. The use of biological resources therefore provides a buffer against poverty as well as a source of economic gain. A number of industries in the country, such as the fishing, hunting, wild flower and wood-harvesting industries, are directly dependent on its biological resources.

Local communities benefit in various ways from the trade in biological resources. For example, the Makuleke community in the Kruger National Park had their land returned to them and are now developing infrastructure for tourists, as well as benefitting from consumptive wildlife resource-use.

South Africa is the fastest-growing tourism destination in the world, with 6,4 million tourists visiting the country during 2002. Overseas arrivals increased by 20,1% (just over 1,8 million people) during 2002.

Cape Town installed one of the first 'penguin' crossings in the world in 2003.

The crossing is aimed at reducing penguin fatalities in the Simon's Town area.

The colony of African penguins making use of the crossing live in a naturally protected area at Boulders Beach, which forms part of the Cape Peninsula National Park.

By June 2003, the estimated penguin population in the area was estimated at 3 600 birds – from just two breeding pairs in 1982.

The main attractions are nature-based tourism facilities such as national parks and private game reserves.

There are some 9 000 privately owned game ranches in South Africa, expanding at a rate of 300 000 ha per annum. The contribution of these areas in maintaining South Africa's unique biodiversity is incalculable.

The following are examples of the success that has been achieved in South Africa, in terms of the conservation of endangered species by various role-players:

White rhinoceros

South Africa hosts the most stable population of the southern white rhinoceros in Africa. Through concerted efforts by conservation agencies such as Ezemvelo KwaZulu-Natal Wildlife and SANParks, the population of this species increased from less than 20 in 1910 to almost 8 000 in 1997, in approximately 60 populations across South Africa. Almost a third of the animals are in private ownership. A significant number of animals have also been relocated to destinations outside the country.

African elephant

In 1910, the elephant population in South Africa was reduced to four remnant populations covering an area of less than 10 000 ha. Due to the efforts of judicious management practices, of among others, SANParks, the number of elephants had increased to more than 11 300 in 1998, in approximately 60 locations throughout the country.

With over 500 bird species, including black coucals, narina trogons, Pel's fishing owls, crowned eagles, black eagles and the African finfoot, the Kruger National Park is a birding paradise. The Park has tapped into its wealth of bird species to boost its income. The Park hosts an annual Big Birding Day, which is becoming a very popular event.

The Park is home to an impressive number of species: 336 trees, 49 fish, 34 amphibians, 114 reptiles and 147 mammals.

Cycads

This genus is very popular among collectors, causing it to be under severe threat. Through actions such as legislation and the refining of *ex situ* conservation efforts, artificial propagation has been achieved. By mid-2002, more than 200 000 seedlings of endangered species of the genus had been sold to the general public, and the threat to the wild populations has largely been reduced.

Cheetah

Through the efforts of formal conservation agencies assisted by private individuals, South Africa has managed to breed large numbers of this species in captivity. Relocation of these animals to protected areas, both in and outside South Africa, is common practice.

Wild dog

The wild dog, *Lycaon pictus*, is the most endangered large carnivore species in South Africa.

On 1 January 2000, there were at least 177 wild dogs living in 25 packs in the Kruger National Park and neighbouring reserves.

Conservation areas

South Africa boasts some 403 terrestrial protected areas, with a total area of 6 638 658 ha or about 5,44% of its total land area. Twenty-two of these protected areas are national parks, and their total area makes up 53,09% of South Africa. A further 13,82% are State forests in terms of the National Forests Act, 1998 (Act 84 of 1998). Provinces are legally responsible for 30,51% of South Africa's protected area estate.

There are a number of management categories of protected areas in South Africa, which conform to the accepted categories of the World Conservation Union (IUCN).

The National Environment Management: Protected Areas Bill, which was tabled in Parliament in August 2003, seeks to establish a representative system of protected areas as part of a national strategy to protect South Africa's biological diversity, and to ensure that

Environmental management

biodiversity is able to bring about sustainable benefits for future generations.

The Bill will repeal the National Parks Act, 1976, (Act 57 of 1976), and provide for the continued existence of SANParks, which will continue to administer the National Parks Land Acquisition Fund.

It also enables the Minister to acquire private land by purchasing land rights for the creation of protected areas.

Four types of protected areas can be declared in terms of the Bill, including nature reserves, national parks and protected environments. It is intended that all terrestrial protected areas in South Africa, other than those established in terms of the National Forests Act, 1998, be catered for in the Bill.

Scientific reserves

Scientific reserves are sensitive and undisturbed areas managed for research, monitoring and maintenance of genetic sources. Access is limited to researchers and staff. Examples of such areas are Marion Island and the Prince Edward Islands near Antarctica.

Wilderness areas

These areas are extensive in size, uninhabited and underdeveloped, and access is strictly controlled since no vehicles are allowed. The highest management priority is the maintenance of the intrinsic wilderness character. Examples of wilderness areas are the Cedarberg Wilderness Area and Dassen Island in the Western Cape, and the Baviaanskloof Wilderness Area in the Eastern Cape.

National parks and equivalent reserves

SANParks manages a system of 20 national parks, representative of the country's important ecosystems and unique natural features. Commercial and tourism-conservation development, and the involvement of local communities, are regarded as performance indicators. These areas include national parks proclaimed in terms of the National Parks Act, 1976 (Act 57 of 1976), provincial parks and nature reserves, and indigenous State forests.

Some of these natural and scenic areas are extensive in size, and include large representative areas of at least one of the country's biomes. Since 1994, parks under SANParks have expanded by 166 071 ha.

The National Parks are: Kruger National Park, Kalahari Gemsbok National Park (part of the Kgalagadi Transfrontier Park), Addo Elephant National Park, Bontebok National Park, Mountain Zebra National Park, Golden Gate Highlands National, Tsitsikamma National Park, Augrabies Falls National Park, Karoo National Park, Wilderness National Lakes Area, West Coast National Park, Tankwa-Karoo National Park, Knysna National Lakes Area, Marakele National Park, Richtersveld National Park, Vhembe-Dongala National Park, Vaalbos National Park, Aghulhas National Park, Namaqua National Park, and Cape Peninsula National Park, whcih incorporates the Cape of Good Hope, Table Mountain and Silvermine Nature Reserves.

There are currently six Transfrontier Conservation Areas (TFCAs) along borders with neighbouring countries, at various stages of development: GLTP, Kgalagadi, Lubombo, Ais-Ais/Richtersveld, Maloti-Drakensberg and Limpopo-Shashe. These are conservation landmarks, significantly promoting regional

---

The Kruger National Park received more than a million tourists between April 2002 and March 2003, the largest number ever in its history.

The Park, which first opened to visitors in 1927, recorded a steep growth after 1994, with a record 954 732 visitors in the 1997/98 financial year.

One of the major events that attracted visitors to the Park was the total solar eclipse that took place on 4 December 2002.

THe far northern section of the Park was the only place in the world from which the eclipse's path of totality was completely visible. The Phabeni Gate was opened to the public in December 2002, creating easy access to the entire southern region.

South Africa Yearbook 2003/04

integration, greater biodiversity, environmental tourism and economic growth.

The proposed GLTP covers South Africa's Kruger National Park, Mozambique's Limpopo National Park and the Gonarezhou National Park in Zimbabwe.

Part of the fence dividing South Africa and Mozambique was removed in December 2002, following the signing of a treaty by President Thabo Mbeki, Mozambican President Joacquim Chissano and Zimbabwean President Robert Mugabe to formally establish the GLTP.

The signing ceremony sealed a two-year process of intensive preparations for the establishment of the 35 000 km^2 Park, referred to as Africa's 'super park'.

It is envisaged that the establishment of the GLTP will eventually lead to the development of a TFCA spanning 99 800 km^2.

President Mbeki and President Sam Nujoma of Namibia signed a treaty between the two neighbouring countries for the establishment of the Ais-Ais/Richtersveld Transfrontier Park on 1 August 2003.

The Park features the world's second largest canyon in the Fish River, a hot spring game park on the Namibian side, and spectacular arid and desert mountainous scenery in the South African part.

South African National Parks launched a R45-million poverty relief project at the Vhembe-Dongola National Park near Musina in Limpopo in May 2003.

Through funding from the Department of Environmental Affairs and Tourism, some 500 jobs will be created at the Park. The funds will also be used to establish a wide range of tourism facilities including rest camps, fences, roads and staff housing.

Mapungubwe was declared a World Heritage Site in July 2003. This means that the Vhembe-Dongola National Park now has international status, as the declaration specifies that the term 'site' means the larger cultural landscape, which includes the well-known Mapungubwe Archaeological Site.

The Park is the third largest TFCA in the Southern African Development Community (SADC) region.

On 22 August 2003, the Minister of Environmental Affairs and Tourism launched the Maloti-Drakensberg Conservation and Development Area in Lesotho. The project was conceived on 11 June 2001 when the two countries concluded an agreement for the purpose of conserving biological diversity and the promotion of sustainable development in the area. This was further bolstered by an injection of funds by the World Bank for reconstruction and development, as a result of which both countries co-signed the Global Environmental Trust Fund Grant Agreement.

South Africa has accepted the duty to make a positive and responsible contribution to the conservation of biodiversity and to the environment on a global scale. This is done through responsible participation in the affairs of the IUCN, Convention on the International Trade in Endangered Species (CITES), Ramsar Convention on Wetlands, the World Wildlife Fund, and other agencies.

National and cultural monuments

These are natural or cultural features, or both, and may include botanical gardens, zoological gardens, natural heritage sites and sites of conservation significance.

In May 1997, South Africa ratified the World Heritage Convention. The South Africa World Heritage Convention Committee is responsible for the identification of possible sites in South Africa and the co-ordination of the Convention.

The World Heritage Convention Act, 1999 (Act 49 of 1999), allows for cultural and natural sites in South Africa to be granted World Heritage status. The Convention obliges the South African Government to guarantee its implementation, ensure legal protection and develop management plans and institutional structures for periodic monitoring.

The Act makes the principles of the Convention applicable to South Africa's World

Environmental management

Size of South African National Parks

Park	Date proclaimed	Area in 1994	Area added since 1994 (ha)	Current size (ha)
Addo Elephant	1931	51 309	23 030	74 339
Agulhas	1999	0	5 690	5 690
Augrabies Falls	1966	11 743	29 933	41 676
Bontebok	1931	2 786	0	2 786
Cape Peninsula	1998	0	13 450	22 100
Golden Gate Highlands	1963	11 633	0	11 633
Kalahari Gemsbok (now part of Kgalagadi Transfrontier)	1931	959 103	0	959 103
Karoo	1979	41 047	36 047	77 094
Knysna National Lakes Area	1985	15 000	0	15 000
Kruger	1926	1 962 362	0	1 962 362
Marakele	1993	37 035	13 691	50 726
Mountain Zebra	1937	6 536	18 127	24 633
Richtersveld	1991	162 445	0	162 445
Tankwa-Karoo	1986	27 064	16 835	43 899
Tsitsikamma	1964	63 942	0	63 942
Vaalbos	1986	22 697	0	22 697
Vhembe-Dongola	1998	0	5 356	5 356
West Coast	1985	32 361	3 912	36 273
Wilderness	1985	10 600	0	10 600
Total				3 592 384

Source: SANParks

Heritage sites and further provides for the adequate protection and conservation of these sites to promote tourism in a culturally and environmentally responsible way.

In December 1999, Robben Island, the GSWLP and the hominid sites at Swartkrans, Sterkfontein and Kromdraai, which had become known as the Cradle of Humankind, were proclaimed World Heritage sites by the United Nations Educational, Scientific and Cultural Organisation.

The Ukhahlamba-Drakensberg Park was nominated as a mixed site. This was the first mixed (natural and cultural) site to be nominated by South Africa, and became the 23rd mixed site worldwide to achieve World Heritage Site status.

The Ukhahlamba-Drakensberg Park has a number of outstanding natural features linked to the geomorphic history of the subcontinent, including the high altitude and unique southern African alpine-tundra vegetation and its associated endemic palaeo-invertebrates. In addition to these natural assets, and located within its original natural setting and ecosystems, is one of the world's greatest rock art collections.

In July 2003, Mapungubwe cultural landscape became the fifth heritage site.

Mapungubwe is situated at the confluence of the Shashe and Limpopo Rivers in Limpopo. The area includes the archaeological sites of Schroda, K2 and Mapungubwe.

Successive capitals of the Mapungubwe civilisation inhabited the area between 900 and 1 290 AD. The kingdom was a sophisticated, class-based society built on wealth generated by controlling trade into the Indian Ocean's trade network. At its peak there were probably 5 000 people living at Mapungubwe, which has been called the 'first southern African kingdom'.

By late 2003, the number of World Heritage Sites stood at 754. A total of 149 were natural sites, 582 cultural sites, and 23 mixed. Twenty-three of these were regarded as sites of outstanding universal value.

Habitat and wildlife management areas

These areas are subject to human intervention, based on research into the requirements of specific species for survival. They include conservancies, provincial, regional or private reserves created for the conservation of species habitats or biotic communities, marshes, lakes, and nesting and feeding areas.

Protected land and seascapes

These areas are products of the harmonious interaction of people and nature, and include natural environments protected in terms of the Environment Conservation Act, 1989 (Act 73 of 1989), scenic landscapes, and historical urban landscapes.

Sustainable-use areas

These areas emphasise the utilisation of products on a sustainable basis in protected areas such as the Kosi Bay Lake system in KwaZulu-Natal. Nature areas in private ownership are proclaimed and managed to curtail undesirable development in areas with high aesthetic or conservation potential.

Conservancies are formed to involve the ordinary landowner in conservation. One or more landowners can establish a conservancy where conservation principles are integrated with normal farming activities.

Wetlands

Wetlands include a wide range of inland and coastal habitats – from mountain bogs and fens and midland marshes to swamp forests and estuaries, linked by green corridors of streambank wetlands.

Wetlands were previously regarded as unproductive and even unhealthy wastelands. Today it is understood that, if well managed, wetlands are essential in meeting the needs of a growing population.

South Africa became a contracting party to the Ramsar Convention in 1975, and the country's Ramsar sites include the Nylsvlei Nature Reserve, Blesbokspruit, Barberspan, Seekoeivlei, the Ukhahlamba-Drakensberg Park, Ndumo Game Reserve, the Kosi Bay System, Lake Sibaya, the turtle beaches and coral reefs of Tongaland, the St Lucia System, Wilderness Lakes, De Hoop Vlei, De Mond State Forest, Langebaan, Verlorenvlei and Orange River Mouth Wetland.

In 2003, the Verloren Valley Wetland in Mpumalanga became the 17th wetland to be registered by Ramsar.

Working for Wetlands is implementing a rehabilitation project in the Verloren Valley Reserve, in partnership with the Mpumalanga Parks Board. The Working for Water Programme is also being implemented in the area.

The Directorate: Biodiversity Management of the Department of Environmental Affairs and Tourism is responsible for the South African Wetlands Conservation Programme. The Programme has been developed to ensure that South Africa's obligations are met in terms of the Ramsar Convention and the aspects concerning aquatic ecology under the Convention on Biological Diversity.

The Programme is aimed at building on past efforts to protect wetlands in South Africa against degradation and destruction, while striving for the ideal of wise and sustainable use of resources, to ensure that the ecological and socio-economic functions of wetlands are sustained for the future.

South Africa is a member of Wetlands International, an international body dedicated to conserving the world's wetlands.

Botanical gardens

The NBI, with its head office at Kirstenbosch National Botanical Garden in Cape Town, is an

Environmental management

autonomous State-aided Institute, which collects, displays and cultivates plants indigenous to South Africa; undertakes and promotes research into indigenous plants and related matters; studies and cultivates endangered plant species; promotes utilisation of the economic potential of indigenous plants; and runs environmental education programmes.

The NBI manages eight botanical gardens in five of the nine provinces. The largest, and the site of the Institute's headquarters, is Kirstenbosch, on the eastern slopes of Table Mountain in Cape Town. It houses 5 300 indigenous plant species, and was voted one of the top seven botanical gardens in the world at the World Botanic Gardens Congress in 2000.

The other gardens are the Karoo Desert in Worcester, Harold Porter in Betty's Bay, Free State in Bloemfontein, Natal in Pietermaritzburg, Lowveld in Nelspruit, Witwatersrand in Roodepoort, and the Pretoria National Botanical Garden. The latter houses the National Herbarium of South Africa, the largest in the southern hemisphere. Here, research is conducted on 750 000 specimens of southern African plants, 150 000 tropical African specimens, 50 000 others from around the world, and 25 000 cultivated specimens. There are also regional herbaria in Durban and at the Kirstenbosch Research Centre.

The NBI has two main libraries, the Mary Gunn Library in Pretoria and the Harry Molteno Library at Kirstenbosch, which are valuable sources of information on southern African flora and related topics.

Some municipalities have botanical gardens which are not controlled by the NBI. These include The Wilds and Melville Koppies in Johannesburg, and the Municipal Durban Botanic Gardens.

The Johannesburg Botanical Garden owns one of the biggest collections of lithops in the world. These are found only in the southern regions of Africa.

During 2002, the NBI set up the Biodiversity Division, which is to play a major role in linking biodiversity management with the socio-economic development needs of the country.

The NBI is about to embark on an extensive capital development programme in the Pretoria, Witwatersrand and Lowveld Botanical Gardens, as well as entering into major research partnerships in the Cape Floral Kingdom and succulent Karoo biome.

The Kirstenbosch National Botanical Garden is in the process of setting up the Centre for Home Gardening, which will feature an indigenous retail nursery.

A new commercial centre, featuring a nursery, will be developed at the Witwatersrand Botanical Gardens.

Botanists at the NBI at the Compton Herbarium, Kirstenbosch have discovered more than 160 new species of southern African plants over the past decade.

These include several species of erica, gladiolus and other *fynbos* plants, two freesias, the second species of amaryllis to be named in 250 years, and, most astonishingly, a new clivia.

Zoological gardens

The National Zoological Gardens of South Africa in Pretoria, or the Pretoria Zoo, celebra-

---

The World Bank announced in March 2003 that it would commit about R62 million towards the creation of a massive transfrontier conservation and development programme involving areas in the Eastern Cape, KwaZulu-Natal, the Free State and Lesotho.

The conserved areas include the Ukhahlamba-Drakensberg World Heritage Site, Golden Gate National Park, QwaQwa National Park, Sterkfontein Dam Nature Reserve and conserved areas within Lesotho.

The programme aims to put a management strategy in place for the whole region as well as create sustainable economic activity for the people who live there.

The conservation bodies from all four provinces, along with South African National Parks, will be involved in the project and will contribute portions of their operating budgets to add to the World Bank funds.

This will bring the total amount to be utilised over the next five years to R264 million.

ted its centenary in October 1999. It is the only zoo in South Africa with national status and is a member of the American Zoo Association, the World Association of Zoos and Aquariums, the Pan-African Association of Zoological Gardens, Aquaria and Botanical Gardens, the International Union of Zooculturists and the International Association of Zoo Educators.

The Pretoria Zoo, considered to be one of the 10 best in the world, extends over an area of about 80 ha. In 2001, the Zoo attracted 488 168 visitors.

It has breeding centres in Mokopane in Limpopo, and Lichtenburg in the North West, where many endangered animal species are bred.

By mid-2003, the Zoo's collection included 526 specimens of 96 mammal species, 1 136 specimens of 157 bird species, 4 007 specimens of 303 fish species, 40 specimens of 14 invertebrate species, 333 specimens of 80 reptile species, and 87 specimens of six amphibian species. The animal collections at the two game-breeding centres include 1 821 specimens of 62 mammal species and 56 specimens of 22 bird species.

The National Zoological Gardens of South Africa undertook the creation of a zoo and animal park at the Emerald Safari Resort and Casino in Vanderbijlpark. The resulting Animal World comprises 314 ha consisting of a game park and zoo, which house, among others, rhino, buffalo, hippo, wild dog and a variety of bird and animal species.

The Emerald Safari Resort has 277 specimens of 40 mammal species, 186 specimens of 49 bird species, 74 species of 25 reptile species, and six specimens of three species of amphibians.

All the animals were provided by the National Zoo and its two satellite breeding centres.

The Johannesburg Zoological Gardens, covering some 54 ha, has an animal collection which includes about 300 species represented by some 1 900 specimens. The animals are kept in open-air enclosures, separated from the public by dry or water moats. The enclosures include the internationally acclaimed gorilla complex, the pachyderm section and the section for large carnivores.

Of particular interest are the African elephants, golden lion tamarins and sitatunga.

The Johannesburg Zoo has gained international recognition for animal-breeding programmes with numerous species, including the red panda, African wild cats and grysbok.

Breeding centres

There are a number of breeding centres in South Africa. The National Zoological Gardens of South Africa is responsible for the management of the Lichtenburg Game Breeding Centre, which covers an area of some 6 000 ha, and the Game Breeding Centre near Mokopane, covering an area of 1 500 ha. The main aim of the two centres is to supplement the Zoo's breeding programme for various endangered animals, and to supplement the Zoo's own animal collection.

The Lichtenburg Game Breeding Centre houses, among others, Père David's deer, pygmy hippopotamus, white rhino, the endangered addax, and scimitar-horned and Arabian oryx. Large herds of impala, springbuck, zebra, blesbuck and red hartebeest also roam the area.

About 32 ha of the wetland area in the Centre have been developed into a system of

---

A breathtaking sandcastle sculpture of Table Mountain and a tapestry of coastal *fynbos* species were featured in South Africa's exhibit at the prestigious Chelsea Flower Show in London in May 2003.

The exhibit, entitled *Cape of Flowers*, was unique with several flora species endemic to Table Mountain being used, including the pride of Table Mountain disa (*Disa uniflora*) and the silverleaf tree (*Leucodendron argenteum*).

A ton of beach sand from Cape Town had to be shipped to London to make the sculpture of Table Mountain and surrounding beaches.

In 2002, South Africa won gold at Chelsea for the 25th consecutive year.

Environmental management

dams and pans, which serves as a natural haven for waterbirds such as spoonbills, kingfishers, ibises and herons.

The Mokopane Game Breeding Centre is home to an abundance of exotic and indigenous fauna such as lemurs, rare tsessebe, roan antelope, cheetah and black rhino.

The renowned De Wildt Cheetah Breeding and Research Centre, situated near Pretoria, is best known for its highly successful captive-breeding programme. De Wildt also breeds a number of rare and endangered African species, the most spectacular of which is the magnificent king cheetah. It also plays a major role in the breeding of wild dogs.

The Hoedspruit Research and Breeding Centre for Endangered Species in Mpumalanga is another well-known breeding centre. The Centre caters for, among others, five species of vulture: Cape griffins, whitebacked, hooded, whiteheaded and lappetfaced vultures.

Aquaria

There are well-known aquaria in Pretoria, Port Elizabeth, Cape Town and Durban.

The Aquarium and Reptile Park of the Pretoria Zoo is the largest inland aquarium in Africa, with the largest collection of freshwater fish. It is also the only aquarium in South Africa that exhibits a large variety of marine fish in artificial sea water.

The Port Elizabeth Oceanarium is the home of seal, dolphin and fish families indigenous to the Eastern Cape coastline. East London also has a smaller aquarium, which is well worth visiting.

At the Two Oceans Aquarium situated at the Victoria and Alfred Waterfront, Cape Town, more than 3 000 specimens represent some 300 species of fish, invertebrates, mammals, birds and plants supported by the waters in and around the Cape coast.

This is the largest aquarium in South Africa, housing more than 300 marine species in impressive and informative displays.

Sea World, comprising a dolphinarium and aquarium, is situated on the beach front at Marine Parade in Durban. The aquarium has a shark and reef tank with large turtles and a variety of fish, including kingfish and stingrays.

Snake parks

The Hartbeespoort Dam Snake and Animal Park on the northern shore of the Hartbeespoort Dam near Pretoria has a fine reptile collection.

The Transvaal Snake Park at Midrand, between Pretoria and Johannesburg, houses up to 150 species of snake and other reptiles and amphibians from southern Africa and elsewhere. The emphasis is on the development of breeding programmes for animals in captivity.

In Durban, the Fitzsimons Snake Park houses more than 100 exotic and indigenous species of snake.

The Port Elizabeth Snake Park has a wide variety of South African and foreign reptiles, including boa constrictors, pythons, crocodiles, lizards and deadly venomous snakes such as cobras, mambas and rattlers.

The Aquarium and Reptile Park complex situated at the Pretoria Zoo houses 80 reptile species from all over the world.

Marine resources

South Africa's coastline covers some 3 000 km. Of this, only a very small portion is protected in terms of being closed to certain activities.

The Chief Directorate: Marine and Coastal Management of the Department of Environmental Affairs and Tourism is the central government agency primarily responsible for the administration of marine fisheries in South Africa. This includes marine research, exploitation control, formulating policy advice, and managing a fleet of research ships, including the *MV SA Agulhas*. This ship also serves as a replenishment ship for the South African

Antarctic base and various Southern Ocean islands.

The research component of Marine and Coastal Management advises on the utilisation of living marine resources and the conservation of marine ecosystems, interacting with decision-makers, role-players, and local and international scientific communities.

Inland fisheries fall under the jurisdiction of the provincial administrations or the national Department of Agriculture. Some aspects of estuarine research and management, as well as all aspects of mariculture (aquaculture in the sea), fall under the control of Marine and Coastal Management.

South Africa's rich coastal waters are an important source of nutrition and sustainable livelihood for many coastal communities. For this reason, the country's marine resources must be carefully managed to avoid over-exploitation, and to ensure that the maximum benefit is derived to achieve sustainable economic growth.

South Africa's fisheries are considered to be among the best-managed in the world. The Department has followed a precautionary approach in the management of fish stocks. This, coupled with a policy of stock-rebuilding, has yielded significant dividends. For example, in the pelagic fish industry, oceanographic surveys indicate that populations of pilchard and anchovy are at record highs. A stock-rebuilding strategy for west coast rock lobster, which was instituted in 1996, appears to have paid off sooner than expected. In 2002, fishery scientists measured an increase in two out of the three indices that are used to determine the status of west coast rock lobster populations. This has resulted in the Total Allowable Catch (TAC) for west coast rock lobster being increased by 25%, and the opening up of further areas for limited commercial fishing.

By mid-2003, the process of allocating medium-term commercial fishing rights had been substantially completed. Some 2 200 fishing rights had been allocated, of which 60% went to historically disadvantaged persons.

In a recent landmark decision, the Supreme Court of Appeal pronounced favourably upon the allocation process. The total number of fishing rights allocated increased from 400 to 2 200, 1 700 of which are allocated to small, medium and micro enterprises. Communities in KwaZulu-Natal and the Eastern Cape, many of whom are women, have been issued with 859 subsistence-fishing rights. In the Eastern Cape, 337 women have received subsistence-fishing rights, and in the Western Cape, 152 limited commercial-fishing-rights have been allocated to women.

At the end of August 2003, it was announced that an additional 341 fishers had been allocated rights in the linefish sector, following an appeal process.

In protecting South Africa's valuable fish stocks, the Department has recorded a number of significant successes.

In February 2003, the first Environmental Court in South Africa was opened. Strategically situated on the south coast, at Hermanus in the Western Cape, this Court has already had an impact on poaching, due to a high rate of successful prosecutions, the imposition of jail sentences, and the seizure of assets.

The deployment of scientific observers on at least 15% of offshore fishing voyages began in South Africa in July 2002. The Offshore Resources Observer Programme is contributing to an improved understanding of fishing operations, and is likely to provide Marine and Coastal Management researchers with a vastly improved set of data with which to manage offshore fisheries.

State of marine resources

Small pelagic fish

South Africa's pelagic fishing industry, which catches pilchards for canning, and anchovy for reduction to fishmeal, a major constituent in animal foods, had a frustrating year in 2002.

Environmental management

Although fishmeal prices were high in 2002, and there was an exceptional abundance of pilchard and anchovy in South African waters, bad weather, mixed shoals, and the poor availability of fish made it nearly impossible for the industry to catch their full allocations.

Demersal fish

Owing to the poor environmental conditions that prevailed in 2002, catch rates in the offshore hake fishery were particularly poor. For the first time in many years, several thousand tons (t) of hake had not been landed by the fishing industry before the close of the season. The TAC for 2003 was reduced slightly from 166 000 t, and there will be a further reduction of 6 000 t over the next two years.

West coast rock lobster

The TAC for the west coast rock lobster fishery increased by 25% in 2002, owing to an improvement in the status of stock.

The completion of the appeal process in May 2002 saw the number of limited commercial-right-holders in the west coast rock lobster fishing industry increase from 321 to 500. Limited commercial fishing rights of between 200 and 1 500 kg each were allocated to historically disadvantaged fishers in five fishing zones between Port Nolloth and Cape Hangklip.

The Department has also opened a new area for the commercial exploitation of west coast rock lobster. Limited commercial rights will be allocated predominantly to historically disadvantaged fishers in Hermanus (40 t), Gans Bay (40 t), and Kleinmond (20 t).

South Africa celebrated World Environment Day on 5 June 2003 under the theme *My Environment, My Life*.

The year 2003 was declared the International Year of Freshwater by the United Nations General Assembly.

Activities organised by the various provinces focused on the importance of wetlands and water.

These included hosting a youth environmental *lekgotla*, anti-litter campaigns, environment marches and clean-up campaigns.

South coast rock lobster

In 2002, Marine and Coastal Management scientists recorded a turnaround in the prospects of the south coast rock lobster fishery, which had been plagued by declining catch rates and annual cuts in the TAC for 12 years. Two consecutive increases in catch rates were recorded in 2001 and 2002.

Fishing rights held by Hout Bay Fishing Industries and a joint venture partner were revoked and reallocated to the remaining right-holders in this fishery on a *pro rata* basis.

Squid

Eastern Cape towns such as St Francis and Humansdorp have benefitted from one of the best squid fishing seasons ever recorded. It is estimated that 4 000 t of squid were landed between the opening of the season on 23 November 2002 and 1 January 2003. Squid shoals moved inshore and were highly available to the fishing fleet between Mossel Bay and East London.

Abalone

The impact that widespread poaching has had on abalone resources is amply demonstrated by the fishery-independent abalone survey that is carried out annually by Marine and Coastal Management scientists. Results indicate that the average density of abalone in the fishing zone between Hawston and Hermanus has dropped to 0,1 abalone per square metre – the lowest level ever recorded. This will impact on the further allocation of fishing rights in this sector.

In October 2003, the Department of Environmental Affairs and Tourism released its final policy on the allocation of commercial abalone fishing rights. Earlier, the Minister had announced a dramatic increase in fines for abalone poaching from the previous maximum of R40 000 to R800 000 as a measure to further deter abalone poaching.

The primary objectives of the policy are to ensure the long-term viability of the South

African commercial abalone fishery, and to sustain jobs in the commercial abalone fishery.

The TAC was reduced from 693 t in 2000 to 430 t for the 2002/03 season. In 2002, the Department determined that more than 1 000 t of abalone had been poached. In the first six months of 2003, the Department confiscated approximately 600 000 abalone (102 t).

The final policy makes provision for the allocation of commercial rights to three different categories. These are: divers; legal entities owned and managed by historically disadvantaged persons that previously held a medium-term commercial abalone right; and abalone-processing factories (i.e. fish-processing establishments that currently have a right to process wild abalone and that previously held a medium term commercial abalone right).

Rights will be allocated for a period of 10 years to divers and legal entities. Rights will be granted to abalone fish-processing factories for a period of three years. At the end of the three-year period, abalone fish-processing factories will not be allocated their own abalone allocations.

By mid-August 2003, the TAC was split into seven zones from Cape Columbine in the west to Cape Agulhas in the east. The Department was expected to divide each of these zones into smaller secondary zones.

Subsistence fishing
A community of approximately 5 200 people benefit directly from exemptions issued in December 2002 to 859 subsistence fishers from the Eastern Cape district of Hamburg, and to the Sokhulu subsistence fishers in KwaZulu-Natal, who harvest brown mussel and red bait. Community monitoring and co-management programmes have been established at Sokhulu and are proving highly successful.

Seabirds
In 2002, the Department drafted a National Plan of Action for reducing the incidental catch of seabirds in longline fisheries, after concern was raised over the number of seabirds, especially albatrosses, that are killed by longline fishing vessels in southern Africa.

The Plan sets out the required mitigation measures to reduce the mortality of seabirds to below an interim target level of 0,05 birds per 1 000 hooks cast by South Africa's longline fisheries for hake, tuna and swordfish, Patagonian toothfish and sharks.

Seaweed
Abalone farms are creating an enormous demand for fresh kelp fronds (leaves). Research into seaweed cultivation for use on abalone farms is being undertaken, to establish whether the nutrient-rich waste water from abalone farms can be effectively utilised to cultivate certain seaweeds for abalone feed. This would have the additional benefit of purifying waste-water, which could then be recirculated on the farm.

New opportunities
The Department plans to develop 12 new fisheries over the next five years. Some of the fisheries that have been earmarked are Eastern Cape abalone; limpets; ornamental fish; east coast rock lobster; sand soldier and Indian Ocean squid in KwaZulu-Natal; as well as a directed monk fishery.

Policies and guidelines for an experimental octopus fishery were developed in 2002, and

---

The Cabinet approved the Southern African Development Community (SADC) Protocol on Fisheries in February 2003.
  The Protocol will be tabled in Parliament for ratification.
  The objective of the Protocol is to promote responsible and sustainable use of living aquatic resources and ecosystems on its coastline in order to promote and enhance food security and human health; to safeguard the livelihood of fishing communities; to generate economic opportunities to ensure that future generations benefit from these renewable resources; and to alleviate poverty.

applications for experimental permits were expected to be called for in 2003.

The termination of the Japanese and Taiwanese fisheries agreements saw the departure of the foreign fleets in January 2003. This has opened the door for the development of the local tuna longline industry, which has struggled to establish itself under difficult conditions. The experimental tuna fishery will be brought to an end and longer-term fishing rights will be allocated to South Africans.

Did you know?
- South Africans buy over a million cans of pilchards every day.
- South Africa is the largest fishing nation in Africa. In 2000, it was ranked by the Food and Agricultural Organisation of the United Nations (UN) as the 27th largest producer of fish in the world, with a total catch of 643 812 t. China, with a production of 16 987 325 t, was ranked as the world's top fishing nation.
- At least 70% of the world's fisheries are either depleted or fully exploited, according to the UN Environment Programme.
- The west coast of southern Africa is home to the largest mainland seal colonies in the world, with nearly two million individual seals recorded in South Africa and Namibia.
- Marine scientists agree that the whole South African coast, sweeping down from the coral reefs of the Indian Ocean to the rich kelp beds of the Atlantic, is one of the richest, most biologically diverse and oceanographically complex marine environments on earth.
- South Africa has the most accessible coelacanth population in the world. A group of seven coelacanths was observed in underwater caves off the coast of Sodwana Bay in April 2002. The latest count, by a team of German scientists using submersible craft, estimates the size of the Sodwana Bay population at 18. Prior to 1938, scientists believed the coelacanth had been extinct for 70 million years.
- Elf or shad are one of South Africa's most popular angling fish. They are pursued by more than 300 000 anglers every year.
- Albatrosses are among the largest of flying birds. The largest is the wandering albatross with a wing span of up to 3,5 m, enabling it to soar for hours in the oceanic air currents.

Legislation

The Coastal Management Bill was drafted in 2002 and was expected to be presented for comment in 2003. The Bill provides for important interventions to regulate, enhance, preserve and rehabilitate sensitive or over-exploited coastal reserves. It also ensures equitable access to South Africa's coastline, and aligns South African legislation with international laws and conventions. The Marine Living Resources Act, 1998 (Act 18 of 1998), is in the process of being amended, to provide increased protection for certain linefish and other species.

Transformation

In his 2003 State of the Nation Address, President Thabo Mbeki referred to the fishing industry as being one of three industries that had shown positive signs with respect to Black Economic Empowerment.

The establishment of a bargaining council for the fishing industry, and the publication of a set of minimum conditions of employment for workers in the deep-sea and inshore trawling industries in 2002, are seen as historic steps forward for the industry.

The Marine and Coastal Management Branch is planning further transformation by working towards the National Charter for the South African Fishing Industry, and increasing the number of historically disadvantaged individuals who are trained in marine sciences every year. The existing recruitment, bursary, internship, and mentorship programmes will be maintained and strengthened.

Harbours

An extensive Harbour Repair and Maintenance Programme was initiated in 2002, following the completion of a full investigation into the state of South Africa's 12 fishing harbours. The National Treasury approved a budget of R83 million for the Programme. Extensive repairs have been carried out at St Helena Bay Harbour, one of the busiest fishing harbours on the west coast, and at the small fishing harbour of Gans Bay on the Cape south coast.

A further R18,3 million will be spent on the repair and improvement of harbours at Laaiplek, Kalk Bay, Hout Bay and Hermanus.

International relations

South Africa, through the Department of Environmental Affairs and Tourism, has adopted the Benguela Fisheries Interaction Training (BENEFIT) Programme and the Benguela Current Large Marine Ecosystem (BCLME) Programme as an integral part of the New Partnership for Africa's Development.

BENEFIT is a joint initiative between South Africa, Namibia and Angola to address fisheries, and other marine scientific investigations of important living marine resources and their interactions with the environment. Training of staff to undertake research and to achieve the levels of expertise necessary to provide advice to fisheries management is also an important objective of BENEFIT, which is generously funded by the Norwegian and German Governments.

While BENEFIT is very much a science-based programme, the BCLME Programme is a management-orientated programme aimed at boosting the infrastructure necessary to address cross-boundary problems associated with fishing, mining, oil exploitation, coastal development, biodiversity and pollution. The BCLME Programme is funded by the Global Environment Facility under its International Waters portfolio, and is implemented by the UN Development Programme.

The following important instruments have been acceded to and are in the process of being ratified:
- Agreement for the Implementation of the Provisions of the UN Convention on the Law of the Sea of 10 December 1982, relating to the Conservation and Management of Straddling Fish Stocks and Highly Migratory Fish Stocks (Straddling Stocks Agreement)
- Agreement on the Conservation of Albatrosses and Petrels
- Convention for the Protection, Management and Development of the Marine and Coastal Environment of the East African Region and Related Protocols (Nairobi Convention)
- Convention for Co-operation in the Protection and Development of the Marine and Coastal Environment of the West and Central African Region and Related Protocol (Abidjan Convention)
- SADC Protocol on Fisheries.

4x4s

There has been overwhelming public support for the implementation of strict measures that prohibit off-road vehicles from being driven on South Africa's beaches. Accordingly, the bird and animal life on South Africa's beaches and sensitive coastal areas has increased notably.

Conservation challenges

South Africa faces many of the problems experienced by developing countries, in which rapid industrialisation, population growth and urbanisation pose a threat to the quality of the environment.

The Department is reforming environmental law to introduce reform in biodiversity conservation, pollution, waste management and environmental planning.

Climatic and atmospheric change

According to the *State of the Environment Report,* South Africa is sensitive to climatic changes, and contributed about 1,2% to global warming in 1990.

The levels of sulphur dioxide, nitric oxide and ozone are, on average, within the accepted South African guidelines for human health and the prevention of direct ecosystem damage. The measured concentrations at ground level are not currently indicating an upward trend.

The Report states that there are, however, occasions, especially in the major urban areas, when the concentrations of sulphur dioxide, nitric oxide, ozone and smoke particles could lead to further health problems in people who have respiratory problems. No trend is apparent in the number of times these levels are being exceeded, but with more people living in urban areas, the impact is likely to increase.

Indoor air quality constitutes a health hazard in poorly ventilated dwellings without chimneys, where coal, wood, paraffin or dung is used as fuel. The electrification of houses is improving this situation, as is the general improvement in housing design and construction brought about by national housing policy.

According to the Report, susceptible terrestrial and freshwater ecosystems are likely to show the adverse effects of acid deposition in a few decades if the current emission rates of sulphur dioxide and nitric oxide continue or increase. The National Assembly approved accession to the Kyoto Protocol of the UN Framework Convention on Climate Change in March 2002. The accession to the Protocol demonstrates South Africa's commitment to further enhance the effectiveness of environmental legislation.

The Kyoto Protocol is a legally binding instrument whereby developed countries undertake to reduce greenhouse gas emissions by at least 5% of their 1990 levels. One of the Protocol's features is the incorporation of market-based mechanisms designed to allow developed countries to achieve their required emission reductions at the least possible cost.

The Department is operating three climatic change projects. A sum of $5 million has been donated to South Africa by the United States of America (USA) in terms of the US-South African Bilateral Agreement on Climate Change Support. These projects are:

Cities for Climate Protection

This project involves the improvement of management capacity in local government. It will run for three years, with a budget of US$1,2 million to help local governments identify and implement actions that meet their objectives, as well as address global climate change.

Demonstration projects linking climate change and sustainable development

Various institutions, including educational institutions, private, and non-profit organisations implement a number of projects on behalf of the Department countrywide. These projects include the promotion of ecovillages in urban and rural areas; rural energisation; renewable energy technology such as biomass gasification and ethanol production; community-based greening and waste recycling; low-tech energy solutions such as thermally efficient and renewable-energy solutions in housing; clean transport systems; carbon sequestration and conservation; and industrial energy efficiency. Some R12,6 million is being spent on these projects.

Climate change, public awareness and education

The objective of this project is to increase public awareness of global climate change in South Africa, and to assist government in its efforts to educate students on the importance of such change within the country.

Erosion and desertification

Most of South Africa's soils are unstable. The country loses an estimated 500 million t of topsoil annually through erosion caused by water and wind.

Approximately 81% of the total land area of South Africa is being farmed. However, only 70% of this area is suitable for grazing. Overgrazing and erosion diminish the carrying-capacity of the veld and lead to land degradation. This process has already claimed more than 250 000 ha of land in South Africa.

The Department of Agriculture administers the Conservation of Agricultural Resources Act, 1983 (Act 43 of 1983), in terms of which various measures are being implemented to prevent or contain soil erosion.

In January 1995, South Africa signed the Convention to Combat Desertification, which was ratified on 30 September 1997. The main objectives of the Convention include co-operation between governments, organisations and communities to accomplish sustainable development, especially where water resources are scarce. The Convention aims to support member countries in Africa to prevent desertification and its consequences. These countries support one another at technical and scientific level, as they share similar climatic conditions. South Africa also acts as co-ordinator for the Valdivia Group for Desertification. The Group consists of countries in the southern hemisphere, namely Australia, New Zealand, Argentina, Chile, Uruguay, South Africa and Brazil, whose aim it is, *inter alia*, to foster scientific and technological co-operation.

Waste management

Towards the end of 2002, government published the *White Paper on Integrated Pollution and Waste Management*, which outlines its new thinking in relation to pollution and waste management.

The Government believes that pollution prevention is one of the most effective means of protecting South Africa's people and the environment. Pollution prevention eliminates costly and unnecessary waste and promotes sustainable development. It aims to reduce risks to human health and the environment by trying to eliminate the causes, instead of treating the symptoms, of pollution. This objective marks a major shift in emphasis from control to prevention.

The White Paper also stresses the need to make pollution prevention a part of everyday activities.

Effective pollution prevention not only focuses on the installation of pollution-abatement equipment in industry, but also on the shared responsibility of all sectors of society to protect South Africa's natural resources, which involves:

- innovation in product design and production
- the encouragement of cost savings through efficiencies and conservation
- insisting on sound management of persistent bio-accumulative and toxic substances, and eliminating their use where necessary.

Both municipalities and provincial governments will play an important role in implementing national strategies addressing waste and pollution management.

Municipalities will be responsible for providing waste-management services, and managing waste-disposal facilities. Specific functions to be carried out by municipalities will include:

- compiling and implementing general waste-management plans
- implementing public awareness
- collecting data for the Waste Information System
- providing general waste-collection services and managing waste-disposal facilities
- implementing and enforcing appropriate waste minimisation and recycling initiatives
- where possible, regional planning and establishment and management of landfill sites, especially for regionally based general waste landfills.

On 6 August 2003, the Cabinet approved the release of the Draft Radioactive Waste Management Policy for public comment.

The Draft Policy is based on internationally accepted standards and focuses on:

- the need for future generations not to be burdened with nuclear-waste disposal
- banning the import or export of nuclear waste.

The Draft Policy furthermore makes provision for the establishment of a fund to enforce the 'polluter pays' principle.

The Department also recommended, during 2003, that the International Convention on the Safe Management of Spent Nuclear Fuel and Radioactive Waste be signed by South Africa.

Medical waste treatment continues to be inadequate in South African hospitals, prin-

Environmental management

cipally because non-hazardous items such as food are often mixed with contaminated medical waste. This dramatically increases the volume of medical waste, and makes the cost of safe disposal prohibitive.

In August 2003, an International Conference on Healthcare Risk Waste Management was held. More than 280 delegates representing 16 countries attended the Conference at Johannesburg's Sandton Convention Centre, aimed at sharing information on the management of healthcare risks in their respective countries.

The Conference, the first of its kind, was a culmination of a two-year feasibility project assessing the *status quo* of health-risk waste management in Gauteng. A pilot project on healthcare waste management was run in Leratong Hospital in Krugersdorp and Itireleng Clinic in Soweto.

The pilot project was implemented through financial and technical support from the Danish Government as part of an ongoing country-to-country support programme for the development and implementation of the National Waste Management Strategy.

The Department of Environmental Affairs and Tourism, in collaboration with the United Nations' Environment Programme and Food and Agriculture Organisation, hosted a workshop in January 2003 to launch the National Implementation Plan (NIP) of the Stockholm Convention on Persistent Organic Pollutants (POPs) and the African Stockpile Project.

South Africa is among the first 14 African countries nominated for the first phase of the obsolete pesticides clean-up and disposal operation through the African Stockpile Project.

The objective is to clean up and safely dispose of all obsolete pesticide stocks from Africa, and establish preventative measures to avoid future accumulation.

The Department is in the process of implementing an NIP that will rid South Africa of the impact of POPs.

The NIP will involve assessing the sources of POPs in the country, the impact of these POPs, the infrastructure available to manage the issue, and the additional capacity required.

The pilot project entailed the re-engineering of the entire healthcare waste management system with considerable capacity-building and training efforts. The project demonstrated improved occupational health and safety for health workers, and that measures are in place for safe segregation, transport and disposal of hazardous healthcare waste. Some of the highlights of the project were:

- the reduction of general waste in the medical waste stream from 25% to 7%.
- the amount of misplaced medical waste disposed at landfill sites being reduced by half
- new equipment to reduce the number and risks of needle stick injuries and exposure to infectious material, being developed and tested
- the pilot also demonstrated that it is possible to eliminate unnecessary overhead expenses incurred because of poor management of medical waste.

A successful Waste Summit was held in Polokwane in Limpopo during September 2001. It formed part of the National Waste Management Strategy and resulted in the Polokwane Declaration on Waste Management. Its vision is to implement a waste-management system which contributes to sustainable development and a measurable improvement in the quality of life, by harnessing the energy and commitment of all South Africans for the effective reduction of waste. The Polokwane Declaration outlines the goal of reducing waste generation and disposal by 50% and 25%, respectively, by 2012, and developing a plan for zero waste by 2022.

These are ambitious plans, but are potentially quite feasible with the introduction of a number of initiatives like eco-industrial parks (there are currently 25 around the world) that function on a zero-waste basis. Here factories are brought together so that they can use each other's waste (by-products) as input or raw materials.

A National Waste Management Workshop was held in Port Elizabeth in July 2003 to discuss issues including the impact of waste and pollution on poor communities, and develop a national programme of action to address the problems surrrounding waste management.

The main themes discussed were capacity-building, education and awareness; how local government deals with waste; financing waste; landfills and waste; and minimum standards.

An agreement containing new regulations governing plastic shopping bags was signed in September 2002 by the Minister of Environmental Affairs and Tourism, and representatives from various labour and business organisations.

The agreement, which came into effect on 9 May 2003, stipulates that the thickness of plastic bags will be 30 microns, but that manufacturers will be allowed to continue using their existing machinery to make bags of 24 micron thickness for the next five years before having to comply with the 30-micron standard.

The agreement states that printing will only be allowed on 25% of the surface area if the ink is not environmentally friendly. In situations where the ink is acceptable, this area can be increased to 50%.

A toll-free line was installed by the Department to deal with queries relating to plastic bags.

The Department of Environmental Affairs and Tourism met with its social partners during June 2003 to review and take stock of the implementation of the plastic bag regulations.

Water-quality management

Quality management of national water resources in South Africa is the responsibility of the Directorate: Water Quality Management of the Department of Water Affairs and Forestry.

Water-quality management involves the maintenance of the fitness of water resources for use on a sustained basis, by achieving a balance between socio-economic development and environmental protection. From a regulatory point of view, water-quality management entails the ongoing process of planning, development, implementation and administration of water-quality management policy; the authorisation of water-uses that may have, or may potentially have, an impact on water quality; as well as the monitoring and auditing of the aforementioned. The evolution of South African society and the imperatives for equity of access to water served as the driving forces behind the water-law reform process, which culminated in the National Water Act, 1998 (Act 36 of 1998).

The Directorate is developing new water-quality policies and implementing various regulatory instruments stipulated by the Act to face up to these new challenges.

The National Water Act, 1998 further enables the Department to manage water-quality through both source-directed and resource-directed measures. Source-directed measures include the issuing of licences to water users with a potential impact on the resource.

The Department has adopted a hierarchy of decision-taking with regard to source-directed water-quality management:
- Pollution prevention: preventing waste production and pollution or degradation of the water resource wherever possible.
- Waste minimisation and remediation: if waste production and pollution or degradation of the water resource cannot be avoided, it must be minimised and remedied.
- Precautionary principle: if there is no alternative to the disposal of waste and/or the discharge of water containing waste, the precautionary principle applies. In applying this principle, the disposal of waste and/or discharge of water containing waste will only be allowed if the receiving environment has the capacity to assimilate the additional waste load.
- Differentiated approach: if the receiving water resource has the capacity to assimilate an additional waste load, i.e. when the requirements of the reserve and the other waste users are not threatened, relaxation from prescribed standards or requirements

may be considered. This approach is followed for all potential sources of pollution (as defined by the Act) and not only for hazardous substances.

The Act requires that all significant water resources be classified in accordance with the prescribed classification system.

The Department of Water Affairs and Forestry, in partnership with the Department of Environmental Affairs and Tourism, contributed to the completion of the Integrated Pollution Control and Waste Management Policy and the National Waste Management Strategy. It focused specifically on its water quality responsibilities within an integrated pollution-control policy model. (See Chapter 23: *Water affairs and forestry*.)

Air pollution

The Air-Quality Management Bill was approved for public comment by the Cabinet in April 2003.

The Bill, which will repeal the Atmospheric Pollution Prevention Act, 1965 (Act 45 of 1965), seeks to give effect to the integrated pollution and waste-management policy to ensure that all South Africans have access to clean air.

The Department of Environmental Affairs and Tourism is in the process of establishing several initiatives aimed at ensuring better air quality.

Durban South, in KwaZulu-Natal, is the second-largest industrial area in South Africa, and home to several fuel refineries, a pulp-and paper-mill, sugar refineries and a number of smaller industries.

By mid-2003, the Department had contributed R4,4 million and the Norwegian Government R5,5 million towards the establishment of a new Air-Quality Management System in Durban South.

It was announced in June 2003 that a health study was to be conducted on the Durban South basin at a cost of R7 million.

The execution of the study, which was approved by the Executive Committee of the eThekwini Municipality, is expected to be undertaken over a period of 18 to 24 months, and will comprise an epidemiological study and a health-risk assessment.

The focus on Durban South is increasingly being seen as a potential model for cleaning other air-pollution hotspots around the country, including the Vaal Triangle, the Witbank-Middelburg area, and Milnerton, near Cape Town.

According to the UN, the transportation sector worldwide now accounts for as much as 73% of global carbon emissions. Vehicles emit huge quantities of carbon monoxide, nitrogen oxides and volatile hydrocarbons.

Most of the petrol used in South Africa contains lead, which poses another serious health risk, particularly for children, as it can hamper their mental development.

Nitrous oxide harms the health of people with cardiac and respiratory weaknesses.

Oxides of nitrogen combined with water vapour create acid rain. Carbon monoxide can kill a person in a matter of minutes if large enough quantities are inhaled, and hydrocarbons harm human health as well as the environment.

The increasing number of vehicles on the country's roads is compunding the country's air pollution challenge.

The Vehicle Emission Strategy, which forms part of the Air-Quality Management Bill, is designed to ensure that emissions from vehicles do not lead to unacceptably poor air quality. The Ambient Air Standards were set to give guidelines in terms of acceptable emissions into the atmosphere, as well as the monitoring and enforcement of transgressors.

Marine pollution

More than 80% of marine pollution originates from land-based sources such as pipeline discharges, rivers and stormwater run-off.

There are many places where water or water containing waste is discharged into the sea. Forty sea outfalls have been formalised through exemptions issued by the Department of Water Affairs and Forestry in terms of the Water Act, 1956 (Act 54 of 1956).

The same principles used for the issuing of other water-use licences apply to licences for sea outfalls. Such effluents include raw and treated sewage, industrial effluents, or a mixture of the two. In the past, many of these discharges were made into the surf zone, or even onto the shore, but the current tendency is to extend the pipelines further offshore. Permit conditions generally include the monitoring of adverse effects of such discharges on the marine environment.

An increasing source of concern is non-point-source pollution, especially that coming from the burgeoning informal settlements that form part of many coastal cities. Such pollution is generally the result of inadequate sanitation and other infrastructure, and is very difficult to control or monitor.

Shipping also contributes significantly to marine pollution, particularly with regard to specific types of pollutants. Of the estimated 6,1 million mt of oil entering the oceans every year, some 45% originates from shipping activities.

The balance comes from industrial discharges, urban run-off, and oil exploration and production – the latter contributing only 2%. Of the pollution emanating from shipping activities, the majority comes from vessel operations, with only 12% from tanker accidents. Nevertheless, due to the notorious sea conditions along its coastline, South Africa has experienced a number of major oil spills, and, as a consequence, has a well-developed response capability. This includes contingency plans, salvage tugs, dispersant spraying vessels, a reconnaissance aircraft, and a stockpile of oil-spill-response equipment.

Other pollutants linked to the operational activities of ships include sewage and garbage, ballast water discharges, air pollution, and cargoes which enter the sea through accidents. Sewage, garbage and air pollution are regulated by annexes to MARPOL, an international convention controlling pollution from ships, to which South Africa is a party. New regulations to control ballast water discharges are being developed. A major concern is the translocation of alien species, including pathogens, which may have serious ecological, social (public health) and economic consequences. South Africa is involved in an international project aimed at implementing international guidelines on ballast water management in developing countries.

Cargoes range from foodstuffs such as rice and maize, to crude oil, toxic waste and plutonium.

Another potential source of marine pollution is the dumping of waste at sea. This activity is regulated under the Dumping at Sea Control Act, 1980 (Act 73 of 1980), and, since 1995, excludes industrial waste. The main categories of waste dumped in South Africa are dredged material from the ports; obsolete vessels; and, occasionally, spoiled cargoes.

Coastal management

The Department of Environmental Affairs and Tourism's Subdirectorate: Coastal Zone Management is the lead agent for coastal management. This requires empowering coastal users, decision-makers, and the people to sustain and manage the coastal zone and its resources appropriately.

The Coastal Management Bill sets out a new approach to managing the nation's coastal resources, in order to promote social equity and make the best economic use of coastal resources, while protecting the natural environment.

The Department of Transport, in partnership with the South African Maritime Safety Authority and the Department of Environmental Affairs and Tourism, is developing a national contingency plan to respond quickly and effectively to oil spills whenever they occur. Part of the plan is an envisaged rescue co-ordination centre.

Environmental management

The *White Paper on Coastal Management* was launched in June 2000. According to the White Paper, the coast has been a driving force in the national economy. Its products account for about 35% of the country's national Gross Domestic Product (GDP) and has enormous development potential.

A number of far-reaching initiatives were undertaken. These include:
- The ruling by the Port Elizabeth High Court in favour of the banning of private 4x4 vehicles on South African beaches. The regulation came into effect in January 2002.
- The removal/bulldozing of illegal cottages on the Wild Coast.
- The declaration of a Whale Sanctuary in Hermanus.
- The restructuring of the fishing-rights dispensation to control the exploitation of coastal and marine resources.

These measures supplement the illustrious programme of action already anticipated in the White Paper. Elements of this programme include the following:
- diversifying coastal economies and optimising benefits for local coastal communities
- promoting coastal tourism, leisure and recreational development
- establishing 'one-stop-shops' for development approvals
- improving public access to the coast and coastal resources
- developing ports and harbours
- improving co-ordination and integration of coastal and marine-resource management
- improving the monitoring and management of coastal pollution
- rehabilitating degraded coastal areas and resources.

The Working for the Coast Programme was launched in October 2000. It has succeeded in upgrading the environment and improving the lives of many people living along the coast. The Programme has created more than 1 500 jobs.

More than 55 teams of workers have been formed along South Africa's coast to upgrade the environment, with many of them having started their own small businesses.

The Department announced in April 2003 that it would be investing R3 million in poverty-relief projects in the Centani region in the Eastern Cape.

It is envisaged that the projects will be driven through the Working for the Coast Programme.

Chemicals

Although relatively small by international standards, the chemical industry is a significant player in the South African economy, contributing about 5% to GDP and providing employment to about 200 000 people. The industry produces 1 301 t of primary and secondary process chemicals annually, making it the largest of its kind in Africa.

Several steps have been taken to align current legislation with the Constitution, 1996 (Act 108 of 1996), and with global chemicals management:
- A special unit has been set up in the Department of Environmental Affairs and Tourism to implement a system aimed at preventing major industrial accidents, as well as systems for emergency preparedness and response.
- The Minister has initiated an integrated safety, health and environment approach for the management of chemicals in South Africa.

On 31 October 2003, the International Blue Flag jury approved eight South African beaches for the 2003/04 season. The Blue Flag eco-label assures visitors that beaches adhere to international standards in water quality, safety and security, environmental information and environmental management. They are:
- Humewood Beach, Nelson Mandela metropole (Port Elizabeth, Eastern Cape)
- Margate Main Beach (KwaZulu-Natal)
- South Beach, Durban (KwaZulu-Natal)
- Hibberdene Beach (KwaZulu-Natal South Coast)
- Ramsgate Beach (KwaZulu-Natal South Coast)
- Marina Beach, San Lameer (KwaZulu-Natal)
- Umhlanga Rocks Main Beach, (KwaZulu-Natal)
- Grotto Beach, Hermanus (Western Cape).

This government-level initiative, funded by the UN Institute for Training and Research, will involve a multistakeholder forum, including labour representatives, and aims to integrate legislation. At present, the laws governing chemicals are fragmented.

The Department embarked on a process to develop the South African National Chemicals Profile. The Profile is intended to contribute to a better understanding of the problems relating to the management and impact of chemicals. It will also help to identify important gaps and weaknesses in the existing system, as a first step in defining whether further efforts may be required.

The development of the Profile was motivated by the recommendations of the International Programme on Chemical Safety, as a follow-up to the Rio Declaration on Environment and Development in 1992.

South Africa has signed the Stockholm Convention on Persistent Organic Pollutants, and the Rotterdam Convention on Prior Informed Consent Procedure for Certain Hazardous Chemicals and Pesticides in International Trade.

Recycling

Almost every type of paper produced in South Africa has a recycled content. Each ton of waste paper recycled saves about 17 pine trees, and a ton of recycled paper saves 3 m^3 of landfill space, meaning that South Africa saves 10 million trees annually.

South Africa follows the USA and Japan as the best collectors of used metal beverage cans in the world. The recovery rate of metal beverage cans sold in South Africa has grown to 63%.

A major role in this regard has been played by the Collect-a-Can project, which was founded in 1993 to reduce litter and optimise the recovery of metal beverage cans. In the process, informal employment has been created for over 30 000 people.

In comparison with other countries, South Africa has a high returnable glass-container market: 33% of all glass containers produced are returnable or reusable, and these are also recycled.

The Minister of Environmental Affairs and Tourism announced, at the 10th anniversary of Collect-a-Can in April 2003, that 37 773 people were earning or supplementing their income through can recoveries, and that more than R270 million had been paid out to collectors over the last 10 years.

Urban conservation

Rapid urbanisation and its concomitant environmental impact are posing serious challenges for South African planners and environmentalists.

Up to 16 000 ha of farmland is lost to urban development each year. Low-density urban sprawl and the rapid growth of informal settlements contribute to increasing competition between urban land-users for diminishing space and resources.

As a result, many informal settlements are located on marginal and environmentally sensitive land, posing serious threats to human well-being and ecosystems.

The environmentally friendly use and development of land can be promoted through official planning processes such as integrated development plans and land-development objectives.

New planning and environmental legislation provides for environmental concerns in urban planning and development. Regulations making environmental-impact assessments compulsory for certain planned developments were promulgated in September 1997.

Environmental injustices

The Department issued a directive under the National Environmental Management Act, 1998 to Guernica Chemicals (previously known as Thor Chemicals) in KwaZulu-Natal in March 2003. They were ordered to clean up, decontaminate and remove the waste at the plant within 30 days. The waste had resulted in

Environmental management

the mercury-poisoning and death of a number of workers, as well as poisoned communities and livestock, damage to the environment, and contaminated groundwater.

The negative effects of asbestos are other environmental-injustice issues that have received attention from the Department.

The Minister of Environmental Affairs and Tourism announced during the parliamentary hearings on asbestos in January 2003 that the Department was committed to implementing the recommendations of the Parliamentary Portfolio Committee on Environmental Affairs and Tourism, stressing that environmental issues would be a priority during 2003.

Efforts that are being undertaken by the South African Government to deal with the asbestos problem include:
- eradicating mine-dumps
- developing occupational health and safety regulations on asbestos
- developing safety standards and establishing a single compensation office
- formulating a code of best practice for the maintenance, demolition and disposal of asbestos-containing material
- abolishing the use of asbestos in road construction
- gradually phasing out asbestos-use in housing.

It was announced in January 2003 that the Department had launched a study with organised labour and business through the National Economic Development and Labour Council, on all the issues surrounding the phasing out of asbestos.

South Africa hosted the SADC meeting on asbestos in February 2003.

International co-operation

South Africa is a signatory to a variety of international agreements dealing with environmental issues.

United Nations Framework Convention on Climate Change (UNFCCC)

South Africa ratified the UNFCCC in 1997. The Convention is a global commitment to take collective responsibility for climate change, and is a mandate for action to address the problem.

The Convention was signed at the Rio Earth Summit in 1992 by Heads of State and other senior representatives from 154 countries (and the European Community), and came into effect on 21 March 1994. As of mid-1998, some 175 states had ratified or acceded to the Convention.

The objective of the Convention is to stabilise greenhouse gas concentrations in the atmosphere at a level that will not have an adverse effect on the climate.

The Convention aims to control the rate of approach to this level over a period of time, in order to:
- allow ecosystems to adapt naturally to climate change
- ensure that food production is not threatened
- enable economic development to proceed in a sustainable manner.

The Convention is guided by four main principles. These are:
- intergenerational equity
- recognition of the specific needs and circumstances of developing countries
- the precautionary principle
- sustainable development, and the need for global co-operation and an open international economic system that will lead to sustainable economic growth.

All countries that have ratified the Convention are required to:
- develop, update and publish national inventories of anthropogenic emissions by sources, and removals by sinks of greenhouse gases (the greenhouse gases exclude those listed in the Montreal Protocol)
- formulate, implement and update national and regional programmes containing measures to mitigate climate change

- promote and co-operate in the development and transfer of technology that controls, reduces or prevents anthropogenic emissions of greenhouse gases
- promote sustainable management, conservation and enhancement of sinks and reservoirs of greenhouse gases
- co-operate in preparing for the adaptation to the impact of climate change
- take climate-change considerations into account where feasible, in relevant social, economic and environmental policies and actions, with a view to minimising the adverse effects on the economy, public health and the quality of the environment
- promote and co-operate in research
- promote and co-operate in the timeous and transparent exchange of information, including scientific, technological, socio-economic and legal information
- promote and co-operate in education, training and public awareness, encourage the widest participation in this process, and report to the Conference of the Parties (COP).

Convention on International Trade in Endangered Species

CITES, also known as the Washington Convention, was negotiated in 1973 when it was realised that international trade in wildlife and wildlife products could lead to the overexploitation of certain species, thereby threatening them with extinction. CITES came into force in South Africa on 13 October 1975. South Africa, together with the other 149 member countries, acts by regulating and monitoring international trade in species which are or may be, affected by this trade.

South Africa views the African elephant, with a population of more than 200 000 in southern African countries, as not endangered. As a result, South Africa is able to sell elephant hides and leather goods, as well as trade in live animals.

Botswana, Namibia, Zimbabwe and South Africa have withdrawn their proposals to sell ivory stocks. South Africa now has an Appendix II listing and a zero quota for ivory. This means that at future COPs, South Africa will not have to campaign for a downlisting, but rather an amendment to request a quota.

The issue at stake for South Africa is not just ivory. It is about the sustainable use of natural resources and its use for poverty alleviation in rural areas.

The agreement on the downlisting of the African elephant will be restricted to the ivory stockpile in the Kruger National Park.

In October 2001, the Department of Environmental Affairs and Tourism invited interested South African citizens and registered South African non-governmental organisations to assist in the preparation for the 12th COP of CITES. The meeting took place in Chile in November 2002.

During this meeting, South Africa submitted three proposals aimed at ensuring the sustainability of its wild fauna and flora. These proposals included:
- the amendment of the annotation to the Appendix II listing of the South African population of African elephant to allow the initial sale of the Kruger National Park ivory stockpile (of 30 t), 18 months after the adoption of the proposal, and a subsequent annual quota of 2 t
- the transfer of the South African population of Cape parrot from Appendix II (species not necessarily in danger of extinction, but which could become so if their trade were not strictly regulated) to Appendix I (species threatened with extinction that are or could be affected by trade)
- transfer of *Aloe thorncroftii* from Appendix I to Appendix II.

Montreal Protocol

South Africa, as a signatory to the Montreal Protocol, has a national obligation to safeguard the ozone layer from complete depletion. If this is not done, the long-term negative impli-

Environmental management

cations for the whole world will be such that life on earth will be threatened.

To date, South Africa has phased out chlorofluorocarbons (CFCs), halons, methyl chloroform and carbon tetrachloride – making it the only developed country in the world that has achieved so much in line with the phase-out schedule for developed countries. It is a known fact that, although South Africa is classified as a developing country, its consumption of these substances is equal to some of the developed countries. It is for this reason that South Africa did not hesitate to comply with the requirements of the Protocol, more especially because it is also a signatory. To demonstrate the country's commitment towards phasing out ozone-depleting substances (ODSs), the following control measures constitute the overall position of South Africa on the Montreal Protocol:
- working groups were constituted under a neutral chairmanship to assist the Government to implement the Protocol
- regulated ODSs can only be imported or exported after applying for an import/export permit through the Department of Trade and Industry under their Import and Export Control Act, 1963 (Act 45 of 1963)
- ODSs can only be imported after an environmental levy of R5 per kg of CFC is paid
- information is disseminated to interested and affected parties
- Africa Networking Meetings, as arranged by the UN Environment Programme, are attended, where views, experiences and problems are shared in an effort to improve and co-operate within the region.

Obligations include:
- ensuring that South Africa, as a party to the Protocol, protects human health and the environment against harm from human activities which modify or are likely to modify the ozone layer
- ensuring the protection of the ozone layer by taking precautionary measures to equitably control total global emissions of substances that deplete the ozone layer, with the ultimate objective of totally eliminating them
- reporting and sending data to the Ozone Secretariat on production, imports, exports and consumption of regulated ODSs as collected from dealers and relevant departments
- representing the country affected and interested parties in meetings or COPs to ensure that their interest and that of South Africa is upheld.

Private-sector involvement

Numerous private bodies are involved in conservation activities. There are more than 400 organisations in the country concentrating on conservation, wildlife and the general environment, and more than 30 botanical and horticultural organisations. Among these are:
- BirdLife South Africa
- Wildlife and Environment Society
- WWF South Africa
- Green Trust
- Earthlife Africa
- Endangered Wildlife Trust
- Wilderness Trust of Southern Africa
- Environmental Justice Networking Forum
- Dolphin Action Protection Group
- Keep South Africa Beautiful
- Trees and Food for Africa
- South African National Foundation for the Conservation of Coastal Birds
- Rhino and Elephant Foundation
- EcoLink.

South Africa Yearbook 2003/04

Acknowledgements

BuaNews
Department of Environmental Affairs and Tourism
Department of Water Affairs and Forestry
Estimates of National Expenditure 2003, published by the National Treasury
National Botanical Institute
National Zoological Gardens of South Africa
South African National Parks
South Africa.info
www.gov.za

Suggested reading

Bethlehem, L. and Goldblatt, M. *The Bottom Line: Industry and the Environment in South Africa.* Rondebosch: University of Cape Town Press, 1997.
Bond, P. *Unsustainable South Africa: Environment, Development and Social Protest.* Pietermaritzburg: University of Natal Press, 2002.
Clarke, J. *Back to Earth. South Africa's Environmental Challenges.* Halfway House: Southern Book Publishers, 1991.
Dovers, S, ed. *South Africa's Environmental History: Cases and Comparisons.* Cape Town: David Philip, 2002
Ecology and Empire: Environmental History of Settler Societies. Editors: T. Griffiths and L. Robin. Pietermaritzburg: University of Natal Press and Keele University Press, 1997.
Environmental Potential Atlas for South Africa. Editors: W. van der Riet and others. Pretoria: Van Schaik for the Department of Environmental Affairs and Tourism, 1997.
Environmental Management in South Africa. Editors: R.F. Fuggle and M.A. Rabie. Rev. ed. Cape Town: Juta, 1996.
Fuggle, R.F. and Rabie, M.A. *Environmental Management in South Africa.* Cape Town: Juta, 1992.
Going Green: People, Politics and 0the Environment in South Africa. Editors: J. Cock and E. Koch. Cape Town: Oxford University Press, 1991.
Hattingh, J. et al, eds. *Environmental Education: Ethics and Action in Southern Africa.* Pretoria: Human Sciences Research Council (HSRC), 2002.
Hosking, S. *Exploring the Case for Increasing Glass Recycling Through Regulation.* Pretoria: HSRC, 2000.
Hulme, D. and Murphee, M. eds. *African Wildlife and Livelihoods: The Promise and Performance of Community Conservation.* Cape Town: David Philip, 2001.
Koch, E. and others. *Water, Waste and Wildlife: The Politics of Ecology in South Africa.* Johannesburg: Penguin, 1990.
Kok, P. and Pietersen, J. *Biodiversity.* Pretoria: HSRC, 2000. (National Research and Technology Foresight Project).
Kok, P. and Pietersen, J. *Environmental Management.* Pretoria: HSRC, 2000.
McDonald, D. ed. *Environmental Justice in South Africa.* Cape Town: University of Cape Town Press, 2002.
Mills, G. and Harvey, M. *African Predator.* Cape Town: Struik, 2001.
Nürnberger, K. *Prosperity, Poverty and Pollution: Managing the Approaching Crisis.* Pietermaritzburg: Cluster Publications, 1999.
Payne, A.I.L. and Crawford, R.J.M. *Oceans of Life off Southern Africa.* 2nd ed. Cape Town: Vlaeberg, 1995.
Phezulu, L. *Leigh Voigt's African Album: A Miscellany of Paintings, Curiosities, Lore and Legend by a Bushveld Naturalist.* Cape Town: David Philip, 1999.
Restoring the Land: Environment and Change in Post-apartheid South Africa. Editor: M. Ramphele. London: Panos, 1991.
Ritchie, J. *The Environment Funding Guide: A Comprehensive Guide to Raising Funds for the Environment.* Cape Town: Papillon Books for Nedbank, c.1997.
South Africa. Editor: J. Haape. 2nd ed. Basingstroke (UK): GeoCentre International, 1995.
Van Oudtshoorn, F. *Guide to the Grasses of South Africa.* Photographs by E. van Wyk and F. van Oudtshoorn. Pretoria: Briza, 1999.
Van Wyk, B. and Gericke, N. *People's Plants: A Guide to Useful Plants of Southern Africa.* Pretoria: Briza, 1999.

Environmental management

Weinberg, P. ed. and photographer. *Once We Were Hunters: A Journey with Indigenous People*. Cape Town: David Philip, 2000.

White Paper on the Conservation and Sustainable Use of South Africa's Biological Diversity. Pretoria: Department of Environmental Affairs and Tourism, 1997.

Wildlife of Southern Africa: A Field Guide to the Animals and Plants of the Region. Editors: V. Carruthers and M. Pearson. Halfway House, Gauteng: Southern Book Publishers, 1997.

JSE
2 GWEN LANE

chapter 10
Finance

The Constitution of the Republic of South Africa, 1996 (Act 108 of 1996), lays down a framework for the division of responsibilities between national, provincial and local government. It prescribes an equitable division of revenue between the spheres of government, taking into account their respective functions. It also creates an independent Auditor-General and an independent central bank, and sets out the principles governing financial accountability to Parliament and the annual budget process.

The objectives of the National Treasury are to:
- advance economic growth and income redistribution through economic, fiscal and financial policies that stimulate investment and trade; create employment; and allocate budget resources to targeted beneficiaries
- prepare a sound and fiscally sustainable national budget and an equitable division of resources between the national, provincial and local spheres of government
- equitably and efficiently raise fiscal revenue as required, through targeted and fair tax policy and other measures that ensure revenue stability and the efficiency and competitiveness of the South African economy

◀ The JSE Securities Exchange is the largest securities exchange in Africa and has a market capitalisation of several times that of all the other African markets combined.

- soundly manage government's financial assets and liabilities through prudent cash management, asset restructuring, financial management and management of the debt portfolio
- promote accountability through effective and reliable financial reporting systems and internal controls
- contribute to improved financial management by promoting and enforcing transparency and effective management of revenue, expenditure, assets and liabilities in all spheres of government.

Fiscal policy framework

The Minister of Finance, Mr Trevor Manuel, presented the Budget for 2003/04 on 26 February 2003. The highlights were:
- The police and the criminal justice sector were allocated R2,7 billion for more police members, streamlining of the justice process and improved protection of women and children.
- An additional R1,7 billion was allocated to universities and technikons, and for increased skills-development spending.
- Personal income tax was cut by R13,3 billion.
- A tax incentive for investment in underdeveloped urban areas was introduced.
- The Child Support Grant (CSG) will be gradually extended to children up to their 14th birthday, providing benefits to about 3,2 million more children. Increased

Consolidated national and provincial expenditure: functional classification[1]

	2002/03 Revised estimate	% of total	2003/04 Budget estimate	% of total	2004/05 Budget estimate	% of total
General government service and unallocable expenditure[2]	20 063	6,5	21 733	6,2	24 700	6,5
Protective services:	53 335	17,2	58 475	16,6	62 647	16,5
Defence and intelligence	20 763	6,7	22 481	6,4	23 203	6,1
Police	20 529	6,6	22 806	6,5	25 083	6,6
Prisons	7 313	2,4	8 077	2,3	8 843	2,3
Justice	4 730	1,5	5 111	1,5	5 518	1,4
Social services:	153 341	49,4	173 496	49,4	190 767	50,1
Education	62 757	20,2	69 063	19,7	74 329	19,5
Health	34 940	11,3	39 077	11,1	42 543	11,2
Social security and welfare	41 966	13,5	48 652	13,8	55 314	14,5
Housing	5 553	1,8	6 548	1,9	7 320	1,9
Community development[3]	8 125	2,6	10 156	2,9	11 261	3,0
Economic services:	36 242	11,7	43 650	12,4	45 585	12,0
Water schemes and related services	4 540	1,5	6 029	1,7	6 169	1,6
Fuel and energy	1 508	0,5	1 696	0,5	1 960	0,5
Agriculture, forestry and fishing	5 729	1,8	6 710	1,9	7 068	1,9
Mining, manufacturing and construction	1 503.3	0,5	1 821	0,5	1 977	0,5
Transport and communications	13 825	4,5	15 537	4,4	16 656	4,4
Other economic services[4]	9 137	2,9	11 857	3,4	11 755	3,1
Interest	47 250	15,2	50 985	14,5	53 079	13,9
Subtotal: main budget	310 231	100,0	348 339	99,1	376 778	98,9
Plus contingency reserves	0	0	3 000	0,9	4 000	1,1
Total estimated expenditure	310 231	100,0	351 339	100,00	380 778	100,0

1) These figures were estimated by the National Treasury and may differ from data published by Statistics South Africa. The numbers in these tables are not strictly comparable to those published in previous years, due to the allocation of some of the unallocable expenditure for previous years. Data for the history years has been adjusted accordingly.
2) Mainly general administration, cost of raising loans and allocable capital expenditure.
3) Including cultural, recreational and sport services.
4) Including tourism, labour and multi-purpose projects.

Source: National Treasury

allocations for primary-school nutrition were announced.
- Pension and disability grants were increased by R60 to R700 a month. The CSG was increased by 14% to R160 a month, effective from April 2003.
- Some R1,2 billion was provided for emergency food-relief projects.
- An additional R38 billion was allocated to provinces to finance higher social grants, textbooks, medicine, road maintenance, and to enhance the Government's response to HIV/AIDS.
- An additional R1,9 billion was allocated to accelerate land restitution.
- A further R1 billion went to expenditure on the National Research and Development Strategy for programmes relating to health, industrial biotechnology, food security and agricultural production.
- Municipalities received an additional R6,5 billion for free basic services, investment in municipal infrastructure, rural water supply and sanitation, and the expansion of employment in community services.
- Sin taxes were increased.

- The *ad valorem* duty on computers, which was 5% of the imported or manufactured price, was scrapped.

Debt management

South Africa's debt, both domestic Rand-denominated bonds and foreign-debt issues, enjoys increasing recognition on international capital markets and continues to attract a diverse range of investors.

This reflects the country's success in adopting sustainable fiscal and macro-economic policies, the evolution of a sound and transparent approach to debt management, the healthy Balance of Payments position, and the maturity of South Africa's financial markets. In recent years, both Standard and Poor's and Moody's Investors' Service upgraded their ratings of South African debt, affirming their confidence in the country's macro-economic and fiscal management. These assessments contribute to broadening South Africa's international investor base, and reinforce the favourable outlook for interest rates and the cost of capital.

South African foreign debt continues to trade at tighter spreads than the Emerging Market Bond Index, indicating that investors share the confidence expressed by international rating agencies, and regard South Africa positively in comparison with its competitors.

The primary objective of domestic-debt management has since shifted to the reduction of the cost of debt to within acceptable risk limits, with diversification of funding instruments and ensuring flexible government access to markets as secondary goals. Recourse to foreign borrowing has been stepped up, allowing the fiscus to contribute to reducing the foreign currency exposure of the South African Reserve Bank in its forward market portfolio.

Domestic-debt-management reforms have addressed several policy and instrument gaps:
- Lower coupon bonds have been introduced, consistent with government's approach to reducing inflation in the years ahead.
- The Public-Sector Borrowers' Forum was established in 2001.
- Co-ordination between monetary policy and liability management has been strengthened through more effective liaison between the National Treasury and the South African Reserve Bank.
- Regular meetings with the primary dealers, the Reserve Bank and the futures and bond exchanges provide a forum for ensuring a transparent and efficient bond market.
- Debt consolidation has reduced fragmentation on the yield curve and improved liquidity of the benchmark issues. Illiquid bonds were consolidated into five liquid benchmark bonds, thereby smoothing the maturity profile and reducing refinancing risks.
- The integrity and efficiency of the Government securities market have been strengthened through buying back illiquid bonds, including diverse 'ex-homeland' bonds of limited issue size.
- Inflation-linked bonds were introduced to diversify government's investor base and to signal confidence in government's macro-economic policy, while also providing an objective measure of inflationary expectations and benchmarks for other issuers.
- The 'Strips' (Separate Trading of Registered Interest and Principal Securities) Programme has been introduced to increase demand for the underlying instruments and encourage active portfolio management.
- State debt costs continue to fall as a share of government expenditure. It was projected to be 4,1% of Gross Domestic Product (GDP) in 2003/04 and is expected to decrease to 3,8% of GDP in 2005/06.

The liquidity in the domestic government-bond market, measured by the increase in the nominal trades, has improved substantially during recent years, especially since the appointment of primary dealers in government bonds in April 1998. The bond market

South Africa Yearbook 2003/04

Terms of trade and exchange rate of the Rand – percentage changes

Period	Terms of trade[1] Including gold (5037Q)	Terms of trade[1] Excluding gold (5036Q)	Nominal effective exchange rate[2]	Real effective exchange rate[3]	US Dollar	British Pound (5314Q)	Euro	Japanese Yen
1996	1,4	-0,7	-11,2	-6,3	-15,1-	14,0	-12,4	-1,5
1997	-1,2	1,2	1,0	6,9	-6,8	-11,1	3,5	3,6
1998	-0,9	-0,7	-11,7	-8,8	-16,2	-17,0	-15,2	-9,3
1999	-2,9	-2,3	-7,6	-4,6	-9,5	-7,3	-4,3	-21,5
2000	-1,9	-2,0	-5,1	-2,9	-11,4	-5,6	2,2	-16,1
2001	0,1	0,3	-14,7	-13,6	-18,9	-14,5	-16,1	-8,5
2002	2,5	0,7	-19,6	-16,0	-17,1	-20,9	-21,9	-15,1

1) Change compared with preceding period.
2) Weighted average exchange rate against most important currencies.
3) Percentage changes of average.

Source: South African Reserve Bank – *Quarterly Bulletin*

turnover increased further to R10,6 trillion and R12 trillion in 2001 and 2002 respectively. The bond yields continued to decline from the highs of 22% in 1998 to single digits in November 2001, but reverted to double digits on the back of the Rand's decline in the last quarter of 2001.

In actively managing its debt portfolio, the National Treasury is responsible for identifying, controlling and managing the risks to which government is exposed. A comprehensive risk-management framework of the National Treasury calls for quantitative analysis to model, monitor and manage risk exposure. The framework provides for a set of benchmarks or reference criteria against which the structure and evolution of the debt portfolio can be tested and understood.

Legislation

The National Treasury tables a significant amount of legislation in Parliament annually.

The legislative workload of the National Treasury can be subdivided into three categories, namely:
- legislation conceptualised and prepared in-house
- legislation prepared by regulatory bodies such as the Financial Services Board (FSB) and the Reserve Bank, with policy direction provided by the National Treasury
- tax legislation prepared in conjunction with the South African Revenue Service (SARS), with policy direction provided by the National Treasury.

Between April 2002 and July 2003, pieces of legislation prepared in-house by the National Treasury included the:
- Social Grants Appropriation Act, 2002 (Act 2 of 2002)
- Burundi Protection Support Appropriation Act, 2002 (Act 3 of 2002)
- Division of Revenue Act, 2002 (Act 5 of 2002)
- Appropriation Act, 2002 (Act 29 of 2002)
- Finance Act, 2002 (Act 48 of 2002)
- Adjustments Appropriation Act, 2002 (Act 73 of 2002)
- Gold and Foreign Exchange Contingency Reserve Account Defrayal Act, 2003 (Act 4 of 2003)
- Food Relief Adjustments Appropriation Act, 2003 (Act 5 of 2003)
- Division of Revenue Act, 2003 (Act 7 of 2003)
- Appropriation Act, 2003 (Act 18 of 2003).

By July 2003, Amendment Bills receiving parliamentary consideration included the:
- Special Pensions Amendment Bill
- Government Employees Pension Laws Amendment Bill
- Financial and Fiscal Commission (FFC) Amendment Bill.

Between April 2002 and July 2003, the following pieces of legislation were prepared by regulatory bodies, with policy direction provided by the National Treasury:
- The Financial Advisory and Intermediary Services Act, 2002 (Act 37 of 2002)
- The Collective Investment Schemes Control Act, 2002 (Act 45 of 2002)
- The Insurance Amendment Act, 2003 (Act 17 of 2003)
- The Banks Amendment Act, 2003 (Act 19 of 2003).

The following regulatory Bills were tabled for parliamentary consideration in 2003:
- The Securities Services Bill
- The Financial Services Ombud Schemes Bill.

Tax legislation prepared in conjunction with SARS, with policy direction provided by the National Treasury, included the:
- Unemployment Insurance Contributions Act, 2002 (Act 4 of 2002)
- Taxation Laws Amendment Act, 2002 (Act 30 of 2002)
- Revenue Laws Amendment Act, 2002 (Act 74 of 2002)
- Gas Regulator Levies Act, 2002 (Act 75 of 2002)
- Exchange Control Amnesty and Amendment of Taxation Laws Act, 2003 (Act 12 of 2003).

At the end of February 2003, the Minister of Finance, Mr Trevor Manuel, became the first Finance Minister to address the International Labour Organisation (ILO) in its 85-year history.

In his presentation to the ILO's Working Party on Social Dimension of Globalisation, in Geneva, Switzerland, Mr Manuel stressed the importance of multilateralism in addressing the challenges of globalisation.

The following tax Bills were tabled for parliamentary consideration in 2003:
- The Mineral and Petroleum Levies Bill
- The Revenue Laws Amendment Bill.

The Debt Collectors Act, 1998 (Act 114 of 1998), as well as its Regulations came into operation on 7 February 2003.

The Act provides for the establishment of the Council for Debt Collectors. The Council will exercise control over the occupation of debt collectors and legalise the recovery of fees or remuneration by registered debt collectors. In the past, a debt collector was not entitled to legally recover any amount from a debtor, and had to rely solely on the contract between him/her and the client for remuneration.

In terms of the Act, no person, excluding an attorney, an employee of an attorney or a party to a factoring arrangement, will be allowed to act as a debt collector unless he or she is registered as a debt collector in terms of the Act.

An employee whose duties are purely administrative, clerical or otherwise subservient to the actual occupation of debt collecting, is also exempted from registering as a debt collector. The Minister may also, in terms of Section 26 of the Act, on the conditions he or she deems fit, exempt any person or category from the provisions of the Act.

After 11 August 2003, a person who acts as a debt collector and who has not been registered as a debt collector in terms of the Act, will be committing an offence.

Once a debt collector has been registered, the Council will have jurisdiction over such a debt collector and can charge him or her and find him or her guilty of improper conduct. The Council has adopted a Code of Conduct which is binding to all registered debt collectors.

The Public Finance Management Act

The Public Finance Management Act (PFMA), 1999 (Act 1 of 1999), came into effect on 1 April 2000 for all departments, constitutional institutions and public entities.

The PFMA, 1999 represents a fundamental change in government's approach to the handling of public finances, as it shifts the emphasis away from a highly centralised system of expenditure control by the treasuries. It holds the heads of departments accountable for the use of resources to deliver services to communities. It will also, in time, change the accounting base from cash to accrual.

The Act emphasises:
- regular financial reporting
- independent auditing and supervision of internal control systems
- improved accounting standards
- greater focus on output and performance
- increased accountability at all levels.

The National Treasury has embarked on several initiatives to assist departments with capacity-building and ensure the successful implementation of the PFMA. These initiatives include:

Internal Audit Framework
The Framework was developed to provide a set of internal audit guidelines that set the tone to create the necessary impetus for a sustainable and effective internal audit mechanism in government. This Framework includes guidelines on risk management and internal controls, and is based on the findings of a skills assessment of internal audit capacity in national and provincial departments.

Asset Management Guidelines
These Guidelines were compiled to provide a contextual view of asset management. The Guidelines also clarify fundamental concepts, with an emphasis on financial management, accounting and reporting of assets.

Provincial Good Practice Programme (PGPP)
In an attempt to provide direct assistance to provinces, the National Treasury initiated the PGPP. The sector-specific Chief Financial Officers' Forums (for the provincial Departments of Education, Health, Housing, Social Development and Transport) were established to improve the efficiency, economy and effectiveness of provincial departments by facilitating peer learning through the identification, documentation and communication of 'good practices' arising from collective experience. The immediate focus of the Programme is the development and use of measurable objectives, internal budget documentation, and the improvement of data quality and consistency. The deliverables of the Programme include the development of good-practice guides, the conducting of good-practice workshops, and the provision of training and support.

Appointment of members to the Accounting Standards Board (ASB)
The appointment of members to the ASB is seen as a positive step towards the implementation of the PFMA, 1999. The formal establishment and functional operations of the Board will contribute extensively towards the implementation of Generally Recognised Accounting Practice in national and provincial departments, public entities, constitutional institutions, municipalities and boards, com-

---

At the end of March 2003, President Thabo Mbeki hosted an *indaba* with leaders of South African big business. The Big Business Working Group is one of the groups that meet biannually with the President and Ministers to discuss matters of common interest.

The purpose of the meeting was to explore ways to accelerate the rate of growth and development in South Africa, and to ensure open and constructive communication between government and large corporations.

Representatives of the Big Business Working Group indicated that the Group was broadly satisfied with government's macro-economic policies such as the fiscal and monetary policy, and trade and industrial policy. While there were issues that will continue to be discussed and negotiated in detail regarding the actual implementation, there was broad agreement on the direction of macro-economic policy and micro-economic programmes.

missions, companies, corporations, and funds of other entities under the ownership control of a municipality.

Aligning Treasury regulations with the *King II Report on Corporate Governance in South Africa, 2002*

In an attempt to ensure that Treasury regulations are consistent with international best practices prevalent in the private sector, these regulations have been aligned with the principles contained in the *King II Report on Corporate Governance in South Africa, 2002*. In this regard, certain concepts of the Report have been modified for adaptation in the Government finance arena, and the Treasury regulations have been amended accordingly.

Validation Board
The National Treasury has established the Validation Board in an attempt to exercise qualitative control over and accredit training material presented by external service-providers. The Board accredits courses that meet the requirements, and departments are accordingly informed as to who is offering courses of an acceptable quality. In this way, departments are made aware of courses that would be beneficial to employees and which would add value to their capacity-building initiatives.

Normative measures for financial management
The National Treasury, in consultation with the Office of the Auditor-General, is in the process of finalising normative measures for financial management. These measures are aimed at:
- contributing towards the improvement of financial management in the public sector
- providing a benchmark for accounting officers, to assist them with the continuous evaluation of the quality of financial management within their departments
- enabling the National Treasury and the Office of the Auditor-General to report on progress made in the implementation of the PFMA, 1999 as well as the status of financial management within a department or in the public sector as a whole.

State expenditure

The National Treasury plays a pivotal role in the management of government expenditure.

The National Treasury determines the financial-management norms and standards and sets reporting policy that guides the Auditor-General in the performance of his/her duties. It also assists Parliament, through the Standing Committee on Public Accounts, their recommendations and formulation of corrective actions. The National Treasury closely monitors the performance of State departments and is obliged to report any deviations to the Auditor-General.

The National Treasury furthermore maintains transparent and fair tendering processes, as well as accounting, logistic and personnel systems. It sets and maintains standards and norms for treasury and logistics, acts as banker for national departments, and oversees logistical control of stocks and assets.

National Treasury

Treasury norms and standards
In terms of Section 216(1)(c) of the Constitution, 1996, the National Treasury must prescribe measures to ensure both transparency and expenditure control in each sphere of government, by introducing uniform treasury norms and standards. These treasury norms and standards aim at deregulating financial controls, by granting accounting officers of spending agencies more autonomy in financial decision-making within the ambits of impending financial legislation.

Budget evaluations
The National Treasury plays an important role in supporting the economic policy to which

government has committed itself. It determines the macro limit on expenditure, which is then matched with requests from departments in line with the affordability and sustainability of services.

Based on this limit, all national departments are requested annually to submit budget proposals for the following financial year to the National Treasury.

Early Warning System

The Early Warning System was first established in 1997. Any likely under- or overexpenditure is brought to the attention of the Cabinet so that the relevant Minister can ensure that appropriate action is taken.

The introduction of the System has also assisted in the monthly monitoring of the expenditure trends of provincial departments, by having provincial treasuries reporting to the National Treasury in a prescribed format. The information derived from the Early Warning Reports is used for advising the Budget Council and the Cabinet. The Minister of Finance is also kept informed on a regular basis of the Early Warning Report results.

Financial policies, systems and skills development

The National Treasury is responsible for the financial-management systems and training of government.

The services delivered support the following areas:
- financial systems, which consist of the Personnel and Salary System, Logistical Information System, Financial Management System, Basic Accounting System and Management Information System
- banking services and financial reporting for government
- financial-management capacity development in national and provincial governments.

Procurement

The Preferential Procurement Regulations, 2001 give substance to the content of the Preferential Procurement Policy Framework Act, 2000 (Act 5 of 2000). This Act and its Regulations are applicable to central and provincial departments and local government.

Tenders are evaluated according to a preference point system where tenderers can score a maximum of 80 or 90 points for price, while 20 or 10 points can be scored for contracting or subcontracting historically disadvantaged individuals (HDIs) and promoting/achieving specified Reconstruction and Development Programme (RDP) goals. A contract is awarded to the tenderer who scores the highest total number of points. The way in which the tender is evaluated, including the RDP goals to be promoted or achieved and the allocated points in this regard, forms part of the tender documents.

The implementation of the Regulations enhances the involvement of HDIs in the public tendering system and contributes to achieving RDP goals, including the promotion of the small-to-medium enterprises sector.

By mid-2003, the National Treasury was in the process of establishing a supply-chain management (SCM) office to assume responsibility for the development of SCM policies and procedures, the regulatory framework for SCM, and the monitoring of compliance with policies and procedures.

South Africa's anti money-laundering system

South Africa has made considerable progress in developing an anti money-laundering and combating terrorist-financing (AML/CFT) environment. In 2001, Parliament passed the Financial Intelligence Centre (FIC) Act, 2001 (Act 38 of 2001), which consolidates previous legislation and introduces new AML/CFT measures. The Act seeks to implement measures that are in accordance with international standards set by the Financial Action Task Force (FATF).

The implementation of the Act is the responsibility of the National Treasury, and during 2003, the FIC was expected to become an autonomous and self-functioning government agency reporting to the Minister of Finance.

Two institutions were created by the Act, namely the Money-Laundering Advisory Council (MLAC), which is intended to provide the Minister with legislative advice, and the FIC. The mandate of the FIC is to track irregular financial practices, especially the proceeds of crime. The Centre receives reports from accountable institutions, and stores and analyses this information. It then makes disclosures or information packages available to law-enforcement agencies for investigation. It may also make this information available to similar bodies in other countries.

The Act identifies a range of 19 different business sectors which it defines as being accountable institutions, and which are most vulnerable to abuse by criminals. These include banks, *bureaux de change*, life-insurance companies, stockbrokers, money remitters, as well as casinos, lawyers, accountants, investment advisors, estate agents and motor dealers.

The Regulations of the Act were approved in December 2002. They introduced reporting and compliance obligations for accountable institutions. All accountable institutions were obliged to submit suspicious transaction reports to the FIC with effect from 3 February 2003. Nearly 1 000 reports were received by mid-2003 and a significant number of disclosures were made to law-enforcement agencies for investigation. The FIC estimated that it would receive 3 000 reports during the 2003/04 financial year.

Additional measures came into effect on 30 June 2003, which included obligations for accountable institutions to identify their clients and keep proper records.

In 2002, South Africa became a member of the Eastern and Southern Africa Anti Money-Laundering Group (ESAAMLG). South Africa has also been attending meetings of the FATF as an observing member, and applied for FATF membership in 2002. As part of this process, South Africa agreed to undergo a mutual evaluation to access its compliance in terms of international standards. This was done in April 2003 as a joint FATF/ESAAMLG process.

The Egmont Group of Financial Intelligence Units invited the FIC to become a member of the Group after it conducted an assessment of the Centre.

Financial and Fiscal Commission

The FFC is one of the innovations of the multiparty constitutional negotiations that took place between 1992 and 1994. The Commission, which came into operation in April 1994, is a statutory institution and permanent expert commission dealing with intergovernmental fiscal relations.

The FFC is responsible for making recommendations to Parliament and the Cabinet on the equitable division of revenue between national, provincial and local governments on an annual basis, giving advice on fiscal policies and taxes which provinces intend to impose, borrowing by local and provincial governments, and criteria to be considered in determining fiscal allocations. Additional responsibilities can be designated by means of appropriate legislation.

Budget Council

The Budget Council consists of the Minister of Finance and the nine provincial executive committee members responsible for Finance. The mission of the Council is to ensure that the country uses the available resources productively, efficiently and equitably, to the advantage of its people.

It recommends to the Cabinet the share each province should receive after taking national priorities and FFC proposals into account.

Macro-economic strategy

The positive performance of the South African economy in the wake of a global slowdown is indicative of a highly resilient economy. The long-term outlook points towards further growth acceleration over the next few years, and reflects a strong improvement in economic fundamentals, that include:
- Benefits associated with stricter fiscal discipline, which has resulted in lower budget deficits, and which will eliminate government dissaving and pave the way for higher fixed investment spending.
- Improved domestic competitiveness in foreign markets. This has led to significant improvements on trade and current account balances.

Government's micro-economic reform strategy identifies six key performance areas or objectives:
- economic growth
- employment
- small business development
- Black Economic Empowerment (BEE)
- competitiveness
- geographic spread of growth and development.

The strategy rests on three pillars:
- The first pillar consists of cross-cutting issues: human resource development (HRD), infrastructure, access to finance, technology, and research and development (R&D).
- The second pillar comprises a set of actions to improve efficiency and lower costs in three input sectors: transport, telecommunications and energy. In addition, access to these sectors needs to be widened to include all South Africans.
- The third pillar consists of growth sectors that demonstrate a high potential for growth and employment, namely tourism, exports, agriculture, information and communications technology, and cultural industries.

Government has adopted an integrated way forward that consists of the following:
- Fine-tuning the micro-economic strategy.
- Continued managed liberalisation and infrastructure investment in key input sectors.
- Increased attention to the cross-cutting issues that underpin the strategy, including:
  - Clarifying the role of individual departments in sectoral HRD strategies.
  - Adopting a research strategy and allocating the necessary resources to implement it effectively. The Cabinet has already adopted a biotechnology strategy and the relevant Cluster was expected to table a relevant document on technology, innovation and boosting investment in R&D.
- Establishing an integrated financing institution focused on BEE and small business.
- An integrated approach to planning and implementation of infrastructure investment by government.
- Developing and implementing an employment-creation framework.
- Strengthening and co-ordinating government products and services to promote key growth sectors.
- An integrated strategy for small business development, emphasising co-ordination and refinement of existing initiatives, addressing access to finance, and a greater focus on micro enterprises.
- Implementing three components of the BEE strategy, namely an enhanced environment for BEE partnership programmes with the private sector; the establishment of a BEE Advisory Council; and a review of government procurement.

By April 2003, Statistics South Africa indicated that there were between two and three million economically active (some of whom are below the tax threshold) entities that were not registered for tax. In the 2003/04 financial year, the South African Revenue Service focused on bringing these elements into the tax net by comparing databases that reflect economic activity with internal databases of registered tax payers.

- Incorporating a specific geographical dimension into the micro-economic reform strategy, to tap the economic and human potential of all nine provinces by co-ordinating current strategies such as the Integrated Sustainable Rural Development Strategy, Urban Renewal Programme, Spatial Development Initiatives, Industrial Development Zones and Integrated Development Plans, as well as regional economic integration and the New Partnership for Africa's Development (NEPAD). (See Chapter 7: *Economy*.)

South African Revenue Service

In accordance with the SARS Act, 1997 (Act 34 of 1997), the Service is an administratively autonomous (outside the Public Service, but within the public administration) organ of State.

It aims to provide an enhanced, transparent and client-orientated service to ensure optimum and equitable collection of revenue. Its main functions are to:
- collect and administer all national taxes, duties and levies
- collect revenue that may be imposed under any other legislation, as agreed upon between SARS and an organ of State or institution entitled to the revenue
- provide protection against the illegal importation and exportation of goods
- facilitate trade
- advise the Minister of Finance on all revenue-related matters.

Tax system

The National Treasury is also responsible for advising the Minister of Finance on tax-policy issues that arise at local, provincial and national government level. In its policy-advice function to government, the National Treasury must design tax instruments that can optimally fulfil their revenue-raising function, achieve economic and allocative functions, and strengthen redistributive and social-policy functions. This must be done in a manner that creates a basis for general political acceptability of the selected tax instruments. In designing tax policies, co-operation between the National Treasury and SARS is of the utmost importance.

As of 2001, South Africa's source-based income tax system was replaced with a residence-based system. With effect from the years of assessment commencing on or after 1 January 2001, residents are (subject to certain exclusions) taxed on their worldwide income, irrespective of where their income was earned. Foreign taxes are credited against South African tax payable on foreign income. Foreign income and taxes are translated into the South African monetary unit, the Rand.

Capital Gains Tax (CGT) was introduced on 1 October 2001. It forms part of the income tax system and includes capital gains made upon the disposal of assets in taxable income.

Value-Added Tax (VAT) is levied at a standard rate of 14% on all goods and services subject to certain exemptions, exceptions, deductions and adjustments provided for in the VAT Act, 1991 (Act 89 of 1991), as amended.

Transfer duty, estate duty, stamp duty, marketable securities tax, customs duty and

---

On 19 August 2003, the South African Revenue Service (SARS), in partnership with the South African National Council for the Blind (SANCB), launched a project to train visually impaired people as call-centre operators.

As part of its Corporate Social Investment Programme, SARS pledged to provide bursaries worth R1 million to 10 students for call centre training, after which they will be employed by the organisation. SARS will also implement an organisation-wide awareness campaign to educate its employees on working with people with disabilities and people with special needs.

Research undertaken by the SANCB shows that visually impaired people are the least employed group in South Africa, with the employment of this group in the corporate sector being as low as 0,28%.

excise duty are also levied by the national Government.

Regional Services Councils levy turnover and payroll taxes. However, these taxes are at fairly low rates. Local governments levy rates on the value of fixed property, to finance the cost of municipal services.

International tax agreements for the avoidance of double taxation

International tax agreements are important for encouraging investment and trade flows between nations. By reaching agreement on the allocation of taxing rights between residence and source countries of international investors, double-taxation agreements provide a solid platform for growth in international trade and investment, by providing a certain tax framework.

In the 2002/03 fiscal year, considerable progress was once again made in reaching agreements with other countries for the avoidance of double taxation in respect of income accruing to South Africa tax payers from foreign sources, or to foreign tax payers from South African sources. By June 2003:
- Comprehensive agreements were in place with Algeria, Australia, Austria, Belgium, Botswana, Canada, Croatia, Cyprus, the Czech Republic, Denmark, Egypt, Finland, France, Germany, Greece, Hungary, India, Indonesia, Iran, Ireland, Israel, Italy, Japan, Korea, Lesotho, Luxembourg, Malawi, Malta, Mauritius, Namibia, the Netherlands, Norway, Pakistan, the People's Republic of China, Poland, Romania, the Russian Federation, the Seychelles, Singapore, the Slovak Republic, Swaziland, Sweden, Switzerland, Thailand, Tunisia, Uganda, the United Kingdom (UK), the United States of America (USA), Zambia and Zimbabwe. An agreement with the UK extends to Grenada and Sierra Leone.
- Limited sea and air transport agreements existed with Brazil, Portugal and Spain.
- Comprehensive agreements were ratified in South Africa with New Zealand and Nigeria.
- Comprehensive agreements were signed but not ratified with Belarus, Rwanda and the Sultanate of Oman.
- Comprehensive agreements were negotiated or renegotiated, but not signed, with Botswana, Bulgaria, Estonia, Ethiopia, Gabon, Germany, Ghana, Kuwait, Latvia, Lithuania, Malawi, Malaysia, Morocco, Mozambique, the Netherlands, Portugal, Qatar, Spain, Swaziland, Tanzania, Turkey, Ukraine, the United Arab Emirates, Zambia and Zimbabwe. Where treaties were being renegotiated, the existing treaties remained effective until a new agreement was finalised.
- Comprehensive agreements were negotiated or renegotiated but had not been finalised with Bangladesh, Brazil, Saudi Arabia and Sri Lanka.

A number of other countries have expressed the desire to negotiate double-taxation agreements with South Africa.

Agreements for mutual administrative assistance between customs administrations

These agreements cover all aspects of assistance, including the exchange of information, technical assistance, surveillance, investigations and visits by officials.

By June 2003:
- agreements were in place with France, the UK and the USA
- agreements had been ratified in South Africa with Algeria, the Czech Republic, Mozambique, the Netherlands and Zambia
- agreements had been negotiated but not signed with Angola, Iran and Norway
- a number of countries had expressed the desire to negotiate similar agreements.

Sources of revenue

Income tax
Income tax is the Government's main source of income and is levied in terms of the Income Tax Act, 1962 (Act 58 of 1962).

Finance

In South Africa, income tax is levied on South African residents on their worldwide income, with appropriate relief to avoid double taxation. Non-residents are taxed on their income from a South African source. Tax is levied on taxable income which, in essence, consists of gross income less allowable deductions as per the Act.

Companies are taxed at a rate of 30%. In addition to this, secondary tax is levied on companies at a rate of 12,5% on all income distributed by way of dividends. A formula tax applies to gold-mining companies. Small-business corporations (annual turnover limit will be increased to R5 million) benefit from a graduated tax rate of 15% on the first R150 000 of taxable income and can write off certain investment expenditure in the year in which it is incurred.

Small businesses also receive double deduction for expenses initially incurred, with respect to a new business capped at the first R20 000 of available deductions.

Main budget estimates and revenue outcome: 2001/02 and 2002/03

R million	2001/02 Budget estimate	2001/02 Actual outcome	2001/02 Deviation	2002/03 Budget estimate	2002/03 Revised estimate	2002/03 Deviation	2001/02 – 2002/03 (%) change
Taxes on income and profits, including:	131 582	147 310	15 728	155 740	162 500	6 760	10,3
Personal income tax	90 122	90 390	268	89 982	93 200	3 218	3,1
Company tax	29 960	42 354	12 394	50 858	54 850	3 992	29,5
Secondary tax on companies	4 200	7 163	2 963	6 500	6 300	-200	-12,0
Tax on retirement funds	6 300	6 191	-109	6 900	6 900	–	11,5
Other	1 000	1 213	213	1 500	1 250	-250	3,0
Taxes on payroll and workforce	2 800	2 717	-83	2 950	3 300	350	21,4
Taxes on property	4 709	4 628	-81	4 585	5 335	750	15,3
Domestic taxes on goods and services, including:	86 740	86 888	148	92 848	97 554	4 706	12,3
Value-Added Tax	60 350	61 057	707	66 200	70 600	4 400	15,6
Excise duties	10 625	10 573	-52	11 067	11 302	235	6,9
Levies on fuel	15 310	14 923	-387	15 166	15 200	34	1,9
Other	455	335	-120	415	452	37	35,0
Taxes on international trade and transactions	9 427	8 680	-747	10 613	9 805	-808	13,0
Stamp duties and fees	1 585	1 767	182	1 770	1 600	-170	-9,5
State miscellaneous revenue	–	307	307	–	–	–	
Total tax revenue	236 843	252 298	15 455	268 506	280 095	11 588	11,0
Departmental revenue	4 657	4 088	-569	3 910	3 589	-321	-12,2
Transactions in assets and liabilities	50	4	-46	30	40	10	
Recoveries of loans and repayments	93	77	-16	900	164	-736	
Grants	–	–	–	130	117	-13	
Less: Southern African Customs Union payments	-8 205	-8 205	–	-8 259	-8 259	–	0,7
Main budget revenue	233 438	248 262	14 824	265 217	275 745	10 529	11,1

Source: Budget Review 2003

Income tax returns are issued annually to registered tax payers after the end of each year of assessment. The year of assessment for individuals covers a period of 12 months which generally commences on 1 March of a specific year and ends on the last day of February the following year. Companies are permitted to have a tax year ending on a date that coincides with their financial year.

However, the Act also provides for certain classes of tax payers to have a year of assessment ending on a day other than the last day of February.

Tax returns must be submitted to SARS within 60 days from the end of the year of assessment or the date of the returns' issue. A tax payer may apply for extension for the rendition of a tax return.

People who owe SARS tax are charged interest at a rate as published in the *Government Gazette* in accordance with the PFMA, 1999. Persons who derive income from sources other than remuneration, e.g. trade, profession or investments and companies, are required to make two provisional tax payments during the course of the tax year and may opt for a third 'topping-up' payment six months after the end of the tax year.

Value-Added Tax

VAT is levied on the supply of all goods and services rendered by registered vendors throughout the business cycle. It is the Government's second biggest source of income.

Effectively, the Tax is levied on the value added by an enterprise. As vendors levy and pay over the tax included in their prices, VAT is borne by the final consumer. VAT is also levied on the importation of goods and services into South Africa by any person. It is levied at the standard rate of 14%, but certain supplies are subject to the zero-rate or are exempt from VAT.

The prices of goods and services must be quoted/displayed on an inclusive basis, which means that VAT has to be included in all prices on products, price lists, advertisements and quotations.

Customs duty

South Africa is a signatory to the Southern African Customs Union (SACU) agreement, together with Botswana, Lesotho, Namibia and Swaziland (BLNS countries). The five member countries of SACU apply the same customs and excise legislation, the same rates of customs and excise duties on imported and locally manufactured goods, and the same import duties on imported goods. The uniform application of tariffs and the harmonisation of procedures simplify trade within the SACU common customs area.

Import duties, including anti-dumping and countervailing duties, are used as mechanisms to protect the local industry.

Customs and excise revenue collected in SACU is shared according to a formula that has been in place since 1969. Following eight years of negotiations, a new SACU Agreement was signed in October 2002. The new revenue-sharing formula was expected to take effect in the 2003/04 financial year and will ensure long-term sustainability of these transfer payments. SACU revenue shares for 2003/04 amounted to R9,7 billion, with an anticipated rise to R11,6 billion and R12,4 billion in 2004/05 and 2005/06 respectively.

South Africa has entered into agreements on mutual assistance between customs administrations. These agreements cover all aspects of assistance, including the exchange of information, technical assistance, surveillance, investigations and visits by officials.

Agreements are in place with France, the UK, Mozambique and the USA. An agreement between South Africa and Algeria has been ratified. Agreements have been signed, but not ratified, with the Czech Republic and the Netherlands. Further agreements have been negotiated, but not signed, with Norway and Zambia.

In 2003, efforts were doubled to improve the effectiveness of customs controls and trade facilitation. One of the highlights includes the commencement of a 24-hour operation for commercial traffic at Beit Bridge, the busiest border post in southern Africa.

Another development will be the implementation of the simplified and harmonised transit procedures in terms of the Southern African Development Community (SADC) Protocol on Trade. The SARS will also step up the fight against customs-evasion through a year-long national enforcement campaign. At the same time, SARS will double efforts to strengthen co-operation with legitimate traders who operate within the terms of the law.

Excise duty

Excise duty is levied on certain locally manufactured goods as well as their imported equivalents. This duty is levied as a specific duty on tobacco, liquor and as an *ad valorem* duty on cosmetics, televisions, audio equipment and motor cars.

Relief from excise duty is available where excisable products are exported. In addition, relief is also available in respect of specific farming, forestry, and certain manufacturing activities.

Excise duties are imposed both as a means to generate revenue for the fiscus, and to change consumer behaviour.

Transfer duty

Transfer duty is payable on the acquisition of property by individuals at progressive marginal rates between 0% and 8%.

Transfer duty on property acquired by a person other than an individual, e.g. a company or trust, is payable at a rate of 10%.

All transactions relating to a taxable supply of goods that are subject to VAT are exempt from transfer duty.

Estate duty

For the purposes of estate duty, an estate consists of all property, including deemed property (e.g. life-insurance policies, payments from pension funds, etc.) of the deceased, wherever situated. The estate of a deceased non-resident consists only of his/her South African assets.

The duty, at a rate of 20%, is calculated on the dutiable amount of the estate. Certain admissible deductions from the total value of the estate are allowed.

Stamp duty

Stamp duty is levied on certain financial transactions.

Marketable Securities Tax (MST)

MST is payable in respect of every purchase of marketable securities by a stockbroker, on behalf of any person, at a rate of 0,25% of the consideration for which such securities are purchased.

Uncertified Securities Tax (UST)

UST is payable in respect of the issue and change in beneficial ownership of any securities, which are transferable without a written instrument and are not evidenced by a certificate. It is levied at a rate of 0,25% and will eventually replace MST.

Skills-development levy

A skills-development levy was introduced on 1 April 2000. This is a compulsory levy scheme for the funding of education and training. SARS administers the collection thereof. The rate was at 1,0% of payroll as from 1 April 2001 and is payable by employers who are registered with SARS for employees' tax purposes, or employers who have an annual payroll in excess of R250 000.

Air passenger departure tax

A tax of R110 per fee-paying passenger departing on international flights and R55 per passenger departing to the BLNS countries is payable.

Organisational performance

The SARS has exceeded its revenue target of R280 billion set during the Budget speech in February 2003. This was announced in Parliament by the Minister of Finance, who said growth in tax revenue collected by SARS in the 2002/03 financial year amounted to R281 billion.

Recent years have seen a marked decline in marginal rates for corporates and individuals, as well as the consolidation of income-tax brackets to eliminate the adverse effects of inflation.

The SARS has had considerable success in targeting and convicting tax evaders, thereby enhancing the overall tax-compliance environment considerably.

Other achievements include:
- The implementation of a new enforcement strategy that targets areas of high risk and aggressive tax-planning practices. This has resulted in significant increases in the total revenue contribution of corporates through sector-specific enforcement action.
- The upgrade of border infrastructure and the introduction of an informal dispute-resolution mechanism for customs.
- The achievement of process efficiencies through the establishment of rapid processing areas, thereby improving turnaround times.
- The appointment of the SARS Commissioner in 2003 – for the third time in a row – as the chairperson of the World Customs Organisation. This was the first time in the history of the Organisation that anyone had occupied the seat for three consecutive terms.

From a customs perspective, SARS has been upgrading border posts in order to improve trade facilitation and better protect the public from trade in dangerous substances. Customs stepped up its anti-smuggling operations and targeted inspections.

Other initiatives in customs include the introduction of centralised registration, refund mobile units and a valuation database. A risk-based audit approach has been introduced, and differentiated service levels will be implemented through an accredited client scheme.

On 27 June 2003, SARS and the United States Bureau of Customs and Border Protection (USBCBP) signed a co-operation agreement in Brussels, Belgium to secure trade between South Africa and the USA.

Subsequently, SARS and the USBCBP commenced with intensive preparations to improve security measures at South African ports to ensure the safety of exports from South and southern Africa.

The agreement forms part of South Africa's commitment to facilitate and boost economic ties between South Africa and the USA. In terms of the agreement, both parties will exchange information and work together to identify, screen, examine and seal high-risk containers, and station customs officials at each other's seaports that handle significant volumes of direct container traffic between the two countries.

Budget estimates and revenue outcome

Audited results show that the actual receipts for 2001/02 were R248,3 billion or 6,4% more than the original Budget estimate. Significant deviations from the original estimates include company tax up by R12,4 billion, secondary tax on companies up by R3 billion, and trade tax down by R747 million.

The revenue outcome of R278,3 billion for the 2002/03 fiscal year was R13 billion higher than the original Budget estimate of R265,2 billion. The main reasons for this increase are the higher-than-estimated increase of price levels in the economy, and higher-than-anticipated growth in the economy. Taxes on income and profits grew at an annual rate of 8,4% and contributed about 60% to the main Budget revenue. Taxes on domestic goods and services and international trade grew at annual rates of 11,1% and 12,2%, respectively.

2003 tax proposals

Sound structural changes since 1994 have created fiscal space for introducing tax-driven stimulus measures that seek to grow the tax base, create sustainable employment opportunities, and alleviate poverty. Personal income-tax relief for the period 1995 to 2002 totalled R48,9 billion. In support of economic activity, a tax holiday scheme was introduced in 1997, the corporate tax rate was reduced to 30% in 1999, and a split rate was introduced for small business in 2000.

Tax policy and enhanced revenue collection continue to contribute materially to improving growth prospects, development and employment creation through personal income-tax relief, encouragement of investment, measures to boost household savings, and reforms to stimulate enterprise development. The 2003 tax proposals provided for:
- personal income-tax relief of R13,3 billion, raising the minimum tax threshold to R30 000 and increasing the take-home pay of wage earners to encourage consumption and saving
- reducing the Retirement Fund Tax to protect savings, especially of low-income earners
- accelerated depreciation allowances for urban development zones, materially addressing urban decay, and the supply of affordable housing to the urban poor
- eliminating the dividend tax from foreign subsidiaries, thus encouraging capital inflow
- reduced excise duties on passenger vehicles and abolition of duties on computers, easing their cost for business and personal use
- inflation-related adjustments to alcohol and tobacco taxes, in keeping with government's social and health policies.

Gambling and lotteries

The gambling industry in South Africa is regulated by the National Gambling Act, 1996 (Act 33 of 1996).

About 50 000 people are directly or indirectly employed in this industry, the majority of which are first-time workers.

Casinos, racing, gambling and wagering, excluding lotteries and sports pools, are functional areas over which the provinces and Parliament have concurrent legislative competence, in terms of Schedule 4 of the Constitution, 1996.

Substantial fixed investment is, and remains, a condition for a casino licence, and investments have to go beyond gambling. The Act provides for a maximum of 40 casinos nationwide. In 2003, 28 casinos were operational throughout the country. Investments of approximately R11,7 billion had been made, which included the establishment of conference centres for public use.

All gambling licences should ensure effective participation of the historically disadvantaged. On average, there is equity holding of 43% by BEE companies.

The Department of Trade and Industry was expected to submit a new Gambling Bill during 2003/04 to clarify the differences existing in legislation and administrative processes between provinces, particularly in respect of horse-racing. The licensing processes, costs, levels of taxation and types of bets allowed vary between provinces, creating confusion in the industry.

In September 1999, the Minister of Trade and Industry signed the National Lottery Licence Agreement with Uthingo Management (Pty) Ltd, the official lottery operator. The National Lottery celebrated its third anniversary in March 2003.

Lottery-ticket sales rose from R88,4 million in 1999/00 to R3,77 billion in 2002/03.

Amounts available for distribution to worthy causes amounted to R10,2 billion in 2000/01, R439,2 million in 2001/02 and R1,021 billion in 2002/03, while in the first three months of 2003, some R177,2 million was allocated.

During the 2002/03 financial year, the largest slice of funds was allocated to charities

– R344 million of a total of R367 million available for distribution. Sport and recreation received R211 million of the R224,6 million available. Spending on arts and culture amounted to R170 million of a distribution amount of R224 million.

Auditor-General

The Auditor-General is appointed statutorily by the President as the independent auditor of the executive authority. The Auditor-General's appointment, conditions of service, powers, duties and related matters are covered by the Constitution, 1996 and the Auditor-General Act, 1995 (Act 12 of 1995).

The Office of the Auditor-General was established in terms of Section 3 of the Audit Arrangement Act, 1992 (Act 122 of 1992). The Office of the Auditor-General gained independence from the executive authority on 1 April 1993 and operates as a juristic body under appropriate parliamentary control, namely the Audit Commission.

The Deputy Auditor-General is the chief executive officer (CEO) and accounting officer, and is responsible for the efficient management and administration of the Office. Six corporate executive managers assist the CEO.

The Office has a personnel complement of 1 400 and a budget of R560 million, and each year audits national and provincial departments, local governments, as well as a number of miscellaneous accounts.

Government auditing involves the investigation and/or evaluation of financial management practices, financial statements, and performance and compliance with the requirements by government and related institutions. The objective is to form an opinion on whether the financial statements fairly present the results of the operations of an auditee at a given time, and whether laws and regulations have been complied with. It also forms an opinion on control, to ensure that public funds and assets are safeguarded, accounting systems are functioning properly, and public monies are spent effectively.

The Office contributed significantly to developments that would improve the regular reporting on national government accounts. These include:

- Accounting for environmental assets, especially fresh water.
- Formulating principles and indicators for municipal performance reporting.
- Finalising and implementing improved municipal-accounting practices.
- Assisting in the preparation of draft formats for the annual financial statements required of accounting officers in terms of the PFMA, 1999.
- Summarising the findings of all national entities into a general report on audit outcomes. This enables the user of the report to view the audit results among Ministerial portfolio lines.

The Institute for Public Finance and Auditing, established in 1999 for the professional development of staff in government, is fully operational and implements an active programme of training. It has implemented a financial management improvement programme which is supported by the European Union.

In accordance with the PFMA, 1999, the Auditor-General has the power to investigate and audit the activities of public entities without the necessary approval of the CEO or board of directors, if he or she considers it to be in the public interest, or upon receipt of a complaint.

All the companies listed in terms of the Act have to report on their financial affairs and performance. Among these are the Post Office, Eskom and Transnet. Provincial auditors are responsible for the management of all audits of provincial governments, specific statutory bodies and municipalities. They are also responsible for related reporting to the provincial legislatures and other provincial and local government institutions.

Financial sector

South African Reserve Bank

The Reserve Bank and the Ministry of Finance form the monetary authority in South Africa. The Reserve Bank has been given a significant degree of autonomy in terms of the Constitution, 1996, and must perform its functions independently. However, the Reserve Bank must hold regular consultations with the Minister of Finance. Its management, powers and functions are governed by the South African Reserve Bank Act, 1989.

The Reserve Bank formulates and implements monetary policy and regulates the supply (availability) of money by influencing its cost. Monetary policy is guided by the objectives of the Reserve Bank, which are formulated to ensure financial stability. Consistent combating of inflation is the cornerstone of the Bank's policy. A formal inflation-targeting monetary-policy framework has been adopted since 2000.

Monetary policy is set by the Bank's Monetary Policy Committee (MPC). The Committee, consisting of the Reserve Bank's governors and other senior officials, usually meets once a quarter, after which it issues a statement indicating its assessment of the economy and policy changes, if any.

The Reserve Bank is responsible for:
- assisting government in formulating and implementing macro-economic policy
- formulating and implementing monetary policy to achieve its primary goal in the interest of the community it serves
- ensuring that the South African money and banking system as a whole is sound, meets the requirements of the community, and keeps abreast of international finance developments
- informing the South African community and all interested parties abroad about monetary policy and the South African economic situation in general.

The Reserve Bank is managed by a board of 14 directors, seven of whom are elected by the shareholders of the Bank and represent commerce, finance, industry and agriculture. The President of South Africa appoints the governor, three deputy governors and three directors.

The Reserve Bank acts as the central bank of South Africa and banker to other banking institutions. It provides accommodation to banks and is the custodian of the statutory cash reserves that all registered banks are required to maintain. It also provides facilities for the clearing and settlement of interbank obligations.

On 9 March 1998, the Bank implemented a system of repurchase transactions (repos) as the main instrument in managing liquidity in the money market. The repo rate is the price at which the central bank lends cash to the banking system. The repo rate has become the most important indicator for short-term interest rates.

The repurchase agreements entered into between the Reserve Bank and other banks are conducted on the basis of an outright buy-and-sell transaction, with a full transfer of ownership of the underlying assets. The system also provides for a marginal lending facility, which replaces the previous discount window. This facility is available to banks at their initiative to bridge overnight liquidity needs.

The marginal lending facility forms an integrated part of the South African Multiple Option Settlement (SAMOS) System, which came into operation in March 1998.

This enables banks to electronically make payments to and receive payments from the Reserve Bank, through their settlement accounts held in the books of the Reserve Bank. Daily settlements of interbank exposures are effected through the SAMOS System.

Payments through the System can only be made if a bank has sufficient funds in its settlement account. Such funds can be obtained through interbank transfers, repurchase transactions, other types of liquidity-creating instruments of the Reserve Bank, or the marginal lending facility. The SAMOS System, however, allows banks to receive funds obtained in the interbank market directly in their settlement accounts in the Reserve Bank's books.

The Reserve Bank uses various instruments to achieve its objectives. These include changes in the repo-rate marginal-lending facility; open-market transactions, including selling its own debentures; changes in requirements with regard to cash reserves of banking institutions; and controlling the liquidity in the money market through repurchase transactions.

The Bank undertakes national and international transactions on behalf of the State, and acts for government in transactions with the International Monetary Fund (IMF).

The Reserve Bank is the custodian of the greater part of South Africa's gold and other foreign-exchange reserves.

The Reserve Bank issues banknotes (printed by the South African Bank Note Company, a wholly owned subsidiary of the Reserve Bank) and controls the South African Mint Company (SA Mint).

Monetary policy

From about 1989, the main objective of monetary policy has been to secure a stable financial environment within which economic decisions are no longer influenced by high and variable inflation.

The Reserve Bank has therefore not applied monetary policy as a short-term counter-cyclical instrument, but has rather aimed at creating financial stability, which is seen as a necessary precondition for growth and development in the long run. To achieve the objective of low and stable inflation, the Reserve Bank adopted a policy framework that was initially anchored by the setting of guidelines for growth in the broad money supply (M3). In later years, the predictability of the relationship between growth in the money supply and growth in the aggregate nominal income became less certain. As changes in the money supply became a less reliable indicator of changes in nominal income in the short-to-medium term, the Bank decided to attach less significance to the growth in M3. Instead, movements in other financial and economic indicators were also thoroughly assessed during deliberations on policy issues. Because changes in money and credit totals are major determinants of inflation in the long run, they were nevertheless still seen as important variables that could be closely monitored by decision-makers.

The framework for monetary policy was tightened and made more transparent by adopting formal inflation targeting. Inflation targeting is aimed at facilitating the reduction of the inflation rate or the maintenance of price stability, and has been successfully adopted by an increasing number of countries in recent years. The National Treasury and the Reserve Bank initially agreed on an inflation target band of 3% to 6% on average for 2002, for the Consumer Price Index excluding mortgage costs (CPIX). This target was left unchanged for 2003 when the Minister of Finance announced new targets in October 2001, and a lower target range of 3% to 5% was introduced for 2004 and 2005.

Amid a global downturn and little domestic pressure on inflation, the CPIX inflation rate had declined to below the upper limit of the 2002 target by September 2001, and at that time it was expected that the downward trend would be sustained, albeit at a slower rate. However, the pressure on the exchange rate, which had been present since 2000, had intensified in the second half of 2001, and the impact that this had on the inflation rate inevitably caused the CPIX to reverse its downward trend. The CPIX inflation rate moved outside the 2002 target to 6,3% in November 2001.

An important challenge for monetary policy during this period was resisting the temptation to use interest-rate policy to defend the currency directly. For this reason, there was no change in the monetary-policy stance during the worst of the exchange-rate movements in November and December 2001. Nevertheless, monetary policy could not be impervious to the impact of exchange-rate changes on the measured inflation rate in an inflation-targeting regime. Although monetary policy can do little to offset the first-round effects of exchange-rate changes on the measured inflation rate, if the depreciation and initial price increase result in or threaten higher wage demands and further price-raising behaviour, then monetary policy could play a role in moderating these second-round effects.

An unscheduled meeting was therefore convened on 15 January 2002 and the repo rate was raised by 100 basis points. The primary reason for this increase was preemptive, with the main concern at the time being the evidence of higher inflation expectations that could feed through to higher wage demands and further price increases. In addition, although excess spending in the economy was still relatively moderate, there were signs of excessive increases in the money supply and credit-extension data.

Following the increase, monetary policy was tightened further during the subsequent three meetings of the MPC. In all cases the repo rate was increased by a further 100 basis points. By March 2002, it was clear that inflation expectations had been adversely affected by the depreciation, and that the impact of the depreciation on prices would not be limited to a once-off unavoidable first-round effect. In addition, there was concern about the continued high rate of growth in the money supply and credit extension, the state of the Balance of Payments, and the beginning of an acceleration in unit labour cost. This was against the backdrop of a world economy recovering from the downturn, with anticipated acceleration in the recovery. It was felt that tightening monetary policy at that stage, if successful in dampening wage and price increases, would avert the need for more drastic increases in the future.

By June 2002, the upward trends of inflation and inflation expectations had maintained their momentum, and unit labour-cost trends and money-supply developments remained unfavourable. By that time, CPIX inflation had moved above the 9% level and production price inflation (PPI) had reached almost 15%. There were, however, some positive indications that could have signalled a reduction in pressure on inflation, and that appeared to signal the peak of the interest-rate cycle at the time. These included the partial recovery of the Rand, the surplus on both the current and financial accounts of the Balance of Payments, the continued low level of capacity utilisation, and the fact that fiscal discipline was being maintained.

This relatively positive outlook appeared to be confirmed with the release of the production price index figures for June, which showed that PPI had declined. It was hoped that this would mark the turning point of the PPI and feed in with a lag to the CPIX. This appeared to bode well for the inflation outlook. Unfortunately, in July 2002, production prices resumed their upward trend. Apart from this setback, a number of factors contributed to the increasingly negative outlook for inflation when the MPC met in September 2002.

At the September meeting, the MPC had to take cognisance of the fact that not only was inflation rising at a faster rate than expected, but inflation pressures were also becoming more broadly based. It was no longer a case of rising food prices, but the price increases were becoming more generalised and had also spread to services. Furthermore, quarter-on-quarter CPIX inflation was even more pronounced. Apart from this, the oil price was keeping petrol prices high, and the risk of an attack on Iraq by the USA was likely to keep these prices at higher levels, with a risk of further acceleration. The weaker exchange rate since June 2002 also clouded the inflation outlook.

Inflation expectations remained high, and there was increasing evidence that wage settlements were significantly higher in the third quarter than had been the case in the first half of the year.

The MPC also had to consider the fact that despite the previous increases in interest rates, growth in the monetary aggregates and credit extension had remained stubbornly high. On the positive side, despite fairly robust growth in demand, it was acknowledged that there was no sign of excess spending or production-capacity constraints. Although inflation was being driven primarily by cost-push factors, it was felt that this, combined with accommodating monetary developments, required a monetary-policy response from the Reserve Bank. The challenge facing the Reserve Bank was to increase real rates sufficiently to achieve its inflation objectives, at a minimum cost to the real economy.

After the September MPC meeting, the outlook for inflation was still uncertain. Although inflation was expected to peak by the end of 2002, factors such as higher wage settlements, high money-supply growth figures, stubbornly high producer prices, and questions over the sustainability of the exchange-rate recovery cast doubt on the strength of the expected downturn in the inflation rate. The outlook for a relaxation of the monetary-policy stance was also influenced by the fact that the targets for 2004 and 2005 were to decline to 3 – 5%, which added to the pressures on monetary policy.

In October 2002, the Minister of Finance announced a revision of the targets for 2004 and 2005. In his Medium Term Budget Policy Statement (MTBPS) he announced that it was decided to modify the targets by maintaining the target at 3 – 6% for 2004, and that the target of 3 – 5% would be suspended until further notice. Subsequently, in the February 2003 Budget speech, it was announced that the target for 2005 would also be maintained at 3 – 6%, and that the target for 2006 would be announced concurrent with the October 2003 MTBPS.

The November MPC meeting was the first meeting in 2002 at which interest rates were not increased. This decision was taken despite the fact that CPIX inflation was still rising, having reached a year-on-year rate of 12,5% in October, and an even higher quarter-on-quarter annualised rate of 12,7% in the third quarter. However, the prices of non-food goods appeared to be levelling off, although service prices, which are traditionally more sticky, were still accelerating.

There was sufficient evidence to suggest that the turning point in inflation had either been reached or was imminent. There were a number of fundamental factors that convinced the MPC not to raise rates further at that stage. These factors, included the significant slowdown in PPI; the strengthening of the external value of the Rand; the decline in international oil prices; slower growth in bank-credit extension; and a deceleration in the pace of growth in the more broadly defined money-supply aggregates. These factors had been a major cause for concern earlier in 2002. In addition, there were other factors which continued to be conducive to a lower inflation environment, including continued excess production-capacity in the economy, the lack of signs of excess spending, and continued fiscal discipline on the part of government.

There were, however, a number of upside risks highlighted by the MPC. The Committee was particularly concerned about high inflationary expectations, the high increases in some administered prices, as well as the faster growth in nominal unit labour cost. This latter factor was of particular concern given the strong relationship between unit labour-cost increases and inflation, and the possibility of a wage/price spiral combined with higher inflation expectations.

The relatively long gap between the November 2002 meeting and the meeting in March 2003 gave the MPC a chance to better assess the sustainability of the improved inflation climate. At the time of the meeting, there were more positive signs that the downward trend in inflation was sustainable. Apart from the fact that the CPIX inflation rate itself had appeared to be on a downward trajectory, PPI had declined significantly.

The Rand's recovery proved to be sustained, and money supply and underlying bank-credit extension-growth continued to moderate. Apart from a decrease in capacity utilisation, the MPC noted that although fiscal policy was expected to be more expansionary in 2003, the projected levels for the Budget deficit over the next three years would not present any difficulties for monetary policy. Two other factors that had improved the inflation outlook since the previous meeting were that the current account recorded a surplus in the fourth quarter, and that food-price increases, a major driver of inflation in the recent past, had shown signs of moderating. Although food-price inflation was still at a higher level than the average inflation rate, indications were that the downward trend would continue.

Despite this positive outlook, the MPC felt that it would be premature to be too complacent about inflation, and left the repo rate unchanged. The Committee was reluctant to reverse the policy stance, because certain risks were identified that could prevent or slow down the expected decline in the inflation rate. The major risk identified was that of the rate of increase in unit labour-cost which had risen considerably in the third quarter of 2003. Furthermore, it was felt that the publicity surrounding a number of recently announced increases in administered prices could have a negative impact on inflation expectations in general. Finally, the uncertainty surrounding the outcome and impact of the war in Iraq made it difficult to predict the short-to-medium term outlook for the recovery in the world economy and the behaviour of oil prices.

The MPC decided to reduce the repo rate by 100 basis points to a level of 11% effective from 15 August 2003.

On 11 September 2003, the repo rate was again reduced by 100 basis points to a level of 10%.

The course of future movements in the repo rate in either direction will continue to be judged by the Committee in the light of the outlook for inflation against the inflation target.

Financial Services Board

The FSB is an independent statutory body financed by the financial services industry itself. It supervises the exercise of control over the activities of financial institutions and financial services, excluding banks and mutual banks. The FSB also promotes programmes and initiatives by financial institutions and bodies, representing the financial-services industry, to inform and educate users of financial products and services. It also acts in an advisory capacity to the Minister of Finance.

The FSB supervises the exercise of control over such institutions and services, in terms of several parliamentary Acts, that entrust regulatory functions to registrars of long-term insurance, short-term insurance, friendly societies, pension funds, collective investment schemes, financial service-providers exchanges and financial markets. These functions converge in the office of the executive officer, acting with the other members of the executive and heads of the various departments of the FSB's administrative infrastructure.

Included in such functions is regulatory control over central security depositories and depository institutions responsible for the safe custody of securities.

The FSB is also responsible for the financial supervision of the Road Accident Fund.

Excluded from the FSB's responsibilities are some areas involving listing requirements or public issues, take-overs and mergers.

The Insider Trading Act, 1998 (Act 135 of 1998), provides for the establishment of the Insider Trading Directorate at the FSB. The Act makes it easier to impose criminal sanctions and, in addition, the FSB can take civil action against offenders.

The executive officer is provided with an armoury of regulatory sanctions, including the cancellation of authorisation to supply financial services.

The executive officer has formal powers of investigation to which criminal sanctions attach in the event of obstruction. He or she can, in certain circumstances, also petition for the winding up of, or placing under judicial management, certain financial institutions such as insurers and pension funds.

These powers of intervention do not, however, take the risk out of an investment made at a financial institution. All investments carry some degree of risk, whether relating to business or general economic conditions.

The Inspection of Financial Institutions Act, 1998 (Act 80 of 1998), gives the FSB greater policing powers. The Act allows the FSB to obtain warrants for searching and questioning third parties who might have information about unregistered financial institutions, such as those providing insurance or investment services.

The FSB is assisted by an advisory board on financial markets, and advisory committees on financial service-providers, long and short-term insurance, pension funds and collective investment schemes. A Financial Services Consumer Advisory Panel was also established to advise the FSB and Registrar of Banks on consumer-protection issues falling within the regulators' jurisdiction.

The FSB maintains a close relationship with all existing industry associations. It liaises with overseas regulatory organisations and is a member of the International Organisation of Security Commissions, the International Association of Insurance Supervisors, the African Association of Insurance Supervisors and the International Network of Pension Regulators and Supervisors.

On the domestic scene, it liaises with bodies such as the Public Accountants and Auditors, Consumers Affairs Committee and various government departments, as well as with prosecuting authorities such as the South African Police Service (SAPS), the Directorate of Special Operations and the National Director of Public Prosecutions.

The banking industry

At the end of December 2002, 42 banks, including 14 branches of foreign banks and two mutual banks, were registered with the Office of the Registrar of Banks. Furthermore, 52 foreign banks had authorised representative offices in South Africa. The banking institutions collectively employed 115 734 workers at 8 438 branches and agencies.

Four major groups dominate the South African banking sector, namely Amalgamated Banks of South Africa (Absa) Group Limited, Standard Bank Investment Corporation Limited, FirstRand Holdings Limited and Nedcor Limited. These groups maintain extensive branch networks across all nine provinces, and together hold 82% of the total assets (R1,101 billion) of the banking sector.

The major banks offer a wide range of services to both individual and corporate customers. One-stop relationship banking, instead of isolated services, has gained importance. Nevertheless, several banks specialise in providing services in merchant banking, securities underwriting or other niche areas.

Industry-wide net income after tax declined to 0,4% of total assets in 2002. As a percentage of equity, industry-wide net income after tax decreased from 9,2% in 2001 to 5,4% in 2002. By the end of 2002, industry-wide net income before taxation had begun to decline to R8,9 billion, compared with R10,5 billion in 2001.

The change in focus of the regulatory authorities, from direct control to deregulation, has been accompanied by an emphasis on proper capitalisation, sound risk-management procedures and greater disclosure.

South Africa adheres to the capital-adequacy guidelines for banks issued by the Basel Committee on Banking Supervision, under the auspices of the Bank for International Settlements. In South Africa, the requirement to maintain capital equal to the full ratio of 10% of risk-weighted assets became effective in October 2001.

By the end of 2002, the banking sector as a whole had a ratio of capital-to-risk weighted assets of 10%.

Many demands are now being made on South African banking institutions to extend their activities to accommodate the banking needs of the underprivileged, and to provide more funds for housing, export financing, agriculture and small-business development. Several initiatives are under way to develop appropriate structures to provide access to finance to all sectors of South Africa's population.

The regulations relating to Banks, which form part of South Africa's banking legislation, were revised during 2002, ensuring South Africa's continued adherence to best practice.

The Bank Supervision Department envisages amending the regulatory framework in order to allow for the establishment of different classes of banking institutions, such as second-tier and third-tier banks.

A project to consider the establishment of narrow and core banks was initiated during 2002/03. The objective is to increase competition in the banking sector, while also creating greater access to basic banking services, such as savings accounts and housing and educational loans to the under- and unbanked.

The Department proposes that such banks be subject to lower-entry criteria, but that their business scope be limited. In order to safeguard the stability of the banking system, it is envisaged that narrow and core banks would be subject to strict conditions, such as being permitted to take retail deposits, but not to trade or invest in, for example, derivatives. Draft legislation was expected in 2003.

The microlending industry

A process of regulating and enhancing the credibility of the microlending industry was initiated by the Minister of Trade and Industry a few years ago.

In May 1999, the Department announced changes to the laws governing the industry. Amendments to the Usury Act, 1968 (Act 73 of 1968), include three provisions: capping interest rates at 10 times the prime lending rate, increasing the loan ceiling from R6 000 to R10 000, and creating a system to compel microlenders to become members of a regulatory authority. Role-players in the industry were required to register with the Micro Finance Regulatory Council (MFRC) by 15 September 1999.

According to an Appeal Court ruling in July 2000, microlenders are not allowed to hold the bank cards and personal identification numbers of their clients as security.

In 2002, the MFRC instituted a Code of Conduct for microlenders aimed at encouraging responsible lending. The guidelines of the Code compel microlenders to assess applicants' levels of financial commitments against the National Loans Register (NLR) before advancing a loan. The NLR was launched in November 2000 by the MFRC to enable assessment of the ability of prospective borrowers to afford repayments on loans.

Microlenders are also required to maintain a register of their appointed agents, who are expected to carry identification cards bearing the lender's name and the MFRC logo.

Creditors who violate the Code of Conduct are penalised and subjected to disciplinary measures in accordance with the MFRC's disciplinary processes.

The Deputy Minister of Trade and Industry, Ms Lindiwe Hendricks, addressed the MFRC National Microlenders Awards ceremony held in Johannesburg in November 2002.

The Awards aim to promote and encourage excellence and innovation in micro-enterprise lending, consumer education and housing finance.

Ms Hendricks said at the ceremony that the Department of Trade and Industry's Unfair Business Practice Unit had investigated numerous complaints about unscrupulous lenders. Between June 1999 and November 2002, the Unit had received close to 7 000 complaints.

Several of these were referred to the SAPS and arrests and convictions have taken place.

Insurance companies

Short-term (non-life) insurance is concerned primarily with risk assessment. The contracts usually run from year to year and can be cancelled by either party. These contracts apply to engineering, guarantee, liability, motor business, accident and health, property, transportation, and miscellaneous insurance. As at 31 March 2003, 96 short-term insurers were registered. The total gross premiums written for 2002 (unaudited figures) amounted to R31,5 billion and the total assets amounted to R38,6 billion (excluding the South African Special Risks Insurance Association Limited).

In essence, long-term insurance consists of life, assistance, sinking fund, health and disability insurance. Long-term insurance and pension and provident funds are concerned with maximising investment results, and life insurance is dominant. As at 31 March 2003, a total of 75 long-term insurers were registered. The total net premiums received and outstanding for 2002 (unaudited figures) amounted to R184,5 billion, while total assets amounted to R802,8 billion.

The Financial Advisory and Intermediary Services Act, 2002 (Act 37 of 2002), contains many of the provisions incorporated in the Policyholder Protection Rules. The FSB is in the process of redrafting these Rules to ensure that there is no duplication of provisions.

The FSB made a submission to the Minister of Finance to remove the statutory ceiling on the payment of commission to intermediaries on commercial and corporate business in the short-term insurance industry. Approval was granted on the grounds that the decapping would only become effective from the date on which intermediaries were licensed, as required in terms of the Financial Advisory and Intermediary Services Act, 2002.

Other financial institutions

Development Bank of Southern Africa (DBSA)

In terms of the DBSA Act, 1997 (Act 13 of 1997), the primary purpose of the Bank is to promote economic development and growth, HRD and institutional capacity-building by mobilising financial and other resources from the national or international private and public sectors for sustainable development projects and programmes. The DBSA operates in South Africa and in all SADC countries.

Its mandate is focused on infrastructure, acting as a catalyst for investments in partnership with the private sector. The Bank's capital structure and financial policy have been changed, and there is a comprehensive approach to risk management.

The capital base of the DBSA has been strengthened by the Government callable-capital amounting to R4,8 billion, which can be accessed as and when required.

The financial resources of the DBSA are made up of the share-capital contribution of the National Treasury, borrowings in the financial markets, repayments on loans granted by it, and internally generated funds. In addition to these resources, it mobilises loan capital from other international sources.

As part of its funding strategy, the Bank has established lines of credit with reputable and highly rated international institutions such as the African Development Bank and the European Investment Bank. It also funds itself from bilateral sources such as the *Kreditanstalt fur Wiederaufbau*, Overseas Economic Co-operation Fund (Japan) and the *Agence Française de Developpement*.

By March 2003, the DBSA had raised R3,2 billion from multilateral and bilateral institutions.

The scale of impact on the Bank's funding operations has been estimated using economic modelling techniques. Employment opportunities generated directly and indirectly through projects co-funded by the DBSA in 2002/03 were estimated at 42 000. The ultimate direct, indirect and induced impact on the economy of projects co-funded by the DBSA in 2002/03 was estimated as having added R8,4 billion to GDP.

The number of households expected to benefit from new infrastructure projects funded or co-funded by the DBSA in 2002/03 was estimated at 717 000. Income flowing to low-income households as a result of projects co-funded by the DBSA in 2002/03 was estimated at R1,2 million.

Land and Agricultural Development Bank

The Land and Agricultural Development Bank (Land Bank) operates as a development finance institution within the agricultural and agribusiness sectors, and is regulated by the Land and Agricultural Development Bank Act, 2002 (Act 15 of 2002). The Land Bank provides a range of financing products to a broad spectrum of clients within the agricultural industry. Financing products include wholesale and retail financing to commercial and developing farmers, co-operatives and other agriculture-related businesses.

The Land Bank's objectives are defined within its mandate, which requires that the Bank should achieve:
- growth in the commercial market
- growth in the development market
- business efficiency:
    - service delivery
    - resource management
- sustainability.

(See Chapter 4: *Agriculture*.)

Participation mortgage-bond schemes

About 14 organisations act as managers of participation mortgage-bond schemes in South Africa. According to the South African Reserve Bank, investments totalled R3,8 billion on 31 December 2002.

Stokvels

Stokvels are co-operative rotating saving schemes that mobilise funds among mostly black communities for a variety of purposes. Rotating saving schemes similar to *stokvels* are also found in other countries such as South Korea, Jamaica, Egypt and Japan. An estimated one million *stokvels* operate in South Africa.

Unit trusts

Equity unit trusts, or so-called open-ended trusts, are investment vehicles that provide a means of participation in the equity, bond and money markets for investors who may not have the time, money or expertise to effect investments successfully in markets on their own.

The price of units is calculated and published daily. Unit-trust management companies create units for sale to the public, either directly or indirectly through independent financial advisors.

Management companies may create units in the trust to meet the demand from the public, or may cancel them when the public sell back their holdings of units to the management company. The management company is obliged to buy back any units offered to it and at a price determined within 24 hours of receiving any notice of a buy-back from an investor.

Various unit trusts in South Africa offer similar ranges of investment plans, varying mainly as to the minimum amounts accepted.

There are two types of investment plans, namely the open-account or lump-sum plan, and the regular savings plan, which caters for regular monthly savers.

By March 2003, 29 management companies managed the assets of 466 separate unit trusts. Most of the companies are owned by South Africa's leading financial institutions. However, a number of independent institutions were registered in 2003. The market value of net assets of the unit-trust industry amounted to R181 billion (excluding intra-industry holdings of assets) at the end of 2002.

Since 1998, foreign collective investment schemes have been allowed to sell their products in South Africa, provided they obtain approval from the FSB. Individual investors utilising their foreign-exchange allowances, as well as institutional investors seeking foreign exposure, are the primary investors. At the end of 2002, 76 foreign schemes managing 401 different portfolios had obtained approval to market in South Africa. These schemes had a total value of R55,5 billion.

The unit-trust industry competes principally with long-term insurance companies, pension and provident funds, and investment trusts, for such investments. The trust deed stipulates the investment objective of each portfolio and constrains the investment managers regarding the type of assets in which they may invest. The other type of registered unit-trust scheme is property unit trusts. They mainly invest in shares of property-owning companies. Their units are listed on the JSE Securities Exchange (JSE) where investors can buy or sell them. By December 2002, there were six management companies managing nine portfolios with a market value of all listed units of R6,4 billion.

Financial intermediaries and advisors

In preparation for the adoption of the Financial Advisory and Intermediary Act, 2002, major sections of which came into effect on 15 November 2002, the FSB underwent restructuring during 2002.

Part of the restructuring was the creation of a Financial Intermediary and Advisory Department which was finalised on 1 August 2002. The Act requires that a wide range of financial-service intermediaries and financial-service advisors in South Africa, in respect of a wide range of financial products which are listed in the Act, obtain a licence to carry out their activities. Only a small portion of financial intermediaries were included in the regulatory framework. The result of the adoption of the Act will entail that up to an estimated 20 000 financial intermediaries and advisors are required to apply for a licence to continue with their activities.

The aims of the Act are:
- enhanced consumer protection
- professionalisation of the financial intermediaries and advisors sector in South Africa.

The financial advisory and intermediary services' licensing process was expected to commence during June 2003. By no later than March 2004, all new licences in terms of the Act should be issued. The mechanisms for enhanced consumer protection provided for in the Act include the setting up of the Office of the Financial Advisory and Intermediary Services Ombud for consumer recourse, and the introduction of extensive, fit and proper criteria for financial-service intermediaries and advisors as well as Codes of Conduct to govern the activities of persons affected by the Act.

Retirement funds and friendly societies

As at 31 December 2002, the FSB supervised

14 239 registered retirement funds and 179 registered friendly societies. These funds exclude the official State funds, Transnet, Telkom and some bargaining-council funds, all of which are not registered in terms of the Pension Funds Act, 1956 (Act 24 of 1956).

The total membership of all pension funds at the end of 2001 was 9 533 846, of which 8 252 092 were active members and 1 281 754 were pensioners, deferred pensioners and dependants. These figures do not reflect the total number of individuals who were members of funds, as some were members of more than one fund.

The total contributions received increased by 17,2% from R52 130 million in 2000 to R61 097 million in 2001. Total contributions to the State, Transnet, Telkom and Post Office funds increased by 15,2%, while total contributions to self-administered, underwritten and industrial funds in the private sector increased by 18%.

Benefits paid increased from R64 930 million in 2000 to R111 206 million in 2001. Amounts paid out in respect of pensions, lump sums on retirement or death, and resignations, were included.

Total assets of the retirement-fund industry in South Africa increased by 20,5% from R694 billion in 2000 to R836 billion in 2001.

The net assets of self-administered funds increased by 12,5% from R329 billion in 2000 to R730 billion in 2001.

Financial markets

Primary capital-market activity

Public-sector borrowers reduced their outstanding domestic marketable bond debt in the first 11 months of the 2002/03 financial year. Net redemptions of fixed-interest securities amounted to R4,2 billion from April 2002 to February 2003, compared with net redemptions of R15,2 billion in the same period of the 2001/02 fiscal year.

In contrast, the outstanding nominal value of private-sector loan stock listed on the Bond Exchange of South Africa (BESA) increased rapidly in 2002 with a marked increase in the second half of the year. Fuelled by, among others, the low cost of funding in the bond market relative to the high cost of borrowing in the money market, and the dearth of public-sector fixed-interest securities, listed private-sector loan stock increased from R28,9 billion in June 2002 to R38,9 billion in December, and expanded further to R40,9 billion in March 2003.

Government raised R10,7 billion through foreign-currency denominated debt issues in the international bond markets in 2002/03, compared with R12,4 billion in 2001/02. In 2003/04, national government raised R10,4 billion in May 2003 through the issuance of a 10-year 1,25 billion Euro global bond at a coupon of 5,25% and a spread of 142 basis points over benchmark German bonds. With this issue, government took advantage of low international interest rates and foreign investors' appetite for high-yielding South African securities.

In 2002, new issues of Eurorand bonds by non-residents in the European bond markets tapered off as the strengthening of the exchange rate of the Rand discouraged unhedged issues. Net issues of Eurorand bonds, to the value of R1,3 billion in the first quarter of 2002, were followed by net redemptions of R2,7 billion in the ensuing three quarters, resulting in overall net redemptions of R1,4 billion for 2002 as a whole.

The total value of equity-capital raised in the domestic and international primary share markets by companies listed on the JSE increased strongly during 2002 as noted by the R28,1 billion raised in the third quarter of 2002. Equity financing amounted to R60 billion in 2002 compared with R24 billion in 2001.

Secondary capital-market activity

The abrupt depreciation of the Rand in December 2001 impacted negatively on the outlook for domestic inflation. From then on, bond yield movements became more sensitive to changes in the exchange-rate of the Rand, and nominal yields reflected the reassessment of the exchange-rate risk premium. The mon-thly average yield on long-term government bonds increased from 10,3% in November 2001 to 12,6% in March 2002. By the end of March 2002, the market settled down and the mon-thly average yield on long-term government bonds declined to 9,9% in February 2003 when it reached its lowest level since 1980. The decline in bond yields was the result of, among others, the appreciation of the exchange value of the Rand and the improved near-term outlook for inflation. However, the bond market rally lost momentum from the beginning of March 2003, in response to the uncertainties created by the US-led invasion into Iraq, a slower than expected moderation of inflation, and increased recourse to funding in the domestic bond market as announced in Government's Budget for 2003/04. The monthly average bond yield increased slightly to 10,0% in March 2003 before declining to 9,9% in April 2003.

Trading activity on BESA declined by almost 2% from a record R12,4 trillion in 2001 to R12,2 trillion in 2002. In December 2002, the nominal value of bonds in issue amounted to R440 billion, with a market capitalisation of R473 billion which included 272 listed bonds of 40 issuers.

Non-resident transactions in the secondary bond market changed from net sales of R25,6 billion in 2001 to, albeit small, net purchases of R0,2 billion in 2002. Sentiment again turned negative as non-residents once more reduced their holdings of South African debt securities by R5,6 billion in the first quarter of 2003. Subsequently, net purchases of bonds to the value of R5,8 billion were recorded in April 2003.

The monthly average price level of all classes of shares listed on the JSE fell by 32% from an all-time high in May 2002 to April 2003. The general decline in share prices was primarily driven by the strength of the exchange rate of the Rand, which reduced the attractiveness of Rand-hedge shares and dampened the prospects of companies with exposure to foreign earnings. The monthly average price level of the resources sector fell by 36% from May 2002 to April 2003.

Turnover in the share market was buoyant in 2002 and the value of listed shares traded on the JSE amounted to a record R808 billion. Liquidity, measured as turnover as a percentage of market capitalisation, reached a new level of more than 46% in 2002 compared with 38% in 2001.

Non-resident portfolio investment in the secondary share market switched from a net inflow of foreign portfolio capital to the value of R5,4 billion in the first half of 2002, to a net outflow of R11,0 billion in the second half of the year. On balance, a net outflow of R5,6 billion was recorded for 2002 as a whole, followed by net sales of R2,0 billion in the first quarter of 2003 despite net purchases in February and March. In April 2003, non-residents increased their share holdings by R1,7 billion.

Money markets

The South African money market is well advanced, with a fairly large number of banks and other institutions actively participating. The South African Reserve Bank implements monetary policy in a system based on a shortage in the money market and uses this to make its repo rate effective in influencing money-market interest rates. The Reserve Bank accommodates private banks through weekly repurchase transactions at fixed-rate tenders with a seven-day maturity. Banks with short or long liquidity positions are accommodated by way of final clearing repurchase or reverse repurchase-auctions at rates that are 1,50 percentage points above or below the fixed repo rate.

Finance

In cases where the Reserve Bank has unintentionally under- or overestimated the market's liquidity requirement, supplementary repurchase or reverse tenders are conducted at the fixed repurchase rate. These tenders are mainly aimed at enabling banks to square off their short or long positions. They are conducted at the Reserve Bank's discretion and occur more frequently than the final clearing repurchase auctions and the regular weekly auctions.

The average daily liquidity requirement of the private-sector banks varied between R12,2 billion in January 2002 and R10,5 billion in November 2002. During the first quarter of 2002, conditions in the money market eased somewhat, in part because of the liquidity assistance the Reserve Bank provided to certain banks when they encountered large-scale deposit withdrawals. This easing was reflected in a decline of the average daily liquidity requirement to R11,0 billion in March 2002. In the ensuing months, liquidity conditions tightened again and the average daily liquidity requirement of private-sector banks increased to R12,2 billion in May, and R11,9 billion in July 2002. In January 2003, the liquidity needs of the private-sector banks declined to R10,6 billion from R11,1 billion in December 2002, but increased again to R11,2 billion in April 2003.

The Reserve Bank ensured the existence of an adequate daily liquidity requirement in 2002 and the first four months of 2003, by actively implementing various intervention techniques. These measures included foreign-currency swap transactions with private-sector parties. The outstanding amount of these transactions rose from R41,1 billion at the end of January 2002 to R54,8 billion at the end of August 2002. During the second half of 2002, the Reserve Bank curtailed the use of foreign-currency swap transactions with private-sector parties as a liquidity-draining instrument. This reduced the outstanding amount of foreign-currency swap transactions with private-sector parties from R54,8 billion at the end of August 2002 to R45,3 billion at the end of December and R30,5 billion at the end of April 2003.

The Reserve Bank increased the outstanding amount of its own debentures from R2,1 billion at the end of January 2002 to R7,7 billion at the end of December. Debentures with a maturity of three months were introduced in August 2002 and gradually increased to R3,0 billion by December 2002, reducing the amount of one-month debentures to R4,7 billion. Outstanding debentures amounted to R8,0 billion at the end of April 2003, divided between R4,4 billion with a one-month maturity and R3,6 billion with a maturity of three months.

The Reserve Bank also allowed the amount of reverse repurchase transactions in government securities to increase, on balance, from R5,8 billion in January 2002 to R8,6 billion in November 2002. This was reduced to R7,6 billion at the end of December 2002 as the strong demand for notes and coin drained an additional amount of R2,2 billion in liquidity from the money market during that month. At the height of the festive season, on 24 December 2002, notes and coin in circulation outside the Reserve Bank amounted to R42,1 billion or some R4,1 billion more than its corresponding peak in 2001.

When notes and coin began to flow back to the Reserve Bank, the reverse repurchase transactions were increased to R10,5 billion at the end of January 2003. These transactions were reduced to R10,0 billion at the end of February, but increased to R10,3 billion at the end of April. Out of that total, R6,3 billion worth of reverse repurchase transactions had a maturity of 28 days and R4,0 billion had a maturity of 91 days. The longer maturity had been introduced in June 2002.

The amount of vault cash that qualifies as a deduction when calculating banks' require cash-reserve deposits with the Reserve Bank was reduced further from 75% to 50% in September 2002. This drained about R1,7 billion from the money market, bringing the cumulative money-market effect of the new vault-cash dispensation to some R3,5 billion since September 2001. The currently prevailing deductible proportion will be reduced by a further 25 percentage points per year over a two-year period.

On 2 April 2002, some changes were made to the composition of the South African Overnight Interbank Average (SAONIA) rate which had been introduced by the Reserve Bank on 5 September 2001. Some changes have since been implemented to improve the SAONIA rate as an indicator of money-market conditions. As an example, the revised SAONIA rate now comprises the average rate on unsecured interbank funding at market rates only, i.e. it excludes the interbank overnight funding raised in terms of special agreements among banks at the prevailing Reserve Bank repurchase rate. The previous SAONIA rate, now called the SAONIA+ rate, covers all unsecured interbank overnight funding, i.e. the weighted average of funding at the repo rate as well as the other funding rates. Since their inception, the SAONIA and the SAONIA+ rates have moved in close proximity to each other and have both displayed limited volatility. Relatively minor fluctuations in the rates usually occur shortly before the start of a new maintenance period when the minimum reserve requirements of the banking system are under review, and occasionally on or close to the last trading day of the month.

The SAONIA rate rose from 8,44% on 10 January 2002 and briefly breached 12% on 28 June 2002, when some private-sector banks had to access the accommodation facilities of the Reserve Bank through the final clearing mechanism. In the ensuing months, the SAONIA rate moved even higher and reached 12,45% on 30 September. In the fourth quarter of 2002, the SAONIA rate firmed even further to fluctuate within a narrow range of between 12,48% and 12,78%, essentially emulating the steady behaviour of the Reserve Bank's repo rate. During the first four months of 2003, the SAONIA rate fluctuated within a range of between 12,31% and 12,88%. The rate amounted to 12,71% on 15 May 2003.

During 2002, the upward trend in other money-market interest rates was generally either in response to actual increases in the repo rate, or to inflation expectations hence anticipated increases in the repo rate. The 9x12-month Forward Rate Agreement (FRA) rate increased from 9,85% on 8 January 2002 to 12,97% on 27 March 2002. During the second quarter of 2002, the 9x12-month FRA rate steadily drifted downwards, signalling market expectations of potentially lower money-market interest rates later. The increase in the Reserve Bank's repo rate on June 2002 was seemingly fully discounted ahead of the announcement by the market, and the FRA rate consequently showed little variation in the aftermath of this tightening of monetary conditions.

October 2002 appeared to mark a turning point in the money-market rates as fears of higher inflation began to dissipate. However, at the beginning of 2003, mounting geopolitical tensions reversed the downward trend in money-market rates. The rate on three-month bankers' acceptances declined from 13,15% on 23 October 2002 to 13,03% on 8 November 2002, and by 11 basis points from 13,04% on 2 January 2003 to 12,93% on 19 March 2003. However, from the end of March, this rate moved higher and stood at 12,98% on 25 April 2003.

The tender rate on 91-day Treasury bills moved lower from 12,78% on 10 October 2002 and briefly fell below the 12%-mark in mid-November. During the second half of November 2002, the tender rate resumed its upward movement, rising from 12,28% at the end of that month to 12,74% on 14 February 2003, and remained around this level in the ensuing period to 14 May. The weekly amount of 91-day Treasury bills offered on tender was increased by R500 million to R1,5 billion from

31 January 2003, contributing to upward pressure on this rate.

The prime overdraft rates and the predominant rate on mortgage loans of the private-sector banks closely followed the changes in the Reserve Bank's repo rate during 2002. When monetary conditions tightened in the first nine months of 2002, these rates increased from 13% in early January 2002 to 17% in September – reaching their highest levels since July 1999.

Exchange control

Exchange control was first introduced in South Africa during World War II. This formed part of the emergency finance measures adopted by the British Sterling Area to prevent large capital outflows and protect foreign reserves.

The measures were at first applicable mainly to South African residents. From 1961, the capital transactions of non-residents were also restricted. In subsequent years, these controls were tightened or relaxed from time to time, depending on domestic and international circumstances.

Exchange control is administered by the Reserve Bank on behalf of the Minister of Finance. The Reserve Bank is assisted in this task by a number of banking institutions, which have been appointed by the Minister of Finance as authorised dealers in foreign exchange. These institutions undertake foreign exchange transactions for their own account with their clients, within limits, and subject to conditions laid down by the Reserve Bank.

The Government is committed to an open capital market and the gradual relaxation of exchange controls. The private individual investment allowance was increased from R400 000 to R500 000 and then to R750 000 in February 2000.

In terms of the announcement made by the Minister of Finance on 26 February 2003, the following liberalisations with regard to exchange control are allowed:

Institutional investors

Part of the process of gradual exchange-control liberalisation and financial-sector strengthening is the shift to a system of prudential regulation governing the foreign portfolio investment of institutional investors, such as long-term insurers and pension funds. Prudential regulations are applied internationally to protect policyholders and pensioners from excessive risk, and typically include restrictions on foreign asset holdings, set at a certain percentage of an institution's total assets or liabilities. As an interim step towards a prudential framework, institutional investors will be:

- Allowed to invest, on approval, up to existing foreign asset limits. These foreign asset limits are 15% of total assets for long-term insurers, pension funds and fund managers, and 20% of total assets for unit-trust companies. The previous restriction based on 10% of the prior year's net inflow of funds will no longer apply. The Exchange Control Department of the Reserve Bank reserves the right, however, to require a staggered transfer of such funds in some cases so as to maintain overall financial stability.
- Required to submit additional information when making an application for a foreign-investment allowance. The shift to prudential regulation requires improved data reporting on individual institutions' foreign investments and the foreign-diversification levels of the industry as a whole. The new dispensation became operational on 1 May 2003, after the National Treasury and Exchange Control Department, in consultation with the FSB, reached agreement with the respective industries on the appropriate revised reporting standards.

South African corporates

The global expansion of South African firms holds significant benefits for the economy – expanded market access, increased exports

and improved competitiveness. In October 2002, the exchange-control allowance for foreign direct investment (FDI) into Africa was increased from R750 million to R2 billion, in line with South Africa's commitment to NEPAD. In order to facilitate the global expansion of South African companies from a domestic base, increased exchange-control allowances for direct investment are now being extended to investment outside Africa. The following new exchange-control limits apply:
- The allowance governing South African corporates' use of South African funds to finance new approved FDI outside Africa is increased from R500 million to R1 billion.
- The allowance for the use of South African funds for investment outside Africa is expanded from just the financing of new approved FDI to include 'top-up' funding for the financing of new approved expansions of existing FDI. This expanded dispensation is maintained in the case of investment in Africa.

The global expansion of South African firms also holds potential benefits in the form of future foreign-income streams. These potential benefits may not have been fully realised owing to tax and exchange-control disincentives to the repatriation of foreign dividends. As part of easing the exchange-control impediments, dividends repatriated from foreign subsidiaries are eligible for an exchange-control credit, which will allow them to be re-exported, upon application, for approved FDIs.

Emigrants' funds

A system of exchange-control allowances for the export of funds when persons emigrate has been in place in South Africa for a number of decades. Emigrants' funds in excess of the emigration allowance were placed in emigrants' blocked accounts in order to preserve foreign reserves. Reflecting the improved strength and resilience of the South African economy, these blocked assets will now be unwound. The imminent elimination of the net open forward position and an increasingly diversified and growing export sector create an environment conducive to dealing with the foreign reserve problems of the past. As such, the following applies:
- The distinction between the settling-in allowance for emigrants and the private individual foreign-investment allowance for residents has fallen away, and there is now a common foreign allowance for both residents and emigrants of R750 000 per individual (or R1,5 million in respect of family units).
- Emigrant-blocked assets were unwound. Amounts up to R750 000 (inclusive of amounts already exited) are eligible for exiting without charge. Holders of blocked assets wishing to exit more than R750 000 (inclusive of amounts already exited) must apply to the Exchange Control Department of the Reserve Bank to do so. Approval is subject to an exiting schedule and an exit charge of 10% of the amount.
- New emigrants wishing to exit more than R750 000 (inclusive of amounts already exited) can similarly apply to the Exchange Control Department to do so, with approval subject to an exiting schedule and an exit charge of 10% of the amount.

JSE Securities Exchange

The JSE was first established to provide a marketplace for the shares of the many mining and financial companies formed shortly after the Witwatersrand gold fields were discovered in 1886. The Exchange dates from November 1887.

It is regulated by the FSB under the Stock Exchanges Control Act, 1985 (Act 1 of 1985), and the Financial Markets Control Act, 1989 (Act 55 of 1989). The JSE in turn regulates its listed companies and brokers by extensive rules and directives. The JSE is the largest securities exchange in Africa and has a market

Finance

capitalisation of several times that of all the other African markets combined.

In November 1995, the JSE permitted ownership by foreign and corporate members for the first time. The move, part of a broader deregulation package designed to entice local and international investors, parallels the London stock market's 'Big Bang' of 1986, although changes were phased in over time. These included closing the open-outcry market floor in favour of automated electronic trading, the introduction of fully negotiable commission, and dual-trading capacity.

The JSE is committed to promoting South Africa both regionally and internationally. In this regard, it has led the process of harmonising the listing requirements of the members of the SADC Committee of Stock Exchanges (COSSE). COSSE envisages an integrated real-time national network of securities markets in the region by 2006. The JSE has offered its trading platform to these members, and the Namibian Stock Exchange has been trading on the JSE's trading platform for the past four years.

On 6 August 2001, the JSE acquired the business and assets of the South African Futures Exchange (SAFEX). SAFEX is now incorporated into the JSE as two new divisions – the Financial Derivatives Division, which covers the equity and interest-rate futures and options markets, and the Agricultural Products Division, which covers commodities futures and options on maize, sunflowers, soya beans and wheat. The rules governing trading and the settlement of trades on SAFEX have remained largely unchanged. This has many long-term advantages for both exchanges.

The 2002/03 financial year brought momentous technological change for the JSE following the completion of most of the 31 projects identified under the Gateway 2002 strategic plan. These changes represent a major milestone in winning local and international investor confidence.

Bond Exchange of South Africa

BESA is an independent financial exchange operating under an annual licence granted by the country's securities market regulator, the FSB. BESA is responsible for regulating the debt securities market in South Africa.

Primary debt markets

Although primarily a government-bond market, BESA also lists Rand-denominated debt securities issued by local government, public enterprises and major corporates. By 31 March 2003, BESA had granted a listing to some 272 bonds issued by 43 borrowers, with a total nominal value of R442 billion (US$1 = R7,88 as at 31 March 2003). Approximately 60% of this debt has been issued by central government. By comparison, there are some half-a-dozen listed corporate issues, including Telkom SA Ltd, Iscor, Absa Bank Ltd, Investec Bank Ltd, Standard Bank of SA Ltd and Sasol Financing. Of the listed bonds, some 84% by value have been immobilised in the Central Depository Ltd.

The evolution of sophisticated bond products in South Africa has been hampered generally by restrictive regulations, the relatively small size of the local market, and weak demand from both borrowers and investors. Vanilla bonds constitute the majority of BESA's listed instruments and variations on this theme include:

- fixed interest-bearing bonds with single and multiple redemption dates
- zero-coupon bonds
- CPI Index-linked bonds
- variable interest-rate bonds/floating rate notes
- strip bonds.

BESA has appointed a Listings Advisory Technical Committee (Listech) to provide ongoing advice on BESA's Listings Disclosure Requirements and Rules. The aim is to ensure that these contribute to the strengthening of investor protection and market confidence.

Market performance

The South African bond market is one of the most liquid emerging bond markets in the world. In 2002, the local market turned over its market capitalisation some 27 times.

Trading volumes recorded on BESA for the full year to 31 December 2002 exceeded R11,6 trillion, a marginal increase over that of 2001.

These local-trade figures for 2002 represent turnover of some 27 times market capitalisation. In addition to the trades concluded by BESA, some R383 billion was traded in the over-the-counter (OTC) off-shore market (for local settlement) during 2002, with a further R418 billion traded OTC, but settled through Euroclear and Clearstream rather than in South Africa.

The daily average turnover in 2002 amounted to some R46 billion per day (spot & repo).

Main indices

BESA, in collaboration with the Actuarial Society of South Africa, has introduced a trio of bond indices that provide a simple yet accurate measure of total returns of representative bond portfolios, and benchmarks for historical performance. These indices (introduced in August 2000) replaced the previous bond indices used in South Africa.

These indices are published daily by the Exchange on its web site (*www.besa.za.com*) and are widely disseminated to all members, the asset-management community and the media. These indices are used by the asset-management industry as the benchmarks for the evaluation of the performance of the funds under management.

Regulation

BESA is a licensed Exchange and together with its member firms must adhere to the Financial Markets Control Act, 1989 and a set of approved rules. As a self-regulatory organisation, BESA undertakes ongoing surveillance over all aspects of bond-market activity in South Africa.

Guarantee Fund

BESA maintains the Guarantee Fund to ensure, as far as possible, the performance of trans-actions entered on the Exchange. The Fund provides members and clients with price-risk cover against a member default, to a maximum aggregate of R190 million. Since inception, no settlement defaults or claims on the Fund have been recorded.

Finance

Acknowledgements

Bond Exchange of South Africa
Development Bank of Southern Africa
Estimates of National Expenditure 2003, published by the National Treasury
Financial Services Board
JSE Securities Exchange
Land Bank of South Africa
National Treasury
Office of the Auditor-General
South African Reserve Bank
South African Revenue Service
www.gov.za

Suggested reading

Abedian, I.A. and T., and Walker, L. *Promises, Plans and Priorities: South Africa's Emerging Fiscal Structures.* Cape Town: Institute for Democracy in South Africa (IDASA), 1997.
Budlender, D. *The Women's Budget.* Rondebosch: IDASA, 1996.
Clark, I., Louw, E. and Myburgh, J. *More Small Business Opportunities in South Africa.* 2nd ed. Cape Town: Zebra Books, 1996.
Dolny, H. *Banking on Change.* Sandton: Penguin, 2001.
Falkena, H.B. *Financial Policy in South Africa.* Halfway House: Southern Book Publishers, 1991.
Falkena, H.B. *Fundamentals of the South African Financial System.* Halfway House: Southern Book Publishers, 1993.
Falkena, H.B. ed. *South African Financial Institutions.* Halfway House: Southern Book Publishers, 1992.
Fölscher, A. and others. *Transparency and Participation in the Budget Process: South Africa: A Country Report.* Cape Town: IDASA, 2001.
Fourie, L.J., Falkena, H.B. and Kok, W.J. eds. *Fundamentals of the South African Financial System.* Students' Edition. Halfway House, Gauteng: International Thompson Publishing, 1996.
Human, P. and Horwitz, F. *On the Edge: How the South African Business Organisation Copes with Change.* Cape Town: Juta, 1992.
Jones, S. *Banking and Business in South Africa.* Basingstoke: MacMillan, 1988.
Kelly, M.V. *Financial Institutions in South Africa – Financial, Investment and Risk Management.* Cape Town: Juta 1993.
Kok, P. and Pietersen, J. *Financial Services.* Pretoria: HSRC, 2000.
Makinta, V. and Schwabe, C. eds. *Development Funding in South Africa: 1998 – 1999*, Pretoria: Human Sciences Research Council (HSRC), 2000.
Whiteford, A. and Van Deventer, D.E. *Winners and Losers: South Africa's Changing Income Distribution in the 1990s.* Pretoria: HSRC and Warton Econometric Forecasting Services, 2000.

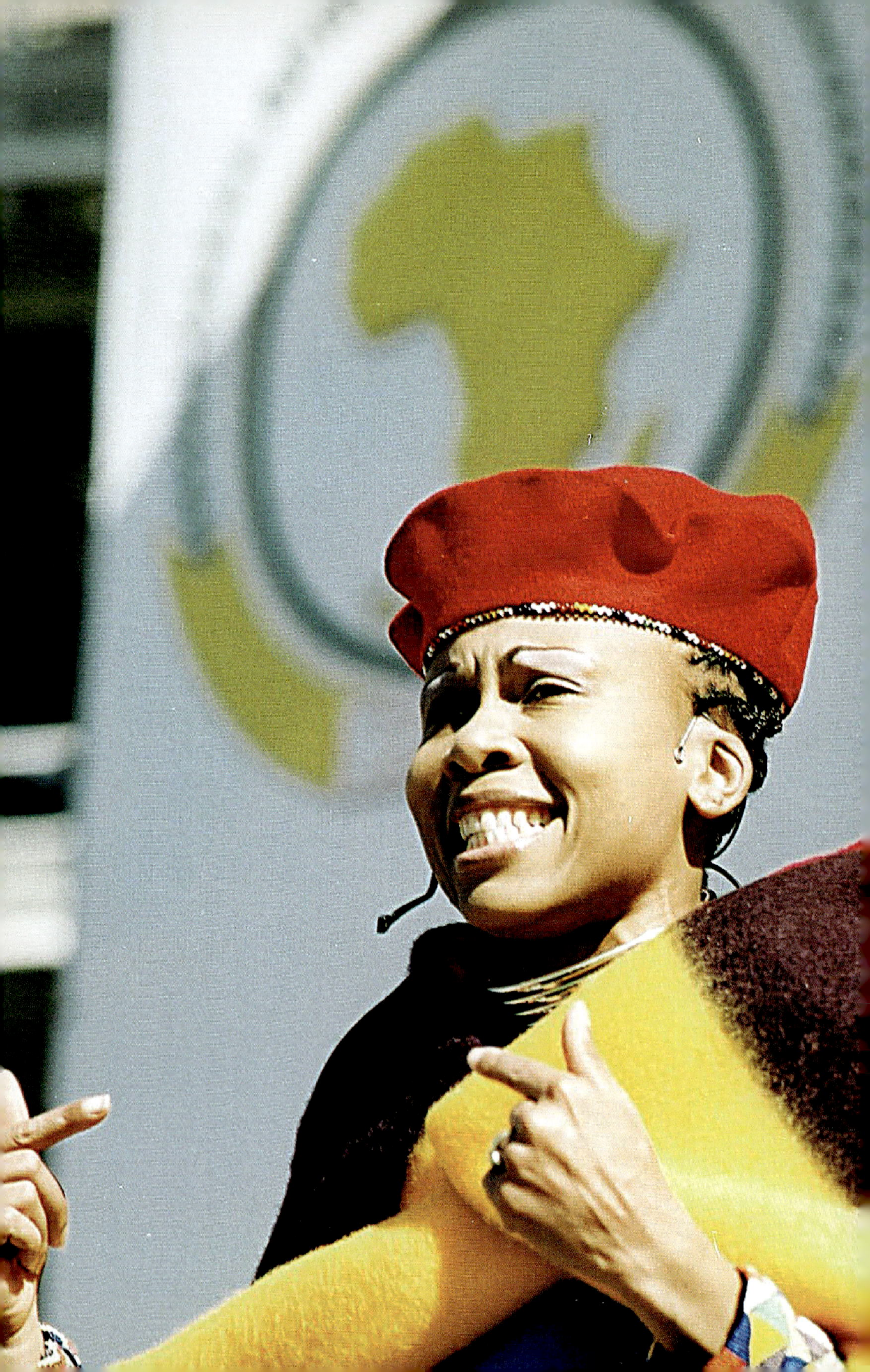

chapter 11
Foreign relations

According to the Constitution of the Republic of South Africa, 1996 (Act 108 of 1996), the President is ultimately responsible for the foreign policy and international relations of South Africa. It is the prerogative of the President to appoint Heads of Missions, receive foreign Heads of Missions and conduct State-to-State relations.

According to the Department of Foreign Affairs' Strategic Plan for 2003 to 2005, the Minister of Foreign Affairs is entrusted with the formulation, promotion and execution of South Africa's foreign policy, and the daily conduct of South Africa's international relations. The Minister assumes overall responsibility for all aspects of South Africa's international relations in consultation with the President.

Other Cabinet Ministers are required to consult the Minister of Foreign Affairs on their international role, among others:

The Department of Foreign Affairs is responsible for:
- monitoring developments in the international environment
- communicating government's policy positions
- developing and advising government on policy options, mechanisms and avenues for achieving objectives
- protecting South Africa's sovereignty and territorial integrity
- assisting South African citizens abroad.

South Africa's diplomatic and consular Missions help to enhance the country's international profile and serve as strategic mechanisms for the achievement of South Africa's international interests.

South Africa maintains diplomatic relations with countries and organisations through 96 missions in 85 countries abroad, and through the accreditation of more than 160 countries and organisations resident in South Africa.

South Africa and Africa

Organisation of African Unity (OAU)/African Economic Community (AEC)/African Union (AU)

The OAU was established on 25 May 1963 in Addis Ababa, Ethiopia, after the signature of the OAU Charter by representatives of 32 governments. South Africa became the 53rd member in 1994. The aims of the Organisation were, among others, to:
- promote the unity and solidarity of African states
- defend their sovereignty, territorial integrity and independence
- eradicate all forms of colonialism in Africa
- promote international co-operation, with due regard for the Charter of the United

◀ On Africa Day, 25 May 2003, thousands of people attended the celebrations at Johannesburg Stadium. Africa Day marked the 40th anniversary of the Organisation of Africa Unity's (OAU) existence. The OAU gave birth to the Africa Union in July 2002.

Nations (UN) and the Universal Declaration of Human Rights.

The Treaty Establishing the AEC, commonly referred to as the Abuja Treaty, was signed on 3 June 1991 and came into force after the requisite ratification in May 1994.

The Abuja Treaty provided for the AEC to be set up gradually by co-ordination, harmonisation and progressive integration of the activities of existing and future regional economic communities (RECs) in Africa.

The implementation of the Abuja Treaty introduced a process to be completed in six stages over 34 years, i.e. by 2028, as follows:
- strengthening existing RECs and creating new ones where needed (five years)
- stabilising tariff and other barriers to regional trade and strengthening sectoral integration, particularly in the fields of trade, agriculture, finance, transport, communications, industry and energy, as well as co-ordinating and harmonising the activities of RECs (eight years)
- establishing a free trade area (FTA) and a customs union at the level of each REC (10 years)
- co-ordinating and harmonising tariff and non-tariff systems among RECs, with a view to establishing a continental customs union (two years)
- establishing an African common market and adopting common policies (four years)
- integrating all sectors, establishing the African Central Bank and a single African currency, setting up the African Economic and Monetary Union, and creating and electing the first Pan-African Parliament (PAP) (five years).

As more and more African countries attained their independence, it became evident that there was a need to amend the OAU Charter to streamline the Organisation.

An Extraordinary Summit was held in Sirte, Libya in September 1999 to amend the OAU Charter, to increase the efficiency and effectiveness of the OAU. This Summit concluded with the Sirte Declaration aimed at:
- effectively addressing the new social, political and economic realities in Africa and the world
- fulfilling the people's aspirations for greater unity in conforming with the objectives of the OAU Charter and the Abuja Treaty
- revitalising the continental organisation to play a more active role in addressing the needs of the people
- eliminating the scourge of conflict
- meeting global challenges
- harnessing the human and natural resources of the continent to improve living conditions.

To achieve these aims, the Summit decided to:
- establish the AU in conformity with the ultimate objectives of the Charter and the provisions of the Treaty establishing the AEC
- accelerate the process of implementing the Abuja Treaty in particular
- shorten the implementation periods of the Abuja Treaty
- ensure the speedy establishment of all institutions provided for in the Abuja Treaty,

South African representation abroad	Total	Foreign representation in South Africa	Total
Embassies/High Commissions	76	Embassies/High Commissions	107
Consulates/Consulates General	12	Consulates/Consulates General	53
Honorary Consulates	54	Honorary Consulates	7
Other (e.g. Liaison Offices)	4	Other (e.g. Liaison Offices)	4
Non-resident accreditations	101	Non-resident accreditations	15
International organisations	7	International organisations	23

Foreign relations

such as the African Central Bank, the African Monetary Union, the African Court of Justice and, in particular, the PAP
- strengthen and consolidate RECs as the pillars for achieving the objectives of the AEC, and realise the AU
- convene an African Ministerial Conference on Security, Stability, Development and Co-operation.

The establishment of the AU was declared on 2 March 2001 at the second Extraordinary Summit in Sirte. The transition period was concluded with the convening of the Inaugural Summit of the AU in Durban from 9 to 10 July 2002. The objectives of the AU are, among others, to:
- achieve greater unity and solidarity between African countries and the peoples of Africa
- defend the sovereignty, territorial integrity and independence of its member states
- accelerate the political and socio-economic integration of the continent
- encourage international co-operation, taking due account of the Charter of the UN and the Universal Declaration of Human Rights
- promote peace, security and stability on the continent
- promote democratic principles and institutions, popular participation and good governance
- promote and protect people's rights
- establish the necessary conditions to enable the continent to play its rightful role in the global economy and in international negotiations
- promote sustainable development at economic, social and cultural level, as well as the integration of African economies
- promote co-operation in all fields of human activity to raise the living standards of African peoples
- advance the development of the continent by promoting research in all fields
- work with relevant international partners in eradicating preventable diseases and promoting good health on the continent.

The main challenge in the first year of the AU's existence was setting up its priority structures and laying down the groundwork for the rest of its proposed structures, as foreseen in the Constitutive Act of the AU.

The principal organs, namely the Assembly of the Heads of State and Government, the Executive Council of Ministers and the Permanent Representatives Committee, are fully functional.

By September 2003, the setting up of the Commission of the AU was in progress.

The former President of Mali, Mr Oumar Alpha Konare, was elected the new chairperson of the Commission, while Mr Patrick Mazimhaka of Rwanda was elected his deputy.

According to an approved quota system, South Africa will be entitled to 22 posts in the new Commission. The process was expected to take up to three years.

The appointment of members of the Commission also heralded the start of the meetings of the Specialised Technical Committees (STCs) which consist of relevant line-function Ministers. The Commissioners and their directorates will support the work of the STCs.

Considerable progress was made on the 'people's organs' of the AU, namely the PAP and the Economic, Social and Cultural Council (ECOSOCC). The PAP Protocol was ratified by 21 member states and required a further six ratifications before entering into force.

ECOSOCC is a meeting of civil society and will come into being once its statutes have been approved.

The Protocol on the Court of Justice was adopted by the Assembly in Maputo, Mozambique in 2003. The Court of Justice will, among others, adjudicate the interpretation of the Constitutive Act of the AU.

The financial institutions – the African Central Bank, the African Monetary Fund and the African Investment Bank – are expected to take longer to operationalise.

Promotion of peace, security and stability on the continent

The AU is responsible for the peaceful resolution of conflict among member states, through such appropriate means as may be decided upon by the Assembly, which may give directives to the Executive Council on the management of conflict, war, acts of terrorism, emergency situations and the restoration of peace.

Apart from the Assembly and the Executive Council, the other principal organ responsible for peace, security and stability will be the Central Organ of the Mechanism on Conflict Prevention, Management and Resolution. The Protocol on the Establishment of the Peace and Security Council of the AU was adopted at the Durban Summit in 2002 to replace the Mechanism on Conflict Prevention, Management and Resolution.

The Peace and Security Council (PSC) of the AU will be established in terms of a Protocol. By September 2003, it had received 15 ratifications. It requires an additional 12 ratifications, giving a simple majority of 27, before it will enter into force. It was expected that this would be achieved by January 2004.

By September 2003, work on its substructures had progressed well. These will involve the African Standby Force, the Panel of the Wise, the Early Warning System, as well as a Peace Fund to support the activities of the PSC. The Rules of Procedure of the PSC will also have to be concluded. Once the PSC has been established, the Executive Council is mandated to vote on its membership – five countries serving three years each and 10 countries serving two years each.

Related to the PSC is the development of the Common African Defence and Security Policy as mandated by the Durban Summit. A Draft Framework has been developed and will need to be considered by the Ministers of Defence and Security.

Socio-economic development and integration of the continent

The AU will also be the principal institution responsible for promoting sustainable development at economic, social and cultural level, as well as the integration of African economies. RECs are recognised as the building-blocks of the AU, necessitating the need for their close involvement in the formulation and implementation of all AU programmes.

To this end, the AU must co-ordinate and take decisions on policies in areas of common interest to member states, as well as co-ordinate and harmonise policies between existing and future RECs, for the gradual attainment of the objectives of the AU.

The STCs are responsible for the actual implementation of the continental socio-economic integration process, together with the Permanent Representatives Committee.

Seven STCs will be established, namely the:

- Committee on Rural Economy and Agricultural Matters
- Committee on Monetary and Financial Affairs
- Committee on Trade, Customs and Immigration Matters
- Committee on Industry, Science and Technology, Energy, Natural Resources and Environment
- Committee on Transport, Communications and Tourism
- Committee on Health, Labour and Social Affairs
- Committee on Education, Culture and Human Resources.

Partnership with civil society

Active involvement of African non-governmental organisations (NGOs), socio-economic organisations, professional associations and civil society organisations is required in Africa's integration process, as well as in the formulation and implementation of programmes of the AU.

New Partnership for Africa's Development (NEPAD)

The adoption of NEPAD is considered to be one of the most important developments of recent times for its conception of a development programme, placing Africa at the apex of the global agenda, by:
- creating an instrument for advancing people-centered and sustainable development in Africa based on democratic values
- being premised on the recognition that Africa has an abundance of natural resources and people who have the capacity to be agents for change, and so holds the key to its own development
- providing the common African platform from which to engage the rest of the international community in a dynamic partnership that holds real prospects for creating a better life for all.

While the principle of partnership with the rest of the world is equally vital to this process, such a partnership must be based on mutual respect, dignity, shared responsibility and mutual accountability. The expected outcomes are:
- economic growth and development and increased employment
- a reduction in poverty and inequality
- diversification of productive activities
- enhanced international competitiveness and increased exports
- increased African integration.

NEPAD is a mandated initiative of the AU. The NEPAD Heads of State and Government Implementation Committee is required to report annually to the Summit of the AU. The chairperson of the AU, as well as the chairperson of the Commission of the AU, are ex-officio members of the Implementation Committee. The Commission of the AU is expected to participate in Steering Committee meetings.

The link between NEPAD and the Southern African Development Community (SADC) Regional Indicative Strategic Development Plan (RISDP) was adopted by the Ministers of Foreign Affairs and Finance at their meeting in Blantyre, Malawi, in September 2001, which came to the conclusion that, in terms of relationships, the SADC is part of and feeds into NEPAD, since the latter is premised on the RECs. The Ministers recognised that NEPAD is a framework and process within the AU, while the SADC is a recognised REC of the Union. The SADC participates, therefore, in both the AU and NEPAD.

A major effort is ongoing to continuously factor NEPAD imperatives into the outcomes of international conferences, such as the Conference on Financing for Development, the World Summit on Sustainable Development (WSSD) and the World Trade Organisation (WTO), to ensure the integration of NEPAD into the multilateral system. In a wider context, countries of the South subscribe to the priorities outlined in NEPAD and have pledged their solidarity and moral support, as well as an appreciation for South Africa's positive role in NEPAD. However, NEPAD does not have a mechanism for South-South co-operation. To this end, improved co-ordination with partners in the South should be pursued.

At the inaugural Heads of State and Government Implementation Committee meeting held in Abuja in October 2001, a 15-member Task Force was established for the implementation of NEPAD. The following three-tier governing structure was accepted:

Heads of State and Government Implementation Committee

Chaired by Nigerian President, Mr Olusegun Obasanjo, with Presidents Abdoulaye Wade of Senegal and Abdelaziz Bouteflika of Algeria as vice-chairpersons, the Implementation Committee comprises 15 states (three per AU geographic region), including the five initiating states: South Africa, Nigeria, Algeria, Senegal and Egypt.

The main function of the Implementation Committee is to set policies, priorities and the Programme of Action of NEPAD.

Steering Committee

The Steering Committee is composed of the personal representatives of the five initiating Presidents, and is tasked with the development of the Terms of Reference for identified programmes and projects, as well as overseeing the Secretariat.

Secretariat

The full-time core staff of the Secretariat, located at the Development Bank of Southern Africa in Midrand, near Johannesburg, provides liaison, co-ordination, administrative and logistical functions for NEPAD.

Five task teams were established to urgently identify and prepare specific implementable projects and programmes. In terms of working arrangements, South Africa is to co-ordinate the Peace, Security, Democracy and Political Governance Initiative; Nigeria, the Economic and Corporate Governance/Banking and Financial Standards/Capital Flows Initiatives; Egypt the Market Access and Agriculture Initiatives; Algeria the Human Resource Development (HRD) Initiative; and Senegal, the Infrastructure Initiative.

During the Ordinary Summit in July 2003 in Maputo, President Thabo Mbeki handed over the leadership of the AU to Mozambican President, Joaquim Chissano.

The second Ordinary Session of the AU Summit of Heads of State and Government took place under the theme *The Implementation of NEPAD as a Contribution to Africa's Development.*

The NEPAD Implementation Committee meeting prepared a report on the progress made in the implementation of NEPAD, and reviewed the status of the NEPAD Secretariat as well as interactions that the African leaders had with leaders of the developed North, with a view to building strategic partnerships to ensure Africa's renewal.

The AU's mechanisms for peer review and conflict resolution reflect commitment to human rights, democratisation, good governance, and peace and security as being in the interest of Africans, irrespective of relations with industrialised countries.

The second meeting of the African Peer Review Mechanism (ARPM) Panel of Eminent Persons took place in Johannesburg, on 3 October 2003.

The ARPM is a process voluntarily acceded to by the member states of the AU as an African self-monitoring mechanism.

The APRM requires that each country develops a Programme of Action within the framework of specific time-bound objectives.

It will enable participating member states to adopt policies and practices that conform to the agreed political, economic and corporate governance values, codes and standards. It will also serve as a critical instrument for advancing reforms in governance and socio-economic development, and in building capacity to implement these reforms.

In September 2003, infrastructure-development projects within the New Partnership for Africa's Development (NEPAD) received a R25-million boost with the signing of an agreement between the Development Bank of Southern Africa (DBSA) and the French Development Agency.

The agreement provides for both parties to mobilise necessary resources, either in foreign or local currencies, for investment in countries within sub-Saharan Africa.

The projects to be taken into consideration will stem exclusively from the transport (road, air, shipping and rail), energy (generation, transmission and distribution), information and communication technologies, as well as water and sanitation sectors.

This facility, in the form of a grant, is assigned to finance NEPAD project studies, or any other preparations.

The DBSA has established the Africa Partnerships Unit to promote the implementation of NEPAD's vision and to provide further stimulus to the Secretariat's endeavours.

The Unit will interact and co-operate with national, regional and international stakeholders to facilitate the implementation of the NEPAD Short-Term Action Plan.

One of the key objectives of the APRM is to identify the deficiencies in implementation, with a view to improving its compliance with the Constitutive Act of the AU by member states.

Conference on Security, Stability, Development and Co-operation in Africa (CSSDCA)

The first Standing Conference of Heads of State and Government on the CSSDCA took place during the 38th OAU Summit in Durban, in July 2002.

The Summit approved the CSSDCA Memorandum of Understanding (MoU) on Security, Stability, Development and Co-operation, affirming the centrality of the CSSDCA process as a policy-development forum, a framework for the advancement of common values, and a monitoring and evaluation mechanism for the AU. The MoU provides the following framework:
- core values concerning security, stability, development and co-operation
- commitments to give effect to these core values
- key performance indicators to evaluate compliance with the commitments in the MoU
- a framework of implementation as a means of carrying out the commitments contained in the MoU
- an agreed mechanism for measuring performance.

While the strategic focus of the CSSDCA process is to ensure good governance in the political and economic realm, as well as to provide the framework for development and co-operation in Africa, NEPAD serves as the socio-economic development blueprint for the AU to implement its objectives. In addition, it serves as the mechanism for accelerating the implementation of the Abuja Treaty. At the same time, its management structures are particularly designed to ensure follow-up and implementation in the transition phase from the OAU to the AU.

Southern Africa

Regional approach
South Africa's foreign policy with regard to the southern African region reflects a commitment to close diplomatic, economic and security co-operation and integration, adherence to human rights, the promotion of democracy, and the preservation of regional solidarity, peace and stability.

Angola
The signing of a ceasefire agreement in Angola on 4 April 2002 with the Union for the Total Independence of Angola (UNITA) ended one of Africa's longest and most devastating wars.

Subsequently, the Government of Angola established the Parliamentary Commission on Peace and Reconciliation (PCPR) with the aim of consulting with community representatives, church groups and civil society on the revival of the peace process.

South Africa, conscious of its obligation to assist with political reconciliation and economic reconstruction, sent Deputy President Jacob Zuma to Luanda during April 2002 to consult with the Angolan Government and to assess the country's political and material needs. The Deputy President also addressed the PCPR and reiterated South Africa's commitment to assist Angola, when called upon, with matters of national reconciliation.

South Africa recognised that the future of democracy and good governance in Angola hinged on the success of the peace process.

A committee was set up, in accordance with a mandate from the Cabinet *Lekgotla* in July 2002, to devise a strategy for South Africa's humanitarian assistance to Angola.

Subsequently, South Africa contributed maize and other humanitarian assistance to that country.

The first meeting of the Joint Commission of Co-operation (JCC) between South Africa and

Angola took place in Pretoria on 28 February 2003. Several agreement proposals were discussed, and an agreement on the waiving of visas for diplomatic and official passports was signed by South Africa's Minister of Foreign Affairs, Dr Nkosazana Dlamini-Zuma, and the Angolan Minister for External Relations, Dr J.B. de Miranda.

During his visit, Minister de Miranda also met with President Mbeki.

Lesotho

In October 2002, the Ministers of Foreign Affairs of Lesotho and South Africa agreed that a donor conference should be convened to assist Lesotho in moving out of its current status of least-developed country, in line with the objectives of a Joint Bilateral Commission for Co-operation (JBCC).

By June 2003, the Department of Foreign Affairs was facilitating the process towards the signing of the JBCC. A donor briefing took place on 10 April 2003 in the capital, Maseru. South Africa was represented by the Deputy Minister of Environmental Affairs and Tourism, Ms Joyce Mabudafhasi. Key players within the donor community as well as the private sector attended. The briefing was aimed at soliciting international funding for various projects in Lesotho, which would promote the objectives of the JBCC.

Twenty-five projects identified by the Lesotho Government, which were introduced in detail to the participants, are aimed at creating employment and alleviating poverty in Lesotho. These include agricultural, tourism, mining and infrastructure-development projects.

A donor conference was envisaged for the latter part of 2003.

In February 2003, the Minister of Safety and Security, Mr Charles Nqakula, led a South African Ministerial delegation to Lesotho for talks on the tightening of security at border posts separating the two countries. The discussions focused on cross-border crimes such as stock theft, rural safety and border control.

The Minister of Environmental Affairs and Tourism, Mr Mohammed Valli Moosa, launched the Maloti-Drakensberg Transfrontier Conservation Project in Lesotho in August 2003.

The Project had been initiated in June 2001 when the two countries concluded an agreement on the conservation of biological diversity and the promotion of the sustainable development of the area.

Botswana

President Mbeki, accompanied by a delegation of six Ministers and senior government officials, paid a State Visit to Botswana from 11 to 13 March 2003. The two countries entered into the Agreement on the Establishment of a Joint Permanent Commission for Co-operation (JPCC), which was signed by the Ministers of Foreign Affairs of the two countries.

The JPCC covers, among others, areas such as agriculture and livestock, water affairs, mining and tourism, environmental co-operation, monetary and financial arrangements, transportation, roads, and infrastructure development.

History was made when President Mbeki became the first foreign President to address the Botswana Parliament on 11 March 2003.

The Minister of Transport, Mr Dullah Omar, and his Namibian and Botswana counterparts, signed a MoU on the development and management of the Trans-Kalahari Corridor (TKC) in September 2003.

The TKC was formally established in 1998 following the completion of the Trans-Kgalagadi Highway in Botswana, which links the three countires by road.

One of the main benefits of the TKC is that it links the three countries with the port of Walvis Bay. The port is the western seaboard in southern Africa and is in the closest proximity to shipping routes and markets in the Americas and Europe.

Foreign relations

Malawi

Malawi was the first independent African country with which South Africa established formal diplomatic, in 1967. Upon South Africa's return to the Commonwealth, relations with Malawi were conducted at the level of High Commission. Current bilateral relations between the two countries are friendly and expanding within the SADC regional context.

Malawi is one of South Africa's main trading partners in the southern African region. Like other African trading partners, the trade imbalance with Malawi is in favour of South Africa.

South African-based companies, following the trend in most African countries, are becoming increasingly interested in linking up with and establishing a presence in Malawi, ranging from the finance, telecommunications and retail sectors to those involved in the construction industry.

Mauritius

Relations with Mauritius are on a very cordial footing, with Mauritius being one of South Africa's largest trading partners within the SADC. Mauritius is also a very popular destination with South African tourists.

Bilateral relations are also targeted at improving co-operation within the SADC framework.

Mozambique

The South African Government supports the democratically elected Government of Mozambique under the leadership of President Chissano, and continues with initiatives aimed at strengthening bilateral relations and the democratic reconstruction and development processes under way in that country.

Continuous bilateral interaction with the Mozambican Government has culminated in the signing of several bilateral agreements, which include, among others, sport and recreation, customs administration, maritime air-search and rescue, air services, agriculture, the protection and utilisation of the water resources of the Inkomati and Maputo water courses, the Trilateral Treaty on the Great Limpopo Transfrontier Park (GLTP), the CFM/Spoornet Concession on the Ressano Garcia railway line, as well as the South Africa-Mozambique Labour Co-operation Agreement.

The close bilateral relations are also facilitating the successful implementation of several phases of Operation Rachel, aimed at the non-proliferation of small arms, which saw more than 1 000 tons (t) of small arms, landmines and unexploded devices destroyed, as well as those of other cross-border security-related operations.

Both the South African and Mozambican Governments view the expansion of the infrastructural links between the two countries as one of the priority bilateral co-operation areas. The rail and road connections between the two countries serve as the main arteries linking the respective economies.

The upgrading of the road, sea and rail links that form part of the corridors between Gauteng, Limpopo, Mpumalanga and Mozambique is central to the promotion of the economies of both countries.

The Maputo Development Corridor Project has already attracted substantial new investments in Mpumalanga, and is expected to boost the Mozambican economy to an equal degree.

In accordance with the SADC's current initiatives and efforts to bring about regional economic integration, South Africa and Mozambique have made substantial progress in the implementation of so-called borderlands and transfrontier conservation initiatives. These are the Lubombo Spatial Development Initiative, the GLTP, as well as the Beira and Nacala Corridors, which are in various stages of development.

The development of these Corridors and borderlands are aimed at exploiting the opportunities and advantages to be derived from countries seeking increased convergence and integration across borders – the sharing of infrastructure, facilities, natural and human resources, as well as enhanced capacity to market the region and lobby internationally for foreign investment in these projects.

A number of quarterly South Africa/ Mozambique bilateral meetings played a pivotal role in the successful implementation of all the respective bilateral macro-economic projects in Mozambique.

Namibia

The relationship between South Africa and Namibia remains close and is marked by co-operation in various areas.

Defence and security co-operation between South Africa and Namibia was further boosted by the second meeting of the South Africa-Namibia Joint Commission on Defence and Security, which took place in Windhoek, Namibia in October 2002.

Economic co-operation was the subject of a Heads of State Economic Bilateral Meeting between President Mbeki and his Namibian counterpart, Dr Sam Nujoma, in Pretoria on 18 March 2003.

In August 2003, Presidents Mbeki and Nujoma signed a treaty in Windhoek for the establishment of the Ai-Ais/Richtersveld Transfrontier Park. The 7 000 km^2 cross-border Park features the world's second-largest canyon in the Fish River, a hot-spring game park on the Namibian side and spectacular arid and desert mountainous scenery on the South African side.

The treaty will result in Namibian and South African tourism authorities encouraging public and private investment in the Park and cross-border tourism, which is expected to grow from 660 000 annual visitors to a million tourists per year.

The signing took place after the fifth Meeting of Heads of State and Government of South Africa and Namibia on Bilateral Economic Co-operation in August 2003 in Windhoek.

Other issues discussed at the Meeting included the:

- Walvis Bay Development Corridor initiative
- Trans-Gariep and Ouzit tourism projects
- Kudu Gas and Western Corridor projects
- implementation of the SADC Trade Protocol and the Southern African Customs Union (SACU) renegotiation.

South Africa is the source of between 80% and 90% of Namibia's imports by value, including virtually all commodities. Bilateral trade between the two countries accounts for two-thirds of Namibia's total foreign trade.

Swaziland

In June 2003, South Africa was planning to establish a JBCC with the Kingdom of Swaziland to structure formal bilateral interaction. Swaziland has made considerable progress towards the creation of a new constitution.

Zambia

Long-standing Zambian support for the liberation struggle in South Africa led to the establishment of a deep mutual bond between the people of South Africa and Zambia.

Trade between the two countries has increased dramatically since the establishment of formal relations on 10 May 1993. Both countries are taking advantage of existing bilateral agreements to foster relations, which is evident in the annual increase of trade and investment flow between them.

Zambia is one of the major supporters of NEPAD and its commitment to peace-keeping efforts by South Africa is a clear indication of the country's interest in the continent.

Uganda

In July 2003, Deputy President Zuma met with President Yoweri Kaguta Museveni of Uganda.

The meeting was the first in the Deputy President's three-day visit to the Great Lakes region, for consultations regarding the Burundi transitional process and the security situation in that country. President Museveni is the chairperson of the Great Lakes Heads of State Regional Initiative of Burundi.

Foreign relations

Kenya

There is a high level of engagement between South Africa and Kenyan institutions aimed at strengthening democratic and constitutional systems.

Kenyan President, Mwai Kibaki, paid an official visit to South Africa in August 2003. Talks between President Mbeki and his Kenyan counterpart focused on political, economic and peace processes, global terrorism, and trade relations. Mr Kibaki was the first Kenyan President to visit South Africa.

On 6 September 2003, Deputy President Zuma attended the funeral of the late Vice-President of Kenya, Mr Michael Kijana Wamalwa.

Kenya is South Africa's largest trading partner on the continent beyond the SADC region.

South African exports to Kenya in 2002/03 totalled R2,3 billion.

Zimbabwe

South Africa and Zimbabwe, besides their geographic proximity, have a common and long history of regional affiliation and cultural ties. The people of Zimbabwe have played an important historic role in support of the liberation struggle in South Africa against the system of apartheid.

South Africa is part of the Commonwealth of Nations, and its policy on Zimbabwe is in line with the decisions made by the Commonwealth Chairpersons' Committee meeting held in March 2002, and informed by specific aspects of the Commonwealth Observer Group Report on the elections in Zimbabwe. South Africa is working with the international community to assist the people of Zimbabwe in solving their problems.

The Joint Commission for Economic, Scientific, Technical and Cultural Co-operation between South Africa and Zimbabwe was revived in November 2002 to strengthen bilateral relations.

South Africa also relies on the SADC Ministerial Task Team on Zimbabwe to continue with their work in the context of existing SADC decisions, which in many instances coincide with those taken by the Commonwealth.

South Africa donated R93,5 milion through the World Food Programme to improve food security in Zimbabwe. The country furthermore donated R12 million to Zimbabwe to purchase vaccine/drugs to curb the spread of foot-and-mouth disease in Zimbabwe and the region.

Development co-operation

Although South Africa is not a donor country, development co-operation with countries in Africa is an integral part of South Africa's foreign policy. Assistance is wide-ranging and includes educational visits by agriculturists, the establishment of viable training centres, conservation of the environment, the rendering of medical assistance, and technology-exchange programmes. Technical and financial assistance, with a view to capacity-building, especially to SADC countries, is a major instrument for promoting economic development, peace and stability, democracy, and the African Renaissance, on a regional basis.

South Africa and the Southern African Development Community

The Government's vision for the southern African region involves the highest possible degree of economic co-operation, mutual assistance, and joint planning consistent with socio-economic, environmental and political realities. Within the region, the SADC will of necessity remain the primary vehicle for South African policy and action to achieve regional economic development.

Originally known as the Southern African Development Co-ordination Conference, the SADC was formed in Lusaka, Zambia, on 1 April 1980, following the adoption of the Lusaka Declaration. The Declaration and Treaty establishing the SADC was signed at the Summit of Heads of State and Government, on 17 August 1992 in Windhoek.

The aim of the SADC is to provide for regional peace and security, sectoral co-operation and an integrated regional economy. The SADC member states are Angola, Botswana, the Democratic Republic of the Congo (DRC), Lesotho, Malawi, Mauritius, Mozambique, Namibia, the Seychelles, South Africa, Swaziland, Tanzania, Zambia and Zimbabwe.

South Africa, through the Department of Foreign Affairs and other relevant departments, continues to actively participate in the work of the SADC Review Committee, as well as contributing towards the SADC Plan of Action for the following 10 years, in particular its RISDP. The effective operationalisation of the SADC's security/stability mechanism underpins the RISDP. Implementation of the RISDP within the context of NEPAD will enhance the standing of the region internationally, and allow it to become the leading regional economic community on the continent.

The SADC Heads of State and Government Summit was held in Dar-es-Salaam, Tanzania, from 25 to 26 August 2003.

At the Summit, President Benjamin Mkapa of Tanzania was elected chairperson of the SADC, and the Prime Minister of Lesotho, Prof. Pakalitha Mosisili, was elected to chair the Organ on Politics, Defence and Security Co-operation. South Africa was elected deputy chairperson of the Organ.

During the Implementation of the Review of the Operations of SADC Institutions, which began in March 2001, the following tasks were completed:
- the establishment of all four directorates at the Secretariat, namely:
  - Trade, Industry, Finance and Investment
  - Food, Agriculture and Natural Resources
  - Infrastructure and Services
  - Human and Social Development, and Special Programmes
- the operationalisation of the Integrated Committee of Ministers
- the mobilisation of resources in the form of human resources from member states, through secondment of officers to the directorates, and funds from international co-operating partners for financing key activities relating to the restructuring exercise
- the establishment of SADC National Committees in most member states
- the completion of the formulation of the SADC RISDP
- the adoption and operationalisation of the study on the implementation of the new SADC structure.

The Summit also approved the RISDP and the Strategic Indicative Plan for the Organ, and called for the co-ordination and rationalisation of the two plans to maximise their inherent synergies.

Implementation of the SADC operational structure was expected to commence in April 2004.

By September 2003, 12 protocols had been ratified and entered into force. These were the:
- Protocol on Immunities and Privileges
- Protocol on Shared Watercourse Systems
- Protocol on Energy
- Protocol on Transport, Communications and Meteorology
- Protocol on Combating Illicit Drugs
- Protocol on Trade
- Protocol on Education and Training
- Protocol on Mining
- Protocol on the Development of Tourism
- Protocol on the Tribunal
- Amendment Protocol on Trade
- Protocol on Fisheries.

Eleven additional protocols still need to be ratified before entering into force.

Implementation of the SADC Trade Protocol

The SADC Protocol on Trade entered into force on 25 January 2000. The objectives of the Trade Protocol are to further liberalise intra-regional trade in goods and services, on the basis of fair, mutually equitable and beneficial trade arrangements; ensure efficient production within the SADC, reflecting the current and dynamic comparative advantages of its members; contribute towards the improvement of a climate for domestic, cross-border and foreign investment; enhance the economic development, diversification and industrialisation of the region; and establish an FTA in the SADC region. At the core of this agreement is the reduction and ultimate elimination of tariffs and non-tariff barriers and the setting up of Rules of Origin. This will happen over a period of eight years, after the ratification of the Protocol by member states.

Since the signing of the Trade Protocol, several rounds of negotiations have taken place. The main issues around which the negotiations centered were modalities for tariff reduction and tariff structure, and customs and trade.

On the issue of customs co-operation and trade facilitation, member states agreed on the harmonisation, simplification and standardisation of SADC customs and trade documentation and procedures.

SADC member states undertook to deposit their instruments of implementation of the SADC Trade Protocol on or before 1 September 2000. South Africa and Mauritius were the first member states to sign and deposit their instruments of implementation. All member states, with the exception of Angola, the DRC and Seychelles, have now deposited their instruments of implementation of the Trade Protocol.

Negotiations are continuing on the outstanding issues of Rules of Origin, particularly in those areas where consensus has not been reached. South Africa maintains the position that each chapter under the Harmonised Systems Code should have a product-specific rule. This formulation will ensure the effective administration of the agreement by customs authorities, and provide exporters with a single, clear set of Rules of Origin for each chapter.

For clothing and textiles, the Rules of Origin tabled by South Africa were based on a two-stage transformation rule similar to the Rules of Origin contained in the South Africa-European Union (EU) Agreement on Trade, Development and Co-operation. In practical terms, it means that clothing will be originated only if the fabrics used are manufactured in the SADC region.

After the Committee of Ministers for Trade directed the SADC trade-negotiating forum to discuss product-specific Rules of Origin and negotiate their specific formulation, the SADC member states that are not part of SACU accepted the product-specific Rules of Origin, with the exception of those applying to the clothing and textile sector.

The SADC Committee of Ministers responsible for Finance and Investment met on 7 August 2003 in Gaborone, Botswana, to discuss developments in the region, consider some MoUs, and review progress on the implementation of the signed MoUs on macro-economic convergence, tax and related matters.

SADC relations with international co-operating partners

The SADC's main international co-operating partners are the EU and the United States of America (USA). The SADC-US Forum was established in 1999 to identify projects of mutual benefit. The Forum meets annually for discussions on the political and security situation in the region, and to identify, evaluate and assess progress in areas of co-operation agreed upon. It is focused on the building of capacity towards the implementation of the SADC Trade Protocol and FTA. The main focus of co-operation of the SADC-US Forum is in the spheres of non-proliferation of small arms and light weapons, and mine action programmes.

Co-operation with other regional role-players such as the Nordic countries and SADC-Mercusor remains to be fully realised.

There is a need for the SADC to establish closer co-operation with other regional economic organisations on the continent, e.g.

the Economic Community of West African States (ECOWAS), to promote cohesion and harmonisation of common approaches to Africa's challenges.

Relations with central Africa

South Africa's diplomatic relations with central Africa have been dominated by attempts to bring peace to the DRC, thereby ensuring greater stability in the whole of the central African region.

It was expected that relations with the region would improve as peaceful conditions returned to the DRC and opportunities for trade and investment with the countries of the world intensified.

Gabon and Equatorial Guinea

A multidisciplinary technical visit of senior officials from the Departments of Foreign Affairs, Housing, Transport, Minerals and Energy, and Justice and Constitutional Development was undertaken to Gabon and Equatorial Guinea, from 28 September to 4 October 2002. The principal objective of the visit was to identify areas of co-operation between South Africa and these two countries.

Rwanda

Relations between South Africa and Rwanda are good. Co-operation between the two countries focuses on the post-conflict reconstruction of Rwanda and has extended to the co-ordination of NEPAD on the continent.

On 12 September 2003, President Mbeki attended the inauguration of Rwandan President, Mr Paul Kagame, following his victory in the country's parliamentary elections on 29 September 2003.

Burundi

South Africa's good relations with Burundi are demonstrated by the leading role the South African Government played in the peace-negotiation process that culminated in the signing of the peace agreement between the Burundi Government and the Forces for the Defence of Democracy on 9 October 2003, which ended years of conflict.

President Mbeki and Deputy President Zuma hosted and facilitated consultations aimed at working out the areas of participation and integration between the two parties in Pretoria, on 5 October 2003.

Democratic Republic of the Congo

Since the beginning of the conflict in the DRC in August 1998, South Africa has played an active role in attempting to bring peace to this vast country and the Great Lakes region of central Africa. South Africa was a major role-player in negotiating and drafting the Lusaka Ceasefire Agreement and was present when the documentation was signed on 10 July 1999.

At the end of 2002, a ground-breaking peace agreement brokered by South Africa was signed between the Governments of the DRC and Rwanda. The agreement paved the way for the withdrawal and disarming of Rwandan troops from the DRC, and the repatriation of the Interahamwe and the Rwandan former army (ex-FAR).

The agreement assigned the role of Third Party to the UN Secretary-General and the South African Government, the latter in its capacity as facilitator and then chairperson of the AU. The Third Party Verification Mechanism (TPVM) was established to act as the Secretariat for the Third Party, and its task was to monitor and verify the implementation of the agreement. The TPVM comprised four representatives from South Africa and two from the UN Secretary-General.

The final plenary session of the Inter-Congolese Dialogue (ICD), attended by 361 delegates, representing the DRC Government, the Congolese Rally for Democracy (RCD-Goma), the Congolese Movement for Liberation (MLC), the unarmed political opposition and civil society, took place at Sun City in the North West in April 2003. During the plenary session, the Global and Inclusive Agreement on the Transition in the DRC and the Transitional Constitution was endorsed. This made provision for the establishment of a transitional government, with the Congolese President, Mr Joseph Kabila, as Head of State for a period of two years.

The Vice-Presidents nominated were Mr Yerodia Abdoulaye Ndombasi of the DRC Government, Mr Azarias Ruberwa of the RCD-Goma, Mr Jean-Pierre Bemba of the MLC and Prof. Arthur Zahidi Ngoma of the unarmed political opposition.

During the closing ceremony on 2 April 2003, about 44 delegates, representing the five components of the ICD, signed the Final Act. The Final Act comprises a Preamble, four Articles, and the 36 Resolutions adopted during the plenary session of the ICD. In the Preamble and Articles, the signatories committed themselves to being bound by the decisions and agreements of the ICD.

The UN Secretary-General, Mr Kofi Annan, in his second report to the UN's Organisation Mission in the DRC (MONUC), which was presented to the UN Security Council on 4 June 2003, recommended that the mandate of the peace-keeping mission in the DRC be extended until 30 June 2004.

Mr Annan further recommended that its military strength be increased to 10 800 members.

At the time, MONUC had about 4 600 troops throughout the DRC, most of whom were unarmed logistical support troops.

Tanzania
Agreements between South Africa and Tanzania include the:
- MoU on Co-operation in Industry and Trade Programmes
- General Agreement on Co-operation in the Economic, Scientific, Technical and Cultural Fields
- Exchange of Notes to Establish Representative Offices.

Relations with North and West Africa and the Horn of Africa

The countries of North and West Africa and the Horn of Africa are becoming increasingly important trading partners for South Africa, as well as important partners within the context of the AU/AEC.

South Africa maintains diplomatic relations with all states in the West African subregion, although it maintains residential diplomatic Missions only in Nigeria, Ghana, Senegal and Côte d'Ivoire. The South African Embassies in Abidjan and Dakar are responsible for South Africa's non-residential relationship with the rest of the West African subregion. The placement of South Africa's diplomatic Missions in this area represents the importance South Africa attaches to those states as partners in Africa, and their use as a platform for the further expansion of South Africa's diplomatic reach into the subregion.

States in West Africa that are on the path towards reinforcing a democratic culture, such as Ghana, Senegal, Benin, Sierra Leone, Cape Verde and Mali, represent a positive development for South Africa. Sierra Leone and Niger, both emerging from difficult periods, also offer potential for democratic consolidation.

South Africa continues to bridge its long-distance relationship with West Africa by engaging in more meaningful actions in the subregion, in terms of political dialogue and economic co-operation. The business community in South Africa is demonstrating a keen interest in the subregion, and has been actively exploring and taking advantage, where possible, of opportunities in mining, infrastructure, telecommunications and financial services, as well as the trade of consumer goods and capital equipment.

Algeria
The third Session of the Binational Commission (BNC) of Co-operation between South Africa and Algeria, the only BNC at Presidential

level in Africa, was held in Algiers from 17 to 23 October 2002.

The BNC serves as a framework for bilateral relations between the two countries in various sectors.

President Mbeki and President Bouteflika expressed satisfaction with the quality of the relations of friendship, solidarity and co-operation that exist between the two countries.

The period 2002/03 witnessed various exchanges between South African and Algerian delegations, in line with commitments made in the Plan of Action. These included, among others, a visit to South Africa by a delegation from the Algerian National Archives, a visit to Algeria by a delegation from the South African Department of Health, and a visit to South Africa by a delegation from the Algerian Ministry of Transport. An Algerian delegation travelled to South Africa in February/March 2003 for the first meeting of the Joint Algeria/South African Committee on Water and Forestry.

On the request of President Mbeki, a South African rescue team was despatched to Algeria to assist with rescue operations following a devastating earthquake in May 2003, which left more than 2 000 people dead and 8 000 injured.

The team comprised members of the fire, rescue, engineering and medical staff of the South African National Defence Force, the South African Police Service, the Tshwane, Ekhurhuleni and Johannesburg Metro municipalities, as well as representatives from two NGOs, Rescue South Africa and Global Relief.

South Africa was one of 38 international rescue teams that assisted with the rescue operations.

The positive relationship between South Africa and Algeria has seen significant growth in South African exports to Algeria, from about R230 million in 2000 to R560 million in 2002.

Cote d'Ivoire

South Africa established full diplomatic relations with Cote d'Ivoire in May 1992.

Given South Africa's firm commitment to the African Renaissance and its attendant features of stability and democratisation on the continent, the events in Cote d'Ivoire, since the rebellion of September 2002, are of major significance. South Africa has pledged to assist Cote d'Ivoire in its process of national reconciliation, and to work through the ECOWAS and the AU in an attempt to assist the country to resolve conflict.

Cote d'Ivoire is South Africa's largest trading partner in Francophone West Africa.

Egypt

Bilateral political and economic relations between Egypt and South Africa have improved greatly in recent years. These improvements were underlined in April 1996 with the convening of the First Annual Joint Bilateral Commission (JBC) Meeting in Cairo.

During 2002, the South African Mission in Cairo focused much of its attention on developments in the Middle East and Egypt's role in the region. Egypt, as a member of the NEPAD Steering Committee, continued to play a role in the implementation and functioning of NEPAD. An Egyptian official was seconded to the NEPAD Secretariat.

The South African Ministries of Intelligence and Water Affairs and Forestry visited Egypt for bilateral and multilateral purposes.

The Mission in Cairo, together with a bilateral desk, arranged for a group of Egyptian journalists to visit South Africa in an attempt to promote the country as a tourist destination.

Several agreements were signed between South Africa and Egypt during the sixth session of the South Africa-Egypt JBC in Pretoria during July 2003.

These included agreements on:
- co-operation between the South African Government and the Egyptian Foreign Ministry

Foreign relations

- co-operation between the Foreign Service Training Institute and the Egyptian Diplomatic Training Institute
- co-operation in the fields of health and pharmaceuticals
- cultural co-operation
- tourism co-operation
- the MoU between the South African Broadcasting Corporation (SABC) and the Egyptian Broadcasting Authority.

Sudan

South Africa reaffirmed its support for Sudan in its quest for peace, at a dinner held in honour of the Sudanese Vice-President, Mr Omar Hassan El-Bashir, in Pretoria in February 2003.

Morocco

The first JBC Meeting with Morocco took place in Pretoria in 1988. Negotiations are under way to finalise dates for the second session of the JBC.

The Moroccan monarch, King Mohammed VI, as Head of State of Morocco, and a Moroccan delegation attended the WSSD in Johannesburg in July and August 2002. Talks took place between King Mohammed VI and President Mbeki during the course of the Summit.

South Africa participated in the fifth Biregional Africa/Europe Meeting, which was held in Rabat, the Moroccan capital, during September 2002.

Mauritania

Mauritanian President, Maaouiya Ould Sid' Ahmed Taya, attended the Inaugural Summit of the AU in 2002 in Durban, as well as the WSSD.

In January 2003, President Taya sent a special envoy to South Africa for consultation on multilateral issues.

Liberia

President Mbeki and the Minister of Foreign Affairs attended the ceremony during which the Liberian President, Mr Charles Taylor, handed over power to the Vice-President, Mr Moses Blah, in Monrovia, Liberia on 11 August 2003.

President Mbeki, in his capacity as then chairperson of the AU, had been involved in efforts to bring about peace and stability in Liberia early in 2003.

Nigeria

South Africa's bilateral and multilateral relationship with Nigeria remains of strategic importance, particularly in the light of the development and promotion of NEPAD. Nigeria serves as the chairperson of the Heads of State and Government Implementation Committee of NEPAD, and is involved in the evolution of mechanisms around the AU.

At bilateral level, trade continues to increase, with the total of two-way trade reaching R3,3 billion in 2001 and R3,7 billion between January and June 2002 alone. South African companies continue to establish themselves in a number of sectors (e.g. hospitality, financial services, communications and energy) in the Nigerian market. The South Africa-Nigeria BNC, which was established in October 1999, held its fourth session in Pretoria in March 2002.

During the session, an additional four agreements (on co-operation in the fields of extradition, mutual legal assistance in criminal matters, immigration and health) were signed, bringing to 15 the total number of bilateral agreements concluded between South Africa and Nigeria.

The fifth Annual Session of the BNC was scheduled to be held in Abuja during the second half of 2003.

Following President Mbeki's State Visit to Nigeria in September 2001, President Obasanjo undertook a return State Visit to South Africa in February 2003, during which the two Heads of State discussed not only the bilateral relations between South Africa and Nigeria, but also issues relating to the promotion and implementation of NEPAD and the institutionalisation of the AU.

In May 2003, President Mbeki attended the inauguration of President Obasanjo, a month after the latter had been elected for a second five-year term.

Ghana

Diplomatic relations between South Africa and Ghana continue to improve. Ghana is a stable democracy with immense potential. The country represents a neutral island of stability with no geopolitical interest in the volatile West African subregion. In recent years, South African imports from and exports to Ghana have increased, placing greater importance on that country as an important trading partner for South Africa. Both countries maintain High Commissions in each other's capitals.

Mali

The Department of Foreign Affairs established a residential diplomatic Mission in Mali's capital, Bamako, in November 2002.

The two countries are involved in a joint Presidential project for the preservation of the ancient manuscripts at the Ahmed Baba Institute of Higher Learning and Islamic Research in Timbuktu. The project was officially launched by the South African and Malian Heads of State during the Africa Day celebrations in Johannesburg, on 28 May 2003.

The project, the first of its kind on the African continent, involves the training of Malian archive officials in South Africa, and the eventual construction of a new centre in Timbuktu, where the ancient manuscripts will be preserved.

In May 2003, the Minister in The Presidency, Dr Essop Pahad, together with the Malian Minister of Education, Mr Mohamed Lamine Traore, launched a trust fund in Pretoria for the preservation of the Timbuktu manuscripts.

The trust fund will finance the building of a library with the necessary technology to preserve the manuscripts. The fund was expected to raise about R36 million over a five-year period.

Economic relations between the two countries are good and South Africa continues to pursue and strengthen such relations. Two mining companies run operations in Mali, namely Anglogold and Randgold.

Various agreements have been signed between Mali and South Africa.

Senegal

Representative offices were established in November 1993 in Pretoria and Dakar. Full diplomatic relations between South Africa and Senegal were established in May 1994. After having closed its Embassy in Pretoria in December 1995, the Senegalese authorities re-established an Embassy in Pretoria during 2001.

The South African Ambassador is resident in Dakar, Senegal. The Ambassador is accredited to Guinea, Mali, Mauritania, Cape Verde, Gambia and Guinea-Bissau on a non-residential basis.

Senegal continues to play a very active role in the development and implementation of NEPAD.

Tunisia

A meeting of senior officials, in preparation for the fourth session of the JBC between Tunisia and South Africa, was held in Pretoria early in 2003.

Parallel to the senior officials' meeting, a meeting of the Tunisian-South African Business Forum was held.

This meeting brought together business leaders from various sectors.

The senior officials' meeting accorded both delegations the opportunity to review the state of bilateral relations between the two countries, and to compare notes on the global and regional situation.

Bilateral co-operation in the following areas was discussed: agriculture, trade and industry,

Foreign relations

arts and culture, minerals and energy, health, immigration, sport, vocational training, and employment.

The delegations noted the good progress made with regard to the implementation of existing agreements.

Libya

The first session of the South African-Libyan JBC was held in Tripoli in June 2002. The session presented an opportunity to further strengthen bilateral relations between the two countries, and jointly promote unity, peace, security and development on the African continent.

Co-operation was discussed in the areas of minerals and energy, agriculture and animal health, transport, communications, trade and industry, investments, tourism, higher education, and arts and culture. At a multilateral level, the AU, NEPAD and the Non-Aligned Movement (NAM) were discussed.

Bilateral agreements signed included the following:
- Agreement on the Reciprocal Protection and Promotion of Investments
- Agreement on Merchant Shipping and Maritime-Related Matters
- Letter of Intent for Co-operation in the Field of Transport and Transportation
- MoU on Air Services
- Protocol of Intent on Co-operation in the Fields of Science and Technology.

The JBC preceded a State Visit to Libya by President Mbeki. The leaders agreed on the necessity of promoting bilateral co-operation between the two countries to realise the mutual aspirations of their people.

Relations with Asia and the Middle East

Asia

South Africa values its relations with Asian countries. Since 1994, South Africa's interaction with Asia has seen a manifold increase. South Africa has 15 residential Missions in the Asian and Australasian region.

Furthermore, 16 countries from this region currently maintain 31 diplomatic, consular and other Missions in South Africa, compared with the three that existed prior to 1994.

Since 1994, South Africa has continued to strengthen its relations with the region through increases in two-way trade; personal exchanges between high-level dignitaries; and the finalisation of new instruments of co-operation in the scientific and technological fields, through technology transfer, investments and overseas development assistance (ODA) in capacity-building.

South Africa's successful transition to democracy also prompted the parties involved in the Sri Lankan peace process to request South Africa to host a round of peace talks between Sri Lanka and the Liberation Tigers of Tamil Eelam, during the latter half of 2003.

For South Africa, as part of the Indian Ocean Rim (IOR), which encompasses the eastern African coastal countries, the Arabian Peninsula, south-east Asia, Australia and the Indian subcontinent, the Indian Ocean Rim Association for Regional Co-operation (IOR-ARC) is considered an important regional economic entity. The IOR-ARC Initiative, currently backed by 19 countries including South Africa, creates an opportunity for countries of the South to serve their economic interests.

On 5 November 2002, President Mbeki delivered the closing address at the closing session of the eighth Association of South-East Asian Nations (ASEAN) Summit in Phnom Pehn, where he briefed Asian leaders on NEPAD.

An Asian and African Subregional Organisations' Conference was held in Bandung, Indonesia, in July 2003 – about 45 years after the historic 1955 Asia-Africa Conference – to promote economic, cultural and political co-operation.

Singapore serves as an important economic and trading hub in the south-east Asian region. South Africa's bilateral trade with Singapore is substantial, with trade in 2002 amounting to R4 billion.

In addition to providing South Africa with valuable opportunities for HRD through its Technical Co-operation Programme, Singapore also enjoys ongoing defence co-operation with South Africa.

Thailand currently chairs the United Nations Conference on Trade and Development (UNCTAD), after having taken over the chairpersonship from South Africa in April 2001. South Africa continues to interact closely with Thailand on the UNCTAD. Bilateral trade in 2002 amounted to R5 billion. Thailand also took over the chairpersonship of the Asia-Pacific Economic Co-operation in December 2002. The year 2002 marked the 10th anniversary of the establishment of consular relations between South Africa and Thailand. High-level visitors from Thailand in 2002 included Princess Chulabhorn Mahidol, who led the Thai delegation to the WSSD.

Vietnam plays an increasingly important role in south-east Asia and has vast economic potential and opportunities for mining, infrastructure development and agricultural and manufacturing companies. Bilateral trade with Vietnam in 2000 amounted to R206 million. South Africa established an Embassy in Hanoi in October 2002. The year 2002 saw a visit by the Vietnamese Vice-Minister of Trade to South Africa, while the Vietnamese Minister of Foreign Affairs also attended the WSSD.

Economic relations with **Malaysia** and **Indonesia** remain important, due to Malaysian investment in South Africa and the size of the Indonesian market. Malaysian investment has focused on the hospitality, telecommunications and energy industries, while trade with Malaysia amounted to R5,6 billion in 2002. Bilateral trade with Indonesia amounted to R2,9 million in 2002.

South Africa and Malaysia enjoy close co-operation within the multilateral field in forums such as the Commonwealth and NAM.

Malaysia continues to be very supportive of South Africa's efforts to enhance South-South co-operation and ensure that the needs of the South are addressed in international forums.

Malaysia has also indicated its support for NEPAD and has sought to promote the Malaysian-initiated Langkawi International Dialogue aimed at expanding co-operation among countries of the South, including those in southern Africa.

Through its intensive Technical Co-operation Programme, Malaysia has provided HRD training opportunities to numerous South Africans across a wide range of disciplines.

Ten years ago there were no South African Missions located in the south and central Asian regions. In fact, South Africa had no diplomatic relations with states in this region. Today, there are resident High Commissions in New Delhi and Islamabad, and a Consulate-General in Mumbai. South Africa has diplomatic relations with Afghanistan, Bangladesh, India, Kazakhstan, Kyrgyzstan, Maldives, Nepal, Pakistan, Sri Lanka, Tajikistan, Turkmenistan and Uzbekistan. In addition, India, Pakistan, Sri Lanka and Bangladesh have resident Missions in South Africa.

The events of 11 September 2001 focused the world's attention on **Afghanistan** and the campaign against international terrorism. South Africa continues to monitor developments, and encourages South African individuals and organisations to become involved in reconstruction efforts in Afghanistan.

During recent months, the South African Liaison Office for Afghanistan was established, headed by the current South African High Commissioner to Pakistan. The Transitional Islamic State of Afghanistan is represented by the Honorary Consul for Afghanistan, who is based in Cape Town.

South Africa has also encouraged peace efforts in Sri Lanka and between India and Pakistan over Kashmir. Late in 2002, delegations from India and Pakistan briefed South

Foreign relations

Africa's Deputy Foreign Minister, Mr Aziz Pahad, and the Deputy President on the status of India-Pakistan relations and the sensitive issue of Kashmir.

A number of South Africans have participated in and benefited from training programmes conducted by countries such as India and Pakistan. Military personnel from Pakistan and India have also benefited from training programmes conducted by the South African Defence College.

A number of South African business delegations have visited Afghanistan, India and **Sri Lanka**. During March 2003, the South Africa-Sri Lanka Business Council was officially opened by the visiting Sri Lankan Minister of Enterprise Development, Industrial Policy, and the Minister of Constitutional Affairs, Prof. Gamini Peiris.

In July 2003, South Africa hosted the fifth session of the South Africa-India Joint Ministerial Commission (JMC) in Pretoria. Trade between the two countries exceeded R6,9 billion in 2002, with the balance in South Africa's favour.

India is currently South Africa's sixth largest trading partner in Asia.

An increasing number of cultural groups from India have recently visited South Africa. In 2003, the South African musical production of *African Footprint* enjoyed a successful tour of India.

The Indian International Film Academy Awards (IIFA) ceremony took place at Sun City, North West in 2002, and was followed with an equally successful IIFA awards ceremony held at the Dome in Randburg in May 2003. South Africa is becoming a destination of interest for Indian film-makers.

The India-South Africa Commercial Alliance met for the second time in Pretoria, in June 2002. A variety of opportunities for bilateral co-operation and increased trade were identified in, among others, the pharmaceutical, engineering, information communications technology (ICT) and chemical sectors. South Africa and India are currently negotiating a Preferential Trade Agreement.

The Indian Ministry of External Affairs launched a Focus Africa Programme during 2002, which is aimed at enhancing economic and commercial ties between India and African countries. India's expertise in areas such as agriculture, ICT and health, offers great potential for NEPAD-related projects.

President Mbeki paid a State Visit to India in October 2003 to foster the already close relationship between the two countries.

The central Asian states of Kazakhstan, Kyrgystan, Tajikistan, Turkmenistan and Uzbekistan are receiving increased attention, and South Africa is considering opening a Mission in the region in the near future. Economic opportunities exist in the region, particularly in the mining sector.

An Air Services Agreement with Maldives awaits signature, as do a Trade Agreement with Bangladesh and a Partnership Forum Agreement with Sri Lanka.

South Africa maintains active and mutually beneficial relations with Australia and New Zealand, and non-residential accreditation in Papua New Guinea, Fiji, Samoa and the Cook Islands.

With regard to **Fiji**, South Africa was, through the appointment of Justice Pius Langa, instrumental in assisting Fiji in the process of democratisation, following the ousting of the legitimate government in a coup in May 2000.

In July 2002, President Mbeki visited Fiji for the African Caribbean and Pacific (ACP) Summit.

South Africa is **Australia**'s 20th largest export market and 22nd largest trading partner. Total exports to Australia in 2002 amounted to R4,4 billion, and imports from Australia amounted to R6,6 billion with the trade balance favouring Australia. Cultural, institutional, political and trade relations have expanded rapidly since 1994.

In the multilateral field, the two countries are members of most of the major southern hemisphere organisations and share similar views on most international issues such as disarmament, agriculture and trade in food products, fishing, protection of marine resources, Antarctica, and fair international trade.

Australia and **New Zealand** are both eager to strengthen relations, especially trade and investment, with South Africa. This will also be pivotal in enhancing relations with southern Africa. New Zealand maintains a High Commission in Pretoria, while the High Commission in Canberra represents South Africa in New Zealand. The establishment of a resident High Commission in Wellington is imminent.

Since 1994, political, economic and social links between the two countries have improved significantly. In 1996, the Cape Town Communiqué was signed, which seeks to strengthen co-operation between South Africa and New Zealand. The political relationship has been further strengthened by numerous high-level delegations that have visited New Zealand, to gain expertise in their different fields and exchange knowledge to enhance capacity-building in central, provincial and local government structures.

Prime Minister Helen Clarke came to South Africa in August/September 2002 for the WSSD and a working visit.

South Africa and New Zealand enjoy wide-ranging multilateral relations. Both are members of the Valdivia Group, which aims to promote southern hemisphere views in international environmental meetings and the enhancement of scientific co-operation.

They enjoy a close working relationship within the context of the Antarctic Treaty and Indian Ocean Fisheries, and also interact within the context of the WTO and the Cairns Group. South Africa and New Zealand also work closely on Commonwealth issues, particularly those affecting Africa.

Bilateral trade between the two countries has been growing steadily since 1994.

South African exports in 2000 totalled R3,5 billion, R3,8 billion in 2001, and R4,2 billion in 2002. South African imports in 2000 totalled R4,9 billion, R5,9 billion in 2001, and R5,7 billion in 2002.

Bilateral relations with the **People's Republic of China (PRC)** have expanded substantially since the establishment of diplomatic relations in 1998.

A broad range of agreements to formalise relations has been concluded between South Africa and the PRC. Of specific importance was the signing of the Pretoria Declaration between President Jiang Zemin and President Mbeki in April 2000. The Declaration served to establish a high-level BNC between the two countries. The inaugural meeting was held in Beijing in December 2001. The second BNC was scheduled to take place in February 2004 in Pretoria. In an effort to address the problem of transnational crime, South Africa and China concluded an Agreement on Extradition and Mutual Legal Assistance in December 2001.

To further facilitate co-operation in this field, the two countries signed the Mutual Legal Assistance in Criminal Matters Agreement in January 2003.

Total bilateral trade between China and South Africa reached R18,74 billion in 2001 with the balance in favour of the PRC.

The establishment of a Consulate-General in Shanghai in November 2002 was expected to stimulate bilateral trade interaction, in particular South African exports to China.

A working visit to South Africa by China's Premier, Zhu Gongji, in September 2002, and an official visit by First Vice-Premier Li Langing in January 2003, added momentum to the development of relations between South Africa and China in almost every arena.

During the Senior Officials' Meeting of the China-Africa Co-operation Forum, held in November 2003 in Addis Ababa, China reaffirmed its support for the objectives of NEPAD.

In an effort to promote tourism to South Africa from China, the authorities in Beijing have granted Approved Destination Status (ADS) to South Africa. The ADS Agreement was signed in October 2002. The first group of Chinese tourists under this dispensation arrived in South Africa in April 2003.

Hong Kong continues to be an important gateway to China and much of South Africa's trade with the PRC is channelled through the territory. A significant number of South African companies and financial institutions maintain offices in Hong Kong, and South African Airways operates direct flights to the territory from Johannesburg.

The African Business Chamber, which was established in 2001, serves as a forum for the discussion of ways in which business-ties between Hong Kong and African countries may be strengthened.

Notwithstanding the absence of diplomatic relations, South Africa and **Taiwan** continue with trade, scientific, cultural and other relations, and Taiwanese investors in South Africa continue to enjoy full protection under South African law, as well as all the other benefits extended to foreign investors.

In 2002, **Japan** and South Africa met for the fifth Japan-South Africa Partnership Forum meeting in Tokyo, during which bilateral and multilateral issues of interest and concern were discussed.

President Mbeki, accompanied by the Minister of Foreign Affairs led a South African delegation comprising senior government officials to the International Conference on Africa Development (TICAD III) in September 2003.

TICAD is an initiative for African development, launched in 1993 through the joint efforts of the Japanese Government, the UN and the Global Coalition for Africa.

The primary goals of TICAD are to:
- promote high-level policy dialogue between African leaders and their trade partners
- mobilise support for Africa's own development efforts
- strengthen co-ordination among all development partners
- promote regional co-operation and integration through support for regional and sub-regional groupings and organisations
- promote South-South co-operation in general, and Asia-African co-operation in particular, through the exchange of experience and knowledge.

NEPAD is set to continue featuring strongly as a central issue in Africa's relationship with Japan.

During 2002, the Japanese implementation of a series of ODA projects continued, especially in the health, education, and safe water-management sectors.

South Africans also benefitted from HRD courses provided by the Japan International Co-operation Agency.

Japan continues to be South Africa's most important trade partner in Asia. Bilateral trade in 2002 totalled R43,9 billion, with the balance in South Africa's favour.

South Korea remains an important trade partner of South Africa in Asia. In 2002, bilateral trade amounted to R10 billion.

South Korea continued to assist South Africa with HRD in specialised sectors in 2002.

The Middle East

In the Middle East, the Department of Foreign Affairs distinguishes between two clearly identifiable subregions. On one hand, there is the Levant, which comprises Israel, Iraq, Jordan, Lebanon, Palestine and Syria, and on the other hand, the Arabian/Persian Gulf Region, consisting of the member states of the Gulf Co-operation Council, namely Bahrain, Kuwait, Oman, Qatar, Saudi Arabia, the United Arab Emirates (UAE), as well as Iran and Yemen.

The Middle East is an important economic region as it occupies a unique geopolitical position in the tricontinental hub of Europe, Asia and Africa. It is the source of 67% of the world's petroleum reserves and commands two of the most strategically important waterways in the world, namely the Arabian/Persian

Gulf and the Red Sea, giving access to the Asian hinterland via the Gulf of Aqaba. South Africa places strong emphasis on the expansion of diplomatic representation and activities in this region, where it was formerly underrepresented, particularly in the area of trade, which has grown significantly since 1994.

The South African Consulate-General in Jeddah, in addition to performing important functions relating to the promotion of trade, also serves the South African Muslim community on their annual pilgrimage to Mecca.

Before 1994, South Africa's relations with the Middle East were characterised by a lack of diplomatic representation in the entire region, with a concentration only on links with Israel. After the advent of democracy in 1994, this changed significantly, to the point where today South Africa is accepted as a meaningful political interlocutor in the region.

South Africa supports a just, equitable and comprehensive peace process in the Middle East and an end to the illegal occupation of land that has led to conflict and violence between the peoples of the region. Peace and security for the Israelis and the Palestinians cannot be achieved without the fulfilment of the inalienable right of the Palestinian people to self-determination within their own sovereign State.

Based on its own experiences, South Africa continues to maintain that violence can never provide solutions to intractable conflicts. Inasmuch as this applies to Palestine and Israel, it also applies to the situation in Iraq. A just solution that involves co-operation between Iraq and the UN is an objective which South Africa continues to work for in its interaction with all parties involved.

South Africa aims to utilise its political access to enhance, broaden and consolidate its commercial and technical links with the region. The Middle East holds great potential for South Africa as an export market, and at the same time serves as a potential strategic source of foreign direct investment (FDI) which is essential if NEPAD is to succeed.

Overall bilateral trade between South Africa and the Middle East increased in Rand terms from R32 059 billion in 2000 to R35 503 billion in 2001. Unfortunately, because of South Africa's energy imports from the region, South Africa has a large deficit in respect of trade with the Middle East. In 2001, the country's trade with that region represented 7,54% of South Africa's total international trade.

South Africa's leading trade partners in the region are Saudi Arabia, Iran, Kuwait, Qatar, Israel and the UAE.

The importance of the Middle East to South Africa can also be seen in the growing number of bilateral agreements that are being concluded between South Africa and countries of the region. These cover the fields of civil aviation, avoidance of double taxation, protection of investments, scientific co-operation, and defence.

The Deputy Minister of Foreign Affairs visited the Middle East and Gulf regions, as well as Saudi Arabia and the City of Kuwait, in mid-2003.

In **Saudi Arabia**, Deputy Minister Pahad met with Dr Hasim Yamani, the Minister of Trade and Industry; Dr Nizar Madani, the Assistant Minister of Foreign Affairs; and Mr Khaled Al-Jarallah, the Under-Secretary for Foreign Affairs in Kuwait.

Discussions focused on post-war Iraq, the Middle East Road Map for Peace, and the impact of both situations on regional and global peace and security.

The Saudi Arabian Government established an interministerial committee, chaired by Minister Yamani, to facilitate the relationship between the two countries.

Deputy President Zuma and Deputy Minister Pahad paid an official visit to **Turkey** in October 2003.

Deputy President Zuma held bilateral discussions with Turkish Prime Minister, Recep Tayyip Erdogan, on the following issues:
- the expansion and consolidation of bilateral political and economic relations
- the operationalisation of the AU and the implementation of NEPAD
- multilateral issues including post-war Iraq, the escalation of conditions in the Middle East, reform of the UN, and the global fight against terrorism.

FDI from Turkey in South Africa amounts to US$60 million.

During the visit, several agreements were signed between the two countries, including agreements on trade and economic co-operation; co-operation in the fields of education, arts and culture, science and technology, sport, recreation and youth affairs; and police co-operation.

On 14 September 2003, the State of **Qatar** and South Africa signed an agreement for the development of a large-scale fuel grade methanol project, targeting an output of 12 000 to 15 000 t per day.

South Africa has consistently called for the immediate implementation of the Middle East Road Map for Peace without preconditions, and states that peace between Israel and the Arab States is in the country's national interest. To this end, an active programme of support has been undertaken under the auspices of the Presidential Peace Initiative. The key strategic engagement of South Africa with the Middle East conflict, as clearly shown by the Spier Presidential Peace Retreat in January 2002, remains the strengthening of 'peace camps' in both Israel and Palestine, sharing the South African experience with a wide section of Israeli and Palestinian civil society and government officials; as well as assisting in the Palestinian reform process and supporting international peace efforts, particularly through the UN.

Relations with the Americas

United States of America

The promotion of economic relations with the USA, particularly in trade and investment, remained a central element of the bilateral relationship in 2002/03. The trade relationship continued to expand, with total trade for 2001 in excess of US$7,25 billion, making the USA South Africa's largest single trading partner. South Africa expanded its exports to the USA in 2001 under the General System of Preferences (GSP) Programme through the African Growth and Opportunity Act (AGOA), the value of which was in excess of US$400 million.

US President George W. Bush visited South Africa in July 2003.

Issues on the agenda for discussion between Presidents Bush and Mbeki included bilateral economic relations between the two countries, NEPAD, conflict on the African continent, Zimbabwe, the global war on terrorism, and HIV/AIDS.

The importance of the AGOA in enhancing trade between the two countries was highlighted. Exports from South Africa to the USA under AGOA increased by 45% during 2002.

The USA pledged support for South Africa's increased fight against HIV/AIDS, committing US$15 billion over a period of five years to the global fight against the pandemic.

Canada

South Africa and Canada enjoy cordial relations. Considerable co-operation also occurs between the two countries on a multilateral level and within international forums.

A number of South African Cabinet Ministers and officials have visited Canada in recent years and have held discussions with their Canadian counterparts on bilateral and multilateral issues. Canada has played a leading role in co-ordinating and formulating the G-8 response to NEPAD.

In November 2003, President Mbeki paid a State Visit to Canada. Canada became the first country to create a fund to support NEPAD.

It has indicated its support for NEPAD in a concrete fashion, through the scrapping of tariffs for least-developed countries and the creation of a C$500 million Fund for Africa.

Furthermore, Canada made available C$6 billion in ODA over a five-year period. Canadian civil society has also indicated strong support for, and interest in, NEPAD.

Trade and investment between the two countries has grown steadily since 1994, with mining remaining the mainstay of the economic relationship.

In 2002, bilateral trade amounted to more than R4 billion per annum.

This includes not only trade in raw material, but also in the field of mining equipment, technology, services and joint ventures. Growth has also occurred in the areas of agroprocessing and ICT.

Canada is active in the field of development co-operation in South Africa. Its technical-assistance programme is aimed at fostering social upliftment, policy development and HRD. The Canadians have made a significant contribution towards good governance and education in South Africa, through a twinning programme that links six Canadian provinces to six South African provinces.

The Caribbean

South Africa's relations with the independent member states of the Caribbean Community have been strengthened and expanded through the fully operational South African High Commission in Kingston, Jamaica. In addition to Jamaica, the High Commission also maintains responsibility for Antigua and Barbuda, The Bahamas, Barbados, Belize, Dominica, Dominican Republic, Grenada, Guyana, Haiti, St Kitts and Nevis, St Lucia, St Vincent and the Grenadines, Suriname, and Trinidad and Tobago.

President Mbeki, accompanied by the Minister of Foreign Affairs and the Minister of Public Enterprises, Mr Jeff Radebe, visited Jamaica in July 2003. The purpose of the State Visit was for President Mbeki, as then chairperson of the AU, to address the Carribean Regional Economic Community in Caricom.

President Mbeki also held bilateral discussions with his Caricom Heads of Government counterparts from the Bahamas, St Vincent and the Grenadines, Haiti, St Kitt and Nevis, and Belize, with a view to boosting bilateral political, economic and cultural relations between South Africa and Jamaica as well as between South Africa and the Caricom.

Latin America

South Africa's relations with the countries of the South American region are entering an important and dynamic period of development. South Africa maintains formal diplomatic relations with all the countries of Latin America.

Latin America's population of about 300 million, as well as its various economic blocs, such as Mercosur (Southern Common Market) and the Andean Community, will ensure the region's increasing importance to South Africa.

There is great potential for co-operation with the Mercosur trading bloc, which consists of Argentina, Brazil, Paraguay and Uruguay, with Bolivia and Chile having associate status. Co-operation in the South Atlantic is further enhanced through the Zone of Peace and Co-operation in the South Atlantic (ZPCSA). The aims and objectives of the ZPCSA include the protection of the marine environment and resources, the promotion of the South Atlantic as a nuclear-free zone, and joint business ventures.

In December 2000, a Framework Agreement for the Creation of an FTA between South Africa and Mercosur was signed by the South African Minister of Trade and Industry, Mr Alec Erwin. The aim of the Agreement was to

Foreign relations

strengthen existing relations, promote the expansion of trade, and establish the conditions for the creation of a future FTA.

Several rounds of discussions towards the establishment of an FTA have taken place since the first talks in Montevideo, Uruguay, in October 2001.

The second South Africa-Cuba JBC took place in November 2002 in Havana, which reviewed existing bilateral co-operation projects and the extension of co-operation to new areas. In April 2002, the first South Africa-Cuba Consultative Mechanism reviewed bilateral and multilateral issues. The Minister of Foreign Affairs visited **Cuba** in January 2003, where she was honoured by the Cuban Government with the Medal of Friendship. The Minister held a bilateral meeting with her Cuban counterpart, Mr Felipe Perez Roque.

Relations with **Brazil** were given further impetus with the inaugural meeting of the South Africa-Brazil JBC in Brasilia, in August 2002. This encompassed political discussions between the respective Foreign Affairs Ministers, as well as discussions on co-operation between line-function departments in a variety of technical fields. The second meeting, held in Pretoria in May 2003, cemented these ties and laid the basis for expanded co-operation.

In November 2003, President Mbeki hosted his Brazilian counterpart, President Lula Da Silva, for bilateral discussions. Brazil is South Africa's largest trading partner in Latin America.

Relations with Europe

South Africa's bilateral relations with Europe have improved and expanded significantly since 1994. Exchanges have continuously increased in terms of high-level political consultation, economic relations and development assistance. South Africa currently maintains diplomatic relations with virtually all countries in Europe. South Africa has 25 Missions in Europe, while these countries are, in turn, represented by more than 50 Embassies and Consulates-General or Trade Missions in South Africa.

Collectively, western Europe is South Africa's largest trading partner and main source of FDI and development assistance. Regular consultations with the EU and its member countries take place with regard to the continued and possible expansion of their constructive involvement in South Africa.

In order to enhance co-operation with European countries, a variety of political and economic mechanisms such as binational and economic commissions have been established with the United Kingdom (UK), France, Germany, Sweden, Spain, Italy and Portugal.

Mechanisms to step up bilateral political consultations have also been created with a number of Nordic countries.

Multilateral interaction with Europe continues on issues such as globalisation, market access, debt relief, the role and reform of the UN Security Council, disarmament and human rights. The establishment of a constructive North-South dialogue is of particular importance to South Africa.

Relations with **Germany** have expanded considerably since the introduction of the South African-German BNC in 1996, as the committees of the Commission now work continuously to enhance political, economic, scientific, cultural and environmental co-operation.

Africa is the main focus of German development co-operation initiatives. Germany has pledged its firm support for NEPAD, with priority areas being conflict prevention and good governance.

The fourth session of the South African-German BNC took place on 30 October 2003 in Pretoria.

South Africa and the **UK** continue to build a special partnership. President Mbeki and Prime Minister Tony Blair met on several occasions in 2002 and there have been numerous meetings between Cabinet Ministers of the two countries. The UK has shown strong support for NEPAD, the AU and conflict resolution in Africa, and has maintained its position as one of South Africa's most significant trade partners, the largest single foreign investor in South Africa, and a major source of tourism.

Bilateral relations between South Africa and **France** are directed by institutionalised mechanisms, such as the MoU for Political Dialogue, as well as joint commissions on trade and industry, arts and culture, and science and technology.

People-to-people relations have expanded dramatically and there have been regular exchanges of cultural, art and sports groups. President Jacques Chirac is a staunch supporter of the AU and NEPAD, especially in the context of the G-8. France demonstrated its commitment to Africa by hosting the Special Summit in the Cote d'Ivoire from 25 to 26 January 2003, the Franco-Africa Summit from 20 to 21 February 2003, and the G-8 meeting with Heads of State of Emerging Market Economies and the NEPAD Heads of State Implementation Committee meeting on 1 June 2003.

On 26 June 2003, Dr Dlamini-Zuma and her French counterpart, Mr Dominique De Villepin, held bilateral discussions in Parliament in Cape Town, before signing an agreement on technical assistance.

President Mbeki paid a State Visit to France in November 2003.

The historic links between South Africa and the Nordic countries have further deepened in recent years. Flowing from the strong grassroots support in these countries for democratisation in South Africa, relations have been established in virtually every field at both public and official levels.

The scope of Nordic development co-operation relations is broad and has benefited civil society and the three tiers of government throughout the country. Relations in the international arena have seen close co-operation on multilateral issues such as the banning of anti-personnel mines.

Two South African-Nordic Summits between President Mbeki and the Nordic Prime Ministers were held in 2000 and 2002 to discuss ways in which to expand relations further. These Summits also pledged Nordic support for the African Renaissance and Nordic involvement in NEPAD.

South Africa maintains excellent bilateral relations with the Benelux countries (**Belgium**, the **Netherlands** and **Luxembourg**). This is, *inter alia*, reflected in the increase in high-level visits, co-operation in multilateral forums, and the number of development-assistance programmes being implemented in South Africa. The commitment of the Benelux countries to the objectives and ideals of the AU and NEPAD is underscored by the close interaction with South Africa in the promotion of peace and security on the African continent. Both the Netherlands and Belgium are providing political and financial support for South Africa's role in conflict-resolution and peace-keeping operations in the Great Lakes region.

In September 2003, Deputy President Zuma paid an official visit to the Netherlands and **Spain**. The Deputy President's delegation included the Minister of Justice, Dr Penuell Maduna, and the Deputy Minister of Foreign Affairs.

In the context of South Africa's key role in conflict resolution, management and prevention, arbitration, as well as peace-keeping on the African continent, the delegation interacted with legal multilateral institutions in the Netherlands, including the Permanent Court of Arbitration, the International Court of Justice, the International Criminal Court and The Hague Convention on International Private Law.

Deputy President Zuma's delegation to Madrid, Spain, included the Minister of Intelligence Services, Dr Lindiwe Sisulu, the Deputy Minister of Trade and Industry, Ms Lindiwe Hendricks, and the Deputy Minister of

Foreign Affairs. The visit focused on deepening economic and political ties between South Africa and Spain.

The Deputy President held bilateral discussions with Spain's First Deputy Prime Minister, Mr Rodrigo Rato, to discuss:
- the current status of, and prospects for, further expansion of bilateral relations, and steps to expand economic ties
- NEPAD and the AU
- conflict resolution and peace-keeping on the African continent.

Spain is one of South Africa's major trading partners. Between 1999 and 2002, Spain invested R2 020 billion in South Africa.

The President of the Republic of **Italy**, Mr Carlo Azeglio Ciampi, received President Mbeki during the G-8 Summit in July 2001. President Ciampi was subsequently invited to pay a State Visit to South Africa in March 2002. This was a successful visit during which Italian support for NEPAD, the WSSD, the fight against HIV/AIDS, increased levels of the ODA and the transfer of technology was pledged.

President Constantinos Stephanopoulos of the **Hellenic Republic**, accompanied by a trade delegation, paid a State Visit to South Africa in October 2002. He expressed support for socio-economic upliftment through NEPAD, increased levels of trade and investment, and targeted ODA projects.

On 26 May 2003, South Africa and **Austria** signed a co-operation agreement on safety and security issues.

A South African delegation, comprising President Mbeki, the Minister of Trade and Industry and the Deputy Minister of Foreign Affairs, travelled to **Switzerland** in June 2003, for bilateral discussions with the Swiss delegation comprising the Swiss President, Mr Pascal Couchepin; the Minister of Foreign Affairs, Ms Micheline Calmy-Rey; and the Minister of Economic Affairs, Mr Joseph Deiss.

A Declaration of Intent on joint co-operation in Africa was signed by Ministers Erwin and Calmy-Rey. The aim of the Declaration is to enhance co-operation on joint initiatives within the context of the AU and NEPAD.

These initiatives include key areas such as humanitarian assistance, international humanitarian law, development assistance, governance, private-enterprise promotion and economic development.

Deputy President Zuma co-chaired the third session of the South Africa-Swedish BNC with his Swedish counterpart, Ms Margareta Winburg, in October 2003.

The BNC focused on discussions centred around its three committees, namely Political Affairs, Economic Affairs, and Social and Development Co-operation Affairs.

South Africa's exports to **Sweden** increased from R231 million in 1999 to R736 million in 2002. Sweden exported goods to the value of R3,31 billion to South Africa in 2002.

Figures provided by the Swedish International Development Agency show that Swedish investments in South Africa since 1994 exceed R800 million in 80 companies employing more than 1 200 people.

Sweden is one of the top five donors to South Africa.

Multilateral diplomacy

South Africa is a full participant in the debates on global issues in international forums and organisations such as the UN, the Commonwealth and NAM. Among the multitude of issues that are dealt with are UN reform; South Africa's role in peace-keeping operations and disarmament issues; the global development debate; negotiations with the EU; the future of NAM; the implementation of Agenda 21 and the treaties that flow from it, such as those on biodiversity and climate change, international drug control, international measures to combat crime, good governance, human rights and humanitarian assistance.

The country's active and full involvement in initiatives such as the renegotiation of the

SACU, the South African-Britain Bilateral Forum and new structures in the WTO, also places South Africa in a good position to ensure that not only trade, but also development is addressed in its international relations.

International organisations

United Nations

Since its readmission to the UN in 1994, South Africa has fully participated in and contributed to international organisations, treaties and conventions concerned with global policies. It has played an active role in several General Assembly working groups tasked with the appraisal of UN reforms as well as the restructuring of the Security Council.

South Africa's name has consistently appeared on the Secretary-General's 'Roll of Honour' of countries that pay their dues timeously.

President Mbeki, accompanied by the Minister of Foreign Affairs, represented South Africa at the 58th Session of the UN General Assembly (UNGA) in New York in September 2003.

President Mbeki addressed the General Debate of UNGA on issues of international, regional and national significance. South Africa will serve as vice-chairperson of the Economic and Financial Committee of UNGA. This follows South Africa's chairpersonship of the Special Political and Decolonisation Committee during UNGA 57.

European Union

South Africa relates to the EU at various levels and in many forums. The most important of these relations is the bilateral relationship, followed by the regional and continental dimensions. South Africa is also a signatory to the Cotonou Partnership Agreement (CPA), which is the basis for co-operation between the ACP group of states and the EU. Bilaterally, the SA-EU Trade, Development and Co-operation Agreement (TDCA) governs South Africa's relations with the EU. At regional and continental levels, several processes relate Africa (South Africa included, and playing a very significant role) to the EU. These include the Berlin Process, Cairo Process, the CPA and NEPAD.

Following the first democratic election in 1994, the South African Government started a process of reintegrating the economy into the world economy. To this end, South Africa needed to urgently spur its economic growth by attracting investments and securing market access for goods and products. The EU Council of Ministers then called for a package of immediate measures to support South Africa's transition to democracy. These measures included granting South Africa improved market access through the GSP in the short term, with an offer to negotiate a long-term trade and co-operation agreement with the EU. Encouraged by this offer, South Africa requested to become a standard beneficiary of both the industrial and agricultural GSP which is offered to developing countries. South Africa also indicated preference to accede to the Lomé Convention, thus benefiting from the unilateral trade regime of the ACP states. The European Commission and the Council of Ministers of the EU rejected South Africa's request for a long-term trade arrangement under the aegis of the Lomé Convention. Instead, the EU Council of Ministers' meeting in June 1995 adopted negotiating directives proposing progressive and reciprocal liberalisation of trade with South Africa, in order to establish an FTA.

After more than 20 formal sessions of negotiations, South Africa and the EU reached broad agreement on the contents of the TDCA in December 1998. The central component of the Agreement revolves around a tariff phase-down schedule for agricultural and industrial products. In terms of the schedule, South Africa will eliminate tariffs on 86% of EU exports to South Africa over a period of 12

Foreign relations

years. The EU, in turn, will eliminate tariffs on 95% of South African exports to the EU over 10 years. In addition to the tariff-liberalisation schedule, agreement was reached on the numerous articles dealing with trade-related issues such as intellectual property rights, competition policy and Rules of Origin. The parties also agreed to co-operate in a number of non-trade fields, such as the fight against drugs and money laundering, and the protection of data.

The finalised SA-EU TDCA was signed on 11 October 1999 and provisionally entered into force in January 2000. The TDCA now has to be ratified by all 15 EU member states. By mid-2003, the TDCA had been ratified by Sweden, Denmark, the Netherlands, Germany, Finland, Spain, Portugal and Ireland.

The TDCA is expected to substantially increase South Africa's trade with Europe. The EU is already South Africa's largest trading partner while South Africa ranks as the EU's 15th largest trading partner.

It was intended that the TDCA would be complemented by three side agreements, namely the Science and Technology Agreement, the Wines and Spirits Agreement (WSA), and the Fisheries Agreement, in addition to the development co-operation instrument, the European Programme for the Reconstruction and Development (EPRD) of South Africa.

The South Africa-EU Science and Technology Agreement was the first agreement to be reached between post-apartheid South Africa and the EU. It was signed in December 1996 and entered into force in November 1997. It allows South African researchers to engage in collaborative research projects funded by the EU. A South Africa-EU Joint Science and Technology Co-operation Committee was established to review collaboration and develop initiatives to intensify co-operation. In order to further biregional dialogue on science and technology between the EU and ACP States, South Africa hosted the first ACP-EU Ministerial Forum on Research for Sustainable Development in Cape Town from 29 July to 1 August 2002. In this regard, the EU also released a total of 50,7 million Euro during the first half of 2003 for research on sustainable development in ACP countries.

The WSA negotiations were officially concluded in June 2000. The WSA provides for the mutual recognition of Geographical Indications and Trademarks. In this regard, a special meeting was held between South Africa and the EU during July 2001, which culminated in a MoU. The latter, in turn, resulted in the conclusion of the WSA, which was signed on 28 January 2002 in South Africa. It has been implemented retroactively from 1 January 2002 to ensure that no benefits are lost from the WSA.

The first round of negotiations on a South Africa-EU Fisheries Agreement took place in Brussels on 5 March 2001. Soon after the negotiations started, both parties realised that they had been given irreconcilable mandates, and negotiations were formally suspended. However, negotiations on the Fisheries Agreement may well be initiated again when the European Commission's (EC) Common Policy on Fisheries is finalised.

European Programme for Reconstruction and Development

The TDCA provides the legal basis for continued EU support for development activities in South Africa, which is channelled through the EPRD. The EPRD is funded directly from the EU budget with an annual budget of 127,5 million Euro, and is the single largest development programme in South Africa financed by foreign donors. From 1995 to 1998, the EU provided 43% of all foreign grant aid to South Africa.

Further assistance is supplied through soft loans from the European Investment Bank. These funds are managed by the Industrial Development Corporation on behalf of government. The second co-operation strategy and implementation framework came to an end in December 2002. The 2003 to 2006 framework of development co-operation will have an indicative financial envelope of approximately 126 million Euro per annum.

South Africa also interacts with the EU as a member of the ACP Group, which consists of 79 countries. South Africa joined the Lomé Convention as a qualified member, as it was excluded from the trade regime as well as its provisions on development assistance. However, South Africans may tender for projects in all ACP countries, and participate fully in all the political instruments of the Convention.

The Lomé Convention governed relations between the ACP Group and the EU. Negotiations for a successor to the Lomé Convention, which expired in February 2000, were concluded, and the CPA was signed on 23 June 2000 in Cotonou. South Africa is again only a qualified member of the CPA, as South Africa's economic relations with the EU are governed by the TDCA.

The CPA differs significantly from its predecessor in that its duration will be 20 years, with a revision clause every five years and a financial protocol for each five-year period.

The most far-reaching changes, however, are to be introduced in the sphere of trade, where non-reciprocal preferences are gradually to be abolished and replaced with WTO-compatible trade arrangements. The present arrangements are to be maintained during a period of trade negotiations that will continue until the end of 2007. Formal negotiations for New Economic Partnership Agreements – as the post non-reciprocal arrangements will be called – started in September 2002 and will have entered into force by January 2008. South Africa is not a direct participant in these negotiations, but assists the ACP in an advisory capacity. In this regard, South Africa hosted the first ACP Trade Ministers' Committee Meeting in Johannesburg, in April 2001, as well as an SADC Ministers of Trade Meeting, in March 2003, to discuss the negotiations at regional level.

One of the key aspects of South Africa's relations with the EU, within the framework of the ACP-EU partnership, is its active participation in the ACP-EU Joint Parliamentary Activities (JPA). South Africa hosted the fourth session of the ACP-EU JPA in March 2002 in Cape Town. At this session, the JPA accepted a resolution on NEPAD, noting that there was considerable scope for the ACP-EU partnership to be effectively aligned with NEPAD. It urged the EC to identify ways in which, both directly and through the ACP-EU partnership, EU programmes could support NEPAD.

South Africa's relations with European parliamentarians are also extensive, and regular exchanges have taken place in this regard. South Africa, then chairperson of the AU, took a lead in ensuring that NEPAD was discussed on an ongoing basis with all EU member states, especially those that are also members of the G-8.

President Thabo Mbeki participated in the Enlarged Dialogue during the G-8 Summit in Evian-les-bains, France, on 1 June 2003.

The overall theme of the Enlarged Dialogue, which brought together G-8 Heads of State and Government and the Heads of State of 12 selected developing countries, was *International Co-operation to Promote Economic Growth and Development.*

Economic development in Africa, sustainable development, and the ongoing global fight against terrorism were discussed.

Other issues on the agenda included:
- macro-economic policies
- development strategies
- trade issues
- promotion of private investment
- prevention of international and regional crises
- Millennium Development Goals (e.g. water and sanitation)
- implementation of healthcare programmes and infrastructure
- consistency of standards imposed by international organisations.

Foreign relations

The Commonwealth
The Commonwealth is a voluntary association of 54 sovereign states with a common political heritage. After the UN, with 185 members, the Commonwealth is one of the world's largest multilateral organisations. It includes members of every major regional institution, economic zone and multilateral organisation.

Its total population exceeds 1 500 million. The link in this union is the common use of the English language as well as elements of the common culture, including sport, inherited from the colonial past.

South Africa rejoined the Commonwealth in 1994 after an absence of 33 years. The Department of Foreign Affairs co-ordinates the policy and objectives of the Government in the Commonwealth.

The successful hosting of the Commonwealth Heads of Government Meeting (CHOGM) in 1999 provided President Mbeki with an opportunity to indicate South Africa's position on development, trade, and the use of ICT. The Fancourt Declaration resulted from discussions at the Retreat of Commonwealth Heads during the CHOGM. The Declaration marked an important milestone in the South African strategy to argue the case of the South and to advance the cause of the African Renaissance.

Commonwealth Heads of Government decided to establish a high-level group, with the aim of reviewing the role of the Commonwealth and advising on how best it could respond to the challenges of the new century. Members of the group are Australia, India, Malta, Papua New Guinea, Singapore, South Africa, Tanzania, Trinidad and Tobago, the UK and Zimbabwe.

The review process has produced a number of proposals and decisions, which will have a major impact on the way the Commonwealth deals with the issues of conflict resolution and poverty reduction from a political, economic/developmental and social perspective.

In his capacity as then chairperson of the Commonwealth, President Mbeki oversaw the successful conclusion of the High-Level Review Group on the Review of the Commonwealth and its governance.

The CHOGM reviewed global political issues, including the international fight against terrorism, HIV/AIDS, debt relief, private capital flows, WTO issues, and barriers to investment in poor countries.

The Non-Aligned Movement
The NAM is the second-largest grouping of countries within the UN, comprising 115 member states. It was founded in 1961 as a global voice for developing countries that felt excluded from international politics dominated by the superpowers of the time. South Africa joined the Movement as a full member in 1994, and assumed chairpersonship in September 1998, during the XII Summit Conference of Heads of State and Government of NAM, held in Durban. The fundamental principles of the Movement include respect for the sovereignty and territorial integrity of all countries, the right to self-determination of all colonised peoples, and economic and cultural equality.

As then chairperson of NAM, South Africa worked hard to strengthen dialogue with the developed countries on issues of interest to developing countries, and worked ceaselessly for multilateralism. At the Ministerial meeting of NAM in Durban, South Africa agreed to reposition the Movement to take advantage of new realities.

The NAM also continues its long-standing support for the rights of the Palestinian people, in international forums such as the UN and the Organisation of the Islamic Conference.

The NAM has persistently called on Israel to end its occupation of East Jerusalem, for the withdrawal of settlers from the occupied Palestinian territories, and to cease military actions in the Palestinian territory.

The NAM Committee on Palestine met twice at Ministerial level with members of the NAM Security Council Caucus in the space of one year, to deliberate on ways to work together with all the influential forces in the Middle East for the attainment of just and lasting peace in the region.

Malaysia took over the chair of NAM from South Africa in February 2003.

South Africa hosted the NAM Foreign Ministers' meeting in the Western Cape in December 2002. Ministers from Algeria, Columbia, Cuba, Egypt, India, Indonesia, Iran, Jamaica, Jordan, Malaysia, Mozambique, Sri Lanka, Zambia, Zimbabwe and the Secretary-General of the League of Arab States, Mr Amre Moussax, attended.

In May 2003, Dr Dlamini-Zuma attended the NAM Ministerial Troika held in France. The NAM Troika comprises South Africa, Malaysia and Cuba. The meeting took place against the background of the decision of the NAM Summit, held in Kuala Lumpur in February 2003, to take the necessary steps to ensure the revitalisation of NAM to meet the challenges of the 21st century. This included lending its support to efforts aimed at pushing back the frontiers of poverty and underdevelopment in developing countries.

United Nations Development Programme (UNDP)

On 12 October 1994, the Government signed the Standard Basic Assistance Agreement with the UNDP. The UNDP has an office in Pretoria, headed by its resident representative, who is also the UN Resident Co-ordinator for all UN operational activities for development in South Africa.

Acknowledgements

BuaNews
Department of Foreign Affairs
www.gov.za

Suggested reading

African Conference on Peacemaking and Conflict Resolution (1995, Durban, South Africa).
 State, Sovereignty and Responsibility: African Resolutions to African Problems. Durban: ACCORD, 1996.
Chakoodza, A. M. *International Diplomacy in Southern Africa from Reagan to Mandela.* London: Third World, 1990.
Change and South African External Relations. Editors: W. Carlsnaes and M. Muller. Johannesburg: International Thompson Publishing, 1997.
Gill, R. et al. eds. *Charting a New Course: Globalisation, African Recovery and the New Africa Initiative.* Johannesburg: South African Institute of International Affairs, 2002.
Mathoma, P., Mills, G. and Stremlau, J. eds. *Putting People First: African Priorities for the UN Millennium Assembly.* Johannesburg: South African Institute of International Affairs, 2000.
Makgoba, M. W. *African Renaissance: The New Struggle.* Sandton: Mfube Publishing; Cape Town: Tafelberg, 1999.
Malan, J.C. *Conflict Resolution Wisdom from Africa.* Durban: ACCORD, 1997.
Mbeki, T. *Africa: The Time Has Come.* Cape Town: Tafelberg; Houghton: Mafube, 1998.
Mills, G. ed. *From Pariah to Participant: South Africa's Evolving Foreign Relations, 1990 – 1994.* Johannesburg: South African Institute of International Affairs, 1994.
Mills, G. *The Wired Model: South Africa, Foreign Policy and Globalisation.* Cape Town: Tafelberg, 2000.
Mollo, J.K. *Diplomacy Protocol.* Oaklands, Johannesburg: The Author, 1997.
Payne, R.J. *The Non-Superpowers and South Africa.* Johannesburg: Witwatersrand University Press, 1990.
Payne, R.J. *Third World and South Africa: Post-Apartheid Challenges.* Westport: Greenwood Press, 1992.
Power, Wealth and Global Order. Editors: P. Nel and P.J. McGowan. Cape Town: University of Cape Town Press, 1999.
Venancio, M. and Chan, S. *Portuguese Diplomacy in Southern Africa, 1974 – 1994.* Johannesburg: South African Institute of International Affairs, 1996.

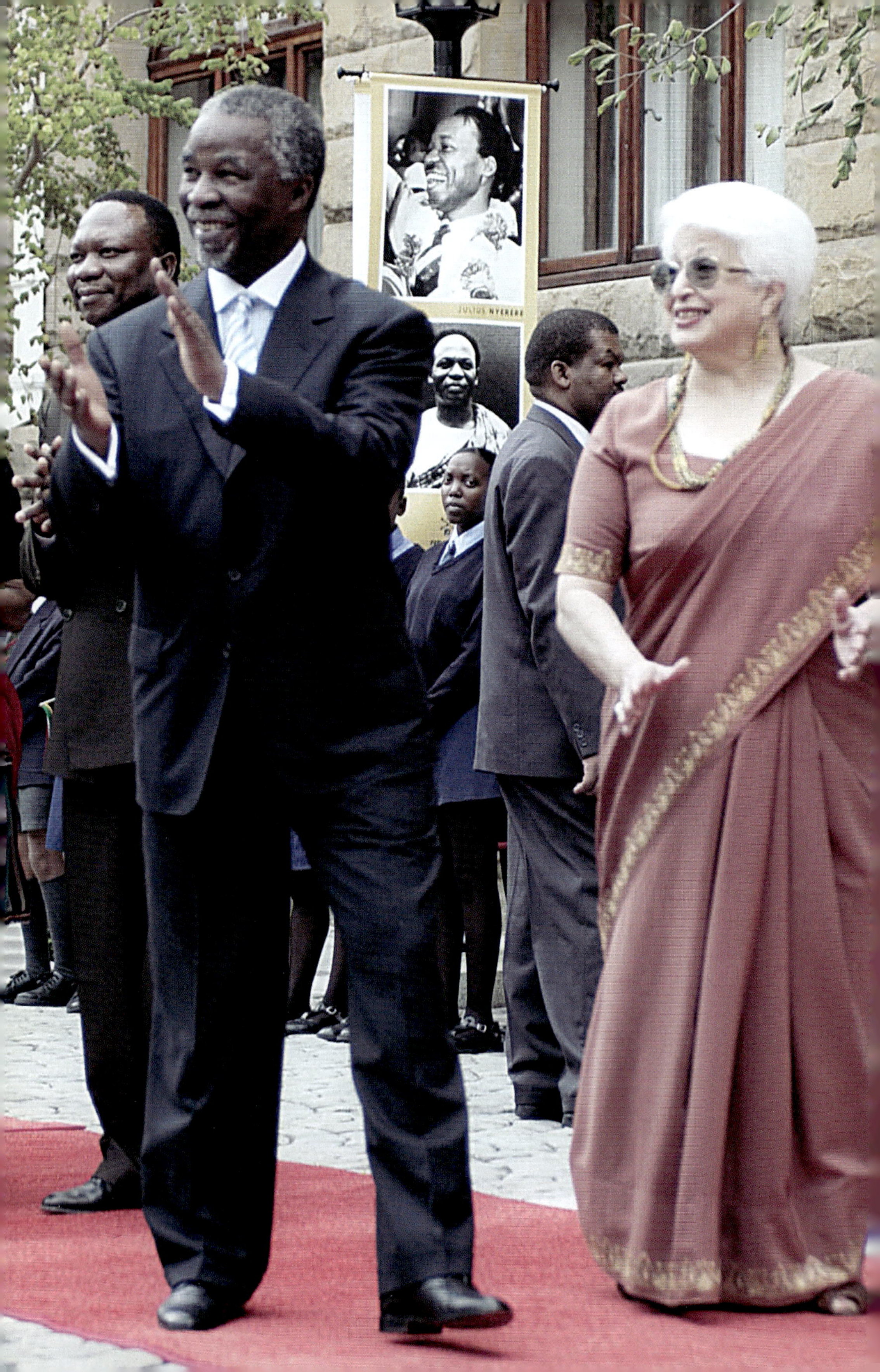
JULIUS NYERERE

chapter 12

Government system

The Constitution

The Constitution of the Republic of South Africa, 1996 (Act 108 of 1996), was approved by the Constitutional Court (CC) on 4 December 1996 and took effect on 4 February 1997.

The Constitution is the supreme law of the land. No other law or government action can supersede the provisions of the Constitution.

South Africa's Constitution is one of the most progressive in the world and enjoys high acclaim internationally.

The Preamble

The Preamble to the Constitution states that the aims of the Constitution are to:
- heal the divisions of the past and establish a society based on democratic values, social justice and fundamental human rights
- improve the quality of life of all citizens and free the potential of each person
- lay the foundations for a democratic and open society in which government is based on the will of the people and every citizen is equally protected by law
- build a united and democratic South Africa able to take its rightful place as a sovereign State in the family of nations.

Fundamental rights

Fundamental rights are contained in Chapter Two of the Constitution and seek to protect the rights and freedom of individuals. The CC guards these rights and determines whether or not actions by the State are in accordance with constitutional provisions.

Government

Government is constituted as national, provincial and local spheres, which are distinctive, interdependent and interrelated. The powers of the law makers (legislative authorities), governments (executive authorities) and courts (judicial authorities) are separate from one another.

Parliament

Parliament is the legislative authority of South Africa and has the power to make laws for the country in accordance with the Constitution. It consists of the National Assembly and the National Council of Provinces (NCOP). Parliamentary sittings are open to the public.

Since the establishment of Parliament in 1994, a number of steps have been taken to make it more accessible. This has been done to make the institution more accountable, as well as to motivate and facilitate pub-

◀ President Thabo Mbeki and the Speaker of Parliament, Dr Frene Ginwala, during the Opening of Parliament in February 2003. The annual opening of Parliament sees the President delivering the State of the Nation Address in which government's programmes of action are outlined.

lic participation in the legislative process. One of these steps has been the creation of a website (www.parliament.gov.za), which encourages comment and feedback from the public.

In 2002/03, 85 Bills were introduced and 69 Acts were produced. A total of 4 202 questions and 2 321 motions were processed. Some 21 806 people visited Parliament in 2002/03.

National Assembly

The National Assembly consists of no fewer than 350 and no more than 400 members elected through a system of proportional representation. The National Assembly, which is elected for a term of five years, is presided over by a Speaker, assisted by a Deputy Speaker.

The National Assembly is elected to represent the people and to ensure democratic governance as required by the Constitution. It does this by electing the President, providing a national forum for public consideration of issues, passing legislation and scrutinising and overseeing executive action.

From 29 to 31 August 2003, President Thabo Mbeki visited the Western Cape as part of *Imbizo*, the Government's programme of interactive governance.

Imbizo is aimed at promoting participatory democracy and partnership with communities for reconstruction and development.

The Premier of the Western Cape, Mr Marthinus van Schalkwyk, and other senior provincial government officials accompanied the President, who also assessed the progress made by the Coalition Government of the Western Cape in delivering services to the people of the province.

President Mbeki visited, among other projects, the crime-prevention command centre in Goodwood, a land-reform project in Koekedouw, the People's Housing Process in Khayelitsha, the Mitchell's Plain Community Health Centre and the Mitchell's Plain Retail Park.

He also held meetings with representatives from Western Cape business, trade-union movements, churches, and non-governmental and community-based organisations.

The *Imbizo* followed a series of similar provincial visits to Limpopo, Eastern Cape, Free State, Gauteng and North West.

In the 1999 national election, the African National Congress gained 266 seats in the National Assembly, the Democratic Party 38, the Inkatha Freedom Party 34, the New National Party 28, the United Democratic Movement 14, the African Christian Democratic Party six, the Pan Africanist Congress three, the United Christian Democratic Party three, the *Vryheidsfront*/Freedom Front three, the Freedom Alliance two, the *Afrikaner Eenheidsbeweging* one, the Azanian People's Organisation one, and the Minority Front one.

From 21 March 2003, for a period of two weeks, members of the National Assembly and provincial legislatures were allowed to defect to other political parties without losing their seats in both houses, in accordance with the Constitution of the Republic of South Africa Amendment Act, 2003 (Act 2 of 2003).

The Act provides for three 'window' periods. The first one was a transitional arrangement consisting of a 15-day period starting on 21 March 2003. The second and third periods will be for 15 days each, from 1 to 15 September in the second and fourth years following the date of a national and provincial election.

The Act also allowed members of the two houses to retain their seats despite a change in membership from the party that nominated them to the Assembly or Legislature.

It also allows for such retention in the event of a merger, subdivision, or a merger of a subdivided party with another party.

The retention of membership will apply if the change of party membership, merger, subdivision and a merger of a subdivided party with another party takes place within specified periods – the so-called 'window' periods. After the last window period ended at midnight on 4 April 2003, the ANC had gained a two-thirds majority. It now has 275 of the 400 seats in the National Assembly.

National Council of Provinces

The NCOP consists of 54 permanent mem-

Government system

bers and 36 special delegates and aims to represent provincial interests in the national sphere of government. Delegations from each province consist of 10 representatives.

The NCOP gets a mandate from the provinces before it can make certain decisions. It cannot, however, initiate a Bill concerning money, which is the prerogative of the Minister of Finance.

The NCOP also has a website, NCOP Online! (www.parliament.gov.za/ncop), which links Parliament to the provincial legislatures and local government associations.

NCOP Online! provides information on draft legislation and allows the public to make electronic submissions.

Thabo Mbeki was born on 18 June 1942 in Idutywa, Queenstown, in the Eastern Cape. He joined the African National Congress (ANC) Youth League at the age of 14 and in 1961 was elected Secretary of the African Students' Association. He was involved in underground activities after the banning of the ANC in 1960, until he left South Africa in 1962. He continued his studies in the United Kingdom (UK) and obtained his MA (Economics) at the University of Sussex. While in the UK, he mobilised the international student community against apartheid and worked at the London office of the ANC for several years. He also underwent military training in what was then the Soviet Union. From 1973, he worked in Botswana, Swaziland, Nigeria and Lusaka and became a member of the ANC's National Executive Committee in 1975. Between 1984 and 1989, he was Director of the ANC's Department of Information. He led the organisation's delegations, which met groups from inside South Africa in Dakar, Senegal and elsewhere. In 1989, he headed the delegation that held talks with the apartheid Government, which led to agreements on the unbanning of political organisations and the release of political prisoners. He also participated in negotiations preceding the adoption of South Africa's Interim Constitution in 1993. Following the first democratic election in 1994, Mr Mbeki was appointed Executive Deputy President. In 1997, he was elected President of the ANC and in June 1999, after the country's second democratic election, he succeeded Mr Nelson Mandela as President of South Africa.

Law-making

Any Bill may be introduced in the National Assembly. A Bill passed by the National Assembly must be referred to the NCOP for consideration. A Bill affecting the provinces may be introduced in the NCOP. After it has been passed by the Council, it must be referred to the Assembly.

A Bill concerning money must be introduced in the Assembly and must be referred to the NCOP for consideration and approval after being passed. If the Council rejects a Bill or passes it subject to amendments, the Assembly must reconsider the Bill and pass it again with or without amendments. There are special conditions for the approval of laws dealing with provinces.

The President

The President is the Head of State and leads the Cabinet. He or she is elected by the National Assembly from among its members, and leads the country in the interest of national unity, in accordance with the Constitution and the law.

The President of South Africa is Mr Thabo Mbeki.

The Deputy President

The President appoints the Deputy President from among the members of the National Assembly. The Deputy President must assist the President in executing government functions. South Africa's Deputy President is Mr Jacob Zuma.

Cabinet

The Cabinet consists of the President, as head of the Cabinet, the Deputy President and Ministers. The President appoints the Deputy President and Ministers, assigns their powers and functions and may dismiss them.

South Africa Yearbook 2003/04

The President may select any number of Ministers from among the members of the National Assembly, and may select no more than two Ministers from outside the Assembly.

The President appoints a member of the Cabinet to be the leader of government business in the National Assembly.

Cabinet, as on 1 December 2003	
Mr Thabo Mbeki	President
Mr Jacob Zuma	Deputy President
Dr Mangosuthu Buthelezi	Home Affairs
Prof. Kader Asmal	Education
Dr Nkosazana Dlamini-Zuma	Foreign Affairs
Mr Mosiuoa Lekota	Defence
Mr Trevor Manuel	Finance
Mr Sydney Mufamadi	Provincial and Local Government
Dr Ben Ngubane	Arts, Culture, Science and Technology
Mr Dullah Omar	Transport
Mr Jeff Radebe	Public Enterprises
Ms Stella Sigcau	Public Works
Dr Zola Skweyiya	Social Development
Mr Charles Nqakula	Safety and Security
Ms Bridget Mabandla	Housing
Mr Alec Erwin	Trade and Industry
Dr Penuell Maduna	Justice and Constitutional Development
Mr Mohammed Valli Moosa	Environmental Affairs and Tourism
Ms Geraldine Fraser-Moleketi	Public Service and Administration
Dr Ivy Matsepe-Casaburri	Communications
Mr Membathisi Mdladlana	Labour
Mr Ben Skosana	Correctional Services
Ms Thoko Didiza	Agriculture and Land Affairs
Mr Ronnie Kasrils	Water Affairs and Forestry
Dr Lindiwe Sisulu	Intelligence
Ms Phumzile Mlambo-Ngcuka	Minerals and Energy
Dr Manto Tshabalala-Msimang	Health
Dr Essop Pahad	Minister in The Presidency
Mr Ngconde Balfour	Sport and Recreation

Deputy Ministers

The President appoints Deputy Ministers from among the members of the National Assembly.

Traditional leadership

According to Chapter 12 of the Constitution, the institution, status and roles of traditional leadership, according to customary law, are recognised, subject to the Constitution.

The Directorate: Traditional Leadership and Institutions in the Department of Provincial and Local Government provides support to traditional leaders and institutions, and is responsible for the development of policy in this regard. It also renders an anthropological service, and provides advice and support to traditional leadership and institutions with regard to governance and development matters. It advises and supports the National House of Traditional Leaders and maintains a database of traditional leaders and institutions.

The *White Paper on Traditional Leadership and Governance*, released in October 2002, deals with the following issues:

- the identification of a role for traditional leadership, as an institution at local level, on matters affecting local communities
- the reform of the entire institution to restore the legitimacy it once enjoyed prior to the distortions introduced by the colonial and apartheid regimes
- the transformation of the institution generally, particularly the restoration of its character as an institution founded on custom, culture and tradition of the people
- reform of the institution so that it embraces some of the basic tenets underpinning the Constitution, such as equality and democracy.

The *White Paper on Traditional Leadership and Governance* was widely consulted on, through workshops and public hearings, with a range of stakeholders, organisations and interest groups.

Government system

Deputy Ministers, as on 1 December 2003	
Mr P W Saaiman	Correctional Services
Mr Joe Matthews	Safety and Security
Mr Aziz Pahad	Foreign Affairs
Ms Buyelwa Sonjica	Arts, Culture, Science and Technology
Ms Susan Shabangu	Minerals and Energy
Mr Mosibudi Mangena	Education
Ms Nosiviwe Mapisa-Nqakula	Home Affairs
Rev. Musa Zondi	Public Works
Mr Mandisi Mpahlwa	Finance
Prof. Dirk du Toit	Agriculture
Ms Joyce Mabudafhasi	Environmental Affairs and Tourism
Ms Lindiwe Hendricks	Trade and Industry
Ms Nozizwe Madlala Routledge	Defence
Ms Cheryl Gillwald	Justice and Constitutional Development
Ms Ntombazana Botha	Provincial and Local Government
Mr Renier Schoeman	Health

The Minister for Provincial and Local Government, Mr Sydney Mufamadi, established the White Paper Task Team and the Political Reference Team to assist with the finalisation of the White Paper in June 2003. Together with the Draft Traditional Leadership and Governance Framework Bill, which was prepared by the Department, the White Paper was presented to the Cabinet on 25 June 2003. Both the White Paper and Bill were approved.

The Bill provides for the establishment of the Commission on Traditional Leadership, Disputes and Claims, which will help resolve disputes regarding the legitimacy of otherwise incumbent traditional leaders.

Section 81 of the Local Government: Municipal Structures Act, 1998 (Act 117 of 1998), was amended during 2000, providing enhanced representation of traditional leaders in municipal councils. They enjoy 20% representation.

Houses of Traditional Leaders

The Constitution mandates the establishment of Houses of Traditional Leaders by means of either provincial or national legislation. Provincial Houses of Traditional Leaders have been established in all six provinces which have traditional leaders, namely the Eastern Cape, KwaZulu-Natal, the Free State, Mpumalanga, Limpopo and the North West.

The National House of Traditional Leaders was established in April 1997. Each provincial House of Traditional Leaders nominated three members to be represented in the National House, which then elected its own office-bearers.

The National House advises national government on the role of traditional leaders and customary law. It may also conduct its own investigations and advise the President at his request.

Provincial government

In accordance with the Constitution, each of the nine provinces has its own legislature, consisting of between 30 and 80 members. The number of members is determined in terms of a formula set out in national legislation. The members are elected in terms of proportional representation.

The Executive Council of a province consists of a Premier and a number of members. The Premier is elected by the Provincial Legislature.

Decisions are taken by consensus, as in the national Cabinet. Besides being able to make provincial laws, a provincial legislature

---

In April 2003, the Minister for Provincial and Local Government, Mr Sydney Mufamadi, called for nominations for the Commission for the Promotion and Protection of the Rights of Cultural, Religious and Linguistic Communities.

The Commission aims to promote respect for and protect the rights of all communities in South Africa.

The names of the 18 members of the Commission were announced at the end of September 2003.

South Africa Yearbook 2003/04

Provincial governments, as on 25 September 2003

Eastern Cape

Rev. Makhenkesi Stofile	Premier
Max Mamase	Agriculture
Nomsa Jajula	Education
Enoch Godongwana	Provincial Treasury, Economic Affairs, Environment and Tourism
Dr Bevan Goqwana	Health
Guguzile Nkwinti	Housing, Local Government and Traditional Affairs
Dennis Neer	Provincial Safety, Liaison and Transport
Gloria Barry	Roads and Public Works
Nosimo Balindlela	Sport, Recreation, Arts and Culture
Neo Moerana	Social Development

KwaZulu-Natal

Lionel Mtshali	Premier
Naredi Singh	Agriculture and Environmental Affairs
Faith Xolile Gasa	Education and Culture
Michael Mabuyakhulu	Economic Development and Tourism
Peter Miller	Finance
Dr Zwelini Mkhize	Health
Dumisane Makhaye	Housing
Inkosi Nyanga Ngubane	Traditional Affairs, Local Government and Safety and Security
Prince Gideon Zulu	Social Services and Population Development
Rev Celani Mtetwa	Public Works
Sibusiso Ndebele	Transport

Free State

Isabella Winkie Direko	Premier
Mann Oelrich	Agriculture
Papi Kganare	Education
Sakhiwe Belott	Environmental Affairs and Tourism
Zingile Dingani	Finance, Expenditure and Economic Affairs
Anna Motsumi-Tsopo	Health Services
Lechesa Tsenoli	Local Government and Housing
Sekhopi Malebo	Public Works, Roads and Transport
Itumeleng Kotsoane	Safety and Security
Beatrice Marshoff	Social Development
Webster Mfebe	Sport, Arts, Culture, Science and Technology

Limpopo

Ngoako Ramatlhodi	Premier
Dr Aaron Motsoaledi	Agriculture
Joyce Mashamba	Education
Thaba Mufamadi	Finance, Economic Affairs, Tourism and Environment
Sello Moloto	Health and Welfare
Joe Maswanganyi	Local Government and Housing
Catherine Mabuza	Office of the Premier
Collins Chabane	Public Works
Dikeledi Magadzi	Safety, Security and Liaison
Rosina Semenya	Sports, Arts and Culture
Dean Farisani	Transport

Gauteng

Mbhazima Shilowa	Premier
Mary Metcalfe	Agriculture, Conservation, Environment and Land Affairs
Trevor Fowler	Development Planning and Local Goverment
Ignatius Jacobs	Education
Jabu Moleketi	Finance and Economic Affairs
Gwen Ramokgopa	Health
Paul Mashatile	Housing
Nomvula Mokonyane	Provincial Safety and Liaison
Mondli Gungubele	Sport, Recreation, Arts and Culture
Angelina Motshekga	Social Services and Population Development
Khabisi Mosunkutu	Transport and Public Works

Mpumalanga

Ndaweni Mahlangu	Premier
Candith Mashego-Dlamini	Agriculture, Conservation and Environment
Jacob Mabena	Finance and Economic Affairs
Craig Padayachee	Education
Sibongile Manana	Health
Simeon Ginindza	Housing and Land Administration
Mohammed Bhabha	Local Government and Traffic
Steve Mabona	Public Works, Roads and Transport
Thabang Makwetla	Safety and Security
Busi Coleman	Social Services and Population Development
Siphosezwe Amos Masango	Sport, Recreation, Arts and Culture

Government system

Northern Cape

Manne Dipico	Premier
Dawid Rooi	Agriculture, Land Reform, Environment and Conservation
Thabo Makweya	Economic Affairs and Tourism
Tina Joemat-Pettersson	Education
Goolam Hoosain Akharwaray	Finance
Dipuo Peters	Health
Pakes Dikgetsi	Housing and Local Government
Connie Seoposengwe	Safety and Liaison
Fred Wyngaardt	Social Services and Population Development
Sebastian Bonokwane	Sports, Arts and Culture
John Block	Transport, Roads and Public Works

North West

Dr Popo Molefe	Premier
Edina Molewa	Agriculture, Conservation and Environment
Darky Africa	Developmental Local Government and Housing
Maureen Modiselle	Economic Development and Tourism
Zacharia Tolo	Education
Martin Kuscus	Finance
Dr Molefi Sefularo	Health
Dimotana Thibedi	Traditional and Corporate Affairs
Nomonde Rasmeni	Safety and Security
Mandlenkosi Mayisela	Social Services, Arts, Culture and Sport
Phenye Vilakazi	Transport and Roads
Jerry Thibedi	Public Works

Western Cape

Marthinus van Schalkwyk	Premier
Johan Gelderblom	Agriculture, Tourism and Gambling
Leonard Ramatlakane	Community Safety
Patrick McKenzie	Cultural Affairs, Sport and Recreation
Adv. Andre Gaum	Education
Johan Gelderblom (Acting)	Environmental Affairs and Development Planning
Ebrahim Rasool	Finance and Economic Development
Tasneem Essop	Transport, Public Works and Property Management
Piet Meyer	Health
Nomatyala Hangana	Housing
Cobus Dowry	Local Government
Marius Fransman	Social Services and Poverty Alleviation

may adopt a constitution for its province if two-thirds of its members agree. However, a provincial constitution must correspond with the national Constitution as confirmed by the CC.

According to the Constitution, provinces may have legislative and executive powers concurrently with the national sphere, over:

- agriculture
- casinos, racing, gambling and wagering
- cultural affairs
- education at all levels, excluding university and university of technology (technikon) education
- environment
- health services
- housing
- language policy
- nature conservation
- police services
- provincial public media
- public transport
- regional planning and development
- road-traffic regulation
- tourism
- trade and industrial promotion
- traditional authorities
- urban and rural development
- vehicle licensing
- welfare services.

These powers can be exercised to the extent that provinces have the administrative capacity to assume effective responsibilities.

Provinces also have exclusive competency over a number of areas, which include:

- abattoirs
- ambulance services
- liquor licences
- museums other than national museums
- provincial planning
- provincial cultural matters
- provincial recreation and activities
- provincial roads and traffic.

The President's Co-ordinating Council (PCC) is a consultative forum where the President discusses issues of national, provincial and

local importance with the Premiers. The forum meets quarterly and addresses issues such as:
- enhancing the role of provincial executives with regard to national policy decisions
- strengthening the capacity of provincial governments to implement government policies and programmes
- integrating provincial growth and development strategies within national development plans
- improving co-operation between national and provincial spheres of government to strengthen local government
- improving co-operation on fiscal issues
- ensuring that there are co-ordinated programmes of implementation and the necessary structures in place to address issues such as rural development, urban renewal and safety and security.

Local government

Local governments have been given a dynamic role. They are no longer purely instruments of service delivery, but are also assigned a key role as agents of economic development.

The relationship between the three spheres of government is outlined in Chapter Three of the Constitution, which requires Parliament to establish structures and institutions to promote and facilitate intergovernmental relations.

In accordance with the Constitution and the Organised Local Government Act, 1997 (Act 52 of 1997), (which formally recognises organised local government and the nine provincial local government associations), organised local government may designate up to 10 part-time representatives to represent municipalities and participate in proceedings of the NCOP.

The largest increases in national government's 2002 Budget were in transfers to the local sphere, rising by 26% a year from 2001/02 to 2004/05. Total allocations rose from R6,6 billion in 2001/02 to R8,8 billion in 2002/03, and will increase to R12,0 billion in 2003/04 and R13,2 billion in 2004/05.

Allocations for local government infrastructure transfers rose from R3,4 billion in 2002/03 to R4,1 billion in 2003/04 and R4,6 billion in 2004/05. This represents an average annual increase of 27% between 2001/02 and 2004/05.

Government's commitment to assisting municipalities with poverty relief, primarily through the provision of free basic services to impoverished households, is made clear by substantial increases in the equitable share grant – from R4,0 billion in 2002/03 to R6,3 billion in 2003/04 and R7,1 billion in 2004/05.

As part of the local government equitable share, R1 122 million (R822 million for free basic services and R300 million for free basic electricity/energy) will be made available to municipalities. The roll-out started on 1 July 2003. Free basic water was rolled out from 1 July 2001.

South African Local Government Association (SALGA)

SALGA represents the interests of local government, in the country's intergovernmental relations system, with a united voice.

SALGA's business plan sets out a series of objectives, namely to:
- promote sound labour-relations practices that can achieve high levels of performance and responsiveness to the needs of citizens
- represent, promote, protect and articulate the interests of local government at national and provincial levels, in intergovernmental processes, and in other policy-making forums
- build the capacity of local government to contribute towards a developmental democratic governance system that addresses and meets basic human needs.

SALGA is funded through a combination of sources. These include a percentage share of the national revenue allocated to local government, membership fees from municipalities, and donations and grants from a variety of sources that fund specific projects.

Municipalities

The Constitution provides for three categories of municipalities.

As directed by the Constitution, the Local Government: Municipal Structures Act, 1998 contains criteria for determining when an area must have a Category A municipality (metropolitan municipalities) and when municipalities fall into categories B (local municipalities) or C (district areas or municipalities). The Act also determines that Category A municipalities can only be established in metropolitan areas.

The Municipal Demarcation Board determined that Johannesburg, Durban, Cape Town, Pretoria, East Rand and Port Elizabeth be declared metropolitan areas.

Metropolitan councils have a single metropolitan budget, common property rating and service-tariff systems, and a single employer body. South Africa has six metropolitan municipalities, namely Tshwane, Johannesburg, Ekurhuleni, Ethekwini, Cape Town and Nelson Mandela, 231 local municipalities, and 47 district municipalities.

Metropolitan councils may decentralise powers and functions. However, all original municipal, legislative and executive powers are vested in the metro council.

In metropolitan areas there is a choice of two types of executive systems: the mayoral executive system where executive authority is vested in the mayor, and the collective executive committee where these powers are vested in the executive committee.

Non-metropolitan areas consist of district councils and local councils. District councils are primarily responsible for capacity-building and district-wide planning.

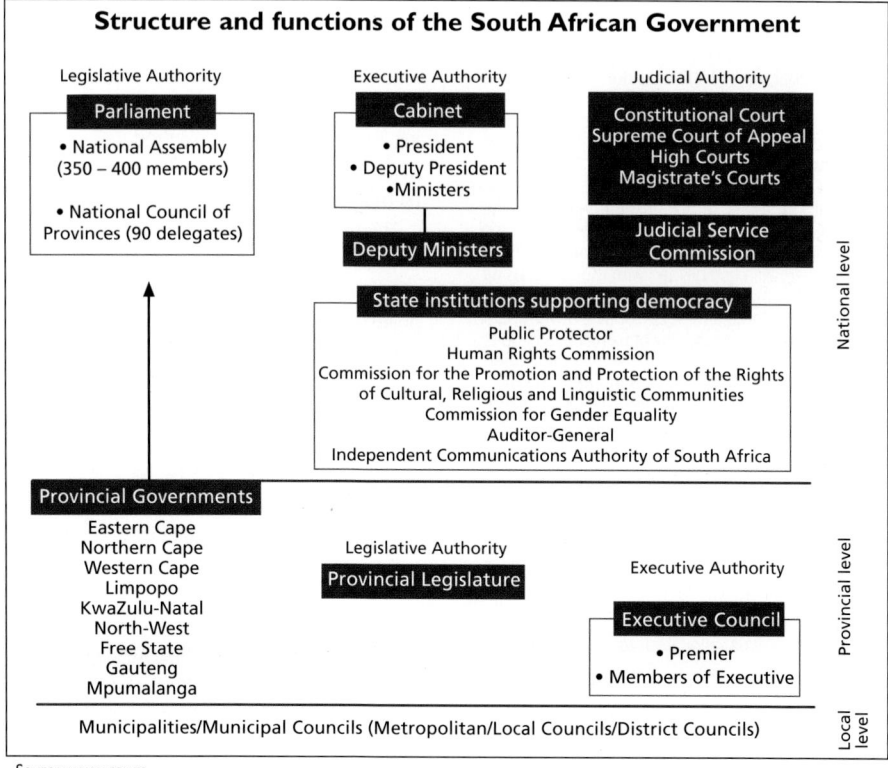

Structure and functions of the South African Government

National level

Legislative Authority
- **Parliament**
  - National Assembly (350 – 400 members)
  - National Council of Provinces (90 delegates)

Executive Authority
- **Cabinet**
  - President
  - Deputy President
  - Ministers
- **Deputy Ministers**

Judicial Authority
- Constitutional Court
- Supreme Court of Appeal
- High Courts
- Magistrate's Courts
- Judicial Service Commission

State institutions supporting democracy
- Public Protector
- Human Rights Commission
- Commission for the Promotion and Protection of the Rights of Cultural, Religious and Linguistic Communities
- Commission for Gender Equality
- Auditor-General
- Independent Communications Authority of South Africa

Provincial level

Provincial Governments
- Eastern Cape
- Northern Cape
- Western Cape
- Limpopo
- KwaZulu-Natal
- North-West
- Free State
- Gauteng
- Mpumalanga

Legislative Authority
- **Provincial Legislature**

Executive Authority
- **Executive Council**
  - Premier
  - Members of Executive

Local level

Municipalities/Municipal Councils (Metropolitan/Local Councils/District Councils)

Source: www.gov.za

Legislation

The Local Government: Municipal Systems Act, 2000 (Act 32 of 2000), established a framework for planning, performance-management systems, effective use of resources and organisational change in a business context.

The Act also established a system for municipalities to report on their performance, and gives an opportunity for residents to compare this performance with others.

Public-private partnerships are also regulated by the Act. It allows municipalities significant powers to corporatise their services, establish utilities for service delivery, or enter into partnerships with other service-providers. The Act provides for the adoption of a credit-control policy by municipalities that will provide for the termination of services in the event of non-payment. Municipalities will have the power to pass bylaws to implement the policy.

Currently, the rationalisation of old-order legislation is being investigated.

To complete the legal framework necessary for the new system of local government, two key pieces of legislation were introduced to Parliament during 2003, namely the Property Rates Bill and the Municipal Finance Management Bill.

The Property Rates Bill proposes the reform of the property-rating regime, bringing in innovation in administration, and thus improving revenue collection at local level. Once enacted, the legislation will be implemented over a four-year period. A process to rationalise 'old order' local-government legislation in consultation with the provinces is also under way, and is expected to be completed in 2004.

The Municipal Finance Management Bill is aimed at modernising municipal budgeting and financial management. It facilitates the development of a long-term municipal lending/bond market. It also introduces a governance framework for separate entities created by municipalities.

The Municipal Finance Management Bill is a critical element in the overall transformation of local government in South Africa. The basic philosophy underlying the approach to municipal finance in the Bill is to allow 'managers to manage and to be held accountable', while councillors are provided with information necessary to set overall policy and priorities for the municipality.

The Bill fosters transparency at the local government sphere through budget and reporting requirements.

Programmes

National and provincial government departments are continuing to formulate programmes that constitute support for local government.

In February 2001, President Thabo Mbeki, in his address to Parliament, announced details of the Integrated Sustainable Rural Development Programme (ISRDP) and the Urban Renewal Strategy (URS). The URS in particular, includes a multidisciplinary approach to dealing with crime.

A number of key stakeholders, such as the National Coalition for Municipal Service Delivery, the Umsobomvu Youth Fund and the World Bank are also partnering with government to support the programmes.

By February 2003, government had made R65 million available for institutional capacity-building in the ISRDP nodes. A number of Planning Implementation Management Support (PIMS) centres were also established with the aim of using them as a support base for the development of local project-management capacities. Government is investigating the possibility of using PIMS centres as a base for the provision of institutional support and training to community development workers.

By February 2003, a total of 350 anchor projects had been identified in a variety of sectors. In the ISRDP, 68% of the projects are infrastructure-related, while projects focusing on social development and capacity-building make up 10% and 14% respectively.

This trend is similar to the URS – 66% of the projects are related to infrastructure, 21% to economic development and 6% to social development.

During the 2002/03 financial year, a total of R960 million was allocated to the implementation of anchor projects in rural nodes. Some R2,1 billion was allocated to municipalities that are home to urban renewal nodes, and part of this was to be used for the implementation of anchor projects.

Consolidated Municipal Infrastructure Programme (CMIP)

The CMIP aims to provide basic levels of service to improve the quality of life of ordinary people. The Programme enhances the developmental impact of the delivery process by focusing on the transfer of skills and promotion of small, medium and micro enterprises, using labour-intensive construction processes and maximising job-creation opportunities. The CMIP also aims to enhance long-term sustainability and rapid improvement of delivery through a capacity-building programme that will strengthen the institutional ability of municipalities, including their local management and operation and maintenance capacities. Tangible results and visible impact on the poor communities, leading to improvement in the quality of life, have been achieved.

By March 2003, approximately six million households that previously had no access or only limited access to a basic level of service were benefiting from the CMIP, receiving water, sanitation, roads, storm water, solid waste, and community lighting facilities. Greater support has been given to rural development, with 53% of CMIP funds allocated to projects in these areas.

The use of labour-intensive construction methods has created about 11 million workdays of temporary and permanent employment for local labourers, particularly for single-headed households, women, youth and the disabled. The CMIP supports the Housing Programme, Integrated Sustainable Rural Development Programme and Urban Renewal Strategy. An amount of R400,7 million has been allocated to the CMIP during the 2003/04 financial year for funding in the nodal areas.

Municipal Infrastructure Investment Unit (MIIU)

The MIIU is a non-profit company created in 1998 to help municipalities find innovative solutions to critical problems in the financing and management of essential municipal services. The MIIU receives grant funding to provide technical assistance to local governments pursuing municipal-service partnerships, including long-term concession contracts, build-operate-transfer agreements, management contracts and other partnerships with public and private entities. Since its establishment, the MIIU has assisted in finalising projects with a contract value of more than R6 billion.

Municipal Systems Improvement Programme

The Municipal Systems Improvement Programme provides direct assistance to municipalities for capacity-building and for implementing new systems required by local-government legislation. Planning, Implementation and Management Support Centres, in district municipalities in particular, are funded to assist with the preparation of Integrated Development Plans (IDPs) in line with municipal budgets. This grant assists municipalities to pilot performance management and monitoring systems, and will complement other initiatives by the National Treasury aimed at building municipal financial-management capacity and implementing budget reforms.

Municipal Infrastructure Grant (MIG)

For the medium term, plans are in the pipeline to rationalise infrastructure transfers to local government and to make the system of transfers more simple, predictable, policy-sensitive and fair. The phased transition to a formula-driven infrastructure grant disbursement mechanism is referred to as the MIG. The MIG will be created through the merger of the CMIP, the Local Economic Development (LED) Fund, the Water Services Project, the Community-Based Public Works Programme (CBPWP) and the Municipal Sports and Recreation Programme (MSRP). The consolidation will be phased in over a three-year period, beginning with an allocation of R50 million in 2003/04 for the piloting of the consolidated MIG in selected municipalities. Although full consolidation is targeted for the 2006/07 financial year, some grants, such as the CMIP which forms the core of the MIG, may be phased in sooner. The inclusion of the LED, CBPWP and MSRP is subject to the Cabinet review of all poverty-relief programmes.

The Grant is intended to assist municipalities with providing basic municipal infrastructure and community services to low-income households and promoting economic development. The MIG is also intended to assist with overcoming the current problems of inequity in grant distributions, as well as flaws in financial-accountability arrangements, as identified by the National Treasury and the Auditor-General.

The MIG is a conditional grant and municipalities will have to achieve a number of output conditions, including the attainment of service-coverage targets and employment creation. The role of national government will be to support, monitor policy outcomes and regulate infrastructure investments.

Local economic development and poverty alleviation

LED programmes are designed to create employment and economic growth with the aim of alleviating poverty through municipality-led initiatives and projects. It is a way of improving links with government's other household, social, and economic-infrastructure programmes.

LED programmes and the Social Plan Grant assisted 109 municipalities with funding for 95 local-development initiatives in 2002/03, creating 1 400 job opportunities.

Integrated Development Plans

In terms of the Municipal Systems Act, 2000, all municipalities are required to prepare IDPs, with the aim of promoting integration by balancing social, economic and ecological pillars of sustainability without compromising the institutional capacity required in the implementation thereof, and by co-ordinating actions across sectors and spheres of government.

It is a process by which municipalities prepare a five-year strategic plan that is reviewed annually in consultation with communities and stakeholders. The Department of Provincial and Local Government is developing a supporting intergovernmental planning framework which will provide greater clarity as to the type and role of appropriate planning at each government level. The framework will entail policy work as well as practical initiatives such as the IDP Nerve Centre, which will provide an information-co-ordination service to strengthen intergovernmental planning.

The Moral Regeneration Movement (MRM) launched the country's Moral Charter Campaign on Friday, 31 January 2003.

The Campaign is aimed at inviting all sectors of society to participate in the process of drawing up a moral charter to encourage good ethical behaviour.

The MRM, which was launched in April 2002, is a multisectoral organisation that co-ordinates the country's moral renewal programmes at every level.

In line with the holistic and intersectoral approach of the MRM, moral regeneration has become an integral part of the work of government.

Some of the moral-regeneration programmes implemented include:
- the promotion of a caring society and building stronger family structures
- a rehabilitation programme for prisoners
- promoting a healthy nation and care and support for people living with HIV/AIDS
- the Values in Education Project which promotes good values from an early age
- promoting *Batho Pele* principles within the Public Service.

The MRM is also participating with other national initiatives such as the Freedom Park Trust in cleansing and healing ceremonies that seek to symbolically repair the soul of the nation.

Collaboration is taking place between the MRM, the South African Chapter of the African Renaissance and the Indigenous Knowledge Systems of South Africa, in linking moral regeneration with the Indigenous Knowledge Project.

Government and communication

The vision of Government Communications (GCIS) is to make an indispensable and widely valued contribution to society, working with government for a better life for all, by meeting government's communication needs as well as those of the public.

It consists of the following Chief Directorates:
- Communication Service Agency, which is responsible for the production and distribution of government information products (including the *South Africa Yearbook* and *Pocket Guide to South Africa*) and the bulk-buying of advertising space.
- Government and Media Liaison, which is responsible for strengthening working relations between the media and government, as well as the international promotion of South Africa. It is also responsible for BuaNews, a government news service.
- Policy and Research, which contributes to the development of policy in the fields of media, communication and information-monitoring of government policy in general from a communication perspective.
- Information Management and Technology, which is responsible for providing access to government information through the website Government Online (*www.gov.za*).
- Provincial and Local Liaison, which provides development communication and information to South Africans to ensure that they have public information that can assist them in becoming active citizens.
- Corporate Services, which provides administration, financial management, and administrative services and human resource administration and development.

GCIS is central in developing communication strategies and programmes for each of the transversal campaigns of government. It also assists departments with specific campaigns and events, as well as setting up departmental communication structures.

GCIS is leading an intersectoral process to set up Multi-Purpose Community Centres (MPCCs) in every municipality in the country, each one providing information on accessing government services, as well as offering some government services at the Centres themselves.

By November 2003, there were 48 operational MPCCs. It is expected that there will be 60 operational MPCCs by March 2004.

A process of establishing MPCCs in each municipality by 2010 is under way. An implementation strategy has been formulated to achieve this objective.

GCIS is also involved in the Media Development and Diversity Agency. It played a major role in the development of the new coat of arms that was launched on 27 April 2000 and the redesign of the National Orders. (See Chapters 5 and 6: *Arts and culture* and *Communications*.)

International Marketing Council (IMC)

The IMC of South Africa is a public-private sector partnership to develop and sustain meaningful co-operation between organisations involved in the marketing of South Africa. Members of the Council's Board act as advocates for South Africa, advise the Cabinet Committee on International Relations, and provide the Council's operational team with strategic guidance.

The IMC's mission involves the following:
- the establishment of a brand for South Africa that positions the country in terms of its investment and creditworthiness, exports, tourism and international-relations objectives
- the establishment of an integrated approach in government and the private sector for the international marketing of South Africa
- the building of national support for the brand within South Africa itself.

In October 2002, the Council launched its slogan, *Alive with Possibility*, which is used to promote South Africa around the world.

The following projects facilitate the work of the Council:
- the Communication Resource Centre enhances South Africa's response to national and international media coverage about the country
- the Information Resource Centre collects, collates and makes accessible a vast spectrum of positive information about South Africa
- launched in August 2002, www.safrica.info is a unique, comprehensive and official national gateway to the country for national and international Internet users
- building national pride is a key focus as the IMC encourages South Africans at home and abroad to fly the flag in thought, word and deed.

The IMC emphasises ongoing relationship-building and campaign integration among the international relations, investment, trade and 'national pride' organisations in South Africa.

In April 2003, the Independent Electoral Commission of South Africa hosted a continental conference on democracy, elections and governance. The theme of the conference was *Strengthening Africa's Partnerships*.

The conference deliberated on the following key issues:
- constitutions and electoral processes
- the role of African observer missions
- resourcing elections
- acceptance of election results
- multiparty democracy and its relevance in Africa
- governance issues.

Some 350 delegates from 48 African countries including representatives of electoral-management bodies, scholars, experts, governments, non-governmental organisations and other civil-society stakeholders attended.

Co-operative governance

The importance of co-operative governance and intergovernmental relations in South Africa is reflected in Chapter Three of the Constitution, which determines a number of principles.

Section 41(2) of the Constitution specifically determines that an Act of Parliament must establish or provide for structures and institutions to promote and facilitate intergovernmental relations. It should also provide for appropriate mechanisms and procedures to facilitate the settlement of intergovernmental disputes. The Department of Provincial and Local Government is developing this framework, and the relevant Bill was expected to be introduced to Parliament during the second half of 2003.

A number of intergovernmental structures promote and facilitate co-operative governance and intergovernmental relations between the respective spheres of government. These include the following:
- The PCC, comprising the President, the Minister for Provincial and Local Government, and the nine Premiers.
- Ministerial Clusters, Directors-General Clusters and the Forum of South African Directors-General, which promote programme integration at national and provincial level.
- Ministerial forums (or MinMecs) between responsible line-function Ministers at national level and their respective counterparts at provincial government level, which normally meet on a quarterly basis. These forums are supported by technical committees.
- A number of intergovernmental forums that facilitate co-operative government and intergovernmental relations.

Elections

The Constitution of South Africa places all elections and referendums in the country in all three spheres of government (national, provincial and local) under the control of the Independent Electoral Commission (IEC), established in terms of the IEC Act, 1996 (Act 51 of 1996).

National and provincial elections were held on 2 June 1999. Registered voters totalled 18,1 million, representing a turnout of 89%. Of the 16 political parties that took part in the national elections, 13 are represented in Parliament, based on the election results.

The next national election will be held in 2004. Voter registration took place in the various voting districts on 8 and 9 November 2003.

Municipal elections

On 5 December 2000, South Africans went to the polls to elect local representatives. Registered voters totalled 18,5 million with a turnout of 48,08%. Seventy-nine parties nominated 30 477 candidates of whom 16 573 were party-list and 13 214 ward candidates. Six hundred-and-ninety were independent candidates.

Disaster management

Disaster management is a continuous and integrated multisectoral, multidisciplinary process of planning and implementing measures aimed at preventing or reducing the risk of disasters; mitigating the severity of the consequences of disasters; emergency preparedness; a rapid and effective response to disasters; and post-disaster recovery and rehabilitation.

The National Disaster Management Centre (NDMC) was constituted to promote an integrated and co-ordinated system of disaster management, with special emphasis on prevention and mitigation by national, provincial and municipal organs of State, statutory functionaries, other role-players and communities. The general responsibilities of the NDMC involve:
- co-ordinating an integrated disaster-management system
- specialising in issues relating to disaster management
- monitoring compliance with the Disaster Management Act, 2002 (Act 57 of 2002), and the National Disaster Management Framework
- acting as a central repository for information concerning disasters, impending disasters and disaster management
- initiating and facilitating efforts to make funding available for disaster management
- liaising and co-ordinating all activities with provincial and local disaster-management offices.

The Disaster Management Act, 2002 was promulgated on 15 January 2003. The implementation of the Act will be phased in over two years, taking into account capacity limitations in provincial and local spheres.

The Public Service

The Public Service continues to build on the policy and regulatory reforms it has put in place since 1994. In particular, the Department of Public Service and Administration continues to implement the wage policy developed in 1999, including a major review of macrobenefits. An incentive policy framework has been developed. A competency framework and performance-management system for the Senior Management Service (SMS) are being implemented. The Human Resource (HR) Development Strategy for the Public Service is under implementation, including a system of learnerships and the internship programme. Minimum standards on the management of HIV/AIDS in the workplace have been promulgated. The Country Corruption Assessment for South Africa was released.

The policy and strategy of *batho pele* (people first) continues to underpin the support provided to other departments by the Department of Public Service and Administration.

Size of the Public Service

By 31 December 2002, the Public Service had

1 040 506 people in its employ, representing a 0,86% difference and an increase of 8 912 from the total employment as on 31 December 2001. With regard to the share of personnel in the Public Service sectors, 62% are attached to the social services sector (health, social development and education), followed by 17,3% in the Criminal Justice Cluster, 13,6% in the Governance and Administration (G&A) Cluster, and 7,1% in the Defence and Intelligence Clusters.

Restructuring of the Public Service

Resolution 7 of 2002 came to an end on 12 September 2003. The aim of this Resolution was to restructure the Public Service in terms of human resources, to enable the most effective and efficient delivery of services. Phase one of the programme has been completed. Phase two deals with excess employees not accommodated during the redeployment. Restructuring in the Public Service, however, is an ongoing process and a framework will be established to guide its ongoing transformation and restructuring.

All excess employees who were unsuccessful in the redeployment process as at 12 September 2003, were placed in a special programme and assigned to defined centres by the employer. By that date, government had 20 958 excess employees, including South African National Defence Force personnel, and 20 313 vacancies. Of the 20 313, there were 5 279 non-funded vacancies and 15 034 funded vacancies. Overall, the majority of excess personnel were from the agricultural sector while the majority of vacancies were in the health sector.

At the beginning of the process the total number of excess employees was 28 744. This number was reduced through internal appointments, voluntary packages (2 507), resignations (746), employment in other departments (2 311) and early retirement (23). Departments further reviewed their human resource plans and further absorbed (2 199) within their respective structures.

A special programme, which was expected to run until May 2003, focused on the re-skilling of employees and also facilitated absorption into future departmental vacancies.

Employees who were not successful in this programme were eligible for the employer-initiated severance package. Employees may, however, choose to exit the Public Service earlier rather than join this special programme, by applying for a severance package.

Macro-organisational issues

Government has a range of institutions that render services to citizens. These institutions are generally referred to as the public sector and range from national and provincial government departments, constitutional institutions, and national and provincial public entities.

The Cabinet has approved a process for the creation of public entities as part of an overarching framework for service delivery.

The Department of Public Service Administration and the National Treasury have developed a business plan to review all public entities reporting to national government departments, excluding constitutional bodies and commissions.

As at 28 February 2003, the recorded number of public entities totalled 336 and in the 2003/04 financial year, national government allocated approximately R15 billion towards these entities.

The review is expected to be finalised by May 2004.

Community Development Workers (CDWs)

In August 2003, the Cabinet approved the roll-out of CDWs. They are an additional type of public servant (different to the mainline public servant or local government official); skilled facilitators who will bridge the gap between government services and the people. These public servants will assist citizens with matters such as birth certificates, identity documents (IDs), social-grant applications and small business start-ups, on their own doorsteps and in their own communities.

Recruitment procedures for CDWs will be customised according to local and other provincial specifications. The job description designed for CDWs calls for a minimum requirement of Grade 12 or equivalent prior learning. CDWs will go through a learnership phase that includes thorough training before their formal appointment. Remuneration will correspond with their levels of appointment and phase of operation.

On 1 October 2003, the South African Management Development Institute (SAMDI) started rolling out training for the CDWs. They will use a specific and practical training intervention that responds to real community issues.

Training will be supplemented by a toolkit that CDWs can use in their day-to-day operations. The training includes a Participatory Rural Appraisal, a technique that broadly covers community-needs assessment, public facilitation, project management, communication and conflict resolution. The training will be enhanced by the inclusion of a simulated project component.

Gauteng will be the first province to deploy the group of 40 trained CDWs, followed by Limpopo, North West and the Eastern Cape.

Strengthening institutional performance

Government's programme of creating a better life for all requires capable institutions that can deliver on priorities identified. The Integrated Provincial Support Programme (IPSP) continues to support five provincial administrations in enhancing the performance of selected institutions. The Programme focuses on service-delivery improvement; capacity-building; learning by doing cross-pollination and the sharing of experiences in the quest to deeply entrench sound public-administration practices; an ethos of good governance; and the delivery of services.

In Limpopo, the IPSP has contributed to a better functioning Department of Public Works, which has won a number of awards for service excellence. The IPSP has also helped to put in place a model for taking services provided by the South African Police Service (SAPS) to remote rural areas, through an effective mobile unit in the former Venda area.

Similar achievements can be reported about other provinces, including turning Ezemvelo KZN Wildlife in KwaZulu-Natal into a capable ecotourism facility. The Eastern Cape managed, through IPSP support, to create a mobile mechanism for registering Child Support Grant beneficiaries in remote rural areas. It has established a solid reliable warehouse for electronically captured social-grant files. About 1,8 million social-grant files have been captured in the province through this system.

A special intervention to support the Eastern Cape Provincial Government with service delivery and governance challenges commenced in November 2002. Turnaround strategies are being implemented in the Departments of Education, Health, Welfare, and Roads and Public Works.

There is also an increasing focus on promoting learning and knowledge management. To this end, a number of platforms have been established, including national and provincial learning networks; an annual learning academy bringing together public-service front-line managers; the annual Public Management Conversation involving local senior managers, academics and selected international contributors; and a *Service-Delivery Review Journal* in which experiences about service-delivery improvement efforts are shared.

Service-delivery improvement

The vision of government is to promote integrated seamless service delivery. This is done within the *Batho Pele* policy of government, as promulgated in 1997. The *batho pele* principles are applied as the basis for service delivery. Various projects are being implemented to give full realisation to the improvement of service delivery. The e-Gateway project aims to establish a single electronic gateway that will facilitate access to all information and services being provided by government.

A key initiative in terms of *batho pele* is to modernise government. As part of the process, the Department has established the Centre for Public-Service Innovation (CPSI) to encourage service-delivery innovation in the Public Service. The work of the CPSI focuses on using innovative means to achieve outcomes in sustainable service-delivery partnerships, influencing the work culture within government and developing an environment supportive of innovation. The role of the CPSI is primarily to function as an enabler, facilitator and champion of innovative ideas.

New service-delivery mechanisms are also being implemented, such as the MPCCs, Shared Services and One-Stop Centres. The Department has also produced the *Directory of Public Services*, which provides information to citizens on the points of service delivery.

> The Acting Director-General of the Public Service Commission at the time, Prof. Richard Levin, presented the results of the Citizen Satisfaction Survey to the Portfolio Committee on Public Service and Administration in April 2003.
>
> The Survey was conducted in the Departments of Education, Health, Housing and Social Development across the nine provinces.
>
> The primary aims of the Survey were:
> - accommodate citizens' desire to be consulted about services rendered to them
> - identify key factors that have an influence on the satisfaction of citizens in general
> - determine the level of services desired by citizens
> - measure actual service delivery against expectations with the aim of identifying gaps
> - identify and highlight areas that have to be prioritised for improvement
> - provide a basis for comparison or benchmarking service delivery within a department and between other departments.
>
> Based on the overall Citizen Satisfaction index score, the Survey revealed that generally citizens felt that their expectations were largely met. However, citizens who participated in Adult Basic Education and Training, life skills education, antenatal care, and social security grants were far more likely to feel that their expectations were being met by the Departments of Education, Health, and Social Development, respectively. Citizens who received services pertaining to outcome-based education (Department of Education), emergency medical services (Department of Health), internal housing-delivery services or a housing subsidy (Department of Housing), or from social workers, non-governmental organisations and social-development projects (Department of Social Development) felt that their expectations were being met.

Labour relations and conditions of service

The results of the Personnel Expenditure Review in 1999 highlighted a need to review a number of public-service practices and systems. The purpose of this Review was to highlight problem areas and help identify opportunities where innovation could result in the release of available resources to fund other development programmes in line with the national reconstruction and development framework.

Certain focus areas were identified in the medium term:
- The review of conditions of service for SMS members. Agreement was reached to determine conditions of service of SMS members outside the normal bargaining structures. A revised and inclusive remuneration structure has been introduced for members of the SMS.
- The review of macrobenefits in the Public Service with special focus on medical aid, housing, leave and pension arrangements, with a view to ensuring efficiency, adequacy, equity and administrative justice. Task teams comprising parties to the Public Service Co-ordinating Bargaining Council (PSCBC) were established to facilitate the review process. In December 2002, an agreement was

concluded on pension restructuring. The Resolution resolves to amend the Rules of the Government Employee Pension Fund to make provision for, *inter alia*, an improved benefit structure, a new employer-contribution arrangement, new arrangements to expedite the appointment of the Board of Trustees, and new arrangements for the recognition of pensionable years of service for former members of the non-statutory forces and employees disadvantaged by past discriminatory employment practices.
- Work has commenced on medical aid restructuring.
- Agreement has been reached to discontinue with rank- and leg-promotion (with effect from 1 July 2001) in favour of a performance-based pay progression system. An Incentive Policy Framework, incorporating pay progression, grade progression and performance incentives has been introduced, effective from 1 April 2003. The first pay progression based on the outcome of performance assessments was effected on 1 July 2003.
- The review of collective bargaining structures in the Public Service to clearly define roles, responsibilities and issues to be negotiated at national, sectoral or departmental level.
- The development of a national strategy to facilitate the mitigation of the impact of HIV/AIDS on service delivery.

Fighting corruption

The Public Service Anti-Corruption Strategy has been approved by the Cabinet for implementation over a three-year period. To inform and support the implementation phase, new anti-corruption legislation has been introduced in Parliament and there are processes to assess departments' capability to deal with corruption, gauge the extent of corruption and build further institutional capacity. Particulars of the Strategy are available on the website of the Department of Public Service and Administration (*www.dpsa.gov.za*).

Senior Management Service

The overall goal of the SMS initiative is to improve government's ability to recruit, retain and develop quality managers and professionals. To this end, the following have been put in place:
- a modernised employment framework consisting of improved terms and conditions of service
- mechanisms to improve interdepartmental mobility of senior managers and professionals
- uniform Performance Management and Development Systems supported by a competency framework
- improved and competency-based recruitment and selection processes
- the institution of a higher ethical conduct through the disclosure of financial interests
- focused training and development interventions.

The second SMS conference was held in September 2003 in Port Elizabeth, Eastern Cape. The theme of the conference was *Towards an Integrated Public Service*.

Human resource management

The Public Service HR management systems propagate the inculcation of a culture of performance, hence the emphasis on strategic and HR planning and the development of human-capital capacity.

The Competency Framework for Senior Managers has been introduced to improve the quality of managers and professionals employed in the Public Service. This Framework links directly with performance management, training and development as well as recruitment and selection. Initiatives are under way to develop a similar competency framework for middle managers and lower ranks. It will also involve submitting proposals on how to accelerate the development of middle managers and prepare them for senior-management positions.

The State as employer has a responsibility to comply with the laws of the country on representivity. To this end, the Public Service Regulations require that heads of departments conduct strategic planning sessions to inform their annual plans (e.g. service-delivery, HR, recruitment, training and development, and change-management strategies) in accordance with their delivery programmes.

Human resource development

The Human Resource Development (HRD) Strategy for the Public Service builds on the foundation put in place by the National Skills Development Strategy and the National HR Development Strategy for South Africa. The Strategy has been approved by the Cabinet for implementation. It aims at addressing the major HR capacity constraints hampering the effective and equitable delivery of public services, and has the following four strategic objectives, namely, to ensure:
- full commitment to promote HR development in all public-service institutions
- the establishment of effective strategic and operational planning in the Public Service
- the establishment of competencies that are critical for service delivery in the Public Service
- effective management and co-ordination of developmental interventions in the Public Service.

The roll-out of the Public Service HRD Strategy commenced in 2003.

HIV/AIDS

Following an assessment of the likely impact of HIV/AIDS on the Public Service, a programme of action was developed, focusing on the following key areas:
- The development of workplace-policy frameworks and the definition of minimum standards. A framework to ensure the establishment of work environments conducive to preventing and mitigating the impact of HIV/AIDS in the workplace was agreed upon at the PSCBC. To provide relevant terms of reference for the users of the framework, minimum standards were defined and promulgated as part of the working-environment provisions in the Public Service Regulations.
- The review of service conditions to ensure that there is consideration of the potential impact on medical-aid provisions, pension arrangements, management of incapacity leave and ill-health retirements, and to ensure that public servants enjoy an acceptable level of care and support.
- The identification and provision of support, capacity development and training as part of the broader processes to manage the impact of HIV/AIDS on the Public Service.
- The review of current legislation and policy documents to eliminate any forms of discrimination and ensure relevance.

A comprehensive implementation strategy was developed, which focuses on the implementation of the workplace-policy framework and minimum standards, facilitating the development and implementation of departmental workplace policies and continuously monitoring and evaluating the progress achieved by departments.

Public-service information

The Department of Public Service and Administration has published the National Minimum Information Requirements (NMIRs), which identify the information required at a strategic level which departments must ensure is kept accurate and up to date. The National Treasury, in conjunction with the Department, developed a diagnostic toolkit to assess a department's compliance with the NMIRs and to identify factors that contribute to the lack of compliance. This toolkit has been applied with success in various departments.

The Department, in partnership with the National Treasury, is engaged in a process to investigate the modernisation and upgrading of HR management-information systems.

Since 2002, departments have had to publish, as part of their annual reports, a statistical report with regard to HR-management practices.

Government Information Technology Officers' (GITO) Council

The GITO Council was created to serve as an information technology (IT) co-ordination and consolidation vehicle in government, and as a radar that will assist in informing the Government, on a continuous basis, when and how to intervene in the interest of enhanced service delivery to citizens. It is premised on the requirement that each government IT officer is part of the executive team in the respective organ of State, and responsible for the departmental or provincial IT strategy and plan.

The GITO Council has been involved in the investigation, formulation and development of an IT security-policy framework, e-government policy and strategy, and IT procurement guidelines. It also monitors government IT projects to eliminate duplication.

The GITO Council has formed a workgroup to investigate and make recommendations on the use of open-source software in government. Another workgroup looked at knowledge management in government.

The Office of the Government Chief Information Officer in the Department of Public Service and Administration has been interacting with departments on their projects and reporting to the GITO Council on a regular basis to facilitate project co-ordination. All e-government projects will be brought in line with the objectives of the Gateway project.

e-Government policy

The Draft e-Government Policy has been subject to bilateral consultations with specific departments to ensure that the concerned departments can implement policy statements.

The Draft Policy outlines the mission and vision of the South African Government with regard to electronic service delivery, challenges and mechanisms of effecting service delivery based on citizens' life expectations/events, and the necessary institutional framework to realise e-government.

e-Government regulations, which will form a new Chapter of the Public Service Regulations, were developed and approved by the GITO Council in November 2001. These Regulations seek to enforce interoperability and information security across all government departments at all levels.

A set of standards to guide government-wide interoperability were agreed upon by the GITO Council in January 2002. A process is under way to develop an e-Government Act to facilitate the implementation of the Gateway project. A study has been done by the Gateway legal advisors who identified the need for legislative intervention to facilitate this process. The e-Government Act is expected to be completed by the first quarter of 2004.

State Information Technology Agency (SITA)

The restructuring of SITA has been completed as approved by the Cabinet. The current structure consists of:
- SITA Holdings, responsible for all the corporate functions and three operating divisions, namely:
  - SITA D, ring-fencing the affairs of the Department of Defence.
  - SITA C, taking care of the affairs of all other national and provincial governments.
  - SITA e-Services, which is responsible for transforming the way in which government conducts its business. It is also the single channel for procurement of government IT and related services through its IT Acquisition Centre.

The SITA Act, 1998 (Act 88 of 1998), has been amended primarily with the purpose of entrenching the basic principles of the IT 'house of values' and to improve the governance of SITA.

The focus of SITA remains on service delivery to its client base through adherence to the principles as embedded in the IT 'house of values'. Improved co-ordination of requirements and interoperability will become the order of the day, resulting in the elimination of duplication and leveraging the buying power of government.

The first phase of the Government Common Core Network has been completed. It provides a single integrated Wide Area Network for all government departments, eliminating the 13 networks in existence. Various other initiatives to achieve economies of scale are in the tender adjudication phase.

SITA remains committed to the promotion of openness and fairness during procurement, and to the socio-economic responsibility of advancing Black Economic Empowerment. Particular attention is given to ensuring the regional distribution of spending, and skills development.

In line with the provisions of the SITA Act, 1998, as amended, national departments and provincial governments continue to integrate their services into SITA.

International and African affairs

The Minister of Public Service and Administration, Ms Geraldine Fraser-Moleketi, is the chairperson of the Pan-African Conference of Ministers of Public Service. At the fourth Conference, participating Ministers and delegations from across Africa approved the Pan-African Governance and Public Administration Programme, to be implemented within the broad framework of the New Partnership for Africa's Development (NEPAD).

The Programme is governed by a Committee of Ministers from across the continent, and is built on the principles of regional co-operation, identification of common needs, and the pooling of available resources. The Programme identified as critical areas of intervention the following: institutional capability development, knowledge and policy learning, data collection and exchange, and innovation and partnership support.

The overall Programme also creates a framework for regional organisations, national management-development institutions and international development partners to collaborate in a manner unprecedented on the African continent.

The Ministry is also active in global organisations involved in public-administration issues and challenges. The Minister actively participates in the Commonwealth Association of Public Administration and Management, the International Institute for Administrative Sciences, and in the activities of the United Nations pertaining to public administration. In addition, the Ministry has established and continues to establish various information-sharing and capacity-development bilateral co-operative agreements with similar Ministries and departments across the globe.

Governance and Administration Cluster

In 1999, the Cabinet established six Committees which clustered the work of the Cabinet and became the locus of policy debates prior to the submission of memoranda to the Cabinet. At the level of directors-general, similar Clusters were established. The focus of the G&A Cluster is mainly, though not exclusively, on supporting the efficient and effective functioning of government, and is therefore primarily concerned with matters internal to government operations.

G&A Cluster priorities for 2002/03 included strengthening integrated governance, including the implementation of the Planning Framework of government; improving the capacity of government, including the transformation of local government; integrated service delivery, including the establishment of MPCCs and the Gateway project; and promoting good governance, including the Cluster's support to NEPAD and the implementation of the Public Service Anti-Corruption Strategy.

Public Service Commission (PSC)

The PSC is the independent monitor and arbiter of the activities, ethos and conduct of the Public Service. The powers and functions of the PSC are set out in Section 196 of the Constitution, 1996. The Commission is required to:
- promote the values and principles of public administration as set out in the Constitution
- monitor, evaluate and investigate human resource practices, service delivery and related organisational matters to assess the extent to which they comply with constitutional values and principles
- support the efforts of the Public Service to promote a high standard of professional ethics
- investigate grievances of officers and recommend appropriate remedies or actions
- report to Parliament and provincial legislatures on its activities.

The PSC is one of a number of institutions whose role it is to support the legislature in enhancing accountability.

The PSC is supported by the Office of the Public Service Commission (OPSC), which implements the policy and programmes of the PSC. The Commission comprises 14 commissioners and has regional offices in all nine provinces.

The work of the OPSC is structured around six key performance areas:

Professional ethics and risk management

The approach of the PSC is to address corruption proactively and in an integrated manner, focusing on the creation of an ethics-management infrastructure. Previous surveys in 2001 reiterated the need to strengthen the ethics-management skills of public servants and the ethics-management infrastructure, as the latter was found to be too basic and therefore potentially ineffective. Many of the elements of an effective ethics infrastructure (code of conduct, fraud prevention plan, risk-management plans and consistent financial disclosures) are present in departments, but are often generic, inappropriate and poorly supported. The effectiveness of the different elements is often compromised by their failure to operate in an integrated and co-ordinated manner.

The implementation of the Anti-Corruption Strategy is co-ordinated by the Anti-Corruption Co-ordinating Committee which is chaired by the Department of Public Service and Administration. Departments are individually tasked with the implementation of the projects identified in the Strategy. The OPSC undertook several activities to implement the Strategy and build the capacity of the Public Service to prevent and fight corruption. These included:
- Auditing of anti-corruption capabilities in national and provincial departments in conjunction with the Department of Public Service and Administration.
- Training in anti-corruption.
- Acting as Secretariat to the National Anti-Corruption Forum (NACF). The NACF is a co-ordinating Forum consisting of representatives from business, civil society and the Public Service. It is convened by the Minister of Public Service and Administration and acts as a co-ordinating structure to lead and monitor the Anti-Corruption Strategy.
- Development of a generic professional ethics statement for the Public Service. The aim of the ethics statement/ethics pledge is to inculcate and maintain a culture of integrity and ethos within the Public Service.
- Ethics awareness and education. An explanatory manual on the Public Service Code of Conduct was developed and published. One million copies were produced and distributed to departments through an intensive workshop programme.

Special investigations

This unit manages the execution of special investigations with relation to the core functions of the PSC. It researches problematic public-administration areas, investigates and audits departmental anti-corruption units, and contributes to the national fight against corruption by participating in cross-sectoral investigations and strategic workshops.

The special-investigations component contributes to the combating of corruption in the Public Service through:
- Investigating cases of corruption in national and provincial government departments. These are either referred to the PSC for investigation or are investigated on the Commission's own initiative.
- Investigating systemic issues of defective administration in government departments.
- Investigating adherence to applicable procedures in the Public Service.
- Making recommendations to remedy, rectify and/or correct issues investigated. Depending on the type of investigation, the recommendation may consist of advice to a department to either discipline official(s) proven to have been involved in corrupt activities, or refer the matter for criminal prosecution. Recommendations may advise departments on the recovery of pecuniary losses suffered or State assets lost. The component may also refer matters for further investigation by another appropriate agency, or engage in cross-sectoral investigations with other agencies.

Management and service-delivery improvement

This unit investigates, monitors and evaluates management practices and service delivery in the Public Service. It also researches and develops innovative methods to enhance management practices and improve service delivery. Based on research and analysis, the Commission produces an *Annual State of the Public Service Report* that provides a comprehensive overview of public-service performance.

To assist in the research process, the Commission has put in place a long-term monitoring and evaluation system for assessing and analysing the performance of the Public Service. The intention of the process is to identify areas where improvements could successfully be effected, thereby contributing to overall management and service-delivery improvement. This system is based on constitutional values and principles.

Another research practice is that of evaluating specific departmental programmes, especially those involving development and that are focused on the poor. The Evaluation of the National Housing Subsidy Scheme showed that it was generally efficient and effective. It was, however, found that a lack of local government capacity, especially in the rural areas, is a major blockage in housing delivery.

Other projects undertaken by the PSC to enhance management practices and service delivery include the following:
- A report on performance management in the Department of Social Welfare and Population Development in KwaZulu-Natal.
- Evaluation of land administration in the Eastern Cape.
- A review of the restructuring needs of the national Department of Transport.
- the Citizen Satisfaction Survey Tools to enhance and complement the Citizen Satisfaction Surveys, the PSC-considered methodologies and tools that will promote the incorporation of the views and perceptions of citizens in the process of service delivery. In co-operation with the Parliamentary Portfolio Committee on Public Service and Administration, Citizens' Forums were conceptionalised and launched.

Another activity of this unit in the promotion of effectiveness and efficiency is to evaluate innovative approaches to service delivery by looking at alternative organisation and governance arrangements. The pilot projects under the MPCC Programme were evaluated an showed that these Centres were in demand.

Labour relations
This unit investigates, monitors and evaluates the application of merit and equity principles and sound human-resource practices and policies. This entails providing advice on grievances in the Public Service and the monitoring of labour relations. It also investigates grievances lodged with the PSC, and monitors and evaluates the application of sound labour-relations principles in national and provincial departments. To this end, the Commission has developed grievance rules for the Public Service that will be set out in the PSCBC Resolution, as well as guidelines on the management of suspensions and those to follow when considering the merits of an appeal in a case of misconduct.

The PSC has also approved a policy for lodging complaints made by members of the public.

Human resource management and development
This unit investigates, monitors and evaluates HR policies and practices in the Public Service.

In terms of its constitutional mandate, the PSC conducts investigations into the application and management of various HR practices. These investigations include the management of leave, overtime, sick leave, and dismissal as a result of misconduct.

Senior management and conditions of service
This unit manages the monitoring and evaluation of conditions of service and the performance management of heads of departments.

The Commission conducts investigations into the management of performance agreements of senior managers and evaluates the application of developed authority regarding conditions of service of executing authorities.

The Commission further facilitates the evaluation of heads of department at national and provincial levels.

Affirmative action
The Government's affirmative action policy for the Public Service emphasises the management of diversity, based on public-service culture, composition, HR management and service-provision practices.

The overall profile of the Public Service is very close to achieving perfect representivity status, edging its way to matching the population profile in terms of both race and gender.

On 31 March 2003, 72,5% of the Public Service was African, 3,6% Asian, 8,9% coloured and 14,7% white. With regard to gender, 52,5% was female and 47,5% male. However, at senior management level 56% was African, 8,2% Asian, 10,1% coloured and 25,6% white. The gender breakdown for senior management was 22,1% female and 77,9% male.

For State-owned enterprises, the composition of the boards with regard to race was as follows: 63% African, 2,5% Asian, 9,9% coloured and 24,7% white. In terms of gender, 76,5% was male and 23,5% female. The breakdown at senior management levels was as follows: 56,5% was white and 43,5% black with a gender breakdown of 75% male and 25% female.

Training
As mandated to provide training and development in the public sector, South African Management Development Institute (SAMDI) trained 22 966 employees in 2002/03. Training was provided in HR management, change management, the Presidential Strategic Leadership Development Programme (PSLDP), service delivery, provisioning management, administration and training development and quality assurance.

The PSLDP, one major flagship programme of SAMDI, enrolled 4 921 delegates who completed training in 2002/03. Of this total, 1 432 were SAPS officials. The Ministerial

Support Staff Programme was launched in January 2002 with the intention of improving the functioning of the offices of political office-bearers. As a result of increased needs owing to the impact of the Programme, a total of 302 delegates were trained in 2002/03.

The Institute continuously engages its international counterparts in its capacity-building programmes to offer world-class interventions that encompass the latest and best practices.

Basic administration skills training for the Department of Home Affairs was also rolled out by SAMDI, through funding by the Public Service Sector Education and Training Authority. A total of 1 277 employees were trained in 2002/03.

The Institute has been involved in the Joint Committee on Collaboration and has engaged with Rwanda, Burundi and Uganda on projects that focus on capacity-building.

In collaboration with the Governance Institutional Development Division of the Commonwealth Secretariat, SAMDI offered a programme on effective negotiation skills to senior managers of the Southern African Development Community.

SAMDI's website (www.samdi.gov.za) was launched in June 2003.

Home Affairs

The Department of Home Affairs provides individual status-determination services.

The Department has a network of offices in all the provinces. Where the establishment of fixed offices is not warranted, mobile offices or units service such areas on a regular pre-arranged basis.

The Department is divided into five functional support divisions and two line-function divisions.

Statutory bodies falling under the Department are the:
- Immigration Advisory Board
- Standing Committee for Refugee Affairs
- Refugee Appeal Board.

The Government Printing Works provides printing, stationery and related services to all government departments, provincial governments and municipalities.

It also publishes, markets and distributes government publications. Based in Pretoria, the Printing Works provides a variety of related services to departments, the printing industry and other African countries, including the manufacture and supply of fingerprint ink to the SAPS, and the printing of postage stamps for the Democratic Republic of the Congo and the Kingdom of Lesotho.

Negotiations on the rationalisation of the services of the Government Printing Works with provincial printing facilities are in progress.

Civic services

The responsibilities of the Chief Directorate: Civic Services comprise mainly population registration and civic services. Population registration entails the recording of personal particulars in the Population Register with a view to the issuing of IDs, identification by means of fingerprints and photographs; and matters pertaining to the status of persons, such as births, marriages and deaths.

Civic services entail the issuing of passports, registration of foreign births, determining citizenship, and issuing certificates of naturalisation or resumption of South African citizenship.

Citizenship matters

South African citizenship is regulated by the South African Citizenship Act, 1995 (Act 88 of 1995), and regulations issued in terms thereof. South African citizenship may be granted by way of:
- an application for naturalisation as a South African citizen
- an application for resumption of South African citizenship
- the registration of the birth of children born outside South Africa to South African fathers or mothers

- an application for exemption in terms of Section 26(4) of the Act.

Population Register

The Population Register is being rewritten, and an associated Document Management System will be developed and rolled out gradually. This will consist of a large database, an online document-storage system, and a query interface for the retrieval and viewing of electronically stored documentation. The System will reduce processing time for each business transaction, while enhancing information integrity.

The rewriting of the Population Register is closely aligned with the implementation of the Home Affairs National Identification System (HANIS), approved by the Cabinet in January 1996. HANIS will significantly improve the accuracy and accessibility of personal identification, but, because of its scale, its successful implementation is the greatest challenge facing the Department. It will automate the manual fingerprint identification system, replace the ID with an identity card, and integrate these systems with the Population Register. It is being established by the MarPless consortium at a cost of just over R1 billion over five years.

The creation of online services and the implementation of HANIS will assist a variety of departments to accurately identify the beneficiaries of the services they offer.

Migration

The Chief Directorate: Migration is responsible for control over the admission of foreigners for residence in and departure from South Africa. This entails:
- processing applications for visas, temporary residence permits and immigration permits
- maintaining a travellers' and foreigners' control system
- tracing and removing foreigners who are considered undesirable or who are in the Republic illegally.

About 150 000 illegal foreigners are repatriated every year.

Mozambique and Zimbabwe are by far the largest sources of illegal immigrants. South Africa is believed to harbour between 2,5 and 4,1 million illegal immigrants.

The Refugees Act, 1998 (Act 130 of 1998), gives effect within South Africa to the relevant international legal instruments, principles and standards relating to refugees; provides for the reception into South Africa of asylum seekers; regulates applications for and recognition of refugee status; and provides for the rights and obligations flowing from such status, and related matters. The Act came into effect on 1 April 2000.

In 2002, the Department received 20 842 asylum applications.

In recent years, the Department has sought to control illegal immigration through a variety of measures:
- The Aliens Control Amendment Act, 1995 (Act 76 of 1995), which provides for a stricter immigration policy. The implementation of visa fees, and other measures, came into effect in 2001.
- The Department is working closely with the South African Revenue Service and the SAPS to ensure effective border control over the medium term.
- A computerised visa system has been instituted to curb the forgery of South African visas and is being expanded to all South African missions abroad.
- The Immigration Act, 2002 (Act 13 of 2002), was enacted during the first half of 2002. It regulates the admission of people into South Africa, as well as their residence in and departure from the country. After a lengthy hearing and court arguments, the new system of migration control came into effect on 8 April 2003. The Immigration Advisory Board has been functioning since May 2003.

Visas

Foreigners who wish to enter South Africa

must be in possession of valid and acceptable travel documents. They must also be in possession of valid visas, except in the case of certain countries whose citizens are exempt from visa control. Such exemptions are normally limited to permits which are issued for 90 days or less and transits.

The visa system is aimed at facilitating the admission of acceptable aliens at the ports of entry. A visa does not afford the holder any right of residence in South Africa. Temporary residence permits reflecting the purpose and duration of the visit are issued at ports of entry for this purpose.

Control of travellers

The travel documents of persons entering or departing from South Africa are examined by immigration officers at recognised ports of entry to determine whether such persons comply with the necessary requirements.

Control of sojourn

Foreigners who are in the country illegally and who are therefore guilty of an offence can be classified into three categories, namely those who:
- entered the country clandestinely
- failed to renew the temporary residence permits issued to them at ports of entry
- breached the conditions of their temporary residence permits without permission, e.g. holiday visitors who took up employment or started their own businesses.

Depending on the circumstances, persons who are in South Africa illegally are either prosecuted, removed, or their sojourn is legalised. Officers at the various regional and district offices of the Department are in charge of tracing, prosecuting and removing illegal foreigners from the country. Employers of illegal foreigners can also be prosecuted.

Permanent residence

It is government's policy to allow immigration on a selective basis. The Department is responsible for:
- Processing applications for immigration permits for consideration
- Admitting persons suitable for immigration, such as skilled workers in occupations in which there is a shortage in South Africa. The Department particularly encourages applications by industrialists and other entrepreneurs who wish to relocate their existing concerns or establish new concerns in South Africa.

The Department is not directly involved in an active immigration drive.

In categories where shortages exist, the normal procedure is for employers to recruit abroad independently, and in most cases, apply for temporary work permits initially.

Regional committees of the Immigration Advisory Board consider applications for immigration permits of prospective immigrants who wish to settle in the relevant provinces. In terms of the new regulations, regions will carry the responsibility of issuing permits as the regional committees used to do in respect of permanent residence, but they will do so also in respect of temporary residence.

Enquiries in this regard can be made to the nearest office of the Department of Home Affairs in South Africa, Missions abroad, or the Director-General of Home Affairs (for attention Subdirectorate: Permanent Residence) in Pretoria.

Temporary residence

In terms of the Aliens Control Act, 1991 (Act 96 of 1991), temporary residence permits are divided into the following categories:
- visitor's permits
- study permits
- work permits
- business permits
- work seeker's permits
- medical permits.

In terms of Section 11 of the Act, aliens wishing to enter South Africa as visitors or for business or medical purposes, must be in possession of a visa, if not exempt from visa control. An immigration officer will issue a temporary residence permit to holders of such visas or to persons exempt from such visa requirements at the port of entry, if such persons meet entry requirements. However, persons wishing to enter the country as work seekers or for work or study purposes must be in possession of the relevant permit that is issued outside the country.

The overriding consideration in dealing with applications for work permits is whether the employment or task to be undertaken cannot be performed by a South African citizen or an approved permanent immigrant already residing in South Africa.

Applications for the extension of temporary residence permits can be submitted to the nearest regional/district office of the Department of Home Affairs prior to the expiry date of the permit. Any enquiries related to temporary residence permits can be directed to the nearest district/regional office of the Department in South Africa, South African diplomatic representatives abroad, or the Director-General of Home Affairs, for the attention of the Subdirectorate: Temporary Residence.

Removal of undesirable persons

In terms of legislation, the Minister of Home Affairs may order the deportation of any person (other than a South African citizen) convicted of any of the offences specified, or if such person is deemed by the Minister to be an undesirable inhabitant of or visitor to South Africa.

The Minister may also order the deportation of any person (other than a South African citizen) if it is deemed to be in public interest.

Acknowledgements

Department of Home Affairs
Department of Provincial and Local Government
Department of Public Service and Administration
Eastern Cape Provincial Government
Estimates of National Expenditure 2003, published by the National Treasury
Free State Provincial Government
Gauteng Provincial Government
Government Communication and Information System
International Marketing Council website
KwaZulu-Natal Provincial Government
Limpopo Provincial Government
National Treasury
Mpumalanga Provincial Government
Northern Cape Provincial Government
North West Provincial Government
Office of the Public Service Commission
South African Local Government Association
South African Management and Development Institute
Western Cape Provincial Government
www.gov.za

Suggested reading

Alexander, N. *An Ordinary Country: Issues in the Transition from Apartheid to Democracy in South Africa.* Pietermaritzburg: University of Natal Press, 2002.
Bond, P. and Khosa, M. eds. *RDP Policy Audit.* Pretoria: Human Sciences Research Council (HSRC), 1999.
Brink, A. *27 April: One Year Later.* Cape Town: Queillerie, 1995.
Budlender, D. *The Women's Budget.* Cape Town: Institute for Democracy in South Africa (IDASA), 1996.
Callant, R. ed. *The First Five Years: A Review of South Africa's Democratic Parliament.* Cape Town: IDASA, 1999.

South Africa Yearbook 2003/04

Centre for Development and Enterprise. *Policy-Making in a New Democracy: South Africa's Challenges for the 21st Century*. Johannesburg: Centre for Development and Enterprise, 1999.
Chikane, F. et al. eds. *Africa: The Time has Come: Selected Speeches by Thabo Mbeki*. Cape Town: Tafelberg Publishers, 1998.
Corrigan, T. *Beyond the Boycotts: Financing Local Government in the Post-apartheid Era*. Johannesburg: South African Institute for Race Relations, 1998.
Craythorne, D.L. *Municipal Administration: A Handbook*. 4th ed. Kenwyn: Juta, 1997.
Crush, J. and Williams, V. eds. *The New South Africans: Immigration Amnesties and their Aftermath*, Cape Town: Southern African Migration Project, 1999.
D'Engelbronner-Kolff, F.M., Hinz, M.O. and Sindano, J.L. *Traditional Authority and Democracy in South Africa*. Windhoek: Centre for Applied Social Sciences, University of Namibia, 1998.
Devenish, G.E. *A Commentary on the South African Constitution*. Durban: Butterworths, 1998.
De Ville, J. and Steytler, N. eds. *Voting in 1999: Choosing an Electoral System*. Durban: Butterworths, 1996.
De Villiers, B. ed. *State of the Nation 1997/98*. Pretoria: HSRC, 1998.
Direct Access to Key People in South Africa, 2000. Johannesburg: Jonathan Ball, 2000.
Du Toit, D. et al. *Service Excellence Governance*. Johannesburg: Heinemann, 2002.
Ebrahim, H. *The Soul of a Nation: Constitution-Making in South Africa*. Cape Town: Oxford University Press Southern Africa, 1998.
Ergas, Z. *Catharsis and the Healing: South Africa in the 1990s*. London: Janus, 1994.
Erkens, R. and Kane-Berman, J. eds. *Political Correctness in South Africa*. Johannesburg: South African Institute of Race Relations, 2000.
Fakir, E. and others. *Provincial Pocketbook: PIMS 2000 Guide to Politics in the Provinces*. Mackenzie, K. ed. Cape Town: IDASA, 2000.
Faure, M. and Lane, J.E. eds. *South Africa: Designing New Political Institutions*. London: Sage Publications, 1996.
Fick, G. et al. eds. *One Woman, One Vote*. Johannesburg: Electoral Institute of South Africa, 2002.
Friedman, S. and Atkinson, D. eds. *Small Miracle: South Africa's Negotiated Settlement*. Randburg: Ravan Press, 1994.
Friedman, S. ed. *South African Review 8*. Johannesburg: Ravan Press, 2000.
Gardner, J. *Politicians and Apartheid: Trailing in the People's Wake*. Pretoria: HSRC, 1997.
Gevisser, M. *Portraits of Power: Profiles in a Changing South Africa*. Cape Town: David Philip, 1996.
Gilliomee, H. and Schlemmer, L. eds. *Bold Experiment: South Africa's New Democracy*. Halfway House: Southern Book Publishers, 1994.
Gilliomee, H. and Simkins, C. eds. *Awkward Embrace: One-Party Domination and Democracy*. Cape Town: Tafelberg Publishers, 1999.
Graham, P. and Coetzee, A. eds. *In the Balance. Debating the State of Democracy in South Africa*. Cape Town: IDASA, 2002.
Hadland, A. and Rantao, J. *The Life and Times of Thabo Mbeki*. Rivonia: Zebra Press, 1999.
Hain, P. *Sing the Beloved Country: The Struggle for the New South Africa*. London: Pluto Press, 1996.
Heyns, S. *Down Government Avenue: PIMS Guide to Politics in Practice*. Cape Town: IDASA, 1999.
Heyns, S. *Parliamentary Pocketbook*. Cape Town: IDASA, 1996.
Houston, G. ed. *Public Participation in Democratic Governance in South Africa*. Pretoria: HSRC, 2001.
Human Resource Development in the Reconstruction and Development Programme. Randburg: Ravan Press, 1995.
Hyden, G. and Venter, D. eds. *Constitution-Making and Democratisation in Africa*. Pretoria: Africa Institute of South Africa, 2001. African Century Publications series 6.
Ismail, N. and others. *Local Government Management*. Johannesburg International Thomson Publications, c. 1997.
James, D. *Songs of the African Migrants: Performance and Identity in South Africa*. Johannesburg: Witwatersrand University Press, 1999.
James, W. and Levy, M. *Pulse: Passages in Democracy-Building: Assessing South Africa's Transition*. Cape Town: IDASA, 1998.
Johnson, R.W. and Schlemmer, L. eds. *Launching Democracy in South Africa: The First Open Election, April 1994*. New Haven: Yale University Press, 1996.
Johnson, R. W. and Welsh, D. eds. *Ironic Victory: Liberalism in Post-Liberation South Africa*. Cape Town: Oxford University Press, 1998.
Klug, H. *Constituting Democracy: Law, Globalism and South Africa's Political Reconstruction*. Cambridge: University Press, 2000.

Levy, N. and Tapscott, C. *Intergovernmental Relations in South Africa: The Challenges of Co-operative Government.* Cape Town: IDASA and the University of the Western Cape, 2001.

Lodge, T. *Consolidating Democracy: South Africa's Second Popular Election.* Johannesburg: Witwatersrand University Press for the Electoral Institute of South Africa, 1999.

Lodge, T., Kadima, D. and Poltie, D. eds. *Compendium of Elections in Southern Africa.* Johannesburg: Electoral Institute of Southern Africa, 2002.

Lodge, T. *Politics in South Africa: From Mandela to Mbeki.* 2nd ed. Cape Town: David Philip, 2002.

Lodge, T. *South African Politics since 1994.* Cape Town: David Philip, 1999.

Maharaj, G. ed. *Between Unity and Diversity: Essays on Nation-Building in Post-Apartheid South Africa.* Cape Town: IDASA and David Philip, 1999.

Mail and Guardian A – Z of South African Politics 1999: The Essential Handbook. Compilers: P. van Niekerk and B. Ludman. London: Penguin, 1999.

Maltes, R. *Election Book: Judgement and Choice in South Africa's 1994 Election.* Cape Town: IDASA, 1995.

Mayekiso, M. *Township Politics: Civic Struggles for a New South Africa.* New York: Monthly Review Press, 1996.

Meredith, M. *South Africa's New Era: The 1994 Election.* London: Mandarin, 1994.

Milazi, D., et al. eds. *Democracy, Human Rights and Regional Co-operation in Southern Africa.* Pretoria: Africa Institute of South Africa, 2002. African Century Publications series 9.

Murray, M.J. *Revolution Deferred: The Painful Birth of Post-Apartheid South Africa.* London: Verso, 1994.

Muthien, Y. ed. *Democracy South Africa: Evaluating the 1999 Election.* Pretoria: HSRC, 1999.

Ndlela, L. ed. *Practical Guide to Local Government in South Africa.* Pretoria: IDASA, 2001.

Nyatsumba, K.M. *All Sides of the Story: A Grandstand View of South Africa's Political Transition.* Johannesburg: Jonathan Ball, 1997.

Rautenbach, I.M. and Malherbe, E.F.J. *What does the Constitution say?* Pretoria: Van Schaik Academic, 1998.

Reddy, P. S. et al. *Local Government Financing and Development in Southern Africa.* Cape Town: Oxford University Press, 2003.

Reynolds, A. ed. *Elections '94 South Africa: The Campaigns, Results and Future Prospects.* Cape Town: David Philip, 1994.

Rule, S. *Democracy South Africa: Public Opinion on National Priority Issues, March 2000.* Pretoria: HSRC, 2000.

Rule, S. *Democracy South Africa: Public Opinion on National Issues, Election 1999.* Pretoria: HSRC, 2000.

Sanders, M. *Complicities: The Intellectual and Apartheid.* Pietermaritzburg: University of Natal Press, 2002.

South Africa Survey, 2000/01. Johannesburg: South African Institute of Race Relations, 2001.

Sparks, A. *Beyond the Miracle: Inside the New South Africa.* Johannesburg: Jonathan Ball, 2003.

Sparks, A. *Tomorrow is Another Country: The Inside Story of South Africa's Negotiated Revolution.* Cape Town: Struik, 1995.

Steytler, N. and others, eds. *Free and Fair Elections.* Cape Town: Juta, 1994.

Sunstein, C.R. *Designing Democracy: What Constitutions Do.* New York: Oxford University Press, 2001.

Sunter, C. *New Century: Quest for the High Road.* Cape Town: Human & Rousseau, 1992.

The Constitution of the Republic of South Africa, 1996. Cape Town: Constitutional Assembly, 1997. Published in the 11 official languages.

Theron, F. and others, eds. *Good Governance for People.* Stellenbosch: School of Public Management, University of Stellenbosch, 2000.

Tutu, D. *Rainbow People of God: South Africa's Victory over Apartheid.* London: Bantam Books, 1995.

Van Niekerk, D., Van der Walt, G. and Jonker, A. *Governance, Politics and Policy in South Africa.* Cape Town: Oxford University Press for Southern Africa, 2001.

Waldmeir, P. *Anatomy of a Miracle: The End of Apartheid and the Birth of a New South Africa.* England: Penguin Books, 1998.

Woods, D. *Rainbow Nation Revisited: South Africa's Decade of Democracy.* London: André Deutsch, 2000.

Wood, E. J. *Forging Democracy From Below: Insurgent Traditions in South Africa and El Salvador.* Cambridge University Press, 2000.

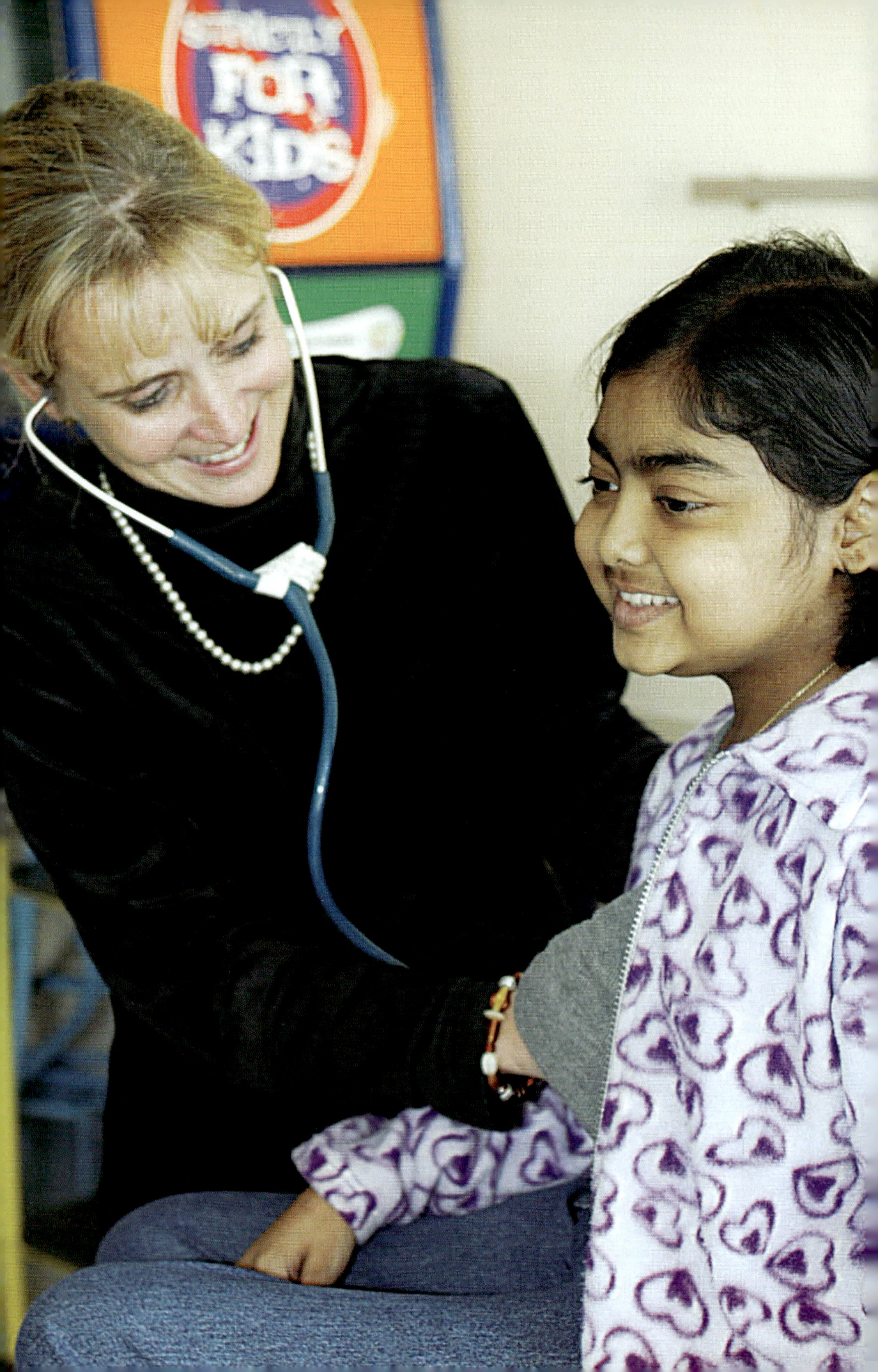
FOR KIDS

chapter 13
Health

The Department of Health is committed to providing quality healthcare to all South Africans, to achieve a unified National Health System and to implement policies that reflect its mission, goals and objectives.

Departmental activities are guided by the *White Paper on the Transformation of the Health System*, adopted in 1997, and the Health-Sector Strategic Framework 1999 to 2004. These outline key objectives such as reducing morbidity and mortality, improving the quality of care, ensuring equity and access, revitalising public hospitals, improving primary healthcare (PHC) and the district health system, reforming legislation, and strengthening human resource development (HRD).

Statutory bodies

Statutory bodies for the health-service professions include the Health Professions Council of South Africa (HPCSA), the South African Dental Technicians' Council, the South African Nursing Council, the South African Pharmacy Council, Allied Health Professions Council of South Africa, and the Council for Social Service Professions.

Regulations in the private health sector are effected through the Statutory Council for Medical Schemes.

◀ By June 2003, some 2662 young professionals were doing community service – contributing critically needed services to the public health sector.

The Medicines Control Council (MCC) is the statutory body charged with ensuring the safety, quality and effectiveness of medicines through a system of registration.

Health authorities

National
The Department of Health is responsible for:
- formulating health policy and legislation
- formulating norms and standards for healthcare
- ensuring appropriate utilisation of health resources
- co-ordinating information systems and monitoring national health goals
- regulating the public and private health-care sectors
- ensuring access to cost-effective and appropriate health commodities at all levels
- liaising with health departments in other countries and international agencies.

Provincial
The provincial Health Departments are responsible for:
- providing and/or rendering health services
- formulating and implementing provincial health policy, standards and legislation
- planning and managing a provincial health-information system
- researching health services rendered in the province to ensure efficiency and quality
- controlling the quality of all health services and facilities

- screening applications for licensing and inspecting private health facilities
- co-ordinating the funding and financial management of district health authorities
- effective consulting on health matters at community level
- ensuring that delegated functions are performed.

Primary healthcare

Government is committed to providing basic healthcare as a fundamental right. To improve the quality of services and consistency of their availability, a comprehensive package of PHC services has been developed and costed, and is being progressively implemented in all health districts, now realigned with the new municipal boundaries. By April 2003, free PHC services were provided at about 3 500 public health clinics nationwide.

The constitutional definition of municipal health services is considerably narrower than the primary care package of services. Local government will therefore have to be engaged through service agreements to provide a more comprehensive service.

The services provided by PHC workers include immunisation, communicable and endemic disease prevention, maternity care, screening of children, Integrated Management of Childhood Illnesses (IMCI) and child healthcare, health promotion, youth health services, counselling services, chronic diseases, diseases of older persons, rehabilitation, accident and emergency services, family planning, and oral health services.

Patients visiting PHC clinics are treated mainly by PHC-trained nurses, or at some clinics, by doctors. Patients with complications are referred to higher levels of care, such as hospitals, if their condition cannot be treated at PHC level.

Persons who are members of a medical aid scheme are excluded from free services.

The National Drug Policy is, to a large extent, based on the essential drugs concept, and is aimed at ensuring the availability of essential drugs of good quality, safety and efficacy to all South Africans.

Health policy

In 1999, the Minister of Health published a reviewed strategic framework to guide work over the following five years. Relevant aspects identified in this 10-point plan are:
- reorganisation of support services
- improvement in the quality of care
- revitalisation of public hospitals
- further implementation of the district health system and primary care
- a decrease in the incidence of HIV/AIDS, sexually transmitted infections (STIs) and tuberculosis (TB)
- resource mobilisation and allocation
- HRD.

In recent years, substantial developments took place in several of these areas:
- a unified National Health Laboratory Service (NHLS) was established to provide laboratory services to the public health sector
- the National Planning Framework, provincial health plans and costing of services have progressed substantially, enabling a longer-term focused rehabilitation and revitalisation programme in the Department
- significant progress in HRD included the submission to the Cabinet of a draft human resource plan for the sector.

By June 2003, 2 662 young professional healthcare workers were doing community service, contributing critically to services in the public sector.

Other achievements of the healthcare system in South Africa include the work of the Medical Research Council (MRC), which responds to a broad spectrum of challenges. Clinics and hospitals have been deracialised, new facilities have been built and many of the existing institutions have been rehabilitated. The National Institute for Communicable Diseases (NICD), backed by increasingly skilled outbreak teams in the provinces, ensures that government is able to respond to any outbreak of disease.

Telemedicine

The South African Government has identified telemedicine as a strategic tool for facilitating the delivery of equitable healthcare and educational services, irrespective of distance and the availability of specialised expertise, particularly in rural areas. In 1998, the Department of Health adopted the National Telemedicine Project Strategy. The Strategy called for the establishment of a National Telemedicine Research Centre and a network of telemedicine links to be implemented in three phases over a period of five years.

In September 1999, the National Telemedicine Research Centre was established as a joint venture of the Department and the MRC.

This exciting project will go a long way towards delivering a solution to the severe problem of inadequate services and geographical challenges that confront the South African healthcare system, as a result of long-standing, previously misplaced priorities.

Implementation of the project is ongoing.

Legislation

The National Health Bill was presented to Parliament in July 2003 and was expected to be passed in the latter half of 2003.

The Bill, which provides a legal framework for a national health system that encompasses public, private, non-governmental and other providers of health services, also sets out the rights and duties of healthcare providers, health workers, establishments and users.

It aims to promote the progressive realisation of South Africans' right to health services and an environment that is not harmful to their well-being. It will also promote the right of children to basic healthcare services.

The most contentious provision of the Bill has been that every health establishment, private or public, requires a certificate of need to operate. The establishment of new hospitals and the expansion of existing facilities would be subject to the issuing of such a certificate.

The central motivation for this provision is the protection of the health-service consumer, not only in terms of the standards of healthcare, but also in terms of the cost of healthcare.

The Mental Healthcare Act, 2002 (Act 17 of 2002), provides for the care, treatment, rehabilitation and administration of persons who are mentally ill. It also sets out the different procedures to be followed in the admission of such persons.

The Traditional Healers Bill was approved by the Cabinet in early 2003 before publication for public comment. It will provide for the registration of traditional healers and the establishment of a statutory body for the regulation of this area of practice.

The recommendations of a task team comprising the Department of Health and officials from the HPCSA and the South African Nursing Council are expected to lead to amendments to the Health Professions Act, 1974 (Act 56 of 1974), and the Nursing Act, 1978 (Act 50 of 1978).

The Medical Schemes Amendment Act, 2002 (Act 62 of 2002), amended the Medical Schemes Act, 1998 (Act 131 of 1998), to extend certain rights of members to their dependants. In addition, the Act:
- explicitly prohibits discrimination on the basis of age
- regulates the practice of reinsurance
- regulates the circumstances under which waiting periods may be applied
- improves the powers of the Council and the Registrar to act in the interest of beneficiaries.

Mandatory medical-scheme cover for certain chronic conditions was expected to come into effect in January 2004.

National School Health Policy

The Minister of Health, Dr Manto Tshabalala-Msimang, launched the National School-

Health Policy and Guidelines on 22 July 2003.

The comprehensive Policy and Guidelines aim to ensure that all children, irrespective of race, colour and location, have equal access to school-health services.

The Policy is in line with the United Nations (UN) Convention on the Rights of the Child recommendations, which affirm that the State has an obligation to ensure that all segments of society, in particular parents and children, are informed and have access to knowledge of child health and nutrition, hygiene, environmental sanitation, and the prevention of accidents.

Department of Health officials will visit all the provinces, especially those with a School-Health Programme, to embark on a major training campaign of PHC nurses.

The nurses will be trained to:
- give health education to children
- impart life skills
- screen children, especially at Grade R and Grade 1, for specific health problems, and at puberty stage as children undergo physiological changes
- detect disabilities at an early age
- identify missed opportunities for immunisation and other interventions.

The Programme, under the theme, *Healthy Children Are Successful Learners*, will be implemented in phases. Some 30% of districts in every province are expected to be covered by the end of 2004, at an estimated cost of about R10 million.

The programme will be extended to cover 60% of districts by 2005, and the whole country by the end of 2007.

Medicines administration

The Medicine and Related Substances Amendment Act, 2002 (Act 59 of 2002), makes provision for, among others, the:
- Definition of the search-and-seizure powers of the MCC in a way that is consistent with the Bill of Rights.
- Extension of regulations applicable to pharmacists to cover other health practitioners licensed to dispense and compound medicines. These include professional fees and the obligation to inform patients about generic drug options.

The Act further states that any party appealing against a decision of the Director-General on the granting of dispensing licences must approach the Minister of Health directly.

Any party appealing against a decision of the MCC on medicines registration will have recourse to an appeal committee established by the Minister.

The Act and its 1997 predecessor of the same name came into effect in May 2003, together with a comprehensive set of regulations.

Health team

Health personnel are a crucial component in realising the Department of Health's vision. Major challenges still exist in attracting health personnel to the rural areas.

Physicians

Some 30 153 doctors were registered with the HPCSA at the end of 2002. These include doctors working for the State, doctors in private practice, and specialists. The majority of doctors practise in the private sector. In selected communities, medical students render health services at clinics under the supervision of medical practitioners.

In terms of the Continuing Professional Development (CPD) system, all doctors, irrespective of earlier qualifications, must obtain a specified number of points to retain their registration. The system requires that doctors attend workshops, conferences, refresher courses, seminars, departmental meetings and journal clubs.

Non-compliance with the requirements of the system could result in the doctor being deregistered.

The use of foreign health professionals has

assisted in relieving the shortage of skilled medical practitioners in many parts of South Africa.

Applications are subject to assessment by the Examinations Committee of the Medical and Dental Professions Board. Those who are admitted have to write an examination, after which they can be registered in the particular category for which they applied and were assessed.

In 2002, there were some 7 203 foreign-qualified doctors working in South Africa.

Newly qualified interns are required to do remunerated compulsory community service at State hospitals for one year. Only after completion of this service are they allowed to register with the HPCSA, and only then are they entitled to practise privately.

The system of community service provides significant relief in rural areas. In 2003, the Department expanded community service to cover physiotherapists, radiographers, occupational therapists, speech and hearing therapists, clinical psychologists, dietitians and environmental health officers.

Oral health professionals

At the end of 2001, a total of 4 503 dentists, 11 dental and oral specialists, 849 oral hygienists and 347 dental therapists were registered with the HPCSA.

At the end of 2002, 4 499 dentists were registered. Since 1 January 1999, dentists have also been subject to the CPD system. The system of community service was extended to dentists in July 2000.

Oral health workers render services in the private as well as the public sectors.

Pharmacists

The Pharmacy Amendment Act, 2000 (Act 1 of 2000), provides for all graduates who wish to register as pharmacists for the first time to work for the State as part of government's plan to provide health services to all communities. The provision came into effect on 20 November 2000. All pharmacists who have registered since that date are obliged to perform one year of remunerated pharmaceutical community service in a public-health facility. Those who have not completed this year of service are not allowed to practise independently as pharmacists. Some 366 pharmacists commenced community service in 2001, compared with 49 in 2000.

A section of the Pharmacy Amendment Act, 2000, which allows non-pharmacists to own pharmacies, came into effect at the same time.

This legislation aims to improve access to medicines, make them more affordable, improve marketing and dispensing practices, and promote consumer interests.

In 2001, 10 782 pharmacists were registered with the South African Pharmacy Council, approximately 7% of whom were employed in provincial and State hospitals.

Nurses

The South African Nursing Council controls nursing education and practice in South Africa.

The key role of the Nursing Council is to protect and promote public interest, including ensuring delivery of quality healthcare. It does so by prescribing minimum requirements for the education and training of nurses and midwives, approves training schools, and registers or enrols those who qualify in one or more of the basic or postbasic categories.

Total of supplementary healthcare practitioners at end of December 2002	
Basic ambulance assistants	9 806
Ambulance emergency assistants	3 466
Environmental health officers	2 228
Medical technologists	3 854
Occupational therapists	2 356
Optometrists	1 969
Physiotherapists	1 019
Psychologists	4 649
Radiographers	4 081

Source: Health Professions Council of South Africa

At the end of 2002, there were 172 869 registered and enrolled nurses and enrolled nursing auxiliaries on the registers and rolls of the Council. The nursing profession represents more than 50% of the total professional human resources of health services.

Similarly, 21 104 persons were registered as student and pupil nurses or pupil nursing auxiliaries on the registers and rolls of the Council.

Supplementary health services

South Africa has a dire shortage of health professionals such as physiotherapists, dietitians and radiographers. By mid-May 2001, there were 89 793 supplementary health professionals registered with the HPCSA.

Allied health professions

In July 2003, the following practitioners were registered with the Allied Health Professions Council of South Africa:
- Ayurveda 114
- Chinese medicine and acupuncture 638
- chiropractors 424
- homeopaths 652
- naturopaths 142
- osteopaths 60
- phytotherapists 23
- therapeutic aromatherapists 1 003
- therapeutic massage therapists 279
- therapeutic reflexologists 1 726

Provincial Health Departments

The function of the provincial Health Departments is to provide and manage comprehensive health services at all levels of care. The basis for these services is a district-based PHC model. The major emphasis in the development of health services in South Africa at provincial level has been the shift from curative hospital-based healthcare to that provided in an integrated community-based manner.

Clinics

A network of mobile clinics run by government forms the backbone of primary and preventive healthcare in South Africa. Clinics are being built or expanded throughout the country. Between 1994 and 2003, upgrading and new clinic-building resulted in 701 additional clinics.

Hospitals

According to the Department of Health, there were 357 provincial public hospitals in 2002.

Ongoing programmes are in place to improve the quality of hospital services. A charter of patients' rights has been developed, as well as procedures to follow when dealing with complaints and suggestions. A service package with norms and standards has been developed for district hospitals and is being extended to regional hospitals. Funding for tertiary health services has been reformed with the introduction of the National Tertiary Services Grant.

In the last two years, funding for the Hospital Revitalisation Programme has taken a great leap forward; the 2003 budget of R717 million, is set to increase by almost R200 million in 2004.

By 2003, there were 27 hospitals on the Department's list, with 18 of these hospital projects involving the construction of entirely new facilities, either to replace an existing hospital or to create a new service.

Hospital revitalisation also involves technology maintenance, replacement and innovation, the development of managers and management systems, and improving the quality of healthcare in general.

The Programme ensures that managers and health workers are able to respond to the

Registered medical interns, practitioners, pharmacists, nurses and dentists, 2001 – 2002

	2001	2002
Dentists	4 454	4 499
Medical interns	1 651	3 004
Medical practitioners	29 310	30 153
Nurses (students included)	190 449	193 973

Source: Health Professions Council of South Africa and South African Nursing Council

needs of clients and treat patients with care and respect in line with the principles of *batho pele* (people first) and the Patients' Rights Charter.

Various provincial budgets for health have increased capital expenditure substantially. This ensures that clinic-building and the routine maintenance of facilities continues even though the national funding is now focused on major projects at fewer hospitals.

According to the National Health Accounts (March 2001), there were 200 private hospitals and a total of 23 076 beds in use in South Africa in 1999. Many of these hospitals are owned and managed by consortia of private physicians or by large business organisations. Private hospital fees are generally higher than those of provincial hospitals.

Emergency medical services

Emergency medical services, which include ambulance services, are the responsibility of the provincial Departments of Health. Emergency care practitioners receive nationally standardised training through provincial colleges of emergency care. Some technikons also offer diploma and degree programmes in emergency care. Personnel can receive training to the level of advanced life-support.

These services also include aeromedical and medical-rescue services.

Personnel working in this field are required to register with the HPCSA, which has a Professional Board for Emergency Care.

The national Department of Health plays a co-ordinating role in the operation, formulation of policy and guidelines, and development of government emergency medical services.

Private ambulance services also provide services to the community, mainly on a private basis. Some of these also provide aeromedical services to the private sector.

The South African Health Services of the South African National Defence Force plays a vital supporting role in emergencies and disasters.

National Health Laboratory Service

The NHLS is a single national public entity that consists of personnel from provincial Health Departments and from the former South African Institute for Medical Research's (SAIMR) laboratory service. It consists of 234 laboratories. Unification of laboratories provides cost-effective and efficient health-laboratory services to all public-sector healthcare providers, private healthcare providers, and to any government institutions that may require such service.

The National Institute for Virology and a section of the SAIMR have been combined to form the NICD. This is also part of the NHLS. The research expertise and sophisticated laboratories at the NICD have made it a testing centre and resource for the African continent, in relation to several of the rarer communicable diseases.

South African Vaccine Producers and State Vaccine Institute

The strategic equity partnership, designed to re-establish the State Vaccine Institute as a local vaccine producer, was concluded in the first half of 2003. The private partner Blovac Consortium combines South African, British and Cuban interests and holds 49% of shares.

The role of local government

Local government has been recognised as a separate sphere of government, thereby endorsing its constitutional status. Some of the services rendered at this level include the following:
- preventive and promotive healthcare, with some municipalities rendering curative care
- environmental health services, including the supply of safe and adequate drinking water, sewage disposal and refuse removal
- regulation of air pollution, municipal airports, fire-fighting services, licensing and abattoirs.

Many local authorities provide additional PHC services. In some instances, these are funded by provincial health authorities, but in major metropolitan areas the councils carry some of the costs.

Government has recognised the need to formalise service agreements between provinces and councils for the running of these services.

Non-profit health sector

Non-governmental organisations (NGOs) at various levels play an increasingly important role in health, many of them co-operating with government to implement priority programmes. They make an essential contribution in relation to HIV, AIDS and TB and also parti-cipate significantly in the fields of mental health, cancer, disability, and the development of PHC systems.

The national Department of Health budgeted more than R75 million in 2003/04 for NGOs. Provincial Health Departments also set aside funding for NGOs operating within their borders. Health NGOs also receive funding from international donors and from the private sector.

Two particularly high-profile and innovative non-profit organisations are Soul City and loveLife. Both focus on health promotion and the use of the mass media to raise awareness on the prevention of illness, and to enable people to manage their health more effectively. Soul City pioneered one of the most successful multimedia edutainment initiatives on any continent and is known for its sound research-based approach. Over a period of nine years, it has addressed a wide range of health issues relevant to all age groups. The centrepiece of its multimedia strategy is the television drama series broadcast on SABC1. The radio series is broadcast on all nine SABC regional stations (in nine of South Africa's official languages). It is also broadcast on many community radio stations. The booklets are serialised in newspapers throughout South Africa in synergy with electronic media. They are also distributed through clinics and other channels. At least three million booklets are distributed per series. The sixth Soul City television series commenced in 2003.

loveLife focuses more on teenage sexuality and relationships and their critical role in the prevention of HIV infection and related conditions. Apart from mass-media advertising campaigns backed by a helpline, loveLife focuses on services for young people. It has a programme to transform existing reproductive-health and communicable-infection services to make them more 'youth friendly', and it has developed drop-in centres where young people can get information and support.

Both Soul City and loveLife have been sponsored by the Global Fund to Fight HIV, AIDS and malaria. They also have a relationship with government and are funded or contracted to provide expertise in developing AIDS awareness programmes (in the case of Soul City) and 'youth-friendly' public facilities (in the case of loveLife).

The Health Systems Trust is another significant health NGO, which conducts research and helps build appropriate delivery systems for PHC. It is funded partly by the Department of Health and has done important work in supporting the development of the district health system, monitoring the quality of care at public-sector clinics and facilitating the introduction of services to reduce mother-to-child transmission of HIV.

The South African Cancer Association and the Council Against Smoking share government's approach to the prevention of many chronic non-communicable diseases. They partnered government in the development of tobacco-control measures and their implementation. The health-promotion activities of these organisations augment government's own, somewhat limited, capacity in these areas.

The more established national health NGOs – such as the St John Ambulance and the South African Red Cross – continue to play an important role. They still focus on emergency care and first-aid capacity but have adapted their services to take account of changing needs, particularly the impact of HIV and AIDS.

Health

Several important organisations in relation to HIV and AIDS are run by people living with HIV or AIDS. The biggest of these is the National Association of People Living with AIDS, which has branches in many areas. There are also many unaffiliated support groups that serve local communities.

Human-rights and health-rights issues in relation to HIV and AIDS have given rise to groups such as the AIDS Law Project and the Treatment Action Campaign, which has pursued a high-profile campaign in support of expanded treatment.

Faith-based organisations (FBOs) are one of the mainstays of hospice, and institutional and home-based care for those infected and affected by HIV and AIDS. The Salvation Army was perhaps the first to become meaningfully involved, but in recent years organisations of other faiths and denominations have become increasingly significant sources of care. Many FBOs are also involved in HIV-prevention programmes.

Traditional 'service' organisations, like the Lions and Rotary, have health projects that boost the public health sector. Fields in which they have made a particular mark are mass immunisation – particularly the Polio-Free Initiative – and reducing the national backlog for cataract surgery.

The involvement of NGOs extends from the national level, through provincial structures, to small local organisations rooted in individual communities. All are vitally important and bring different qualities to the healthcare network.

Costs and medical schemes

The Council for Medical Schemes regulates the private medical-scheme industry in terms of the Medical Schemes Act, 1998 and is funded mainly through levies on the industry in terms of the Council for Medical Schemes Levies Act, 2000 (Act 58 of 2000). In addition, it receives funding from the Department, which will increase from R2,6 million in 2002/03 to R3,0 million in 2005/06.

Tariffs for admission to private and provincial hospitals differ. Cost differences also exist between various provincial hospitals, depending on the facilities offered. All provincial-hospital patients pay for examinations and treatment on a sliding scale in accordance with their income and number of dependants. If a family is unable to bear the cost in terms of the standard means test, the patient is classified as a hospital patient. His or her treatment is then partly or entirely financed by the particular provincial government or the health authorities of the administration concerned.

By April 1999, 168 private medical schemes were registered in terms of the provisions of the Medical Schemes Act, 1967 (Act 72 of 1967).

The Medical Schemes Amendment Act, 2001 (Act 55 of 2001), improves the regulatory capacity of the Registrar for Medical Schemes and regulates reinsurance. It provides for:
- Improved protection for members. The Act addresses the problem area of medical insurance, by revisiting the provision on waiting periods, and specifically protecting patients against discrimination on grounds of age.
- Promoting efficient administration and good governance of medical schemes by insisting on the independence of individuals in certain key positions.

Chris Hani-Baragwanath Hospital in Soweto, Gauteng, the world's largest hospital, will receive state-of-the-art facilities as part of a R700-million project which is to be undertaken over a period of six years.

Phase one of the project has commenced and includes the establishment of a new renal dialysis unit, a speech therapy and audiology centre, a paediatric admission ward, and bulk stores.

During 2002, the Hospital acquired two new computed tomography scanners, a cardiac catherisation laboratory and a R25-million digital angiography suite, and undertook extensive modernisation of equipment for the Intensive Care Unit.

- Introducing mechanisms to address problematic practices in the marketing of medical schemes and brokerage of services.

The consumer is further protected by additional powers that are assigned to the Minister in terms of the Act. These include the power to:
- regulate managed-healthcare contracts
- impose penalties on medical schemes or administrators for the late payment of claims.

Community health

The most common communicable diseases in South Africa are TB, malaria, measles and STIs.

The appropriate and timeous immunisation of children against infectious diseases is one of the most cost-effective and beneficial preventive measures known.

The mission of the South African Expanded Programme on Immunisation is to reduce death and disability from vaccine-preventable diseases by making immunisation accessible to all children. Immunisations against TB, whooping cough, tetanus, diphtheria, poliomyelitis, hepatitis B, hermafluous influenza type-B and measles are available free of charge to all children up to the age of five years. A tetanus vaccine is administered to women at risk during pregnancy, to protect their newborn infants against neonatal tetanus. Other services include the control of rabies and certain endemic diseases, such as malaria.

In 2002, 72% of children were fully immunised at one year of age, representing a significant increase compared with 63% in 1998.

Polio and measles
All suspected measles cases are actively investigated. Blood and urine specimens are collected to confirm whether the cases are real measles. To date, less than 5% of suspected measles cases proved to be real measles.

Measles decreased dramatically from about 22 000 cases and 53 deaths in 1992, to 37 laboratory-confirmed cases and no deaths in 2000, a direct result of the Measles Elimination Strategy. Polio remains a major problem in Africa, although the last confirmed case in South Africa occurred in 1989.

The year 2003 was a crucial year in South Africa's bid to be declared polio-free in 2005, as it had to sustain certain standards set by the World Health Organisation (WHO) for three consecutive years.

On 30 May 2003, the Minister of Health launched the countdown to a polio-free South Africa as part of a global initiative to heighten awareness about efforts to eradicate polio by 31 December 2005.

The South African Government has implemented the necessary strategies, as recommended by the WHO, to become certified free of polio.

National immunisation campaigns were conducted in 1995, 1996, 1997 and 2000, and a polio-focused campaign is expected to take place throughout the country in 2004.

Three committees have been formed, as required by the WHO, to monitor the polio-eradication process. These are the National Certification Committee, the Laboratory Containment Committee, and the Polio Expert Committee.

South Africa, Lesotho and Swaziland have established an Intercountry Certification Committee to ensure that polio-free certification in the region occurs before December 2005.

A toll-free line is available for the reporting of any suspected polio cases: 0800 111 408.

Integrated Management of Childhood Illnesses
IMCI promotes child health and improves child survival as part of the National Plan of Action for Children. It is being instituted as part of the Department of Health's policy on the National Health System for Universal Primary Care.

The core intervention is integrated case management of the five most important causes of childhood deaths and of common associated conditions.

Implementation of the IMCI strategy in South Africa involves improvement in:
- the case-management skills of health staff through the provision of locally adapted guidelines on IMCI, and activities to promote their use
- the health system required for effective management of childhood illnesses
- family and community practices.

The IMCI material has been adapted for South Africa, and implementation and training are ongoing.

South Africa was the first country to include prevention and management of HIV and AIDS in its IMCI guidelines.

Malaria

Malaria is endemic in the low-altitude areas of Limpopo, Mpumalanga and north-eastern KwaZulu-Natal. The highest-risk area is a strip of about 100 km along the Zimbabwe, Mozambique and Swaziland border. The disease should therefore be viewed as a regional rather than a country-specific problem. The risk areas are divided into high-, intermediate- and low-risk areas.

The number of malaria cases and related deaths in South Africa started to rise from approximately 27 000 cases and 160 deaths, in the mid-1990s, peaking at 62 000 cases and 420 deaths in 2000.

To deal with the problem, the Department of Health first identified problem areas that needed to be addressed, including parasite resistance, vector-insecticide resistance and community-compliance issues. The Department took drastic measures to address these factors, which included changing the drugs and insecticides used, as well as massive education and awareness campaigns within the affected communities.

As a result of these actions, the number of malaria cases dropped by 59% in 2001 and a further 42% in 2002. The malaria deaths in 2001 declined by 74% and a further 21% in 2002 compared with the 2000 malaria season.

Malaria-control teams of the provincial Departments of Health are responsible for measures such as education, treatment of patients, residual spraying of all internal surfaces of dwellings situated in high-risk areas, and detection and treatment of all parasite carriers. It was decided to continue with a programme of controlled and restricted use of DDT because of the growing resistance to pyrethroid insecticides.

The MRC has produced the first district malaria-distribution maps for the country, which have direct implications for focused and cost-effective control measures.

Nearly 35 000 homesteads and facilities have been plotted in collaboration with the Department of Health. The risk map for the entire country is updated annually in collaboration with the Department. The MRC maintains a website (*www.mrc.ac.za*) containing, among others, maps compiled by the Mapping Malaria Risk in Africa project. The initiative has seven regional centres throughout Africa.

The MRC's South African Traditional Medicines Research Group is investigating plants used by traditional healers for the treatment of malaria, TB, skin disorders and immune-system stimulation. Two plants that are effective against malaria parasites have been identified, and the active compounds in one of the plants have been identified and isolated. Anti-TB chemical entities, in traditional medicines, have also been isolated.

The Department of Health is in the process of implementing the Rollback Malaria Strategic Plan. The goal of the Plan is to integrate the Malaria-Control Programme into PHC so that community and district malaria activities can be strengthened and sustained.

South Africa is one of the signatories to the Abuja Declaration, committing itself to reducing malaria morbidity and mortality by 50% by 2010.

Since the onset of the Lubombo Spatial Development Initiative (SDI), of which South Africa is a partner with Mozambique and

Swaziland, there has been an overall reduction of 40% in malaria cases in 2001, followed by a 70% reduction in 2002 from the baseline study conducted in 2000 in the Lubombo SDI areas.

The South African Government has pledged the amount of R5 million to the project for two years and will continue to support the project in 2004. The project managed to secure a five-year grant to the value of US $22 million from the Global Fund to Fight AIDS, TB and malaria.

These resources will be used to intensify the project, including the expansion of the spraying programme in Mozambique, introducing more effective malaria drugs in all the partner countries, increasing malaria control infrastructure, and training scientists and officials in effective malaria control.

The WHO honoured South Africa for its role in the Lubombo SDI with an award for best malaria control in southern Africa. South Africa has committed itself to playing a role in the New Partnership for Africa's Development (NEPAD) and malaria control is one of the major programmes in this regard.

The *Race Against Malaria* Campaign, launched on 10 April 2003, is one of the initiatives to bring partners across southern Africa together in pursuit of better health.

South Africa's rally team joined counterparts from the nine malaria-affected countries of southern Africa, on a two-week drive to Dar es Salaam in Tanzania, during which the teams raised awareness about malaria and distributed insecticide-treated nets, drugs, and education and communication material.

Preliminary negotiations have started with Zimbabwe to explore the possibility of cross-border malaria control, and malaria-control experts are being sent to other Southern African Development Community countries to provide technical assistance and strengthen control programmes in the subregion.

Tuberculosis

South Africa has to cope with 188 000 new TB cases a year. The country remains one of the 22 high-burden TB countries, even though free testing is available at public clinics countrywide.

On World TB Day on 24 March 2003, South Africa's first National TB advocacy and social-mobilisation campaign was launched – it was also the first such campaign globally. It was announced that more than R8 million would be made available over a period of two years to address the problem of HIV/TB infection.

The Department of Health has implemented the Directly Observed Treatment Strategy (DOTS), advocated by the International Union against TB and the WHO. The focus is on curing infectious patients at the first attempt, by ensuring that:

- they are identified by examining their sputum under a microscope for TB bacilli
- they are then supported and monitored to ensure that they take their tablets
- the treatment, laboratory results and outcome are documented
- the right drugs are given for the correct period
- TB control receives special emphasis in terms of political priority, finances and good district health management.

Treatment is free of charge at all public clinics and hospitals in South Africa.

A TB team has been set up at national level, while all provinces have TB co-ordinators. A reporting system, which tracks the outcome of all infectious patients, has been implemented countrywide.

Demonstration and training areas have been set up countrywide. Training manuals, posters and charts have been developed, and courses presented. Communication between clinics and laboratories has improved, and treatment guidelines for drug-resistant TB have been developed.

Government's National Medium-Term Development Plan for the National TB Control Programme aims to achieve the following specific targets by 2005:

- a cure rate of between 80 and 85% among smear-positive TB cases

- decreasing the treatment interruption rate to less than 10%
- detecting 70% of estimated new smear-positive TB cases.

HIV/AIDS

The Government's policy on HIV and AIDS is set out in the five-year Strategic Plan adopted in 2000 and the Cabinet statements of 17 April 2002, 9 October 2002 and 8 August 2003.

The national action system is defined as the Partnership Against AIDS. The Partnership is represented by the South African National AIDS Council (SANAC), which has contributed substantially to co-ordinating various sectors at the highest level.

Government's commitment to intensifying implementation of the Plan is backed by very large budgets for the HIV/AIDS programme. In 2002/03, government provided large additional allocations for an enhanced response to HIV/AIDS and TB. These allocations, estimated at more than R1 billion for 2002/03, were again strengthened in the 2003 Budget.

Additional allocations of R3,4 billion for the next three financial years strengthen key national programmes (such as condom distribution), as well as bolster provincial budgets to extend prevention programmes and treatment. Dedicated funding for HIV/AIDS (excluding allocations from the provincial equitable shares) is set to increase more than tenfold from R342 million in 2001/02 to R3,6 billion in 2005/06.

The Cabinet convened a special meeting on 8 August 2003 to consider the Report of the Joint Health and Treasury Task Team on treatment options to enhance comprehensive care for HIV/AIDS in the public sector.

The Cabinet decided that the Department of Health should, as a matter of urgency, develop a detailed operational plan on an anti-retroviral (ARV) treatment programme.

The Task Team was assisted by a team of experts from the Clinton Foundation AIDS Initiative.

On 19 November 2003, Cabinet, in principle, approved the Operational Plan for Comprehensive Treatment and Care for HIV and AIDS, which it had requested the Department of Health to prepare. Among others, the Plan provides for ARV treatment in the public health sector as part of government's comprehensive strategy to combat HIV and AIDS.

Awareness and life skills campaigns

Government campaigns are continuously increasing awareness about HIV, AIDS, STIs and TB.

Research surveys indicate a high level of awareness among South Africans. The Human Sciences Research Council (HSRC) study, released in November 2002, showed that prevention messages regarding condom-use were working, especially as the young are taking abstinence and faithfulness to heart.

During 2002/03, awareness advanced mainly through the *Khomanani* Campaign and the life skills and HIV/AIDS education programme in schools.

The *Khomanani* Campaign, for which government provided R98 million, aims to move the nation to act, so that individuals see themselves as part of a caring community, proactively addressing the HIV, AIDS and TB epidemics.

Condom supplies

Condoms are available free of charge at all clinics.

During 2002, government distributed 350 million male condoms free of charge. This rose to 400 million in 2003/04. Government will increase the supply through non-traditional outlets – like clubs, shebeens and spaza shops – and double the number of sites where female condoms are available (the number of such sites has already increased from 27 in 2000 to over 200 in 2002).

In 2003, government spent R123 million on the distribution of approximately 22 million male condoms and 100 000 female condoms every month.

Improved access to voluntary HIV counselling and testing (VCT)

Ensuring access to confidential and voluntary HIV counselling and testing is one of the essential elements of the Strategic Plan, as it provides an important entry into other health interventions, e.g. TB and STI treatment. This goal focuses on expanding access to VCT in both the private and public sectors.

By the end of 2002, VCT was available at 982 sites throughout the country, including the sites of the Preventing Mother-to-Child Transmission (PMTCT) programme. VCT services were expected to be available in 80% of public health facilities by the end of 2003/04. To this end, the conditional grant for HIV/AIDS to the provinces, including expanding VCT and PMTCT, was increased from R210 million in 2002/03 to R334 million in 2003/04.

Preventing mother-to-child transmission of HIV

The PMTCT programme that provides Nevirapine to mother and baby is expanding. The original research sites continue to function, providing a full package of care, and helping to answer critical operational questions such as the impact of infant-feeding options and the significance of drug resistance.

Most provinces are extending this comprehensive package to more facilities. By 2003, about 658 hospitals and clinics were providing the service.

All doctors working in the public-sector maternity services may offer Nevirapine to HIV-positive pregnant women, provided that adequate HIV testing and counselling facilities exist. Provinces are therefore also focusing on upgrading testing and counselling services to take into account the needs of PMTCT.

Rape survivors

The decision taken by the Cabinet in April 2002, to offer ARVs to victims of sexual assault as part of a comprehensive package of support, is being implemented. The post-exposure prophylaxis programme includes counselling on the effectiveness and risks of using ARVs for this purpose.

Supplementary funding was approved for this programme in 2002 and increased funding was included in 2003 in the conditional grants to provinces.

All provinces are working according to national protocols. In some provinces, the focus is on multidisciplinary crisis or victim-empowerment centres, while in others, the service is offered through the emergency rooms of general hospitals.

Vaccine

The South African AIDS Vaccine Initiative (SAAVI) was established in 1999 to develop and test an effective, affordable and locally relevant vaccine for South Africa. The SAAVI has made unusually fast progress for a biotechnology project of this nature.

The Cabinet received a report in July 2003 on the progress of SAAVI with regard to developing a vaccine against HIV and AIDS. Clinical trials on South African products are expected to start in 2004, while trials on other products developed in collaboration with international partners were expected to start in 2003 – pending approval from the MCC and Ethics Committee.

The Department of Health has increased its funding to SAAVI from R5 million to R10 million a year. This is matched by R10 million a year from the Department of Science and Technology (bringing the total Government contribution to R20 million annually), while Eskom contributes R15 million a year.

South Africa is also involved in trials of candidate vaccines that have been developed outside the country.

Training

The Integrated Training Grant for 2003/04

helped ensure collaboration between provincial and academic institutions to standardise both undergraduate and in-service training.

Through a partnership with the Foundation for Professional Development, health workers will be trained in issues relating to HIV, AIDS, STIs and TB. This includes a component on managing patients on ARVs. This training will target 100 health workers per province annually for three years.

Government began setting up Centres of Excellence in 2003. Their main function will be to develop curricula on HIV, AIDS and TB care, and to align the skills of healthcare workers with the requirements of national treatment guidelines.

Home/community-based care

By March 2003, there were 466 Home/Community-Based Care Programmes in the country, reaching some 370 170 people. There were 9 553 volunteers attached to these programmes.

Additional funds were made available in 2003/04 through the conditional grants for strengthening the Home/Community-Based Care Programmes. Apart from the health grant, a conditional grant of R66 million was allocated to the Department of Social Development to focus on home/community-based care, specifically addressing the issues of orphans and vulnerable children; and social relief including food parcels, counselling and child care.

Reproductive health

According to the Maternal Mortality Report, released by the Minister of Health in February 2003, HIV/AIDS, malnutrition, substandard healthcare and other non-pregnancy related infections are the chief contributing factors to the country's increasing death rate among pregnant women.

HIV/AIDS remains the most common cause of maternal deaths, responsible for 31,4% of all cases.

The release of the Report coincided with International Women's Day.

Entitled, *Saving Mothers 1999 – 2001*, the Report was commissioned by the Health Ministry four years ago because of the growing concern about rising maternal deaths.

The Report shows that women in their first pregnancy and those who have had five or more pregnancies are at as much risk of maternal death as 35-year-olds and older women.

High blood-pressure complications are responsible for 20% of maternal deaths during pregnancy, uncontrolled bleeding (obstetric haemorrhage) 13,9%, pregnancy-related sepsis 12,4%, and pre-existing medical conditions account for 7% of maternal deaths.

Other factors include lack of emergency transport, especially in predominantly rural areas, substandard healthcare, and lack of adequate health personnel, resources and information.

The Report recommends, as part of the remedial treatment to reduce maternal deaths, that staffing and equipment norms be improved, emergency-transport facilities and termination-of-pregnancy services be made available to pregnant women, and blood be made available at all health centres where Caesarean services are performed.

The Department of Health has developed a card for women's reproductive health to improve continued care and to promote healthy lifestyles. The card is retained by the patient and facilitates communication between health services.

Antenatal care is provided free of charge. However, some women do not use this service effectively. The Department is convinced that a lack of information could be a contributing factor. Therefore, the Department is addressing the problem by empowering women with quality information that will enable them to make informed choices and decisions affecting their reproductive rights and health.

A Pregnancy Education Week is held annually in February, during which talks and workshops are conducted in rural and urban areas to educate women on their reproductive rights and related issues.

The Contraception and the Youth and Adolescent Health Policy Guidelines promote access to health services for the vulnerable groups, by improving the capacity of health and other workers to care for women and children.

The Guidelines are aimed at the provision of quality care, preventing and responding to the needs of the youth, and promoting healthy lifestyles among all youths. The promotion of a healthy lifestyle includes programmes or activities on issues such as:
- life skills
- prevention of substance and alcohol abuse
- provision of a smoke-free environment.

The focus is on the positive potential of young people as opposed to the problems they manifest.

Eight critical areas within the Youth and Adolescent Health Policy Guidelines have been identified, namely:
- sexual and reproductive health
- mental health
- substance abuse
- violence
- unintentional injuries
- birth defects and inherited disorders
- nutrition
- oral health.

The Guidelines for Maternity Care deal with the prevention of opportunistic infections in HIV-positive women, and the provision of micro-nutrient supplements to help ensure the well-being of mothers. They also require health workers to delay the rupture of membranes in labour, avoid suctioning of the newborn by using scalp electrodes, and avoid traumatic procedures such as amniocentesis.

The Guidelines for the Cervical Cancer-Screening Programme are set to reduce the incidence of cervical cancer by detecting and treating the pre-invasive stages of the disease. According to the Cancer Registry, cervical cancer is the second most common cancer in women, comprising 16,6% of all cancers. It is the most common cancer in black (31,2%) and coloured women (22,9%), second most common cancer in Asian women (8,9%), and fourth most common cancer in white women (2,7%).

The Cancer-Screening Programme is set to screen at least 70% of women in their early thirties within 10 years of initiating the Programme. The policy allows for three free pap tests with a 10-year interval between each test. Pilot sites for the screening of cervical cancer have been set up in Limpopo, Gauteng and the Western Cape. The project will be rolled out to all provinces.

The Department is also involved in a programme promoting the participation of men in reproductive health and in the prevention of domestic violence and HIV/AIDS.

The Choice on Termination of Pregnancy Act, 1996 (Act 93 of 1996), allows abortion on request for all women in the first 12 weeks of pregnancy, and in the first 20 weeks in certain cases. The Act came into effect on 1 February 1997. Designated facilities have to meet the minimum criteria as recommended by the Minister of Health. These include trained staff, the availability of an operating theatre and appropriate surgical equipment, drugs, and infection-control measures. Termination-of-pregnancy services are provided free of charge within the comprehensive reproductive health services.

A total of 45 449 abortions were performed in State hospitals during 2001. There was a significant decrease in the maternal mortality rate from unsafe abortions – from over 64% in 1994 to 9,5% in March 2002. However, deaths from septic abortions do still occur and this is cause for concern. Amendments to the Choice on Termination of Pregnancy Act, 1996 are planned to facilitate better access to termination services.

The Department of Health continues to support training in abortion care and contraception provision. There was an increase from

239 trained providers in March 2001 to 366 trained providers in March 2002. There was also an increase in the number of functioning designated facilities, from 33% in March 2001 to 48% in March 2002.

The Subdirectorate: Women's Health has developed Contraception Service-Delivery Guidelines. The Subdirectorate is reviewing the National Guidelines on the Management of Survivors of Sexual Offences, and developing a policy on the management of survivors of sexual offences.

Traditional medicine

In August 2003, South Africa launched the Institute for African Traditional Medicines to research African herbs, and evaluate their medicinal value as part of the Government's campaign to fight HIV, AIDS, TB and other debilitating diseases.

The Institute serves as a reference centre at the Council for Scientific and Industrial Research (CSIR) and will work in partnership with the MRC and the WHO.

The launch of the Institute was the result of a research programme initiated by the Department of Health and the MRC to test the effectiveness, safety and quality of traditional medicines, as well as to protect people from unscrupulous conduct and unproven medical claims within the traditional healing sector.

According to the MRC, an estimated 80% of the population in southern Africa use traditional therapies, with many people reportedly deriving benefits from their use.

The WHO has stated that traditional medicines need to be evaluated for safety and effectiveness before they can be incorporated into or excluded from national health policies. The MRC has put in place systems to safeguard the intellectual property rights of individuals or communities who may bring forward such agents for evaluation.

The MRC will conduct tests to evaluate such medicines, develop substances that could be used for chronic conditions – including immune boosters – and provide information on these medicines to the general public.

Tobacco control

It is estimated that about 25 000 South Africans die each year from tobacco-related diseases.

Regulations of the Tobacco Products Control Amendment Act, 1999 (Act 12 of 1999), include:
- a ban on all advertising for tobacco products from 23 April 2001
- all public places must be smoke-free, but employers and restaurateurs can set aside 25% of their space for smokers, and this space must be separated by a solid partition
- a fine of R10 000 for those who are caught selling or giving cigarettes to children.

The Tobacco Products Control Amendment Act, 1999 has earned the Ministry of Health notable worldwide recognition with the awarding of the Luther L. Terry Award in August 2000.

The Department of Health has set up a tobacco hotline for the general public to lodge smoking-related complaints. More than 12 500 complaints were received in less than a year.

Complaints can be lodged at the hotline on (012) 312 0180. People who want to quit smoking can contact the National Council Against Smoking's Quit Line on (011) 720 3145.

The Department's approach to reducing tobacco is multipronged. While encouraging communities and individuals to take control of their health, government has also assumed a greater responsibility through education, policy and law enforcement.

The results of these interventions are encouraging. In 1998, South Africa recorded a significant drop in adult tobacco consumption. According to the South African Demographic Health Survey Report, adult smoking dropped from 34% in 1996 to 24% in 1998.

A similar trend was noted among high-school-leavers in two surveys conducted by the MRC in 1999 and 2002, (as part of the Global Youth Tobacco Survey).

The 2002 Survey showed that schoolgoing teenagers were less likely to smoke than they had been in 1999.

This was attributed to a halt in exposure to the advertising, promotion and sponsorship of tobacco products.

The Survey revealed, among other things, that the percentage of:
- teenagers interviewed who had ever smoked (even one or two puffs) dropped from 46,7% in 1999 to 37,6% in 2002
- frequent smokers (who had smoked on at least 20 days in the 30 days preceding the interview) dropped from 10,1% in 1999 to 5,8% in 2002
- those who recalled seeing tobacco adverts dropped from 77,9% (magazines and newspapers) and 85% (billboards) in 1999 to 69,5% and 78% in 2002
- those who had been offered free cigarettes by a tobacco-industry representative was down from 29,7% to 22%.

By the year 2006, the levels of nicotine and tar contents of cigarettes will be reduced even further.

Restrictions on the tar level will be reduced from the current 15 milligrams (mg) to 12 mg, while nicotine will decrease from 1,5 mg to 1,2 mg in all cigarettes sold in South Africa.

South Africa has strongly endorsed, and was one of the first signatories to the Global Framework Convention on Tobacco Control. The Convention is the first global health treaty and was adopted by 192 countries of the World Health Assembly in May 2003.

Alcohol and substance abuse

Foetal Alcohol Syndrome (FAS) is one of South Africa's most common birth defects. It is caused by a mother's consumption of alcohol during pregnancy. Rates in South Africa are the highest recorded anywhere in the world. In the Northern Cape, one in 10 children starting school shows signs of the Syndrome and in the Western Cape, one in 20.

According to a report by the MRC's Alcohol and Drug Abuse Research Group, released in April 2002, alcohol remains the dominant substance of abuse in South Africa. Across the five sites in the South African Community Epidemiology Network on Drug Use, between 46% (Cape Town) and 69% (Mpumalanga) of patients in specialist substance-abuse treatment centres have alcohol as their primary substance of abuse. In Port Elizabeth in 2001, 57% of trauma patients had breath-alcohol concentrations at or above 0,05 grams (g) per 100 millilitres (ml) (the legal limit for driving), compared to 31% in Cape Town and 22% in Durban. Up to 74% of violence-related trauma patients were alcohol-positive in Port Elizabeth, and in Cape Town, up to 45% of persons injured in transport accidents tested positive for alcohol.

Use of cannabis (dagga) and mandrax (methaqualone) alone or in combination (white pipes) continues to be high. The increase in treatment-demand for cocaine addiction which was reported in Cape Town, Durban and Gauteng, has not continued and there has been a levelling off in treatment demand. In Gauteng, however, there has been an increase in the proportion of females reporting cocaine/crack as their primary drug of abuse. Nine per cent of trauma patients in Cape Town tested positive for cocaine in 2001 (up from 3% in 1999/00). An increase in arrests for dealing in cocaine were reported in three of the four sites for which data were available, and large seizures were reported by the South African Police Service's Forensic Science Laboratory in the Western Cape (166 kilograms (kg)).

Over time, there has been a dramatic increase in treatment demand for heroin as the primary drug of abuse in Cape Town and Gauteng. In Cape Town, this is particularly evident among females younger than 20 years of age. Heroin is mainly smoked, but an increasing proportion of patients with heroin as their primary drug of abuse report some injection (36% of patients in Gauteng and 51% of patients in Cape Town).

The abuse of over-the-counter and prescription medicines such as slimming tablets, analgesics (especially products containing codeine), and benzodiazepines (e.g. valium) continues to be an issue across sites, but treatment-demand indicators are stable, except in Mpumalanga where an increase was reported. All sites for which age data are available have shown an increase in treatment-demand by persons younger than 20 years of age.

The Central Drug Authority was established in 2000 and is in the process of operationalising the Drug Master Plan. Key government departments are represented on this body, which reports to Parliament annually. (See chapter 19: *Social development*).

Violence against women

The Department has implemented a series of concrete measures to eliminate violence against women and children.

The Department is raising awareness and promoting intersectoral and interregional co-operation in this area. On 25 November 2003, Government launched the *16 Days of Activism on No Violence Against Women and Children* Campaign.

On 20 March 2003, the Foundation for Human Rights launched a fund for the money raised during the Campaign. The money will be disbursed through the Foundation for Human Rights to NGOs assisting victims and survivors of violence.

The Domestic Violence Act, 1998 (Act 116 of 1998), was enacted in December 1999, and mass campaigns have been held to create community awareness of the Act. Sexual-offence guidelines have been distributed to provinces for implementation.

Training of health providers in victim empowerment and trauma management is ongoing. A national pilot project on secondary-level services for victims of violence and other psychological crises is ongoing in Mpumalanga, KwaZulu-Natal and the Eastern Cape.

Violence prevention

The Department of Health is playing an important role in violence prevention. PHC professionals are being trained in victim empowerment and trauma support and advanced training of healthcare professionals for the management of complicated cases of violence is being carried out in the Secondary-Level Victim Empowerment Centres, established by the Department in some provinces. Violence-prevention programmes in schools are also running in some provinces.

A Crime, Violence and Injury Lead Programme, co-directed by the MRC and University of South Africa's Institute for Social and Health Sciences, has been designed to improve the population's health status, safety, and quality of life, through public health-orientated research aimed at preventing death, disability and suffering arising from crime, violence and unintentional incidents of injury. The Lead Programme's overall goal is to produce research on the extent, causes, consequences and costs of injuries, and on best practices for primary prevention and injury control.

Birth defects

It is estimated that 150 000 children born annually in South Africa are affected by a significant birth defect or genetic disorder.

The Department of Health's four priority conditions are albinism, Down's syndrome, FAS and neural tube defects. Implementation of policy guidelines for the management and prevention of genetic disorders, birth defects and disabilities will reduce morbidity and mortality resulting from genetic disorders and birth defects. This will involve decentralisation of training, expansion of the sentinel sites for birth-defect monitoring, and collaboration with NGOs in creating awareness.

South Africa, through the Birth Defects Surveillance System, is a member of the

International Clearing House for Birth Defects Monitoring Systems. In the long term, this should result in diagnoses being more accurate and the data collected on birth defects more reliable. Links have been made with those sentinel sites reporting on perinatal mortality, as congenital anomalies have been shown to be among the top three causes of perinatal mortality at some sentinel sites.

The Department of Health participates in various campaigns to create awareness, including:
- Albinism Awareness Month (September)
- National Inherited Disorders Day (1 October)
- Down's Syndrome Day (20 October)
- World Haemophilia Day (17 April)
- World TB Day (24 March)
- World Breastfeeding Week (1 – 17 August)
- World No-Tobacco Day (31 May).

Regular meetings are held with NGOs to discuss collaborative issues.

Chronic diseases, disabilities and geriatrics

The Department continues to focus on the development of guidelines for the clinical management of priority chronic diseases, diseases of lifestyle, eye care, cancers, and cataract surgery. Patient education and information, including education on their rights and responsibilities, are also emphasised. Booklets, posters, audiotapes and videotapes with appropriate informative health messages are available at clinics.

The Department promotes the rights of patients as well as the need for them to take responsibility for their own health. This includes a new area to be researched, i.e. therapeutic education, whereby barriers to patient compliance will be identified and addressed.

Healthcare professionals from each province have been trained in the management of asthma, hypertension, diabetes and eye health. This includes training in a health-compliance model to improve patient compliance.

The Department aims to reduce avoidable blindness by increasing the cataract-surgery rate.

Government introduced free health services for people with disabilities in July 2003.

Beneficiaries of the new policy include people with permanent, moderate or severe disabilities, as well as people who have been diagnosed with chronic irreversible psychiatric disabilities.

Frail older people and long-term institutionalised State-subsidised patients also qualify for these free services.

People with temporary disabilities or a chronic illness that does not cause a substantial loss of functional ability, and disabled people who are employed and/or covered by relevant health insurance, are not entitled to these free services.

Beneficiaries receive all in-and-out-patient hospital services free of charge. Specialist medical interventions for the prevention, cure, correction or rehabilitation of a disability are provided, subject to motivation from the treating specialist and approval by a committee appointed by the Minister of Health.

All assistive devices for the prevention of complications, cure or rehabilitation of a disability are provided. These include orthotics and prosthetics, wheelchairs and walking aids, hearing aids, spectacles and intra-ocular lenses. The Department of Health is also responsible for maintaining and replacing these devices.

There is still a backlog in the supply of wheelchairs and hearing aids. The National Department of Health spent about R30 million to ensure that people who were on the waiting list received these devices during 2003/04.

The population of older persons (60 years and older) was estimated to be over three million in 2001. Over 60% were women. The Department continues to develop national policy guidelines on the management and control of priority diseases/conditions of older persons to improve their quality of life and accessibility to healthcare services. These include the development of exercise posters and pamphlets and the development of guidelines that focus specifically on older persons, e.g. National Guidelines on Falls in Older Persons, Guidelines on Active Ageing, National Guidelines on Stroke and TIA (transient ischemic attacks), and National Guidelines on Osteoporosis. The National Strategy on Elder Abuse, together with the National Guidelines on the Management of Physical Abuse of Older Persons, have been implemented in all the provinces. These raise awareness of abuse in all its subtle forms.

Occupational health

The introduction of legislation such as the Occupational Health and Safety Act, 1993 (Act 181 of 1993), and the Mines Health and Safety Act, 1996 (Act 29 of 1996), has done much to focus the attention of employers and employees alike on the prevention of work-related accidents and diseases. The Compensation for Occupational Injuries and Diseases Act, 1993 (Act 30 of 1993), places the onus on medical practitioners who diagnose conditions which they suspect might be a result of workplace exposure, to report these to the employer and relevant authority.

The Medical Bureau for Occupational Diseases has a statutory function under the Occupational Diseases in Mines and Works Act, 1973 (Act 78 of 1973), to monitor former mineworkers and evaluate present miners for possible compensational occupational lung diseases until they either die or are compensated maximally.

Mental health

The promotion of mental health is one of the cornerstones of the health policy of South Africa.

There are 18 State institutions with some 10 000 beds.

Private psychiatric hospitals and clinics cater for patients requiring hospitalisation for less severe psychiatric illnesses. General hospitals have some psychiatric beds. A further 7 000 beds are hired from the private sector for treatment of long-term chronic psychiatric and severely intellectually disabled patients.

In keeping with government policy of promoting care of the severely intellectually disabled within the community, these persons receive care-dependency grants to reimburse their families for out-of-pocket expenses, thus allowing the person to remain with his or her family in the community. These grants are administered by the Department of Social Development. In recent years, the focus of treatment has shifted from medication only, except where necessary, to patient rehabilitation.

A comprehensive psychiatric community service is managed by health authorities countrywide. Where possible, consultations are undertaken by multidisciplinary teams comprising psychiatrists, psychiatric nurse practitioners, psychologists, pharmacists, social workers and occupational therapists.

According to the Mental Healthcare Act, 2002, mental health is to become a health issue like any other. The purpose is to bring community services closer to mentally-ill patients instead of simply placing them in institutions.

The Act focuses on a strong human rights approach to mental health. It also makes the process of certifying a person more complex, and introduces a 72-hour assessment period before a person can be certified. Previous legislation relied on psychiatrists and doctors to make the decision, but the new Act recognises that there are not enough psychiatrists, especially in rural areas. According to the Act, a mental healthcare practitioner may make such a decision. It also introduces a review board, comprising a mental healthcare practitioner, a legal expert and a community representative to examine the certified patient's case. The patient and their family will be able to appeal to the board, and all certified cases will be reviewed at least once a year.

Quarantinable diseases

The Port Health Service is responsible for the prevention of the introduction of quarantinable diseases into the country as determined by the International Health Regulations Act, 1974 (Act 28 of 1974). These services are rendered at sanitary airports (Johannesburg, Cape Town and Durban International Airports) and approved ports.

An aircraft entering South Africa from an epidemic yellow-fever area must make its first landing at a sanitary airport, and passengers travelling from such areas must be in possession of a valid yellow-fever vaccination certificate. Every aircraft or ship on an international voyage must also obtain a pratique from a port health officer upon entering South Africa.

During the Severe Acute Respiratory Syndrome (SARS) outbreak in 2003, the Port Health Service played a key role in creating awareness among travellers arriving from affected countries.

South Africa had one possible case of SARS, a traveller returning from China who showed many clinical signs of SARS, but who died without any laboratory confirmation of this.

Consumer goods

Another function of the Department, in conjunction with municipalities and other authorities, is to prevent, control and reduce possible risks to public health from hazardous substances or harmful products present in foodstuffs, cosmetics, disinfectants and medicines; from the abuse of hazardous substances; or from various forms of pollution.

Food is controlled to safeguard the consumer against any harmful, injurious or adulterated products, or misrepresentation as to their nature, as well as against unhygienic manufacturing practices, premises and equipment.

Nutrition

The Department of Health has instituted various interventions to address micronutrient deficiencies and to enhance households' access to nutritious foods.

During 2002, the Department started providing Vitamin A supplements to all children aged between six and 60 months and all mothers, within six to eight weeks after delivery. These supplements are also provided to pre-school children who suffer from severe undernutrition, persistent diarrhoea, measles and severe eye infection. Iron supplementation and anti-helminth treatment are also provided to anaemic pre-school children as part of the IMCI.

Folic acid supplements are provided to women within the first three months of pregnancy, and all pregnant women receive iron supplements.

Breast milk is a rich source of micronutrients, especially Vitamin A. The Department is taking various actions to promote, support and protect breast-feeding. These include the Baby-Friendly Hospital Initiative, which seeks to create an enabling environment for breast-feeding. By April 2003, there were 59 baby-friendly health facilities where mothers were encouraged and supported with the process of breast-feeding.

The Department is also busy drafting regulations on the marketing of breast-milk substitutes, with the view of curbing the sometimes irresponsible marketing of infant formulae by some baby-food manufacturers.

The Food Fortification Programme was launched in April 2003.

With effect from 7 October 2003, millers are compelled by law to fortify their white and brown-bread flour and maize meal with specific micronutrients.

The regulations on food fortification stipulate mandatory fortification of all maize meal and wheat flour with six vitamins and two minerals, including Vitamin A, thiamine, riboflavin, niacin, folic acid, iron and zinc.

Environmental health practitioners at local government level will be responsible for compliance monitoring and law enforcement. Fines of up to R125 000 can be imposed upon millers who fail to comply.

The Department received a grant of US$2,8 million from the Global Alliance for Improved Nutrition. The money will be used to improve implementation of the Programme, including providing support to small-scale millers to comply with fortification requirements, and training environmental officers to monitor implementation of the Programme

The Food Fortification Programme is a result of a long and intensive process of stakeholder consultation and preparatory studies. The contribution of members of the Fortification Task Group, especially the milling and baking industry, consumer organisations, professional food and nutrition organisations, and various academics, has been invaluable in developing this Programme.

In selecting food vehicles, the Department also considered the organisation and capacity of the industry that should fortify and deliver fortified foods to consumers. An industry situation analysis showed that at least 85% of maize meal and 97% of wheat flour could be fortified centrally. Furthermore, a database of 580 small millers was compiled. These millers were visited to discuss the Programme and to determine their technical and capacity constraints. Extensive stability tests and organoleptic trials on fortified maize meal and bread were also conducted.

The Department has ensured that the fortification levels as indicated in the regulations do not change the taste and colour of food. The levels are consistent with those in other countries.

In formulating the Programme, the Department also consulted consumers to establish their views on fortification. Consumer research conducted in 2002 indicated that 81% of consumers in peri-urban, rural and deep rural areas were positive about fortification.

Provision has been made for the use of a voluntary food-fortification logo and an officially approved claim, *Fortified for Better Health*, to indicate that a particular maize meal or wheat flour is fortified according to the regulations.

This means that fortification levels will provide, per 200 g raw maize meal or wheat flour, at least 25% of the daily requirement of most nutrients for a person 10 years or older.

For instance, fortified maize meal will provide a child of between four and six years with an additional 46% (from the previous 36%) of the daily requirement of Vitamin A, bringing it to 82% of the total daily requirement.

The Primary School Nutrition Programme has proved its worth in delivery over a period of nine years. In 2002, the Cabinet made a series of recommendations to strengthen this Programme. As a result, the budget allocation for the Programme was increased substantially from R592 million to R809 million.

An estimated five million children in 15 000 schools have benefitted from this Programme.

It is within this context that the Integrated Nutrition Programme (INP) aims to ensure optimum nutrition for all South Africans by preventing and managing malnutrition. A co-ordinated and intersectoral approach, focusing on the following areas or broad strategies, is thus fundamental to the success of the INP:
- disease-specific nutrition support, treatment and counselling
- growth monitoring and promotion
- nutrition promotion
- micronutrient malnutrition control
- food-service management
- promotion, protection and support of breast-feeding
- contribution to household-food security.

The INP targets nutritionally vulnerable/at-risk communities, groups and individuals for nutrition interventions, and provides appropriate nutrition education and promotion to all.

South Africa Yearbook 2003/04

Acknowledgements

Allied Health Service Professions Council of South Africa
Department of Health
Estimates of National Expenditure 2003, published by the National Treasury
Health Professions Council of South Africa
Medical Research Council website
National Health Laboratory Service
South African Nursing Council
South African Pharmacy Council
www.gov.za

Suggested reading

Arden, N. *African Spirits Speak: A White Woman's Journey into the Healing Tradition of the Sangoma.* Rochester, Vermont: Destiny Books, 1999.
Baldwin-Ragaven, L., De Gruchy, J. and London, L. *An Ambulance of the Wrong Colour: Health Professionals, Human Rights and Ethics in South Africa.* Cape Town: University of Cape Town Press, 1999.
Barnett, T. and Whiteside, A. *AIDS in the Twenty-First Century. Disease and Globalisation.* Hampshire: Palgrave Macmillan, 2002.
Bayer, R. and Oppenheimer, G.M. *AIDS Doctors: Voices from the Epidemic.* Cape Town: Oxford University Press, 2002.
Booysens, S.W. ed. *Introduction to Health Services Management.* Kenwyn: Juta, 1996.
Campbell, C. *Letting Them Die – Why HIV/AIDS Intervention Programmes Fail.* London: International African Institute and Cape Town: Double Storey Books, 2003
Campbell, S. *Called to Heal: Traditional Healing Meets Modern Medicine in Southern Africa.* Halfway House: Zebra Press, 1998.
Couvadia, H. M. and Benatar, S. eds. *Tuberculosis With Special Reference to Southern Africa.* Cape Town: Oxford University Press, 1992.
Crewe, M. *AIDS in South Africa: The Myth and the Reality.* London: Penguin, 1992.
De Haan, M. *Health of Southern Africa.* 6th ed. Cape Town: Juta, 1988.
De Miranda, J. *The South African Guide to Drugs and Drug Abuse.* Cresta, Randburg: Michael Collins Publications, 1998.
Dennil, K. and others. *Aspects of Primary Health Care.* Halfway House, Gauteng: Southern Book Publishers, 1995.
Dreyer, M. and others. *Fundamental Aspects of Community Nursing.* 2nd ed. Halfway House: International Thomson Publishing, 1997.
Engel, J. *The Complete South African Health Guide.* Halfway House, Gauteng: Southern Book Publishers, 1996.
Evian, C. *Primary AIDS Care: A Practical Guide for Primary Health Care Personnel.* 3rd ed. Johannesburg: Jacana, 2003.
Felhaber, T. ed. *South African Traditional Healers' Primary Health Care Handbook.* Traditional aspects compiled by I. Mayeng. Cape Town: Kagiso, 1997.
Gow, J. and Desmond C. eds. *Impacts and Interventions: the HIV/AIDS Epidemic and the Children of South Africa.* Pietermaritzburg: University of Natal Press, 2002.
Gumede, M.V. *Traditional Healers: A Medical Doctor's Perspective.* Johannesburg: Skotaville, 1990.
Hammond-Tooke, W.D. *Rituals and Medicines: Traditional Healing in South Africa.* Johannesburg: Donker, 1989.
Hattingh, S. and others. *Gerontology: A Community Health Perspective.* Johannesburg: International Thomson Publishing, 1996.
Holland, H. *African Magic: Traditional Ideas that Heal a Continent.* Sandton: Penguin, 2001.
Kibel, M. and Wagstaff, L. eds. *Child Health for All: A Manual for Southern Africa.* Cape Town: Oxford University Press, 1992.
Kok, P. and Pietersen, J. *Health.* Pretoria: Human Sciences Research Council (HSRC), 2000.
Mashaba, T.G. *Rising to the Challenge of Change: A History of Black Nursing in South Africa.* Kenwyn: Juta, 1995.
Mbuya, J. *The AIDS Epidemic in South Africa.* Johannesburg: The Author, 2000.
Mendel, G. *A Broken Landscape: HIV and AIDS in Africa.* Johannesburg: M & G Books, 2002.

Health

Nadasen, S. *Public Health Law in South Africa: An Introduction*. Durban: Butterworths, 2000.
Reddy, S.P. and Meyer-Weitz, A. *Sense and Sensibilities: The Psychosocial and Contextual Determinants of STD-Related behaviour*. Pretoria: Medical Research Council and HSRC, 1999.
South African First Aid Manual: The Authorised Manual of the St John's Ambulance and the South African Red Cross Society. 3rd ed. Cape Town: Struik, 1997.
Van Rensburg, H.C.J. *Health Care in South Africa: Structure and Dynamics*. Pretoria: Academica, 1992.
Van Wyk, B.E. and Gericke, N. *Medicinal Plants of South Africa*. Pretoria: Briza Publications, 1999.
Webb, D. *HIV and AIDS in Africa*. London: Pluto; Cape Town: David Philip, 1997.
Whiteside, A. and Sunter, C. *AIDS: The Challenge for South Africa*. Cape Town: Human & Rousseau, 2000.
Wood, M. *No Turning Back*. London: Michael Wood Memorial Fund, 2001.

Guy Stubbs/Touchline Images

chapter 14
Housing

Access to housing and secure accommodation is an integral part of government's commitment to reduce poverty and improve people's quality of life.

Since the launch of the *White Paper on Housing* in December 1994, housing has undergone fundamental changes. Some 1 985 545 housing subsidies have been approved and 1,5 million housing units constructed, providing more than six million poor people with secure tenure and safe homes.

However, resource constraints and changing demographics now necessitate a more rigorous focus on quality, rather than the former quantity-driven approach. Housing policy and strategy have therefore been adjusted to accommodate this new focus.

The Housing Programme will in future also emphasise pressure relief. It balances urban and rural development, counters housing fraud and facilitates urban renewal, especially in inner cities. Attention will furthermore be paid to monitoring and performance evaluation to assess the elements of the national housing strategy. Initially, housing policy placed too much emphasis on ownership, but it has been recognised that the lack of a co-ordinated rental housing policy is a shortcoming.

◀ Since 1994, some 1 985 545 housing subsidies have been approved and 1,5 million housing units constructed, providing more than six million poor people with secure tenure and safe housing.

The Human Settlement Redevelopment Programme impacts on the lives of people and communities in a physical, social, economic and environmental context. The Programme will fill the gap in the development needs of dysfunctional and disadvantaged communities, which cannot be addressed through existing, alternative government programmes.

Recognising the need to align national, provincial and local budgets and planning processes, and budget co-ordination across national departments, this Programme of pilot projects was initiated in 1999. Its aim is to improve the quality of the urban environment and to address the legacy of dysfunctional urban structures, frameworks and imbalances. To achieve this, the Department of Housing introduced a system of multi-year housing development plans to be applied coherently across the three spheres of government. These plans are to be updated annually on a rolling basis. They have to take into account current housing needs and backlogs, as well as available resources, and on that basis, prioritise the needs of the various national housing programmes.

The need was identified for a programme to assist municipalities to initiate Human Settlement Redevelopment Projects, which will focus on correcting imbalances and dysfunctionalities of the human settlement patterns by:
- addressing the nature and underlying reasons for dysfunctionality

- providing a source of funding to correct such dysfunctionality and acting as catalyst to gear other sources
- co-ordinating sources of development funding to promote holistic and integrated development
- adding value to projects that can be funded through other processes and programmes.

The following broad categories of projects are considered under the Programme:
- Infrastructure-upgrading initiatives to facilitate the redevelopment of depressed areas or to improve access to employment and business opportunities.
- Land-intervention initiatives to counter spatial distortion and enhance the integration of human settlement.
- Replanning and redevelopment of existing human settlements, which could entail slum clearance, acquisition of property, planning of redevelopment initiatives and resettlement of people.
- Consolidation initiatives where previous housing/development initiatives resulted in unsafe, inappropriate or substandard development in need of enhancement.
- Provision of essential community facilities and amenities.
- Special development-needs projects to satisfy Presidential requests that may entail cross-functional co-operation and co-ordination and require extraordinary solutions outside of approved government programmes. Lately, the focus of these programmes has, to a large extent, fallen on the Urban Renewal Strategy and the Integrated Sustainable Rural Development Programme (ISRDP).

There has been a steady growth in transfers to the Programme, from R1 million in 1999/00 to an expected R122,5 million in 2005/06.

The Minister of Housing, Ms Brigitte Mabandla, announced during her 2003/04 Budget vote speech that the Department would continue its well-established approach of giving priority to the reduction of poverty and vulnerability, and make a meaningful contribution to economic growth, especially to the empowerment of the historically marginalised groups. The Department has pledged to continue to respond to the challenges facing beneficiaries with disabilities and those living with and affected by HIV/AIDS, as well as working towards the empowerment of emerging developers and contractors. It aims to bring as many women contractors and black professionals as possible into the housing sector.

The Department also aims to extend and strengthen its contribution to the Growth and Development Strategy by accelerating its drive towards the development of small, micro and medium enterprises in this industry. Since housing has the potential to create thousands of jobs and sustainable communities, the Department focuses on the following areas:
- Promoting marginalised women in construction by setting aside at least 10% of the provincial expenditure for housing projects to be handled by women developers or contractors.
- Incorporating integrated land development that encourages all national housing programmes to promote development with all the necessary infrastructure in order to develop sustainable communities.
- People-centred housing development, which focuses on the promotion of the People's Housing Process (PHP), whereby communities actively participate in the provision of their own housing.
- Rural housing that effectively deals with the housing backlog outside of the cities, 31% of which involves rural households.
- Rental housing, which is currently provided through the institutional housing subsidy instrument and has been identified as a national expenditure priority to provide beneficiaries with an alternative tenure option.
- Upgrading informal settlements, whereby housing projects are approved to target the elimination of specific informal settlements.
- Savings-linked subsidies to encourage people to save towards their housing developments.

- Housing subsidies for people with disabilities.
- Emergency housing programmes through which provincial Housing Departments can make provision for unforeseen emergency housing needs. The Department has resolved to set aside 0,5% to 0,75% of provincial annual allocations for this purpose.

Legislation and policy

Rental Housing Act, 1999 (Act 50 of 1999)

The Rental Housing Act, 1999 ensures that more houses are provided for rental purposes and regulates the behaviour of unscrupulous landlords so that tenants do not pay exorbitant rents.

It also provides for a special tribunal to mediate between landlords and tenants in the event of disputes. It outlaws the eviction of long-standing tenants from their homes without mediation.

The Act came into effect on 1 August 2000. Three Rental Housing Tribunals have been set up in Gauteng, Western Cape and North West.

Other provinces are in the process of establishing similar Tribunals. The Act gives the Tribunals the power to make rulings in line with those of a Magistrate's Court.

Home Loan and Mortgage Disclosure Act, 2000 (Act 63 of 2000)

The Home Loan and Mortgage Disclosure Act, 2000 provides for the establishment of the Office of Disclosure and the monitoring of financial institutions serving the housing-credit needs of communities. It requires financial institutions to disclose information, and identifies discriminatory lending patterns. The Act is aimed at promoting equity and fairness in lending and disclosure by financial institutions, and will be implemented as soon as the Regulations of the Act have been promulgated.

The Act aims to encourage banks and financial institutions to grant home loans to all its clients. It compels banks and financial institutions to disclose annual financial statements so that their lending practices in respect of home loans can be monitored.

Housing Consumer Protection Measures Act, 1998 (Act 95 of 1998)

In terms of the Housing Consumer Protection Measures Act, 1998, residential builders have to register with the National Home-Builders Registration Council (NHBRC) and are obliged to enrol all new houses under the NHBRC's Defect Warranty Scheme. The first phase of the Act came into effect on 4 June 1999, making the NHBRC a statutory body.

The aim of the Act is to protect homeowners from inferior workmanship. Builders are responsible for design and material defects for three months, roof leaks for a year, and any structural failures of houses for five years. NHBRC inspectors may assess workmanship during and after the building process.

Banks are compelled by law to insist on home-builder registration and enrolment prior to granting a mortgage loan or finance.

All new government-subsidised housing units constructed as part of approved projects have enjoyed protection against shoddy workmanship by housing contractors since April 2002. Through the Housing Consumer Protection Measures Act, 1998, properties that were built with funding from the Government's housing subsidy grant only, now enjoy protection against structural defects and must comply with minimum technical norms and standards.

Previously, this was the responsibility of the poor, because their properties did not qualify for such protection. The NHBRC ensures that registered builders deliver within the minimum housing standards.

Housing Amendment Act, 2001 (Act 4 of 2001)

The Housing Amendment Act, 2001 removes some of the inefficiencies in the institutional arrangements covered in the Housing Act, 1997 (Act 107 of 1997). The Amendment Act, 2001 abolished Provincial Housing Development Boards, transferring their powers, duties, rights and obligations to the provincial members of executive councils responsible for housing. The Act empowers the Minister of Housing to determine a procurement policy on housing development and puts regulatory measures in place to restrict the sale or alienation of State-subsidised housing.

Draft Social Housing Bill

The Department developed a Social Housing Policy discussion document in 2001, as a basis for the development of a Social Housing Policy document and Bill for the sector.

The Social Housing Policy was finalised in 2003 and implementation was planned for 1 April 2004. This initiative is closely linked to government's Medium Density Housing Programme, which will also be implemented with effect from 1 April 2004.

The Programme will cater for the needs of single persons with special housing needs. Other categories of persons currently excluded from accessing government's housing-assistance programmes will also benefit.

The Social Housing Policy aims to establish a sustainable social housing process and provides for the establishment of a Social Housing Corporation to regulate and oversee the social housing development and maintenance process.

The discussion document focuses on creating an enabling environment for the growth and development of the social housing sector in South Africa. It provides a definition and grounding principles for the sector and introduces a revised funding and regulating framework.

The Social Housing Bill will enable the establishment of a Social Housing Accreditation Board for the accreditation and ongoing monitoring of social housing institutions. It will ensure that robust institutions are established to develop and manage housing stock. The Board should provide confidence for financial institutions interested in investing in the sector.

Community Reinvestment (Housing) Bill

The Community Reinvestment Bill was expected to be finalised by the end of 2003. The legislation is a sequel to the Home Loan and Mortgage Disclosure Act, 2000 and will provide for mechanisms to ensure that more home loans are allocated to low- and medium-income borrowers. However, the Bill will not compel housing finance institutions to take risks in meeting their community-reinvestment obligations.

Public-Sector Hostel Redevelopment Programme

The Public-Sector Hostel Redevelopment Programme Policy provides for:
- the funding of redevelopment initiatives to create humane living conditions in hostels
- hostel inhabitants to be involved in redevelopment initiatives and the ongoing administration of the redeveloped complexes
- the upgrading of dilapidated complexes and/or the redevelopment of hostels into family units or a combination of single sex units and family accommodation on a rental and/or ownership basis.

During a media briefing in March 2002, then Minister of Housing, Ms Sankie Mthembi-Mahanyele, said that the Hostel Redevelopment Policy was being reviewed. The fundamental objective of the policy review process is to move away from the so-called redevelopment of hostels to an approach where sustainable rental housing stock will be created and maintained.

Pilot projects totalling R12 million were conducted in Gauteng, KwaZulu-Natal, the Western Cape and the Free State.

A special task team was established, comprising technical and policy experts from the nine provincial Housing Departments, key municipalities that own public-sector hostels, and the national Department of Housing. The fundamental policy changes already identified by the task team comprise the following:
- The Public-Sector Hostel Redevelopment Policy should be converted into a policy framework for the creation of sustainable rental housing stock. This stock should augment government's new emphasis on the provision of medium-density housing stock and rental housing options such as those to be provided within the Presidential Job Summit initiative.
- As a substitute for the current funding limit, a flexible minimum standard, linked to standard finishing norms and costing parameters, should be introduced.

The revision process has been concluded. The replacement of the funding limit is being finalised.

By May 2002, the Government had spent R775 million on the upgrading of hostels.

Funding

For 2002/03, the Department received a total amount of R3 739 624 billion to finance national and provincial housing programmes.

The allocation is made annually on the basis of a formula that takes into account the backlog in each province, the number of households in various income categories of the subsidy scheme, the ratio between urban and rural housing, and the performance of the relevant provincial government.

The PHP recognises the efforts and initiatives of those who prefer to build their own houses and are prepared to commit their resources, skills and energies to this task. It provides technical, financial and other support to these people. Funding is administered through the provincial Housing Departments, while the People's Housing Partnership Trust (PHPT) helps build the capacity to speed up delivery.

Capacity-building

One of the major constraints in housing delivery is the lack of capacity, which entails an efficient workforce and the installation of appropriate technology, equipment and systems for monitoring, evaluation and reporting purposes.

The Department continues to provide support and assist provinces to ensure effective and efficient implementation of the National Housing Programme. The strategy and guidelines for housing capacity-building, as well as guidelines for provincial housing-capacity business plans were developed during 2003.

As part of the Department's endeavour to keep abreast with developments and changes in respect of capacity-building for improved service delivery, further workshops were conducted on the National Housing System, policies, legislation and programmes.

National Housing Code workshops were held at both national and provincial level, aimed at capacitating internal and provincial officials, including municipal officials and councillors, and increasing knowledge on housing policies, programmes and legislation.

National Housing Capacity-Building and Training Programme

The Programme has undergone major transformation and improvement since its inception in 1998. By June 2003, a total of 5 590 participants had been trained. Initially, the University of the Witwatersrand (Wits) School of Public Management and Development played a central role as the only service-provider. In 1999, the Programme was decentralised and courses were offered in all nine provinces by tertiary institutions based in each province, through Wits. These changes were the result of continuous monitoring and reviews conducted during the implementation of the course, as well as input from the Capacity-Building Task Team established to oversee the effective and efficient implementation of the Programme.

Courses are designed to cater for the capacity needs of all officials employed in the national, provincial and local governments, including councillors. Out of the 1 287 participants trained in 2002, 48% came from municipalities, which indicated a gradual improvement compared with 45% in 2001.

There has been a gradual increase in the number of women participating in these courses. In 2002, the percentage of women participants was 50%.

Formal education and training in housing

During 2001, an investigation was conducted in all the provinces to obtain the views of housing practitioners regarding the professionalism of the housing sector. The Cabinet approved the establishment of a Professional Housing Institute on 29 May 2002.

In line with the Skills Development Act, 1998 (Act 97 of 1998), the Department facilitated and co-ordinated the establishment of the Housing Standard Generation Body (SGB). The Housing SGB was expected to register with the South African Qualifications Authority in 2003.

The Housing SGB commits itself to the generation of standards and qualifications to ensure quality education and training programmes in the sector.

Through this process, the needs of housing practitioners and consumers will be accommodated and lifelong learning encouraged.

Work with regard to SGB activities and processes has commenced. The activities have been divided into two subgroups, one focusing on housing consumer education and the other on professional qualifications.

Consumer education

The Housing Consumer Education Task Team was established in 2002. Its primary function is to:
- develop the National Housing Consumer Education Framework
- collect and present training material for the purpose of developing the Framework
- facilitate and promote the acceptance of the Framework by stakeholders
- assist in investigating viable funding mechanisms for housing education.

The Framework has been developed and discussed with various stakeholders. It will serve as a guideline for the development and implementation of the Housing Consumer Education and Training Programme. The envisaged Training Programme will cover training modules in line with the Framework, a Train the Trainer Programme, and the development and implementation of four pilot projects targeting 1 000 units.

Housing Scholarship Programme

The Department launched the Scholarship Programme in 2002, targeting matriculants who wish to pursue a career in housing. Ten students were awarded scholarships for the 2003 academic year. Owing to limited resources, the Department approached the Construction Education and Training Authority (CETA) for funding assistance. The Department, in conjunction with CETA, intends to embark on an internship programme to provide students with the opportunity and scope to gain practical experience and facilitate their learning.

Housing subsidies

Individual ownership subsidies are allocated to help beneficiaries acquire ownership of fixed residential property (housing opportunities) for the first time.

New housing-subsidy programmes are being developed and certain existing programmes have been enhanced, including rental and social-housing subsidies. The

Housing

housing-subsidy programmes, including project-linked subsidies, are also being revised to introduce a procurement prescript compliant regime, consolidation subsidies, PHP, rural subsidies and institutional subsidies. The Department also started the phasing-out of subsidy subprogrammes to address the subsidies of the previous dispensation.

With effect from April 2003, the Department increased housing subsidies by between 11,4% and 14,8% to counter the effects of inflation. The subsidy for beneficiaries earning from zero to R1 500 rose by R2 800, from R20 300 to R23 100.

Beneficiaries earning between R1 501 and R2 500 received a R1 500-subsidy increase, from R12 700 to R14 200. The subsidy for beneficiaries earning between R2 501 and R3 500 rose from R7 000 to R7 800.

Subsidies for the indigent, including the aged, people with disabilities and the health-stricken, were increased from R22 800 to R25 580.

The consolidation subsidy for beneficiaries earning R1 500 was increased from R10 900 to R12 521, and for indigents from R13 400 to R15 000.

The Department has designed the housing scheme to effectively cater for people with disabilities. People with visual impairment and other disabilities will get an additional amount to the normal subsidy to make their homes more accessible and comfortable, according to their physical needs. By May 2003, the Department was exploring mechanisms to include an additional subsidy to cater for people with HIV/AIDS, in line with government's Home-Based Care Policy.

It will also assist in providing shelter for areas where home-based care might not be available, in conjunction with the Department of Social Development.

Financial support to poor communities is provided as part of the Consolidated Municipal Infrastructure Programme.

The Department has also developed the Emergency Housing Policy to deal with emergency housing needs caused by natural and other disasters, as well as people living under stressful conditions, on flood-plains and in adverse geotechnical conditions.

Various events, such as severe floods in 2000 and 2001, led to the development of the Policy.

The Department established a dedicated fund through which to render financial assistance in the form of grants to those affected, from 2004. The purpose of the proposed programme is to provide assistance in the form of secure access to land, basic engineering services and or/shelter in a wide range of situations of emergency housing needs, through the allocation of grants to municipalities instead of housing subsidies to individuals.

Since 1 April 2002, all housing-subsidy beneficiaries are required to contribute either in kind or financially. The National Savings Programme for Housing is administered by the National Urban Reconstruction and Housing Agency (NURCHA) and seeks to assist beneficiaries to accumulate the financial contribution required.

Contribution in kind entails participation in PHP projects and therefore the building of their own houses.

Qualifying subsidy beneficiaries who fall within the R0 to R1 500 income category and

---

In January 2003, the National Urban Reconstruction and Housing Agency (NURCHA) signed a funding agreement with Rand Merchant Bank, the Overseas Private Investment Corporation (OPIC) and the Open Society Institute of New York (OSI).

The agreement was endorsed by then Minister of Housing, Ms Sankie Mthembi-Mahanyele, and the United States Trade Representative, Mr Robert Zoellik.

OPIC and OSI have jointly created a $20-million guarantee that will release R200 million in bridging finance loans for small housing contractors and developers. These loan funds, administered by NURCHA, should support the construction of 100 000 houses over the next five years.

who will not participate in the PHP, are required to make a financial contribution of R2 479, to enable the final approval of a housing-subsidy application. The contribution assists with improving or increasing the size and value of the house, and encourages beneficiaries to value their homes and maintain them in a habitable condition.

Due to the exemption of the PHP projects from the NHBRC warranty cover, beneficiaries who opt to construct or manage the construction of their own homes are not required to contribute R2 479. Beneficiaries of the PHP, in the income category R0 to R1 500 per month, qualify for a subsidy of R23 100.

Where a beneficiary of special assistance for the aged, disabled and the indigent qualifies for a consolidation subsidy, the subsidy amounts to R15 000. If the individual qualifies for a consolidation subsidy, but does not fall into one of the abovementioned categories, he or she is obliged to make the required contribution of R2 479. However, consolidation-subsidy beneficiaries who participate in the PHP are not obliged to make the financial contribution.

The immediate outcome of the success of the approach of people constructing their own homes has been the increase in the number of PHP projects or self-building, and the emergence of more, bigger and better structures.

In an effort to enhance the capacity of the programme, the Department has sought additional assistance from 38 Cuban architects and designers who were deployed in the provinces as part of supporting the increased demand for this type of housing delivery. Cuba's approach to housing contruction is similar to that of South Africa.

Project-linked subsidies
Project-linked subsidies give individuals the opportunity to own houses in approved projects. From the introduction of project-linked subsidies until March 2002, 2 510 housing projects, representing 1 247 974 housing opportunities, were approved. Accordingly, the same number of project-linked subsidies has been reserved.

Individual subsidies
The individual subsidy affords people access to housing subsidies to acquire ownership of an existing property or a property in a project not approved as part of a project-linked subsidy project. A person may also buy a serviced site linked to a house-building contract. The individual subsidy can be used in two different ways:
- on a non-credit basis, where only the subsidy amount is used to acquire a property
- on a credit-linked basis, where a home loan is also obtained from a mortgage or non-traditional lender to buy a property.

Consolidation subsidies
Through the consolidation subsidy, there were people who received housing assistance from government in the form of ownership of serviced sites, including serviced sites under the auspices of the Independent Development Trust.

Those beneficiaries who received assistance may apply for a further benefit from government to improve their housing circumstances. The consolidation subsidy is granted for the provision or upgrading of a top structure on such a site.

As of April 2003, the subsidy category is R12 521 for a monthly income up to R1 500. Such beneficiaries must also contribute either in kind or financially.

Institutional subsidies
Subsidies are available to institutions creating affordable housing stock to allow eligible people to live in subsidised residential properties with secure tenure. The properties will often be rented, but tenure forms based on share blocks, deeds of sale or full ownership are not excluded.

Housing

In an approved project, an institution is entitled to receive R20 300 for each residential property that will be occupied by qualifying beneficiaries. Cost recovery is required with respect to the management and administration of projects that receive institutional housing-subsidy support.

Relocation assistance
Government's initiatives to stabilise the housing environment resulted in the development of a relocation-assistance mechanism. It provides an alternative to defaulting borrowers who were three months in arrears on 31 August 1997, and where the rehabilitation of their mortgage loans was not affordable.

The relocation instrument provides for the conclusion of a rental arrangement on a monthly basis to stay on the relevant property, pending relocation to an affordable property. The Government provides assistance in the form of a Relocation Assistance Grant, equal to the subsidy for which a person would normally qualify, while banks provide a mortgage loan that the individual can afford. The process has been commonly termed 'rightsizing'.

By March 2002, relocation assistance had been approved to enable 2 870 beneficiaries to acquire affordable housing.

A shortage of alternative housing is, however, delaying progress. In an effort to alleviate this problem, the company managing the initiative, Servcon Housing Solutions (Pty) Ltd, was given the opportunity to establish a housing-construction entity. The construction company will focus on the building of houses to accommodate beneficiaries who wish to relocate to affordable houses.

Discount Benefit Scheme
The Discount Benefit Scheme promotes home-ownership among tenants of State-financed rental stock, including formal deed-of-sale housing and serviced sites.

In terms of the Scheme, tenants receive a maximum discount of up to R7 500 on the selling price or outstanding loan balance of a property. Often the discount equals the selling price of the property, which is then transferred free of charge to the tenant. Some one million households qualify for assistance under the Discount Benefit Scheme. By March 2002, a total of 396 546 beneficiaries had received their title deeds through the Scheme.

Housing institutions

National Home-Builders Registration Council
The NHBRC was established in terms of the Housing Consumer Protection Measures Act, 1998. The Council protects the interests of consumers and regulates the home-building industry.

Before the commencement of the Act, the National Home-Builders Regulation Council was established as a Section 21 company. Its main objective was to promote the common interests of persons occupied in the business or profession of home-building, through the regulation of the home-building industry.

In August 1995, the NHBRC (Pty) Ltd also established the National Home-Builders Registration Council Fund (Pty) Ltd. The main objective of this company was to establish an indemnity fund to promote the interests of contactors, by making funds available through the NHBRC on an *ex gratia* basis to finance the rectification of defects in housing units in circumstances where contractors were either unable or not liable to do so.

On 26 March 2001, a statutory council was established in accordance with the provisions of the Housing Consumer Protection Measures Act, 1998. The two former Section 21 companies were consequently dissolved and all their assets and liabilities were transferred to the statutory council.

By the end of March 2003, the NHBRC had registered 6 845 home-builders. Approximately 58% of these were renewals. The actual increase in respect of new entrants into the home-building industry for the 2003 financial year was about 42% of the total number of registered home-builders. By the end of March 2003, there was an increase of 21% in registered home-builders.

Despite the increases in interest rates in 2002, the NHBRC recorded a 17% increase in the enrolment of new homes. The total number of enrolments by the end of 2002 was 41 580. The main driver of the increase in enrolling new homes has been public awareness. More and more members of the public want to purchase homes which are enrolled with the NHBRC.

The NHBRC's major source of revenue is the enrolment of new homes. Almost 83,8% of its income comes from enrolled homes, followed by 13% generated from interest on investments. Registration of home-builders constitutes 2,99% of its total revenue. The remaining balance of about 0,13% is gene-rated from document sales and a grant from the national Department of Housing to cover administrative costs relating to the entry of the NHBRC Warranty Scheme into the housing-subsidy sector.

National Housing Finance Corporation (NHFC)

The NHFC was established as a result of a Cabinet decision in May 1996, as envisaged in the *White Paper on Housing*, to search for new and better ways to mobilise finance for housing from sources outside the State, in partnership with the broadest range of organisations.

The mission of the NHFC is to ensure:
- Development and appropriate funding of institutions providing affordable housing finance at retail level. Such finance is aimed at the lowest possible income levels able to afford credit on a sustainable and commercial basis.
- Development and appropriate funding of institutions offering a variety of tenure options for residential purposes, in the under- and unserviced segments of the housing market.
- Sustained and growing mobilisation of savings in the housing process, through appropriate intermediaries.

The NHFC Business Plan states that it aims to create housing opportunities for low- and moderate-income families by:
- funding or underwriting the funding of intermediaries and institutions to promote broader access to housing
- building adequate and sustainable capacity within the organisations it funds
- partnering organisations and institutions to deliver innovative housing-finance solutions.

Between May 1996 and March 2003, the NHFC approved facilities totalling more than R1,471 million, and disbursed R1,152 million.

Alternative tenure has been involved in the establishment of 28 institutions since the establishment of the Housing Institutions Development Fund in 1998. Economic pressures, particularly in 2002/03, resulted in a number of these institutions showing financial strain and defaulting on the repayment of loans advanced by the NHFC. A turnaround strategy for these clients has been developed.

The Home Ownership Division of the NHFC offers 'on-balance sheet' and 'off-balance sheet' lending, and is working towards developing a more appropriate pricing structure for its products, particularly on its loan buy-in programme.

Many clients of the Incremental Housing Division were affected by the turmoil in the micro-finance industry, particularly with the failure of Unibank and Saambou. This resulted in a number of clients requesting the restructuring of loans. An exercise is being conducted into the feasibility of consolidating three of the clients into a larger, more viable entity.

In the last quarter of 2002, the Division received a number of applications from micro-lenders who wanted to expand into housing lending, with assistance from the NHFC. The Division expects to meet its budget of providing 20 000 loans in 2004.

Housing

The Job Summit Housing Project continues with the first houses being built in Witbank, Mpumalanga. There has, however, been a decision by the stakeholders to appoint transaction advisors to explore the best funding option for the project. A decision in this regard is expected within the first quarter of 2004.

At the Presidential Job Summit held in October 1998, government, the private sector and labour resolved that there was a need for a National Presidential Lead Project on Rental Housing at sufficient scale to pilot affordable mass housing delivery and alternative forms of tenure, especially rental housing. The Presidential Pilot Project on Rental Housing was conceived to provide 50 000 rental units over multiple financial years.

The NHFC was appointed as management agent for the programme. An amount of R225 million in poverty-relief funding has been transferred to the NHFC for the purpose of the partial funding of phases one to three of the project.

By mid-2003, three projects selected for the first phase of the Presidential Pilot Project on Rental Housing were in various stages of implementation. Two of the three, Johannesburg (notably the Kliptown subproject) and Witbank (eMalahleni) had completed their show units. These units will serve the dual purpose of physically launching the Presidential Pilot Project on Rental Housing, and further enhancing end-user processes, such as unit selection based on individual affordability levels.

The first pilot project for Gauteng was launched by President Thabo Mbeki in Fordsburg in 2002.

In Durban, the Roosfontein subproject is being prioritised and it is anticipated that the remaining units, to be constructed as part of the first phase in KwaZulu-Natal, will target inner city infill and refurbishment projects.

National Urban Reconstruction and Housing Agency (NURCHA)

NURCHA was formed as a partnership between the South African Government and the Open Society Institute (OSI) of New York, United States of America (USA), in May 1995 to arrange finance for housing. It is a tax-exempt, non-profit-making company.

By March 2003, NURCHA had arranged financing for 550 projects and the completion of 124 000 houses.

Through its savings programme, 40 000 people had been encouraged to open savings accounts and 12 400 people had become regular savers, accumulating funds towards their housing needs.

Operational expenses are funded by an initial allocation from government and a grant from the OSI. NURCHA's mission is to expedite housing delivery in the short-to-medium term for low-income households.

Programmes

The NURCHA uses a variety of interventions to arrange and package finance for those delivering housing to low-income families:
- Bridging-finance guarantees: NURCHA offers guarantees to financial institutions, making bridging-finance loans available for housing or related infrastructure.
- Bridging-finance loans: The NURCHA offers bridging-finance loans to support the construction of credit-linked housing in the R30 000 to R150 000 price range.
- Loans through financial intermediaries: In order to assist contractors and developers who are unable to access bridging finance from a bank, NURCHA has entered into agreements with financial institutions and intermediaries that have specifically tailored products to ensure the appropriate flow of finance to projects. Applicants requiring this form of funding are normally smaller contractors who also require financial-management support.
- Bridging finance for rental housing: NURCHA provides bridging finance for the construction or upgrading of rental stock in the affordable housing market sector.

- National Savings Scheme: The Scheme has been recognised by the Ministry of Housing as a vehicle for the administration of new home-owners' own contribution to subsidy-linked projects. The Scheme is run in collaboration with deposit-taking institutions under agreement with NURCHA, and is geared to be of assistance and support to developers, contractors, municipalities and other role-players engaged in the delivery of low-income housing.

Servcon Housing Solutions

Servcon was established as a joint venture between the Department of Housing (representing government) and the Council of South African Banks (COSAB) in 1994.

Servcon was mandated to provide exclusive management services in respect of the designated portfolio, comprising 33 306 properties in possession (PIPs) and non-performing loans (NPLs) with a value of R1,277 billion, for a period of eight years from 1 April 1998 to 31 March 2006.

The mission of Servcon is to normalise the lending process by managing NPLs and PIPs in areas where the normal legal process has broken down, in terms of the normalisation programme agreed to by the Department and COSAB.

Servcon has four programmes, namely:
- the repurchase/rescheduling programme that assists those who can afford an existing property by providing a mechanism to reassess the property and arrive at a reasonable buy-back or new-debt amount
- the subsidised rental programme that gives the occupant time to adjust to paying again after a period of non-payment
- rightsizing, which is designed for the owner/ex-owner who cannot afford a property or the rental option, by offering assistance to procure and finance in whole or in part, an alternative affordable house
- special assistance, which is provided to the aged and disabled, such as providing relocation assistance *in situ*, i.e. without having to relocate.

Servcon receives funding from the Department on a quarterly basis. The funding goes towards 50% of the operating costs of Servcon, and 50% of interest on the value of the undischarged guarantee to the banks.

By 31 March 2003, Servcon had managed to exceed the financial mandate by successfully disposing of 54,2% (target 52,5%) of properties. The number of properties has declined from 33 322 to 19 398 with a value of R714 million.

Banks are reimbursed for their costs by the Department on a quarterly basis and 50% of

Servcon's progress up to 31 March 2003

Province	No. of properties	Total properties SDO*	%	Rightsizing signed	Other leases	Total agreements signed
Eastern Cape	1 641	936	57,0	488	147	705
Free State	1 879	480	25,5	180	152	486
Gauteng	22 265	12 038	54,1	4 117	3 240	13 820
KwaZulu-Natal	536	319	59,5	92	51	260
Mpumalanga	1 523	1 111	72,9	435	150	761
North West	1 389	652	46,9	546	182	834
Northern Cape	51	41	80,4	0	3	7
Limpopo	97	79	81,4	3	4	15
Western Cape	3 925	1 768	45,0	530	717	2 127
National total	**33 306**	**17 424**	**52,3**	**6 391**	**4 646**	**19 164**

* Satisfactorily disposed of

interest on the value of the undischarged guarantee to the banks.

Thubelisha Homes

Thubelisha Homes is a Section 21 company established in 1998 by the Department of Housing and Servcon. It commenced operations in 1999.

Thubelisha Homes' mandate is to procure or develop housing stock appropriate for rightsizing purposes.

To achieve this, Thubelisha Homes has to:
- determine the number, nature and location of the required housing stock
- secure funding to finance rightsizing housing stock
- procure or develop and finance relevant rightsizing stock
- evaluate the clients for 'rightsizing' stock and grant credit to qualifying clients
- sell houses to approved 'rightsizing' clients under cost-effective and appropriate terms
- communicate its role effectively to key stakeholders on an ongoing basis and obtain their support for the programmes.

Rightsizing is a process initiated by the Record of Understanding between certain banks and the Government, whereby occupants of bank-owned PIPs or NPLs are assisted to relocate to more affordable homes.

These clients are permitted to occupy their existing homes temporarily while paying a pre-determined and affordable rental to Servcon. Relocation assistance equivalent to the capital subsidy is available to Thubelisha via the provincial Housing Departments, to procure new homes for the clients.

Thubelisha was initially capitalised with a R50-million grant from government to assist with bridging finance and working capital. A division of the First Rand Group, which provides a treasury function for Thubelisha, manages this fund.

In addition to ensuring the effective implementation of the rightsizing programme, Thubelisha's other core strategic objectives are to:

- increase the utilisation of female contractors on their projects
- integrate the aged and clients with disabilities from the municipal waiting lists into their projects
- facilitate the delivery of houses on their projects through a managed PHP
- implement an accredited emerging-contractor development programme

By May 2003, Thubelisha had delivered over 4 500 houses in six provinces to qualifying families, with another 10 000 planned over the next three years.

Future operations will include houses being delivered through the PHP as well as an accredited Contractor Development Programme.

Social Housing Foundation (SHF)

The SHF was established as a Section 21 company by the Department of Housing in 1997. It is mandated by the Department to develop and build capacity for social housing institutions and to develop a policy framework for the sector.

The strategic objectives of the organisation, based on its mandate, mission and vision, are to:
- provide social-housing-sector strategic information
- mobilise resources for the social housing sector
- facilitate the capacitation of sectoral participants
- promote the social housing sector
- facilitate sectoral stakeholder alignment
- achieve SHF business service excellence.

The SHF and the social housing sector have shown significant growth and development in recent years. By mid-2003, 59 social housing institutions had been established throughout South Africa and 33 500 housing units provided.

The international experience in social housing is extensive, spanning several decades. Other countries have therefore been keen to include a component on social housing as part of their development-assistance packages to the South African Government.

The most significant agreement relating to social housing is that between the European Commission (EC) and the South African Government.

The EC has pledged 20 million Euros (about R200 million) for social housing over the next five years.

The EC programme has been strengthened with a considerable amount of work conducted around building the internal staff capacity, systems, procedures and manuals of the SHF. Three social housing institutions were successful in applying for grant funding for capacity-building and development, and plans for a number of additional institutions are in the pipeline.

The SHF's relationship with the US Agency for International Development (USAID) finally came to an end on 31 March 2003.

Through this programme, grant funding was made available to 19 emerging social housing institutions, a number of best practice workshops were held, several publications were produced, and training facilitated for tenants, management, boards and other role-players within the greater social housing sector. A total of R3,78 million was received from USAID for these initiatives.

During 2002, the SHF signed a new agreement with the Royal Norwegian Embassy which undertook to provide 9 million krone over a three-year period for the furthering of co-operative housing in South Africa. It is envisaged that co-operative housing institutions will be established through this programme.

The Technical Assistance Programme with the Dutch Ministry of Housing, which started in the 2001/02 financial year, continues with a technical advisor completing his contract in Pietermaritzburg, KwaZulu-Natal. Negotiations are under way for another advisor to be placed in another institution in 2004.

The following was achieved through the SHF's own efforts and assistance from its donors:
- Research into and production of a handbook on HIV/AIDS in the social housing environment.
- Contributions to the social housing policy at national level, which were expected to enable legislation during 2004.
- Further research into projects such as tenure options, communal living and needs assessment. Further research into topics relevant to the sector continued in the 2003/04 financial year.
- Skills development and a number of social-housing-related training courses being conducted for provinces, local government and social housing institutions.
- The development of the Job Summit Division within the SHF and its work to promote accredited housing institutions. These are pilot projects that will be rolled out into the social housing sector as a whole.
- Facilitation of the process for the establishment of a national social housing federation.
- Hosting a National Housing Summit on tenure options.

South African Housing Fund

The South African Housing Fund aims to provide adequate funds to enable provincial governments to establish and maintain habitable, stable and sustainable residential environments.

This includes the provision of:
- permanent residential structures with secure tenure and privacy, and which provide adequate protection against the elements
- potable water, adequate sanitation facilities and domestic electricity supply.

Housing funds for national housing programmes are budgeted for and appropriated in the South African Housing Fund Programme. Since 2000/01, the funds have been allocated through the conditional-grant mechanism to the nine provinces, in accordance with the provisions of the Housing Act, 1997. Housing funds are reflected in the revenue funds and expenditure appropriations of provinces, enhancing provincial accountability. The allocation to the provinces is calculated according to a formula based on equity, taking into account the housing backlog in, and income profile of, each province.

The conditions attached to the funds are based on the provisions of the Housing Act, 1997 and are agreed upon between the Department and the provinces. The Department developed guidelines to facilitate the process of transferring funds from the Housing Fund to provinces, and to guide reporting processes in terms of the Housing Act, 1997, the Public Finance Management Act, 1999 (Act 1 of 1999), and the Division of Revenue Act, 2000 (Act 16 of 2000).

People's Housing Process

The National Housing Policy: Supporting the PHP was adopted by the Minister of Housing in 1998. The Policy focuses on poor families in both urban and rural areas, using capital subsidies to allow people to build their own homes.

It also assists people in obtaining access to technical, financial, logistical and administrative support to build their own homes, on either an individual or a collective basis.

Peoples' Housing Partnership Trust

The broad mandate of the PHPT is aligned with the National Housing Policy: Supporting the PHP, which stipulates and defines the PHPT mandate as capacitating and engaging with national, provincial and local governments and civil society to meaningfully participate and support the PHP. In order to create adequate capacity for the PHP, the Department established the PHPT in June 1997 to implement the Capacitation Programme to Support the PHP.

The main objective of the Programme is to develop capacity at all levels of government, non-governmental organisations and community-based organisations and communities to support the PHP.

The PHPT has five programmes:
- communication
- training
- research and development to develop a database of information which is easily accessible
- technical advisory services to establish and manage a support programme
- corporate services to ensure efficient and effective functioning.

The PHPT is funded by the United Nations (UN) Development Programme, the UN Centre for Human Settlement and the US Agency for International Development. Government assists the PHP by way of subsidies, facilitation grants and housing-support funding.

Rural Housing Loan Fund (RHLF)

The RHLF focuses on its core business of providing loans, through intermediaries, to low-income households for incremental housing purposes. Incremental housing is a people-driven process and the RHLF's core business is to empower low-income families in rural areas to access credit that will enable them to unleash the force of their self-help savings and local ingenuity to build and improve their shelters over time.

In 2002/03, the RHLF's retail lenders provided 10 936 housing loans to rural households. The RHLF exceeded its financial projections by 29% and disbursed R62 million to rural areas.

Since its inception, RHLF-funded intermediaries have provided more than 45 000 loans to rural borrowers for incremental housing and home improvement, totalling R220 million.

Market research indicates that 87% of people in rural areas earn less than R2 500 per month and this income band constituted 68% of RHLF end-users at the end of March 2003. This indicated that the RHLF, working with retail financiers, continued to make significant impact in alleviating poverty and improving the living conditions of the working poor.

In 2002/03, like all retail-finance operators and banks, RHLF clients were hit by bad debts, declining disposable incomes and more complicated debit-order repayment systems. Higher interest rates, coupled with soaring fuel and food prices inevitably led to the erosion of disposable income of the target market and aggravated an already difficult banking and lending environment.

In 2003/04, the RHLF embarked on a strategy to consolidate unsustainable retail operations to take advantage of an expected improvement in the economic climate and expand impact into those provinces that have fewer distribution channels.

Urban renewal

The Special Integrated Presidential Project for Urban Renewal was identified as one of the first Presidential Lead Projects.

The aim of the Project was to kick-start development in major urban areas, focusing on violence-torn communities and those in crisis.

It was developed to ensure an integrated approach to the provision of infrastructure, housing, community and recreation facilities, and job opportunities. It aimed to transform previously disadvantaged communities and create sustainable and habitable living environments.

In addition, the Project has been viewed as an ideal opportunity to promote the business-planning concept and to give provincial governments the opportunity to improve co-ordination.

Several such projects within 31 communities have been identified as beneficiaries. The projects are:
- Eastern Cape: Duncan Village and Ibhayi
- Free State: Thabong
- Gauteng: Katorus
- KwaZulu-Natal: Cato Manor
- Limpopo: Mahwelereng
- Mpumalanga: Masoyi and Siyabuswa
- Northern Cape: Galeshewe
- North West: Molopo River Basin
- Western Cape: Integrated Service Land Project in the Cape Metropolitan Area.

These projects include the provision of housing, hostel upgrading, infrastructure upgrading (such as roads and the provision of electricity and street-lighting), and the provision and upgrading of social infrastructure. The projects include child-care facilities, schools, clinics, sports fields, libraries, police stations, centres for the aged, post offices and playgrounds.

Providing areas for markets, community gardens and skills training creates opportunities for business development. These activities are planned and implemented in an integrated manner to ensure sustainable and habitable living environments.

Urban Upgrading and Development Programme (UUDP)

The UUDP is a joint bilateral undertaking between South Africa and Germany, which was established in 1994 between the national Department of Housing and German Technical Co-operation.

The Department is playing a key facilitation and co-ordination role in the implementation of the Programme in the Free State and Eastern Cape. Assistance to the two provinces and the housing institutions has involved:
- support to the Masilonyana Municipality in the Free State in bridging the buffer zone by promoting the integration of the Masilo township with the former town through territorial marketing
- support for the implementation of the PHP projects in Mount Fletcher, Elliotdale and Tarkastad in the Eastern Cape
- support for the national review of the PHP by the PHPT
- the piloting of a municipal housing-sector plan as part of the Integrated Development Plan of the local municipality of Mohokare in the Free State.

Settlement policy and urban development

In June 1996, South Africa made a commitment at the Habitat II Conference in Istanbul, Turkey, to implement the Habitat Agenda. The Agenda is the guiding international policy for human settlements.

The Department of Housing is charged with the responsibility of co-ordinating the implementation of the Agenda. To do this, national policies that support the principles and the vision of the Agenda should be in place.

The Urban Development Framework is essentially the key policy document that will guide the implementation of the Habitat Agenda in South Africa. Besides the Framework, the Department has taken the opportunity offered by the Global Urban Observatory, and initiated an Urban Indicators Programme and a Local Best Practice Strategy.

The Minister of Housing launched the African Solutions Network, a website hosted by the Department, that features:
- information about the African Solutions Conference and others in the region, which deal with issues relating to sustainable development
- contact details of individuals and organisations active in the field of sustainable human-settlement development
- a database of relevant good practices
- information on technologies, building material and practices that support sustainable human-settlement development
- links to relevant research databases to source the latest research relating to sustainable human settlement.

The African Solutions Network also provides links to other websites and resources on the Internet.

Another initiative driven by the Department, which relates to Habitat II, is the Environmentally Sound Low-Cost Housing Task Team. The Team has been tasked with promoting environmental efficiency in the housing sector, and is working on the development of standards and guidelines, incentive programmes, a financing mechanism and general awareness-raising initiatives.

Acknowledgements

Department of Housing
Estimates of National Expenditure 2003, published by the National Treasury
Social Housing Foundation
Thubelisha Homes
National Urban Reconstruction and Housing Agency
www.gov.za

Suggested reading

Bond, P. *Cities of Gold: Townships of Coal: Essays on South Africa's New Urban Crisis*. Trematon, New Jersey: African World Press, 2000.
Bundy, C. *Rise and Fall of the South African Peasantry*. 2nd ed. Cape Town: David Philip, 1988.
Harrison, P. et al. eds. *Confronting Management: Housing and Urban Development in a Democratising Society*. Cape Town: University of Cape Town Press, 2003.
Housing and the World of Work. Produced by the National Housing Initiative in association with AECI and Matthew Nell and Associates. Auckland Park, Johannesburg: National Business Institute, 1998.
James, W. ed. *Houses for Africa: An Inspirational Source Book for Building and Finishing Your Home*. Johannesburg: Emden Publishing, n.d.
Keegan, T. J. *Facing the Storm: Portraits of Black Lives in Rural South Africa*. Cape Town: David Philip, 1988.
Khan, F. and Thring, P. *Housing Policy and Practice in Post-Apartheid South Africa*. Johannesburg: Heinemann, 2003.
Rust, K. and Rubenstein, S. eds. *A Mandate to Build: Developing Consensus Around a National Housing Policy in South Africa*. Johannesburg: Ravan Press, 1996.
South African Home Owners Buyers' Guide: Design, Building, Renovating, Decorating, Garden and Outdoor, 1998/99. Johannesburg: Avonwold, 1998. Annual.

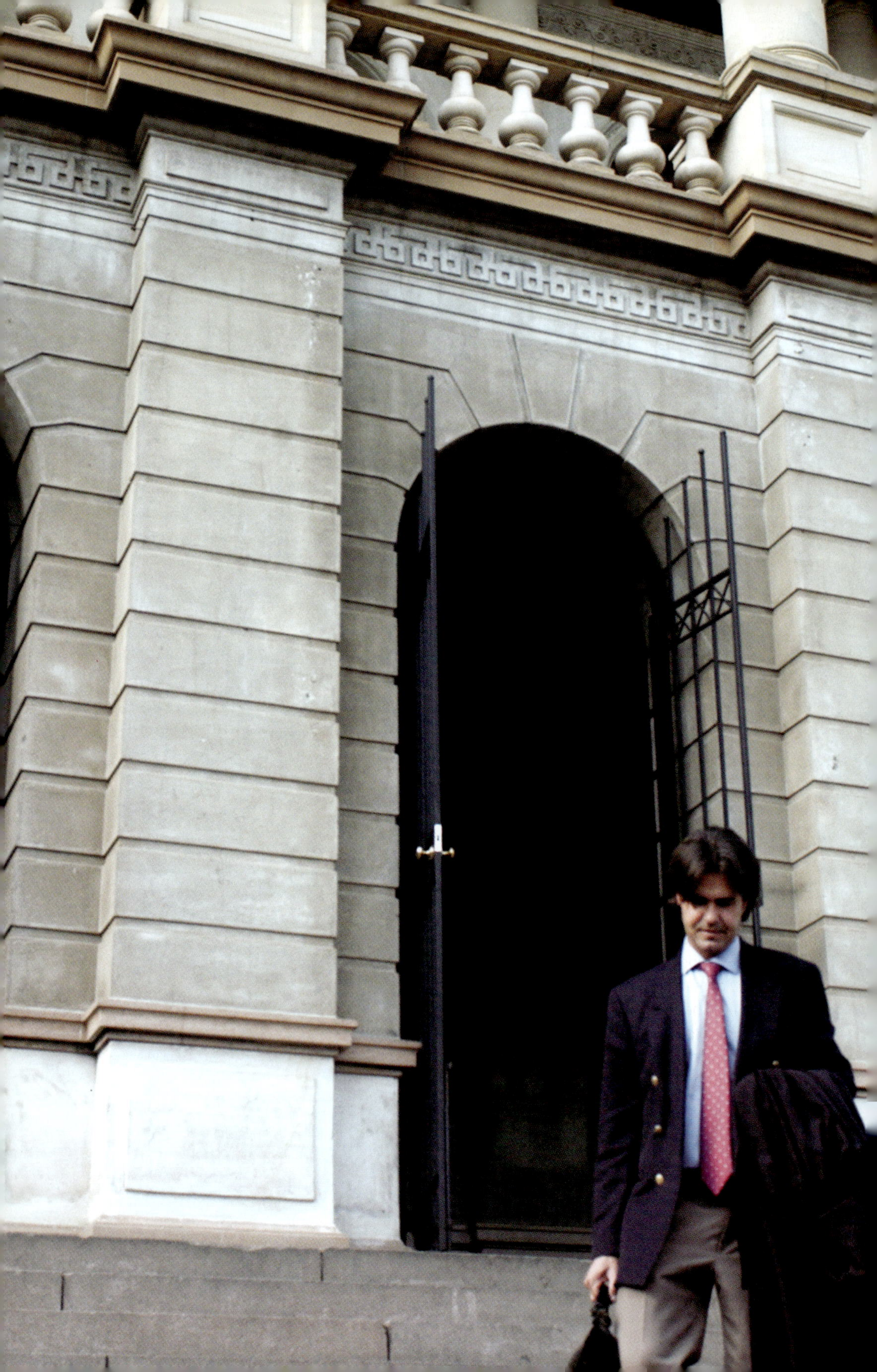

chapter 15
Justice and correctional services

Administration of justice

The Constitution of the Republic of South Africa, 1996 (Act 108 of 1996), is the supreme law of the country and binds all legislative, executive and judicial organs of the State at all levels of government.

In terms of Section 165 of the Constitution, the judicial authority in South Africa is vested in the courts, which are independent and subject only to the Constitution and the law.

No person or organ of State may interfere with the functioning of the courts, and an order or decision of a court binds all organs of State and persons to whom it applies.

The Department of Justice and Constitutional Development is responsible for the administration of the courts and constitutional development.

It is the mission of the Department to uphold and protect the Constitution and the rule of the law. The Department is accountable to the public and the State in rendering accessible, fair, speedy and cost-effective administration of justice in the interest of a safer and more secure South Africa. The Department aims to achieve this by promoting constitutional democracy, providing appropriate legal services and the sound management of courts, and alternative dispute-resolution mechanisms.

It performs these functions in conjunction with judges, magistrates, the National Director of Public Prosecutions (NDPP) and the Directors of Public Prosecutions (DPPs), who are independent.

The Department's responsibilities include the provision of adequate resources for the proper and efficient functioning of the criminal and civil justice systems. It provides legislation and administrative support for the establishment of institutions required by the Constitution.

Transformation of the justice system

One of the biggest challenges facing government was, and still is, the successful transformation of the justice system.

Restructuring of the Department

The Department of Justice and Constitutional Development is undergoing a restructuring process. The Department's goals are to:
- Improve service delivery to internal and external clients to enhance client satisfaction.
- Ensure that business is conducted efficiently and in a cost-effective manner, with the primary focus on courts and other

◀ The judicial authority in South Africa is vested in the courts, which are independent and subject only to the Constitution and the law.

services rendered to the State and the public. This includes improving productivity in the courts and making justice more accessible and affordable.

For the purpose of restructuring, the following core business units have been identified under the leadership of the Minister of Justice and Constitutional Development, Dr Penuell Maduna:
- Court Services
- Masters' Offices
- Legal Services
- Legislative and Constitutional Development.

Various other units have been identified in support of these business units, namely:
- the Office of the Chief Financial Officer
- Human Resource Development
- Information and Systems Management, which includes information technology services
- Public Education and Communication.

National Prosecuting Authority of South Africa (NPA)

The NPA structure includes the National Prosecuting Services (NPS), the Directorate: Special Operations (DSO), the Witness-Protection Programme, the Asset Forfeiture Unit (AFU) and specialised units such as the Sexual Offences and Community Affairs Unit and the Specialised Commercial Crime Unit.

In terms of the NPA Amendment Act, 2000 (Act 61 of 2000), the DSO is a distinct and autonomous agency.

The NPA has made steady progress in achieving its priorities. Generally, productivity in courts is increasing, but this has to be viewed in the light of substantial increases in the number of new cases. Between January 2002 and December 2002, the lower courts finalised a total of 833 594 cases, of which 421 213 were withdrawn. Outstanding cases on the lower courts' rolls decreased from 195 638 in January 2002 to 180 953 by the end of December 2002. Over the same period the conviction rate was 81%. The High Courts finalised 1 684 cases between January 2002 and the end of September 2002. Of these, 288 were rape cases referred by the lower courts, for which the High Court must give at least the minimum sentence; with 1 130 receiving a verdict of guilty (81%). There was an outstanding roll of 1 048 cases and 1 827 new cases were registered.

Office of the National Director of Public Prosecution

The Office of the NDPP is the head office of the NPA. The prosecuting authority vests in the NDPP. This authority can be and has been delegated to other members of the NPA. They have the power to:
- institute and conduct criminal proceedings on behalf of the State
- carry out any necessary functions incidental to instituting and conducting such criminal proceedings
- discontinue criminal proceedings.

Directorate: Special Operations

The DSO pursues its objectives, and complies with its legislative mandate through the application of numerous legislative tools. In addition to the NPA Act, 1998, other statutes include the Prevention of Organised Crime Act, 1998 (Act 121 of 1998), International Co-operation in Criminal Matters Amendment Act, 1996 (Act 75 of 1996), and the Extradition Amendment Act, 1996 (Act 77 of 1996).

The DSO is committed to the investigation of matters that are national in scope, and concentrates on those crimes that threaten national security and economic stability. The more complex and protracted the investigations and higher up the criminal target, the more appropriate the matter would be for DSO selection. In many instances, these high-impact investigations fall outside the scope and capacity of the South African Police Service (SAPS).

The following three delineated areas fall within this strategic focus: organised corrup-

Justice and correctional services

tion, transnational organised crime, and serious and complex financial crime.

The DSO has specifically initiated investigations in respect of transnational drug syndicates, such as West-African and Chinese drug syndicates with strong international links. It has developed operational liaison with international law enforcement agencies such as the United States (US) Federal Bureau of Investigation and Drug Enforcement Administration, United Kingdom's (UK) Scotland Yard, and UK Customs and Excise, which allows for international collaboration.

In the area of serious and complex financial crime, DSO investigations are evidence of its intention to penetrate crime markets that have in recent years been out of the reach of traditional law enforcement. The DSO has initiated investigations into organised public-office corruption. It has developed an ambitious, though realistic strategy, based on a customised model of successful overseas anti-corruption programmes.

By September 2002, the DSO had finalised 210 prosecutions over a period of 18 months. Eighty-five of these were finalised in the last seven months with a 93% conviction rate. In those seven months, an additional 43 major case investigations were initiated, bringing the total number of projects on its books to 500, one-third of which had already appeared before the courts.

The Department of Justice and Constitutional Development raised more than R700 000 for civil organisations fighting women and child abuse through the National Signature Pledge held during the *16 Days of Activism for No Violence Against Women and Children* Campaign in 2002.

Over 580 000 people, including President Thabo Mbeki and several sporting and international personalities, supported the Campaign.

The money was disbursed to the different non-governmental organisations by the Foundation for Human Rights.

The Campaign was repeated in 2003.

Asset Forfeiture Unit

In terms of Chapters 5 and 6 of the Prevention of Organised Crime Act, 1998, the AFU can seize and forfeit property that is the proceeds of crime, or property that has been used to commit a crime.

The AFU has two major strategic objectives, namely to:
- develop the law by taking test cases to court and creating the legal precedents necessary to allow for the effective use of the law
- build capacity to ensure that asset forfeiture is used as widely as possible to make a real impact in the fight against crime.

The use of asset forfeiture to fight crime has been one of government's important innovations. By June 2003, the AFU had initiated over 300 cases and frozen nearly R500 million worth of criminal assets. There was more than R25 million in the Criminal Assets Recovery Account, which will be used to fight crime.

Special Investigating Unit

A special investigation and tribunals unit was appointed in March 1997 to probe corruption and maladministration in government.

Sexual Offences and Community Affairs Unit

This Unit focuses on violent and indecent offences committed against women and children, as well as on family violence, child support and child justice. It ensures that these cases are prioritised, monitors the quality of delivery, and ensures that victims and witnesses receive decent treatment in courts.

The Unit also seeks to improve the investigation and prosecution of rape cases. To this end, four multidisciplinary rape care centres, known as the Thuthuzela Care Centres, have been established.

The Centres comprise police investigators, medical personnel, social workers, prosecutors and community volunteers who assist in addressing the underreporting of rape cases.

These teams have also contributed to speeding up and humanising rape investigations, developing accurate data-collection tools, and building better co-operation and communication between victims and the justice system.

In June 2002, the Unit began training prosecutors in the handling of domestic violence. It also recruited and trained maintenance prosecutors. In addition, prosecutors countrywide have been trained to deal with child-justice matters. Since the inception of child-justice committees co-ordinated by prosecutors, some 9 990 offenders have been diverted from the criminal justice system (CJS).

Sexual offences

By July 2003, 40 Sexual Offences Courts had been established countrywide.

The fight against sexual offences is a national priority. The Department of Justice and Constitutional Development is busy with a programme of providing facilities at courts where child witnesses, especially in child-abuse cases, can testify in a friendly and secure environment without the risk of being intimidated.

New child-witness rooms are furbished with one-way glass partitions adjacent to the courtrooms. Where it is impossible to provide such rooms in existing buildings, other rooms away from the courts are utilised by providing a closed-circuit television link.

Significant progress has been made in this regard. Some 35 rooms have been provided with one-way glass partitioning, while 178 closed-circuit television systems have been installed.

Twenty of the Sexual Offences Courts are blueprint-compliant while a further 20 Regional Courts are dedicated to hearing mainly sexual offences cases.

The Department of Justice and Constitutional Development, the NPA, the Department of Social Development and the SAPS have established a close working relationship and have developed a national strategy for the accelerated roll-out of Sexual Offences Courts.

The Office of the NDPP and the Department of Justice and Constitutional Development have identified several additional areas for the creation of these Courts. Similar court structures have been included as a standard requirement for all future building projects.

National Prosecuting Services

The mission of the NPS is to raise the levels of productivity in the NPA and make it efficient and credible.

The unit has to ensure proper planning of court rolls, prioritisation, proper preparation and arrangement for all cases to be heard, and the avoidance of unreasonable delays.

Between 2000 and 2002, District Court rolls decreased to 127 per court, and to 106 in Regional Courts.

In addition, there has been a dramatic increase in cases finalised with a verdict of guilty.

The conviction rate in District Courts is over 80%, and in Regional Courts approximately 70%.

By mid-2003, integrated justice system (IJS) Court Centres had been established at 39 lower courts throughout the country. The IJS Project has resulted in improved case preparation and reduced case-cycle times. Court statistics show that the average cycle time of cases has declined from 110 to 74 days. The Court Management Information System (MIS) reports aspects such as the number of cases finalised per courtroom and per judicial officer, cases withdrawn as a proportion of cases disposed of, and the number of new cases per courtroom and per judicial officer. Encouraged by the initial results, the Department decided to extend the Southern Gauteng Pilot Project to the rest of the courts in Gauteng and all the courts that have IJS Court Centres.

Specialised Commercial Crime Unit

The Pretoria-based Specialised Commercial

Justice and correctional services

Crime Unit was established in 1999 to bring specialisation to the investigation, prosecution and adjudication of commercial crimes.

Three new courts and offices were established in the Johannesburg and Pretoria central business districts for specialised commercial crime cases.

The Johannesburg and Pretoria Courts will eventually be followed by similar courts in Durban and Cape Town.

Before the establishment of the Specialised Commercial Crime Courts, only 6% of all perpetrators prosecuted were convicted, compared with the 23% conviction rate at the Pretoria Court.

The Specialised Commercial Crimes Unit had a conviction rate of more than 95% in 2002.

Witness-Protection Programme

The Office for Witness Protection falls under the auspices of the NPA. The Office is responsible for the protection of witnesses in terms of the Witness Protection Act, 1998 (Act 112 of 1998), and its regulations.

It also makes provision for placing a person related to the witness under protection at the request of the witness, prospective witness or a person who has given evidence or is required to give evidence in criminal proceedings or before a commission of inquiry.

The 2003/04 budget for witness protection amounted to R36 524 million.

The Programme does not offer incentives to witnesses of serious crimes such as those offered by the SAPS.

Instead, the Programme offers sustenance in the form of a food allowance, replacement of salary if employment has been lost, free accommodation including all municipal services, a clothing allowance, transport, a housing allowance for school-going children, medical expenses, etc.

At the end of March 2003, there were 326 potential testifying witnesses admitted to the Programme. The total number of people in the Programme is 704, including family members. The average gross monthly expenditure stands at R1 775 million.

Between January and March 2003, the following was realised through the involvement of the Witness-Protection Programme: some 87 cases were finalised, 114 witnesses testified, the number of accused persons stood at 183, while 141 convictions took place, 42 persons were acquitted, and the combined jail terms amounted to 2 626 years and 72 life sentences.

Community Courts

In May 1999, South Africa's first Community Court, aimed at alleviating the burden placed on the justice system by petty crimes and social disputes, was launched at the Kyalami Metro Council in Gauteng. The pilot project is guided by members of the SAPS, the Department of Justice and Constitutional Development, and non-governmental organisations (NGOs). It promotes community participation in justice administration and policing.

The South African Law Reform Commission (SALRC) is finalising a report on Community Courts.

During 2002/03, the Department delivered new Community Courts at an unprecedented rate. Some R211 138 million was spent on establishing new courts at Botshabelo, Queenstown, Kroonstad, Khutsong, Khayelitsha, Blue Downs, Patensie and Middledrift. Ongoing extensions at various other Courts ensured that the capital budget was put to the best possible use.

Courts for Income Tax Offenders

In October 1999, the South African Revenue Service (SARS) opened a criminal courtroom at the Johannesburg Magistrate's Office dedicated to the prosecution of tax offenders. The Court deals only with cases concerning failure to submit tax returns or to provide information requested by SARS officials. It does not deal with bigger cases such as tax fraud.

Another SARS court is operating twice a week at the Magistrate's Office in Roodepoort.

Discussions to decentralise and expand such a Court to the bigger centres in the country have taken place between SARS and the Department.

In terms of Section 22(8) of the NPA Act, 1998, the NDPP may authorise any competent person to conduct prosecutions in respect of statutory offences. Representatives from the NPA and SARS are engaged in discussions to appoint suitable officials to deal exclusively with the prosecution of income-tax offenders.

Family Court Pilot Projects

A specialised Family Court structure and extended Family Advocate services are priority areas for the Department.

The Family Court Blueprint was developed by the Family Court Task Team in 2002 to support the existing five pilot projects in becoming fully fledged successful Family Courts, and thereafter the rolling out of Family Courts to other magisterial districts. The establishment of Family Courts in South Africa is motivated by three broad aims, namely to:
- give wide and specialised protection and help to the family as the fundamental unit in society
- bring about access to justice for all in family disputes
- improve the quality and effectiveness of service delivery to citizens who have family law disputes.

The Family Court Blueprint recommended that 17 interim projects be established to strengthen the existing pilot projects. The Department is implementing these recommendations as part of the restructuring of the Courts.

Municipal Courts

Municipal Courts are being set up in the larger centres of South Africa in conjunction with municipalities. They are Magistrate's Courts but deal only with traffic offences and contraventions of municipal by-laws.

They are set up in a partnership agreement in that administrative and infrastructural support is supplied by the municipality, while magistrates are provided by the Department. Pretoria, Johannesburg, Port Elizabeth and Nelspruit either have Municipal Courts already or are in the process of setting up these Courts. These Courts assist in addressing the backlogs and severe workloads of the other lower courts.

Equality Courts

The role of Equality Courts, which are to be rolled out countrywide, is to enforce the provisions of the Promotion of Equality and Prevention of Unfair Discrimination Act, 2000 (Act 4 of 2000).

The Act outlaws unfair discrimination and allows for the creation of Equality Courts within the Magistrate's and High Courts, each to be presided over by an equality court officer.

The Act further authorises the Minister of Justice and Constitutional Development to appoint an Equality Review Committee to monitor the implementation of the Act's provisions.

By June 2003, 62 Equality Courts were in operation.

State Legal Services

State Legal Services provides government with legal services and facilitates constitutional amendments through three subprogrammes.
- Legal Services to the State provides for the work of the State Attorney and State law advisors. The former acts as attorney, notary and conveyancer for government. State law advisors provide legal opinions, scrutinise and amend international agreements and draft legislation and attend relevant Parliamentary Portfolio Committees as legal advisors for all national departments.
- The Legislative and Constitutional Development Unit is responsible for promoting, maintaining and developing the Constitution and its values by researching, developing and promoting appropriate legislation. It

includes the research activities of the SALRC, which involve extensive reviews of wide areas of law and legal practice. The Unit established a section for statutory-law revision in 2002, which researches and develops legislation, researches possible future legislation, and develops reports for the Minister on a range of issues.
- The Master of the High Court is responsible for the administration of deceased and insolvent estates, companies and close corporations in liquidation, trusts and the Guardians Fund, as well as the property of minors, persons under curatorship and absent persons.

Human rights

Human rights, in terms of Chapter Two of the Constitution, bind all legislative and executive bodies of State at all levels of government.

They apply to all laws, administrative decisions taken and acts performed during the period in which the Constitution is in force. In terms of the Constitution, every person has basic human rights such as:
- freedom from discrimination
- a right to life.

Crime prevention

The Department of Justice and Constitutional Development is one of the four core departments in the Criminal Justice Cluster that has been tasked with the implementation of the National Crime Prevention Strategy (NCPS). This is government's official strategy to combat, control and prevent crime. (See Chapter 17: *Safety, security and defence.*)

The main responsibilities of the Department in the implementation of the NCPS are:
- promoting legislation to create an effective CJS
- creating an effective prosecution system
- creating an effective court system for the adjudication of cases
- co-ordinating and integrating departmental activities of all role-players involved in crime prevention.

Integrated Justice System

The IJS Board was established in 1997 to integrate the activities of departments in the Justice Cluster in a co-ordinated manner.

The underlying principle in establishing this System is the re-engineering of business processes through the necessary technology to ensure effective interaction and transition between the respective departmental responsibilities.

Six major developments are being undertaken, namely the:
- Development of a framework detailing the business processes that will be re-engineered in an integrated manner. By July 2003, the project was nearing completion, the results of which are going to be used to finalise the design of the initial build of the integrated business process, for subsequent release and implementation.
- Establishment of the necessary infrastructure to enable the IJS. Each department has been tasked with the responsibility of ensuring that the required infrastructure is put in place for the deployment of the IJS elements.
- Establishment of the Virtual Private Network. This task has been assigned to the State Information Technology Agency.
- Identification System that has been procured. The project consists of an Automated Fingerprint Information System (AFIS), the National Photographic Identification System (NPIS), and a database of all DNA samples. By July 2003, these systems were largely complete. However, they still have to be placed within the IJS framework to facilitate the management of the person through the justice process, which not only includes the offender, but also the victim and witnesses.

- Development of the necessary business-intelligence capacity within the Justice Cluster, which was expected to move into a new phase during 2003/04.
- Integrated Case-Flow Management System, which includes Case, the Person (offender, victim and witness) and the Exhibit business processes. These processes are seen to be the primary business capabilities which are to be supported by the main functionalities of work flow, document management, scheduling and event notification.

Improved governance was one of the most significant achievements during 2002/03 as well as the following:
- Framework development – by July 2003, the project was almost concluded.
- Business enablement – a core strategy has been developed and demonstrated.
- Reference-data management – initial requirements have been delivered.
- Business intelligence – two business areas were ready for implementation by July 2003.
- Identification service – the NPIS enhancement is nearing completion. Since its implementation in September 2002, AFIS has reduced the backlog in fingerprint searches from 84 891 to 32 169.
- Inmate tracking (offender/persons management).
- Improved database capacities.
- The Court Process Project (CPP) – a functional baseline has been established for court processes across departments.
- The CPP roll-out to 13 police stations in the Durban Magistrate's Court area is showing good progress.

The CPP provides for the automation of civil and criminal case-management systems. The objective is to implement it in all 450 Magistrate's Courts countrywide, together with the associated Community Safety Centres, prisons and social development institutions.

In relation to the Department, the 2003/04 priorities of the IJS – focusing on promoting service-delivery excellence in the CJS – are to increase the efficiency of the courts, especially the handling of sexual-assault crimes. The Department is recruiting court managers to take over the administrative function of magistrates following the decision to separate administrative and judicial functions.

Courts are working longer hours, and between 1999 and 2001 there was a 49% increase in the number of daily court sittings. As a result, the number of cases finalised in courts has increased since 2001.

To deal with case backlogs, 3 027 Saturday and additional court days were introduced. Between January 2002 and March 2003, these courts finalised 27 570 cases. More courts are being encouraged to sit over weekends to reduce unacceptable case backlogs.

There has been a positive reversal in the ratio between sentenced and other prisoners, owing to the overall improvement in court efficiency. During 2002, 18 new permanent judges were appointed and further appointments are being processed. An amount of R20 million was set aside to increase the number of magistrates and prosecutors to cope with escalating court rolls.

For 2003/04, an amount of R229 million was allocated for capital works and R35 million for the upgrading of existing infrastructure. Construction of new court buildings is under way in Tembisa, Benoni, Boksburg, Scottburgh, Atteridgeville, Randburg, Pretoria North, Atamelang, Sasolburg and Sebokeng.

e-Justice

The e-Justice Programme was developed to transform the Department into an equal role-player in the IJS. The Programme is a multi-year development that consists of four components. These are the:
- Digital Nervous System (DNS) Project, which entails rapid infrastructure deployment throughout all the Department's offices. The Project was scheduled for completion by December 2002, but the baseline deadline

Justice and correctional services

could not be met and has been extended to 2004.
- Financial Administration System, which consists of four projects involving the automation of the Guardian's Fund, bail, maintenance, and the State Attorney's trust accounts. The development phases of the projects have been completed and roll-out was due to start in 2003.
- MIS, which is designed to provide essential information necessary to manage the Department. The MIS has been incorporated into and will now be a subproject of the DNS.

Legislation

In terms of the Constitution, legislative authority is vested in Parliament, which consists of the National Assembly and the National Council of Provinces (NCOP). South African legislation is constantly revised to meet changing circumstances in a dynamic and developing society. This is done on the advice of the legal sections of various government departments and the SALRC, after consultation with all interest groups.

Since April 1994, the Department has promoted more than 100 Bills. The Department's legislative programme was dominated by three main themes, namely, legislation to give effect to the spirit of the new constitutional dispensation, legislation to address the crime problem prevailing in South Africa, and legal reform.

The Department of Justice and Constitutional Development's Maintenance Outreach Programme was launched by the Deputy Minister of Justice, Ms Cheryl Gillwald, in Cape Town in March 2003.
The Outreach Programme is aimed at educating people about their rights and responsibilities with regard to maintenance and child support, appointing maintenance investigators to improve the payment of maintenance and progress in the modernisation of systems for the collection and distribution of maintenance.

The most important pieces of legislation promoted in recent years include the following:

Implementation of the Maintenance Act, 1998 (Act 99 of 1998), and the Domestic Violence Act, 1998 (Act 116 of 1998)

The Department implemented the Maintenance Act, 1998 and the Domestic Violence Act, 1998 in November 1999 to make a difference to the lives of vulnerable women and children. The Department has also started appointing contract maintenance investigators in 55 of the Maintenance Courts.

Promotion of Access to Information Act, 2000 (Act 2 of 2000)

The Open Democracy Bill was introduced to Parliament in August 1998. Amendments were made and Parliament finally approved the Promotion of Access to Information Bill, 2000 in January 2000. The Promotion of Access to Information Act, 2000 grants the right of access to information referred to in Section 32 of the Constitution.

The Act generally promotes transparency, accountability and effective governance of all public and private bodies.

The Act, with the exception of a few sections, came into force on 9 March 2001.

The Promotion of Access to Information Amendment Act, 2002 (Act 54 of 2002), was published in the *Government Gazette* in January 2003. The aims of the Amendment Act are to amend the definition of 'court' in the principal Act and to provide for the training of presiding officers in Magistrate's Courts. The Department has approached the Minister to designate all Magistrate's Courts as Access of Information Courts.

Promotion of Administrative Justice Act, 2000 (Act 3 of 2000)

The Act is aimed at the provision of lawful, reasonable and procedurally fair administrative action as contemplated in Section 33 of the Constitution.

The Act, with the exception of Sections 4 and 10, came into force on 30 November 2000.

The Promotion of Administrative Justice Amendment Act, 2002 (Act 53 of 2002), was published in the *Government Gazette* in February 2003. The aims of the Amendment Act are to amend the definition of 'court' in the principal Act and to provide for the training of presiding officers in the Magistrate's Courts for purposes of the Act.

Promotion of Equality and Prevention of Unfair Discrimination Act, 2000 (Act 4 of 2000)

The objectives of the Act include the prevention and prohibition of unfair discrimination, redress for discrimination, the promotion of equality and progressive eradication of discrimination.

The Promotion of Equality and Prevention of Unfair Discrimination Amendment Act, 2002 (Act 52 of 2002), was published in the *Government Gazette* in January 2003. The objectives of the Amendment Act are to further provide for the training and designation of presiding officers of Equality Courts for purposes of the Act, to provide for the designation of Magistrate's Courts as Equality Courts, to further regulate the training of clerks for Equality Courts and to provide for related matters.

The Department is in the process of approaching the Minister to designate Magistrate's Courts as Equality Courts.

Child Justice Bill

Article 40(3) of the Convention on the Rights of the Child requires State parties 'to promote the establishment of laws, procedural authorities and institutions specifically applicable to children alleged as, accused of, or recognised as having infringed the penal law'.

The Government, having ratified the Convention on the Rights of the Child in 1995, recognised that the situation regarding such children in South Africa was unsatisfactory, and decided to bring about change.

A Juvenile Justice Project Committee, appointed by the SALRC, drafted a comprehensive Bill. The proposed legislation will create a new system for dealing with children accused of crimes that will:

- set a minimum age of criminal capacity
- ensure individual assessment of each child
- establish procedures to divert as many children as possible away from courts and institutions
- set up new Child Justice Courts with trained personnel
- provide a creative range of sentencing options
- develop a system of review and monitoring for the system.

The Bill encourages the release of children into the care of their parents and entrenches the constitutional injunction that prison should be considered as the last resort.

The Child Justice Bill was presented to the Portfolio Committee on Justice and Constitutional Development on 20 February 2003. Public hearings were held and several submissions were received.

Amendments to the Bill were made on the request of the Portfolio Committee. Although substantial redrafting of certain sections has been requested, the main policy direction of the Child Justice Bill remains intact. It was expected that the Bill would be passed before the end of 2003.

Constitution of the Republic of South Africa Amendment Act, 2001 (Act 34 of 2001)

This Amendment Act amends the Constitution of the Republic of South Africa, 1996 so as to change the title of the President of the Constitutional Court (CC) to that of Chief Justice; provide for the Offices of the Deputy Chief Justice, President of the Supreme Court of Appeal and Deputy President of the Supreme Court of Appeal; and provide for the extension of the term of office of a Chief Justice. The Amendment Act also makes provision for municipal borrowing powers, and to

Justice and correctional services

enable a municipal council to bind itself and a future council in the exercise of its legislative and executive authority to secure loans or investments for the municipality concerned.

Criminal Procedure Second Amendment Act, 2001 (Act 62 of 2001)

The Act emanates from a report of the SALRC (as part of its investigation into the simplification of the criminal justice process) and aims to amend the Criminal Procedure Act, 1977 (Act 51 of 1977), to allow a prosecutor and an accused person to enter into a plea and sentence agreement.

Regulation of Interception of Communications and Provision of Communication-Related Information Act, 2002 (Act 70 of 2002)

This Act aims, among other things, to regulate the interception of certain communications, the monitoring of certain signals and radiofrequency spectrums, and the provision of certain communications-related information. The Act also regulates the making of applications for, and the issuing of, directions authorising the interception of communications and the provision of communications-related information under certain circumstances. It further provides for the execution of directions and entry warrants by law-enforcement officers and the assistance to be given by postal service-providers, telecommunications service-providers and decryption key holders in the execution of such directions and entry warrants.

Constitution of the Republic of South Africa Second Amendment Act, 2003 (Act 3 of 2003)

The objectives of the Amendment Act include amending the Constitution so as to simplify the process of review by the NCOP where national executive interventions have taken place in provincial affairs, and simplifying the process of review by the NCOP where provincial executive interventions have taken place in local affairs. The Act also changed the name of the Northern Province to Limpopo.

The Republic of South Africa Third Amendment Bill, 2003

The Bill amends the Constitution of the Republic of South Africa, 1996 in two respects:
- provision is made for a single High Court of South Africa, consisting of the divisions, with the areas of jurisdiction, as determined by an Act of Parliament
- provision is made for the appointment of a second Deputy President of the Supreme Court of Appeal.

The amendments contained in the Bill are required in order to constitutionally sanction certain corresponding provisions of the Superior Courts Bill, 2003. The Superior Courts Bill will largely be giving effect to item 16(6) of Schedule 6 to the Constitution, in terms of which all courts must be rationalised with the view to establishing a judicial system suited to the requirements of the Constitution. This Bill aims to rationalise and consolidate the laws pertaining to the CC, the Supreme Court of Appeal and the High Courts, referred to collectively as the Superior Courts. It will also merge the Labour Court and the Labour Appeal Court with the proposed High Court of South Africa and the Supreme Court of Appeal, respectively.

Compulsory HIV-Testing of Alleged Sexual Offenders Bill, 2003

The purpose of the Bill is to provide a speedy and uncomplicated mechanism whereby the victim of a sexual offence can apply to have the alleged offender tested for HIV and have the test results disclosed to the victim.

The Bill emanates from the SALRC's fourth interim report on *Aspects of the Law Relating to AIDS*. In its report, the Law Commission noted the vulnerability of women and children being infected with HIV as a result of rape and other sexual offences.

In accordance with the Bill, the HIV-testing of the alleged offender should take place within a specific period after the alleged sexual offence was committed. The victim, or any interested person on behalf of the victim, may apply to a magistrate for an order that the alleged offender be tested for HIV.

The application may also be made as soon as possible after a charge has been laid, and may be made before or after an arrest.

Criminal Procedure Amendment Bill, 2003

The purpose of the Bill is to further regulate appeals against decisions of lower courts in criminal cases. The Bill provides that any person convicted of any offence in a lower court who wishes to appeal against the conviction, sentence or order, must apply to the relevant lower court for leave to appeal against any conviction, sentence or order. The Bill further provides for a petition procedure to the High Court having jurisdiction, in the case where an application for leave to appeal has been refused.

Public Protector Amendment Bill, 2003

The main purpose of the Bill is to further regulate the appointment of the Deputy Public Protector.

The Public Protector Act, 1994 (Act 23 of 1994), provides for the appointment of Deputy Public Protectors by the Cabinet member responsible for the administration of justice. There have been arguments that this erodes the independence of that office, as such a person (Deputy Public Protector) may eventually assume the duties of the Public Protector. The amendments to the Bill propose that only one Deputy Public Protector be appointed, and that he or she, as is the case with the Public Protector, be appointed by the President with the involvement of Parliament. Amendments that regulate the remuneration and other terms and conditions of employment, vacancies in office, and removal from office of the Deputy Public Protector, are also included in the Bill.

Sexual Offences Bill

The Bill emanates from an investigation by the SALRC. The aim of the Bill is to address mounting public concern about the high levels of rape and other sexual offences in South Africa.

According to statistics released by the Crime Information Analysis Centre of the SAPS, 52 425 rape cases were reported between April 2003 and March 2003.

The Bill proposes that all types of sexual penetration should be considered unlawful when they occur under coercive circumstances, including the application of force, threats and the abuse of power.

The Criminal Law (Sexual Offences) Amendment Bill, which seeks to improve the approach to dealing with sexual offences, was adopted for submission to Parliament in July 2003.

Court and other legal structures

Constitutional Court

The CC is situated in Johannesburg and is the highest court in all constitutional matters. It deals only with constitutional matters and issues connected with decisions on constitutional matters, including whether Acts of Parliament and the conduct of the President and Executive are consistent with the Constitution, including the Bill of Rights. Its decisions are binding on all persons, including organs of State, and on all other courts. The Court consists of the Chief Justice of South Africa, the Deputy Chief Justice and nine other justices. Justice Arthur Chaskalson is the Chief Justice and Justice Pius Langa is the Deputy Chief Justice.

The Department of Justice and Constitutional Development aims to promote better case-flow management at the CC. Targets set

Justice and correctional services

include increasing the number of cases finalised by 5%, and increasing the number of court hours worked per day.

Supreme Court of Appeal

The Supreme Court of Appeal, situated in Bloemfontein, is the highest court in respect of all other matters. It is composed of the President and Deputy President of the Supreme Court of Appeal and a number of judges of appeal determined by an Act of Parliament. The Supreme Court of Appeal has jurisdiction to hear and determine an appeal against any decision of a High Court.

Decisions of the Supreme Court of Appeal are binding on all courts of a lower order, and the decisions of the High Courts are binding on Magistrate's Courts within the respective areas of jurisdiction of the divisions.

High Courts

In terms of Item 16(6)(a) of Schedule 6 to the Constitution, 'all courts, their structure, composition, functioning and jurisdiction, and all relevant legislation, must be rationalised with a view to establishing a judicial system suited to the requirements of the Constitution'. The Minister of Justice and Constitutional Development must, after consultation with the Judicial Service Commission (JSC), manage this process.

When the post-apartheid Government came to office in May 1994, there were only one black male judge and two white female judges.

By July 2003, out of 214 judges of the Superior Courts, there were 128 white males (60%), 14 white females, 42 indigenous African males, eight indigenous African females, eight coloured males, one coloured female, 11 Asian males and two Asian females. Some 60% of the Superior Court judges are post-apartheid appointments. This result has been achieved through the application of a rigorous appointment procedure conducted by and under the auspices of the Judicial Service Commission.

Presently there are 10 court divisions: Cape of Good Hope (with its seat in Cape Town); Eastern Cape (Grahamstown); Northern Cape (Kimberley); Orange Free State (Bloemfontein); Natal (Pietermaritzburg); Transvaal (Pretoria); Transkei (Umtata); Ciskei (Bisho); Venda (Sibasa), and Bophuthatswana (Mmabatho). Each of these divisions, with the exception of Venda, is composed of a Judge President and, if the President so determines, one or more Deputy Judges President, and as many judges as the President may determine from time to time.

There are also three local divisions: the Witwatersrand Local Division (Johannesburg), Durban and Coast Local Division (Durban), and South-Eastern Cape Division (Port Elizabeth). These courts are presided over by judges in the provincial courts concerned.

A provincial or local division has jurisdiction in its own area over all persons residing or being in that area. These divisions hear matters that are of such a serious nature that the lower courts would not be competent to make an appropriate judgment or impose a penalty. Except where minimum or maximum sentences are prescribed by law, their penal jurisdiction is unlimited and includes life imprisonment in certain specified cases.

The Department aims to increase the number of cases finalised by the High Courts to 1 000 cases a day. The Department also hopes to increase the number of court hours worked per day.

Decisions of the CC, the Supreme Court of Appeal and the High Courts are an important source of law. These Courts are required to uphold and enforce the Constitution, which has an extensive Bill of Rights binding all organs of State and all persons. The Courts are also required to declare any law or conduct that is inconsistent with the Constitution to be invalid to the extent of that inconsistency, and to develop the common law in a manner consistent with the values of the Constitution and the spirit and purpose of the Bill of Rights.

The Land Claims Court and the Labour Court have the same status as the High Court. The Land Claims Court hears matters on the restitution of land rights that people lost after 1913 as a result of racially discriminatory land laws. The Labour Court adjudicates matters relating to labour disputes, and appeals are made to the Labour Appeal Court.

By mid-2003, the Department was engaged in consultations with the judiciary and key stakeholders regarding the rationalisation of the High Courts in terms of the Superior Courts Bill. The objective is to ensure that High Courts are distributed in accordance with political and constitutional boundaries.

By mid-2003, the rationalisation of the Labour Court was at an advanced stage, with legislation being prepared to integrate that Court and the Labour Appeal Court into the High Court and the Supreme Court of Appeal.

Circuit local divisions

These are itinerant courts, each presided over by a judge of the provincial division. These courts periodically visit areas designated by the Judge President of the provincial division concerned.

Regional Courts

The Minister of Justice and Constitutional Development may divide the country into magisterial districts and create regional divisions consisting of districts. Regional Courts are then established at one or more places in each regional division to hear matters within their jurisdiction.

Unlike the High Court, the penal jurisdiction of the Regional Courts is limited by legislation.

Magistrate's Courts

Magisterial districts have been grouped into 13 clusters headed by chief magistrates. This system has streamlined, simplified and provided uniform court-management systems applicable throughout South Africa, in terms of judicial provincial boundaries. It facilitated the separation of functions pertaining to the judiciary, prosecution and administration; enhanced and developed the skills and training of judicial officers; optimised the use of the limited available resources in an equitable manner; and addressed the imbalances in the former homeland regions. The Department now communicates through cluster heads.

In terms of the Magistrates Act, 1993 (Act 90 of 1993), all magistrates in South Africa fall outside the ambit of the Public Service. The aim is to strengthen the independence of the judiciary. Although the Regional Courts have a higher penal jurisdiction than Magistrate's Courts (District Courts), an accused person cannot appeal to the Regional Court against the decision of a District Court, only to the High Court.

By March 2003, there were 370 magistrate's offices, 51 detached offices, 107 branch courts and 234 periodical courts in South Africa, with 1 772 magistrates.

The Department has set several targets aimed at promoting case-flow management in the lower courts. These include finalising 40 cases per month per District Court and 15 cases per month per Regional Court during 2003/04.

A further target set is increasing the number of court hours worked per day to five hours per District Court and four hours per Regional Court during 2003/04.

Civil jurisdiction

Except when otherwise provided by law, the area of civil jurisdiction of a Magistrate's Court is the district, subdistrict or area for which the Court has been established. South African law as applied in the Western Cape is in force on Prince Edward and Marion Islands which, for the purpose of the administration of justice, are deemed to be part of the Cape Town magisterial district.

On 1 May 1995, the civil jurisdictional limits of Magistrate's Courts were increased for both liquid and illiquid claims, from R50 000 and R20 000 respectively, to R100 000. In addition to the considerable increase, the previous distinction between jurisdictional limits with regard to the different causes of action was abolished.

Unless all the parties in a case consent to higher jurisdiction, the jurisdiction of a Magistrate's Court is limited to cases in which the claim value does not exceed R100 000 where the action arises out of a liquid document or credit agreement, or R50 000 in all other cases.

Small Claims Court

Cases involving civil claims not exceeding R3 000 are heard by a commissioner in the Small Claims Court. Thirty-five such Courts have been created since 1994, with a focus on rural and previously disadvantaged areas. By July 2003, there were 142 courts countrywide, of which 25 were designated to rural areas.

The commissioner is usually a practising advocate or attorney, a legal academic or other competent person, who offers his or her services free of charge.

Neither the plaintiff nor the defendant may be represented or assisted by counsel at the hearing. The commissioner's decision is final and there is no appeal to a higher court.

Other civil courts

An authorised African headman or his deputy may hear and determine civil claims arising from indigenous law and custom, brought before him by an African against another African within his area of jurisdiction. Courts constituted in this way are commonly known as Chief's Courts. Litigants have the right to choose whether to institute an action in the Chief's Court or in a Magistrate's Court.

Proceedings in a Chief's Court are informal. An appeal against a judgment of a Chief's Court is heard in a Magistrate's Court.

Criminal jurisdiction

Apart from specific provisions of the Magistrate's Courts Act, 1944 (Act 32 of 1944), or any other Act, jurisdiction with regard to sentences imposed by District Courts is limited to a period of not more than three years' imprisonment or a fine not exceeding R60 000. The Regional Court can impose a sentence of not more than 15 years' imprisonment or a fine not exceeding R300 000.

Any person charged with any offence committed within any district or regional division may be tried either by the Court of that district or the Court of that regional division. Where it is uncertain in which of several jurisdictions an offence has been committed, it may be tried in any of such jurisdictions.

Where, by any special provision of law, a Magistrate's Court has jurisdiction over an offence committed beyond the limits of the district or regional division, the Court will not be deprived of such jurisdiction.

A Magistrate's Court has jurisdiction over all offences except treason, murder and rape. The Regional Court has jurisdiction over all offences except treason. However, the High Court may try all offences. Depending on the gravity of the offence and circumstances pertaining to the offender, the DPP decides in which court a matter will be heard. He or she may even decide on a summary trial in the High Court.

Prosecutions are usually summarily disposed of in Magistrate's Courts, and judgment and sentence passed. The following sentences may, where provided for by law, be passed upon a convicted person:
- imprisonment
- periodical imprisonment
- declaration as a habitual criminal (Regional Court and High Court)
- committal to an institution established by law
- a fine with or without imprisonment as alternative, correctional supervision or a suspended sentence
- declaration as a dangerous criminal (Regional Court and High Court)
- a warning or caution
- discharge.

The sentencing of 'petty' offenders to do community service as a condition of suspension, correctional supervision or postponement in appropriate circumstances has become part of an alternative sentence to imprisonment.

Where a court convicts a person of any offence other than one for which any law prescribes a minimum punishment, the court may, at its discretion, postpone the passing of sentence for a period not exceeding five years and release the person convicted on one or more conditions, or pass sentence but suspend it on certain conditions.

If the conditions of suspension or postponement are not fulfilled, the offender may be arrested and made to serve the sentence. This is done provided that the court may grant an order further suspending the operation of the sentence if the offender proves that circumstances beyond his or her control or any other good and sufficient reason prevented him or her from complying with the conditions of suspension.

Other criminal courts

In terms of statutory law, jurisdiction may be conferred upon a chief or headman or his deputy to punish an African person who has committed an offence under common law or indigenous law and custom, with the exception of certain serious offences specified in the relevant legislation. The procedure at such trials is in accordance with indigenous law and custom. The jurisdiction conferred upon a chief and a magistrate does not affect the jurisdiction of other courts competent to try criminal cases.

Legal practitioners

The legal profession is divided into two branches – advocates and attorneys – who are subject to a strict ethical code.

Advocates are organised into Bar associations or societies, one each at the seat of the various divisions of the High Court. The General Council of the Bar of South Africa is the co-ordinating body of the various Bar associations. There is a law society for attorneys in each of the provinces. A practising attorney is *ipso jure* a member of at least one of these societies, which seek to promote the interests of the profession.

The Law Society of South Africa is the co-ordinating body of the various independent law societies.

In terms of the Right of Appearance in Courts Act, 1995 (Act 62 of 1995), advocates can appear in any court, while attorneys may be heard in all of the country's lower courts and can also acquire the right of appearance in the Superior Courts. An attorney who wishes to represent his or her client in the High Court is required to apply to the registrar of a provincial division of the High Court. Such an attorney may also appear in the CC. All attorneys who hold an LLB or equivalent degree, or who have at least three years' experience, may acquire the right of audience in the High Court.

The Attorneys Amendment Act, 1993 (Act 115 of 1993), provides for alternative routes for admission as an attorney. One of these routes is that a person who intends to be admitted as an attorney and who has satisfied certain degree requirements prescribed in the Act is exempted from service under articles or clerkship. However, such a person must satisfy the society concerned that he or she has at least five years' appropriate legal experience.

State law advisors give legal advice to Ministers, government departments and provincial administrations, as well as to a number of statutory bodies. In addition, they draft Bills and assist the Minister concerned with the passage of Bills through Parliament. They also assist in criminal and constitutional matters.

In terms of the NPA Act, 1998, State advocates and prosecutors have been separated from the Public Service in certain respects, notably the determination of salaries.

Justice and correctional services

The State Attorney derives his or her power from the State Attorney Act, 1957 (Act 56 of 1957), and protects the interests of the State in the most cost-effective manner possible. He or she does this by acting on behalf of the State in legal matters covering a wide spectrum of the law.

The State Attorney is involved in the drafting of contracts where the State is a party, and also acts on behalf of elected and appointed officials acting in the performance of their duties, e.g. civil and criminal actions instituted against Ministers and government officials in their official capacities.

Masters of the High Court

The Masters of the High Court are involved with the administration of justice in estates of deceased persons and those declared insolvent, the liquidation of companies and close corporations, and the registration of trusts.

The key statutory functions of the Masters are the following:
- controlling the administration of deceased and curatorship estates
- controlling the administration of insolvent estates and the liquidation of companies and close corporations
- controlling the registration and administration of both testamentary and *inter vivos* trusts
- managing the Guardian's Fund, which is entrusted with the funds of minors, mentally challenged persons, unknown and/or absent heirs, and creditors for administration on their behalf
- assessing estate duty and certain functions with regard thereto
- the acceptance and custodianship of wills in deceased estates
- acting as an Office of Record.

The computerisation of the Guardian's Fund has reached an advanced stage and will revolutionise the administration of trust funds for minors. The Guardian's Fund grew by 18% in 2003.

Master's Business Unit

The Master's Business Unit was launched in Pretoria in October 2002, creating a structure for the Master's Division of the High Court. The Unit is responsible for the overall control of Master's Offices in the country, creating uniformity in Master's Offices, overall control of the Guardian's Fund, strategy and research, and the creation of new offices.

The Unit was expected to open offices in Johannesburg, Polokwane, Durban and Port Elizabeth in 2003.

Rules Board for Courts of Law

The Rules Board is a statutory body, empowered to make or amend rules for the High Courts, the Supreme Court of Appeal and the lower courts.

It also develops rules and court procedure to ensure a speedy, inexpensive civil justice system, which is in harmony with the Constitution and technological developments, and accessible to all South Africans.

Justice College

The Justice College is tasked with the vocational training of all officials of the Department. The College also presents training to autonomous professions such as magistrates and prosecutors.

Office of the Family Advocate

The Office of the Family Advocate functions in terms of the Mediation in Certain Divorce Matters Act, 1987 (Act 24 of 1987).

The Family Advocate, assisted by family counsellors, reports to the court and makes recommendations which will serve the best interest of children in cases where there is litigation relating to children in divorce actions or applications for the variation of existing divorce orders.

Inquiries take place at the request of the court, one or both parties to the litigation, or on the initiative of the Family Advocate, in which case authorisation of the court must be obtained.

Family advocates operate in the provincial and local divisions of the High Court.

The Hague Convention on the Civil Aspects of International Child Abduction Act, 1996 (Act 72 of 1996), came into effect in October 1997 and the Natural Fathers of Children Born out of Wedlock Act, 1997 (Act 86 of 1997), in September 1998. The promulgation of these Acts extended the service delivery of the Office of the Family Advocate countrywide.

The Office of the Family Advocate provides support services for the Family Court pilot projects. Most offices are involved in mediation training for a large contingent of social workers and other mental-health professionals.

The Office of the Family Advocate co-ordinates community-outreach programmes to assist children involved in family disputes.

Legal aid

The Legal Aid Board is an independent statutory body established in terms of the Legal Aid Act, 1969 (Act 22 of 1969).

The Legal Aid Board provides tax-subsidised legal help to those in greatest need. It does so in accordance with the Constitution and the Bill of Rights. As a progressive and independent public defender, the Board is committed to the building of a just society where each person respects the constitutional rights of others.

The Legal Aid Board's work covers both civil and criminal cases. Its criminal work supports each person's right of innocence until proven guilty. The Constitution guarantees accused criminals the right to a fair trial and this is done through the Board. In its civil work, the Board places special emphasis on providing legal advice and protecting and defending the rights of women, children and the landless.

The Board's half-a-billion Rand budget contributes to:
- finalising over half of all matters in courts
- protecting the rights of people through timely legal advice
- defending the rights of households through impact litigation.

In civil matters, legal applicants are obliged to qualify in terms of a means test. In criminal matters, the means test is used as a point of departure, but the final test is whether or not the accused is able to afford the cost of his/her own legal representation.

Criminal matters handled by the Legal Aid Board include all matters in which substantial injustice would result if legal representation were not provided at State expense. Subject to the ability of the accused to provide his/her legal representation, all matters in the High Court, all matters in the Regional Courts, many matters in the District and Magistrate's Courts, and less serious matters where the accused, if convicted, would be unlikely to be sentenced to more than three years' imprisonment, are excluded from the scheme.

Minor civil claims, the institution of claims sounding in money (for which contingency-fee arrangements are legal) and civil claims, which do not have reasonable prospect of success, are also excluded from the civil legal-aid scheme.

The Board used to provide legal aid and representation mostly by instructing legal practitioners in private practice. This has proved to be unsustainably expensive and subject to abuse. The Legal Aid Board is moving towards a scheme in which salaried legal practitioners employed by the Board provide most legal aid and representation. By the end of 2004, the Board plans to have a national network of 60 Justice Centres throughout South Africa. By the end of April 2003, 44 Justice Centres had been established.

Legal aid may also be provided through co-operation agreements with NGOs and universities which provide legal services. Co-operation agreements are an important part of the Legal Aid Board's Access to Justice Strategy. The Board is committed to rendering quality legal services and is consequently eager to participate in the further development of the justice system through continued co-operation with its partners. It assists approximately 250 000 applicants a year.

Office of the Public Protector

In terms of the Constitution and the Public Protector Act, 1994, as amended, the Public Protector is independent of government and is responsible for investigating any conduct in State affairs, or in the public administration in any sphere of government, that is alleged or suspected to be improper or to result in any impropriety or prejudice. The Public Protector is required to report and take remedial action on that conduct. The purpose of the Office is to strengthen and support constitutional democracy in South Africa.

The Public Protector enjoys wide discretion regarding the manner in which any dispute is resolved and methods may include mediation, conciliation and negotiation as well as formal methods of investigation, such as the issuing of subpoenas, taking evidence under oath, and cross-examination. The Public Protector may, after the issue of a warrant by a magistrate or judge, enter any building or premises to investigate a complaint, and may seize anything on those premises which in his or her opinion has a bearing on the investigation.

The Public Protector can make recommendations to the public body involved, and may refer any indications of a criminal offence to the relevant authority responsible for prosecutions. The Public Protector is prohibited from inquiring into the decisions of a court of law. No person or institution may hinder the Public Protector in the execution of his or her duties.

Any person may submit complaints to the Public Protector. Except in special circumstances, the Public Protector will not investigate a complaint unless it is reported within two years of the occurrence of the incident or matter concerned. Reports on the findings in any investigation are made public, unless the Public Protector is of the opinion that exceptional circumstances require that the report be kept confidential. The Public Protector submits annual reports to Parliament on its activities and functions. If necessary, reports on the findings of certain investigations are also submitted to Parliament.

The Office of the Public Protector has provincial offices in all provinces, except Gauteng, where the national Office fulfils that function. In 2002/03, the Office received 15 680 new cases and 13 108 cases were carried forward from 2001/02. Of these, 21 707 cases were finalised in 2002/03.

Magistrate's Commission

The Magistrate's Commission was established to ensure that the appointment, promotion, transfer or discharge of, or disciplinary steps against judicial officers in the lower courts take place without favour or prejudice, and that the applicable laws and administrative directions in connection with such actions are applied uniformly and correctly.

The Commission also attends to grievances, complaints and misconduct investigations against magistrates. It advises the Minister on matters such as the appointment of magistrates, promotions, salaries and legislation.

The Commission has established committees to deal with appointments and promotions; misconduct, disciplinary inquiries and incapacity; grievances; salary and service conditions; and the training of magistrates.

South African Law Reform Commission

It is generally accepted that legal systems and rules should be revised and reformed on a continuous basis. Law reform is necessary to ensure that the principles underlying the legal system are just and in line with governing social views and values.

With a view to extending the basis for consultation and involving interested parties and the community at an earlier stage in the process of law reform, shorter documents –

which precede the publication of discussion papers – are compiled for general information and comment. The object is to stimulate and activate debate in respect of relevant matters, and to give direction to the reform which is to follow. The Commission's line of thinking is also evident from the community-orientated nature of the investigations included in its programmes.

Judicial Service Commission

In terms of the Constitution, the Chief Justice and the Deputy Chief Justice, and the President and Deputy President of the Supreme Court of Appeal are appointed by the President after consulting the JSC. Other judges are appointed by the President on the advice of the JSC.

In the case of the Chief Justice and the Deputy Chief Justice, the leaders of the parties represented in the National Assembly are also consulted.

The JSC was established in terms of Section 178 of the Constitution to perform this function and also advises government on any matters relating to the judiciary or the administration of justice.

When appointments have to be made, the Commission gives public notice of the vacancies that exist and calls for nominations. Suitable candidates are short-listed by the Commission and invited for interviews. Professional bodies and members of the public are afforded the opportunity to comment before interviews or make representations concerning the candidates, to the Commission. The Commission has determined criteria and guidelines for the making of appointments, which have been made public.

The interviews are conducted as public hearings and may be attended by anyone who wishes to do so. Following the interviews, the JSC deliberates and makes its decisions in private. Its recommendations are communicated to the President, who then makes the appointments.

In terms of Section 177 of the Constitution, a judge may be removed from office only if the JSC finds that the judge suffers from an incapacity, is grossly incompetent, or is guilty of gross misconduct.

The Commission considered it desirable that a formal system for the handling of complaints against judges be established by legislation. After discussions with the judiciary, draft legislation dealing with aspects such as control over discipline, leave, salaries and a complaints mechanism regarding the lower judiciary in order to strengthen the independence of the judiciary, is being prepared.

South African Human Rights Commission (SAHRC)

The Constitution makes provision for a Human Rights Commission consisting of a chairperson and 10 members. The appointment of commissioners is regulated by the Constitution.

The SAHRC, launched on 21 March 1996, comprises a Commission and a Secretariat. The aim of the Commission is to promote a culture and respect for human rights, to promote the protection, development and attainment of human rights, and to monitor and assess the observance of human rights in South Africa.

The SAHRC has the power to:
- investigate and report on the observance of human rights
- take steps to secure appropriate redress where human rights have been violated
- carry out research and educate.

The Commission has established standing committees that advise and assist the Commission in its work. The committees are:
- International Standards
- NGO and Community-based Organisation Liaison
- Disability
- Children
- Government and Parliamentary Liaison.

The Secretariat implements the policy of the Commission and ensures the promotion and

Justice and correctional services

protection of rights by handling complaints of human rights-violations; monitoring observance of human rights; and education, training and public information.

Strategic objectives
To effectively execute the constitutional mandate and give effect to its mission statement, the strategic objectives of the SAHRC are to:
- raise awareness on human rights and the role of the Commission, and to provide an internal and external communication service
- contribute to the development of a sustainable culture of human rights and democracy through training and by translating human-rights standards into tangible and deliverable education and training outcomes
- investigate individual and systemic complaints of human-rights violations and provide redress
- provide a research and documentation facility designed to advance human rights, especially social and economic rights
- establish the Commission as a resource and focal point for human rights in South Africa in collaboration with other institutions on the continent.

Within the parameters of its business plan, the Commission has focused on:
- socio-economic rights
- equality, with specific focus on child rights, HIV/AIDS, disability, racism, older persons, and health
- the administration of justice.

National Centre for Human-Rights Education and Training (NACHRET)
NACHRET was established in April 2000. The Centre provides a platform for debate on human-rights issues aimed at enhancing an understanding of these issues and practices. The Centre also provides training and builds capacity both in South Africa and on the continent with regard to human rights themes, challenges and issues.

Commission on Gender Equality (CGE)
Chapter 9 of the Constitution provides for the establishment of, among others, the CGE. Section 187 of the Constitution specifically grants the CGE powers to promote respect for gender equality, and promote the protection, development and attainment of gender equality. The composition, functions and objectives of the CGE are outlined in the CGE Act, 1996 (Act 39 of 1996).

The CGE comprises 11 commissioners, one chairperson and 37 members of the Secretariat who fall within four departments and are based in six provinces. The other three provinces are serviced from the Johannesburg office. The CGE is responsible for:
- gathering information and conducting education on gender equality
- monitoring and evaluating the policies and practices of State organs, statutory and public bodies, as well as the private sector, to promote gender equality
- evaluating Acts in force, or proposed by Parliament, affecting or likely to affect gender
- investigating any gender-related complaints
- liaising with institutions, bodies or authorities with similar objectives
- conducting research to further the objectives of the CGE.

The CGE works in partnership with various civil-society structures and other organisations with similar objectives.

Attending to gender-inequality complaints is one of its core functions. The CGE received 904 complaints in 2001/02, of which 29% related to gender-based violence and 52% involved maintenance cases.

The flagship theme of the CGE during 2003 was *Gender and Poverty*. There are other themes for which the CGE implements programmes, namely:
- *Gender and Good Governance*
- *Gender-Based Violence*
- *Gender, Culture, Religion and Tradition.*

Some of the activities that were performed include:
- conducting research on:
  - women and access to social security
  - women and access to economic opportunities
  - monitoring the implementation of the Employment Equity Act, 1998 (Act 55 of 1998)
  - Unemployment Insurance Fund maternity benefits
  - implementation of the Maintenance Act, 1998 and addressing systemic problems
  - Spatial Development Initiatives.

One of the noteworthy activities recently finalised by the CGE is Integrated Development Planning, whereby the CGE monitored and evaluated whether or not local government has gender-responsive approaches to service provision, and developmental plans that have a positive impact on women.

The CGE supports strategic interventions in litigation, with the aim of encouraging law reform.

The CGE also monitors most Bills that are introduced in Parliament to ensure that gender sensitivity is considered and that the rights of women are integrated.

Truth and Reconciliation Commission (TRC)

The TRC's date of dissolution was determined as 31 March 2002 by way of proclamation in the *Government Gazette*. The dissolution was ordered by the President in terms of Section 43(3)(b) of the Promotion of National Unity and Reconciliation Act, 1995 (Act 34 of 1995).

President Thabo Mbeki presented government's recommendations arising from the work of the TRC and tabled the final TRC report in Parliament on 15 April 2003.

The Department of Justice and Constitutional Development hosted a one-day consultative workshop for the business sector and civil society to discuss the various recommendations of the TRC prior to the tabling of the final report.

According to the TRC, some 22 000 individuals or their surviving family members appeared before the Commission. Of these, 19 000 required urgent reparations, and virtually all of them, where the necessary information was available, were attended to as proposed by the TRC with regard to interim reparations.

With regard to final reparations, during 2003/04, government planned to provide a once-off grant of R30 000 to those individuals or survivors designated by the TRC. This was over and above other material commitments.

A Joint Committee of Parliament considered the recommendations of the TRC and government, as presented to Parliament. The recommendations, as approved by Parliament, were referred to President Thabo Mbeki. The publication of the regulations in the *Government Gazette* will pave the way for the disbursement of final reparations to those eligible, from the President's Fund.

International affairs

The functions of the Directorate: International Affairs in the Department of Justice and Constitutional Development consist mainly of identifying and researching legal questions that relate to matters pertaining to the administration of justice between South Africa and other states.

The Directorate is involved in direct liaison and negotiations at administrative and technical levels with foreign states in an effort to promote international legal co-operation and for the possible conclusion of extradition and mutual legal-assistance agreements.

The Directorate also aims to establish greater uniformity between the legal systems of southern African states, especially the Southern African Development Community (SADC), and thus promote and establish an efficient administration of justice in the southern African region.

Justice and correctional services

The Directorate co-ordinates human rights issues at international level under the auspices of the United Nations (UN) and the African Union (AU).

The functions of the Directorate can be divided into six broad categories:
- the establishment of regular liaison with SADC states
- the co-ordination of all Commonwealth matters pertaining to the administration of justice
- interaction with other international bodies, such as the UN, the Hague Conference and the International Institute for the Unification of Private Law
- interaction with foreign states outside the SADC region
- negotiation of extradition and mutual legal-assistance agreements with other countries
- preparation of Cabinet and Parliament documentation for ratification of human-rights treaties, including report-writing.

Extradition and Mutal Legal-Assistance (in Criminal Matters) Treaties (MLATs)

On 21 May 2003, South Africa had extradition agreements, ratified by Parliament, with the following countries:
- Botswana
- Lesotho (ratified on 7 November 2001)
- Malawi
- Swaziland
- USA (ratified on 9 November 2000)
- Canada (ratified on 3 April 2001)
- Australia (ratified on 9 November 2000)
- Israel
- Egypt (ratified on 11 November 2002)
- Algeria (ratified on 11 November 2002)
- Nigeria (ratified on 11 November 2002)
- China (ratified on 11 November 2002).

The following treaties were negotiated, but bave not yet been signed:
- Zambia (Extradition and MLAT)
- Argentina (Extradition)
- Hungary (Extradition)
- Namibia (Extradition and MLAT)
- Hong Kong (Extradition and MLAT)
- Brazil (MLAT).

South Africa has MLATs with the following countries:
- Canada (ratified on 3 April 2001, entered into force on 5 May 2001)
- USA (ratified on 9 November 2000, entered into force on 25 June 2001)
- Lesotho (ratified on 7 November 2001)
- Egypt (ratified on 11 November 2002)
- Algeria (ratified on 11 November 2002)
- Nigeria (ratified on 11 November 2002)
- France (ratified on 11 November 2002).

An MLAT with China was recently signed but has not yet been ratified.

The Department is preparing for negotiations for the conclusion of extradition and MLATs with various countries including the United Arab Emirates, Iran, India, Peru, Uruguay, Thailand and Chile.

South Africa has also designated Ireland, Zimbabwe, Namibia and the UK in terms of Section 3(2) of the Extradition Act, 1962 (Act 67 0f 1962).

South Africa's accession to the Council of Europe's Convention on Extradition entered into force on 13 May 2003. A request was also directed to the Council of Europe that South Africa accede to the Convention on Mutual Legal Assistance (MLA).

The AU Convention on Extradition was finalised during a meeting of legal experts held in Ethiopia in April 2001.

Human-rights issues

Southern African Development Community

The Directorate participated in the negotiation and preparation of the establishment of the Legal Sector and the SADC Protocol on the Tribunal. Heads of State and Government signed both Protocols in August 2000. The Protocols have been submitted to Parliament for approval to ratify.

The Directorate also participated in the negotiation and the finalisation of the SADC Protocol Against Corruption. The Cabinet has approved this Protocol and it is before Parliament for ratification.

African Union
The Directorate: International Affairs hosted the 31st Ordinary Session of the African Commission on Human and Peoples' Rights in May 2002. The Protocol to Establish the African Court was signed by South Africa in June 2002.

The Directorate has prepared the First Periodic Country Report on the African Charter on Human and People's Rights.

Commonwealth
With regard to the Commonwealth Heads of Government meeting, the Directorate had to provide input on a variety of issues regarding the Senior Law Officials meeting. It also formed part of an interdepartmental committee that had to determine the substance of South Africa's input to the Commonwealth Heads of Government meeting.

United Nations
The Directorate has prepared three human-rights country reports for submission to the relevant UN Committees. The reports relate to the Convention Against Torture or other Cruel, Inhuman or Degrading Treatment or Punishment, the International Convention on the Elimination of All Forms of Discrimination, and the International Covenant on Civil and Political Rights (ICCPR).

The Directorate was responsible for promoting South Africa's accession to the First and Second Optional Protocols to the ICCPR.

National Action Plan (NAP)
The Directorate was part of the process of drafting an interim report on the NAP for the promotion and protection of human rights pertaining to the justice mandate.

Hague Conference
After numerous calls for South Africa to become a member of the Hague Conference on Private International Law, the Directorate prepared documents for the Cabinet and Parliament for approval to ratify the Hague Statute. South Africa became a member of the Conference on 15 February 2002.

The Hague Conference seeks to foster co-operation between states on private law matters. This is done by elaborating on conventions and inviting states to become party to these conventions.

International Criminal Court (ICC)
A South African delegation comprising the Departments of Justice and Constitutional Development and of Foreign Affairs attended the UN Preparatory Commission Sessions during April and June/July 2002, which saw the finalisation of the outstanding instruments of the ICC, in particular the Fifth Year Budget of the ICC, and the procedure for the nomination and election of judges, prosecutors and deputy prosecutors.

On 11 March 2003, the Minister of Justice and Constitutional Development and his delegation attended the inauguration ceremony of the Court in The Hague, Netherlands.

As required by the Rome Statute of the ICC, South Africa has promulgated the Implementation of the Rome Statute of the ICC Act, 2002 (Act 27 of 2002).

This Act provides for a framework to:
- ensure the effective implementation of the Rome Statute of the ICC in South Africa
- ensure that South Africa conforms with the obligations set out in the Statute
- address the crime of genocide, crimes against humanity and war crimes
- address the prosecution in South African courts of persons accused of having committed the said crimes in South Africa and beyond the borders of South Africa in certain circumstances
- deal with the arrest of certain persons

accused of having committed the said crimes and their surrender to the ICC in certain circumstances
- address co-operation by South Africa with the ICC.

South African judge Ms Navi Pillay was appointed one of the first judges of the ICC in March 2003.

Correctional services

Safe custody of prisoners

The aim of the Department of Correctional Services is to contribute towards maintaining and protecting a just, peaceful and safe society by enforcing court-imposed sentences, detaining offenders in safe custody, and promoting the social responsibility and human development of all offenders and persons subject to community correction programmes.

A re-engineering project, called *Gearing for Rehabilitation*, was introduced in 2002/03 to evaluate systems, processes and structures, and align them with the core business of the Department.

The project has moved beyond a substantial review of rehabilitation and has identified key service-delivery areas, namely:
- corrections
- development
- security
- care
- facilities
- after-care.

This comprehensive approach entails all aspects of the Department's core business, ranging from corrections, which profile and risk-assess individuals, to after-care, which focuses on pre-release reintegration programmes for offenders. This substantial undertaking also involves developing new policy for the types of rehabilitation programmes offered and the training of prison personnel.

The *Gearing for Rehabilitation* process was aligned to the broader transformation and restructuring of the Public Service.

This process saw the development of an updated departmental strategic plan and, stemming from that, a new organisational structure. The updated structure of the Department consolidated the nine provinces into six geographical regions and the previous 148 management areas into 48 such areas.

During 2003/04, the budget allocation for the Department of Correctional Services was spent as follows:
- R3 554 million on incarceration
- R398 million on the rehabilitation of offenders
- R260 million on community corrections
- R1 547 million on facility management and capital works
- R2 455 million on administration.

By 31 March 2003, the Department had a personnel force of 33 385 with 189 748 offenders incarcerated in 241 prisons countrywide. By April 2003, there were approximately 48 000 parolees and 24 500 probationers under the Department's supervision within the system of community corrections.

Incarceration

The Incarceration Programme finances the detention of prisoners in safe custody until they can be lawfully released. The Programme provides for the healthcare and physical needs of offenders in terms of norms and standards that comply with the Constitution.

Offender population and accommodation

The Department strives to provide adequate prison accommodation that complies with accepted standards. Offenders are housed in 241 prisons countrywide, which include:
- eight prisons for female offenders only
- 13 youth correctional facilities
- 134 prisons for male offenders only
- 72 prisons for both male and female offenders
- 14 prisons temporarily inactive (closed down for renovations).

In prisons where male, female and juvenile offenders are accommodated, female and juvenile offenders are housed in separate designated sections.

Overcrowding in South Africa's active prisons is problematic. A long history of inadequate funding to renovate existing prisons and build new ones makes this problem difficult to address.

The prisons can accommodate some 111 241 offenders, but by June 2003, the prison population stood at 185 748. This constituted 127 604 sentenced and 58 144 unsentenced prisoners. Capacity then stood at 111 241, indicating overcrowding by 74 507 or about 67%. The figures showed a slight decrease in the prisoner population which may be attributed to several strategies being adopted by the Department.

To deal with overcrowding in prisons, the Departments of Correctional Services and of Justice and Constitutional Development have initiated:
- transferring unsentenced juveniles to places of secure care
- converting certain prison sentences to correctional supervision
- identifying, renovating and upgrading existing facilities
- placing awaiting-trial persons under community corrections
- piloting integrated action by departments to review cases and reduce the average detention cycle times of awaiting-trial offenders.

Apart from these initiatives, the Department is addressing overcrowding on a continuous basis in conjunction with the other role-players in the CJS. One strategy is the use of Saturday courts to address the backlog with regard to awaiting-trial offenders. The implementation of the electronic court process will also go a long way towards streamlining court processes.

The Department will continue to release offenders serving minor offences after they have served a set minimum sentence.

It will further enhance rehabilitation by placing it at the centre of all activities, striking a balance between rehabilitation and safe custody.

The aim is to provide education, skills development, personal development and spiritual enlightenment to address offending behaviour and to release offenders as productive and law-abiding citizens.

It is expected that the already overcrowded prisons will come under greater strain in the next few years as the effects of the new offender-release policy and the Criminal Law Amendment Act, 1997 (Act 105 of 1997), are felt.

In terms of the new release policy, no offender may be considered for parole before he or she has completed at least half of his or her sentence.

The Criminal Law Amendment Act, 1997 makes provision for much harsher sentences for serious crimes.

These changes are expected to place an even greater burden on the prisons since it is likely to increase the average length of prison sentences.

Safety and security

In general, the Department has been quite successful in bringing down the number of escapes during the last few years. However, owing to one unfortunate incident at Bizana Prison in the Eastern Cape in December 2002, when 98 offenders escaped during an evacuation operation as a result of a serious fire threat, there was an increase in the number of escapes from 223 in 2001/02 to 281 in 2002/03.

The Department has put in place various measures aimed at combating escapes. These include the optimal utilisation of existing security aids and equipment, continued evaluation of security directives, upgrading of personnel training, disciplinary action against negligent personnel, rewarding offenders who report on or warn of planned escapes, and the installation of electronic fences and X-ray scanners in high-risk prisons.

Ninety-four prisoners escaped between January and August 2003, compared to 166 in the same period during 2002, representing a 43% reduction.

Classification

Offenders undergo safe-custody classification upon admission to determine the level of security required to detain them.

Offenders are classified into minimum, medium or maximum custodial categories. Variables taken into account include the type of crime committed, the length of the sentence, and previous convictions. The safe-custody classification of every offender is reviewed regularly, and if his or her behaviour, or any other aspect affecting his or her security risk, justifies it, reclassification takes place.

Categories

There are five categories of offenders in South African prisons, namely:
- unsentenced offenders (mainly offenders standing trial on a charge and detained in prison pending the conclusion of the judicial process)
- short-term offenders (offenders serving a sentence of less than two years)
- long-term offenders (offenders serving sentences of two years and longer)
- unsentenced children/juveniles and youths between the ages of 14 and 25
- sentenced children/juveniles and youths between the ages of 14 and 25.

Young offenders

In terms of the Constitution, a child is a person under the age of 18 years. The Department regards a person between the ages of 14 and 25 years as a youth. The Department is responsible for the detention, treatment and development of sentenced juveniles.

Section 7(2)(c) of the Correctional Services Act, 1998 (Act 111 of 1998), stipulates that children must be kept separate from adult offenders and in accommodation appropriate to their age, as young offenders are predisposed to negative influence. The aim of this separation is the provision of distinctive custodial, development and treatment programmes, as well as religious care, in an environment conducive to the care, development and motivation of youths to participate and to develop their potential.

Sentenced young offenders are also kept separate from unsentenced ones.

By June 2003, there were about 26 000 young people between the ages of 14 and 21 in the system, and about 49 000 between the ages of 21 and 25. The nature of serious offences committed or allegedly committed by about 4 500 children under the age of 18 who were awaiting trial or sentenced was alarming. There were 2 000 economic-related offenders under 18; 1 800 aggressive crime offenders; 500 sexually related offenders under the age of 18; and 200 for drug-related and other types of offences.

There are 13 youth correctional facilities in the country, namely Hawequa, Brandvlei, Drakenstein Medium B and Pollsmoor Medium A (Western Cape); Leeuwkop, Emthonjeni and Boksburg (Gauteng); Rustenburg (North West), Durban and Ekuseni (KwaZulu-Natal); Groenpunt and Kroonstad (Free State); and Barberton Town Prison (Mpumalanga).

The development and support of youth offenders form an essential part of their incarceration. The aim of rendering professional services (education, reskilling, learning a trade, moral and spiritual enlightenment, and personal development) is to rehabilitate youth offenders, contribute towards their behavioural change, and prepare them for their reintegration into the community.

The focus is on the promotion and development of leadership qualities. A holistic approach is followed in which:
- young offenders are motivated to actively participate in their own development and the realisation of their potential
- a culture and atmosphere of development prevails
- sound discipline and co-operation between personnel and offenders, and among offenders, is fostered and maintained.

Mother-and-child units

Mother-and-child units have been established in eight female prisons nationally. By June 2003, there were 208 infants under the age of five in prison with their mothers. Policy on such infants clearly stipulates that mothers and children are kept in a separate unit within the prison, where the surroundings and facilities are complementary to the sound physical, social and mental care and development of children.

The policy also stipulates that the admission of an infant with a mother is permitted if no other suitable accommodation and care are available at that stage, and that it should be regarded as a temporary measure only.

The right of the mother to have her child with her during admission promotes a positive relationship between mother and child. Policy emphasises that the mother should be taught good child-care practices for her own self-esteem and self-confidence and for the benefit of the child.

The privilege system

The main objectives of the privilege system are to encourage offenders to display good behaviour, engender a sense of responsibility in them, and ensure their interest and co-operation in treatment programmes.

The system consists of primary and secondary privileges. Primary privileges are aimed at the retention, maintenance or furthering of family ties to, among other things, facilitate reintegration into the community. These privileges are divided into A, B and C groups. The entry level for all new admissions is the B group and, depending on behaviour, an offender may be promoted or demoted to either the A or C privilege group.

Secondary privileges are aimed at leisure-time activities such as participation in sports and watching television. No sentenced offenders are allowed to receive food from outside prison or to use private electrical appliances.

Physical care and hygiene

Physical care of offenders is regarded as an important responsibility of the Department, and includes healthcare, nutrition and accommodation. The Department endorses the fundamental rights and privileges of all offenders.

In accordance with the Correctional Services Act, 1998, an independent judicial inspectorate regularly inspects all prisons and reports on conditions and the treatment of offenders.

The policy and administrative framework for the maintenance of an adequate, affordable and comprehensive healthcare service is based on the principles of Primary Health Care (PHC). The service includes mental, dental and reproductive health, ancillary healthcare, health-promotion management of communicable diseases (including HIV/AIDS and sexually transmitted infections [STIs]) and referrals where necessary, through the acknowledgement of national and international norms and standards, within the limits of available resources.

The approach to healthcare in South African correctional facilities focuses on:
- the strict pursuance of ethical codes by health professionals
- regular health-quality inspections
- strict compliance with rules of confidentiality and privacy with regard to the medical records of patients
- the continuous evaluation and upgrading of medical emergency services.

The Department of Correctional Services foresees a system in which offenders are treated in the same way as other patients in the State sector through the PHC programme.

Offenders in need of medical attention are, as far as possible, treated in State hospitals. The use of private hospitals for offenders is permitted in cases where public hospitals are unable to provide access to healthcare and only after approval by the Provincial Commissioner of Correctional Services.

The Department's policy on healthcare caters for the following:

- prevention, which involves the promotion of safe sexual practices, management and control of STIs, provision of condoms and access to voluntary counselling and testing
- treatment, care and support
- respect for human rights
- awareness campaigns and commemoration of HIV/AIDS calendar events
- partnerships with other government departments, the private sector, NGOs and educational institutions
- peer-led education programmes to introduce behavioural changes among peers
- the appointment of employee-assistance practitioners to implement employee-wellness programmes
- principles of universal precautions, which provide personnel with guidelines and procedures regarding the handling of all body fluids.

The Department's objective is to maintain a high standard of personal hygiene by ensuring that the following are provided to offenders:
- toilet and bathing amenities with warm water
- suitable clothing and comfortable shoes
- adequate bedding
- a clean and healthy environment
- a safe water-supply
- promotion of a smoke-free prison environment.

Nutrition

The Department is committed to maintaining the health and strength of those entrusted to its care by satisfying their nutritional needs according to the Recommended Daily Allowance for food intake. The main objectives are to provide:
- all offenders with three nutritious meals per day and with a therapeutic diet when prescribed by a medical doctor
- religious and cultural diets.

There are four types of ration scales in the Department, namely for:
- adult male and female offenders
- pregnant and breast-feeding women
- children
- babies.

The proposed ration scales are compiled and amended by a nutritionist and evaluated by qualified and registered dieticians at the Department of Health and NGOs, before approval by management.

Provision of rehabilitation services

The aim of rehabilitation is to provide treatment and development programmes to offenders in partnership with the community to enhance personal and social functioning, and to prepare them for reintegration into the community as productive, well-adapted and law-abiding citizens.

A multidisciplinary team, consisting of social workers, psychologists, chaplains, educators, correctional officers and others (external community), addresses the basic needs of offenders by means of comprehensive assessments and various needs-based programmes.

The development and rehabilitation processes, which enable offenders to improve their mental health, social functioning, competencies, knowledge, skills and spiritual well-being, are focused on the following key strategies, namely to:
- positively combat illiteracy within the prison environment
- actively engage the community to assist with development programmes for the people entrusted to the Department's care
- develop and implement a needs-based development programme
- establish training centres at large prisons as well as capacity-building in small prisons
- market rehabilitation programmes to offenders and the community
- promote and implement restorative justice principles to ensure the involvement of offenders, victims and the community in the rehabilitation process.

On average, the budget for rehabilitation increases by 8,3% per annum from R264,8 million in 1999/00 to R427,5 million in 2005/06.

As part of the Department's rehabilitation initiatives, a total of 22 360 offenders were trained in a variety of skills in 2002. The further establishment of training centres in the various provinces is aimed at equipping offenders with basic technical skills in a variety of fields such as brick-making, brick-laying, woodwork, welding, garment-making, etc. Training is also provided in business skills to equip individuals to operate their own small businesses upon release.

Institutional Committees

Institutional Committees at each prison are responsible for ensuring a professional and co-ordinated approach towards the incarceration, treatment, training and development of all offenders. This is implemented by means of a multidisciplinary approach in which all role-players are involved, i.e. those concerned with custodial, training, educational, psychological, religious-care and social-work functions, recreational sport and library projects, as well as self-sufficiency and skills programmes.

Institutional Committees have statutory decision-making competency with regard to the safe custody of offenders, individual participation, subgroup and group programmes, as well as the prompt rewarding of positive behaviour.

Education and training of offenders

All offenders have a right to basic education and training. The aim is to enhance the education level and improve the skills of offenders to facilitate their reintegration into the community. Services are provided to sentenced and unsentenced offenders in collaboration with external partners (government institutions, training boards, NGOs, etc.) and are in line with the provisions of the South African Qualifica-tions Authority and the National Qualifications Framework. Some 37 427 offenders were involved in education and training programmes during the 2002 academic year.

Education and training programmes include:
- Adult Basic Education and Training
- mainstream education (Grades 10 to 12)
- correspondence studies
- technical studies
- vocational training
- occupational skills training
- instruction in recreation
- life-skills training and development
- entrepreneurial skills training
- computer-based training.

The main emphasis is on the provision of literacy and numeracy programmes, which include training in occupational, life and entrepreneurial skills, and should enhance the chances of the successful reintegration of the offender into the community and labour market.

Twelve of the 14 new training centres were completed by 31 March 2003. The two remaining training centres nearing completion are in the Odi and Polokwane Management Areas. These centres will provide training opportunities to offenders and equip them with skills not only to be employable, but also to enable them to start their own small businesses after their release.

Psychological services

Psychological services are provided for sentenced offenders, persons under correctional supervision and probationers to maintain or improve their mental health and quality of life.

The Department aims to address the needs of all sentenced offenders.

Psychologists held 4 430 individual sessions, 806 group sessions and 117 family-counselling sessions during 2002/03. In areas where there are no departmental psychologists, the Department uses the following procedures to address the emotional needs of offenders:
- external registered psychologists can be contracted in if a medical practitioner has referred the offender for psychological treatment
- offenders can see a private psychologist at their own expense

- final-year students who are busy with their MA degrees in clinical or counselling psychology provide services without remuneration under the supervision of various universities.

Psychologists also provide a programme intended to change old habits, attitudes and beliefs. The Investment in Excellence Programme, a non-traditional education curriculum that enhances individual and/or group potential, is also presented.

Social Work Services

Social Work Services aim to provide professional services to help offenders cope more effectively with their problems with social functioning, and to prepare them for reintegration into the community.

Treatment programmes offered by Social Work Services comprise structured programmes on issues such as life skills, family care and marriage, alcohol and drug abuse, orientation, sexual offences, trauma, pre-release and HIV/AIDS.

By March 2003, the Department employed 460 social workers. The social workers conducted 87 532 individual counselling sessions with juvenile and adult offenders in 2002/03. An important challenge is the growing number of people living with HIV/AIDS, as not all social workers possess the necessary training to qualify them as HIV/AIDS counsellors.

Research on the rehabilitation of offenders found that there was a need for rehabilitation interventions to be systematic and needs-based. This led to the development of a framework/model of intervention that aims to assist in the consistent and intensive assessment and evaluation of offenders' needs and rehabilitation programmes.

All social workers in the Department have been trained on the model of intervention to assist in the consistent assessment of offenders and provision of needs-based rehabilitation programmes. All social workers are implementing the intervention model.

However, other structured programmes are still being offered as a preventative measure, e.g. the programme on HIV/AIDS to young offenders.

Religious care of offenders

Religious-care services are rendered through needs-based programmes within a multi-disciplinary context to persons who are in the care of the Department. This is done in partnership with churches or faiths and other role-players with the aim of rehabilitating offenders and reintegrating them into the community.

It also aims to contribute to changing the offender's behaviour, based on a lifestyle which is in accordance with the acceptable values and norms of their faith.

Religious-care services are rendered to sentenced and unsentenced offenders, probationers, parolees and personnel on an *ad hoc* basis. Religious-care programmes take the form of large group gatherings, small group sessions and personal interviews. Structured needs-based spiritual-care programmes addressing the specific needs of offenders are provided.

The Department employs full-time chaplains and part-time religious workers from various religious backgrounds.

The extent of religious counselling is reflected by the 46 719 religious services, 38 571 group sessions and 77 434 individual sessions held for offenders in 2002/03.

Quarterly meetings are held with the chaplains of the South African National Defence Force and the SAPS to discuss issues of common concern. Meetings are also held with the Departments of Foreign Affairs and of Social Development concerning South African offenders abroad.

The Department is a member of the International Prison Chaplains' Association. A working relationship also exists with Prison Fellowship International, and contact is maintained with the chaplains of Zimbabwe, Namibia, Botswana and Zambia.

Provision is made for offenders to observe the main religious festivals and holy days such as Ramadan, Passover, Good Friday and Christmas. Religious literature, including the *Bible* and the *Qur'an*, is supplied to offenders.

In line with the Vienna Declaration on Crime and Justice, the Department has embraced the restorative-justice approach with the aim of reducing crime and promoting healing between offenders, victims and the community. The process to conduct public awareness and education campaigns has begun to raise awareness of the implementation of restorative-justice programmes and policies. This project intends to facilitate the mediation process between victims of crime and offenders, in an attempt to bring about restitution and reparation. This will be done by means of developing restorative-justice and victim-empowerment programmes.

Release of offenders

The Correctional Services Act, 1998 provides for the creation of independent regional correctional supervision and parole boards throughout the country, with greater powers to consider and approve which offenders, serving sentences exceeding 12 months, should be granted parole. In the interest of protecting the community, the Department has abolished the concept of remission of sentence.

The Parole and Correctional Supervision Amendment Act, 1997 (Act 87 of 1997), deals with parole and correctional-supervision policy and also provides for a non-parole period. In terms of the Correctional Services Act, 1998, offenders are not considered for parole until they have served at least half of their original sentences or the non-parole period, whichever is the longer period.

The Parole and Correctional Supervision Amendment Act, 1997 empowers courts to build a non-parole period into the sentence of any convicted criminal. This period may be as much as two-thirds of the total sentence. A person declared a habitual criminal may not be considered for parole before having served at least seven years in prison. An offender serving a life sentence may not be considered for parole until at least 25 years have been served.

Reintegration into the community

The Department aims to equip offenders with the skills required for effective reintegration into society after release. Offenders sentenced to longer than six months' imprisonment undergo a basic pre-release programme before release. Aspects receiving attention include how to secure employment, personal finance management and street law.

Specialists from the community are also involved in the presentation of the programme. Care and support for an offender are prerequisites for placement in the community. Before offenders are placed, they are assisted with obtaining employment and accommodation, or at least care and support. Community involvement in supporting offenders after placement is encouraged.

Offenders are provided with financial and material assistance before they are released from prison.

Community corrections

Supervision of parolees

Parolees are subject to certain conditions as well as supervisory measures aimed at gradually reintegrating them into the community.

To achieve these goals, parolees are allocated to a supervision official of the Department, who ensures that they are regularly monitored. Contravention of parole conditions leads to stricter conditions and increased supervision or reimprisonment for a part of or the entire remainder of the parole period.

Volunteers from the community are encouraged to assist the Department in the monitoring of parolees.

Based on their risk profile, parolees are placed in minimum, medium or maximum supervision categories. These supervision categories are also applicable to probationers. Awaiting-trial persons under community corrections are classified as maximum categories.

Parolees are confined to their homes according to their monitoring categories. Monitoring includes visits to the parolee's home and workplace, liaison over the telephone, and reports to the Community Corrections Office.

Parliament approved amendments to the Correctional Services Act, 1998 to address concerns about the lack of community involvement in the parole system. According to the amendments, the composition of the new Parole Boards includes three permanent members from the community: the chairperson, members from the Departments of Correctional Services and of Justice and Constitutional Development, as well as the SAPS.

The victim may also participate or be represented at the parole hearings, to allow, for the first time, the direct participation of victims in the justice system instead of them being called upon only as prosecution witnesses.

The Department aims to increase the number of personnel responsible for managing and controlling persons sentenced to community corrections, in order to decrease the number of probationers and parolees each officer must supervise.

In 2002/03, 5 413 parole absconders were traced. They have either been referred back to court to receive alternative sentences or sent back to prison to serve the remainder of their sentences.

Correctional supervision

The Correctional Services Act, 1998 ensures that all probationers and parolees are subject to the same conditions.

In terms of the Act, parolees must do community service. Correctional supervision aims to control and rehabilitate those who can serve their sentences in the community. Offenders who pose a real threat to the community and who have chosen crime as a career, however, do not qualify for correctional supervision.

A person sentenced to correctional supervision is placed under the control of a correctional supervision official. This official ensures that the probationer complies with whichever of the following conditions he or she may be subject to:
- house arrest
- community service, rendered free of charge
- victim's compensation
- restriction to a magisterial district
- prohibition on alcohol usage or abuse
- participation in certain correctional programmes.

If the set conditions are violated, the probationer can be referred to the court of first hearing for consideration of an alternative sentence or, in certain cases, be admitted directly to prison to serve the remainder of his/her sentence.

Section 117(e) of the Correctional Services Act, 1998 makes it an offence for a probationer or parolee to abscond from the system of community corrections. If found guilty by court, they may receive an additional sentence of up to 10 years' imprisonment.

The community corrections population, comprising parolees and probationers, versus the sentenced prison population on 31 March 2003 was 38%.

Day parole

A small number of offenders are placed on day parole because they are institutionalised or have a doubtful prognosis and pose a high security risk to the community. These offenders are gradually resettled into the community as a bridging measure, instead of being released upon termination of sentence. Day parolees have to comply with certain conditions. Contravention leads to withdrawal of privileges, stricter conditions or suspension of day parole.

Certain categories of offenders are allowed to spend weekends at home. Inmates may temporarily leave prison for compassionate leave, consolidation of family ties, preparation for release, and for reasons that involve reintegration of the offender into society.

The offender has to observe strict conditions, which include abstaining from drugs and alcohol, being in the care of a specific person and at a specific address, personally accepting liability for any event that might result in expenses for the State, and not being found guilty of any misconduct.

Facility management and capital works

The Correctional Services Act, 1998 empowers the Minister to enter into joint ventures with the private sector to design, construct, finance and operate any prison or part of a prison.

Two such prisons were procured by the Department of Public Works on behalf of the Department of Correctional Services, using private-sector capital and expertise for their financing, designing, construction, operation and maintenance.

The first privately operated prison is the Mangaung Maximum Security Prison near Bloemfontein. The 3 024-bed Kutama Sinthumule Maximum Prison at Makhado (formerly Louis Trichardt) in Limpopo, is the second facility to be built and operated by a private-sector company in South Africa.

The Department has adopted a unit-management approach that involves dividing prisons into smaller, manageable units, which encourages the management of the offender, as opposed to the management of the prison. In line with this approach, a new concept of prison design is being implemented. It entails smaller housing units for offenders, clustered together, to ensure safe custody and control, and which enable multiskilled unit staff to be actively involved in rehabilitation programmes.

The concept of unit management was being implemented at 101 prisons by 31 January 2003, representing 41,9% of prisons. The Department aims to extend this to all prisons by 2005 to improve service delivery and the rehabilitation of offenders.

Construction started on four new prisons in 2003/04. It is envisaged that these will be completed by 2005/06, providing accommodation for an additional 12 000 offenders.

The Minister of Correctional Services, Mr Ben Skosana, announced in 2003 that 'new generation' prison facilities for medium- and low-risk categories will be built to add an additional 30 000 beds during the Medium Term Expenditure Framework period.

Construction started in 2003 and it is envisaged that they will be operational by 2005/06. The four new prisons will be located in Leeuwkop, Nigel, Klerksdorp and Kimberley. Repairs and renovations continue in 12 prisons in KwaZulu-Natal, Eastern Cape and the North West and accommodation will be available for 863 more offenders.

The Repair and Maintenance Programme has also been embarked upon. The Programme addresses backlogs in maintenance and inhumane conditions under which offenders are incarcerated. During 2001/02, 22 prisons were renovated.

Prisons are divided into three priority groups, each in various stages of progress. The Department identified 33 prisons in need of repair and maintenance work in 2003/04.

Administration

The Administration Programme funds the overall management of the Department. It includes policy formulation by the Minister, the National Commissioner, and other members of senior management, and facilitates prison inspections by the Inspecting Judge.

The budget of the Programme accounted for about 32% of the budget of the Department in 2003/04, and remains at approximately this level throughout the medium term. Over the medium term, the budget for administration will grow by an average of 6,6% a year, mainly because the Department will focus on increasing its anti-corruption capacity and investment in human resource development.

Human resources

Employees of the Department of Correctional Services are not entitled to strike and conditions of employment have to be negotiated with labour unions in a bargaining council.

The major unions active in the Department are the Police and Prisons Civil Rights Union, the Public Servants' Association and the Democratic Nursing Association of South Africa.

Community involvement

The Subdirectorate: Community Involvement facilitates the involvement of members of the community in correctional matters and provides expanded capacity for the Department. The objectives of the Subdirectorate are to:
- promote co-responsibility for offender management and crime prevention
- share responsibility for the rehabilitation and reintegration of offenders into the community
- maximise the use of public and private resources.

The Department actively participates in the initiative of the NCPS to establish Community Safety Centres. The aim of these Centres is to provide integrated services to the disadvantaged communities in South Africa. The Departments of Correctional Services, Health, Social Development, Justice and Constitutional Development and the SAPS provide these integrated services to the community under one roof. Two Community Safety Centres were opened at Nsimbini in KwaZulu-Natal and at Leobeng in Limpopo.

The Department has embarked on a poverty-alleviation programme that entails the deployment of offender-generated goods and services for poverty alleviation, disaster relief and rural development.

In 2002, the Deputy President, Mr Jacob Zuma, launched the first poverty-alleviation programme at the Zonderwater Prison near Cullinan in Gauteng. A piece of land was identified that will be cultivated by offenders. The produce will go to a needy old-age home, an orphanage and a local school-feeding scheme.

A similar project was subsequently launched at Thohoyandou Prison at Vondwe Village, Limpopo. Here, the Department also assisted a local primary school by supplying the labour and expertise for the building of three additional classrooms, the repainting of the school and the renovation of school benches.

The poverty-alleviation project at the Manguang Maximum Security Prison has provided underprivileged schools and people with disabilities in the area with more than 8,4 tons of vegetables. An amount of R12 000 was also donated to a hospice in Bloemfontein.

Anti-corruption

In 2002/03, 270 reports on corruption in the Department of Correctional Services were received. As a result, 55 officials were dismissed, 175 officials disciplined, and 23 officials criminally convicted, while 17 cases were still being finalised. At the request of the Minister, the President appointed an independent commission of inquiry, the Jali Commission, to investigate corruption, maladministration, violence and intimidation in nine management areas. Two interim reports on Westville Prison were received. A retired judge will be appointed to head the internal investigations on the recommendations.

The scope of the Jali Commission was extended to include the Grootvlei management area in the Free State.

The Jali Commission convened in Durban-Westville, Pietermaritzburg, Grootvlei, St Albans, Pollsmoor and Johannesburg management areas and has since brought out six interim reports which recommend the institution of disciplinary steps against a number of officials.

In Durban-Westville, seven officials were charged with drug smuggling, corruption and negligence. Six of them were dismissed and the seventh received a final warning. In Pietermaritzburg, 19 officials were dismissed for falsifying their qualifications, while at Grootvlei, 18 officials were dismissed on charges of corruption and negligence, one resigned, and hearings against two others are still outstanding.

The Department is awaiting further reports of the Jali Commission, following investigations in other areas. The Commissioner is ensuring that the response to the interim recommendations results in the development of a sustainable and clean investigative and disciplinary capacity within the Department, to ensure that internal regulatory policies are complied with and that corruption, gross negligence and crime are eradicated. Since no investigative unit can solve the situation alone, management has been tasked with ensuring an appropriate style of management to eliminate opportunities for criminal activity and corruption within the Department of Correctional Services.

Three important milestones were reached in terms of the Department's commitment to rooting out corruption, namely:
- the approval of a National Risk-Management Plan and Anti-Corruption Strategy to assist the management of the Department to focus on the continuous improvement of the efficiency and effectiveness of the Depart-ment
- the establishment of a formal Anti-Corruption Unit in the organisational structure of the Department for the sound management of the Department's Anti-Corruption Strategy
- research conducted by private consultants on the assessment of the levels of corruption and the scope and extent thereof in the Department.

Acknowledgements

BuaNews
Commission on Gender Equality
Department of Correctional Services
Department of Justice and Constitutional Development
Estimates of National Expenditure 2003, published by the National Treasury
South Africa.info
South African Law Reform Commission
www.gov.za

Suggested reading

Abel, R. L. *Politics by Other Means: Law in the Struggle Against Apartheid, 1980 – 1994.* London: Routledge, 1995.
Ajibola, B. and Van Zyl, D. *The Judiciary in South Africa.* Cape Town: Juta, 1998.
Albertyn, C. and others, eds. *Introduction to the Promotion of Equality and Prevention of Unfair Discrimination Act (Act 4 of 2000).* Johannesburg: Witwatersrand University Press, 2001.
Andrews, P. and Ellman, S. eds. *The Post-Apartheid Constitution: Perspectives on South Africa's Basic Law.* Johannesburg: Witwatersrand University Press, 2001.
Asmal, K., Asmal, L. and Roberts, R. S. *Reconciliation through Truth: A Reckoning of Apartheid's Criminal Governance.* 2nd ed. Cape Town: David Philip, 1997.
Bell, T. *Unfinished Business: South Africa, Apartheid and Truth.* Observatory: Redworks, 2001.
Mamdani, M. ed. *Beyond Rights Talk and Culture Talk: Comparative Essays on the Politics of Rights and Culture.* Cape Town: David Philip, 2000.
Chanock, M. *The Making of South African Legal Culture, 1902 – 1936: Fear, Favour and Prejudice.* Cambridge: University Press, 2001.
Chubb, K. and Van Dijk, L. *Between Anger and Hope: South Africa's Youth and the Truth and Reconciliation Commission.* Johannesburg: Witwatersrand University Press, 2001.

Justice and correctional services

Cries without Tears: An Anthology of Writings from Rehabilitating Offenders. Johannesburg: Corrective Action Holdings and Sandton: Sizwe, 1999.
Coleman, M. ed. *Crime against Humanity: Analysing the Repression of the Apartheid State.* Johannesburg: Human Rights Commission; Cape Town: David Philip, 1998.
Corder, H. ed. *Democracy and the Judiciary.* Cape Town: Institute for Democracy in South Africa, 1989.
Directory of Human Rights Organisations. Compiler: C. Sibanyoni. Pretoria: Human Sciences Research Council (HSRC), 1999.
Edelstein, J. *Truth and Lies: Stories from the Truth and Reconciliation Commission in South Africa.* Johannesburg: M & G Books, 2001.
Goldstone, R. *For Humanity: Reflections of a War Crimes Investigator.* Johannesburg: Witwatersrand University Press, 2000.
Gutto, S. *Equality and Non-Discrimination in South Africa: The Political Economy of Law and Law-Making.* Cape Town: New Africa Books, 2001.
James, W. G. and Van de Vijver, L. eds. *After the TRC: Reflections on Truth and Reconciliation.* Cape Town: David Philip, 2000.
Jeffrey, A. *The Truth about the Truth Commission.* Johannesburg: South African Institute of Race Relations, 1999.
Krog, A. *Country of My Skull.* Johannesburg: Random House, 1998.
Hund, J. ed. *Law and Justice in South Africa.* Cape Town: Centre for Intergroup Studies, 1986.
Law of South Africa (LAWSA), Encyclopaedia of South African Law. Durban: Butterworth, 1976 – (Continuously updated and revised.)
Leggett, T. *The Market for Drugs and Sex in South Africa.* Cape Town: New David Philip Publishers, 2001.
Lewis, D. *Parliamentary Support Programme: A Review, 1996 – 2001.* Cape Town: Parliamentary Support Programme, 2002.
Lewis, S. *Dealing with Rape.* Johannesburg: Sached, 1997.
Lobban, M. *White Man's Justice: South African Political Trials in the Black Consciousness Era.* Oxford: Clarendon Press, 1996.
Murray, C. and Nijzinky, L. *Building Representative Democracy: South Africa's Legislatures and the Constitution.* Cape Town: Parliamentary Support Programme, 2002.
Murray, J. *The Law in South Africa: A Practical Guide.* 5th ed. Gardenview: Legal and General Publishers, 2002
Ncube, W, ed. *Law, Culture and Tradition: Children's Rights in Eastern and Southern Africa.* London: Ashgate, 1998.
Orr, W. *From Biko to Basson: Wendy Orr's Search for the Soul of South Africa as a Commissioner of the Truth and Reconciliation Commission.* Johannesburg: Contra, 2000.
Pistorius, M. *Catch Me a Killer: Serial Murders: A Profiler's True Story.* Sandton: Penguin, 2000.
Pistorius, M. *Strangers on the Street: Serial Homicide in South Africa.* Sandton: Penguin, 2002.
Rautenbach, F. *Liberating South African Labour from the Law.* Cape Town: Tafelberg, 1999.
Shaw, M. *Crime and Policing in Post-Apartheid South Africa: Transforming Under Fire.* Cape Town: David Philip, 2002.
Steinberg, J. *Farm Murders, Crime.* Johannesburg: Jonathan Ball, 2002.
Truth and Reconciliation Commission. Report. Cape Town: Juta, 1998. 3 vols.
Truth and Reconciliation Commission of South Africa Report vols 6 and 7. Cape Town: Juta, 2003. 2 vols.
Tshiwula, L. *Crime and Delinquency.* Pretoria: Kagiso Publishers, 1998.
Vale, P. *Security and Politics in South Africa: The Regional Dimension.* Cape Town: University of Cape Town Press, 2003.
Villa-Vicencio, C. and Verwoerd, W. *Looking Back, Reaching Forward: Reflections on the Truth and Reconciliation Commission of South Africa.* Cape Town: University of Cape Town Press, 2000.

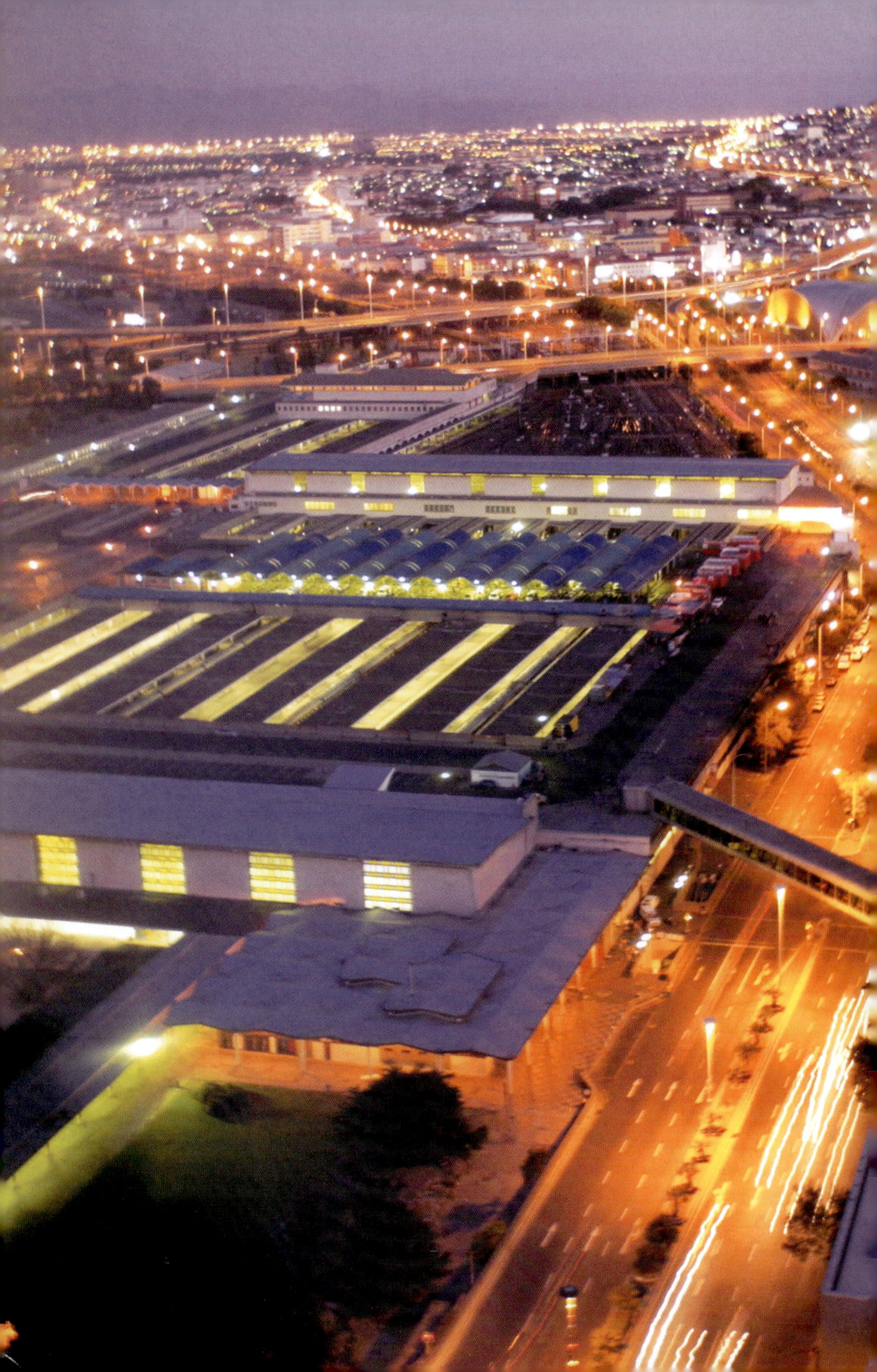

chapter 16
Minerals and energy

Mining continues to play an important role in the national economy. Preliminary 2002 figures indicated that mining contributed R30,6 billion or 8,5% of gross value added, an improvement of R13,86 billion from 2001. The preliminary figures also indicated a 1,5% rise in employment in the mining sector from 407 154 in 2001 to 413 087 in 2002. Sales of primary mineral products accounted for 34,3% of South Africa's total export revenue during 2001.

Earnings from platinum surpassed gold for the first time in 100 years. Total revenue from platinum-group metals (PGMs) in 2001 was $3,88 billion compared with the gold revenue of $3,37 billion for 2001.

South Africa continues to export a very high proportion of its raw mineral resources.

There is still a lot of potential for growth in the exploitation of minerals in the country, especially where the country is ranked number one in terms of reserves. For example, in manganese, chrome and the PGMs, South Africa has 80%, 72,4% and 55,7% of world reserves respectively.

The Department of Minerals and Energy is the primary government institution responsible for formulating and implementing policy. It reports to and advises the Minister of Minerals and Energy who, in consultation with the Cabinet, takes final responsibility for policy.

◀ South Africa, which supplies two-thirds of Africa's electricity, is one of the four cheapest electricity producers in the world.

Within the Department, the Electricity and Nuclear Branch is responsible for electricity and nuclear-energy affairs; the Hydro Carbons and Energy Planning Branch is responsible for coal, gas, liquid fuels, energy efficiency, renewable energy and energy planning, including the energy database; while the Mineral Development Branch manages, among others, mineral prospecting and mining rights.

The Mine Health and Safety Inspectorate (MHSI) is responsible for the application of mine health and safety legislation.

Policy

The Minerals and Petroleum Resources Development Act, 2002 (Act 28 of 2002), aims to:
- recognise that mineral resources are the common heritage of all South Africans and collectively belong to all the peoples of South Africa
- promote the beneficiation of minerals
- guarantee security of tenure for existing prospecting and mining operations
- ensure that mining contributes to rural development and supports those communities affected by mining operations
- ensure that historically disadvantaged persons participate more meaningfully in the mining industry
- promote junior and small-scale mining
- uphold good environmental practices and sustainable development

- ensure increased access to geological and mining information.

The following concerns have been addressed:
- the Act ensures that new order rights are registrable, transferable, tradable and bondable
- existing operators are guaranteed security of tenure
- prospecting rights will be valid for a maximum period of five years and renewable for a further maximum period of three years
- mining rights are valid for a maximum period of 30 years and renewable for a further period of 30 years.

The cancellation of new rights will only take place if there is a breach of the terms and conditions of the right of tenure by the holder, and only after the holder had been given enough notice to rectify such a breach.

The Draft Mining Titles Registration Amendment Bill, 2003 has been published for comment.

The Department of Minerals and Energy played a leading role in the establishment of the Kimberley Process, which aims to prevent conflict diamonds from getting into the global diamond-market industry and to protect legitimate trade.

The Kimberley Process was initiated by a Working Group of representatives from 39 African diamond-producing and trading countries in 2000, after non-governmental organisations, supported by some governments, threatened to boycott diamonds from conflict-ridden areas.

The Kimberley Process Certification Scheme (KPCS), which was launched and accepted by 52 governments in Interlaken, Switzerland in November 2002, was officially implemented on 1 January 2003. In essence, these countries have agreed that they will only allow for the import and export of rough diamonds if they come from or are being exported to another Kimberley Process partici-pant.

Participants welcomed the resolutions adopted respectively by the United Nations (UN) Security Council in January, and by the UN General Assembly in April 2003, which expressed strong support for the KPCS. The Working Group on Diamond Experts discussed ways and means of improving the manner in which the national certification schemes of participants interact.

By May 2003, all the world's diamond industries and approximately 70 countries were participating.

The Bill will amend the Mining Titles Registration Act, 1967 (Act 16 of 1967), to regulate the registration of mineral and petroleum titles and other rights, and to effect certain amendments necessary to ensure consistency with the Mineral and Petroleum Resources Development Act, 2002.

The Broad-Based Socio-Economic Empowerment Charter for the South African Mining Industry, which has the support of the mining houses and labour unions concerned, was approved by the Cabinet in October 2002.

Targets of the Charter include 15% ownership of mines by historically disadvantaged South Africans within five years, 40% of historically disadvantaged South Africans in both junior and senior management positions in five years, 26% ownership within 10 years, and 10% participation by women within five years. The objectives of the Charter are to:
- promote equitable access to the nation's mineral resources for all South Africans
- substantially and meaningfully expand opportunities for historically disadvantaged South Africans, including women, to enter the mining and minerals industry and to benefit from the exploitation of the nation's mineral resources
- utilise the existing skills base for the empowerment of historically disadvantaged South Africans
- expand the skills base of historically disadvantaged South Africans to serve the community
- promote employment and advance the social and economic welfare of mining communities and the major labour-sending areas
- promote beneficiation of South Africa's mineral commodities.

The proposed Scorecard for the Charter has been introduced, giving effect to the provisions contained in the Charter.

The Scorecard is designed to facilitate the application of the Charter in terms of the requirements of the Mineral and Petroleum

Resources Development Act, 2002 for the conversion of all the 'old order rights' into new rights within a five-year conversion window period, while recognising the full 10-year period.

Mine environmental management

Mine environmental management forms an integral part of mineral-resource management. The following national priorities have been identified:
- The strengthening of enforcement to prevent mining legacies from happening. This relates to the implementation of the Mineral and Petroleum Resources Development Act, 2002 and other short and long-term strategies to strengthen environmental enforcement.
- Identifying mine-pollution 'hot spots' and implementing additional measures, norms and standards to address and manage the pollution problems within these areas.
- Rehabilitating the mine legacies of the past.

In order to facilitate the implementation of these priorities, the *Phephafatso* Strategy (meaning 'clean-up' in Tswana) is being finalised. The Strategy is not only an initiative of the Department of Minerals and Energy, but a co-operative government initiative supported by the mining industry, various parastatals and other role-players.

In order to address mine-water pollution problems within the Witwatersrand gold-mining 'hot spots', the Department, in conjunction with the Council for Geoscience and other government departments, is developing a comprehensive strategy to address the polluted underground water that has been a hindrance for many years. In line with the 'polluter pays' principle, the dedicated involvement of the gold-mining industry, local authorities and other role-players must be obtained.

This strategy currently includes measures to prevent water ingress into mines.

Such preventative measures will reduce the impact on the environment and substantially decrease mining costs within the Witwatersrand gold-mining area. For the prevention of water ingress, a work programme aimed at engineering interventions in the central and East Rand mining basins was expected to be implemented in 2003/04.

Mining outcomes of the World Summit on Sustainable Development (WSSD)

Representatives from nearly 200 countries assembled at the WSSD in Johannesburg in September 2002 to reaffirm their commitment to sustainable development.

As a follow-up to the WSSD outcomes for mining, the Department of Minerals and Energy finalised a strategy with specific programmes, plans and time frames to achieve the objectives and priorities with regard to the implementation of the Johannesburg Plan for Implementation.

The WSSD outcomes for mining include:
- poverty eradication
- changing the unsustainable patterns for consumption and production
- protecting and managing the natural resource base for economic and social development
- globalisation
- initiatives for sustainable development in Africa.

Apart from the national processes being established to take the WSSD outcomes forward, international processes and structures such as the African Mining Partnership will be established to champion, among others, the New Partnership for Africa's Development's (NEPAD) mining and mineral-related initiatives. The Global Mining Dialogue is also being established to promote the WSSD mining outcomes in the international arena.

Rehabilitation of mines

Government follows an integrated and co-operative approach with regard to the rehabilitation of the asbestos legacies of the past. Specific responsibilities regarding the management of asbestos pollution have been assigned to specific government departments, namely the Departments of Environmental Affairs and Tourism, Minerals and Energy, Water Affairs and Forestry, Trade and Industry, Health, and Labour.

Addressing asbestos legacies has always been a priority for the Department. In accordance with the Asbestos Rehabilitation Priority Index database, 145 derelict and ownerless asbestos dump complexes have been identified for rehabilitation.

In recent years, the Department has implemented a dedicated programme for the rehabilitation of derelict and ownerless asbestos mines/dumps.

Only 84 derelict and/or ownerless asbestos dump complexes in South Africa still need to be rehabilitated. It is also envisaged that the rehabilitation will be finalised within the next 10 years at a cost of R100 million. The Department spent R17 million during 2002/03 at the old Voorspoed Asbestos Mine, Koegas, Neweng and the Whitebank Complex in the Northern Cape.

With regard to the rehabilitation of abandoned and ownerless gold, coal and other mines in South Africa, the Department is in the process of identifying and developing a database. The Department of Minerals and Energy, in co-operation with the Department of Water Affairs and Forestry and other role-players, implemented urgent short-term rehabilitation measures at the burning Transvaal and Delagoa Bay Colliery near Witbank in 2002/03, which included the construction of:
- safety pathways over the site, and access control
- a storm-water diversion system to prevent storm water flowing through the site and becoming acidic.

Investigations regarding the methods of rehabilitating the Transvaal and Delagoa Bay Colliery have been finalised.

These methods include remining, blasting and collapsing, flooding and ashing. A combination of the above methods was agreed on as the preferred rehabilitation option. The rehabilitation of the Colliery will serve as a trial case for the successful rehabilitation of the other abandoned and ownerless coal mines in South Africa.

Excellence in Mining Environmental Management (EMEM) Award System

The EMEM Award System was implemented in March 2000 to motivate the mining industry to excel in environmental management and to recognise those mining companies which have excelled in their field. The EMEM Awards are awarded to regional and national companies. The winners of the 2002 National EMEM Awards were Richards Bay Minerals and Serina Koalin (Pty) Ltd.

Mining industry

During 2001, the mining industry directly contributed 7,5% to gross value added, and an estimated 10,3% through associated multiplier effects. The declining trend in mining's contribution to gross value added in recent years has been reversed since 2001, with the highest levels recorded since 1996, mainly as a consequence of the strong performance in the PGM sector.

Mining contributed 10,1% to South Africa's gross fixed capital formation during 2001, while sales of primary mineral products accounted for 34,3% of total exports. The inclusion of various processed mineral products such as ferro-alloys and aluminium increased this contribution to more than 40% in 2001.

Employers and trade unions in the mining industry have agreed to establish various measures that will help create jobs and alleviate poverty. The parties committed themselves to co-operate, to ensure that skills development becomes a priority in the industry.

Over the last few years, South African mining houses have transformed into large focused mining companies that include Anglo Platinum, Anglogold, De Beers, Implats and Iscor.

Minerals and energy

The Government is the only shareholder of Alexkor, a diamond mine situated on the west coast in Namaqualand. The Alexkor Limited Amendment Act, 2001 (Act 29 of 2001), was promulgated in November 2001. The Act provides for the sale or disposal of shares held by the State.

In June 2003, government announced that it had resolved to defer the finalisation of the bidding process for the disposal of a 51% interest in Alexkor, pending the outcome of a land claim by the Richtersveld community.

In October 2003, the Constitutional Court returned the land and mineral rights owned by Alexkor to the Richtersveld community who were forcibly removed from the land in the 1920s.

Mineworkers

Gold mining, with 47,4% of the mining industry's labour force, was the largest employer in 2002, followed by PGM mining with 27%. The coal industry employed 12%.

Taking into account the multiplier effect of the supply and consumer industries, including dependants, many millions rely on the mining industry for their livelihood.

Over the past five years, South Africa's gold mines have been plagued by diminishing economic reserves and consequent cost controls. Since 1990, more than 200 000 workers in the gold-mining industry alone have lost their jobs through retrenchments.

This trend was reversed in 2002, with a 1,5% increase in employment in the mining sector.

Mine health and safety

The Mine Health and Safety Inspectorate (MHSI), as an integral part of the Department of Minerals and Energy, was established to protect the health and safety of employees and other persons at mines.

Proposed key measures for the prevention of machinery-related accidents were identified by the Minister of Minerals and Energy, Ms Phumzile Mlambo-Nqcuka, during the National Union of Mineworkers (NUM) Policy Conference in February 2003.

These include:
- the maintenance of track work to prevent derailment
- the development of a traffic-control system to prevent the collision of vehicles
- a clearance of at least 500 mm between rolling stock and any object to allow sufficient space for pedestrians.

In the next three years, the MHSI will focus on addressing hazards relating to mine falls, machinery and occupational health. Work will also continue on supporting human resource development in the industry, inquiries into recent major accidents, developing and improving occupational health and safety databases, and supporting work to bring about the integration of occupational health and inspectorates at national level.

Key events planned include, among others, convening the Mine Health and Safety Summit, which will involve government, employers and labour discussing concerns, trends and policy; hosting a conference of mine health and safety research organisations; and a series of workshops on implementing new legislation, particularly legislation relating to occupational health.

The 30th International Conference of Safety in Mines Research Institutes was held in Johannesburg from 6 to 8 October 2003. The Conference was presented by the South African Institute of Mining and Metallurgy and the MHSI.

An independent review of the MHSI was commissioned to assess the performance of the industry since the Leon Commission of Inquiry in 1994 and the promulgation of the Mine Health and Safety Act, 1996 (Act 29 of 1996).

The review recommended that the MHSI:
- consider a number of changes in structure and approach, such as establishing a policy unit
- increase the number of inspectors in the field

- develop a more effective recruitment and staffing strategy
- develop the outlook and expertise of inspectors
- develop a more effective and standardised approach to enforcement.

The fatality rate for 2002 was 0,74 per 1 000 people at work, corresponding to 288 deaths during the year. This is a small improvement on 2001's rate of 0,75 (also 288 deaths).

The number of people employed in the mining industry rose in 2002. The reportable injury rate for 2002 was 11,5, corresponding to 4 453 injuries. The corresponding figures for 2001 were 12,34 and 4 728. Against a backdrop of expansion in the gold, platinum and small-mining areas, and particularly serious capacity problems in the platinum and small-mining sector, these results reflect a considerable effort on the part of the MHSI and industry stakeholders to halt deterioration in safety performance.

By March 2003, the MHSI had conducted 3 200 accident investigations and 14 500 inspections and audits.

Audits and inspections are apportioned to various mines according to their risk profile. In 2002/03 the Inspectorate issued 3 464 instructions in terms of Sections 54 and 55 of the Mine Health and Safety Act, 1996 to rectify, stop work and rectify, or review control/management systems.

Extra funding will be allocated to the promotion of mine health and safety over the next three years to provide for:
- the Tripartite Mining Industry HIV and AIDS Committee and programmes in the mining industry
- the receipt and storage of medical records when mines close
- exit medical examinations for employees of liquidated mines.

Human resource development

The overall aim of the Mining Qualifications Authority (MQA) is to facilitate the development of appropriate knowledge and skills in the mining, minerals and jewellery sectors, to:
- enable the development and transformation of the sector
- contribute to the health, safety and competitiveness of the sector
- improve access to quality education and training for all
- redress past inequalities in education and training.

The MQA has been established as a Sector Education and Training Authority (SETA) under the aegis of the Department of Labour. The responsibilities of the MQA are to:
- develop and monitor the implementation of a sector skills plan
- register skills-development facilitators at workplaces within the sector
- approve work skills plans and annual training reports of companies in the sector
- develop unit standards and qualifications
- maintain the quality of standards, qualifications and learning provision in the sector
- establish, register, administer and promote learnerships
- administer existing apprenticeship systems
- administer and disburse skills-development levies.

The African Mining Partnership (AMP) was formed at the African Mining Ministers' Forum in Cape Town during February 2003.

The AMP's main mandate is to support the New Partnership for Africa's Development, as well as mining and mineral-related initiatives.

Other priority issues include finding methods to ensure that Africa's mineral wealth stays on the continent, as well as ways to stop non-Africans from exploiting natural resources.

It was decided to identify four projects in which Africa has fairly large dispersed resources.

Also tabled at the Forum was the exploration of various ways of utilising small-scale mining as a vehicle for the alleviation of poverty, economic empowerment of women in the mineral sector, and, in particular, regional economic growth.

It was agreed that each member country should develop legal and financial strategies to enable this sector, including industrial minerals, to gain access to finance and international markets.

Minerals and energy

By December 2002, the Minerals and Energy Education and Training Institute had trained 240 students, 78 of whom were women.

Chamber of Mines

Established in 1889, the Chamber of Mines consists of independent mining finance corporations, individual mines and mining companies. The members account for more than 85% of South Africa's mineral output.

The Chamber of Mines provides an advisory and service function to its members and to the industry on a co-operative basis, in areas such as industrial relations; education and training; security and healthcare; technical, legal and communication services; and the provision of statistical data.

The following services to the South African mining industry and, in some instances, also to customers outside the mining industry, are provided by subsidiary companies: training; examination administration; visits to operational gold mines; the monthly newspaper *Mining News*; mine-rescue services; environmental management services; and centres for human development.

Other areas of industry networking include:
- the Employment Bureau of Africa (TEBA)
- TEBA-Bank, providing efficient and cost-effective banking services for mineworkers
- Rand Mutual Assurance, providing workers' compensation benefits for accidental injury or death arising out of and in the course of employment
- Rand Refinery Ltd, the world's largest gold refinery
- the Nuclear Fuels Corporation (NUFCOR), one of the world's largest continuous producers of uranium oxide
- Colliery Technical Services, which includes the Colliery Training College
- Rescue Drilling Unit
- Collieries Environmental Control Services
- the Council for Scientific and Industrial Research' (CSIR) Mining Technology Division (Miningtek).

South Africa's mineral reserves, 2002

Commodity	Unit	Reserves	%	World ranking
Alumino-silicates	Mt	51	37,4	1
Antimony	kt	250	6,4	4
Asbestos	Mt	Moderate		
Chrome ore	Mt	5 500	77,5	1
Coal	Mt	55 333	10,7	5
Copper	Mt	13	2	13
Diamonds*	kcar			
Fluorspar	Mt	80	18,2	3
Gold	t	36 000	40,4	1
Iron ore	Mt	2 300	3,4	10
Lead	Mt	3,0	2,1	7
Manganese ore	Mt	4 000	80	1
Phosphate rock	Mt	2 500	5,3	4
Platinum-group metals	t	70 000	70,0	1
Silver	kt	10	*	
Titanium minerals	Mt	220	30	2
Uranium	kt	284	9,1	4
Vanadium	kt	12 000	31,6	2
Vermiculite	Mt	80	40	2
Zinc	Mt	15	3,5	5
Zirconium minerals	Mt	14	19,4	2

Mt = megaton, kt = kiloton, t = ton, car = carats
* Confidential information, kcar = kilocarats

Source: Minerals Bureau

Junior and small-scale mining

The economic impact of small-scale mining is difficult to measure, as most of this mining is illegal and criteria to monitor these operations have not yet been developed. One of the most crucial tasks facing government is to legalise small-scale mining by assisting in upgrading these operations into economically viable business units. This task is ongoing and for the period April 2001 to March 2002, the National Steering Committee of Service-Providers to the Small-Scale Mining Sector (NSC) received over 200 applications of which 16 projects were approved.

The NSC is focusing on identifying small-scale mining operations in recognised poverty nodes to enhance economic development in these mainly rural areas. A number of areas have been singled out for attention.

The NSC has also played a pivotal role in the regeneration of economic activity in former mining and labour-sending areas currently in a state of economic decline, e.g. in Namaqualand in the Northern Cape, Ndedwe in KwaZulu-Natal, Indwe and Port St Johns in Alfred Nzo, and O.R. Tambo municipalities in the Eastern Cape, State projects in Sekhukhune in Limpopo, and Zeerust in North West.

The Minister of Minerals and Energy announced in her 2003/04 budget speech the establishment of the Small-Scale Mining Committee (SSMC). The SSMC will be responsible for setting up a diamond-processing plant in the Northern Cape, a phosphate mine in the Western Cape, and implementing coal and brick-making projects in the Eastern Cape.

The projects are expected to create some 1 500 direct jobs.

Mineral wealth

South Africa's mineral wealth is found in diverse geological formations, some of which are unique and extensive by world standards. Some of the country's minerals include:

- Gold – the unique and wide-spread Witwatersrand Basin yields some 98% of South Africa's gold output.
- Diamonds (in kimberlites, alluvial and marine) – the country is among the world's top producers.
- Titanium – heavy mineral-sand occurrences containing titanium minerals are found along the coasts.
- Manganese – enormous reserves of manganese are found in the sedimentary rocks of the Transvaal Supergroup.
- PGMs and chrome – these minerals occur in the Bushveld Complex in Mpumalanga, Limpopo and North West. More than half of the global reserves of chrome and platinum are found in this deposit.
- Coal and anthracite beds occur in the Karoo Basin in Mpumalanga, KwaZulu-Natal and Limpopo.
- Copper phosphate, titanium, iron, vermiculite and zirconium are found in the Phalaborwa Igneous Complex in Limpopo.

South Africa's reserves of seven commodities rank highest in the world. These are:

South Africa's mineral production, 2002*

Commodity	Unit	Production	%	World rank
Aluminium	kt	707		7
Alumino-silicates	kt	161,8	36,9	1
Antimony	t	5746	4,1	3
Asbestos	kt	•	*	*
Chrome ore	kt	6 436	49,5	1
Coal	Mt	221,5	5,8	6
Copper	kt	130		
Diamonds	kcar	-	-	-
Ferrochromium	kt	2 351		
Ferromanganese	kt	934		
Ferrosilicon	kt	184		
Fluorspar	kt	232	5	3
Gold	t	399	15,7	1
Iron ore	Mt	36	3,3	8
Lead	kt	49	1,7	8
Manganese ore	kt	33 22	17,1	2
Nickel	kt	38,5	2,9	9
Phosphate rock	kt	-	-	-
Platinum-group metals	kg	239 761	65,9	1
Silicon metal	kt	42	1,0	7
Silver	t	113	0,6	
Titanium minerals	kt	2 643	53,9	2
Uranium	t	998		
Vanadium	kt	25	37,6	2
Vermiculite	kt	210	58	1
Zinc in minerals	kt	64	0,7	
Zirconium minerals	kt	425	46,7	1

Mt = megaton, kt = kiloton, t = ton, car = carats kcar = kilocarats
*Preliminary data •Production ceased - Confidential information

Source: Minerals Bureau

Minerals and energy

South Africa's primary and processed mineral sales, 2002*

Commodity or sector	Unit	Local sales (FOR)** Mass	Local sales (FOR)** Value (R' million)	Export sales (FOB)*** Mass	Export sales (FOB)*** Value (R' million)	Total sales Mass	Total sales Value (R' million)
Gold	t	4,5	453,4	393,1	40 935	397,5	41 388
Coal	Mt	156,5	1 169,5	69,2	164,0	225,7	30 611,0
Platinum Group Metals	t	-	4 369	208	30 459	~	34 828
Base minerals	Mt	1,9	3 871	0,9	4 920	2,8	8 791
Ferrous minerals	Mt	16,4	2 174,8	26,5	5 661,9	42,9	7 836,7
Industrial minerals	~	60,2	3 957,9	1,5	1 537,9	61,7	5 495,8
Other minerals	~	-	323,7	-	7 039	~	10 443
Processed minerals	Mt		5 293		18 269		23 563

*Preliminary
~ Various mass and volume units (e.g. carats, barrels and tons)
** FOR – Free on rail values
*** FOB – Free on board values

Source: Minerals Bureau

- manganese
- chromium
- PGMs
- gold
- vanadium
- alumino-silicates
- vermiculite.

The small domestic market for most commodities means that South Africa's mineral industry is export-orientated: for vermiculite it contributes 95% of world exports, vanadium 76%, alumino-silicates 51%, ferrochromium 57%, PGMs 51%, chrome ore 24%, and manganese ore and ferromanganese 23% and 25% respectively.

South Africa is the world's largest exporter of these commodities, as well as of gold, ziconium and antimony. Other important export commodities include coal and titanium minerals.

Because of this vast mineral resource base, South Africa is, to a large degree, self-sufficient with respect to the supply of minerals.

However, some minerals and mineral products need to be imported due to an insufficiency of local resources or the fact that their deposits in South Africa cannot be economically exploited.

Another factor is that certain specialised grades and products are not produced in South Africa.

The more notable imports into South Africa in 2002 were diamonds, alumina and other non-ferrous minerals, certain ferro-alloys and coking coal.

South Africa's total primary minerals increased by 17,1% to R115,2 billion in 2002. Total processed mineral sales increased by 8,4% in 2002 to some R24,5 billion.

The combined total for primary and processed mineral sales is estimated to have increased by 15,5% in 2002 to R139,7 billion.

Domestic primary mineral sales revenue increased in 2002 by 18% to R29,8 billion.

The value of exports of primary minerals in 2002 increased by 19,8% to R107,8 billion.

The Directorate: Mineral Economics (Minerals Bureau) of the Department of Minerals and Energy monitors and analyses all mineral commodities with regard to South African and world supply and demand, marketing and market trends.

Full details of South Africa's mineral industry (including the individual commodities) and its recent performance are provided in the Directorate's annual review.

South Africa Yearbook 2003/04

South Africa's 'heavyweight' mineral exports, 2002*

Commodity	Export mass in kt
Aluminium	522
Alumino-silicates	90
Chrome ore	651
Chrome alloys	2 189
Coal	69 200
Dimension stone	677
Fluorspar	197
Iron ore	24 304
Manganese ore	1 539
Manganese products	690
Phosphate rock	197
Silicon products	103
Titanium products	270
Vermiculite	170
Zirconium products	486

*Preliminary data

Source: Minerals Bureau

The recent performance of the more important individual commodities and of the different mineral sectors is summarised as follows.

The Department of Minerals and Energy has increased the funding allocated annually to assist with the development of the small-scale mining sector from R5,1 million in 2002/03 to R15 million for the 2003/04 financial year.

During 2002/03, there were 13 projects in different stages of development. The projects employed 740 people, with the bulk of them, 593, being women. A total of R6,8 million was spent in developing these projects. Strides were made at the brick-making project in KwaZulu-Natal.

The Mining Qualifications Authority enabled young people to study for tertiary qualifications in mining through a total of 135 scholarships mainly to previously disadvantaged South Africans. This is done to ensure that the mining industry has the required number of skills, and that people from previously disadvantaged backgrounds are prepared to seize opportunities made available by the Mining Charter, which states that in five years, 40% of junior and senior managers in the mining industry should be historically disadvantaged South Africans.

Gold

World supply and demand for gold decreased by 1,5% to 3 978 tons (t) in 2002.

The average gold price traded at a five-year high of $310/oz.

World mine supply decreased by 36 t to 2 587 t, but South African gold production increased for the first time since 1993. According to provisional 2002 data, gold output in 2002 rose by 0,7% to 397 t and gold revenue increased by 22,4% to £3,94 billion.

The country's first new underground gold mine in 20 years, Avgold's Target Mine, was officially opened in March 2002.

ARMgold, the country's largest black-controlled gold producer, listed on the JSE Securities Exchange in May 2002. During 2002, the company was South Africa's largest, and the world's 11th-largest producer of gold.

Coal

Revenue from coal increased by $163 million, or 5,7%, in 2001 to regain the $3-billion level that was last exceeded in the 1995 to 1998 period. World coal prices strengthened considerably towards mid-year, but sales volumes were relatively unchanged. Just over 30% of the sales volume was exported, accounting for 63% of the sales revenue.

Investments in new coal-mining and transport infrastructural developments are still awaiting prospects of sustained strong activity and firm prices.

Platinum-group metals

South African PGM production increased by 4,7% to 240 t in 2002, but PGM revenue decreased by 14,6% to $3,31 billion. The average platinum price for 2002 was 2,0% higher at $540/oz, while the average palladium price was 44,1% lower at $337/oz.

A noteworthy feature has been the dramatic increase in domestic sales revenue over five years, from almost zero to $415 million in 2002, largely to supply a developing manufacturing business providing automotive exhaust catalysis systems for world markets.

PGM-mining investments in progress, committed and proposed, involving new mines, extensions, mineral processing plants and smelters will be substantial over the next five years. New entrants, often representing previously disadvantaged community interests, are mostly participating through joint ventures with established major operators.

Base minerals

Refined copper, nickel, cobalt, titanium and zirconium concentrates dominate this sector, with support from zinc, lead and arsenic concentrates. The sector contributes some 12% and 4% respectively to total primary local sales and total primary export sales. About 44% of total revenue is local sales for further added-value operations.

World prices for base minerals stabilised in 2002, and most base metal annual average prices were somewhat below their 2001 levels. Demand was also weak. It was anticipated that the recovery of base metal demand and prices would start towards the end of 2003.

Provisional statistics, however, indicate that South Africa's base mineral sales excluding titanium and zirconium minerals increased slightly by $12 million or 2,4% to $503 million. This increase is largely attributed to increased sales by volume.

Ferrous minerals

This sector consists of the ores of iron, manganese and chrome, dominated by iron ore. It has been a leading performer in the primary minerals industry in recent years, with revenue in Dollar terms growing at almost 3% annually. Demand depends on the fortunes of the world's steel and stainless steel industries.

Recessionary economic conditions in the developed world during 2001 impacted negatively on ferrous minerals demand and prices. Improved iron ore sales were insufficient to offset this trend. Overall, ferrous mineral sales fell by $28 million, or 3,5%, below the 2000 revenue.

Industrial minerals

This sector comprises a wide variety of mineral products, from which 70% of revenue is local sales. In Dollar terms, domestic activity appears to be decreasing alarmingly, with total sales decreasing by 9,1% in 2001 to $523 million. In Rand terms, local sales increased by 14,1% to the value of R4,0 billion, and export sales increased by 4,3% to R1,5 billion.

During 2002, 80% of local sales comprised limestone and lime (26%), phosphate rock concentrate (data withheld), aggregate and sand (25%) and sulphur (5%).

Exports were dominated by dimension stone (46%), vermiculite and fluorspar (15% each), andalusite (9%) and phosphate rock concentrate (data withheld).

South African industrial mineral statistics do not include beach sands (ilmenite, rutile and zircon), chromite and manganese ore used in non-metallic applications (e.g. pigments, chemicals and batteries) and antimony trioxide (used in flame retardants), all of which are included in this sector in other parts of the world.

Processed minerals

Ferro-alloys and aluminium dominate this sector, with solid support from titanium slag, phosphoric acid, vanadium, zinc metal and low-manganese pig-iron. Through investment in beneficiation, it has been the outstanding performer in the mineral industry over the last 16 years, with revenue in Dollar terms growing at 5,5% annually.

Weaker international prices during 2002 were responsible for processed mineral sales falling some 5,5% compared with 2001.

Other minerals

This sector is dominated by diamonds, with support from hydrocarbon fuel, uranium oxide and silver. Sales revenue was boosted enormously in 2000 by diamond sales that were held back from 1999, and by a strategy to amortise commercial diamond inventories.

In 2002, the sector sales amounted to just under $1 billion, down from 2001 as a result of the stronger Rand against the Dollar. Almost two-thirds of sales were exports, and a strong share of the local sales arose from products of the domestic hydrocarbon wells, which are not directly exported.

New investment potential remains strong in this sector, which has recovered enormously by new investments in operations since 1994, compensating for the rapid demise in the demand for uranium oxide in nuclear applications since the late 1980s.

Energy

Energy in the economy

Energy comprises approximately 15% of Gross Domestic Product (GDP), creating employment for about 250 000 people. The total electricity sales by Eskom in 2002 grew by 1,5% to 187 957 gigawatt-hour (GWh). Total liquid-fuels sales in 2001 grew by 0,3% to 20 934 million litres (ML). These figures demonstrate the growth of the South African economy and the importance of energy as a key driver of the country's economy.

Its energy intensity is above average, with only 10 other countries having higher commercial primary energy intensities. This high-energy intensity is largely a result of the economy's structure, with large-scale, energy-intensive primary mineral beneficiation industries and mining industries dominating.

In addition, there is a heavy reliance on coal for the generation of most of the electricity and a significant proportion of the liquid fuels consumed in the country. Furthermore, South Africa's industry has not generally used the latest in energy-efficient technologies, mainly as a result of relatively low energy costs.

Government has been persistently engaging members of the Organisation of Petroleum Exporting Countries through diplomatic channels to increase production.

Energy efficiency

Significant potential exists for energy efficiency improvements in South Africa in all economic sectors, the largest potential being in industry, which uses 68% of all electricity.

The savings potential of the industrial sector could be as high as 50% for a number of reasons: the low cost of electricity is only a temporary phenomenon, energy-efficient technologies are more easily available than in the past and the payback periods are short. However, maximum benefits for the national economy will only realise if energy efficiency is practised across all sectors, including mining, households, commercial buildings and transport.

The energy-efficiency strategy to be pursued by government envisages achieving a target of 5% improvement over the next 10 years through enabling instruments and interventions. These include economic and legislative means, norms and standards and appliance labelling, energy audits and management, promotion of energy-efficient technologies, as well as the promotion of public awareness and information about the benefits of energy-efficiency measures.

Interventions will be grouped into three phases according to the payback period aimed at implementing 'easy gain' measures in the first phase and 'long-term gains' in the third phase.

The barriers to implementing energy efficiency in the past have been the low cost of electricity and the lack of knowledge among the public about the benefits of energy-efficient technologies, but the situation is set to change. The commitment to sustainable development and cleaner energy utilisation, the low cost of energy-efficient technologies and, above all, the cost-effectiveness of energy efficiency (including demand-side management on behalf of the electricity utilities) compared with the great expenditure involved in building new power-generation capacity, are driving government policy in a new direction.

Energy demand by the economic subsector

Households

Energy consumed by households represents some 22% of the country's net use. Most household energy is obtained from fuel wood (65% of net energy), primarily in rural areas, with the remainder coming from coal (9%), illuminating paraffin (8%), and a small amount from liquid petroleum gas.

Rural households comprise the majority of poor homes and are characterised by severe poverty. In terms of basic energy services, their energy 'poverty' is exacerbated by the increasingly widespread scarcity of fuel-wood resources. Wood and paraffin are their main energy sources, with few having access to electricity.

Productive sectors

Industry and mining are the most important subsectors in terms of energy consumption. These sectors mainly use electricity and coal as energy sources.

The balance comes largely from coke and blast-furnace gases and small amounts of heating oils.

The mining industry depends heavily on electricity. Mineral and metal processing uses large amounts of electricity and coal, mostly in large-scale mineral beneficiation processes. Base metals, the largest single industrial energy-consuming subsector, is also by far the most energy-intensive one.

The food sector shows a high total use and relatively high intensity, although, in terms of value added, its energy requirements are very modest in comparison with the basic mineral and metal industries. The chemical and paper and pulp industries also consume large amounts of energy at high intensities.

Transport

Liquid fuels such as petrol and diesel account for 92% of energy used for transport. Rail transport accounts for less than 5% of the total national electricity consumption. Petrol sales account for more than half of the total sales of local petroleum products.

The total volume of liquid fuels sold during 2002 in South Africa was 21 267 ML, in comparison with 20 934 ML sold in 2001.

The demand for petrol and diesel has remained relatively static over the last five years. The demand for jet fuel has, however, grown steadily since 1994 as a result of increased business and tourism activities.

Government has accepted a process of managed liberalisation for the liquid fuel industry.

The Petroleum Products Act, 1977 (Act 120 of 1977), will be amended to institute a licensing dispensation for participants in the liquid fuel industry.

A regulatory regime for the petroleum pipeline industry will be established.

Coal

South Africa's indigenous energy resource base is dominated by coal. Many of the deposits can be exploited at extremely favourable costs and, as a result, a large coal-mining industry has developed.

The country ranks as the world's sixth-largest coal producer. In addition to the extensive use of coal in the domestic economy, large amounts are exported mainly through the Richards Bay Coal Terminal. South Africa is ranked the fourth-largest exporter of steam coal.

South Africa's coal comes from collieries ranging from among the largest in the world to small-scale producers with output in the range of between 5 000 and one million t per month. As a result of mergers and purchases, operating collieries were reduced to 55 in 2001. Of these, a relatively small number of large-scale producers supply coal primarily to the electricity and synthetic fuel producers.

About 54% of South African coal-mining is done underground and about 46% is produced by open-cast methods.

The coal-mining industry is highly concentrated, with three companies, Ingwe (Billiton), Anglo Coal and Sasol, accounting for 82% of saleable coal production. Production is concentrated in large mines, with 13 mines accounting for 74% of production.

South African coal for local electricity production is among the cheapest in the world. The beneficiation of coal, particularly for export, results in more than 60 megaton (Mt) of coal discards being produced annually.

Thirty per cent of raw coal mined for the export market, and between 15% and 25% of the raw coal mined for local demand (excluding power-station coal), is not marketable and therefore discarded.

Total discards on the surface could reach 2 300 Mt by the year 2020, should none of this material be utilised. As a result, the Department of Minerals and Energy is investigating ways to promote and encourage the economic use of the discards.

Nuclear power

Nuclear science employs approximately 3 000 skilled people in diverse areas such as electricity generation, isotope production and non-destructive material studies for industry.

It positions South Africa at the forefront of medical applications of radioisotopes such as cancer diagnostics and therapy, and enables it to absorb and apply new nuclear technologies developed elsewhere in the world. It also gives South Africa the competitive advantage to play a leading role in Africa in the application of nuclear techniques in health, food, agriculture and environmental management.

South Africa has 34 nuclear medicine-imaging centres, of which 75% are privately owned. These centres together perform between 25 000 and 30 000 diagnostic procedures per annum. In addition, 30 oncology clinics and hospitals are equipped with teletherapy and accelerator equipment used in nuclear therapy to treat life-threatening diseases.

The South African nuclear industry is mainly governed by the Nuclear Energy Act, 1999 (Act 46 of 1999), and the National Nuclear Regulator (NNR) Act, 1999 (Act 47 of 1999). The legislation has established the South African Nuclear Energy Corporation Ltd (NECSA), previously called the Atomic Energy Corporation, responsible for nuclear technology, and the NNR, previously called the Council for Nuclear Safety.

Other relevant legislation that also play a regulatory role in the nuclear industry are the Hazardous Substances Act, 1993 (Act 131 of 1993), the Mine Health and Safety Act, 1996, the Minerals Act, 1989 (Act 30 of 1989), the National Environmental Management Act, 1998 (Act 107 of 1998), the Water Act, 1998 (Act 36 of 1998), and the Dumping at Sea Act, 1980 (Act 73 of 1980).

The Minister of Minerals and Energy is responsible for the governance of the nuclear industry and related matters. NECSA and the NNR report to the Minister. Apart from the Minister's authority over radioactive waste and irradicated nuclear fuel, the Minister also regulates matters pertaining to nuclear non-proliferation.

Nuclear energy policy was formulated as part of the *White Paper on Energy Policy*, 1998. In terms of this policy, government will investigate what long-term contribution nuclear power can make to the country's energy economy and, secondly, how the existing nuclear industrial infrastructure can be optimised.

In September 2003, the Deputy Minister of Minerals and Energy, Ms Susan Shabangu, released the Draft Radioactive Waste-Management Policy and Strategy for public comment. The purpose of the Draft Policy is to establish a comprehensive radioactive waste-governance framework, by formulating a policy and implementation strategy in consultation with all stakeholders.

The Radioactive Waste Management Policy and Strategy outlines government's thinking on radioactive waste management and reflects the following:
- international and national principles for the safe management of radioactive waste
- responsibilities of government, radioactive waste generators and regulators
- basic principles and evaluation/authorisation processes for radioactive waste-management plans
- management structures to service the radioactive waste-management obligations of the Minister of Minerals and Energy
- a national radioactive waste-classification scheme
- a long-term radioactive waste-management fund
- undertakings to investigate the best long-term option for spent-fuel management.

Nuclear Energy Corporation

The NECSA was established as a public company in terms of the Nuclear Energy Act, 1999 and is wholly owned by the State. Apart from several ancillary functions, the main functions of NECSA are to undertake and promote research and development (R&D) in the fields of nuclear energy and radiation science and technology; to process source material, special nuclear material and restricted material; and to co-operate with persons in matters falling within these functions. Apart from its main operations at Pelindaba, west of Pretoria, NECSA also operates the Vaalputs radioactive waste-disposal facility in the Northern Cape.

NECSA is divided into six divisions, two of which are corporatised in structure and commercial in nature, two focusing on R&D and other non-commercial tasks, and two providing support services to the other four and to any other companies which now, or in the future, will operate from NECSA's Pelindaba complex.

The new structure contains two corporatised divisions to allow one to concentrate on nuclear business and the other on the group's high-tech non-nuclear business.

The former is called Nuclear Technology Products (NTP) and is responsible for the production and sale of radioisotopes and for radiation services. Radioisotopes, which are exported worldwide by NECSA, are essential for nuclear medicine and many industrial applications.

In September 2003, the Minister of Minerals and Energy announced that NTP had exported 86% of its sales of R131 million to 40 countries on five continents during 2002/03.

A chemical plant for the production of an advanced fluorine-based gas for use in the global semi-conductor industry has been established and commissioned on the Pelindaba site. The plant will generate in excess of R60 million per annum in foreign exchange over the next 10 years.

During 2003, NTP signed seven agreements involving product and business initiatives with the large Canadian multinational, MDS Nordion Inc.

NTP was the winner of the prestigious Technology Top 100 award in its category for 2002 and also received a special award from MTN for its role in successfully commercialising key domestic nuclear technology.

The non-nuclear commercial division will be corporatised as HTP Marketing and Manufacturing (Pty) Ltd. It focuses on commercial activities involving chemicals and gases – including fluorine beneficiation products and services.

The third of NECSA's divisions is called Nuclear Technology and houses the strategic core business functions of the group. It is here that R&D, training, skills transfer, as well as work that has relevance to the Pebble-Bed Modular Reactor (PBMR) project at Koeberg in the Western Cape, take place.

The fourth of the group's divisions is Nuclear Services. This is a non-commercial division that is geared to perform State obligatory tasks, including the management of nuclear licences, management of decontamination, decommissioning functions, the ownership of the Safari-1 Research Reactor, as well as all safeguard functions and work with related international agencies, such as the International Atomic Energy Agency (IAEA).

The last two divisions of NECSA are Corporate Services, which supports the management of the other divisions, and Facilities Management, which is the landlord of the Pelindaba complex.

NECSA employs some 1 400 people in such diverse areas as physics engineering, chemistry and electronics.

Safari-1 is the most commercialised such reactor in the world with ISO 9001 accreditation, and is earning South Africa millions of Rands' worth of foreign revenue.

NECSA develops and utilises nuclear technology as part of the National System of Innovation. The Corporation also serves the State's nuclear institutional obligations. Its growth strategy, Vision 2010, is aimed at contributing to national and regional socio-economic development, in line with NEPAD.

In addition, NECSA is actively involved in training the healthcare sector in the safe and optimal use of nuclear material and technology. It also provides a 24-hour emergency service for nuclear-related accidents throughout Africa.

It (among other things) produces radioisotopes that are used to fight diseases and to accurately measure critical process parameters such as levels, mass, density and quality, and thus help keep the wheels of industry turning.

NECSA houses and operates the first gamma-irradiation facility in Africa. The facility, which was commissioned in 1971, is used to sterilise a range of products such as peat moss used as a growth medium in the seed industry.

NECSA is accredited by the IAEA as a regional designated centre, servicing the rest of Africa in radioactive waste management. The Corporation has been given the responsibility of developing a low-cost radioactive waste-disposal facility – known as the Borehole Nuclear Waste Disposal System – to be used for the disposal of radioactive waste from hospitals on the continent.

Annually, NECSA dispatches top nuclear scientists to help condition and store spent radium sources in countries such as Zimbabwe, Madagascar, Tunisia, Sudan and Mauritius. Other projects include dam-leakage detection and the auditing of radiotherapy and nuclear medicine facilities in countries that include Libya, Nigeria and Ethiopia.

Radiation techniques are benefiting farmers across the continent – its use in agriculture increases crop quality and improves cattle production, thus raising income potential.

Other projects undertaken by NECSA include helping authorities curb the growing illegal trade in elephant and rhino horns, by using radiation techniques to identify the origins of the ivory. The dating of archaeological artifacts is yet another example of the useful and peaceful application of nuclear technology.

Eskom Koeberg Nuclear Power Station

Koeberg's two reactors have operated safely since their commissioning in 1984 and 1985 respectively. Koeberg supplies 1 800 megawatt to the national grid when both reactors are operating at full power, contributing approximately 6% of South Africa's electricity. Koeberg meets the full electricity demand of the Western Cape and was built mainly for economic reasons. It would be approximately 6% more costly to supply electricity to the Western Cape from the power-stations in the northern part of the country owing to losses during transmission.

With most of South Africa's electricity-generating stations situated on the Highveld coalfields, Koeberg provides a necessary 'anchor' for the supply network.

Uranium mining
The Nuclear Fuels Corporation is the uranium sales organisation in South Africa. In 1986, South Africa produced approximately 1 436 t of uranium at four production centres.

Nuclear-safety regulation
The NNR is the prime safety regulator and is responsible for the protection of persons, property and the environment against nuclear damage through the establishment of safety standards and regulatory practices. It exercises regulatory control related to safety over the siting, design, construction and operation of nuclear installations and other actions.

The Department of Environmental Affairs and Tourism announced in June 2003 that the environmental impact of the proposed PBMR at Koeberg, and the manufacturing and transportation of nuclear fuel to and from Pelindaba, was acceptable from an environmental impact point of view, subject to certain conditions.

One of these conditions was adherence by the Department of Minerals and Energy to finalise the Radioactive Waste-Management Policy and Strategy. This was achieved in September 2003.

Possible expansion
Nuclear power has not been excluded as a possible energy-supply option for the future. However, energy policy requires that decisions to construct future nuclear power-stations will be taken within the context of an integrated energy-planning process, and will be subject to consultation with all stakeholders. This integrated energy-planning process has been initiated by the Department of Minerals and Energy.

Eskom has completed a feasibility study of the PBMR with the objective of establishing whether such technology could form part of Eskom's expansion planning, and what advantages/disadvantages it would have compared with other options.

Liquid fuels
South Africa's consumed 21 267 ML of liquid-fuel products in 2002. Thirty-six per cent of the demand is met by synthetic fuels (synfuels) produced locally, largely from coal and a small amount from natural gas. The rest is met by products refined locally from imported crude oil.

The petrol price in South Africa is linked to the price of petrol in United States (US) Dollars in certain international markets for petrol. This means that the domestic price is influenced by supply and demand for petroleum products in the international markets, combined with the Rand/Dollar exchange rate.

During 2002/03, there were various petrol-price increases as a result of increased prices for petroleum products in relevant international markets and the deterioration in the Rand/Dollar exchange rate. However, 2003 also saw some price cuts.

The National Petroleum, Gas and Oil Corporation of South Africa (PetroSA) was officially launched in Cape Town in October 2002.

The formation of the Corporation was the result of a merger between Mossgas, Soekor and other assets managed by the Strategic Fuel Fund.

The work on the merger began in 1998 with the adoption of the *White Paper on Energy Policy*.

As the national petroleum company in South Africa, PetroSA is responsible for the exploration and exploitation of oil and natural gas, as well as the production and marketing of synthetic fuels produced from offshore gas at the world's largest commercial gas-to-liquids plant in Mossel Bay.

PetroSA's commitment to the safety and health of its workers led to the company winning the National Association of Clean Air Award for clean air and environmental care at its Mossel Bay refinery operation.

During the State of the Nation Address in February 2003, President Thabo Mbeki announced that with effect from April 2003, the Basic Fuel Price Formula would be phased in to replace the In Bond Landed Cost Pricing Mechanism.

It is expected that the new pricing mechanism will save fuel users more than R1 billion annually.

The Petroleum Products Amendment Bill was introduced in Parliament on 13 May 2003, and the Petroleum Pipeline Bill on 17 April 2003.

The Department of Minerals and Energy extablished a monitoring team in 2002 to evaluate the sustainability of Black Economic Empowerment (BEE) deals in liquid fuels and the validity of BEE groups.

Sasol

The Sasol group of companies comprises diversified fuel, chemical and related manufacturing and marketing operations, complemented by interests in technology development, oil and gas exploration, and production.

Its principal feedstocks are obtained from coal, which the company converts into value-added hydrocarbons through Fischer-Tropsch process technologies.

The company supplies 41% of South Africa's liquid fuel needs. It also provides 200 000 direct and indirect jobs, contributes R34 billion annually to South Africa's GDP, and produces 23% of the country's required coal.

Through Sasol Petroleum International and Sasol Synfuels International, the group also has interests in Mozambique, Congo, Equatorial Guinea, Gabon, Nigeria and Qatar.

Among its recent international developments is an agreement signed with the Mozambican Government for the development of natural gas fields in that country, and the construction of a pipeline to South Africa.

> Sasol was named Global Coal Company of the Year for 2002 by the Platts-Business Week Global Energy Awards.

The project, a joint venture between Sasol and the Governments of South Africa and Mozambique, involves the construction of a pipeline running for 865 km from the natural gas fields of Pande and Temane in Mozambique to Secunda in South Africa.

The initial capacity of the pipeline is 120 million giga-joules per year, equivalent to 4 000 MW.

The first gas was expected to be delivered to Secunda by February 2004.

Sasol listed its American Depository Receipts on the New York Stock Exchange on 9 April 2003.

Sasol now operates in 23 countries on all continents, producing hundreds of fuel and chemical products for customers in more than 100 countries.

Indigenous oil and gas resources and production

The Petroleum Agency of South Africa (PASA), the Department of Minerals and Energy's Agency responsible for the promotion of oil and gas exploration, has been successful in further encouraging international exploration companies to evaluate the country's oil and gas opportunities.

As a result of increased exploration activities, a better understanding of the potential for commercial oil and gas is being developed. PASA is following this up with a detailed possible resource study.

The EM gas-field complex off Mossel Bay started production in the third quarter of 2000, and will ensure sufficient feedstock to PetroSA to maintain current liquid-fuel production levels at 36 000 barrels (bbls) of petroleum products a day until 2009.

Parallel exploration is being carried out in various other sections of the Bredasdorp Basin off the coast of Mossel Bay in the Western Cape to find reserves for PetroSA beyond 2009.

PetroSA's gas-to-liquid plant supplies about 7% of South Africa's liquid-fuel needs. The

Minerals and energy

products are supplied to oil companies that market them under their own brand names.

PetroSA also produces anhydrous alcohols and speciality fuels that are exported and earn the company more than R500 million per year.

PetroSA's new oilfield, Sable, situated about 150 km south off the coast of Mossel Bay, is expected to produce 17% of South Africa's oil needs.

The field, which came into operation in August 2003, was initially projected to produce 30 000 to 40 000 bbls of crude oil a day and 20 million to 25 million bbls in the next three years.

The net savings in foreign exchange to the country would be equivalent to PetroSA's bottom-line profit of between $10 million and $15 million a year.

PetroSA holds 60% working interest in Sable, while Dallas-based partner company Pioneer Natural Resources holds the remaining 40%.

PetroSA has offered 9% of its Sable interest for sale to a BEE group.

Import and export of fuel products

The import of refined products is restricted to special cases where local producers cannot meet demand. It is subject to State control with a view to promoting local refinery utilisation.

When overproduction occurs, export permits are required and generally granted, provided that both South Africa's and other Southern African Customs Union members' requirements are met.

More diesel than petrol is exported, owing to the balance of supply and demand of petrol and diesel relative to refinery configurations. Although petrol and diesel make up 55% of total liquid-fuel exports, South Africa is also the main supplier of all other liquid fuels to Botswana, Namibia, Lesotho and Swaziland.

Gas

In addition to coal gas and liquid petroleum gas, South Africa produced some 15 234 t of natural gas and 271 billion t of associated condensate in 2002.

The entire gas and condensate output is dedicated to PetroSA's liquid-fuel synthesis plant, and accounts for about 1,5% of total primary energy supply. Gas manufactured from coal accounts for 1,2% of net energy consumption, while liquid petroleum gas accounts for about 0,5%.

Natural and coal gas play separate roles in the energy system, with natural gas being used solely as a feedstock for production of synthetic fuels, and coal gas as an industrial and domestic fuel.

However, current development of regional gas fields will lead to natural gas becoming a more important fuel in South Africa.

Infrastructure

South Africa's gas infrastructure stretches from Sasolburg in the northern Free State, through the industrial areas of Vereeniging, Johannesburg and the East Rand, and from Secunda to Witbank and Middelburg, to Newcastle, Richards Bay and Durban.

Through the Sasol Gas Division, Sasol Oil markets industrial pipeline gas produced by Sasol Synthetic Fuels and Sasol Chemical Industries to about 700 industrial customers. These customers are mostly in the greater Johannesburg-Pretoria region and the industrial areas of Witbank-Middelburg and Durban.

South Africa will host the 18th World Petroleum Congress in 2005.

The Congress, considered the world's biggest and most prestigious meeting in the oil industry, is expected to attract more than 20 Energy Ministers and 5 000 representatives from the oil, gas and related industries, governments, and academics from across the globe.

The South African International Oil and Gas Exhibition will run parallel with the 2005 Congress.

It promises to be the largest exhibition of its kind on the African continent, with some 4 000 exhibitors and 25 000 visitors expected.

Its pipeline network consists of about 1 500 km of underground pipelines.

Most of the remaining 10% of gas sales in South Africa is on-selling of Sasol gas by Metro Gas in Johannesburg, which owns 1 300 km of distribution pipe, and supplies 12 000 domestic and 3 000 industrial customers.

The privatisation of Metro Gas was completed in 2000. It is now owned by Egoli Gas (Pty) Ltd, a joint venture company owned by Cinergy Global Power Inc. Egoli Gas intends to invest R276 million in Metro Gas.

Petronet owns and operates a gas pipeline, known as the Lily Line, which is approximately 600 km long and transports methane-rich gas from Sasol's Secunda plant as far as the Durban area. Easigas (Shell) has a small liquid petroleum gas/air pipe network in Port Elizabeth. A privately owned company in Port Elizabeth distributes a small amount of liquid petroleum gas/air blend by pipe.

Industrial customers use 87% of the gas, and domestic consumers the rest. The supply of cost-competitive pipeline gas is complemented by the fuel oils range of low-sulphur residual and distillate fuel oils derived from coal and other synthesised forms, as well as crude oil.

PASA markets offshore gas exploration and exploitation.

Sasol announced in February 2003 that it would invest R15 million as part of a project to help government set up 10 Integrated Energy Centres over the next three years, in an effort to make energy more accessible and affordable to the country's rural poor.

The project stems from the Integrated Sustainable Rural Development Strategy (ISRDS). Energy products will be delivered directly to the Integrated Energy Centres that will become sole wholesalers and distributors.

Embalenhle in Mpumalanga, and QwaQwa in the Free State, have been identified as the first two sites. The other eight sites will be determined in line with the nodes identified in the ISRDS and will be set up in KwaZulu-Natal, the Eastern Cape, Free State, Northern Cape, Limpopo and Mpumalanga.

The Gas Act, 2001 (Act 48 of 2001), aims to:
- promote the orderly development of the piped-gas industry
- establish a national regulatory framework
- establish the National Gas Regulator as the custodian and enforcer of the national regulatory framework.

To facilitate the movement of gas across international borders, a cross-border gas trade agreement with Mozambique has been signed.

In 2000, the Cabinet approved the establishment of a national gas-development company, iGas, within the Central Energy Fund (CEF) Group. The task of this company is to enter into joint ventures for gas-transmission pipeline projects.

During 2002/03:
- the Gas Regulator Levies Act, 2002 (Act 75 of 2002), was assented to by President Mbeki. The Act provides for the establishment of a gas regulator
- the Cabinet approved the rationalisation of the regulators of the gas, electricity and petroleum pipelines sectors into a single National Energy Regulator.

Other initiatives included:
- the development of the Draft Gas Infrastructure Plan, which outlines how gas resources will be developed to produce energy for South Africa
- the South Africa/Mozambique Cross-Border Gas Commission, which has commenced its sittings
- the text of the South Africa/Namibia Cross-Border Agreement, which was agreed upon
- the production of the first Integrated Energy Plan, which also makes provision for gas.

In August 2003, the Minister of Minerals and Energy launched the Ibhubezi Gas Field at Redisson, Seapoint, Cape Town.

The introduction of natural gas is in compliance with the *White Paper on Energy Policy* by diversifying primary energy supply. Natural gas has the least negative environmental impact of the fossil fuels.

Ibhubezi Gas Field is presently the only field discovered off the west coast of South Africa containing potentially commercial volumes of gas. This gas would be supplied to a gas-to-electricity project in the Western Cape and to the PetroSA's manufacturing plant in Mossel Bay. The volume of gas already discovered in the Ibhubesi Gas Field is too small to guarantee a production life of 20 years needed to match market demand.

Electricity

South Africa, which supplies two-thirds of Africa's electricity, is one of the four cheapest electricity producers in the world. Ninety-two per cent of South African electricity is produced from coal. Generation is currently dominated by Eskom, the national wholly State-owned utility, which also owns and operates the national electricity grid. Eskom currently supplies more than 95% of South Africa's electricity.

In global terms, the utility is among the top seven in generating capacity, among the top nine in terms of sales, and has the world's biggest dry-cooling power-station.

Eskom was incorporated as a public company on 1 July 2002, as it is financed by net financial market liabilities and assets as well as reserves.

While Eskom does not currently have exclusive generation rights, it has a practical mono-poly on bulk electricity. It also operates the integrated national high-voltage transmission system and supplies electricity directly to large consumers such as mines, mineral beneficiators and other large industries. In addition, it supplies directly to commercial farmers and, through the Integrated National Electrification Programme (INEP), to a large number of residential consumers. It sells in bulk to muni-cipalities, which distribute to consumers within their boundaries.

During 2002, Eskom electrified 211 628 homes against government's target of 205 371 homes, thereby exceeding the target by 6 257 homes.

Restructuring of the electricity supply industry (ESI)

The recommendations approved by the Cabinet and which represent government's position on the ESI, are the following:
- To meet government's developmental and social objectives, Eskom retains no less than 70% of the existing electricity-generating market sector.
- That the introduction of private-sector participation in the generation sector be increased to 30% of the existing electricity-generating market sector.
- That the involvement of BEE within the generation sector be about 10% of the existing generation capacity by no later than 2003.
- To ensure a meaningful participation of the private sector in electricity in the medium term, Eskom should not be allowed to invest in new generation capacity in the domestic market, other than in existing capacity.
- To ensure non-discriminatory and open access to the transmission lines, and taking into consideration the financial stability of Eskom, government, in the medium term, establishes a separate State-owned transmission company that will be independent of generation and retail businesses, with a ring-fenced transmission-system and market-operation functions. Initially, this transmission company will be a subsidiary of Eskom Holdings and will be established as a separate State-owned company before any investments are made in current or new-generation capacity.
- Over time, a multimarket model electricity-market framework will ensure that transactions between electricity generators, traders and power purchasers take place on a variety of platforms, including bilateral deals, and future and day-ahead markets.
- A regulatory framework is in place that will ensure the participation of independent

power producers, and that diversified primary energy sources be developed within the electricity sector without hindrance.
- The planning and development of transmission systems will be undertaken by the transmission company, subject to government policy guidelines.
- Over time, and taking cognisance of the strategic objectives of the region, the Southern African Power Pool (SAPP) must develop into an independent system operator for the southern African regional grid system, so that public and private generating companies can participate in the Pool.
- Adapting the role of the regulatory system, which will include the reform of the legal framework defining the role of the National Electricity Regulator (NER), the development of a new framework for licensing, the adaptation of price-setting, and the creation of the capacity to monitor the effectiveness of the reformed ESI and ensure security of supply.

Restructuring of the electricity distribution industry (EDI)

The EDI restructuring process differs from most of the other State restructuring activities, as it addresses a number of diverse stakeholders, of which the most important are:
- Eskom
- electricity departments of municipalities
- provinces (related to their governance of municipalities)
- consumers, ranging from very large and electricity-intensive to small
- labour
- a number of government departments.

The normal State restructuring process needs to be modified at the entry level for EDI restructuring in such a manner that the ESI and the EDI restructuring process are interlinked.

The EDI Holdings Company will be responsible for the next phase, which is to move from the current fragmented EDI structure to the implementation of regional electricity distributors (REDs).

The recommendations approved by the Cabinet and which represent government's position on the EDI are the following:
- Endorsing the thrust of the revised EDI Restructuring Blueprint Report.
- The number of six REDs as both the Government's policy direction and the end-state model for the restructured EDI.
- The EDI restructuring implementation plan, especially the time frames, the establishment of the EDI Holdings Company and the transition, will ensure that Eskom and stronger municipalities support the weaker municipal distributors, and that RED 3 and RED 6 receive transitional financial support from the EDI Holdings Company. During 2003/04, the Company was expected to start transforming the EDI. Significant progress in the transformation of the supply industry was also expected to begin in 2003/04.
- Ongoing consultations with stakeholders such as new municipalities, the NER, Eskom, organised labour, customers, and provincial and local governments.
- The Minister of Provincial and Local Government will convene a meeting of relevant Ministers to deal with the issue of debt owed by local authorities to Eskom.

By May 2003, the industry was worth R30 billion and employed more than 30 000 personnel. The work on demarcating the six new REDS has been completed. The REDS will own the distribution business of Eskom and municipalities.

National Electricity Regulator

Established in 1995, the NER is a statutory body funded from a small levy imposed on electricity generators.

Legislation requires anybody wishing to generate, transmit or supply electricity to apply to the NER for a licence. This is issued on the basis of criteria which aim to promote and maintain a viable ESI. During 2002, the NER approved a general price increase of 8,439%.

In 2002/03, the NER:

Minerals and energy

- Continued to play a key role as a member of government's Electricity Distribution Industry Restructuring Committee (EDIRC). It also provided advice to government on the 'managed liberalisation' of the generation and transmission sectors, as part of the lead-up to a competitive market structure.
- Participated in and provided specific input to the following working groups:
  - ESI working groups (led by the Department of Public Enterprises)
  - EDI working groups (led by the Department of Minerals and Energy).
- Facilitated a process to ensure that the National Integrated Resource Plan (IRP) is published annually. The first National IRP for 2001/02 was published in December 2002.
- Regulated price increases applied for by licencees (including Eskom), resulting in customers enjoying considerable savings as a result of lower-than-applied-for electricity price increases.
- Managed the process to ensure that the Wholesale Electricity Pricing System (WEPS) is ready for implementation. In addition, the WEPS tariffs modelling and simulation were tested and confirmed. WEPS is intended to regulate the wholesale price of electricity in South Africa when REDs are introduced.
- Broadened the Independent Power Producer (IPP) policy and licensing framework to include renewable IPPs and demonstration plants.
- Implemented the NER Power Quality Directive, resolved disputes between suppliers and customers, and dealt with customer complaints so that customers could have recourse at no or little cost.
- Developed the Draft Energy Efficiency Policy.
- Developed the Transmission Grid Code in consultation with industry stakeholders. These stakeholders represent entities that are foreseen to become Grid Code participants. The Grid Code Advisory Committee was established to advise the NER Board on matters relating to the drafting and amendment of the Grid Code.
- approved the first non-grid licences for concessionaires to implement non-grid electrification projects.

Furthermore, the NER was elected deputy chairperson of the South African Regulator's Forum, which was launched in March 2002.

National and regional co-operation

The NER was also elected the first chairperson of the formalised African Forum for Utility Regulators (AFUR). The NER was also the founding member of the Regional Electricity Regulators' Association (RERA) and the South African Utility Regulators' Association (SAURA), which were launched in September and October 2002 respectively. The NER is the chairperson of SAURA and a chairperson of one of RERA's portfolio commitees.

The main purpose of RERA is to provide a platform for co-operation between independent electricity regulators within the Southern African Development Community (SADC) region.

In deciding to set up RERA, members recognised:

- the need to co-operate in and promote the development of regulatory capacity-building in the region
- the increasing interconnections of the electricity systems between SADC countries, and the continuous increase in regional electricity trade, driven by the benefits of economies of scale and shared resources
- that the successful integration of electricity systems requires clear frameworks to facilitate the development of harmonised market structures, system operations and institutional arrangements
- the need to harmonise regional policies and strategies to promote infrastructure investment in the ESI across the region.

Integrated National Electrification Programme

The INEP remains the flagship of the Department of Minerals and Energy.

The EDI initiated and initially funded the Programme in the early 1990s. Between 1994 and 2003, a total of 3,8 million households were connected to the extended national electricity grid. According to Census 2001, the percentage of households using electricity has increased from 57,6% to 69,7%.

The Department of Minerals and Energy has taken over direct control of the INEP, with electrification funds flowing through the Department since 2001/02 instead of being funded by the ESI (mainly Eskom).

During 2002/03, a further 24 776 households, 974 schools and nine clinics were grid-electrified at a cost of R950 million. With more emphasis placed on integration with other infrastructures and service-providers, this pace will continue until universal access is reached, which is targeted for 2012.

To reach the more remote and sparsely populated rural areas where grid extension becomes expensive, a non-grid electrification programme using photovoltaic-based solar home systems was launched, involving private-sector service-providers. During 2002/03, a basic electricity service was provided to 6 300 rural households.

President Mbeki announced in the State of the Nation Address in 2003, that poor households, in areas connected to the grid, would receive up to 50 kilowatt (kW) of free basic electricity. In non-grid areas, such households are provided with a subsidy of up to 80% of the market cost to provide them with access to electricity.

As part of government's commitment to delivering basic services, the Department is helping to put in place mechanisms to ensure the supply of free electricity to poor households. The funds for this will flow through the equitable share of local government from 2003/04. Total extra funding for free basic electricity in the next Medium Term Expenditure Framework period is R1,4 billion. This should ensure the delivery of about 50 kW hours free each month to poor households.

Government aimed to establish 275 000 grids and 13 900 non-grid household connections, and provide 1 349 schools and clinics with electricity by March 2004.

Mini-grid hybrid systems

In recent years, much attention has focused on developing a project-implementation plan of a mini-grid for the Hluleka Nature Reserve in the Eastern Cape. The main role-players are the NER, CSIR, Shell, the Department of Minerals and Energy, and the Eastern Cape Provincial Government. An integrated approach resulted in a design consisting of an energy system, a water-purification system and a telecommunications system. The energy system will make use of renewable energy, solar water-heaters and liquid petroleum gas.

Additionally, two villages adjacent to Hluleka Nature Reserve have been identified as sites for pilot mini-grid hybrid systems. Emphasis has been placed on the linking of these mini-grids to new economic activities in collaboration with the Agricultural Research Council. High-value crops have been planted in a number of demonstration plants in co-operation with entrepreneurial farmers. The plan is to evaluate the mini-grid systems with a view to exporting the value-added crops out of the region, thus generating income.

After starting with the identified sites next to Hluleka Nature Reserve, additional sites for mini-grid hybrid systems will be attended to in the Eastern Cape, KwaZulu-Natal and Limpopo.

An integrated framework for a national strategy to roll out hybrid mini-grids will be developed as part of the analysis of the pilot study.

Southern African Power Pool

The Minister of Minerals and Energy participated in the opening of the SAPP in Zimbabwe in November 2002. It is the first formal international power pool in Africa.

The objectives of the SAPP are, among others, to:

Minerals and energy

- co-ordinate and co-operate in the planning and operation of electricity power systems to minimise costs, while maintaining reliability, autonomy and self-sufficiency
- increase interconnectivity between SADC countries to increase the reliability of power supplies
- facilitate cross-border electricity trading
- fully recover costs of operations, and equitably share benefits, including reductions in generating capacity and fuel costs, and improved use of hydro-electric energy.

Member countries include Angola, Botswana, Lesotho, Malawi, Mozambique, Namibia, Swaziland, Tanzania, Zambia, Zimbabwe and the Democratic Republic of the Congo.

Biomass

Fuel wood, which comes mainly from natural woodlands, is the primary source of energy used by households in most rural areas for the purposes of cooking and heating. In some areas, this is already almost completely depleted and in others it is under heavy pressure.

The total annual sustainable supply of wood from natural woodlands in communal rural areas is estimated at about 12 Mt. However, probably no more than half of it is usable as fuel wood. In addition to these sources, residues from commercial forestry total about 4,2 Mt per year. Much of this, as well as wood from bush clearing on commercial farmland, is increasingly being used as fuel.

To be effective, planning for a sustainable fuel-wood supply requires decentralisation, understanding of local conditions and flexibility.

Supply-side interventions focus on satisfying a range of local needs and the realisation that community forestry does not involve only the planting of trees, but community participation, which is central to all activities.

Planning must ensure their integration into broader rural development, land use, natural resource management, and agricultural and energy planning. Interventions should build on the best indigenous practices identified. (See Chapter 23: *Water affairs and forestry*.)

Renewables

Renewable energy sources, other than biomass, have not yet been exploited to the full in South Africa. There are a number of initiatives to expand their use.

The *Draft White Paper on the Promotion of Renewable Energy and Clean Energy Development* was released in August 2002. The White Paper addresses four key strategic areas, namely:

- financial instruments to promote the implementation of sustainable renewable energy through the establishment of appropriate financial instruments
- legal instruments to develop, implement, maintain and continuously improve an effective legislative system to promote the implementation of renewable energy
- technology development to promote, enhance and develop technologies for the implementation of sustainable renewable energy
- building capacity and education to develop mechanisms to raise awareness of the benefits and opportunities renewable energy offers.

Technological feasibility studies will be conducted for possible implementation in the medium to longer term. These include:

- grid-connected wind farms
- wind farm/pumped storage as a means of addressing peak loads on the national electricity grid
- the local production and commercial dissemination of solar cookers which is a collaborative project between the German development agency GTZ and the Department of Minerals and Energy
- solar thermal power generation – which is a collaborative programme with Eskom, also involving the SolarPACES programme of the International Energy Agency

- small-scale hydropower – a scoping study aimed at developing an implementation strategy
- landfill gas exploitation
- rural water supply and sanitation.

The Minister of Minerals and Energy announced in September 2003 that the Department's Renewable Energy Strategy and Implementation Plan would be approved and implemented within a year with assistance from the World Bank and the Prototype Carbon Fund.

The aim is to consume an additional 10 000 GWh of renewable energy by 2013, which will be achieved through renewable energy power-generation and other sources such as biodiesel, solar-water heating, etc. The Energy SETA is expected to develop renewable energy technology (including biodiesel) and education and training unit standards with the help of the Department of Minerals and Energy.

The CEF is expected to install some 250 domestic solar water-heaters as part of the CEF/GEF (Global Environment Facility) Solar Water-Heating Programme, aimed at the commercialisation of domestic solar water-heating.

Solar

Most areas in South Africa average more than 2 500 hours of sunshine per year, and average daily solar-radiation levels range between 4,5 and 6,5 kWh/m^2 in one day.

The southern African region, and in fact the whole of Africa, is well endowed with sunshine all year round. The annual 24-hour global solar radiation average is about 220 W/m^2 for South Africa, compared to about 150 W/m^2 for parts of the USA, and about 100 W/m^2 for Europe and the United Kingdom, making the local resource one of the highest in the world. The solar resource is by far the most readily accessible in South Africa. It lends itself to a number of potential uses.

The country's solar-equipment industry is developing. Annual photovoltaic panel-assembly capacity totals 5 MW, and a number of companies in South Africa manufacture solar water-heaters.

The *White Paper on Energy Policy* identifies universal access to electricity as one of the primary goals of South Africa's energy policy.

To achieve this goal, it was decided to integrate non-grid technologies into the INEP as complementary supply-technologies to grid extension.

A pilot programme has been launched to establish a limited number of public-private sector institutions in conjunction with the relevant municipalities to provide electricity services on an integrated basis. The service-provider will own and maintain the systems, allowing longer-term financing to ameliorate monthly payments. It will provide the service against a fee, payable as a monthly tariff.

Once the underlying managerial and funding issues have been resolved, the process will be expanded to cover all the rural areas.

Solar power is increasingly being used for water-pumping through the rural water provision and sanitation programme of the Department of Water Affairs and Forestry.

Solar water-heating is used to a certain extent. Current capacity installed includes domestic 330 000 m^2 and swimming pools 327 000 m^2 (middle to high income), commerce and industry 45 000 m^2 and agriculture 4 000 m^2.

In 2002/03, some 5 300 solar home systems were installed by the Department of Minerals and Energy, representing a 3% increase from 2001/02.

Solar-passive building design

Houses and buildings in South Africa are seldom designed from an energy consumption or energy-efficiency perspective. The energy characteristics of low-cost housing are particularly bad, resulting in high levels of energy consumption for space heating in winter. The net result is dangerously high levels of indoor and outdoor air pollution in the townships, due mainly to coal burning.

Research has shown that low-cost housing could be rendered 'energy smart' through the utilisation of elementary 'solar passive building design' practice. This can result in fuel savings of as much as 65%. Such savings on energy expenditure will have a major beneficial impact on the household cash-flow situation. Energy-efficient homes may be constructed at the same direct cost (and lower life-cycle cost) as energy-wasteful houses. The challenge is to develop awareness and to ensure implementation of basic energy-efficiency principles.

National solar water-heating programme

Water-heating accounts for a third to half of the energy consumption in the average household. In South Africa, this derives mainly from electricity, it being the most common energy-carrier employed. Avoidance of this expenditure on household budgets could lead to significant improvements in the disposable incomes of the lower-income sector.

Furthermore, the equivalent of a large coal-fired power-station (2 000 MW+) is employed to provide hot water on tap to the domestic sector alone. Since the inception of the accelerated domestic electrification programme through grid extension, a major distortion of the national load curve has emerged, with the early evening load peak growing significantly.

Modelling indicates that the introduction of solar water-heating can ameliorate the situation substantially.

Switching from electrical to solar water-heating can, therefore, have significant economic and environmental benefits.

There are economic benefits for home-owners in reducing their energy bills. Expensive generation capacity to address load peaks will be obviated, and the introduction of new base-load capacity will be postponed. Benefits for the country include reducing greenhouse gas (GHG) emissions, and the release of scarce capital for other pressing needs.

Wind

Wind as an energy source is only practical in strong and steady wind areas. South Africa has fair wind potential, especially along the coastal areas. At present, however, wind is not used to generate electricity in this country. For the future it presents itself as a competitive energy source.

Wind power is primarily used for water-pumping, with about 300 000 windmills being used for watering livestock and supplying communities with water.

The first wind-energy farm in Africa was opened at Klipheuwel in the Western Cape on 21 February 2003.

The experimental wind farm, property of Eskom, will explore the use of wind energy for bulk electricity-generation.

Wind energy is environmentally friendly and helps reduce global warming and GHGs.

A further useful aspect of the experimental farm is the ability to update the wind atlas of South Africa that will be used for, among others, identifying other suitable areas for wind-power facilities.

The first turbine was commissioned in August 2002, the second in December 2002, and the third was commissioned at the launch in February 2003.

Hydro

South Africa has limited potential for large-scale hydroelectric power owing to its limited water resources. Although the country's total hydro potential is estimated at 3 500 MW, the economically feasible potential is much lower.

The current total installed large-scale hydropower generation-capacity (larger than 10 MW), is 2 061 MW. The installed capacity of plants smaller than 10 MW totals some 65 MW.

River flows in South Africa are not constant, varying between floods and very low flows. For this reason, the running of river schemes is generally not a feasible option. Relatively large and expensive storage dams are normally required, even for small hydro-stations.

South Africa has two conventional hydro-electric power-stations and two pumped storage schemes. Pumped storage-generation involves the construction of two adjacent reservoirs, or dams, one at a significantly higher elevation than the other. During periods of low demand on the Eskom grid, normally at night and over weekends, excess energy is used to pump water from the lower reservoir to the higher reservoir via underground tunnels. During peak demand periods, such as early mornings and evenings, the process is reversed. The stored water is allowed to flow back via the tunnels to the lower reservoir through hydraulic turbines, driving generators. Apart from a small quantity of water lost to evaporation, pumped storage schemes, like conventional hydro-stations, do not consume water. Once one of the reservoirs is filled, the same active volume is used over and over again.

Energy and the environment

Energy and the global environment
On a global scale, South Africa's contribution to GHG emissions is small. On a per-capita basis, however, it is well above global averages and that of other middle-income developing countries.

Furthermore, the economy is carbon-intensive, producing only US$259 per ton of carbon dioxide emitted, as compared with US$1 131 for South Korea, US$484 for Mexico and US$418 for Brazil.

Sources of greenhouse gas emissions
The energy sector is a major source of GHG because of the heavy reliance on coal for electricity generation, the Sasol oil-from-coal process, and a dearth of other indigenous energy resources, such as hydro and wind energy. In addition, 57% of the coal-mining methane emissions can be attributed to these two uses of coal.

Energy and the national environment
There is some contention regarding the polluting effects of the energy sector, particularly in the Mpumalanga Highveld – the location of most of Eskom's coal-powered stations and the largest Sasol plants.

As is the case internationally, there is ongoing debate about the desirability of nuclear energy.

Energy and the household environment
Coal is used by about 950 000 households countrywide. This brings with it indoor air-pollution problems, which have a serious health impact. It has been found that some people's exposure, especially to particulate matter, can exceed World Health Organisation (WHO) standards (180 mg.m^{-3}) by factors of six to seven during winter, and two to three in summer. A national programme has been established, with the objective of introducing low-smoke alternatives into the townships.

Fuel wood is used by three million rural households as their primary energy source. Studies have shown that fuel-wood users are exposed to even higher levels of particulate emissions than coal users. In one study, exposure levels were found to exceed the WHO lowest-observed-effect level by 26 times. The Department participates in a National Housing Interdepartmental Task Team and has contributed towards the development of norms and standards for solar-passive and thermally-efficient housing design.

The Department is investigating the introduction of improved woodstoves and other alternatives, such as solar cookers and biogas, in an attempt to address these pollution problems.

More widespread is the use of paraffin by low-income households, rural as well as urban. Paraffin has, however, associated

Minerals and energy

health and safety problems. The distribution of child-proof caps and the dissemination of information on the safe storage and use of paraffin are some of the measures being taken by the Department and other role-players to address the problem.

Institutions involved
Apart from the Department of Minerals and Energy, the Departments of Health, Environmental Affairs and Tourism, and Water Affairs and Forestry, are involved to greater or lesser degrees in the monitoring of and legislation on pollution.

Acknowledgements

Central Energy Fund
Chamber of Mines of South Africa
Department of Minerals and Energy
Eskom
Estimates of National Expenditure 2003, published by the National Treasury
National Electricity Regulator
Nuclear Energy Corporation of South Africa
PetroSA
South Africa.info
www.gov.za

Suggested reading

Allen, V.L. *History of Black Mineworkers in South Africa.* Keighley: Moor Press, 1992.
Anhaeusser, C.R. ed. *Century of Geological Endeavour in Southern Africa.* Johannesburg: Geological Society of South Africa, 1997.
Cruse, J. and James, W. eds. *Crossing Boundaries: Mine Migrancy in a Democratic South Africa.* Claremont, Cape Town: Institute for Democracy in South Africa. 1995.
Flynn, L. *Studded with Diamonds and Paved with Gold Mines.* Mining Companies and Human Rights in South Africa. London: Bloomsbury, 1992.
Gustafsson, H. and others. *South African Minerals: An Analysis of Western Dependence.* Uppsala: Scandinavian Institute of African Studies, 1990.
Kamfer, S. *Last Empire: De Beers, Diamonds and the World.* London: Hodder & Stoughton, 1994.
Katz, E. *The White Death: Silicosis on the Witwatersrand Gold Mines, 1880 – 1910.* Johannesburg: Witwatersrand University Press, 1994.
Lang, J. *Bullion Johannesburg: Men, Mines and the Challenge of Conflict.* Johannesburg: Jonathan Ball, 1986.
Lang, J. *Power Base: Coal-Mining in the Life of South Africa.* Johannesburg: Jonathan Ball, 1995.
Roberts, J.L. *A Photographic Guide to Minerals, Rocks and Fossils.* London, Cape Town: New Holland, 1998.
South Africa Minerals Yearbook, 1997. University of the Witwatersrand: Minerals and Energy Policy Centre, 1997.
Wilson, M.G.C. and Anhaeusser, C.R. eds. *The Mineral Resources of South Africa: Handbook.* Pretoria: Council for Geoscience, 1998.
Walton, J. and Pretorius, A. *Windpumps in South Africa: Wherever You Go, You See Them; Whenever You See Them, They Go.* Cape Town: Human & Rousseau, C, 1998.
Ward, S. *The Energy Book for Urban Development in South Africa.* Noordhoek: Sustainable Energy Africa, 2002.

Johann van Tonder / PictureNET Africa

chapter 17
Safety, security and defence

Internal security and crime prevention are primarily the responsibility of the South African Police Service (SAPS), while the South African National Defence Force (SANDF) is responsible for defending South Africa against external military threats.

Safety and security

In accordance with the South African Constitution, 1996 (Act 108 of 1996), the Minister of Safety and Security is responsible for policing in general and is required to account to the Cabinet and Parliament on all matters relating to policing. Important features of the Minister's responsibility are the determination of national policing policy and the provision of civilian oversight. The following three structures fall under the Minister of Safety and Security.
- Secretariat for Safety and Security
- Independent Complaints Directorate (ICD)
- SAPS.

Based on its legislative mandate, the Department of Safety and Security has identified the following key objectives for the medium term, namely to:

◀ The Department of Defence strives towards representivity at all levels in terms of gender and race. By March 2003, 15% of the Force was female.

- enhance the safety and security of South Africans
- ensure proper investigation of criminal cases and the provision of sound crime intelligence
- protect prominent people
- manage the SAPS, including its resources, development and operations more efficiently.

These objectives have been aligned with the goals of the Integrated Justice System and the Justice, Crime Prevention and Security (JCPS) Cabinet Cluster, which co-ordinates joint crime-prevention initiatives.

A review of strategic priorities in 2000 resulted in a medium-term plan, the Strategic Focus, 2000 – 2005.

The Department of Safety and Security has set four key strategic priorities for this period.

The first priority is to combat organised crime, focusing on crimes relating to drugs, trafficking in firearms, vehicle theft and hijacking, corrupt police officials, and organised commercial crime.

The second priority is concerned with the levels of serious and violent crime. In this regard, the Department has developed strategies to counter the proliferation of firearms, which fuels high levels of violent crime; improve safety and security in high-crime areas; combat specific crimes – such as taxi and gang violence, and faction fighting; and maintain security at major public events.

The third priority focuses on developing strategies to reduce the incidence of crimes against women and children, while also improving the investigation and prosecution of these crimes.

The fourth priority is to improve service delivery at police stations.

The Department has also identified human resource and budget management as key organisational priorities. These priorities were implemented by means of the National Crime-Combating Strategy (NCCS).

The NCCS involves the establishment of crime-combating task groups targeting serious and violent crime in designated high-crime zones. Operational interventions are intelligence-driven and based on the specific crime patterns of each zone.

The SAPS also collaborated with other departments in the JCPS Cluster to focus resources on addressing the incidence of crime and public disorder. The JCPS Cluster concentrates on programmes like the development and transformation of Cluster departments; crime prevention; and crime combating, which includes combating organised crime, crimes against women and children, corruption, improved intelligence, border control, regional and international co-operation, security, prosecution and the judiciary, detention (e.g. addressing the overcrowding of prisons), and the reduction of illegal firearms.

Secretariat for Safety and Security

In terms of the SAPS Act, 1995 (Act 68 of 1995), the functions of the Secretariat for Safety and Security are, among others, to:
- advise the Minister
- promote democratic accountability and transparency in the SAPS
- provide the Minister with legal services and advice on constitutional matters
- monitor the implementation of policy
- conduct research on any policing matter in accordance with the instructions of the Minister, and evaluate the performance of the SAPS.

During 2003, the Secretariat emphasised the importance of moral regeneration in efforts to combat crime, in the belief that a major problem affecting criminality is moral degeneration. The Moral Regeneration Movement (MRM) calls on all cardinal role-players – the family, church, school system, government departments, various constitutional commissions such as the National Youth Commission (NYC), the Commission on Gender Equality, and business – to come on board.

Independent Complaints Directorate

The ICD was established in terms of the Interim Constitution of South Africa, 1993 (Act 200 of 1993), to investigate complaints of alleged criminality and misconduct against members of the SAPS.

The primary role of the ICD is to ensure that complaints about offences and misconduct committed in the SAPS are investigated in an effective manner. It is governed by Chapter 10 of the SAPS Act, 1995.

The ICD has additional mandates in respect of monitoring the implementation of the Domestic Violence Act, 1998 (Act 116 of 1998), by the SAPS, and in respect of civilian oversight over municipal policing services.

The ICD is mandated to investigate all deaths in police custody or as a result of police action. An investigation is conducted to determine whether there are any indications of criminal conduct by the police. Where there are no indications of criminal conduct, the matter is left to the police themselves to investigate, while the ICD monitors/supervises the investigation. If information is subsequently received indicating that there was criminal conduct on the part of the police, the ICD will take control and conduct a full investigation.

Upon completion of an investigation, the ICD may make recommendations to the

Director of Public Prosecutions about the prosecution of any SAPS member(s) implicated. It may also make recommendations to the SAPS management with regard to the departmental prosecution of a police member.

The ICD is compelled by law to investigate complaints or reports of deaths in police custody, or as a result of police action.

The ICD reports to Parliament through the Minister of Safety and Security. However, it is operationally independent from the SAPS.

The number of complaints handled by the ICD in 2002/03 amounted to 4 443, representing an increase of 31,9% compared with 2001/02.

The number of deaths in custody or as a result of police action during 2002/03 was 528, representing a decrease of 9,7% compared with 2001/02 when 585 deaths were recorded.

Persistent interventions by the ICD and SAPS management have led to the decrease in the number of deaths in custody or as a result of police action. The decrease also confirms a growing human-rights ethic within the SAPS.

South African Police Service

Strategic overview and key objectives

The key aims and programmes of the SAPS are based on the objectives provided for in Section 205 of the Constitution. The SAPS has a responsibility to:
- prevent, combat and investigate crime
- maintain public order
- protect and secure South Africans and their property
- uphold and enforce the law.

The vision of the SAPS is to create a safe and secure environment for all South Africans.

The values held by the SAPS are to:
- protect everyone's rights and be impartial, respectful, open and accountable to the community
- use its powers in a responsible way
- provide a responsible, effective and high-quality service with honesty and integrity
- evaluate its service continuously and make every effort to improve it
- use its resources in the best way possible
- develop the skills of all its members through equal opportunities
- co-operate with the community, all levels of government and other role-players.

The SAPS came into being in 1994 after the amalgamation of the 11 independent policing agencies that existed before the nation's transition to democracy.

The Service-Delivery Improvement Programme (SDIP) of the SAPS seeks to improve service delivery to communities at local level in line with the principles of *batho pele* (meaning putting people first), and equipping police-station managers with the necessary practical tools. The objectives of the SDIP are to inculcate a culture of participative management in the organisation and to encourage the community's involvement in safety issues.

SAPS activities are administered by means of five programmes:

Administration
Administration provides for the formulation of policy and the management of the SAPS, and includes provision for capital works and the medical benefits of SAPS employees.

Crime Prevention
Crime Prevention provides for the functions of police stations nationally, and for specific functional services such as the Dog, Equestrian, Radio Control and Diving Units.

Operational Response Services
Operational Response Services provides for the policing of South Africa's national borders, and for specialised policing services associated with maintaining public order, crowd management and the high-risk functions performed by the Special Task Force.

Detective Service and Crime Intelligence

Detective Service and Crime Intelligence provide the infrastructure required for investigative and intelligence work and the examination of forensic evidence. They provide training to investigators and manage the Criminal Record Centre (CRC).

Protection and Security Services Division

Protection Services provides for the protection of foreign and local dignitaries.

Given the integrated nature of policing, identified policing priorities are not contained individually or collectively in any single programme. Rather, they underpin the operational activities undertaken at all levels and across all divisions of the SAPS within the context of the entire financial programme structure.

Divisions

National Evaluation Services

This division is responsible for supporting management in the assessment of service-delivery standards and performance related to service delivery.

Protection Services

The SAPS fulfils its responsibility to protect both local and foreign prominent persons, using resources allocated to Protection Services. The Presidential Protection Unit provides protection to the President, Deputy President and former Presidents and their spouses.

Financial and Administration Services

This division is responsible for rendering a financial and administrative support function to the management of the SAPS.

Logistics

This division is responsible for fleet and facility management and all other logistical support.

Career Management

The function of this division is to render a people-centred human resource service to all personnel and to ensure their optimal utilisation.

Legal Services

Legal Services renders a legal support function to management. The division is responsible for national standards and policy relating to crime operations, property and assets, legislation, contracts and agreements, policy standards and litigation.

Personnel Services

Personnel Services is responsible for managing personnel-related matters in support of the operational priorities of the SAPS.

By April 2003, the SAPS had a staff complement of 132 121 employees. In compliance with the human resource plan, the personnel strength at station level was expected to increase by approximately 11 300 employees to 67% of the total staff complement during 2003/04.

The ratios for race and gender were 74% blacks and 26% whites and 74% males and 26% females.

The SAPS planned to enlist 9 550 entry-level constables and 4 010 civilians during the 2003/04 financial year.

Training

The division presents functional training that consists of basic training (entry-level) and training in protection services, dog handling, public order, border policing, functional skills, human rights and community policing. Recruits undergo a 12-week basic training course, followed by a four-week tactical firearms-training course and a three-week field-training mentorship course.

Support training consists of financial, logistical, career, management, adult basic education and basic diversity training.

Crime Prevention

Crime Prevention is regarded as a line-function division of the SAPS, specifically responsible for the prevention of crime, by addressing the root causes of crime, e.g. socio-economic factors, and by uplifting the community through rural-development and urban-renewal projects.

Crime Prevention aims to reduce opportunities to commit crime by optimising visible policing. Furthermore, the division is responsible for developing, maintaining and monitoring policy standards and directives regarding crime prevention and uniformed services in general. Police Emergency Services and Social Crime Prevention resort under this division.

Police Emergency Services

Police Emergency Services focuses on enhancing the skills and knowledge of all personnel performing rapid-response services (10111 Centres and Flying Squad), hostage negotiators, police divers and members of the Dog and Equestrian Units.

Rapid Response Services

Advanced technological equipment has been installed at various 10111 Centres to enhance service delivery to the community. A capacity-building programme has been developed and implemented to recruit, select and train rapid-response personnel.

Hostage Negotiation

Hostage negotiators respond to hostage and suicide incidents. The SAPS presented various courses in hostage and suicide negotiation during 2002, equipping members with skills to deal with hostage- and suicide-related incidents. An introduction to the management of hostage incidents was addressed in the Southern African Regional Police Chiefs Co-operation Organisation's (SARPCCO) Middle Management Programme.

Inland Water Policing

Police divers participated in a number of operations, most of which entail the recovery of drowned people. The recovery of evidence disposed of in water is an important activity of police divers.

Police divers and vessel handlers also assist in crime prevention and water-safety activities. Members from the various provinces have been trained as police divers, diver supervisors and vessel handlers in swift water-rescue techniques.

Dog and Equestrian Units

The SAPS is not only responsible for the training of dogs and dog handlers to perform specialised policing functions, but also breeds these specialised dogs and provides veterinarian services to the dogs and horses. Continuous training of dogs, horses, dog handlers and horse riders is done.

Social Crime Prevention

This component manages projects/programmes that address situational, community-based and social factors that contribute or precipitate crime, by integrating services and knowledge.

Programmes of the Social Crime Prevention component aim to:
- improve victim support and assistance services, particularly for victims of domestic violence and rape
- build capacity for local crime-prevention-strategy development, particularly within the framework of rural development and urban renewal
- build skills for resilience and resistance to crime among young people
- develop and implement strategies to deal with factors contributing to crime.

Operational Response Services

Operational Response Services is responsible for maintaining public order, conducting high-risk operations, combating rural and urban terror, executing search-and-rescue flights, stabilising volatile situations and preventing cross-border crime.

Public Order Policing Units include the Special Task Force, Intervention Units, Border Police and the Air Wing.

The effective policing of the country's borders, and the prevention and detection of transnational crime, are priorities. Border policing covers 53 land-border posts, 10 air-border posts and nine sea-border posts.

Successes include:
- Excellent and structured co-operation with related role-players such as the Department of Home Affairs and the Customs Offices of the South African Revenue Service.
- Support from Business Against Crime (BAC).
- The development of a well-defined strategy of border-line control for SAPS entry over a six-year period, as the SANDF withdraws over the same period.
- The upgrading of the SAPS capacity at land ports of entry to detect crime, i.e. stolen vehicles. This includes new technology and project-driven training.
- The envisaged upgrading of service delivery at identified air and seaports of entry on a project-driven basis. This includes technology, procedures, infrastructure and training.

The Operational Co-ordination Component also falls under this division. It has the following subcomponents:
- Operational Planning and Monitoring ensures the implementation of all national joint operations, be they interdepartmental or the various branches of the SAPS working together in joint operations. The component and its operational co-ordinators have no (vertical) line functions in terms of policing, such as crime prevention, but do have a lateral or horizontal responsibility across all line functions to ensure effective co-ordinated execution of operations as directed by the National Crime Combating Forum.
- Operational Advisory Support renders an advisory support service (secretarial service) to a host of meetings both at interdepartmental and departmental levels.
- Operational Research aims to ensure the development of operational doctrines and concepts, especially with regard to joint operations.

This subsection is required to do operational research to enable the development of critical areas identified and new areas that will be identified continuously.

This is carried out in co-operation with any other research capacity in the SAPS and the SANDF, but also involves external expertise. It also aims to improve the understanding of the problems confronting the SAPS and the security forces in general, to enable more effective planning and operations.

Detective Service

The Detective Service is responsible for maintaining an effective crime-investigation service. The division's main functions involve investigations into serious, violent, commercial and organised crime.

The Detective Service has the following units and subprogrammes:
- General Investigations.
- Organised Crime.
- Commercial Crime.
- CRC.
- Forensic Science Laboratory.
- Laboratory Information Management System.
- Family Violence, Child Protection and Sexual Offences Units (FCS). By mid-2003, there were 32 Child Protection Units and 13 Family Violence and Sexual Offence Units in the main centres and 156 other towns across the country. The 839 members of the FCS received 40 604 cases (7 894 enquiries and 32 710 case dockets) for investigation in 2002.
- National Bureau for Missing Persons. As a community-orientated service, its main purpose is to render support to investigating officers. This entails the running of a database where all the particulars of a missing

Safety, security and defence

person such as tattoos, scars, hair and eye colour, etc. are stored. This database is situated on a mainframe and is accessible to every police official in the country.

The Bureau has state-of-the-art computer equipment, which enables it to, for example, obtain a photo of a missing child suspected of being kidnapped and broadcast it on national television within a short period of time.

In June 2001, the SAPS became the first police service in Africa to launch a missing children website (za.missingkids.com). It became the 11th country in the world to harness computer technology in the search for missing children.

Crime Intelligence

Illicit drugs play a major part in the commission of violent crime. An interdepartmental task team co-ordinated the implementation of a multidimensional anti-drug strategy. This strategy forms part of the Drug Master Plan which is being co-ordinated by the Central Drug Authority (CDA).

Under the auspices of the CDA, the United Nations (UN) Office on Drugs and Crime, the Secretariat for Safety and Security, other relevant government departments and the NYC piloted an anti-drug campaign in Mamelodi, east of Pretoria, in 2002. On 26 June 2003, the same campaign was launched in Cape Town.

The SAPS has focused its attention on the 'supply' part of the 'demand and supply' dimensions of the drug phenomenon. The 'demand' dimension is also being addressed by the MRM.

The South African Police Service deployed a team of experts in Nairobi, Kenya to assist Kenyan police and private security officials during an International Cricket Council World Cup Cricket match in February 2003.

The 43-member team comprised the Special Task Force, a bomb disposal unit, detectives and the Intervention Unit, as well as experts in crowd control. Apart from cross-border operations in the past, this was the first large-scale international operation of its kind.

Examples of successes achieved by the SAPS include the launch of disruptive operations in targeted drug hot spots throughout South Africa. Clandestine laboratories are continuously being identified and neutralised. The focus has moved to manufacturers, suppliers and pushers as opposed to addicts and users.

During 2002, about 6 758 individuals involved in drug-related offences were arrested, and illicit substances to the value of R330 million seized.

By September 2003, police had made major inroads in the fight against drug peddling by confiscating drugs worth more than R500 million.

Police projects

Information Systems Management (ISM)

The ISM of the SAPS conducts various projects to support and enhance the administration, analysis and management of crime and criminal information in support of crime investigation and prevention. The following critical projects relating to the development and/or the implementation of application-software systems, have been undertaken:
- a Geographic Information System at priority stations
- the Laboratory Information Management Systems at the Forensic Science Laboratory
- the Automated Fingerprint Information System (AFIS) at the CRC
- the Analysts Notebook application at the Crime Intelligence and Organised Crime Units
- the Loss Management System for Financial Services
- replacement of equipment for the production of SAPS identity cards
- a workshop system at SAPS garages.

Automated Fingerprint Information System

The AFIS became operational in 35 decentralised Local Criminal Record Centres in September 2002.

The automation of the process has contributed towards an increase in accuracy, productivity and service delivery. Faster response times lead to more previous-conviction reports being produced. For a period of 35 days in 2001, it was only possible to produce 163 369 previous-conviction reports. However, since the introduction of the AFIS, it has become possible to produce 293 386 previous-conviction reports for the same period.

The CRC has also experienced an increase in the identification of scene-of-crime fingerprints. A total of 3 481 more identifications of scene-of-crime fingerprints were made in 2002 than in 2001.

One of the greatest technological advances that the SAPS intends recording in its crime-combating strategy relates to the fact that the expanded AFIS will include palm-print identification. Concomitant with this will be a new programme of live-scanning facilities that will enable the electronic scanning of fingerprints. A pilot project utilising hand-held scanners has been completed.

Community involvement

The implementation of the Crime Prevention Development Programme continued during 2002/03. The Programme facilitates the development and implementation of community-based crime-prevention strategies. The Programme has made a significant contribution towards intersectoral co-operation, and serves as a tool for local service-providers such as local government to integrate community-based crime-prevention strategies in their core business. Communities have been able to participate through applying indigenous knowledge during the conceptual phase of projects.

The Programme was successfully completed in the urban-renewal nodes of KwaMashu and Inanda in KwaZulu-Natal.

It is being extended to the following areas:
- Limpopo (Thohoyandou and Bolobedu)
- KwaZulu-Natal (KwaDukuza, Mtubatuba and Umhlathuze)
- Eastern Cape (Motherwell and Mdantsane)
- Mpumalanga (Driefontein).

The projects are aimed at enhancing the existing crime-prevention partnerships between the SAPS, municipalities, private security firms, business and local communities.

The SAPS has developed a strong focus on partnership policing. This involves mobilising the community to become involved in various projects to counteract crime. Community Policing Forums are featuring more prominently and playing a major role in safeguarding the country. The year 2002 was proclaimed the Year of the Volunteer and some 70 000 members of the community volunteered their services at police stations across the country.

Demonstration projects initiated during 2002, aimed at reducing social-fabric crimes, were continued in the areas of Driefontein (Mpumalanga) and Bolobedu (Limpopo). Multidisciplinary committees to manage the project were established, research to establish the local causes of crime in the relevant areas undertaken, and the respective project plans approved by the responsible structures. These multisectoral committees, through strong partnerships with all stakeholders, led to intervention strategies that focus on the key causes of crime in the areas. A similar project in Nongoma (KwaZulu-Natal) is in its inception phase.

Sector policing

Sector policing provides an ideal opportunity for community involvement in local safety and security needs, in the form of participation in the Sector Crime Forums and police-community projects at sector level. Policing areas become smaller, manageable geographic areas under the supervision of a sector commander.

Sector policing will be phased in at some 1 139 police stations in South Africa. According to the SAPS Strategic Plan, it will be implemented at 145 priority police stations by the end of the 2004/05 financial year.

Safety, security and defence

Intervention training workshops for sector commanders from the 14 Presidential and 50 priority stations commenced during 2002/03 and by mid-2003, some 300 members had been introduced to the concept. Further training for another 300 sector commanders/deputies, including reservists, was planned for 2003/04. By August 2003, a formal training curriculum for sector policing was being developed and the National Instruction on Sector Policing was nearing completion.

Co-operation between the sector commanders and their sector communities through consultants and joint projects has enhanced healthy police-community relations. The involvement of reservists and community volunteers in sector policing, as well as the platform created through the Sector Crime Forums, has strengthened this partnership.

The policy on the South African Reserve Police Service has opened more doors for community involvement by specifically creating a category for community members wanting to be involved in sector policing.

Community Safety Centres

The SAPS is dedicated to the upliftment of previously disadvantaged communities. The building of Community Safety Centres has consequently been introduced as an enabling mechanism. The focus of the Centres is on delivering basic and easily accessible services to communities, especially in deep rural and informal settlement areas.

In the execution of their duties, many South African Police Service (SAPS) members distinguish themselves by performing deeds of bravery in dangerous circumstances, and in so doing save the lives of others while endangering their own.

Between January 2002 and April 2003, 18 police members were honoured for their acts of outstanding and exceptional bravery and awarded the SAPS Cross for Bravery in the different categories (Cross for Bravery [Gold] – one recipient, Cross for Bravery [Silver] – six and Cross for Bravery [Bronze] – 11.).

The innovative concept of Community Safety Centres brings all relevant departments under one roof and involves the SAPS, the Departments of Justice and Constitutional Development, Correctional Services, Health, and Social Development. Community Safety Centres have been completed and are fully operational in Thembalethu in the Western Cape, Ntsimbini in KwaZulu-Natal, Leboeng in Limpopo, and Khutsong in Gauteng. By mid-2003, Community Safety Centres were under construction in Galeshewe in the Northern Cape, Thabong in the Free State and Tshidilamlomo in the North West.

The Centres are a result of the National Crime Prevention Strategy (NCPS) and the Reconstruction and Development Programme. The idea behind the Centres is the creation of a safe and stable environment which is conducive to socio-economic development.

The Minister of Public Works, Ms Stella Sigcau, and the Minister of Safety and Security, Mr Charles Nqakula, handed over a Community Safety Centre to the community of Centane in the Eastern Cape in July 2003.

The Centane Community Safety Centre boasts a police-services point, logistics and finance office, crime-investigation services, two Magistrate's Courts, Correctional Services parole officers and cells, a Victim Support Centre, and other auxiliary services such as a clinic with a delivery room, a four-bed ward, a one-bed ward, five consulting rooms, a day-care centre for children and housing for staff.

Victim-Empowerment Programme (VEP)

Government recognises the importance of addressing the needs of victims of crime and violence in South Africa. To meet these needs, a national VEP was launched. It aims to make the country's criminal justice system more understandable and accessible to victims.

The VEP further aims to address the negative aspects of crime and violence through the provision of counselling and other support services. The SAPS, as the first and often the only criminal justice agency to come into contact with victims, has a vital role to play in the empowerment of victims.

The *White Paper on Safety and Security: 1999 - 2004* also emphasises the need for improved services to victims. The Department of Safety and Security views victimisation as a violation of human rights.

It subscribes to the UN Declaration of Basic Principles of Justice for Victims of Crime and Abuse of Power, which clearly states that victims have the right to be treated with respect and dignity; the right to offer and receive information; the right to legal advice; and the right to protection, compensation or restitution.

Victim empowerment has also been included as a national priority in the annual priorities and objectives of the SAPS and forms an integral part of community policing.

Victim-friendly facilities

Early in the 2002/03 financial year, an audit was conducted to determine provincial needs for victim-friendly facilities. A three-year implementation plan was then developed for the incremental provision of such facilities, prioritising those stations responsible for 50% of reported incidence of gender-based violence such as rape and domestic violence.

These facilities are of particular benefit to victims, as they enable statements of victims to be taken in a private and victim-friendly environment. By mid-2003, victim-friendly facilities had been established at 130 stations throughout the country.

In 2002, preventative activities were undertaken at the 20 stations with the highest reported incidence of rape and domestic violence.

These include encouraging members of the public to report domestic violence and rape cases.

Rural Safety Committee and banking-sector agreements

The concern over the incidence of attacks on farms has led to the establishment of a Rural Safety Committee.

The banking sector is working with the SAPS to curb bank robberies and cash-in-transit heists. The SAPS reached an agreement with the banking sector to develop a formal mechanism for combating banking-related crimes and cash-in-transit robberies.

Telephone Interpreting Service for South Africa (TISSA)

The SAPS is an important partner in the project that will allow a full-scale telephone interpreting service to be established in the country. TISSA is a government-approved project aimed at giving effect to the linguistic human rights enshrined in the Constitution.

TISSA makes it possible for all South Africans to have immediate access to information and government services in an official language of their choice. TISSA has been implemented at many police stations around the country. By making use of this interpreting service, information-gathering by the SAPS will become increasingly accurate, and collaboration between the SAPS and the community in fighting crime will be enhanced.

Youth programmes

To acquaint children with the SAPS, it launched, among others, the Captain Crime Stop Project. The friendly Captain Crime Stop pays regular visits to schools countrywide. The aim of the Project is to educate children about crimes and

---

The Movement Control System, which was introduced in 1998, is now fully computerised and installed at all South Africa's border posts and airports.

The computerised System enhances policing to be more effective in tracing unwanted persons, goods and stolen vehicles, and monitors the movements of suspect persons or vehicles at border posts and other ports of entry. The principal shareholder of the System is the Department of Home Affairs.

Safety, security and defence

to provide them with tips for personal safety, while showing them that the SAPS is an organisation that serves and protects the community.

A national Crime Stop number (08600 10111) and the national emergency number (10111) are available to report information on criminals and their activities.

Children and youths are affected by crime both as perpetrators and as victims. Reported criminal victimisation of children by other children is also of concern. Recognising the importance of early intervention in changing criminal behaviour, the SAPS supports the Department of Education's Safe Schools Programme.

The objectives of the partnership include:
- reducing firearm violence in schools
- assisting young people to become resilient to crime and violence through SAPS presentations.

The Youth Violence-Prevention Programme has joined hands with various national departments and bodies such as the NYC and the National Consultative Forum to develop and implement a holistic and integrated Youth Crime-Prevention Programme.

Firearm-free zones at schools
By the end of December 2002, applications had been received from 21 schools to be declared as firearm-free zones. These applications were submitted to Legal Services for promulgation in the *Government Gazette*.

Operation *Sethunya*
On 1 April 2003, the SAPS launched Operation *Sethunya*. Its main focus is to combat the illegal possession, trafficking and use of firearms by individuals in organised crime.

In the first two months of the Operation, the SAPS confiscated 7 975 firearms and 1,5 million rounds of ammunition, while some 1 026 persons were arrested countrywide for the illegal possession of firearms and ammunition. During 2002/03, some 38 426 State-owned firearms and 20 191 confiscated firearms were destroyed.

International obligations and involvement in Africa
The Department of Safety and Security has an obligation to ensure peace and stability in South Africa, on the continent and internationally. These obligations are achieved through international conventions and forging partnerships with security establishments.

The skills of the SAPS in certain specialised fields have already been recognised by various countries in the world, e.g. by being asked to provide an advanced training course in high-risk operations to police members from the United Arab Emirates and Oman.

The Department also continues to forge and strengthen partnerships with police institutions on the African continent in order to advance the objectives of the New Partnership for Africa's Development (NEPAD) and the African Union (AU). To this end, the Department is actively involved in peace initiatives in the Democratic Republic of the Congo (DRC) and Burundi, and has received requests for training support from various African countries, including Mozambique, Kenya and Nigeria.

Joint operations between the police services in southern Africa, co-ordinated by SARPCCO, have had a major impact on cross-border crime. These efforts will be enhanced by the completion of an integrated organised crime-threat analysis among the SARPCCO police services, and the implementation of joint projects and operations based on the analysis.

According to a report released in November 2003, South Africa is the world leader in solving serial murders. In other countries it takes an average of two years to arrest a serial killer. In South Africa, there have been numerous cases where a killer was arrested within six weeks of the crime. Since 1936, police have chased 60 serial murderers. They were unsuccessful in only 16 cases. Everyone who was arrested was convicted.

International relations

The SAPS has co-operation agreements with France, Argentina, Chile, Brazil, the Russian Federation, Hungary, Egypt, China, Nigeria, Mozambique, Portugal, Swaziland and the People's Republic of China.

Negotiations are ongoing to include more countries on its list of international partners against organised crime.

SARPCCO is a police co-operation agreement involving 12 southern African countries, which is an important instrument in the fight against organised crime.

South Africa is among 179 countries whose police structures are affiliated with Interpol. It has 12 liaison officers based at South African Missions abroad, to interact on a continuous basis with its counterparts in the detection of international crime. International Liaison serves as a 24-hour nodal point in respect of all crimes committed against and by the diplomatic corps, requests for protection duties throughout the country, visits by foreign delegates to the SAPS and general enquiries in by foreign Missions and diplomatic-accredited international organisations.

The SAPS regularly participates in UN activities such as:
- The UN Crime Prevention and Criminal Justice Programme. The National Commissioner of the SAPS, Mr Jackie Selebi, is the Government rapporteur to the UN Commission on Crime Prevention and Criminal Justice.
- The negotiations of the UN Single Convention Against Terrorism.
- The implementation of UN Security Council Resolution 1373, in particular the work of the Counter Terrorist Committee in New York.

South Africa has signed and ratified the Southern African Development Community (SADC) Protocol on Drug Trafficking. It has also signed the SADC Protocol on the Control of Firearms, Light Weapons and Other Related Materials.

The SAPS has agreements with six international donor countries to the value of approximately R500 million. The aims of the projects range from operational initiatives to human resource capacity-building (training, skills development, etc.), technical assistance and physical resources.

Defence

The Constitution, the Defence Act, 2002 (Act 42 of 2002), the *White Paper on Defence and the Defence Review* mandate the Department of Defence. These laws and policies direct and guide the functions of the Department of Defence and the SANDF.

The mission of the Department of Defence is to defend and protect South Africa, its territorial integrity and its people in accordance with the Constitution and the principles of international law regulating the use of force.

To achieve its mission, it is essential that the Department of Defence is managed strategically. As part of this process, certain factors have been identified that are fundamental to achieving success. These are known as the mission success factors of the Department and involve the following:
- national consensus on defence
- excellent strategic direction
- excellent resource management
- effective combat and support forces
- professionalism in the conduct of operations
- successful implementation of the transformation process.

On 22 September 2003, the Minister of Safety and Security, Mr Charles Nqakula, tabled the South African Police Service's Annual Report and Crime Statistics for the 2002/03 financial year.
The statistics indicated, among others, that:
- murder decreased by 1,3% in 2002/03, with a marked decrease of 29,5% since 1994/95
- rape decreased by 5,7%
- hijacking of motor vehicles decreased by 20,2%
- bank-related robberies, including cash-in-transit robberies, decreased by 15,4%
- car-theft decreased by almost 6%
- aggravated robberies, including street, business and house robberies, increased by 11,6%.

Ongoing transformation has drastically changed the functions of the Department from offensive to defensive. It has gradually withdrawn from its involvement in support of the police and other protection agencies.

As a key player in regional peace efforts, the Department, under the auspices of NEPAD, plays an important part, participating in a variety of initiatives aimed at securing peace and stability on the continent.

The SANDF's budget was increased by more than R1 billion to R20,05 billion in the 2003/04 financial year. The Medium Term Expenditure Framework estimate puts the allocation for 2005/06 at R22,5 million.

In 2003/04, the South African Army was allocated R3,1 billlion, the South African Air Force (SAAF) R2,1 billion, the South African Military Health Service (SAMHS) R1,2 billion, and the South African Navy R1,05 billion. Defence Intelligence received R153 million.

Defence Secretariat

In terms of the Defence Act, 2002, the Defence Secretariat is responsible for the following:
- supporting the Secretary for Defence in his/her capacity as the head of the Department, the accounting officer for the Department and the principal departmental advisor to the Minister of Defence
- performing any functions entrusted by the Minister to the Secretary for Defence, in particular those necessary or expedient to enhance civil control by
  - Parliament over the Department of Defence
  - Parliamentary committees overseeing the Department of Defence
  - the Minister of Defence over the Department of Defence
- providing the SANDF with comprehensive instructions regarding the exercise of powers
- monitoring compliance with policies and directions issued by the Minister of Defence to the SANDF, and reporting thereon to the Minister
- ensuring discipline of, administrative control over, and management of employees, including effective utilisation and training
- instituting departmental investigations as may be provided for by law.

Legislation

Defence Bill
The Bill aims to regulate the defence function. Discussions on this Bill by the Portfolio Committee on Defence continued in 2002/03.

National Conventional Arms Control Committee (NCACC) Bill
This Bill is intended to establish the NCACC as a legal body. The Committee controls the services and brokering of conventional arms.

Armaments Corporation of South Africa (Armscor) Bill
This Bill will replace the Armaments Development and Production Act, 1968 (Act 57 of 1968). It will be aligned with current national and defence policy, which pronounces the role, function, accountability, management and operations of Armscor.

Military Discipline Bill
The Bill consolidates various separate legislative instruments such as the Military Discipline Supplementary Measures Act, 1999 (Act 16 of 1999), Chapter XI, and the First Schedule of the Defence Act, 1957 (Act 44 of 1957). The Bill is intended to obviate future constitutional challenges by eliminating those provisions of current legislation not in line with the Constitution.

Prohibition on Anti-Personnel Mines Bill
The Bill aims to give effect to the International Mines Ban Treaty to which South Africa is a party. It is intended to provide for appropriate legal and administrative measures to suppress any activity that may be in contravention of provisions of the Treaty. The Bill also prescribes

penal sanctions against those who contravene the Treaty or engage in prohibited activities.

In 1996, South Africa prohibited the export of all types of landmines and, in 1997, it prohibited the use, development, production and stockpiling of anti-personnel landmines. By 1998, some 312 000 anti-personnel landmines held by the Department of Defence had been destroyed.

South Africa plays a leading role in demining, training de-miners and improving the cost-efficiency of operations.

Functions of the South African National Defence Force

The Constitution provides for the SANDF to be deployed for service in:
- the defence of the country and its people, for the protection of its sovereignty and territorial integrity
- compliance with the international obligations of the country to international bodies and other states
- the preservation of life, health or property
- the provision or maintenance of essential services
- the upholding of law and order in the country in co-operation with the SAPS, under circumstances set out in legislation, where the SAPS is unable to maintain law and order on its own
- the support of any State department for the purpose of socio-economic upliftment.

Tasks of the South African National Defence Force

The SANDF's military strategic objectives are to:
- defend against aggression
- promote security
- support the people of South Africa.

At operational level, forces have to be structured and prepared to deal with specific tasks. Each of these places demands on the capabilities of the Department of Defence. The tasks of the SANDF are as follows:
- defending against aggression:
  - providing core defence capabilities for the defence of South Africa against external military threats, and the execution of military operations in defence of South Africa, its interests and its citizens when so ordered by the President in his/her capacity as Commander-in-Chief of the SANDF
- promoting security:
  - promoting regional security through defence co-operation within the SADC
  - promoting international security through military co-operation in support of South Africa's foreign policy
  - providing a military capability for participation in regional and international peace-support operations
- supporting the people of South Africa:
  - providing defence capabilities against internal threats to the constitutional order, and the execution of such operations in a state of emergency when so ordered by the President

---

The Government formed a partnership with Business Against Crime (BAC) in 1996.

The partnership covers a broad spectrum and includes the Integrated Justice System, the Criminal Justice Strengthening Programme, the Service-Delivery Improvement Programme of the South African Police Service (SAPS), the installation of surveillance systems, dealing with organised crime, co-operation in respect of white-collar crime and corruption, and the *Tisa Thuto* Project which teaches school learners non-violent methods of conflict resolution and positive morality, including life skills and personal values.

The BAC has supported government as consultant and facilitator by, among other things, influencing strategy, policing and priorities; supporting a mutually agreed-upon vision, transferring business skills; developing working solutions that deliver results; and developing public-private partnerships.

Successes of the partnership include the installation of surveillance systems in urban areas, which has resulted in an 80% decrease in street crime in these areas, while also improving the SAPS' response time to one minute. Video footage obtained from these surveillance systems is admissible evidence in a court of law.

Safety, security and defence

- providing and applying forces for land, air and maritime border protection against non-military threats
- providing capacity to maintain law and order in co-operation with the SAPS on an ongoing basis, which will remain necessary until the SAPS is able to fulfil the task without assistance from the military other than in exceptional circumstances
- providing surveillance and enforcement support to relevant authorities for the protection of marine resources, control of marine pollution, and maritime law and enforcement
- providing air-traffic control services in support of civil aviation authorities
- providing military support for the preservation of life, health and property in emergencies where the scale of the emergency temporarily exceeds the capacity of the relevant civil authority
- providing emergency capabilities for the maintenance of essential services which have been disrupted temporarily and where the capacity of the relevant civil authority is exceeded
- providing medical and health services in support of relevant authorities
- providing search-and-rescue support for relevant authorities in accordance with domestic agreements and South Africa's international obligations
- providing an air transport service for Very Important Persons (VIPs) and other officials in accordance with approved policy
- providing support for other State departments for missions to the Antarctic and southern oceans
- providing hydrographic services to South African mariners in compliance with the international obligations of the country
- providing an infrastructure for the management of the Service Corps
- providing a communication-security service for other State departments.

Corporate Strategy

The Department of Defence's Corporate Strategy is based on the National Security Strategy.

The Corporate Strategy consists of the Business Strategy and the Military Strategy. The Business Strategy informs the way in which the Department conducts its business as a State department, while the Military Strategy indicates the way in which the SANDF prepares for and executes its missions. The Military Strategy has a number of strategies emanating from it, namely the Force Employment Strategy, Provide Force Strategy and its supporting strategies.

Business Strategy

The Business Strategy of the Department consists of those strategies, plans and measures taken to ensure:
- that the military forces are fully supported, equipped, maintained and administered while in barracks and when deployed on missions of any nature
- alignment with the policies and priorities of government in respect of governance and administration
- the effective, economic and efficient utilisation of resources to improve accountability
- the continuous improvement of the quality of departmental service delivery, personnel, equipment and facilities.

The Business Strategy enables the execution of the Military Strategy and its substrategies, the Force Employment and Force Preparation strategies.

Military Strategy

The Military Strategy of South Africa is derived from the Constitution, the *Defence Review*, *White Paper on Defence* and the National Security Strategy.

The National Security Strategy is derived from implied national interests, the Department of Foreign Affairs and JCPS Cluster objectives.

Missions

The SANDF uses a mission-based approach to achieve the military strategic objectives of the Department of Defence. This approach uses wartime and peacetime missions to direct the peacetime strategy for force preparation, and to guide joint and combined force preparation and force employment for incidences of conflict. The prioritised missions envisaged for the next 10 years include:
- borderline control
- co-operation with the SAPS
- defence against a biological and/or chemical onslaught
- defence against an information onslaught
- disaster relief and humanitarian assistance
- international or regional humanitarian intervention
- international or regional observers
- international, regional or subregional peace-building and peace-making
- international or regional peace enforcement
- international or regional search-and-rescue
- maintenance of the health status of members of the SANDF
- maritime support
- pre-emptive operations
- Presidential healthcare
- Presidential tasks
- protection of foreign assets
- repelling of conventional and non-conventional onslaught
- show-of-force
- special operations
- subregional disaster-relief and humanitarian assistance
- support to military diplomacy
- support to government departments
- VIP transport.

Military strategic concepts

The military strategic concepts describe the procedures to be followed to meet the military strategic objectives:
- Provision of mission-essential training: The SANDF is to educate, train and develop its soldiers in the essential skills required to execute the tasks necessary to accomplish its missions. It focuses on force training/preparation and is aligned with the allocated budget.
- Capability of establishing a mission-trained force: The SANDF is to have the capability to establish a mission-trained force that can engage in specific missions. The force must be relatively small, but must ultimately be prepared according to the missions and capabilities required.
- Selective engagement where possible: The SANDF will execute all the missions as ordered, but will be selective in the courses of action it will follow, the force levels it will field, as well as the capabilities and resources it will provide and maintain. It focuses on the conscious taking of calculated strategic and operational risks.
- Strategic positioning: This entails the establishment of early-warning mechanisms, such as the placement of military attachés and involvement in subregional institutions to enhance peace and security in the region. This supports development initiatives such as NEPAD.

Military strategic capabilities

The capabilities of the SANDF constitute the means of the Military Strategy and consist of:
- command and control, communications, computers, information, intelligence, infrastructure, reconnaissance and surveillance
- light mobile
- conventional warfare
- support.

Organisational structure

Defence administration

The Department of Defence adheres to the

Safety, security and defence

principles of civil control and oversight through the Minister of Defence, Mr Mosiuoa Lekota, the Joint Standing Committee on Defence (JSCD) and the Defence Secretariat.

While the Minister is responsible for providing political direction to the Department, the JSCD ensures that the Executive Authority (Minister of Defence) remains accountable to Parliament. However, for day-to-day administration and co-ordination of strategic processes, the Minister of Defence relies on the Defence Secretariat, which is the civilian leg of the Department. The Defence Secretariat is headed by the Secretary for Defence.

The functions of the Chief of the SANDF include, but are not limited to:
- executing defence policy
- directing the work of Defence Headquarters
- responsibility for the overall functioning of the SANDF
- serving as the principal advisor to the Minister and President on military, operational and administrative matters within his/her competence.

The Inspector-General provides management information to the Secretary for Defence. This is derived from performance and regulatory internal audits that are based on the risks derived from the Department of Defence Risk Register and results depicted from survey analyses.

The Directorate: Anti-Fraud (DAF) was established to conduct forensic investigations, detect and implement prevention measures within the Department of Defence to eliminate fraud and corruption.

Since its establishment in January 2003, the DAF has achieved positive results in assisting the Military Police Agency and the Chief: Military Legal Services to deal with cases of fraud and corruption within the Department. In July 2003, 16 fraud cases of subsistence and travel, home-owners' allowance, forgery of leave, irregular medical aid, medical prescriptions and cheque fraud, as well as several corruption cases were finalised.

During the same period, the DAF completed 10 detection reviews and two investigations with the assistance of whistle-blowers.

SANDF members have been encouraged to blow the whistle on fraud and corruption by contacting the DAF on the toll-free number 0800 767 323 (0800 SOS DAF).

A deliberate effort has been launched to enhance the quality of the Internal Audit function in pursuit of both superior performance delivery and good governance. To this effect, an International Standards Organisation Certification (9001:2000) was attained towards the end of 2002. This historic achievement has brought the Defence Inspectorate on par internationally with regard to production delivery.

Policy and planning

One of the subprogrammes of the Defence Administration Programme is the Division: Policy and Planning. The Division comprises three subprogrammes, namely Defence Policy, Human Resource Policy and Strategic Management. The functions of this subprogramme include, but are not limited to, the following:
- providing expert input relating to general defence policy to the Minister of Defence, Deputy Minister of Defence, Secretary for Defence and the Chief of the SANDF

On 25 April 2003, the old South African National Defence Force (SANDF) emblem was phased out. On 29 April 2003, the Chief of the SANDF, General Siphiwe Nyanda, presented the new SANDF flags and emblem to the senior echelons of the SANDF.

The new emblem incorporates a nine-pointed star, representing the warm sun of Africa and the nine provinces. The star is also used in divisional emblems and flags to reflect a common corporate identity.

The emblem reinforces the idea of military identity, authority and dignity.

The four Services of the SANDF – Army, Military Health Service, Navy and Air Force – are represented in their respective traditional colours.

- responsibility for the strategic management, planning and strategic control processes of the Department
- managing the policy-formulation process of the Department
- drawing up, promulgating and presenting the departmental plan to Parliament
- the integration and performance analysis of management systems in the Department
- interpreting input and influences that could effect the overall national defence strategy
- regulating conventional arms transfers in accordance with government policy
- co-ordinating the drawing-up of national contingency plans for a state of national defence (war).

Operations

Conventional

In the event of a conventional military threat against South Africa, the broad joint concept of operations will be as follows:
- land operations: the SANDF will conduct offensive, proactive and reactive land operations directed at stopping and destroying the enemy before it can penetrate South African territory
- air operations: enemy air power will be neutralised mainly through defensive counter-air operations assisted by air-mobile land operations aimed at destroying the enemy air force on the ground
- maritime operations: enemy maritime forces will be attacked at range, while the defence of own and friendly shipping will be enhanced by defensive patrols and escort
- SAMHS operations: during conventional operations, the SAMHS deploys its mobile formation in direct support of land, air and maritime operations.

Non-conventional

The broad non-conventional concepts of operations are as follows:

- support to the SAPS in the maintenance of law and order will be provided by general support tasks and focused rapid-reaction operations directed at priority crime and the conduct of special operations
- border control will be exercised on land, sea and air by high-technology surveillance supported by rapid-reaction forces
- general area protection will be provided by a combination of high-density and rapid-reaction operations.

Operational commitments

These include:
- The achievement of international and regional defence co-operation aims.
- The execution of limited peace operations.
- Effective land, sea and air border control.
- The maintenance of law and order in support of the SAPS, with special attention to the combating of taxi violence, robberies and heists.
- Control of the South African maritime areas of responsibility, including the Exclusive Economic Zone (EEZ).
- When requested, providing support to civil authorities within the scope of regulations regarding the following:
  - the preservation of life, health and property
  - the maintenance of essential services
  - the provision of medical and health services
  - search-and-rescue operations
  - missions to the Antarctic and the southern oceans
  - diplomatic initiatives.
- Air-transport missions, including VIP flights and departmental scheduled flights.
- Area-defence operation missions.
- Multinational and joint-force preparation missions.
- Special forces missions.
- Borderline control – the SANDF deploys forces in support of the SAPS along South Africa's international borders. This is in line

with a Cabinet decision and a subsequent agreement between the Department of Defence and the SAPS. The defence legislation has not yet been completed and therefore the SANDF must still deploy in terms of the SAPS powers. Once the defence legislation has been completed, clarity in terms of the role of the SANDF along the borderline will be achieved. SANDF deployment consists of an average of nine infantry companies patrolling selected stretches of the borderline as the situation demands, supported by elements of the SAMHS and the SAAF. The SAAF contributes aircraft to deploy land forces along the land borders where necessary and carries out reconnaissance flights along the land and sea borders where they assist the South African Navy patrolling the EEZ. The Navy patrols the coastline, assisting the Department of Environmental Affairs and Tourism with the prosecution of illegal fishermen, while also maintaining a presence at sea and thereby deterring other criminal activities such as drug smuggling. The SAAF further assists the Civil Aviation Authority and the SAPS border component in reducing the incidence of illegal aircraft flights into the country which, in most cases, are involved with smuggling of some kind.

Other defence commitments

Other defence commitments of the Department of Defence are to:
- achieve a reasonable level of military diplomacy through:
  - the placement and control of defence attachés
  - the preparation and servicing of Memoranda of Understanding
  - participation in international and regional defence structures, such as the UN, AU, SADC and the Interstate Defence and Security Committee
- achieve international obligations of the Department of Defence according to international agreements such as the following:
  - search-and-rescue
  - hydrography
- provide communication-security services to other State departments
- administer the National Key Points Act, 1980 (Act 102 of 1980)
- provide healthcare for the President and Deputy President.

Management of transformation

Since 1996, the Department of Defence has been undergoing a formal transformation process through which the Transformation Project was registered. The Project's goals are to:
- maximise defence capabilities through an affordable and sustainable force design and structure
- minimise defence costs by business process, i.e. engineering and restructuring of especially the support structures
- institutionalise appropriate leadership, command and management practices, philosophy and principles
- align defence policies, plans and management with the overall government transformation and administrative-reform initiatives
- ensure compliance with the Public Finance Management Act (PFMA), 1999 (Act 1 of 1999) as amended by Act 29 of 1999 and National Treasury regulations.

After comprehensive research, a set of seven shared values for the Department was approved. These values are:
- military professionalism
- human dignity
- integrity
- leadership
- accountability
- loyalty
- patriotism.

Force employment

In accordance with the Force Employment Strategy approved in 2002, the force employment structures are being revisited to make provision for rationalised level-3 operational structures to enhance command and control, cost-efficiency and functional differentiation at levels 2, 3 and 4 of the Joint Operations Division. This will ensure that the core strategic objectives of the Department are effectively addressed. It is foreseen that the five permanent Regional Joint Task Force Headquarters will be replaced by nine smaller Level-4 Regional Joint Task Force Tactical Headquarters, one in each province.

If required, temporary Joint Task Force Headquarters may be created for specific operations. Combat-ready units are prepared, provided and supported, as required.

Bases

Bases are lower-level structures provided by all the Services. Units are generally clustered in or around bases and share common facilities and services.

Bases exercise administrative control, but not command over attached units. In some cases, base commanders may also be type-formation commanders or task-force commanders for specific local operations or exercises.

One force

The 'one force' concept comprises the Regular and Reserve Force components of the SANDF.

The Regular Force consists of highly trained soldiers to operate and maintain a core capability, sophisticated equipment and defence systems.

The Reserve Force is the former part-time component of the SANDF. They are trained to bolster the core defence commitment. Other components are the Army Conventional Reserve, the Army Territorial Reserve, which includes the commandos, the SAAF, the Naval Reserve and the SAMHS Reserve. The Army Territorial Reserve operates mainly in co-operation with other government departments, especially the SAPS. Approval has been granted for the expansion of the Defence Reserve Force divisions to include offices in 10 regions. These offices will carry out the mandate of Chief of Defence Reserve at regional level.

This is aimed at involving Reserve Force members in the command, management and decision-making processes, and providing them with enhanced career-development opportunities.

Force preparation

The Chiefs of the Services (Army, SAAF, Navy and SAMHS) are responsible for the 'provide forces' processes of their respective Services. Formations are basic building-blocks in this process.

Each formation has its own commander. A formation includes, where practical, all units and support elements relating to a specific user-system type. It is capable of providing a fully supported user system to a commander responsible for the exercising and combat-readiness of land, air, maritime and military-health capabilities, such as a brigade or division commander.

A formation can provide the same service to a task-force commander appointed by the Chief of Joint Operations.

This is a considerable improvement in cost-effectiveness, while it also provides the best way of retaining core defence capabilities, especially expertise in critical mass function. Some examples of formations established by the different Services are:
- Army – infantry, artillery or armour formations
- SAAF – direct combat system
- Navy – the fleet
- SAMHS – military-health formations.

A formation's specific geographical location depends on where its combat and support units are concentrated.

Force support

Support formations are intermediate structures with their own formation commanders. Their task is to provide combat support to type formations and other system structures. Their nature and functions are generally

Safety, security and defence

similar to those of type formations, except that they do not provide combat-ready forces.

Important developments

Integration
The termination of the Integration Intake Bill together with a constitutional amendment and an amendment to the Demobilisation Act, 1996 (Act 99 of 1996), aims to formally and legally bring the integration and demobilisation process to an end.

Provision is made, however, for members whose names are on the Certified Personnel Register and are granted amnesty to be considered for integration.

Subject to the promulgation of the draft legislation, a final intake of former non-statutory force members will be undertaken.

A Code of Conduct, which will be signed by all top management members, has been formulated.

The Code is intended to capture the core values of the SANDF and is a vision of military professionalism in South Africa. It provides a normative basis for unity, morale and discipline.

Military veterans
The Military Veterans Affairs Act, 1999 (Act 17 of 1999), came into effect on 1 February 2001, and the regulations in terms of the Act have been approved by the Minister of Defence for promulgation.

The South African National Defence Force Commando system will be replaced by a revised South African Police Service (SAPS) Reservist System based on the amended National Instruction for Reservists.

This System is linked to various initiatives which form part of the National Crime-Combating Strategy normalisation phase, such as the drastic increase in the SAPS personnel figures over the next three years from 2003, the restructuring of specialised investigation units, the implementation of sector policing, and the establishment of crime-combating units for each police area.

The Minister has appointed the Chairperson and members of the Advisory Board on Military Veterans' Affairs from nominations received from the recognised military veterans' organisations. The President is designated the Patron-in-Chief of all military veterans in terms of the Act.

The Board was involved in preparations for the launch of the new Military Veterans' Federation and hosting the World Veterans' Federation Congress in December 2003. Military veterans and the Department of Defence are involved in the Freedom Park Project at Salvokop in Pretoria, which will commemorate and celebrate the history of South Africa's struggle for freedom. (See Chapter 5: *Arts and culture*.)

Humanitarian relief
As in the past, the SANDF participated in various disaster and human-relief operations throughout South Africa and the region in 2002/03.

The SANDF, through the SAMHS, assisted in stabilising a severe cholera outbreak in KwaZulu-Natal. The organisation also became involved in the management, containment and combat of a major foot-and-mouth disease outbreak.

Downsizing and rightsizing
The transformation of the Department's human resources entails two macroprocesses, namely a reduction in the number of personnel (downsizing) and the attainment of the desired composition and ratios (rightsizing).

The *Defence Review* guidelines, financial limitations and Parliamentary approval will determine the final force design and shape of the Department, as well as the size and composition of its human resources.

The Department strives towards representivity at all levels in terms of gender and race. The Department's baseline target for race is 65% African, 10% coloured, 0,75% Indian and 24% white. By March 2003, the Force had 62%

Since 1994, unions have emerged among certain government departments initially referred to as essential services. These unions exist through provisions of the Labour Relations Act, 1995 (Act 66 of 1995), and exclude the military personnel in the Department of Defence.

The battle to legalise unions in the South African National Defence Force (SANDF) was precipitated by the leadership of the South African National Defence Union (SANDU) at the Constitutional Court (CC) as a result of the refusal of the SANDF to recognise trade unions.

The CC found it unconstitutional to deprive uniformed members the right to join trade unions or any organisations looking after their interests. At the end of May 1999, the Court ordered the Minister of Defence to promulgate regulations concerning the relationship between the members of the SANDF and the Department of Defence as the employer.

Consequently, the regulations granting labour rights to members of the SANDF were promulgated and published in the *Government Gazette* on 20 August 1999 as Chapter 20 of the General Regulations for the SANDF and Reserve. These Regulations provide for the formation of military trade unions (MTUs) and apply to members of the Permanent Force and the Auxiliary Service. Various MTUs were formed and registered with the right to recruit members within the SANDF to meet the threshold required for formal registration as an MTU by the Registrar of MTUs. Individual members are required to accept the rights and limitations in respect of their labour rights as specified in the Regulations. Subject to the provisions of these Regulations, a member is entitled to exercise his or her labour rights as contemplated in Section 23 of the Constitution, on an individual basis or collectively through an MTU. No member may join or belong to any trade union other than an MTU.

The limitations are that members may not participate in a strike or secondary strike or incite other members to strike or to participate in a secondary strike. Members are prohibited from participating in peaceful and unarmed assemblies, demonstrations, pickets and petitions in support of a strike or secondary strike relating to any defence matter.

The Regulations also provide for organisational and bargaining rights with regard to MTUs.

Subject to the provisions of the Regulations, the following MTUs are permitted to recruit members in the SANDF: SANDU, the Armed Force Union of South Africa, the South African National Defence Forum and the Military Trade Union of South Africa. A number of other groupings are organising and are expected to be recognised shortly. The first MTU was registered in July 2000.

African, 12% coloured, 1% Asian and 25% white, while 85% of the Force was male and 15% female.

The baseline target for the employment of people with disabilities is 2% but owing to rightsizing this is not viable. By September 2003, the Department of Defence was employing 446 persons with disabilities. To achieve the target, the Department would have to employ 1 400 persons with disabilities.

Reserve Force

For political, strategic and economic reasons, the SANDF is an all-volunteer force consisting of a Regular Force core and a sufficiently large Reserve Force. This Force can be further augmented by a controlled reserve consisting of trained personnel who have done military service and are no longer active in the SANDF, but who can be utilised for 'hostilities only' on a voluntary basis.

The basic structure of the system is highly cost-effective and allows for flexibility in force levels according to the operational requirement. The system is non-discriminatory and females have an equal opportunity to serve in combat mustering.

The size and structure of the Reserve Force is derived from the force design and structure of each of the Services and makes provision for combat, combat support and support-force structure elements as well as staff officers at all levels. Approximately 85% of the Reserve Force component of the SANDF is in the South African Army and consists of two main elements, namely conventional and territorial units.

As an integral and essential part of the SANDF, the Reserve Force component will, during mobilisation or in times of war, provide a substantial expansion capability to the personnel component of the SANDF.

As the intended prime source from which the Reserve Force is to be staffed in future, a Military Skills Development (MSD) Programme has been introduced in the SANDF. The MSD

Programme is similar to voluntary national service. Members are selected to undergo training and serve in the armed forces for a period of two years, after which those who are not selected for extension of full-time service have an obligation to serve in the Reserve Force for a period of five years.

The Reserve Force of the SANDF is organised in the classic military array of regiments, battalions and maintenance units, while the establishment of the Reserve Force Formation in the SAMHS facilitates the detachment of elements as required.

As an integral part of the SANDF, the Reserve Force is under the command of the Chiefs of the respective services. Units function from independently managed headquarters under the command of a Reserve Force unit commander. At corporate level, a dedicated staff division renders a Reserve Force Marketing and Policy Advice Service to the Department of Defence.

The Reserve Force of the SANDF are trained to the same level of competency as their Regular Force counterparts and have the opportunity to advance through the ranks in their respective units by attending the appropriate courses for functional development and promotion.

Members of the Reserve Force may volunteer for service outside the borders of South Africa, e.g. to be deployed for peace-support operations.

Reserve Force members are paid for services rendered whether it be training or operations. Members may be called upon to serve for a specific period (continuous service) or for short periods which may vary from a few hours, to a day or a few days at a time (non-continuous service).

Resettlement

The Directorate: Personnel Separation has executed programmes at various levels in terms of the Department's Human Resource Strategy 2010. The Directorate is serving as a nodal point for redeployment and resettlement.

The Department of Defence has established a Personnel Rationalisation Advisory and Co-ordinating Committee for the management of this process, in order to ensure efficient and cost-effective support programmes for both the resettlement and redeployment of the Department's members and employees affected by separation.

The Directorate has established and implemented a Social Plan, which addresses the reskilling and psychosocial needs of the Department's members and employees.

Professional multidisciplinary teams execute this support programme.

The Department of Defence has set in place the Human Resource Planning Instruction that guides the process of interdepartmental transfers of redeployable members and employees.

Peace support

According to the *White Paper on South African Participation in International Peace Missions*, the SANDF continues to prepare for support in peace missions. Since 1999, the SANDF has established a reserve of military observers for deployment. These members are available as UN military observers, military liaison officers (MLOs) and staff officers in Mission Headquarters. Trained personnel can be deployed to any AU or SADC mission for the same purposes.

Since September 1999, one MLO has been deployed in Kampala, Uganda, as part of the UN Mission for the DRC (MONUC I). Members rotate every six months.

Since March 2001, members of the SANDF have been deployed to the AU Mission for Ethiopia and Eritrea (OLMEE), and the UN Mission in those countries. By mid-2003, five SANDF members were deployed in OLMEE, including a senior military representative and MLOs.

The SANDF also contributes to the second phase of the UN Mission for the DRC (MONUC II) in terms of specialised elements.

Some 160 members of the SANDF are deployed all over the DRC and these specialised elements include cargo-handling teams, emergency operational care orderlies, fire-fighting teams, military police and staff officers in the MONUC headquarters.

Since May 2003, some 1 300 members of the SANDF have been deployed for MONUCs Phase III in the eastern DRC.

SANDF members are also occupying posts as staff officers in the MONUC Headquarters in Kinshasa.

Since October 2001, some 700 South African soldiers have been deployed in Burundi to provide protection to the politicians who returned from exile to join the transitional institutions that were put in place on 1 November 2001. These South African soldiers became part of the AU Mission in Burundi on 1 May 2003.

The contingent will eventually comprise about 1 600 South African soldiers as part of the 3 200-strong AU Mission in Burundi, consisting of soldiers from South Africa, Mozambique and Ethiopia.

Requirement of main equipment

The Department of Defence has completely revised and consolidated its policies for the acquisition of weapon systems. Whereas the old approach placed emphasis squarely on the local satisfaction of systems and technological needs, the new direction takes into account the fact that South Africa is part of the global environment within which opportunities should be exploited to the benefit of the Department of Defence.

The Ground-Based Defence System (Phase 1) was contracted for delivery from 2004 to 2006.

The rapid-deployment logistical vehicles for paraforces and special forces were delivered at the end of 2002.

By November 2003, the first three South African Navy valour-class patrol corvettes had been officially named and launched.

The *SAS Amatola* was launched and christened by Ms Zanele Mbeki, the First Lady, on 2 June 2002. The vessel was transferred to South Africa in November 2003 for the fitment of her weapons and combat suites.

The *SAS Isandlwana* was launched and christened by Ms Nozizwe Madlala-Routledge, the Deputy Minister of Defence, on 5 December 2002. The vessel will be handed over to the Navy, after fitment of her weapons and combat suites, in August 2005.

The *SAS Spioenkop* was launched and christened by Ms Thandi Modise, Chairperson of the Parliamentary Standing Committee on Defence, on 4 June 2003. The vessel will be handed over to the South African Navy in December 2005.

The fourth corvette, *SAS Mendi*, was expected to be launched and christened in December 2003 for final handover to the Navy in February 2006.

These ships are the first new warships for South Africa in 16 years and are specifically designed for South African conditions.

South Africa is acquiring three types of 209 submarines from Germany. The first boat is due for commissioning and trials in July 2005, with delivery to South Africa expected by the end of 2005.

The submarines will be delivered at approximately 12-month intervals, with the final delivery expected by December 2008.

Inkwazi, which means 'fish eagle', is the name given to the Boeing Business Jet which the SAAF accepted into service in January 2003. *Inkwazi* provides the South African Government with a VIP intercontinental air-transport capability.

The first four of nine C130 Hercules mid-life aircraft have been delivered to the SAAF after a life-extension programme. The final delivery is expected by October 2004.

Ministerial approval has been received for the procurement of four maritime helicopters for the SAAF for operational deployment on the South African Navy corvettes.

The following major projects will commence in the next five years:
- new tactical radios
- new power-supply equipment
- new telecommunications infrastructure
- human centrifuge.

Provision was made by the Government in 2003/04 for the procurement of Westland Super Lynx multirole naval helicopters to be carried on board the patrol corvettes.

Facilities, land and environment

Facilities, Land and Environmental Management in the Department of Defence strives for the efficient management of these entities.

The Department has adopted the process of base conversion. The focus is on the role and responsibilities of the military process of conversion aimed at assisting role-players in closing down and re-using military bases in a sustainable manner. The *Military Integrated Training Range Guidebook* provides military environmental managers with a process that will ensure long-term continuation of environmentally sound management practices, while simultaneously enhancing the ability of the defence sector to sustain long-term and cost-effective range operations.

The Department continues to demonstrate its responsibility as custodian of land entrusted to it through active co-operation in the land redistribution and restitution policies of government. It co-operated in a pilot study regarding the closing down and re-use of redundant military bases for the purposes of alternative economic land-use initiatives. These are aimed at achieving co-operative environmental governance as advocated in national environmental policies.

Over the past decade, the Department has been rationalising its land portfolio and has made one-third (close to a quarter million hectares) of its original estate available for non-military use.

Armaments

Armaments Corporation of South Africa

The primary function of Armscor is to acquire defence products, mainly for the SANDF, and to co-manage, with the SANDF, the development of technologies for future weapon systems and products. It also manages the disposal of excess, forfeited, redundant or surplus defence material for the SANDF and subsidiary companies, which directly support defence technology and acquisition strategies.

Armscor's other functions include providing tender-board functions; acting as procurement secretariat; providing financial, quality and asset-management services; as well as legal services, project security and arms-control compliance assurance.

The net value of the Armscor Group's assets of R381,3 million on 31 March 2003 was slightly higher than the previous year's R356,1 million. Investments and cash form a substantial part of the assets and are reserved to finance specific future obligations, such as the replacement of capital equipment and promotion activities.

Armscor Business and its subsidiaries have been restructured into the following divisions:
- The Institute for Maritime Technology (Pty) Ltd, which aims to satisfy strategic needs for technomilitary support, products and services, and to establish applicable technology and systems to further the interests of the SANDF.
- Gerotek Test Facilities (Pty) Ltd, which is a global leader in vehicle-testing and related services, such as product-testing, consultancy and armour development.
- Alkantpan (Pty) Ltd, which offers an all-purpose weapon and ammunition test range, compiles specifications and analyses test data.
- Protechnik Laboratories (Pty) Ltd, which conducts research and development in the field of chemical defence, such as the

protection of personnel working in chemically hazardous environments.
- The South African Defence Export Support Organisation, which promotes export opportunities for the defence-related industry in order to retain strategic technologies and expertise for the SANDF and sustain the South African incorporated export drive.
- Hazmat Protective Systems (Pty) Ltd, which manufactures and markets protective equipment for use in chemical or biological warfare, as well as industrial respirators and breathing equipment.
- AB Logistics, which provides services such as freight clearing and forwarding, chartering of aircraft/vessels, travel arrangements and other related services.
- The Defence Institute, which assists the defence community in developing informed solutions in decision-making problems over the full life cycle of defence capabilities. It provides decision-support services at a strategic, operational and technical level and renders engineering and management services.

The activities of Armscor are financed mainly by an annual transfer payment from the Department of Defence, interest received on investments, the hiring of some of their buildings, commission from stock sales, and income from subsidiaries.

Acquisition of arms is totally transparent. Armscor publishes the monthly *Contracts Bulletin*, which contains all requests for proposals and tenders awarded. An electronic bulletin, updated daily, is available to industry via a computer network.

During March 2003, the Defence Council of the SANDF approved the running and management of the transformation process of the Simon's Town Naval Dockyard by Armscor. The decision was necessitated by the need to provide effective and professional logistical support to the Navy, and to utilise and manage the Dockyard's capacity on a sound economic and commercial basis.

The transformation process will be jointly managed by Armscor, the Secretary of Defence and the South African Navy.

Denel Group of South Africa

Established in 1992 and registered under the South African Companies Act, 1973 (Act 61 of 1973), Denel (Pty) Ltd operates as a profit-driven company.

The State is currently the sole shareholder, although the Government's restructuring programme of State-owned enterprises is under way. This has already resulted in a majority stake (51%) in Denel's Airmotive division being sold to the French company Turbomeca, part of the SNECMA group. Denel currently retains 49% in the new company called Turbomeca Africa.

The group employs approximately 10 500 people in several predominantly defence-related divisions. Recognised as a world leader in artillery systems, Denel's defence capabilities were established over 50 years ago when some of its oldest manufacturing divisions were formed.

The group specialises in:
- aviation and guided weapons
- ordnance
- commercial and information technologies.

With a broad range of products and systems exported and supported worldwide, Denel also has alliances and joint ventures with major international aerospace and defence companies.

The modernisation of the SANDF's major defence systems afforded Denel an opportunity to secure some offset contracts.

In terms of the Defence Industrial Participation and non-defence-related National Industrial Participation activities, Denel supplies aerostructures for Gripen and Hawk aircraft to BAE Systems and Saab. It has started licence manufacturing of the Agusta A119 Koala helicopters for AgustaWestland and is providing aircraft parts to the Boeing Company for Boeing 747 and B767 commercial airliners.

Safety, security and defence

Denel's Eloptro division manufactures periscopes for Zeiss Optronik in Germany, destined for Greece and South Korea's navy submarines.

Like many other South African companies, Denel is also benefiting from new technology transfers, as well as training and skills-development programmes provided by international suppliers. Some of its staff, mainly from previously disadvantaged communities, receive aviation technical training in Sweden, Italy and the United Kingdom.

Export sales now account for more than 50% of Denel's turnover, exceeding 80% in certain manufacturing divisions. Its order cover in 2002 amounted to some R9 billion.

Denel's leading ordnance technologies, including projectiles and the M90 bimodular charge system for 155-mm artillery guns, find ready export markets in the North Atlantic Treaty Organisation (NATO) and elsewhere.

Some of its subsystems such as the Arachnida weapon-management system, laser rangefinders and thermal-imaging equipment now operate within the NATO environment. Finland's Navy selected the sophisticated *Umkhonto* naval missile, developed by Denel's Kentron division.

Denel's Mechem division is successfully executing humanitarian landmine clearance, notably in the DRC, northern Iraq and Afghanistan, often in terms of UN contracts.

Denel systems and products that have been designed, developed and maintained for the domestic and international market, iclude:
- aerospace (the Oryx tactical transport helicopter, as well as the Rooivalk attack helicopter)
- unmanned aerial vehicles and target drones
- airborne observation and electro-optical systems
- innovative landmine-clearing technologies
- small- to medium-calibre ammunition
- infantry weapons
- world-leading integrated artillery systems.

From Denel's proven capabilities in defence-technology development and manufacturing, it has also emerged as a leader in commercial fields such as property development, innovative food technology, industrial manufacturing and information technology.

In June 2003, Denel was contracted on behalf of Boeing by the Satellite Application Centre of the Council for Scientific and Industrial Research (CSIR) to provide critical mission assistance during the launch of the Mars Exploration Rover (MER).

By deploying one of its mobile telemetry systems to Oshakati in Namibia, Denel's OTB advanced test range near Bredasdorp in the Western Cape was able to monitor and relay data of the Delta 11 launcher's second and third-stage separation shortly after lift-off. The MER was launched, after two delays, on 10 June 2003, on its seven-month journey to Mars.

On 24 September 2003, Denel announced a R75-million contract to sell a high-tech helmet-tracking system to Europe's BAE Systems and Saab.

The contract forms part of South Africa's Gripen and Hawk procurement deals. South Africa is in the process of buying 28 Gripen fighter jets from Saab as part of the arms procurement deal.

The two export contracts involve the sale of the advanced helmet-tracking system for NATO's latest jet fighters, the Eurofighter-Typhoon, and for components of the Gripen helmet-display system.

Denel and BAE were expected to supply 620 Typhoons with 800 advanced helmet systems and 200 Gripen fighters with 250 components of the helmet-display system.

Through special sensors, the system allows a pilot to control weapons and take readings of targets' location and distance by simply looking at the instrument panels.

Once the pilot has spotted the target, the weapons-guided system picks up on the target and directs the missile or canon by itself. The system, which can also be operated at night with an infrared display, also provides pilots with information on way-points, height, speed and warnings.

National Conventional Arms Control Committee

The NCACC consists of Ministers and Deputy Ministers, and oversees policy and sets control mechanisms for the South African arms trade. It ensures that arms-trade policies conform to internationally accepted practices.

Companies interested in exporting arms have to apply for export permits, after which the Ministry of Defence processes the application.

Each application is also sent for scrutiny to the relevant government departments, such as Foreign Affairs or Trade and Industry. The application is then referred to the various Directors-General to make their recommendations, whereafter the NCACC makes the final decision.

An independent inspectorate ensures that all levels of the process are subject to independent scrutiny and supervision, and conducted in accordance with the policies and guidelines of the NCACC. The inspectorate submits periodic reports to the Standing Parliamentary Committee on Defence.

Between 25 June and 1 August 2003, military units of the South African Defence Force and the United States of America (USA) conducted a routine bilateral training exercise, dubbed Exercise Flintlock.

The aim of the Exercise was to conduct a multinational airborne-focused field-training exercise in South Africa as an element of peace-support operations.

The Exercise included a broad spectrum of military activities, such as combat life-saving procedures, live firing of weapons, day and night-time low-level flying, and airdrops of personnel and equipment.

The Exercise provided the US forces with a new diverse environment in which to train, while the South African forces had the training opportunity to enhance their peace-support and humanitarian operation capabilities.

Intelligence services

There are two civilian intelligence structures, namely the National Intelligence Agency (NIA) and the South African Secret Service (SASS).

The NIA's mission is to proactively, professionally and impartially manage and provide the Government with domestic intelligence and counter-intelligence to enhance national security and defend the Constitution, the interests of the State and the well-being of the people of South Africa.

The NIA concentrates on the following areas and intelligence themes:
- international terrorism, which involves:
  - monitoring South Africa's compliance with international terrorism treaties
  - monitoring local support of international terrorist groups
  - monitoring international terrorism and related trends with a view to ascertaining their impact on South Africa.
- domestic terrorism, which involves:
  - urban terrorism
  - extremism
  - cyber terrorism.

The SASS is South Africa's foreign-intelligence capacity. It is concerned with providing clients with accurate, policy-relevant and timeous foreign intelligence collected abroad with the intention to inform, forecast and advise on real and potential threats and opportunities to the country. The purpose of the intelligence process is to promote, enhance and protect the national and security interests of the country and its people.

Executive control is exercised by a civilian Ministry and a Cabinet committee.

The civilian intelligence services are accountable to the Minister of Intelligence, who reports to the Cabinet through the Cabinet Committee on Security and Intelligence Affairs.

Parliament has also appointed a mechanism, the Joint Standing Committee on Intelligence, legislated in the Intelligence

Services Control Act, 1994 (Act 40 of 1994), which is able to order investigations into the intelligence community's activities.

In addition, the Constitution provides for protection against State abuse through the Public Protector and the Human Rights Commission. (See Chapter 15: *Justice and correctional services*.)

The objective of the intelligence community is to provide evaluated information with the following responsibilities in mind:
- safeguarding the Constitution
- promoting the interrelated elements of security, stability, co-operation and development, both within South Africa and in relation to southern Africa
- upholding the individual rights enunciated in the chapter on Fundamental Rights (the Bill of Rights) contained in the Constitution
- intensifying collection efforts on crime in support of the SAPS' crime intelligence task
- promoting South Africa's ability to face foreign threats and to enhance its competitiveness in a dynamic world
- achieving national prosperity while making an active contribution to global peace and other globally defined priorities for the well-being of humankind.

The National Strategic Intelligence Amendment Act, 1998 (Act 37 of 1998), allows South Africa to conduct a counter-intelligence service overseas, under the SASS.

The Act also gives the Minister of Intelligence a seat on the National Intelligence Co-ordinating Committee and more clearly defines his/her powers and functions.

The Minister is also accountable to the Cabinet for co-ordinating intelligence by the national intelligence structures.

The South African Academy of Intelligence (SANAI), situated at the Mzwandile Piliso Campus in Mafikeng, North West, opened its doors on 28 February 2003.

The SANAI is responsible for providing training to members of the intelligence community and other related departments.

The Academy is involved with the management and running of a cadet programme which seeks to attract the best of the youth. The cadet programme will be driven by a systemic process of talent-spotting, head-hunting, and focused and dedicated training of the youth, to bring much-needed skills into the intelligence community.

During 2002/03, the Electronic Communications Security Company was established to develop cutting-edge electronic communications technology and secure South Africa's communications sector.

One of the Company's first tasks is to conduct security audits of prioritised government departments at provincial and local level. This is a strategic intervention aimed at ensuring that e-commerce in South Africa can thrive without difficulty in reaction to threats posed by intrusion, cyber crime or cyber sabotage.

In an effort to unmask cyber criminals' plans, the Office of Interception Centres will be established.

These Centres will target those who seek to undermine South Africa's national security, commit crimes, and steal and sell strategic information belonging to the country.

The Centres will interface with telecommunications operators to provide law-enforcement agencies with judiciary-approved intercepting products and services, as approved by Parliament through the Regulation of Interception of Communication and Provision of Communication-Related Information Act, 2002 (Act 70 of 2002).

The Interception Act, 2002 prohibits the manufacturing, possession, selling and use of interception devices. The only structures that may manufacture, possess or sell these devices are law-enforcement agencies and those private security companies registered in terms of the Private Security Industry Regulation Act, 2001 (Act 56 of 2001). These authorised groups can intercept communications for the sole purpose of combating crime and providing emergency services.

South Africa Yearbook 2003/04

Acknowledgements

Armscor
Denel
Estimates of National Expenditure 2003, published by the National Treasury
Independent Complaints Directorate
Secretariat for Safety and Security
South African National Defence Force
South African Police Service
www.gov.za

Suggested reading

A Navy for Three Oceans: Celebrating 75 Years of the South African Navy. Roggebaai: BP Southern Africa, 1997.
Batchelor, P. and Willet, S. *Disarmament and Defence: Industrial Adjustment in South Africa.* Oxford: Stockholm International Peace Research Institute. Oxford University Press, 1998.
Bornman, E. and others. *Violence in South Africa: A Variety of Perspectives.* Pretoria: Human Sciences Research Council (HSRC), 1998.
Bremer, J.D. *Black and Blue: Policing in South Africa.* Oxford: Clarendon Press, 1994.
Brogden, M. and Shearing, C. *Policing for a New South Africa.* London: Routledge, 1993.
Cawthra, G. *Policing South Africa: The South African Police and the Transition from Apartheid.* Cape Town: David Philip, 1993.
Cock, J. and Mackenzie, P. eds. *From Defence to Development: Redirecting Military Resources in South Africa.* Cape Town: David Philip for the Group for Environmental Monitoring, 1998.
Davis, D. and Slabbert, M. eds. *Crime and Violence in South Africa: Critical Studies in Criminology.* Cape Town: David Philip, 1985.
Du Plessis, L. and Hough, M. eds. *Managing African Conflicts: The Challenge of Military Intervention.* Pretoria: HSRC, 2000.
Du Plessis, L. and Hough, M. eds. *Protecting Sub-Saharan Africa: The Military Challenge.* Pretoria: HSRC, 1999.
Emmett, T. and Buthcart, A. eds. *Behind the Mask: Getting to Grips with Crime and Violence in South Africa.* Pretoria: HSRC, 2000.
Gamba, V., Meek, S. and Potgieter, J. eds. *Society Under Siege: Crime, Violence and Illegal Weapons.* Halfway House: Institute for Security Studies, 1997.
Gutteridge, W. and Spence, J.E. *Violence in Southern Africa.* London: Frank Cass, 1997.
Hansson, D. and Van Zyl-Smit, D. eds. *Towards Justice? Crime and State Control in South Africa.* Cape Town: Oxford University Press, 1990.
Kok, P. and Pietersen, J. *Safety and Security of Citizen and Society.* Pretoria: HSRC, 2000.
Louw, M.N. and Bouwer, J.S. *The South African Air Force at War: A Pictorial Appraisal.* 2nd ed. Johannesburg: Chris van Rensburg Publications, 1995.
Machel, G. *Impact of War on Children.* London: Hurst, 2001.
Manganyi, N. and du Toit, A. eds. *Political Violence and the Struggle in South Africa.* Halfway House: Southern Book Publishers, 1990.
Marsh, R. *With Criminal Intent: The Changing Face of Crime in South Africa.* Kenilworth: Ampersand Press, 1999.
Matthews, M.L. and others, eds. *Policing the Conflict in South Africa.* Gainesville: University Press of Florida, 1995.
McKendrick, B. and Hoffman, W. eds. *People and Violence in South Africa.* Cape Town: Oxford University Press, 1990.
Melville, N. *The Taming of the Blue: Regulating Police Misconduct in South Africa.* Pretoria: HSRC, 1999.
Minaar, A. and Hough, M. eds. *Conflict, Violence and Conflict Resolution: Where is South Africa Heading?* Pretoria: HSRC 1997.
Myerson, L. *Hijackings, Burglaries and Serious Crime: How to Protect Your Family, Your Home and Your Valuables.* Sandton: LAD, 1995.
Reyneke, E. compiler. *Small Arms and Light Weapons in Africa.* Pretoria: Institute for Security Studies, 2000.
Safe, Secure and Streetwise: The Essential Guide to Protecting Yourself, Your Family and Your Home from Crime. Cape Town: Reader's Digest Association, 1997.

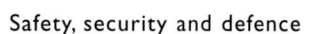

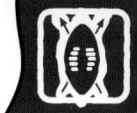

Schonteich, M. *Unshackling the Crime Fighters: Increasing Private-Sector Involvement in South Africa's Criminal Justice System*. Johannesburg: South African Institute of Race Relations, 1999.
Seegers, A. *The Military in the Making of Modern South Africa*. London: Taurus Academic Studies, 1996.
Smith, L. *A Guide to a Safer Lifestyle: A Practical Guide to Surviving the Urban Jungle*. Johannesburg: Chris van Rensburg, 2000.
The Pride of the Nation: A Short History of the South African Air Force, 1920 – 1995. Compilers: C.J. Nöthling and D. Becker. Pretoria: The Air Force, 1995.
Van der Merwe, H.W. *Peace-Making in South Africa: A Life in Conflict Resolution*. Cape Town: Tafelberg, 2000.

Barry Lamprecht/*Die Burger*

chapter 18
Science and technology

Policy

The vision of the Department of Science and Technology is to enable the creation of prosperity and well-being in South Africa, and to achieve enduring and equitable benefits from science and technology (S&T) for all South Africans.

Over the past five years, the science vote has increased by 27,6%. The Innovation Fund is a major initiative introduced by the *White Paper on Science and Technology*, published in 1996. It promotes large-scale projects, involving participation from throughout the National System of Innovation (NSI). It focuses attention on the major themes of government, namely competitiveness, quality of life, environmental sustainability and the harnessing of information technology (IT) to address the needs of society and the economy.

National S&T policy is the responsibility of the Minister of Arts, Culture, Science and Technology.

The intellectual framework for policy is the NSI, in which a set of functioning institutions, organisations, individuals and policies interact in the pursuit of a common set of social and economic goals.

◀ Upon its completion in 2004, the Southern African Large Telescope (SALT) at Sutherland in the Northern Cape will be the most powerful optical/infra-red telescope in the southern hemisphere.

National Research and Development (R&D) Strategy

In 2002, the Cabinet approved the Department of Science and Technology's National R&D Strategy, which allows for the enhancement of the NSI. The R&D Strategy identifies the need to pay greater attention to human resource development (HRD) as a wealth and employment creator, to bring innovation to the fore in all the Department's activities, and to facilitate S&T performance across government. Delivering increased economic growth and improved quality of life are the two key outcomes of the R&D Strategy.

National Advisory Council on Innovation (NACI)

Government has a constant need for informed advice on the development and implementation of S&T policy and the stimulation of innovation. The NACI is responsible for carrying out inquiries, studies, policy research and consultations in respect of the functioning of the NSI, as requested by the Minister.

The Council enables the Department to consolidate and develop the NSI in an informed and proactive manner. It provides a focused mechanism to access and target critical S&T research and information, for the purpose of socio-economic development.

The members of the NACI are broadly representative of government and the higher education, business and non-profit sectors.

Public understanding of science, engineering and technology (Puset)

Getting information about science across to different sections of the population is a big challenge. The Department's efforts in this regard include the following:

- The dire need for science reporting in South Africa compelled the Department of Science and Technology, in conjunction with the American Association for the Advancement of Science (AAAS), to establish the Science Radio Journalism Fellowship Programme. The objective is to build a critical mass of science radio journalists who can communicate science to South Africans in their indigenous languages. Between 2001 and 2003, several fellowship awards were granted. During the four-week programme, fellows receive state-of-the-art training in science radio journalism at the AAAS headquarters in Washington DC, United States of America (USA). Fellows from the journalism community learn how to research, write and produce science stories, while those from the science community are taught how to communicate effectively with the media.
- The Reference Group of Women in S&T is aimed at the creation of an environment in which women contribute to, participate in, and share benefits equally with their male counterparts in the science, engineering and technology (SET) fields, whether from a policy-making or a research perspective.
- National Science Week 2003 kicked off with the launch of the Science Train. During the Week, the Train took various science exhibits with the theme *Taking Science, Engineering and Technology to Our People* to four areas. It was announced during National Science Week that the Department of Science and Technology, in conjunction with the Department of Agriculture, would invest R15 million over a three-year period for the promotion of public awareness and understanding of biotechnology.
- The Department hosted the first meeting of the International Public Communication of Science and Technology Network in Africa, and the second in the southern hemisphere, in Cape Town in late 2002.

The Minister of Arts, Culture, Science and Technology, Dr Ben Ngubane, launched a computer-literacy pilot project in the Eastern Cape in December 2002. This education project, designed to be as user-friendly and accessible as possible, is in line with government's commitment to rural development, as it affords children in rural areas access to a multimedia kiosk equipped with various computer applications, including the Internet, and an assistant to guide the children's learning processes.

International S&T co-operation

The Department of Science and Technology is committed to building strong international relations and innovatively benefiting from, and contributing to, the SET sectors of other countries. It manages over 30 S&T bilateral agreements with different countries and is a key player in many multilateral forums, including the Commonwealth; the African, Caribbean and Pacific Group of States; the European Union; and the Organisation for Economic Co-operation and Development. South Africa also played a key role in deliberations during the 2002 World Summit on Sustainable Development (WSSD).

The main areas of S&T co-operation between South Africa and its international partners are material science; manufacturing technology; biotechnology; environmental management; sustainable exploitation of natural resources and minerals; medical research and public health; engineering science and advancement of technologies; water-supply projects; and agriculture, mathematics and science education.

The National Research Foundation (NRF) manages the implementation of the agreements, which range from 60 active projects with France to eight projects with the People's

Science and technology

Republic of China. Other countries in which active projects are under way include Belgium, Germany, Hungary, Sweden, Poland, Italy, India, Norway, Nigeria, the Russian Federation, the United Kingdom (UK) and the USA.

By mid-2003, preparations were under way for research collaboration with countries such as Egypt, the Ukraine, Belarus, Algeria, Morocco, Tunisia and Pakistan, subject to the finalisation of the requisite Framework Programmes of Co-operation. New agreements are also being negotiated with countries such as Chile and Brazil.

Implementing S&T policy and the objectives of the NSI

The establishment of the interdepartmental Science and Technology Co-operation Committee (SATCCOM), representing all relevant departments and with the chairperson and Secretariat provided by the Department of Science and Technology, was approved by the Cabinet. It promotes and guides the participation of government departments in international S&T co-operation.

SATCCOM is provided with an overview of the management, promotion and utilisation of R&D and S&T within government departments with an S&T component.

The Department has embarked on the establishment of a database on international co-operation in SET. Major international initiatives include the South African Coelacanth Conservation and Genome Resource Programme, launched at Sodwana Bay, KwaZulu-Natal. Research is co-ordinated by the South African Institute for Aquatic Biodiversity (SAIAB) in Grahamstown and involves several Southern African Development Community (SADC) neighbours.

Another international initiative is the establishment of a long-term ecological research site in southern Africa. This site will join an international network of ecosystem observatories, which help regions manage natural resources in a sustainable manner.

The Satellite Laser Ranging System at Hartebeesthoek, near Krugersdorp in Gauteng, is operated in conjunction with the National Aeronautics and Space Administration in the USA.

The South African Large Telescope (SALT) under construction at Sutherland in the Northern Cape is a multimillion-Rand project involving Germany, Poland, the USA, New Zealand and the UK.

Upon its completion, SALT will be the largest single optical telescope in the southern hemisphere.

Science and Technology Agreements Committee (STAC) Fund

Since its inception in 1996, STAC has, through the offices of the NRF, effectively serviced intergovernmental S&T agreements and multilateral activities.

Lead Programmes Fund

This Fund enhances existing international co-operation in the fields of biotechnology, new material, information and communications technology (ICT), environmental management, rural development and urban renewal. The Fund has successfully leveraged international R&D support and established viable consortia be-tween, among others, South African science councils, the *Centre de Coopération Inter-nationale en Recherche Agronomique pour le Développement* (France), ALCOA (USA), Rolls Royce (UK), and the IVL Swedish Environmental Research Institute.

Southern African Development Community Fund

The main priority areas include water management, cross-border pollution, food technology, indigenous knowledge systems, ICT, soil management and HIV/AIDS.

Technology diffusion and transfer

In September 2002, the *Tshumisano* Technology Stations Trust was launched. The Trust is a partnership programme with the German Agency for Technical Co-operation and the Committee of Technikon Principals. The Trust was established to further the Technology Stations Programme (TSP).

The TSP provides skills-development training to small, medium and micro enterprises (SMMEs) to enhance their innovation capacity and competitiveness, while exposing university of technology (until recently technikon) students to practical situations facing businesses. It aims to address the product and process technology needs of SMME manufacturing and the service industry, through technology transfer, development and diffusion.

Seven stations are operational in the fields of electronics and electrical engineering, complemented by IT as imbedded in electronic processes and products; metals value adding, product development and rapid prototyping; chemicals (at two universities of technology); composites; automotive components; and textiles and clothing. The *Tshumisano* Trust is set to stimulate job creation, skills transfer and application, a culture of innovation, and increased social and economic investment.

In March 2003, the Deputy Minister of Arts, Culture, Science and Technology, Ms Buyelwa Sonjica, announced the launch of the South African Reference Group on Women in Science and Technology (SARG).

SARG, which consists of academics and businesspeople in the field, has two major objectives, namely, developing strategies that address identified obstacles and challenges that women face when entering the field of science and technology due to various socialisation, educational, environmental and cultural barriers; and achieving gender mainstreaming within research and development agendas, by ensuring that all these projects consider women as beneficiaries or end-users of the products generated.

National Biotechnology Strategy (NBS)

The NBS was approved by the Cabinet in 2001 and forms an important component of the R&D Strategy. It addresses new developments in biotechnology and the country's vulnerability with respect to the exploitation of South Africa's biodiversity and indigenous knowledge, and the advent of new technologies.

By February 2003, implementation of the Strategy had gained momentum with the establishment of Biotechnology Regional Innovation Centres (BRICs).

The Department received proposals by consortia comprising academic institutions, private institutions and research councils to form three BRICs representing specific regions in the country. The BRICs promote R&D, entrepreneurial services, technology platforms, intellectual-property management and business incubation. Each Centre specialises in specific areas of technology within the national development imperatives, local expertise and market opportunities.

There are three key Centres that will leverage bio-technology opportunities:
- Biopad BRIC in Gauteng focuses on animal health and industry/environmental-related biotechnology
- Ecobio BRIC in KwaZulu-Natal focuses on human health and bioprocessing, with a plant biotechnology focal area to contribute to plant biotechnology
- Cape Biotech Initiative BRIC in the Western Cape focuses on human health and bioprocessing.

These Centres combine business, academic and research capabilities to target areas that are directly relevant to South Africa's needs, as well as providing a platform for global economic participation. The key areas of activity include human health, industrial biotechnology, food security and agricultural production. These activities complement existing strategies in ICT and new developments to support the advanced manufacturing industry.

Science and technology

Godisa Programme

The Departments of Science and Technology and of Trade and Industry, with the support of the EU, launched the Godisa National Incubation Programme in 2001. The Godisa Programme aims at encouraging technology transfer and capacity-building to enable small business to compete in the global economy.

Godisa aims to address:
- outdated technologies employed by SMMEs
- low engagement rates of SMMEs in value-adding activities
- the high failure rate of start-up SMMEs
- poor access to facilities for testing and promoting SMMEs.

Godisa supports eight technology-transfer centres in five provinces, focusing on a multitude of technology platforms and markets, such as biotechnology, life sciences, medical devices, software, embedded systems, fine and performance chemicals, small-scale miners and hydroponics for cut-flower exports. This technology has very real local and international benefits and leads directly to job creation, increased levels of competency and enhanced international competitiveness.

By mid-2002, the following centres had been established:
- Softstart Software Technology Incubation in Pretoria (IT)
- KwaZulu-Natal Innovation Support Centre in Durban (IT)
- Zenzele Technology Demonstration Centre in Johannesburg (mining)
- Egoli Biotechnology Incubator in Johannesburg (biotechnology)
- Mbombela Horticultural Incubator in Nelspruit (horticulture)
- Arcon Technology Incubator (life science) in Cape Town
- Chemin Fine Chemicals Incubator in Port Elizabeth (chemicals).

The Godisa Programme is set to become the National Incubation Programme and a National Centre of Excellence.

The establishment of the Timbali Technology Incubator under the Godisa Programme stems from opportunities that were identified in the Mbombela Investment Strategy and the report on the South African Floriculture Cluster.

Timbali is responsible for creating the technology basis that will focus on the establishment and development of a financially feasible export-based cut-flower industry in the Mbombela region in Mpumalanga.

This will be achieved through technology transfer to flower-growers selected from the previously disadvantaged community, with emphasis on training in horticulture, business, finance and mentoring.

Poverty-Reduction Programme

The Department of Science and Technology believes in a multipronged approach to fight poverty.

For this reason, the Department has established a Poverty-Reduction Programme focusing on the agroprocessing area, with great potential for achieving sustainable reductions in poverty levels in rural and peri-urban areas. Its mechanism is the establishment of small and micro business ventures within targeted communities once skills transfer has taken place.

The Programme emphasises the transfer of skills, the utilisation of low-cost labour-

---

The Deputy Minister of Arts, Culture, Science and Technology, Ms Buyelwa Sonjica, and the Deputy Minister of Science and Technology of the People's Republic of China, Ms Wu Zhongze, signed an agreement on future scientific and technological collaboration, during the second session of the Science and Technology Joint Committee between South Africa and China, which was held in Pretoria in March 2003.

To enhance scientific and technological development, the China-Africa Engineering Association was established in 1997 in South Africa to promote engineering and scientific information exchange between the two countries. It also focused on promoting and organising exchange programmes for engineering experts and scholars from China to visit South Africa.

intensive technologies, stimulating demand and securing orders within the South African domestic market, establishing and maintaining product-quality standards, and the practice of general good business management. The Programme has established a variety of projects:
- The honeybee, widely found in South Africa, has been significantly underutilised for honey production. The Department funded the cost of training communities across the country to keep honeybees and make honey, sweets and candles from the wax. All the new production units sell their honey under the brand name.

  The Agricultural Research Council (ARC) won the *Impumelelo* 2002 Platinum Innovation Award in recognition of the Bee-Keeping for Poverty-Relief Programme, which epitomises the goals of the Departments of Science and Technology, of Social Development and of Agriculture. In addition to the revenue from honey, the Programme has also led to the production of crafts and other products, such as handcrafted containers for honey, beeswax candles, sewing and the making of protective clothing, and honey distribution and transport. The Programme was implemented in 35 rural and peri-urban areas all over South Africa. Programme implementation projects in Muldersdrift, Atteridgeville and Stinkwater in Gauteng were selected to be showcased during the WSSD as best-practice projects in the *Greening the WSSD* initiative.
- A similar project is that of small-scale and community-based oyster-mushroom farming to promote food security. This is a new initiative and is in the planning phase.
- A range of projects train people in the skills of paper-making and product development. These projects use natural fibres from the waste of large commercial farming operations or from the farming operations of small, resource-poor, emerging farmers. One of the projects involves, for instance, a group of about 15 rural women who are using sugar-cane waste and a low-cost technique for pulping it to make paper by hand. Further processing enables them to make the packaging for the crafts that they sell to tourists. The group has moved from the informal sector and selling its products on the street, to a production premises where manufactured goods are sold to tourist shops and businesses requiring paper packaging.

By February 2003, the Department had spent a total of R40 million on enabling vulnerable and impoverished communities and individuals across the country to learn useful and wealth-creating skills. A further R30 million has been budgeted for 2004.

Science councils

The statutory science councils are a key part of South Africa's NSI. Through them, government is able to directly commission research in the interest of the nation and support technology development in its pre-competitive phase.

National Research Foundation

As the Government's national agency responsible for promoting and supporting basic and applied research as well as innovation, the NRF upholds excellence in its investments in knowledge, people, products and infrastructure. The NRF provides services and grants to support research and postgraduate research training, vital to the development of S&T in South Africa. It is the NRF's vision to be a key instrument in creating an innovative and knowledge-driven society where all citizens are empowered to contribute to a globally competitive and prosperous South Africa.

Funding from the NRF is largely directed towards academic research, developing high-level HR, and supporting the nation's national research facilities.

The South African Environmental Observatory Network (SAEON) was established in 2002/03. The NRF was mandated by the Department of

Science and Technology to develop a long-term ecological research programme for South Africa. Relevant government departments and science councils support the programme, and the Department has provided the core funding of R11,8 million over three years. The function of SAEON is to establish a network of environmental observatories/research sites and network information-management systems, to monitor long-term climate and environmental change in southern Africa.

The NRF's Research and Innovation Support Agency (RISA) invests funds, granted mainly by parliamentary vote, to institutions, teams and individuals engaged in research.

The total budget allocation from the Department of Science and Technology for the NRF for 2003/04 was R377 million. Of this, R113 million went to the national facilities; R9 million to the Foundation for Education, Science and Technology (FEST); and R221,6 million to RISA. A total of R34 million was used for departmental ring-fenced activities such as the STAC and SAEON, and for giving researchers access to the National Laser Centre.

The NRF's parliamentary grant is supplemented by joint ventures with other funding partners.

On 18 September 2003, the African Institute for Mathematical Sciences (AIMS) programme was launched in Muizenburg, Cape Town.

AIMS is aimed at strengthening scientific and technological capacity across the African continent. It focuses, among others, on a unique, intensive nine-month postgraduate course, developing a strong foundation in mathematical and computing research skills.

Some of the courses include:
- the art of scientific approximation
- mathematical problem-solving
- probability and statistics
- mathematical modelling
- methods of mathematical physics.

A total of 30 students from various African countries such as Algeria, South Africa, Morocco and Kenya, and visiting lecturers will be accommodated at the AIMS educational centre, allowing for maximum interaction.

The Square Kilometre Array (SKA) bid

South Africa, with the NRF as the lead agency, is gearing up to bid to become a host country for the mammoth SKA radio telescope, the world's largest radio-telescope project under consideration by international science bodies. South Africa is proposing to host the core array of the SKA, or part of the peripheral array.

The SKA project is an ambitious effort between institutions from 11 countries. The instrument will have multiple receiving surfaces and will provide radio astronomers with one million m^2 of collecting area, making it 100 times more sensitive than today's leading telescopes. The Northern Cape is considered to be one of the best potential locations for the SKA.

The South African SKA Steering Committee submitted a preliminary bid proposal in May 2003. The bidding process is expected to take two or three years to finalise. The International SKA Steering Committee hopes to choose the site for the SKA in 2005. Construction will hopefully start in 2010 and the SKA should start operating in 2015. The SKA is expected to cost US$1 billion, with the USA, Europe and the rest of the participating countries contributing a third each.

Technology for Human Resources for Industry Programme (THRIP)

The THRIP is a joint initiative between industry, research and educational at institutions, and the Department of Trade and Industry. The Programme is managed by the NRF on behalf of the Department of Trade and Industry. During 2003, some R404 million was invested in R&D activities designed to improve the competitiveness of the South African industry. This was 32% more than the amount in 2002. Of this investment, R158,5 million came from the Department of Trade and Industry (through THRIP) and the remainder, from industry (47% large and 53% SMMEs).

Some 266 THRIP projects were supported in 2003, with an average value of almost

R600 000 each (THRIP investment only). The projects cover a wide range of technology areas in the natural sciences and engineering. Some specific areas include agriculture and forestry, bioprocessing, food, healthcare, new material, mining, manufacturing and power.

The THRIP supports interventions focusing on improving the industry's competitiveness. In addition to supporting focused research and technology development with well-defined output, THRIP funds contributed towards the training of more than 2 651 students in 2003. Of these, more than 1 000 (39%) were black students, and more than 750 (28%) were women.

Innovation Fund

The Innovation Fund is designed to encourage large-scale, collaborative research and technology-development programmes; a multi-disciplinary approach to problem-solving; and application-based research. The Fund's economic and S&T policies recognise the process of innovation, one of the agents driving technological change. Many countries believe innovation is primary to economic growth. The Innovation Fund is an investment by government that gives effect to this concept.

Under the management of the NRF, the Fund directs large grants (between R1 million and R5 million per year) to consortia of researchers for the final-stage research process in which knowledge is translated into new or improved products, productivity processes and services. The Fund assists in the conversion of research ideas into commercially useful end-products, by funding necessary items such as equipment, R&D expertise, access to managerial skills, the securing of intellectual-property rights, and the construction of prototypes.

The Innovation Fund is a policy instrument to lever economic and social resources. It seeks to address socio-economic challenges by harnessing South Africa's S&T competencies to simultaneously develop and maintain cutting-edge global competitiveness and address the needs of citizens unable to assert themselves in the marketplace.

The Fund has focused on ICT, biotechnology, new material and fauna and flora in its previous calls for proposals. The Innovation Fund will support projects to the value of R161 million over the next three years.

Research and Innovation Support Agency

The NRF's RISA has a suite of funding programmes that are in line with South Africa's priorities and needs. They are:
- unlocking the future and advancing and strengthening strategic knowledge
- distinct South African research opportunities
- economic growth and international competitiveness
- sustainable livelihoods and the eradication of poverty
- conservation and management of ecosystems and biodiversity
- ICTs and the information society
- the socio-political impact of globalisation and its challenge for South Africa
- education and indigenous knowledge systems.

Collectively, these themes form the conceptual landscape within which most of the granting activities of RISA take place.

Research Capacity-Development (RCD) programmes

Institutional RCD programmes focus on boosting historically black universities and universities of technology that are committed to the research process. In addition, the *Thuthuka* Programme supports individual researchers.

It comprises the subprogrammes Researchers in Training, Women in Research, and Research Development for Black Academics. All the NRF's RCD initiatives aim to boost the output of high-level black HR (both academics and research students at all

Science and technology

higher education institutions); develop a postdoctoral research culture; strengthen weak, yet critically important disciplines; improve gender equity; and renew outdated research equipment.

Student support
The NRF provides two complementary types of postgraduate student support, namely:
- free-standing bursaries, scholarships and fellowships
- grantholder-linked bursaries.

Free-standing bursaries, scholarships and fellowships are awarded directly to students on a competitive basis, while grantholder-linked bursaries are granted to researchers within their NRF support package and may be awarded to students selected by the NRF grantholder.

The NRF offers a limited number of travel grants for research abroad.

Knowledge management
The NRF's research-information programme comprises:
- NEXUS, a set of research and knowledge networking databases containing information about South African research projects, professional associations, researcher networking, conferences and research organisations
- the South African Data Archive, an archive of computerised raw quantitative data of large-scale regional, national and international research projects
- the South African Network of Skills Abroad, which connects skilled people living abroad, who wish to make a contribution to South Africa's economic and social development, with local experts and projects.

International Science Liaison (ISL)
The ISL aims to forge and maintain strategic and intellectual alliances between individuals, institutions and organisations in the national and international science-research community, to support the international competitiveness of the country. The NRF manages some 19 S&T agreements signed between South Africa and other countries.

The South African International Council for Science (ICSU) Secretariat, which is administered by the NRF, serves the South African scientific community and most of the ICSU unions and affiliates. The ISL maintains contact with ICSU and similar bodies to facilitate South African participation in relevant and important international scientific activities.

Through the Africa Interaction Programme, the ISL expands scientific co-operation between scientists in South Africa and their counterparts in the rest of Africa.

Foundation for Education, Science and Technology
FEST's mission and mandate are to promote public understanding of science among all South Africans through open and constructive dialogue between the scientific community and society. Its vision is to give effect to the African Renaissance, by empowering people with knowledge of SET to help them improve their lives.

As of December 2002, FEST was incorporated into the NRF. Its products include the popular science magazines *Archimedes* and *EasyScience*, and it houses the Museum of Science and Technology. FEST is responsible for a range of other activities and events aimed at the youth, including science weeks and science and language olympiads. FEST was selected by the Department of Science and Technology to launch a programme on the public understanding of biotechnology, which the Department will fund for three years.

National research facilities
The NRF is responsible for managing South Africa's five national research facilities. These are the:
- Hartebeesthoek Radio Astronomy Observatory (HartRAO)
- SAIAB in Grahamstown

- iThemba Laboratory for Accelerator-Based Sciences in Faure, Western Cape
- South African Astronomical Observatory (SAAO) in Cape Town, Western Cape, and Sutherland in the Northern Cape, and SALT
- Hermanus Magnetic Observatory (HMO).

Hartebeesthoek Radio Astronomy Observatory

HartRAO is South Africa's national research facility for radio astronomy and space geodesy. It operates, maintains and develops internationally recognised research facilities for local and international astronomers and scientists. The Observatory's unique geographic location is pivotal in a variety of global programmes.

The Observatory's 26-metre (m) telescope operates as a single dedicated instrument in a variety of fields, while participating in global networks of radio telescopes. The facility takes part in global geodetic projects to study the dynamics of the earth's crust and the rotation and orientation of the earth in space.

The Space Geodesy Programme has been expanded to include the operation of a regional network of global positioning system (GPS) stations as part of the International GPS Service, and a sophisticated satellite laser-ranging system. The Observatory is one of only six fundamental stations for space geodesy in the world, and the only one in Africa.

HartRAO will invest heavily in new equipment over the next three years. The SKA, an International GPS Service station, and a high-performance microwave telescope are some of the equipment needed to effectively continue the work of the facility in future.

South African Institute for Aquatic Biodiversity

The SAIAB is a leading centre for the study of fish and biodiversity in Africa and the surrounding seas. The Institute is responsible for the national collection of fish (more than 450 000 specimens) and promotes knowledge and awareness of fish and aquatic conservation. The collection catalogue includes a computerised database, a library and information services.

In 2002, the South African Coelacanth Conservation and Genome Resource Programme was launched at Sodwana Bay. The SAIAB co-ordinates the research project, which promotes co-operation in marine biodiversity conservation, environmental education and capacity-building. Countries such as Mozambique, Tanzania and Madagascar are participating in the Programme. The International Coelacanth Conference was held in South Africa in October 2003.

The Institute's educational programmes include illustrated lectures and guided tours of, among others, the experimental fish farm.

Exciting developments at the SAIAB include the expansion of the Coelacanth Programme beyond South Africa, the setting up of incubator groups through the Coelacanth Programme, and the development of a cryogenic tissue-storage facility.

iThemba LABS

iThemba LABS provides modern research facilities to users in science, medicine and industry. iThemba LABS has established itself as a major commercial centre for radiation medicine and is forging strategic partnerships with the private and public sectors to leverage capital, skills and the expertise required for an initiative of this magnitude.

By establishing a major oncology centre, iThemba is creating more space for training in physics and radiation sciences. The Major Radiation Medicine Centre (MRMC), as the proposed oncology centre is known, was endorsed by leading international oncologists during a visit to iThemba LABS during 2002.

The MRMC will become the centrepiece of cancer control in southern Africa and an internationally recognised centre of excellence in cancer treatment, research and training. iThemba LABS will invest in equip-

Science and technology

ment for therapy, while initial 'seed money' funding of R10 million is required for the MRMC project.

A good example of iThemba LABS boosting its income sources is its radionuclide sales, which achieved record levels of over R6,5 million in 2002. The income generated from such initiatives is ploughed back into research, infrastructure and HRD in radiation science.

South African Astronomical Observatory and Southern African Large Telescope

The SAAO in Cape Town and Sutherland has seven telescopes at Sutherland used for optical and infra-red observations. It provides an international facility for research in astronomy in Africa and educates and informs the community.

The US$30-million SALT, an 11-m optical telescope, is currently under construction at Sutherland and will be commissioned during 2004. SALT will be managed by the SAAO on behalf of the SALT Foundation, an international consortium with partners from South Africa, Germany, New Zealand, Poland, the UK and USA. It is being funded by the five international partners and the South African Government, which has committed R50 million over five years.

SALT will collect light and infra-red rays with a mirror mosaic of 91 hexagonal segments, each 1 m wide, making it the largest single optical telescope in the southern hemisphere. During 2002, the SAAO was extensively involved in the establishment of a postgraduate astronomy/space-science programme. The completion of the SALT in 2004 makes it imperative that the next generation of South African and African astronomers and astrophysicists is produced and appropriately prepared. The scholarship programme in astronomy and astrophysics is an initiative designed to meet this challenge. It is focused on accelerating the development of astronomers and astrophysicists from historically disadvantaged communities.

A SALT Collateral Benefits Plan was designed to maximise benefits from the investment of public funds in the construction and operation of the project. The main thrusts are industrial empowerment, educational empowerment, public outreach, direct educational benefits, science education visitor centres, and SALT as an African facility.

Hermanus Magnetic Observatory

The HMO is of strategic importance as a player in space and earth sciences, as well as geospatial information.

The HMO comprises the:
- Space Physics Group, which conducts fundamental and applied research of the earth's magnetic field and space environment
- Geomagnetism Group, responsible for the continuous monitoring of the geomagnetic field and providing models and information
- Technology Group, which provides quality-controlled magnetic-field and sensor-related services and carries out commercial contract work
- Education and Science Awareness Group, which focuses particularly on school children.

In November 2002, the HMO was awarded accreditation as an Aircraft Processing and Testing Organisation, as well as an Aviation Training Organisation, by the South African Civil Aviation Authority. This opens doors to the wider aviation fraternity in southern Africa. At present, the HMO is the only local organisation with the infrastructure to do magnetic compass calibrations, aircraft compass swing base surveys and magnetic-effect tests on avionics equipment.

Agricultural Research Council

The ARC is a statutory parastatal body established in terms of the Agricultural Research Act, 1990 (Act 86 of 1990). It is committed to the promotion of agriculture and related sectors through research, and technology development and transfer.

Through its wide network of research institutes and experimental farms, the ARC provides a strong scientific base and a broadly distributed technology-transfer capacity for the entire agricultural industry in South Africa. In support of national and household food security, ARC research empowers both commercial and resource-poor farmers.

Farmers are provided with appropriate technologies to improve production. Training of farmers and agricultural extension staff in new technologies is an integral component of the ARC's activities.

Rural development

The ARC collaborates with government and the Independent Development Trust in the development of government's Integrated Sustainable Rural Development Strategy (ISRDS).

The ARC advises the M-17 group of Ministers under the chairpersonship of the Deputy President on the development of a planning tool, based on geographic information systems (GIS).

To share information and assess the use-options of resources in a particular area, the South Africa Integrated Spatial Information System is being developed to provide a user-friendly framework for informed decision-making.

The Agricultural Georeferenced Information System (AGIS) was launched during the WSSD. This marked the establishment of an official information system for agriculture in South Africa.

The AGIS is cross-sectional and delivers information for natural resource use and management to provide decision-support systems for effective planning and management to ensure sustainable development.

The organisational website is also linked to AGIS, which was developed by the ARC in collaboration with the national Department of Agriculture and the nine provincial Departments of Agriculture. Agricultural information is made available to all users via the Internet and other electronic media.

The impact and wide scope of the ARC's sustainable rural development thrusts are evident in all provinces. The ARC empowers people through research, information and appropriate training that address economic and social challenges.

ARC-generated technologies also underpin SMMEs that aim to create new job opportunities through agribusiness. Its research impacts on agriculture and related disciplines such as applied S&T, health and nutrition, food safety, education, the environment and natural-resource conservation.

Partnerships

The ARC interfaces with national, provincial and local governments as well as various agricultural unions and farmers' associations in South Africa. Apart from research collaboration with these stakeholders, the ARC also partners other science councils.

By mid-2003, the ARC had 36 competitive bidding projects on which institutions collaborated with a range of local, regional and international research partners – six Innovation Fund projects; seven THRIP projects; one EU project; 11 projects funded by donor and international organisations; six regionally funded projects, mainly in association with the Consultative Group for International Agricultural Research research centres; and five binational projects, one each with Poland, India and Sweden, and two with Hungary.

At a regional level, the ARC is involved in the agricultural research activities of the SADC, with links to other African role-players in the Special Programme for African Agricultural Research.

The ARC is active in over 65 regional networks and has 137 research projects with international partners, involving one or more countries.

The ARC is also active in international collaboration, especially with universities in the USA, UK, Europe, Australia, New Zealand and Africa. It has Memoranda of Understanding with numerous scientific role-players in other countries.

Science and technology

The ARC's Institutes have localised research and demonstration trials at about 40 sites. These include strategic research farms and satellite stations located within some provincial Departments of Agriculture.

ARC-Institute for Soil, Climate and Water

This Institute in Pretoria, Gauteng, promotes the characterisation, sustainable utilisation and protection of natural resources.

Research activities cover soil science, agrometeorology, water utilisation and analytical services.

ARC-Institute for Agricultural Engineering

Situated in Pretoria, the Institute is active in agricultural mechanisation, resource conservation, farm structures, irrigation, alternative energy, aquaculture and product-processing.

Research is directed at a wide range of clients, from subsistence farmers using animal traction to commercial farmers and manufacturers requiring scientific performance evaluations of advanced equipment. Innovative energy sources and applications are developed for rural areas.

The Agricultural Research Council (ARC) developed an improved method for combating the foot-and-mouth disease (FMD) virus and preparing the FMD vaccine. The ARC patented the method in both India and Brazil. The ARC patent for a vaccine for Newcastle disease is limited to South Africa. Two other patents in the pipeline are related to a lactate-utilising bacterium for the prevention of lactic acidosis in ruminants, and a new dosing system.

One of the ARC's largest contributions involves the breeding of new plant cultivars that are better adapted to South African production conditions than imported cultivars or races.

By mid-2003, the ARC held registered plant-breeder's rights on 291 cultivars of the major plant types commercially produced in South Africa. Export figures over the last 20 years indicate the growth in production and international demand for South African cultivars.

ARC-Plant Protection Research Institute

The ARC-Plant Protection Research Institute in Pretoria concentrates on national agricultural and environmental problems. It is committed to the promotion of economic and environmentally acceptable pest control. Research focuses on biosystematics, ecology and epidemiology of vertebrates, as well as fungi, and pathogenic and useful bacteria and viruses.

The Institute researches the control of pests and invasive plants through effective pesticide management, as well as biological and integrated control strategies. A variety of services is provided.

The Institute also houses the Plant Genetic Resource Unit.

ARC-Grain Crops Institute

This Institute, situated in Potchefstroom, North West, is responsible for research into the improvement and cultivation of grain crops such as maize, sorghum and millet, as well as oil-and-protein seeds such as sunflower, ground-nuts, soya beans, dry beans, cowpeas, sweet white lupin and bambara. Research activities involve plant-breeding, evaluation of cultivars, grain quality, plant physiology and other production factors.

ARC-Small Grain Institute

The ARC-Small Grain Institute in Bethlehem, Free State, concentrates on the improvement and cultivation of small grain crops such as barley, wheat, oats, triticale and rye. Research activities include plant-breeding, evaluation of cultivars, grain quality, plant physiology, tillage, weed science, plant pathology, entomology and yield potential.

ARC-Institute for Industrial Crops

This Institute in Rustenburg, North West, is involved in all fundamental and applied research in the interest of the tobacco and cotton industries. Research is also conducted on other fibre crops such as hemp, sisal and flax that have potential as new crops in rural areas.

ARC-Institute for Tropical and Subtropical Crops

The ARC-Institute for Tropical and Subtropical Crops in Nelspruit, Mpumalanga, is responsible for research into all aspects of the cultivation of tropical and subtropical fruits.

Other crops on which production research is conducted include tea, coffee, spices such as ginger, and pecan, macadamia and cashew nuts. Lesser-known exotic crops being evaluated are pitanga, feijoa, annona types, carambola and jaboticaba.

ARC-Roodeplaat Vegetable and Ornamental Plant Institute

Situated outside Pretoria, this Institute concentrates on a wide range of horticultural crops. Research is conducted on commercial vegetables such as onions, potatoes, tomatoes and sweet potatoes. Traditional and indigenous vegetables receiving attention include amaranthus, cassava, plectranthus, Zulu round potato, pigeonpeas, cowpeas and bambara.

Research on the production and development of ornamentals and indigenous flora such as *fynbos*, woody ornamentals and bulbs has led to a new growth industry.

ARC-Infruitec/Nietvoorbij

ARC-Infruitec/Nietvoorbij in Stellenbosch, Western Cape, is responsible for research on the cultivation and post-harvest technology of deciduous fruit.

Other assigned crops are berry fruits, tree-nut crops, *rooibos* tea, honeybush tea, dates, olives, kiwi fruit and hops. It is also responsible for research on the cultivation of table, raisin and wine grapes, as well as on the production of wine and brandy.

ARC-Animal Improvement Institute

The ARC-Animal Improvement Institute at Irene, outside Pretoria, provides the livestock industry with technologies for the improved quality of animals.

It has established genetic and physiological methods to identify and study superior breeding material to improve the efficiency of the national herd.

ARC-Animal Nutrition and Animal Products Institute

Situated at Irene near Pretoria, this Institute develops environment-friendly technologies to promote animal production through improved nutrition.

Research is conducted on beef and dairy cattle, sheep, pigs, goats and poultry. The Institute also evaluates technologies to enhance the quality of meat and dairy products.

ARC-Onderstepoort Veterinary Institute

The ARC-Onderstepoort Veterinary Institute, north of Pretoria, is responsible for the prevention and control of animal diseases. It also provides a public health service with regard to animal products such as milk, meat and eggs.

The Institute conducts research on specialised diagnostics, parasitology, toxicology and related disciplines. Various vaccines and other biological products are developed and produced. The Institute also houses a high-security facility for research into infectious diseases such as foot-and-mouth disease and African swine fever. It serves as a regional centre for diagnostic services, advice and training.

ARC-Range and Forage Institute

The Institute, situated in Pretoria, focuses on the development of holistic and integrated land-use strategies. It provides guidelines for sustainable livestock and rangeland management systems.

Council for Scientific and Industrial Research (CSIR)

The CSIR is the largest community and industry-directed scientific and technological research, development and implementation organisation in Africa.

Science and technology

It delivers scientific and technological services in areas where industry, parastatals or government clients require support, as well as innovative leadership in the development of new technologies which can be further developed and exploited by the private sector.

Approximately 7 000 clients are served every year, and 60% of the CSIR's income is funded externally.

The CSIR's functions are centred in eight market-orientated business units:
- Food, Biotechnology and Fine Chemicals Technology
- Building and Construction Technology
- Defence Technology
- Water, Environment and Forestry Technology
- ICT
- Manufacturing and Materials Technology
- Mining Technology
- Roads and Transport Technology.

The CSIR-based South African National Cleaner Production Centre (NCPC), an initiative financed jointly by the Swiss and Austrian Governments to enhance the competitiveness and productive capacity of the national industry, through the adoption of cleaner production techniques and the transfer and development of environmentally acceptable technologies, was officially inaugurated in February 2003. The Centre is hosted at the CSIR's Process Technology Centre, which is part of the CSIR Manufacturing and Materials Technology business unit. The NCPC was launched during the WSSD.

The activities of the business units are aimed at:
- supporting the technological competitiveness of the South African industry in both the formal and informal sectors
- providing technological solutions to improve the quality of life of urban and rural communities
- providing scientific and technological support for decision-making in the private and public sectors.

The CSIR focuses on team work, building relationships, forging strategic alliances and working with consortia. It is strongly committed to serving the national imperatives of crime prevention, HIV/AIDS, HRD, job creation, regional integration, rural development and urban renewal. In these endeavours, it draws on skills from across the organisation and collaborates with partners in science councils and other agencies, including local, provincial and national government.

The CSIR is empowered by the Measuring Units and National Measuring Standards Act, 1973 (Act 76 of 1973), as amended by the Measuring Units and National Measuring Standards Amendment Act, 1998 (Act 24 of 1998), to maintain all national measurement standards through its National Metrology Laboratory.

Internationally, the CSIR works with 18 African countries, has co-operation agreements with major R&D organisations and companies, and is a registered consultant with the World Bank, the African Development Bank, United Nations Development Programme and others.

The CSIR is well-positioned to provide services to Africa in support of the New Partnership for Africa's Development (NEPAD). The combination of its scientific and technical expertise, its understanding of the African continent, and its developing strategic-relationship network with key African private, public and official development-assistance sectors, make the organisation an ideal partner to support Africa's economic development through specific interventions. These are primarily aimed at the environment, ICTs, infrastructural services and manufacturing. The CSIR also supports the utilisation of indigenous knowledge systems as well as capacity-building to secure Africa's position in the knowledge economy.

Long-term relationships with multinational companies and knowledge-intensive organisations have resulted in five-year compound growth of almost 26% in international external income.

The CSIR and the South African San Council reached an agreement in March 2003 to share the benefits that are anticipated to arise from the potential commercial success of a CSIR patent that followed the R&D of a new technology relating to the Hoodia plant. Clinical trials continue internationally on the product (dubbed P57), which – if successful – will form the basis of a new obesity treatment.

In terms of the agreement, the CSIR will pay the San 8% of all milestone payments it receives from its licensee, UK-based Phytopharm plc, as well as 6% of all royalties that the CSIR receives once the drug is commercially available. Milestone payments are subject to agreed technical-performance targets of P57 during its clinical development over the next three to four years, and royalties are based on sales, which are not set to commence before 2008. This benefit-sharing model ensures that the San will receive equitable benefits if the drug is successfully commercialised, and is based on established international benefit-sharing models for the pharmaceutical industry.

The potential income stream will be deposited into a San Hoodia Benefit Sharing Trust, established by the CSIR and the San.

Mintek

Mintek, South Africa's national mineral research organisation, was established in 1934 to ensure the sustainability and growth of the minerals industry through technology development and transfer. This role has expanded internationally, and today Mintek is one of the world's leading technology organisations specialising in mineral processing, extractive metallurgy and related areas. Working closely with industry and other R&D institutions, Mintek provides service-test work, process development, consulting and innovative products to clients on six continents.

Mintek is an autonomous statutory organisation and reports to the Minister of Minerals and Energy. About 37% of the annual budget of R220 million is funded by the State, with the balance provided by contract R&D, sales of services and products, technology-licensing agreements, and joint-venture operating companies. Mintek has some 500 permanent staff members, over half of whom are scientists, engineers and other technical R&D personnel.

Mintek's objectives are to research, develop and transfer novel and improved techniques to industry for processing, extracting, refining, and utilising minerals and mineral products to:
- enhance the competitiveness of South Africa's minerals industry in the global market
- promote job creation, economic growth and regional development
- assist local mining and engineering companies to expand internationally.

Specific goals include:
- promoting increased beneficiation of South Africa's minerals and mineral commodities by developing competitive and innovative processing technology and equipment
- strengthening South Africa's international position as a supplier of mineral technologies, capital goods and services
- developing regional strategies for the mineral processing sector, concentrating on value-addition, capacity-building and broad-based development.

Mintek achieves its objectives in the following ways:
- providing essential services (information, consulting and experimental)
- increasing the competitiveness of industry by developing appropriate technology to cut costs and improve recoveries
- developing 'breakthrough' process technologies and novel uses for metals and their products
- marketing its commercial products and technologies to industry
- establishing strategic partnerships and joint ventures
- participating in regional development initiatives and SADC activities and projects
- maintaining and expanding international scientific links

Science and technology

- developing the HR potential of the region through educational and training activities.

Mintek offers a complete range of process development services, from preliminary bench-scale investigations to large-scale piloting and integrated flowsheet development in support of bankable feasibility studies. Engineering design, plant construction and commissioning are carried out in conjunction with international partners. Comprehensive laboratory and piloting facilities for sample preparation, milling, flotation, physical separation, smelting, leaching, pressure leaching, and metal recovery and purification are supported by internationally accredited analytical laboratory and mineralogical services.

To ensure focus and market orientation, Mintek's R&D activities are grouped into programmes that are based largely on industry structure:
- The Gold Industry Programme focuses on developing and introducing improved technologies, such as biotechnology and ion-exchange processes, to simplify processing and increase recoveries, particularly from ores that are difficult to treat. A major joint venture with industry and other research groups is exploring new industrial uses of gold.
- The Platinum-Group Metals (PGMs) Industry Programme aims to increase the cost-effectiveness of PGM production and stimulate industrial demand for the PGMs.
- The Ferrous Metals Industry Programme develops products and technical services to increase the cost-effectiveness of steel, stainless steel and ferro-alloy production, as well as improved alloys.
- The Non-Ferrous Metals Industry Programme includes the processing of aluminium, cobalt, copper, lead, magnesium, nickel and zinc. A major emphasis is on the introduction of cleaner technologies.
- The Industrial Minerals Industry Programme includes a major R&D effort towards the beneficiation of titaniferous raw materials, which constitute one of the country's most significant mineral resources. Mintek's research into waste management and environmental problems also fall under this programme.

Promoting industrial growth

Mintek is promoting a number of major new industrial projects based on mineral beneficiation, and utilising both existing and newly developed technologies. These include the production of hot briquetted iron from Sishen ore fines utilising natural gas, the recovery of PGMs from chromite tailings, the production of ferronickel and electrolytic manganese dioxide, and the establishment of a local magnesium industry using a novel thermal-production route being developed in conjunction with industry partners.

Regional development

Mintek carries out surveys, evaluations and commodity and market studies to support initiatives by governmental, international, regional or industry associations. It also identifies and evaluates potential development projects, assesses and provides technology, and conducts feasibility studies. Mintek supports the activities of the SADC Mining Co-ordination Unit and was closely involved in developing the economic growth strategy for NEPAD.

Mintek is a founder member of the National Steering Committee (NSC) of Service-Providers to small mines, which assists artisanal and small-scale miners on matters such as mineral rights, better technology, raising finance for equipment, and marketing. A Technology Demonstration Centre, Zenzele, established in co-operation with the EU and the Department of Science and Technology, assists with the implementation of mineral-beneficiation techniques, hosts workshops and seminars, and assesses likely deposits for small-scale exploitation.

Environment

Mintek continues to focus on the develop-

South Africa Yearbook 2003/04

ment of environmentally responsible technologies for the recovery and recycling of metals from metallurgical residues. A major programme is in place to monitor cyanide species after discharge in various locations around gold plants, from both an environmental and a processing point of view. Mintek's environmental technologies and services are provided to industry via a co-operative agreement with an established environmental consulting group.

Education

There is a shortage of engineers and scientists within Mintek's field of expertise in South Africa.

The undergraduate bursary scheme assists in supplying Mintek with a steady stream of suitable new graduates and also in fulfilling Mintek's commitment to promote education in the mineral-related engineering disciplines. The postgraduate bursary scheme is a source of researchers at MSc, MTech and PhD levels.

The EngTrain and TechTrain programmes focus on university and university of technology students who require in-service training to complete their qualifications. Mintek continues to support pre-tertiary activities to encourage young people to pursue careers in S&T. The two primary efforts in this regard are Minquiz, the annual national competition for secondary schools, and the Edumap Programme at the College of Education, University of the Witwatersrand, which affords young people from disadvantaged educational backgrounds the opportunity to prepare for tertiary education in engineering and commercial subjects.

Mintek's Adopt-a-School initiative, from which Kwadeba High School in Soweto benefits, was launched in 2001. Mintek supplies surplus laboratory equipment, and assists in ensuring that the school's science laboratories are functioning. Winter tutorials in mathematics and science are organised during school vacations. In 2002, the school's matriculation pass rate was 81%.

Human Sciences Research Council (HSRC)

The HSRC of South Africa is a statutory body established in 1968. It supports development nationally, in the SADC, and in Africa. It primarily conducts large-scale, policy-relevant, social-scientific projects for public-sector users, non-governmental organisations and international development agencies.

Over the last couple of years, the HSRC has undergone major restructuring, aligning its research activities and structures with South Africa's national-development priorities, notably poverty reduction through economic development, skills enhancement, job creation, the elimination of discrimination and inequalities, and effective service delivery.

It also seeks to contribute to the R&D Strategy of the Department of Science and Technology, especially through its mission to focus on the contribution of S&T in addressing poverty.

With its new structures and greatly expanded research complement of more than 130 top researchers and 100 support staff in five different centres, the HSRC is well-equipped to respond flexibly and comprehensively to current and emerging needs. Its 10 multidisciplinary research programmes, focused on user needs, are spread across five centres in different parts of South Africa.

Research programmes

The HSRC is responsible for the following research programmes:

Assessment Technology and Education Evaluation (ATEE)

The ATEE provides assessment, evaluation expertise and information aimed at improving the development and utilisation of resources (human and physical) in the education and training system, with the primary focus on schools and the industrial sector.

The programme focuses on school reform and change; science, mathematics and technology education; psychological assessment and methodology; modelling; and analysis. Future plans include addressing language-policy and implementation issues.

Democracy and Governance (D&G)

The D&G focuses on the two broad areas of democratic consolidation and local-government development and delivery. Projects falling under the ambit of democratic consolidation include work on electoral systems, intergovernmental relations and civil society, good governance, and issues relating to human rights and non-racialism.

Future projects in this area will include a democratic auditing project, intended as a response to NEPAD initiatives such as the African Peer Review Mechanism. Projects planned for 2003/04 deal with issues such as community-based information systems, determinants of non-payment of service delivery in the Tshwane metropolitan area, service delivery to farm workers in the Free State, and municipal land management.

Employment and Economic Policy Research (EEPR)

The EEPR focuses on themes that will contribute to the development of know-how in constructing an employment-planning framework for policy co-ordination.

The focus is not only on the labour market. The ultimate purpose is to enable government to address the growing crisis of unemployment and underemployment that are contributing to unacceptable levels of poverty and inequality in the middle-income economy.

The research programme has established a number of strategic partnerships that will add value to the work undertaken by the programme. Research projects in this programme are strongly aligned with the National Human Resource Development Strategy, as well as the Integrated Manufacturing Strategy of the Department of Trade and Industry.

Current and completed research projects in the EEPR address strategic aspects of sustainable development and quality of life, including public-private partnerships, SMME development, small-scale mining and the jewellery sector. Central research themes in the EEPR programme include labour-market analysis and HIV/AIDS in industry.

Human Resource Development

HRD undertakes research on the supply-side of strategic HRD planning by focusing on the provision of post-school education and training, particularly in the further and higher education and training bands, including public and private institutions.

Research on the demand-side examines the characteristics of skills in demand, those in short supply and those that will be needed in future. Linked to this is the research on the State's new science and industrial policies, aiming to identify the implications of new knowledge and innovation requirements on the education and training system. The programme also aims to develop appropriate analytical models to enable the matching of demand- and supply-side perspectives without falling short of the limitation of previous models of HR planning.

Integrated Rural and Regional Development (IRRD)

The IRRD emphasises poverty reduction as an overarching research theme. A multidisciplinary and multi-institutional task team prepares research proposals to support the mission *S&T for Poverty Reduction*, while the Southern African Regional Poverty Network provides a platform for policy-relevant discussions among key stakeholders and decision-makers in the region.

Other areas covered in the IRRD research programme include agrarian reform, rural non-farm development and regional resource flows. The programme also focuses on priorities articulated in the agendas of NEPAD, the WSSD and the ISRDS.

Knowledge Management (KM)

The KM provides key research input to the national R&D Strategy, with particular reference to strategic planning and capacity-development issues.

The programme has three main thrusts:
- NSI, which entails both policy and evaluation studies of the way that the system operates
- Government and Knowledge Economy, which considers the way information is managed and used across government, including the necessary enabling and regulatory environment
- Becoming an Innovative Research Organisation that considers how the work processes of the HSRC must and will change.

Social Aspects of HIV/AIDS and Health (SAHA)

The SAHA focuses on studying key socio-cultural, political, economic and demographic determinants that increase or reduce vulnerability to HIV-infection, through facilitating or hindering change in risky behaviour; enable or retard progress towards care; and prevent or enable mitigation of the impact of HIV/AIDS in South Africa and the SADC region. The public-health component of the programme focuses on health-system issues necessary for disease control within a social development context. The SAHA research programme has succeeded in attracting substantial funding for research, networking and grant-management purposes.

Following a commissioned situation analysis of HIV/AIDS in six countries, the SAHA made recommendations on appropriate, co-ordinated and research-based intervention programmes in the SADC region, focusing on orphans and vulnerable children. The HSRC has subsequently been appointed to manage a multi-year, multimillion-Rand research-based intervention programme.

Surveys, Analysis, Mapping and Modelling (SAMM)

The SAMM is a cross-cutting entity that brings together the HSRC's capacity in surveys, quantitative and qualitative analyses, GIS, statistical and econometric modelling, and data management. It assists other research programmes to meet their development research needs in a flexible and user-driven way. The HSRC's survey work has gained a clear competitive advantage following the strategic investment in the development of a master sample, funded by a grant from the Swedish Development Co-operation.

Social, Cohesion and Integration is a science and humanities research programme devoted to the promotion of excellence, leadership and public discourse in the arts, sports, religion, media, history and sciences. The programme is pioneering debates on the significance of the international Human Genome initiative for Africa. A major international conference on the human genome was held in March 2003.

Cross-cutting research initiatives

The majority of research projects housed in the 10 research programmes are multidisciplinary, multi-year projects. The interdisciplinary nature of these projects encourages collaboration between the different research programmes, as well as with researchers and research institutions outside the HSRC.

The output of the HRSC's research projects includes reports for users, occasional papers and scholarly articles in peer-reviewed journals or books. These are disseminated in print through an online bookshop, and published electronically on the HSRC's website *www.hsrcpublishers.ac.za*

Medical Research Council (MRC)

The MRC was established in 1969 by an Act of Parliament. Its mission is to improve the nation's health status and quality of life, through relevant and excellent research aimed at promoting equity and development.

The MRC is an autonomous body, but reports to the national Department of Health.

It receives 60% of its budget from the Department of Science and Technology. Its Head Office is in Cape Town, with provincial offices in Pretoria and Durban.

The MRC's research activities are aligned with the health priorities of the nation, in line with the national S&T Imperatives and the health priorities defined by the Department of Health under the philosophy of Essential National Health Research. Activities are grouped into the following six national programmes:

National Programme for Research in Molecules to Disease

This group undertakes research on human and microbial genetics, genomics, bioinformatics, cell and molecular biology, tissue engineering, oesophageal cancer, molecular hepatology, microbacteriology, and liver and bone disease.

National Programme for Health Systems and Policy Research

The scientists in this Programme conduct research on health systems, clinical epidemiology, biostatistics, health policy, burden of disease, and telemedicine.

National Programme for Infection and Immunity Research

The research units in this Programme are involved in research on tuberculosis, malaria, immunology of infectious diseases, diarrhoeal diseases, inflammation and amoebiasis, genital ulcer diseases, respiration and meningeal pathogens, and South African traditional medicines.

It also incorporates the MRC National HIV/AIDS Lead Programme, whose divisions co-ordinate the South African AIDS Vaccine Initiative; various aspects of biomedical research, including mother-to-child transmision and microbicides; and prevention of transmission through behavioural change. (See Chapter 13: *Health*.)

National Programme for Non-Communicable Disease Research

This group undertakes research on heart disease (both laboratory, clinical and public health research), nutritional intervention, diabetes, crime, violence and injury, anxiety and stress disorders, dental issues, medical imaging, chronic diseases of lifestyle and cancer epidemiology.

National Programme for Environment and Development Research

In this entity, research is undertaken on health promotion, health and development, exercise and sports science, occupational and environmental health, alcohol and drug abuse, and technology transfer.

National Programme for Women and Child Health Research

The MRC's 47 research units within these six national programmes employ over 300 scientists engaged in 600 research projects, supported by 200 support staff members.

This Programme undertakes research on many aspects of women's health, including high blood pressure during pregnancy, healthcare strategies in maternal and infant health, perinatal mortality, gender and health, mineral metabolism and nutritional intervention.

Twenty-seven of the units are situated at medical schools and research institutes – six of these in historically disadvantaged institutions. The MRC also funds 350 short-term researchers at academic institutions throughout South Africa.

It has a new research-grant management system, using electronic databases and software to ensure equitable and efficient disbursement of health-research funding.

The MRC is becoming increasingly Africanised in terms of its research and organisational philosophy, its gender and ethnic profile, and its collaboration with other African countries. It is also becoming increasingly internationalised through collaboration with most of the world's leading health-research agencies, including the National Institute of Health and Centre for Disease Control and Prevention in the USA, the Gates Foundation, the World Health Organisation, the Wellcome Trust, the Pasteur Institute, the Kenya Medical Research Institute, and the Blair Institute in Zimbabwe.

It works with national and provincial Departments of Health to ensure its research findings feed into policy formulation and healthcare practice.

South African National Health Knowledge Network

The South African National Health Knowledge Network was established in 1999 at the MRC with funding from the Government's Innovation Fund.

It operates under the tradename SA HealthInfo and is available on the Internet (www.sahealthinfo.org), providing a one-stop interactive forum or resource for quality-controlled and evidence-based health-research information.

This Internet portal caters for three types of audiences: health researchers and healthcare professionals, health consumers and related organisations, and policy-makers. It also serves as a gateway to other trusted health resources.

A new portal for HIV/AIDS in southern Africa, www.afroaidsinfo.org, was launched on World AIDS Day 2002 and serves South African researchers, health professionals, educators, policy-makers and the general public. The project has secured external funding from the XIII International AIDS Conference organisers and BMS Secure the Future. The HIV/AIDS portal is endorsed by the Department of Health.

In response to the needs of researchers, and in line with government's biotechnology focus, as well as NEPAD, the MRC has initiated a process to establish an African Biotechnology Information Centre in collaboration with a consortium of universities.

The Knowledge Network also provides a unique access point to online full-text publications.

Council for Geoscience (CGS)

The CGS is a statutory body established in terms of the Geoscience Act, 1993 (Act 100 of 1993), to manage the functions of the Geological Survey of South Africa. The main functions of the CGS are:
- the systematic documentation of the surface of the earth within the borders of South Africa; the compilation of geological, geophysical, geochemical and other geoscientific information; and the publication of this information in the form of maps and documents
- geoscientific research on rocks, minerals, ores, fossils, etc. in South Africa, and the publication of research-results in national and international journals
- the collection and conservation of all geoscientific information and data on South Africa in national collections and electronic databases
- the supply of geoscientific services and advice to the national and provincial governments, to ensure informed decisions regarding the optimal and efficient use of the earth's surface.

The objectives of the CGS are to:
- minimise the geological and geoscientific investment risk for national and international entrepreneurs in the South African mining sector (the quality of available geological information, which is known as the 'geological risk grading', contributes to about 61% of the investment risk in any country)
- supply the country with basic geoscience data to establish a safe, cost-effective physical infrastructure without sterilising valuable mineral resources
- supply basic knowledge to ensure safe, cost-effective and environmentally acceptable urbanisation and housing development

Science and technology

- carry out research on raw material needed to clothe, transport, feed and provide shelter for the nation.

To accomplish these functions and objectives, the CGS maintains a specialised workforce, consisting of earth scientists supplemented by technical, support and administrative staff at its headquarters in Pretoria, as well as branch offices in the nine provinces.

To perform its functions, the following national institutions are maintained by the CGS:
- The National Geoscience Library in Pretoria is probably the most comprehensive geoscience library on the African continent. It includes the National Geoscience Map Library, which contains a collection of South African and African geoscience maps.
- The National Core Library contains a representative stratigraphic borehole core collection, representing most of the lithological units located within the borders of South Africa. This collection is housed at Donkerhoek, east of Pretoria.
- The Geoscience Museum in Pretoria contains a unique collection of minerals and fossils, catering for the earth-science education of the public, especially schoolchildren.
- An extensive laboratory to analyse rock and soil samples, using various specialised techniques.

The geoscience information and services provided by the CGS are particularly important for sustainable development. In South Africa's arid region, the management of groundwater resources (both the quantity and quality thereof) is aimed at providing enough clean water to communities.

A new map series, the 1:50 000 geotechnical map series, covering the rapidly developing areas of South Africa, can be used to locate land that is geotechnically suitable for development, and free of geohazards such as sinkholes. These maps also show the locations of building-material resources.

Through its membership of the NSC, the CGS helps mining entrepreneurs, particularly those from previously disadvantaged groups, to exploit South Africa's mineral resources in a cost-effective and environmentally friendly way.

The CGS plays a leading role in the SADC and has been chairing the Geological Subcommittee for several years. Several geoscience publications covering the region have been produced by this Subcommittee.

An exciting service is provided by two microlight aircraft capable of performing high-resolution aerial geophysical surveys.

In addition to its national responsibilities, the CGS is also active internationally, mainly in Africa. Geological and metallogenic maps of, among others, Angola, the Democratic Republic of the Congo, Mozambique, Gabon and Morocco have been produced.

A map indicating seismic activity in sub-Saharan Africa has also been produced, as well as a publication on the gold deposits in the SADC region.

A digital edition of the Metallogenic Map of South Africa, at a scale of 1:1 000 000, was recently released. A metallurgic map of Africa, at a scale of 1:5 000 000, is being printed, and a digital version of this map will also be available in CD-ROM format.

The CD-ROM supplies information on all known mineral deposits and occurrences in South Africa.

South African Bureau of Standards (SABS)

The core business of the SABS is the production, maintenance and dissemination of standards. In terms of the Standards Act, 1993 (Act 29 of 1993), the objectives of the SABS include:
- promoting standardisation in industry and commerce
- undertaking educational work in connection with standardisation
- administering compulsory standards on behalf of the State

- collaborating with relevant international organisations to protect and advance South Africa's interests
- assisting government departments, public bodies, and provincial and local government in the preparation of any specification or code of practice they require.

The SABS provides standardisation services that improve South Africa's competitiveness. It consists of Standards, Regulatory, R&D and the Design Institute. It is further split into SABS Holdings, which comprises seven revenue-generating companies. The support rendered to government includes testing certification for local manufacturers and their products destined for overseas markets, to avoid double testing.

The Certification Strategic Business Unit of the SABS runs a product certification scheme; several quality-system certification schemes, such as the SABS ISO 9000 Quality-Management Certification Scheme and SABS ISO 14001 Environmental-Management Certification Scheme; and a consignment inspection service.

The extensive state-of-the-art testing capability of the SABS forms the backbone of the organisation's commercial activities and contributes a significant portion of turnover. Goods can be inspected, tested and analysed against private, voluntary or compulsory standards, while precision-measuring and scientific equipment can be tested and calibrated for clients in both the public and private sectors.

Consequently, most of the 66 testing laboratories within the SABS are accredited by the South African National Accreditation System for the competent performance of tests in accordance with ISO/IEC Guide 25, the general requirements for the competence of calibration and testing laboratories.

The SABS is a founding member of the independent South African Quality Institute, which was established in 1991.

By means of its focused training programmes, the SABS actively assists industry in creating an overall awareness of quality and the environment. It provides a countrywide service in training quality-system and environmental auditors.

The core business units of the SABS are financed by monies allocated for that purpose under the science vote and administered by the Department of Science and Technology. Inspections and tests, which are carried out for the private sector, industry, national, provincial and local government, as well as the certification of products and systems, are funded on a commercial basis by fees charged for services rendered.

The Regulatory Divisions' prime objective is to align South Africa's requirements with international requirements, and to become actively involved in the creation of international standards. The Division has jurisdiction in the following areas:
- legal metrology: it ensures consumer protection in the area of measurement as it controls the accuracy of measuring instruments and the quantity of contents in prepacked goods
- automotive: the Division sees to the safety of the public by ensuring that vehicles meet legal requirements
- electrotechnical: the Division is primarily concerned with the safety of the public in electrotechnical fields by ensuring that they meet legal requirements
- food and associated industries: it ensures that fish products and canned-meat products are safe for human consumption.

Other scientific and research organisations and structures

Biotechnology Partnership for Africa's Development (Biopad)

Biopad was initiated early in 2003 by a community of biotechnologists and professionals as a means to put South Africa among the world leaders in the application of biotechnology.

Sasol

Although the Sasol Group is best known for its petrol, diesel, kerosene, liquid petroleum gas, power paraffin, illuminating paraffin, fuel oils and gas, it is also a major producer of ethylene, propylene, ammonia, phenols, sulphur, road tar, pitch, creosote, alcohols, ketones, solvent blends, alpha olefins, fertilisers, explosives and waxes.

Sasol Technology's R&D Division is responsible for the R&D function of the Sasol Group.

Continuous R&D in recent years has enabled Sasol to launch two major, more cost-effective technological innovations: the Sasol Advanced Synthol Process and the Sasol Slurry Phase Distillate (SSPD) Process. The SSPD process technology evolved from Sasol's extensive expertise in the field of low-temperature FischerTropsch process technology.

Besides the production of high-quality and more environmentally friendly diesel, the proprietary technology can also manufacture high-quality kerosene and naphtha from natural gas.

Iscor

The technology arm of the minerals and metals company Iscor Limited, ITEC, provides technical and research support for the company.

Areas of operation include minerals beneficiation, new extraction methods and high-temperature metallurgical processes. ITEC is also involved in environmental control through research into novel warp recycling and effective use of waste material.

Eskom

Eskom's Technology Services International group is a multidisciplinary industrial laboratory and consulting organisation. It undertakes testing, investigation studies, project management, engineering services and applied research for Eskom and other customers.

R&D and demonstration in Eskom are focused on supporting sustainable development. In 2002, investment in technical research, development and demonstration projects amounted to R625 million, which represented 1,2% of total revenue. It is estimated that in 2002, research provided a return of 5:1 in terms of avoided costs and direct-costs reduction. In addition, non-quantifiable benefits in social, environmental and customer satisfaction were realised.

During 2002, highlights of R&D and demonstration activities included the final commissioning of both the first sub-Saharan wind farm in the Western Cape, and the first solar dish stirling system outside of the USA, in partnership with the Development Bank of Southern Africa.

National Health Laboratory Service (NHLS)

The NHLS conducts research into the prevention and treatment of human diseases.

The NHLS was established on 1 October 2001 to form a single public health laboratory service in South Africa. The NHLS comprises about 240 laboratories countrywide, including the former South African Institute for Medical Research, the National Institute for Virology, all provincial diagnostic pathology laboratories (excluding those in KwaZulu-Natal), and tertiary laboratories used by universities' medical schools. It has approximately 4 000 employees and consists of four divisions: Research, Diagnostic Laboratory Services, Production (serum and laboratory reagents) and Teaching and Training. The NHLS conducts medical research as well as pathology laboratory tests for all provincial hospitals, excluding those in KwaZulu-Natal. Research is conducted on diseases and health dangers that are of specific importance to South Africa.

Bureau for Economic Research

The Bureau for Economic Research at the University of Stellenbosch, Western Cape, is an independent and objective economic research organisation rendering a service to organisations ranging from small one-person businesses to policy-makers at the highest level of government.

National Institute for Tropical Diseases

The National Institute for Tropical Diseases in Tzaneen, Limpopo, is responsible for the ongoing assessment of the malaria-control programmes carried out by various authorities in South Africa.

Control methods are assessed, and recommendations made to the appropriate authorities with regard to equipment, insecticide usage and application. A malaria reference service is also provided. Tests for malaria are carried out by the Institute, and statistical analysis of data pertaining to the programme is undertaken.

General research areas

Antarctic research

South Africa has been involved in Antarctic research since 1957. It is one of the 12 original signatories to the Antarctic Treaty and plays an active role in Antarctic matters. The South African National Antarctic Programme (SANAP), which is run by the Directorate: Antarctica and Islands of the Department of Environmental Affairs and Tourism, provides logistical support to the annual science programme that is conducted in Antarctica and on the islands. It manages three bases, one on a mountain top at Vesleskarvet in Dronning Maud Land, Antarctica; a second on Marion Island in the south Indian Ocean; and a third on Gough Island, a British territory in the South Atlantic Ocean.

The country also ratified the Madrid Protocol on Environmental Protection to the Antarctic Treaty, which was implemented on 14 January 1998.

Relief voyages, which bring new over-wintering staff and supplies to the South African National Antarctic Expedition (SANAE) IV base, Marion Island and Gough Island, were all successfully carried out during 2002. SANAP continues to support the South African Weather Service by maintaining stations at all three bases. The Programme also assists with the deployment of weather buoys and the servicing of an automatic weather station at the South Sandwich Islands.

The Minister of Environmental Affairs and Tourism, Mr Mohammed Valli Moosa, led a multidepartmental delegation to Antarctica in January 2003. This was the first time that a South African Cabinet Minister had visited the Antarctic and SANAE IV base. Accompanying the Minister was a Norwegian delegation, led by that country's Minister of the Environment. A letter of intent, which heralds closer co-operation between South Africa and Norway in the Antarctic, was signed by the two Ministers at the Norwegian Antarctic station, Troll, during the four-day visit.

The purpose of the Minister's visit was to assess the research programmes and the scientific infrastructure in place at SANAE IV, and investigate the possibility of improved international co-operation, parti-cularly in the areas of cost sharing, revenue generation, and joint projects and activities. A clear understanding of the complexities of supplying and operating the Antarctic operation was achieved during the visit.

The SANAE IV base at Vesleskarvet can accommodate 20 over-wintering team members and 60 summer take-over personnel.

The main research conducted at the base is Antarctic magnetosphere, ionosphere ground-base observations, and research into cosmic rays.

A research base was established on Marion Island shortly after its annexation in 1947, and since then the base has been expanded and changed on an *ad hoc* basis. The base is used for collecting weather data, as well as for research into the exceptional biodiversity and natural systems.

Science and technology

The buildings on Marion Island have deteriorated to such an extent that they can no longer be economically maintained and repaired. The Directorate: Antarctica and Islands therefore proposed that a new modern research base be built to cater for the safe accommodation of personnel and for scientific research.

To ensure that the environmental impact of the new base is minimised, the Directorate has appointed independent environmental consultants to carry out environmental scoping.

Approval to rebuild the research station at Marion Island has been obtained, and an environmental-impact assessment was completed in 2002. Construction of the new base was expected to begin in the 2003/04 financial year.

The lease agreement between the UK and South Africa to build, maintain and staff a permanent base on Gough Island was to be renewed in 2003/04.

During 2002/03, the Departments of Environmental Affairs and Tourism and Science and Technology agreed to form a partnership and work together in the areas of Antarctic science, research support and funding. The objective is to broaden the scientific base, increase participation by historically disadvantaged individuals in SANAP, and revitalise Antarctic research.

As part of the Department's goal of exposing the Antarctic Programme to the South African public, 16 learners, including nine from historically disadvantaged backgrounds, accompanied the *SA Agulhas* on a voyage to the Antarctic in February 2003.

Mine-safety research

The activities of the Safety in Mines Research Advisory Committee are aimed at the advancement of the safety of workers employed on South African mines. The Committee is a statutory tripartite subcommittee of the Mine Health and Safety Council. It has a permanent research management office managing the fields of research, namely rock engineering, engineering and mine occupational health.

Energy research

The Chief Directorate: Energy of the Department of Minerals and Energy manages a policy-directed research programme. This includes transport energy, renewable energy and energy for developing areas, coal, electricity, energy efficiency, energy economy and integrated energy-policy formulation.

Agricultural research

Agricultural research is conducted by the ARC, several universities and a variety of organisations in the private sector. Provinces are responsible for farm management and technological development. These activities are aimed at improving managerial efficiency on farms.

The Directorate: Agricultural Water-Use Management of the national Department of Agriculture co-operates with provinces to steer research in the engineering aspects of agriculture.

Biannual meetings are held to debate and agree on research needs, programmes and budgeting. Efforts are made to ensure that the bulk of research serves the needs of small-scale producers.

Research initiatives have been integrated into the various industries in line with the overall objectives of each particular agricultural sector.

Water research

Water research in South Africa is co-ordinated and funded by the Water Research Commission (WRC) in Pretoria. The WRC was established in 1971 through the Water Research Act, 1971 (Act 34 of 1971), following a period of water shortage. It was deemed to be of national importance to generate new knowledge and to promote the country's water research purposefully, owing to the view held that water would be one of South Africa's most limited resources in the 21st century.

Being a water-stressed country, South Africa progressively needs to find innovative ways of managing water resources to ensure that the basic needs of its citizens are met, that social and economic development is not restricted through a lack of or a poor quality of water, and that sustainability of water resources and of water-dependent ecosystems is achieved.

The WRC has the mandate to perform the following functions:
- promote co-ordination, co-operation and communication in the area of water research and development
- establish water research needs and priorities
- stimulate and fund water research according to priority
- promote effective transfer of information and technology
- enhance knowledge and capacity-building within the water sector.

The Water Research Act, 1971 provides for the establishment of the Water Research Fund which derives income primarily from levies on water consumption.

The WRC funds R&D under contract with other organisations. In view of the broad scope of water research, a wide spectrum of research-providers are involved in WRC research contracts. They are drawn from universities, universities of technology, statutory research agencies, government departments, local authorities, non-governmental organisations (NGOs), water boards, consultants and industry.

In supporting the creation, dissemination and application of knowledge, the WRC focuses on five key strategic areas:
- water-resource management
- water-linked ecosystems
- water use and waste management
- water utilisation in agriculture
- water-centred knowledge.

The WRC strategy also calls for specific mechanisms to address key strategic issues of national importance. These issues are dealt with in four cross-cutting domains:

- water and society
- water and the economy
- water and the environment
- water and health.

The organisations most active in water research are:
- universities (51,57% of the total number of contracts)
- consultants (21,97%)
- the CSIR (11,32%)
- water boards (3,77%)
- the ARC (4,14%)
- universities of technology (2,83%)
- government departments (3,46%)
- municipalities (1,26%).

The main areas of research are surface hydrology, groundwater, hydrometeorology, agricultural water utilisation, water pollution, municipal effluents, industrial water and effluents, drinking water, membrane technology, water ecosystems, hydraulics, mine-water management, water policy, developing communities, and the transfer of information technology.

The Division: Water, Environment and Forestry Technology (Environmentek) of the CSIR specialises in research into water quality, including technology to meet effluent and water-quality standards and to establish reclaimed water as an additional water source. Environmentek is a world leader in research into activated sludge processes and the biological monitoring of water to detect potentially toxic substances. It is also involved in research on the effects of afforestation and veld management on the quantity and quality of catchment water-yield.

Environmental research

The Chief Directorate: Environmental Management of the Department of Environmental Affairs and Tourism annually finances several research and monitoring programmes.

The programmes comprise subjects such as waste management and pollution, nature conservation, river management, the coastline and marine environment, and the atmosphere.

Some programmes are conducted in collaboration with the NRF, while others are undertaken on behalf of the Department by the CSIR. Universities also carry out research on behalf of the Department.

Research on human-environment interaction sponsored by the Department is coordinated by the HSRC.

In addition, institutes of the ARC are concerned with environmental research insofar as environmental problems impact on agriculture or are caused by agricultural practices.

The Department's National Environmental Potential Atlas (ENPAT) provides a visual overview of South Africa's environmental resources. The most important advantage of ENPAT is that environmental implications of land-use decisions are available before any actions are initiated. ENPAT-National contains two main data types, namely environmental and population data. The Atlas also identifies possible conflict areas in the utilisation of natural resources.

The South African Weather Service functions under the Department of Environmental Affairs and Tourism.

The Weather Service delivers public good services, mainly for the protection of life and property, as well as commercial services to the private sector as stipulated in the Weather Service Act, 2001 (Act 8 of 2001).

The public-good services are funded by government while commercial services are paid for by the user. The public-good services include weather and climate forecasting, a weather disaster warning system, services to subsistence farmers and fishers, the provision of information and advice to government, meeting regional and international treaty and agreement obligations, maintaining a national meteorological library, technical and scientific training in meteorology, and undertaking research to improve services.

The Weather Service operates the Global Atmosphere Watch (GAW) station, situated at Cape Point in the Western Cape. The GAW is an initiative of the World Meteorological Organisation and serves as an early-warning and forecasting system for changes in the background chemical composition and related physical characteristics of the atmosphere.

Atmospheric-ozone monitoring at Irene, near Pretoria, is maintained throughout the year.

The NRF directs the multidisciplinary Conservation and Management of Ecosystems and Biodiversity Focus Area, primarily in collaboration with universities and museums, to promote and support research on living resources and the terrestrial, freshwater, marine, coastal and atmospheric ecosystems.

Some 170 projects are approved annually, and global issues such as climate change and biological diversity are also included. The sustainable use of natural resources is a priority area, resulting in a growth of projects relying on sociology and the humanities. The NRF also supports a range of environmental research network organisations such as the Arid Zone Ecology Forum, the *Fynbos* Forum, the Indigenous Plant-Use Forum, the South African Network for Coastal and Oceanic Research (SANCOR) and the Savanna Ecology Forum.

Fisheries research

Research into South Africa's fish resources, their conservation and judicious exploitation is carried out by research personnel of the Chief Directorate: Marine and Coastal Management, a division of the Department of Environmental Affairs and Tourism, and by several universities and NGOs. Research is designed to provide parameters for estimates of stock sizes and sustainable yields for the different fisheries.

Coastal and marine research

The Chief Directorate: Marine and Coastal Management advises on the utilisation of marine living resources and the conservation of marine ecosystems, by conducting and supporting relevant multidisciplinary scientific research and monitoring the marine environment. Sustainable use and the need to preserve future options in the utilisation of marine ecosystems and their resources are guiding objectives in the research and advice of the organisation.

The NRF supports marine and coastal research in partnership with the Department of Environmental Affairs and Tourism and SANCOR.

Private-sector involvement

South Africa's gold-mining industry works at deeper levels and under more difficult circumstances than any other mining industry in the world. The research on gold-mining conducted by the CSIR's Mining Technology is concerned primarily with ensuring the health and safety of the workforce, and includes the areas of rock engineering and the underground environment. Mining Technology's coal-mining research takes place on a smaller scale than that of gold-mining, because the coal-mining industry can make use of various overseas developments. Areas in which research is undertaken include strata control, mining, maximising extraction of coal, and the underground environment.

Research is also carried out by a large number of industrial companies with facilities to meet their specific needs.

The more important ones are Anglo American Corporation of South Africa (applied metallurgy, processing of precious metals, base metals and coal), Agricura (synthesis and testing of veterinary remedies, insecticides, herbicides and entomology), Cullinan Holdings (refractories and electrical porcelain), De Beers Industrial Diamond Division (manufacture and application of synthetic diamonds and other super-hard material), Johannesburg Consolidated Investment Company (metallurgy, mineralogy, chemistry and chemical engineering), National Chemical Products (chemistry, microbiology and animal nutrition), Metal Box Company of South Africa (corrosion mechanism and microbiology), Tellumat (development of electronic instruments), Rembrandt Group (development and improvement of tobacco and liquor products), South African Pulp and Paper Industries (wood technology, paper manufacture and water treatment) and Standard Telephones and Cables SA (long-distance transmission of information and lightning protection).

Science and technology

Acknowledgements

Agricultural Research Council
*Bua*News
Chamber of Mines of South Africa
Council for Geoscience
Council for Scientific and Industrial Research
Department of Environmental Affairs and Tourism
Department of Science and Technology
Eskom
Estimates of National Expenditure 2003, published by the National Treasury
Human Sciences Research Council
Iscor
Medical Research Council
Mintek
National Department of Agriculture
National Health Laboratory Service
National Research Foundation
Sasol
South African Bureau of Standards
SouthAfrica.info
Water Research Commission
www.gov.za

Suggested reading

Austin, B. *Schonland.* Johannesburg: Witwatersrand University Press, 2001.
Basson, N. *Passage to Progress: The Council for Scientific and Industrial Research's (CSIR) Journey of Change, 1945 – 1995.* Johannesburg: Jonathan Ball, 1995.
Crouch, M. ed. *Sparkling Achievements.* Johannesburg: Chris van Rensburg Publications, 2001.
Kingwill, D. *The CSIR: The First 40 Years.* Pretoria: CSIR Docel, 1990.
Kok, P. and others. *Development Research in South Africa.* Pretoria: Human Sciences Research Council, 1994.
Liebenberg, L. *Tracking: The Origin of Science.* Cape Town: David Philip, 1990.
Macrae, C. *Life Etched in Stone: Fossils of Southern Africa.* Johannesburg: Geological Society of South Africa, 1999.
Prout-Jones, D. *Cracking the Sky.* Pretoria: UNISA, 2002.
Sasol. *Sasol Facts 1998.* Johannesburg: Sasol Corporate Communications, 1998.
Wilson, M.S.G. and Anhaeusser, C.R. eds. *Council for Geoscience, Handbook no 16, Mineral Resources of South Africa*, 1998.

mpcc
Mashishing Multipurpose Community
mpcc
programme
OF GOVERNMEN

LELO LOMXH
EZINDAWEN
SEMAKHA

chapter 19

Social development

The Department of Social Development is responsible for developing and monitoring the implementation of social policy that both creates an enabling environment for, and leads to the reduction in, poverty. The Department ensures the provision of social protection and social-welfare services to all South Africans. It works in partnership with non-governmental organisations (NGOs), faith-based organisations (FBOs), the business sector, organised labour and other role-players in the spirit of *batho pele*.

The Department provides implementation support to the provincial Departments of Social Development, and monitors and evaluates the range of social-development programmes. Responsibility for most of the service delivery rests with provincial Departments.

There has been a substantial increase in the social development budget from R19,4 billion in 1999/00 to R31,2 billion in 2002/03.

In January 2000, the Minister of Social Development, Dr Zola Skweyiya, identified 10 priorities to be addressed over a five-year period:
- Restoring the ethics of care and human development in all welfare programmes. This includes the rebuilding of family, community and social relations to promote social integration.
- Developing and implementing an integrated poverty-eradication strategy that provides direct benefits for those who are in need, within a sustainable development approach.
- Developing a comprehensive social-security system that links contributory and non-contributory schemes, prioritising the most vulnerable households.
- Responding to the brutal effects of all forms of violence against women and children, including strategies to deal with perpetrators.
- Providing a range of services to support community-based care and support for people living with HIV/AIDS as well as those affected, such as AIDS orphans.
- Developing a national strategy to reduce youth criminality and unemployment within the framework of the National Crime Prevention Strategy.
- Making social-welfare services accessible and available to people in rural, peri-urban and informal settlements, as well as ensuring equity in service provision.
- Redesigning services for people with disabilities to promote their human rights and economic development.
- Basing welfare work on a commitment to co-operative governance that includes working with different spheres of government and civil society.
- Training, educating, redeploying and employing a new category of workers relevant to addressing the development challenges of South Africa.

◀ By September 2003, about 6,5 million people were receiving social grants at a cost of about R2,5 million per month. Of these about two million were recipients of Old-Age Grants.

Recent years have seen significant progress in developing and strengthening the system of social grants (government's key instrument for direct poverty relief), expanding the social safety net, as well as improving administration. In addition, since 1998/99 there has been a progressive shift from the traditional welfare model to a social-development model, placing more emphasis on addressing the structural causes of poverty and responding to their social manifestations.

Examples of significant recent progress in strengthening the social-grant system are:
- The Department of Social Development has surpassed the target of registering three million children for the Child Support Grant (CSG) by April 2004. By 31 July 2003, some 3,4 million children had been registered.
- The administration of social security has been rationalised with the introduction of assessment panels for Disability Grants, the simplification of the review of eligibility, and the removal of the three-month limitation on arrear payments to beneficiaries.
- Norms and standards for social-grant delivery have been developed and planning is under way for its phased implementation over a three-year period.

With regard to social-welfare services, ongoing initiatives include:
- Developing new policy in line with the recommendations of the Ministerial Committee on the Abuse, Neglect and Ill-treatment of Older Persons, adopted by the Cabinet in February 2001.
- Revising the financing subsidies for welfare organisations.
- Establishing the Advisory Board on Social Development to advise the Minister on a range of social-development issues and serve as a consultative mechanism.
- The implementation of the National Integrated Plan for Children Infected and Affected by HIV/AIDS, focusing on home- and community-based care initiatives, which started in 2000 in partnership with the Department of Health, is gathering momentum.

Legislation

Older Persons Bill

The investigation by the Ministerial Committee on the Abuse, Neglect and Ill-Treatment of Older Persons revealed an alarming level of abuse, neglect and ill-treatment of the elderly by families, institutions and government services. The Cabinet adopted the recommendations of the Committee and implementation of these recommendations is in progress.

The main recommendations of the Committee include:
- significantly improving social-assistance service delivery to older persons
- accelerating the transformation of residential homes for older persons
- increasing the support for community-based care and non-residential services to older persons
- introducing new legislation that complies with the Constitution, 1996 (Act 108 of 1996), and with the international conventions on the rights of older persons.

The Older Persons Bill was adopted for submission to Parliament in July 2003.

The Bill strives to maintain and increase the capacity of older persons to support themselves and contribute to the well-being of those around them.

The main objectives of the Bill are to:
- maintain and promote the status, well-being, safety and security of older persons
- maintain and protect the rights of older persons as recipients of services
- regulate the registration of facilities for older persons
- combat the abuse of older persons.

New child-care legislation

The South African Law Reform Commission (SALRC) is drafting new comprehensive child-care legislation to replace the Child Care Act, 1983 (Act 74 of 1983), which is inconsistent with the Constitution and the United Nations (UN) Declaration on the Rights of the Child.

On 7 December 2002, the SALRC approved the report and draft Child Care Bill in its investigation into the Review of the Child Care Act, 1983, concluding an investigation that commenced in 1997.

Issues covered in the report and Draft Child Care Bill include recommendations that:
- childhood begins at birth
- the age of majority be lowered to 18 years of age
- more than one (even more than two) persons be allowed to acquire and manage parental rights and responsibilities, or components thereof, in respect of the same child at the same time
- mothers and married fathers be accorded such parental rights and responsibilities automatically, while some unmarried fathers and other persons will have to apply to court to acquire such rights and responsibilities
- a Child and Family Court be established at regional court level
- a register of persons unsuitable to working with children be created
- children of all ages be provided with confidential access to condoms
- the common law defence to reasonable chastisement be repealed
- municipalities establish and administer child- and youth-care centres
- child-headed households be recognised by law
- a child grant be payable on a universal basis in respect of all children in need of care and protection.

Social Assistance Bill

The aim of the Social Assistance Bill is to provide for the rendering of social assistance to persons, the mechanisms for the rendering of such assistance, the establishment of an inspectorate for social assist-ance, and matters connected therewith.

The Portfolio Committee on Social Development held public hearings on the Social Assistance Bill and the Social Security Agency Bill on 22 and 23 September 2003.

The proposed Social Assistance Bill will provide for the establishment of the National Social Security Agency which will help to improve the administration and delivery of social grants. Through the amendment of the Social Assistance Bill, the Department of Social Development seeks to ensure easier access to government services with regard to the provision of social assistance to individuals and families that are in dire need.

In July 2003, the Cabinet approved the process of establishing the National Social Security Agency.

Social assistance

The Regulations for Social Assistance were amended to relax conditions that impeded easy access to grants and to promote administrative justice. Some of the amendments involve the following:
- The removal of the pensions medical officer for the approval of Disability and Care Dependency Grants, and the introduction of panels to assess applicants for these Grants, in terms of both medical and social factors.
- The payment of grants, if approved, accrues from the date of application for all grant types except for the Foster Care Grant, in which case accrual begins from the date of the court order.
- The review of grants has been streamlined. Only applicants who declare their means of income at the time of the application are required to have an annual review of their grant. Those who have no means are only required to submit a life certificate on an annual basis to verify that they are alive. Those who collect their grants through biometrics and have no means are neither

required to submit life certificates nor to have their grants reviewed.
- Previously, the Care Dependency Grant was only available to parents and foster parents of children. It is now also available to custodians and guardians. Personal income has replaced household income as the means-test indicator, thus increasing the income exclusion level for applicants.

Payment of social grants

More than four million social grants were paid in March 2002 to means-tested recipients in certain categories of older persons, persons with disabilities, and families with children. These payments have been relatively effective in reaching the rural poor, a group which is difficult to reach with other government services and programmes.

By September 2003, about 6,5 million people received social grants at a cost of about R2,5 billion per month. Of these, 3,8 million received the CSG and about two million, Old-Age Grants.

The CSG, which was introduced in March 1998 to widen the safety net, continues to increase its take-up rate. In the first year of the CSG's implementation, there were just over 58 000 children receiving payment. By July 2003, this had increased to 3,4 million children. The aim of government is to register all children eligible for CSGs by 2005.

With the registration of over three million children, each child receiving R160, the Government is spending over R480 million per month. More than half of unregistered children and eligible people are in the poorest provinces, namely Free State, Limpopo, KwaZulu-Natal and the Eastern Cape.

In his State of the Nation Address in February 2003, President Thabo Mbeki announced that the age of children eligible for the CSG would be progressively increased to include children up to the age of 14 years.

The increase will be implemented in phases over the next three years. During the 2003/04 financial year, the focus was on ensuring that all children between the ages of seven and nine were registered, while during 2004/05, children between the ages of nine and 12 years will be registered. Beneficiaries between 12 and 14 years are expected to be registered in 2005/06.

Government has set aside R11 billion for the age extensions, which will result in an additional 3,2 million children receiving the CSG.

A further large proportion of the beneficiaries of social grants are the elderly. Women qualify at the age of 60 years and men at the age of 65.

The Disability Grant is paid to people who have been assessed as permanently or temporarily disabled.

Foster Care Grants are paid to caregivers of children who have been placed with them by the courts. Caregivers of disabled children up to the age of 18 years are eligible for the Care Dependency Grant. Once the child turns 18 years, he or she is eligible for the Disability Grant.

The total budget allocation for the payment of social assistance by the provincial Departments of Social Development was R21,4 billion for 2001/02 and this was expected to reach R25,2 billion in 2002/03.

Other grants provided by the Department of Social Development include the War Veterans Grant and Grant-in-Aid.

Amounts of grants per month as at 1 April 2003	
Grant Type	Amount
Old-Age Grant	R700
Disability Grant	R700
War Veterans Grant	R718
Foster Care Grant	R500
Care Dependency Grant	R700
Child Support Grant	R160
Grant-in-Aid	R150

Social development

Improving the existing system of social assistance

Improvements made by government with regard to social security include:
- increasing the amounts of all types of grants above the inflation rate as a form of poverty alleviation
- increasing the eligibility age of the CSG to 14 years over the next three years as a way of progressively realising and prioritising children's socio-economic rights as enshrined in the Constitution
- implementing programmes to ensure easy access to grants, including improved communication and reaching out to communities
- improving the administration of grants (intensification of the Implementation of Norms and Standards).

Poverty-Relief Programme

In addition to the provision of social assistance, the Department also manages the Poverty-Relief Programme. This Programme is funded through a special allocation from the Poverty-Relief, Infrastructure and Job Creation Fund of the National Treasury and aims to assist communities in a range of developmental projects.

The Programme entrusts State resources to communities to undertake and dictate development for themselves by themselves.

Steady progress is being made with the Poverty-Relief Programme.

Since 1997, the Department has administered more than R563 million, providing support to over 3 600 community-based projects.

Most of the projects are located in the Eastern Cape, KwaZulu-Natal and Limpopo.

The Poverty-Relief Programme targets vulnerable groups, namely women, children, youth, the elderly and people with disabilities. Over a three-year period, it is estimated that 60 000 people would have earned wages generated through poverty-relief projects. For the coming years, the Department has prioritised the areas of food security, centres for engaging older persons in economic activities, support for community-based initiatives in the area of HIV/AIDS, youth-skills development in the context of urban renewal, economic empowerment of women, support for initiatives that integrate the capacities of persons with disabilities into the Poverty-Relief Programme, and income-generating projects.

The feeding of children, through the Poverty-Relief Programme, particularly orphans and those people infected and affected by HIV/AIDS, is growing.

One of the projects is the Carol Shaw Memorial Project based in Zuurbekom, west of Johannesburg.

Communities are also using poverty-relief funds to generate income, by selling surplus produce from their food projects, such as the Skills Dynamic Project based in Richards Bay, KwaZulu-Natal, which feeds poor families in the area and sells eggs from its poultry project.

The *Nyumba Ya Kwethu* Youth and Children's Project takes care of orphaned children of former South African exiles.

In February 2003, the Minister of Social Development commended the *Inyosi* Bee-Keeping Poverty-Relief Project in the Eastern Cape for receiving the *Mpumelelo* Trust Award.

The Award is given to organisations for creating jobs and improving the lives of poor rural communities, especially women.

The Project focuses on bee-keeping and the production of wax products and has created employment for over 500 people from poor communities. The Project received R2,4 million from the Department during the 2002/03 financial year.

During 2003, a total of R71 million was allocated to the Department of Social Development for poverty relief, targeting mostly unemployed women and the youth in especially rural areas.

In order to mitigate the impact of HIV/AIDS on the poorest of the poor, the Department disbursed R65 million to support community- and home-based care programmes during 2003.

Food security

Government is committed to focusing more on social spending to further push back the frontiers of poverty and advance the cause of building a better life for all.

In October 2002, the Cabinet allocated R400 million to counteract soaring food prices, famine and food insecurity in South Africa and the Southern African Development Community (SADC) region.

Some R170 million was sent to the World Food Programme to assist neighbouring countries devastated by famine.

The larger portion of the allocation, R230 million, was used for the Food Emergency Scheme that was benefiting over 240 000 poor households by July 2003. Families without an income and those who spent a maximum of R200 per month on food and basic household essentials received food parcels.

The focus is shifting towards more sustainable ways, such as food production through the provision of starter packs, registration for social grants, linking families and communities to the income-generation programmes of government and the private sector, training and capacity-building, studying the lessons of the pilot and its costs, and escalating beyond the pilot phase.

These would further enhance the realisation of the Millennium Declaration Goals and the goals of the 2002 World Summit on Sustainable Development to have reduced poverty by half in 2015.

In 2003, government committed R1,2 billion to finance the Scheme over the next three years.

The main objectives of the Scheme include:
- providing food parcels as emergency food relief to poor households, especially those headed by children
- linking eligible persons from these households and communities to social assistance and social security
- enhancing better nutrition among the vulnerable sectors of society
- ensuring that vulnerable children, especially orphans, are linked to the School Nutrition Programme
- protecting the poorest households from surging food prices by enhancing the capacity of communities and households to provide for themselves
- enhancing partnerships and co-operative governance in the fight against hunger and poverty.

The Scheme forms part of government's Integrated Food Security and Nutrition Programme (IFSNP).

The five elements of the IFSNP are the:
- Development of comprehensive food-production and trade schemes to enhance the capacity of communities to produce food for themselves through the setting up of both household and communal food gardens.
- Initiation of a community-development scheme aimed at providing employment to local communities through community-based and community-owned public works programmes. This involves the setting up of community-based income-generating projects and activities to ensure sustainable food security.
- Development of a nutrition and food programme that focuses primarily on the improvement of nutrition levels in communities, to ensure that every child has at least one nutritious meal a day.
- Development of a fully funded communication strategy to ensure the maintenance of government's communication lines with all of its people.
- Building of a safety net and Food Emergency Scheme to ensure that the poorest families, especially children and child-headed households, have food on the table.

Responding to the impact of HIV/AIDS

The national Department of Social Development has developed a social-development framework for an integrated and co-ordinated response to HIV/AIDS. The framework includes sourcing reliable research and information; the provision of social protection to those infected and affected, especially children; protection of children's rights; provision of services; special programmes such as the Home-Based/Community-Based Care Programme; empowerment of women; and the capacitating of officials to deal with HIV/AIDS. The Department's response to HIV/AIDS is underpinned by working in partnership with other government departments, NGOs, community-based organisations (CBOs), FBOs, the business sector, volunteers and international agencies.

The Department received an allocation of R65,9 million for HIV/AIDS programmes in 2003.

During 2003, the Department focused on strengthening home- and community-based care, with the emphasis on child-headed households and strengthening partnerships with NGOs, FBOs, CBOs and civil-society structures. By mid-2003, some 300 centres, supporting 75 000 children and their families, had been established through this programme.

In February 2003, the Minister of Social Development addressed representatives from the United Nations Population Fund (UNFPA) from across the southern African region on HIV/AIDS, and poverty and population issues affecting the region, at a five-day Southern African Region Cluster meeting held in Cape Town.

The Minister announced that the R72 million injected by the UNFPA would be used to support government in reducing the impact of HIV/AIDS, strengthening integrated rural-development programmes and promoting best practices through regional integration.

The Programme will focus on three main areas, namely:
- reproductive health and rights
- advocacy and the mobilisation of resources
- strengthening population and development capacity.

The Programme will target developments in the Eastern Cape, KwaZulu-Natal and Limpopo.

On 9 October 2003, the Minister visited several HIV/AIDS projects caring for children around Durban, KwaZulu-Natal, to assess the needs and services rendered by government. These projects are taking care of about 300 children affected by HIV/AIDS and those who have been abandoned.

During their meeting on 15 August 2003, the Minister of Social Development and the provincial members of executive councils (MECs) for Social Development (MINMEC) committed themselves to fully supporting the Cabinet's decision on the roll-out of anti-retroviral treatment.

A task team was subsequently set up to study the implications of the decision and advise the Minister accordingly. (See Chapter 13: Health.)

Home-based/community-based care

The Department is implementing the Home-Based/Community-Based Care Programme in conjunction with the Departments of Health and of Education. The integrated Programme provides life skills for children and youths, voluntary testing and counselling services, and a range of care and support services focusing on families and children orphaned through the AIDS-related death of their parents. There has been significant progress with regard to the initial implementation of home- and community-based care and support.

Government has embarked on other programmes to mitigate the impact of HIV/AIDS, which include the following:
- Nutritional care and support guidelines for people living with HIV and AIDS have

been developed and distributed, together with national guidelines on home- and community-based care.
- Government increased its budget on the conditional grant allocation for home- and community-based care from R28 million in 1999 to R180 million in 2003.
- Besides this massive conditional grant, NGO funding nationally has spent R7 million on home- and community-based care from a total NGO budget of R22 million which covers all other HIV and AIDS-related interventions that are provided by NGOs.
- By August 2003, 10 000 caregivers had been trained in home- and community-based care. The number of home- and community-based care projects doubled from 466 in 2001 to 892 in August 2003.

Partnerships with international organisations, NGOs, CBOs, and FBOs in the fight against HIV and AIDS are being strengthened.

The Department of Social Development also supports a number of community-initiated care and support projects. With the increasing demand for these services by families and children infected and affected by HIV/AIDS, the Department will be expanding this project over the next three years. Special attention is being given to integrate the Home- and Community-Based Care and Support Programme into all programmes of the Department, nationally and provincially.

In order to mitigate the impact of HIV/AIDS on the poorest of the poor, the Department disbursed more than R65 million in 2003 to support Community- and Home-Based Care Programmes.

Of this, KwaZulu-Natal received the biggest allocation of R11,9 million, followed by Mpumalanga with R9,8 million, Gauteng with R9,6 million and the Free State with R9,2 million. The balance was allocated to the remaining provinces. The provincial Departments have established and supported more than 300 centres.

Services for children infected or affected by HIV/AIDS

Services provided to children infected or affected by HIV/AIDS include the provision of food parcels and clothing, counselling, support, provision of day care and after school/drop-in centres, placement of children in foster and/or residential care, and addressing their education and health needs.

The Department spent R48 million during 2002/03 to ensure that children infected and affected by HIV/AIDS had access to services that included alternative care, social grants, counselling, food security, and protection from abuse and other forms of maltreatment.

The HIV/AIDS drop-in centres established by the Department of Social Development received a budget of R16,4 million in 2003/04. Each food parcel these centres provide costs about R300. The drop-in centres were identified through the HIV/AIDS database of Home- and Community-Based Care Centres. Each province has identified drop-in centres to be contracted to provide cooked meals to identified beneficiaries. These beneficiaries are classified as people who are not able to cook for themselves, e.g. as in the case of child-headed households.

The National Conference on Co-ordinated Action for Children Infected and Affected by HIV/AIDS was held in June 2002.

The Conference culminated in a plan of action to ensure that stakeholders, at all levels, work in a co-ordinated way to protect the rights

---

On 11 October 2003, the Traditional HIV/AIDS Home-Based Care (THABC) Project in Robega Village in Phokeng in the North West launched a Drop-In Centre and soup kitchen.

The Department of Social Development provided funds for the project, aimed at feeding children and poor families in the area.

Since 2001, the THABC has supplied about 60 families with food packages, made lunch boxes for about 50 scholars and cooked supper for about 130 orphans on a daily basis.

of children who are infected and affected by HIV/AIDS and to ensure that the rights of children to food, shelter, social services and grants, education, health, counselling, alternative care, protection and non-discrimination are enhanced. This includes engaging in a national capacity-development process for communities to identify and care for orphans and other vulnerable children, to create a community, district, provincial and national database, and to track the process of accessing social grants and essential services. A Plan of Action to pursue these objectives has been developed.

The Department has developed an integrated and consolidated Five-Year National Social Development Strategic Plan which is being implemented in partnership with other stakeholders such as the United Nations Children's Fund (UNICEF).

Developing capacity

The Department, in collaboration with the South African Management Development Institute, has developed a curriculum for planners, analysts and researchers in the public sector (national, provincial and local governments) to develop a common basic understanding of the impact of HIV/AIDS on service delivery. The programme was launched in the second half of 2001 and is expected to reach 3 000 officials over a period of three years. The programme is being presented in all provinces and is run by universities across the country. Over 1 500 planners from all three spheres of government had attended the course by March 2003.

The first-ever Volunteer Conference was held from 5 to 7 September 2003 in Johannesburg.

Its aim was to form a co-ordination body for volunteering in South Africa.

The Conference, which was co-ordinated by Volunteer South Africa, deliberated on:
- voluntary work as an essential element of civic life and civic responsibility
- the role of the media in promoting volunteering
- partnerships in volunteering.

Research

On 8 October 2003, the Department of Social Development and the UNFPA released the State of the World's Population Report 2003.

The report, with the theme *Making One Billion Count: Investing in Adolescents' Health and Rights*, aims to prepare and inform adolescents and youths on issues of poverty, inequality and HIV/AIDS.

The Report states that challenges facing South Africa include the improvement of gender practices, eradicating poverty, fighting crime, providing education, and combating sexually transmitted diseases, including HIV/AIDS.

The Report aims to stimulate and generate public debate on the challenges and risks faced by adolescents. It finds that investing in young people yields generous returns for generations to come.

According to the Report, failure to invest in the youth perpetuates poverty, inequality, unsustainable population growth and HIV/AIDS. Young women are often worst affected. Expanding their opportunities and ensuring their reproductive health and rights, free from violence and discrimination, are critically important for sustainable human development.

Partnerships

Since 2000, the Department has strengthened its partnership with national and international organisations involved in the fight against HIV/AIDS. The Department chairs the National AIDS Children's Task Team (NACTT), a multisectoral task team focusing on the care and support of children infected and affected by HIV/AIDS.

United Nations Children's Fund

UNICEF conducted studies on caring for vulnerable children and children orphaned through AIDS-related illnesses, as well as studies on the cost-effectiveness of six models of care for vulnerable children. The Department has implemented the results of the UNICEF studies in its design of programmes for children. UNICEF has indicated interest in providing further support to the Department in fast-tracking the Home-Based and Community-Based Care Programme.

Save the Children Fund
This organisation provides secretariat and other assistance to the NACTT and has undertaken research on abused children and children affected by HIV/AIDS. It has compiled a directory of services and children's organisations.

Faith-based organisations and the business sector
The Department has strengthened its partnership with churches and other FBOs, the business sector, volunteer organisations and individuals to assist with the Poverty-Relief, HIV/AIDS and social-grant-registration programmes.

Promoting and protecting rights of vulnerable groups

Children and youths
In addition to providing social assistance to children through the CSG and the Foster Care Grant, the Department facilitates the provision of services to children and youths through the provincial Departments of Social Development and NGOs.

Child abuse and neglect
Fighting child abuse and neglect is a priority of the Department, as illustrated by the following initiatives:
- developing a computerised Child-Protection Register
- facilitating the development of protocols on the management of child-abuse and neglect cases
- facilitating the development of an intersectoral Child-Abuse and Neglect Strategy

- representing South Africa in international social-service organisations.

Integrated Justice System (IJS)
The IJS Project ensures the integration of the management of cases and offenders through four departments, namely the South African Police Service (SAPS), and the Departments of Justice and Constitutional Development, of Correctional Services and of Social Development, supported by enabling technologies. A number of projects have been initiated to this end. These include the Awaiting-Trial Prisoner Project.

Children awaiting trial in any residential-care facility are a priority of the Department of Social Development. Active participation from the provincial social-service representatives and management teams has yielded positive results. An interdepartmental committee of senior officials monitors the cases of children awaiting trial.

The computerised Child-Protection Register has been developed, and technological improvements in the SAPS Crime Administration System enable the four Departments to track children through the System and assist in the monitoring of their cases. The Court Process Project provides for the electronic management of court processes from arrest to final court appearances. The Project is increasing efficiency and reducing court delays. The Department of Social Development runs six pilot sites.

Women
Social-development services to women are another priority. This derives from the premise and concern that the inequality that exists between men and women in South Africa is deeply entrenched and has characterised South African society for many decades. Women are subject to discrimination, exploitation and violence despite the Constitution, which affirms the democratic values of human dignity, equality and freedom. An unprecedent-

Social development

ed effort is therefore required to ensure that the status of women is elevated to protect their rights and speed up gender equality.

Economic empowerment

The Department established the Flagship Programme: Developmental Programmes for Unemployed Women with Children under Five Years. This provides economic and development opportunities and services to unemployed women with children under the age of five years, living in deep rural areas and previously disadvantaged informal settlements. Sixteen projects have been designed to create income that is distributed among the parti-cipating women.

The various projects include activities such as eating houses, overnight facilities, car washes, beauty salons, vegetable gardens, garment-making, poultry and egg production, bread-baking, leather works, offal-cleaning, child-minding and paper-and-fabric printing. Some 727 women and 646 children are benefiting from the Programme. The Flagship Programme has developed a creative form of early childhood intervention, which provides developmentally appropriate education to children younger than five to increase their chances of healthy growth and development.

A partnership between the Department and Transnet has led to the donation of old containers to communities in rural areas. These are repaired and refurbished for use by the communities as one-stop service centres or multi-purpose centres from which a range of services can be provided.

Three Social-Service Centres, housed in containers, were opened in the Northern Cape in February 2003.

The Centres, estimated to be worth more than R100 million, were provided by Transnet as part of a long-standing partnership with the provincial Department of Social Services and Population Development. The containers will serve the communities of the remote and underdeveloped Brandvlei, Galeshewe and Delportshoop, by providing services such as the registration of eligible persons for social grants, social work, poverty relief and capacity-building by NGOs.

People with disabilities

By July 2003, 1 029 167 beneficiaries had received social assistance in the form of the Disability Grant. The Department also provides assistance to people with disabilities through the Poverty-Relief Programme and subsidies to national councils. The national councils supported by the Department are the:
- National Council for Persons with Physical Disabilities
- Deaf Federation of South Africa
- South African National Epilepsy League
- South African Federation for Mental Health
- Cancer Association of South Africa.

During 2000/01, the Department reviewed the procedures for assessing applicants for the Disability Grant and proposed amendments to the regulations of the Social Assistance Act, 1992 (Act 20 of 1992). The amendments provide for the use of community-based assessment panels as an alternative to district surgeons, who are not easily accessible to people in rural areas. The Committee of Inquiry into a Comprehensive Social Security System made recommendations to improve social protection for people with disabilities.

Victim-Empowerment Programme (VEP)

The VEP facilitates the establishment and integration of interdepartmental/intersectoral programmes and policies for the support, protection and empowerment of victims of crime and violence, with special focus on women and children.

It also ensures that the implementation of such programmes and policies is monitored and evaluated.

Some 120 projects have been established since the inception of the VEP in 1999. The projects provide trauma support and counselling services to the victims of violence and crime. Some of these projects focus on empowering community workers and professionals with skills and knowledge for the effective delivery of services to such victims.

One such meaningful project, which has been provided with technical and financial support through the VEP, is the Stop Abuse Help-Line of the Johannesburg Life Line.

Other organisations that are financially supported by the VEP include the National Network on Violence Against Women, the Ilitha Psychological Services NGO in Fort Hare, the Soshanguve Trauma Centre, University of South Africa's Department of Industrial Psychology, Themba Lesizwe NGO, and the Walk the Talk Challenge from Durban to Cape Town.

One-stop centres for abused women and children

The VEP is a major component of the joint agreement between the Department of Social Development and the UN Office for Drug Control and Crime Prevention, for the establishment of one-stop centres for women and children who are victims of abuse, especially domestic violence. Two such centres are already operating as pilot projects in the Eastern Cape and Mpumalanga.

The centres were handed over to the provincial Governments in September 2002 and February 2003, respectively, to ensure their sustainability.

Anti-rape strategy

The Interdepartmental Management Team (IDMT) comprises representatives from the Departments of Health, of Safety and Security, of Social Development, and the Sexual Offences and Community Affairs Unit of the National Directorate of Public Prosecutions. The IDMT was tasked by the Departments' Ministers to develop an anti-rape strategy for the prevention of sexual violence against women and children.

In March 2002, the Cabinet approved the strategic framework for an interdepartmental anti-rape strategy. The Justice and Crime Prevention Cluster and the Social Cluster Departments have begun to jointly implement the strategy.

The SAPS has also established partnerships with several other community-based role-players, including businesses. These links have improved the implementation of crime-prevention initiatives, e.g. the implementation of the Government's Anti-Rape Strategy.

Non-profit organisations (NPOs)

The Non-Profit Directorate of the Department of Social Development registers organisations under the NPO Act, 1997 (Act 71 of 1997).

The primary purpose of the Act is to encourage and support organisations in a wider range of the work they do, by creating an enabling environment for NPOs to flourish, and setting and maintaining adequate standards of governance, accountability and transparency.

An NPO is defined as a trust, company or association of persons that has been established for public purpose and of which the income and property are not distributable to its members or office bearers except as reasonable compensation for services rendered.

This includes NGOs, CBOs, FBOs, Section 21 companies, trusts and any voluntary organisations.

The registration process to attain NPO status takes two months on average and is free of charge. The benefits of registration include improving the credibility of the sector, as NPOs can account to a public office and receive help in accessing benefits such as tax incentives and funding opportunities.

Social development

Statutory bodies

National Development Agency (NDA)

The NDA was transferred from the Ministry of Finance to the Ministry of Social Development in October 2001. It is a statutory development agency whose primary focus areas are to contribute towards the eradication of poverty and its causes, and to strengthen the capacity of civil-society organisations to combat poverty.

Its primary sources of income are an annual allocation from the Department of Social Development (R96 million in 2002/03 to over R103 million in 2003/04) and donor funding.

Relief boards

The Fund-Raising Act, 1978 (Act 107 of 1978), provides for relief boards to provide social relief to people in distress as a result of disasters or displacement from another country.

The Disaster Relief Board paid out R49,7 million to victims in the 2002/03 financial year and completed the processing of more than 19 000 claims from victims of the 2001 floods in the Western Cape.

Central Drug Authority (CDA)

Strategic and business plans have been developed specifically to facilitate the implementation of the South African National Drug Master Plan (NDMP) that was adopted by the Cabinet in 1999. The business plan takes cognisance of the basic proposals and priorities identified in the NDMP to counter the drug problem effectively, e.g. the need to comprehensively mobilise national and provincial departments towards taking account of drug-abuse issues in their activities and budgets, and to reduce the supply of and demand for drugs.

With regard to drug-demand reduction, various initiatives have been undertaken. For example, the launching of an ongoing national anti-drug awareness programme has been negotiated; information sheets have been developed and distributed; and numerous media interviews have been conducted on burning issues such as the decriminalisation of the use of dagga (cannabis).

With regard to drug-supply reduction, the CDA has, for example, approached members of the liquor industry in view of increasing self-regulation. Directly and indirectly, CDA members have participated in local efforts against drug syndicates, and in the efforts of the SADC, the African Union and international agencies in countering the drug problem on the African continent and abroad.

The groundwork has also been laid for the establishment of a national database on drug issues and a national clearing-house, specifically to ensure evidence-led future initiatives.

By March 2003, the CDA was planning to establish a national network of provincial and local drug forums in all nine provinces.

These will ensure good communication and the involvement of all stakeholders, including community members and grassroots organisations.

As part of the commemoration of the International Day Against Drug Abuse, the Minister of Social Development, together with the CDA and UN Office for Drug Control, launched the *Ke Moja* Anti-Drug Campaign in Cape Town on 24 June 2003. The Minister also gave a special address to Parliament on the impact of drugs in South African society, particularly on the youth.

South Africa Yearbook 2003/04

Acknowledgements

BuaNews
Department of Social Development
Estimates of National Expenditure 2003, published by the National Treasury
National Development Agency
www.gov.za

Suggested reading

Barnard, D. and Terreblanche, Y. eds. *PRODDER: The Southern African Development Directory 1999/00*. Pretoria: Human Sciences Research Council (HSRC), 1999.
Cassiem, S. and others. *Are Poor Children Being Put First? Child Poverty and the Budget*. Cape Town: Institute for Democracy in South Africa, 2000.
Donald, D., Dawes, A. and Louw, J. eds. *Addressing Childhood Adversity*. Cape Town: David Philip, 2000.
Eckley, S.A.C. *Transformation of Care for the Aged in South Africa*. In: *Social Work Practice*, 2, 1996, pp 47 – 51.
Fraser-Molekti, G. *Giving the Youth their Due*. In: *SA Now*, Vol I no 4 1996, pp 7 – 12.
Gray, M, ed. *Developmental Social Work: Theory and Practice in South Africa*. Cape Town: David Philip, 1999.
Hart, G. *Disabling Globalisation: Places of Power in Post-Apartheid South Africa*. Pietermaritzburg: University of Natal Press, 2002.
Isbister, J. *Promises Not Kept: The Betrayal of Social Change in the Third World*. 4th ed. West Hartford. Connecticut, Kumarian Press: 1998.
Kok, P. and Pietersen, J. *Youth*. Pretoria: HSRC, 2000.
Laubscher, J. ed. *Interfering Women. No Place: National Council of Women of South Africa, n.d. History of the National Council of Women of South Africa, 1909 – 1999*.
Leggett, T., Miller, V. and Richards, R. eds. *My Life in the New South Africa: A Youth Perspective*. Pretoria: HSRC, 1997.
Luirink, B. *Moffies: Gay and Lesbian Life in Southern Africa*. Cape Town: David Philip, 2000.
Magubane, B. M. *African Sociology: Towards a Critical Perspective*. Trenton, N.J: Africa World Press, 2000.
Marais, H.C. and others. eds. *Sustainable Social Development: Critical Issues*. Pretoria: Network Publishers, 2001.
May, J. ed. *Poverty and Inequality in South Africa: Meeting the Challenge*. Cape Town: David Philip, 1999.
Mazibuko, F.N.M. *Policy Analysis as a Strategy of Welfare Policy Development: The White Paper Process, 1996*. In: *Social Work Practice*, 32, 1996, p 234 – 241.
Midgley, J. *Promoting a Developmental Perspective in Social Welfare*. In: *Social Work Practice*, 32, 1996, p 1 – 7.
Morris, A. *Bleakness and Light: Inner-City Transition in Hillbrow*. Johannesburg: Witwatersrand, 1999.
Mothers and Fathers of the Nation: The Forgotten People? Department of Social Development, 26 February 2001.
Pistorius, P. ed. *Texture and Memory: The Urbanism of District Six*. Cape Town: Cape Technikon, 2002. 2nd ed.
Report of the Land Committee on Child and Family Support. August 1996.
Role of the Private Practice of Social Work in the Transformation and Restructuring of Welfare in South Africa. In: *Social Work Practice*, 2, 1996, pp 43 – 46.
Sadik, N. ed. *Population Policies and Programmes. Lessons Learnt from Two Decades of Experience*. New York: New York University Press, 1991.
Sarandon, S. *Children of AIDS: Africa's Orphan Disaster*. Pietermaritzburg: University of Natal Press, 2001.
Seleoane, M. *Socio-Economic Rights in the South African Constitution*. Pretoria: HSRC, 2001.
Sono, T. *Race Relations in Post-Apartheid South Africa*. Johannesburg: South African Institute of Race Relations, 1999.
The Apartheid City and Beyond: Urbanisation and Social Change in South Africa. London: Routledge; Johannesburg: University of the Witwatersrand, 1992.
The Road to Social Development: Department of Social Development, April 2001.
The State of South Africa's Population: 2000: National Population Unit, Department of Social Development, September 2000.

The Women, Gender and Development Reader. Editors: N. Visvananathan and others. Cape Town: David Philip, 1997.
Vergnani, L. *Getting Rid of the Welfare Dinosaurs.* In: *Landing Edge,* 6, 1996, pp 29 – 33.
Women Marching into the 21st Century: Wathint' Abafazi, Wathint' Imbokodo. Pretoria: HSRC, 2000.
Wylie, D. *Starving on a Full Stomach.* Charlottesville: University Press of Virginia, 2001.
Zegeye, A. ed. *Social Identities in the New South Africa. (After Apartheid, Vol. 1).* Cape Town: Kwela Books, 2001.

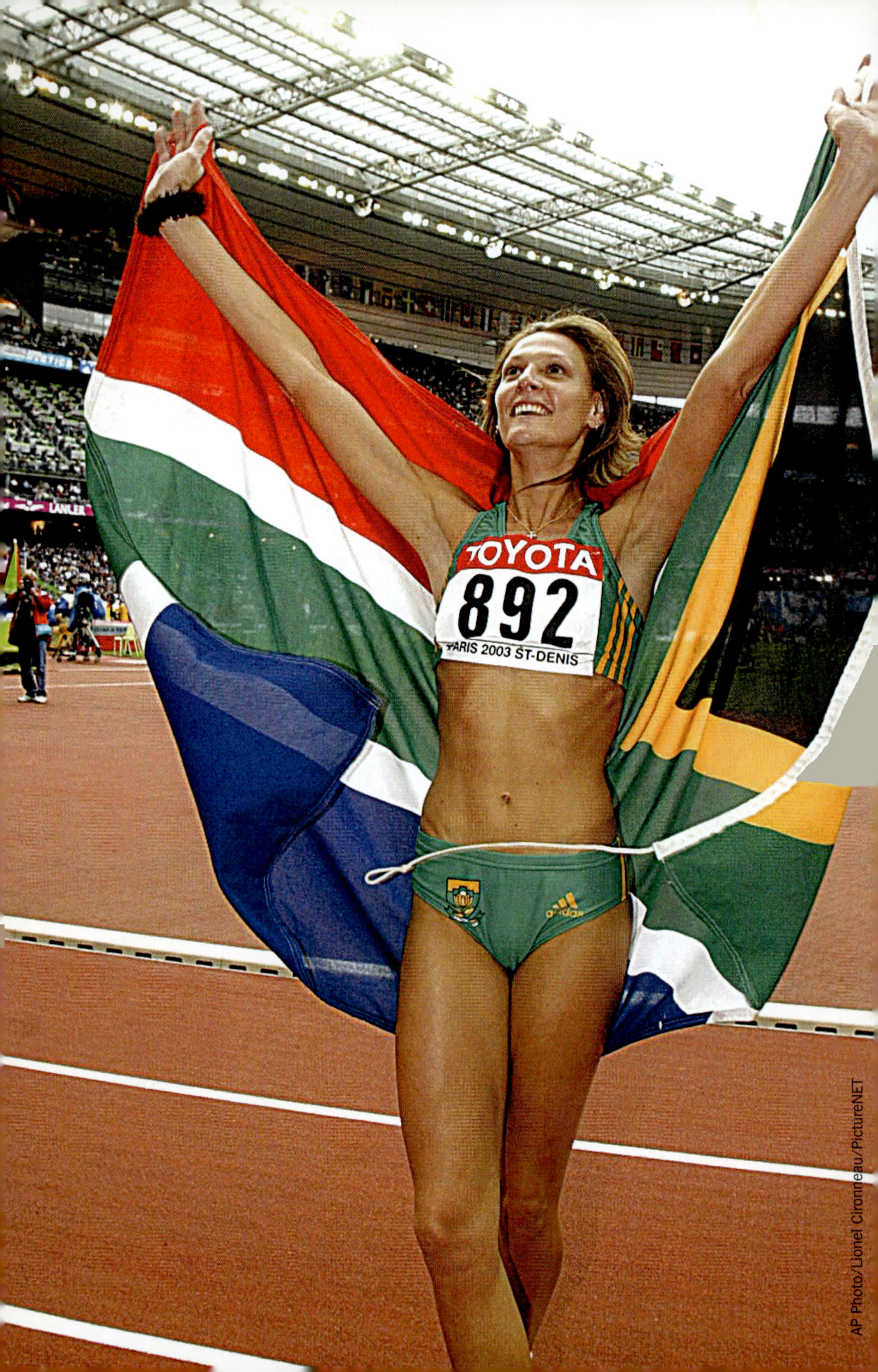

AP Photo/Lionel Cironneau/PictureNET

chapter 20

Sport and recreation

In giving effect to the theme of sport and recreation in South Africa, namely *Getting The Nation To Play*, there is a huge responsibility on stakeholders (including all spheres of government) to actively contribute towards raising the levels of participation in organised sport and recreation, which are currently estimated at between 7% and 20%. In this regard, emphasis is directed at increasing the levels of participation of historically disadvantaged and marginalised groups, including black South Africans, women, the youth, rural communities and people with disabilities.

According to a survey done in 2000, there was an increase in the contribution of sport and recreation to the Gross Domestic Product (GDP) of South Africa from 1,9% in 1997 to 2% in 2000. Its estimated worth was some R15 913 million. If capital expenditure is included, the contribution rises to R16 765 million or 2,1% of GDP. According to the survey, sport and recreation provided employment for some 34 325 full-time and 6 140 part-time workers, and makes use of 8 000 volunteers.

Within South Africa, the overall responsibility for policy, provision and facilitation of sport and recreation delivery, resides with Sport and Recreation South Africa (SRSA) and the South African Sports Commission (SASC).

The key objectives of the SRSA are to:
- increase participation in sport and recreational activities
- raise the profile of sport and recreation, particularly among decision-makers
- increase the probability of South Africa's sportspersons and teams achieving success in major international competitions
- place sport and recreation at the forefront of efforts to address issues of national importance such as unemployment, poverty, economic development, and individual and community health.

These objectives are being pursued in co-operation with the SASC, to which several of the objectives of the former Department of Sport and Recreation were transferred in terms of the SASC Act, 1998 (109 of 1998), as amended.

The SASC is responsible for the delivery of sport and recreation through its programmes and those of its clients (the national federations).

Provincial governments are responsible for:
- making sport and recreation accessible to all people in their respective provinces
- providing the infrastructure required for sport and recreation and its maintenance
- optimising the usage of facilities through better management and capacity-building
- policy development within the context of the national sport and recreation policy, with the principal agents being provincial federations and macrobodies

◀ Hestrie Cloete was chosen as the Female World Athlete of the Year 2003. She recorded 22 wins in 26 high-jump competitions during 2003.

- implementing recreation policy through the Provincial Recreation Councils (PRORECs)
- funding these agencies
- upgrading facilities created by local governments for national and provincial events
- ensuring the existence of programmes that develop the human-resource potential in sport and recreation
- effecting international agreements as reached by the SRSA, for the purpose of sharing technology, skills transfer and the development of sport and recreation.

The SRSA is directly responsible for:
- Managing the vote for sport and recreation in the national government.
- Supporting the Minister of Sport and Recreation.
- Co-ordinating and contributing to the drafting of legislation on sport and recreation.
- Interpreting broad government policy, translating government policy into policies for sport and recreation, revising such policy if and when necessary, and monitoring the implementation thereof.
- Aligning sport and recreation policy with the policies of other government departments in the spirit of integrated planning and delivery.
- Providing legal advice to all stakeholders in sport and recreation from a government perspective.
- Subsidising clients of the SRSA in accordance with the Public Finance Management Act, 1999 (Act 1 of 1999), its concomitant regulations, as well as the SRSA funding policy, monitoring the application of such funds and advising clients on the management of their finances.
- Managing inter- and intra-governmental relations.
- Acknowledging the outstanding contributions of sportspeople to the South African society on behalf of the President, through the annual Presidential Sports Awards.
- Procuring resources from abroad for sport and recreation, through the appropriate structures in National Treasury.
- Communicating sport and recreation-related matters from a government perspective.
- Co-ordinating and monitoring the creation and upgrading of sport and recreation infrastructure through the Building for Sport and Recreation Project (BSRP). Projects have been identified in line with the Integrated Sustainable Rural Development Strategy and the Urban Renewal Strategy.

The main focus of the Project is the erection of outdoor and indoor facilities and the rehabilitation and upgrading of existing facilities. Key elements of this Project are the provision of training in facility management, and the implementation of sustainable maintenance projects.

The majority of the projects are located in rural poverty nodes.

Between 1994 and 2001, the Reconstruction and Development Programme Fund provided for the completion of 138 basic outdoor sports facilities to the value of R49,5 million and one indoor facility in each province at a total cost of R40,7 million. This amount included construction, marketing, facility management and training initiatives. During the same period, 26 projects with a total value of R1,2 million were completed countrywide with resources from the Central Sport and Recreation Fund.

The R90-million budget in 2002/03 provided for the upgrading and building of 85 facilities. It was estimated that approximately 5 500 jobs would be created in the process. A total number of 100 community sports councils and clubs were established and empowered to run and manage the facilities.

The Minister of Sport and Recreation, Mr Ncgonde Balfour, announced a R129-million allocation for the BSRP during his 2003/04 Budget speech in April 2003.

Some 113 projects were expected to benefit from the funding which was distributed as follows:
- Western Cape (R8,71 million for 13 facilities)
- Eastern Cape (R22,08 million for 25 facilities)
- KwaZulu-Natal (R23,01 million for 17 facilities)
- Mpumalanga (R9,91 million for 12 facilities)

- Gauteng (R10,8 million for 10 facilities)
- Limpopo (R19,2 million for nine facilities)
- North West (R10,25 million for 10 facilities)
- Free State (R9,66 million for 15 facilities)
- Northern Cape (R6,57 million for two facilities).

Between 2000 and 2002, the SRSA provided jobs for 6 500 people, with an average income of R4 500, during the building phases of its various projects.

Since 1993, the SRSA has spent some R450 million on building and upgrading facilities countrywide.

In the last two years, 142 facilities were completed. There is still a huge backlog in terms of facility provision to disadvantaged communities. The Project will in future be pursued through the Municipal Infrastructure Development Programme of the Department of Provincial and Local Government, while the SRSA will continue to play a policy-development and oversight role, and ensure that programmes are implemented at the sites.

Sport and recreation benefit from the proceeds of the National Lottery, subject to the Lotteries Act, 2000 (Act 10 of 2000). The Distribution Agency for Sport and Recreation was established to create and consolidate thriving, sustainable, mass-based sport and recreational structures and programmes, especially in disadvantaged rural communities.

Sports Tourism Project

The primary motivation of the Project is to exploit the substantial benefits that the tourist industry presents for job creation in South Africa. The International Cricket Council (ICC) Cricket World Cup hosted in South Africa in February and March 2003 attracted some 20 000 foreign spectators. This led to the creation of 3 500 jobs during the World Cup.

The SRSA hopes to enhance the sustainability of the Project through:

- promoting 'home-grown' events such as the Comrades Marathon, Dusi Canoe Marathon, *Argus* Cycle Tour, Midmar Mile (swimming), Berg and Breede River Canoe Marathons and the Two Oceans Marathon, which attract large numbers of international participants and spectators
- working closely with South African Tourism and the Department of Environmental Affairs and Tourism to promote more attractive tourist packages for spectators who want to accompany touring sports teams to South Africa
- assisting agencies, in line with a major events strategy and the hosting and bidding regulations, to attract major international sports events to South Africa.
- marketing South Africa's sport and recreation facilities, such as golf courses and beaches, abroad.

The Minister of Sport and Recreation announced during his budget vote in April 2003 that the SRSA had conducted socio-economic impact studies on international sports events hosted by South Africa.

These included the World Surfing Games, which according to the studies, brought in revenue of more than R11 million.

It was also determined that the 2002 *Argus* Cycle Tour generated more than R300 million countrywide, with the City of Cape Town benefitting by more than R200 million.

A study on the impact of the Cricket World Cup shows that the economic impact of the tournament in terms of South African economic activity was estimated at R2,0 billion. The estimated economic impact of the Cricket World Cup in terms of net foreign spend in the country was R1,1 billion.

In the latter half of 2003, Sport and Recreation South Africa was finalising the first draft of the Safety at Sports Stadiums Bill. The Bill seeks to ensure that sports events taking place at stadiums all over the country are safe, organised and secure. The Bill also seeks to ensure that stadiums comply with the highest safety standards possible. It was envisaged that the Bill would go through the Cabinet and parliamentary processes early in 2004.

Young Champions Project

The Young Champions Project was launched in Mamelodi, Pretoria, on 18 January 2003; in Khayelitsha, Cape Town, on 7 June 2003; and in KwaMashu, Durban, on 16 August 2003.

The Project is a joint effort of the SRSA, the SASC, the South African Police Service, provincial and local departments responsible for sport and recreation, the Office of the Public Prosecutor, the Department of Justice and national and provincial sports federations.

It forms part of the SRSA's commitment to playing a role in implementing a People's Contract for Moral Regeneration, by encouraging youth, especially those in crime nodes, to take part in sport.

The Project will set up sustainable local sports leagues in the identified areas.

It will also focus on addressing the problem of substance abuse among the youth.

At the end of September 2003, a delegation from South Africa presented the *South African 2010 Bid Book* to the President of the *Federation Internationale de Football Association* (FIFA), Mr Sepp Blatter. The *Bid Book* contains all the guarantees required by FIFA as South Africa makes its bid to host the 2010 Soccer World Cup.

The 2010 Soccer World Cup Bid Committee has commissioned an economic impact study that looks very promising in terms of the potential benefits of hosting the event in South Africa.

They predict that 2,72 million tickets will be sold, generating revenue to the tune of R4,6 billion.

Capital expenditure on the upgrades of stadiums and other infrastructure will amount to R2,3 billion and the event will lead to direct expenditure of R12,7 billion while contributing R21,3 billion to the country's Gross Domestic Product. Some 159 000 new employment opportunities will be created and some R7,2 billion will be paid to government in taxes.

Staging the Soccer World Cup in South Africa in 2010 will create significant direct and indirect economic benefits for the country's economy.

A team from FIFA visited South Africa in November 2003 to assess the country's infrastructure.

South African Sports Commission

The SASC Act, 1998 provides for a commission to administer sport and recreation under the guidance of the responsible Minister. In terms of the Act, the Commission must respect the autonomy of sport and recreational organisations while acting in an advisory capacity to the Minister. It also co-ordinates the provision of facilities and community centres via a national facility plan, in consultation with the relevant authorities.

The Commission started operating on 1 April 2000.

The allocation to the SASC increased from R24,7 million in 2002/03 to 28 million in 2003/04.

The vision of the SASC is to lead South Africa to sporting excellence. The responsibilities of the SASC include:
- improving the quality of international events hosted by South Africa
- enhancing the bidding for and hosting of international events
- assisting federations and organisations that have been granted permission to host international events
- establishing internal dispute-handling mechanisms with national federations
- identifying talented athletes to ensure that South African teams are fully representative
- providing life-skills development and training
- providing information, and financial and logistical resources
- identifying priority sports on which the country's resources will be focused.

Recognition of sport and recreational bodies

The SASC has drafted regulations to administer the recognition of sport and recreational bodies, as contemplated in terms of the proposed National Sport and Recreation Amendment Bill.

Sport and recreation

The Bill will:
- amend the National Sport and Recreation Act, 1998 (Act 110 of 1998)
- provide for the registration of all women in sport and recreation with the SASC
- provide for penalties for sport and recreational bodies that do not obtain prior approval from the SASC before participating abroad
- provide for the ring-fencing by sport and recreational bodies of a percentage of all income derived from the sale of television rights, for development
- empower the Minister to intervene in disputes
- provide for the submission by all sport and recreational bodies of statistics of their total membership to the SASC.

In 2003, a new structure for karate was put in place after much division within the sport.

A professional league in basketball was also expected to be revived, while other codes such as lifesaving have been fully unified. A transformation monitoring committee is in place to ensure progress in this regard.

Hosting of and bidding for major international sports events

The SRSA and SASC have drafted regulations and administer and control the hosting of and bidding for major international sports events. A city and/or national federation that intends to bid for and host such an event is compelled to obtain written authorisation from the Minister beforehand.

National colours

The SASC has drafted regulations to administer the awarding of national colours.

In pursuance of its vision, the SASC seeks to create a nation of world-class sportsmen and women by improving opportunities for all South Africans. It also works in partnership with stakeholders by striving to meet their human-resource and infrastructure needs.

Indigenous games

The Indigenous Games Project was launched on 24 February 2001 to promote and popularise those activities that have a particular appeal to vast sectors of the South African community, especially in rural areas. The eight games are: *morabaraba, intonga, diketo, kgati, dibeke, jukskei, ncuva* and *kho-kho*.

The SASC is in the process of establishing a national structure for all indigenous games federations.

The first national Indigenous Games Festival was held in Polokwane, Limpopo from 10 to 12 October 2003.

At least 600 participants from the nine provinces took part.

Sports Information and Science Agency (SISA)

SISA was officially launched in November 1995 and is now a project of the SASC. It is committed to the establishment, co-ordination and application of a world-class information, scientific and technological resource base, with skills, capabilities, facilities and equipment to provide services to athletes, coaches, technical officials and administrators.

The first initiative taken was the establishment of a network of accredited institutes based at tertiary-education institutions. These institutes are capable of delivering professional services to sportspeople in the areas of sports nutrition, sports psychology, sports vision, sports medicine and exercise science.

The High Performance Programme (HPP) is one of many successful SISA initiatives. Between 600 and 800 elite athletes benefit from the HPP each year.

The following scientific services are provided to elite athletes nominated to be part of SISA's HPP:

Physical evaluation

This involves an evaluation of the overall physical fitness of high-performance athletes. It includes, among others, an assessment of cardiorespiratory endurance, muscular endurance, speed, muscular strength, power, flexibility, body composition and sports-specific physical evaluations.

Sports-psychology assessment
Psychological assessments are conducted with the aim of improving the athletes' mental skills before, during and after competition. The focus areas include achievement motivation, visualisation, self-confidence, concentration and goal-setting.

A sports-specific mental-skills inventory forms the basis of the assessment. The results of this assessment are strictly confidential and are only revealed to the athlete concerned.

Sports-nutrition assessment
The main aim of nutritional assessments is to improve the knowledge of the athletes to optimise sports performance, aid post-exercise recovery and maintain their health (prevent infection and fatigue).

This assessment includes a general nutritional information questionnaire, food-frequency questionnaire, typical training day's intake, and a typical competition day's intake. The athletes' fluid requirements, nutrition supplements, and menu and meal-planning are also addressed.

Sports-medicine screening
The medical screening includes a general medical assessment, a musculoskeletal assessment and a sports-specific assessment. An injury history and haematology screening is also recorded.

Sports-vision assessment
Sports-vision screening assists in determining visual abilities for the design of a programme for the enhancement of visual performance.

The assessment includes an evaluation of general ocular health, visual acuity, colour discrimination, depth perception, hand-eye co-ordination and visual concentration.

Sports technology
In 1999, a joint venture with the Council for Scientific and Industrial Research (CSIR) extended the range of services provided by SISA to include the following:
- game tactics and strategy
- virtual reality (simulation of events or situations)
- material science to improve equipment, playing areas, facilities and apparel
- communication systems to improve performance levels and to provide decision-making support to athletes, coaches, technical officials and administrators.

Dispute-Resolution Centre
The SASC established the Dispute-Resolution Centre in April 2001 in response to the national federations' need for fast, economical and private dispute-resolution mechanisms.

The Centre has, together with dispute-resolution experts, designed a set of rules that provide for strict, fair and expeditious hearings. These rules may be used when the Centre for Arbitration, under the aegis of the Arbitration Foundation for Southern Africa, refers a matter.

Projects

Junior *Dipapadi*
The Sports Pioneers Programme and Movers in Action have been merged into one programme, called Junior *Dipapadi*.

Junior *Dipapadi* aims at giving all children from the ages of three to 14 years the opportunity to participate in sport and recreation. Children are introduced to a variety of sports codes through play at beginner level. The project is divided into three subcomponents:

Super Start
The Super Start Programme has been developed in recognition of play and movement experience for children between three and six years of age. It promotes participation in

enjoyable physical activity at an early age, to encourage learning and social integration and enhance self-image. Skills such as balance, co-ordination and rhythm are developed.

Playsport
Playsport is a fundamental motor-skills programme for primary-school children. It focuses on the acquisition of basic skills, providing teachers with the resources and strategies to address the motor skills of throwing, kicking, striking, locomotion, ball control, trapping and tracking.

Modified Sport
Modified Sport is a co-ordinated way of adapting adult sport for children so that they can develop skills, experience success, and enjoy their introduction to sport. This means changing playing conditions, equipment and rules to suit the needs of young people.

The rules, equipment and dimensions of playing fields are modified to make it attractive for young people to participate in the sport.

The cornerstones of this phase are mass participation, safety and fair play, as well as skills development.

The SASC launched its first Modified Sports Festival in KwaZulu-Natal on 26 October 2002.

On 29 March 2003, about 1 000 youngsters participated in the Modified Sports Festival held at the Concordia Sports Ground in Springbok in the Northern Cape.

The event featured mini netball, rugby, soccer, volleyball, cricket and various fun activities.

Transformation in sport

Sports Transformation Charter
Following a series of workshops on transformation in sport in all nine provinces, the Transformation Charter was drafted, which guides all macrobodies, national and provincial federations and clubs on the need to transform sport by making it accessible to all South Africans. The Charter is complemented by performance agreements that national federations enter into with the Minister of Sports and Recreation. The main focus of the Charter and the performance agreement is to:
- increase participation levels in sport and recreation
- make sport and recreation accessible to all South Africans
- ensure that provincial and national teams reflect South African society as whole
- ensure that all sport and recreation bodies meet their affirmative-action objectives
- promote greater involvement of marginalised groups, such as women, people with disabilities, people living in rural communities and the youth, in sport and recreation.

Ministerial Task Team into High-Performance Sport

A Ministerial Task Team was appointed in December 2000 by the Minister of Sport and Recreation to investigate high-performance sport. Its findings are expected to result in the major restructuring of South African sport.

With the approval of the Cabinet, South African sport will in future be governed by a two-tier system, comprising a fully fledged goverment department and a non-governmental sports confederation. These two structures will take full responsibility for all levels of sport, including mass participation and high performance.

A national academy will concentrate on delivering athletes for international competition, while existing provincial academies will identify and nurture talent to feed into the national academy. The new system of governance is expected to be implemented by April 2005.

The report of the Task Team will ultimately inform the formulation of a Plan for Sport which will constitute the new *White Paper on Sport and Recreation*.

A team will be appointed to develop the plan.

Presidential Sports Awards

Natalie du Toit, who impressed with her performance at the 2002 Commonwealth Games in Manchester, England, was among those honoured by President Thabo Mbeki with a gold medal during the 2003 Presidential Sports Awards.

Other gold-medal recipients included golfers Ernie Els and Retief Goosen, high jumper Hestrie Cloete, and athlete Malcolm Pringle.

A total of 47 sport stars were honoured during the ceremony.

Silver-medal winners included cricketers Makhaya Ntini and Herschelle Gibbs, rugby player Joe van Niekerk, surfing star Travis Logie, and swimmers Scott Field, Nathan Oliver and Christiaan Du Plessis.

Eighteen disabled athletes were honoured during the 2003 Presidential Sports Awards – two received gold medals, while the others received 16 out of the 28 silver medals.

Sports organisations

National Olympic Committee of South Africa (NOCSA)

The core business of NOCSA, in terms of the Olympic Charter, is to ensure the participation of South African athletes in the Olympic Games and the execution of its high-performance mandate.

This comprises talent-identification capacity-building (Operation Excellence Programme) and fast-tracking delivery. NOCSA's main mandate is to ensure commendable performances in the Olympic Games.

About 41 national federations fall under the NOCSA umbrella body, 28 of which represent Olympic sports. Three are winter Olympic sports.

In May 2003, NOCSA and the 2004 Olympic partners visited Athens, Greece, to view hospitality facilities available for the 2004 Games. Athletes have been hard at work under the Operation Excellence Programme. Through this Programme, athletes are provided with an annual grant to cover their basic costs. They are also supported with equipment, and money for training camps, international participation and the services of an international coach, if needed. Among the athletes gaining from Operation Excellence are Terence Parkin, Zaida Jardine, Ryk Neethling, Nzimeni Msutu, Mbulaheni Mulaudzi, Hestrie Cloete and Morne Nagel.

Disability Sport South Africa (DISSA)

DISSA is the controlling body that recognises the right of the disabled to participate in sports activities at all levels.

It is responsible for the selection and funding of South African national teams attending the Paralympic Games or any world championships recognised by the International Paralympic Committee (IPC). It is the South African member of the IPC.

The strategic objectives of DISSA include:
- ensuring increased opportunities for participation by promoting the inclusion of the disabled community with sports federations, sponsors and other stakeholders
- supporting athletes, coaches and officials through the Sports Commission's HPP
- creating opportunities through mass-participation programmes for coaches, athletes, technical officials, classifiers and volunteers.

DISSA's programmes are broadly defined in terms of talent identification and high performance.

DISSA aims to provide athletes with an opportunity to achieve consistent success in major international competitions, in co-operation with the able-bodied and hearing federations at national level.

The delivery of DISSA's sports-development programmes are achieved through:
- effective and efficient distribution of funding, both for capital and revenue programmes, with straightforward application procedures

Sport and recreation

and thorough monitoring and evaluation of projects
- support for the education and training of volunteers, coaches, technical officials, classifiers and administrators
- efficient support services, delivered either in-house or by external contractors
- a desire to create an excellent organisation with a commitment towards continuous improvement and innovation.

DISSA works closely with the South African Commonwealth Games Association, the All Africa Games, and the South African Federal Council on Disability.

DISSA also has close contact with the national sports federations and is committed towards supporting their development as the responsible bodies for all athletes, including those with disabilities.

Through the merger of the South African Sport Association for the Intellectualy Impaired and Special Olympics South Africa, Sport for the Intellectually Disabled (SID) was born. A delegation from SID met Special Olympics International during the World Games in June 2003, to get their buy-in to the process and support for three brands under DISSA, namely Paralympics, Deaflympics and Special Olympics.

Boxing South Africa

Boxing South Africa was established in terms of the South African Boxing Act, 2001 (Act 11 of 2001), and is partly funded with public money. Its function is to promote boxing and protect the interests of boxers and officials. Its main purposes are to:
- consider applications for licences from all stakeholders in professional boxing
- sanction fights
- implement the regulations pertaining to boxing
- promote the interests of all stakeholders in boxing.

Boxing South Africa's new academy was launched in August 2003.

The Boxing Academy was kickstarted using part of the R27 million invested in boxing by cellular provider Vodacom. The Academy will be spearheaded by SISA, in conjunction with the University of Pretoria's High-Performance Centre.

The first phase of implementation started in August 2003, with nine hand-picked promoters from across the country honing their promotional skills in courses at the High Performance Centre.

The Academy will also offer boxers high performance, physical fitness, and athletics and life skills.

South African Institute for Drug-Free Sport (SAIDS)

The main objectives of the SAIDS are to promote participation in sport which is free from the use of prohibited substances, to encourage the development of programmes in respect of the dangers of using drugs in sport, and to provide leadership in the development of a national strategy concerning doping in sport.

The SRSA has drafted the South African Institute for Drug-Free Sport Amendment Bill to:
- reprioritise the objectives of the Institute
- strengthen the powers and duties of the Institute.

The Bill is expected to be promulgated during 2004.

Between April 2002 and March 2003, the Institute conducted 2 800 drug tests on South African athletes from 54 sporting disciplines, of which there were 42 (1,77%) positive test results. The majority of these positive results were for the following prohibited substances:
- stimulants (31%)
- anabolic agents (47,6%)
- diuretics (14,3%).

In addition to its national testing programme, the SAIDS was subcontracted to conduct 292 in- and out-of-competition tests for international sports federations, the World Anti-Doping Agency (WADA) and other national anti-doping organisations.

South Africa Yearbook 2003/04

Funding for the Institute will increase from R3,3 million in 2002/03 to R4,0 million in 2005/06.

The Institute was appointed to conduct doping-control programmes at two major international events outside the borders of South Africa, namely the Women's Rugby World Cup, which was held in Barcelona, Spain, and the 2002 Africa Military Games held in Kenya.

The Institute has 55 fully trained and certified doping control officers (DCOs) based throughout South Africa and 12 trainee DCOs who were certified by mid-2003. Since May 2003, the Institute has implemented a recruitment and training programme for chaperones.

The Institute produced and distributed education and information material to sports federations, athletes and coaches, and conducted an average of three lectures and workshops a month to its various target markets. The Institute also developed a sports-drug education programme for school learners in collaboration with Bridges, a drug education and intervention non-governmental organisation. During 2002 and early 2003, a series of pilot workshops were held nationally to assess the reaction and get input from school sports coaches. The programme was expected to be launched in 2003 with the assistance of funds for this project allocated to the Institute by the Lottery Board.

In September 2002, the Institute became one of only nine national anti-doping agencies worldwide to be certified by the International Organisation for Standardisation (ISO) in compliance with International Standards for Doping Control, and one of only three national anti-doping agencies to have been certified against the latest, updated and improved ISO 9001:2000 Standard.

South African golfing legend Gary Player was honoured for his contribution to the world of golf (on and off the course) with a Lifetime Achievement Award at the Laureus Sport Awards in Monaco in May 2003.

The Institute has entered into Reciprocal Testing Agreements with Australia, Norway and the Netherlands.

The WADA has agreed to establish a regional office for Africa in Cape Town. The office will take responsibility for all WADA activities on the continent.

Recreation

The result of co-operation between Recreation South Africa, the South African National Recreation Council and the SRSA is the South African National Games and Leisure Activities (SANGALA) Programme. The programme was launched in February 1996 to involve South Africans in healthy recreational activities in the nation-building process.

SANGALA consists of the following:
- Community, which targets the broad community without any differentiation in age or status.
- Training, which specialises in the training of community recreational leaders.
- Corporate, which is aimed at middle and senior management in both the private and public sectors.
- Senior, which encourages physical activity among senior citizens. More than 200 000 senior citizens participate annually in this project.
- Street, which is a life-skills project for homeless children.
- RecRehab, which is a project for the rehabilitation of youth and women in prisons, and trains leaders to present recreational activities in prison. More than 1 000 prisoners participate in activities countrywide.

PRORECs are responsible for networking with recreational service-providers to ensure participation at grassroots level.

The emphasis of recreation delivery is on provincial and local levels, where people participate in a variety of recreational activities, including indigenous games.

2003 sports highlights

Cricket

Cricket World Cup 2003

The opening ceremony of the 2003 ICC Cricket World Cup on 8 February dazzled audiences across the globe, as 4 500 performers turned Newlands Stadium in Cape Town into the best celebration Africa had to offer.

The impressive extravaganza was made possible by the dedication of a cast of volunteers, ranging from eight to 86-years-of-age, and top South African performers such as Johnny Clegg, Rebecca Malope, Yvonne Chaka Chaka, the Soweto String Quartet and Lekgoa.

The showcase was broadcast to a worldwide television audience of over one billion people.

The 2003 Cricket World Cup ran for 44 days from the opening ceremony to the final in Johannesburg on 23 March. A total of 54 cricket matches were played – a record for the ICC Cricket World Cup.

A total of 14 countries participated in the tournament, namely South Africa, Australia, Pakistan, India, England, Zimbabwe, Netherlands, Namibia, Sri Lanka, New Zealand, West Indies, Bangladesh, Kenya and Canada.

The 2003 Cricket World Cup was won by Australia, who beat India by 125 runs at the Wanderers Stadium.

Breaking records

Makhaya Ntini became the ninth South African bowler to take 100 Test wickets – this feat was achieved during the second Test match against Bangladesh at Dhaka in October 2003.

Graeme Smith became the youngest captain to score a Test century at Birmingham, England, in July 2003. Having also added 368 for the first wicket in the Test against Pakistan at Cape Town earlier in 2003, Herschelle Gibbs and Smith became the second pair to have made two triple-century partnerships in Test cricket for any wicket.

Tennis

Mercedes Benz Cup

Wayne Ferreira overcame a nagging hip injury and searing heat to beat top-seeded Lleyton Hewitt 6-3, 4-6, 7-5 in the final of the Mercedes Benz Cup in Los Angeles, United States of America (USA).

His victory made Ferreira the first South African to win the 77-year-old tournament.

Golf

Nedbank Golf Challenge

Ernie Els claimed his third Nedbank title with an astounding nine-under-par course-record, 63, in the final round at Sun City in the North West, in December 2002. He ended with 21 shots under par.

Mercedes Golf Championship

Els won the Mercedes Golf Championship in Hawaii in January 2003 with a final round of 65.

Els' outstanding performance also earned him a new record for a PGA Championship in the American series, with a total of 261 for the four rounds, 31 strokes under par.

Heineken Classic

Els continued his winning streak in Melbourne, Australia in February 2003, when he played a round of 65 to win the Heineken Classic.

Els' spectacular win featured an average tee-shot of 317,3 yards.

European Masters

Els won his sixth major championship for the season when he finished with 267, 17 under par at the European Masters in Crans-Sur-Sierre, Switzerland, September 2003.

It was Els' 15th European Tour and his 46th Championship worldwide.

HSBC World Match-Play Championships

In October 2003, Els successfully defended the HSBC World Match-Play Championship title in Wentworth, United Kingdom (UK), beating fellow European Tour member Thomas Bjorn by 4 and 3 in a 36-hole final.

Champion Tour (Seniors Tour)
In October 2003, Hale Irwin won the Champion Tour (Seniors Tour) with 37 wins out of 200 starts. He also came second 35 times and third 19 times.

Qatar Masters
Darren Fichardt closed with a 69 for a four-round total of 275, 13 under par in March 2003, to win the Qatar Masters, his second title on the European Tour.

Chrysler Classic
In November 2003, Retief Goosen won the Chrysler Classic by three shots. He finished the tournament with 12 under par. Vijay Singh took second place.

World Gold Championships
In November 2003, Trevor Immelman and Rory Sabbatini won the World Cup at Kawaih Island by four strokes.

President's Cup
In November 2003, President Mbeki officiated as honorary chairperson at the President's Cup, a golf event between a team from the USA and an international team at the Fancourt Golf Estate in George, Western Cape. In an unprecedented finish, the US and international teams, led by Tiger Woods and Ernie Els respectively, finished level and shared the cup.

Motorsport

Dakar Rally
Giniel de Villiers from the Proudly South African Team braved 8 602 km of difficult terrain between Marseille, France and Sjarm-el-Sjeikh in Egypt to finish fifth overall in the 2003 Dakar Rally. It was the first time that the young South African had participated in the gruelling 19-day race.

Only 61 of the 134 vehicles that set out from the starting line managed to reach the finish.

Boxing
Corrie Saunders scored a sensational second-round knockout win over Vladimir Klitschko in Hanover, Germany, in March 2003, to claim the World Boxing Organisation heavyweight title.

The 38-year-old Saunders turned professional in 1989.

Hockey

Afro-Asian Games
Susan Webber's five-goal streak led to South Africa's rousing 12-0 victory over Kazakhstan, in the Afro-Asian Games women's field hockey competition held in Hyderabad, India, in October 2003.

All Africa Games
In October 2003, the women's hockey team qualified for the 2004 Olympic Games in Athens, by defeating Nigeria 10-0 to claim gold at the 8th All Africa Games in Nigeria.

Surfing
Heather Clark braved the waves in Fiji in April 2003, managing to finish second at the Roxy Pro.

It was Clark's second consecutive second-position finish. This secured Clark a seventh position ranking among the world's top 10 female surfers.

In May 2003, she finished second in the Magnolia Girls Pro Six-Star Association of Surfing Professionals World Qualifying Series women's event in Portugal.

Swimming
Swimming South Africa hosted a leg of the Swimming World Cup in Durban in December 2003.

It was the first time that a leg of the World Cup was held in Africa.

Sport and recreation

South Africa was one of the nine countries chosen out of the 16 that bid for the event.

Other successful applicants were Korea, Australia, France, Sweden, Russia, Germany, the USA, Mexico and Brazil.

Natalie du Toit, who wowed sport enthusiasts with her brave recovery after losing a leg in an accident, and her subsequent remarkable performance at the Commonwealth Games in Manchester in 2002, shattered the world record in the 100 m freestyle exhibition race at the 10th Fina World Championship in Barcelona, Spain.

Du Toit took the honours in 1 minute 2,72 seconds, bettering the previous world record of 1:02,89.

She was invited to participate in the exhibition event by the IPC, based on her number one ranking following her performance in Manchester.

Du Toit also took the silver medal in the closely contested women's 800-m freestyle event behind Sharon Austin of the Seychelles, at the Afro-Asian Games in October 2003.

Special Olympics

The 40-athlete strong South African Special Olympics team brought home 37 medals from the Special Olympics held in Dublin, Ireland, in June 2003.

The South Africans won eight gold, seven silver and three bronze medals in athletics, while the soccer team claimed two bronze medals in the five-a-side and the 11-a-side events.

The golfers brought home two medals of each colour.

The gold-medal winners were Mzewakhe Sithole, Thulani Stambola, Johannes Nhlapo, Shelboy Pitsi, Kevin Gibbs, Gail Bugana, Sam Mphela, Willem Swanepoel and Jennifer Higgins.

Athletics

Golden League

Long-legged Hestrie Cloete dazzled the crowd at the Golden League meet in Berlin, Germany, during August 2003, when she broke her own Africa record with a jump of 2,05 metre (m), marking the best jump of her athletic career.

Cloete's previous personal best was 2,04 m, which she achieved in Monaco in 1999.

World Athletics Championships

Jacques Freitag set the pace for the South African team when he cleared 2,35 m in the men's high jump, earning his first gold at the World Athletics Championships in Saint-Denis, Paris, in August 2003.

His female counterpart, Hestrie Cloete broke her own Commonwealth and Africa records by clearing a height of 2,06 m, earning her the gold and title of world champion in the women's high jump. Cloete became the first women in the history of athletics to keep her title after two events. She first won the title at Edmonton, Canada, in 2001.

In September 2003, Cloete was chosen as the female World Athlete of the Year 2003. She recorded 22 wins in 26 high-jump competitions during 2003.

Other outstanding performances by the South African team included Okkert Brits' silver medal in the men's pole vault, and a bronze for the 800-m athlete Mbulaheni Mulaudzi.

Equestrian

Federation Equestre Internationale (FEI) Children's World Cup Challenge

One of the most touching success stories in South African sport in 2003 was that of Bongani Mvumvu from Cape Town, who became the world champion at the FEI Children's World Cup Challenge, in Hargen, Germany, during August 2003.

It was the first time Mvumvu had ever competed at international level.

Soccer

Africa Cup of Nations

Bafana Bafana qualified for the Africa Cup of

Nations tournament, to be played in Tunisia in February 2004, when they beat Burundi 2-0 at the Louis Rwagasore stadium in Bujumbura in July 2003.

South African Football Association Awards

In October 2003, Banyana Banyana midfielder Antonio Carelse won the South African Football Association's Women's Player of the Year Award.

Abongile Nkamane from Ajax Cape Town scooped the Junior Player of the Year Award. He was a key member of the national under-12 championship team which won an international junior tournament in France in 2003.

Danone Nations Cup

In September 2003, South Africa's under-12 soccer team, the Tsetse Flies, won the Danone Nations Cup in France.

The world champions beat Portugal 2-0 in the final game in Paris. The South Africans scored 28 goals and conceded none in the 32-country tournament.

The team returned home with an impressive string of victories, having kickstarted their winning streak when they beat the USA 5-0. The South Africans went on to beat Holland 12-0, Portugal 2-0, Poland 2-0, England 1-0, Austria 3-0, and beat Portugal again 3-0.

Besides clinching the title of world champions and the award for the tournament's best defence, the Tsetse Flies' Monama Motsamela also walked off with the Player of the Tournament Award.

Squash

World Masters Squash Championship

The South African team squashed their opponents to win the most medals at the World Masters Squash Championship in Espoo, Finland, in August 2003.

The team won a total of six gold and four silver medals.

The medal winners included Craig van der Wath, Alan Colburn, Brian Heath, Angie Clifton Parks, Pauline Douglas and Jean Grainger.

Cycling

World Downhill Cycling Race

Mountain biker Greg Minnaar from Pietermaritzburg became the first South African in 110 years to become a world champion at the Downhill Cycling Race in Lugano, Switzerland, in August 2003. The only previous South African to boast this achievement was Laurens Meintjies from Port Elizabeth, who won the title in 1893 in Chicago, USA.

All Africa Games

South Africa glittered at the 2003 Africa Games in Abuja, Nigeria, in October 2003. The swimming team did especially well, earning several gold medals. The gold-medallists included Natalie du Toit, who won the 800 m freestyle event, Romy Altmann (breaking the Africa record in the 100 m backstroke), Kurt Muller (50 m breaststroke) and the women's 4x100 m freestyle relay team. Johannes Kekana won gold in the men's marathon, after recording two hours, 25:01 minutes.

Nigeria won the Games with 85 gold medals, four ahead of Egypt's 81. South Africa came third with a total of 63 gold medals.

Rugby

South Africa participated in the Rugby World Cup 2003 in Australia. They lost to England 6-25, beat Georgia 46-19, beat Samoa 60-10, but lost to New Zealand by 29-9 in the quarter-finals.

2004 sports events

South African sports fans are looking forward to, among others, the following sports events in 2004:

- Africa Cup of Nations, Tunisia (February)
- South African Games (April in Buffalo City, Eastern Cape).
- Olympic Games, Athens, Greece (August)

Sport and recreation

Acknowledgements

Estimates of National Expenditure 2003, Published by the National Treasury
South Africa.info
South African Sports Commission
Sport and Recreation South Africa
www.gov.za

Suggested reading

Alfred, L. *Lifting the Covers: The Inside Story of South African Cricket*. Cape Town: Spearhead, 2001.
Alfred, L. *Testing Times: The Story of the Man Who Made South African Cricket*. Cape Town: Spearhead Press, 2003.
Attitudes and Impressions about Sports Sponsorships among Major South African Companies. Pretoria, 2000. Sports Information and Science Agency (SISA).
Berkowitz, A. and Samson, A. *Supersport Factfinder*. 5th ed. Cape Town: Don Nelson, 1997.
Bryden, C. *Story of SA Cricket, 1990 – 1996*. Cape Town: Inter-African Publications, 1997.
Burke, L. and others. *The Complete South African Guide to Sports Nutrition*. Cape Town: Oxford University Press, 1998.
Chesterfield, T. and McGlew, J. *South Africa's Cricket Captains*. Cape Town: Zebra Press, 2002.
Cottrell, T. *Old Mutual's Runner's Guide to Road Races in South Africa*. Parklands: Guide Book Publications, 2003.
Cottrell, T. and others. *Comrades Marathon Yearbook*. Halfway House: Southern Books, 1998.
Cottrell, T., Laxton, I. and Williams, D. *Comrades Marathon: Highlights and Heroes, 1921 – 1999*. Johannesburg: Jonathan Ball, 2000.
Desai, A. et al. *Blacks in Whites: A Century of Cricket Struggles in KwaZulu-Natal*. Pietermaritzburg: University of Natal Press, 2002.
Evans, G. *Dancing Shoes is Dead*. London: Doubleday, 2002.
Griffiths, E. *Bidding for Glory: Why South Africa Lost the Olympic and World Cup Bids, and How to Win Next Time*. Johannesburg: Jonathan Ball, 2000.
Griffiths, E. *The Captains*. Johannesburg: Jonathan Ball, 2001.
Grundelingh, A. and others. *Beyond the Tryline: Rugby and SA Society*. Randburg: Ravan Press, 1995.
Jarvie, G. *Class, Race and Sport in SA's Political Economy*. London: Routledge and Kegan Paul, 1985.
Knowles, R. *SA Versus England: A Test History*. Cape Town: Sable Media, 1995.
Lambson, B. *The South African Guide to Cricket with Barry Lambson and Brian Basson*. Editor: M. Collins. Cresta: Michael Collins Publications, 1998.
Leppan, L. *South African Book of Records*. Cape Town: Don Nelson, 1999.
National Sport and Recreation South Africa, White Paper: Getting the Nation to Play. Pretoria, 1998.
Nauright, J. *Sport, Cultures and Identities in South Africa*. Cape Town: David Philip, 1998.
Odendaal, A. *The Story of an African Game*. Cape Town: David Philip, 2003.
South African Rugby Annual, 2003; edited by Andy Colquhoun. Cape Town: South African Rugby, 2003.
SISA. *Drug-Related issues in South African sport – an awareness study*, 2000.
SISA. *HIV/AIDS in Sport – Play it safe*, 1999.
SISA. *Sport Facility Provision in South Africa – A Prioritising Model*, Pretoria, 1999.
SISA. *Strategic Framework*, Pretoria, 2000.
SISA. *Impact of Sport on the South African Economy*, Pretoria, 2000.
SISA. *Research on the Participation of Women in Sport in South Africa*, 1997.
SISA. *A Summary of the Contribution of Sport to the South African Society*. Pretoria, 2000.
Stangen Sports Record RSA, 1990. Randburg: Resources Dynamics, 1990.
Taking Sport into the Future. 2001. South African Sports Commission.
Who's Who of South African Rugby. Cape Town: Don Nelson, 1996.
Winch, J. *Cricket in Southern Africa: Two Hundred Years of Achievements and Records*: Rosettenville, Johannesburg: Windsor, 1997

Guy Stubbs/Touchline Images

chapter 21
Tourism

Tourism is South Africa's fastest growing industry and contributes about 7,1% of the Gross Domestic Product.

South Africa is the fastest-growing tourism destination in the world, with 6,4 million tourists having travelled to the country during 2002.

Overseas arrivals increased by 20,1% (just over 1,8 million) during 2002.

All of South Africa's key markets posted double-digit growth for the year, with Europe up 24,2% and North America up 9,2%. There was also an increase of 20,7% in travel from Asia, and 14,5% from Australasia.

Africa, contributing the bulk of foreign arrivals into South Africa (1,06 million) grew by 2,1% with close to 35 000 additional arrivals from Kenya, identified as one of South Africa's key emerging markets.

The United Kingdom (UK) and Germany led the influx of European tourists with 442 910 and 248 990 arrivals respectively.

The majority of travellers from Asia were from China (some 36 957), representing an increase of 24,5% from 2001. Travel from Australia increased by 15,1%.

Arrivals from the United States of America (USA) increased by 7% – an increase that was very welcome given the tough conditions affecting travel from that market.

◀ Tourism employs about 3% of South Africa's workforce and is regarded as potentially the largest provider of jobs and earner of foreign exchange.

December 2002 recorded the highest monthly foreign tourist arrivals. More than 650 683 foreign tourists visited the country in comparison with the 575 831 recorded in December 2001, recording a 15,8% growth – the highest since 1998.

Arrivals from Africa increased by 7,8% to almost 4,4 million, despite the significant decrease from Lesotho, though this was offset by significant increases from Zimbabwe (22,1%) and Botswana (21,6%).

Tourist arrivals from Europe increased by 10,9% over January to March 2002, North America increased by 8,9%, while those from Australia were up 13,5%. Asia enjoyed 19,4% growth, boosted in no small part by 14 339 Indian visitors cheering on their cricket team during the 8th International Cricket Council (ICC) Cricket World Cup.

The 2003 first quarterly tourist-arrival statistics showed an increase of 11,3% compared with the same period in 2002 (January to March).

South Africa maintained its 2002 performance in the first quarter of 2003, despite adverse global conditions which included the war on Iraq, recession in three of the world's major economies and the outbreak of Severe Acute Respiratory Syndrome. This compared favourably with many of South Africa's competitors, who recorded sharp decreases across the board during the same period.

Tourism employs an estimated 3% of South Africa's workforce, and is regarded as potentially the largest provider of jobs and earner of foreign exchange. It is projected that in 2010, the South African tourism economy will employ more than 1,2 million people (directly and indirectly).

Tourism is the fourth-largest industry in South Africa, supporting some 6 500 accommodation establishments.

Certain factors in South Africa's favour, which are expected to further tourism growth, include:
- national tourism assets of incomparable quality in certain segments
- a diversity of tourism products, especially adventure, ecotourism and cultural attractions
- exceptional value for money relative to key competitors, partly owing to foreign-exchange rates

---

South Africa received several international tourism accolades in 2002.

In September 2002, South Africa was rated as a preferred tourist destination by the French travel industry, with over 21 000 tour operators and retail agents giving the country the thumbs-up at TOP RESA, the annual travel and tourism trade show held in Deauville, France.

The United Kingdom (UK) travel publication *Conde Nast Traveller* awarded South Africa top place as the overall value-for-money long-haul destination.

The *Conde Nast* Awards are voted for by the readers of the influential magazine that focuses on well-travelled high-income earners in the UK. This is how South Africa fared in the following categories:
- Best Overall Global Destination Country (short-and-long haul): South Africa was rated 10th in the world, taking top global honours for value for money
- Best Overseas City: Cape Town was voted number 14, taking top honours for hospitality and value for money
- Best Overseas Leisure Hotels (Africa and Middle East): South Africa had four hotels in the top 10: Singita (10th), Londolozi (8th), Cape Grace (3rd) and the Mount Nelson (2nd)
- Best Overall Tour Operators: South African Tourism has relationships with seven of the top 10: British Airways Holidays, Carrier, Trailfinders, Kuoni, ITC Classics, Abercrombie & Kent and Elegant Resorts.

- positive global perceptions of peaceful political transition in South Africa.

The fastest-growing segment of tourism in South Africa is ecological tourism (ecotourism), which includes nature photography, bird-watching, botanical studies, snorkelling, hiking and mountaineering.

National and provincial parks in South Africa, as well as private game reserves, involve local communities in the conservation and management of natural resources. These communities are not only benefiting financially from ecotourism, but are also becoming aware of their responsibility to the environment.

The high foreign-exchange value of ecotourism enables significant economic value to be assigned to ecological resources, in this way helping to promote their conservation.

Community tourism is becoming increasingly popular, with tourists wanting to experience South Africa in the many rural villages and townships across the country. (See Chapter 5: *Arts and culture*.)

Tourism policy

At national level, the Tourism Branch in the Department of Environmental Affairs and Tourism leads and directs tourism-policy formulation and implementation towards national tourism growth. It works in partnership with South African Tourism, the provincial tourism authorities, the tourism industry and other relevant stakeholders. It aims to ensure and accelerate the practical delivery of tourism benefits to the broad spectrum of South Africans, while maintaining sustainability and quality of life.

The *White Paper on Tourism* provides a policy framework for tourism development and entails the following programmes:
- a special empowerment programme for capacity-building
- establishing a tourism-infrastructure investigations programme that will culminate in

identified public-infrastructure-investment programmes
- mobilising funds to aggressively market South Africa as a tourism destination in international markets, through a focused marketing strategy
- launching a domestic tourism and travel campaign.

A collaborative tourism action (cluster) process, which will provide the framework for taking tourism into the next millennium, has been launched. The process aims to achieve collective action among key stakeholders, to enhance tourism marketing, investment, skills and infrastructure development.

The Tourism Forum was established in December 1998 as an advisory body to the Minister of Environmental Affairs and Tourism. It comprises leadership drawn from government, business, public institutions and labour, with the common purpose of ensuring growth and development of the tourism sector. The Forum agreed to support the following key strategic areas:
- sustainable funding mechanisms
- information systems
- human resource development (HRD) programmes
- international marketing
- the *Welcome* Campaign.

The Department has embarked on a legislative reform process to reflect the guidelines set out in the White Paper.

The Tourist Guides Awards, which aim to recognise the contribution made by South Africa's tourist guides in promoting the country as a must-see destination, were launched at the Tourism Indaba in Durban in May 2003.

The initiator of the Awards, the Department of Environmental Affairs and Tourism, will consult with relevant stakeholders to develop criteria for the competition.

The Department and the various provincial tourism authorities will be responsible for the co-ordination and launching of the Awards in their respective provinces.

The winners will be announced on World Tourist-Guide Day, 21 February 2004.

The Tourism Transformation Strategy was approved by Cabinet in November 2001. More emphasis is being placed on developing black-owned businesses within the tourism industry, by raising the proportion of government expenditure going to these businesses from 30% in 2001/02 to 50% in 2004/05.

A database of black-owned tourism enterprises was compiled to assist government departments with meeting affirmative-procurement targets.

A public-private tourism transformation forum to promote Black Economic Empowerment (BEE) was established, with representatives from the Departments of Environmental Affairs and Tourism, of Trade and Industry and of Labour, the Tourism Business Council, the Development Bank of Southern Africa and the Industrial Development Corporation.

Other initiatives launched by the Department in 2002 to promote tourism included the formulation of an information booklet outlining the funding opportunities and assistance programmes available to small, medium and micro enterprises (SMMEs) within the tourism industry, the launch of a handbook on tourism-support programmes for SMMEs, and brochures and posters to create awareness about illegal tour guiding.

Poverty-relief funding

By early 2003, some R232 million had been committed and spent on tourism-development projects aimed at creating jobs and alleviating poverty in South Africa.

Almost R69 million had been invested in poverty-relief funding in respect of tourism, with over R10 million invested in the Free State alone.

By mid-2003, poverty-relief investment stood at a total of R290,6 million, of which R27,3 million was expected to be invested in the Free State. These poverty-relief projects promote the development of community-owned tourism products, such as lodges and the development of tourism infrastructure, including roads, information centres and tourism signage.

These poverty-relief projects are categorised into product development, infrastructure development, capacity-building and training, the establishment of SMMEs, and business-development projects.

Some 76 tourism craft projects, set up in all nine provinces in 2000/01, were expected to create 8 600 job opportunities.

Marketing

Welcome Campaign

Launched in December 1999 by the Minister of Environmental Affairs and Tourism, Mr Mohammed Valli Moosa, the *Welcome* Campaign encourages all South Africans to embrace tourism and share South Africa's rich natural and cultural heritage. The Campaign is run as a national general-awareness campaign, through roadshows and community-outreach programmes.

South Africa's Tourism Month culminated in World Tourism Day celebrations in Upington in the Northern Cape on 26 September 2003.

The theme of World Tourism Day was *Tourism as a Driving Force for Poverty Alleviation, Job Creation and Social Harmony.*

The Minister of Environmental Affairs and Tourism, Mr Mohammed Valli Moosa, encouraged South Africans to travel and discover the beauty and diversity of the country, which is a preferred tourism destination.

One of the significant activities during Tourism Month 2003 was South African Tourism's ground-breaking partnership with South African Airways and the South African Broadcasting Corporation to bring focus to the nationwide *Licence to Discover South Africa* TV competition.

Other Tourism Month activities included local media tours, festivals, exhibitions, a schools' competition and the launching of several empowerment projects.

The success of South Africa's gravity-defying tourism growth bodes well for the industry's efforts in contributing to sustainable job creation and Gross Domestic Product growth.

Central to this commitment is the strategy of co-operation that has seen a total of 172 tourism projects funded by the Department since 2001.

Key events in which the Campaign has featured include the World Summit on Sustainable Development (WSSD) and the ICC Cricket World Cup.

Underpinning the Campaign is the message that tourism is the fastest-growing contributor to South Africa's future economic prosperity and plays a key role in job creation and socio-economic upliftment.

Another facet of the Campaign is Tourism Month. This annual promotion, held in September, is designed to promote a culture of tourism among all South Africans.

SA Host

SA Host, a basic customer-service training programme, was introduced in December 2001. The programme was originally developed in Canada and has been successfully run in 14 countries. It educates trainers to run the programme for learners who, if successful, are awarded a certificate and a lapel badge. SA Host's target was to train 5 000 learners by December 2003. The following has also been achieved:

- the Customer-Service Training Course and the Leader-Development Programme were aligned with the National Qualifications Framework
- a national trainer and three regional trainers were trained and are operating in Gauteng and the Western Cape
- some 30 trainers were trained to run the programme (63% previously disadvantaged, 70% female, and 70% in SMMEs).

The Department of Environmental Affairs and Tourism has provided funds to set up a further seven regional trainers throughout South Africa.

International and local marketing

The launch of the Tourism Growth Strategy by South African Tourism in May 2002 gave proper direction and content to the industry. It also positioned Team South Africa and South Africa as a world-class destination. The

Strategy seeks to increase tourist volumes, spend, and length of stay, and improve seasonality and geographic spread.

The Tourism Growth Strategy, which has been endorsed by the Cabinet, is based on detailed market research, and identifies priority markets for tourism and the target-market segments within these priority markets.

Priority markets have been identified in Europe (Britain, France, Italy, Germany, Spain and the Netherlands), Asia (India, China and Japan) and Africa (Southern African Development Community, Nigeria and Kenya).

The Strategy is not only about increasing arrivals, but is also underpinned by other core principles, such as:
- increasing the length of time tourists spend in South Africa
- increasing the spending of tourists within South Africa
- ensuring that tourists travel throughout the country, and not just in a few provinces
- facilitating transformation and BEE in the tourism industry.

The Cabinet approved the International Tourism Growth Strategy in June 2003. The Strategy includes an analysis of core markets and their segments, as well as broad proposals on matters like air travel. The Strategy also focuses on a marketing strategy, visa arrangements, security and local transport infrastructure.

The implementation of the Strategy will further raise the importance of tourism as a critical economic-growth driver and source of employment opportunities.

South African Tourism has overseen the launch of four integrated global marketing campaigns featuring value-for-money packages during South Africa's traditional low season – the *My South Africa Story* Campaign in the USA, *Live the Moment* in India, *The Great Urban Getaway* Campaign in Kenya and Tanzania, and the *Sunsation* Campaign in the UK. Plans are in the pipeline to extend and expand these Campaigns into other core markets such as Germany and France.

South Africa has also made its mark as a world Meetings, Incentives, Conferences and Exhibitions (MICE) destination.

South African Tourism has leveraged the opportunities afforded by a number of high-profile events, including the 2002 WSSD – the largest gathering of its kind in the history of the United Nations (UN).

This event demonstrated to the world that as a stable democracy, South Africa has the capacity to provide secure, state-of-the-art meeting places and support services for world leaders to hold high-level talks.

The success of the WSSD and a series of very successful major international conferences, hosted in different venues in South Africa, culminated in the hosting of the longest and largest Cricket World Cup in the history of the tournament.

Another highlight was the signing of the official Memorandum of Understanding between South Africa and the People's Republic of China, paving the way for increased tourism activity with what is forecast to be the world's largest tourist market by 2010.

South African Tourism's e-business platform was also successfully launched in 2002, with the number of website hits increasing from 12 000 at first, to more than two million per day. The programme has been expanded to include the development of a national database of over 30 000 products, indicative of the growth of this industry.

The 2003 Tourism Indaba was held in Durban, KwaZulu-Natal, during May 2003.

The Indaba, Africa's largest annual travel and tourism exhibition, showcases products from international and national tour operators, hotel groups, travel agents and tourism boards.

The 2003 Indaba recorded a 8,8% increase in the number of delegates attending (more than 1 700), 263 of which were small, medium and micro enterprises.

When Durban first hosted the event in 1990, some 200 companies and 527 international delegates and media attended.

South Africa signed a Declaration of Intent on tourism co-operation with Spain in February 2003.

The signing is a confirmation of the importance that both countries bestow on tourism in terms of economic development, exploration of historical and cultural heritage, and co-operative relations.

Tourism Enterprise Programme (TEP)

The Department of Environmental Affairs and Tourism, the Business Trust, and Ebony Consulting International launched the R129-million TEP to promote growth in the tourism industry.

By September 2003, the TEP had assisted 1 200 SMMEs and created 10 000 jobs. The primary objective of the Programme is to develop skills capacity and the participation of 75% of historically disadvantaged enterprises within the tourism economy.

Human resource development

Tourism HRD is considered one of the pillars of the development of a new responsible tourism culture in South Africa.

The Department has supported the full introduction of travel and tourism and hospitality studies as a subject in schools. Travel and tourism was introduced in 2000 in all schools wanting to offer the subject from Grades 10 to 12.

The Tourism and Hospitality Education and Training Authority (THETA) comprises the following sectors:

- hotels
- provision of short-stay accommodation
- restaurants, bars, canteens and other catering services
- travel agencies and related activities
- destination management
- motor-car rental services
- conservation, game parks and zoological establishments
- gaming and gambling.

The South African Tourism Institute (SATI) was established with the assistance of the Spanish Government, which provided some R13 million for the project.

SATI initiated a number of projects that will create a supportive learning environment for teachers, high-school learners and employees in the tourism industry.

SATI focuses on teacher-development programmes with the intention of enhancing the delivery quality of the travel and tourism and hospitality subjects.

The project began with 14 schools and 800 learners in 1996, growing to 368 schools and 40 000 learners in 2002.

SATI trained over 600 educators on tourism, provided 200 learners from disadvantaged backgrounds with tourism internships, and created tourism awareness in over 540 schools.

There is also emphasis on capacity-building of Department of Education officials as well as educators.

A loan and bursary scheme established for higher education had benefited 45 students by mid-2002, with almost 90% of awards going to the previously disadvantaged. This scheme is operated by the National Student Financial Aid Scheme.

A SATI resource centre has been established, containing electronic and physical resources on many aspects of tourism and its related industries. The centre is open to the public. (See *www.sati.web.za*.)

Other developmental projects are also under way that include working with tourism

---

> The South Africa Fundi Tourism Expert Course, launched at the Tourism Indaba 2003, is aimed at making international travel agents and tour operators experts on what the country has to offer, thereby increasing South Africa's market share.
> The material of the eight-week course covers a wide spectrum of subjects, which include basic facts about South Africa, a comprehensive overview of South Africa's products, general infrastructure and detailed coverage of provinces, towns and cities.

Tourism

departments and industry to develop levels of customer service and staff training.

SATI, in conjunction with the *Sunday Times* and with the endorsement of the Minister of Environmental Affairs and Tourism, launched an eight-week educational initiative, which allowed readers to set up and successfully operate their own bed-and-breakfast establishment or guest-house.

A partnership between the South African business community, via the Business Trust and the Department of Labour, is aiming to train 17 000 people, most of them unemployed, between 2000 and 2004. The Tourism Learnership Project aims to elevate skills, service and productivity levels in the tourism, conservation and hospitality subsectors. By August 2002, some 21 learnerships had been registered. The project is supported by almost 150 companies in developing the 1 500 employed and 2 000 unemployed learners.

A learnership consists of structured workplace learning and structured off-the-job learning. On successful completion, a national qualification is awarded.

The Department of Environmental Affairs and Tourism has commissioned tourism hospitality, education and sports training authorities to train tour guides, with the specific aim of empowering the unemployed and previously disadvantaged individuals.

By May 2003, there were 5 645 registered tour guides in South Africa, 1 058 of whom were black.

Hints for the tourist

Every person wishing to enter South Africa must be in possession of a valid passport for travel to South Africa and, where necessary, a visa.

The Immigration Act, 2002 (Act 13 of 2002), stipulates that all visitors to South Africa are required to have a minimum of one blank page (both back and front) in their passport to enable the entry visa to be issued.

If there is insufficient space in the passport, entry will be denied.

Enquiries can be directed to South African diplomatic representatives abroad or the Department of Home Affairs in Pretoria. Visas are issued free of charge. Visitors who intend travelling to South Africa's neighbouring countries and back into South Africa are advised to apply for multiple-entry visas. Passport-holders of certain countries are exempt from visa requirements. Tourists must satisfy immigration officers that they have the means to support themselves during their stay and that they are in possession of return or onward tickets. They must also have valid international health certificates.

Visitors from the yellow-fever belt in Africa and the USA, as well as those who travel through or disembark in these areas, have to be inoculated against the disease.

Malaria is endemic to parts of KwaZulu-Natal, Mpumalanga and Limpopo. It is essential

---

Southern Africa has become one of the most popular big-game hunting regions in the world. It offers a great variety to trophy hunters, including the Big Five, namely elephant, white rhino, lion, leopard and buffalo, as well as 26 species of antelope.

Hunting proclamations of the various provinces differ and are promulgated annually. The hunting season is normally during the winter months, from May to the end of July.

Most species may be hunted legally by non-land-owners during the hunting season, provided they have the written consent of the landowner and a valid hunting permit issued by the appropriate conservation authority.

Trophy hunting by overseas clients is subject to uniform legislation throughout South Africa, and all hunters are required to be accompanied by registered professional hunters and have their hunts arranged by approved hunting outfitters.

All nine provinces provide schedules of ordinary, protected and specially protected game. Ordinary game may be hunted under licence during an open season. Protected game may be hunted only under permit and licence, the fee depending on the species. Specially protected game, which includes grysbok, klipspringer, red hartebeest, giraffe, black rhinoceros, pangolin and antbear, may not be hunted at all.

to take precautions when visiting these areas.

Foreign tourists visiting South Africa can have their value-added tax (VAT) refunded, provided the value of the items purchased exceeds R20. VAT is refunded on departure at the point of exit.

South Africa's transport infrastructure – airlines, railroads, roads, luxury touring buses (coaches) and motor cars – is such that tourists can travel comfortably and quickly from their port of entry to any other part of the country. A number of international airlines, including South African Airways, operate regular scheduled flights to and from South Africa. Several domestic airlines operate in the country. There are also mainline trains to all parts of the country. (See Chapter 22: *Transport*.)

A brochure entitled *Helpful Hints to Make Your Stay Enjoyable and Safe* is distributed to tourists at international airports.

Accommodation

The tourist accommodation industry in South Africa provides a wide spectrum of accommodation, from formal hotels to informal holiday flats and cottages, game lodges and reserves, guest-houses, youth hostels and bed-and-breakfast establishments.

A variety of promotional material on South Africa is available. Comprehensive guides and maps cover all the regions and aspects of interest to tourists, including accommodation. Various useful tourism websites can be found on the Internet. (See also Suggested reading, p.616.)

The Tourism Grading Council of South Africa (TGCSA) was appointed in September 2000 to inspect the standards in the hospitality and accommodation industry.

The voluntary grading system, which was launched in 2001, uses internationally recognised star insignia to rate accommodation establishments initially, and will be extended to include relevant businesses in classified sectors of the tourism industry. Once graded, establishments will be encouraged to utilise the star system for marketing and advertising purposes.

Since its inception in 2001, the TGCSA has been directly responsible for an additional R76,5 million being invested in hotels, lodges, guest-houses, bed-and-breakfast and self-catering establishments.

Management at 34 hospitality establishments that have adopted TGCSA's National Star-Grading Scheme decided to invest the R76,5 million in refurbishing and other infrastructure spending.

Grading assessors undergo training to receive the National Certificate in tourism grading. The awarding of such a qualification is a world-first. Assessors are then accredited with THETA and registered with the TGCSA before being recommended to the industry. Larger group hotels with their own internal assessors will also be accredited with THETA. Independent auditors conduct random audits. These auditors also assist in ensuring that the assessors adhere to a Code of Conduct.

By March 2003, more than 1 200 accommodation establishments had been graded as part of the Star-Grading System. Forty-eight independent assessors, including 15 from historically disadvantaged backgrounds, have been trained and accredited to undertake grading on behalf of the TGCSA. The star grading is the only system recognised by government and the Tourism Business Council.

By March 2003, the Council was working with representatives from the Meetings Incentive, Conference and Exhibitions Industry (MICE) industry to develop customer-orientated, practical and relevant star-grading criteria for the sector.

South Africa will be one of the first countries in the world to have national grading criteria for the MICE venues sector.

Implementation of the star-grading criteria for caravan and camping facilities was expected to commence during the middle of 2003.

The TGCSA is also in the process of developing star-grading criteria for backpacker and hostel establishments, conference venues, restaurants, tour operators and tourist transport service-providers.

By April 2003, the TGCSA was engaging representatives from the food and beverage industry (coffee shops, restaurants, bars, etc.) in developing star-grading criteria for the sector.

Tourist safety

South African Tourism has launched several initiatives aimed at ensuring the safety of travellers to the country.

These include a partnership initiative with the oil company Engen and the Tourism Information and Safety Call Line, which provides tourists with information on what to do in an emergency and where to locate services.

The line, 083 123 2345 is operational 24 hours per day.

The Department of Environmental Affairs and Tourism has established a National Tourism Safety Network, which is a multi-stakeholder structure comprising provincial representatives, the South African Police Service (SAPS), metro police, organised local government, community policing structures, South African Tourism and other key stakeholders.

The forum has so far developed a Tourism Safety Communications Strategy that is presently being implemented by provinces. It has also redrafted the *National Tourism Safety Tips* for visitors and established agreement in the industry to distribute only the new documents to tourists.

The Mpumalanga Provincial Government announced in April 2003 that it would be spending R1,4 million to establish permanent tourism-safety monitors.

The Tourism-Safety Monitors Project was launched in December 2002 as a pilot project aimed at preventing and curbing criminal attacks against both domestic and foreign visitors. Some 85 youth were trained and placed at more than 10 tourist points in the province.

The Western Cape Government established the Western Cape Tourism Safety Forum, a task team joining tourism bureaux, the SAPS and community-safety authorities.

Together they ensure that tourists who are involved in incidents of crime receive humanitarian support.

On 15 and 16 October 2003, the provincial Government hosted the Tourism Safety Conference in Cape Town to discuss issues around tourism safety.

The Conference harnessed the collective thinking of tourism and safety stakeholders to come up with consistent and co-ordinated actions.

Tourism in the provinces

Western Cape

The Western Cape continues to be one of the most favoured destinations for foreigners. It is estimated that tourism accounts for about 9,1% of the Western Cape's regional product and employs a similar proportion of the formal workforce.

The Western Cape Tourism Board serves eight different regions.

Cape Metropolitan Area

The Cape Metropolitan Area is divided into six different local areas, namely Cape Town, the South Peninsula, Blaauwberg, Helderberg, Tygerberg and Oostenberg. Tourist life in the city of Cape Town centres around the Victoria & Alfred (V&A) Waterfront, a working harbour offering everything from upmarket shopping malls, arts and craft markets, theatres and live music, to museums.

Major attractions in the city include the Bo-Kaap Museum, the Castle of Good Hope, the Company's Garden, the District Six Museum, flea markets, the Grand Parade, the Houses of Parliament, the South African Cultural History Museum and the South African National Gallery.

Also worth a visit are historical buildings in the Bo-Kaap and District Six.

The Gold of Africa Museum was opened in February 2002. Established by Anglo Gold, it is home to a celebrated collection of more than 350 gold artefacts.

Air flips and trips are available, as well as many boat and yacht trips from Table Bay Harbour, including trips to **Robben Island** (proclaimed a World Heritage Site and also the place where former President Nelson Mandela was imprisoned for a number of years), which is fast becoming one of South Africa's premier tourist attractions.

The Nelson Mandela Gateway to Robben Island is situated in the Clock Tower Precinct at the V&A Waterfront. The Gateway houses interactive multimedia exhibitions, an auditorium, boardrooms, a new Robben Island Museum shop and a restaurant.

Table Mountain is a popular site for visitors and provides the majestic backdrop to the vibrant and friendly Mother City. It can be reached by an ultra-modern cableway. The Mountain forms part of the Cape Peninsula National Park.

Newlands is home to the Kirstenbosch National Botanical Garden. In summer, various open-air concerts are held and visitors can bring their own picnic baskets.

At the South African Rugby Museum, visitors can view the history of the sport back to 1891.

The Rhodes Memorial is situated at **Rondebosch** on the slopes of Table Mountain. It was built of granite from the Mountain as a tribute to the memory of Cecil John Rhodes, Prime Minister of the Cape from 1890 to 1896.

The University of Cape Town is worth a visit for its historic Middle Campus and many buildings designed by Sir Herbert Baker.

At **Cape Point**, part of the Cape Peninsula National Park, there are many drives, walks, picnic spots and a licensed restaurant. Care has been taken to protect the environmental integrity of this 22 100-hectare (ha) reserve of indigenous flora and fauna.

Simon's Town's naval atmosphere and Historic Mile are major attractions in the area. A statue of the famous dog and sailor's friend, Able Seaman Just Nuisance, stands at Jubilee Square.

Other attractions include the South African Naval Museum and the Warrior Toy Museum. One of only two mainland jackass-penguin breeding colonies in the world can be found at Boulders Beach.

Hout Bay is well-known for its colourful working harbour. Seafood outlets, round-the-bay trips to the nearby seal colony, shell and gift shops, and a famous harbourfront emporium attract many visitors. Duiker Island, opposite The Sentinel, is a seal and sea-bird sanctuary. The World of Birds Wildlife Sanctuary is one of the largest bird parks in the world and provides a home for some 3 000 birds. Visitors can walk through the large landscaped aviaries.

Against the backdrop of the magnificent Hottentots Holland and Helderberg Mountains, the Helderberg region is a paradise for tourists. Hiking and bird-watching in the Helderberg Nature Reserve, the historic Vergelegen Wine Farm and the Helderberg Wine Route offer something for everyone. Golfers can play a round at the popular Erinvale Golf Course, while a scenic viewpoint on Sir Lowry's Pass offers uninterrupted views across False Bay.

In **Oostenberg**, visitors can enjoy some fine wine and flower farms, such as Zevenwacht Wine Estate with its graceful Cape Dutch homestead. At Tygerberg Zoo, visitors can see a collection of exotic animals. Endless stretches of quiet beaches provide popular surfing and windsurfing spots. Big Bay in

---

The Buffelsfontein Visitor Centre at Cape Point, officially known as the Cape of Good Hope section of the Cape Peninsula National Park, was officially opened in January 2003.

The Centre houses a full complement of artefact displays, state-of-the-art audio-visual equipment and information material covering all aspects of the area's natural and cultural wealth.

Tourism

Bloubergstrand is a surfer's paradise and is host to an international windsurfing event. Rietvlei Nature Reserve is a unique wetland area, boasting over 110 bird species, including pelicans and flamingos.

Century City with the massive Canal Walk shopping mall (over 350 stores) is a tourist haven.

Canal Walk Century City is the largest shopping centre in Africa, with close to 400 shops and home to the largest movie complex in South Africa.

A state-of-the-art olympic-size ice-rink, an amusement park and an upmarket casino are on offer at GrandWest Casino and Entertainment World.

Ratanga Junction, Africa's first full-scale theme park, is situated next to Century City. It offers adrenaline-pumping thrill rides, roller coasters, kiddie rides, and snake and bird shows.

Tygerberg is a vibrant and fast-growing area with a well-developed business centre, numerous sports fields, an international indoor cycle track, well-kept golf courses, a racecourse and a casino.

South Africa's Blue Train is one of the world's most luxurious railway services. The Train runs between Cape Town and Pretoria, to Hoedspruit in Mpumalanga and along a section of the Garden Route between Cape Town and Port Elizabeth. A trip to the Victoria Falls in Zimbabwe is also offered.

Each Blue Train compartment has a bathroom *en suite*, featuring either a bath or shower, a telephone, television and individually controlled air-conditioning. A video channel allows guests to access short documentaries about the area through which the Train is travelling, while a large screen in the club car provides an eye-view of the track ahead, courtesy of a camera mounted onto the front of the locomotive.

Features include CD players and video machines in the luxury compartments. Professionally trained personnel are on call for guests 24 hours a day.

The 380-m long Train has 18 carriages, accommodates 84 passengers and 27 staff members, and travels at a maximum speed of 110 km/h.

Garden Route region

The Garden Route has a well-developed tourist infrastructure, making the region popular all year round.

The pont at **Malgas** is the only remaining pont in the country, ferrying vehicles and livestock across the Breede River. Whale-watching attracts tourists at **Witsand** and **Port Beaufort** from June to November. The area also has a few free-range ostrich farms.

The Grootvadersbosch Nature Reserve outside **Heidelberg** comprises the popular Bushbuck Trail, a wilderness trail and two mountain-bike trails.

Riversdale is one of South Africa's most important *fynbos* export areas. Other attractions include the Julius Gordon Africana Museum.

At the historical Strandveld Architectural Heritage Site at **Still Bay**, visitors can watch tame eels being fed. Ancient fish-traps can be seen at Morris Point and the harbour.

At the aloe factories at **Albertinia**, aloe juices are extracted for medicine and high-quality skin-care products.

Nearby, bungee-jumping on the Gourits River Gorge, hiking, mountain-biking and angling are popular pastimes.

At **Mossel Bay**, the Point, a well-liked area for surfers, also features a natural pool formed by rock – a popular swimming place at low tide. The St Blaize trail starts here and it is the ideal spot to watch the whales and dolphins at play in season. There is plenty to do in Mossel Bay, such as suntanning on the 24-km beach, shark diving and hiking.

The harbour at Mossel Bay is one of the most modern commercial and recreational harbours on the southern Cape coastline. The Information Centre at PetroSA (formerly Mossgas) informs visitors about the project and the production of synthetic fuels from Mossel Bay's offshore gas fields. Other attractions include the Attequas Kloof Pass, Anglo-Boer/South African War blockhouses and the Bartholomew Dias complex.

Great Brak River offers a historic village with many opportunities for whale and dolphin watching along the extensive coast. Game farms hosting four of the Big Five enrich the wild and bird life.

George is at the heart of the Garden Route and the mecca of golf in the southern Cape, as it is home to the renowned Fancourt Country Club and Golf Estate and various other acclaimed golf courses. Board the Outeniqua Choo-Tjoe on its daily trip along the coastline between George and Knysna (except Sundays) at the Outeniqua Transport Museum, where one can enjoy a variety of enterprises. Visitors can also board the Power Van here, and enjoy a glimpse of the Garden Route Botanical Garden.

The George Museum with its timber history as theme offers ongoing exhibitions. The Montagu and Voortrekker Passes are national monuments, providing spectacular views of the Outeniqua Nature Reserve, which offers several hiking trails.

The George Airport, the Outeniqua Pass, the railway line and the N2 offer excellent access and make George the ideal hub from which to explore the Garden Route and Little Karoo.

Victoria Bay and **Wilderness** are popular for their safe bathing and unspoilt nature. Wilderness is the western gateway to the southern Cape lakes area. It's a nature lover's paradise, best known for its beaches, lakes, placid lagoon and lush indigenous forests. Bird watchers flock to the Langvlei and Rondevlei Bird Sanctuaries in the Wilderness National Park, which host over 230 different bird species. Other activities include biking, abseiling, horse-riding, paragliding, scenic drives, canoeing, scuba diving and fishing.

Sedgefield borders Swartvlei Lagoon, the largest natural inland saltwater lake in South Africa. Activities include beach horse-riding, hiking, angling and bird-watching.

Knysna has officially become South Africa's favourite destination. What makes it unique is the fact that the town nestles on the banks of an estuary, guarded by The Heads (two huge sandstone cliffs) surrounded by indigenous forests, tranquil lakes and golden beaches.

This natural wonderland is home to the largest and smallest of creatures, from the Knysna seahorse to the Knysna elephants, rare delicate butterflies and the endemic Knysna loerie, a colourful forest bird. Over 200 species can be found in the abundant *fynbos* and forest settings.

Knysna is also famous for its delectable home-grown oysters, enjoyed with locally brewed beer in quaint pubs and restaurants. An eclectic mix of art galleries showcases the diversity of talent in the area. The area also offers lagoon cruises, forest hikes, golf and adventure sports. A visit to the Knysna Quays is a must.

Plettenberg Bay is adventure country, offering boat-based whale watching, black water tubing, hiking, and forest and cycling trails. Look-Out Beach is one of the Blue Flag beaches in South Africa.

The Keurbooms River Nature Reserve at Plettenberg Bay offers a canoeing trail, and the Robberg Nature Reserve is a treasure trove of land, marine, geological and archaeological wealth.

The Tsitsikamma National Park offers many scenic walks and trails, including the world-famous Otter Trail. It also boasts the only underwater trail in Africa. The Park is South Africa's first proclaimed marine reserve.

There are several bungee-jumping spots in the area, including the highest bungee jump in the world at the Bloukrans River Bridge. Other popular activities include boat cruises, trout-fishing, whale watching, diving, sea-kayaking, gliding, golfing, abseiling and canoeing.

Klein

The Klein is a semi-desert area broken by unexpected lush river valleys. Excellent wines and port are produced in the **Calitzdorp** and **De Rust** areas.

Oudtshoorn, the world's ostrich-feather capital, is the region's main town. The Swartberg Nature Reserve and Pass are also worth a visit. The *Klein Karoo Nasionale Kunstefees* is held in the town annually. Some 29 km from Oudtshoorn lie the remarkable Cango Caves, a series of spectacular subterranean limestone caverns. Bearing evidence of early San habitation, the 30-cave wonderland boasts magnificent dripstone formations. Between 200 000 and 250 000 people visit the Caves annually.

Amalienstein and Zoar are historic mission stations midway between Ladismith and Calitzdorp. Visitors can go on donkey-cart and hiking trails through orchards and vineyards, while the Seweweekspoort is ideal for mountain-biking, hiking, and protea and *fynbos* admirers.

Calitzdorp boasts four wine estates, three of which are open to the public. The spring water of the Calitzdorp Spa is rich in minerals and is reputed to have medicinal properties. The Gamka Mountain Reserve is home to the rare and endangered Cape mountain zebra.

De Rust lies at the southern entrance to Meiringspoort. The Meiringspoort Gorge extends 20 km through the Swartberg Mountain Range. Halfway through, a beautiful 69 m-high waterfall can be seen. Wine farms in the area are open to the public.

Ladysmith is home to the Towerkop Cheese Factory. There are various hiking trails, mountain-biking trails and 4x4 trails in the area. The Anysberg, Klein Karoo and Towerkop Nature Reserves can also be visited.

Uniondale, on the main route between George and Graaff-Reinet, features the largest water-wheel in the country, the Old Watermill. Uniondale Poort is a scenic drive linking Uniondale with Avontuur in the Langkloof Valley.

At **Vanwyksdorp**, visitors can see how *fynbos* is dried and packed for the export market. Donkey-cart rides take visitors to Anglo-Boer/South African War grave sites.

Central Karoo region

The Central Karoo forms part of one of the world's most interesting and unique arid zones. This ancient, fossil-rich land with the richest desert flora in the world, also has the largest variety of succulents found anywhere on earth. There are over 9 000 plant species in the Karoo, and the Beaufort West area alone is home to more species than the whole of Great Britain.

Beaufort West, the oldest town in the Central Karoo, is often referred to as the 'Oasis of the Karoo'. The local museum features a display of awards presented to pioneer heart transplant surgeon, the late Prof. Chris Barnard, a son of this town. Close by is the Karoo National Park, which is home to a huge range of game as well as the highly endangered riverine rabbit.

The village of **Matjiesfontein**, a national monument, offers tourists a peek into the splendour of Victorian England. The village houses a small railway museum, a private motor museum and the largest privately owned museum in South Africa.

The vastness of the Great Karoo can best be experienced at **Murraysburg**, an ecotourist and hunter's paradise, while the geology of the region can be studied at **Laingsburg**, a tiny village once almost completely wiped out by floods.

Prince Albert is a well-preserved town which nestles at the foot of the Swartberg Mountains. The Fransie Pienaar Museum offers interesting cultural-history displays, a fossil room and an exhibit of the old gold-mining activities of the 19th century. The Museum has a license to distil and sell *witblits* (white lightening). Prince Albert is the closest town by road to Gamkaskloof.

The Hell, a little valley in the heart of the Swartberg Mountains, was the home of one of the world's most isolated communities for almost 150 years. Today, it is a nature reserve and national monument managed by Cape Nature Conservation. It is accessed from the peak of the Swartberg Pass.

Winelands region

Whether it is its magnificent natural beauty, its rich cultural heritage or its world-renowned wines, the Winelands region is synonymous with the best that the Cape has to offer. Splendid mountains, gabled Cape Dutch homesteads and lush vineyards provide a splendid backdrop to the towns of Stellenbosch, Paarl, Wellington, Franschhoek and the Dwarsrivier Valley.

Franschhoek, originally known as Oliphantshoek, was named after the arrival of Huguenots who were predominantly French. The Huguenot Monument was built in 1944 to commemorate the 250th anniversary of their arrival in 1688. The Huguenot Museum depicts the genealogical history of these families. Visitors can also enjoy various hiking trails and historical walks, as well as the *Vignerons de Franschhoek* wine route.

Paarl lies between the second-largest granite rock in the world and the Du Toit's Kloof Mountains and is famous for its architectural treasures found along a 1-km stretch of the Main Street featuring, among others, Cape Dutch and Victorian architecture.

The *Afrikaanse Taalmonument* is situated on the slopes of the Paarl Mountain while the *Afrikaanse Taalmuseum* is in the centre of the town.

Visitors can also visit various animal attractions like the Drakenstein Lion Park, Animal Zone or Le Bonheur Crocodile Farm. The Paarl Mountain and Nature Reserve, rich in its natural beauty, is known for its enormous 500 million-year-old granite rocks. The Dwarsrivier Valley boasts a leisurely drive from Stellenbosch through the Helshoogte Pass, so named because of its dangerous curves.

Enter the Banhoek Valley, to which unruly slaves were banished from the castle in the late 1700s. These slaves found freedom in the secluded mountain areas. They interacted with other slaves on the already established farms and started their own settlements. Today Kylemore is one of these small *dorpies*. Further down the road is the little town of **Pniel**. When slaves were emancipated in 1834, those who were not tradesmen or entrepreneurs were quite adept at fruit farming, but had no land to tend. A concerned philanthrophic organisation bought land on which a mission station was established in 1843. Places of interest include the Freedom Monument, which was erected in 1992 – a symbol to commemorate the freed slaves who were the first settlers at the mission station.

Stellenbosch is the second-oldest town in South Africa, and is also known as the *Eikestad* (city of oaks). Various historical walks will delight visitors. Dorp Street consists of one of the longest rows of old buildings in the country. The Stellenbosch Village Museum consists of four homesteads and gardens ranging from the late 17th to the middle 19th centuries.

A number of nature reserves provide excellent hikes. The town hosts various festivals, including the Simon van der Stel Festival, which takes place in October each year to commemorate the birthday of the founder of Stellenbosch, and the Stellenbosch Food and Wine Festival.

At the Oude Libertas Amphitheatre, visitors can enjoy concerts, and ballet between December and March. The Spier Summer Arts Festival also livens up sultry summer nights from November to March at the Spier Wine Estate near Stellenbosch. The Stellenbosch Wine Route comprises over 100 wine estates.

Wellington, which is steeped in history and tradition, has a magical atmosphere that will captivate you once you discover the town, its

---

The Western Cape walked away with all the awards at the 2002 Engen Town of the Year Competition.

Cape Town was named the City of the Year, while the prize for the town category went to Knysna. Montagu, situated midway between Cape Town and Knysna, took the trophy for the village category.

people and its myriad attractions. Apart from fine cuisine and pleasant accommodation, visitors can explore its rich inheritance of historic buildings, experience *fynbos* hikes, horse riding and mountain biking. Bain's Kloof Pass is regarded as the proud legacy of all inhabitants of the Drakenstein Valley and is of great importance for tourism.

Flower lovers will certainly enjoy the chrysanthemum show in May, the longest running such show in South Africa. More than 90% of South Africa's vine-cutting nurseries are found in Wellington. The town is also the home of South Africa's dried-fruit industry.

Tourism-related projects

The Ikhwezi Community Centre, situated between Paarl and Wellington, empowers disadvantaged women and children through craft projects. Handmade articles such as beautifully coloured woven rugs and tapestries, patchwork quilts, hand-embroidered linen and children's clothing are sold at the Centre. Cultural dancing, a marimba band and traditional Xhosa and Malay food are available.

Homestays have been developed in the Winelands region, where guests can become part of the host's family and experience community life.

Kayamandi, Cloetesville, Idas Valley and Jamestown in the greater Stellenbosch area, offer cultural experiences, with the vibrant townships offering genuine African hospitality. With a local resident of the township as the guide, enjoy a drive around the township, take a tour of the hostels, experience African contemporary music, or simply sip a homemade beer.

West Coast

The West Coast comprises the Olifants River Valley, the Swartland and the coastal areas bordering the Atlantic.

Within the first two months of the first good winter rains, wild flowers on the West Coast explode in a brilliant array of colour. The area is famous for its abundance of seafood and cultural-historical heritage sites.

The town of **Darling** draws visitors to its country museum and art gallery, annual wild flower and orchid shows, basket factory and wine cellars. The entertainment venue *Evita se Perron* is situated at the old Darling Railway Station and offers top entertainment from local entertainers.

The *Hartbeeshuisie* at **Hopefield** is a replica of the original reed-built houses of the area.

Langrietvlei, a national monument, boasts a Guernsey and Hereford stud, a honey farm and hiking trails.

Langebaan is a popular holiday destination. The West Coast National Park, an internationally renowned wetland which houses about 60 000 waterbirds and waders, attracts thousands of visitors each year.

The Park is also the site where the oldest anatomically modern fossilised human footprints, were discovered. The site at the farm Elandsfontein near Hopefield where the human skull cap referred to as the 'Saldanha Man' was discovered, and the Park, form part of the West Coast Fossil Route.

The West Coast Fossil Park is situated 110 km north of Cape Town. Visitors to the Park can learn about the animal life and climate changes that occurred in the Western Cape five million years ago. The Park is also used for research programmes.

The Langebaan Lagoon forms part of the Park and is zoned for specific activities. The Postberg section of the Park, across the Lagoon, is famous for its wild flowers, blooming mainly during August and September. Bird watching, fishing, hiking, horse-riding and whale watching (in spring) are some of the activities on offer.

Cape Columbine at **Paternoster** is the last manned lighthouse built on the South African coast. The Columbine Nature Reserve is home to many seabird species.

Saldanha is a water-sport enthusiast's paradise. Other attractions include Doc's Cave, a landmark on the scenic breakwater drive, and the Hoedjieskoppie Nature Reserve. There are various hiking trails in the SAS Saldanha Nature Reserve.

The annual Harvest Festival of the Sea at Saldanha commemorates those people who lost their lives at sea.

St Helena Bay is best known for the Vasco Da Gama Monument and Museum. Fishing (snoek in season), hiking, bird and whale-watching opportunities also draw many visitors.

Vredenburg, the business centre of the area, offers shopping opportunities, cinemas and other essential services. The golf course just outside the town is very popular and boasts a bird hide where various species can be viewed.

Lambert's Bay is a traditional fishing village with Bird Island as a tourist attraction. It is a breeding ground for jackass penguins, Cape cormorants and other sea birds. Visitors can also watch southern right whales from June to November.

The picturesque town of **Doringbaai** with its attractive lighthouse is popular for its seafood. The crayfish factory in town can be visited by appointment.

Strandfontein, situated about 8 km north of Doring Bay, is essentially a holiday and retirement resort. The interesting location of the town and its breathtaking view of the ocean present a priceless panorama.

At **Velddrif/Laaiplek**, visitors can indulge in some *bokkom* (a West Coast salted-fish delicacy) at factories along the Berg River. Tourists can also visit the salt-processing factory or the West Coast Art Gallery in town.

Yzerfontein is famous for its unspoilt beaches, *fynbos*, beautiful views and whale-watching. Another major attraction is the historical lime furnaces.

Olifants River Valley/West Coast

During winter, the Olifants River Valley is filled with the heady scent of orange blossoms. The citrus area in the Valley is the third-largest in South Africa. The wine route from Citrusdal to Lutzville boasts a selection of internationally acclaimed wines. The world-renowned *rooibos* tea is also produced here.

Citrusdal is famous for its citrus products and wines. The Citrusdal Museum depicts the pioneering days of the early colonists.

The Goede Hoop Citrus Co-op is the largest single packing facility in South Africa.

The annual Citrusdal Outdoor Calabash features, among others, 4x4 outings, lectures and visits to rock-art sites, and an arts and crafts market.

The *Sandveldhuisie* is a recently built example of a typical Sandveld dwelling. There are several recognised mountain-biking routes, walking, hiking and canoeing trails, and a skydiving club. The Cederberg Wilderness Area features the elephant's foot plant, the rare snow protea, and the best examples of San rock art in the Western Cape.

Visitors to **Clanwilliam** can visit the *rooibos* and *velskoen* factories, the grave of the well-known South African poet Louis Leipoldt, and the Englishman's Grave. Various historical buildings can also be viewed. The Clanwilliam and Bulshoek Dams are popular among watersport enthusiasts.

At **Wupperthal**, the oldest Rhenish Mission Station, at the foot of the Cederberg Mountains, a self-help footwear-development project is under way. Workers sell the *velskoens* to retailers, primarily in Gauteng and the Western Cape. Proceeds from 4x4 trails in the area go to community coffers for new hiking trails and building more overnight huts and guest-houses.

Graafwater is situated in an area well known for its potato produce. Tourists can visit the *Heerenlogement*, an overhang used as an overnighting site by early settlers.

Klawer was named after the wild clover growing in the area. During the flower season, the area is a kaleidoscope of colour. Visitors can go on a hiking trail along the Doring River, as well as on a river-rafting trail.

Lutzville and **Koekenaap** are synonymous with wine and flowers in season.

Visitors can also view the Sishen-Saldanha Railway Bridge. Where the railway line spans the Olifants River, it is divided into 23 sections, each 45 m long. The 14 100-ton deck was pushed into position over teflon sheets with hydraulic jacks from the bridgehead. It is the longest bridge in the world built using this method.

Vanrhynsdorp houses the largest succulent nursery in South Africa. The Latsky Radio Museum houses a collection of old valve radios, some dating back to 1924. Bird watching, mountain biking, day walks, hiking and 4x4 trails abound. The Troe-Troe and Rietpoort Mission Stations are a must-see for historians.

Vredendal is the centre of the Lower Olifants River Valley. Major attractions include marble-processing and manufacturing, industrial mines (dolomite and limestone), the KWV Grape Juice Concentrate Plant and Distillery, and the South African Dried Fruit Co-op. The town is also home to the Vredendal Wine Cellar, the largest co-operative wine cellar under one roof in the southern hemisphere.

Swartland region

The Swartland is best known for its wheat production.

Malmesbury is the biggest town in the Swartland. Major attractions include Bokomo Mills, the Malmesbury Museum, the Sugarbird glazed fruit factory and the historical walkabout.

The Riebeek Valley is known for its scenic beauty. The area has become a popular haven for well-known artists of various disciplines. Wines at various cellars and olives can be tasted. Steeped in South African history, it is the birthplace of both Genl Jan Smuts and Dr DF Malan. Smuts House is open to the public.

Elands Bay is a popular holiday resort and surfer's paradise. Khoi and San rock art can be viewed at Elands Bay Caves.

Moorreesburg and **Koringberg** are major wheat-distributing towns. Visitors can visit the Wheat Industry Museum, one of only three in the world. Bird watching, hiking, 4x4 routes, clay-pigeon shooting, mountain-bike trails, canoeing and waterskiing at Misverstand are popular activities in and around the town.

Piketberg offers arts and craft, fauna and flora, wine culture and recreation.

The Goedverwacht and Wittewater Moravian Mission Stations are situated close to Piketberg.

Porterville is famous for its Disa Route (best in January and February). The Groot Winterhoek Mountain Peak in the Groot Winterhoek Wilderness Area is the second-highest in the Western Cape. There are several walking trails. The Dasklip Pass is popular with hang-gliders.

Overberg region

The **Hangklip-Kleinmond** area comprises Kleinmond, Betty's Bay, Pringle Bay and Rooiels. It is a popular holiday region, ideal for whale watching, and includes the Kleinmond Coastal Nature Reserve and the Harold Porter Botanical Garden.

The Penguin Reserve at Stoney Point is one of two breeding colonies of the jackass penguin on the African continent.

South Africa's first international biosphere reserve, the Kogelberg Biosphere Reserve, was proclaimed by the UN Educational, Scientific and Cultural Organisation in 1999. The 90 000-ha Reserve includes 23 000 ha of marine environment. It runs along the coast from Gordon's Bay to the Bot River Vlei, stretching 2 km out to sea, and inland to the Groenlandberg, the mountains near Grabouw.

Hermanus is a popular holiday resort, famous for the best land-based whale watching in the world. The coastline offers miles of white sandy beaches, restaurants, sports facilities and a unique 12-km cliff path.

Stanford is one of the few villages in South Africa where the market square has been retained. The central core of the village has been proclaimed a national conservation area. A total of 124 bird species has been recorded to date.

Gansbaai is known for its excellent rock and boat angling, diving, shark-cage diving and whale watching. The Danger Point Lighthouse, named as such because of the ships that have been wrecked and lives that have been lost on this dangerous coast is open to the public.

De Kelders is the only freshwater cave on the African coast. Spectacular views of southern right whales can be enjoyed from the cliffs at De Kelders and along the coast to Pearly Beach. Also popular are white shark tours, diving safaris and fishing trips.

Elim was founded by German missionaries in 1824, with its only inhabitants being members of the Moravian Church. Visitors are welcome to attend services. The Old Watermill (1833) has been restored and declared a national monument.

Popular sites in **Napier** include the Militaria Museum and Rose Boats and Toy Museum. At the latter, unique handmade tin-plate steamboats can be seen driven by copper and brass rose boats. Old toys and trains are also on display.

Kleinsanddrif farm, situated half-way between Bredasdorp and Napier, offers guided tours by tractor and trailer up the picturesque mountain range. *Fynbos* and many species of birds, including the engandered blue crane, South Africa's national bird, can be seen.

At **Bredasdorp**, the historical farm Nacht Wacht can be visited for a real Overberg farm experience.

De Mond Nature Reserve boasts rare bird species including the Damara tern and giant tern.

Geelkop Nature Reserve, which is about 450 ha in size, derives its name from the mass of yellow flowering plants, particularly leucadendrons, which cover the hill during spring. The Reserve offers a half-day hiking trail and scenic circular drives.

The lighthouse at **L'Agulhas**, which forms part of the Agulhas National Park, is the country's second-oldest working lighthouse. It celebrated its 150th anniversary in 1999. It houses a restaurant and a museum. About 1 km from the lighthouse is the southernmost point of Africa, Cape Agulhas. This is also the meeting point of the Indian and Atlantic Oceans.

The Agulhas National Park is home to a rich and diverse plant population, which includes some 2 000 indigenous species comprising more than 110 *Red Data Book* species. The Agulhas Plain is home to a variety of wetlands, as well as the endangered Cape platanna and microfrog, and rare coastal birds such as the African oystercatcher. The Darmara fern finds the area ideal for breeding.

Visitors can also view the ancient tidal fish traps constructed by the Khoi-Khoi people.

Struisbaai has the longest white coastline in the southern hemisphere. Hiking trails are on offer and boat-based whale watching can be enjoyed from the Struisbaai Harbour.

Arniston was named Waenhuiskrans by the local fishers in honour of the huge sea cave capable of housing several ox-wagons. For outsiders it was named after the Arniston, a ship wrecked here in 1815. The Waenhuiskrans Cave can be explored at low tide.

The De Hoop Nature Reserve on the way to Swellendam includes an internationally renowned wetland and bird sanctuary. The marine reserve is a winter retreat for the southern right whale and the Western Cape's only Cape griffen vulture colony. There is a mountain-bike trail and an environmental education centre. The red Bredasdorp lily and many species of protea and erica are found in the Heuningberg Nature Reserve.

Swellendam is well-known for its youngberries and eclectic architecture. The Drostdy Museum consists of a group of buildings containing a huge selection of period furniture.

The Bontebok National Park, about 7 km from Swellendam, provides sanctuary to, among others, the threatened bontebuck.

Suurbraak is a mission village situated in the folds of the Langeberg Mountains, alongside the Buffelsjachts River about 5 km from the majestic Tradouw Pass.

Barrydale can be approached from three directions: the Overberg and Garden Route via the magnificent Tradouw Pass, Montagu and the fertile Tradouw Valley, or Oudtshoorn through the starkly beautiful Klein Karoo. Known for its world-class wine, Barrydale offers the visitor fruit and fresh air in abundance.

Situated on the N2, about 160 km from Cape Town, **Riviersonderend** offers beautiful mountain and river scenery, a nine-hole golf course and sightings of the blue crane.

Caledon is famous for its natural mineral waters, hot springs and wild-flower shows. The Southern Associated Maltsters is the only malt producer for the South African lager beer industry and the largest in the southern hemisphere.

Genadendal is the oldest Moravian village in Africa, with church buildings and a school dating back to 1738. The Genadendal Mission and Museum Complex documents the first mission station in South Africa.

Greyton is a peaceful town in a beautiful mountain setting where various outdoor activities can be enjoyed.

The Theewaterskloof Dam outside **Villiersdorp** is the seventh-largest dam in the country. The Villiersdorp Wild Flower Garden and Nature Reserve boasts an indigenous herb garden and a reference library.

The **Grabouw/Elgin** district produces about 60% of South Africa's total apple exports. The Valley is also renowned for cultivating fresh chrysanthemums, roses and proteas. The Elgin Apple Museum is one of only two in the world. Houwhoek Pass is a beautiful mountain pass and the Elgin Valley road-side farm stalls are known for their fresh produce. Sir Lowry's Pass offers spectacular views of False Bay from Gordon's Bay to Cape Point.

Breede River Valley region

At the foot of the majestic Langeberg Mountains lies **Ashton**, an important wine-producing and food-processing centre. Besides being home to four wineries and two large canneries, Ashton also offers cruises down the Breede River, amazing rock formations at the spectacular Cogmans Kloof, and beautiful day walks in the surrounding foothills, allowing the visitor to take a closer look at the region's *fynbos*.

Known as 'beautiful valley', **Bonnievale** lies in a fertile valley along the Breede River. Lush vineyards and peach and apricot orchards meander through the town against the backdrop of imposing mountains. The tranquil atmosphere, moderate climate, scenic beauty, excellent wines and well-known Bonnievale sausage all make for an enchanting visit. Other attractions include the Myrtle Rigg Church, the Parmalat Cheese Factory, and cruises on the Breede River.

The vast fertile basin in which **Ceres** lies is one of the richest agricultural areas in the Western Cape. Surrounded by mountains that are heavily capped with snow in winter, Ceres is encircled by streams from the Breede River. Hiking trails, 4x4 routes, mountain biking and nature reserves are on offer.

De Doorns is situated in the heart of the Hex River Valley, the largest producer of table grapes in southern Africa. The many historical buildings and homesteads, San rock paintings, the kaleidoscope of autumn colours and the Hex River 4x4 Route are all ingredients that make a visit to the Valley a truly unforgettable experience. The legend of the *heks* or witch of the Hex River Valley adds to the mystery surrounding this breathtaking area.

The picturesque village of **Gouda** is renowned for the Parrotts Den Pub, a living museum, in the Gouda Hotel.

McGregor has a wealth of fascinating white-washed, thatched cottages and well-preserved Victorian houses, making it one of the best-preserved examples of mid-19th century architecture in the Western Cape. Besides the Boesmanskloof Hiking Trail, there are other walks and hikes, bird watching and fabulous star-filled night skies.

Montagu, gateway to the Klein Karoo, lies in a fertile valley and is blessed with typical Klein Karoo landscapes as well as the spectacular Cogman's Kloof with its unique rock formations. Renowned for its muscadel wines, mineral springs and unique tractor-trailer rides that take the visitor to the summit of the Langeberg Mountains for a breathtaking view of the Robertson and Koo Valleys, Montagu also offers hiking trails, 4x4 routes, mountain biking and some of the best rock climbing in the world.

Prince Alfred Hamlet is the gateway to the Gydo Pass, known for its scenic views. This quaint village lies in an important deciduous-fruit-farming area.

Hidden amidst vineyards and wine estates lies the picturesque town of **Rawsonville**, renowned for its array of award-winning wines. Tourists can enjoy an afternoon drive along the awe-inspiring Slanghoek Valley, with its lush vineyards and breathtaking views, or relax in the warm-water mineral springs at Goudini Spa.

Known as 'the valley of wine and roses', **Robertson** is one of the most beautiful areas in South Africa. Surrounded by vineyards, orchards, delectable fruit and radiant roses, Robertson produces connoisseur-quality wines and is also known for its thoroughbred horses.

Known for its hiking trail and Vermeulens *Velskoen* Factory, **Saron**, meaning 'the plains', has a charm of its own.

When the railway to the north was built, **Touwsriver** became the first major locomotive depot after Cape Town. The Astronomical Survey Monument serves as a reminder of the British expedition that studied the transit of Venus in 1882. The nature reserve is a hiker's paradise and home to abundant wildlife. San paintings can be seen in this area, also known for its Karoo hospitality.

The picturesque village of **Tulbagh** is known for its heritage and historical homesteads. Church Street, home to 32 national monuments, constitutes the largest concentration of national monuments in one street in South Africa. Other attractions include wineries, hiking trails, mountain biking, horse riding, fishing or a train ride through the scenic Nuwe Kloof Pass.

Wolseley is situated on an extraordinary watershed. This phenomenon, one of only a few in the world, together with the various hiking trails, mountain biking, trout-fishing, farm visits, wine-tasting and waterfalls, make a visit to the town an unforgettable experience. An added attraction is the blockhouses dating back to the Anglo-Boer/South African War.

In the heart of the Breede River Valley lies **Worcester**, encircled by majestic mountains. Museums, art galleries and the town's architectural heritage make it well worth a visit. Visitors can experience life as the pioneers lived, in years gone by, at the Kleinplasie Living Open-Air Museum. Brandies and world-renowned wines can be enjoyed. The indigenous semi-desert vegetation as well as the landscaped gardens of the Karoo National Botanical Gardens will enthral the visitor with their beauty. Hiking trails, fishing opportunities and 4x4 routes abound.

Northern Cape

The Augrabies Falls National Park remains one of the main attractions of the Northern Cape. The province also boasts four of the country's major parks, namely the Kgalagadi Transfrontier Park, and Richtersveld, Namaqua and TankwaKaroo National Parks. Game-viewing drives reveal a variety of bird life, and animals such as klipspringers, steenbuck, various wildcats and otters. The popular three-day Klipspringer Trail encompasses all the major landmarks in the southern section of the Park, including some amazing rock formations.

The Big Hole in **Kimberley** is the largest hand-dug excavation in the world. The Kimberley Tram Service dates from the beginning of the century and still transports passengers from the City Hall to the Mine Museum.

Underground mine tours are a big attraction, as are the famous ghost tours, during which many historical buildings are seen from a different perspective.

Hand and mechanical diamond-digging by private diggers can be viewed by appointment.

The McGregor Museum houses invaluable collections of the archaeological finds in the area, as well as San art works. A San settlement can be visited.

The house where Sol Plaatje (African National Congress founding member and human-rights activist) lived in Kimberley, houses a library of Plaatje's and other black South African writers' works and several displays, including a portrayal of black involvement in the Anglo-Boer/South African War.

A life-sized statue of Plaatje was erected in the Garden of Remembrance at the new Northern Cape Legislature during 2003.

A township tour to **Galeshewe** provides a fresh perspective on South Africa's socio-historical realities. Pan African Congress founder, Robert Sobukwe's house in Galeshewe is also worth a visit.

A cultural centre at Wildebeestkuil outside Kimberley features !Xun and Khwe artwork for sale and a tour of rock engravings by this indigenous people.

A short distance from Kimberley is the mining town **Barkley West**, which, due to its proximity to the Vaal River, is a favourite spot for many a water-sport enthusiast and angler.

Tucked along the Vaal River near Barkley West lies the Vaalbos National Park. Named after the camphor bush which is dominant in the region, the Park conserves part of a transitional vegetation zone where typical Karoo and Kalahari thornveld and grassveld meet.

The Park is not only home to large raptors, but is also a breeding centre for endangered African herbivores such as rhino, roan, sable and disease-free buffalo.

The Orange River Wine Cellars Co-op in **Upington** offers wine-tasting and cellar tours.

The South African Dried Fruit Co-operative is the second-largest and one of the most modern of its kind in the world. Tours of the plant are offered.

Moffat's Mission in **Kuruman** is a tranquil place featuring the house of missionary Robert Moffat, the church he built, and several other buildings. Moffat translated the Bible into Setswana – the first African language in which the Bible was made accessible.

The printing press on which he printed the first 2 000 copies can still be viewed. The church can seat 800 people and is still in use. David Livingstone married Moffat's daughter and started many famous travels from this mission station.

The Wonderwerk Cave at Kuruman features extensive San paintings that may be viewed by appointment.

The Kalahari Raptor Centre cares for injured birds and many of these majestic birds can be seen at close quarters.

Hand-built irrigation canals at **Kakamas** are still in use today. The Orange River Wine Cellar Co-op Rockery Route runs between Keimoes and Kakamas.

Kanoneiland is a settlement on the biggest island in the Orange River, in the Green Kalahari region.

At **Keimoes**, the Orange River flows at its widest. The Tierberg Nature Garden offers spectacular views of the Keimoes Valley and the many islands in the Orange River. The original irrigation canal system is still in use. The Orange River Wine Cellar Co-op's largest cellar is situated here.

Kenhardt is the oldest town in the Lower Orange River area. The Quiver Tree Forest and Kokerboom Hiking Trail consist of between 4 000 and 5 000 quiver trees. The Verneukpan Tourist Route leads visitors to the rare phenomenon of the remains of a permanent San settlement and the track on which Sir Malcolm Campbell once attempted to shatter the land-speed record.

Namaqualand, the land of the Nama and San people, annually puts on a spectacular show in spring. A floral splendour covers vast tracts of desert. The flowers sprout and survive for a brief period before they wilt and disappear just as suddenly, in the face of blistering heat and dry conditions.

Another marvel is the Witsand Nature Reserve about 70 km west of **Postmasburg**. A 100-m high dune of brilliant white sand can be seen. It stretches for about 9 km and is about 2 km wide. The dunes are in vivid contrast to the red Kalahari sand, olive-green thorns and hazy blue Langberg Mountains.

The province offers several hiking trails, horse trails, mountain biking, canoeing, white-river rafting and combination trails.

Free State

Bloemfontein

The *Eerste Raadsaal* (First Parliament Building) was built in 1849 as a school. It is Bloemfontein's oldest surviving building still existing in its original condition and is still in use as the seat of the Provincial Legislature.

The National Afrikaans Literary Museum and Research Centre houses a repository of works by prominent Afrikaans authors. Exhibits in the Afrikaans Music Museum and the Theatre Museum (part of the Centre) include old musical instruments, sheet music, costumes, photographs and furniture.

The National Museum is notable for its wide collection of fossils, cultural-historical exhibits and archaeological displays, including the Florisbad skull, which was discovered in the 1930s at the Florisbad spring, about 50 km north of Bloemfontein.

The National Women's Memorial is a sandstone obelisk, 36,5 m high, which commemorates the women and children who died in concentration camps during the Anglo-Boer/South African War from 1899 to 1902. The War Museum not only gives insight into the War through its unique art collection, dioramas and exhibits, but also brings the visitor closer to understanding the background against which the War took place. Visitors are also afforded a glimpse into life in the concentration and prisoner-of-war camps. The research library contains an extensive collection of Africana.

The Old Presidency dates back to 1885 and was the official residence of three Presidents of the former Republic of the Orange Free State. The Presidency houses a museum depicting their respective terms of office, and a cultural centre for art exhibitions, theatrical productions and musical events.

King's Park Rose Garden contains over 4 000 rose bushes. Bloemfontein hosts an annual rose festival.

The Observatory Theatre in Bloemfontein's game reserve is a unique attraction.

The Sand du Plessis Theatre and art gallery at Oliewenhuis are also worth visiting.

Transgariep region

Bethulie used to be a London Missionary Society station. The original mission buildings still stand.

The Pellissier House Museum depicts the history of events in the area.

The Gariep Dam, more than 100 km long and 15 km wide, is part of the Orange River Water Scheme. Situated between the Dam and Bethulie lies the Gariep Dam Nature Reserve. On the southern side of the Dam lies the Oviston Nature Reserve.

Philippolis was founded as a London Missionary Society station in 1824 and was the first mission station in the province.

The Tussen-die-Riviere Nature Reserve reputedly supports more game than any other sanctuary in the Free State. It is reserved for hunters in autumn and winter.

Trails in the region include horse trails, hikes, mountain-bike trails and day walks.

Eastern Highlands region

The Basotho Cultural Village in the QwaQwa National Park is a living museum where visitors can witness the Sotho traditions and lifestyles in the chief's kraal.

Clocolan is known for its cherry trees, with its blossoms providing a spectacular sight in spring. San rock paintings and engravings are found in the area.

Clarens is often described as 'the jewel of the Free State', owing to the spectacular scenery. San paintings are found on farms in the area. Close by, the Highlands Route meanders along the foothills of the Maluti Mountains. One can also explore the magnificent mountain scenery by bike.

Ficksburg is known for its cherry and asparagus farms. A cherry festival is held annually in November. The town is a gateway to the Mountain Kingdom of Lesotho.

The Golden Gate Highlands National Park is known for its beautiful scenery and is a very popular holiday destination. A vulture restaurant enables visitors to observe these scavengers closely. San paintings can also be viewed.

The Highlands Route follows the Lesotho border via **Ladybrand** and ends at **Zastron** in the south. San caves and rock art are some of the main features of the Route.

The Seekoeivlei Nature Reserve is listed as a Wetland of International Importance and is home to endangered bird species such as the blue and wattled cranes.

Riemland region

Bethlehem lies on the banks of the Jordaan River and was founded by the *Voortrekkers* during the 1840s. The museum in Miller Street depicts the history of the area. The banks of the Jordaan River form part of the Pretoriuskloof Nature Reserve – a sanctuary for birds and small game.

Van Reenen's Pass winds through the Drakensberg, and was originally used by migrating herds of zebra, hartebeest, blesbuck and wildebeest. The Llandaff Oratory in the nearby village of **Van Reenen** is believed to be the smallest Roman Catholic church in the world.

At **Harrismith** there are various memorials in honour of those who fought in the Anglo-Boer/South African War and World War I. Of particular interest is a memorial for the Scots Guards and Grenadier Guards. Platberg, the 2 394-m 'flat mountain', is the town's landmark. A well-known race, claimed by some to be the toughest in the country, is run annually up, along and back down the mountain. Sterkfontein Dam is ideal for water sports and fishing. Other attractions include the Kerkenberg Monument, Harrismith Wildflower Gardens, and the blockhouse which was used to guard water supplies during the Anglo-Boer/South African War.

The Riemland Museum in **Heilbron** depicts the heritage and the agricultural activities of the region.

The QwaQwa district is a traditional home to the Southern Sotho people. Karakul carpets, mohair, wall hangings, copper, glassware and brass are made and sold at **Phuthaditjhaba**. The Metsi Matsho and Fika Patso Dams are renowned for trout fishing.

Welkom is known for its gold mines. It is also the only city in the country that makes use of traffic circles instead of traffic lights.

Winburg is the oldest town and first capital of the former Republic of the Orange Free State. The Voortrekker Museum, using life-size models, depicts the daily routine of the *trekkers*. A concentration camp cemetery is situated close by.

Sasolburg originated in 1954 with the establishment of Sasol, the synthetic fuel producer.

Eastern Cape

The Eastern Cape is situated along the south-eastern coast of South Africa and is the only province in South Africa, and one of the few places on earth, where all eight biomes (major vegetation types) converge.

With approximately 820 km of unspoilt coastline, the beaches of the Eastern Cape are among the most impressive anywhere, stretching from the Tsitsikamma National Park along the south coast, through St Francis Bay, Jeffreys Bay and Algoa Bay, up to the pristine Wild Coast and south-eastern coast to Port Edward. Added to the diverse coastal experiences are a number of national parks and private game reserves, which collectively cover an area greater than the Kruger National Park.

East London, South Africa's only river port, was originally established as a supply port to serve the military headquarters at King William's Town. The city's own waterfront development, Latimer's Landing, is situated on the banks of the Buffalo River. The East London Aquarium houses approximately 400 different species of marine and freshwater animals.

The East London Museum depicts the natural environment and rich heritage of the region. Best known for the prehistoric coelacanth, the Museum also displays reconstructions of the extinct dodo of Mauritius, along with the only extant dodo egg in the world.

Port Elizabeth is a superb holiday destination, offering a diverse mix of eco-attractions. The Algoa Bay National Sailing Week is held annually in May. There are various scuba-diving sites. Other attractions include national parks and game reserves; the traditional healing village, Kaya Lendaba; bird watching; air tours; canoeing; various mountain-bike and horse-riding trails; and organised outdoor excursions. Tourists can visit various museums and memorials, go on the Donkin Heritage Trail, take a ride on the famous Apple Express and visit the Oceanarium.

Tucked away in the dense valley-bushveld of the Eastern Cape is the Addo Elephant National Park, which provides sanctuary to some 350 elephants, as well as buffalo, black rhino, plenty of birds and several species of antelope.

Grahamstown is sometimes referred to as the City of Saints, because of the more than 40 churches found in the town. The National Arts Festival is held annually. Every year during this time, Grahamstown is transformed into a dedicated arts venue where performers, visual artists, audiences, writers and craftspeople fuse in a celebration of creative energy. In 2002, the Festival was attended by 102 000 people, representing an increase of 5,2% compared with 2001.

Other attractions include various museums and historical buildings, the oldest post-box in South Africa, botanical gardens, the Cathedrals of St Michael and St George, nature reserves and hiking trails.

The Wild Coast draws many anglers. Catches include musselcracker and sardines. Southern right whales and their calves are regularly spotted from May to November. Common and bottlenose dolphins are often seen close to shore. **Coffee Bay** is popular among surfers, anglers and shell collectors. The new alignment of the N2 national route along the Wild Coast and the establishment of the Pondoland National Park will open up investment opportunities.

To the south, the Hole in the Wall is a prominent landmark. Waves continuously crash through the huge hole in the cliff. The coast on both sides of the cliff is notorious for the number of ships that have been wrecked there. In addition to fishing, the giant sand dunes and rich oyster beds, the Wild Coast is renowned for its beautiful beaches.

Visitors to the rural village of **Qunu** are shown the plot where former President Mandela's childhood home once stood, as well as his parents' graves.

Inland, the Owl House in **Nieu-Bethesda** displays the creative talent of the late Helen Martins. Statues of mermaids, wise men, camels and churches create a wonderland in the garden. Everything was built with broken bottles, bits of mirror and cement.

Over 200 houses in **Graaff-Reinet** have been restored to their original Victorian look, and have been proclaimed national monuments. The Old Library Museum houses the Lex Bremner Fossil Collection of Karoo reptile fossils and a collection of Khoi and San art reproductions. Urquhart House has a popular genealogical research centre.

The first evidence of the presence of dinosaurs in South African can be viewed at **Maclear**.

The Eastern Cape has a variety of official conservation areas such as the Mkambati Nature Reserve, Mountain Zebra National Park and Addo Elephant National Park.

Limpopo

Limpopo is well endowed with cultural diversity, historic sites and tourist attractions.

Waterberg

The Nylsvley Nature Reserve has one of the greatest concentrations of waterfowl and bushveld birds in South Africa. More than 400 species frequent the area.

The **Mokopane** vicinity has several nature reserves. The Arend Dieperink Museum has a fine cultural-historical collection and the Makapan Caves are notable for their fossils. The Caves are being developed into an archaeological site.

The Makapansgat Caves and limeworks near Mokopane represent an archeological site of global importance.

The **Thabazimbi** district has a large concentration of private game reserves and is one of the fastest-growing ecotourism areas in the country. The Marakele National Park is home to some rare yellowwood and cedar trees and the world's largest colony of Cape vultures. It is a leader in the conservation of the black rhino outside of the Kruger National Park and the KwaZulu-Natal parks.

Bela-Bela is known for its hot springs. There are a number of game reserves and leisure resorts in the area.

The springs at **Tshipise** attract more than a million visitors every year.

The Waterberg Range is rich in indigenous trees, streams, springs, wetlands and bird life. Cliffs known as 'the palace of the vultures' harbour a large breeding colony of Cape vultures. **Modimolle** is the main town in this region.

Capricorn district

The Bakone Malapa Open-Air Museum outside **Polokwane** is a traditional Northern Sotho kraal. Men and women practise traditional skills such as making baskets, clay pots, furniture and utensils, and preparing hides.

Zion City at Moria near Polokwane is the headquarters of the Zion Christian Church, which attracts more than a million pilgrims every Easter.

Polokwane itself hosts a great variety of museums and art galleries.

Soutpansberg region

The Mapungubwe Archaeological Site, situated 80 km west of **Musina**, lies within the boundaries of the Vhembe/Dongola National Park. It is one of the richest of its kind in Africa. Excavations in the 1930s uncovered a royal graveyard, which included a number of golden artefacts.

The Schoemansdal Voortrekker Town and Museum, west of **Louis Trichardt,** is built on the site of an original *Voortrekker* village and depicts their lifestyle between 1848 and 1852.

Also worth visiting is the Big Tree (the largest known baobab in southern Africa), Tshatshingo potholes, the mystical lake of Dzivhafundudzi and the holy forest at Phiphidi.

Mopani district

The Modjadji Nature Reserve, north of **Tzaneen**, is named after the legendary Rain Queen, Modjadji, who is believed to have settled in the area early in the 16th century. The Reserve encompasses the world's largest concentration of the cycad species *Encephalartos transvenosus*, also known as the Modjadji palm.

The Hans Merensky Nature Reserve and Mineral Spa on the southern banks of the Great Letaba River supports a large variety of game. More than 200 bird species have been recorded there.

At the Tsonga Kraal Open-Air Museum, arts, crafts and traditional huts reflect the Tsonga lifestyle of 100 years ago.

The Kruger National Park (northern section) is one of South Africa's biggest tourist attractions. The Park is home to a huge number and wide variety of amphibians, reptiles and birds, and 147 mammal species, including the Big Five.

Thulamela, in the northern part of the Kruger National Park, was opened to guided groups in June 1997. This followed seven years of archaeological excavations, which brought to light the skeletons of two ancient royals and a multitude of artefacts, including gold bangles, beads and a double gong.

North West

North West has five geographically distinct areas, namely the Central, Eastern, Bophirima, Rustenburg and Southern districts.

Central district

The Historic Route of **Mafikeng** includes an Anglo-Boer/South African War siege site, the Molema House where Sol Plaatje lived while writing his *Mafikeng Diary*, and the Mafikeng Museum.

The Lichtenburg Game Breeding Centre and the Botsalano Game Reserve are well worth a visit.

The Groot Marico region is known as *mampoer* country and visitors can embark on a *mampoer* and tobacco route. The Kortkloof Cultural Village is dedicated to the Tswana people.

Other attractions include the Wondergat, the Bosbult Monument which commemorates a battle during the Anglo-Boer/South African War, the Kaditshwene Iron Age Village Ruins and various hiking trails.

Eastern district

The Hartbeespoort Dam is a popular spot for weekend outings, breakfast runs and yachting. The Hartbeespoort Cableway offers a breathtaking view of the Dam and surrounding areas.

The Hartbeespoort Reptile and Animal Park is situated on the banks of the Dam.

Cultural experiences in the area include the popular Mapoch and Gaabo Motho Cultural Villages as well as the Ring Wagon Inn.

The De Wildt Cheetah Breeding and Research Centre specialises in the breeding of cheetah and other endangered wildlife species. Other places of interests include the Borakalalo Game Reserve, the Margaret Roberts Herb Farm and the Phaladingwe Nature Trail.

The Vredefort Dome is a crater 40 km across, caused by the collision of a meteorite with the earth many years ago. It features unique fauna and flora. A variety of hiking and mountain-bike trails are offered.

Bophirima district

The Taung Skull Site and the Blue Pools are renowned for the Taung skull found in the Buxton quarries. This region is popular with adventure-seekers – especially the 4x4 routes and hunting farms.

Rustenburg district

The Pilanesberg National Park supports over 7 000 head of game, including the Big Five and 350 bird species. Guided day and night game drives are available.

The Madikwe Game Reserve is home to the biggest game-relocation programme ever. Over 10 000 animals of 27 major species have been reintroduced under Operation Phoenix. A hot-air balloon ride, day and night game drives and bushwalks are available. Sun City and the Palace of the Lost City are very popular tourist attractions offering gambling, golf, extravaganza shows, water sport and an artificial sea.

There are various hiking trails in the region. The Heritage Route starts at the Sterkfontein Caves World Heritage Site and ends at Pilanesberg.

Southern district

The OPM Prozesky Bird Sanctuary in **Potchefstroom** has over 200 bird species and is situated adjacent to the Mooi River. The Oudorp Hiking Trail takes visitors through the old part of Klerksdorp where 12 *Voortrekker* families settled.

Other attractions in the region include the Potchefstroom Lakeside Resort, the Faan Meintjies Nature Reserve in Klerksdorp, mine tours at Orkney, the Diggers Route at Wolmaransstad, and the Bloemhof Dam Nature Reserve.

Mpumalanga

Mpumalanga – 'the place where the sun rises' – epitomises every traveller's dream of the true African experience. Located in the north-eastern part of South Africa, the province is bordered by Mozambique to the east and the Kingdom of Swaziland to the south and east.

The climate and topography vary from cool highland grasslands at 1 600 m above sea level, through the middleveld and Escarpment, to the subtropical Lowveld towards the Kruger National Park and many private game reserves. Scenic beauty, climate and wildlife, voted the most attractive features of South Africa, are found in abundance in the province.

Attractions range from game viewing and bird watching to scenic drives across the valleys and peaks of the vast Drakensberg Escarpment, and include agritourism and industrial tourism, adventure tourism and cultural experiences. Historical sites and villages, old wagon routes and monuments mark events and characters who passed this way in search of adventure and wealth.

The cultural heritage of the province is varied and exciting. The Ndebele beadwork and house-painting in the north-west, the arts and crafts of the Lowveld and the different traditional villages all over the province offer a unique insight into the history of the people.

The Maputo Development Corridor links Gauteng with the Maputo Harbour in Mozambique, opening new tourism opportunities for Mpumalanga.

Its serenity and natural ambience, enthralling landscapes, majestic waterfalls, kaleidoscope of cultures, imposing mountains, unequalled scenic beauty, and enchanting flora and fauna make Mpumalanga a favourite tourist destination.

Mpumalanga offers attractions and activities ranging from game viewing, bird watching, trout fishing, white-water river rafting, hiking, paragliding, abseiling, 4X4 trails, hot-air ballooning and riveting cultural villages to historical sites and monuments testimony to events of yesteryears.

The province has recently been demarcated into tourism regions, each with its own unique features and an array of attractions to ensure a rewarding holiday to visitors.

Nelspruit

Nelspruit is the capital of Mpumalanga and the commercial and administrative hub of the Lowveld. The Nelspruit Historical Trail is an hour-long route stretching from the Promenade Centre to the Civic Centre.

The Blue Train runs between Pretoria and Nelspruit from May to September on a trip called the Lowveld Experience. Rovos Rail's trains also visit Nelspruit.

The Green Heritage Hiking Trail in the Nelspruit Nature Reserve is one of several walks in the Reserve and one of many in the region.

Not to be missed is the Lowveld Botanical Garden, as well as the Reptile Park, both situated near the Emnotweni Casino. The Lowveld National Botanical Garden features many rare

Lowveld species, which include the country's best collection of indigenous ferns, 500 tree species and the famous rare cycads.

The Sudwala Caves, PR Owen Dinosaur Park, and the artists' village of White River should also not be missed.

Panorama
Barberton features many reminders of the early gold-rush era. Museums include Belhaven, Fernlea House and Stopforth House. The only known verdite deposits in the world are found in the rocks of the Barberton district. Verdite has been used by sangomas for promoting fertility. An annual Diggers Festival is held in September.

The Blyderiviersspoort Nature Reserve near **Graskop** is characterised by striking rock formations and a rich diversity of plants. Within the Reserve, the Bourke's Luck Potholes were formed by river erosion and the action of flood water.

The spectacular Blyde River Canyon is a 26-km-long gorge carved out of the face of the Escarpment, and is one of the natural wonders of Africa. The Canyon is the third-largest in the world but the only green canyon, and hosts three rivers which feed the Blydepoort Dam at **Swadini**. God's Window provides a magnificent view of miles of thickly forested mountains, the green Lowveld and the Canyon. The Blyderiviersspoort Hiking Trail is one of the most popular in the country. A number of other hiking trails are also available.

The southern section of the Kruger National Park falls within this region. The Park is a major tourist attraction, locally and internationally. The main camps have an excellent range of facilities. Game viewing is easier in winter, and guided wilderness trails as well as hiking trails are available. Tourists are also taken on open-vehicle game drives.

Kaapsehoop is a quaint historical village known for the wild horses that frequent the district. Blue swallows are regular visitors from September to April.

The **Lydenburg** Museum is situated in the Gustav Klingbiel Reserve, which is the site of archaeological ruins from the Later Iron Age. The Lydenburg Heads were discovered in this area.

The Mac Mac Pools and Falls outside **Sabie** are worth a visit. The 69-km Prospector's Trail starts at the Mac Mac Forest Station and leads to the Bourke's Luck Potholes.

At the Montrose Falls in **Schoemanskloof**, the Crocodile River cascades 12 m into a series of rock pools. It is also the starting point of the annual Lowveld Crocodile Canoe Marathon, held in February.

Pilgrim's Rest is a living museum and a replica of the early gold-mining town. The Alanglade House Museum offers guided tours of the former mine-manager's house, while the Diggings Museum just outside the town arranges guided tours of gold-panning activities. This area was the setting for *Jock of the Bushveld*, the novel by Sir Percy Fitzpatrick about the experiences of a man and his dog as they share adventures in the world of African gold-mining. The Dredzen Shop Museum consists of a store stocked with a range of items in use nearly a century ago. The Pilgrim's Rest Festival is held annually in December.

Mount Sheba Nature Reserve, south of Pilgrim's Rest, is best known for its indigenous forest – one of few left in the region.

Sabie is the centre of the largest man-made forest in South Africa.

The Cultural-Historical Forestry Museum depicts various aspects of the country's forestry industry. The Bridal Veil, Horseshoe and Lone Creek Falls just outside Sabie are worth a visit.

Cultural
The Highlands Meander is a mecca for fly-fishers. It is in the placid and pristine waters of this region that one can find various stocks of fish, with trout as the major drawcard. The Meander offers a myriad of activities like rock climbing, bird watching, mountain biking and an abundance of historical sites.

It is in this region at the Verloren Vlei Nature Reserve (**Dullstroom**) that one can have the rare glimpse of the three endangered crane species (the blue, wattled and crowned cranes).

The Loskop Dam Nature Reserve is one of the country's largest reserves and offers game watching, boating and fishing.

The Highlands Meander is famous for its trout-fishing opportunities. Bird-watching, walking trails and horse trails are also popular. The Steenkampsberg Nature Reserve, outside **Dullstroom**, provides sanctuary for the rare wattled crane. The annual Trout Festival is held in October.

Horse-riding and trout-fishing are popular in the Highlands Meander area. A large number of hiking trails are available, such as the Elandskrans Trail, which includes a 30-minute train ride between **Waterval-Boven** and **Waterval-Onder**.

Cultural heartland

It is in this region of cultural heartland that one can immerse oneself in the true cultural heritage of Mpumalanga. Here, one can learn about the proud and welcoming amaNdebele people, revered for the striking geometric patterns on their houses and clothing. This region also has illuminating historical sites like Botshabelo Historical Village.

Cosmos country

Cosmos country covers parts of what is known as the energy belt of Mpumalanga, which is home to a number of power stations that supply most of the energy to other African countries. This region also boasts the world's largest underground coal-mining complex and the Sasol plant renowned for its technology of extracting oil from coal, a unique process in the world.

The carpet of cosmos flowers that blossoms in late summer also lures visitors to this region.

Wild frontier

Wild frontier is deemed the cradle of life, owing to the astonishing archaelogical discoveries dating back to almost three billion years ago in the imposing mountains of this region.

Visitors to this region can have a rare glimpse of the inimitable San paintings embossed in some rocks.

The region also holds rich historical sentiments centered around the monument of Samora Machel constructed in the village of Mbuzini. Due to the location of this region, visitors can have a rare opportunity to visit two other countries (Swaziland and Mozambique) in a short space of time.

Grass and wetlands

Grass and wetlands is indeed a paradise, with a variety of bird species to see. This region stretches across the deep valleys and mountains of the east where thermal springs bubble to the surface.

There are 270 pans and lakes within a 20-km radius of Lake Chrissie. In this region visitors can take part in the unusual 'frogging expedition' or simply gaze at the stars during 'star gazing weekends'.

Lowveld Legogote

This region offers visitors plenty attractions, from the daring explorations of the Sudwala Caves, the natural ambience of the Lowveld Botanical Garden, and the nostalgic horse rides in the historical village of Kaapsehoop, to the craftsmen and artists' haven of White River, or the glimpse of a collection of reptiles at the Crocriver Enviro Park, which is Africa's largest reptile park.

The region also features the Kruger National Park, which stretches across Mpumalanga into Limpopo.

Adventurers can take part in the four night/five-day Lebombo 4X4 Overland Trail, which stretches from the Crocodile River in the south to the mighty Limpopo.

Gauteng

The Gauteng Provincial Government is to

contribute more than R300 million over the next few years towards developing tourism sites in the province. These include a Big Five nature reserve east of Pretoria, developing infrastructure in the Leeufontein Nature Reserve and Roodeplaat Dam Reserve, and improving the Cradle of Humankind Heritage Site near **Krugersdorp**.

Gauteng offers a vibrant business environment and many tourist attractions, including a rainbow of ecological and cultural diversity.

The Vaal Dam covers some 300 km^2 and is a popular venue for water sport. Numerous resorts line the shore. The Dam also attracts a great diversity of birds.

Vanderbijlpark was built during the late 1940s by the Iron and Steel Corporation to accommodate its employees.

The Sterkfontein Caves near Krugersdorp are the site of the discovery of the skull of the famous Mrs Ples (now believed to be Mr Ples), an estimated 2,5-million-year-old hominid fossil, and Little Foot, an almost complete hominid skeleton some 3,3-million years old.

The Caves comprise a series of caverns with many stalactites and stalagmites and a huge underground lake. Guided tours are available. The Wonder Cave, about two billion years old, is one of South Africa's most impressive natural assets. In 1999, Sterkfontein and its environs were declared a World Heritage Site.

The Krugersdorp Game Reserve provides sanctuary for several game species, including four of the Big Five. The African Fauna and Bird Park houses various species of wildlife and birds.

The South African National Railway and Steam Museum at Randfontein Estates Gold Mine outside Krugersdorp houses some of the country's old steam locomotives, a diesel-electric locomotive, and more than 50 vintage passenger coaches. Train rides are offered once a month.

A team of Lippizaner stallions performs every Sunday at the South African National Horsemanship Centre, **Kyalami,** near Johannesburg.

Visitors to **Roodepoort** can go on walks and trails through the Kloofendal Nature Reserve, or enjoy a picnic or show at the popular Kloofendal Amphitheatre. The Witwatersrand National Botanical Garden boasts a 70-m high waterfall.

Forty kilometres north of Pretoria lies a ring of hills a kilometre in diameter and 100 m high. These hills are the walls of an impact crater left by an asteroid that hit there some 200 000 years ago. The Tswaing Meteorite Crater is similar in size to the well-known Barringer meteor crater in Arizona, USA. The Crater walls at Tswaing were originally about twice as high as they are today.

There is a museum adjacent to the Crater. A path leads from the museum to the Crater, along the rim, and down to the central lake. The Crater is covered with indigenous trees and bushes and attracts a variety of bird life.

The old mining town of **Cullinan** developed around the Premier Diamond Mine and many turn-of-the-century houses still stand. The Mine has produced some of the world's most famous diamonds, including the Cullinan, the world's largest at 3 106 carats.

The Willem Prinsloo Agricultural Museum outside Cullinan centres around a farmstead dating from 1880. Traditional farming activities are demonstrated, and annual events include a prickly-pear festival, a *mampoer* festival and the Agricultural Museum Show.

Johannesburg

The Adler Museum of the History of Medicine depicts the history of medicine, dentistry and pharmacy in South Africa. The Pharmacy Museum in Melrose houses a large variety of medicines, including more than 670 traditional medicines that have been collected throughout southern Africa.

There is also a display of old prescription books and dictionaries used by pharmacists in 1755.

Museum Africa in Newtown tells the story of life in South Africa from the Stone Age to the

Nuclear Age and beyond. The museum is located in the old fruit-and-vegetable building next to the Market Theatre.

The Market Theatre Complex comprises three theatres, an art gallery, restaurants and pubs. Kippies Jazz Bar is a popular venue for live jazz.

Lesedi Cultural Village in the Swartkops Hills north of Johannesburg gives visitors the opportunity to meet families of different tribes. Visitors can spend the night with a family of their choice.

The Phumanegna Zulu Kraal is an authentic Zulu kraal with traditional Zulu people living and working there.

The Melville Koppies in Johannesburg was once the site of a Stone Age African village and iron-smelting works. The flora includes 80% of the species recorded on the Witwatersrand. It is open to the public from September to April.

Gold Reef City is a reconstruction of Johannesburg during the gold-rush era. Attractions include a Victorian funfair, pubs, miners' houses, a brewery, restaurants, a hotel and a stock exchange. Visitors can take a trip down an old mine shaft and watch molten gold being poured.

The Apartheid Museum near Gold Reef City tells the story of the legacy of apartheid through exhibitions consisting of film footage, photographs, text panels and artifacts.

At Santarama Miniland and Entertainment World visitors can explore models of South Africa's most popular beacons, such as Robben Island, Johannesburg International Airport, East London Harbour, the Castle of Good Hope in Cape Town, and the Union Buildings in Pretoria.

The South African Museum of Military History houses an impressive collection of weaponry and uniforms from the two World Wars. The South African Transport Museum (Heidelberg) relates to all aspects of South Africa's transport services.

A large, well-established park surrounds Zoo Lake, which is frequented by breeding bird colonies. Other attractions include jazz concerts, rowing boats for hire, a tea garden and a restaurant.

Soweto (an acronym for South Western Townships) is a popular tourist destination. It is estimated that some 1 000 foreign tourists visit Soweto every day.

The two-bedroom house where former President Mandela lived before his incarceration has been declared a national monument and converted into a museum.

Another venue worth visiting is the Hector Petersen Museum, which commemorates the people who died following the student uprising of 16 June 1976. The museum was named after the young boy, who was the first person to be shot dead by police on that day.

Pretoria

Many historical buildings can be seen in the city, which is known for its jacaranda trees.

Church Square is centred around a statue of Paul Kruger, President of the former *Zuid-Afrikaansche Republiek*, and includes buildings such as the Old Raadsaal and the Palace of Justice.

The Kruger House Museum contains the personal belongings of President Kruger. Melrose House is a beautiful example of Victorian architecture. The Peace Treaty of Vereeniging, which ended the Anglo-Boer/South African War, was signed here in 1902.

Demonstrations at the Pioneer Open-Air Museum include milking cows, making butter and candles, baking bread and grinding coffee beans.

Other museums include the Police Museum, the Science and Technology Museum, the Coert Steynberg Museum and the Transvaal Museum of Natural History.

The Voortrekker Monument also houses a museum and commemorates the Great Trek. Some 260 steps lead to the dome, where spectacular views of the city can be enjoyed.

Fort Schanskop has been refurbished and boasts a 375-seat amphitheatre.

The Union Buildings were designed by Sir Herbert Baker and completed in 1913. They were the setting for the presidential inauguration of Nelson Mandela in 1994, and of Thabo Mbeki on 16 June 1999.

The Sammy Marks Museum just outside Pretoria dates from 1885. Rooms in the house are filled with Victorian paintings, furniture, silver and porcelain. There is a tea garden and restaurant on the premises.

The General Smuts House Museum in Irene, south-east of Pretoria, contains the original furnishings of the Smuts family. A popular arts and craft market is held here on certain Saturdays.

The Rietvlei Nature Reserve is notable for its 73 grass types, 147 different herbs, a large number of game and over 140 bird species. In July 2000, five hippos were released into the Reserve, the first hippos to roam the area in more than 100 years.

The Mapoch Ndebele Village, north of Pretoria, is being restored by its residents and the National Cultural History Museum. To develop the project into a viable, living tourist village, the 50 families staying there have undergone tourist-guide and business training. It is the first living cultural village in South Africa owned and managed by its residents.

Mamelodi is a dynamic black community set against the majestic backdrop of the Magalies-berg mountain range. The township was established on the farm Vlakfontein in 1945, whose name was changed to Mamelodi in 1962. The Department of Environmental Affairs and Tourism, together with the Mamelodi Heritage Forum, launched the Mamelodi Heritage Route at the Solomon Mahlangu Freedom Square in Mamelodi, in September 2000.

KwaZulu-Natal

KwaZulu-Natal continues to attract the largest number of local tourists, catering for 44% of the domestic-tourist market in 2000.

Durban and surroundings

The Tourist Junction in Durban's historical station building provides access to tourist information, accommodation bookings for Ezemvelo KwaZulu-Natal Wildlife (formerly KwaZulu-Natal Nature Conservation Service) and South African National Parks, and theatre bookings.

The Golden Mile skirts the main beaches of the Indian Ocean. Attractions include an amusement centre, paddling pools, paved walkways and fountains.

The Durban area has more than 50 reserves, developed parks and specialised gardens, the most renowned being the Municipal Botanical Garden.

Seaworld on Durban's beach front is home to a wide variety of sea life, including sharks, dolphins and seals. Fish and sharks are hand-fed, and dolphin and seal shows are held daily.

The Fitzsimons Snake Park offers lectures and venom-milking demonstrations.

MiniTown is a model city depicting Durban's best-known buildings.

Museums include the Natural History Museum, the Natural Science Museum, the Old House Museum and the Old Fort.

The *Shree Ambalavaanar Alayam* Temple (The Second River Temple) in **Cato Manor** was the first Hindu temple on the African continent. It is a national monument.

The Juma Mosque is the largest mosque in the southern hemisphere. Daily tours are available.

Annual events in and around the city include the popular Comrades Marathon between Durban and Pietermaritzburg, an international surfing competition, and the July Handicap horse-race.

Umhlanga Rocks, just north of Durban, is notable for its ski-boating facilities. The annual Ski Boat Festival takes place in April. The Natal Sharks Board offers shark dissections and interesting displays. Guided tours of the Hawaan Forest are on offer. Hawaan is the last relic of coastal forest in the region and contains rare indigenous trees.

The Umgeni River Bird Park overlooks the Umgeni River and ranks among the world's best. Many varieties of birds, indigenous and exotic, inhabit walk-in aviaries.

Dolphin Coast

The coastline between the Umdloti and the Tugela Rivers is aptly called the Dolphin Coast, as Indian Ocean bottlenose dolphins can be seen here all year round. The larger humpback dolphins are also found here, but are rarely seen.

Many of the first Indian immigrants settled here, and the area's markets, mosques and temples bring an authentic eastern flavour to the region.

Tongaat is an area where sugar was first planted in 1854. The town's Indian ambience is accentuated by two prominent Hindu temples – the *Juggernath Puri* and *Vishwaroop* temples.

Other coastal towns on the Dolphin Coast include Shaka's Rock, Salt Rock, Ballito, Verulam, Stanger, Darnall and Umdloti.

Zululand and the North Coast

The Hluhluwe-Umfolozi Park is one of the largest game parks in South Africa and hosts the Big Five as well as the elusive cheetah and wild dogs.

The eMakhosini Valley, birthplace of King Shaka, is the venue for a new tourism- and economic-development project. Known as Makhosini, 'the Valley of Zulu Kings', the joint public-private sector project aims to preserve the culture and history of the Zulu people. The project was launched in October 1998. Construction of the first lodge in the Valley, called Nexele's House, started at the end of March 2000. Tourism KwaZulu-Natal has injected a sum of R1,36 million as seed capital for the development of the lodge.

The eMakhosini Memorial Site, where seven Zulu Kings are buried, was unveiled in May 2003.

Ulundi lies at the hub of the old Zulu Kingdom. The KwaZulu Cultural Museum houses interesting displays relating to Zulu history and archaeology. The beehive huts and the layout of the original Zulu village have been reproduced.

Umgungundlovu used to be the royal capital of King Dingaan and is being reconstructed. A tour provides the opportunity to observe Zulu building techniques and experience the social life of the Zulu people.

Authentic Zulu villages such as Shakaland, Kwabhekithunga Kraal and Stewart's Farm offer accommodation and the opportunity to experience traditional Zulu culture.

The Lubombo Corridor is one of the Spatial Development Initiatives spearheaded by government to unlock economic potential in previously neglected areas. The Corridor will stretch from the St Lucia Wetland Park in KwaZulu-Natal, along the Indian Ocean coastline, to Ponta do Ouro in Mozambique, and will embrace the Jozini Dam and game reserves in Swaziland. The area supports 3 048 different plant and animal species and six ecosystems. In addition to 25 major tourist attractions, there are 11 game reserves and the World Heritage Site, the Greater St Lucia Wetland Park, as well as Border Cave, which is in a cliff-face in the Lubombo mountains, near the Swaziland border. The Cave has long been one of the most important sites for archaeologists seeking the beginnings of modern human beings.

The Greater **St Lucia** Wetlands have some of the highest forested dunes in the world. The St Lucia Lake and its surroundings comprise a wetland of global importance. It is a fishing and bird-watcher's paradise.

The Kosi Bay Nature Reserve is part of the Coastal Forest Reserve between Mozambique and **Sodwana Bay**. The adjacent Indian Ocean provides exciting snorkelling and fishing opportunities. On offer is a four-day guided walking trail around the estuarine system. Lake Sibaya is South Africa's largest natural freshwater lake, covering some 77 km². Bird-watching and walks through the coastal forest are major attractions.

Sibaya Lake Lodge, the first South African ecotourism development jointly owned by private enterprise and the local community, was officially launched in September 1999. The development is administered by the Kwa-Chithumuzi Tourism and Development Trust.

Maputuland is a region of coral, unspoilt beaches, freshwater lakes, sand forests, wetland systems and bushveld. Activities include game-viewing, snorkelling, diving, boat cruises, canoeing and walking safaris.

The coral reef in the Sodwana Bay National Park attracts hundreds of scuba-divers throughout the year, and in summer powerboaters arrive for some of the best marlin-fishing in the world.

South Coast and interior

The Banana Express is a narrow-gauge steam train running between Port Shepstone and Paddock and back (39km) twice a week. A shorter route is also available.

Amanzimtoti is popular for its safe swimming beaches and various other activities and attractions.

The Hibiscus Coast stretches between Umkomaas and the Wild Coast. Margate is the largest resort town along this Coast, and is very popular during the holidays. The Hibiscus Festival is held in July.

The Oribi Gorge Nature Reserve encompasses forest, rivers, rapids and ravines.

Prolific bird life, including five kingfisher species and seven eagle species, inhabits the Reserve, along with a variety of mammals.

Port Edward is known for its safe swimming and good fishing opportunities. Nearby, the Umthamvuna Nature Reserve is noted for its beautiful scenery, bird life and many rare plant species.

The Shell Museum at Shelly Beach is well worth a visit to see its large display of shells.

Other popular coastal towns include Port Shepstone, Ramsgate, St Michael's-on-Sea, Uvongo and Scottburgh.

Sardine fever strikes the South Coast around the end of June every year, with people flocking to the beaches to scoop the sardines up, while anglers wait for the game fish to arrive.

Midlands

Pietermaritzburg boasts various museums, including the Voortrekker Museum, the Natal Museum and the Natal Steam Railway Museum, which offers steam-train rides on the second Sunday of every month.

The Albert Falls Public Resort Nature Reserve and the Albert Falls Dam provide opportunities for sailing, canoeing and fishing.

Bird watching, horse riding and hiking are also popular pastimes.

The Howick Falls are situated in the Valley Nature Reserve, where the river tumbles down 100 m in a single fall. The Midlands Meander is a scenic drive between Hilton and Mooi River with about 70 ports of call en route, ranging from art studios, potters and painters, to herb gardens and cheese-makers.

Midmar Dam is zoned for yachting and powerboating. The 1000-ha Midmar Game Park is inhabitated by rhino, zebra, a wide variety of antelope species, and waterfowl.

Drakensberg

Ezemvelo KwaZulu-Natal Wildlife's trout hatcheries are located in the Kamberg Reserve.

The Lotheni Nature Reserve is notable for its trout-fishing facilities (angling permits are required). Relics of the area's history have been preserved in the Settler Museum.

The Himeville Nature Reserve has two lakes stocked with trout. The Swamp Nature Reserve close by attracts a variety of waterfowl, including the rare wattled crane.

The Ndedema Gorge is located in the Mdedelelo Wilderness Area near Cathedral Peak, and contains examples of Khoi and San art.

Tourism

Sani Pass is the only road between KwaZulu-Natal and the Kingdom of Lesotho. The Giant's Cup Hiking Trail, starting at the foot of the Pass, is described as one of South Africa's finest. Giant's Castle Game Reserve is especially known for its more than 5 000 San paintings on the walls of the caves. The Bushman Site Museum is well worth a visit.

The Reserve is a bird-watcher's paradise, and a bird hide facilitates the viewing of cliff-dwelling species.

The Royal Natal National Park offers many scenic highlights, including the Amphitheatre, Mont-aux-Sources and the Tugela Falls.

The Kamberg Rock Art Centre, situated in the Ukhahlamba-Drakensberg Park, offers visitors a glimpse of more than 40 000 San Bushman images.

The Ukhahlamba-Drakensberg Park is one of 23 World Heritage Sites worldwide.

The 230 000 ha of protected area contains 500 known sites of San rock art. The Kamberg San Rock Art Trail and Interpretive Centre offer visitors information about the world of the San, and the opportunity to walk to the game pass shelter to view outstanding examples of their art in the company of a trained guide.

The Drakensberg mountain range forms the north-western border of KwaZulu-Natal.

A variety of wildlife including antelope, predators, small mammals and reptiles can be seen here.

The whole area is a bird sanctuary, and the endangered lammergeier (or bearded vulture) can be spotted. The highest concentration of walks and trails in South Africa is found here.

Many of these trails lead to sites once inhabited by the San, whose legacy of rock art can be viewed.

Northern Natal and battlefields

White and black rhino, elephant, crocodile, giraffe, cheetah and leopard, among others, can be seen at the Itala Game Reserve.

The KwaZulu-Natal Battlefields Route has the highest concentration of battlefields and related military sites in South Africa. The Battlefields Route starts at Estcourt and winds north through Colenso and Ladysmith to Newcastle and Volksrust, and eastwards to Utrecht, Glencoe, Dundee, Nqutu, Paulpietersburg, Vryheid, Babanango and Ulundi.

All the towns along the Route have their unique charm and range of attractions: arts and craft, scenic hiking trails, farm resorts, Zulu culture and roadside stalls. Game viewing, natural hot springs, horse trails and water sport can also be enjoyed.

The Chelmsford Nature Reserve near Newcastle is a bird-watcher's paradise.

Power boating and carp fishing are added attractions. Game includes springbuck, zebra, rhino and blesbuck. Other interesting places to visit are Majuba Hill and O'Neill's Cottage.

The Ladysmith Siege Museum provides insight into the Battles of Colenso, Spioenkop, Vaalkrans and Tugela Heights. Guided tours to nearby battlefields such as Wagon Hill are arranged by museum staff. Other attractions in Ladysmith include the Statue of Fandhi, the All Saints Church, the Soofi Mosque and the Spioenkop Dam and Nature Reserve.

Near Dundee, tourists can visit various battlefields, including Blood River, Isandlwana, Rorke's Drift and Talana. The Talana Museum depicts various facets of the coal industry, as well as local Zulu, Boer and British history.

Rorke's Drift was the setting for one of the most famous battles of the War. The main attrraction is the Rorke's Drift Battle Museum.

South Africa Yearbook 2003/04

Acknowledgements

Department of Environmental Affairs and Tourism
Eastern Cape Provincial Government
Free State Provincial Government
Gauteng Provincial Government
KwaZulu-Natal Provincial Government
Limpopo Provincial Government
Mpumalanga Provincial Government
Northern Cape Provincial Government
North West Provincial Government
South African National Parks
South African Tourism
Western Cape Provincial Government
www.gov.za

Suggested reading

Ballard, S. *South African Handbook*. 2nd ed. Bath (UK): Footprint Handbooks, 1997.
Barbour, A. *Fodor's South Africa*. New York: Fodor, 1996.
Beckett, D. *Madibaland*. Johannesburg: Penguin Books South Africa, 1998.
Bell, G. *Somewhere Over the Rainbow: Travels in South Africa*. London: ABACUS, 2001.
Braak, L.E.O. *Kruger National Park: A Visitor's Guide*. Revised edition. Cape Town: Struik, 1998.
Brett, M. and Mountain, A. *Touring Atlas of Southern Africa*. Cape Town: Struik, 1997.
Brett, M. and others. *South Africa*. London: Dorling Kindersley, 1999.
Bulpin, T.V. *Discovering Southern Africa*. 6th ed. Cape Town: Tafelberg, 2001.
Butchart, D. *Wild about Johannesburg: All-in-One Guide to Common Animals, Plants of Gardens, Parks and Nature Reserves*. Halfway House: Southern Book Publishers, 1995.
Connolly, D. *Connolly's Guide to Southern Africa*. 5th ed. Scottburgh: Connoly Publishers, 1992.
Crewe-Brown, M. *Traveller's Companion to South Africa*. 2nd ed. Johannesburg: CBM Publishing, 1994.
Deacon, H. *The Essential Robben Island*. Cape Town: Mayibuye Books and David Philip, 1997.
Dennis, N. and Scholes, B. *The Kruger National Park: Wonders of an African Eden*. London, Cape Town: New Holland, 1994.
Derwent, S. *Guide to Cultural Tourism in South Africa*. Cape Town: Struik, 1999.
Detert, L. ed. *Automobile Association (AA) Hotels, Lodges, Guest-Houses, B&Bs, 2002/03 edition*. Johannesburg: Automobile Association, 2002.
Duncan, P. *Thomas Cook Traveller's South Africa*. Basingstoke, Hampshire (UK): AA Publishing, 1996.
Du Plessis, H. *Tourism Destinations: Southern Africa*. Cape Town: Juta, 2000.
Erasmus, B.P.J. *On Route in South Africa: A Region by Region Guide to South Africa*. Johannesburg: Jonathan Ball, 1995. Also available in Afrikaans as *Op Pad in Suid-Afrika*.
Federated Hotel Association of Southern Africa. *Hotelier and Caterer Buyers' Guide. 1996 – 1997*. Cape Town: Ramsey Son and Parker, 1997.
George, R. *Marketing South African Tourism and Hospitality*. Cape Town: Oxford University Press, 2001.
Haw, S., Unsworth, A. and Robertson, H. *Rediscovering South Africa*. Cape Town: Spearhead, 2001.
Isaacson, R. *The Healing Land: A Kalahari Journey*. London: Fourth Estate, 2001.
Jordaan, M.J.S. *Tourism in South Africa*. 2nd ed. Bloemfontein: The Author, 2001.
Joyce, P. *South Africa*. 2nd ed. London: New Holland Publishers, 1996. (*Globetrotter Travel Guide*.) First published in 1994.
Keyser, H. *Tourism Development*. Cape Town: Oxford University Press, 2002.
Kok, P. and Pietersen, J. *Tourism*. Pretoria: Human Sciences Research Council, 2000.
Koornhof, A. *Dive Guide: South Africa*. London: New Holland Publishers, 2000.
Leigh, M. *Touring in South Africa*. 2nd ed. Revised and updated by Brian Johnson Burker. Cape Town: Struik, 1993.
Levy, J. *Complete Guide to Walks and Trails in Southern Africa*. 3rd ed. Cape Town: Struik, 1993.
Loubser, J. ed. *Tourist and Leisure Destinations 2002/03*. Cape Town: Comparex Africa, 2001.

Tourism

Loubser, J. ed. *Western Cape Tourist and Leisure Road Atlas.* Cape Town: Lapa Publishers, 2000.
Magubane, P. *Soweto*; text by C. Smith. Cape Town: Struik, 2001.
Maylam, P. and Edwards, I. eds. *The People's City: African Life in the Twentieth Century.* Pietermaritzburg: University of Natal Press, 1996.
National Parks of South Africa. Photography by A. Bannister. Text by B. Ryan. Cape Town: Struik, 1993.
New South African Book of the Road. 2nd ed. Cape Town: AA Motorist Publications, 1995.
O'Hagan, T. *Wild Places of Southern Africa.* 3rd edition. Cape Town: Struik, 2001.
Olivier, W. *Guide to Backpacking and Wilderness Trails.* Halfway House: Southern Book Publishers, 1991.
Olivier, W. and Olivier, S. *Overland Through Southern Africa.* Cape Town: Struik, 1998.
Paynter, D. and Nussey, W. *Kruger: Portrait of a National Park.* Halfway House: Southern Book Publishers, 1992.
Places to Visit in Southern Africa. Cape Town: AA Motorist Publications, 1995.
Reader's Digest Illustrated Guide to the Game Parks and Nature Reserves of Southern Africa. 3rd ed. Cape Town: Reader's Digest Association, 1997.
Saayman, M. *Tourism Marketing in South Africa.* Potchefstroom: Leisure Consultants and Publications, 1997.
South Africa: The Rough Guide. 2nd ed. London: Rough Guides, 1999.
South Africa Focus: South African Tourism Directory. Johannesburg: Africa Focus, 1997.
Southern African Travel Guide. 31st edition. Rosebank, Cape: Promeo, 2001.
Stern, J. *Engen Guide to Adventure Travel in Southern Africa.* Halfway House: Southern Book Publishers, 1997.
Stuart, C. and Stuart, T. *Guide to Southern African Game and Nature Reserves.* 4th ed. Cape Town: Struik, 1997.
Sycholt, A. *A Guide to the Drakensberg.* Cape Town: Struik, 2002.
Van der Merwe, P. and Saayman, M. *Managing Game Farms from a Tourism Perspective.* Potchefstroom: Leisure Consultants and Publications, 2002.
Van der Walt, B. *The Enchanting World of the Drakensberg Mountains.* Potchefstroom: Institute for Contemporary Christianity in Africa, 2003.
Weinberg, P. *Once We Were Hunters: A Journey with Africa's Indigenous People.* Cape Town: David Philip, 2000.

AKE 1163 A

SAA ✈ SAL
SOUTH AFRICAN AIRWAYS · SUID-AFRIKAANSE LUGDIENS

AKE 1163 SAA

chapter 22

Transport

The Department of Transport's vision is one of a transport system that builds a better life for all. Its mission is to promote affordable transport access and mobility that is safe, reliable and internationally competitive.

The Department's main objective is to formulate, co-ordinate, implement and monitor transport strategies and policies in general, and to enhance safety, improve public transport and develop transport infrastructure.

The other key objectives include:
- facilitating access and affordability of public transport to the commuting public
- planning, developing and maintaining transport infrastructure to improve mobility and quality of life and contribute to economic development
- promoting sector and enterprise reforms to create a reliable, safe and competitive transport system.

Policy

Transport infrastructure in South Africa is deeply affected by the disparities arising from previous patterns of spatial development, with people, particularly the poor, often having to travel long distances.

This reduces the economic efficiency of the transport system and has a high social cost because transport consumes a relatively large proportion of the disposable income of the poor.

Coupled with this is the high rate of transport accidents, on both roads and rail. Overcoming these problems is the central challenge facing the Department of Transport. The Department is working to improve and expand infrastructure, and through subsidies, reduce the costs of public transport.

Transport policy is built on the framework set out by the Moving South Africa project, which began in 1997, and the National Land Transport Transition Act, 2000 (Act 22 of 2000).

These set out a vision of an efficient public transport system with the use of targeted subsidies, and the provision of a high-quality, comprehensive infrastructure.

The Department is continuously reviewing, developing, monitoring and evaluating its policies and strategies.

Public-transport subsidies

Transport subsidies are a potentially important tool for improving efficiency, access and equity. In the past they have been targeted loosely and implemented selectively, but the Department is trying to target subsidies at those with the greatest need – vulnerable

◀ In 2003, South African Airways won the following awards: Best African Airline, Best Domestic Airline, Best International Airline flying to South Afric (ASATA Diners Club), Best Airline in Africa, Best Cabin Crew in Africa (Skytrax), Best Airline based in Africa (the Official Airline Guide) and Top Airline in Africa (the British weekly magazine, *Travel Bulletin*).

groups such as learners, people with disabilities, the aged, the unemployed and the employed poor – to maximise economic and social gains.

The strategy also seeks to integrate transport that is accessible to people with disabilities, and to promote the provision of accessible transport across all modes of public transport.

Significant additional funds have been allocated to the Department – over R1,5 billion – to help to deliver more effective and efficient public transport.

The Department is continuing to improve the efficiency of bus subsidies. It has already converted 30% of bus-subsidy contracts to more efficient, competitive tenders, and the remaining 70% were expected to be converted during 2003/04. It is also reforming contract provisions to ensure greater value for money for the Department. The passenger rail network also receives significant amounts of money.

In 2003, the Department of Transport commissioned Statistics South Africa to conduct a nationwide survey on travel patterns and modes of transport used by the majority of citizens, to help government to intervene properly in the allocation of subsidy and transport spending.

By July 2003, the Department was conducting a strategic review of public-transport policy and strategy, including the development of a policy on the targeting of public-transport subsidies for bus and commuter rail. The Department allocates R4 billion per annum to public-transport subsidies for bus and commuter-rail transportation.

Subsidised bus services currently operate in 36 local authorities in the country. Most subsidies are funded from the Department of Transport's budget, while provincial budgets provide for additional subsidies in certain areas.

During the 2001/02 financial year, almost 380 million subsidised passenger trips were recorded, while subsidised buses covered approximately 362 million kilometres (km). On average, each subsidised bus passenger received approximately R198 in subsidies per month, constituting some 6,7% of the average household income.

Black Economic Empowerment (BEE)

By June 2003, the Department of Transport was engaged in a process of developing a BEE Strategy for the transport sector.

The objective of the process is to identify the challenges, set targets, and develop a monitoring and evaluation framework for the implementation of the Strategy.

The process includes stakeholders from all the key subsectors, such as maritime, aviation, rail, road construction, minibus-taxis, buses and road freight.

The proposed BEE targets will require provinces to set aside a minimum of 30% of services to be contracted to companies with at least 50,1% previously disadvantaged individuals (PDIs). Of the remaining 70% of services, a minimum of 35% PDI equity ownership

---

By June 2003, the curriculum for traffic-officer training was being revised to extend it from six months to one year.

The proposed change is expected to take place in 2004. The revised course will meet the South African Qualifications Authority's registration requirements.

The course content will be modernised and more subjects that are relevant to the operational responsibilities of traffic officers, such as first aid and trauma-management skills, will be introduced.

The revised basic course will further close the gap between metro and traffic courses as it will have the same legal content as the South African Police Service course. All 10 traffic training colleges have been evaluated for the first time in six years.

Certain metropolitan police departments have replaced traditional traffic departments. In such cases, traffic policing duties and functions have also been taken over.

will be required, together with 10% subcontracting of services to small, medium and micro enterprises (SMMEs)/PDIs.

The process of developing a Maritime Transport BEE Strategy has been under way since the end of May 2003.

A steering committee was nominated, with the objective of overseeing the formulation of the Draft Maritime Transport BEE Strategy.

By September 2003, the Draft Strategy was available for comment from industry.

Non-motorised transport

Greater emphasis will be placed on the promotion of non-motorised transport, primarily with a view to increasing transport mobility and accessibility, mainly in rural areas. In his budget vote speech in June 2002, the Minister of Transport, Mr Dullah Omar, announced that the Department would roll out the Non-Motorised Transport (NMT) Programme in the Kgalagadi and Botlhabela Presidential rural nodes. This Programme has four subcomponents:

- The promotion of ownership and usage of various rural transport operations (e.g. human/animal-drawn carts) in low-income rural areas and at local project level.
- The creation and/or improvement of appropriate, safe on- and off-the-road rural-transport infrastructure (on-the-road includes access roads, low-level access bridges, etc. and off-the-road includes footpaths, side-tracks, as well as various safety gadgets).
- Alleviating rural poverty by promoting the economic as well as strong industrial dimension of NMT project operations and infrastructure (e.g. SMMEs). This will be achieved by exploiting to the maximum local expertise in the running and sustaining of the Programme.
- Impact assessment and programme evaluation. The main objective of this component is to provide meaningful contributions to the rural transport strategy.

Transport safety

Increased emphasis will be placed on safety issues in all transport modes. The Road to Safety Strategy, transportation of dangerous goods by road, the establishment of a Maritime Rescue Centre, the setting-up of the Railway Safety Regulator and the Road-Traffic Management Corporation (RTMC) are examples of this. The RTMC Bill, which improves the structure and systems of the Board, was approved for submission to Parliament in December 2002.

Each province had to identify 10 hazardous locations and prioritise three for improvement. Work is under way to improve safety in those locations.

New Partnership for Africa's Development (NEPAD)

From a transport point of view, key issues in creating an effectively co-ordinated African response to global market challenges are

---

By June 2003, a total of 16 pedestrian roadshows were held, aimed at promoting pedestrian road safety through the use of music artists and role models and the distribution of retro-reflective material such as sashes and bandanas.

Between April 2002 and June 2003, the Western Cape built two pedestrian bridges – one on the N2 and the other on the R300. Other pedestrian bridges were constructed in Hammanskraal and Witbank in Gauteng.

By June 2003, there were 2 826 scholar patrols, with 162 in the Eastern Cape, 65 in the Northern Cape, 185 in Mpumalanga, 48 in the North West, 109 in KwaZulu-Natal, 1 467 in Gauteng, 96 in Limpopo, 285 in the Free State and some 200 in the Western Cape. The Department of Transport has centralised the administration and control of all scholar patrols including equipment and uniforms. Some 20 000 scholar patrol bibs have been distributed in all nine provinces.

Of the envisaged 26 Junior Traffic Training Centres, 20 had been completed and six were under construction by June 2003.

The Centres are aimed at educating children through simulating the real road environment. In the most rural areas, trailers, which will act as Centres, will be distributed to the different provinces.

market access, mobility, and systems integration. These are the factors that, in the overall environment of increasingly effective governance, make sustained economic and social development possible.

The Department is contributing actively to the practical realisation of both NEPAD and Southern African Development Community (SADC) development goals in several major areas, by promoting:
- efficient and effective maritime transport services
- rail-systems integration
- road-systems development and infrastructure maintenance.

Agencies

The Department of Transport has established four bodies to move certain elements of government's operational activities to commercial agencies. They are the South African National Roads Agency Ltd (SANRAL), the South African Maritime Safety Authority (SAMSA), the Cross-Border Road Transport Agency (CBRTA), and the Civil Aviation Authority (CAA).

The agencies perform functions and services previously provided by the national Department of Transport, in a fully commercial environment. They have been assigned clearly defined responsibilities and functions, and each agency has entered into a formal performance agreement and Memorandum of Understanding (MoU) with the Government as shareholder.

South African National Roads Agency Ltd

The SANRAL was created out of the need for the national Department of Transport to separate its roles as policy-maker and operator. The SANRAL, a commercially driven company with the Minister of Transport as its single shareholder, manages and operates the national road network on behalf of government.

The SANRAL was established in April 1998 as an independent, statutory company. It is responsible for the design, construction, management and maintenance of South Africa's national road network, both toll and non-toll. It is also charged with raising the finances required to develop and manage the road network, an asset worth an estimated R40 billion.

The SANRAL's responsibilities are to:
- strategically plan, design, construct, operate, rehabilitate and maintain South Africa's national roads
- deliver and maintain a world-class primary-road network
- generate revenue from the development and management of its assets
- undertake research and development to enhance the quality of the country's roads
- upon request of the Minister and in agreement with a foreign country, provide, operate and maintain roads in that country.

South African Maritime Safety Authority

The Authority is a statutory body that reports to the Minister of Transport. Its responsibilities include the promotion of safety of life and property at sea, the prevention of sea pollution by pollutants emanating from ships, and the co-ordination of overall technical operations. It also develops policy on legal issues, foreign relations, marine pollution and certain specific safety matters.

SAMSA's main functions are to:
- provide shipping competence and pollution services in a regional context
- manage marine incidents, casualties and wrecks, and participate in search-and-rescue missions
- control standby tugs and pollution stores
- maintain seafarers according to standards of training and staffing criteria
- provide a shipping-administration support service
- manage the registration of ships

- manage a coastal patrol service
- manage vessel traffic, including navigation aids
- provide lighthouse services.

Funding comes from, among others, levies on ships calling at South African ports, direct user charges, and government service fees.

Cross-Border Road Transport Agency

The Agency regulates and controls access to the cross-border road-transport market by the road-transport industry. It also aims to facilitate the establishment of co-operative and consultative relationships and structures between public and private-sector institutions, with an interest in cross-border transport.

The CBRTA is furthermore involved in the collection, processing and dissemination of relevant information; the provision of training and capacity-building; and the promotion of entrepreneurship, with the focus on SMMEs with an interest in cross-border road transport.

The functions of the Agency include:
- advising the Minister of Transport on cross-border transport matters and assisting in the process of negotiating and renegotiating cross-border road-transport agreements on request
- regulating the road-transport industry's access to the cross-border road-transport market
- facilitating ongoing co-operative and consultative relationships and structures between the public and private sectors in support of cross-border road-transport operations
- undertaking road-transport law enforcement.

The main source of income for the CBRTA is fees charged for cross-border permits.

Civil Aviation Authority

The CAA was established on 1 October 1998 following the enactment of the CAA Act, 1998 (Act 40 of 1998). The Act provides for the establishment of a stand-alone authority charged with promoting, regulating and enforcing civil aviation safety and security.

The primary purpose of the CAA is to promote, regulate and support high levels of safety throughout the civil aviation industry. Its core activities relate to overseeing aviation safety for operations, aircraft, personnel, airports and airspace. The CAA receives transfers as subsidies and user charges for Ministerial directives on aircraft-accident investigations. These declined from R10 million in 2000/01 to R5,4 million in 2002/03. In the medium term, they are projected to grow to R6,4 million by 2005/06.

The CAA receives most of its revenue from industry-user fees and levies.

Transnet Limited

Transnet Limited was established on 1 April 1990. It is a public company, of which the South African Government is the sole shareholder. The company is recognised as a dominant player in the southern African transport infrastructure. Its activities are not restricted to southern Africa but extend beyond its borders into Africa and the rest of the world.

It handles 176 million tons (Mt) of rail freight per year, 2,8 Mt road freight and 194 Mt of freight through the harbours, while 13,8 million litres (ML) are pumped through its petrol pipelines annually.

The company through South African Airways (SAA) flies 6,1 million domestic, regional and international passengers per year. In total, Transnet is worth R72 billion in fixed assets and has a workforce of some 80 000 employees.

Transnet Limited consists of nine main divisions, a number of subsidiaries and related businesses:
- Spoornet focuses on the transportation of freight, containers and mainline passengers by rail
- the National Ports Authority (NPA) focuses on the provision of total port infrastructure and marine-related services, the manage-

ment of port activities in a landlord capacity, and the regulation of the port systems
- South African Port Operations (SAPO) focuses on port-terminal and cargo operations in commercially viable business units
- Petronet focuses on the transportation of petroleum products and gas through a high-pressure long-distance pipeline network
- Freightdynamics is a strategic road-freight business with a national network of operations
- Propnet manages a profitable property development, and handles the management and investment function of Transnet's vast property portfolio
- Metrorail is a commuter rail transport business
- Transtel is the telecommunications unit of Transnet
- Transwerk is involved in engineering activities and is one of South Africa's leading manufacturers and refurbishers of railway rolling stock.

Road transport

National roads

In terms of the National Roads Act, 1998 (Act 7 of 1998), government is responsible for overall policy, while road-building and maintenance is the responsibility of SANRAL.

In October 2003, Johannesburg International Airport (JIA), Africa's biggest and busiest airport, was named the Best Airport in Africa for the second consecutive year by the Skytrax survey.

The Skytrax survey is one of the largest airport surveys of airline passengers, and is commissioned and undertaken by Skytrax of London.

Travellers from 80 countries submitted more than 1,6 million eligible nominations.

The Airports Company South Africa recorded a strong result in the survey, with Cape Town International Airport claiming second position and Durban International fifth.

About 12 million people pass through the JIA in a year.

Air-traffic movements increased by 175 509 (16%) from 1992 to 2002, and the number of passengers had increased by 103% to more than 12 million by 2002.

The Department continues to work on improving the road network, ensuring that it is well-maintained and safe. A new National Roads Plan is being developed, indicating the importance of roads to the economy.

The South African road network comprises some 534 076 km of roads and streets.

Responsibility for the network is carried by the Department with SANRAL, the nine provinces, and local authorities.

The national road system links all the major centres in the country to one another as well as to neighbouring countries. There is a national road network of 9 400 km, with plans to extend this to 20 000 km of primary roads. Toll roads, which are serviced by 31 mainline toll plazas, cover about 2 200 km. The network includes 1 437 km of dual-carriage freeway, 440 km of single-carriage freeway, and 56 967 km of single-carriage main road with unlimited access. South Africa has the longest road network of any country in Africa.

The Cabinet approved a five-year road infrastructure strategy to prevent the further deterioration of the country's road network.

The SANRAL is very involved in improving the country's primary road network. Although the issue of tolling is very contentious, the existing concession roads are combined with a private-sector investment value of R5,2 billion, of which R1,37 billion is in the form of foreign direct investment. Approximately 1 350 km of national roads are being upgraded and maintained without making any demands on tax-based revenue.

The Department is developing the Road-Infrastructure Strategic Framework that will give effect to the national vision of road transport in South Africa, taking into consideration the socio-economic environment, national imperatives, policy goals, institutional arrangements, funding mechanisms, current realities and future scenarios, as well as the needs and perceptions of the road user. The outcome will be a review of the principal issues facing the development of road infrastructure and a sustainable strategy for the future.

In line with the resolution of the Growth and Development Summit held in June 2003, the Department has embarked on a new initiative to integrate labour-intensive road-construction programmes. This initiative aims to mobilise the road subsector to maximise the amount of jobs that can be created through labour-intensive construction methods.

This is expected to ensure that the road subsector contributes meaningfully to the Expanded Public Works Programme, which is a key vehicle for creating jobs for unemployed people who cannot get access to the formal economy.

The Minister of Finance, Mr Trevor Manuel, announced at the tabling of the Medium Term Budget Policy Statement, in November 2003, that R20 million would be allocated to the Department of Transport for urgent road repair at a number of border posts.

Provincial roads

The planning, construction and maintenance of roads and bridges, other than those falling under the SANRAL or local governments, is the responsibility of provincial governments. The national Department of Transport is always ready to assist provincial and local governments to improve and develop the state of their roads.

It is estimated that the funding required to address the backlog for rural roads is R56 billion for all provincial roads and R8 billion for roads under the National Roads Agency.

Provincial budgets for infrastructure and road development increased by 7,5% from R4,7 billion in 2002/03 to R5,1 billion in 2003/04.

Spatial Development Initiatives (SDIs)

The SDI programme uses public resources – particularly project planning, scoping and logistical co-ordination skills – to leverage private-sector involvement. SDIs are recognised as an effective means of stimulating economic growth by exploiting the existing economic potential within an area. The Department's involvement in this project is focused on infrastructure provision, BEE, skills transfer and the creation of sustainable jobs.

The SDIs are Lubombo, West Coast, Fish River, Maputo Development Corridor, Wild Coast, Platinum, Phalaborwa and Richards Bay.

Municipal roads

The construction and maintenance of most roads and streets within the municipal boundaries of cities and towns is the responsibility of the municipality concerned.

Toll roads

Toll roads cover some 2 200 km and are serviced by 31 toll plazas, including concessioned roads.

The viability of every toll road is determined over a 30-year period to assess the private-sector funding which can be sustained and served. The performance of all toll roads is within the forecast, and in many cases roads perform better than forecast. It is envisaged that all new major toll-road projects will be financed through the Build, Operate and Transfer principle. This allows greater private-sector involvement in the financing, building, operation and maintenance of toll projects. When the concession period expires, the facility is transferred back to the State at no cost.

Construction of the N4 Maputo Corridor Toll Road has been completed and includes 70 km of new road, 112 km of rehabilitation, and 240 km of road-widening. The new Road is one of the few privately financed cross-border toll roads in the world. Ownership of the N4 Maputo Corridor Toll Road, for which Trans African Concessions is the concessionaire for 30 years, will revert to the South African and Mozambican Governments after the concession agreement expires. It is the first international toll road in Africa.

The Bakwena Platinum Highway near Rustenburg, which closes the link between the Maputo Harbour in Mozambique and Walvis Bay in Namibia, is the first high-quality transcontinental route in sub-Saharan Africa.

The road reduces export and shipping times by as much as 10 shipping days, while the distance by road between Johannesburg and Windhoek is shortened by some 500 km. Other benefits of the Highway include injecting R3 billion into the economy, creating 3 000 direct jobs during the construction period, and opening doors for foreign direct investment.

An analysis of the project also revealed that the project would contribute at least R2,2 billion per annum to the Gross Domestic Product. Of this amount, at least 61% (R1,35 billion) will manifest in the region itself.

The project was also named 'Deal of the Year' by adjudicators under the auspices of Project Finance International.

Construction on the N3 toll road commenced in 1999, on the 418-km road from Heidelberg in Gauteng to Cedara in KwaZulu-Natal. The Harrismith section of the road has been open to the public since April 2001, while the Heidelberg-Villiers section opened in December 2001.

This project injected R3,5 billion into the economy, of which a payment of R1,38 billion allowed government to excise its debt obligation. The project includes a 100-km section over the De Beers Pass, which will be built in 2010, depending on the traffic volumes at that time.

Toll roads funded by the SANRAL include the N1-South extension in the Free State between Kroonstad, Welkom and Bloemfontein, at an investment value of about R180 million. Future projects in this category include an N17-East toll road in Gauteng and Mpumalanga; N4 East toll road below the Hans Strijdom offramp, outside Pretoria and the Gauteng-Mpumalanga border; and an N1 North extension in Limpopo. The roads' total investment value is estimated at R863 million. A new toll road was expected to be erected between Empangeni and Richards Bay in KwaZulu-Natal in 2003. The R1,2-billion project includes the design, construction, financing, operation and maintenance of a 19,2-km stretch of the John Ross toll highway.

Road-traffic signs

A revised road-traffic-sign system, which closely conforms to international standards, has been phased in since November 1993.

The revised system involves changes to the colours of some of the regulatory and all of the warning signs, changes in design parameters, the modernisation of text and symbols, and the addition of new signs, signals and markings. Many of the new signs make use of symbols rather than text to eliminate language problems and reduce observation time.

South Africa prepared a road-signs manual for the SADC in terms of the 1998 Protocol on Transport, Communications and Meteorology. South Africa has since started phasing in new SADC-aligned signs on its roads and other cross-border roads. The previous system was concurrently legal with the new system until 31 December 2000, by which date all the old signs had to be phased out and replaced with new signs.

To simplify the navigation task for tourists, foreigners and drivers in unfamiliar areas, as well as to promote global uniformity, it was

---

South Africa hosted the Paris-based Independent Association of Road Congresses' (PIARC) 22nd World Road Congress in Durban from 19 to 25 October 2003.

The aim of the Congress was to promote international co-operation and technology transfer among members of PIARC, which include 100 countries – two-thirds of which are from developing countries – and 2 000 individual members.

Transport

agreed that drivers should make use of route maps (readable in any language) and route numbers to guide them towards their destinations (all major routes and main streets in urban areas are numbered and displayed on readily available maps).

Credit-card format (CCF) licences

The CCF driving licence was introduced on 1 March 1998. A period of five years was determined by Notice in the *Government Gazette*, for each motorist, based on their birth month, to apply for the conversion before 31 August 2002.

The Department of Transport extended the deadline for the conversion of the old book-style driving licence to the CCF to 28 February 2003.

However, due to an unprecedented number of outstanding applications, the final deadline was extended to 30 April 2003.

The CCF driving-licence is valid for five years. Motorists who failed to convert could either be fined or have their current driving licences nullified.

By April 2003, a total of 7 025 million CCF driving licences had been produced. All driving-licence records are centralised into the database of the online National Traffic Information System.

The introduction of modern technology to limit human intervention in driving-licence testing is in line with the strategy to fight fraud and corruption.

By September 2003, the Department was working on a computerised learner's-licence testing procedure which involves the use of an audio-visual, user-friendly computerised system to compile test questions and the marking of thereof.

The system was expected to be introduced at 330 learner driving-license testing centres in all 11 official languages. Other technology in the pipeline will limit human intervention in the process of eye-testing and the capturing of fingerprint information on the CCF.

Public transport

In terms of the Constitution of South Africa, 1996 (Act 108 of 1996), legislative and executive powers in respect of public transport are a provincial competency. National government, however, is responsible for policy formulation, monitoring and strategic implementation. The national Department of Transport continues to administer subsidies for buses and other subsidised forms of public transport.

National Transport Register

The establishment of the National Transport Register is a requirement of the National Land Transport Transition Act, 2000 (Act 22 of 2000).

The purpose of the Register is to integrate the land-transport systems, i.e. the Subsidy-Management System (SUMS), the Land-Transport Permit System (LTPS) and the Registration Administration System (RAS). The primary goal of the LTPS is to facilitate the issue of public road-carrier permits, to regulate entry into the road-carrier markets.

The objective is to facilitate the processing of permit applications and enable the Local Road Transportation Boards (Provincial Permit Boards) to provide an efficient service to the industry. In achieving this goal, the System supports the Boards with:
- registering applications
- generating and verifying advertisements
- capturing objections and appeals
- generating agendas
- verifying vehicle information
- generating permits and permit transfers.

The primary goal of the RAS is to facilitate the registration of minibus-taxi associations with the Provincial Registrar to formalise the industry. They support the Registrar with:
- registering members and associations
- registering vehicle particulars of members
- registering corridor particulars of associations
- management reporting.

The primary goal of the SUMS is to manage claims received from provincial departments for bus contracts, and to manage payment.

Urban transport

Metropolitan Transport Advisory Boards govern urban areas which have been declared metropolitan transport areas. Both short- and long-term programmes for adequate transportation development are drawn up by the core city of each area and are revised and adjusted annually.

Nine such core areas exist, namely Johannesburg, Cape Town, Pretoria, Durban, Pietermaritzburg, Port Elizabeth, the East Rand, Bloemfontein and East London.

The planning of transport for metropolitan and major urban areas must be done in accordance with a growth-management plan, and travel modes should not compete with each other. In urban areas, passenger road-transport services are provided by local governments, private bus companies which operate scheduled bus services between peripheral areas and city centres, and minibus-taxis.

The Department will support provincial Departments of Transport and Public Works in the construction of intermodal facilities and in their efforts to achieve integration between bus and taxi operations.

The minibus-taxi industry has shown phenomenal growth during the last few years, leading to a decrease in the market share of the bus and train as modes of transport.

Motor vehicles

On 31 December 2001, there were some 6,9 million registered vehicles in South Africa, more than 3,98 million of which were motor vehicles. The number of private motor vehicles continues to grow at a rate of 1,7% per annum.

Minibus-taxis

There are close to 127 000 minibus-taxis in South Africa, which provide 65% of the 2,5 billion annual passenger trips in urban areas, and a high percentage of rural and intercity transport.

The South African National Taxi Council (SANTACO) is the umbrella body for all provincial taxi organisations and strives to regulate, formalise and stabilise the industry. The Council acts as a mediator in disputes between taxi organisations and plays a role in eliminating the causes of taxi violence.

In May 1999, the Government signed an MoU with SANTACO, paving the way for the replacement of the industry's ageing fleet and its absorption into South Africa's formal economy.

The Memorandum commits SANTACO to act against violent elements in the industry, participate in the regulation of the industry by ensuring its members have legal operations, and implement a programme of acceptable labour practices. Government, in turn, is bound by the Memorandum to find an acceptable solution to the industry's recapitalisation crisis, legalise illegal operations within agreed parameters, and provide taxi operators with extensive training.

Taxi Recapitalisation Programme

The aim of the Taxi Recapitalisation Programme is to replace the current ageing taxi fleet with new, safer and purpose-built 18- and 35-seater vehicles.

In terms of Section 31 of the National Land Transport Transition Act, 2000, the Minister of Transport can determine a date from which existing minibus-taxis will not be used as public transport vehicles.

Key to the Programme will be a strong empowerment element involving the establishment of taxi co-operatives to liaise with financiers, distribute the new vehicles, and provide the facilities for a compulsory maintenance programme. The co-operatives will be established after extensive consultation with local taxi organisations.

The aim is to ensure that the new vehicles are manufactured locally, and to tap into

South Africa's highly diversified components-manufacturing sector.

On 8 October 2003, the Pretoria High Court granted the KwaZulu-Natal Taxi Council (KWANATACO) an interdict to prevent SANTACO from signing the Memorandum of Agreement (MoA) with government.

KWANATACO contended that it was not properly consulted by SANTACO and therefore wanted to be part of the decision-making process.

The MoA deals with frameworks and guidelines on the implementation of the Programme, and the relationship between government and SANTACO in the implementation process. Government is expected to start roll-out of the vehicles by mid-2004, with an average delivery of approximately 25 000 vehicles per year over the next four years.

On 8 October 2003, government confirmed that the Taxi Recapitalisation Programme would proceed as planned. The interdict brought against SANTACO will not affect the Taxi Recapitalisation Programme being finalised by government.

Subsequent to the court's interdict, negotiations between government, SANTACO and the industry have continued, resulting in collective endorsement of the Programme.

Bus transport

A network of public and privately owned passenger bus services links the major centres of South Africa and also serves commuters in the deep rural areas. The Cabinet has approved measures intended to improve public-transport safety. These include the intensification of law enforcement, lowering the maximum speed limit for buses and minibus-taxis to 100 km/h, and a fitness-testing programme for buses.

An informal consultation process is under way with freight and public transport employers' associations and trade unions. This will be followed by formal negotiations to build consensus around self-regulatory measures and legislative or regulatory changes deemed necessary for tighter fleet-safety management.

International models being explored emphasise the need for a formal safety fitness-rating methodology. A vehicle operator will receive a safety rating when an accredited or authorised safety specialist conducts an on-site review of the operator's compliance with applicable safety and hazardous material regulations. In terms of the formal compliance review, the operator will then be awarded one of three ratings: satisfactory, conditional or unsatisfactory.

To meet safety-fitness standards, the carrier will have to demonstrate that it has adequate safety-management controls in place to reduce the risks associated with:
- inadequate levels of financial responsibility
- inadequate inspection, repair and maintenance of vehicles
- Professional Driver's Permit standard violations
- the use of unqualified and fatigued drivers
- improper use of motor vehicles
- unsafe vehicles operating on highways
- failure to maintain collision registers and copies of collision reports
- motor-vehicle crashes
- driving and parking violations
- violation of hazardous materials regulations.

The operator of a vehicle that has received an unsatisfactory safety rating will have a specified period of time from the effective date of rating notice to improve the safety rating to 'conditional' or 'satisfactory'.

If these improvements do not occur, the carrier will be prohibited from operating commercial motor vehicles or transporting passengers for reward.

The Department of Transport has been working closely with the South African Bureau of Standards (SABS) to ensure that the emergency exits of buses and taxis meet required standards and allow passengers to escape without difficulty in emergencies.

The Department has requested the SABS to pay specific attention to the relevant safety standards, adequacy and competence in and out of water, day and night.

This includes the ability of young children and the aged to break through emergency windows.

The SABS has also been requested to look at the locations of all emergency exits and the education of passengers on how to use them.

The Department has intensified its education campaign on how to use emergency exits and is engaging manufacturers in ensuring that more visible and reflective material are used to identify emergency exits.

Realising that the majority of small bus operators do not have formalised structures which government could consult with on issues that affect the bus industry, a process to facilitate the formalisation of the industry was started in 2003.

Cross-border transport

Multilateral
The SADC Protocol on Transport, Communications and Meteorology provides a comprehensive framework for regional integration across the entire spectrum of the transport, communications and meteorology sectors. The general objective is to promote the provision of efficient, cost-effective and fully integrated infrastructure and operations in these fields.

The Protocol also specifically addresses road transport, and aims to facilitate the unimpeded flow of goods and passengers between and across the territories of SADC member states. It wants to promote the adoption of a harmonised policy, which lays down general operational conditions for carriers.

Cross-border transport within the Southern African Customs Union (SACU) is undertaken in terms of the SACU MoU. The Memorandum facilitates transport between member countries through, among others, the use of the single-permit system.

The MoU provides the framework for cooperation between the signatory countries, which has resulted in the establishment of technical working groups for, among others, traffic standards, road-user charges and passenger transport.

The activities of the passenger-transport working group led to the establishment of Joint Route Management Committees (JRMCs) for certain cross-border passenger routes within the SACU. The JRMCs comprise representatives from the public and private sectors of the countries concerned, and are aimed at jointly managing the routes in consultation with all stakeholders.

Bilateral
The main thrust of bilateral agreements is to facilitate and encourage cross-border road transport in support of regional trade.

This is promoted through the entrenchment of the principle of extra-territorial jurisdiction, the entrenchment of a strategic public-private sector relationship, and the establishment of consultative mechanisms that are sufficiently flexible to promote the joint management of implementation.

The Maputo Development Corridor between South Africa and Mozambique is a good example.

The two Governments also signed agreements dealing with road freight and passenger transport between the two countries, which will facilitate the movement of goods and people by road and eliminate bureaucratic proceedings at border posts.

The project also includes the upgrading and modernisation of the railway line between the two countries and of Maputo Harbour, at a cost of about R150 million.

During a bilateral meeting with the South African Minister of Transport, on 24 October 2003, the United Kingdom's Minister of Transport, Mr David Jamieson, accepted South Africa's request for assistance on road-traffic management expertise to address the carnage on South Africa's roads.

Both Ministers agreed that there was a need for the two countries to work together in exploring the latest methods and technical skills in an effort to decrease the country's high road-fatality rate.

On 29 September 2003, the Minister of Transport and his Namibian and Botswana counterparts signed an MoU on the development and management of the Trans-Kalahari Corridor (TKC).

The TKC was formally established in 1998 following the completion of the Trans-Kgalagadi Highway in Botswana. The TKC links the three southern African countries by road.

One of the benefits of the TKC is that it links the hinterlands of Botswana, Namibia and South Africa (especially Gauteng) with the Port of Walvis Bay. This Port is the western seabord port in southern Africa and closest to shipping routes to and from markets in the Americas and Europe.

The development of the TKC has the potential of significantly reducing transaction costs for SADC exporters and importers. This is expected to enable economic operators to become increasingly internationally competitive by enhancing their ability to exploit the benefits of preferential trade agreements with the United States of America (USA) and European Union.

Domestic

The CBRTA fosters investment in the cross-border road-transport industry and provides high-quality cross-border freight and passenger road transport services at reasonable prices. The Agency works on a cost-recovery basis and any profits from cross-border permit fees are ploughed back into the system through a price reduction on permits in the following financial year. It also encourages small-business development in the industry.

Goods transport

Since the mid-1980s, the southern African road transport industry has grown considerably.

Approximately 80% of all freight carried in South Africa is conveyed by road, while nearly 7% of the Gross National Product is spent on freight transport.

About 69% of road-freight tonnage is carried by firms or operators transporting freight in the course of their business, and 29% by firms transporting goods for reward.

The Department is working with provincial counterparts and major stakeholders on the Overload-Control Infrastructure Programme which deals with reckless overloading. The Programme is based on the construction of a strategic network of traffic-control centres and fixed weigh stations on major roads, supported by mobile weigh stations on alternative roads in the main freight corridors. As part of the Department's freight-transport strategic intervention of promoting a modal shift from road to rail, joint-venture projects with the Eastern Cape and KwaZulu-Natal Departments of Transport have been embarked upon to revive rail lines that have been classified as low and light-density lines.

Road-traffic safety

South Africa's road-vehicle collision and fatality rates compare poorly with those of most other countries. Every year, about 10 000 people are killed and 150 000 injured in approximately 500 000 accidents. The cost of road-traffic accidents is estimated at more than R13 billion a year.

Greater road-safety awareness has been generated through the activities of the *Arrive Alive* Campaign, which is part of the Road to Safety Strategy (2001 – 2005).

The Strategy involves the creation of the RTMC that will be responsible for vehicle registration, traffic information systems, public communication and traffic law enforcement.

The RTMC Act, 1999 (Act 20 of 1999), provided for the establishment of the RTMC. Recognising the importance of the regulation of public transport and road traffic for the

development, safety and quality of life of all South Africans, the RTMC was created to:
- enhance the overall quality of road-traffic management and service provision
- strengthen co-operation and co-ordination between the national, provincial and local spheres of government in the management of road traffic
- maximise the effectiveness of provincial and local government efforts, particularly in road-traffic law enforcement
- create business opportunities, particularly for the previously disadvantaged sectors, to supplement public-sector capacity
- guide and sustain the expansion of private-sector investment in road-traffic management.

The process for adjudicating road-traffic offences has been reformed and is now administrative, rather than judicial. The Road Traffic Infringement Agency will serve as the collection agency for outstanding traffic fines and adjudicate contested traffic offences. This is supposed to be a more efficient and effective system for administering traffic offences.

The Constitution authorises provinces to exercise legislative and executive powers pertaining to road-traffic safety, while the promotion thereof is primarily the responsibility of the Department of Transport. The Road Traffic Safety Board (RTSB) endorses and acts as guardian of the Road Traffic Management Strategy (RTMS); assists in the identification, formulation and prioritisation of projects; monitors progress; and gives direction in the implementation of the RTMS. The RTSB is made up of members of all three spheres of government as well as traffic stakeholders in the private sector. The Ministers of Education, of Health, of Justice and Constitutional Development, of Provincial and Local Government, of Safety and Security and of Transport serve on the Board.

Three Acts provide for the national co-ordination of regulation and law enforcement, the registration and licensing of motor vehicles, and the training and appointment of traffic officers. These are the RTMC Act, 1999 (Act 20 of 1999), the National Road-Traffic Amendment Act, 1999 (Act 21 of 1999), and the Administrative Adjudication of Road-Traffic Offences Amendment Act, 1999 (Act 22 of 1999).

The Administrative Adjudication of Road-Traffic Offences Amendment Act, 1999 provides for a more efficient system of collecting traffic fines and for the introduction of a points demerit system, linked to the CCF driver's licence. In terms of the Act, a motorist's driver's licence will be suspended when he or she has 12 penalty points against his or her name. For every point over and above 12, the motorist's licence will be suspended for three months. Points can easily be accumulated, for example, four points each for exceeding the speed limit by 50%, driving an unregistered vehicle, refusing to undergo a blood or breathalyser test, or driving a vehicle without registration plates. The use of hand-held cellphones in vehicles is not allowed and non-compliance could cost a motorist two points.

When a licence is suspended for a third time, it will be cancelled and the motorist will again have to undergo a driver's test. In more serious cases, a court may forbid a motorist to drive on a public road ever again. However, the system in no way detracts from the accused's

---

The eighth International Symposium on Heavy-Vehicle Weights and Dimensions will be held in South Africa from 14 to 18 March 2004.

The theme of the Symposium, an intercontinental forum for researchers, policy-makers and industry leaders in the field of freight transportation by road, is *Loads, Roads and the Information Highway.*

The issues expected to be discussed are safety, maintenance, efficiency, vehicle configuration and components, economic and operational issues, standards and regulations, emissions, fuels, life cycle and recycling as well as the effect of heavy vehicles on pavements.

constitutional right to a fair trial. The points demerit system is to be implemented in phases.

Arrive Alive
Government's *Arrive Alive* Road-Safety Campaign aims to:
- reduce the number of road-traffic accidents in general, and fatalities in particular, by 5%, compared with the same period the previous year
- improve road-user compliance with traffic laws
- forge an improved working relationship between traffic authorities in the various spheres of government.

Greater attention is being given to pedestrian safety, as 40% of deaths on South African roads are pedestrians. Pedestrian road-safety messages are being featured on billboards and a contract was negotiated with the Premier Soccer League to advertise road-safety messages on screens in big soccer stadiums.

The remedial engineering projects are supported by appropriate education efforts aimed at adults and children, and by public awareness and enforcement campaigns to ensure compliance with the new or changed facilities. The Council for Scientific and Industrial Research is responsible for the evaluation of these 90 projects and for preparing a report on the effectiveness of the Campaign.

South Africa's rate of pedestrian fatalities is unacceptably high. Factors that have exaggerated the problem in South Africa include lack of infrastructure such as adequate pavements or road-crossing facilities, lack of education in road usage, a traffic mix with vehicles and pedestrians sharing the road, poor town and transport planning of facilities such as schools and community halls, and an absence of law enforcement.

Important strides have been made in integrating road-safety awareness education into the mainstream school curriculum, as a set of basic life skills that can be continuously expanded and deepened over time.

The implementation of road-safety education has been planned and prepared in detail by task teams from the Departments of Transport and of Education.

Pupils at pre-school level through to 9 are being exposed to systematic, practical road-safety education within the framework of the 'life-skills' component of their curriculum.

During April 2003, the Cabinet approved a number of priority projects to deal with the scourge of road accidents in the country.

These included Integrated Law Enforcement, the establishment of a Central Accident Bureau, and Visibility and Community-Based Co-ordinating Structures.

On 13 October 2003, the Minister of Transport, Mr Dullah Omar, launched a pilot project of the National Public Traffic Call Centre in Limpopo.

The Public Traffic Call Centre aims to give easy access to all public road-transport passengers on buses and minibus-taxis to report unsafe vehicles and reckless and negligent driver behaviour, as well as fraud and corruption.

The Call Centre will also provide the public road-user with the opportunity to report blatant moving violations, such as ignoring red traffic lights and illegal and unsafe overtaking and overloading, as well as fraud and corruption at vehicle-testing stations and driving-licence testing centres.

Incidents and accidents can also be reported to the Centre, which will also be a source of limited road-traffic information, such as road and traffic conditions. Reports on courteous, good and helpful driver-behaviour can also be submitted.

The information collected by the Centre will be utilised for advising the registered owner of the vehicle, by letter, of the nature and location of the alleged offence.

The Centre will prepare and distribute reports to the South African Police Service and relevant traffic authorities on the routes and/or locations where stolen vehicles and vehicles with false registration plates were observed, where regular traffic offences occur, and where cases of fraud and corruption were observed.

Road-traffic control

The Department of Transport is responsible for co-ordinating and harmonising traffic control (law enforcement) in South Africa. This is done in conjunction with the provinces, which have legislative and executive powers in this regard. The aim is to enhance traffic quality, promote voluntary compliance of road users with rules and regulations, reduce the incidence of traffic offences, prevent accidents, ensure effective adjudication, and implement improved management.

An important facet of the Department's work is the development of a standardised management system for traffic control at micro level, to assist traffic authorities in managing their internal and external environments optimally, and to achieve the highest levels of traffic quality, subject to the limited availability of resources.

The traffic-management model has been implemented by approximately 100 provincial and local traffic authorities.

Road-traffic law enforcement is the responsibility of the respective local and provincial traffic authorities as well as metro police services in metropolitan areas. Vehicles are allocated to shifts and specifically designated tasks, e.g. road patrols. In some provinces, two officers are allocated to a vehicle, while in other provinces, one officer may be allocated to a vehicle. The time of day also plays a role, e.g. night operations require at least two officers per vehicle for security reasons.

Roadblocks are held on a continuous basis by provincial and local traffic authorities. Roadblocks take many forms, from formal joint roadblocks with the South African Police Service (SAPS), the South African National Defence Force (SANDF) and other role-players, to standard driver and vehicle roadside checks, run by traffic officers to check on driving licences, alcohol usage by drivers, vehicle licences, tyres, lights, brakes, outstanding fines, etc.

No reservist traffic officers or volunteers have been appointed to date, due to constraints in terms of their powers, duties and responsibilities with regard to the Criminal Procedure Act, 1997 (Act 51 of 1997). However, the matter is being investigated.

Generally, traffic wardens fulfil their duties within local and municipal traffic authorities. Provincial authorities are expected to appoint more full-time traffic officers to fulfil all the tasks required of a traffic law-enforcement officer.

Road Accident Fund (RAF)

The RAF compensates victims of motor-vehicle accidents under the terms and conditions provided for in the relevant legislation. The Fund receives a dedicated RAF levy, which is imposed on petrol and diesel.

The Fund is in regular contact with the National Treasury and Department of Transport on proposed increases dependent upon the number of claims received, as recent trends have seen a mismatch between the Fund's revenue from the levy and the amount required to settle all the claims lodged. The Fund has proposed a quarterly review of the levy to keep pace with the cost of claims received.

The RAF Commission, appointed by government to recommend improvements to the accident-compensation system, has proposed the introduction of a no-fault system under a completely new body.

The RAF has proposed a more evolutionary approach starting with legislative amendments to stabilise the current system, while a no-fault system is being considered for the long term.

This is informed by the fact that a no-fault system would require billions of Rand more than the current system and lengthy preparatory work before it can be implemented.

Some of the most critical legislative amendments proposed by the RAF to normalise the financial position of the current system are:
- instalments rather than lump-sum payments in some categories of compensation

- caps on non-residents' claims
- introduction of medical tariffs and provision of managed healthcare.

Steps not requiring legislative amendments to improve the cash flow of the RAF include investment in road safety – principally through *Arrive Alive* – to limit the high number of accidents in the country.

Since 2001, the RAF has been vigorously fighting fraud and corruption bedevilling the system. A new claims-management system has been introduced to detect fraud, and forensic-investigation partnerships with the SAPS and the Scorpions have resulted in the arrest of hundreds of people.

All RAF staff undergo security clearances before appointment, and staff involved in fraud and corruption are dealt with severely.

In 2003, the RAF introduced a project called *Tip-Offs Anonymous*, which allows members of the public to report fraudulent behaviour and service-providers who approach them and try to convince them to defraud the RAF.

The RAF has also embarked on a campaign to inform all South Africans on their right to compensation, and to encourage them to claim directly without using attorneys as intermediaries.

In 2002, at least five million information sheets in all the official languages were distributed countrywide. By the end of 2003, at least 12 new information offices were expected to be opened nationally, to educate the public about the Fund, assist claimants to lodge claims on their own without using attorneys, and update claimants on the status of their claims.

Rail transport

The Department has embarked on a comprehensive recapitalisation programme to improve rail safety and revive rail transport as a viable public-transport alternative.

Two contracts were entered into with the industry to refurbish 236 coaches at a cost of R615 million over two years, with final delivery expected at the end of 2003.

The South African Rail Commuter Corporation (SARCC) ensured, through its Tender Policy and Procedures, that the allocation of the refurbishment coaches to suppliers significantly contributed to BEE, while maintaining acceptable standards of safety and comfort.

A total of R884 million has been invested in the upgrading, remodelling and refurbishment of rail commuter stations countrywide over the past few years.

A further R1,6 billion of private-sector investments, covering more than 120 developments, has also been allocated for upgrading land and properties surrounding rail commuter stations.

The cumulative total economic impact of job creation and economic activity through the Station Investment Programme exceeded R3,7 billion. The SARCC, in consultation with representatives of communities and the informal traders sector, has commenced a programme to turn the stations into major community and economic hubs contributing to the economic development of South Africa.

In 2002, the Department of Transport, the

The Gautrain Rapid Rail Link project aims to alleviate the severe traffic congestion in the Johannesburg-Tshwane corridor – a corridor in which the traffic volume is growing at 7% per year. It is forecasted that the initial demand for the Gautrain service will be 104 000 passenger-trips per day.

The key objectives of the Gautrain Project include economic growth, development and job creation, alleviation of traffic congestion, promotion of business tourism, and the improvement of city sustainability.

A feasibility study showed that 57 000 jobs would be created during construction, 2 200 jobs would be created as part of the operation and maintenance of the system, and 39 500 would further be created as part of the urban change. It also indicated a projected R6-billion increase in business sales, which would contribute to an increase of between 0,7% and 1% in the Gauteng Gross Geographic Product.

The preferred bidder was expected to be announced in January 2004.

SARCC and Metrorail developed a new two-pronged Safety and Security Strategy for the rail commuter system.

The Strategy has been implemented, as a pilot project, in the entire Western Cape Metropolitan rail network since October 2002 with very positive results.

On the technical and institutional side, the system involves alarms, and helicopter surveillance capability for the co-ordination of safety and security actions. Improved co-ordination between rail security efforts and SAPS interventions is a priority and forms an integral part of the total Strategy.

Based on the assessment of the pilot project, the Strategy is expected to be rolled out to other metropolitan rail commuter networks across the country.

The second element of the Strategy is that of engaging communities along the rail corridors to protect rail assets, by promoting the concept of 'community ownership'. The system draws the community to assist rail security personnel and the SAPS in proactively identifying and neutralising criminal elements.

The National Railway Safety Regulator Act, 2002 (Act 16 of 2002), is the enabling legislation for the setting up of an independent Railway Safety Regulator, reporting and accountable to the Minister of Transport.

The Regulator will oversee safety by means of conducting audits and inspections; undertaking occurrence investigations; analysing occurrence statistics, operator safety plans and accident reports; and issuing notices to operators to cease an activity or to improve an unsafe activity. Failure to respond to a notice could result in the operator, including the top management and even the board, being prosecuted.

The Board of the Railway Safety Regulator was inaugurated in the second half of 2003.

The implementation of the National Land Transport Transition Act, 2000 resulted in a focus by newly elected metropolitan or unicity authorities on their obligations and rights relative to commuter rail. Most of the bigger cities have already started processes to ensure the establishment of appropriate structures, such as metropolitan transport authorities to control commuter-rail concessions within their sphere of authority.

Spoornet

Spoornet is the largest division of Transnet, a commercialised business with the State as shareholder. Spoornet's core business lies in Freight Logistics Solutions (FLS) designed for customers in numerous industry-based business segments, mining, and heavy and light manufacturing sectors.

Spoornet is the largest railroad and heavy haulier in southern Africa, with an annual turnover of R9 billion generated by the transportation of 180 Mt of freight. The company has a 60% market share of the 170 billion Mt km cargo available in South Africa. To serve these markets, it utilises some 30 600 km of track, 3 253 locomotives and 114 433 wagons, and 2 102 passenger coaches.

Spoornet maintains an extensive rail network across South Africa and connects with rail networks in the sub-Saharan region. Its infrastructure represents 80% of Africa's rail infrastructure.

Spoornet's future investment in infrastructure will be focused on renewal and where appropriate, capacity expansion. Significant parts of infrastructure, namely signalling and electrification infrastructure, are reaching the end of their design lifespans. Renewal is expected to concentrate on the application of new, cheaper and more effective technologies.

Planned investment expenditure for the next 15 years is about R1 billion per annum to address the estimated backlog of R15 billion.

Freight Logistics Solutions

In line with current market demands, Spoornet's vision is to be the leader in FLS. To achieve this vision, the company has devolved from its rail competencies to warehousing, transport (including long haul, trans-shipment and feeder services), inventory management, freight forwarding, clearing and other logistical services. Logistics incorporates all the freight transportation modes such as road, rail, airfreight, ocean and barge. It includes warehousing, inventory management, fleet operations, freight forwarding and customs-brokerage services. The software and information technology used to support the flow of goods to market is also part of the logistics mix.

Spoornet consists of five business units, each with its own core business focus.

General Freight Business (GFB)

GFB is the largest Spoornet business unit in terms of revenue, customer accounts and the number of people employed. It handles in excess of 52% of Spoornet's freight tonnage per annum.

GFB conveys about 96 Mt of commodity freight a year, serving customers in specialised diverse industrial commodity markets, namely mining, and light and heavy manufacturing. Structures provide for a sales force dedicated to customers in specific business sectors under a relationship/one-on-one philosophy.

COALlink

COALlink focuses on the provision of world-class transportation for South Africa's export coal, from the Mpumalanga coalfields to the Richards Bay Coal Terminal at the Port of Richards Bay.

Coal exports constitute an integral part of the South African export industry. South Africa is second only to Australia in terms of tons of coal exported. South Africa is the world leader in terms of steam-coal exports. COALlink was formed in 1997 through the ring-fencing of the rail operation over the coal-export line, and augmenting the structure with a business component and other support functions. This initiative ensured that South Africa remains at the forefront of the world steam-coal export market. Mercer Management Consultants benchmarked the coal-line operation in 1994 against similar operations worldwide. The study rated the bulk export logistics supply chain as 8% more efficient than global best practice.

A major milestone in the history of the coal-export industry in South Africa was reached in December 2000 when the billionth ton of coal was transported over the coal line and exported through the Richards Bay Coal Terminal. The coal line celebrated 25 years of existence in April 2001.

Orex

Orex, a specialist business unit of Spoornet, deals in the haulage of iron ore over the 861-km track from Sishen to Saldanha Bay. The line is dedicated to the movement of iron ore from the mines in the far Northern Cape to the steel industries in the Western Cape, and for the export of the ore through the Port of Saldanha Bay. The success of this bulk logistics operation depends on close co-operation with the Port and its facilities.

The average tonnage of iron ore transported per year increased from 17,5 Mt for the period 1990/92 to 1994/95, to 21,6 Mt for 1999/00. A benchmark study rated this seamless operation as 38% more efficient than global best practice.

Orex not only transports iron ore, but has also become an international player in providing a diverse range of heavy-haul logistics solutions for growing local and international markets. The line celebrated its 25th anniversary in May 2001.

Shosholoza Meyl

Shosholoza Meyl provides an affordable intercity passenger service between major destinations in South and southern Africa. Approximately four million passengers utilise this service per year.

It operates daily long-distance passenger services between Johannesburg, Durban, East

London, Port Elizabeth, Bloemfontein, Kimberley and Cape Town. Services also connect main centres in South Africa with destinations in southern Africa, namely Bulawayo in Zimbabwe, Maputo in Mozambique, and Mbabane, Swaziland.

Shosholoza Meyl ensures access for any person or enterprise that wishes to charter a train. Significant time and effort are spent on the design of the train service to fit each client's needs and requirements. The type of coaches that can be hired varies from traditional sleeper coaches to lounge cars, dining cars, and open-plan coaches that can be used for parties or lecture rooms. For the more selective traveller, *Shosholoza Meyl* offers a new class of travel called *Premier Classe*. It consists of two sleeping coaches and one dining/lounge car for the exclusive use of these guests. The sleeping coaches and air-conditioned lounge/dining car can accommodate up to 20 people.

In April 2003, *Shosholoza Meyl*'s facilities at Johannesburg's Park Station were relaunched, after being upgraded at a cost of R50 million. The upgrading of the Station and the Pretoria and Durban platforms focused on improving passenger flow, baggage handling, communication, a passenger-information system and access control from waiting areas to the platforms and trains.

Shosholoza Meyl requires an additional R450 million to refurbish coaches that are on average 25 years old. It receives an annual R175-million subsidy from Spoornet.

LuxRail

LuxRail's primary focus is on the prestigious operation of the Blue Train and caters for a growing international tourist market. For over half a century, South Africa's Blue Train has enjoyed an international reputation as one of the world's paramount travelling experiences. It was voted the world's leading luxury train by some 250 000 travel agents in 181 countries at the 2001 World Travel Awards. The Blue Train wine list has, for the past few years, consistently received the Annual Diners Club Award of Approval.

A lounge car at the rear of the Train complements the Blue Train experience, by allowing guests to use it as an observation car. The observation car is designed to be converted from a lounge into a 22-seater conference facility with computer, overhead projection, video and slide facilities.

The Blue Train travels from Pretoria to Cape Town, the Victoria Falls and Hoedspruit, and on the famous Garden Route between Port Elizabeth and Cape Town.

LuxRail also manages contracts with other luxury-train operators utilising Spoornet's infrastructure, such as Rovos Rail and Spier on the wine route in the Western Cape.

Social-investment activities

Spoornet contributes to the social fabric of South Africans. Notable social-investment activities include the following: AIDS awareness, Mr ChooChoo Safety Education Campaign, the Spoornet Rugby Excellence Programme, and Saturday schools for Spoornet employees' children, which improve their performance in mathematics and science, and offer supplementary courses such as study skills, career guidance and computer literacy. These classes are designed to support the national school curriculum.

Metrorail

Metrorail, a division of Transnet, is tasked with the operation of the SARCC's assets to provide an efficient commuter service. Metrorail ser-vices urban areas only. It operates in the Witwatersrand area, Pretoria, the Western Cape, Durban, Port Elizabeth and East London.

Metrorail operations have made steady progress in implementing far-reaching efficiency-improvement projects. This has enabled Metrorail to save the fiscus about 70% of the projected savings of R108 million. At the same time, it has produced healthy returns to its shareholder.

Together with the SARCC, major safety projects have been identified, and significant portions of the R355-million capital fund will be spent on refurbishing or renewing safety-critical signalling installations. The investment in the refurbishment of rolling stock is continuing, and the increased infrastructural investment, as announced by the Ministers of Finance and Transport, should also see improvements in other parts of the railway infrastructure.

The Department has developed a strategic framework for the concessioning of rail services – the current Metrorail service contract is already based on concessioning principles.

The Minister of Transport announced that concessioning would not occur during 2003 as originally planned. This is to give the country an opportunity to review the principles around concessioning, and develop a programme to address the challenges around infrastructure-investment in the railway industry. It also has implications for the pilot concessioning project that was due to start in 2002. In the meantime, Metrorail and the SARCC continue to conduct their relationship in terms of a business agreement that is firmly based on worldwide concessioning principles.

Metrorail is responsible for some 17% of all public transport in South Africa, which amounts to transporting approximately two million people to and from work daily. It serves 473 stations with 2 400 train services. Operating assets to the value of R69 million are managed on behalf of the State.

These include mobile ticket-selling points, customer-care programmes for all frontline staff, station upgrades, and a zone-fare structure.

South African Rail Commuter Corporation

The SARCC is a State corporation, established in 1990 to provide commuter rail services for the people of South Africa. It falls directly under the Department of Transport but has its own autonomous board of control. It owns all the commuter rail infrastructure and its rolling stock is valued at R70 billion. Its main sources of revenue are subsidies to cover operational losses and capital expenditure.

The Corporation received a R366-million operational subsidy and R490,2-million capital subsidy in 2001/02. The SARCC operates two major businesses – Rail Commuter Services and Property Management. Rail Commuter Services is operated as a social responsibility programme requiring considerable government subsidisation. The assets that were transferred to the SARCC included property with a net potential of R2 000 million in the main metropolitan areas.

The Corporation's role as concessionaire is to establish and monitor service standards, safety and security levels, and operating efficiencies. More than two million people use the commuter rail service daily.

The SARCC has 478 commuter train stations in Johannesburg, Pretoria, Durban and Cape Town.

The *White Paper on National Transport Policy* will lead to far-reaching changes in the way commuter rail services are structured in future. According to the White Paper, public and private operators will in future be able to bid competitively for the right to operate a rail line, service or network concession.

This has meant a change in the mission of the SARCC to one that ensures the 'provision of effective, efficient and sustainable rail commuter services under concessioning agreements'.

Intersite

Faced with managing a property portfolio of more than 478 stations worth some R2,6 billion, the SARCC formed a property-management company in 1992, called Intersite Property Management Services, to perform this task on its behalf. Intersite aims to develop railway stations into transport nodes that link taxi, bus and rail services in an integrated public-transport system.

Since 1990, Intersite has completed 61 station upgrades at a cost of R414 million. Nine were completed in the Western Cape at a cost of R75 million, 10 in the Eastern Cape at R9 million, eight in KwaZulu-Natal at R60 million, seven in northern Gauteng at R40 million, and 27 in southern Gauteng at R230 million.

Several intermodal transport facilities were also completed.

The objectives of interchange developments are to create an intermodal road/rail/bus/taxi transport environment for the commuting public, to enhance commuter rail stations and precincts, and to support government initiatives to integrate all modes of transport.

Money earned from the commercial aspects of Intersite's developments is ploughed back to reduce the subsidy provided by government.

Civil aviation

Airports

The Cabinet approved the *Green Paper on National Policy on Airports and Airspace Management* in February 1998. The document lays down principles for the development of airports, calls for the sustainability of public-owned airports to be assessed and for action to be taken where necessary. The Green Paper establishes criteria, ranging from economic activity to the implementation of air-traffic control that should be used to determine which airports could be named as possible international airports.

International airports are those airports where the necessary facilities and services exist to accommodate international flights. The current international airports are: Johannesburg, Cape Town, Durban, Bloemfontein, Port Elizabeth, Pilanesberg, Lanseria, Gateway (Polokwane), Kruger Mpumalanga and Upington.

The Kruger Mpumalanga International Airport, near Nelspruit, is the most recent addition, having been officially opened in October 2002. The Airport is run by the international power and automation group ABB. In April 2003, the Cabinet approved the status of the Kruger Mpumalanga Airport as an international airport. The Airport was opened in October 2002 and is expected to receive international flights from Europe, the USA and the East. It assumed the international status of the smaller Nelspruit Airport, which was downgraded to national status.

The Airports Company of South Africa (ACSA), which was officially established on 23 July 1993, owns and operates South Africa's nine principal airports, including the three major international airports in Johannesburg, Cape Town and Durban.

ACSA also operates the Pilanesberg International Airport in the North West on a concession basis. Before the formation of ACSA, airports countrywide were owned and operated by the State.

In April 1998, *Aeroporti di Roma* (ADR), an Italian airport-management firm, won a competitive bid to become ACSA's strategic equity partner, and paid R819 million for 20% of the company's shares.

ACSA's flagship development, the new R750-million domestic terminal at Johannesburg International Airport (JIA), was opened for operations in March 2003.

This is the largest terminal in Africa and will increase the Airport's total capacity to more than 18 million passengers annually. JIA is ACSA's success story and accounts for over half of the throughput of all ACSA airports. It has overtaken Cairo in terms of passenger traffic. Passenger traffic has climbed steadily over the past couple of years, with the figures now averaging 12 million passengers a year.

The Airport's greatest success lies in its commercial transformation. The dramatic R210-million duty-free retail mall contributed largely to JIA increasing its net operating income by more than 120%, fuelled by growth in non-aeronautical revenues over three times greater than aeronautical revenues.

Cape Town International Airport now boasts a world-class international terminal with capacity for up to five million passengers a year.

ACSA has committed R1 billion to the upgrading and development of Cape Town International Airport, including extensions to existing terminal buildings, the construction of parkades, two new satellite terminals, and an expanded runway system.

Cape Town International's new R120-million international departures terminal, officially opened in February 2003, boasts a total area of 21 000 m^2 – of which 2 360 m^2 is retail space, accommodating 13 shops. The new terminal is capable of accommodating up to 1 300 passengers in peak hours, or a million passengers a year, which is three times the capacity of the previous departures terminal.

The terminal building at Durban International Airport has been upgraded with the reconfiguration of the international and domestic terminal into an arrivals and departures terminal. Parking facilities have also been revamped and upgraded.

In April 2002, Cabinet decided that the Durban International Airport will relocate to La Mercy, about 50 km outside Durban.

Construction of the new Airport, to be known as the King Shaka International Airport, is set to begin in early 2004.

The new Airport forms part of the planned R2,2-billion Dube Trade Port at La Mercy. The project incorporates an Industrial Development Zone (IDZ), a cyberport and a multimodal transport node.

About R100 billion was budgeted for capital expenditure in the Medium Term Expenditure Framework. The amount included R55 billion for infrastructure projects.

A national Ministerial committee, which includes the Ministers of Trade and Industry, of Finance, of Transport and of Public Enterprises, has been established to drive implementation and guide the detailed business plan and financial structuring of the project.

By 2007, ACSA is expected to have spent R185 million on infrastructural developments at the seven smaller airports. Port Elizabeth, the largest and busiest of the seven, will receive the bulk of the capital expenditure amounting to R88 million for, among other things, a new instrument landing system (ILS), terminal upgrade, and equipment upgrade and replacement. The terminal upgrade was expected to be completed in April 2004.

The ACSA will spend about R14 million on Bloemfontein Airport for terminal revamp, upgrade of fire-fighting equipment, as well as runway rehabilitation, while the East London Airport will receive R23 million for a new ILS and fire-fighting equipment.

Kimberley and George Airports will each receive R6 million for terminal refurbishment, replacement and upgrade of equipment, and R17 million for terminal upgrade, an ILS, and equipment replacement.

Given its strong although seasonal freight traffic, about R14 million has been budgeted for cargo-apron extension, fire fighting and general equipment replacement, while R21 million has been set aside for strengthening of the runway, terminal extension and equipment improvement at Pilanesberg International Airport.

The Air-Traffic Navigation Service (ATNS) is responsible for the efficient running of South Africa's air-traffic control systems and the maintenance of navigation equipment, which includes the deployment of air-traffic controllers and aviation technical staff.

A joint operations centre at the JIA is the nerve centre of all airport communications and operations.

From here, all activities related to maintenance and building management are co-ordinated. The centre serves as a control office, crisis control centre for emergencies, and information technology centre.

The ATNS will increase the number of air-traffic controllers at the airport by 30% over the next 13 months.

Scheduled airlines

Domestic services
Twenty scheduled domestic airlines are currently licensed to provide air services within South Africa. These airlines provide internal flights, which link up to the internal and international networks of South African Airways (SAA), British Airways (BA)/Comair, Interair, SA Express and SA Airlink.

International services
SAA, BA/Comair, SA Express, SA Airlink and Interair operate scheduled air services within South Africa and the Indian Ocean islands. In addition to serving Africa, SAA operates services to Europe, Latin America and the Far East.

Scheduled international air services are also provided by Air Afrique, Air Austral, Air Botswana, Air France, Air Gabon, Air Madagascar, Air Malawi, Air Mauritius, Air Namibia, Air Portugal, Air Seychelles, Air Tanzania, Air Zimbabwe, Airlink Swaziland, Alliance Express, BA, Cameroon Airlines, Delta Airlines, El Al, Egyptair, Emirates, Ethiopian Airlines, Ghana Airways, Iberia, KLM, Kenya Airways, LAM, LTU, Lufthansa, MK Airlines, Malaysia Airlines, Martinair Holland, North-West Airlines, Olympic Airways, Quantas, Royal Air Maroc, Saudi Arabian Airlines, Singapore Airlines, Swissair, Taag, Thai International, Turkish Airlines, Uganda Airlines, United Airlines, Varig, Virgin Atlantic, Yemenia, Zambian Air Services and Zambian Skyways.

Aviation safety and security
South Africa complies with the International Civil Aviation Organisation's (ICAO) recommended practices on aviation security. South Africa serves on the council of the ICAO.

Aviation safety in South Africa was audited by the ICAO at the Minister's request. The ICAO's recommendations are currently being implemented. South Africa is also participating in the development and establishment of an Upper Airspace Control Centre for the SADC. This initiative proposes that a single centre hosted by a SADC state will provide air-navigation services to all aircraft flying above 24 500 feet.

The ATNS is working on upgrading ageing radar display and processing systems at the JIA. The upgrade will expand control centres countrywide and incorporate 'automatic sequencing' of traffic into Johannesburg and Cape Town. This will ensure separation and a consistent flow of arrivals, which in turn will enhance efficiency and reduce costs for airlines. The total cost of the project, which is due for completion in 2004, is R228 million.

By early June 2003, SAA, SA Airlink and British Airways/Comair all operated the airborne collision-avoidance systems and were fully compliant with all requirements. Other South African registered airlines were taking steps to be compliant by the implementation date of 30 June 2003.

Emphasis is being placed on improved international access to and from South Africa by air, the expansion of the bilateral air-services framework, the implementation of the Yamoussoukro Declaration, effective monitoring of airline activities, and the efficient licensing and regulation of domestic and international air services. Other aims include promoting:
- safer skies: this involves ensuring that adequate safety and upper-air space-control regimes are in place across the continent, supported by efficient air-traffic and navigational services and systematic human resource development programmes
- efficient and effective aviation networks: this involves regulating as necessary to make air transport more affordable, creating regional hubs and air-carrier alliances, and supporting one another to establish a high-quality African airports network.

Ports

Commercial ports play a crucial role in South Africa's transport, logistics and socio-economic development. Approximately 98% of South Africa's exports are conveyed by sea.

On 16 September 2003, the Minister of Transport tabled the NPA Bill in the National Assembly.

Specific objectives of the Bill are to:
- provide for the establishment of the NPA to own, manage, and control ports on behalf of the State
- provide for the transfer of ports, land and other rights and obligations from Transnet to the Authority
- provide for the establishment of the Ports Regulator
- ensure equity in the access of ports facilities in a non-discriminating manner
- authorise the NPA to enter into various forms of contracts, including concessions
- provide for the licensing of port services and facilities
- authorise the charging of fees
- amend other laws that have a bearing on the activities of the ports.

The Bill has its origin in the *White Paper on National Commercial Ports Policy*, adopted by the Cabinet in March 2002.

The aim of the White Paper is to ensure affordable, internationally competitive, efficient and safe port services, based on the application of commercial rules in a transparent and competitive environment and applied consistently across the transport system.

The White Paper proposes that, in order to ensure that South African ports continue to contribute to international competitiveness, the separation of the port authority and port operations components will provide impetus to ongoing efforts to upgrade facilities and equipment.

By far the largest, best-equipped and most efficient network of ports on the African continent, South Africa's seven commercial ports have a significant role to play. They are not only conduits for the imports and exports of South Africa and neighbouring countries, but also serve as hubs for traffic emanating from and destined for the east and west African coasts. The NPA, a division of Transnet Limited, is the largest port authority in greater southern Africa, controlling seven of the 16 biggest ports in this region, namely Richards Bay, Durban, East London, Port Elizabeth, Mossel Bay, Cape Town and Saldanha.

The NPA was born out of the restructuring of Portnet, the port-management division of Transnet. The NPA's responsibility has been broadly defined as attending to the maintenance and development of port infrastructure.

The restructuring of Portnet into the NPA and SAPO came about after government's realisation of the benefits of public and private partnerships. While government plans to retain ownership of the country's port infrastructure, it is envisaged that individual terminals will ultimately be leased or concessioned to private operators.

A R4,3-billion investment has been set aside for use by the NPA in addressing infrastructural backlog, its primary responsibilities being landlord and maritime services.

Landlord services focus on the needs of cargo owners and terminal operators – from project conception, to terminal design, assessment of environmental factors and the concluding stages whereby a lease is signed with the terminal operator through which the cargo will pass.

Maritime services include the improvement of efficiency in shipping services, the dredging of navigational waterways, and ensuring a safe shipping environment by means of vessel-tracing services, pilotage and lighthouse services.

The ports provide:
- pilotage, tug and berthing services
- bulkhandling installations to handle dry

and liquid bulk, complemented by storage facilities
- container-handling facilities
- multipurpose terminals for the handling of breakbulk and containers
- access to rail and road links
- ship-repair facilities
- feeder services.

Lighthouse services operate 45 lighthouses along the South African coastline.

The NPA has vessel-traffic systems in all ports, which ensure improved safety of navigation within the port and port limits, and enhance the service provided to the port user.

Marine services operate 24 large tugs, eight work boats, four pilot boats and 14 launches in the seven commercial ports of South Africa. Twenty-four-hour services are provided in the Ports of Durban and Richards Bay.

The **Port of Richards Bay**, although a young port by international standards, and initially built for bulk exports, has rapidly developed and diversified into other cargo-handling forms. The Port is presently South Africa's leading port in terms of dry bulk volumes, and is capable of handling a diverse group of commodities from steel to forest products.

With increased traffic to and from the Far East and Australia, an upgrade was essential. More than R500 million was allocated to reduce vessel turnaround time, improve quality control, upgrade terminal-handling equipment, and increase storage capacity. The Port handles in excess of 80 Mt per year, representing 55% of South Africa's seaborne cargo trade.

It also offers easy access to South Africa's national and rail network with substantial growth capacity in the rail network link.

For industrial investors, there is an abundance of prime industrial land, both immediately adjacent to the Port and further inland. The Port hosts five cargo-handling terminals, of which three are privately operated and two are operated by SAPO. The privately operated terminals are the Richards Bay Coal Terminal; Island View Storage, which handles bulk liquids and liquefied gases; and Fedmis, which exports phosphoric acid.

The **Port of Durban** is a full-service general cargo and container port. It is the busiest port in southern Africa and is also the most conveniently situated port for the industrialised Durban/Pinetown and Gauteng areas and overborder traffic.

As South Africa's premier cargo and container port, the Port of Durban handles over 55 Mt of cargo per year. Durban has abundant shipping opportunities, both in terms of frequency and destinations served.

It is especially effective as a hub port for cargo to and from the Far East, Europe and the Americas, serving South Africa as well as west and east African countries. The Port is the premier port for a wide range of commodities, including coal, mineral ores, granite, chemicals, petrochemicals, steel, forest products, citrus products, sugar and grain.

The Port handles more than 1,2 million containers per annum, with an increase of 6% to 7% each year.

On 31 July 2003, the Durban Container Terminal (DCT) handled 2 555 container vehicles through its gates – the highest number handled in a 24-hour period in the history of the DCT.

The **Port of East London** is situated at the mouth of the Buffalo River on the east coast of South Africa, and is the only commercial river port on the South African coastline.

With a well-developed infrastructure, the Port has become one of the major motor vehicle export and import terminals in South Africa.

The **Port of Port Elizabeth**, with its proximity to heavily industrialised and intensively farmed areas, has facilities for the handling of all commodities – bulk, general and container cargo.

Being at the centre of the country's motor-vehicle-manufacturing industry, the Port imports large volumes of containerised components and raw material for this industry. The bulk of exports comprises agricultural products. Apart from agricultural produce, manganese ore, motor-vehicle-industry-related products and steel are exported.

The **Port of Mossel Bay**, primarily serving the fishing and oil industries, also offers limited commercial cargo activity.

This Port is the only South African port that operates two offshore mooring points within port limits. Both mooring points are utilised for the transport of refined petroleum products.

The NPA is building the modern deepwater port while the Coega Development Corporation is developing the entire land-side infrastructure for the IDZ.

The area is already well-serviced by existing transport networks and a skilled labour force.

The **Port of Cape Town** is a full-service general-cargo port. It is renowned for its deciduous fruit and frozen-products exports. The fishing industry based at the Port of Cape Town is of major proportion.

The Port of Cape Town is strategically positioned and ideally situated to serve as a hub for cargoes between Europe, the Americas, Africa, Asia and Oceania. The Port provides a complex network of services to its clients and a favourable environment for all stakeholders, so as to maximise the benefit to the local and national economy.

Integrated intermodal cargo systems, ship repair, bunkering facilities and the reefer trade are all examples of these services.

Saldanha Port is a deep-water port and is the largest natural port in southern Africa. The Port is unique in that it has a purpose-built railroad serving a bulk-handling facility, which is connected to a dedicated jetty for the shipment of iron ore.

Saldanha also serves as a major crude-oil importation and transhipment port.

About R600 million is being spent on upgrading and expanding Saldanha Bay's steel and iron ore handling facilities. This includes acquiring new equipment and increasing workspace efficiency. A number of projects have been initiated to help address environmental and ecoresponsibility issues.

Pipelines

Petronet owns, maintains and operates a network of 3 000 km of high-pressure petroleum and gas pipelines. During 2001/02, Petronet transported 13,8 billion litres of fuel from coastal and inland refineries to the main business centres in Gauteng and surrounding areas, and some 334 million m^3 of gas from Secunda to KwaZulu-Natal. Petronet's customers are the major oil companies in South Africa.

Maritime affairs

Maritime administration, legislation and shipping

South Africa's maritime administration and legislation is the responsibility of the Department of Transport, and is controlled on its behalf by SAMSA in terms of the SAMSA Act, 1998 (Act 5 of 1998).

The broad aim of SAMSA is to maintain the safety of life and property at sea within South Africa's area of maritime jurisdiction and to ensure the prevention of sea pollution by oil and other substances emanating from ships.

The Department of Environmental Affairs and Tourism is responsible for the combating of pollution, and has specific means at its disposal, such as the *Kuswag* coast watch vessels, with which to perform this function.

The Port of East London's car terminal, which opened in 2000, reported a 29% increase in vehicle imports and exports moving through it in 2002. It moves 44 000 vehicles a year and this number was expected to rise to 55 000 units in 2003/04.

SAMSA is responsible for the introduction and maintenance of international standards set by the International Maritime Organisation (IMO) in London, with respect to:
- ship construction
- maritime training and training curricula
- watch-keeping
- certification of seafarers
- manning and operation of local and foreign ships
- maritime search-and-rescue
- marine communication and radio navigation aids
- pollution prevention.

SAMSA has an operations unit, a policy unit and a corporate support division to handle all financial, human resource and information technology issues.

Other functions include the registration of ships, the establishment of a coastal patrol service, and the management of marine casualties and wrecks.

SAMSA is steadily improving its capacity to monitor safety standards on foreign vessels. Over the past year, 700 ships calling at South Africa's seven major ports were inspected. Vessels not in compliance with international safety standards were detained until the deficiencies were corrected.

The South African Marine Corporation (Safmarine), Unicorn Lines and Griffin Shipping are South Africa's predominant shipping lines. Their fleets of container, oil tanker, general cargo and bulk cargo vessels operate not only between South African ports, but also as cross-traders to other parts of the world.

Training

On 9 September 2003, President Thabo Mbeki officially opened the South African Maritime Training Academy (SAMTRA) at Simonstown in the Western Cape.

SAMTRA is expected to provide advanced training to the broader maritime sector, including the merchant navy, harbour-craft operations, the fishing industry and the South African Navy.

The South African Merchant Navy Academy, General Botha, established at Granger Bay, is integrated with the Cape Peninsula University of Technology (formerly called Cape Technikon), with a similar training facility at the Durban Institute of Technology (formerly called Natal Technikon). Deck and engineering students and officers complete their academic training at the Cape Peninsula University of Technology and the Durban Institute of Technology, while lower classes of certificates are offered at the Training Centre for Seamen, situated in the Duncan Dock area in Cape Town.

This training institution also caters for deck, engine-room and catering department ratings.

SAMSA is responsible for setting all standards of training certification and watch-keeping on behalf of the Department of Transport, while the Maritime Education and Training Board is responsible for the accreditation of all maritime courses.

Other maritime training organisations offer a wide range of courses that have been developed within the South African maritime industry. These are situated mainly in the Ports of Cape Town and Durban and, to a lesser degree, in Port Elizabeth.

Search-and-rescue services

The Department of Transport is responsible for the provision of a search-and-rescue function in South Africa.

The search-and-rescue programme has been in existence since 1948.

The South African Search-and-Rescue Organisation (SASAR) has been established to provide South Africa with a world-class search-and-rescue capability.

SASAR is a voluntary organisation functioning under the auspices of the Department of Transport.

Its main function is to search for, assist and, if necessary, rescue survivors of aircraft accidents or forced landings, vessels in distress, and accidents at sea. It is also charged with co-ordinating the resources made available to the Department by various government departments, voluntary organisations, and private aircraft and shipping companies for search-and-rescue purposes. The executive committee of SASAR, in conjunction with the relevant officials of the Department, is responsible for formulating policy and procedures.

The Department of Transport, the SANDF, Telkom, Portnet, SAMSA, CAA, ATNS, SAPS, the Independent Communications Authority of South Africa, SAA and the Department of Provincial and Local Government are members of SASAR and contribute their services and/or facilities.

Voluntary organisations such as the 4x4 Rescue Club, Mountain Club of South Africa, Hamnet and the National Sea Rescue Institute are also members of SASAR.

The South African Maritime and Aeronautical Search-and-Rescue Act, 2002 (Act 44 of 2002), is being implemented.

The Department was engaged in the following in 2003/04:
- inculcating a safety culture in the fishing industry
- developing appropriate legislation to inform and guide the port-sector reform process, which is near completion
- developing a framework for better working conditions in the maritime industry in conjunction with the Department of Labour
- developing a maritime multilateral strategy
- setting up a Maritime Resource Centre
- creating awareness of the importance of maritime transport in the economy
- undertaking a Marine-Pollution Prevention Programme to prevent incidents of oil and chemical spills at sea
- evaluating the levels of investment in maritime infrastructure necessary for the reconstruction and development of African economies
- conducting a maritime legislation-review process
- promoting safety in the maritime industry
- promoting SASAR through education and training, raising public awareness, raising funds for SASAR's member organisations, and being on par with international standards
- improving the search-and-rescue information systems by computerising the SASAR assets manual
- developing and reviewing search-and-rescue policies in order to comply with ICAO and the IMO
- revising the current institutional search-and-rescue framework.

The Department of Transport is charged with the negotiation and conclusion of bilateral search-and-rescue agreements with countries bordering on the vast area of responsibility, which is laid down by both the ICAO and the IMO, and is approximately 28,5 million km^2.

South Africa has contributed significantly to search-and-rescue in the southern oceans with the establishment of the Cospas-Sarsat System. It comprises three segments, namely:
- radio beacons, carried by ships and aircraft
- a space segment
- a ground segment.

Satellite services are provided free of charge in terms of the International Cospas-Sarsat Agreement, but individual countries must provide and pay for the ground segment that comprises:
- Local User Terminals (LUTs) that process relayed distress signals to provide a beacon location and then transmit alert messages to the Mission Control Centre (MCC)
- the MCC, which then validates and exchanges alert data and technical information and redistributes it to search-and-rescue authorities.

South Africa was accepted as a member of the International Cospas-Sarsat Programme as Ground Segment Provider with effect from 1 November 2000.

This enables its LUT/MCC to be integrated into the global Cospas-Sarsat System. The following countries will be served by the LUT/MCC: Angola, Botswana, Burundi, the Democratic Republic of the Congo, Lesotho, Malawi, Mozambique, Namibia, Rwanda, Swaziland, Uganda, Zambia and Zimbabwe.

Maritime safety

South Africa has been identified as a focal point for a regional search-and-rescue centre. During 2003/04, the Department set aside R3,5 million for the establishment of a dedicated Maritime Rescue Co-ordination Centre. The process is at an advanced stage.

Transport

Acknowledgements

Air Traffic and Navigation Services
Airports Company South Africa
Civil Aviation Authority
Department of Transport
Estimates of National Expenditure 2003, published by the National Treasury
National Ports Authority of South Africa
South African Rail Commuter Corporation
Spoornet Ltd
Transnet Ltd
South African National Roads Agency Ltd
Road Accident Fund
www.gov.za

Suggested reading

Burkett, D. *Jetlag: South African Airways in the Andrews Era.* Sandton: Penguin, 2001.
Byrom, J. *Fields of Air: Triumphs, Tragedies and Mysteries of Civil Aviation in Southern Africa.* Rivonia, Sandton: Ashanti, 1993.
Development Bank of Southern Africa. *Infrastructure: A Foundation for Development. Development Report 1998.* Midrand: Development Bank of Southern Africa, 1998.
Du Toit, A. *South Africa's Fighting Ships, Past and Present.* Rivonia, Sandton: Ashanti, 1992.
Harris, C.J. and Ingpen, B.D. *Mailships of the Union-Castle Line.* Cape Town: Fernwood, 1994.
Infrastructure Mandates for Change: 1994 – 1999. Pretoria: Human Sciences Research Council (HSRC), 2000.
Ingpen, B.D. *South African Merchant Ships: An Illustrated Recent History of Coasters, Colliers, Containerships, Tugs and Other Vessels.* Cape Town: Balkema, 1979.
Khosa, M. ed. *Empowerment Through Service Delivery.* Pretoria: HSRC, 2000.
Moore, D. *Sunset of Steam: A Tribute in Colour to the Golden Years of Steam Locomotives in South Africa.* Johannesburg: Chris van Rensburg, 1990.
Nöthling, C.J. and Becker, D. *Pride of the Nation: A Short History of the South African Air Force.* Pretoria: South African Air Force, 1995.
Robbins, D. *Blue Train.* Johannesburg: Penguin, 1993.
Schnettler, F. *A Century of Cars.* Cape Town: Tafelberg, 1997.

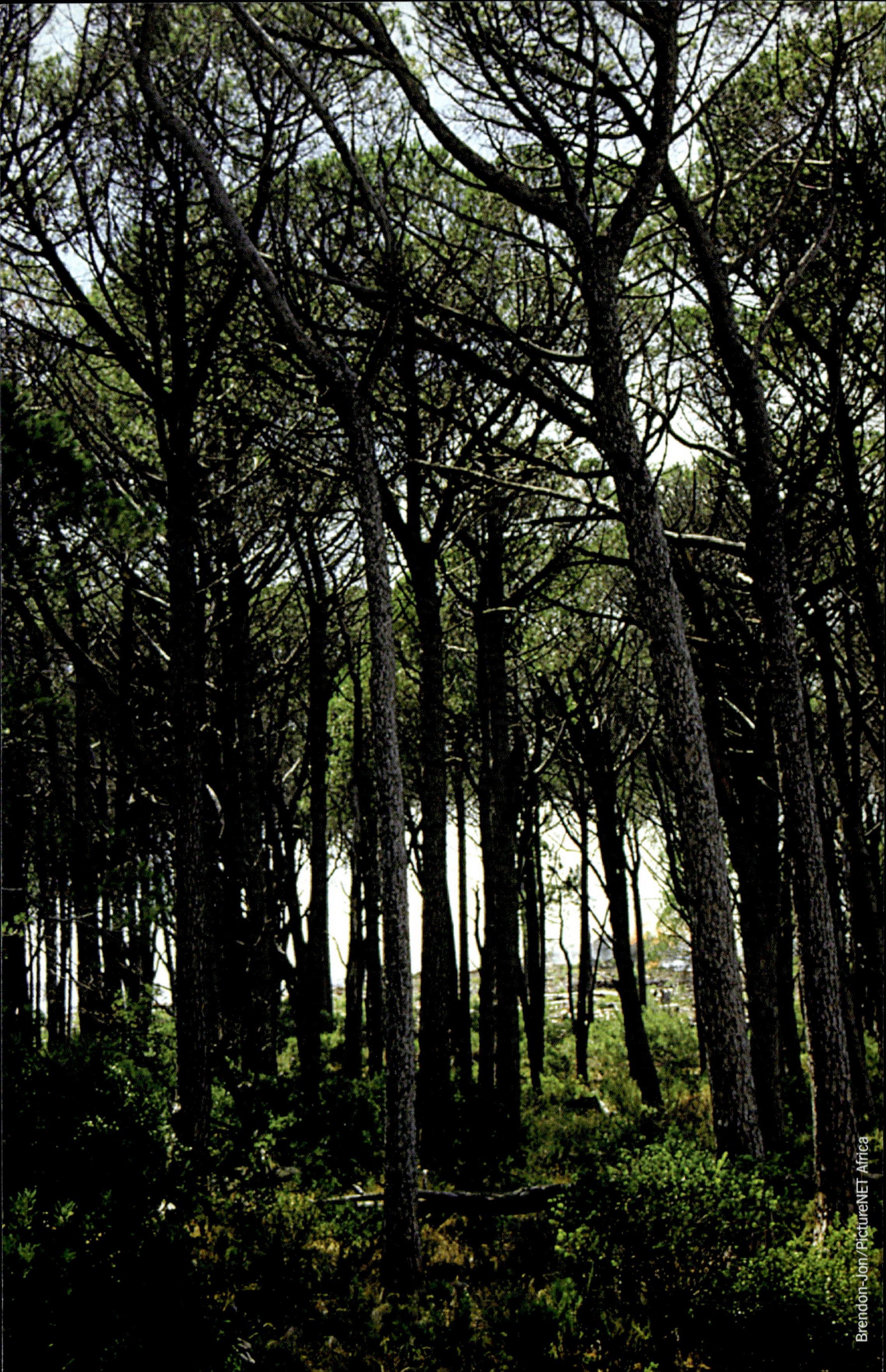

Brendon-Jon/PictureNET Africa

chapter 23

Water affairs and forestry

South Africa is a water-stressed country and water planners and managers are being faced with increasingly complex issues.

The country is largely semi-arid and prone to erratic, unpredictable extremes in the form of droughts and floods. Water is most abundant in the geographically small escarpment areas, which run in a narrow strip from the north-east of the country down the eastern and southern seaboards, remote from the major demand centres in the hinterland. Many large storage dams have been constructed to regulate the natural variable flow of rivers and facilitate water transfers between catchments.

Rivers are the main source of water in South Africa. Countrywide, the average annual rainfall is about 500 millimetres (mm), compared with a world average of about 860 mm. On average, only some 9% of rainfall reaches the rivers as run-off. Sixty-five per cent of the country receives less than 500 mm per year, which is generally accepted as the minimum amount required for successful dry-land farming. Twenty-one per cent of the country, mainly in the arid west, receives less than 200 mm a year.

◀ The commercial forestry industry in South Africa is committed to practising sustainable forest management and has one of the largest areas of Forest Stewardship Council-certified plantations of any country in the world.

The Orange River Basin is the largest river basin in South Africa with a total catchment area of one million square kilometres (km^2), almost 600 000 km^2 of which is inside South Africa, with the remainder in Lesotho, Botswana and Namibia.

On average, South African rivers receive about 50 billion cubic metres (m^3) of water per annum with a further six billion m^3 available from underground aquifers. This translates into 1 400 m^3 on average per person per annum. Of this 56 billion m^3, 21 billion m^3 is utilised. Of this volume, 52% is used for agriculture and irrigation, 4% for forestry, 4% for industry, 10% for domestic use, with 19% allocated to ensuring a sustainable environment.

Apart from erratic rainfall and the low ratio of run-off, which affects the reliability and variability of river flow, the average annual potential evaporation is higher than the rainfall in all but a few isolated areas where rainfall exceeds 1 400 mm per year. Only about 32 000 million m^3 of the annual run-off can be economically exploited using current methods. Usable run-off is further reduced by land uses such as commercial afforestation and sugar cane, and by high evaporative losses from the numerous storage dams throughout the country.

Farm dams, of which there are a large number, can seriously reduce the flow of

South Africa Yearbook 2003/04

rivers and streams during the dry season and also delay the run-off water at the onset of the rainy periods.

Furthermore, rainfall, and to a greater extent run-off, is poorly distributed in relation to the areas of greatest economic activity. Accordingly, water is transported over great distances from areas of relative abundance to areas of increasing demand. For instance, water supplies in the populous and economically important industrial hub in Gauteng are supplemented by transfers from the better-watered east.

The aim of the Department of Water Affairs and Forestry is to ensure the availability and supply of water on a national level and to promote forestry development.

Some 6,2 million people have access to a basic supply, obtaining water from sources that are further than 200 metres (m) away. However, the service needs to be improved to meet Reconstruction and Development Programme standards. The focus of the Department is to bring water to within 200 m of these households.

The past few years have seen a number of achievements in the management of water resources in South Africa and the implementation of the internationally acclaimed National Water Act, 1998 (Act 36 of 1998).

Key achievements include:
- developing conservation and demand-management strategies for the industrial, agricultural and domestic sectors
- promoting water conservation and integrated water resource management
- developing resource learning and support material
- launching the Women in Water Awards
- integrating water-related issues in the outcomes-based curriculum
- a formal networking, consultation and communication strategy
- the pilot cholera education project
- continued participation in the United Nations Habitat Co-ordinated Water for African Cities project at various levels
- registering significant abstract uses of raw water for the proper management of scarce water resources and for the implementation of the national pricing strategy as promulgated in 1999
- developing the licensing system for all Section 21 water users
- introducing the new raw-water pricing strategy on government water schemes, and developing a pricing strategy for waste discharges
- developing strategies to deal with the impact on water quality of mining and industrial developments and dense settlements, and introducing an environmental-assessment tool

Major dams of South Africa

	Full supply capacity ($10^6 m^3$)	River
Gariep	5 341	Orange
Vanderkloof	3 171	Orange
Sterkfontein	2 616	Nuwejaarspruit
Nuwejaarspruit Vaal	2 603	Vaal
Pongolapoort	2 445	Pongolo
Bloemhof	1 264	Vaal
Theewaterskloof	480	Sonderend
Heyshope	451	Assegaai
Woodstock	380	Tugela
Loskop	361	Olifants
Grootdraai	354	Vaal
Kalkfontein	318	Riet
Goedertrouw	304	Mhlatuze
Albert Falls	288	Mgeni
Brandvlei	284	Brandvlei
Spioenkop	277	Tugela
Umtata	253	Mtata
Driekoppies	250	Lomati
Inanda	241	Mgeni
Hartbeespoort	212	Crocodile
Erfenis	207	Groot Vet
Rhenosterkop	204	Elands
Molatedi	200	Groot Marico
Ntshingwayo	198	Ngagane
Zaaihoek	192	Slang
Midmar	175	Mgeni

Source: Department of Water Affairs and Forestry

Water affairs and forestry

- creating 20 000 work opportunities through the Working for Water Programme, and developing strategies to provide general and financial support to small-scale and emerging farmers.

Water for all

According to the Constitution of South Africa, 1996 (Act 108 of 1996), it is every person's right to have access to clean water.

According to the 2001 Census, five million people still need access to a basic supply of water or are without the bare minimum supply. These are people who take water directly from dams, pools, streams, rivers or springs, or purchase water from water vendors.

Households with access to water increased from 80% in 1996 to 85% in 2001.

Community Water Supply and Sanitation (CWSS) Programme

The Department of Water Affairs and Forestry's CWSS Programme was initiated in 1994 to achieve the constitutional objective of ensuring that all South Africans have access to sufficient water and a healthy living environment, with the focus on rural areas.

One aim of the CWSS Programme is to capacitate local government and promote the sustainability of water-service projects.

President Thabo Mbeki joined the celebrations on 5 July 2003 at the Umzinyathi village outside Durban, KwaZulu-Natal, when the nine-millionth connection of safe water, since South Africa became a democracy in 1994, was celebrated.

In 2002/03, some 1,2 million people received water-supply infrastructure and 65 105 toilets were built.

This translates to 390 630 people who received sanitation through the CWSS Programme.

In the process, temporary employment was provided to 98 000 people, 11 300 of which received formal training.

Government is on target to eradicate the backlog in water infrastructure and sanitation facilities by 2008 and 2010, respectively.

Census 2001 also highlighted the following trends, which could have an impact on the Department's programmes:
- rapid urbanisation, with many municipalities facing challenges typical to cities in a developing country
- additional households will necessitate the provision of additional sanitation infrastructure.

The National Sanitation Programme, which includes the Housing and Municipal Infrastructure Programmes, continues to accelerate, with improved sanitation provided to an estimated 2 260 000 people in 2002. The Department spent about R221 446 000 providing toilets for 65 105 households.

Some R321 million was allocated in 2003/04 to provide sanitation to 120 000 households, as part of the national target of 300 000 households for the combined Programme. Through community-based labour-intensive approaches, the Programme is expected to generate over 6 000 jobs annually and plough R50 million into rural economies.

The Department intends to eradicate the bucket system in 430 000 households by 2006.

The Department continues to collaborate with the Departments of Health and of Education to improve sanitation in schools and clinics. Some R40 million will be spent on clinic-sanitation programmes and R150 million on school sanitation.

In August 2003, the Minister of Water Affairs and Forestry, Mr Ronnie Kasrils, handed over 29 boreholes worth R1 million to the communities under the Greater Groblersdal Municipality – Dennilton, Phokwane, Leeufontein, Doornlaagte, Driefontein, Elandsdoorn, Tafelkop and Naganeng.

The boreholes form part of government's efforts to provide people with clean drinking water and curb the spread of waterborne diseases such as cholera.

South Africa Yearbook 2003/04

The Department has set aside R116 million for refurbishment, plus another R210 million in the next two years of the Medium Term Expenditure Framework (MTEF), R93 million for capacity-building and R25 million for strengthening the Department's oversight role.

Municipal Infrastructure Grant (MIG)

To eradicate backlogs in access to water and sanitation by 2008 and 2010 respectively, future funding for water and sanitation is expected to increase.

The MIG is intended to facilitate and ensure more effective and integrated service delivery.

Free basic water

The Free Basic Water Policy was launched in July 2001.

By June 2003, 78% of the country's municipalities were implementing the Policy, providing more than 27 million people with free basic water.

Provincial support units, staffed by trained free-basic-water specialists, were established.

Medium-term targets of the Department of Water Affairs and Forestry include supplying an additional one million people with basic water and 300 000 households with basic sanitation every year.

The Department also aims to expand the Free Basic Water Policy to 85% by March 2004.

Water policy

South Africa is developing a multidisciplinary approach to managing the country's scarce water resources, based not only on technical considerations, but also on economic, social, political and environmental considerations. This new approach to integrated water resource management is enshrined in the National Water Resource Strategy, which was published in August 2002 for public comment.

The draft Strategy outlines the framework for water resource management as required by the National Water Act, 1998, and describes, among other things, how the Government intends to implement water-resource protection measures. These measures are being implemented and include the determination of the reserve-water required to meet basic human needs and ecological-flow requirements for aquatic ecosystems, as a standard prerequisite before any other water use is authorised.

The Strategy also describes provisions for water-use and how it will be authorised, water conservation, demand management, water pricing, the institutional arrangements for water resource management, infrastructure development, monitoring and information systems, and public safety in water matters.

In November 2000, the Minister of Water Affairs and Forestry, Mr Ronnie Kasrils, signed a partnership agreement with Roundabout Outdoor and the United States' Kaiser Family Foundation for the installation of 100 merry-go-rounds, which use the energy of children at play to pump water to rural communities.

Water tanks are installed a few metres away from the play pumps, sporting HIV/AIDS-prevention messages aimed specifically at young women who frequently collect water for their households. The tanks also carry paid advertising by companies such as Unilever, Colgate-Palmolive and Telkom, which covers the cost of maintaining the play pumps.

In 2001, play pumps were installed in 40 rural villages throughout South Africa. The Kaiser Family Foundation donated US $250 000 in 2001 to install an additional 60 play pumps countrywide.

Tapping the energy of children at play, the pumps can generate some 1 400 litres of water per hour, saving young women time and energy they would otherwise have spent walking to and from more remote water resources.

The play pumps also help prevent diseases such as cholera that can stem from open-water supplies.

International donor money continues to come in from the World Bank, and the latest contributor to join the project is the ClearWater Project. Roundabout Outdoor has 130 sites already established and during National Water Week 2003, the SABMiller (until recently South African Breweries) donated a cheque of R5 million for 110 more sites.

These sites are in the Eastern Cape, KwaZulu-Natal, Mpumalanga, North West and Limpopo.

Water affairs and forestry

Considered to be South Africa's 'blueprint for survival', the Strategy sets out proposed strategies to achieve equity, sustainability and efficiency in the use of the country's water resources.

It also outlines plans for investment in new dams and related infrastructure over the next 25 years, and proposes arrangements with neighbouring countries for managing shared rivers.

The Strategy also describes how government will deal with water allocations, water pricing and pollution control, and outlines how the demands for water will be met in future, as well as the institutions that will be established to allow the public to participate in water resource management.

Public safety, and ways to manage disasters such as droughts and floods and their impact, are also addressed.

The Strategy will ensure that water resources are used to meet the needs of the people, create jobs and support sustained economic development while ensuring that aquatic ecosystems are protected.

National Water Week 2003 was celebrated from 17 to 23 March under the theme *Water is our Future* – focusing on protecting and respecting South Africa's water resources.

Water Week 2003 coincided with the launch of the International Year of Fresh Water in South Africa, as well as the Third Water Forum in Japan.

A call was made to all South Africans during the Week to maintain and improve the quality and quantity of freshwater available for current and future generations.

As part of the Water Week celebrations and activities, the Minister of Water Affairs and Forestry, Mr Ronnie Kasrils, awarded the annual *Baswa le Meetse* Youth in Water Arts Award to learners who produced inspiring educational messages to the public about water and sanitation through theatre and the arts.

The Award was complemented by the existing school-based 2020 Vision for Water Education Programme.

Minister Kasrils also awarded the annual National Women in Water Awards. These Awards serve to honour women who have distinguished themselves in water resource management.

The Strategy was expected to be finalised in November 2003.

Water Services Act, 1997 (Act 108 of 1997)

The Water Services Act, 1997 aims to:
- ensure and define the rights of access to basic water supply and basic sanitation services
- set out the rights and duties of consumers and those who are responsible for providing services
- allow the Minister of Water Affairs and Forestry to set national standards (including norms and standards for tariffs) to ensure sufficient, continuous, affordable and fair water services
- promote the effective and sustainable use of financial and natural resources
- regulate contracts for the fair and transparent provision of water services
- create effective and financially viable statutory institutions to assist local government to fulfil its obligations under the Act.

In addition, a potentially powerful provision of the Water Services Act, 1997 requires the production by Water-Service Authorities (the designated municipalities) of Water-Service Development Plans, within the framework of the Integrated Development Plans, now required by municipal legislation. In a similar manner, tariff regulations cover areas (also addressed by legislation) governing municipal finances, highlighting the need for a coherent interface between generic municipal regulation and sector-focused regulation.

In addition to regulating the Water-Service Authorities, the Water Services Act, 1997 provides a comprehensive framework for the oversight and regulation of the Water Boards, established as a family of regional public utilities under the authority of the Minister of Water Affairs and Forestry. It also provides a framework for the collection and publication of information about water services, which may come to be one of the more powerful regulatory tools available to national government.

National Water Act, 1998

The National Water Act, 1998, provides for:
- integrated management of surface water and groundwater
- sustainable use of groundwater within the average annual replenishment rates
- sustainable use of surface and groundwater
- devolution of surface and groundwater to catchment and local level
- government to play a support role through functions such as promoting awareness, information provision and capacity-building.

The Act does not differentiate between surface water and groundwater with respect to allocation, protection and conservation. The Act aims to control the use of water resources, protect them from being impacted on or exploited and polluted, and ensure that every person has equitable access to water resources.

On 1 October 1999, the Department of Water Affairs and Forestry started a registration drive for users of large amounts of untreated raw water.

The new measures do not apply to users of borehole water for domestic purposes, those who use it to grow food for subsistence, or those who use it to water a few head of cattle. It affects those who draw water from a dam, stream or underground aquifer and use it for irrigation, mining, industrial use and feedlots.

Water users had to register before 30 June 2001 or face paying a late registration penalty of the greater of R300 or 10% of outstanding water charges. The registration of users of raw water provides the knowledge base needed to manage the country's water resources more effectively. From 1 April 2002, the process also saw management charges levied on commercial users of water.

By May 2002, about 46 000 water users had been registered, accounting for about 90% of the country's water use.

New water use is now subject to licensing. An assessment of the environmental requirements of the rivers and streams concerned is conducted before a licence can be issued.

The implementation of the National Pricing Strategy for raw water began in 2002, to ensure that, as far as possible, the costs of the management of water resources and water-supply infrastructure are borne by water users.

Billing through the Water Administration and Resource Management System to all water users started in the 2002/03 financial year to recover the appropriate costs. The majority of the water users are paying the water-resource charge or cost for which they are accordingly billed. However, there is still a considerable underrecovery of costs.

Draft Water Services White Paper

The *Draft Water Services White Paper* was released for public comment by the Minister of Water Affairs and Forestry in February 2003.

The Draft White Paper seeks to address government's beliefs that:
- everyone is entitled to a basic supply of 25 litres of clean water per day, or 6 000 litres per household per month
- no one should be without a water supply for more than seven days per year – if a public supply is interrupted for more than 24 hours, the municipality should liaise with residents and arrange for emergency supplies

---

The Department of Water Affairs and Forestry was awarded with a Best Practice Certificate for its initiative 'Partnership in Service Delivery for Sustainable Rural Water Provision' by the United Nations Human Settlement Programme (UN-Habitat) in January 2003.

The International Award for Best Practice aims to identify and promote best practices in development from around the world.

Government aims, through the initiative, to eliminate the backlog of water in South Africa within a period of 10 years. The target is for every citizen to have at least 25 litres of clean water available within 200 metres of their households.

Water affairs and forestry

- people who cannot afford to pay for water are still entitled to a free basic water supply
- it is a criminal offence to connect to a public water supply without municipal permission
- people who are unable to pay their water bill should make arrangements with their municipality
- municipalities may restrict people to the free basic amount, but may not withhold the basic supply
- municipalities must inform people before they discontinue their services and must also have a consumer service where people can lodge complaints.

The White Paper provides a comprehensive review of policy with respect to the water-service sector in South Africa and provides a policy framework for the next 10 years.

The White Paper addresses the full spectrum of water-supply and sanitation services and all relevant institutions. It will replace the 1994 *White Paper on Water Supply and Sanitation*. The *White Paper on Basic Household Sanitation* of 2001 will also be amended to ensure compatibility with the new White Paper.

Water resource management

Water resource management in South Africa has undergone major revision along with the reform of water policy and legislation. The National Water Act, 1998 provides the principles for water resource management. The objective of this policy is to manage water resources in an integrated manner that will ensure a healthy, stable water-resource base to meet the current and future needs of South Africa.

The definition of water quality has been extended from the classical microbiological and physicochemical status to encompass a more comprehensive consideration of water resources as dynamic aquatic ecosystems, including indicators such as biotic diversity and the status of riverbank or riparian habitat. Water resource quality provides an indication of the status of water resources and the ability of resources to provide sustained access for use. Recognising that protection and conservation are not goals in themselves, the policy reflects the reality that certain effects are associated with equitable water use.

Water resource management provides a protective framework that is intended to safeguard water resource quality against unsustainable practices, through a system of pollution source controls and resource-protection measures. Source-directed measures include a range of regulatory controls aimed at the sources of impact on water resources, such as limitations on:

- abstractions
- the volumes and minimum quality standards for water containing waste being discharged.

Resource-directed measures focus on ecosystems because these provide people with goods and services such as water supply, waste transport, processing and dilution, natural products (e.g. reeds, fish and plants), nature and biodiversity conservation, flood control, recreation, a 'sense of place', and places for religious rituals or spiritual needs. Resource-directed measures are therefore designed to protect the resource to ensure that adequate ecosystems continue to supply people with these goods and services.

Claire Reid, the South African Youth Water Prize winner, was awarded the prestigious Stockholm Junior Water Prize in Stockholm, Sweden, on 12 August 2003.

Claire, a Grade 11 learner at St Teresa Mercy School in Rosebank, Johannesburg, won a R37 000-scholarship and a crystal sculpture, which was awarded by the Crown Princess Victoria on behalf of the Stockholm Water Foundation.

Claire developed the so-called Water Wise Reel Gardening System, a seed-planting system that cuts down water usage by as much as 80% by reducing water leakage into the soil. It also keeps seeds moist, so that they can germinate without using additional water.

A classification system will provide the basis for setting appropriate resource-quality objectives and pollution-source controls for the management of the resource. Water use will be allocated according to the resource class, including the use of certain water resources for disposal of waste discharges. Water resources classified as particularly sensitive or environmentally important will be stringently controlled, with water-use allocations limited to minimise detrimental effects.

While recognising that water resources cannot be protected from all detrimental effects on quality, it is not realistic to seek to prevent all effects on economically important water resources. Controlled effects will be permitted and managed within a system of waste-minimisation technologies, pollution prevention, recycling and re-use of water. A system of economic incentives will form part of the management approach, through the introduction of the Waste Discharge Charge System (WDCS) in a phased manner intended to foster the use of low-waste or zero-waste technology.

The WDCS will be based on the waste loading discharge by polluters of a particular water resource.

Voluntary as well as mandatory measures for water conservation are intended to ensure that water is used efficiently, as are demanding management strategies, which increasingly form part of water supply, management and development decision-making. The establishment of formal structures for integrated management of water resources at catchment and local level will bring a new dimension to the management of water resource quality. Stronger user representation of all interest groups will ensure equitable allocations among the user groups, as both the costs and benefits of utilising water resources are realised by the stakeholders. Decision-making will be devolved to the appropriate level, allowing those most affected by the decisions to provide primary input through catchment-agency structures.

Water management institutions

The National Water Act, 1998 sets out the framework for the management of water resources in South Africa. This framework provides for the establishment of water management institutions, which include Catchment Management Agencies (CMAs) and Water-User Associations (WUAs). The core purpose of CMAs is to ensure the sustainable use of water resources in line with the purpose of the Act, which is underpinned by the principles of equity, efficiency, sustainability and representivity.

The country has been divided into 19 Water Management Areas which will each be managed by a CMA. The Inkomati CMA will

---

In September 2003, the 31st Ordinary Session of the Tripartite Permanent Technical Committee (TPTC) considered a report on the drought situation in the southern Africa region.

The TPTC comprises Swaziland, Mozambique and South Africa.

At the 29th Ordinary Session in December 2002, the TPTC noted the scarcity of water in the Inkomati River Basin and mandated the Inkomati System Operation Task Team to monitor the situation.

Following an evaluation of the drought situation, the 30th Ordinary Session held in April 2003 decided to:
- declare a situation of drought in the Inkomati River Basin
- set up a task team to implement measures to manage the use of the waters of the Inkomati River and develop practical measures to mitigate the effects of the drought
- instruct the task team to, among other things, prioritise the supply of water to priority users and ensure effective management of water in the Inkomati River.

At the 31st Ordinary Session, the Task Team reported that it had visited areas affected by the drought on the Mozambican portion of the River, which resulted in measures being adopted to achieve an adequate flow at the Mozambique/South Africa border.

South Africa reported at the meeting that to achieve those flows, restrictions of more than 50% of allocations had been imposed on local irrigators.

Water affairs and forestry

be the first to be established in the country, closely followed by an additional three CMAs in the following two years.

The departmental co-ordinating committee, established by the Departments of Water Affairs and Forestry and of Agriculture and Land Affairs, continues to support the plight of emerging farmers. Continued efforts are being made to ensure that these farmers are empowered to establish WUAs and that they function in a sustainable manner.

Numerous Catchment Management Forums have been established nationally to ensure active participation in the management of local water resources so as to acquire optimal social and economic benefits.

These forums ensure that integrated water resource management is implemented. They also play an important role in establishing statutory institutions such as CMAs and WUAs.

During 2002/03, a proposal to establish a CMA in the Inkomati Water Management Area was published for public comment as an important step towards establishing this institution.

In June 2003, the Department of Water Affairs and Forestry announced that a total of 1 577 water and sanitation schemes operated by the Department would be transferred to 84 municipalities.

Some 1 544 departmental schemes valued at R9,95 billion were surveyed before their transfer to local government.

The transfer team comprises the Department of Water Affairs and Forestry, the National Treasury, the Department of Provincial and Local Government and the South African Local Government Association.

The Department's target is to complete all transfers by June 2005, with 90 schemes expected to be transferred in the 2003/04 financial year.

By June 2003, negotiations were under way for the transfer of the 8 094 departmental staff who operated the schemes. Conditional grants (subsidies), which will be phased out by June 2011, will be incorporated into the equitable share allocations to local government.

By June 2003, some 50 Irrigation Boards had been transformed into 25 WUAs. Three Water Boards had been transformed into three WUAs, and eight new WUAs had been established. A further 31 constitutions for WUAs were being evaluated.

Water Boards

The Water Boards were established as service-providers that report to the Minister of Water Affairs and Forestry. These Boards manage water services within their supply areas and provide potable water at cost-effective prices.

By March 2003, some 15 Water Boards were in operation.

Working for Water Programme

The Working for Water Programme is a labour-intensive initiative to clear invasive alien plants. These introduced species have a negative impact on South Africa's water security, biological diversity, the ecological functioning of natural systems, the productive use of land and the intensities of fires and floods.

The Programme has a marked influence on employment opportunities, training and capacity-building, community empowerment, social development and the creation of secondary industries. It focuses on the most marginalised – the poor, rural communities, women, the disabled and those living with HIV/AIDS.

The Working for Water Programme is a multidepartmental initiative led by the Departments of Water Affairs and Forestry, of Environmental Affairs and Tourism and of Agriculture. It started in 1995 with a budget of R25 million and has grown into one of government's key poverty-relief-fund initiatives.

The Working for Water Programme hosted its first Inaugural Research Symposium in Cape Town in August 2003.

The Symposium aimed at highlighting ongoing research, while eliciting responses from the broader research community on innovative approaches in dealing with the problem of alien invader plants.

By August 2003, over one million invader plants had been cleared while over 15 million person days of employment had been created.

A collaborative research partnership between Working for Water and the Agricultural Research Council's (ARC) Plant Protection Research Institute to conduct research into the identification and screening of biological agents was expected to be signed in 2003.

Flood and drought management

In terms of the South African Disaster Management Policy, there is a major move in focus from reactive to preventive disaster management. This will inevitably move the South African flood-management focus from structural to non-structural, such as attaching special value to floodplain zoning and flood warnings.

Dams and water schemes

A number of new projects were and are being undertaken by the Department of Water Affairs and Forestry. Departmental policy ensures that water-demand management programmes are implemented before embarking on new infrastructure development.

One of the most ambitious binational water projects ever to be undertaken is the Lesotho Highlands Water Project between South Africa and Lesotho. The completion of the first phase was celebrated in January 1998. The first phase of the project is composed of 1A and 1B. The main components of 1A are the construction of dams at Katse and Muela, an 82-km water-transfer tunnel and a hydroelectric plant at Muela. Phase 1B includes the construction of the Mohale Dam and tunnel, and the Matsoku tunnel and weir. The latter was inaugurated in October 2001. By June 2003, the Lesotho Highlands Water Project was progressing well with the Mohale Dam nearly a quarter full.

Planning studies and an environmental-impact assessment have been compiled on the proposed Skuifraam Dam on the Berg River near Franschhoek in the Western Cape. The Dam was also reviewed against the World Commission on Dams' Guidelines, with satisfactory results.

The Levuvhu Water Scheme will provide nine million people in Limpopo with drinking water. Construction of the Nandoni Dam started in May 1998. The total cost of the project will amount to R750 million. The Scheme will also stabilise the water supply for irrigation, and alleviate water shortages in the Kruger National Park. It will be run by the Department of Water Affairs and Forestry's CWSS Programme while municipalities gain the experience and capacity needed to handle the provision of services.

Progress is being made in the establishment of a commission in the Orange-Senqu Basin between Lesotho, Namibia and South Africa. The country is also engaged in a number of collaborative projects with Mozambique and Swaziland. An interim water-sharing agreement was signed in August 2002 as a first step towards the implementation of full basin-management arrangements, as provided for in the Southern African Development Community (SADC) Protocol on Shared Rivers.

The Minister of Water Affairs and Forestry announced during a parliamentary media briefing in February 2003 that the Olifants River would be developed to cope with the increasing water demand generated by platinum-mining developments in Limpopo and Mpumalanga.

During the first phase of the development, the Flag Boshielo Dam, situated on the river near Marble Hall in Mpumalanga, will be raised

---

The Department of Water Affairs and Forestry/Unilever WASH Partnership was launched in October 2003.

The WASH Partnership involves delivering safe water and adequate sanitation, and educating people on hygienic practices.

The key message of WASH is that proper handwashing at critical times plays a major role in reducing diseases such as diarrhoea.

by 5 m at an estimated cost of R180 million. This will increase its storage capacity from 100 million m³ to 188 million m³, allowing 72 million m³ of water to be used annually, compared with the present 56 million m³. The project is expected to be completed by October 2005.

During the second phase, a large dam will be built, either at Rooipoort, or on the Steelpoort River, a tributary of the Olifants River.

Construction on this phase will start in 2006 and is expected to be completed by 2010. The dam yield will be between 50 and 70 million m³, depending on the final design, and is estimated to cost between R700 and R900 million.

In the interim, the additional water secured by raising the Flag Boshielo Dam will be made available to new mining ventures near Burgersfort in Mpumalanga. This will enable water entitlements, currently leased on a temporary basis by the mining ventures, to be returned to small farmers on the irrigation schemes downstream of the Flag Boshielo Dam, which are being rehabilitated.

Drainage and hydrology

Worldwide, 31% of all rainfall returns as run-off to the sea through rivers. In South Africa, with its abundant sunshine and high evaporation rate, the figure is a mere 9%.

The average annual run-off of all South African rivers amounts to approximately 50 billion m³. This is only half the run-off of the Zambezi River and roughly equal to that of the Nile River at Aswan in Egypt or the Rhine River at Rotterdam in the Netherlands. South Africa lies in a drought belt. Rainfall is seasonal and is influenced by topography. The slopes of the eastern plateau, which cover 13% of the surface area of South Africa, account for nearly 43% of the total run-off. The Orange River System, which drains almost the entire plateau – 48% of the total surface area of the country – accounts for only 24% (about 12 060 million m³) of the total average annual run-off to the sea.

Truly perennial rivers (those that flow all year round) are only found over one quarter of South Africa's surface area – mainly in the southern and south-western Cape and on the eastern plateau slopes.

Rivers that flow only during the rainy season are found over a further quarter of the surface area. Rivers in the western interior are episodic, that is, they flow only sporadically after infrequent storms, while their beds are dry for the rest of the year.

Research on river ecosystems is funded by the Water Research Commission (WRC) and the National Research Foundation. (See Chapter 18: *Science and technology*.)

A key objective of the River Health Programme (RHP) is to 'package' and disseminate information on river health in such a way as to serve ecologically sound management of rivers in South Africa, and inform and educate the people of South Africa regarding the health of rivers.

During the past two years, and in collaboration with the Department of Environmental Affairs and Tourism, the WRC and the Council for Scientific and Industrial Research's (CSIR) Environmentek, a new and sophisticated template has been developed for river-health reporting.

Specific objectives of this reporting format are to:
- provide information to government and agencies for improved decision-making in river management
- compare environmental performances of different areas
- increase public awareness of environmental and development issues
- empower people and organisations to improve their environment and quality of life for themselves and future generations.

The RHP primarily uses biological indicators (e.g. fish communities, riparian vegetation, aquatic invertebrate fauna) to assess the health of river systems. The rationale for using biological monitoring is that the integrity of the biota inhabiting river ecosystems provides a direct, holistic and integrated measure of the integrity or health of the river as a whole.

The RHP serves as a source of information on the ecological state of ecosystems in the country, in order to support the rational management of these natural resources.

The objectives of the RHP are therefore to:
- measure, access and report on the ecological state of aquatic ecosystems
- detect and report on spatial and temporal trends in the ecological state of aqua
- identify and report on emerging problems regarding aquatic ecosystems
- ensure that all reports provide relevant scientific and managerial relevant information on aquatic ecosystem management.

Lakes and pans

Except for Lake Fundudzi, which was formed by a huge landslide in the Soutpansberg in Limpopo, there are no true inland lakes in the country. Coastal 'lakes' are found at Wilderness on the Cape south coast, and at St Lucia, Sibaya and Kosi Bay on the KwaZulu-Natal coast. Although they are seldom without water, Lakes Chrissie and Banagher near Ermelo in Mpumalanga differ little from the innumerable 'pans' to be found in a wide belt from the Northern Cape through the western Free State to the North West.

Groundwater resources

Groundwater, despite its relatively small contribution to bulk water supply (13%), represents an important and strategic water resource in South Africa.

Owing to the lack of perennial streams in the semi-desert-to-desert parts, two-thirds of South Africa's surface area is largely dependent on groundwater. Although irrigation is the largest user, the supply to more than 300 towns and smaller settlements is also extremely important. Through government's commitment to meeting the basic water needs of communities, groundwater has also become a strategic resource for village water supply in the wetter parts of the country, because of its cost-effectiveness in a widely scattered small-scale-user situation.

Underground water sources also contribute to river flow. This requires reserving a significant part of groundwater resources for the protection of aquatic ecosystems in terms of the National Water Act, 1998. The maximum quantity of groundwater that can be developed economically is estimated at about 6 000 million m^3 a year.

A national groundwater mapping programme and the development of a national groundwater information system form part of the new strategy. A number of important secondary maps, such as national exploitation potential, groundwater importance, classification and groundwater pollution-vulnerability maps have also been produced.

Forestry

Indigenous forests are indispensable to the country's heritage, beauty, wildlife and environment, while commercial forests provide jobs and economic opportunities for many people in the rural areas. Forestry represents a massive investment in the country and plays an important role in the rural-development strategy.

South Africa has developed one of the largest planted forests in the world. Production from these plantations approached 15,1 million m^3, valued at almost R11,86 million, in 2001. Together with the processed products, the total industry turnover was approximately R2,7 billion in 2001, including R2,0-billion worth of wood-pulp.

More than 11,8 million tons (pulpwood, mining timber, matchwood and charcoal) and 3,2 million m^3 (sawlogs, veneer and poles) were sold in this period.

Collectively, the forestry sector employs about 151 000 people. An equivalent of about 60 000 full-time staff are employed in the primary sector (growing and harvesting), while the balance are employed in the processing industries (sawmilling, pulp and paper, mining timber and poles, and board products).

The organised forest industry claims that each job created within the sector results in four others in supporting industries, through the multiplier effect. The sector thus contributes about 600 000 jobs to the economy.

About half of the 1 100 indigenous tree species found in South Africa grow along the south and east coasts and on the southern and south-eastern slopes of inland mountains. The other half is spread over the interior plateaux.

The yellowwood tree (*Podacarpus*) is South Africa's national tree. Yellowwood trees can grow to a height of more than 40 m with a girth of 8 m, and can live up to 800 years. The Big Tree near the Storms River Bridge (46 m), the King Edward VII in the Knysna Forest (46 m), and the Eastern Monarch in the Amatola Mountains (44 m) are the best-known giants.

Arbour Day celebrated its 131st anniversary in 2003. Every year, National Arbour Week is celebrated at the beginning of September to encourage the greening of South Africa. Two different Trees of the Year are nominated annually: a common variety and a scarcer, possibly endangered, species. The 2003 Trees of the Year were the Kiaat (*Pterocarpus angolensis*) and the Red Current (*Rhus chirindensis*).

In 2003, Arbour Week was celebrated under the theme *Trees are our Heritage – Mehlare ke Bohwa Bja rena*.

At the launch of National Arbour Week 2003 in Johannesburg, the Minister of Water Affairs and Forestry, Mr Ronnie Kasrils, called on the public to help prevent veld and forest fires.

The Minister also announced at the launch that he had proposed a way forward for saving the Jacaranda tree, by asking the Minister of Agriculture and Land Affairs, Ms Thoko Didiza, to list the tree under Category 2 of the Conservation of Agricultural Resources Act, 1983 (Act 43 of 1983), which means that it will be maintained in a similar way to industrial plantations, but within the boundaries of South African cities. In addition, research is being developed with government funding to develop an infertile seed, so that Jacarandas will not be able to propagate themselves.

The Jacaranda was previously listed as a prohibited tree.

Managing the forests

The Department of Water Affairs and Forestry is pursuing a reform programme in the forestry sector which will eventually see the Government leasing all State-owned forest land to private-sector operators.

The Department will thus move from the management of plantations towards promoting, regulating and developing the forest industry. The forestry policy of the Department focuses on several elements:
- overall policy on the place of forestry in the management of land, water and other natural resources
- industrial forestry
- community forestry
- the conservation of natural forests and woodlands
- South Africa's response to global concerns about forests
- research, education and training
- South Africa's relationship with SADC members, and bilateral relations with countries beyond the SADC.

The policy has been applied, tested and developed in accordance with the following principles:
- sustainable forest development
- forests and forest resources are to be treated as national assets
- democratisation
- gender equity
- people-driven development
- recognition of the scarcity of water resources
- a competitive and value-adding forest sector
- decent employment conditions.

The overall goal of the Department is to promote a thriving forestry sector, to be utilised for the lasting benefit of the nation, and developed and managed to protect the environment.

The Department of Water Affairs and Forestry has been involved in a strategic transformation and restructuring process during the past two years. To this end, the forestry division has been restructured into two main functional areas, namely Forestry Operations and Policy and Regulation.

The Policy and Regulation branch has four management components:
- Forestry Policy and Strategy is responsible for developing an appropriate policy and strategy framework for sustainable forest management (SFM) in South Africa, and for promoting the Department's sector leadership role in forestry, both nationally and inter-nationally
- Technical and Information Services is responsible for developing forestry norms and standards, technical guidelines, criteria and indicators for SFM, managing systems for forestry information, and providing technical advice to the Department's regions and other sector institutions
- Participatory Forestry is responsible for providing assistance, advocacy and promoting and formulating programmes and guidelines for the implementation of participative forestry to serve the livelihoods of poor, rural and marginalised urban communities, in terms of using indigenous forests, exotic plantations and associated resources.
- Forestry Regulation is responsible for ensuring effective regulation under the National Forest Act, 1998 (Act 84 of 1998), and the National Veld and Forest Fire Act, 1998 (Act 101 of 1998), including overseeing the management of State forests by commercial entities and/or public bodies.

The Forestry Operations Branch has two management components:
- Forestry Transfers co-ordinates and supports the Department's regional operations in transferring the management of commercial plantations (as well as indigenous forests) to other private (or public) institutions.
- Forestry Support co-ordinates and monitors the operations of the regional clusters in line with the Department's forestry policy, and co-ordinates the implementation of national forestry programmes.

The following are some highlights of the progress made in the restructuring of the State's forest assets:
- Late in 2001, the remaining 22 800 hectares (ha) of forest plantation in the KwaZulu-Natal package was sold to the Siyaqhubeka Consortium comprising Mondi Ltd and Imbokodvo Lemabalabala, a black empowerment company representing communities living near the forest plantations. This area was sold for R100 million in addition to the lease rentals, which were valued at R48 million.
- Late in 2001, the Eastern Cape North package (57 000 ha) was sold for R45 million to Singisi Forest Products, which is a consortium involving Hans Merensky Holdings and community groups living in the areas adjacent to the forest. The involvement of the communities has been facilitated by the Eastern Cape Development Corporation.
- The largest package to be put out to tender in the restructuring process was the Komatiland Forests package.

  The bid price was R446 million, or R335 million for 75%. The Department of Public Enterprises announced the shortlisted bidders in May 2003. The preferred bidder was expected to be announced in December 2003. Komatiland operates 20 plantations that occupy approximately 129 000 ha in Mpumalanga, Limpopo and KwaZulu-Natal. It also operates two sawmills, a veneer-slicing plant and an export facility in Richards Bay.
- The Eastern Cape South package, consisting of approximately 15 000 ha of forests, has been offered for sale.
- The South African Forestry Company Ltd's

Water affairs and forestry

(SAFCOL) commercial forest operations and sawmills in the Western and southern Cape have been restructured into a single package and transferred to a special-purpose vehicle company called Mountain to Oceans (MTO) Forestry (Pty) Ltd.

- Forestry will be phased out on 12 000 ha, on the eastern and western shores of Lake St Lucia. Of the area to be phased out, SAFCOL will clear-fell about 6 600 ha over the next five years. The land will be transferred to the Greater St Lucia Wetland Authority and will be incorporated into the conservation area falling under the World Heritage Site. This will encourage tourism investment through the Lubombo Spatial Development Initiative.
- Forestry operations will be phased out on 15 000 ha in the Boland area of the Western Cape and 30 000 ha in the southern Cape currently managed by SAFCOL. These plantations are not commercially viable and timber no longer represents the best land-use option in these areas. This will open up opportunities for other land uses including agriculture (particularly fruit and grapes), tourism and conservation. The process of conversion will be carefully managed over a period of 10 to 15 years.

With the conclusion of the Singisi and Siyaqhubeka deals by the beginning of 2002, SAFCOL's plantation area stood at 179 000 ha, and that of the Department of Water Affairs and Forestry at 158 000 ha.

The latter area will gradually reduce as the Department's title deeds are transferred into SAFCOL's name. As part of the restructuring process, the Department's plantations were split into category A, B and C plantations. The category A plantations were regarded as being commercially viable and were amalgamated into the SAFCOL plantation packages. No final decision has however been taken regarding the future of the category B and C plantations which are regarded as being non-commercially viable.

The remaining forestry areas (3 000 ha in the Western Cape and 30 000 ha in the southern Cape) will continue to be operated on a sustainable basis. Negotiations are under way with a preferred bidder, Cape Timber Resources (CTR) (Pty) Ltd.

The Department agreed in March 2003 to transfer management control over the Tokai and Cecilia State Forests situated within the area, for the establishment of the Cape Peninsula National Park. The forestry operations will be managed by MTO, and South African National Parks (SanParks) will manage the recreation and conservation functions.

SanParks will continue to accommodate MTO's commercial forestry activities, but will manage the plantations on a multiple use and sustainable basis within a broader conservation framework. The parties will work on a detailed agreement, which will involve the Departments of Water Affairs and Forestry and of Environmental Affairs and Tourism, the MTO, and the Cape Peninsula National Park.

As with the lease agreements for other State forests in the Cape, MTO will retain access to the timber-producing sections of the two plantations for the next 70 years. Conservation and commercial timber production will therefore co-exist on the same area, managed in an integrated and mutually beneficial manner by a single management authority.

By mid-2003, the process of transferring indigenous forests in the Knysna/Tsitsikamma area to SanParks was at an advanced stage of negotiations. Both the process of arriving at an appropriate legal mechanism for the transfer and negotiations for the transfer of employees are at an advanced stage. In terms of the legal mechanism agreed on, the Department of Water Affairs and Forestry will transfer to SanParks through a delegation agreement provided in Section 547 of the National Forests Act, 1998. This will ensure that SanParks will manage the area according to all the provisions of the National Forests Act, 1998.

South African Forestry Company Limited
SAFCOL, a wholly-owned State enterprise

comprising the Department of Water Affairs and Forestry's forestry assets at the time, was formed in 1992.

Its objectives were to enhance the development of the local forestry industry and to optimise the State's forestry assets through running the business on accepted commercial management practices and sustainable forestry-management principles. At the time of its creation, SAFCOL managed 256 000 ha of world-class softwood sawlog plantations, and six small sawmills and pole-treating plants. Its annual roundwood production of 3,3 million m^3 represented a significant contribution to the industry's total output and provided the sawmilling industry with 75% of its fibre requirements.

The decision by government to restructure its forestry assets, not just those managed by the Department of Water Affairs and Forestry, but also those managed by SAFCOL, has had a marked impact on the company since 2001. Two special-purpose vehicles to assist in the restructuring process were formed, namely MTO and Komatiland Forests in Mpumalanga.

Once the process is complete, SAFCOL will remain in existence, its task being to manage the removal of plantations from commercial production.

With all the assets of SAFCOL expected to be sold by 31 March 2004, the company will remain as a holding company of the minority interests in the privatised entities, on behalf of government, its shareholder.

Industry and exports

The industry was a net exporter to the value of over R5,7 billion in 2002, more than 97% of which was in the form of converted value-added products. This trade surplus represented 26,4% of the country's entire trade surplus of R4,2 billion in 2002.

The forest-products industry ranks among the top exporting industries in the country, having contributed 3,58% to the total exports and 1,99% of total imports in 2002.

Capital investment in the industry amounted to some R17,8 billion in 2002. Investment totalled R16,3 billion in 2001 and R9,7 billion in 1999.

The value of forest-product exports has grown significantly over the past decade, from R2,3 billion in 1992 to R11,2 billion in 2002, a growth of 379%. In real terms (taking inflation into account), this growth was 129%, or a compounded real growth of 7,8% per annum over that period. As imports did not increase to the same extent as exports, the net trade balance in foreign trade in forest products increased even more, by 523% in nominal terms (198% in real terms) to R5,6 billion in 2002.

In 2002, paper exports were the most important (R4,254 billion or 38% of the total), followed by solid wood products (R3,780 billion or 34% of the total), pulp (R2,894 billion or 26% of the total), and other products (R0,275 billion or 2% of the total). Woodchip exports, which are exported mainly to Japan, accounted for 52% (R1,964 billion) of the total solid wood products exports.

Total sales from primary processing plants in 2001 amounted to some R11,9 billion. However, when the value of paper sales are included (this is a secondary processing activity), this figure increases to R22 billion.

In 2001, the forestry industry contributed 8,7% to agricultural Gross Domestic Product (GDP), and the forest products industry contributed 7,1% of the country's manufacturing GDP. The total contribution to the entire South African GDP in that year amounted to 1,2%.

Stringent environmental codes of practice are implemented in all plantation and processing activities. The Chief Directorate: Forestry of the Department of Water Affairs and Forestry promotes optimal development of forestry and arboriculture in South Africa.

The National Forests Advisory Council (NFAC) was established in terms of the National Forests Act, 1998. It advises the Minister of Water Affairs and Forestry on all aspects of forestry in the country. The NFAC is actively involved in developing local criteria, indicators and standards for SFM and makes recommendations on how public access to State-owned forests can be improved.

Sustainable forest management

The commercial forestry industry in South Africa is committed to practising SFM and is a world leader in forest certification. This is demonstrated by the fact that over 1 million ha, or over three-quarters of the entire area of commercial forestry plantations in South Africa, are currently certified by the Forest Stewardship Council (FSC) and the ISO 14001 certification schemes as being sustainably managed.

South Africa now has one of the largest areas of FSC-certified plantations of any country in the world. This is a remarkable achievement considering that there were no certified plantations in 1996. Although not all these forests are owned by the large forestry companies, the rapid expansion in this certified area has been facilitated by the fact that all these large companies have their own specialist environmental departments which ensure, among other things, that their land is managed according to their own stringent environmental codes of practice. To promote transparency, members of the public are invited to join company staff when these regular audits are done.

There has also been a large increase in the number of non-corporate growers who have become certified. This has been for a number of reasons, among others, the acceptance by the FSC of 'group-certification schemes' and the availability of local FSC auditors, both of which have reduced the cost of certification considerably. Another development has been the recent accreditation of the South African Bureau of Standards by the FSC to conduct farm management unit-certification audits on their behalf.

As part of its commitment to the practice of SFM, the forestry industry is also involved in the NFAC's Committee for SFM, whose primary responsibility it is to develop criteria, indicators and standards for SFM, tailored to meet South Africa's specific conditions.

The Institute of Natural Resources, which was contracted by the Committee for SFM to develop these criteria has, after an extensive consultative process, developed a draft set which is to be tested infield. The industry is fully supportive of this process and has invited the Department to test the criteria in its plantations.

Through the Forestry Industry Environmental Committee, a set of environmental guidelines was published in 1995 to encourage and facilitate timber growers to practise SFM through the implementation of best environmental practices.

These guidelines were not only highly acclaimed, but widely used both within South Africa and abroad. A second updated, and far more comprehensive and user-friendly edition of the guidelines was published in July 2002. These are being used by the certification agents for the auditing of the physical environment component of their FSC audits.

The indigenous forests of the southern Cape received FSC certification, which is a first for the continent for high forests. This is a major step towards the sustainable management of the country's natural forests.

Legislation

The restructuring of the forestry sector is supported by the National Forests Act, 1998 and the National Veld and Forest Fire Act, 1998.

The National Forests Act, 1998 provides a framework for the development of principles, criteria, indicators and standards for SFM. The criteria, indicators and standards that are being developed for SFM are currently being piloted for testing.

The Act ensures that the public has reasonable access to State forest land for recreational, cultural, spiritual and educational purposes. In addition, provision is made for the protection of indigenous forests, as well as support for community forestry.

The National Veld and Forest Fire Act, 1998 bans open-air fires when the risk of veld blazes in an area is high. It also introduces the concept of voluntary fire-protection associations formed by landowners. It furthermore obliges the Minister of Water Affairs and Forestry to operate a national fire-rating system in consultation with the South African Weather Service and fire associations. The Act also allows the Minister to impose minimum fire-fighting requirements on landowners.

Indigenous high-canopy forest

There are approximately 530 000 ha of indigenous high forest in South Africa, amounting to about 0,45% of the country's land surface.

The Department is responsible for the management of between 180 000 ha and 200 000 ha of these forests, which occur mainly on the eastern and southern slopes of mountain ranges from the Soutpansberg in Limpopo to the Cape Peninsula in the Western Cape.

High forest is normally found in isolated pockets, varying in size from only a few hectares to several thousand hectares.

The largest area of high forest (36 000 ha) lies within a strip some 220 km long and 26 km wide between the Outeniqua and Tsitsikamma Mountain Ranges and the sea, extending from Mossel Bay in the Western Cape, through Knysna, to the Humansdorp district in the Eastern Cape. High forest occurs mainly in patches in mountain kloofs. In the Eastern Cape, indigenous forests occur along the coast and on the Amatola and Transkei Mountain Ranges.

Forests in KwaZulu-Natal and the former Transkei area of the Eastern Cape are generally small, and those that are easily accessible have been heavily exploited in the past.

Although similar in composition to those of the Keiskamma area, these forests also include some of the tropical tree species from the northern parts of South Africa.

In Mpumalanga and Limpopo, high forest occurs in patches in the mountain ranges along the eastern edge of the Highveld plateau, while the largest areas are in the Woodbush and Soutpansberg Ranges.

The single largest part of the indigenous high forest (about 15%) is managed by the Chief Directorate: Forestry according to certain multiple-use objectives.

Systematic timber harvesting occurs in areas of the production management class. Harvesting is concentrated on overmature trees, with logs being sold by tender and/or on public auction. On average, 3 750 m^3 of round logs are harvested annually (150 m^3 of stinkwood, 750 m^3 of yellowwood, 2 500 m^3 of Australian blackwood and 350 m^3 of other species). Timber harvesting in Knysna amounts to 2 600 m^3. Another valuable product of the indigenous forests of South Africa is the seven-week fern (*Rumohra adiantiformis*), which is harvested in the Knysna and Tsitsikamma Forests.

Scrub forest and woodlands

This vegetation covers extensive areas in the low-lying, drier areas of Limpopo, KwaZulu-Natal and Mpumalanga. Some areas of savanna and woodlands have been denuded for agriculture and firewood. Most tree species of the scrub forests and woodlands grow slowly and do not reach great heights. The woodlands are, however, a valuable source of fuel, fencing material and other products. They provide protection for the soil, and shelter and fodder for livestock. The tree growth along much of the coast is classified as coastal scrub, with the exception of patches of high forest at Alexandria and along the Eastern Cape coast.

Planted forests

During the 1930s, government started to establish extensive plantations to make South Africa self-sufficient in its timber requirements, and to provide more job opportunities in a diversified economy during the depression years. Commercial plantations of exotic species proved to be a sound investment and the private sector established large plantations of pine, eucalyptus and wattle trees.

The private sector owns 971 098 ha (or 72%) of the total plantation area of 1 351 176 ha as well as virtually all the processing plants in the country. The remaining 28% (380 663 ha) is under public ownership. The extent of public ownership will decrease significantly once the restructuring process is complete.

In 2002, the capital investment in these plantations stood at R15 billion, 55% of which is attributable to investment in trees. A further 23,3% was tied up in land, 13% in roads, 7,2% in fixed assets and 1,4% in machinery and equipment.

The forestry industry is promoting rural development and economic empowerment through a small-grower afforestation programme. Currently, there are more than 20 000 small emerging black timber growers, the vast majority of whom operate through schemes run under the auspices of Sappi Forests (Project Grow), Mondi Forests (Khulanathi) and the Wattle Growers Association. Combined, these growers, most of whom are women, cultivate 48 000 ha of plantations.

Plantation yields

Of the 1 351 176 ha of plantations in 2001, 52% were softwood species and 48% hardwood species. Thirty-seven per cent of the plantation area was managed mainly for saw-log production, 56% for pulpwood and 4% for mining timber, while the balance of 3% was grown for the production of poles, matchwood (poplar) and other minor products. Plantation yields vary from an average of 16 m^3 per ha per annum for softwood, to 21 m^3 per ha per annum for eucalyptus and 10 m^3 per ha per annum for wattle (timber and bark). Likewise, the rotation ages vary from a maximum of 30 years in the case of pine saw-logs, to six to 10 years in the case of eucalyptus pulp and mining timber. The production from plantations amounted to some 16,6 million m^3 in 2001.

Primary wood-processing

South Africa currently has 167 primary wood-processing plants, 161 of which are owned by the private sector and only six of which are owned by local and State authorities. Of these, some 92 are sawmills; 14 mining-timber sawmills; 29 pole-treating plants; 17 pulp, paper and board mills; two match factories, and four charcoal plants. The total roundwood intake in 2001 was 16,7 million m^3 valued at R2,7 billion. The value of sales of timber products produced by these primary processing plants totalled R11 867 million. An amount of some R17,8 billion was invested in primary roundwood-processing plants (at book value). At market value, this increased to an estimated R25 billion.

The two main pulp-and-paper manufacturing companies in South Africa, Sappi and Mondi, rank among the largest in the southern hemisphere and own assets in many parts of the world.

Research and training

South Africa has world-class forestry-research infrastructures and personnel, with almost 2% of the forestry industry turnover (private and public sectors) devoted to research. The priority fields of research include tree-breeding through applied silviculture, climate and soils, environmental impact and management solutions, forest biology, hydrology and forest protection.

Forestry research is mainly undertaken by the Institute for Commercial Forestry Research, Environmentek (CSIR), the University of Stellenbosch, the Plant Protection Research Institute of the ARC, the Forestry and Agricultural Biotechnology Institute at the University of Pretoria, the University of Natal (Pietermaritzburg), and the Port Elizabeth University of Technology (Technikon), George (Saasveld Campus). All major forestry companies also undertake in-house applied research.

Degrees in forestry are offered by the Faculty of Agricultural and Forestry Sciences at the

University of Stellenbosch, the University of Natal (Pietermaritzburg) and the University of Venda. Diplomas and limited degree courses in forestry disciplines are also offered at the Port Elizabeth University of Technology, George (Saasveld Campus). The Natal University of Technology offers a diploma in Pulp and Paper Technology. The Fort Cox College of Agriculture and Forestry offers a diploma in social forestry.

Skills training is provided by a number of industry-sponsored and in-house training centres. Industry-sponsored bursaries are available, as are company-sponsored bursaries for study at these institutions.

Community forestry

According to the *White Paper on Sustainable Forest Development in South Africa*, community forestry is designed and applied to meet local social, household and environmental needs and to favour local economic development. It is implemented by communities or with the participation of communities, and includes tree-centered projects in urban and rural areas, woodlots and woodland management by communities and individuals. Community forestry has gained impetus through more focused core functions, particularly in urban greening and forest enterprise development.

Participatory Forest Management (PFM) in the Department of Water Affairs and Forestry has emerged as an integrated approach that contributes to achieving the goal of the SFM of South African forests.

Elements of PFM were initially developed for indigenous State forests, but the aim is to use PFM as an approach for the management of all forest types where feasible (indigenous forests, plantations, woodlots and woodlands) and different types of ownership and management (State, provincial, communal, private and community) exist.

The PFM Policy covers all forest resources in South Africa that are under the jurisdiction of the National Forests Act, 1998. For forest land under State ownership, custodians are requested to adhere to the principles of SFM, including the PFM Policy.

The PFM Policy involves keeping in line with and supporting other policy developments on local economic development, the protection and management of natural resources and biological diversity, transfer of management of government assets, forest-enterprise development, and support for previously disadvantaged individuals and the constitutional rights of all South Africans.

The more detailed approach and priorities for the actual implementation of PFM are guided by the forthcoming strategies for PFM and for Forest Enterprise Development.

PFM is aimed to be:
- the best practice for the management of all State forests
- a key element in the management of the State-owned commercial plantations managed under a private lease
- part of the scope for forest enterprise development
- implemented with communities in the management of woodlots and woodlands.

The PFM policy is subject to policy directions as set out in the:
- *White Paper on Sustainable Forest Development in South Africa*
- National Forestry Action Programme
- National Forests Act, 1998
- Framework for the PFM Programme
- Policy and Guidelines on Access to State Forests
- Policy and Strategy for Management Devolution of State Natural Forests to other Agents.

Food and Trees for Africa (FTFA)

FTFA is the sub-Saharan African partner of the International Global Releaf greening organisation.

In 2003, the FTFA trained some 637 community and government representatives, planted 29 398 trees with a survival rate of more than 80%, and facilitated some 34 urban greening projects in the greater Johannesburg area.

The Urban Greening Fund is managed by the FTFA, the Departments of Water Affairs and Forestry and of Agriculture, and the Institute of Environment and Recreation Management. It was set up with donor funds, which included R1,2 million from the Department of Water Affairs and Forestry.

It is a collective fund that supports partnerships aimed at sustainable development through tree planting, parks and food gardening projects and environmental education.

Organisations, companies and individuals can contribute to the Fund to help disadvantaged South Africans to create a greener, healthier and more secure food life.

Eduplant

EduPlant, the national schools programme funded by the Eskom Development Foundation, contributes to the upliftment of schools throughout South Africa by assisting disadvantaged schools to grow their own food. EduPlant provides greener environments conducive to learning. It focuses on permaculture and has received a R2-million grant from the Department of Water Affairs and Forestry.

Acknowledgements

Council for Scientific and Industrial Research website
Department of Water Affairs and Forestry
Estimates of National Expenditure, 2003, published by the National Treasury
Forestry South Africa
South African Forestry Company Limited
South Africa. info
Water Research Commission
www.gov.za
www.trees.org.za

Suggested reading

Bate, R. and Tren, T. *The Cost of Free Water.* Johannesburg: Free Market Foundation, 2002.
Davies, B.R. and Day, J. *Vanishing Waters.* Cape Town: University of Cape Town Press, 1998.
Keith, P. and Coates Palgrave, M. *Everyone's Guide to Trees of South Africa.* 4th revised ed. Cape Town: Struik, 2002.
McCullum, H. ed. *Biodiversity of Indigenous Forests and Woodlands in South Africa.* Maseru: Southern African Development Community/International Union for the Conservation of Nature and Natural Resources/Southern African Research and Documentation Centre, 2000.
Van Wyk, B. and Van Wyk, P. *Field Guide to the Trees of Southern Africa.* Cape Town: Struik, 1997.
Venter, F. and Venter, J. *Making the Most of Indigenous Trees.* Pretoria: Briza Publications, 1999.

Addendum

Contact information as at 15 November 2003

National government departments and organisational components

Agriculture
Website: www.nda.agric.za
Private Bag X250
Pretoria 0001
Tel: (012) 319-6000
Fax: (012) 323-2959

Arts and Culture
Website: www.dac.gov.za
Private Bag X897
Pretoria 0001
Tel: (012) 337-8000
Fax: (012) 323-8308

Communications
Website: http://docweb.pwv.gov.za
Private Bag X860
Pretoria 0001
Tel: (012) 427-8000
Fax: (012) 427-8016

Correctional Services
Website: www.dcs.gov.za
Private Bag X136
Pretoria 0001
Tel: (012) 307-2000
Fax: (012) 328-6149

Defence
Website: www.mil.za
Private Bag X910
Pretoria 0001
Tel: (012) 355-6200
Fax: (012) 347-7445

Education
Website: www.education.gov.za
Private Bag X895
Pretoria 0001
Tel: (012) 312-5911
Fax: (012) 325-6260

Environmental Affairs and Tourism
Website: www.environment.gov.za
Private Bag X447
Pretoria 0001
Tel: (012) 310-3911
Fax: (012) 322-2682

Foreign Affairs
Website: www.dfa.gov.za
Private Bag X152
Pretoria 0001
Tel: (012) 351-1000
Fax: (012) 351-0253

Government Communications (GCIS)
Website: www.gcis.gov.za
Private Bag X745
Pretoria 0001
Tel: (012) 314-2911
Fax: (012) 323-3831

Health
Website: www.doh.gov.za
Private Bag X828
Pretoria 0001
Tel: (012) 312-0000
Fax: (012) 312-0911

Home Affairs
Website: www.home-affairs.gov.za
Private Bag X114
Pretoria 0001
Tel: (012) 314-8911
Fax: (012) 323-2416

Housing
Website: www.housing.gov.za
Private Bag X644
Pretoria 0001
Tel: (012) 421-1311
Fax: (012) 341-8510

Independent Complaints Directorate
Website: www.icd.gov.za
Private Bag X941
Pretoria 0001
Tel: (012) 392-0400
Fax: (012) 320-3116

Justice and Constitutional Development
Website: www.doj.gov.za
Private Bag X81
Pretoria 0001
Tel: (012) 315-1111
Fax: (012) 326-0991

Labour
Website: www.labour.gov.za
Private Bag X117
Pretoria 0001
Tel: (012) 309-4000
Fax: (012) 309-4082/320-2059

Land Affairs
Website: http://land.pwv.gov.za
Private Bag X833
Pretoria 0001
Tel: (012) 312-8911
Fax: (012) 323-3693

Minerals and Energy
Website: www.dme.gov.za
Private Bag X59
Pretoria 0001
Tel: (012) 317-9000
Fax: (012) 322-3416

National Intelligence Agency
Website: www.nia.org.za

Private Bag X87
Pretoria 0001
Tel: (012) 427-4000
Fax: (012) 427-4651

National Treasury
Website: www.treasury.gov.za
Private Bag X115
Pretoria 0001
Tel: (012) 315-5111
Fax: (012) 315-5234

The Presidency
Website: www.gov.za/president/index.html
Private Bag X1000
Pretoria 0001
Tel: (012) 300-5200
Fax: (012) 323-8246
and
Private Bag X1000
Cape Town 8000
Tel: (021) 464-2100
Fax: (021) 462-2838

Provincial and Local Government
Website: www.dplg.gov.za
Private Bag X804
Pretoria 0001
Tel: (012) 334-0600
Fax: (012) 334-0603

Public Enterprises
Website: www.dpe.gov.za
Private Bag X15
Pretoria 0001
Tel: (012) 431-1000
Fax: (012) 431-0139

Public Service and Administration
Website: www.dpsa.gov.za
Private Bag X916
Pretoria 0001
Tel: (012) 314-7911
Fax: (012) 323-2386/324-5616

Public Service Commission
Website: www.psc.gov.za
Private Bag X121
Pretoria 0001
Tel: (012) 328-7690
Fax: (012) 325-8319

Public Works
Website: www.publicworks.gov.za
Private Bag X65
Pretoria 0001
Tel: (012) 337-2000
Fax: (012) 323-2856

Science and Technology
Website: www.dst.gov.za/homepage.asp
Private Bag X894
Pretoria 0001
Tel: (012) 337-8297/8001
Fax: (012) 325-2768

Secretariat for Safety and Security
Website: www.gov.za/sss/
Private Bag X922
Pretoria 0001
Tel: (012) 393-2500
Fax: (012) 393-2536/2557

Social Development
Website: www.socdev.gov.za
Private Bag X901
Pretoria 0001
Tel: (012) 312-7500
Fax: (012) 312-7943

South African Management Development Institute
Website: www.samdi.gov.za
Private Bag X759
Pretoria 0001
Tel: (012) 314-7911
Fax: (012) 321-1810

South African Police Service
Website: www.saps.org.za
Private Bag X94
Pretoria 0001
Tel: (012) 393-5488/9
Fax: (012) 393-5002

South African Revenue Service
Website: www.sars.gov.za
Private Bag X923
Pretoria 0001
Tel: (012) 422-4000
Fax: (012) 422-6848

South African Secret Service
Private Bag X5
Elarduspark 0047
Tel: (012) 427-6110
Fax: (012) 427-6428

Sport and Recreation
Website: www.srsa.gov.za
Private Bag X896
Pretoria 0001
Tel: (012) 334-3189
Fax: (012) 326-4026

Statistics South Africa
Website: www.statssa.gov.za
Private Bag X44
Pretoria 0001
Tel: (012) 310-8911
Fax: (012) 310-8500/8495

Trade and Industry
Website: www.dti.gov.za
Private Bag X84
Pretoria 0001
Tel: 0861 843 384 (General enquiries)
Tel: (012) 310-9791
Fax: (012) 322-2951

Transport
Website: www.transport.gov.za
Private Bag X193
Pretoria 0001
Tel: (012) 309-3000
Fax: (012) 328-5926

Water Affairs and Forestry
Website: www.dwaf.gov.za
Private Bag X313
Pretoria 0001
Tel: (012) 336-7500/326-8264
Fax: (012) 336-8850

Parliamentary information

National Assembly
Website: www.parliament.gov.za
PO Box 15
Cape Town 8000
Tel: (021) 403-2364/6
Fax: (021) 403-2371

National Council of Provinces
Website: www.parliament.gov.za
PO Box 15
Cape Town 8000
Tel: (021) 403-2110/5/3221
Fax: (021) 461-9460

Provincial governments

Eastern Cape
Website: www.ecprov.gov.za

Private Bag X0047
Bisho 5605
Tel: (040) 609-2207/639-1415
Fax: (040) 635-1166

Free State
Website: *www.fs.gov.za*
PO Box 20538
Bloemfontein 9300
Tel: (051) 405-5799
Fax: (051) 405-4803

Gauteng
Website: *www.gpg.gov.za*
Private Bag X61
Marshalltown 2107
Tel: (011) 355-6000
Fax: (011) 836-9334

KwaZulu-Natal
Website: *www.kwazulu.net*
Private Bag X54336
Durban 4000
and
Private Bag X01
Ulundi 3838
Tel: (035) 874-4003/4
Fax: (035) 874-4012

Limpopo
Website: *www.limpopo.gov.za*
Private Bag X9483
Polokwane 0700
Tel: (015) 295-3910
Fax: (015) 291-4808

Mpumalanga
Website: *www.mpumalanga.mpu.gov.za*
Private Bag X11291
Nelspruit 1200
Tel: (013) 766-2641
Fax: (013) 766-2494

Northern Cape
Website: *www.northern-cape.gov.za*
Private Bag X5042
Kimberley 8300
Tel: (053) 839-5100
Fax: (053) 839-4917

North West
Website: *www.nwpg.gov.za*
Private Bag X65
Mafikeng 2745
Tel: (018) 387-3000
Fax: (018) 387-3008

Western Cape
Website: *www.westerncape.gov.za*
Private Bag X9043
Cape Town 8000
Tel: (021) 483-4705/6
Fax: (021) 483-3421

Government structures, bodies, commissions and task groups

Agricultural Research Council
Website: *www.arc.agric.za*
PO Box 8783
Pretoria 0001
Tel: (012) 427-9700
Fax: (012) 342-2231

Armaments Corporation of South Africa
Website: *www.armscor.co.za*
Private Bag X337
Pretoria 0001
Tel: (012) 428-1911
Fax: (012) 428-5635

Central Energy Fund
Website: *www.cef.org.za*
PO Box 786141
Sandton 2146
Tel: (011) 535-7000
Fax: (011) 784-0472

Commission for Conciliation, Mediation and Arbitration
Website: *www.ccma.org.za*
Private Bag X94
Marshalltown 2107
Tel: (011) 377-6698
Fax: (011) 834-7386

Commission on Gender Equality
Website: *www.cge.org.za*
PO Box 32175
Braamfontein 2017
Tel: (011) 403-7182
Fax: (011) 403-7188

Commission on the Restitution of Land Rights
Website: *http://land.pwv.gov.za/restitution*
Private Bag X833

Pretoria 0001
Tel: (012) 312-9244
Fax: (012) 321-0428

Commission on the Promotion and Protection of the Rights of Cultural, Religious and Linguistic Communities
c/o Department of Provincial and Local Government
Private Bag X804
Pretoria 0001
Tel: (012) 334-0891
Fax: (012) 334-0614

Competition Commission
Website: *www.compcom.co.za*
Private Bag X23
Lynnwood Ridge 0040
Tel: (012) 482-9000
Fax: (012) 482-9002/3

Constitutional Court
Website: *www.concourt.gov.za*
Private Bag X32
Braamfontein 2017
Tel: (011) 359-7458
Fax: (011) 403-6524

Council for Geoscience
Website: *www.geoscience.org.za*
Private Bag X112
Pretoria 0001
Tel: (012) 841-1911
Fax: (012) 841-1203/21

Council on Higher Education
Website: *www.che.org.za*
PO Box 13354
Tramshed 0126
Tel: (012) 392-9100
Fax: (012) 392-9110

Denel (Pty) Ltd
Website: *www.denel.co.za*
PO Box 8322
Centurion 0046
Tel: (012) 428-0823
Fax: (012) 428-0989

Development Bank of Southern Africa
Website: *www.dbsa.org*
PO Box 1234
Halfway House 1685
Tel: (011) 313-3911
Fax: (011) 313-3086

Directorate: Special Operations and Serious Economic Offences
Private Bag X752
Pretoria 0001
Tel: (012) 845-6000
Fax: (012) 845-7130

Eskom
Website: www.eskom.co.za
PO Box 1091
Johannesburg 2000
Tel: (011) 800-8111
Fax: (011) 800-4299

Film and Publication Board
Website: www.fpb.gov.za
Private Bag X9069
Cape Town 8000
Tel: (021) 465-6518
Fax: (021) 465-6511

Financial Intelligence Centre
Website: www.fic.gov.za
Private Bag X115
Pretoria 0001
Tel: (012) 315-5427
Fax: (012) 315-5828

Financial and Fiscal Commission
Website: www.financialandfiscal.co.za
Private Bag X69
Halfway House 1685
Tel: (011) 315-7100
Fax: (011) 207-2344

Financial Services Board
Website: www.fsb.co.za
PO Box 35655
Menlo Park 0102
Tel: (012) 428-8000
Toll-free: 0800 110443/202087
Fax: (012) 347-0221

Government Printing Works
Private Bag X85
Pretoria 0001
Tel: (012) 334-4500
Fax: (012) 323-9746

Independent Communications Authority of South Africa
Website: www.icasa.org.za
Private Bag X10002
Sandton 2146
Tel: (011) 321-8200
Fax: (011) 444 1919

Independent Development Trust
Website: www.idt.org.za
PO Box 73000
Lynnwood Ridge 0043
Tel: (012) 845-2000
Fax: (012) 348-1089

Independent Electoral Commission
Website: www.elections.org.za
PO Box 7943
Pretoria 0001
Tel: (012) 428-5700
Fax: (012) 341-5292

International Marketing Council
Website: www.imc.org.za
PO Box 3207
Houghton 2198
Tel: (011) 483-0122
Fax: (011) 483-0124

Judicial Service Commission
Private Bag X258
Bloemfontein 9300
Tel: (051) 447-2769
Fax: (051) 447-0836

Land Bank and Agricultural Bank of South Africa (Land Bank)
Website: www.landbank.co.za
PO Box 375
Pretoria 0001
Tel: (012) 312-3999
Fax: (012) 312-3617

Land Claims Court
Website: www.law.wits.ac.za/lcc/index.html
Private Bag X10060
Randburg 2125
Tel: (011) 781-2291
Fax: (011) 781-2218

Mintek
Website: www.mintek.co.za
Private Bag X3015
Randburg 2125
Tel: (011) 709-4111
Fax: (011) 793-2413

Municipal Demarcation Board
Website: www.demarcation.org.za
Private Bag X28
Hatfield 0028
Tel: (012) 342-2481/2
Fax: (012) 342-2480

National Advisory Council on Innovation
Website: www.naci.org.za
PO Box 1758
Pretoria 0001
Tel: (012) 392-9352
Fax: (012) 392-9353

National Archives of South Africa
Website: www.national.archives.gov.za
Private Bag X236
Pretoria 0001
Tel: (012) 323-5300
Fax: (012) 323-5287

National Arts Council of South Africa
Website: www.nac.org.za
PO Box 500
Newtown 2113
Tel: (011) 838-1383
Fax: (011) 838-6363

National Crime Prevention Strategy
Private Bag X922
Pretoria 0001
Tel: (012) 393-2550
Fax: (012) 393-2538

National Development Agency
Website: www.nda.org.za
PO Box 31959
Braamfontein 2017
Tel: (011) 403-6650
Fax: (011) 403-2514/5

National Director of Public Prosecutions
Website: www.ndpp.gov.za
PO Box 752
Pretoria 0001
Tel: (012) 317-5000
Fax: (012) 321-0968

National Economic Development and Labour Council
Website: www.nedlac.org.za
PO Box 1775
Saxonwold 2132
Tel: (011) 328-4211
Fax: (011) 447-2089

National Gambling Board
Website: www.ngb.org.za
Private Bag X27
Hatfield 0028
Tel: (012) 342-8665
Fax: (012) 342-8664

National Homebuilders' Registration Council
Website: www.nhbrc.org.za
PO Box 461
Randburg 2125
Tel: (011) 348-5701
Fax: (011) 787-4310

National House of Traditional Leaders
Private Bag X804
Pretoria 0001
Tel: (012) 301-1054
Fax: (012) 326-1019

National Housing Finance Corporation
Website: www.nhfc.co.za
PO Box 31376
Braamfontein 2017
Tel: (011) 644-9800
Fax: (011) 484-0081

National Nuclear Regulator
Website: www.nnr.co.za
PO Box 7106
Centurion 0046
Tel: (012) 674-7100
Fax: (012) 663-5513

National Peace Accord Trust
Website: www.peaceaccord.org.za
PO Box 485
Modderfontein 1645
Tel: (011) 606-2850
Fax: (011) 606-2836

National Programme of Action for Children in South Africa
Website: www.children.gov.za
The Presidency
Private Bag X1000
Pretoria 0001
Tel: (012) 300-5200
Fax: (012) 321-4566

National Prosecuting Authority
Website: www.npa.gov.za
Private Bag X752
Pretoria 0001
Tel: (012) 845-6000
Fax: (012) 804-7300

National Youth Commission
Website: www.nyc.gov.za
Private Bag X938
Pretoria 0001
Tel: (012) 325-3702
Fax: (012) 324-4759

Office of the Auditor-General
Website: www.agsa.co.za
PO Box 446
Pretoria 0001
Tel: (012) 426-8000
Fax: (012) 426-8333

Pan South African Language Board
Website: www.pansalb.org.za
Private Bag X08
Arcadia 0007
Tel: (012) 341-9638
Fax: (012) 341-5938

Public Investment Commission
Private Bag X187
Pretoria 0001
Tel: (012) 328-3766
Fax: (012) 341-1065/440-1736

Office of the Public Protector
Website: www.polity.org.za/govt/pubprote/index.html
Private Bag X677
Pretoria 0001
Tel: (012) 322-2915/6
Fax: (012) 322-5093

Petroleum Oil and Gas Corporation of South Africa (Pty) Ltd
Website: www.petrosa.com
Private Bag X14
Mossel Bay 6500
Tel: (044) 601-2911
Fax: (044) 601-2390

Rand Water
Website: www.randwater.co.za
PO Box 1127
Johannesburg 2000
Tel: (011) 682-0966
Fax: (011) 682-0663

South African Diamond Board
PO Box 16001
Doornfontein 2023
Tel: (011) 334-8980
Fax: (011) 334-8898

South African Airways
Website: www.saa.co.za or www.flysaa.com
Private Bag X13
Johannesburg International Airport
1627
Tel: (011) 978-1000/2500
Fax: (011) 978-3507

South African Forestry Company Ltd
PO Box 1771
Silverton 0127
Tel: (012) 481-3733
Fax: (012) 481-3566

South African Human Rights Commission
Website: www.sahrc.org.za
Private Bag X2700
Houghton 2041
Tel: (011) 484-8300
Fax: (011) 484-8403

South African Law Commission
Website: www.law.wits.ac.za/salc/salc.htm
Private Bag X668
Pretoria 0001
Tel: (012) 322-6440
Fax: (012) 320-0936

South African Local
Government Association
Website: www.salga.org.za
PO Box 2094
Pretoria 0001
Tel: (012) 338-6700
Fax: (012) 338-6747

South African Nuclear
Energy Corporation
Website: www.necsa.co.za
PO Box X582
Pretoria 0001
Tel: (012) 305-5750
Fax: (012) 305-5751

South African Post Office
Ltd
Website: www.sapo.co.za
PO Box 10000
Pretoria 0001
Tel: (012) 401-7000
Fax: (012) 401-7707

South African Rail
Commuter Corporation
Website: www.sarcc.co.za
Private Bag X02
Sunninghill 2157
Tel: (011) 804-2900
Fax: (011) 804-3852/3

South African Reserve Bank
Website: www.resbank.co.za
PO Box 427
Pretoria 0001
Tel: (012) 313-3911
Fax: (012) 313-4296

South African Sports
Commission
Website: www.sasc.org.za
PO Box 11239
Centurion 0046
Tel: (012) 677-9784/5
Fax: (012) 677-9852

South African Tourism
Website: www.southafrica.net
Private Bag X10012
Sandton 2146
Tel: (011) 778-8000
Fax: (011) 778-8001

Special Investigating Unit
Website: www.siu.org.za
PO Box 893
East London 5200
Tel: (043) 726-9705
Fax: (043) 726-9261/9

State Information
Technology Agency
(Pty) Ltd
Website: www.sita.co.za
PO Box 26100
Monument Park 0105
Tel: (012) 482-3000
Fax: (012) 482-2100

State Tender Board
Website: www.treasury.gov.za
Private Bag X49
Pretoria 0001
Tel: (012) 315-5111
Fax: (012) 315-5301

Telkom SA Ltd
Website: www.telkom.co.za
Private Bag X74
Pretoria 0001
Tel: (012) 311-3911
Fax: (012) 323-6733

Trade and Investment
Council
Website: www.tisaglobal.com
PO Box 902
Groenkloof 0027
Tel: (012) 428-7905
Fax: (012) 428-7898
(012) 428-7853

Transnet Ltd
Website: www.transnet.co.za
PO Box 72501
Parkview 2122
Tel: (011) 308-2524
Fax: (011) 308-2312

Truth and Reconciliation
Commission
Website: www.doj.gov.za/trc/index.html
Private Bag X81
Pretoria 0001
Tel: (012) 315-1807
Fax: (012) 323-3595

Water Research
Commission
Website: www.wrc.org.za
Private Bag X03
Gezina 0031
Tel: (012) 330-0340
Fax: (012) 331-2565

Government Communication and Information Centres

Eastern Cape
Eastern Cape Provincial Office
Private Bag X608
East London 5200
Tel: (043) 722-2602/09/12
Fax: (043) 722-2615
E-mail: lungisa@gcispe.ecape.gov.za

Free State
Free State Regional Office
PO Box 995
Bloemfontein 9300
Tel: (051) 448-4504/5/6
Fax: (051) 430-7032
E-mail: tshenolo@gcis.ofs.gov.za

Kroonstad Satellite Regional
Office
PO Box 995
Bloemfontein 9300
Tel: (056) 213-2795/6
E-mail: kroonstad@intekom.co.za

Gauteng
Gauteng Regional Office
Private Bag X16
Johannesburg 2000
Tel: (011) 834-3560
Fax: (011) 834-3621
E-mail: peter@gcisjhb.pwv.gov.za

KwaZulu-Natal
KwaZulu-Natal Regional Office
Private Bag X54332
Durban 4000
Tel: (031) 301-6787/8
Fax: (031) 305-9431
E-mail: malcolm@gcisdbn.kzntl.gov.za

Limpopo
Limpopo Regional Office
PO Box 2452
Polokwane 0700
Tel: (015) 291-4689
Fax: (015) 295-6982
E-mail: selomo@gcisptb.norprov.gov.za

Mpumalanga
Mpumalanga Regional Office
PO Box X2856
Nelspruit 1200
Tel: (013) 753-2397

Fax: (013) 753-2531
E-mail: sydwel@gcisnls.mpu.gov.za

Northern Cape
Northern Cape Regional Office
Private Bag X5038
Kimberley 8300
Tel: (053) 832-1378/9
Fax: (053) 832-1377
E-mail: mariusn@gcis.ncape.gov.za

Upington Satellite Regional Office
PO Box 2872
Upington 8800
Tel: (054) 332-6206
Fax: (054) 332-6218
E-mail: upingtongic@intekom.co.za

North West
North West Regional Office
Private Bag X2120
Mafikeng 2745
Tel: (018) 381-7068/71
Fax: (018) 381-7066
E-mail: mareka@gcismmb.nwp.gov.za

Western Cape
Western Cape Regional Office
Private Bag X9007
Cape Town 8000
Tel: (021) 421-5070
Fax: (021) 419-8846
E-mail: brent@gcisct.wcape.gov.za

Multi-Purpose Community Centres

Eastern Cape
Centane MPCC
Tel: (047) 498-1207
Fax: (047) 498-1207

Cofimvaba MPCC
PO Box 456
Cofimvaba 5380
Tel: (047) 874-0454
Fax: (047) 874-0454
E-mail: cofimvaba@intekom.co.za

Sandrift MPCC
Tel: (041) 484-2022

Sterkspruit MPCC
PO Box 18
Lady Grey 9755
Tel: (051) 611-0042
Fax: (051) 611-0042
E-mail: sterkspruit@intekom.co.za

Tombo MPCC
PO Box 182608
Port St Johns 5120
Tel: (047) 564-1131
Fax: (047) 564-1129
E-mail: tombo@intekom.co.za

Zalu Hill MPCC
PO Box 182608
Port St Johns 5120
Tel: (047) 564-1139
Fax: (047) 564-1129

Free State
Botshabelo MPCC
Tel: (051) 532-1508
E-mail: botshabelo@intekom.co.za

Namahadi MPCC
PO Box 17942
Witsieshoek 9870
Tel: (058) 789-1147
Fax: (058) 789-3586
E-mail: namahadi@telkomsa.net

Sediba MPCC
Tel: 082 550 8512

Gauteng
Diepsloot MPCC
Tel: (011) 834-3560

Faranani MPCC
PO Box 70021
Tsakane 1550
Tel: (011) 738-8753
E-mail: faranani@intekom.co.za

Ipelegeng MPCC
Tel: (011) 982-5810
Fax: (011) 982-6400
E-mail: sowetompcc@intekom.co.za

Mamelodi MPCC
19481 Makhubela Street
Mamelodi West
Tel: (012) 805-9085
E-mail: mamelodi@intekomsa.net

Vaal/Sebokeng MPCC
Private Bag X029
Vanderbijlpark 1900
Tel: (016) 988-1960
Fax: (016) 988-1960
E-mail: sebokeng@intekom.co.za

Soshanguve MPCC
Nafcoc Shopping Centre
Section F Soshanguve
Tel: (012) 799-5005
E-mail: soshanguvempcc@intekom.co.za

Tembisa MPCC
Tembisa Civic Centre
Igqagqa Section Tembisa
Tel: (011) 920-1120
E-mail: thembisa@intekom.co.za

Zithobeni MPCC
Tel: (013) 937-0133

KwaZulu-Natal
Bhamshela MPCC
Kwamthiyane Ngcogongcongo Road
Bhamsela
Tel: (032) 294-9076
Fax: (032) 294-9075
bamshela@intekom.co.za

Dududu MPCC
Private Bag X54332
Durban 4000
Tel: (039) 974-0989
Fax: (039) 974-0989

Dukuza MPCC
Private Bag X1620
Bergville 3350
Tel: (036) 438-6103
Fax: (036) 438-6136

Mbazwana MPCC
PO Box 231
Mbazwana 3974
Tel: (035) 571-10070
Fax: (035) 571-0023
E-mail: mbazwana@intekom.co.za

Mtshezi/Imbabazane MPCC
PO Box 750
Escort 3310
Tel: (036) 353-3212
Fax: (036) 353-3212

Tugela Ferry MPCC
Main Road
Tugela Ferry Village
Tel: (033) 493-0282
Fax: (033) 493-0724

Limpopo
Atok MPCC
Tel: 082 296 0285
Kgautswane MPCC
PO Box 9
Ohrigstad 1122
Tel: (013) 231-7515
Leboeng MPCC
Tel: 073 198 6714

Makhuva MPCC
PO Box 30
Shangwani 0816
Tel: (015) 812-5601
Fax: (015) 812-5601
E-mail: makhuva@intekom.co.za

Mapela MPCC
Tel: 082 975 8303

Vaalwater MPCC
Tel: 082 975 8303

Mpumalanga
Kgolomodumo MPCC
Tel: 073 238 3365

Matsamo MPCC
PO Box 601
Shongwe Mission 1341
Tel: (013) 781-0666
E-mail: matsamo@intekom.co.za

Mpuluzi MPCC
PO Box 1408
Fernie 2339
Tel: (017) 888-0014
E-mail: mpuluzi@intekom.co.za

Tholulwazi MPCC
Tel: (017) 683-3000
Fax: (017) 683-0385

Northern Cape
Calvinia MPCC
PO Box 8190
Calvinia
E-mail: calviniampcc@telkomsa.net

Colesberg MPCC
PO Box 101
Colesberg 5980
Tel: (051) 753-2170
Fax: (051) 753-2182

Galeshewe MPCC
Private Bag X5016
Kimberley 8300

Tel: (053) 872-2644
Fax: (053) 872-2673

Pescodia MPCC
62 Sparrow Street
Pescodia
Kimberley 8309
Tel: (053) 873-1072
Fax: (053) 873-1298

North West
Lebotlwane MPCC
Moretele District Municipality Offices
4065B Mathibestad
Tel: (012) 424-40032
Fax: (012) 701-5330

Morokweng MPCC
Private Bag X1006
Morokweng 8614
Tel: (053) 998-3346
Fax: (053) 761-1068

Western Cape
Bonteheuwel MPCC
Bonteheuwel
Cape Town 8000
Tel: (021) 695-5425
Fax: (021) 695-5425

George/Tembalethu MPCC
Tembalethu 6530
Tel: (044) 880-1711
Fax: (044) 880-1165

Gugas Thembe MPCC
PO Box 6 Washington
Langa Cape Town 7455
Tel: (021) 695-3328
Fax: (021) 695-3325

Hartebeeskraal/Atlantis MPCC
1 Nottingham Street Atlantis
Cape Town 7349
Tel: (021) 572-1872
Fax: (021) 572-1872

Langebaan MPCC
Tel: (022) 772-2622

Masibambane/Vanrhynsdorp MPCC
1 Mandela Street
Vanrhynsdorp 8170
Tel: (027) 219-1917
Fax: (027) 219-1917

Waboomskraal MPCC
Sandklaar Road
Thembalethu
George 6530
Tel: (044) 886-0040

Worcester MPCC
Mobuntu Centre
c/o Mtwazi and Nkentsha Streets
Zweletemba
Worcester 6854
Tel: (023) 348-2600
Fax: (023) 345-1031

Zolane MPCC
6th Avenue
Nyanga East 7755
Tel: (021) 386-8656
Fax: (021) 386-1032

Foreign representatives in South Africa

Albania (Republic of)
[Honorary Consulate]
PO Box 2000
Witkoppen 2068
Tel: (011) 467-0946
Fax: (011) 467-0952
E-mail: nrose@icon.co.za

Algeria (Democratic People's Republic of) [Embassy]
PO Box 57480
Arcadia 0007
Tel: (012) 342-5074/5
Fax: (012) 342-5078/6479
E-mail: sefa@mweb.co.za

Angola (Republic of)
[Embassy]
PO Box 8685
Pretoria 0001
Tel: (012) 342-4404
Fax: (012) 342-7039
E-mail: embaixada@angola.org.za

Argentina (Republic of)
[Embassy]
PO Box 11125
Hatfield 0028
Tel: (012) 430-3513/6
Fax: (012) 430-3521
E-mail: argembas@global.co.za

Australia [High Commission]
Website: www.australia.gov.au
Private Bag X150

Pretoria 0001
Tel: (012) 342-3740
Fax: (012) 342-8442
E-mail: ian.wilcock@dfat.gov.au

Australia [High Commission]
– during parliamentary session
PO Box 4749
Cape Town 8000
Tel: (021) 419-5425/9
Fax: (021) 419-7345

Austria (Republic of)
[Embassy]
PO Box 95572
Waterkloof 0145
Tel: (012) 452-9155/9121
Fax: (012) 452-9121
E-mail: pretoria-ob@bmaa.gv.at

Austria (Republic of)
[Embassy]
– during parliamentary session
PO Box 6887
Roggebaai 8012
Tel: (021) 421-1440/1
Fax: (021) 425-3489
E-mail: kapstadt-gk@bmaa.gv.at

Bangladesh (People's Republic of)
[High Commission]
410 Farenden Street
Sunnyside
Pretoria 0002
Tel: (012) 343-2105/7
Fax: (012) 343-5222
E-mail: bangladoot@global.co.za
or banglacom@global.co.za

Belarus (Republic of)
[Embassy]
PO Box 4107
Pretoria 0001
Tel: (012) 430-7664/7707/9
Fax: (012) 342-6280
E-mail: sa@belembassy.org

Belgium (Kingdom of)
[Embassy]
Website: www.diplobel.org
625 Leyds Street
Muckleneuk
Pretoria 0002
Tel: (012) 440-3201/2
Fax: (012) 440-3216
E-mail: pretoria@diplobel.org

Belgium (Kingdom of)
[Embassy]
– during parliamentary session
Northgate 29 Boshof Avenue
Newlands
Cape Town 7700
Tel: (021) 683-0400
Fax: (021) 683-0401

Benin (Republic of)
[Embassy]
PO Box 26484
Arcadia 0007
Tel: (012) 342-6978
Fax: (012) 342-1823
E-mail: embbenin@yebo.co.za

Bosnia and Herzegovina
[Embassy]
Website: www.bosniaandherzegovina.embassy.republicofsouthafrica.cjb.net
PO Box 11464
Hatfield 0028
Tel: (012) 346-5547/7366
Fax: (012) 346-2295/2762
E-mail: bih@mweb.co.za

Botswana (Republic of)
[High Commission]
PO Box 57035
Arcadia 0007
Tel: (012) 430-9640
Fax: (012) 342-4783

Brazil (Federative Republic of)
[Embassy]
Website: www.brazil.co.za
PO Box 3269
Pretoria 0001
Tel: (012) 426-9400
Fax: (012) 426-9494
E-mail: braspret@cis.co.za

Bulgaria (Republic of)
[Embassy]
PO Box 26296
Arcadia 0007
Tel: (012) 342-3720/1
Fax: (012) 342-3721
E-mail: embulgsa@iafrica.com

Burundi (Republic of)
[Embassy]
PO Box 12914
Hatfield 0028
Tel: (012) 342-4881/3
Fax: (012) 342-4885
E-mail: ambabusa@mweb.co.za

Cameroon (Republic of)
[High Commission]
Website: www.cameroon.co.za
PO Box 13790
Hatfield 0028
Tel: (012) 342-2477
Fax: (012) 342-2478
E-mail: hicocam@cameroon.co.za

Canada [High Commission]
Website: www.cic.gc.ca
Private Bag X13
Hatfield 0028
Tel: (012) 422-3000
Fax: (012) 422-3052

Canada [High Commission]
– during parliamentary session
Website: www.cic.gc.cd
PO Box 63
Cape Town 8000
Tel: (021) 423-5240
Fax: (021) 423-4893
E-mail: cptwn@dfait-maeci.gc.ca

Central African Republic
[Honorary Consulate-General]
PO Box 2774
Kempton Park 1619
Tel: (011) 970-1355
Fax: (011) 970-1352
E-mail: johan@eriksons.co.za

Chile (Republic of) [Embassy]
PO Box 2449
Brooklyn Square 0075
Tel: (012) 460-8090/4482
Fax: (012) 460-8093
E-mail: chile@iafrica.com

Chile (Republic of)
[Embassy]
– during parliamentary session
PO Box 2067
Cape Town 8000
Tel: (021) 421-2344/6
Fax: (021) 425-3034
E-mail: chilecpt@iafrica.com

China (People's Republic of)
[Embassy]
Website: www.chinese-embassy.org.za
PO Box 95764
Waterkloof 0145
Tel: (012) 342-4194/5560
Fax: (012) 342-4244/4154
E-mail: reception@chinese-embassy.org.za

Colombia (Republic of)
[Embassy]
Private Bag X12791
Hatfield 0028
Tel: (012) 342-0211/4
Fax: (012) 342-0216
E-mail: emcolsf@mweb.co.za

Comores (Federal Islamic Republic of the) [Embassy]
203 Anna Marie Building
419 Leyds Street
Sunnyside 0002
Tel: (012) 344-5429
Fax: (012) 321-2032

Congo (Democratic Republic of the) [Embassy]
PO Box 28795
Sunnyside 0132
Tel: (012) 343-2455
Fax: (012) 344-4054
E-mail: rdcongo@lantic.co.za

Congo (Republic of)
[Embassy]
PO Box 40427
Arcadia 0007
Tel: (012) 342-5507/8
Fax: (012) 342-5510
E-mail: congo@starpost.com

Costa Rica (Republic of)
[Honorary Consulate]
PO Box 68140
Bryanston 2021
Tel: (011) 705-3434
Fax: (011) 705-1222
E-mail: ricacost@netactive.co.za

Cote d'Ivoire (Republic of)
[Embassy]
PO Box 13510
Hatfield 0028
Tel: (012) 342-6913/14
Fax: (012) 342-6713

Croatia (Republic of)
[Embassy]
PO Box 11335
Hatfield 0028
Tel: (012) 342-1206/1598
Fax: (012) 342-1819
E-mail: vrhjar@iafrica.com

Cuba (Republic of)
[Embassy]
PO Box 11605
Hatfield 0028
Tel: (012) 346-2215
Fax: (012) 346-2216
E-mail: sudafri@iafrica.com

Cyprus (Republic of)
[High Commission]
PO Box 14554
Hatfield 0028
Tel: (012) 342-5258
Fax: (012) 342-5596
E-mail: cyprusjb@mweb.co.za

Czech (Republic of)
[Embassy]
Website: www.icon.co.za/˜czmzv
PO Box 3326
Pretoria 0001
Tel: (012) 342-3477
Fax: (012) 342-2033
E-mail: capetown@embassy.mzv.ca

Denmark (Kingdom of)
[Embassy]
Website: www.denmark.co.za
PO Box 11439
Hatfield 0028
Tel: (012) 430-9340
Fax: (012) 342-7620
E-mail: pryamb@um.dk

Denmark (Kingdom of)
[Embassy]
– during parliamentary session
Website: www.denmark.co.za
PO Box 5596
Cape Town 8000
Tel: (021) 419-6936/7
Fax: (021) 419-9527

Equador (Republic of)
[Honorary Consulate]
PO Box 98291
Sloane Park 2152
Tel: (011) 240-0509
Fax: (011) 240-0419
E-mail: tkummert@inobsvez.co.za

Egypt (Arab Republic of)
[Embassy]
PO Box 30025
Sunnyside 0132
Tel: (012) 343-1590/1
Fax: (012) 343-1082
E-mail: egyptian.icon.co.za

Eritrea (State of) [Embassy]
PO Box 11371
Queenswood 0121
Tel: (012) 333-1302
Fax: (012) 333-2330
E-mail: eremb@lantic.co.za

Estonia (Republic of)
[Honorary Consulate]
16 Hofmeyer Street
Welgemoed
Belville 7530
Tel: (021) 913-3850
Fax: (021) 913-2579

Ethiopia (Federal Republic of) [Embassy]
PO Box 11469
Hatfield 0028
Tel: (012) 346-3542
Fax: (012) 346-3867
E-mail: mamietm@iafrica.com

Finland (Republic of)
[Embassy]
Website: www.virtual.finland.fi
PO Box 443
Pretoria 0001
Tel: (012) 343-0275
Fax: (012) 343-3095
E-mail: sanomat.pre@formin.fi

Finland (Republic of)
[Embassy]
– during parliamentary session
Website: www.virtual.finland.fi
PO Box 693
Cape Town 8000
Tel: (021) 461-4732
Fax: 461-5768
E-mail: anu.brady@formin.fi

France (Republic of)
[Embassy]
Website: www.ambafrance-za.org
807 George Avenue
Arcadia 0083
Tel: (012) 429-7000
Fax: (012) 429-7029
E-mail: france@ambafrance-za.org

Gabon (Republic of)
[Embassy]
PO Box 9222
Pretoria 0001
Tel: (012) 342-4376/7
Fax: (012) 342-4375

Germany (Federal Republic of) [Embassy]
PO Box 2023
Pretoria 0001
Tel: (012) 427-8977
Fax: (012) 427-8982
E-mail: germanyembassy
pretoria@gonet.co.za

Germany (Federal Republic of) [Embassy]
– during parliamentary session
PO Box 4273
Cape Town 8000
Tel: (021) 424-2410
Fax: (021) 424-9403
E-mail: info@germanyconsulate
capetown.co.za

Ghana (Republic of)
[High Commission]
PO Box 12537
Hatfield 0028
Tel: (012) 342-5847/9
Fax: (012) 342-5863
E-mail: ghcom27@icon.co.za

Greece (Hellenic Republic)
[Embassy]
1083 Church and Athlone Streets
Arcadia 0083
Tel: (012) 430-7351/2/3
Fax: (012) 430-4313
E-mail: embgresaf@global.co.za

Greece (Hellenic Republic)
[Embassy]
– during parliamentary session
PO Box 3232
Cape Town 8000
Tel: (021) 424-8160/1
Fax: (021) 424-9421
E-mail: grconcpt@mweb.co.za

Granada (Republic of)
[Honorary Consulate]
3rd Floor Digital House
Park Lane 2196
Tel: 083 461 6559
Fax: (011) 787-6407

Guatemala (Republic of)
Honorary Consulate]
PO Box 222
Sunninghill 2157
Tel: (011) 804-5080
Fax: (011) 804-4844
E-mail: marcelr@exatrade.co.za

Guinea (Republic of)
[Embassy]
PO Box 13523
Hatfield 0028
Tel: (012) 342-7348
Fax: (012) 342-8467
E-mail: guinea@diplobel.org.za

Guinea-Bissau
[Honorary Consulate]
PO Box 9689
Edenglen 1613
Tel: (011) 622-3688
Fax: (011) 622-5351

Guyana (Co-operative Republic of)
[Honorary Consulate]
PO Box 1877
Randburg 2125
Tel: (011) 789-9760
Fax: (011) 789-9763
E-mail: raebenz@compuserve.com

Holy See
[Nuncio of the Vatican]
PO Box 26017
Arcadia 0007
Tel: (012) 344-3815/6
Fax: (012) 344-3595
E-mail: nunziosa@iafrica.com

Hungary (Republic of)
[Embassy]
PO Box 27077
Sunnyside 0132
Tel: (012) 430-3020/30
Fax: (012) 430-3029
E-mail: hunem@cis.co.za

India (Republic of)
[High Commission]
PO Box 40216
Arcadia 0007
Tel: (012) 342-5392
Fax: (012)430-8326
E-mail: hcipta@iafrica.com

India (Republic of)
[High Commission]
– during parliamentary session
PO Box 3316
Cape Town 8000
Tel: (021) 419-8110
Fax: (021) 419-8112
E-mail: indiactn@iafrica.com

Indonesia (Republic of)
[Embassy]
PO Box 13155
Hatfield 0028
Tel: (012) 342-3350/4
Fax: (012) 342-3369
E-mail: indonemb@lantic.co.za

Iran (Islamic Republic of)
[Embassy]
PO Box 12546
Hatfield 0028
Tel: (012) 342-5880/1
Fax: (012) 342-1878
E-mail: office@iranembassy.org.za

Iraq (Republic of)
[Embassy]
PO Box 11089
Hatfield 0028
Tel: (012) 362-2012
Fax: (012) 362-2027

Ireland [Embassy]
Website: www.embassyireland.org.za
PO Box 4174
Pretoria 0001
Tel: (012) 342-5062
Fax: (012) 342-4752
E-mail: pretoria@iveagh.irlgov.i.e

Israel (State of) [Embassy]
PO Box 3726
Pretoria 0001
Tel: (012) 342-2693/7
Fax: (012) 342-1442
E-mail: embofisr@iafrica.com

Israel (State of) [Embassy]
– during parliamentary session
PO Box 180
Cape Town 8000
Tel: (021) 457-0271/5
Fax: (021) 461-0075

Italy (Italian Republic)
[Embassy]
Website: www.ambital.org.za
796 George Avenue
Arcadia 0083
Tel: (012) 430-5441/4
Fax: (012) 430-5547
E-mail: ambipret@iafrica.com

Italy (Italian Republic)
[Embassy]
– during parliamentary session
Website: www.ambital.org.za
2 Grey's Pass Gardens

Cape Town 8001
Tel: (021) 423-5157/8
Fax: (021) 424-5559

Ivory Coast (Cote d'Ivoire) Republic of) [Embassy]
PO Box 13510
Hatfield 0028
Tel: (012) 342-6913/4
Fax: (012) 342-6713
E-mail: ambacr.pret@frenchdoor.co.za

Japan [Embassy]
Private Bag X999
Pretoria 0001
Tel: (012) 452-1500
Fax: (012) 452-3800/1
E-mail enquiries@embjapan.org.za

Jordan (Hashemite Kingdom of) [Embassy]
Website: www.embjord.co.za
PO Box 55755
Hatfield 0007
Tel: (012) 342-8026/7
Fax: (012) 342-7847
E-mail: embjord@embjord.co.za

Kenya (Republic of)
[High Commission]
PO Box 35954
Menlo Park 0102
Tel: (012) 362-2249/50/1
Fax: (012) 362-2252
E-mail: kenrep@mweb.co.za

Korea (Democratic People's Republic)
[Embassy]
7 Salome Court
Bourke Street
Pretoria 0001
Tel: (012) 343-4384

Korea (Republic of)
[Embassy]
PO Box 939
Groenkloof 0027
Tel: (012) 460-2508/9
Fax: (012) 460-1158
E-mail: korrsa@smartnet.co.za

Kuwait (State of) [Embassy]
Private Bag X920
Pretoria 0001
Tel: (012) 342-0877/430-3534
Fax: (012) 342-0876
E-mail: safarku@global.co.za

Latvia (State of)
[Honorary Consulate]
4 Lafeyette Road
Sandton 2196
Tel: (011) 783-9445
Fax: (011) 783-9450
E-mail: neishlos@icon.co.za

Lebanon (Lebanese Republic) [Embassy]
PO Box 941
Groenkloof 0027
Tel: (012) 346-7020
Fax: (012) 346-7022
E-mail: stelebsa@iafrica.com

Lesotho (Kingdom of)
[High Commission]
PO Box 55817
Arcadia 0007
Tel: (012) 460-7648
Fax: (012) 460-7649
E-mail: lesothoh@global.co.za

Liberia (Republic of)
[Embassy]
PO Box 25917
Monument Park 0105
Tel: (012) 342-2242
Fax: (012) 342-2306
E-mail: libempta@pta.lia.net

Libya (Socialist People's Libyan Arab Jamahirya)
[Libyan Arab People's Bureau]
PO Box 40388
Arcadia 0007
Tel: (012) 342-3902
E-mail: (012) 342-3904
E-mail: libyansaf@yebo.co.za

Lithuania (Republic of)
[Honorary Consulate]
PO Box 1737
Houghton 2041
Tel: (011) 486-3660
Fax: (011) 486-3650
E-mail: lietuvos@iafrica.com

Lithuania (Republic of)
[Honorary Consulate]
PO Box 596
Cape Town 8000
Tel: (021) 419-6153
Fax: (021) 419-7411
E-mail: smiewitz@iafrica.com

Luxembourg (Grand Duchy of) [Honorary Consulate]
PO Box 78922

Sandton 2146
Tel: (011) 463-1744
Fax: (011) 463-3269
E-mail: motlana@iafrica.com

Madagascar (Republic of)
[Consulate-General]
PO Box 786098
Sandton 2146
Tel: (011) 442-3322
Fax: (011) 442-6660
E-mail: bauno@infodoor.co.za

Malawi (Republic of)
[High Commission]
PO Box 11172
Hatfield 0028
Tel: (012) 342-1759
Fax: (012) 342-0147
E-mail: mhc@easun.co.za

Malaysia [High Commission]
PO Box 11673
Hatfield 0028
Tel: (012) 342-5990/3
Fax: (012) 430-7773
E-mail: mwpretoria@ishoppe.co.za

Maldives (Republic of)
[Honorary Consulate]
PO Box 398
Plumstead 7801
Tel: (021) 761-5038/797-9940
Fax: (021) 761-5039

Mali (Republic of) [Embassy]
876 Pretorius Street (Block B)
Arcadia 0083
Tel: (012) 342-7464/0676
Fax: (012) 342-0670
E-mail: malipta@iafrica.com

Malta (Republic of)
[Honorary Consulate]
PO Box 1351
Morningside 2057
Tel: (011) 706-3052
Fax: (011) 706-0301
E-mail: maltaconsulate@intekom.co.za

Mauritius (Republic of)
[High Commission]
1163 Pretorius Street
Hatfield 0083
Tel: (012) 342-1283/4
Fax: (012) 342-1286
E-mail: mhcpta@smartnet.co.za

Mexico (United Mexican State) [Embassy]
PO Box 9077
Pretoria 0001
Tel: (012) 362-2822/29
Fax: (012) 362-1380
E-mail: embamexza@mweb.co.za

Morocco (Kingdom of)
[Embassy]
PO Box 12382
Hatfield 0028
Tel: (012) 343-0230/49
Fax: (012) 342-0613
E-mail: sifmapre@icon.co.za

Mozambique (Republic of)
[High Commission]
PO Box 40750
Arcadia 0007
Tel: (012) 401-0300
Fax: (012) 326-6388
E-mail: highcomm@iafrica.com

Myanmar (Union of)
[Embassy]
PO Box 12121
Queenswood 0121
Tel: (012) 341-5207/3985
Fax: (012) 341-3867
E-mail: euompta@global.co.za

Namibia (Republic of)
[High Commission]
PO Box 29806
Sunnyside 0132
Tel: (012) 481-9100
Fax: (012) 343-7294

Netherlands (The Royal)
[Embassy]
Website: www.dutchembassy.co.za
PO Box 117
Pretoria 0001
Tel: (012) 344-3910/5
Fax: (012) 343-9950
E-mail: nlgovpre@cis.co.za

Netherlands (The Royal)
[Embassy]
– during parliamentary session
PO Box 346
Cape Town 8000
Tel: (021) 421-5660/3
Fax: (021) 418-2690
E-mail: nlgovkaa@cis.co.za

New Zealand
[High Commission]
Website: www.immigration.govt.nz
Private Bag X17
Hatfield 0028
Tel: (012) 342-8656
Fax: (012) 342-8640
E-mail: nzhc@global.co.za

Nigeria (Federal Republic of) [High Commission]
PO Box 27332
Sunnyside 0132
Tel: (012) 342-0805/0663/8
Fax: (012) 342-0718
E-mail: nhep@iafrica.com

Norway (Kingdom of)
[Royal Norwegian Embassy]
PO Box 11612
Hatfield 0028
Tel: (012) 342-6100
Fax: (012) 342-6099
E-mail: embpta@noramb.co.za

Norway (Kingdom of)
[Royal Norwegian Embassy]
– during parliamentary session
PO Box 5620
Cape Town 8000
Tel: (021)425-1687
Fax: (021) 419-3568
E-mail: embctn@noramb.co.za

Oman (Sultanate of)
[Commercial Office]
PO Box 2142
Fourways 2055
Tel: (011) 884-0999
Fax: (011) 884-0835
E-mail: sultanateofoman@mweb.co.za

Pakistan (Islamic Republic of) [High Commission]
PO Box 11803
Hatfield 0083
Tel: (012) 362-4072
Fax: (012) 362-3967
E-mail: pakicom@global.co.za

Palestine National Authority
[Embassy]
PO Box 56021
Arcadia 0007
Tel: (012) 342-6411
Fax: (012) 342-6412
E-mail: palembsa@intekom.co.za

Panama (Republic of)
[Embassy]
2nd Floor Dover House
44 Orange Street
Cape Town 8001
Tel: (012) 426-0691/2
Fax: (012) 426-0693
E-mail: ptyembsa@infotech.co.za

Paraguay (Republic of)
[Embassy]
PO Box 95774
Waterkloof 0145
Tel: (012) 347-1047/8
Fax: (012) 347-0403
E-mail: embapar@iafrica.com

Peru (Republic of)
[Embassy]
PO Box 907
Groenkloof 0027
Tel: (012) 342-2390/1
Fax: (012) 342-4944
E-mail: emperu@iafrica.com

Phillipines (Republic of The)
[Embassy]
PO Box 2562
Brooklyn 0075
Tel: (012) 346-0451/2
Fax: (012) 346-0454
E-mail: pretoriape@mweb.co.za

Poland (Republic of)
[Embassy]
PO Box 12277
Queenswood 0121
Tel: (012) 430-2631/2
Fax: (012) 430-2608
E-mail: amb.pol@pixie.co.za

Portugal (Republic of)
[Embassy]
PO Box 27102
Sunnyside 0132
Tel: (012) 341-2340/1/2
Fax: (012) 341-3975
E-mail: portemb@satis.co.za

Portugal (Republic of)
[Embassy]
– during parliamentary session
PO Box 314
Cape Town 8000
Tel: (021) 421-4560/2
Fax: (021) 425-4809

Qatar (State of)
[Embassy]
355 Charles Street
Arcadia 0007
Tel: (012) 346-4329

Romania (Republic of)
[Embassy]
PO Box 11295
Brooklyn 0011
Tel: (012) 460-6940/1
Fax: (012) 460-6947
E-mail: romembsa@global.co.za

Russian Federation (The)
[Embassy]
PO Box 6743
Pretoria 0001
Tel: (012) 362-1337/8
Fax: (012) 362-0116
E-mail: ruspospa@mweb.co.za

Rwanda (Republic of)
[Embassy]
PO Box 55224
Arcadia 0007
Tel: (012) 460-0709/361/403
Fax: (012) 460-0708
E-mail: rwasap@rwanda.co.za

Sao Tome e Principe (Democratic Republic of)
[Honorary Consulate]
PO Box 28
Franschoek 7690
Tel: (021) 876-2494
Fax: (021) 876-3237
E-mail: office@chamonix.co.za

Saudi Arabia (Kingdom of)
[Royal Embassy]
PO Box 13930
Hatfield 0028
Tel: (012) 362-4230/4242
Fax: (012) 362-4230/4248
E-mail: reosa4@lantic.net

Senegal (Republic of)
[Embassy]
PO Box 2948
Brooklyn Square 0075
Tel: (012) 460-5263
Fax: (012) 346-5550
E-mail: rosenhos@mweb.co.za

Serbia and Montenegro
[Embassy]
Po Box 13026
Hatfield 0028
Tel: (012) 460-5626/6103
Fax: (012) 460-6003

Seychelles (Republic of)
[High Commission]
PO Box 12337
Hatfield 0028
Tel: (012) 342-0534
Fax: (012) 342-0362
E-mail: mwhicom@iafrica.com

Singapore (Republic of)
[High Commission]
PO Box 11809
Hatfield 0028
Tel: (012) 430-6035
Fax: (012) 342-4425
E-mail: spore@cis.co.za

Slovakia (Slovak Republic)
[Embassy]
PO Box 12736
Hatfield 0028
Tel: (012) 342-2051/2
Fax: (012) 342-3688
E-mail: slovakem@mweb.co.za

Spain (Kingdom of)
[Embassy]
PO Box 1633
Pretoria 0001
Tel: (012) 344-3875/7
Fax: (012) 343-4891
E-mail: embespza@mail.mae.es

Spain (Kingdom of)
[Embassy]
– during parliamentary session
37 Shortmarket Street
Cape Town 8001
Tel: (021) 422-2326/7
Fax: (021) 422-2328
E-mail: conspccabo@mail.mae.es

Sri Lanka (Democratic Socialist Republic)
[High Commission]
Website: www.srilanka.co.za
410 Alexander Street
Brooklyn 0181
Tel: (012) 460-7690/79
Fax: (012) 460-7702
E-mail: srilanka@global.co.za

Sudan (Republic of)
[Embassy]
Website: www.sudan.co.za
PO Box 25513
Monument Park 0105
Tel: (012) 342-4528/7903
Fax: (012) 342-4539
E-mail: sudan@pop.co.za

Swaziland (Kingdom of)
[High Commission]
PO Box 14294
Hatfield 0028
Tel: (012) 344-1910
Fax: (012) 343-0455

Sweden (Kingdom of)
[Embassy]
Website: www.swedeniafrica.com
PO Box 13477
Hatfield 0028
Tel: (012) 426-6400
Fax: (012) 426-6464
E-mail: sweden@iafrica.is.co.za

Switzerland (Swiss Confederation) [Embassy]
PO Box 2289
Pretoria 0001
Tel: (012) 430-6707
Fax: (012) 430-6771
E-mail: vertretung@pre.rep.admin.ch

Switzerland (Swiss Confederation)
[Embassy]
– during parliamentary session
PO Box 1546
Cape Town 8000
Tel: (021) 418-3669
Fax: (021) 418-1569
E-mail: vertretung@cap.rep.admin.ch

Syrian Arab Republic
[Embassy]
PO Box 12830
Hatfield 0028
Tel: (012) 342-4701/4566
Fax: (012) 342-4702
E-mail: syriaemb@lantic.net

Taipei
[Liaison Office in South Africa]
PO Box 649
Pretoria 0001
Tel: (012) 430-6071
Fax: (012) 430-5816
E-mail: embroc@icon.co.za

Tanzania (United Republic of) [High Commission]
PO Box 56572
Arcadia 0007
Tel: (012) 342-4393/71
Fax: (012) 430-4383
E-mail: tanzania@cis.co.za

Thailand (Kingdom of)
[Embassy]
PO Box 12080
Hatfield 0028
Tel: (012) 342-4600/5470/4516/06
Fax: (012) 342-4805
E-mail: thaipta@global.co.za

Tunisia (Republic of)
[Embassy]
PO Box 56535
Arcadia 0007
Tel: (012) 342-6282/3
Fax: (012) 342-6284
E-mail: asdrubal@mweb.co.za

Turkey (Republic of)
[Embassy]
Website:
www.turkishembassy.co.za
PO Box 56014
Arcadia 0007
Tel: (012) 342-6053/7
Fax: (012) 342-6052
E-mail: pretbe@global.co.za

Uganda (Republic of)
[High Commission]
PO Box 12442
Hatfield 0028
Tel: (012) 342-6031/3
Fax: (012) 342-6206
E-mail: ugacomer@cis.co.za

Ukraine [Embassy]
PO Box 57291
Arcadia 0007
Tel: (012) 460-1946
Fax: (012) 460-1944
E-mail: dniepro@mweb.co.za

United Arab Emirates
[Embassy]
PO Box 57090
Arcadia 0007
Tel: (012) 342-7736
Fax: (012) 342-7738
E-mail: uae@mweb.co.za

United Kingdom of Great Britain and Northern Ireland
[Her Britannic Majesty's High Commission]
Website: www.britain.org.za
255 Hill Street
Arcadia 0083
Tel: (012) 483-1200
Fax: (012) 483-1302
E-mail: bhc@icon.co.za

United Kingdom of Great Britain and Northern Ireland
[Her Britannic Majesty's High Commission]
– during parliamentary session
Website: www.britain.org.za
91 Parliament Street
Cape Town 8001
Tel: (021) 461-7220
Fax: (021) 461-0017
E-mail: britain@icon.co.za

United States of America
[Embassy]
Website: www.usembassy.state.gov/southafrica
PO Box 9536
Pretoria 0001
Tel: (012) 342-1048
Fax: (012) 342-2244/2199
E-mail: ptalib@pd.state.gov

United States of America
[Embassy]
– during parliamentary session
Website: www.usembassy.state.gov/southafrica
PO Box 6773
Roggebaai 8012
Tel: (021) 421-4280
Fax: (021) 425-4151/421-4269
E-mail: ptalib@pd.state.gov

Uruguay (Oriental Republic of) [Embassy]
Website: www.uruguay.co.za
PO Box 3247
Pretoria 0001
Tel: (012) 362-6521/2
Fax: (012) 362-6523
E-mail: urusud@pixie.co.za

Uruguay (Oriental Republic of) [Embassy]
– during parliamentary session
Website: www.uruguay.co.za
PO Box 4774
Cape Town 8000
Tel: (021) 425-1847
Fax: (021) 425-3308
E-mail: conursud@iafrica.com

Venezuela (Republic of)
[Embassy]
PO Box 11821
Hatfield 0028
Tel: (012) 362-6593
Fax: (012) 362-6591

Vietnam (Socialist Republic of) [Embassy]
Website: www.vietnam.co.za
PO Box 13692
Hatfield 0028
Tel: (012) 362-8119
Fax: (012) 362-8115
E-mail: vnto@worldonline.co.za

Yemen (Republic of)
[Embassy]
Website:
www.yemenembassy.org.za
PO Box 13343
Hatfield 0028
Tel: (012) 430-9044
Fax: (012) 430-9100
E-mail: ghamdan@tla.lia.net

Yugoslavia (Federal Republic of) [Embassy]
PO Box 13026
Hatfield 0028
Tel: (012) 460-5626/6103
Fax: (012) 460-6003
E-mail:
yuembpta@worldonline.co.za

Zambia (Republic of)
[High Commission]
Website:
www.zamnet.zm/zamnet
PO Box 12234
Hatfield 0028
Tel: (012) 326-1854
Fax: (012) 326-2140
E-mail: zahpta@mweb.co.za

Zimbabwe (Republic of)
[High Commission]
PO Box 55140
Arcadia 0007
Tel: (012) 342-5125
Fax: (012) 342-5126
E-mail: zimpret@lantic.co.za

Representatives of the Republic of South Africa abroad

African Union and United Nations Economic Commission for Africa
[South African Mission]
PO Box 1091
Addis Ababa
Tel: 09251 171 30415
Fax: 09251 171 1330
E-mail:
sa.embassy.addis@telekom.net.et

Algeria (Democratic People's Republic of)
[South African Embassy]
30 Rue Capitan Hocine Slimane
El Biar Algiers 16000
Tel: 092132 123 0384
Fax: 092132 123 0827
E-mail: sae@gecos.net

Angola (Republic of)
[South African Embassy]
Caixa Postal 6212
Luanda
Tel: 092442 33 0593/4189/9126
Fax: 092442 39 8730
E-mail: saemb.ang@netangola.com

Argentina (Republic of)
[South African Embassy]
Avenida Marcelo T de Alvaear 590
Piso 8 Capital Federal
Buenos Aires 1050
Tel: 0954 11 4317 2900
Fax: 0954 11 4317 2951
E-mail: embasa@ciudad.com.ar

Australia
[South African High Commission]
Website: www.rsa.emb.gov.au
Rhodes Place State Circle
Yarrlumla
Canberra ACT 2600
Tel: 0961 26273 2424/7
Fax: 0961 26273 3543
E-mail: info@rsa.emb.gov.au

Austria (Republic of)
[South African Embassy]
Sandgasse 33
A-1190 Vienna
Tel: 09431 320 649351
Fax: 09431 320 649351
E-mail: saembvie.political@aon.at

Belgium (Kingdom of)
[South African Embassy]
26 Rue de la Loi bt-7/8
Brussels
Tel: 0932 2285 4400
Fax: 0932 2285 4430
E-mail: embassy.southafrica@belgium.online.be

Botswana (Republic of)
[South African High Commission]
Private Bag 00402
Gaborone
Tel: 09267 30 4800/1/2
Fax: 09267 30 5501
E-mail: sahcgabs@botsnet.bw

Brazil (Federative Republic of) [South African Embassy]
Website: www.africadosulemb.org.br
Avenida das Nacoes Lote 6
70406-900 Brasilia-DF
Tel: 0955 61312 9500
Fax: 0955 61322 8491
E-mail: saemb@solar.com.br

Bulgaria (Republic of)
[South African Embassy]
Apartment 27 Block 1
Alexander Zhendov Street 1113
Sofia
Tel: 09359 2971 3425/2663
Fax: 09359 2971 3103
E-mail: saembsof@techno-link.com

Burundi
[South African Liaison Office]
BP 3384 Bujumbura
Burundi
Tel: 09257 24 4064/5
Fax: 09257 24 4650
E-mail: gerautenbach@yahoo.com

Canada
[South African High Commission]
Website: www.docuweb.ca/SouthAfrica
15 Sussex Drive
Ottawa Ontario KIM1M8
Tel: 091 613 744 0330
Fax: 091 613 741 1639
E-mail: rsafrica@sympatico.ca

Chile (Republic of)
[South African Embassy]
Website: www.embajada-sudafrica.cl
Casilla 16189 (PO Box)
Santiago 9
Tel: 0956 2231 2860/3
Fax: 0956 2231 3185
E-mail: saembcon@interaccess.cl

China (People's Republic of)
[South African Embassy]
5 Dongzhimenwai Dajie
Beijing 100600 PRC
Tel: 0986 106532 0171/6
Fax: 0986 106532 0177
E-mail: safrican@163bj.com

Congo (Democratic Republic of the)
[South African Embassy]
Boite Postale 7829
Kinshasa 1
Tel: 09243 884 8287
Fax: 09243 880 4152

Cote D'Ivoire
[South African Embassy]
Villa Marc Andr
Rue Monseigneur R ne Koussi
Cocody President
Abidjan 08
Tel: 09225 2244 5963/7534
Fax:L 09225 2244 7450
E-mail: ambafsudpol@aviso.ci

Cuba (Republic of)
[South African Embassy]
Ave Sta no 4201 esq 42
Miramar Plaza
Havanna
Tel: 0953 724 9671/6
Fax: 0953 724 1101
E-mail: rsacuba@ceniai.inf.cu

Cyprus (Republic of)
[South African Honorary Consulate-General]
PO Box 21312
Nicosia 1506
Tel: 09357 237 4411
Fax: 09357 237 7011

Czech Republic
[South African Embassy]
PO Box 133
Prague 10
Tel: 0942 02 6731 1114/2575
Fax: 0942 02 6731 1114/1395
E-mail: saprague@terminal.cz

Denmark (Kingdom of)
[South African Embassy]
PO Box 128
Dk-2900 Hellerup
Copenhagen
Tel: 0945 3918 0155
Fax: 0945 3918 4006
E-mail: sa.embassy@southafrica.dk

Egypt (Arab Republic of)
[South African Embassy]
18th Floor Nile Tower Building
21/23 Giza Street

Cairo
Tel: 09202 571 3034/5
Fax: 09202 571 7241
E-mail: saembcai@tedata.net.eg

Ethiopia (Federal Democratic Republic of)
[South African Embassy]
3rd Floor Nile Tower Building
PO Box 1091
Addis Ababa
Tel: 09251 171 3034/5
Fax: 09251 171 1330
E-mail: sa.embassy.addis@telcom.net.et

European Union
[South African Mission]
Website: http://ambassade.net/southafrica/index.html
26 Rue de la Loi B7/8
Brussels 1040
Tel: 0932 2285 4400
Fax: 0932 2285 4402
E-mail: embassy.southafrica@belgium.online.be

Finland (Republic of)
[South African Embassy]
Rahapajankatu 1A5
Helsinki 00160
Tel: 09358 96860 3100
Fax: 09358 96860 3160
E-mail: saeinfo@welho.com

France (Republic of)
[South African Embassy]
50 Quai d'Orsay 75343
Paris Cedex 07
Tel: 0933 15359 2323
Fax: 0933 15359 2333
E-mail: 10754.1762@compuserve.com

Gabon (Republic of)
[South African Embassy]
BP 4063
Libreville
Tel: 09241 77 4530/1
Fax: 09241 77 4536
E-mail: saegabon@internetgabon.com

Germany (Federal Republic of) [South African Embassy]
Website: http://suedafrika.org
Postfach 080461
Berlin 10004
Tel: 0949 30220 73090
Fax: 0949 3022 073190
E-mail: botschaft@suedafrika.org

Ghana (Republic of)
[South African High Commission]
PO Box 298 Trade Fair
Accra
Tel: 09233 2176 2380/4480/3880
Fax: 09233 2176/4484
E-mail: sahcgh@iafricaonline.com.gh

Greece (Hellenic Republic of)
[South African Embassy]
Website: www.southafrica.gr
PO Box 61152
GR115-10
Athens
Tel: 0930 210 610 6645
Fax: 0930 210 610 6640
E-mail: embassy@southafrica.gr

Hong Kong
[South African Consulate-General]
27/F Great Eagle Centre
Room 2706-10
23 Harbour Road
Wanchai
Hong Kong
Tel: 09852 2577 3279
Fax: 09852 2890 1975
E-mail: sacghgk@netvigator.com

Hungary (Republic of)
[South African Embassy]
Website: www.sa-embassy.hu
PF 259
Budapest 1364
Tel: 0936 1392 0999
Fax: 0936 1200 7277
E-mail: saemb@elender.hu

Iceland (Republic of)
[South African Embassy]
PO Box 3084
123 Reykjavik
Tel: 09354 562 3300
Fax: 09354 520 3399

India (Republic of)
[South African High Commission]
Website: sahc-india.com
B18 Vasant Marg Vasant Vihar
New Delhi 110 057
Tel: 099111 614 9411/9
Fax: 099111 614 3605
E-mail: highcommissioner@sahc-india.com

Indonesia (Republic of)
[South African Embassy]
Website: www.saembassy-jakarta.or.id
Suite 705
7th Floor Wisma GKBI
Ji Jend Sudirman no 28
Jakarta
Tel: 0962 21 574 0660
Fax: 0962 21 574 0661
E-mail: saembpol@indo.net.id

International Monetary Fund and World Bank – Washington DC
[South African Permanent Mission]
Suite 380 3201 New Mexico Avenue NW
Washington DC 20016
Tel: 091 202 364 8320
Fax: 091 202 354 6008

Iran (Islamic Republic of)
[South African Embassy]
No 5 Yekta Street
Vali-e-Asr Avenue
Tajrish
Tehran
Tel: 0998 21270 2866/9
Fax: 0998 21271 9516
E-mail: saemb@neda.net

Ireland
[South African Embassy]
2nd Floor Alexandra House
Earlsfort Centre Earlsfort Terrace
Dublin 2
Tel: 09353 1661 5553
Fax: 09353 1661 5590
E-mail: information@saedublin.com

Israel (State of)
[South African Embassy]
Website: www.safis.co.il
PO Box 7138
Tel Aviv 61071
Tel: 09972 3525 2566
Fax: 09972 3525 3230
E-mail: saemtel@isdn.net.il

Italy (Italian Republic)
[South African Embassy]
Website: www.sudafrica.it

Via Tanaro 14
Rome 00198
Tel: 0939 0685 2541
Fax: 0939 0685 254300/4301
E-mail: sae@flashnet.it

Jamaica
[South African High Commission]
7th Floor First Life Building
60 Knutsford Blvd
Kingston 5
Jamaica
Tel: 091 876 960 3750/4
Fax: 091 876 929 0240
E-mail: sahc@kasnet.com

Japan [South African Embassy]
Website: *www.rsatk.com*
414 Zenkyoren Building 279
Hirakawa-cho
Choyoda-ku
Tokyo 102-0093
Tel: 0981 3 3265 3366/9
Fax: 0981 3 3265 1108
E-mail: sajapan@rsatk.com

Jordan (Hashemite Kingdom of)
[South African Embassy]
PO Box 851508 Sweifieh 11185
Anman
Tel: 099626 592 1194
Fax: 099626 592 0080
E-mail: saembjor@index.com.jo

Kenya (Republic of)
[South African High Commission]
17/18th Floor Lonrho House
Standard Street 762-709
Nairobi
Tel: 09254 2320 63100
Fax: 09254 2320 63236
E-mail: sahc@africaonline.co.ke

Korea (Republic of South)
[South African Embassy]
Website:
www.saembassy.dacom.net
1-37 Hannam-Dong Yongsan-ku
Seoul 140-885
Tel: 0982 2792 4855
Fax: 0982 792 4856
E-mail:
sae@saembassy.dacom.net

Kuwait (The State of)
[South African Embassy]
Website:
www.southafricaq8.com
Block 10 Salwa Street
House 91 Villa no 3

Mishref
Tel: 09965 561 7988/8456
Fax: 09965 561 7917
E-mail:
saemb@southafricaq8.com

Lesotho (Kingdom of)
[South African High Commission]
10th Floor Lesotho Bank Tower
Kingsway
Maseru
Tel: 09266 2231 5758
Fax: 09266 2231 0127
E-mail: sahcls@lesoff.co.za

Libya (Socialist People's Libyan Arab Jamahiriya)
PO Box 1230
Tripoli
Tel: 09218 21333 7006
Fax: 09218 21333 9250

Malawi (Republic of)
[South African High Commission]
PO Box 30043
Lilongwe 3
Tel: 09265 773 722/597/036
Fax: 09265 772 571/771 042
E-mail: sahc@malawi.net

Malaysia (Federation of)
[South African High Commission]
12 Lorong Titiwangsa
12 Taman Tasik Titiwangsa
Setapark
Kuala Lumpur 53200
Tel: 0960 34024
4456/4026/5700
Fax: 0960 3424 9896
E-mail: azmansth@tim.net.my

Mali (Republic of)
[South African Embassy]
c/o Residence Kome
Room 016
Hamdallaye
ACI-2000 Bamako
E-mail: bamako@foreign.gov.za

Mauritius (Republic of)
[South African High Commission]
PO Box 908
Port Louis
Tel: 09230 212 6925/6/8/9
Fax: 09230 212 6936/9346
E-mail: sahc@intnet.mu

Mexico (United Mexican States)
[South African Embassy]
Aportado Postal 105-219
Colonia Polanco

11581 Mexico DF
Tel: 09525 55282 9260/65
Fax: 09525 55282 9259
E-mail: safrica@prodigy.net.mx

Morocco (Kingdom of)
[South African Embassy]
34 Rue des Saadiens
Rabat
Tel: 092 037 706760
Tel: 092 037 70656
E-mail: sudaf@mtds.com

Mozambique (Republic of)
[South African High Commission]
Caixa Postal 1120
Maputo
Tel: 09258 149 1614/0059
Fax: 09258 149 3029
E-mail: sahc@tropical.co.mz

Namibia (Republic of)
[South African High Commission]
c/o Nelson Mandela Avenue
and Jan Jonker Streets
Windhoek
Tel: 09264 61205 7111
Fax: 09264 6122 4140
E-mail: sahcwin@iafrica.com.na

Netherlands (The Royal)
[South African Embassy]
Website: *www.southafrica.nl*
Wassenaarseweg 40 2596 CJ
The Hague
Tel: 0931 70 392 45014/5920
Fax: 0931 70 346 0669/361 4958
E-mail: info@zuidafrika.nl

Nigeria (Republic of)
[South African High Commission]
Plot 676
Vaal Street
Maitama
Abuja
Tel: 09234 9413 3862/3776
Fax: 09234 9413 3829
E-mail: sahc_abuja@yahoo.com

Nigeria (Republic of)
[South African High Commission]
Number 4 Maduike Street
SN Ikoyi
Lagos
Tel: 09234 9413 3862/3776
Fax: 09234 9413 3574/3829
E-mail: safrica@nigol.net.ng

Norway (Kingdom of)
[South African Embassy]
PO Bos 2822 Solli
0204 Oslo
Tel: 09472 327 3220
Fax: 09472 244 3975
E-mail: sa-emb@online.no

Oman (Sultanate of)
[South African Embassy]
PO Box 231
Al Harthy Comples
Sultanate of Oman
Muscat
Oman
Tel: 0968 694 791
Fax: 0968 694 792

Oman (Sultanate of)
[South African Honorary Consulate]
PO Box 171 PC 115
Madinate Al Sultan Qaboos
Tel: 0968 604551
Fax: 0968 604329

Pakistan (Islamic Republic of)
[South African High Commission]
Website: www.southafrica.org.pv
48 Khayaban-e-Iqbal Sector
F-8/2
Islamabad
Tel: 09925 1226 2354/5
Fax: 09925 1225 0114
E-mail: sahcisl@isb.comsats.net.pk

Palestine National Authority
[South African Representative Office]
Website: www.sarep.org
PO Box 567 Ramallah West Bank
Palestine
Tel: 09972 2298 7355/7929
Fax: 09972 2298 7356
E-mail: info@sarep.org

Palestine National Authority
[South African Representative Office]
Al-Hurrieh Building
Doha Street
Gaza City
Tel: 09(0) 970 8284 1313/23
Fax: 09(0) 970 8284 1333
E-mail: info@sarep.org

Peru (Republic of)
[South African Embassy]
PO Box 27-013 L27
Lima
Tel: 09511 440 9996
Fax: 09511 422 3881
E-mail: saemb@terra.com.pe

Poland (Republic of)
[South African Embassy]
IPC Business Centre 6th Floor
U1
Koszykowa 54 Warsaw 00-675
Tel: 0948 22625 6228
Fax: 0948 22625 6270
E-mail: saembassy@supermedia.pl

Portugal (Republic of)
[South African Embassy]
Avenida Luis Bvar 10
1069-024 Lisbon
Tel: 09351 1319 2200
Fax: 09351 1 353 5713
E-mail: ambsa@embaixada-africadosul.pt

Qatar (State of)
[South African Embassy]
PO Box 24744
Doha
Tel: 0974 485 7111
Fax: 0974 483 5961
E-mail: saembdoha@qatar.net.ga

Russian Federation
[South African Embassy]
Website: www.chat.ru/˜soafrica
Granatny Pereulok 1
Building 9
103102 Moscow
Tel: 097 095 540 1177
Fax: 097 095 540 1178
E-mail: southafrica@embassy-moscow.ru

Rwanda (Republic of)
[South African Embassy]
Website: www.saembassy.kigali.org.rw
Tel: 09250 583 185/8
Fax: 09250 511 758
E-mail: saemkgl@rwanda1.com

Saudi Arabia (Kingdom of)
[South African Embassy]
PO Box 94006
Riyadh 11693
Tel: 09966 1456 2983/2982

Fax: 09221 1454 3727
E-mail: embriyad@cyberia.net.sa

Saudi Arabia (Kingdom of)
[South African Consulate-General]
Suleiman Al Tajjel Street
Off Palestine Street
Al Hamra District
Jeddah 21483
Tel: 09 9662 667 0459
Fax: 09 9662 663 1034
E-mail: info@southafrica.com.sa

Senegal (Republic of)
[South African Embassy]
PO Box 21010
Dakar-Ponty
Dakar
Tel: 09221 865 1959
Fax: 09221 864 2359
E-mail: ambafsud@sentoo.sn

Singapore (Republic of)
[South African High Commission]
Website: www.singnet.com.sg˜satrade2
15th Floor Odeon Towers
331 North Bridge Road
Singapore 188720
Tel: 0965 6339 3319
Fax: 0965 6339 6658
E-mail: sinsahc@sahc.iep.net.sg

Slovenia
[South African Honorary Consulate]
Przakova 4
Llubjana 514
Tel: 09386 1200 6300
Fax: 09386 1200 6434
E-mail: janex.pergar@kompas.si

Spain (Kingdom of)
[South African Embassy]
Website: www.sudafrica.com
Bdifficio Lista Calle Claudio Cbello 91-6
cor of Jortega Y Gasset
Madrid 28006
Tel: 0934 91436 3780
Fax: 0934 91577 7414
E-mail: embassy@sudafrica.com

Swaziland (Kingdom of)
[South African High Commission]
PO Box 2507
Mbabane H100
Tel: 09268 404 4651/4

Fax: 09268 404 4335
E-mail: sahc@iafricaonline.sz

Sweden (Kingdom of)
[South African Embassy]
Website:
www.southafricanemb.se
Linnegatan 76
Stockholm 11523
Tel: 0946 824 3950
Fax: 0945 8660 7136
E-mail: saemb.swe@telia.com

**Switzerland
(Swiss Confederation)**
[South African Embassy]
Website: www.southafrica.ch
29 Alpenstrasse
3006 Berne
Tel: 0941 31350 1313
Fax: 0941 31350 1310/1311
E-mail:
ambassador@southafrica.ch

Switzerland
[South African Permanent
Mission in Geneva]
Website: www.southafrica.ch
65 Rue du Rhome
Geneva 1204
Tel: 0941 22849 5454
Fax: 0941 22849 5434/5400
E-mail: geneva-
sa.consulate.itu.ch

Taiwan
[Liaison Office of South Africa]
PO Box 18-140
Taipei
Tel: 09886 22715 3251/4
Fax: 09886 22712 5109
E-mail: saemail@email.gcn.net.tw

Tanzania (United Republic of)
[South African High Commission]
PO Box 10723 Msaki
Dar es Salaam
Tel: 09255 22 260 1800
Fax: 09255 22 260 0684
E-mail: sahcdar@raha.com

Thailand (Kingdom of)
[South African Embassy]
6th Floor The Park Place
Building
231 Soi Sarasin
Lumpini
Bangkok 10330

Tel: 0966 2253 8473/6
Fax: 0966 2253 8477
E-mail: saembbkk@loxinfo.co.th

Tunisia (Republic of)
[South African Embassy]
V Rue Achtart
Nord-Hilton
Tunis
Tel: 09216 7179 8449
Fax: 09216 7180 1918/1170
E-mail: sae@emb-safrica.intl.tn

Turkey (Republic of)
[South African Embassy]
Website: www.southafrica.org.tr
PO Box 30
Eucukesat 06662
Ankara 06700
Tel: 0990 312 446 4056/3626
Fax: 0990 312 446 6434
E-mail: saemb@ada.net.tr

Turkey (Republic of)
[South African Honorary
Consulate]
Alarko Holding Building
Muallim Naci Cad. 113-115
Ortakoy
Istanbul
Tel: 0990 212 227 5200/15
Fax: 0990 212 260 2378/178

Uganda (Republic of)
[South African High
Commission]
PO Box 22667
Kampala
Tel: 09256 4134 3543
Fax: 09256 4134 8216
E-mail: sahc@infocom.co.ug

Ukraine
[South African Embassy]
PO Box 7
Central Post Office
22 Kreschchatik Street
01004 Kyiv
Tel: 0938044 227
7172/4451/34789
Fax: 0938044 227 220 7206
E-mail: saemb@utel.net.ua

United Arab Emirates
[South African Embassy]
PO Box 29446
Abu Dhabi
Tel: 099712 633 7565
Fax: 099712 633 3909
E-mail: saemb@emirates.net.ae

United Arab Emirates
[South African Consulate]
Khaleed bin al Waleed Street
3rd Floor New Sharaf Building
Bur Dubai
Dubai
Tel: 0997 14397 5222
Fax: 0997 14397 9602

**United Kingdom of Great
Britain and Northern
Ireland**
[South African High Commission]
Website:
www.southafricahouse.com
South Africa House
Trafalgar Square
London WC2N 5DP
Tel: 0944 207 451 7299
Fax: 0944 207 451 7284
E-mail:
general@southafricahouse.com

United Nations – New York
[South African Permanent
Mission]
333 East 38th Street
9th Floor New York
NY 10016
Tel: 091212 213 5583
Fax: 091212 692 2498
E-mail: soafun@worldnet.att.net

United Nations – Geneva
[South African Permanent
Mission]
65 Rue de Rhome
Geneva 1204
Tel: 0941 22 849 5454
Fax: 0941 22 849 5432
E-mail: mission@south-
africa@ties.itu.int

**United Nations
(International Atomic
Energy Agency)**
[South African Permanent
Mission]
Sandgasse 33
Vienna
A-1190
Tel: 0943 222 320 6493
Fax: 0943 222 320 7584

United States of America
[South African Embassy]
Website: www.saembassy.org
3051 Massachusettes Avenue
NW

Washington DC 20008
Tel: 091202 232 4400
Fax: 091202 265 1607
E-mail:
executive@saembassy.org

United States of America
[South African Consulate-General]
9th Floor
333 East 38th Street
New York 10016
Tel: 091 212 213 4880
Fax: 091 212 883 0653
E-mail:sacg@southafrica-newyork.net

United States of America
[South African Consulate-General]
200 South Michigan Avenue
6th Floor Suite 600
Chicago IL 60604
Tel: 091 312 939 7929/7932/7143
Fax: 091 312 939 2588
E-mail:
sacgpolchicago@sacg.xohost.com

United States of America
[South African Consulate-General]
Suite 600
6300 Wilshire Boulevard

Los Angeles
California 90048
Tel: 091 323 651 0902
Fax: 091 323 651 5969
E-mail: sacgla@link2sa.com

Uruguay (Oriental Republic of)
[South African Embassy]
PO Box 498
Montevideo 11000
Tel: 09598 623 0161
Fax: 09598 623 0066
E-mail: safem@netgate.com.uy

Uzbekistan (Republic of)
[South African Embassy]
19 A Korakum Street
Tashkent
Tel: 099 9871 137 0171
Fax:099 9871 137 2546
E-mail: mtimcke@mail.tps.uz

Venezuela (Republic of)
[South African Embassy]
PO Box 2613 Carmelitas
1010 Caracas DF
Tel: 0958 212 991 4622/6822
Fax: 0958 212 991 5555
E-mail: rsaven@ifxnw.com.ve

Vietnam
[South African Embassy]

Central Building 3F
31 Hai Ba Trung Street
Hanoi
Tel: 084 4936 2000/1
Fax: 084 4936/1991
E-mail: hanoi@foreign.gov.za

Yemen (Republic of)
[South African Honorary Consulate]
Al Qiyadah Street
Sana'a
Tel: 0967 122 4051
Fax: 0967 122 1611
E-mail: zubieri@y.net.ye

Zambia (Republic of)
[South African High Commission]
Private Bag W369
Lusaka
Tel: 09260 126 0999
Fax: 09260 126 3001
E-mail: sahc@zamnet.zm

Zimbabwe (Republic of)
[South African High Commission]
7 Elcombe Street
Belgravia
Harare
Tel: 09263 475 3147/9/3150/3
Fax: 09263 475 7908
E-mail:
sahcomm@harare.iafrica.com

Legislation

2003 (as at 15 November 2003)
Appropriation Act, 2003 (Act 18 of 2003)
Banks Amendment Act, 2003 (Act 19 of 2003)
Bophuthatswana National Provident Fund Repeal Act, 2003 (Act 13 of 2003)
Constitution of the Republic of South Africa Amendment Act, 2003 (Act 2 of 2003)
Constitution of the Republic of South Africa Second Amendment Act, 2003 (Act 3 of 2003)
Deeds Registries Amendment Act, 2003 (Act 9 of 2003)
Division of Revenue Act, 2003 (Act 7 of 2003)
Electoral Laws Amendment Act, 2003 (Act 34 of 2003)
Exchange Control Amnesty and Amendment of Taxation Laws Act, 2003 (Act 12 of 2003)
Financial and Fiscal Commission Amendment Act, 2003 (Act 25 of 2003)
Food Relief Adjustments Appropriation Act, 2003 (Act 5 of 2003)
Geoscience Amendment Act, 2003 (Act 11 of 2003)
Gold and Foreign Exchange Contingency Reserve Account Defrayal Act, 2003 (Act 4 of 2003)
Insurance Amendment Act, 2003 (Act 17 of 2003)
Judicial Matters Amendment Act, 2003 (Act 16 of 2003)
Judicial Officers (Amendment of Conditions of Service) Amendment Act, 2003 (Act 28 of 2003)
Local Government: Municipal Structures Amendment Act, 2003 (Act 1 of 2003)
National Development Agency Amendment Act, 2003 (Act 6 of 2003)
National Road Traffic Amendment Act, 2003 (Act 20 of 2003)
Pensions (Supplementary) Act, 2003 (Act 8 of 2003)
Promotion of National Unity and Reconciliation Amendment Act, 2003 (Act 23 of 2003)
Public Protector Amendment Act, 2003 (Act 22 of 2003)
Sefalana Employee Benefits Organisation Repeal Act, 2003 (Act 14 of 2003)
Special Pensions Amendment Act, 2003 (Act 21 of 2003)
Usury Amendment Act, 2003 (Act 10 of 2003)

White Papers

2003 (as at 13 November 2003)
Draft White Paper on National Child Labour Action Programme, 29 July 2003
e-Education Draft White Paper, August 2003
White Paper on Traditional Leadership and Governance (Gazette 25438, Notice 2336),
    10 September 2003

2002 (as at 13 November 2003)
Discussion Document towards a *White Paper on Water Services* (Gazette 23377, Notice 538),
    3 May 2002
Draft White Paper on Water Services, October 2002
White Paper on National Commercial Ports Policy (Gazette 23715, Notice 1409), 8 August 2002
White Paper on the Promotion of Renewable Energy and Clean Energy Development: Part One: Promotion of Renewable Energy, 23 August 2002
White Paper on Traditional Leadership and Governance (Gazette 23984, Notice 2103),
    29 October 2002

Index

A

Aardklop 116
ABC's Competitive Index 88
ABSA Group Museum and Archives 124
Abuja Treaty 306, 383
accommodation, tourists 588-589
Accounting Standards Board (ASB) 272-273
Acorn Incubator 181
Adjustments Appropriation Act, 2002 (Act 73 of 2002) 270
Administrative Adjudication of Road Traffic Offences Amendment Act, 1999 (Act 22 of 1999) 632
adolescent health
  see youth, health
Adult Basic Education and Training (ABET) 199, 209-211, 222
Adult Basic Education and Training (ABET) Act, 1998 215
Adult Basic Education and Training (ABET) Act, 2000 (Act 52 of 2000) 214-215, 222
advertising 156-158
  agencies 156
  awards 156-157
  ethics 157-158
  international exposure 157
  marketing communication awards 157
  online and offline 157
Advertising Benevolent Fund 156
Advertising Standards Authority (ASA) 157-158
aerial photography 97
  archive 97

affirmative action 365
Afghanistan 324-325
Afgri 82
Africa
  cellular networks in 138
  foreign relations with 305-311
  radio 144
  trade with 90, 169-171
Africa Day 125, 141
Africa Growth and Opportunity Act (OGOA) 173
African-Caribbean-Pacific (ACP) countries 336
African Connection Project 134
African Economic Community (AEC) 305-311
African elephant conservation 240, 262
African Film and Broadcast Conference 120
African Independent Churches (AICs) 6
African Languages Literacy Museum 120
African Mining Partnership (AMP) 460
African National Congress (ANC) 44-45
  election results, 1994 45
  history 39
African Reference Framework Project 96
African Renaissance 32, 46-47, 315, 320
Africans 1
African Solutions Network 415
African Telecommunications Union (ATU) 134
African Union (AU) 47, 305-311, 440
African Window
  see National Cultural

  History Museum
Africare 88
Afrikaans
  Afrikaans: Buro van die Woordeboek van die Afrikaanse Taal (WAT) 4
  churches 6
  museum 120, 122, 594
  National Lexicographic Unit 4
  newspapers 150-151
  official language 1-2
  radio 144
Afrikaanse Taalmuseum 122, 594
Afrikaner breed 75
Afrikaner nationalism 39-40, 44
Afrikaners 1
Afrino breed 76
aged, social assistance 392-393
Agency for Career Opportunities, Telkom 136
Agenda 21 69
Aggeneys 18
Agribusiness Confidence Index 88
agribusinesses 87-88
  see also agricultural co-operatives
Agribusiness Promotion and Industry Relations (APIR) 83-84
Agricultural Business Chamber (ABC) 87-88
agricultural colleges 89
agricultural co-operatives 87-88
  see also agribusinesses
agricultural engineering, training facilities 90
agricultural museums 124
agricultural pests 79-80
Agricultural Pests Act, 1983

(Act 36 of 1983) 79, 92
agricultural production
 aquaculture 76-77
 bee-keeping 76-77
 field crops 70-75
 game-farming 76-77
 gross value of, 2002 70
 horticulture 70-75
 input 77
 livestock 75-76
agricultural products 71
 exports 66
 GDP, contribution to 67-68
 standards 81
Agricultural Products
 Standards Act, 1990 (Act
 119 of 1990) 81, 92
Agricultural Research Act,
 1990 (Act 86 of 1990) 89,
 527
Agricultural Research Council
 (ARC) 89-90, 123, 527-530
 ARC-Animal Improvement
  Institute 530
 ARC-Animal Nutrition and
  Animal Products Institute
  530
 ARC-Grain Crops Institute
  529
 ARC-Institute for Industrial
  Crops 529
 ARC-Infruitec/Nietvoorbij
  530
 ARC-Institute for
  Agricultural Engineering
  529
 ARC-Institute for Soil,
  Climate and Water 69, 529
 ARC-Institute for Tropical
  and Subtropical Crops 530
 ARC-Onderstepoort
  Veterinary Institute 92, 530
 ARC-Plant Protection
  Research Institute 529,
  660
 ARC-Range and Forage
  Institute 530
 ARC-Roodeplaat Vegetable
  and Ornamental Plant
  Institute 92, 530
 ARC-Small Grain Institute
  529
 BioStore database 76
 crop estimation
  techniques 71

livestock 75-76
partnerships 528-529
Porcinarium, Irene 123
rural development 528
Agricultural Risks Insurance
 Bill 83
agricultural
 sector/agriculture 65-101
 see also Department of
 Agriculture
 Department of Land Affairs
 bee-keeping 76-77
 business 87-88
 capacity-building
  programmes 88-89
 census, 2003 67
 colleges 89
 credit and assistance
  83-89
 disaster management 83
 drought management 660
 economic empowerment
  88-89
 economy 67-68
 engineering 90
 exports 66, 68
 field crops 70-75
 financing 86-87
 food security 81-83
 game-farming 76-77, 587
 GDP 68
 GDP 2001-2002 162
 horticulture 70-75
 import and export control
  92-93
 labour legislation 203
 Land Affairs, Department
  of 93-101
 land conservation 69
 land distribution 81
 livestock 75-76
 marketing 80-81
 museums 75, 122, 124,
  610
 negotiations 90-92
 pest control 78-80, 92-93
 production 71-76
 production input 77
 research 543
 risk insurance 83
 risk management 83
 risk management
  insurance 83
 schools 89
 Strategic Plan for South

African Agriculture 65-67
 sustainable resource-use
  and management 68-70
 trade relations 90-92
 training and research
  89-90
 veterinary service 77-78
 Western Cape 10-11
Agri SA 67, 87
Agulhas Current 9
Agulhas National Park 238
Ai-Ais Hot Springs Game
 Park, Namibia 17
Ai-Ais-Richtersveld
 Transfrontier Conservation
 Park 17
AIDS
 see HIV/AIDS
Air Force
 see South African Air Force
Air Force Base Zwartkop,
 Pretoria 123
airlines 642
air passenger departure tax
 281-282
air pollution 257
Air-Quality Management Bill
 257
Airport Company of South
 Africa (ACSA) 640-641
airports 640-642
Air-Traffic Navigation Service
 (ATNS) 641-642
Albertinia 591
alcohol/substance abuse
 390-391
Alexander Bay 18
Alexandra 115
Alexandria 13
Algeria 319-320
Algoa Bay 13
Aliens Control Act, 1991 (Act
 96 of 1991) 368
Aliens Control Amendment
 Act, 1995 (Act 76 of 1995)
 367
*Alien Weeds and Invasive
 Plants* 79
Aliwal North 13
allied health professionals
 378
Allied Health Service
 Professionals Council of
 South Africa 373, 378
amaryllis bulb production 74

695

Amalienstein 593
Amanzimtoti 614
Amatola Forestry (Pty) Ltd 188
Americas
　foreign relations with 329-331
　trade with 172-173
A nation at work for a better life for all 224
ANC Youth League, history 40
Anglo-Boer/South African War of 1899-1902 Project
　history 37-38
　Museum 122, 124
Angola 8, 311-312
Angora goat-farming 13, 76
Angus breed 75
animal, national
　see national animal
Animal Disease Information System for South Africa 78
animal diseases, control of 77-78
Animal Diseases Act, 1984 (Act 35 of 1984) 77, 92
Animal Health Act, 2002 (Act 7 of 2002) 77
animal products
　agricultural production, 2002 70
　import and export 92-93
Antarctica
　mapping of 96
　research 542-543
　South African National Antarctic Expedition (SANAE) 542
　South African National Antarctic Programme (SANAP) 542
anthem
　see national anthem
anti-retroviral treatment, rape victims 386
apartheid
　ending of 42-44
　history of 40-42
　Museum, Johannesburg 124
Appropriation Act, 2001 (Act 18 of 2001) 270
Appropriation Act, 2003 (Act 18 of 2003) 270
aquaculture 76-77

aquaria 247
ARC
　see Agricultural Research Council
architecture 118
archives and heraldry 125
　see also National Archives
Argentina 91
Ariel Technologies 132
arivia.kom 132
armaments 509-512
Armaments Corporation of South Africa (Armscor) Bill 497, 509-510
Armscor Business 509
Arniston 598
Arrive Alive Campaign 631, 633
Arts Alive International Festival, Johannesburg 115
arts and culture
　education and training 112-113
　initiatives 112
　museums 123
arts and culture organisations 108, 110-111
　Arts and Culture Trust 111
　Business Arts South Africa 111
　National Arts Council (NAC) 110
　National Heritage Council 108
　Performing Arts Companies 110-111
　South African Heritage Resources Agency (SAHRA) 108, 118
　South African Geographical Name Council (SAGNC) 108, 110
　Arts and Culture Trust (ACT) 110
　Awards 111
ArtsCape Theatre, Cape Town 111
arts festivals 115-116
Ashton 599
Asia
　foreign relations with 323-327
　trade with 174-175
Asians
　see Indians/Asians

Assegai Awards 157
Asset Management Guidelines 272
Associated Magazines 149
Associated Press 153
Association of Marketers 156-157
Asymmetric Digital Subscriber Lines 136
Atlantic Ocean 10
　Northern Cape 16
atmospheric changes
　see climatic/atmospheric changes
Atmospheric Pollution Prevention Act, 1965 (Act 45 of 1965) 257
Attorneys Amendment Act, 1993 (Act 115 of 1993) 432
Auditor-General 267, 284
Augrabies Falls 17
Augrabies Falls National Park 17, 237, 600
Australasia, trade with 174-175
Australia 85
　foreign relations with 325-326
　trade with 174
Australian Agency for International Development 85
Austria 333
Automated Fingerprint Identification System (AFIS) 423, 491-493
Autopage Cellular 138
aviation 640-642
aviation safety/security 642
Awesome Africa Music Festival, Durban 116
Ayrshire breed 75
Azanian People's Organisation 45

B

Bakone Malapa Museum, Polokwane 26, 124
balance of payments 166-167
　financial account of, 1996-2002 164
Banana Express 614
Band A households
　food security 81-82

696

banking industry 290-291
Banks Amendment Act, 2003 (Act 19 of 2003) 271
Baobab tree 108
Bapedi, living museum 26
Barberton 24-25, 608
Barkley West 601
barley industry/production, in 2002 71
Barrydale 599
base minerals 465
Basic Conditions of Employment Act, 1997 (Act 75 of 1997) 201, 203-205
Basotho Cultural Village, QwaQwa Nature Reserve, Harrismith 114
Batho Pele - People First - Campaign 357-358
Bathurst 13
battlefields 124, 615
Battle of Blood River/Ncome Project 112
BDFM Publishers (Pty) Ltd 150
Beaufort West 10-11, 593
beef farming 75-76
bee-keeping 76-77
Beeld 150
Beit Bridge 26
Bela-Bela 26-27, 605
Belgium
 foreign relations with 332
 trade relations with 90
Benelux countries 332
Benguela Current 8-9, 11
Benguela Current Large Marine Ecosystem (BCLME) Programme 252
Benguela Fisheries Interaction Training (BENFIT) Programme 252
Benoni 22
Bergville Maize Milling Co-operative 88
Bethel 25
Bethlehem 18, 603
Bethulie 602
Big Hole, Kimberley 124
Biko, Steve 42-43
Bill of Rights
 see Constitution of the Republic of South Africa
Bill on the Commission for the Promotion and Protection of Cultural, Religious and Linguistic Communities 5
Binational Commissions (BNCs) 169
biological diversity 235-239
 Desert biome 239
 Fynbos biome 238
 Grassland biome 237-238
 Nama-Karoo biome 237
 Savanna biome 237
 Succulent Karoo biome 238
 Thicket biome 239
 values, provinces 236
biomass 479
BioStore database 76
Biotechnology Partnership for Africa's Development (Biopad) 540
Biotechnology Regional Innovation Centres (BRICs) 520
bird, national
 see national bird
Birdlife South Africa 263
birth defects 391-392
Bisho 13
Black Business Supplier Programme (BBSP) 197
Black Consciousness Movement 42-43
black economic empowerment (BEE) 183, 196-197
 electricity sector 475
 energy sector 472
 Land Bank 86-87
 macro-economic strategy 276-277
 SA Post Office 140
 SITA 362
 Ten-Year Review 59
 transport 620-621
Blesbokspruit 23
Bloemfontein 18
 Deeds Office 93, 100
 Macufe 116
 museums 120, 122-124
 Performing Arts Council of the Free State 111
 provincial archives repositories 125
 Supreme Court of Appeal 18
 tourist attractions 602
Bloemhof 20
Blombos Cave 31
Bloubergstrand 591
blue crane, national bird 108-109
Blue Flag beaches 259
Blue IQ projects 21-22
Blue Train 190, 591, 638
Blyderivierspoort Nature Reserve 608
Board of Tariffs and Trade (BTT) 169
Boardwalk, rural craft 119
Boer goat farming 76
Bo-Kaap Museum 12, 589
Boksburg 22
Boland, climate 11
Bond Exchange of South Africa (BESA) 301-302
bond market 301-302
Bonnievale 599
Bonsmara breed 75
Boomplaas Cave, Oudtshoorn 118
Bophirima 20, 606
Bop-TV 145
border control, Ten-Year Review 60
Border Technikon 221
botanical gardens 244-245
Botha, PW 43-44
Botshabelo Mission Station and Traditional Village, Middelburg 114
Botswana 8, 20, 26, 170
 foreign relations with 312
 national parks 16-17
Boxing South Africa 573
Brahman breed 75
Brainworks Incubator 181
Brakpan 22
Brazil
 foreign relations with 331
 free trade agreement with 91
bread basket 11
Bredasdorp 11, 598
Breede River Valley region 599-600
breeding centres 246-247
bridging finance, housing 409-410
Brink, Andre P 116
British Aerospace (BAE)

Systems 189
British colonial era 33-35
Brits 20-21
Broad-Based Black Economic Empowerment Strategy 196-197
Broad-based Socio-Economic Empowerment Charter 456
broadcasters 120-121
broadcasting 142-146
   policy and legislation 142-143
   radio 144-145
   role-players 144-146
   television 145-146
Broadcasting Act, 1999 (Act 4 of 1999) 142-143
Broadcasting Amendment Act, 2002 (Act 64 of 2002) 143
   Code of Conduct for Broadcasters 143
   regional television licences 143
Broadcasting Complaints Commission of South Africa 153
Broadcasting Monitoring Complaints Committee (BMCC) 145
Broadcast Production Advisory Body 143
broiler production 76
Bronkhorstspruit 23, 124
Brown Locust Early Warning System 80
Buddhism 7
Budget Council 275
Budget estimates and revenue outcome 2001/02-2002/03 279, 282
Building for Sport and Recreation Project (BSRP) 566
built environment professions 195
Bureau for Economic Research 541-542
Bureau of Heraldry 125
Burger, Die 149-150
Burundi 318
Burundi Protection Support Appropriation Act, 2002 (Act 3 of 2002) 270
Bus Factory, Newtown, rural craft 119
bus transport 629-630
Bushman
   see San
Bushveld 25-27
Business Against Crime (BAC) 497
Business Arts South Africa (BASA) 110-111
Business Day 111, 147, 150
Business Express 168
Business Partners Ltd 186-187

C

cabbages production 73
Cabinet 343-344
   as on 1 Dec 2003 344
Cable News Network Award for Best Report 155
Cadastral Information System (CIS) 94
cadastral spatial data 94-96
Cairns Group 90, 175-176
Calabash 116
Caledon 11, 73, 599
Calitzdorp 592-593
Call of South Africa
   see national anthem
Camperdown 73
Canada 329-330
cancer screening 388
Cango Caves 10-11
Cannes International Advertising Festival 157
Capacity-Building Task Team 404
Cape Agulhas 8
Cape Argus 150
Cape Colony 35
Cape Craft and Design Institute 120
Cape Malays 34
Cape Metropolitan Area, tourist attractions 589-592
Cape parrot 262
Cape Peninsula
   climate 11
   National Park 590
   University of Technology 221
Cape Point 12, 590
Cape Talk MW 144
Cape Technikon 221
Cape Times 150
Cape Town 11
   agriculture 76
   air pollution 257
   ArtsCape Theatre 111
   City Ballet 117
   Deeds Office 93, 100
   harbour/port 10, 645
   International Airport 10
   International Convention Centre 12
   Kirstenbosch National Botanical Garden 12, 244-245
   museums 122-123
   North Sea Jazz Festival 116-117
   provincial archives repositories 125
   rainfall 9
   Table Mountain 10, 12
   Two Oceans Aquarium 247
   University of Cape Town Ballet Company 117
   urban renewal projects 115
Cape Town International Convention Centre 12
Capricorn district 605
Care Dependency Grants 552
Caribbean 330
Carnarvon 16
Carolina 25
Cartographic Renaissance 98
Catholic Newspapers & Pub Co Ltd 151
Cato Manor 612
   urban renewal projects 414
cattle
   livestock numbers, 2001-2002 75
   ranches 75
Caxton 149
Caxton Publishers and Printers Ltd 150
Cedara Agricultural College 89
Cedarberg 74
Cell C 131, 137-138
cellular networks
   see mobile communications
censors 121

Census 2001 1
Central Africa 318-319
Central Drug Authority (CDA) 391, 491, 561
Central Karoo region 13, 593-600
Centre for Public-Service Innovation (CPSI) 358
Centres of Excellence (CoEs), Telkom 137
Ceres 73, 599
Chamber of Mines 461-462
Channel Africa 144
Charolais breed 75
cheetah conservation 240
chemicals 259-260
chemical industry 259-260
Chemin Incubator 181
Chief Albert Luthuli Legacy Project, Stanger 112
Child Care Act 1983 (Act 74 of 1983) 551
child/children
  abuse/neglect 558
  employment 204-205
  in prison 558
  Integrated Justice System Project 338
  labour, eradication of 204-205
  missing, web site 491
  services for HIV-infected 556-557
  social assistance 558
  support grants 550, 552
Child Justice Bill 426
Child Justice Courts 426
Child Labour Intersectoral Group 202
Child Support Grants (CSGs) 550, 552
China 90-91
Choice on Termination of Pregnancy Act, 1996 (Act 93 of 1996) 388
Chris Hani Baragwanath Hospital 22, 381
Chris Hani district 70
Christian churches 5-7
Christiana 20
chronic diseases 392-393
Church Square, Pretoria 22
churches 5-7
  African traditionalists 7
  Afrikaans churches 6

Christian churches 5-7
  Roman Catholic Church 6-7
  Zion Christian Church 6
cinema attendance 121
Cinema Nouveau 121
Citizen, The 148, 150
Citizen Post Offices (CPOs) 134
Citizen Satisfaction Survey 358, 364
Citrusdal 596
citrus fruit production 73
  in 2002 71
City of Saints
  see Grahamstown
City Press 147, 149-150
civil aviation 640-642
Civil Aviation Authority (CAA) 622-623
Civil Aviation Authority (CAA) Act, 1998 (Act 40 of 1998) 623
civil courts 431
civil jurisdiction 430-431
Clanwilliam 596
  rock heritage project 119
Clarens 603
Classic FM 144
climatic features, of South Africa 9
clinics 378
Clocolan 603
Coastal Management Bill 251, 258
Coega IDZ 14, 179-180, 234
coal 482
  mining industry 19-20, 24-25
  revenues from 464
  use in energy supply 467-468
COALlink 637
coastal and marine environment 247-252
coastal and marine research 247-248, 545-546
coasts 247-248
  of South Africa 8
  temperatures 9
Coast-to-Coast highway 21
Coat of Arms
  see National Coat of Arms
Code of Advertising Practice 158

Code of Conduct for Broadcasters 143
Code of Conduct on the Employment of People with Disabilities 203
Code of Good Practice Key Aspects of HIV/AIDS and Employment 203
Codex Alimentarius 83
Coert Steynberg Museum, Pretoria 122
Coffee Bay 604
Colesberg 16
Collect-a-Can project 260
Collective Investment Schemes Control Act, 2002 (Act 45 of 2002) 271
Collondale Cannery 74
coloureds 1
Commission for Conciliation, Mediation and Arbitration (CCMA) 202
Commission for International Trade Administration (CITA) 169
Commission on Gender Equality (CGE) 437-438
Commission on the Restitution of Land Rights 101
Commonwealth 337, 440
Commonwealth Business Council 179
Commonwealth Heads of Government Meeting (CHOGM) 337
Commonwealth Writers Prize for Africa 116
Communal Land Rights Bill 100
communications and culture
  access to, Ten-Year Review 58
Communist Party (CP)
  history of 39
community
  Courts 421
  policing, Ten-Year Review 60
community-based care
  HIV/AIDS 387, 555-556
Community-Based Public Works Programme (CBPWP) 192-193
Community Development

Workers (CDWs) 356-357
community forestry 670-671
community health 382-394
  alcohol/drug abuse
    390-391
  birth defects 391-392
  chronic diseases,
  disabilities and geriatrics
    392-393
  consumer goods 394
  HIV/AIDS 385-387
  Integrated Management of
    Childhood Illnesses
    382-383
  malaria 383
  mental health 393
  occupational health 393
  polio and measles 382
  quarantinable diseases
    394
  reproductive health
    387-389
  tobacco control 389-390
  traditional medicine 389
  tuberculosis 384-385
  violence against women
    391
  violence prevention 391
community involvement, of
  SAPS 492
Community Press Association
  of Southern Africa 148, 152
Community Production
  Centres (CPCs) 192-193
community radio stations
  144
Community Reinvestment
  (Housing) Bill 402
Community Safety Centres
  493
community service 377
Community Services Network
  145
Community Water Supply
  and Sanitation (CWSS)
  Programme 653-654
Companies Act, 1973 (Act 61
  of 1973)
  Performing Arts
    Companies 110
Companies and Intellectual
  Property Registration Office
  (CIPRO) 192
Compensation for
  Occupational Injuries and

Diseases Act, 1993 (Act 30
  of 1993) 393
Competition Act, 1998 (Act
  89 of 1998) 182-183
Competition Appeal Court
  183
Competition Board 183
Competition Commission
  183
competition policy 182-183
Competition Second
  Amendment Act, 2000 (Act
  39 of 2000) 183
Competition Tribunal 183
Compulsory HIV-Testing of
  Alleged Sexual Offenders
  Bill, 2003 427-428
computer-aided design
  initiative, CSIR 119
Conde Nast Awards 582
Conference on Security,
  Stability, Development and
  Co-operation in Africa
  (CSSDCA) 311
Congress of South African
  Trade Unions 43
conservation areas 240-244
  habitat/wildlife
    management areas 244
  national and cultural
    monuments 242-244
  national parks/reserves
    241-242
  protected land/seascapes
    244
  scientific reserves 241
  sustainable-use areas 244
  wetlands 244
  wilderness areas 241
conservation challenges
  252-261
  air pollution 257
  chemicals 259-260
  climatic/atmospheric
    change 252-253
  coastal management
    258-259
  environment injustices
    260-261
  erosion and desertification
    253-254
  marine pollution 257-258
  recycling 260
  urban conservation 260
  waste management

    254-256
  water quality management
    256-257
Conservation of Agricultural
  Resources Act, 1983 (Act 43
  of 1983) 69, 84, 253
Conservative Party (CP) 44
consolidated housing
  subsidies 406
Consolidated Municipal
  Infrastructure Programme
  (CMIP) 351, 405
Consolidated Municipal
  Infrastructure Programme
  (CMIP) Amendment Act, 2001
  (Act 34 of 2001) 426-427
Consolidated Municipal
  Infrastructure Programme
  (CMIP) Amendment Act,
  2003 (Act 2 of 2003) 342
Constitutional Court (CC) 112,
  428
Constitution Hill Project,
  Johannesburg 112
Constitution of the Republic
  of South Africa, 1996 (Act
  108 of 1996) 52
  Deeds Registries 93-94
  educational rights 209
  freedom of worship 5
  fundamental rights 341
  government 341
  languages/rights 1-5
  law-making 343
  media freedom 142
  preamble 341
  press freedom 142
  Press Freedom Index 142
Constitution of the Republic
  of South Africa Second
  Amendment Act, 2003 (Act 3
  of 2003) 427
Construction Education and
  Training Authority (CETA) 404
construction industry 194-195
  women in 195
Construction Industry
  Development Board (CIDB)
  194-195
Construction Industry
  Development Board Act,
  2000 (Act 38 of 2000) 194
Construction Industry
  Development Programme
  192

Consumer and Corporate Regulation Division, Department of Trade and Industry 192
consumer goods 394
Consumer Magazine Awards 156
Consumer Price Index, 1995-2001 165
Consumer Price Inflation 164-165, 204
control boards 80
Convention on Biological Diversity 69, 92
Convention on International Trade in Endangered Species (CITES) 262
Convention on Persistent Organic Pollutants 255
Convention on the Safe Management of Spent Nuclear Fuel and Radioactive Waste 254
Convention to Combat Desertification (CCD) 69, 254
Co-operative Bill 88
Co-operative Development Initiative 88
co-operative governance 354
corporates, South Africa 299-300
Correctional Services see Department of Correctional Services
Correctional Services Act, 1998 (Act 111 of 1998) 448-450
corruption 359
  Ten-Year Review 53, 61
Cosmos country 609
Cote d'Ivoire 320
Cotonou Agreement 172
cotton production 73
Council for Geoscience (CGS) 538-539
Council for Medical Schemes 381
Council for Medical Schemes Levies Act, 2000 (Act 58 of 2000) 381
Council for Quality Assurance in General and Further Education and Training (UMALUSI) 211
Council for Scientific and Industrial Research (CSIR) 23, 530-532
  computer-aided design initiative 119
  cultural industries project 114
  development projects 180
  Environmentek 98, 669
  National Product Development Centre 119
  roads 633
  rural craft projects 119
  traditional medicine 389, 531-532
Council for Social Service Professions 373
Council for the Built Environment (CBE) 195
Council of Commonwealth Postal Administrations 142
Council of Culture Ministers 105
Council of Education Ministers (CEM) 210
Council of South African Banks (COBAB) 410
Council of the International Telecommunications Union 134
Council on Higher Education (CHE) 211-212
Country of My Skull 118
Courier and Freight Group (CFG) Pty Ltd 141
courts/legal structures
  Community 421
  Constitutional 112, 428
  criminal courts 432-433
  equality 422
  family 422
  High 429-430
  income tax offenders 421-422
  Magistrate's 430
  municipal 422
  regional 430
  Sexual Offences 420
  Small Claims 168, 431
  Supreme Court of Appeal 429
Court Process Project (CPP) 424
Cradle of Humankind Heritage Site 22
Cradock 13
crafts/crafts industry 119
  Cultural Industries Growth Strategy projects 114-115
Create SA 110
Create SA Project 113
  emerging designers 120
  web site 113
Credit Guarantee Insurance Corporation (CGIC) 177
Cricket World Cup 2003 141
crime/s
  high priority, Ten-Year Review 60
  prevention 423
  prevention measures 487
  prevention, Ten-Year Review 59-60
  statistics, 2002/2003 496
Crime Intelligence 491
Crime, Violence and Injury Lead Programme 391
criminal courts 432-433
criminal jurisdiction 431
Criminal Justice Cluster 356, 423-424
Criminal Law Amendment Act, 1997 442
Criminal Law Amendment Bill 428
Criminal Procedure Amendment Bill, 2003 428
Criminal Procedure Second Amendment Act, 2001 (Act 62 of 2001) 427
Criminal Record Centre (CRC) 488
CropLife International 77
crop production 67-68
Cross-Border Road Transport Agency (CBRTA) 622-623
cross-border transport 630-631
cross-media control 143-144
CT Media 151
CTP/Caxton Publishers 147-148
Cuba 331
Cullinan 22-23, 610
cultural heartland 609
Cultural Industries Growth Strategy 114-115
cultural industries projects 114-115
Cultural Institutions Act, 1998 (Act 119 of 1998) 122

National Museums Division 122
cultural monuments 242-244
cultural organisations
  see arts and culture organisations
cultural tourism 113-114
cultural villages 114
Culture-Helping-Culture Campaign 111
Curriculum 2005 218
customs duty 280-281
cut flowers 75
CyberTrade Xchange 136
cycads conservation 240

D

Daily Dispatch 150
Daily News 150
dairy breeds 75
dairy farming 75
16 Days of Activism on No Violence Against Women and Children Campaign 391
Defect Warranty Scheme 401
dams 660-661
  major 652
dance/dance festivals 117
Darling 595
Datavia 132
De Aar 16
De Beers Consolidated Mines 18
De Beers Museum, Kimberley 124
Debt Collectors Act, 1998 (Act 114 of 1998) 271
debt management 269-270
deciduous fruit 72, 81
  in 2002 71
declared museums 122
De Doorns 599
deeds
  offices 93-94, 100
  registration 93-94
Deeds Registration System (e-DRS) 99
  properties on, 2001-2003 100
Deeds Registration Trading Account 99
Deeds Registries 93-94, 99
  Document Copy System 94

document-tracking systems (DOTS) 94
DeedsWeb 99
defence
Defence Act, 2002 (Act 42 of 2002) 496
Defence Bill 497
Defence Secretariat 497
Defiance Campaign 42
De Kelders 598
De Klerk, FW 43-44
Demarcation Board 98
Demobilisation Act, 1996 (Act 99 of 1996) 505
Democratic Alliance 45
democratic elections
  1994 44
  1999 45
Democratic Republic of Congo 170
  foreign relations with 318-319
Denel (Pty) Ltd 132, 510-512
  restructuring of 189-190
Department of Agriculture 65-93
  see also agriculture/agricultural sector
  Directorate: Agribusiness Promotion and Industry Relations (APIR) 83-84
  Directorate: Agricultural Production Input 89
  Directorate: Agricultural Resource Conservation 89
  Directorate: Animal Health 77, 89, 92
  Directorate: Domestic Marketing 80
  Directorate: Farmer Settlement and Development 81
  Directorate: Food and Safety and Quality Insurance 78
  Directorate: Genetic Resources 92
  Directorate: International Relations 90
  Directorate: International Trade 90
  Directorate: Marketing 72, 91
  Directorate: Onderstepoort Biological Products (OBP) 78

  Directorate: Plant Health and Quality 79, 81-82, 89, 92-93
  Directorate: Public Veterinary Health 89
  Directorate: Veterinary Services 90
  Inspection Service 69
  institutional capacity-building 89
  pest control 78-80
  Subdirectorate: Key Soil Conservation Works 84
Department of Arts and Culture 104-127
  anthem 105-107
  architecture 118
  archives and heraldry 125
  arts and culture initiatives 112
  arts and culture organisations 108, 110-111
  art festivals 115-116
  coat of arms 106
  crafts 119
  Cultural Industries Growth Strategy 114-115
  cultural tourism 113-114
  dance 117
  design 119-120
  education and training 112-113
  flag 106
  film 120-121
  funding 104
  indigenous languages, promotion of 2
  literature 120
  museums and monuments 121-125
  music 116-117
  national symbols 105-109
  orders 106, 108-109
  photography 119
  policy and legislation 105
  rock art 118-119
  symbols 108-109
  Telephone Interpreting Service of South Africa (TISSA) 3
  theatre 116
  visual arts 118
  web site 110
Department of

702

Communications 129-159
 media 142-158
 policies 130-131
 postal sector 138-142
 telecommunications 131-138
Department of Correctional Services 441-452
 see also prisons, prisoners
 anti-corruption measures 451-452
 community involvement 451
 community corrections 448-450
 incarceration 441-442
 Museum, Pretoria 123
 offenders, categories 443-444
 physical care/hygiene 444-445
 privilege system 444
 rehabilitation services 445-448
 safe custody 441
 safety and security 442-444
Department of Defence
 see South African National Defence Force
Department of Education 209-229
 Directorate: Inclusive Education 223
 education structures 209-210
 financing 213-214
 highlights since 1994 227-228
 HIV/AIDS policy 225
 Human Resource Development Strategy 224-225
 library and information services sector 228-229
 Ministry of Education 209-210
 national and provincial departments 210
 partnerships and international relations 225-227
 policy 214-224
 School Register of Needs 224

statutory bodies 210-213
Department of Environmental Affairs and Tourism 70, 233-263
 see also tourism
 aquaria 247
 biological diversity 235-239
 botanical gardens 244-245
 breeding centres 246-247
 conservation challenges 252-261
 Environmental Impact Assessments (EIAs) 234
 genetic diversity preservation 239-244
 international co-operation 261-263
 mapping 96
 marine resources 247-251
 private-sector involvement 263
 snake parks 247
 state of the environment 234, 252
 tourism 581-615
 tourism policy 582-587
 tourists, hints for 587-589
 zoological gardens 245-246
Department of Finance
 see National Treasury
Department of Foreign Affairs 305-338
 international organisation 334-338
 multilateral diplomacy 333-338
 relations with America 329-331
 relations with Asia and the Middle East 323-329
 relations with Europe 331-333
 South Africa and Africa 305-323
Department of Health 373-395
 community health 382-394
 costs 381-382
 health authorities 373-374
 health teams/personnel 376-381
 legislation 375

medical schemes 381-382
nutrition 394-395
policy 374-376
statutory bodies 373
Department of Home Affairs 366-369
 Chief Directorate: Civic Services 366
 Chief Directorate: Migration 367
 civic services 366
 citizenship matters 366-367
 deportation 369
 migration 367
 permanent residence 368
 sojourn, control of 368
 temporary residence 368-369
 travellers, control of 368
 visas 367-368
Department of Housing 399-415
 see also housing
 capacity-building 403-407
 consumer education 404
 education and training 404
 funding 403
 housing institutions 407-414
 legislation and policy 401-402
 settlement policy and urban development 414-415
 web site 415
 urban renewal 414
 use of DeedsWeb 99
Department of Justice and Constitutional Development 417-441
 administration of justice 417-423
 court and other legal structures 428-438
 crime prevention 423
 human rights 423
 Integrated Justice System (IJS) 423-425
 international affairs 438-441
 legislation 425-428
 restructuring 417-418
Department of Labour 201-205
 see also labour

703

Code of Good Practice 201
Commission for
 Conciliation, Mediation
 and Arbitration (CCMA)
 202
Directorate: Collective
 Bargaining 201-202
Directorate: Employment
 Equity 202-203
Directorate: Employment
 Standards 203-205
Department of Land Affairs
 85, 93-101
 see also land reform
 aerial photography archive
 97
 Branch: Land and Tenure
 Reform 99
 cadastral surveys 94-95
 Chief Directorate: Cadastral
 Surveys 94
 Chief Directorate: Deeds
 Registration 94
 Chief Directorate: Land
 Reform Implementation
 Management and
 Co-ordination 99-100
 Chief Directorate: Surveys
 and Mapping 95-97
 Chief Registrar of Deeds
 99
 Commission on the
 Restitution of Land Rights
 101
 deeds offices 93-94, 100
 deeds registration 93-94,
 100
 Deeds Registry 93-94
 land reform, implementation,
 management
 and co-ordination 99-101
 spatial planning and
 information 97-99
 surveys 96-97
 surveys and mapping
 95-97
Department of Minerals and
 Energy 455-483
 biomass/fuelwood 479
 Chamber of Mines 461
 electricity 475-479
 energy 466-473
 gas 473-475
 mineral wealth 462-466
 mining industry 458-461

renewables 479-481
small-scale mining
 461-462
Department of Provincial and
 Local Government
 see local government,
 provincial government
Department of Public Service
 and Administration
 see also public service
 construction industry
 194-195
 Expanded Public Works
 Programme (EPWP)
 193-194
 strategic asset
 management 195-196
Department of Public Works
 81, 192-196
 Community Production
 Centres (CPCs) 192-193
Department of Science and
 Technology 517-546
 policy 517-522
 research areas 542-546
 research organisations
 540-542
 science councils 522-540
 technology transfer
 519-520
Department of Social
 Development 549-561
 abused women 558-559
 children 558
 disabled 559
 HIV/AIDS 555-558
 legislation 550-551
 non-profit organisations
 (NPOs) 560
 poverty-relief programme
 553-554
 social assistance 551-553
 statutory bodies 561
 youth 558
 women 558-559
 Victim Empowerment
 Programme (VEP) 559-560
 vulnerable groups
 protection 558-559
Department of Trade and
 Industry 168-205
 black economic
 empowerment 196-197
 competition policy 182-183
 consumer and corporate

regulation 192
employment and skills
 development 197-201
enterprise and industry
 development 178-182
public works programmes
 192-196
small, medium and micro
 enterprises 183-187
State assets restructuring
 187-191
trade relations 169-178
web site 196
Department of Transport
 619-648
 agencies 622-623
 civil aviation 640-642
 maritime affairs 645-648
 pipelines 645
 policy 619-622
 ports 643-645
 public transport 627-635
 rail transport 635-640
 road transport 624-627
 Transnet Limited 623-624
Department of Water Affairs
 and Forestry 651-671
 Directorate: Water Quality
 Management 256
 forestry 662-671
 policy 654-657
 Water for All 653-654
 water resources
 management 657-662
 Working for Water
 Programme 79
Deputy Ministers 344
 Arts, Culture, Science and
 Technology 105
 as on 1 Dec 2003 345
Deputy President 343
De Rust 592-593
 agriculture 71
desertification 253-254
Desert Karoo Botanical
 Garden, Worcester 245
design industry 119-120
Detective Service 490
Detective Service and Crime
 Intelligence 488
Development Bank of
 Southern Africa (DBSA)
 292-293
Development Bank of
 Southern Africa Act, 1997

(Act 13 of 1997) 292
development co-operation 315
Development Facilitation Act, 1995 (Act 67 of 1995) 98
Diamond Fields Advertiser 150
diamond mining 20
difaqane 33
Digital Advisory Body 143
Digital Broadcasting Advisory Body 143
Digital Partnership Programme 218
biological diversity 235-239
　desert biome 239
　forest biome 238-239
　fynbos biome 238
　grassland biome 237-238
　Nama-Karoo biome 237
　savanna biome 237
　succulent Karoo biome 238
　thicket biome 239
diplomatic normalisation, Ten-Year Review 60
disabilities 392-393
Disability Grants 552
disabled, social assistance 559
Disability Sport South Africa (DISSA) 572-573
disaster management 355
Disaster Management Act, 2002 (Act 57 of 2002) 355
Disaster Management Programme 80
Disaster Relief Board 561
Discount Benefit Scheme 407
discriminatory laws
　repeal of, Ten-Year Review 58
Dispatch Media (Pty) Ltd 150-151
Disposal Act, 1961 (Act 48 of 1961) 81
Dispute-resolution Centre 570
distance education 221
District Six Museum 12, 589
diversity
　see biodiversity
Division of Revenue Act, 2000 (Act 16 of 2000) 413

Division of Revenue Act, 2002 (Act 5 of 2001) 270
Division of Revenue Act, 2003 (Act 7 of 2003) 270
Dohne breed 76
Dog and Equestrian Units 489
Dolphin Action Protection Group 263
Dolphin Coast 613
domestic airlines 642
domestic expenditure 163-164
domestic output 162-163
Domestic Violence Act, 1998 (Act 116 of 1998) 391, 425, 486
domestic workers, labour legislation 203-204
Doring Bay 596
Dorper breed 76
Douglas 71
Downstream Aluminium Centre for Technology 181
Draft Drought Management Strategy 83
Draft Food Security Bill 82
Draft Mining Titles Registration Amendment Bill, 2003 456
Draft Social Housing Bill 402
Draft Water Services White Paper 656-657
Draft White Paper on e-Education 217-218
Draft White Paper on the Promotion of Renewable Energy and Clean Energy Development 479
drainage and hydrology 661-662
Drakensberg 8, 12, 14-15
　Escarpment 16, 24-25
　tourist attractions 614-615
Drakensberger breed 75
driving licences, credit-card 627
drug abuse
　see also substance abuse
drought management 83
Drug-free Sport Amendment Bill 573
Drug Master Plan 391, 491
Dube Trade Port project 16
Dukuduku 15

Dullstroom 609
Dumping at Sea Control Act, 1980 (Act 73 of 1980) 258, 468
Duncan Village 414
Dundee 15
Durban 14
　agriculture 76
　air pollution 257
　Botanical Garden 245
　Fitzsimons Snake Park 247
　harbour/port 14-15, 644
　industries 15
　International Airport 14, 15
　Local History Museum 123
　museums 123
　provincial archives repositories 125
　Sea World 247
　temperatures 9
　tourist attractions 612-613
　urban renewal projects 115
Dwesa 13

E

Early Childhood Development (ECD) 210-211, 223-224
Early Warning System 274
East Cape Weekend 150
East Coast Radio 145
Eastern Cape 12-14
　agriculture 13-14, 72-76, 82, 84-85, 89
　airports 13-14
　education 13
　fishing 13-14, 248-250
　forests 13-14
　GDP 13
　GGP 13
　harbours 14, 251-252
　industry 14
　land claims 101
　languages 13
　people/population 13
　provincial government as on 25 Sep 2003 346
　sport 566
　statistics 13
　tourist attractions 13, 604-605
　unemployment 13
　urban rural projects 414

Urban Upgrading and
  Development Programme
  (UUDP) 414
Eastern Cape Technikon 221
Eastern Cape University of
  Technology 221
East London
  airport 13
  harbour/port 13
  IDZ 14
  Museum 123, 604
  pineapple-processing plant
  74
  tourist attractions 604
Earthlife Africa 263
Eastern Highlands region 603
EcoLink 263
e-commerce 130
economy
  competition policy 182-183
  consumer and corporate
  regulation 192
  Department of Trade and
  Industry 168-205
  domestic expenditure
  162-163
  domestic output 162-163
  employment and skills
  development 197-202
  enterprise and industry
  development 178-182
  export and investment
  promotion 176-178
  foreign trade and
  payments 166-168
  growth 161-162
  labour relations 201-205
  manufacturing 160-161, 182
  multilateral economic
  relations 175-176
  performance, Ten-Year
  Review 58
  price inflation 164-165
  public works programmes
  192-196
  restructuring of State
  assets 187-191
  small, medium and micro
  enterprises 183-187
  trade relations 169-178
Economy Cluster, Ten-Year
  Review 58-59
EDI Blueprint 191
education/training 209-229
  see also Department of

Education
  access to, Ten-Year Review
  53
  arts and culture 112-113
  departments, national and
  provincial 210
  finance/financing 213-214
  highlights since 1994
  227-228
  HIV/AIDS 225
  Human Resource
  Development Strategy
  224-225
  learners with special
  needs 222-223
  library and information
  sector 228-229
  Ministry of Education
  209-210
  partnerships and
  international relations
  225-226
  policy 214-224
  School Register of Needs
  224
  statutory bodies 210-213
  structures 209-210
Education For All (EFA) 227
Education Labour Relations
  Council (ELRC) 212
Education Laws Amendment
  Act, 2002 (Act 50 0f 2002)
  215
*Education White Paper 3 on
  Higher Education (1997)* 214
*Education White Paper 3 on
  Higher Education:
  Programme for the
  Transformation of Higher
  Education* 220
*Education White Paper 4 on
  Further Education and
  Training (1998)* 214
*Education White Paper 5 on
  Early Childhood
  Development* 223
*Education White Paper 6 on
  Special Needs Education:
  Building an Inclusive
  Education and Training
  System* 223
EduPlant 671
e-Education 217-218
e-Gateway project 358
Egoli

  see Johannesburg
EgoliBio 181
e-Government Act 361
e-government services 130
  Draft 2-Government Policy
  361
Egypt 320-321
e-Justice Programme
  424-425
Elands Bay 597
elections 354-354
electricity 475-478
  access to, Ten-Year Review
  53
  co-operation 477
  distribution industry,
  restructuring 198, 476
  mini-grid hybrid systems
  478
  supply industry,
  restructuring 190, 475-476
Electronic Communications
  and Transactions Act, 2002
  (Act 25 of 2002) 130
elephant's trunk 16
Elgin 599
Elim 598
Elliot 12
Elsenburg Agricultural
  College 89
eMakhosini Valley 613
emergency housing 405
Emergency Housing Policy
  405
emerging farmers 80, 85
emigrants' funds 300
employment and skills
  development 197-201
  Ten-Year Review 58
Employment Conditions
  Commission (ECC) 202-203
employment creation,
  challenges facing SA
  Government 62
Employment Equity Act, 1998
  (Act 55 of 1998) 202-203
Employment Equity Registry
  203
Employment of Educators
  Act, 1998 (Act 76 of 1998)
  214-215
empowerment
  challenges facing SA
  Government 62
  in workplace, Ten-Year

Review 59
Endangered Wildlife Trust 263
energy 466-473
 and the environment 482-483
 biomass 479
 coal 467-468
 contribution to the economy 466
 demand 467
 efficiency 466-467
 electricity 475-479
 gas 473-475
 household consumption 467
 hydropower 481-482
 liquid fuels 471-473
 nuclear 468-471
 productive sectors 467
 proposals regarding renewables 479-482
 research 543
 sector, restructuring 190
 solar 480-481
 transport use of 467
 wind 481
Engelenburg House Art Collection, Pretoria 122
English
 English: Dictionary Unit for South African English (DSAE) 4
 enterprise and industry development 178-182
 literary museum 120
 National Lexicographic Unit 4
 newspapers 150-151
 official language 1-2
 people 1
 radio 144-145
Enterprise Organisation 180
Environmental Affairs and Tourism
 see Department of Environmental Affairs and Tourism
Environmental Impact Assessments (EIAs) 234
Environmental Implementation Plans (EIPs) 234
environmental injustices 260-261

Environmental Justice Networking Forum 263
Environmentally Sound Low-Cost Housing Task Team 415
environmental management
 see also conservation
 aquaria 247
 biological diversity 235-239
 botanical gardens 245
 breeding centres 246-247
 conservation challenges 252-261
 energy industry 482-483
 genetic diversity preservation 239-244
 international co-operation 261-263
 marine resources 247-252
 private-sector involvement 263
 research 544-545
 snake parks 247
 state of the environment 234, 252
 zoological gardens 245-246
environmental research 544-545
Equality Courts 422
Equitable Shares Formula (ESF) 213
Equatorial Guinea 318
Ermelo 24-25, 76
erosion 253-254
Eshowe 15
Eskom 132, 475, 541
 restructuring of 190
Eskom Conversion Act, 2001 (Act 31 of 2001) 190
Eskom Koeberg Nuclear Power Station 470
estate duty 281
Estate Duty Act, 1955 (Act 45 of 1955)
Estcourt 15
 Glenbella Project 100
e-strategy 130
e.tv 146
Europe
 foreign relations with 331-333
 trade with 85, 171-172
European Free Trade Association 90

European Programme for Reconstruction and Development (EPRD) 335-336
European Union (EU) 171
 relations with 334-335
 social housing, assistance 412
 Trade Development and Co-operation Agreement (TDCA) 72
 trade with 172
Excellence in Mining Environmental Management (EMEM) Award System 458
Exchange Control Amnesty and Amendment of Taxation Laws Act, 2003 (Act 12 of 2003) 271
exchange control 299-300
exchange rates 165-166
 of Rand 270
excise duty 281
Expanded Public Works Programme (EPWP) 193-194
Export Credit Finance Guarantee Scheme 177
Export Finance Scheme for Capital Projects 178
Extradition Act, 1962 (Act 67 of 1962) 439
Extradition Amendment Act, 1996 (Act 77 of 1996) 418

F

faith-based organisations (FBOs) 549, 558
Far East 85
Family Advocate 433-434
Family Court Pilot Projects 422
family courts 422
Farmers' Charter 70
farming
 see agriculture
Ferrous Metals Industry Programme 533
ferrous minerals 465
Fertilizers, Farm Feeds, Agricultural Remedies and Stock Remedies Act, 1947 (Act 36 of 1947)
 Draft Bill 77
FET Act, 1998

Ficksburg 18, 603
field crops 71-75
　agricultural production, 2002 70
Fietas
　see Vrededorp
Fiji 325
Film and Publications Act, 1996 (Act 65 of 1996) 121
Film and Publication Board 121, 153
film and television
　Cultural Industries Growth Strategy projects 115
film distributors 121
film industry 120-121
　Film and Production Board 121
film offices 120
finance/financing
　agriculture 86-87
　Auditor-General 267, 284
　banking industry 290-291
　Bond Exchange of South Africa 301-302
　Budget Council 275
　education 213-214
　exchange control 299-300
　Financial and Fiscal Commission 275
　financial institutions 292-295
　Financial Intelligence Centre
　financial markets 295-296
　financial sector 285-286
　Financial Services Board 289-290
　gambling and lotteries 283-284
　insurance companies 292
　JSE Securities Exchange 300-301
　macro-economic strategy 276-277
　micro-lending industry 291-292
　monetary policy 286-289
　money markets 296-299
　South African Revenue Service 277-283
Finance Act, 2002 (Act 48 of 2002) 270
financial advisors 294
Financial Advisory and Intermediary Services Act, 2002 (Act 37 of 2002) 271, 294
Financial and Fiscal Commission (FFC) Amendment Bill 271
financial institutions 292-295
financial intermediaries 294
financial markets 295-296
financial sector 285-286
Financial Services Board (FSB) 289-290
Financial Services Ombud Schemes Bill 271
First Rand Group 411
firearms, illegal
　Ten-Year Review 60
First National Bank Dance Umbrella 117
fiscal policy framework 267-269
fish, national
　see national fish
Fish River SDI 14
fisheries, research 545
fishing industry/sectors 8
　commercial 248-251
　Eastern Cape 14, 249
　harbours/ports 251-252
　pelagic fishery 248-249
　real value added 68
　Western Cape 11
Fish River Canyon 17
flag
　see National flag
Flagship
　Institutions/museums 122
flood management 660
flower, national
　see national flower
Foetal Alcohol Syndrome 390
Food and Allied Workers' Union (FAWU)
Food and Trees for Africa (FTFA) 670-671
Food Pricing Monitoring Committee (FPMC) 82
Food Relief Adjustments Appropriation Act, 2003 (Act 5 of 2003) 270
food safety 68
food security 81-83, 554
Food Security Strategy 81
Foodstuffs, Cosmetics and Disinfectants Act, 1972 (Act 54 of 1972) 68
Foot and Mouth Disease (FMD) 77
Foreign Affairs
　see Department of Foreign Affairs
Foreign Correspondents' Association of South Africa 153
foreign relations, with
　Africa 305-323
　Americas 329-331
　Asia 323-327
　Europe 331-333
　Middle East 327-329
　multilateral diplomacy 333-338
　southern Africa 311-315
foreign trade and payments 166-168
forest biome 238-239
forestry industry/sector 25, 27, 662-671
　Department of 651-671
　community-based 670-671
　exports 666-667
　legislation 667-668
　policy 654-657, 664
　real value added 68
　research and training 669-670
　restructuring 188-189
　sustainable management 667
　wood processing 669
　yields 669
forests
　indigenous/high 15, 662, 668
　management 663-668
　planted 668-669
　scrub 668
Fort Cox Agricultural College 89
Foster Care Grants 551-552
Foundation for Education, Science and Technology 122, 525
France 332
Franschhoek 594
free basic water 654
Free Basic Water Policy 654
Freedom Day, celebrations in 2004 111
Freedom of Commercial

Speech Trust 153
Freedom of Expression Institute (FXI) 152
Freedom Park Monument 46
Freedom Park Project, Pretoria 112
Free State 18-20
  agriculture 18-19, 71-73, 75-76, 89
  climate 18
  GDP 19
  GGP 19
  land claims 101
  languages 18-19
  manufacturing 19-20
  mining 19
  people/population 18-19
  provincial government as on 25 Sep 2003 346
  sport 567
  tourist attractions 602-603
  unemployment 18
  urban renewal projects 414
  Urban Upgrading and Development Programme (UUDP) 414
Free State Consolidated Goldfields 19
Free State Land Reform Provincial Office 98
Free State Regional Land Claims Commission 98
Free State Botanical Garden, Bloemfontein 245
Free-to-air television 146
free trade agreements 91
freight/courier services, of SA Post Office 141
Freightdynamics 624
Freight Logistics Solutions (FLS) 636-637
frost, humidity and fog 9
fuel products, trade 473
fuel wood 479, 482
Fuji Photographer of the Year 155
Fund-raising Act, 1978 (Act 107 of 1978) 561
Furniture Technology Centre (Furntech) 181
Further Education and Training (FET) 209-212, 219-220
  colleges 219-220
  Curriculum 219

Further Education and Training (FET) Act, 1998 214-215
Future Airspace Management Efficiency Programme 96
Fynbos 10
  production 74-75

G

Gaabo Motho Cultural Village, Mabopane 114
Gabon 318
Galeshewe 601
  urban renewal projects 414
galjoen, national fish 108-109
gambling and lotteries 283-284
game farming 76-77, 587
  Eastern Cape 14
Gansbaai 598
Garden Route 591-592
gas 473-475
Gas Act, 2001 (Act 48 of 2001) 474
Gas Regulator Levies Act, 2002 (Act 75 of 2002) 271, 471
gas resources/production 472-473
Gautrain Rapid Rail Link 635
Gauteng 21-24
  agriculture 23-24, 72, 74-76
  climate 23
  economy 21-24
  education 23
  GDP 23
  GGP 21
  industry 23-24
  National Land Cover 2000 Project 96
  land claims 101
  languages 23
  manufacturing 23
  people/population 23
  Provincial Administration 98
  provincial government as on 25 Sep 2003 346
  sport 567
  technology 23
  tourist attractions 609-612
  unemployment 21

urban renewal projects 414
Gemsbok National Park, Botswana 16
Genadendal 599
General Education and Training (GET) 209, 211, 218-219
General Freight Business (GFB) 637
General Smuts House Museum, Pretoria 612
genetically modified crops 68
Genetically Modified Organisms (GMO) Act 1997, (Act 15 of 1997) 68
Genetically Modified Organisms and Indigenous Knowledge Systems 92
genetic diversity, preservation of 239-244
  African elephant 240
  Cheetah 240
  Cycads 240
  White rhinoceros 240
genetic modification 68
geographical names 108, 110
Geographic Information System (GIS)
  soil/climate surveys, use in 68-69
geography 8
George 10, 592
  climate 11
  Furniture Technology Centre (Furntech) 181
geospatial metadata 98
geriatrics 392-393
Germany 331
Germiston 22
Getting The Nation To Play 565
Ghana 322
Gill Greenworld 85
Girls' Education Movement (GEM) 217
Glen Agricultural College 89
Glenbella Project 100
global positioning systems (GPS) 96
  TrigNet 95
goats, livestock numbers 2001-2002 75
Godisa National Incubation Programme 521
Gold and Foreign Exchange

Contingency Reserve Account Defrayal Act, 2003 (Act 4 of 2003) 270
Golden Horse Shoe 26
goldfields, discovery of 36
Gold Industry Programme 533
gold mining industry 464
   Free State 19
   North West 20
gold refineries 19
Goodhouse Agricultural Corporation 85
Goodhouse Paprika Project 85
goods transport 631
Gordonia 17
Gough Island 543
Gourits River
Governance and Administration Cluster 362-363
Governance Cluster 356
   Ten-Year Review 52-53
Government
   and communication 353
   co-operative governance 354
   disaster management 355
   elections 354-355
   International Marketing Council (IMC) 353-354
   Public Service 355-356
   structure and functions 349
   Ten-Year Review 50-63
Government Communications (GCIS) 353
Government Employees Pension Laws Amendment Bill 271
Government Information Technology Officers' (GITO) Council 361
Government of National Unity 45
   see also Government, South Africa
Government Printing Works 189, 366
government system 341-369
   Cabinet 343-344
   Constitution 341
   Deputy Ministers 344
   Deputy President 343

   Houses of Traditional Leaders 345
   Government 341
   law-making 343
   Parliament 341-343
   President 343
   provincial government 345-348
   traditional leadership 344-345
Graaff-Reinet 13, 605
Graafwater 596
Grabouw 599
Grahamstown 13
   museums 120, 122-123
   National Arts Festival 115-116
   South African Institute for Aquatic Biodiversity 122-123
   tourist attractions 604
grain-crop production 71
Grant-in-Aid 552
Graskop 608
Grassland biome 237-238
grasslands 609
Great Brak River 592
Greater St Lucia Wetland Park 15, 237
Great Escarpment 8
Great Karoo 10-13
Great Limpopo Transfrontier Park (GLTP) 234
Great North Road 26
Great Trek 34
Green Paper on National Policy on Airports and Airspace Management 640
Green Revolution
   see Unlocking Agricultural Potential programme
Green Trust 263
Greyton 599
Greytown 73
Groblersdal 25
Groot Constantia 124
Grootfontein Agricultural College 89
Grootfontein Agricultural Development Institute 89
Gross Domestic Expenditure (GDE)
   see domestic expenditure
Gross Domestic Product (GDP) 161, 259

   agricultural sector 67-68
   contribution of tourism 581
ground-nut production/industry
   in 2002 71
groundwater resources 662
Growth and Development Summit (GDS), 2003 46
Guernsey breed 75
Guidelines for Cervical Cancer-Screening Programme 388
Guidelines for Maternity Care 388
Guarantee Fund 302

H

Habitat Agenda 415
habitat/wildlife management areas 244
halfmens
   see elephant's trunk
Hammarsdale 15
Hangklip-Kleinmond area 597
Hansard 3
Harbour Repair and Maintenance Programme 251-252
harbours/ports 10, 251-252
Harding 15
Harmony Gold Refinery, Virginia 19
Harold Porter Botanical Garden, Betty's Bay 245
Hartebeesthoek 94 datum 97
Hartebeesthoek Radio Astronomy Observatory 525-526
Harrismith 603
   Basotho Cultural Village 114
Hartbeespoort Dam 79
   Rainbow Cultural Village 114
   Snake Park and Animal Park 247
   tourist attractions 606
Hazardous Substances Act, 1993 (Act 131 of 1993) 468
Hazyview, Shangana Cultural

Village 114
Haymake Investments 85
Heads of Education Departments Committee (HEDCOM) 210-211
health
 see also Department of Health
 access to, Ten-Year Review 53, 58
health authorities 373-374
health personnel/teams 373, 376-381
 registered 373
 statistics 377-378
health policy 375-376
Health Professions Act, 1974 (Act 56 of 1974) 375
Health Professions Council of South Africa (HPCSA) 373
Health-Sector Strategic Framework 373
Healthy Children Are Successful Learners 376
Hector Petersen Memorial Site, Soweto 22
Heidelberg 591
 Grootvadersbosch Nature Reserve 591
Heidelberg 23
Heilbron 603
Hellenic Republic 333
Herald 150
heraldry
 see archives and heraldry
Hereford breed 75
Heritage Chief Directorate 110
heritage reclamation festivals 115
Heritage SA 118
Hermanus 597
Hermanus Magnetic Observatory 527
High Courts 429-430
Higher Education (HE) 220-222
 institutional restructuring 221
 restructuring/transformation 221
Higher Education Act, 1997 (Act 101 of 1997) 211, 214, 220
Higher Education Amendment Act, 2002 (Act 63 of 2002) 215
Higher Education Amendment Bill, 2003 215
Higher Education Quality Committee (HEQC) 211-212
Highlands Meander 608-609
Highveld 25
Highveld Stereo 145
Hillbrow, Old Fort Prison 112
Hindu/s 5
 religion 7
history 30-49
 Anglo-Boer/South African War and its aftermath 37-38
 apartheid 40-42
 British colonial period 33-35
 early colonial period 32-33
 end of apartheid 42-44
 first decade of 44-47
 mineral revolution 35-37
 segregation 38-40
HIV
 see HIV/AIDS
HIV/AIDS
 access to care, Ten-Year Review 53
 care 555-556
 condom supplies 385-386
 in education 225
 government initiatives against 555-558
 home/community-based care 387, 405, 555-556
 Managing HIV/AIDS in the Workplace 201
 Mother-to-child transmission prevention 386
 non-governmental organisations (NGOs) 380-381
 Partnership Against AIDS 385
 Public Service 360
 rape survivors 386
 services for children 556-557
 social housing 412
 Tirisano programme 215-216
 training 386-387
 vaccine 386
 voluntary counselling and testing (VCT) 386
HIV/AIDS Vaccine Initiative, Ten-Year Review 61
Hluhluwe-Umfolozi Park 237, 613
Hluleka Nature Reserve 478
Hoedspruit Research and Breeding Centre for Endangered Species 247
holidays, public 2
Holstein breed 75
Home Affairs National Identification System (HANIS) 367
home-based care
 HIV/AIDS 387, 405, 555-556
 programme 405
Home Loan and Mortgage Disclosure Act, 2000 (Act 63 of 2000) 401-402
homelands
 history 39
 under Interim Constitution 45
hominid sites 31
honeybush tea production 73-74
honey industry 77
Hoodia plant 531-532
Hopefield 595
Horn of Africa 319-323
horses, export of 11
horticulture 71-75
 agricultural production, 2002 70
hospitality industry, restructuring of 189
hospitals 378-379
Hostage Negotiation 489
hostels, redevelopment 402-403
Hottentots
 see Khoekhoe people
house museums 124
Houses of Traditional Leaders 398-415
housing 398-415
 see also Department of Housing
 access to, Ten-Year Review 58
 capacity-building 403-407
 delivery 403-404
 educational training in 404

legislation 401-403
Housing Act, 1997 (Act 107 of 1997) 402, 413
Housing Amendment Act, 2001 (Act 4 of 2001) 401-402
Housing Consumer Education and Training Programme 40
Housing Consumer Education Task Team 404
Housing Consumer Protection Measures Act, 1998 (Act 95 of 1998) 401-402, 407
housing funding 403-404
housing institutions 407-409
Housing Institutions Development Fund 408
Housing Programme 399-401
Housing Scholarship Programme 404
Housing Standard Generation Body (SGB) 404
housing subsidies 404-407
Hout Bay 590
Howick Falls 614
Human Resource Development Strategy in education 224-225
human rights 423
Human Sciences Research Council (HSRC) 534-536
Human Settlement Redevelopment Programme 399-401
hydropower 481-482

I

Ibhayi, urban renewal projects 414
Ifa textile project, Thohoyandou 119
Ilanga 150
illiteracy 222
Immigration Act, 2002 (Act 13 of 2002) 367, 587
Immigration Advisory Board 367
income tax 278-282
Income Tax Act, 1962 (Act 58 of 1962) 278
Independent Broadcasting Authority (IBA) 131

Independent Broadcasting Authority (IBA) Code of Advertising Practice 153, 158
Independent Broadcasting Authority (IBA) Code of Conduct for Broadcasting Services 153
Independent Communications Authority of South Africa (ICASA) 129-131, 144
  cross-media control 143-144
  training programmes 133
Independent Communications Authority Act, 2000 (Act 13 of 2000) 486-487
Independent Electoral Commission (IEC) 354-355
  Strengthening Africa's Partnerships Conference 354
Independent Electoral Commission (IEC) Act, 1996 (Act 51 of 1996) 355
Independent Newspapers (Pty) Ltd 147, 150-151
Independent on Saturday, The 150
India
  foreign relations with 325
  free trade agreement with 91
Indian Ocean
  Eastern Cape 13
  KwaZulu-Natal 14-15
  Western Cape 10
Indians/Asians 1
  history 35
indigenous forests 10, 15, 662, 668
Indigenous Games Project 569
indigenous languages 1-2
  promotion of, by Department of Arts and Culture 2
individual housing subsidies 406
Indonesia 324
Industrial Development Corporation (IDC) 186
Industrial Development Zones (IDZs) 14
  Coega IDZ 14
  West Bank IDZ 14

industrial minerals 465
Industrial Minerals Industry Programme 533
Industrial Participation Policy and Guidelines 181
information and communication technologies (ICTs) *see also* information technology, communications in education 217-218
information communications technology cluster in Western Cape 12
Information Core for Southern African Migrant Pests (ICOSAMP) network 80
Information Systems Electronics and Telecommunications Technologies Sector Education and Training Authority (SETA) 147
information technology
  aravia.kom 132
  Institute for Satellite and Software Applications 133
  Knowledge Management Unit 132
  Presidential International Advisory Council on Information Society and Development 132
  Presidential National Commission on Information Society and Development 132-133
  State Information Technology Agency (SITA) 132
Inkatha Freedom Party (IFP)
  election results, 1994 45
Inkululeko Project, land redistribution 100
Inland Water Policing 489
innovation and technology 180-181
Innovation Fund 524
Insider Trading Act, 1998 (Act 135 of 1998) 290
Inspection of Financial Institutions Act, 1998 (Act 80 of 1998) 290
Institut Des Hautes et de la Recherche Islamique

(IHERI-AB) 125
Institute for African
  Traditional Medicines 389
Institute for Tropical and
  Subtropical Crops 25
Institute for Satellite and
  Software Applications (ISSA)
  129, 131, 133
institutional housing
  subsidies 406-407
institutional investors 299
institutional support
  framework 184-187
Insurance Amendment Act,
  2003 (Act 17 of 2003) 271
insurance companies 292
Integrated Development
  Plans (IDPs) 97, 352
Integrated Food Security and
  Nutrition Programme (IFSNP)
  81, 554
Integrated Justice System
  (IJS)
  child protection 558
  Ten-Year Review 59
Integrated Management of
  Childhood Illnesses 382-383
Integrated Manufacturing
  Strategy (IMS) 168
Integrated National
  Electrification Programme
  (INEP) 475, 477-478
Integrated Nutrition
  Programme (INP) 395
  access to, Ten-Year Review
  53
Integrated Provincial Support
  Programme (IPSP) 357
Integrated Service Land
  Project 414
Integrated Sustainable Rural
  Development Programme
  (ISRDP) 83, 130, 192
intelligence services 512-513
Intelligence Services Control
  Act, 1994 (Act 40 of 1994)
  513
Inter-African Phytosanitary
  Council 83
Interim Constitution of South
  Africa, 1993 (Act 200 of
  1993) 45, 486
Internal Audit Framework 272
international airlines 642
International Civil Aviation
  Organisation (ICAO) 642
international co-operation
  environmental
  management 261-263
  labour projects 203
  SA Post Office 142
  SAPS 496
  telecommunications
  134-135
  Ten-Year Review 60-61
International Co-operation in
  Criminal Matters
  Amendment Act, 1996
  (Act 75 of 1996) 418
International Criminal Court
  (ICC) 440-441
International Design Indaba,
  2003 120
International Federation of
  Arts Council and Culture
  Agencies 110
International Grains
  Convention 90-91
International Health
  Laboratory Service (NHLS)
  541
International Health
  Regulations Act, 1974 (Act
  28 of 1974) 394
International Investment
  Council 178
International Marketing
  Council (IMC) 353-354
International Monetary Fund
  (IMF) 166, 286
International Network of
  Business Arts Associations
  111
International Plant Protection
  Convention (IPPC) 82, 92
International Science Liaison
  (ISL) 525
International Terrestrial
  Reference Frame 97
international trade and
  economic development 169
International Trade and
  Economic Development
  Division 169
International Trade in
  Endangered Species (CITES)
  417-418
Internet 133-134
  Protocol 136
Intersite 639-640
invader plants, control of
  78-79
Invasive Aquatic Plants 79
Irene, Taurus Livestock
  Improvement Co-operative
  76
Iscor 541
isiNdebele
  *isiNdebele: IsiHlathululi-
  Mezwi SesiNdebele* 4
  National Lexicographic
  Unit 4
  official language 1-2
isiXhosa
  isiXhosa: isiXhosa NLU 4
  National Lexicographic
  Unit 4
  official language 1
isiZulu
  *isiZulu: Isikhungo
  Sesichazamawi SesiZulu* 4
  National Lexicographic
  Unit 4
  newspapers 148, 150
  official language 1
  radio 145
Isolezwe 148, 150
ISRDP/Urban Rural Strategy
  initiatives 134
Italy
  foreign relations with 333
  trade relations with 90
iThemba LABS 526-527
Iziko Museums, Cape Town
  122

J

Jali Commission 451-452
Japan 327
Jersey breed 75
Jew/s 5
  religion 7
JLB Smith Institute of
  Ichthyology
  see South African Institute
  for Aquatic Biodiversity
Job Summit Housing Project
  409
Johannesburg 23
  Arts Alive International
  Festival 115
  Art Gallery 123
  Bus Factory, Newtown 119

Constitution Hill Project 112
Deeds Office 93, 100
International Airport 22, 624
JSE Stock Exchange 24
Lesedi Cultural Village 114
Market Theatre 111, 116
museums 122-124
The Dance Factory 117
tourist attractions 22, 610-611
Wits Theatre 117
Zoological Gardens 246
Johnnic Publishing Ltd 147, 149, 152
journalism awards 154-155
JSE Securities Exchange 24, 300-301
  agribusinesses 88
  listing of Telkom 136
Judicial Service Commission (JSC) 429, 436
Juniorcare 85-86
Junior *Dipapadi* 570
justice
  see also Department of Justice and Constitutional Development
Justice College 433
justice, crime prevention and security
  Ten-Year Review 59-60
justice system 169
  transformation of 417-418
juveniles
  see youth, children

K

Kaapsehoop 608
Kakamas 17, 601
Kalahari 17, 20, 70, 76
Kalahari Gemsbok National Park 16
Kanoneiland 601
Karoo, game farming 76-77
Karoo National Park 237
Kathu 18
Katorus, urban renewal projects 414
Kaya FM 145
Keep South Africa Beautiful 263

Keimoes 17, 601
Keiskammahoek 13
Keiskamma Valley 12
Kempton Park 22
Kenhardt 16, 602
Kenya
  foreign relations with 315
  free trade agreement with 91
Kgalagadi 70
Kgalagadi Transfrontier Park 17, 237, 600
Khaya Lendaba, Port Elizabeth 114
Khoekhoe people 31
Khoi and San National Language Body 4
Khoi
  people 1
  language promotion by PaNSALB 3
  motto, Coat of Arms 106
  National Language Body 4
  rock art 118
Khoisan communities 32-33
  history 31
Khoisan Project 112
Khomanani Campaign 385
Khula Enterprise Finance 59, 184-185
Khubedu Project, land redistribution 100
Kimberley 17
  airport 16
  Big Hole 124, 601
  Deeds Office 93, 100
  diamond mining 18
  museums 123-124
  tourist attractions 601
  William Humphreys Art Gallery 122
Kimberley Process 456
king protea, national flower 108-109
King II Report on Corporate Governance in South Africa, 2002 273
King Shaka, stamps 141
King Shaka International Airport 16
King William's Town 13
  Deeds Office 93, 100
Kirstenbosch National Botanical Garden, Cape Town 12, 244-245

Kirstenbosch Research Centre
Klasies River Caves 119
Klawer 596
Klein 592-593
Klein Karoo 11
Klein Karoo Co-operative 76
Klein Karoo Nasionale Kunstefees, Oudtshoorn 115
Kleinplasie Museum, Worcester 124
Klerksdorp 20-21
Kliptown 22
Knowledge Management Unit 132
Knysna 10, 592
Koekenaap 597
kokerboom
  see tree aloe
Komatiland Forests (Pty) Ltd 188
KoMjekejeke Cultural Village, Pretoria 114
Koppies 19
Koringberg 597
Kosi Bay 15
Koster 20
Krog, Antjie 118
Kromdraal hominid site 22
Kroonstad 18
Kruger House Museum, Pretoria 122-124, 611
Kruger Mpumalanga Airport 24
Kruger National Park 26, 77, 237, 240-241, 262
  tourist attractions 241, 606
Kruger, Pres Paul 124
  Kruger House Museum, Pretoria 123-124
Krugersdorp 22, 610
Kuruman 16, 118, 601
Kwaito music 116
KwaZulu-Natal 14-16
  agriculture 15-16, 70-73, 75-76, 82, 84-85, 89
  airport, Durban 14
  animal diseases 78
  battlefields routes 615
  climate 10, 16
  forests 15-16
  GDP 15
  GGP 15
  harbour, Durban 15
  history 35

industry 15-16
land claims 101
land redistribution 100
languages 15
Midlands region 16, 614
National Land Cover 2000 Project 96
people/population 15
provincial government as on 25 Sep 2003 346
sport 566
statistics 15
tourist attractions 612-615
Unlocking Agricultural Potential programme 16
urban renewal projects 414
Xoshindlala Programme 16
Kyalami 610
Kyoto Protocol on Global Change 92, 253

L

labour
  see Department of Labour
Labour Appeal Court 430
Labour Court 202, 430
labour legislation
  Code of Good Practice 201
  Ten-Year Review 58, 201
labour relations 201-205
Labour Relations Act, 1995 (Act 66 of 1995) 201-202
labour tenants, land redistribution 100
Ladismith/Ladysmith 15, 18
  tourist attractions 593
Laduma 149
Ladybrand 603
L'Agulhas 598
Laingsburg 593
Lake Chrissie 24
Lake Sibaya 614
lakes 662
Lambert's Bay 596
La Mercy 16
land administration/affairs
  see Department of Land Affairs
Land and Agricultural Development Bank 86-87, 293
  see also Land Bank
Land and Agricultural Development Bank Act, 2002 (Act 15 of 2002) 86, 293
land and its people 1-27
  land 8-10
  people 1-7
  provinces 10-27
Land and Tenure Reform Branch 95
Land and Tenure Reform Programme 100
Land Bank 85-87
  see also Land and Agricultural Development Bank
  black economic empowerment (BEE) 86-87
  corporate and development finance 86
  Land Redistribution for Agricultural Development (LRAD), planning agreement 99
  Land and Agricultural Development Bank Bill, 2002
  microfinance 87
  products and services offered 86
  Step Up scheme 87
Land Bank Act, 1944 (Act 13 of 1944) 86
LandCare Programme
  see National LandCare Programme
Land Claims Commissions 95
Land Claims Court 101, 430
Land Cover Classification Standard 99
Landrace breed 76
land redistribution 65, 99-101
  labour tenants 100
Land Redistribution Agricultural Development Grants 85
Land Redistribution for Agricultural Development (LRAD) 86, 99
  Grants and Services Document 99
  Nkomazi Project 99
  Programme 99
land reform
  see also Department of Land Affairs
  Grants and Services Document 99
  Offices 99
  Ten-Year Review 58
Land Type Survey 68
land-use management 97-100
Land-use Management Bill 97-98
Langebaan 595
Langkloof 12
Langkloof Valley 13, 72
language policy 2
languages 1-5
  national language bodies 4
  National Language Policy Framework (NLPF) 2
  National Language Service (NLS) 2, 4
  National Lexicography Units 4
  official 1-2
  Pan South African Language Board (PaNSALB) 3-4
  Pan South African Language Board Amendment Act, 1999 (Act 10 of 1999) 4
  policy 2
  rights, protection of 4-5
  South African Languages Bill 2
  Telephone Interpreting Service of South Africa 3
  usage in government 3
Large White breed 76
Latin America
  foreign relations with 330-331
  trade with 173
Laurence Olivier Awards 116
law-making 343
Law Society of South Africa 432
Lead Programmes Fund 519
Learnership Campaign 198
Legacy Project 112
legal aid 434-435
legal practitioners 432-433
Lesedi Cultural Village, Johannesburg 114
Lesotho 8, 15, 18

food aid to 73
foreign relations with 312
National Land Cover 2000 Project 96
plateau 8
trade with 90
Letaba 73
Levubu 73
Liberia 321
library and information services sector 228-229
Library Association of South Africa (LIASA) 229
Libya 323
Lichtenburg 20
  Game Breeding Centre 246-247, 606
Limpopo 25-27
  agriculture 27, 71-76, 82, 84-85, 89
  climate 10, 27
  economy 26-27
  GDP 26
  GGP 26
  National Land Cover 2000 Project 96
  languages 26
  people/population 26
  provincial government as on 25 Sep 2003 346
  sport 567
  statistics 26
  tourist attractions 26, 605-606
  unemployment 26
  urban renewal projects 44
Limpopo River 8, 25
liquid fuels 471-473
Liquor Products Act, 1989 (Act 60 of 1989) 81, 92
literature 120
livestock 75-76
  numbers, 2001-2002 75
local content
  in media 143-144
local government/s 348-352
  health services 379
  legislation 350
  municipalities 349
  programmes 350-352
  South African Local Government Association (SALGA) 348
Local Government: Municipal Structures Act, 1998 (Act 117 of 1998) 349
Local Government Municipal Systems Act, 2000 (Act 32 of 2000) 350, 352
locusts outbreaks 79-80
Loerie Awards 156
Loerie Education Trust Fund 156
Loskop Dam 79
Lotteries Act, 2000 (Act 10 of 2000)
  sport 567
Louis Trichardt 605
loveLife 380
Lowveld 24-25
  agriculture 72-73
Lowveld Agricultural College 89
Lowveld Botanical Garden, Nelspruit 245
Lowveld Legogote 609
Lubombo Corridor SDI 613
  cultural tourism 113-114
  malaria control 384-385
  rural craft 119
lucerne production 71
Lutzville 597
Luxembourg 332
LuxRail 638
Lydenburg 608

M

Mabopane
  Gaabo Motho Cultural Village 114
Maclear 605
macro-economic strategy 276-277
Macufe, Bloemfontein 116
Madzhivhandila Agricultural College 89
Mafikeng 606
Mafikeng Airport 21
Mafikeng IDZ 21
Magaliesburg
  Tlholego Cultural Village 114
Magazine Publishers Association SA 152
magazines 149
  distribution 149, 152
  sales statistics 149
Magistrates Commission 435
Magistrate's Courts 430
Magistrate's Courts Act, 1944 (Act 32 of 1944) 431
Magwa 13
Mahwelereng, urban renewal projects 414
Mail and Guardian 150, 152
mail volumes 141
Maintenance Act, 1998 425
Maintenance Courts 425
Maintenance Outreach Programme 425
maize meal, subsidised 82
maize production
  in 2002 70-71
Makhado 26-27
Makhosini Cultural Village and Tourism Initiative, Umgungundlovu 114
malaria 383-384
Malawi 170
  food aid to 73
  foreign relations with 313
  trade with 90-91
Malaysia 324
Malelane 24
Malgas 591
Mali 125
  foreign relations with 322
Malmesbury 11, 597
Mamelodi 612
Mandela, Nelson 40, 42, 44-45
Mandeni 15
Mandla Matla Publishing Co (Pty) Ltd 150
Mangethe, land claims 101
manufacturing 182
  Free State 19-20
  Gauteng 23
  GDP, 2001-2002 162
  North West 20-21
Mapoch Ndebele Village, Winterveld 114, 612
mapping
  see surveys and mapping
Mapping Malaria Risk in African Project 383
Mapungubwe Archaeological Site 26, 31, 243
Mapungubwe Hill 26
Maputo 24
  Corridor 24, 26, 625, 630
  Port 21, 26
Maputo Corridor SDI

cultural tourism 113-114
marabi music 116
Margate 15
Marico 21
Marine Living Resources Act, 1998 (Act 18 of 1998) 251
marine pollution 257-258
marine resources
  see also fishing industry
  harbours/ports 251-252
Marion Island 8, 543
  mapping of 96
  scientific reserves 241
maritime affairs 645-648
  administration 645-646
  safety 648
  search and rescue services 646-648
  training 646
marketable securities tax (MST) 281
Market Theatre, Johannesburg 111, 116
marketing/branding
  communications awards 157
  Ten-Year Review 60-61
Marketing Act of 1968 80
Marketing of Agricultural Products Act, 1996 (Act 47 of 1996) 80, 82
Masekela, Hugh 116
Masifunde Sonke 222
Masoyi, urban renewal projects 414
Mass Democratic Movement 43
Masters of the High Court 433
Matjiesfontein 593
Mauritania 321
Mauritius 170
  foreign relations with 313
Maximum Residue Limits (MRLs) 79
Mbeki, Thabo 45, 47, 409
Mbuzini, Samora Machel Monument 112
McGregor 600
McGregor Museum, Kimberley 17, 123, 601
measles 382
Measuring Units and National Measuring Standards Act, 1973 (Act 76 of 1973) 531
Measuring Units and National Measuring Standards Amendment Act, 1998 (Act 24 of 1998) 531
meat examiners, training facilities 90
meat inspections 90
meat inspectors, training facilities 90
Meat Safety Act, 2000 (Act 40 of 2000) 78, 92
media 142
  advertising 156-158
  broadcasting 142-143
  companies 120
  cross-media control 143-144
  diversity 155-156
  freedom 142
  Independent Communications Authority of SA 144-146
  journalism awards 154
  local content 143-144
  news agencies 153
  organisations and role-players 152-153
  print 147-152
  signal distribution 146-147
  training centres 153-154
Media24 Ltd 147-151
Media, Advertising, Publishing, Printing, Packaging Sector Education Training Authority (MAPPP SETA) 113, 115, 154
Media Development and Diversity Agency (MDDA) 155-156
Media Development and Diversity Agency Act, 2002 (Act 14 of 2002) 155
Media Institute of Southern Africa 153
Mediation in Certain Divorce Matters Act, 1987 (Act 24 of 1987) 433
Media Workers' Association of South Africa 152
Medical Bureau for Occupational Diseases 393
Medical Research Council (MRC) 374, 536-538
  malaria control 383
  national programmes 537-538
Medical Schemes Act, 1967 (Act 72 of 1967) 381
Medical Schemes Act, 1998 (Act 131 of 1998) 375, 381
Medical Schemes Amendment Act, 2002 (Act 62 of 2002) 375
Medical University of South Africa (Medunsa) 221
medicines administration 376
Medicine and Related Substances Amendment Act, 2002 (Act 59 of 2002) 376
Medicines Control Council (MCC) 373
Medium Density Housing Programme 402
Meiringspoort 593
Melrose House, Pretoria 124
Mendi Decoration for Bravery 108-109
mental health 393
Mental Health Care Act, 2002 (Act 17 of 2002) 375, 393
MERCOSUR, trade with 90-91
Mercury, The 150
Merino breed 76
Merino Land Sheep breed 76
Messina
  see Musina
Metcash South Africa 82
metropolitan councils 349
Metrorail 624, 638-639
Mexico 85
mfecane 33-34
M&G Media (Pty) Ltd 150
Michaelis Collection 122
Micro-Economic Reform Strategy (MRS) 177
Micro Finance Regulatory Council (MFRC) 291
micro-lending industry 291-292
  housing finance 408
Middelburg 25, 181
  Botshabelo Cultural Village 114
  Ndebele Museum 124
Middle East
  foreign relations with 327-329

trade with 85
Middleveld 24, 73
Midi Television 146
Midmar Dam 614
Midrand 23
migratory pest control 79-80
MIH Group 146
Military Discipline Bill 497
military history museums 124
military trade unions 506
Military Veterans Affairs Act, 1999 (Act 17 of 1999) 505
milk production 75
Mineral and Petroleum Levies Bill 271
mineral exports, 2002 464
mineral production, 2002 462
mineral reserves, 2002 461
Mineral Revolution 35-37
minerals 465-466
　base 465
　ferrous 465
　Free State 19
　industrial 465
　KwaZulu-Natal 15
　Limpopo 27
　Northern Cape 18
　processed 465
Minerals Act, 1989 (Act 30 of 1989) 468
Minerals and Petroleum Resources Development Act, 2002 (Act 28 of 2002) 455
minerals sales, 2002 463
Mine Health and Safety Act, 1996 468
Mine Health and Safety Inspectorate (MHSI) 455
Mining Qualifications Authority (MQA) 460-461, 464
mines 18
　environmental management 457-458
　health and safety 459-460
　rehabilitation of 457-458
　research 546
　safety research 543
Mines Health and Safety Act, 1996 (Act 29 of 1996) 393, 459
Minister of Arts, Culture, Science and Technology 105

Mineworkers 459
minibus-taxis 628
mini-grid hybrid systems 478
Minimum Data Content of the Framework Data Standard 99
mining industry 458-461
　Free State 19
　GDP, 2001-2002 162
　museums 124
　Northern Cape 18
　North West 20
　small-scale mining 18
Mining Titles Registration Act, 1967 (Act 16 of 1967) 456
Ministerial Task Team into High-Performance Sport 571
Minister of Agriculture and Land Affairs
　land restitution 101
　on food security 81-82
Minister of Education 209-210
Minister of Health, on food security 81
Minister of Housing 402
Minister of Social Development, on food security 81
Mintek 532-534
M-Net All Africa Awards 146
M-Net television 145-146, 153
mobile communications 137-138
Mobile Telephone Network
　see MTN
Modified Sport 571
Modimolle 26-27, 79, 605
Modjadji Nature Reserve 605-606
Mohair production 76
Mokopane 26
Mokopane Game Breeding Centre 247
Molopo River Basin, urban renewal projects 414
Mondi Paper Magazine Awards 154
monetary policy 286-289
money-laundering 274-275
money markets 297-299
Montagu 600
Montreal Protocol 92, 261-263

monuments
　see national/cultural monuments
Mopani district 605-606
Moorreesburg 597
Moral Regeneration Movement (MRM) 352
Morgan's Bay Festival 116
Morocco 321
Mossel Bay 74, 591
　Port 645
Mother City
　see Cape Town
motor cars/vehicles 628
Motor Industry Development Plan (MIDP) 182
Mountain to Oceans (MTO) Pty Ltd 188
Mozambique 8, 14, 21, 24, 26, 170
　food aid to 73
　foreign relations with 313-314
　trade with 91
Mozambique-Agulhas Current 8
Mpumalanga
　agriculture 25, 70, 71-76, 84, 89
　airports 24
　climate 10, 25
　Development Tribunal 98
　fields 24
　forests 25
　GDP 25
　GGP 25
　National Land Cover 2000 Project 96
　land claims 101
　land redistribution 100
　languages 25
　people/population 24-25
　provincial government as on 25 Sep 2003 346
　sport 566
　statistics 25
　temperatures 9
　tourist attractions 24, 607-608
　unemployment 25
　urban renewal projects 414
Mpumalanga Stainless Steel Initiative 181
MRC National HIV/AIDS Lead Programme

718

Mrs/Mr Ples 123
MTN 131, 137-138
MultiChoice Africa (MCA) 146
MultiChoice VUKA! Awards 156
multilateral diplomacy 333
multilateral economic relations
   Ten-Year Review 61
Multimedia Network 147
Multiple Across-Country Evaluation 75
Multi-Purpose Community Centres (MPCCs) 53, 134, 192, 353
Multi-Year Programme of Work 235
Municipal Courts 422
municipal elections 355
Municipal Infrastructure Grant (MIG) 351-352, 654
Municipal Infrastructure Investment Unit (MIIU) 351
municipal roads 625
Municipal Systems Improvement Programme 351
municipalities 349
Murraysburg 593
Museum Africa, Johannesburg 123
museum flagships 122
Museum of the Council for Geoscience, Pretoria 123
Museum of the Department of Correctional Services 123
museums/monuments 121-125
   living, in Limpopo 26
Music Industry Development Initiative Trust 115
Music Industry Task Team 115
Music in Public Places 116
music/music industry 116-117
   Cultural Industries Growth Strategy projects 115-116
Musina 26, 605
Muslim/s 5, 7
Mutton Merino breed 76

N

N1 Corridor 25
Namibia 8, 17, 21, 170
   foreign relations with 314
Nama-Karoo biome 16, 237
Namaqua Development Corridor 17
Namaqualand 16
Namaqua National Park 238
Napier 598
Nashua Mobile 138
Natal
   see KwaZulu-Natal
Natal Botanical Garden, Pietermaritzburg 245
Natal Museum, Pietermaritzburg 122-123
Natal Witness 151
National Action Plan 440
National Action Programme 69
National Adult Basic Education and Training (ABET) Board 222
National Advisory Council on Innovation (NACI) 517
National African Farmers' Union (NAFU) 67, 88
National Agricultural Marketing Council (NAMC) 80
National Agricultural Research Forum 67
National Airspace Committee 96
national animal 108
national anthem 105-107
National Anti-Corruption Forum (NACF) 53, 363
National Arbor Week 663
National Archives, Pretoria 125
   web site 125
National Archives of South Africa Act 1996 (Act 43 of 1996) 125
National Archives Repository, Pretoria 125
National Arts Council (NAC) 110
National Arts Festival 115
National Assembly 45, 341-342
National Association of Broadcasters 153
National Biodiversity Institute 236
National Biotechnology Strategy (NBS) 520
national bird 108-109
National Board for Further Education and Training (NBFET) 212
National Botanical Institute (NBI) 233
National Campaign Against Corruption 52
National Centre for Human Rights Education and Training (NACHRET) 437
National Cleaner Production Centre (NCPC) 531
National Coat of Arms 106
national colours 569
National Commission on Special Needs in Education and Training (NCSNET) 222-223
National Committee on Education Support Services (NCESS) 222-223
National Conventional Arms Control Committee (NCACC) 512
National Conventional Arms Control Committee (NCACC) Bill 497
National Co-ordinating Office of the Manufacturing Advisory Office (NAMAC) 185
National Council of Provinces (NCOP) 341-343
National Council of Trade Unions 43
National Crafts Development Initiative 119
National Crime-Combating Strategy (NCCS) 59, 486
National Crime Prevention Strategy (NCPS) 423, 549
   Ten-Year Review 59-60
National Cultural History Museum (NCHM) 122, 124
natural/cultural monuments 242-244
National Curriculum Framework 218
national days 234
National Development Agency (NDA) 561
National Directorate of Public Prosecutions (NDPP) 417
National Disaster

Management Framework 355
National Drug Master Plan (NDMP) 561
National Drug Policy 374
National Early Childhood Development (ECD) Pilot Project 223
National Economic Development and Labour Council (NEDLAC) 46, 202
National Education Policy Act, 1996 (Act 27 of 1996) 209-210, 214
National Electricity Regulator (NER) 476-477
National Electronic Media Institute of South Africa (NEMISA) 129
　media training centres 154
National Emerging Red Meat Producers' Organisation 89
National Empowerment Fund (NEF) Trust 186
National Energy Regulator 474
National English Literacy Museum, Grahamstown 122
National Environmental Management Act, 1998 (Act 107 of 1998) 233-234, 260, 468
National Environmental Management: Biodiversity Bill 236
National Environment Management: Protected Areas Bill 240
National Evaluation Services, SAPS 488
national expenditure, classification of 268
National Fibre Centre 181
National Film and Video Foundation (NFVF) 110, 120
National Film and Video Foundation (NFVF) Act, 1997 (Act 73 of 1997) 120
National Film, Video and Sound Archives, Pretoria 125
national fish 108-109
national flag 106
national flower 108-109
National Forests Act, 1998 (Act 84 of 1998) 240-241, 667
National Gambling Act, 1996 (Act 33 of 1996) 283
National Health Accounts 379
National Health Bill 375
National Health Laboratory Service (NHLS) 379
National Heritage Council 108
National Heritage Council Act, 1999 (Act 11 of 1999) 108
National Heritage Resources Act (SAHRA), 1999 (Act 25 of 1999) 108
National Home-Builders Registration Council (NHBRC) 401, 406-408
National Home-Builders Registration Council (NHBRC) Fund (Pty) Ltd 407
National Home-Builders Registration Council (NHBRC) Warranty Scheme 408
National Housing Capacity-Building and Training Programme 403-404
National Housing Code Workshops 403
National Housing Consumer Education Framework 404
National Housing Finance Corporation (NHFC) 408-409
National Housing Finance Corporation (NHFC) Business Plan 408
National Housing Policy 413
National Housing Programme 403
National Housing Summit 412
National Industrial Participation Programme (NIPP) 181-182
National Institute for Communicable Diseases (NICD) 374-375
National Institute for Tropical Diseases 542
National Intelligence Agency (NIA) 512
National LandCare Programme (NLP) 70, 84-86
　Juniorcare 85-86
　Soilcare 85
　Veldcare 85
　Watercare 85
National Land Cover 2000 Project 96
National Land Transport Transition Act, 2000 (Act 22 of 2000) 627-628
national language bodies 4
National Language Policy Framework (NLPF) 2-3
National Language Service (NLS) 2, 4
National Network Operations Centre 135
National Lexicography Units 4
National Library of South Africa (NLSA)
　Cape Town division 228
National Loans Registry (NLR) 291
National Lottery
　support for arts 111
National Lottery Licence Agreement 283
National Monuments Council 108
National Museum, Bloemfontein 122-123
National Norms and Standards for School Funding 213-214
National Nuclear Regulator (NNR) Act, 1999 (Act 47 of 1999) 468
National Olympic Committee of South Africa (NOCSA) 572
national orders 106, 108-109
　Mendi Decoration for Bravery 108-109
　Order of Baobab 106, 108-109
　Order of Companions of OR Thambo 108-109
　Order of Ikhamanga 108-109
　Order of Luthuli 108-109
　Order of Mapungubwe 106, 109
national parks/reserves 241-242
National Parks Act, 1976 (Act 57 of 1976) 241

National Parks Land
  Acquisition Fund 241
National Party (NP)
  election results, 1994 45
  election results, 1999 45
  history 39-41, 44
National Petroleum, Gas and
  Oil Corporation of South
  Africa
  see PetroSA
National Plan for Higher
  Education 214, 220-221
National Planning Framework
  53
National Plant Protection
  Organisation of South Africa
  92
National Ports Authority (NPA)
  191, 643-644
National Policy on
  Agricultural Land and
  Resource Management
  84-85
National Policy on Religion
  and Education 217
National Post Provisioning
  Norms 213-214
National Presidential Lead
  Project on Rental Housing
  405
National Product
  Development Centre, CSIR
  119
National Professional
  Teachers' Organisation of
  South Africa 225
National Prosecuting
  Authority (NPA) 418-422
  Asset Forfeiture Unit (AFU)
    419
  Community Courts 421
  Courts for Income Tax
    Offenders 421-422
  Directorate: Special
    Operations 418-419
  Equality Courts 422
  Family Court Pilot Projects
    422
  Municipal Courts 422
  National Prosecuting
    Services (NPS) 420
  Office of the National
    Director of Public
    Prosecution 418
  Sexual Offences and
    Community Affairs Unit
    419-420
  Sexual Offences Courts
    420
  Special Investigating Unit
    419
  Specialised Commercial
    Crime Unit 420-421
  Witness-Protection
    Programme 421
National Prosecuting
  Authority (NPA) Amendment
  Act, 2000 (Act 61 of 2000)
  418
National Prosecuting
  Services (NPS) 420
National Public Traffic Call
  Centre 633
National Public Works
  Programme (NPWP) 192
National Qualifications
  Framework (NQF) 113
  in education 209-210
National Railway Safety
  Regulator Act, 2002 (Act 16
  of 2002) 636
National Register of Oral
  Sources 125
National Research and
  Development Strategy 517
National Research
  Foundation (NRF) 522-527
national roads 18, 624-625
National Roads Act, 1998
  (Act 7 of 1998) 624
National Savings Programme
  for Housing 405
National Savings Scheme
  410
National School-Health Policy
  and Guidelines 375-376
national security
  challenges facing SA
    Government 62
National Skills Authority
  (NSA) 199
National Skills Development
  Strategy (NSDS) 198
National Skills Fund (NSF)
  198-200
National Small Business Act,
  1996 (Act 102 of 1996) 184
National Small Business
  Amendment Bill 184
National Spatial Information
  Framework 99
  standards 99
National Sport and
  Recreation Act, 1998 (Act
  110 of 1998) 569
National Sport and
  Recreation Amendment Bill
  568-569
National Strategic
  Intelligence Amendment Act,
  1998 (Act 37 of 1998) 513
National Strategy for Small
  Business 183
National Student Financial
  Aid Scheme (NSFAS) 210,
  212-213
national symbols 108-109
National System of
  Innovation (NSI) 517
National Transport Register
  627
National Treasury 267-302
  Auditor-General 267, 284
  Budget Council 275
  debt management 269-
    270
  exchange control 299-300
  Financial and Fiscal
    Commission 275
  financial institutions
    292-295
  Financial Intelligence
    Centre (FIC) Act, 2001
    (Act 38 of 2001) 274-275
  financial markets 295-296
  financial sector 285-286
  Financial Services Board
    289-290
  fiscal policy framework
    267-269
  gambling and lotteries
    283-283
  insurance companies 292
  JSE Securities Exchange
    300-301
  legislation 270-273
  macro-economic strategy
    276-277
  micro-lending industry
    291-292
  monetary policy 286-289
  money-laundering 274-275
  money markets 296-299
  SA Revenue Service
    277-283

State expenditure 273-274
national tree 108-109
National Urban
 Reconstruction and Housing
 Agency (NURCHA) 405,
 409-410
National Veld and Forest Fire
 Act, 1998 (Act 101 of 1998)
 667-668
National Water Act, 1998 (Act
 36 of 1998) 70, 256-257,
 652, 656, 658
National Water Week 655
National Zoological Gardens
 of South Africa, Pretoria
 245-246
   Aquarium and Reptile Park
   246
   funding of 105
Natives Land Act, 1913 39
Natives (Urban Areas) Act,
 1923 39
Nat Nakasa Award 154-155
Natural Fathers of Children
 Born out of Wedlock Act,
 1997 (Act 861 of 1997) 434
Ncome Monument 112
Ncome Museum 112
Ndebele Museum,
 Middelburg 124
Nelson Mandela
 home of, Soweto 22
Nelson Mandela Bridge 22
Nelson Mandela Gateway 12
Nelson Mandela Metropolitan
 University 221
Nelson Mandela Museum,
 Umtata 112, 122-123
Nelspruit 24-25
   Deeds Office 93, 100
   International Airport 24
   tourist attractions 607-608
Netherlands 332
New African Capital 147
New African Investments
 Limited (Nail) 147
New African Media 147
New African Publications
 (NAP) Pty Ltd 151
Newcastle 15
New Digital Partnership for
 South Africa 131
Newlands 590
New National Party (NNP)
 elections, 1999 45

news agencies 153
Newspaper Association of
 Southern Africa 152
newspapers 147-148
   circulation 148-149
   contact information
   150-151
   daily and weekly 150-151
   publishers 150-151
   statistics 148
New Partnership for Africa's
 Development (NEPAD) 47, 61,
 168-170, 309-311, 336, 362,
 495
   agriculture, role in 66
   CSIR 531
   cultural project 125
   Department of Transport
   621-622
   malaria control 384
   mining 457
New York Stock Exchange
 listing of Telkom 136
New Zealand 326
Ngodwana paper mill 25
Ngome 15
Nguni
   languages, television 143
   people 1
Nguni breed 75
Nieu-Bethesda 604-605
Nigel 23
Nigeria
   foreign relations with
   321-322
   free trade agreement with
   91
   Stock Exchange, listing of
   M-Net 145
Nkomazi Project 99-100
Nkosi Sikelel' iAfrika
 see national anthem
Non-Aligned Movement
 (NAM) 44, 337-338
Non-Ferrous Metals Industry
 Programme 533
non-governmental
 organisations (NGOs)
   in education 225-226
   in health 380-381
   in social development 549
non-motorised transport 621
Non-Motorised Transport
 Programme 621
non-performing loans

410-411
non-profit organisations
 (NPOs)
   in social development 560
Normalised Difference
 Vegetation Index 79
North Africa 319-323
North America 172-173
North-east Asia 174-175
Northern Cape 16-18
   agriculture 17-18, 71-73,
   75-76, 85
   airports 16
   climate 16
   GDP 17
   GGP 17
   industry 17-18
   land claims 101
   languages 17
   mining 18
   people/population 17
   provincial government as
   on 25 Sep 2003 347
   sport 567
   statistics 17
   tourist attractions 16-17,
   600-602
   unemployment 17
   urban renewal projects 414
Northern Cape State
 Regional Land Claims
 Commission 98
Northern Flagship Institution,
 Pretoria 122-123
Northern Gauteng Technikon
 221
Northern Province
 see Limpopo
Northern Sotho Museum
 see Bakone Malapa
 Museum
North Sea Jazz Festival
 116-117
North West 20-21
   agriculture 21, 71-73,
   75-76, 84-85, 89
   education 20
   GDP 20-21
   GGP 20-21
   land claims 101
   languages 21
   manufacturing 20-21
   mining 20
   people/population 20-21
   provincial government as

722

on 25 Sep 2003 347
regions of 20
sport 567
statistics 20-21
Technikon 221
tourist attractions 606-607
unemployment 21
urban renewal projects 414
North West Economic
 Development and Industrial
 Strategy 21
North West 2012
 Development Plan 21
North West University 221
Ntsika Enterprise Promotion
 Agency 59, 184
Nuclear Energy Act, 1999
 (Act 46 of 1999) 468
Nuclear Energy Corporation
 of South Africa (NELSA)
 469-470
nuclear power 468-471
Nu-Metro 121
nurses 377-378
Nursing Act, 1978 (Act 50 of
 1978) 375
nutrition 394-395
  Food Fortification
   Programme 395
Nylstroom
  see Modimolle

O

Occupational Diseases in
 Mines and Works Act, 1973
 (Act 78 of 1973) 393
occupational health and
 safety 200-201
  training of labour
   inspectors 201
Occupational Health and
 Safety Act, 1993 (Act 181 of
 1993) 200-201, 393
oceans, of South Africa 8-9
Odendaalsrus 18-19
Office of the Family Advocate
 434
Office of the Public Protector
 435
Office of the Surveyor-
 General 94
  Client Service Centres
   94-95

official languages 1-2
 National Lexicography
  Units 4
 promotion by PaNSALB 3
Okiep 18
Old-Age Grants 552
Older Persons Bill 550
Old Fort Prison, Hillbrow 112
Olifants River Valley 596-597
Onderstepoort Veterinary
 Institute 23
onion production 73
Oostenberg 590
open-air museums 124
Operational Response
 Services, SAPS 487, 489-490
Operation Crackdown
 Ten-Year Review 59-60
Operation *Sethunya* 495
Operation Tsipa
Oppikoppi 116
oral health professionals 377
Oral History Project 125
Orange River 8, 16-18, 72, 85
Orange River Basin 651
Orange River System 18
Orange River Valley 17
 temperatures 9
ORBIT 20
orchestras 117
Order of Baobab 106-108
Order of Companions of OR
 Thambo 108-109
Order of Ikhamanga 108-109
Order of Luthuli 108-109
Order of Mapungubwe, 106,
 108
orders
 see national orders
Orex 637
Organisation of African Unity
 (OAU) 47, 61, 305-311
organised crime, Ten-Year
 Review 60
Organised Local Government
 Act, 1997 (Act 52 of 1997)
 348
Oriental tobacco 73
Orkney 20
ornamental plants
 production 74
ostrich farming 10-11, 76
 Eastern Cape 14
Oudtshoorn 10-11, 593
 agriculture 71

Boomplaas Cave 118
*Klein Karoo Nasionale
 Kunstefees* 115, 593
Overberg region 11, 597-599
Owen Sitole Agricultural
 College 89
outcomes-based education
 (OCE) 218

P

P4, jazz radio 144-145
Paarl 594
 Afrikaanse Taalmuseum
  122
Pan-Africanist Congress (PAC)
 42
Pan-African Postal Union 142
Pan-African
 Telecommunications Union
 (PATU) 134-135
Panorama 608
pans 662
PaNSALB
 see Pan South African
  Language Board
Pan South African Language
 Board (PaNSALB) 3-4
Pan South African Language
 Board (PaNSALB) Act, 1995
 (Act 59 of 1995) 4
Pan South African Language
 Board (PaNSALB)
 Amendment Act, 1999 (Act
 10 of 1999) 4
paprika factory, Springbok 85
Paraguay, free trade
 agreement with 91
Parliament 341-343
Parole 448-450
participation mortgage-bond
 schemes 293
Participatory Forest
 Management (PFM) 670
Parys 18
pass laws 39
Paternoster 595
Pechiney 14
Pendoring Awards 157
Peninsula Technikon 221
Pension Funds Act, 1956 (Act
 24 of 1956) 295
People's Housing Partnership
 Trust (PHPT) 403, 413

People's Housing Process (PHP) 407-408, 413
People's Republic of China (PRC)
　foreign relations with 326-327
Performing Arts Council of the Free State, Bloemfontein 111
Perishable Products Export Control Board (PPECB) 89
permanent residence 368
Personnel Expenditure Review, 1999
pest control 78-80
　agricultural pests 79-80, 92-93
　invader plants 78-79
pesticides 79
Petroleum Pipeline Bill 472
Petroleum Products Amendment Bill 472
Petronet 624, 645
PetroSA 471, 473
Phalaborwa 26
Phalaborwa SDI 25
pharmacists 377
Pharmacy Amendment Act, 2000 (Act 1 of 2000) 377
philatelic services 141
Philippolis 602-603
photography 118
Phuthaditjhaba 18, 603
physicians/doctors 376-377
Piet Retief 24
　land redistribution 100
Pietermaritzburg 14-15
　agriculture 76
　museums 122-123
　provincial archives repositories 125
　tourist attractions 614
Pietersburg
　see Polokwane
pig farming/industry 76
　livestock numbers, 2001-2002 75
　museum 123
Piketberg 597
Pilgrim's Rest, Mpumalanga
　mining museum 124
　tourist attractions 608
　pineapple
　processing plants 74
　production 73-74

Pioneer Museum, Pretoria 122, 611
pipelines 645
Planning Professions Act, 2002 (act 36 of 2002) 98
Plant Pathogenic and Plant Protecting Bacterial Culture 79
plant products, import and export control 93
platinum group metals (PGMs) 464-465
Platinum-Group Metals Industry Programme 533
platinum mining 20
Platinum SDI 21
Playhouse Company, Durban 111
Playsport 571
Ples, Mrs
　see Mrs/Mr Ples
Plettenberg Bay 592
Pniel 594
Police Emergency Services 489
Police projects 491-495
Policy and Guidelines for the Integration of Environmental Planning into Land Reform 98
Policy Framework for School Libraries 229
Policy on Drug Abuse in Schools 216
polio 382
Polokwane 26-27, 605
　Bakone Malapa Museum 26, 124, 605
Polokwane Declaration on Waste Management 255
Pondoland 72
Pongola 73
population groups 1
Population Register 367
population statistics 1
Porcinarium, Irene, Pretoria 123
port 72
Port Beaufort 591
Port Edward 14
Port Elizabeth 14, 259
　agriculture 76
　airport 13
　Boardwalk, rural craft 119
　Khaya Lendaba Cultural

Village 114
　museums 123
　National Fibre Centre 181
　Oceanarium 247
　port/harbour 13, 644-645
　provincial archives repositories 125
　Snake Park 247
　Technikon 221
　tourist attractions 604
　urban renewal projects 115
Porterville 597
Port Health Service 394
Port Nolloth 18
　temperatures 9
Port Shepstone 15
Port St Johns 13
　Festival 116
ports, restructuring of 191
post 151
postal codes 141
postal delivery standards 141
Postal Regulator 139
PostCoder software 141
Post Office
　see South African Post Office
Post Office Act, 1958 (Act 44 of 1958) 139
postal addresses, provision of 141-142
postal crime 140
postal network 141
postal sector 138-142
　international/regional co-operation 142
　policy and legislation 138-139
　postal services regulatory framework 139
　South African Post Office 139-142
Postal Services Act, 1998 (Act 124 of 1998) 139
Postbank 140, 142
　restructuring of 142
Postmasburg 602
Post Weekend 147
potato-processing industry 73
potato production 73
　in 2002 71
Potchefstroom 20, 607
　Agricultural College 89
　OPM Prozesky Bird

Sanctuary 607
Potgietersrus
  see Mokopane
poultry farming/industry 76
Poverty Alleviation Fund for Job Creation in the Arts and Culture Industry 116
Poverty-Reduction Programme 521-522
poverty relief/alleviation tourism industry 583-584
Poverty-Relief Programme 553
Preferential Procurement Policy Framework Act, 2000 (Act 5 of 2000) 274
Premier Foods 82
President 343
Presidential Jobs Summit, 1998 46
Presidential International Advisory Council on Information Society and Development 132
Presidential Pilot Project on Rental Housing 409
Presidential Sports Awards 572
Presidential Strategic Leadership Development Programme (PSLDP) 365-366
Presidential Mechanisation Lead Projects 89
Presidential National Commission on Information Society and Development 132-133
press freedom 142
Press Freedom Index 142
Press Ombudsman 152
press organisations 153
Pretoria 22
  Art Museum 123
  Deeds Office 93, 100
  Engelenburg House Art Gallery 122
  Freedom Park Project 112
  KoMjekejeke Cultural Village 114
  museums 114, 122-124
  National Archives 125
  News 150
  Northern Flagship Institution 122

provincial archives repositories 125
Salvokop 112
Technikon 221
tourist attractions 22, 611-612
urban renewal projects 115
Pretoria National Botanical Garden, Pretoria 245
Pretoria Zoo
  see National Zoological Gardens of South Africa
Prevention of Corruption Bill 53
Prevention of Organised Crime Act, 1998 (Act 121 of 1998) 418-419
price inflation 164-165
  see also consumer price inflation
Prieska 16
primary debt markets 301-302
primary capital market activity 295
primary health care (PHC) 373-374
  access to, Ten-Year Review 53
Primary School Nutrition Programme 395
Primedia 147
Prince Albert 593
Prince Alfred Hamlet 600
Prince Edward Island 8
Printers Ltd 147
Print Industries Cluster 115
Print Industries Cluster Council 120
Printing Industries Federation of South Africa 153
print media 147-152
  circulation 148-152
  distribution 149-152
  magazines 149
  newspapers 147-149
  online media 152
Print Media SA (PMSA) 152
prisoners
  classification/categories 443
  education/training 446
  incarceration 441-442
  mother and child units 444

nutrition 445
overcrowding 441-442
overcrowding, Ten-Year Review 60
physical health/hygiene 444-445
privilege system 444
psychological services 446-447
rehabilitation services 445-448
reintegration into the community 448
release of 448
religious care 447-448
safe custody of 441
safety and security 442
social work services 447
young offenders 443
prisons 441-442
Private Security Industry Regulation Act, 2001 (Act 56 of 2001) 513
private security sector labour legislation 204
processed minerals 465
production price index, 1995-2001 165
Production Unit Code Registration 81
Professional Housing Institute 404
Professional Photographers of South Africa 153
Programme of Action, history 42
Prohibition on Anti-Personnel Mines Bill 497-498
project-linked housing subsidies 406
Promotion of Access to Information Act, 2000 (Act 2 of 2000) 53, 425
Promotion of Administrative Justice Act, 2000 (Act 3 of 2000) 425-426
Promotion of Equality and Prevention of Unfair Discrimination Act, 2000 (Act 4 of 2000) 422, 426
properties
  on Deeds Registration System Database, 2001-2003 100
properties in possession

(PIPs) 410-411
Propnet 624
protea cultivation 74-75
Protection and Security Services Division, SAPS 488
protocols, between SADC and SA 316
Proud to be a Teacher Campaign 212
provinces 10-27
   under Interim Constitution 45
Provincial and Local Government
   see Department of Provincial and Local Government
provincial archives repositories 125
provincial expenditure, classification of 268
Provincial Geographical Names Committees (PGNCs) 110
Provincial Good Practice Programme (PGPP) 272
provincial governments
   as on 25 September 2003 346-348
provincial health services 378-379
provincial roads 625
Provision of Land and Assistance Act, 1993 (Act 126 of 1993) 99
Public Finance Management Act (PFMA), 1999 (Act 1 of 1999) 197, 271-273, 413, 521
   SANDF 503
   sport funding 566
public holidays 2
Public Internet Terminals (PITs) 134
Public libraries 228-229
public-private partnerships 226
Public Protector 428
Public Protector Act, 1994 (Act 23 of 1994) 428
Public Protector Amendment Bill, 2003 428
Public Sector Hostel Redevelopment Programme 402-403
Public Service 355-366

affirmative action 365
challenges facing 62
Code of Conduct 53
conditions of service 358-359
corruption, fighting 359
corruption, Ten-Year Review 52
ethics 363-364
HIV/AIDS 360
human resource development 360, 365
human resource management 359-360, 365
information 360
institutional performance 357
labour relations 358-359, 365
macro-organisational issues 356
public service information 360-361
restructuring of 356
senior management service 365
service delivery improvement 357-358, 364-365
service delivery, Ten-Year Review 53
Service Management Service 359
size 355-356
training 365-366
transformation, Ten-Year Review 52-53
Public Service Commission (PSC) 363-364
Public Anti-Corruption Strategy 359
Public Switched Telecommunications Services 135
public transport 627-635
public transport subsidies 619-620
public works programmes 192-196
publishing
   Cultural Industries Growth Strategy projects 115
Punt Geselsradio 145

Q

Qunu 604
QwaQwa 70
QwaQwa National Park 603
   Basotho Cultural Village 114, 603
quarantinable diseases 394

R

Race Against Malaria Campaign 384
Radio Act, 1926 (Act 20 of 1926) 144
radio 144-146
   Channel Africa 144
   community radio stations 145
   history 144
   private radio stations 144-145
   radio 144
   Radio 702 145, 153
   Radio Algoa 145
   Radio Jacaranda 145
   Radio KFM 145
   Radio News 144
   Radio Oranje 145
   Radio Sesotho 144
   Radio South Africa 144
   Radio Xhosa 144
   Radio Zulu 144
   Springbok Radio 144
Rainbow Cultural Village, North West 114
rail transport 635-640
rainfall, of South Africa 9
Ramsay Son & Parker 149
Rand Afrikaans University 221
rand exchange rates 270
Rand Refinery 19
rape survivors
   anti-retroviral treatment 386
Rapid Response Services 489
Rapport 151
Raptor Awards 157
Rawsonville 600
RCP Media 150-151
Real Gross Domestic Expenditure, 2001-2002 163

Real Gross Domestic
 Product, 2001-2002 162
real yellowwood
 national tree 108-109
Reconstruction and
 Development Programme
 (RDP) 51
recreation 574
recycling 260
refugees
 see also illegal immigrants
Refugee Appeal Board 366
Refugees Act, 1998 (Act 130
 of 1998) 367
Regional Courts 430
Regional Food Security
 Training Programme (RFSTP)
 83
Regional Industrial
 Development Programme
 176
regional integration
 Southern Africa, Ten-Year
 Review 61
Registrar of Brands 89
Registrar of Livestock
 Improvement and
 Identification 89
Registrar for Medical Scheme
 381
Regulations of Interception of
 Communication and
 Provision of
 Communication-Related
 Information Act, 2002 (Act
 70 of 2002) 427, 513
relief features, of South Africa
 8
religion/s
 African Independent
 Churches (AICs) 6
 African traditionalists 7
 Afrikaans churches 6
 Christian churches 5-7
 religious groups 5
 Roman Catholic Church
 6-7
 statistics based on Census
 2001 7
 other Christian churches 7
 other 7
religious groups 5
relocation assistance 407
Relocation Assistance Grants
 407

renewable energy sources
 479-480
Rental Housing Act, 1999
 (Act 50 of 1999) 401
Rental Housing Tribunals 401
Reporters Without Barriers
 142
reproductive health 387-389
Research and Innovation
 Support Agency (RISA) 524
research areas 540-542
Research Capacity
 Development (RCD)
 programmes 524-525
research organisations
 540-542
Restitution Act, 1994 (Act 22
 of 1994) 101
restitution claims 101
restructuring
 Denel 189-190
 energy sector 190
 forestry 188-189
 Government Printing
 Works 187
 hospitality industry 189
 ports 191
 South African Airways (SAA)
 191
 Spoornet 190-191
 state assets, of 187-191
 Telkom 188
retirement funds 294-295
Revenue Laws Amendment
 Act, 2002 (Act 74 of 2002)
 271
Revenue Laws Amendment
 Bill 271
Review of the Financing,
 Resourcing and Costs of
 Education in Public Schools
 216
Rhino and Elephant
 Foundation 263
Rhodes University 221
Richards Bay 14
 Downstream Aluminium
 Centre for Technology 181
 industries 15
 Port 644
Richmond 15
Richtersveld National Park 17,
 238-239
Riemland region 603
Rietvlei Nature Reserve 612

Right of Appearance in
 Courts Act, 1995 (Act 62 of
 1995) 432
rightsizing, housing stock 411
River Health Programme
 (RHP) 661-662
rivers 661
Riversdale 591
Riviersonderend 599
Road Accident Fund (RAF)
 634-635
road traffic safety 631-633
road traffic signs 626-627
road transport 624-627
Robben Island 12, 590
 World Heritage Site 122
Robben Island Museum,
 Cape Town 122
Robertson 600
rock art 118-119
 in Coat of Arms 106
Roggeveld 8
Rollback Malaria Strategic
 Plan 383
Rome Declaration 83
Rondebosch 590
Roodepoort 22, 610
rooibos tea production 74
Rosslyn 23
RSA Classification and
 Labelling System 77
RTMC Act, 1999 (Act 20 of
 1999) 631-632
Rules Board for Courts of
 Law 433
Rural Safety Committee 495
Rustenburg 20-21, 606-607
rural development 528
Rural Housing Loan Fund
 (RHLF) 413-414
Rural Safety Committee 495

S

SA Agulhas 247
Saambou 408
SABC
 see South African
 Broadcasting Corporation
Sabie 24-25, 608
SADC Food Security Training
 Programme 82-83
 Regional Advisory
 Committee 83

SADC Multidisciplinary Festival, Pretoria 115
SADC Trade Protocol 316-317
SA-EU TDCA 91
SAFCOL
  see South African Forestry Company Limited
Safety at Sports Stadiums Bill 567
Sahara Desert 8
SA Host 584-585
Saldanha Bay 8, 10, 595-596
  port/harbour 10, 645
Saldanha Steel project 12
Saldanha-Vredenburg area 12
Salvokop, Pretoria 112
Sammy Marks Museum, Pretoria 122, 124, 612
Samora Machel Monument, Mbuzini 112
Samora Machel Project 112
San 17, 531-532
  people 1, 31
  language promotion by PaNSALB 3
  National Language Body 4
  rock engravings 17-18, 118
Sani Pass 615
sanitation, access to, Ten-Year Review 53
Sanlam Community Press Awards 154-155
SanParks 241-242, 665
Santa Gertrudis breed 75
SAPPI Magazine Publishers Association of South Africa Pica Awards 154
Saron 600
Sasol 20, 472, 541
Sasolburg 18-19, 603
satellite broadcasting 146
satellite museums 122
Saturday Dispatch 147, 151
Saturday Star 147, 151
SAT-3/WASC/SAFE submarine cable system 135
Saudi Arabia 328
Savanna biome 237
Savant 133
Save the Children Fund 558
Saving Mothers 1999-2001 387
Schoemanskloof 608

school admission policy 219
Science and Technology 517-546
  see also Department of Science and Technology
  international co-operation 61, 518-519
  museum 122
  policy 517-522
  research areas 542-546
  research organisations 540-542
  science councils 522-540
  Public Understanding of (PUSET) 518-519
Science and Technology Agreements Committee (STAC) Fund 519
Science and Technology Co-operation Committee (SATCCOM) 519
science councils 522-527
scientific reserves 241
seabirds 250
search and rescue services 646-648
seaweed 250
secondary capital market activity 295-296
Second National Operator (SNO) 130-131
Secretariat for Safety and Security 486
Section 21 Domain Name Authority 130
Sector Education and Training Authorities (SETAs) 59, 181, 197-199
  Cultural Industries Growth Strategy projects 115
  education 211, 224
  mining 460
sector policing 492-493
Secunda 25
Securemail 140-141
Securities Services Bill 271
security, Ten-Year Review 59-60
Sedgefield 592
segregation, history of 38-40
Sekhukhune district 70
Sentech 129-130, 146-147, 218
Sepedi 322
  official language 1-2

television 143
Servcon Housing Solutions (Pty) Ltd 407, 410-411
  progress up to 31 March 2003 410
Sesotho
  National Lexicographic Unit 4
  official language 1
  radio 144-145
  Sesotho sa Lebowa: Sesotho sa Lebowa Dictionary Unit 4
  Sesotho: Sesiu sa Sesotho NLU 4
  television 143
Setswana
  National Lexicographic Unit 4
  official language 1-2
  Setswana: Setswana NLU 4
sexual assault crimes, Ten-Year Review 60
Sexual Offences and Community Affairs Unit 419-420
Sexual Offences Bill 428
Sexual Offences Courts 420
Seychelles 170
Severe Acute Respiratory Syndrome (SARS) 394, 581
Shangana Cultural Village, Hazyview 114
sheep
  farming 76
  livestock numbers, 2001-2002 75
sherry 72
Shosholoza Meyl 637-638
signal distribution 146-147
signal distributors 146-147
sign language
  promotion by PaNSALB 3
  videophone facility for 3
Simmentaler breed 75
Simon's Town 590
Singapore 323-324
Sishen Mine, Kathu 18
Sisulu, Walter 40
siSwati
  National Lexicographic Unit 4
  official language 1
  siSwati: Silulu SesiSwati

728

NLU 4
SITA Holdings 361
Sithengi 120
Siyabuswa, urban renewal projects 414
Sizakala Campaign 201
skills development 197-201
  Ten-Year Review 59
Skills Development Act, 1998 (Act 97 of 1998) 113, 115, 197, 404
skills development levy 281
skills research 181
small business
  challenges facing 62
  Ten-Year Review 59
Small Business Council 59
Small Claims Court 168, 431
small, medium and micro enterprises (SMMEs) 183-187
  see also small business
  e-commerce 130
  tourism industry 584
Small Medium Manufacturing Enterprise Development Programme 176
small-scale farming/farmers 70, 89
small-scale mining 461-462
snake parks 247
social assistance 551-553
Social Assistance Bill 551
Social Cluster
  food security 81
  Ten-Year Review 53, 58
social development/assistance
  see Department of Social Development
Social Development Funding Window (SDFW) 199
social grants 53
  amounts as at 1 Apr 2003 552
  payment of 552-553
Social Grants Appropriation Act, 2002 (Act 2 of 2002) 270
social housing 411-412
Social Housing Accreditation Board 402
Social Housing Corporation 402
Social Housing Foundation (SHF) 411-412
Social Housing Policy 402
social services
  broadening of access to, Census 2001 52-53, 58
  challenges facing 62
  programmes output, 1994-2002 52
social transition
  challenges facing SA Government 62-63
Soccer-Luma 151
Sodwana Bay 251, 613-614
Software Evaluation Centre (SEC) 133
Soilcare 85
soil conservation/degradation 69
  see also agriculture
Soil Conservation Scheme 69
sojourn control 368
solar energy 480-481
Son 148
Sophiatown
  heritage reclamation festivals 115
sorghum production/industry 70, 72
Soshanguve 22
Sotho-Tswana people 1
Soul City 380
South Africa
  climate 9
  challenges facing 61-63
  coastline 8
  economy 160-207
  fog/frost/humidity 9
  oceans/seas 8
  people/population 1-5
  rainfall 9
  relief features 8
  SADC, and 315-318
  sunshine 9-10
  temperatures 9
South African Advertising Research Foundation (SAARF) 148
South African AIDS Vaccine Initiative (SAAVI) 386
South African Air Force Museum, Pretoria 123
South African Airways (SAA) 623
  restructuring 191
Restructuring Task Team 191
South African Astronomical Observatory (SAAO) 526, 528
South African Boxing Act, 2001 (Act 11 of 2001) 573
South African Breweries (SAB) Journalism Awards 154-155
South African Broadcasting Corporation (SABC) 110, 129, 140, 153
  objectives, as set out in Broadcasting Act 143
  restructuring 143
  television 145
South African Bureau of Standards (SABS) 23, 99, 539-540
South African Citizenship Act, 1995 (Act 88 of 1995) 366-367
South African Company Registration Office 192
South African Constitution
  see Constitution of the Republic of South Africa
South African Council for Educators (SACE) 212
South African Council for Educators (SACE) Act, 2000 (Act 31 of 2000) 212, 215, 223
South African Council for Town and Regional Planners 97
South African Council of Churches (SACC) 6
South African Cultural History Museum, Cape Town 122-123
South African Customs Service 92
South African Customs Union (SACU) 169, 171
South African Democratic Teachers' Union 225
South African Dental Technicians' Council 373
South African Development Trust 81
South African Dried Fruit Co-op 18
South African Environmental Observatory Network

(SAEON) 522-523
South African Expanded Programme on Immunisation 382
South African Forestry Company Limited (SAFCOL) 664-666
South African Game Ranchers' Organisation 76
South African Geographic Names Council (SAGNC) 97, 108, 110
South African Geographical Names Council Act, 1998 (Act 118 of 1998) 108
South African Guild of Motoring Journalists 153
South African Heritage Resources Agency (SAHRA) 108, 118
South African Honeybush Tea Association 74
South African Housing Fund 412-413
South African Human Rights Commission (SAHRC) 436-437
South African Institute for Aquatic Biodiversity, Grahamstown 122-123, 526
South African Institute for Drug-Free Sport (SAIDS) 573-574
South African Languages Bill 2
South African Law Reform Commission (SALRC) 435-436, 550
South African Literacy Agency 222
South African Local Government Association (SALGA) 98, 348
South African Management and Development Institute (SAMDI) 365
South African Maritime Safety Agency (SAMSA) 258, 622-623, 645-646
South African Maritime Safety Agency (SAMSA) Act, 1998 (Act 5 of 1998) 645
South African Maritime Training Academy (SAMTRA) 646

South African Milk Federation 75
South African Mint Company (SA Mint) 286
South African Museum, Cape Town 122-123
South African Museum for Military History, Johannesburg 124-125
South African Music Awards, 2003 117
South African Music Directory 117
South African Music Week 117
South African National AIDS Council (SANAC) 385
South African National Antarctic Expedition (SANAE) 542
South African National Antarctic Programme (SANAP) 542
South African National Chemicals Profile 260
South African National Defence Force (SANDF) 190, 217, 496-509
   armaments 509-512
   downsizing and rightsizing 505-506
   equipment 508
   facilities 509
   force employment 503-505
   functions 498
   humanitarian relief 505
   integration 505
   intelligence services 512-513
   legislation 497-498
   Military Strategy 499-500
   military veterans 505
   operations 503-503
   organisational structure 500-502
   peace support 507-508
   Reserve Force 506-507
   resettlement 356, 507
   tasks 498-499
   transformation 503
South African National Editors' Forum (SANEF) 152
South African National Foundation for the Conservation of Coastal Birds 263
South African National Gallery 122-123, 589
South African National Games and Leisure Activities (SANGALA) Programme 574
South African National Health Knowledge Network 538
South African Literacy Initiative (SANLI) 222
South African National Museum for Military History, Johannesburg 122
South African National Parks (SanParks) 233, 237
   size 243
South African National Roads Agency Ltd (SANRAL) 622, 624
South African National Taxi Council (SANTACO) 628-629
South African-Norwegian Education and Music Education Programme 110
South African Nursing Council 373, 375, 377
South African Pest Control Association (SAPCA) 80
South African Pharmacy Council 373, 377
South African Police Service (SAPS) 485-496
   Administration 487
   Africa, involvement in 495-496
   Career Management 488
   Crime Intelligence 488, 491
   Crime Prevention 487, 489
   crime statistics, 2002-2003 496
   Detective Services 488, 490-491
   Dog and Equestrian Units 489
   Evaluation Services 488
   Financial and Administrative Services 488
   Hostage Negotiation 489
   Inland Water Policing 489
   International relations 496
   Legal Services 488

Logistics 488
Museum, Pretoria 611
National Crime Prevention Strategy (NCPS)
Operational Response Services 487, 489-490
Personnel Services 488
Police Emergency Services 489
projects 491-495
Protection Services 488
Rapid Response Services 487
Reserve Force 506-507
Reservist System 505
Training 488
South African Police Service (SAPS) Act, 1995 (Act 68 of 1995) 486
South African Port Operations (SAPO) 624
South African Post Office 129, 139-142
　address provision 141-142
　business re-engineering 140
　counter service 140
　delivery standards and service performance 141
　freight and courier services 141
　mail volumes 141
　philatelic services 141
　postal crime 140
　postal network 141
　Postbank 142
　principal activities 140
　products and services 140
　Securemail 140-141
South African Press Association (SAPA) 153
South African Property Owners' Association 98
South African Qualifications Authority Act, 1995 (Act 58 of 1995) 113, 209
South African Qualifications Authority (SAQA) 211
　housing standards 404
　media industry 154
South African Rail Commuter Corporation (SARCC) 635, 639-640
South African Reference Group on Women in Science and Technology (SARG) 520
South African Reserve Bank 285-286
　money markets 296-299
South African Revenue Service (SARS) 367, 421
　Courts for Income Tax Offenders 421-422
　organisational performance 282
　sources of revenue 270, 277-283
South African Revenue Service Act, 1997 (Act 34 of 1997) 277
South African Schools Act, 1996 (Act 84 of 1996) 210, 214-215
South African Secret Service (SASS) 512-513
South African Sports Commission (SASC) 565-571
South African Sports Commission (SASC) Act, 1998 (Act 109 of 1998) 565
South African Teachers' Union 225
South African Telecommunications Regulatory Authority (SATRA) 131
South African Tourism 584-585
South African Tourism Institute (SATI) 586-587
South African Typographical Union 153
South African Union of Journalists (SAUJ) 152
South African Vaccine Producers and State Vaccine Institute 379
South African Veterinary Council 89
South African War
　see Anglo-Boer War
South African Weather Service 545, 668
South African Wine and Spirit Export Association 72
South African Women Entrepreneurs Network (SAWEN) 176, 185
South Asia 174
South-east Asia 174
southern Africa
　foreign relations with 311-315
　South Africa and 315-318
Southern African Customs Union (SACU) 90
SACU Agreement 91
Southern African Development Community (SADC) 90, 168
　Free Trade Agreement 171
　international co-operation 317-318
　maize producers 71
　National Action Programme 69-70
　Protocol of Fisheries 250, 252
　Protocol on Trade 91, 316-317
　region 21
　regional integration, Ten-Year Review 61
　relations with 315-318
　Secretariat 91
　trade with 170-171
Southern African Development Community Fund 519
Southern African Large Telescope (SALT) 527
Southern African Power Pool (SAPP) 476, 478-479
Southern African Transport and Communications Commission 142
Southern Cross, The 151
Southern Flagship 122
　see also Iziko Museums
South Korea 327
South Sotho Museum, Witsieshoek 124
Soutpansberg region 26, 605
Sowetan 148, 151
Sowetan Sunday World 147, 149, 151
Soweto 22
　Chris Hani Baragwanath Hospital 381
　tourist attractions 611
　uprise (1976) 43
Spain, foreign relations with 332-333
Spatial Data Discovery Facility (SDDF) 98

Spatial Development
  Frameworks (SDFs) 98
Spatial Development
  Initiatives (SDIs) 179
  Coega 179
  cultural tourism 113-115
  East London 179
  Fish River 14, 179
  KwaZulu-Natal 179
  Lubombo Corridor 179
  Maputo Development
    Corridor 179
  Saldanha 179
  transport 179, 625
  West Coast 12
  Wild Coast 14, 179
spatial information 97-99
Spatial Information Bill 98
spatial planning 97-99
Spear of the Nation
  see Umkhonto we Sizwe
Special Bursary Scheme
  Chief Directorate: Surveys
    and Mapping, of 95-96
Special Integrated
  Presidential Project for
  Urban Renewal 414
Special Investigating Unit 419
Specialist Press Association
  153
Special Pensions
  Amendment Bill 271
Special Programme for
  African Agricultural Research
  91
Special Programme for Food
  Security 83
Specialised Commercial
  Crime Unit 420-421
Species Identification Service
  76
Speed Services Couriers 141
sponsorships, Telkom's
  strategy 137
Spoornet 190-191, 636-639
Sport and Recreation SA
  (SRSA) 565-578
sport/s 565-574
  events, 2004 578
  2003 highlights 575-578
  High Performance
    Programme 569-570
  Ministerial Task Team into
    High-Performance Sport
    571

organisations 572-574
Presidential Sports Awards
  572
tourism 567
transformation in 571
Sports Information and
  Science Agency (SISA) 569-
  570
Sports Transformation
  Charter 571
Springbok 16
  mining 18
  Radio 144
  paprika factory 85
springbuck, national animal
  108-109
Springs 22-23
Square Kilometre Array (SKA)
  bid 523
Sri Lanka 325
stamp duty 281
Standards Act, 1993 (Act 29
  of 1993) 539
Standerton 24
Stanford 597
Stanger
  Chief Albert Luthuli Legacy
    Project 112
Star, The 148, 151
state agricultural land 81
state assets
  challenges facing SA
    Government 62
  restructuring of 187-191
  restructuring, Ten-Year
    Review 59
State Attorney Act, 1957 (Act
  56 of 1957) 433
State expenditure 273-274
State Herald 106
State Information Technology
  Agency (SITA) 132, 361-362
  Deeds Registries 93-94
State Information Technology
  Agency (SITA) Act 361-362
state land 100
State Legal Services 422-423
State Library
  see National Library of
    South Africa
State of the Environment
  Report 252
state-owned enterprises
  (SOEs)
  development role of 191

restructuring of 187-191
State Security Council 43
State-subsidised housing
  402
State Theatre, Pretoria 111
state veterinarians 89-90
State Veterinary Services
  77-78
statistics (Census 2001)
  population 1
  religions 7
Stellaland 21
Stellenbosch 10, 124, 594
Stem van Suid Afrika
  see national anthem
Step Up scheme 87
Sterkfontein hominid site 22
Sterkfontein Caves World
  Heritage Site 31, 607, 610
Ster Kinekor 121
Still Bay 591
St Helena Bay 251, 596
St Lucia 613
  Estuary 15
  Greater St Lucia Wetland
    Park 15, 237
St Lucia Wetlands
  cultural industries project
    114-115
stokvels 293
Stone Age
  paintings/engravings 118
Strandfontein 596
Strategic Asset Management
  Partner 195-196
Strategic Empowerment
  Programme for Women in
  Construction 195
Strategic Investment
  Programme (SIP) 182
Strategic Plan for South
  African Agriculture 65-67
strikes/industrial action,
  statistics 202
Struis Bay 598
Stutterheim 13
Subcommittee for Plant
  Protection 83
subsistence fishing 250
substance abuse 390-391
subtropical crops 73
subtropical fruit production
  73, 81
  in 2002 71
Succulent Karoo biome 238

Sudan 321
sugar industry 72
sugar production 72
Suikerbosrand 124
Sunday Independent, The 147, 151
Sunday Sun 147, 149, 151
Sunday Times 147, 149, 151
Sunday Tribune 151
Sunday World 147, 151
sunflower seed production/industry in 2002 71
sunshine 9-10
Sun, The 148
Superior Courts Bill 427
Super Start Programme 570-571
supplementary health services 378
Supreme Court of Appeal 429
surveys and mapping 95-97
 Special Bursary Scheme 95-96
Sussex breed 75
sustainable resource use/management 68-70
sustainable use areas 244
Sutherland 16, 519
Suurbraak 599
Swadini 608
Swartberg Mountains 593
Swartkrans hominid site 22
Swartland region 11, 597
Swartvlei Lagoon 592
Swaziland 8, 15-16, 24, 170
 food aid to 73
 foreign relations with 314
 National Land Cover 2000 Project 96
 trade with 90
Sweden 333
Swellendam 598
Switzerland 333

T

Table Mountain, Cape Town 10
 cableway 12
Taiwan 327
Taletso 20
TalkPlus 136

Tambo, OR 40, 108
Tankwa-Karoo National Park 238
Tanzania 170
 foreign relations with 319
Taung child 31
Taung Skull Site 606
Taurus Livestock Improvement Co-operative 76
Taxation Laws Amendment Act, 2002 (Act 30 of 2002) 271
Tax Holiday Scheme 176
taxi industry 628-629
 violence, Ten-Year Review 60
tax proposals for 2003 283
Taxi Recapitalisation Programme 628-629
tax
 see South African Revenue Service
tax system 277-278
 double taxation 278
teacher unions 225
technikons
 institutional restructuring 221
Technikon South Africa 221
Technikon Witwatersrand 221
Technology Business Incubator 181
Technology for Human Resources for Industry Programme (THRIP) 523-524
Technology for Women In Business (TWIB) 177, 185
Technology Transfer Centre (TTC) 180-181
telebanking 129
telecommunications 131-138
 Citizen Post Offices (CPOs) 134
 information technology 132-133
 international co-operation 134-135
 Internet 133-134
 mobile communications 137-138
 Multi-Purpose Community Centres (MPCCs) 134
 Public Internet Terminals (PITs) 134

 regulators and licensing 131-132
 Telkom 135-137
Telecommunications Act, 1996 (Act 103 of 1996) 130-131, 138
Telecommunications Amendment Act, 2001 (Act 64 of 2001) 130, 132
tele-education 129
telemedicine 129, 375
Telephone Interpreting Service of South Africa (TISSA) 3, 494
teleshopping 129
television 145-146
 channels 120
 free-to-air 146
 M-Net 145-146
 SABC 145
 satellite broadcasting 146
Telkom 129, 131, 135-137, 140
 Centres of Excellence (CoEs) 137
 economic empowerment 137
 Foundation 136-137, 218
 restructuring 188
 sponsorships 137
temperatures, of South Africa 9
temporary residence 368-369
Ten-Year Review 47, 50-63
terrorism, Ten-Year Review 60
Thabazimbi 26
Thailand 324
theatre 116
The Dance Factory, Johannesburg 117
Theiler Veterinary Science Museum, Onderstepoort, Pretoria 123
The One City Festival 116
Thicket biome 239
Thintana Communications LLC 136
Thor Chemicals 260
Thohoyandou, Ifa textile project 119
Thubelisha Homes 41
Thabong, urban renewal projects 414
Thuso Mentorship Network 185

Thulamela archaeological
  site 31, 606
Timbali Incubator 181
Timbuktu Manuscripts 125
Timbuktu Manuscripts
  Project 125
Times Media 150-151
Tirisano programme 215-216,
  225
Tlholego Cultural Village,
  Magaliesburg 114
tobacco control 389-390
Tobacco Products Control
  Amendment Act, 1999 (Act
  12 of 1999) 389
toll roads 625-626
tomatoes production 73
Tompi Seleka Agricultural
  College 89
Tongaat 613
tourism 581-615
  accommodation 588-589
  cultural 113-114
  in provinces 589-615
  hints for the tourist
    587-589
  human resource
    development 586-587
  marketing 583-587
  policy 582-587
  poverty-relief funding
    583-584
  Ten-Year Review 61
  top attractions 589-615
Tourism and Hospitality
  Education and Training
  Authority (THETA) 586
Tourism Enterprise
  Programme (TEP) 586
Tourism Forum 583
Tourism Indaba 585
Tourism Month 584
Tourism Transformation
  Strategy 583
Tourism Safety
  Communications Strategy
  589
tourists, hints for 587-589
Touwsrivier 600
Town and Regional Planner's
  Act of 1984 98
Trade and Investment
  Framework Arrangement
  (TIFA) 173
Trade and Investment South

Africa (TISA) 170, 177-178
Trade Development and
  Co-operation Agreement
  (TDCA) 171
trade reforms, Ten-Year
  Review 58
trade relations
  Africa, with 169-171
  Americas, with 172-173
  Asia, with 174-175
  Europe, with 171-172
  Ten-Year Review 61
Traditional Healers Bill 375
traditional leaders
  Houses of 345
  leadership 344-345
traditional medicine 389
training centres, media
  153-154
transfer duty 281
Transfrontier Conservation
  Areas (TFCAs) 241
transfrontier game parks 17
Transgariep region 602-603
Trans-Hex 18
Transnet Limited 132,
  623-624
transport 619-648
  see also Department of
  Transport
  agencies 622-623
  civil aviation 640-642
  infrastructure 619
  maritime affairs 645-648
  pipelines 645
  policy 619-622
  ports 643-645
  public transport 627-635
  rail transport 635-640
  road transport 624-627
  Transnet Limited 623-624
Transtel 624
Transvaal Museum of Natural
  History, Pretoria 122-123
Transvaal Snake Park,
  Midrand 247
Transwerk 624
tree, national
  see national tree
tree aloe 16
Trees and Food for Africa 263
TrigNet 95
Trinity Broadcasting Network
  153
Truth and Reconciliation

Commission (TRC) 45-46, 438
Tshipise 605
Tshivenda
  National Lexicographic
  Unit 4
  official language 1
  television 143
  Tshivenda: Tshivenda NLU
  4
Tshumisano Programme
  519-520
Tshwane University of
  Technology 221
Tsolo Agricultural College 89
Tsongakraal, Letsitele,
  Northern Province 124
Tsonga Open-air Museum,
  Tzaneen 26, 606
Tsonga people 1
Tswaing Meteorite Crater
  Museum, Pretoria 122-124,
  610
tuberculosis 384-385
  access to control
  programme, Ten-Year
  Review 53, 58
Tulbagh 600
Tunisia 322-323
Turkey 328-329
Tutu, Archbishop Desmond
  45
Tygerberg 591
Tzaneen 26-27, 605-606

U

Uganda 314
UIP 121
Uitenhage 13-14
Ucingo Investments 136
Ukhahlamba-Drakensberg
  Park 243
Ulundi 14-15, 613
  provincial archives
  repositories 125
Umgeni River Bird Park 613
Umgungundlovu 613
  Makhosini Cultural Village
  and Tourism Initiative 114
Umhlanga Rocks 15, 612-613
Umkhonto we Sizwe 42
Umtata
  airport 13
  Deeds Office 93, 100

museums 112, 123
uncertified securities tax (UST) 281
unemployment, Sep 2002 203
Unemployment Insurance Amendment Bill 200
Unemployment Insurance Act, 2001 (Act 63 of 2001) 200
Unemployment Insurance Contributions Act, 2002 (Act 4 of 2002) 204, 271
Unemployment Insurance Fund (UIF) 200
Unibank 408
Union Buildings, Pretoria 612
Uniondale 593
Unique Feature Identification Standard 99
unit trusts 293-294
United Democratic Front 43
United Kingdom (UK) 331-332
United Nations (UN) 43, 440
 foreign relations with 334
United Nations Children's Fund (UNICEF) 557-558
United Nations Conference on Environment and Development (UNCED) 69
United Nations Development Programme (UNDP) 338
United Nations Food and Agriculture Organisation (FAO) 70
United Nations Framework Convention on Climate Change (UNFCC) 69, 261-262
United Party, history 40
United States of America
 foreign relations with 329
 trade relations with 90
 trade with 85
Universal Postal Union (UPU) 142
Universal Service Agency (USA) 129, 131-132
Universal Service Fund 132
universities, institutional restructuring 221
University of Cape Town 221
University of Cape Town Ballet Company 117

University of Fort Hare 13, 221
University of Johannesburg 221
University of Limpopo 221
University of North West 221
University of Potchefstroom 221
University of Pretoria 23, 221
University of Port Elizabeth 221
University of South Africa (UNISA) 23
 African Languages Literacy Museum 120
University of Transkei 221
University of the North 221
University of the Witwatersrand 221
Unlocking Agricultural Potential programme in KwaZulu-Natal 16
Upington 16-17, 601
uranium mining 471
urban conservation 260
Urban Development Framework 415
Urban Renewal Neighbourhood Branding Project 114
urban renewal 414
 Cultural Industries Growth Strategy projects 115
urban transport 628-630
Uruguay 91
Usury Act, 1968 (Act 73 of 1968) 291
Uthingo Management (Pty) Ltd 283

V

Vaal Dam 24
Vaal River 17-18, 24
Vaal River System 18
Vaal Triangle 23-24, 257
Vaalharts Irrigation Scheme, Warrenton 18
Validation Board 273
Value Added Tax (VAT) 280
Vanderbijlpark 22, 610
Van Reenen 603
Vanrhynsdorp 597
Vanwyksdorp 593

vegetable production 73
 in 2002 71
Vehicle Emission Strategy 257
Veldcare 85
Velddrif/Laaiplek 596
Venda people 1
Venterstad 73
venture capital 180
Venture Capital Fund 180
Vereeniging 22
Verwoerd, HF 41
veterinary services 77-78
veterinary surgeons, training facilities 89
Victim-Empowerment Programme (VEP) 493-494, 559-560
Victoria and Alfred Waterfront 12, 589
Victoria Bay 592
Vietnam 324
Villiersdorp 599
violence
 see also crime
 against women 391
 prevention initiatives 391
Virginia 19
Virginia tobacco production 73
visas 587
Vista University 221
visual arts 118
Vodacom 131, 136-138
 journalism awards 154-155
Volksblad, Die 151
Voortrekker Monument, Pretoria 611
Voortrekker Museum, Pietermaritzburg 122
Voortrekkers, history of 34, 40
Vrededorp, heritage reclamation festivals 115
Vredenburg 10, 596
Vredendal 597
Vryburg 21
 Deeds Office 93, 100
Vryheid 15
Vuselela 20

W

Wakkerstroom, land redistribution 100

war graves, upkeeping 125
Warmbaths
  see Bela-Bela
War Museum of the Boer Republics, Bloemfontein 122, 124
Warrenton 18
War Veterans Grants 552
Washington Convention
  see Convention on International Trade in Endangered Species
water
  access to, Ten-Year Review 53
  Department of 651-671
  Directorate: Water Quality Management 256
  policy 654-657
  Water for All 653-654
  water resources management 657-662
  Working for Water Programme 79
Water Act, 1956 (Act 54 of 1956) 258
  see also National Water Act
Water Act, 1998 (Act 36 of 1998) 468
Water Boards 659
Watercare 85
Water for All 653-654
water management institutions 658-659
water research 543
Water Research Act, 1971 (Act 31 of 1971) 543
Water Research Commission (WRC) 543-544
water resources management 657-662
water schemes 660-661
Water Services Act, 1997 (Act 108 of 1997) 655-656
Waterberg 26, 605
water quality management 256-257
Waterval-Boven 609
Waterval-Onder 609
weed control 79
Weed Control Scheme 69
Weekend Argus 149, 151
Welcome Campaign 583-587
welfare
  see Department of Social Development
Welkom 18-19, 603
Wellington 594-595
Wepener 18
West Africa 319-323
West Bank IDZ 14
West Coast Investment Initiative 12
West Coast 8, 595-597
  Fossil Park 595
Western Cape 10-12
  agriculture 10-11, 71-76, 89
  climatic regions 11
  economic growth 11-12
  education levels 10
  floral kingdom 10
  GDP 10-12
  GGP 11
  industry 11-12
  information communications technology cluster 12
  languages 10-11
  marine fishery 10-11
  oceans 10
  population 11
  printing and publishing industry 12
  Provincial Administration 98
  provincial government as on 25 Sep 2003 347
  rainfall 9
  sport 566
  statistics 10-11
  tourism 12, 589-600
  tourist attractions 12, 589-600
  unemployment 10-11
  urban renewal projects 414
White Paper on Preparing the Western Cape for the Knowledge Economy of the 21st Century 11
wetlands 244, 609
  mapping of Wetlands GIS project 96
Whale Hall, South African Museum, Cape Town 123
wheat production, in 2002 70-71
White Paper on Arts, Culture and Heritage 113
White Paper on Broadcasting 143
White Paper on Broadcasting Policy 146
White Paper on Coastal Management 259
White Paper on Defence and the Defence Review 496
White Paper on Energy Policy 190, 468, 471, 474, 480
White Paper on Housing 399, 408
White Paper on Integrated Pollution and Waste Management 254
White Paper on National Commercial Ports Policy, 2001 191, 643
White Paper on National Transport Policy 639
White Paper on Postal Policy 139
White Paper on Preparing the Western Cape for the Knowledge Economy of the 21st Century 11
White Paper on Science and Technology 517
White Paper on South African Participation in International Peace Missions 507
White Paper on Spatial Planning and Land-use Management 97
White Paper on Sport and Recreation 571
White Paper on Sustainable Forest Development in South Africa 670
White Paper on the Conservation and Sustainable Use of South Africa's Biological Diversity 236
White Paper on the Transformation of the Health System 373
White Paper on Tourism 582
White Paper on Water Supply and Sanitation 657
White rhinoceros conservation 240
Whites 1
wholesaler and retail sector labour legislation 204
Wild Coast 12

cultural tourism 113-114
SDI 14
wild dog conservation 240
Wilderness 592
    areas 241
    National Park 592
Wilderness Trust of Southern Africa 263
wild frontier 609
Wildlife and Environment Society 263
Willem Prinsloo Agricultural Museum, Pretoria 122, 124, 610
William Fehr Collection 122
William Humphreys Art Gallery, Kimberley 122-123
Winburg 603
wind energy 481
Windybrow Theatre, Johannesburg 111
Wine and Spirits Agreement 72
wine and spirits production/industry 72-73
Winelands region 10-11, 16, 594-595
Witbank 24-25, 257
Witness Protection Act, 1998 (Act 112 of 1998) 421
Witness-Protection Programme 421
Wiitsieshoek, South Sotho Museum 124
Wits Theatre 117
Witwatersrand National Botanical Garden, Roodepoort 245
Wolseley 600
women
    economic empowerment 559
    in construction 195
    social assistance 558-559
Women's Monument Project, Pretoria 112
Wonderwerk Cave 118, 601
wool production 76
Worcester 10, 73, 600
    Kleinplasie 124, 600

Workplace Challenge Programme 181
World Food Programme (WFP) 73
Working for Water Programme 79, 659-660
World Committee for Food Security 83
World Economic Forum (WEF) 176
World Food Summit Plan of Action 83
World Heritage Convention 242
World Heritage Convention Act, 1999 (Act 49 of 1999) 242
World Heritage Sites 22, 243-244
    Cradle of Humankind 22
    Greater St Lucia Wetlands Park 15, 237
    hominid sites 22, 31, 243
    Robben Island Museum 122, 243
World Summit on Sustainable Development (WSSD) 235, 518, 584-585
World Summit on the Information Society (WSIS) 135
World Trade Organisation (WTO) 90, 169, 175
World Trade Organisation Agreement on the Application of Sanitary and Phytosanitary Measures (WTO-SPS) 82, 92
WTO-Marrakech Agreement 90
Wupperthal 596
WWF South Africa 263

X

Xhosa
    history 34
    Radio 144
Xitsonga

National Lexicographic Unit 4
    official language 1
    television 143
    Xitsonga: Xitsonga NLU 4
Xoshindlala Programme in KwaZulu-Natal 16

Y

10-Year Review
    see Ten-Year Review
Year of Further Education and Training project 20
Y-FM 145
Yiyo Lena 82
Young Champions Project 568
youth
    see also children, juveniles
Youth and Adolescent Health Policy Guidelines 388
Youth Entrepreneurship Programme 89
Yzerfontein 596

Z

Zambia 170
    food aid to 73
    foreign relations with 314
Zastron 603
Zebediela 27
Zeerust 79
Zijamele Farmers Co-operative training programme 88
Zimbabwe 8, 26, 170
    food aid to 73
    foreign relations with 315
    trade with 90-91
Zion Christian Church 6
Zoar 593
zoological gardens 245-246
Zulu
    Radio 144
    War (1879) 36